LESLY'S PUBLIC RELATIONS HANDBOOK
Second Edition

Contributors

RICHARD A. ARMSTRONG
RICHARD A. ASZLING
J. CARROLL BATEMAN
HERBERT M. BAUS
HAROLD BRAYMAN
MACE BROIDE
VIRGINIA BUTTS
ROBERT O. CARLSON
RICHARD R. CONARROE
WILLIAM W. COOK
MARTIN M. COOPER
JOHN M. COURIC
DON FABUN
GAYLORD FREEMAN
ALEC GALLUP
GEORGE GALLUP, JR.
D. PARKE GIBSON
RONALD I. GOW
CARL F. HAWVER
ROBERT W. HEFTY
THOMAS M. HOPKINSON
HOWARD PENN HUDSON
LOREN J. KALLSEN

KENNETH A. KOYEN
JOHN F. KRAFT
JAMES M. LAMBIE, JR.
PHILIP LESLY
TERRY MAYER
EUGENE MILLER
JAMES F. MINEHAN
PAUL R. NELSON
HUGH C. NEWTON
WILBUR J. PEAK
DAVID J. PHILLIPS
WILLIS PLAYER
HOWARD A. PRAEGER
CHARLES H. PROUT
MICHAEL RADOCK
REBEL L. ROBERTSON
MORRIS VICTOR ROSENBLOOM
MORTON J. SIMON
ROBERT W. TAFT
ROBERT N. THURSTON
JOSEPH A. VARILLA
MARVIN C. WILBUR
JEANE RIDGE YOUNG

LESLY'S PUBLIC RELATIONS HANDBOOK

Second Edition

Edited by
PHILIP LESLY

President
The Philip Lesly Co.
Chicago

PRENTICE–HALL, INC., Englewood Cliffs, N.J.

To All Those
Who Have Raised My Sights

Prentice-Hall International, Inc., *London*
Prentice-Hall of Australia, Pty. Ltd., *Sydney*
Prentice-Hall of Canada, Ltd., *Toronto*
Prentice-Hall of India Private Ltd., *New Delhi*
Prentice-Hall of Japan, Inc., *Tokyo*
Prentice-Hall of Southeast Asia, Pte., Ltd., *Singapore*
Whitehall Books, Ltd., *Wellington, New Zealand*

©1978, by
PRENTICE-HALL, INC.
Englewood Cliffs, N.J.

*All rights reserved. No part of this
book may be reproduced in any form or
by any means, without permission in
writing from the publisher.*

Library of Congress Cataloging in Publication Data

Lesly, Philip.
   Lesly's Public relations handbook.

   Bibliography: p.
   Includes index.
   1. Public relations. I. Title. II. Title:
Public relations handbook.
HM263.L46   1978   659.2   77-27118
ISBN 0-13-530741-4

Printed in the United States of America

FOREWORD

By
Gaylord Freeman

Honorary Chairman
The First National Bank of Chicago

These are uneasy times for anyone who manages an organization. A good manager inherently seeks to make the task manageable—to set out the elements of the operation so they can be seen and evaluated and directed. He wants to base his decisions on tables of figures he can assess, reports on the facts to be weighed, timetables for needed facilities, personnel, and budgets. The emergence of management technology that was so widely heralded in the first part of the century, and has been adopted almost everywhere, has helped transform the face of our world and has turned the pyramid of poverty-and-wealth around in advanced countries.

But even while the miracles of our advanced web of institutions have increased, recent trends make it clear that the real problems facing managers—and all of society—are no longer in the tangible areas of management technology, but in the attitudes of people.

We are in the midst of a revolution of attitudes. Throughout history, men faced shortages in the essentials of life. Our outlook and our institutions developed to provide security against want, predators, and untreatable disease. Now in the Western world we begin to see that our greatest dangers stem from abundance. The mechanisms and techniques that man's genius has developed have begun to outrun themselves. The approaches used in converting a hostile wilderness may no longer appeal to men who believe they face a hostile manmade cosmos.

All the beliefs and concepts that shaped our civilization since man first began to write are now being questioned or assaulted. Which will evolve and survive, and which will be replaced or reshaped? What kind of human society will come out of this cauldron of ideas?

In the individual organization, these questions take on day-to-day importance. Plans of the utilities to function vigorously and meet public needs depend as much on the attitudes of people about land use, pollution, and transportation as on their technical or financial capabilities. Plans of banks to serve the public without being inundated by paper or throttled by inert regulation depend on the attitudes of people and their Congressmen. The ability of our schools to function depends on the community's attitudes as much as on the skills of teachers.

What we do next in every aspect of our society does not depend primarily on advanced techniques of production or finance. It depends on reconciling the drives of millions of persons with the orderly development of very complex systems needed to keep society viable. What industry can do, what banks can do, what education and medicine and government can do depends on whether people understand and will cooperate with the plans that are developed.

We now live in the most powerful, most complex system ever known. It is made up of countless interacting institutions and organizations. Will this conglomeration of elements drift ever faster without guidance, or will some sort of new consensus evolve?

This depends on how managers of our organizations *see the patterns* evolving, how they *shape their policies* to serve these patterns, and how well they *communicate* to achieve understanding and support.

These three factors are the elements of public relations. Recognition of their importance is behind the rapid growth of public relations and public affairs in the consideration of managers. This book—whose precursor, *Public Relations Handbook,* for more than 20 years set the pattern for this burgeoning field—is most timely. It embodies concepts and guidelines for meeting the new challenges at all levels.

It is fortunate that a public relations counsel of Philip Lesly's stature has added editorship of this book to the scope of his activities. He has applied to it experience, perceptiveness, creativity, and judgment. This book illuminates all aspects of this vital field, and draws clear guidelines for carrying out its functions.

Lesly's Public Relations Handbook should be a valuable aid to managers and practitioners in the field, a compendium of ideas and tools whose time is here.

Preface to the Second Edition

All of human society today pivots on communication. Public relations deals with understanding and using mass communication. So this book—encompassing all the principles and practices of public relations—deals with many of the basics of how human society functions in the late Twentieth Century.

The vast and rapid changes of recent years have had an even greater impact in human affairs than in science and technology. A few years ago social changes tended to come singly and slowly; now they occur in all areas at the same time, and in rapid sequence. All institutions and elements of society are interlinked; as each changes, it wreaks changes on others. The whole human spectrum is therefore an ever-changing shape.

Understanding human institutions and the attitudes of their members has emerged as one of the greatest needs of our time. This understanding, plus knowledge of how to cope with these attitudes and direct them, is the rationale of public relations. It is axiomatic, therefore, that the kaleidoscopic change of the past few years has brought significant changes in the public relations field.

The basic principles of the field remain as valid as when they evolved between 1920 and 1950; but much of the emphasis and the execution have changed dramatically.

This is especially important in the realm of public relations practice, whether for a single corporation, an entire industry, a nonprofit organization, a government, or any other institution. The gap between theory and the multifaceted, constantly changing operations in the field has grown tremendously. This is true in all aspects of the art: sensing trends and the climate of attitudes; developing policy; planning; programming; execution of activities; and feedback and evaluation.

Vast experience and expertness. No classic survey or academic approach by one or a few people can be complete or up-to-date when disciplines are multiplying and complexity is intensifying. It must encompass the latest and most-expert knowledge of many proved practitioners, combined into a diverse but unified composite.

That is what *Lesly's Public Relations Handbook* does. Though the 1971 volume had its ancestry in three editions of *Public Relations Handbook* edited by me and published by Prentice-Hall—a work that promptly on its first publication in 1950 became the pre-eminent authority among practitioners throughout the world—in a true sense it was a new volume. In recognition of this primacy and to identify it as a new work based on this heritage, Prentice-Hall titled the new work *Lesly's Public Relations Handbook*. That work involved many additions and changes. This Second Edition of the new volume carries on the constant evolution of the treatment necessary to meet the field's needs. It adds two subjects not covered before, Working with State Government and Public Relations for the Professional Organization, and includes many additions and changed treatments of other aspects of the field. Many references to organizations, media, and other institutions have been brought up to date.

Encompassing "public affairs." One of the most important changes has been increased prominence given to various elements of public relations under the general term "public affairs."

Like so many ideas that come before the business community, public affairs has acquired a momentum of enthusiasm that causes some confusion. Though there is little agreement on what the public affairs area embraces, in some circles "Public Affairs" has been given an aura as if it were a science of its own.

In this new *Handbook,* the public affairs functions are included in Section II, "What Public Relations Includes." The editor identifies the subjects of Chapters 3 through 9 and 13 and 19 as the likely perimeters of public affairs. The organization of this book, then, serves to show how closely intertwined these are with the total scope of public relations—and defines the parts in terms of where they fit in the whole.

It is hoped that this organization and treatment will help clarify and orient the public affairs functions realistically, just as the *Handbook* helped to do that for public relations as a whole from the time of its introduction in 1950.

It is significant that five of the eight elements identified as having public affairs implications were included as part of the general field of public relations as far back as that first *Public Relations Handbook*.

Development of the field. When the First Edition of *Public Relations Handbook* was published there were strong signs that the public relations field was maturing in America after one of the most rapid developments of any significant discipline. During the previous 30 years after the primary concepts of the field were formulated, general outlines and objectives had been well established, but specific practices and techniques had far outrun the ability of practitioners to set them on the record in an explicit form. It was about 1945 that the first truly helpful and meaningful literature in the field, beyond the establishment of concepts, became available. By the time the first *Handbook* was published, it was possible to lay down standards for practice as well as concept.

The 28 years since the appearance of that book have been a phenomenon for public relations. With precipitous accumulations of problems between groups demanding techniques for developing understanding, the development of the public relations field has been remarkable not only in the United States but also in many other countries, where that growth is now being duplicated.

The *Handbook* met with gratifying success both in the United States and elsewhere. The hunger and need for understanding techniques to make free societies and economies work better is evident everywhere outside the Communist empires.

Throughout the history of the field there have been many threatened diversions of its character and purpose. In recent years these have included charges that the Watergate scandals, various ventures in foreign affairs, and efforts of various industries to forestall attack were "public relations ploys" or "facades" or "smokescreens" to divert public attention from the facts. They have also included continued efforts by various unscrupulous persons to cloak their machinations with the title of public relations. These annoy professionals in the field, but they do not alter its basic nature, importance, or growing role in society. Instead, they prove more firmly the wisdom of setting out the principles and content of the field and establishing its standards. The *Handbook* and this successor have been a means of guiding practitioners and making known to others what public relations truly is. The result is that after years of attacks, misdirected assumptions, and other barbs, the field continues to grow in importance and sophistication.

The contributors form a distinguished group; besides being able practitioners of their specialities they have succeeded to high positions in their own spheres.

Organization of the information. Because this is a reference work, to be used many times for many purposes, the essential information to be sought on a specific major subject has been combined in a single chapter. Although somewhat similar information on a few overlapping subjects may appear in two or more chapters, unnecessary duplication has been avoided. However, because a complete section on the techniques of communication has been included, these are touched on in other chapters only as they apply specifically to their subjects.

Many of the illustrations and lists of sources that appear in individual chapters are applicable to others. For instance, some illustrations in the chapter on nonprofit organizations are just as meaningful for corporations, government, or other organizations. Accordingly, by going through the whole book to gain the essence of these illustrative materials, the reader can add to what he gains from any one chapter. Cross references are indicated where more information appears in another chapter. In these ways the resources of the whole volume are applied to the subject of each chapter without requiring full and close study of the whole at one time.

Since public relations deals primarily with ideas, it requires keen understanding and perception, as well as experience, to translate its abstract concepts into tangible reference information. Also, because of its very broad scope, involving at some point or another almost all relationships of people, it is a difficult subject for which to establish rules and patterns. Yet the contributors to this volume have succeeded in solving both problems. The treatment naturally varies in concreteness with the nature of the subject being treated.

This handbook is not in the same pattern as the handbook or manual for the chemist or the mechanic, which sets up tables and charts that can be followed by most technicians at any time. It is a guide, a sourcebook, a reminder, and a stimulator that will enable anyone with imagination and intelligence to chart a course and be sure he or she is proceeding along sound lines.

PREFACE TO THE SECOND EDITION

It is hoped that this new *Handbook* will continue to raise and define the standards and practices of public relations as it continuously fills burgeoning needs throughout the world; and that by giving guidance to those who establish public relations programs as well as giving direction to those who have public relations responsibilities, *Lesly's Public Relations Handbook* will help bring the conciliatory principles and practices of public relations into universal practice among groups of people.

PHILIP LESLY

Acknowledgments

For helping to make this handbook complete, acknowledgment is due to all organizations whose material is used to illustrate points made in the text, or whose activities are cited as examples.

Thanks are also given to Ruth and Craig Lesly for their research and assistance with proofreading and checking at various times; to such members of The Philip Lesly Company organization, not otherwise credited in the book, who helped make its completion possible, as Susanne Scharding, Veronica Woerner, Sherry A. Martin, Lorraine Bordeaux Lynch, Eileen Sharpe, Robin Samelson, and others; and Don Campbell, W. Henry Johnston, Charles H. Prout, Prince Yurka Galitzine, Charles Tisdall, Joseph A.P. Clark, Dr. Ray E. Hiebert, Diane Levin, Will Budd, Douglas Mueller, Richard Toohey, Francis L. Murphy, Raymond Hoewing, Linda Hartwick, Armand G. Arel, Martha Payne, John Pelgrene, Don Bates, Scott Cohen, Erwin van Swol, Alan Carter, Mildred Simpson, Daniel Z. Henkin, Norman Herington, Herbert Schmertz, Daisy Colle, Robert Sandberg, Milton Fairman, Robert L. Barbour, Dr. Rex F. Harlow, Stuart Chant-Sempill, Samuel P. Bates, Robert D. Buehler, James Rosevear, Edward Uzemack, Clifford Sapp, Dr. Paul Hartsuch, Robert McCumber, Robert J. Hoover, Dean Markusch, Theodore Mecke, T. George Harris, Virginia M. Barnes, Romney Wheeler, Arthur Wynne Jr., Irving Settel, Fred Isley, John Verstraete, and Alan Sturdy for their help in making arrangements for some of the material used.

Thanks are also due to those who provided material for the earlier book that has been helpful in this one, including Alice Shelley, Russell Van Cleve, Weston Smith, Patricia Coleman, Marjorie Hoobler, Sol Dolgin, and Barbara McNear; and to *Public Relations Journal, Journal of Marketing,* Harry Coleman & Company, *The Public Relations Quarterly,* Allied Chemical Company, Nekoosa-Edwards Paper Company, General Electric Company, Consumers Power Company, Warner & Swasey Company, Marshall Field & Company, The Conference Board, Dayton-Hudson Company, International Telephone and Telegraph Company, Hercules Inc., Marathon Oil Company, Charles Francis Press, American Smelting and Refining Company, Atlantic Richfield Company, American Medical Association, American Medical Political Action Committee, American Stock Exchange, National Airlines, J C Penney, Air Transport Association, and Prentice-Hall, Inc. for permission to reprint copyrighted material. Some materials in the section on communications techniques are based on work by Herbert M. Baus, besides those bearing his name.

P.L.

Table of Contents

FOREWORD by Gaylord Freeman v

PREFACE TO THE SECOND EDITION vii

Section I. WHAT PUBLIC RELATIONS IS AND DOES

1. **The Nature and Role of Public Relations—PHILIP LESLY** 3

   The development of public relations, • Adjustment in an age of revolutions, • Who does public relations work? • How public relations serves various organizations, • Phases of public relations, • The universe of public relations, • What public relations accomplishes, • The benefits of these activities

2. **The Nature of Effective Communications—PHILIP LESLY** 12

   Forms of communication, • Effective and ineffective communication, • Complexity of communication, • How to influence behavior

Section II. WHAT PUBLIC RELATIONS INCLUDES

3. **The Dynamics and Role of Public Affairs—TOM M. HOPKINSON** 27

   Historical background, • Business and society, • Social audit, • The corporate role, • Changing directions, • Relationship to public relations, • Career training, • How to organize, • Major components, • Problems and barriers, • Information sources, • Public affairs budgets, • Role of outside counsel, • Associations and nonprofit institutions, • What it accomplishes, • Trends for tomorrow

4. **Dealing with Forces for Change Through Government Action— DAVID J. PHILLIPS** 37

   Criticism as a signal of change, • Defining the direction of change, • The role of public relations

5. **Working with Federal Government—HOWARD PENN HUDSON** 40

   A change in the climate, • Tools and techniques, • Activities of Washington public relations, • Investigations and hearings, • Other techniques, • Lobbying and foreign agent registration, • Who does public relations work in Washington?

6. **Working with State Government—RICHARD A. ARMSTRONG** 51

   The need, • The prognosis, • State government relations, • Influencing the executive, • Elected officials, • Non-elected officials, • Approaches to state government relations, • The techniques, • Emerging techniques, • Needs and challenges, • How to maintain effec-

6. **Working with State Government—RICHARD A. ARMSTRONG (cont.)**

tive surveillance, • How to gain management support, • How to get started, • Sources and resources, • Corporate program information, • State government information

7. **Community Relations—WILBUR J. (BILL) PEAK** 64

What community relations is today, • Its importance to business, • What's at stake for business?, • The community speaks out, • The structure of a community (people), • Community strengths and weaknesses, • Setting priorities, • You've come a long way, • Applied community relations, • Planning, • Organizing, • Action, • Communicating, • Evaluating, • Coming into or leaving a community, • Trends

8. **Having a Voice in Politics—MACE BROIDE** 80

Politics is civic service—and good business, • Voting, politics, and government—related but different, • Political party organization and structure, • The precinct : basic election unit, • Political clubs, • The nominating process, • The political campaign, • Financing campaigns, • Political action committees, • Some practical ideas on donations, • Your role in politics

9. **Working and Communicating with Minority Groups—D. PARKE GIBSON** ... 88

Understanding minority group attitudes, • Determining the organization's position, • Telling the story, • Working with groups, • Tailoring the material, • Creating target material

10. **Winning Public Support for an Idea or Cause—HUGH C. NEWTON** 96

Government and our way of life, • The corporate approach, • Organizations to foster a cause, • Winning public support, • The basic principles, • Planning a public opinion campaign, • The use of polls, • Timing and execution

11. **Financial Public Relations** 105

    I. Basic Planning and Programs—EUGENE MILLER

Requisites for the financial public relations man, • Establishing a program, • Communicating with shareholders, • Extra mailings of annual reports, • Other stockholder publications, • Shareholder annual meetings, • The post annual meeting report, • Stockholder letters, • Financial publicity, • Financial and business publications, • Syndicated financial columns, • Directories for management changes, • Primary investment services and financial statistical bureaus, • Tips on dealing with the press, • Publicity during the registration period, • Security analysts, • Other communications outlets, • Proxy fights and tender offers, • Guides to effective disclosure, • Home comings and open houses, • Shareholder surveys, • Long-term effectiveness

12. **Financial Public Relations** 136

    II. Takeover Efforts and Disclosure Regulations—PHILIP LESLY

Disclosure policies, • SEC disclosure requirements

13. **Industry Relations—HAROLD BRAYMAN** 156

The need for cooperation, • Specifics on improving industry relations, • Being helpful to others

TABLE OF CONTENTS xiii

14. Employee Relations and Communications—JOSEPH A. VARILLA 162

Interests of employees, • Techniques for communicating, • Increasing challenges

15. Company Publications—DON FABUN 166

What is it supposed to do?, • Setting up clearance channels, • What kind of a publication?, • What should the format be?, • Letterpress or offset?, • What kind of an editor?, • How should the publication be designed?, • "Market testing" a new publication, • The use of photographs, • What kind of material should be presented?, • Where does the material come from? • Feedback mechanisms, • How often should a publication appear? • Distributing the employee magazine, • Where to get professional help, • Changing trends in employee publications

16. Public Relations and Labor Matters—ROBERT W. HEFTY 176

Major challenge: the restless employee, • The importance of timing, • Preparing for negotiations, • Guarding proprietary information, • A good tool: background "briefing," • Principal responsibilities, • How to help newsmen, • Organizing for the job, • Reporting the results, • Handling the strike

17. The Role of Public Relations in Marketing—ROBERT N. THURSTON 185

The role of public interest in marketing, • The new public relations role, • Public relations in the promotional process

18. Building Effective Dealer Relations—RONALD I. GOW 192

The importance of dealer relations, • The role of communications, • Researching the audience, • Dealer communications media, • Content of dealer communications, • Helping dealers through training and customer service

19. Consumer Relations—RICHARD A. ASZLING 198

Development of consumerism, • Response by business, • Four challenges to public relations

Section III. HOW AN ORGANIZATION UTILIZES PUBLIC RELATIONS

20. The Utility and Its Public—HOWARD A. PRAEGER and JAMES A. MINEHAN 211

The unique nature of utilities, • Specific areas of concern, • Community involvement, • Relations with specific groups, • Special considerations for telephone utilities, • Intra-industry relations, • Meeting growth with adequate supply, • Strategy and techniques, • Utility public relations checklist

21. Public Relations for the Business and Professional Association— J. CARROL BATEMAN 230

Organizing for public relations in the association, • Seven basic steps in developing a program, • Techniques of association public relations, • Differences from corporate public relations

22. Public Relations for Financial Organizations—PHILIP LESLY 245

Basic principles and differences, • Special considerations, • Implications for other institutions

23. **Public Relations for Retailers**—TERRY MAYER 250

Specific characteristics of retailing, • Various types of programs, • Gearing to current events, • Defining the store's distinctiveness, • Windows as image builders, • Appealing to youth, • Employee communications, • Store-wide promotions and events, • Communication by mail, • Investor relations, • Community relations, • Minority group relations, • Emergency situations, • Magazine tie-ins and editorial credits

24. **Public Relations for the Nonprofit Organization**—REBEL L. ROBERTSON .. 263

Prime publics of nonprofit agencies, • Public relations and policy making, • Making the public relations operation successful, • Budgeting, • Special considerations of media and nonprofit public relations, • Special events and their public relations value, • Metropolitan coordination, • How to raise money, • Emergency public relations, • Perspective

25. **Public Relations for Religion and Religious Groups**—MARVIN C. WILBUR .. 277

Organizing an effective religion public relations program, • Financing the program, • Setting up a communication center, • Organizations that can help

26. **Public Relations for Educational Institutions**—MICHAEL RADOCK 284

The changing world of university relations, • Qualifications for the higher education public relations man, • The internal publics, • Communication with students, • New techniques for education, • External publics, • Handling crises, • Program evaluation

27. **Public Relations for Newspapers**—VIRGINIA BUTTS 299

28. **Public Relations for Broadcasters**—JOHN M. COURIC 304

Ambassadors to the community, • Charting the course, • Scope of station plans, • Involving the community, • Relations with governments, • Professional standards, • Building broadcasting with broadcasting

29. **The Public Relations of Government**—CARL F. HAWVER 311

Freedom of information, • The role of public relations in government, • The publics of government, • The size and cost of government information programs

30. **Public Relations for the Professional Organization—
RICHARD R. (DICK) CONARROE** 322

Marketing strategy needed, • The values of public relations, • Start with a plan, • The periodic audit, • Twelve basic tools, • Getting the job done

31. **Publicity for Travel and Tourism**—KENNETH KOYEN 332

32. **Public Relations for Political Candidates**—JOHN F. KRAFT and
MORRIS VICTOR ROSENBLOOM 340

Effects of funding laws, • Fund raising and money making, • The candidate, • Party structure, • The issues: how to find them, • The tools to be used

33. **International Public Relations** 350

    I. **The Developing Need**—PHILIP LESLY

Multinational business communication, • Governments' activities

TABLE OF CONTENTS xv

34. International Public Relations 353

      II. Functioning Abroad—WILLIS PLAYER

Universal differences, • Major considerations, • Staff and counsel abroad

Section IV. ANALYSIS AND PREPARATION

35. The Role of Research in Public Relations 361

      I. Purposes and Types—ROBERT O. CARLSON

Many techniques available, • Evaluating research, • New directions, • Conclusions

      II. Guidelines and Techniques—GEORGE GALLUP, JR. and ALEC GALLUP

Four essential ingredients of surveys, • Importance of research know-how, • What should a survey cost?

36. Fact-Finding for Public Relations—WILLIAM W. COOK 370

Reducing the element of chance, • Qualitative distinctions in fact-finding, • Knowledge of sources is essential, • Information services

37. Analysis, Planning, and Programming—PHILIP LESLY 383

Establishing the essentials, • Elements of planning, • Typical corporate priority schedule

Section V. THE TECHNIQUES OF COMMUNICATION

38. Preparations for Communicating—HERBERT M. BAUS and PHILIP LESLY 391

Planning the publicity program, • News and publicity, • Planning publicity, • Arranging for approvals, • Organizing the files, • Special events, • Product publicity, • Media of publicity, • Controlling rumors, • Press clipping bureaus, • Broadcast and composite reports

39. Relations with Publicity Media—PHILIP LESLY 416

Patterns of working with media, • News conferences, briefings, and introductions, • The exclusive story, • Handling inquiries from media, • Handling emergencies, • Other principles

40. Publicity in Newspapers—HERBERT M. BAUS AND PHILIP LESLY 428

Daily and Sunday newspapers, • Home-town press, • Special newspaper classifications, • News syndicates, • Feature syndicates, • Photograph syndicates, • Distribution services, • Public relations newswires, • Clipsheets, press books, and press kits, • Mechanics of press publicity, • Photographs and illustrations, • Photography files

41. Publicity in Magazines—HERBERT M. BAUS 448

How to deal with magazine editors, • Magazines' timing, • Classifications of magazines, • General magazines, • Weekly newspaper magazines, • News and illustrated magazines, • Special magazines, • City and state magazines, • Business magazines

42. Books and Other Publications—HERBERT M. BAUS AND PHILIP LESLY . 460

Paperback books and minibooks, • Publicity through cartoon booklets, • Special publications, • Reading rack booklets

43. Television and Radio Publicity—PHILIP LESLY 465

Working with broadcast media, • Broadcasters and activism, • Structure of broadcast media, • Types of programming, • Arranging for broadcasts, • How to approach broadcasting people, • How to be effective in TV interviews, • Syndicating self-produced programming, • Source file on broadcasting, • A diversified broadcasting effort, • Capitalizing on broadcast coverage

44. Public Television and Radio—JEANE R. YOUNG 476

Local and national opportunities, • Reaching the community, • Underwriting costs and practices, • Local stations

45. Publicity in the Movies—MARTIN M. COOPER 481

New pattern of film as a medium, • Publicity opportunities today, • Taking advantage of publicity opportunities

46. Sponsored Motion Pictures and Other Audio/Visual Media—LOREN J. KALLSEN 486

Sponsored motion pictures, • TV releases and other films, • Slidefilms and slides, • Some visual and/or audio aids

47. Using Advertising for Public Relations Communications—PHILIP LESLY 494

Special nature of ads as communication, • Effective uses of advertising, • Broadcast media, • Ineffective uses of advertising

48. Direct Communications Methods—HERBERT M. BAUS AND PHILIP LESLY 504

Speakers' bureaus, • The telephone as a public relations device, • Communicating through activism, • Word of mouth, • Letters, • Post cards, • Newsletters, • Extension home economists, • Other direct media, • Signs, • Fairs and exhibits, • Displays, • Public address systems

49. Working with Influential Groups—HERBERT M. BAUS 517

Schools as a medium of communication

50. How to Write for Readership—JAMES M. LAMBIE, JR. 526

Why do we need good readership? • How can we achieve it? • The evils of fancy talk, • Summary

51. How to Use Graphics and Printing—PAUL R. NELSON 537

Why printing is important in public relations, • What to use when, • How and when to distribute printed matter, • Printing processes and techniques, • Preparing copy for printing, • Typography, • Printing types, • Calculating space and copy fitting, • Engravings

Section VI. THE PRACTICE OF PUBLIC RELATIONS

52. Organization and Function of the Corporate Public Relations Department— CHARLES H. PROUT 567

Scope of public relations function, • Functions of the Public Relations Department • Public relations in the corporate organization, • Organization of the department, • Public relations salaries, • Board of Directors participation, • Role of the public relations firm

53. The Place and Function of the Public Relations Counsel—PHILIP LESLY 576

Who is a public relations counsel? • How he works with a client, • What the counsel has to offer, • Limitations of professional counsel, • Payments : When and how much, • Organizing to serve a client, • Educating the client, • The work is confidential, • The counsel is a businessman

54. Considerations of Law in Public Relations—MORTON J. SIMON 589

Increasing public relations interest in the law, • Government attitudes, • Major classifications of legal exposures, • Tabulation of specific legal areas, • Relative degree of legal danger, • The dangers of deception, • Public issue advertising, • Lobbying, • The practitioner in politics, • Treatment and use of research materials, • International public relations operations, • Public relations and litigation, • Liability of public relations people, • The lawyer/law dichotomy, • The public relations/legal team, • Recommendations in brief

Section VII. EMERGING PRINCIPLES AND TRENDS

55. Emerging Principles and Trends—PHILIP LESLY 601

The intangibles in a world of tangibles, • Trend away from oversimplification, • Awareness of fallacies about communication, • The changing role of the media, • The name as an image factor, • The edifice as a visible symbol, • Trends and future requirements, • Evaluation of public relations, • Moves toward professionalism, • Growing need for broad scope

Appendix

Bibliography 617

Public relations, • Public relations periodicals, • Public affairs, • Publicity, • Public opinion and polling, • Communications, • Propaganda, • Management and policy, • Political public relations, • Journalism, • Television and radio, • Internal communications, • Films and audio/visual, • Graphic arts, printing and production, • Semantics and usage, • Public speaking, Advertising, • Fund raising

Glossary 624

Codes of Ethics 637

Code of the Public Relations Society of America, • An official interpretation of the PRSA Code of Professional Standards for the Practice of Public Relations as it applies to financial public relations, • Institute of Public Relations (Great Britain) Code of Professional Conduct, • International Public Relations Association Code of Conduct (adopted in Venice, May 1961)

Associations **642**
  International and regional public relations societies, • *National public relations societies,*
  • *Specialized associations*

Index **647**

LESLY'S PUBLIC RELATIONS HANDBOOK
Second Edition

SECTION I

What Public Relations Is and Does

1

The Nature and Role of Public Relations

PHILIP LESLY, president of The Philip Lesly Company, Chicago, is one of the leading authorities in the field of public relations and a practitioner who has served many leading organizations, companies, and industries.

Before going to college, having attracted attention as organizer and editor of the country's only daily high school newspaper, he landed a job with the editorial staff of the Chicago Herald and Examiner. Two years later, at eighteen, he was awarded a scholarship to Northwestern University, from which he was graduated Magna Cum Laude and possessor of a Phi Beta Kappa Key.

He entered professional public relations work immediately after leaving college, and two years later was vice president of one of the country's larger counseling firms. Since then, with a brief time-out in the Navy Language School, he has planned, directed, and carried out public relations programs for scores of corporations, trade associations, and nonprofit organizations. He has received three Awards of Merit of the Public Relations Society of America. His firm, headquartered in Chicago, now concentrates on counsel and major creative contributions to major clients. It formerly was one of the largest full-service firms, with multiple offices in the U.S. and abroad.

His first book, which was a milestone in the field, was Public Relations: Principles and Procedures (Chicago: Richard D. Irwin, Inc., 1945). He was then 27 years old. In 1947 he published Public Relations in Action, a volume of case studies (New York: Ziff-Davis). This volume's predecessor, Public Relations Handbook, first published in 1950, quickly became the most widely used volume on the subject throughout the world. He was one of the first group of members to receive accreditation by PRSA. He has lectured widely and written for many publications and is author of the bimonthly "Managing the Human Climate." His The People Factor (Dow Jones-Irwin, 1974) has been widely quoted.

THE DEVELOPMENT OF PUBLIC RELATIONS

Public relations is a phenomenon and a necessity of our times. It has been created by the forces that increased the tempo of the world, casting people into many diversified groups, all seeking different objectives yet all having to work together toward common advantages and progress. The growing complexity of civilization has created problems undreamed of when social, economic, political, and religious classifications were simple and distinct.

Change has been magnified by the combined forces of technology, education, mobility, and especially communication. Widespread literacy is less than 500 years old; and well into the Twentieth Century the only media of communication were speech and print. Then in quick succession came the motion picture, recordings, radio, television, and other electronic media. The explosion of communications led to an implosion of the once vast and remote world. Suddenly it is all there to see, to experience, to judge; a person's scope of awareness and judgment has been multiplied thousands of times. Diverse, instant communication has changed the world of man much more than man has changed his institutions for living in that world.

These forces that have changed the world in just a century have been leveling forces. They have greatly exalted the position and importance of the mass of people; and they have greatly reduced the power and control of those who are leaders. Today, as never before in history, people are led by their own consent; they are their own masters, guided only by their own opinions as expressed through the *mores* and demands of the groups to which they belong—such as "farmers," "wage-earners," "Catholics," "youth," and so on. The command of a king or a tycoon is no longer the word of law, automatically obeyed. It is now necessary first to attain the acceptance, if not the support, of those being ordered.

The change has occurred very quickly. In the same way, the science or business or profession of public relations (its true status has not been established yet) has appeared almost full-blown and is today a very significant actuality in all the important associations among diverse groups of our civilization.

Public relations started as publicity—now just one of its phases—because, as it became harder for people with different backgrounds to understand and know about each other, the first necessity was for one group to tell others about itself. In developing, public relations has come to include a great many other functions besides telling about someone or some group. It also tells the group what others think of it; it helps the group determine what it must do to get the good will of others; it plans ways and means of winning that good will; and it carries on activities designed to win it. In the process of doing these things, it encompasses a great many functions, concepts, and techniques—including the range of functions in "public affairs" that help an organization come into confluence with the social forces affecting it.

These functions, concepts, and techniques are the subject of this book. Its purpose is to put down for the benefit of everyone what they are, so that the efforts of different groups to get along better can be expedited; so anyone who has any public relations responsibility or function—and this, in a broad sense, includes everyone—can know the ways to protect and develop good will; and so the "profession" of public relations can develop in an orderly manner, for the benefit of everyone who practices it as well as of those whom it serves.

There are many definitions of public relations, as can be expected for a field that has so many aspects and that reaches into almost every facet of human society. For simplicity as well as completeness, however, public relations can be defined as *helping an organization and its publics accommodate to each other*.

That definition conveys the vital fact that the essence is mutual accommodation, rather than one-sided imposition of a viewpoint. It recognizes that a key factor facing every organization is the insistence of each individual in modern free societies on having a say about every organization and institution that affects his or her life.

ADJUSTMENT IN AN AGE OF REVOLUTIONS

The increasing importance of the individual has been both the effect and the cause of education. As a person acquires more rights, he acquires more education. This, in turn, makes him understand his environment better, so that he can formulate new desires and devise plans for achieving them. When an individual gains education he learns what he can do, and aspires, works, and organizes to get what he wants. Since the individual when multiplied enough times has become a powerful influence, the forces that guide him in developing his desires, attitudes, and opinions—the forces, in a word, that educate him—are naturally important. When we also consider that every activity in modern life has as its most essential ingredient, people—that proper handling of people is the most essential of any organization's activities—we begin to appreciate the scope and influence of public relations, the "science" that deals with the person's opinions and with the relationship of an organization with the people it involves.

Need for mass educational devices. Such a development has not only been created by the necessity of the groups that use it, but is a social necessity as well. As science gives us greater control over matter, machines, and methods, we must learn with increasing effectiveness to control people. Public relations, as a means of interchanging attitudes, can greatly expedite the social adaptations required by our material advancement, without molding public opinion into rigid and totalitarian patterns.

The explosion of communications is more than an accelerator of change, although it is certainly that. It has created a whole new pattern of human dynamics. Its impact is as important as the discovery of writing and then of printing. It is truly a revolutionary force.

There have never been so many revolutions, of so

many types, going on at once. There are revolutions of people who feel oppressed, attempting to gain their national independence; revolutions of modernization, with backward peoples attempting to propel themselves into the latest stage of industrialization; revolutions by minorities for social, civil, and economic rights; revolutions in trade concepts, with the West German expecting to sell his cars in Frankfort, Kentucky, as well as in Frankfurt, Germany, and new trade alliances reshaping concepts of how the world does business.

There is the very real "quiet revolution" that has made more changes in human life since 1945 than in all previous history.

We have a revolution in morality and human values. The revolution of individualism—which would allow the person full license to consume, to procreate, to pollute—conflicts with a growing awareness that mankind as a whole must restrain consumption, procreation, and pollution. And there is the revolution in life styles and multiplicity of career choices that has created a segmented society, at the same time the old segmented pigeonholes into which humanity fitted—farmer or city dweller, nobility or commoner—have been broken down.

Every revolution results in loss of status for those who are out of tune with its changes, and elevates those who are alert to them. The current upheavals are basically revolutions in public attitudes. Public relations, as the discipline that deals with public attitudes, is gaining rapidly in international attention and dedication.

The leveling process in our society has progressed to the point where the Bourbon era is about over. The younger leaders in business management, politics, and other affairs are aware of the importance of public attitudes. They are either aware of public relations, or are receptive when it comes to their attention. As they replace the gradually disappearing handful of Bourbons who remain, the concept of public relations will continue to increase in importance.

The changes have created a "human climate" in which all organizations must exist. For each organization, understanding and coping with the human climate is as vital as dealing with the weather climate is to the farmer.

WHO DOES PUBLIC RELATIONS WORK?

The functions of an organization's public relations are the responsibility of every executive and, indeed, of every member of the organization. They cannot be assigned to a specialist and forgotten, to take care of themselves. For this reason, the contents of this handbook are the concern and part of the requisite working tools of every executive.

For direction and carrying out of the functions, however, organizations call on men and women who by training are equipped to serve as public relations specialists. So far, there have been two primary types of practitioner who have specialized in this field:[1]

First, the person who serves as an employee of the organization, being part of its internal structure and subject to its controls. His title is often Director of Public Relations, and often he has a staff to assist him. He may be a vice-president and perhaps have public affairs, advertising, investor relations, and other functions in his portfolio. It is likely that he reports to a top executive of the organization.

Second, the public relations counsel, who is retained by the organization, and works closely with it, but does not become part of its internal structure. He provides an objective approach to the public relations of the organization, serving just as professional attorneys, engineers, and accountants do. Usually the counsel has a staff.

How they work together. The director of public relations and the public relations counsel may function together for an organization, or either of them may be found separately performing all the functions involved.

Where they are both involved, there are two common arrangements: The staff of the organization conducts many of the activities and is the coordinating force within the organization, while the counsel provides guidance, the benefit of experience, creativity, contacts, and various services for which he and his staff have experience, skill, and resources. Usually in this arrangement, the counsel advises management officials of the organization as well as the Director of Public Relations.

Or the Director of Public Relations serves as liaison within the organization, while the counsel and his staff perform most of the functions required.

There seems to be a trend toward both of these arrangements, in preference to the public relations department alone or the counsel's services alone. The type of dual arrangement varies with the nature of the organization, the problems involved, and other factors.

---

[1] For a discussion of the procedures in a public relations structure, see Chaps. 51 and 52.

Developing capable workers. Since the profession has developed so rapidly, without a framework within which to train workers, there continues to be a severe shortage of capable public relations people, qualified to perform all the functions of the true counsel and practitioner. The educational system (which often lags behind the requirements of the rest of society) is awakening to this need and is beginning to offer training. More than 300 colleges in the U.S. now offer one or more courses in public relations. The demand among the students is indicative of the widespread recognition of the profession's future.

The continuing development in our society of problems requiring the mutual understanding of many groups, and the need for accelerating the social processes, hold great promise that the use of public relations principles and techniques will continue to grow until every organization will follow its precepts. It is today such an important factor in the operation of any enterprise that it is a matter of interest and significance to every executive.

HOW PUBLIC RELATIONS SERVES VARIOUS ORGANIZATIONS

Whether an organization's public relations are sound depends on the type of organization and on its situation at any time. But broad outlines of the factors that influence public relations may be set up according to basic classifications of types of organization.

Since the factors to be considered in other categories are treated by specialists in later chapters, we shall concentrate this analysis on the business corporation.

Public relations and good will.[2] Perhaps the most important force affecting all organizations and governments today is the opinion of people. Businessmen realize this when they talk of "good will." Business good will today means not only the attitude of the consumer toward the company's products, but also the attitude of the employees, the community, the Government, the stockholders, the dealers and distributors, the suppliers, and others. All of these groups are vital to the success of a company; the good will of every one of them is indispensable. This is equally true for all other types of organization.

---

[2]Portions of the remainder of this chapter are adapted from the brochure, *Public Relations—A Function of Management,* by Harry Coleman & Co., Chicago, for whom Mr. Lesly developed the text.

The value of good will is most evident when it is absent. The productivity of employees may be lower than in competitors' plants; morale may be poor; turnover and absenteeism may be abnormally high—the result is higher costs, lower production, inability to compete with companies that have a higher level of good will among their employees. Frequently strikes are symptoms of neglected good will among employees. Difficulty in getting workers, failure to attract enough good dealers, a high volume of complaints from customers, fast turnover of stockholders and frequent stockholder complaints, resentment of the community toward the company and its operations all are signs that the attitude of these groups is at an unsatisfactory level. An organization that becomes the target for attacks by activist groups protesting alleged pollution, job discrimination, or exploitation of consumers; that is singled out for review by government agencies or Congressional committees; or that is vulnerable to "takeover" efforts or financial raids may be showing signs of blindness to attitude trends and ineptness in anticipatory planning. Just as a person appreciates the value of protecting his health when he becomes ill, so an organization can best recognize the necessity for fostering good will when it suffers from one of these problems. In the same way, prevention of disorders is much wiser than waiting for them to appear before seeking the remedy.

For this reason, management executives today realize that along with production, sales, accounting, finance, engineering, their businesses must have the most expert assistance in developing and maintaining good will—or "public relations" as it is most commonly called.

The fostering of good public relations goes beyond winning favor among various groups by telling them what an organization is doing. Expert public relations recognizes that everything the organization does affects the opinion of someone.

PHASES OF PUBLIC RELATIONS

Public relations today involves complete analysis and understanding of all the factors that influence people's attitudes toward an organization. It usually has seven phases:

(1) Analyzing the general climate of attitudes and the relation of the organization to its "universe." Every institution functions within a "universe" or system, and is dependent on everything that happens to this totality. It is vital to understand as well as possible the trends within this system and how the organization may be affected by them. Included in this is "pulse feeling" of the attitudes toward the organization and toward the field it is in, among the various publics it may have relations with.

(2) **Determining the attitude of any group toward the organization.** This may be the employees, the customers, the stockholders, or some other segment of the public. When the attitudes are known, it is possible to see where the organization is misunderstood and where its policies and actions are creating unfavorable opinion.

(3) **Analyzing the state of opinion.** It may be that investigation discloses unrest among a group of employees—unrest that may well break out into very serious uprisings. Or the stockholders may express the desire to know more about the company and its products. Or consumers may not identify products with the manufacturer. Analysis will aid in making plans to improve the opinion of the various groups about which the company is concerned.

(4) **Anticipating potential problems, needs, or opportunities.** From analysis and surveys it sometimes is possible to detect in advance what may develop in the attitudes of various groups. Then plans or actions can be recommended to meet those circumstances at the most advantageous time and under favorable circumstances.

(5) **Formulating policy.** Analysis may indicate that certain policies of the company should be modified to improve the attitude held by certain groups. Often the change involves eliminating causes of misunderstanding and misinterpretation.

(6) **Planning means of improving the attitude of a group.** With an understanding of what people think of the organization and a clarification of the organization's policies on matters that affect public opinion, the groundwork has been laid. Next comes the programming of activities that will explain the company and its products, will overcome misunderstandings, and will promote good will.

(7) **Carrying out the planned activities.** The tools of public relations—publicity, institutional advertising, printed materials, employee activities, stockholder reports, company publications, and other things—are then employed to do the job. With proper preliminary planning and guidance, these become the most tangible phase of a company's public relations activity.

(8) **Feedback, evaluation, and adjustment.** Conditions are changing constantly; the public relations functions both contribute to this change and are affected by it. So it is important to constantly get readings from the publics that are being ap-

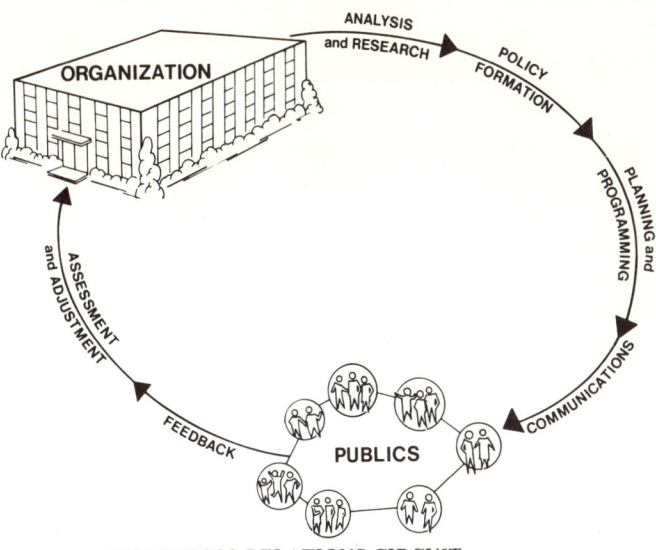

THE PUBLIC RELATIONS CIRCUIT

Figure 1-1. Schematic diagram of an optimum process in public relations. It is continuous, not oriented to single events or objectives; interacting, with each phase affecting the conception and execution of every other phase; and proportioned, with no one element (such as communications) functioning predominantly.

proached. These help to assess the results and developments, and to adjust the public relations program—and often the entire policy of the organization—accordingly.

This scientific approach to an organization's good will goes far beyond the familiar publicity releases and hit-or-miss efforts to please employees or members. It is a task for highly skilled specialization and talent. It demands high-caliber thinking by a number of experts; experience in the ways of public opinion and the techniques of influencing it; and the facilities to do everything that must be done in a well-planned program.

For this reason, most substantial corporations and other organizations in America and an increasing number in other free countries are calling on well-established specialists to serve as public relations counselors and directors. Thus they obtain the best brains for analysis and planning; the benefit of experience based on a large number of other programs; the staff of specialists necessary to achieve peak results in every bit of activity; and the extensive facilities required to carry on all the necessary functions.

THE UNIVERSE OF PUBLIC RELATIONS

Confusion has been caused by both the broad scope of what public relations encompasses and the use of a variety of terms as substitutes or euphemisms—such as corporate affairs, communications, external affairs, and—most commonly—public affairs.

THE UNIVERSE OF PUBLIC RELATIONS

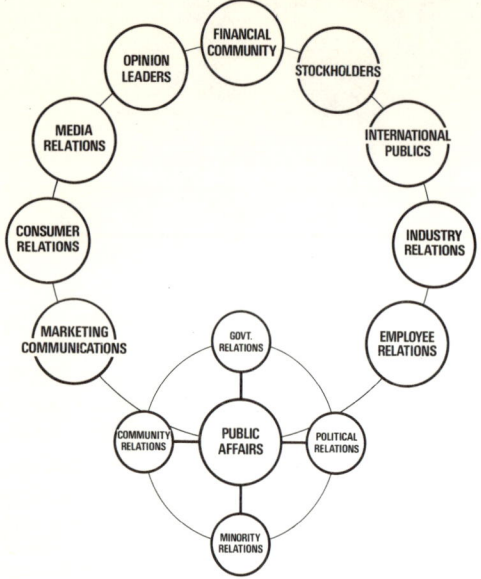

THE UNIVERSE OF PUBLIC RELATIONS

Figure 1-2. This diagram represents the various functions and publics that make up the "universe" of public relations. All the large circles are "planets"—including "public affairs"—and the small circles are satellites of "public affairs," which is one of the planets. The satellites are related to public affairs, but are also part of the total public relations cosmos.

For clarification, Figure 1-2 depicts what the "universe" of public relations embodies.

In this book the elements of public relations that fall into the category of public affairs are covered in Chapters 3-9, 13, and 19—all integral to the total scope of public relations.

WHAT PUBLIC RELATIONS ACCOMPLISHES

There are many objectives that may be achieved through expert public relations activity. Any one of them, any group of them, or all of them may be the basis for an organization's public relations program. Professional public relations directs every activity toward reaching a selected objective; extraneous efforts are avoided—mere volume of press clippings is meaningless. Objectives that may be sought include:

(1) Prestige or "favorable image" and its benefits
(2) Promotion of products or services
(3) Good will of the employees or members
(4) Prevention and solution of labor problems
(5) Fostering the good will of communities in which the organization has units
(6) Good will of the stockholders or constituents
(7) Overcoming misconceptions and prejudices
(8) Forestalling attacks
(9) Good will of suppliers
(10) Good will of the government
(11) Good will of the rest of the industry
(12) Good will of dealers and attraction of other dealers
(13) Ability to attract the best personnel
(14) Education of the public to the use of a product
(15) Education of the public to a point of view
(16) Good will of customers or supporters
(17) Investigation of the attitude of various groups toward the company
(18) Formulation and guidance of policies
(19) Fostering the viability of the society in which the organization functions
(20) Directing the course of change.

THE BENEFITS OF THESE ACTIVITIES

Prestige or "image." The familiarity and reputation of its name is among the greatest assets of any organization—whether it deals directly with the public or not. Everyone is influenced by reputation in choosing everything he buys and in every association he makes. The prominence of a name is taken as a sign of success, because reputation in industry can rarely be won without true accomplishment. Whether a company makes chewing gum or emery wheels, prestige will help to sell its goods, attract dealers, back up sales efforts, attract the best employees, please the stockholders, provide a bulwark against price-cutting competitors, and clear the way for introduction of new products. Phrasemakers from time to time promote other terms to define prestige: "Corporate image," "public personality," and others. A company's prestige determines the "climate" of receptivity toward all its messages—making them more or less effective than their intrinsic merit would warrant.

Promotion of products or services. Telling people

about products and interesting them in purchasing requires more than advertising and sales efforts. People's tastes and desires are developed by the unobtrusive influences about them—the things they read, radio and television, what they see in the movies, what they hear others talk about. These unobtrusive, nonselling influences have an immeasurable effect on their desire to buy. They support the direct-selling activities of advertising and merchandising, giving them an added dimension. They associate product names with the prestige of the company. The many ways in which public relations people can create desires are indispensable to the modern sales program.

Good will of the employees or members. Workers who feel that they are important parts of a worthwhile activity, who identify themselves with the creation of good things for others, and who understand the workings of their company, are likely to be satisfied employees. Giving them a sense of identification and satisfaction is the means toward employee good will. This involves expert analysis of the employee situation, preparation of plans to create good will, and activities to carry out these plans. The tools to choose from are many: employee publications; industrial recreation activities; presentation of awards for service and achievement; identifying symbols for all workers; plant community publicity of all kinds; developing the support of local churchmen, teachers, and club people; educational material for the employees, such as inserts in pay envelopes, periodical reports to employees, printed material on the nature of business, and the facts on earnings.

Prevention and solution of labor problems. Public relations can assist in stabilizing labor conditions through the type of employee relations activity just mentioned, and by special educational activities based on the conditions in the plant, the industry, and the union involved; by creating good will in the community, so that an atmosphere entirely favorable to the company is created that provides a barrier to the destructive efforts of agitators; by working closely with the industrial relations officer, providing aids that help him in his dealings with the union and by telling the company's story to the people and workers when a dispute threatens or breaks out.

The use of public relations as a labor-stabilizing aid is preventive as well as curative, and is most beneficial when it is carried on continuously rather than only when strike clouds appear.

Fostering the good will of communities in which the organization has units. The attitude of the community frequently determines the attitude of the workers toward the company. Workers are closely identified with the community and they unconsciously absorb the tenor of the locality's attitude. Not only does high standing in the community provide a bulwark of morale against unsettling influences, but it also attracts the better workers from the area when they join the labor force. High regard of the community also is invaluable when special assessments are being considered, when special privileges such as parking permits and zoning regulations are desired, when tax rates are being set, and in all other dealings that the company has with the local authorities.

Good will of the stockholders or constituents. When the investors in a company understand and appreciate its operations, they are more likely to retain their stocks for a long period, giving the corporation's securities a desirable stability. Stockholder confidence also is felt by other segments of the public, particularly when the stock is widely held. This confidence usually is reflected in higher market values for the company's stock—important in negotiating mergers as well as in seeking additional capital.

Professional attention to annual reports and periodic communications to the stockholders, as well as sound relations with the financial community and careful placement of news about the company in the financial sections of newspapers and in business publications, goes a long way toward winning loyalty among stockholders.

Overcoming misconceptions and prejudices. Investigation sometimes reveals that unfounded opinions about an organization are injuring its efforts to win good will, or actually hampering its operations. Prejudices that may exist because misinformation has been spread also threaten the success of a business. Analysis of the situation, plans for meeting it, and the dissemination of correct information can clear up these difficulties.

Forestalling attacks. Most people in the Western world today have been conditioned by television, where instant action applied to any "problem" brings a quick "solution"—in dramatic shows, in countless commercials, even in news and documentary programs. In this climate, activism has become an alluring means of seeking quick fulfillment of expectations. Resort to "action" meets the participants' view of how things get done, and feeds the hunger of media for "movement" and controversy. All types of groups, including Congressional committees and regulatory agencies, use the tactics of activism against all types of organizations. Forestalling these attacks and blunting their effects is increasingly a function of analysis, planning, and action of public relations.

Good will of suppliers. The importance of being on good terms with sources of supply is demonstrated during major strikes, when materials are scarce. Suppliers always have an important influence on the attitudes of others toward a company—prospective employees, customers, financial leaders, and so on. Formulating policies that build a reputation for good dealing and creating an opinion that the company will be an increasingly good customer because of its growing success are effective means of gaining the favorable attention of suppliers.

Good will of government. In most cases, the attitudes of government officials and public servants are based on what they know and hear about a company. In America the government is moved by the opinions and attitudes of the public; the soundness of a company's public relations usually determines its relations with public officials. If they are kept informed and if they feel that an organization operates in the public interest, government executives are less likely to make unreasonable demands or issue unfair restrictions. Good will of the government requires two factors: good will of the public and a sincere effort to keep government agencies informed about the company.

Good will of the rest of the industry. The respect of competitors is a great tribute to an organization, and has a marked influence on the attitude of others. It also leads to helpful cooperation, and strengthens a company's position in its dealings with trade associations and other industrial organizations.

Good will of dealers and attraction of other dealers. Keeping dealers informed is a necessary function of every business that does not sell directly to the customer. Retailers and wholesalers are anxious to know what the manufacturer is doing or planning, so they can make plans with a degree of assurance. Providing public relations aids for dealers, such as publicity material they can use locally, helps to win good will; and it is through the dealers that a company can perform its most effective work in building good will among consumers. Dealers must be educated to identify products with the manufacturer—and the prestige of the manufacturer must be made as great as possible. Frequently the public relations executive works closely with the sales staff in coordinating all dealings with dealers and wholesalers.

Ability to attract the best personnel. No organization's future is any better than the caliber of future executives it is able to attract. Research tends to confirm what many experts have long believed: that young people whose abilities and promise give them a choice of employers tend to choose those whose standing with the business world and the public are highest. Making a company or organization known and respected is necessary to assure its healthful development.

Education of the public to the use of a product. When an entirely new and unheralded product or service is to be promoted, it is necessary to capture the imagination of the public in order to make the item attain steady sales. There are numerous examples of products that have won a regular place on the American purchasing list by effective campaigns of educating the public to their use. Such things as oranges, sunglasses, musical instruments, bicycles, automatic washing machines, electric razors, and men's toiletries indicate how effective these campaigns can be. When a company brings out a new type of product, public relations must support advertising and the sales staff in capturing the public's imagination.

Education of the public to a point of view. When an organization seeks to win support for its method of operation, its principles, the system that supports it, or any other viewpoint, its most effective means are the channels of reaching the public that are constantly being utilized by public relations people. A utility, for instance, can systematically tell the people why private ownership benefits them; a store may wish to make the people understand its "no credit" policy; a manufacturer of automobiles may explain why it must recall cars to check possible defects. The guidance and assistance of the public relations organization assure effectiveness, favorable reactions, and low cost of such educational efforts.

Good will of customers or supporters. Establishing means of good relationships at the point where the purchaser meets the company or its product is one of the most important steps in building a company's good will. The manner in which the purchaser is treated, the services and information made available to him, and the handling of his complaints are crucial to his satisfaction with the product. Such considerations are part of the full-scale public relations program.

Investigation of the attitude of various groups

toward the organization. Taking the pulse of various groups' attitudes is an important phase of the good will program. It is important in planning to know what the employees think, how people regard the company in relation to its competitors, what they feel the company's weaknesses and strengths are. Often opinion research reveals unsuspected opportunities for developing neglected potentialities. This research is aside from the market analysis carried on by the sales and advertising departments.

Formulation and guidance of policies. Everything done by an organization that influences any group—employees, consumers, stockholders, the community, the general public—should be examined in advance for its possible effects on opinions and attitudes. The guidance and counsel of a public relations person who is constantly in touch with public reactions is as important to proper policy-forming as the attorney or the financial expert. Prevention of errors is a most important phase of good public relations.

Fostering the viability of the society in which the organization functions. As an element of the community (which includes the nation and, indeed, the world), the organization is an institutional citizen. It has a citizen's responsibilities to the community. Its ability to function will depend on the state of the community. Ability to attract personnel to any area is strongly influenced by the conditions there. Accordingly, most corporations find that the best public relations functions benefit the cosmos they operate in, benefit their own ability to function and grow, and project a favorable impression to their publics.

Directing the course of change. At its best, public relations is a bridge to change. It is a means to adjust to new attitudes that have been caused by change. It is a means of stimulating attitudes in order to create change. It seeks to help an organization see the whole of society together, rather than from one intensified viewpoint. It provides judgment, creativity, and skills in accommodating changing groups to each other.

Each of these objectives can be a basis for a program of its own, and increasing specialization is leading to segmented attention being given to each phase in many organizations. Yet *the reputation of every organization is indivisible*. It must be conceived and attended to in total before the proper perspective can be given to any elements of the total public relations spectrum. What is done in any one phase has early effects on many other phases. Each of these phases fits into the total of the organization's public relations considerations. Each of them, or any narrow group of them, is subordinate to the complete complex of factors that make up the rapport of the organization with the human ecology it deals with.

From this picture of the widely diversified factors in expert public relations, it can be seen that today public relations is a highly skilled field, requiring people, techniques, and facilities able to meet all the conditions involved.

In the chapters that follow, men and women who are experts in their fields outline the techniques and facilities necessary for successful development of good public relations in the major areas of human activity.

2

The Nature of Effective Communications

Philip Lesly

The ability to communicate is such a basic part of the human experience that it makes possible everything that distinguishes man from the rest of creation. The ability of one person to interrelate with another through exchange of ideas is a first step in differentiating the human being from other beings. The ability to record thoughts and information for others to respond to sooner or later is the basis for the accumulative thrust of all experience and knowledge. And the ability of one individual or group to deal with other groups through communications processes is integral to the entire social nature of the human species.

So there is hardly any subject more basic to understanding human processes and succeeding in human endeavors. Yet it is only recently that anything resembling scientific inquiry into this field has been active; and the definition of its basic principles is still in its early stages.

Recognition of the power of effective communication, however, goes back to antiquity. It was already well defined when Plato wrote in his *Dialogs:*

"Gorgias. What is there greater than the word which persuades the judges in the courts, or the Senators in the Council, or the citizens in the assembly, or at any other political meeting? If you have the power of uttering this word, you will have the physician your slave, and the trainer your slave, and the money maker of whom you talk will be found to gather treasures, not for himself, but for you who are able to speak and to persuade the multitude."

Communication is basic to the everyday existence of every modern individual and of every organization of any size. Even at the most primitive levels, man needs to know what the weather is likely to be, what supply of food can be expected, the movings of nearby tribes and herds, and many other things. Every organization needs to know what is going on among all the groups that impinge on it and how to reach the various publics it deals with. The degree of complexity of a society can be measured in terms of how much information, opinion, and speculative knowledge is needed to keep it operating with reasonable consistency.

Although we have seen in Chapter 1 that public relations encompasses much more than communication, the essence of public relations is in the broad definition of the term "communications." It incorporates (1) sensing the state of rapport or lack of it with the public involved; (2) interpreting that state in terms of the organization and its objectives; (3) assimilating the implications of this interpretation and adjusting the posture and thrust of the organization accordingly; (4) developing the thoughts and messages that represent what the organization wants to project to the public, and (5) transmitting those thoughts.

FORMS OF COMMUNICATION

Since communication encompasses so much of the spectrum of human activity, full treatment of it (even in its present partially developed state) fills libraries. For simplification, we can say that there are six major forms of human communication:

1. Oral
2. Written
3. Signs and symbols

4. Gestures (such as finger movements, facial expressions, etc.)
5. Non-verbal sound, such as music, drum signals, etc.
6. Combinations of any of these, such as oral language, music, and visual happenings on television; or oral language and gestures in conversation

Communication as it involves the public relations man encompasses all of these forms, although it is predominantly *mass* communication rather than exchanges between individuals.

EFFECTIVE AND INEFFECTIVE COMMUNICATION

Largely because most comments about the communications process have been prepared by communicators, such as Plato, the potency of the communications process has been overrated through the centuries. While it's true that often deliberate communications processes bring about monumental developments and changes, it is also true that a great deal of communications effort either fails or reacts to the detriment of the source. It is in seeking understanding of causes of effectiveness and ineffectiveness that the researches and conjectures about communication have taken place. Whether the communication actually occurs—whether the conceptualized ideas and information originating with the sender are received in similar form by the intended recipient—depends on a number of conditions and circumstances. These include:

1. The *predisposition* of the intended recipient. This is a composite of his heritage, his outlook on life and on the subject of the communication that has accumulated through his lifetime, his fears, training, group memberships, and so on.
2. The innate propensity to believe what is comforting to one's psyche or that shields it from guilt or fear.
3. The basic needs of the individual, such as individual worth, group acceptance, self-admiration, security, skill, knowledge, and power.
4. The basic need for harmony between the individual's needs and desires, and the social demands and pressures on him, including conscience and other forces. The person inherently moves toward acceptance of what enhances harmony and shields himself from what might create dissonance within him.
5. What Stuart Chase[1] refers to as the fidelity of the message. Does it reach the recipient in the shape in which it was sent? This involves the physics of transmission—sound waves, light waves, and so on; the clarity of both transmission and reception, including such matters as whether accents are recognizable or colors are clear; and the semantics involved: Do sender and auditor give the same precise meanings to words and symbols?
6. The skill and experience of the communicator—*the overriding factor in all communications efforts.* Masterful skills can work wonders; ineptness or amateurishness can create directly opposite results. Is he sharply attuned to "getting inside the skin" of the recipient, understanding how he will receive and respond to any messages? Is he a master at formulating and projecting messages so they will reach the recipient under optimum circumstances and be readily decoded into the desired form?

It can thus be seen that in many instances the barriers against a communications transfer are greater than the influences favoring it.

As pointed out by J.A.C. Brown[2]: "The will to believe is more potent than any mere experience and emotion is stronger than reason in the vast majority of people." Berelson and Steiner[3] in their summation of findings from many studies reached this conclusion.

> People tend to misperceive or misinterpret persuasive communications in accordance with their own predispositions, by evading the message or by distorting it in a favorable direction.
>
> For example, anti-Semites tend to misread the tolerance propaganda put out by Jewish groups; political partisans misinterpret the position of their candidate to bring it more nearly into line with their own position on the issues; partisans on both sides tend to judge neutral speeches as favoring their own point of view; partisans are more likely than others to accept as "fact" those news reports supporting their own position.

[1] Chase, Stuart, *Danger—Men Talking,* Parents' Magazine Press, 1969.
[2] *Techniques of Persuasion,* by J.A.C. Brown, Penguin, 1967.
[3] *Human Behavior,* by Bernard Berelson & Gary A. Steiner, Harcourt, Brace & World, 1964, p. 536. This book is highly recommended.

The propensity for screening incoming communications to shape them to one's own predilection was found in early studies by Douglas Waples of what people get out of their reading: "What reading does to people is not nearly so important as what people do to reading."[4]

Influence of group membership. Emphasizing one element of the predisposition of the individual—his identification with various groups—Berelson and Steiner concluded: "On matters involving group norms, the more attached people are to the group, or the more active within it, the more their membership determines their response to communications."[5]

W. Phillips Davison[6] points out:

> As a result of . . . cultural and individual selective mechanisms each person gives his attention to different portions of the stream of communication. If, for example, a group made up of people with varying interests and from a number of countries is given fifteen minutes to examine a newspaper and each individual is then asked to write down the headlines of the stories he remembers, it is usually found that every person recalls a different list. Each will be likely to remember items dealing with his own country, and most will recall items dealing with their own professional or non-professional interests.

The predisposition not only determines to a large extent what the communication is perceived by the recipient to be, but also the degree to which he exposes himself to an idea. Berelson and Steiner found[7] that "people are more likely to talk about controversial matters with like-minded people than with those who do not share their views."

Those who are already interested in a subject and inclined toward it are the ones who are most open to receive new communications about it: "Those who read about a topic also tend to listen, and those who pay attention at one time also tend to pay attention at another."[8]

Out of this pattern J.A.C. Brown[9] spoke of " . . . the Law of Primacy . . . that the earlier an experience the more potent its effect since it influences how later experiences will be interpreted . . ."

Varying receptivity. There is also a wide range of what might be called *susceptibility* to being moved by communications. "People with low self-esteem (i.e., those persons high in measures of social inadequacy, inhibition of aggression, and depressive tendencies) are more likely to be influenced by persuasive communications than are those with high self-esteem; but those with acute neurotic symptoms (i.e., neurotic anxiety or obsessional reactions) are more likely to be resistant. Those low in self-esteem are easily persuasible by others because they lack character of their own; the neurotic are too disturbed, too self-concerned, or too negativistic to pay attention or to care."[10]

Although the recent predominance of television as an influential force in shaping the communications habits of the populace may be changing this, Berelson and Steiner[11] found that "the higher the education, the greater the reliance on print; the lower the education, the greater the reliance on aural and picture media."

Among the most important variable factors determining where communications are effective is the rapport between the source and the intended recipient.

> The more trustworthy, credible or prestigious the communicator is perceived to be, the less manipulative his intent is considered to be and the greater the immediate tendency to accept his conclusions. However, within reasonable limits, the credibility of the source has little or no influence on the transmission of *factual* information.
>
> When the audience has little or no prior knowledge of the communicator's trustworthiness, it tends to decide a question on the basis of the content itself—i.e., the conformity of the content to predispositions. When the audience does expect or attribute manipulative intent . . . it develops resistance to acceptance of the message.[12]

Accordingly, Berelson and Steiner concluded:[13] "The effect of communication programs that try to convert opinions on controversial issues is usually

---

[4]"The Relation of Subject Interests to Actual Reading," Library Quarterly, 2, 1932, pp. 42-70.

[5]op. cit., p. 539.

[6]Davison, W. Phillips, "The Nature of Effective Communications," Third Ed., *Public Relations Handbook*, Prentice-Hall, 1967.

[7]ibid, page 529.

[8]ibid, page 532.

[9]op. cit., page 39.

[10]Berelson and Steiner, op. cit., p. 548.

[11]ibid, page 533.

[12]ibid, pp. 537-8.

[13]ibid, page 542.

slight. If the issue matters to the audience, predispositions block the conversion. If the issue does not matter, it gets little attention."

Klapper said:[14] "Communications research strongly indicates that persuasive mass communication is in general more likely to reinforce the existing opinions of its audience than it is to change such opinions."

Edward R. Murrow, the late television commentator and head of the United States Information Agency, pointed out that he who seeks to influence opinion can accelerate a trend in public opinion, but he cannot reverse it.

And Brown[15] came to the conclusion that "... there is every reason to believe (that) well-meant but incompetently conceived propaganda ... can ... have positively undesirable (results) or even ... lead to effects diametrically opposed to those desired."

Research in this field has advanced to the point, therefore, where observers are now conscious of how much more difficult it is to communicate than was commonly believed. Much communications activity appears to communicate but actually fails to reach, to be observed by, to motivate the intended audience; and often it backfires completely. It is vital, therefore, for any user of communication, which means everyone, to recognize the complexities and pitfalls involved and to narrow the range of error before proceeding.

COMPLEXITY OF COMMUNICATION

For many years it was generally felt that the essence of mass persuasion was exposure of an idea, a name, or a product to the desired audience. Success was thought to be measured by the number of people reached and the number of times exposure was attained. As we have seen, developing knowledge of how the human mind responds to efforts to reach it indicates the inadequacy of the exposure theory. Some of the major factors that determine the effectiveness of any communications effort, aside from exposure, are now known to include:

(1) The mental posture of the intended audience. There is a very wide range of mental capacities, even within any specified group or classification of people. For simplification, however, we may generalize that most people tend to have either "abstract" or "concrete" minds. The abstract thinker is the writer, the artist, the idea man, who lives with intangibles, is excited by unseen prospects, and seeks the unknown and the new. The concrete thinker is the production man, the accountant, the lawyer—the practical man who generally must feel or see something before he recognizes its existence; who is trained to resist as untrustworthy anything that cannot be measured or calculated.

Both of these types are essential to the proper working of society and indeed to the success of any substantial organization. Yet when a suggestion for a course of action is presented to a mixed group of both types, the task of the communicator is most difficult. When any idea, concept, product, or service is exposed to a group made up of both types, the range of acceptance by the individuals can vary from complete to entirely negative.

Wherever possible and practical, it is the task of the communicator to determine the mental posture of the various elements in the public he seeks to reach, to separate the "abstracts" from the "concretes," and to frame his communications in the appropriate form for each group. With the "concretes" he may utilize charts, tabulations, diagrams, photographs, mock-ups and models, and any other devices that tend to make his message tangible. For the "abstracts" he needs to stimulate the imagination, inspire the enthusiasm, and whet the appetite.

(2) Increased education, a greater share in running things, and other liberating factors have elevated the sophistication of the American people, who have assumed an attitude of skepticism toward communications seeking to influence them. As pointed out by *Business Week*:[16]

> People are suspicious of hogwash. They are pausing to evaluate. They feel they have been fooled and don't want to be fooled again.

Rodney Campbell[17] points out: "There is an increasing requirement for factual presentation of significant information and an increasing impatience with trivia, with hard sell, with propaganda. There is a new age of actualism dawning."

As a result, patently insincere communications not only are ineffective but build resistance that will prevent acceptance of future efforts.

(3) With audiences sophisticated and skeptical of

---

[14]Klapper, Joseph T., *The Effects of Mass Communication,* Free Press, 1960, pp. 49-50.

[15]op. cit., page 10.

[16]Business Week, No. 1514 (September 6, 1958), p. 126.

[17]In communication to the author, April, 1970.

efforts to influence them, with the great diversity of mental "bents" that must be accounted for, and with the vast number of would-be communications directed toward each individual every day, the function of public relations is to inject ideas and information into that broad stream of communication. There they will be caught up with all the other ideas and information, be affected by them, and course their way into the screening processes of the audience. The skill of the public relations man is in selecting the means and the context of the information he puts into the stream of communication, in making it appeal to the recipient in his own frame of reference; in timing; in juxtaposition with all the other things being made known and appealing for his interest. The effectiveness of the public relations function will depend on how well information and ideas it communicates are adopted by the individual, so that they become part of his own body of thought from which he draws his attitudes. Because of its need for these talents, public relations demands the abilities and skills of true scientists of public opinion, rather than information producers, ballyhoo artists, or other narrowly specialized technicians.

(4) For some time there has been a theory that there is at least a two-step flow of communications, through what have come to be known as "opinion leaders." The concept was first clearly expressed by Lazarsfeld, Berelson, and Gaudet[18] when they suggested that "Ideas often flow *from* radio and print *to* the opinion leaders and *from* them to the less active sections of the population."

This concept of the flow of influence is diagrammed in Figure 2-1.

As pointed out by Klapper[19] in discussing this study:

> The "opinion leaders" who exercise such influence were found to be widely dispersed through all social classes, and to be much like the persons they influenced. "Compared with the rest of the population, (however), opinion leaders were found to be considerably more exposed to the radio, to the newspapers, and to magazines; that is, to the formal media of communication." . . .
>
> These specific others, or "opinion leaders," or "influentials" may serve a following of one, of three or four, or of somewhat more, but they

[18]Lazarsfeld, Berelson, and Gaudet, *The People's Choice*, New York: Columbia University Press, 1948.

[19]op. cit.

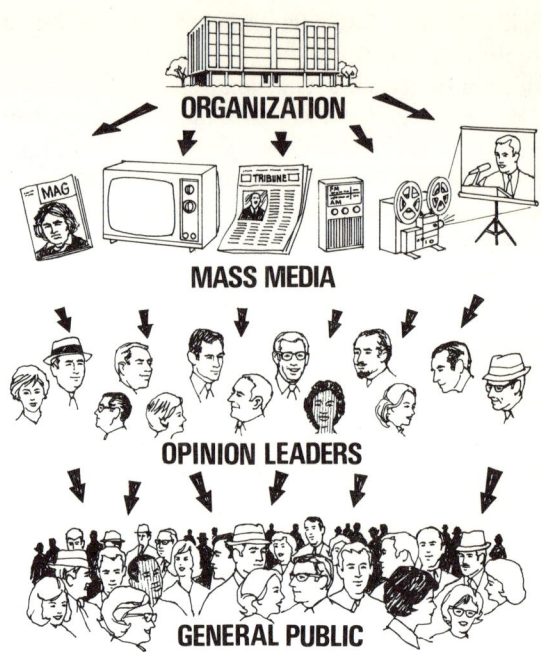

Figure 2-1. The traditional concept of the flow of influence, based on a theory propounded in 1948.

> typically do so in reference to only one topic; the fashion leader, for example, is not likely to be a marketing leader, nor is the physician who influences others to adopt a new drug more likely than his colleagues to influence their views on public issues. . . The leader, however, is typically found to be more exposed than are his followers to the media appropriate to his sphere of influence . . . After the follower has been influenced by the opinion leader, mass communication may provide material which the follower selectively attends or perceives to buttress his newly adopted opinion.

While the concept of the "opinion leaders" is revealing, the problems involved in locating them are generally insurmountable. Because they are not clearly identifiable by position or otherwise, on the basis of this theory it remains necessary to concentrate on the mass media from which the opinion leaders tend to derive the fuel for the development of the opinions they pass on to others. A mass medium need not, however, be a national magazine, a newspaper, or a television show, for a specialized publication read by a few thousand specialists in a given profession, a group of women's club members, or a group of church leaders may be the avenue whereby the ideas are brought to the attention of the opinion leaders among the readers. However, there is evidence that some media are

THE NATURE OF EFFECTIVE COMMUNICATIONS

far more suited to imparting information and ideas to opinion leaders in the areas they cover than are others, and this provides the public relations man with the area of selectivity for his communications.

(5) Now seeming to counterbalance the two-step process is the rise of instant visibility of events and issues. Television brings "reality" and "meaning" directly into the lives of the mass audience. Sensing this, Presidents since Kennedy have geared their approach to reaching people directly through TV appearances.

The impact of television, as well as a great increase in educational levels, affluence, and free time, has transformed the way influence is generated. It is now clear that there are at least three separate groups in the "leader" category and that most of them are increasingly removed from close contact with the general public. They are:

1. *Vocal Activists*, who devote themselves to propounding a cause.
2. *Opinion Leaders*—mass media and key educators.
3. *Power Leaders*—legislators, government officials, judges, and regulators who have the power to take actions that affect organizations and society.

The focal group increasingly is the Power Leaders. They can actually make things happen, and increasingly they feel they should initiate actions that affect private organizations and individuals rather than move only when public demands or needs are felt. The vocal activists, media, influential individuals and groups, and the general public have input to the Power Leaders but have little power themselves.

However, the input that gets to the Power Leaders is much greater from the vocal activists and the opinion leaders than from the public and most private organizations.

The present pattern of the flow of influence is diagrammed in Figure 2-2.

As a result of this new pattern, the Power Leaders—responding to the far heavier input from vocal activists and opinion leaders than from the private sector or general public—often greatly overrate the actual dissatisfaction among the public on any given issue. They tend to assume that the disproportionate impressions they receive from the small articulate groups are what the public at large feels. Often in responding to these strong inputs with alarm and proposals for new government

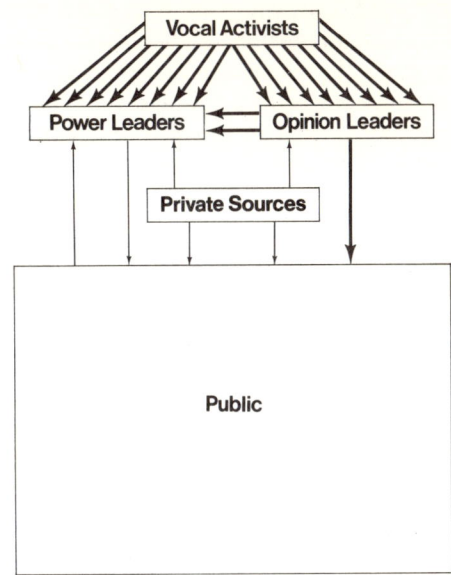

Figure 2-2

controls, they stimulate greater public dissatisfaction than would exist otherwise.

(6) As the proportion increases of people who have grown up with television as the primary influence, the whole pattern of how ideas are established has changed. People who are oriented to instant visual involvement tend to be impatient with complicated interplay between elements of society. They have less patience with "working things out." They see all problems resolved in a thirty-minute drama and all commercials assuring answers to desires. This tends to create a euphoric certainty that all things are attainable readily and quickly, and a resultant frustration when answers don't come easily, but, instead, problems grow. Communicating with these people requires graphic, action orientation.

(7) The primacy of visibility determines the level of importance given to any subject. When activism against the Vietnam War was high in late 1969, America was losing about 85 men a week. At the same time, more than 1,000 people a week were lost in automobile accidents. But the war was highly visible and had been made into an emotional issue. Automobile accidents are seldom shown on TV, a camera is rarely focused on bereaved relatives, a mother is not shown receiving a folded flag from the casket of a son who died in a smashed car. The toll in Vietnam was terrible, but it was its visibility that

made it a flaming issue on the streets while the slaughter on the highways got minor attention.

(8) It must be remembered that in most cases the person selects the media to which he really exposes himself. Appearance of a message in a medium to which he has elected to expose himself predetermines a likely disposition toward at least recognizing and considering that message.

This is increasingly a vital factor in weighing the comparative value of *discretionary* media exposure (editorial material in newspapers and magazines, broadcast content of TV and radio, theatrical motion pictures, books) and *imposed* media exposure (advertisements, TV and radio commercials, literature not requested by the recipient, commercial motion pictures, propaganda speeches). Without willing exposure by selection of the medium, many people cannot be reached by many messages, regardless of how much is spent or how massive the efforts to impose the message on them.

However, where the message is not critcal to the person's psychic assurance, as pointed out by Herbert E. Krugman,[20] under certain circumstances, with massive communications efforts, it is possible to get a specific concept to take hold.

(9) As pointed out by Elihu Katz,[21] there is great variation in how diffusible various messages will be. Some matters involve much more risk or danger to the respondent's psychic equilibrium, and some demand more extensive and pervasive changes than others. It is not possible to judge precisely what a person may assimilate by studying what he has previously assimilated because no two messages involve the same degree of effect on his psyche.

(10) There is what is called the "source effect" in communications. As pointed out in a milestone study by Theodore Levitt of Harvard:[22]

> "... a company's generalized reputation has an important bearing on how its sales prospects make buying decisions."

As noted in Chapter 1, it is probable that this effect of reputation—the net effect of the total public relations of the organization—influences the attitudes of prospective shareholders and employees, government officials, civic leaders, and all other publics.

---

[20]*The Obstinate Audience,* Donald E. Payne, editor—Foundation for Research on Human Behavior, Ann Arbor, Mich., 1965.

[21]ibid.

[22]Theodore Levitt, *Industrial Purchasing,* Cambridge: Harvard University Graduate School of Business, 1965.

(11) For communication to take place, the audience must be in what might be called a "posture of receptivity." As we have seen, the adoption of a message by its object results from a complex combination of preconditioning influences. Aside from those that make up the character of the recipient himself, there are the many previous exposures to the source of any given message. This is of extreme importance in public relations; it's becoming recognized that the favorable inclination of an individual toward all messages from a given source is the result of his total experience with that source. The character of the organization as exemplified by its actions, the sincerity and trustworthiness of its previous statements, the value provided in its products or services, and other influences set the stage for the enthusiasm or rejection with which the organization's communication is met.

This means, of course, that when effective public relations have been practiced for an organization—when its actions and its statements have developed a positive image and a degree of good will—not only is a reservoir of support developed, but every other message from that source will receive much more acceptability. In practice, for instance, this results in very expensive advertising investments returning far greater benefits per dollar when the "posture of receptivity" has been developed through good public relations practice. The welcome a company's salesmen receive when they call on prospective customers; the interest of a prize college senior in talking with the company's personnel recruiters; the eagerness with which the investment public greets a new offering of securities—all become far more favorable as a result of the modest costs of the sound public relations program.

(12) As we will see in Chapter 47, it is now known to be very unlikely that ideas can be sold through direct, overt messages similar to the hard-sell advertising that is effective in selling products if there is no previous "posture of receptivity" to the idea. Where a negative opinion exists or there is indifference, obvious efforts to inject one's opinions into the minds of others is at best ineffective and at worst increases resistance.

(13) There is a "threshold of consciousness" that must be reached and passed before an idea becomes a factor in the attitude of an individual or a group. With millions of subjects attempting to intrude upon the consciousness of each individual, the process through which a concept passes from complete obscurity through the various stages of aware-

HOW PHYSICIANS GET THEIR INFORMATION

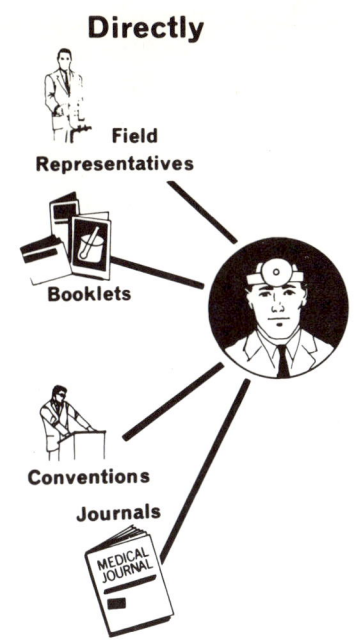

Figure 2-3. Information and influence reach persons from many directions. This part of a two-phase diagram indicates those that are directed specifically at the physician.

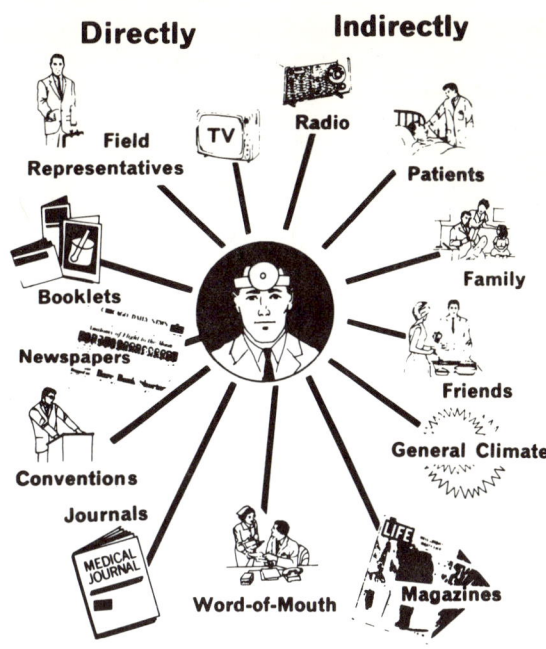

Figure 2-4. When the many indirect avenues to the physician are added, the "multiple-channel effect" surrounds him with the subject and his awareness is greatly increased.

ness in one's mind, until at last it "is there" and an influence, is one of the great unexplored areas of psychology. There is no doubt, however, that every idea that comes to have an influence passes through the screen of resistance that the individual must erect to block out the great majority of clamoring ideas seeking his attention, to become a part of his mental reality and resources. Whether it is one of thousands of attractive girls who somehow becomes what the public knows as Raquel Welch, or a conception of social change requiring a broadening of one's horizons to encompass formerly foreign interests, it is only through a multitude of impressions coming from many directions that the threshold is crossed and the concept imbeds itself.

(14) From this we can discern that establishing an idea in the public mind calls for a "multiple-channel approach." If the idea of owning a boat is expressed a dozen times by one's teen-age son, for instance, it is quite different from having twelve different respected people, in a dozen different situations and circumstances, talk enthusiastically about the fun and excitement of boating. When a multiple combination of impressions impinges on one's attention, the impression is created that the idea is all-pervading, that it is "the thing to do." It therefore has considerably greater influence. The same number of messages is likely to be far more effective if they are directed through many channels—newspapers, radio commentators, television programs, inclusion in motion pictures, word-of-mouth discussion, club meetings, and other channels—than repeatedly through the same means. It is no longer likely that successful communication can be confined to a company newspaper, or just advertisements in the local press, or any other one or two outlets. Public relations to be effective must be as versatile and as all-encompassing of communications channels as the available resources and talents will permit.

When Ivy Lee, Edward L. Bernays, and other early practitioners were formulating their methods, the world of communication was simple and confined. In the U.S. three wire services, a few magazines, and a few major newspapers constituted the key channels of communication. The educated public that exposed itself to ideas or took a part in events was a small fraction of the population. Under these conditions, one staged event or one article in a magazine could alter public opinion.

Today we are experiencing an explosion of the scope that influencing of public opinion must cover.

Besides the wire services and major newspapers, there are many more magazines, plus the multiplying forces of television, radio, motion pictures, and mass-distributed books. A majority of the population represents the public to be reached, and it is educated, diffuse, and skeptical. Except for an extremely rare occasion such as the first landing on the moon or the assassination of President Kennedy, no one event achieves general recognition immediately.

People must be reached by many channels, over a period of time, in the contexts of many diverse outlooks and windows on the world.

(15) The more closely a communication is beamed to a specific audience or single recipient, the more likely it is to be received and accepted. "Communications directed to particular audiences are more effective than those directed to the 'public at large,'" concluded Berelson and Steiner.[23]

(16) The more sharply the key point of a communication is focused for the recipient, the more likely he is to grasp it. At the same time, it must not be condescending or seem to insult his intelligence. The recipient should be led to draw the conclusion and yet not feel that his conclusions are being imposed upon him. Berelson and Steiner's research showed: "Especially on complex matters, the explicit drawing of conclusions by the communicator is more effective in bringing about audience acceptance than relying upon the audience to draw its own conclusions from the material presented—and presumably this is the more so the less intelligent or the less educated the audience."[24]

(17) The early reaction to events may disguise their actual effects. Great publicity and furor may seem to create public opinion because of their immediacy, visibility, and force. But often there is a reaction against that furor that is more substantial and lasting. The uproar caused by the Students for a Democratic Society in 1968—especially in disrupting the Democratic convention—was aimed at grabbing public attention and radicalizing millions of young people. The tumult they created was one of the most-exposed news events in recent years. Yet studies made by the University of Michigan after the election showed that more young people had been moved to voting for right-wing candidates than had been moved to follow the SDS. Much of the public desire to "cool off" the racial issues at the start of the '70s was due to reaction against the trumpeted violence of the Black Panthers.

(18) The number and types of media have expanded greatly and there is a vast range of subjects that clamor for the individual's attention. The days when a person read or at least looked at everything exposed to him are over. The individual is free to choose the communications he will expose himself to. Thus there is almost complete separation between *discretionary* and *imposed* exposure to media.

When the person chooses to expose himself to the subject matter of a TV show or a magazine article, for instance, he[25] makes his own choice of what he will be interested in . . . what he will consider affecting his attitudes. When efforts are made to impose messages on him (advertising, self-pleading literature, captive presentations), today's independent person often resists. He has his guard up against being influenced by what he hasn't chosen to expose himself to.

It is necessary to make the person's self-interest so visible, immediately, he feels the urge to expose his psyche to the message.

(19) There are a number of ways that efforts to communicate actually have the opposite effect and "discommunicate." They result in failure or even a counterproductive reaction. The most common forms of "discommunication" are:

• *Putting art ahead of communication.* The purpose of graphic materials in public relations is to aid the communication process. When artists or designers emphasize their creativity or personality at the expense of conveying the message, discommunication results. This takes various forms: Type treatments that defy legibility repel the audience instead of communicating. (See Figure 2-5.) Multiple, repeated fast cuts in films thwart the audience's efforts to make out what's shown. Multimedia presentations often drown the audience in impressions, but communicate too little. Color combinations are chosen deliberately to affront the eye but make the subject or words illegible. Stylized artwork or photos often convey no message to the reader.

Artwork is helpful if it conveys an impression in addition to its inherent meaning; but impression for the sake of impression is phony and fails.

• *The lure of "controlled" communication.* It is

---

[23]op. cit., p. 540.
[24]ibid., p. 552-3.

[25]The male pronoun is used only because of the restriction of the English language. It applies equally to females.

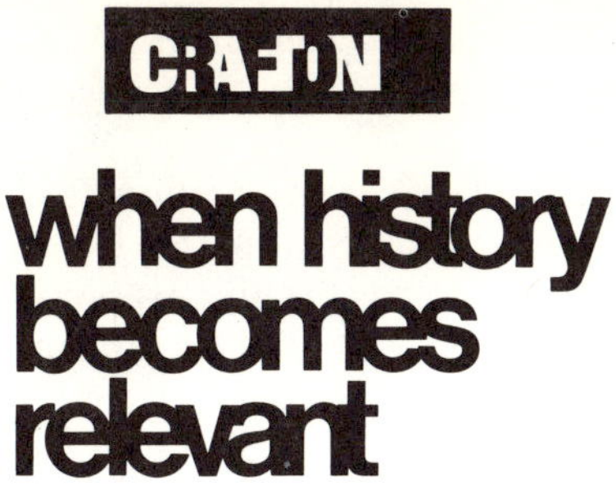

CRAFON
when history becomes relevant

Figure 2-5. These are two examples, from one issue of one magazine, of how overreaching for effect in typography can reduce legibility and thereby interfere with communication.

tempting to try to project information and ideas to the audience exactly as one would like them, rather than through the screening of third parties such as editors. However, we have seen that imposed communication materials are far less effective than those the audience is exposed to by choice or in another context. Thus idea advertising,[26] literature not requested by the recipient, and other "controlled" materials often discommunicate.

• *Names that communicate nothing.* The name of an organization, like that of a person, is a primary source of the impression it makes. Efforts to devise "neutral" names discard this vital source of impression and often cause only confusion.[27]

• *The snobbery of jargon.* Segments of society are being separated by the languages they create. Special terminologies that result from increasing specialization make it harder for various groups to understand each other. But increasingly there is another factor: snobbery. People who want to make sure others recognize they are on a different level deliberately develop jargon that sets them apart. Examples are "motivational deprivation" for laziness; "an interrelated collectivity" for group; "conceptualize" for imagine. Often when a jargon term becomes well known it is changed: "dementia praecox" became "schizophrenia" and "infantile paralysis" became "poliomyelitis."

• *Euphemisms.* Efforts to becloud a subject are treated by today's forthright and skeptical public as evasions. Examples are: "Assigned to committee for reconsideration" for rejected; "discontinued" or "laid off" or "given early retirement" for fired; "deaccession" for unloading an unprofitable division; and "inventory shrinkage" for losses by theft.

[26]See Chap. 47.
[27]See Chap. 55.

• *Condescension.* Communication is a form of courtship: the source is a suitor who presses his case with logic, ardor, charm, and persuasion to overcome the indifference or reticence of his intended. A suitor who is intent on demonstrating his superiority over his love object and disdain for her interests is likely to remain celibate. Yet people who are supposed to be professional communicators, seeking to beguile their audiences, often repel them. They show that the viewer is a target for their own objectives. When a communicator is eager to exhibit his own stature and superior intellect, he shows he is manipulating the audience rather than serving it. He shows condescension for his readers or viewers rather than respect. That exhibits the primacy of his ego over his purpose. Ego is singular, likely to be massaged in solitude. Communication is plural, involving interaction with others, and makes it possible to win over multitudes. Ego is the enemy of communication.

• *The lost art of expression.* Many recent studies have shown that the ability to express oneself both in writing and speech has been declining steadily. While the complexities of society increase and make the need for clear expression greater than ever, the prevalence of sloppy and even semi-literate communication material has been growing. Probably the most vital single attribute of the communicator is exceptional skill in expression. This goes beyond mere competence in putting together manuscripts that contain the necessary information and arguments. Some people use language like underwear, merely to cover the subject; others use it like lingerie, to show it at its best. They are the ones who sway attitudes and make things happen.

In addition to the treatment of writing skill in Chapter 50, this advice by George Orwell, author of *1984* and *Animal Farm,* from *Shooting an Elephant and Other Essays* is pertinent to all public relations persons:

> A scrupulous writer, in every sentence that he writes, will ask himself at least four questions, thus: What am I trying to say? What words will express it? What image or idiom will make it clearer? Is this image fresh enough to have an effect? And he will probably ask himself two more: Could I put it more shortly? Have I said anything that is avoidably ugly?

To this should be added: Who am I trying to reach and what is that audience's orientation?

• *Embracing what's new but a step backward.* As seen in Figure 2-6, modern *sans serif* type, now wide-

Both the development of far-off sources and the implementation of emerging technologies will, however, require time—a matter of years, in most cases—and tremendous sums of money. For these and other reasons, we require both short-term and long-term plans. The short-term objective is to acquire as much gas as possible which is now available or shortly will be, and to adjust summer sales and storage patterns to provide maximum capability for meeting the peak-day and winter season needs of present customers. The objective of the long-term planning is to obtain large new reserves with which to backstop present customer commitments well into the future, and hopefully, to serve more of the prospective new customers who are now or will be seeking service.

assistance for medical research and medical education; active participation in industry efforts to lower medical costs; sponsorship of innovative programs to care for the medically indigent; and experimental research into new methods of health care delivery — such as Health Maintenance Organizations, outpatient clinics, etc.

Figure 2-6. San serif type (top) has a modern appearance and is effective in headlines and other short treatments. However, serif type (below) is easier to read and more restful in the body type of booklets and other printed material.

ly used for printed materials, is harder to read and more tiring than *serif* type, which is more traditional.

(20) From the evolving principles we can sum up the necessary elements that lead to *conviction* and *motivation* in the mind of the object of communication. The primary elements are:

• *Acceptability*. Unless the source of the information is respected and objective, communication is unlikely to take place. The statement or claim must reach the person when he is pre-set to acceptance—when he has opened his mind to a spokesman he is willing to have invade the privacy of his inner convictions. An unknown or suspected spokesman causes him to close his mind and even to resent the person who makes the effort to change his thinking.

• *Compatibility*. The message must relate to the recipient's posture of thought and identity. People reject or distort whatever is alien to their heritage, background, and sources of self-assurance. They respond to what reinforces their conception of themselves and their view of the world.

• *Intensity*. The degree of impact of the message is determined by the prominence it receives in competition with many other efforts to capture the attention. Information presented casually or in a mass of other information has much less impact than information presented prominently and in isolation.

• *Visibility*. The communication that is most nearly real, that involves the person by making him almost a part of it, has the greatest power to sway him. In early days it was the drama and the "revivalist" platform artist that were most activating; today it is television and the film.

• *Pervasiveness*. When a subject appears to be all around him, a person tends to accept it and take it for granted. It becomes part of the atmosphere in which he lives. He finds himself surrounded by it and absorbs the climate itself of the idea.

• *Variety of impressions*. Pervasiveness results from encountering a subject in a wide variety of ways. As we have seen, this multiple-channel approach to persuasion is vital.

• *Persuasiveness*. No amount of impact, variety, or pervasiveness will influence attitudes and opinions unless the context of the communications is persuasive. It must be most deftly developed to reach into the subconscious of the person and tune to his urges, interests, and desires. Mere expression of the communicator's point of view will not succeed; it must be attuned to the mental and emotional bent of the audience.

HOW TO INFLUENCE BEHAVIOR

Although there clearly are a great many barriers to motivating an audience to accept the viewpoint of the communicator, the full weight of history and everyday experience indicates that it is often achieved.

Davison[28] points out:

> There seem to be several reasons why, in spite of the powerful tendency to maintain stable behavior patterns, a communicator can influence people's actions and attitudes under certain conditions. The most important of these reasons, which overlap somewhat with each other, are the following:
>
> (1) Most people are on the lookout for changes in those aspects of their environment that are relevant to them. If they are informed of such a change they may adjust their behavior or attitudes appropriately, especially if this adjustment does not conflict with other established behavior or attitude patterns.

[28]op. cit.

(2) In spite of their efforts to keep informed about things that are important to them, people are not always able to acquire the information they want. The stream of communications may be inadequate. They may wish to do something and not know how.
(3) In very few cases is there *complete* harmony within the body of habits, attitudes, and information that a person has acquired through his previous experience. People are often predisposed in two or more directions at the same time. Communications can sometimes reinforce one tendency so that it prevails over the others.
(4) Many people have a large number of interests and cannot keep track of them all equally. Communications can focus attention on particular subjects, sometimes at the expense of others.
(5) Similarly, some attitudes are latent. A predisposition exists but does not result in action unless it is triggered. Communications can perform this triggering function.
(6) People are faced constantly with the necessity of acquiring information and developing attitudes on new subjects. Communications can provide the desired information and can furnish a basis for the new attitudes.
(7) Even deeply rooted behavior patterns sometimes prove unable to satisfy basic needs. When this happens, due to a radical change in environment or other reasons, people are faced with the necessity of developing new behavior patterns if they wish to avoid serious maladjustment. Communications can then exert a powerful effect by suggesting other patterns of adjustment.

Exploring each of these can provide useful clues:

Reporting changes in the relevant environment. A clearly seen change can most readily bring about a change in viewpoint. Perhaps the most striking example is the attitude of Americans toward the Japanese and German peoples, both of which had been the objects of hatred during World War II. Within a few years, observations showing that both groups had become like Americans in economic and social outlook and especially in supporting comparatively democratic regimes brought about what would seem to be remarkable conversions.

Much advertising is devoted to focusing prospects' attention on new products or features that are intended to change the person's attitude toward that class of product.

Enhancing existing patterns of behavior. Determining what information people want and providing it is a frequently effective means of gaining their good will and support. Much of American aid to underdeveloped countries has been in providing information on better farming practices, improved health procedures, and other matters of clear benefit to the recipients.

Selectively reinforcing existing attitudes. Many objectives of an individual may be in conflict, although kept below the conscious level. For instance, he may want both better schools and lower taxes. By selectively focusing on the strong points of one of these, the communicator may enable the person to settle on that one in his mind even though he must give up the desirability of the other one.

Focusing attention. The more complex society becomes, the greater the number of exposures to viewpoints that confront the individual. Often these are not in harmony with each other. By focusing on any one of them and bringing it to the fore in the individual's mind, it can take dominance over the others. For instance, there often are many issues in an election campaign that are of some interest to a voter. A candidate who focuses on one of them to the point of making that voter strongly aware of his self-interest in it is able to get his vote even though he may not conform to the voter's viewpoint on the other issues.

Activating existing attitudes. A person may be a silently loyal alumnus of his college but do nothing to help it. If communications bring his loyalty to the active stage, he may be persuaded to contribute funds, recommend the school to the prize high school students in his area, and attend its football games.

Developing new interests and attitudes. A person may have never thought of participating in skiing. Yet he may see a thrilling and beautiful motion picture of skiing in the Swiss Alps and be motivated to undertake the sport.

Suggesting new patterns of behavior. When confronted with a major change in condition, an individual develops a strong receptiveness to information that will help him accommodate. For instance, a young man who is drafted into the Army may have given no thought to the procedures of military service and how to thrive. Finding himself about to be in uniform, he may be a prime audience for information that will help him in the new environment he faces.

SECTION II

What Public Relations Includes

3

The Dynamics and Role of Public Affairs

TOM M. HOPKINSON is president of T.M. Hopkinson & Co., a New York headquartered consulting organization specializing in public affairs and corporate and financial communications. Before establishing his own firm in 1968 he was a public affairs analyst with the Conference Board.

Earlier he was an executive with two major New York public relations counseling firms where he dealt with corporate relations problems in a variety of industries. Before entering public relations Hopkinson was a reporter for the Baltimore Sun.

Since 1963 he has been a contributing editor of The Public Relations Quarterly. He has contributed many articles to professional and business journals and chapter material to public relations and marketing textbooks.

Hopkinson has been an active member of the Public Relations Society of America since 1959. In 1969-1970 he served as chairman of the Government Advisory Committee of the professional organization's Counselor's Section. He is listed in "Who's Who in the East" and holds B.A. and M.B.A. degrees from Yale and New York University respectively.

After birth in the 1950's, the growing pains of adolescence in the 1960's, and some hard-won maturity in the 1970's, the practice of public affairs as an organized function of business management is a phenomenon of our times whose eventual role in and importance to the business organization has yet to be fully defined.

In hundreds of business and other organizations it is still in such a relatively early stage of development that its very definition and relationship to other operating departments undergoes almost continual change.

A working definition of public affairs might say that it is the management function responsible for studying and analyzing the corporation's relationship to the total environment in which it operates and then interpreting the significance of public issues to the corporation and counseling on the proper company response to them. It naturally follows that the public affairs unit would also be responsible for the development and execution of any activities that such counsel might create.

HISTORICAL BACKGROUND

Aside from lobbying activities, in the first half of this century the American business community generally tended to avoid involvement with most phases of our political process. As has often been stated, the average business executive considered politics to be "dirty business."

During this same time span industry enjoyed tremendous growth and its decisions and actions had a growing impact on all phases of American society. And, as might have been predicted, as business grew, its regulation by government at the local, state, and federal levels multiplied accordingly.

In 1952 the public affairs movement received an

early boost when President Eisenhower strongly urged businessmen to take an active part in our political process. Two years later, in 1954, the Washington-based Public Affairs Council was established as the formal organization to educate business executives about public affairs programming.

During the '50's and '60's, led by the pioneering efforts of such companies as General Electric, Ford, and Johnson & Johnson, for example, a number of blue chip corporations joined the fledgling public affairs movement. In some of these early programs business activity could be attributed to the collective business community's desire to counter the sharply increased political activity of the labor unions.

In any event, it is today estimated that more than 500 business organizations have formal public affairs programs.

BUSINESS AND SOCIETY

Partly evolving from the new and sometimes radical social unrest of the '60's, the role of business in our society has come under new attack.

Almost daily it seems that national opinion surveys publish reports about the loss of credibility of American business and the simultaneous loss of public faith in the traditional structure of our free enterprise system.

The long-simmering Watergate scandals of the business-sponsored Nixon Administration and disclosures of assorted business wrong-doing—from illegal political contributions to bribery of overseas private and public officials—are all obvious reasons for a decline in business' believability.

In response business bemoans the economic ignorance of the American public and the public's attendant failure to understand and/or appreciate the vital contribution of business to the overall economic well-being of individual citizens.

In an article[1] appearing shortly before he became Secretary of the Treasury in the Carter Administration, W. Michael Blumenthal, former chief executive officer of the Bendix Corporation, said in effect that business morality has not deteriorated but society has changed. The basic causes of the questionable and illegal corporate activities are to be found in causes other than the profit motive or the actual structure of modern business.

[1] "Business Morality Has Not Deteriorated—Society Has Changed," *The New York Times,* January 9, 1977, section F, p. 9.

Instead, he said, they can be traced to drastic changes in society and to unwillingness of many business leaders to recognize or adjust to these changes. In Mr. Blumenthal's opinion the skill to anticipate social change is becoming increasingly critical to business.

Communicating a similar message in somewhat different words, Reginald E. Jones, president of General Electric, said "... the basic strategy for corporate survival is to anticipate the changing expectations of society and serve them more effectively than competing institutions."

Whether this phase of corporate activity is officially labeled public affairs, public relations, corporate relations, or external relations, it is the management function that will be studied in this chapter. And, during the past three decades, it is the particular management function that is increasingly given the responsibility for providing intelligent counsel on how the business corporation may best respond to the complex problems mentioned of business' social climate.

SOCIAL AUDIT

Increased governmental and public concern with business' social responsibility may be spawning a new kind of business accounting wherein social scientists would do the accounting instead of accountants. It is commonly referred to as the "social audit."

The term simply describes an accounting or measuring of corporate performance in non-economic areas. How stringent are a company's policies for pollution control? Beyond providing employment and paying taxes in a company's various operating areas, what contributions to society does the corporation actually make? In equal employment hiring, does a corporation merely meet government regulations or does it volunteer to go beyond what the law says it has to do? These are the kind of questions that a social audit might examine.

In trying to determine what is good and/or desired business behavior in such social areas, a number of special interest groups such as Ralph Nader's various organizations and the Council on Economic Priorities, for example, have appointed themselves monitors of such corporate behavior.

For diverse reasons, it is much too early to forecast whether the "social audit" will become a lasting and useful technique to help corporations chart their relationships with their many diverse publics. Despite considerable publicity in the business press, the only point that most observers would probably agree on today is that social accounting is indeed a popular current concept among business consultants.

THE CORPORATE ROLE

In the same way that the definition of public affairs will vary—and sometimes to a large degree—from corporation to corporation, so will its role in these respective organizations. But this must be expected when individual companies have different objectives and face different kinds of problems in the socioeconomic and political arenas.

Just as the specific function of public affairs will change from company to company, its overall role in business life has undergone considerable evolution since its initial appearance.

Originating from the desire and need to make business and the individual business executive more intelligent and effective forces in the American political process, public affairs initially concerned itself almost exclusively with government and legislative relations activity. At the local, state, and federal levels of government, business organizations for the first time gave official status to the important task of establishing and maintaining effective two-way communications with government.

In the early days of public affairs programming, in addition to legislative relations, the corporate function consisted of two other major components—political action and/or education programs and courses in economic education. The first was designed to prepare and stimulate the individual citizen for a more active role in politics. The economic education was aimed at correcting what many businessmen considered an appalling ignorance of basic economics on the part of many Americans.

Broader viewpoint. In the mid-1960's, however, a few business leaders began to take a broader view of the collective social responsibility of business. However, a catalyst, in the form of the 1967 urban riots, was required before the business community really began to expand the role of corporate public affairs.

As stated in a major business periodical, "Business began to re-define its relationship with society. Publicly indicted for pollution, deceptive packaging, unsafe products, or discrimination, companies started raising their sights and standards."[2]

Due to a combination of the factors cited above, toward the end of the 1960's the role of public affairs—with definite emphasis on urban problem solving—had mushroomed overnight to encompass programs of almost staggering diversity. A research report, including the responses of 356 corporations, published by the Conference Board[3], gives an excellent picture of the business community's pioneering efforts in many urban-oriented public affairs areas. For example, these new business concerns included jobs and job training for the disadvantaged, housing, transportation, law and order, health, education, and economic development.

Unfortunately, and as some observers had forecast, all too often the results of such activities would primarily have to be labelled chaotic and unproductive.

Finally, with two decades of trial, error, and experiment to learn from, it is still difficult to arrive at a definitive definition of the role of public affairs in the business corporation. (The same remark could easily have been made about public relations in the 1940's.)

CHANGING DIRECTIONS

Because the corporate public affairs function is involved with the organization's relationship to the total societal environment in which it operates—and because this environment is continually changing—it is natural that the objectives and priorities of public affairs programming also tend to be in a state of steady change.

By the latter half of the 1970's, many programs had shifted away from establishing urban concerns as the top priority by many corporations. Problems relating to urban minorities were not overlooked but were placed in a broader perspective.

In 1976 a comprehensive and well-publicized study of the Conference Board[4] said that the lack of public confidence in business is the paramount external problem facing corporate management. The survey polled more than 500 executives from 368

---

[2]"The corporation: Moving decisions down to where the action is," *Business Week,* December 6, 1969, p. 138.

[3]"Business Amid Urban Crisis," Barbara J. Flower, National Industrial Conference Board, N.Y., 1968.

[4]*Managing Corporate External Relations: Changing Perspectives and Responses,* Phyllis S. McGrath, The Conference Board, 1976.

Critical Issues — Today and Tomorrow
As Viewed by 185 Chief Executives and 303 External Relations Executives
(ranked by frequency of mention)

Note: The following "issues" represent a consensus of the responses to the question: What do you see as the most critical issues facing your company and American business with regard to relations with external publics — today, and three to five years from now? (Because no list of choices was provided, the responses should be evaluated as volunteered responses.)

Issue	Today		Three to Five Years from Now	
	CEO	External Relations Executive	CEO	External Relations Executive
Business credibility	1	2	5	2
Government overregulation	2	1	1	1
The economy	3	3	3	4
Corporate finance	4	5	2	5
Survival of free enterprise system	5	7	9	9
Demands of special interest groups (consumers, environmentalists, minorities, etc.)	6	4	10	3
Taxation	7	9	7	12
Energy	8	6	4	6
International management	9	8	6	7
Increased expectations of the public, or social issues	10	10	11	13
Media	11	*	*	11
Labor	12	12	13	*
Investor relations	*	11	*	10
People problems (employee relations, human resources, etc.)	*	*	8	8
Skills of future executives and nonexecutives	*	*	12	*

*Mentioned by an insignificant number of respondents. In addition, the tabulation does not include several other issues mentioned too infrequently to merit ranking.

Figure 3-1. Responses to a study by The Conference Board of what chief executives of corporations considered the most critical issues facing them.

corporations. The survey revealed the following rating of public affairs concerns and issues:

RELATIONSHIP TO PUBLIC RELATIONS

For a number of different reasons there is no fixed relationship between the two corporate functions of public affairs and public relations. As might be expected, it will differ from company to company. In one organization, the former may report to the latter and in the next situation, the pattern will be reversed. In many other instances, the two functions will work alongside each other and both report to an executive in charge of corporate relations, corporate services, or some such title.

Since individual corporations have widely varying definitions for each of the two management functions and accordingly assign different responsibilities to each function, it is only natural that corporate organization charts will follow the same patterns.

Sensing trends and attitudes is the starting point of public relations. This precedes judgments on what an organization's involvement in public affairs needs to be.

Relating to the organization's publics through various forms of communication is the functioning level of public relations. This carries out the policies that evolve from consideration of public affairs.

In the total context of all facets of an organization's relations with all of its publics, the interrelationship of each phase is clearly seen. The elements of what various organizations see as "public affairs" fit into the whole logically.

Thus it appears that the public affairs functions are part of the total spectrum covered in this book, integral to the complex web of public relations.

CAREER TRAINING

There is no single academic or career background that should serve as the training ground for the practice of public affairs. Because of the new management function's broad concerns with so many facets of business and its governmental and societal relationships, the disciplines that are capable of providing a suitable background are correspondingly wide in scope.

From without the corporate structure, some of the more popular backgrounds for business public affairs officers include: government; politics; nonprofit organizations—with possible emphasis on foundations and research organizations; academic institutions; and journalism. Corporate functions that have served as a training ground for many of today's public affairs executives include legal, public relations, industrial relations, community relations, and employee relations.

During the past several years, to meet the growing demand for knowledge and professional expertise, a number of organizations providing information, educational, and consulting services have developed to help the executive charged with his organization's public affairs responsibility. Some of these existing services are noted later in the section entitled "Information Sources."

HOW TO ORGANIZE

In much the same way that the public affairs function will have a different relationship to the public relations function from one organization to the next, the way corporations organize their overall public affairs activities will vary tremendously when you examine different companies.

As in other phases of corporate organization planning, the way any corporation structures its formal public affairs function should be determined by specific corporate problems, objectives, and/or needs.

Despite the variety of models of corporate organization charts depicting public affairs operations, The Conference Board survey of external relations discovered a definite trend toward placing all external relations activities under one executive.

THE DYNAMICS AND ROLE OF PUBLIC AFFAIRS

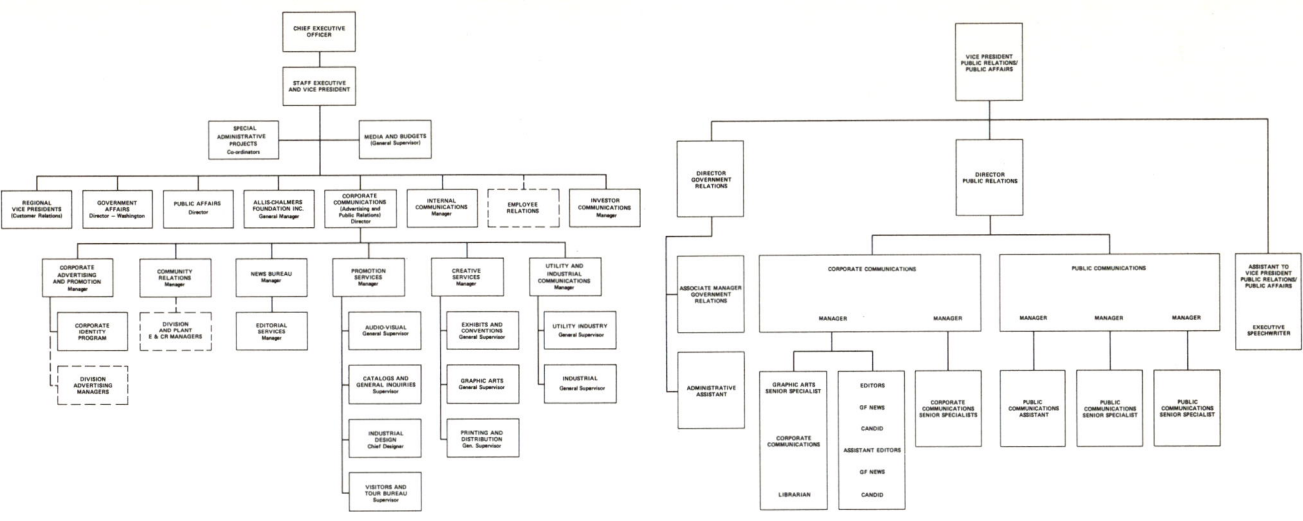

Figure 3-2. A coordinated corporate structure—in the Allis-Chalmers Company—cited in *Organizing for External Relations*, published by The Conference Board.

Figure 3-3. A structure that combines public affairs and government relations with public relations—at General Foods Corporation—cited in The Conference Board's *Organizing for External Relations*.

In that survey 176 of 303 respondents reported such an integrated organizational approach.

Four concepts. Four different organizational concepts collectively account for most of today's corporate public affairs activity. They are:

1. Coordinated organization with all communications functions reporting to one top staff executive. (See the Allis-Chalmers chart as noted in Conference Board survey.)
2. Central coordination with exceptions.

Another approach calls for most public affairs and communications activities to report to one top executive with one or two exceptions.

The most notable exception is customer or consumer relations, which may report through marketing. A second exception is sometimes investor relations (especially institutional relations as opposed to shareholder relations, for example). This function will often report to financial management.

3. Use of committees and boards.

As a prime example of this technique, the Bank of America utilizes a board-level public policy committee. It consists of six senior vice-presidents and its operating arm is a "social policy department."

This unit is given the official responsibility for coordinating, administering, and monitoring socially oriented programs throughout the bank.

Along similar guidelines, at the Stop & Shop grocery chain 27 consumer boards handle all areas of consumer and customer affairs.

4. Regional representation.

In the area of state government relations, the utilization of regional public affairs executives becomes important.[5] In all other subject areas—e.g., consumer, environmental—regional staff is much less in evidence.

In many corporations, the manager of Federal government affairs is located in Washington, D.C. This executive may report to the company's local office there (if they have one) or he may report to the corporate staff executive in charge of public affairs or government relations.[6]

In a 1974 survey[7] that drew 198 responses to this particular question, the Washington-based Public Affairs Council found that major corporations handled their *state relations programs* as follows:

1. Executed primarily through central public affairs staff (51).
2. Mainly rely on line or staff executives supervised and coordinated by corporate staff

[5]See Chapter 6.
[6]See Chapter 5.
[7]"1974 Survey of Corporate Public Affairs," Public Affairs Council, Washington, D.C., 1974.

(42). This has been the trend during the past several years.
3. A combination of regional government relations staff and regional line or staff executives (25).
4. Mostly rely on regional government relations "reps" alone (17).

Personnel. The size of the public affairs staff will vary to a large degree from corporation to corporation. A few industrial giants count more than 50 employees. The Public Affairs Council study found that more than half its respondents reported staffs numbering between 1 and 5 people.

MAJOR COMPONENTS

As might be expected, the different responsibilities of a corporate public affairs department will also vary considerably from organization to organization. And since the professional dimensions of the craft are constantly broadening and changing, the activities assigned to public affairs are accordingly undergoing continual change.

In addition to the evolutionary nature of many of the tasks practiced under the banner of corporate public affairs, a number of these responsibilities are shared with another corporate unit such as public relations, personnel, or legal, for example. There is no universal model.

As noted earlier, goals and priorities of most corporate public affairs departments are, by the nature of the function, in a continual state of change.

Accordingly, the components of any one organization's public affairs department—e.g., consumer affairs, Federal government relations, political education, etc.—undergo corresponding change in budgets, personnel, and overall importance to management.

In the Public Affairs Council study, respondents said that the following areas of activity would receive greater priority in the immediate future:

1. Federal government relations (126)[8]
2. State government relations (116)
3. Advising senior management (116)
4. Urban affairs/social responsibility (79)
5. International government relations (78)
6. Employee citizenship (52)
7. Contributions/philanthropy (45)

[8]Number in parentheses represents the number of respondents who said that particular function would receive greater attention.

Government relations. Business corporations have obviously been involved with local, state, and federal government relations long before the term "public affairs" was coined. Analyzing and interpreting government and legislative issues, counseling management, and communicating the company position to government bodies has been and will continue to be a vital aspect of all corporate public affairs programming within the total framework of the organization's relations.

In recent years, however, some corporations have re-evaluated their governmental relations philosophy. Basically, these companies have replaced their traditional negativism regarding anything connected with government with attempts to establish better two-way communications and cooperative action to jointly solve major public problems.[9] As examples of such changed business thinking, some companies during the past few years have initially become involved or have increased their earlier participation in such activities as:

1. Helping install modern methods and techniques in local government operations—either as business volunteers or on a contract basis
2. Support of charter revision or constitutional proposals affecting city, county, or state governments to simplify governmental structures, to make tax bases more equitable, or to encourage economic growth
3. Serving as volunteers on White House commissions and task forces in the spirit of business "volunteerism"
4. Granting employees leaves-of-absence to run for political office and/or to serve in advisory or administrative posts at the local or state government level
5. Participation in various kinds of "interchange" programs where business and government middle-management executives have a chance to observe the operational routine of their opposite numbers and/or actually swap jobs for a limited period
6. Participation in new evolving patterns of business-government relations as evidenced by such public-private joint ventures as COMSAT and in cooperative efforts to

[9]For a more detailed treatment of changing business-government relations see this author's article "What Is the Business of Business," *The Public Relations Quarterly*, Winter, 1968. Also see Chapters 4-8.

provide housing and jobs for urban disadvantaged citizens.

Minority/urban interests. Following the 1967 urban riots in more than 70 U.S. cities, many corporate organization charts quickly sprouted "urban affairs" units that just as quickly plunged into all kinds of would-be urban problem solving. By the early 1970's some of these business efforts—many of which received considerable national publicity—had become even more important or a regular part of company programming.[10] Conversely, some were eventually reduced in scope and others dropped entirely.

In outline form, some of these urban activities include the following:

- Education and job training programs (either alone or in conjunction with government) to help disadvantaged citizens
- Part-time jobs, on-the-job training, special summer jobs and training courses
- Serving as job counselors to high school students and other volunteer programs to upgrade local educational systems
- New and special recruiting methods to reach inner-city youth
- Review, adjustment, and modification of existing hiring standards to increase job opportunities
- Volunteer efforts to help improve urban/regional transportation problems
- Assisting in programs to provide urban housing with emphasis on middle or low-income housing units
- Day care centers for children of working parents
- Ex-offender programs
- Minority economic development
- Working with government officials and others to fight juvenile delinquency, improve law enforcement, and otherwise assist in crime prevention
- Volunteer efforts to upgrade medical, recreational, or cultural facilities
- Industrial development in urban poverty areas (viz., building facilities et al)

Political and economic education. During the preceding two decades hundreds of American companies have conducted programs to enable employees to learn how they can become more active—and effective—in the political party of their choice.[11] Many of these organizations have used course materials such as "Action Course in Practical Politics" prepared by the Chamber of Commerce of the United States. In recent years the Chamber has also published "Campaign Finance" (a compilation of Federal, state, and local laws regarding political campaign financing and contributions) and "Guidelines for Corporate Political Action Committees." Some of the material covers topics such as:

1. The individual in politics
2. Political party organization
3. The political precinct
4. The political campaign
5. Political clubs
6. The political leader's problems
7. Political meetings
8. Businessmen in politics

In the field of economic education for corporate employees, one of the most popular courses ("Understanding Economics") is also prepared by the U.S. Chamber. A ten-session course of one-and-a-half-hour sessions is designed for small groups of 14-20 people. The Chamber says that it is intended for business organizations, local and state chambers of commerce, trade and professional associations, and student groups, among others. Its component parts are:

1. Why economics?
2. Business ups and downs
3. Why prices?
4. Government and the economy
5. Productive resources
6. International economics
7. Money and finance
8. Science, technology, and the economy
9. National income
10. The power of choice

It is imperative that business organizations utilizing such political and economic education programs be completely non-partisan in their approach. Observers, especially in the early days of such activity, sometimes accused business of violating such guidelines. As far back as 1951, for example, a research study by the Brookings Institution said economic education programs in general were "superficial .... loaded with self-interest .... and ineffective."[12]

---

[10]See Chapter 7.

[11]See Chapter 8.

[12]See "Why Economic Education Is Failing," by Philip Lesly, *Management Review,* Oct., 1976.

If such courses are slanted in favor of one political party or against government participation in any phase of the nation's economic life, for example, it is highly probable that they will lose most of their believability and effectiveness.

Other economic education activities include community open houses with ample opportunity for question-and-answer sessions, increased use of special annual reports for employees, and greater utilization of paid corporate advertising to discuss economic issues.

Environmental problems. Business involvement with far-ranging and ever-increasing environmental problems outside the urban arena continue to multiply. There is more and more focus on America's deteriorating physical environment and its relationship to this nation's methods of industrial production.

As the business sector becomes so involved, public affairs professionals will have to contend with such ever-expanding areas of responsibility. Some of these new and/or emerging concerns include:

- Air and water pollution
- Conservation problems (depletion of the nation's natural resources for industrial use)
- Land use and beautification (litter; esthetics of utility company installations; waste disposal, etc.)
- Ecology problems (viz., control of pesticides, other toxic agents that can disturb the natural patterns of nature and animal life)

Consumerism. Many of the new public affairs problems facing business grow directly out of society's complaints about one or more business practices.

Of all such issues the problem of "consumerism" may prove to be the most complex and difficult for business to handle intelligently. Starting in the early 1960's with consumer criticism of food and consumer goods packaging and today covering almost every single product line available, these consumer complaints are quickly picked up by Government officials and lawmakers as well as many other business critics. Such issues as truth-in-packaging, truth-in-lending, new safety codes for household products, and automobile safety, for example, have all become part of our daily business concerns.

To learn the real reasons behind such consumer problems and to take positive action, some corporations have created permanent apparatus to deal with the problem. Some of these new procedures include innovative consumer and shareholder research, new marketing codes, and new formats for business-government cooperation in solving the problem.

Public issues. For many years a number of American corporations have dedicated themselves to communicating their thinking clearly on a wide range of public issues that might include government regulation of business, Federal tax policy as it applies to corporate dividends, and economic education, for example. Such corporate messages appear in such media as print advertising or in shareholder communications such as annual or quarterly reports.

In recent years, however, Mobil Oil Corporation has probably added a new dimension to the communications technique of speaking up on issues that the corporation deems important to its own business interests or to the collective business community. Mobil's most visible communications vehicle has been the Op-Ed page of *The New York Times* where the company runs an on-going series of institutional ads. On a programmed basis Mobil communicates directly with the mass media when it believes that oil industry news has been presented unfairly or incorrectly.

Other concerns. Other kinds of public affairs activity that vary from industry to industry and from corporation to corporation include new equal employment programs for women and minority groups, job enrichment programs for employees, programs designed to improve the physical working environment, and the problems of complying with the changing requirements of the Occupational Safety Health Administration (OSHA).

PROBLEMS AND BARRIERS

The main problems in professional public affairs are no more or no less difficult to solve than are the environmental problems that put pressure against the corporate structure and demand a business response. Some operating problems facing the department include:

- Identifying in advance those social problems that are relevant to a particular corporation
- Being the most inexact of any management function, results of public affairs activities are accordingly the most difficult to measure
- When corporate budgets are tight, public affairs may be an early victim

THE DYNAMICS AND ROLE OF PUBLIC AFFAIRS

- Some chief executives do not really believe in the function
- Business executives often live in a public affairs vacuum and lead personal lives that largely isolate them from any real perception of many public affairs problems

INFORMATION SOURCES

There are a number of organizations and publications providing informational and educational public affairs source material. The organizations listed here conduct and publish research studies, report case histories and other public affairs developments, and hold seminars and conferences. The following list covers a few of the major organizations and publishers:

1. Organizations:

   - American Enterprise Institute for Public Policy Research (AEI)
     1150 Seventeenth Street, N.W.
     Washington, D.C. 20036

   - The Brookings Institution
     1775 Massachusetts Avenue, N.W.
     Washington, D.C. 20036

   - Chamber of Commerce of the U.S.
     Public Affairs Dept.
     1615 H Street, N.W.
     Washington, D.C. 20006

   - The Conference Board
     Public Affairs Research Division
     845 Third Avenue
     New York, New York 10022

   - National Association of Manufacturers
     Public Affairs Division
     1776 F Street, N.W.
     Washington, D.C. 20006

   - Public Affairs Council
     1220 Sixteenth Street, N.W.
     Washington, D.C. 20036

2. Sources of Information/Periodicals:

   - Business Periodicals Index
     (available in public libraries, other such institutions)

   - Business & Society Review
     870 Seventh Avenue
     New York, New York 10019

   - Potomac Associates
     1707 L Street, N.W.
     Washington, D.C. 20036

   - The Public Affairs Information Service (index)
     (available in public libraries, other such institutions)

   - Public Relations Journal
     Public Relations Society of America
     845 Third Avenue
     New York, New York 10022

   - Public Relations Quarterly
     44 W. Market St.
     Rhinebeck, N.Y. 12572

   - PR Reporter
     P.O. Box 600
     Exeter, N.H. 03833

   - Public Relations Review
     College of Journalism
     University of Maryland
     College Park, Md. 20742

PUBLIC AFFAIRS BUDGETS

As in almost every aspect of public relations, operating budgets will show wide differences when one organization is compared with another. The individual components of the budget (salaries, office expenses, publications, visual aids, fees for staff attendance at seminars and workshops, and so on) will be somewhat similar to others in a public relations budget. In the 1974 poll of the Public Affairs Council, of 106 respondents answering 32 reported annual budgets under $100,000 and 31 claimed budgets of $100,000 to $200,000. Seventeen noted expenditures of $200,000 to $500,000, nine said their corporations spent $500,000 to $1,000,000, and 17 corporations said their annual public affairs budgets exceeded $1,000,000.

ROLE OF OUTSIDE COUNSEL

Consultants in this field function like those in any other field of business. They are called on by business corporations, trade associations, and nonprofit institutions, for example, to help solve a specific problem or they are asked to provide counsel and service on a continuing basis.[13] Such

---

[13]See Chapter 53.

consulting firms may take the place of an internal department or work closely in conjunction with such a unit.

Many counselors in the field tend to specialize in one particular area of the function (urban affairs, state government relations, political education programs, and so on). Conversely, there seem to be few who are capable of working across the board in a number of public affairs disciplines.

ASSOCIATIONS AND NONPROFIT INSTITUTIONS

The practice of public affairs, like any other formal management function such as marketing or accounting, for example, is obviously not limited in its application to a corporation. During the past decade or so, a number of trade associations, universities, hospitals, and other organizations (both profit and nonprofit) have added the title of public affairs executive to their rosters.

In some instances it is merely a new label for past functions, perhaps regrouped. In many other organizations, however, the public affairs departments are concerned with many of the same activities and public issues that are described in this chapter.

WHAT IT ACCOMPLISHES

Measuring the results of business public affairs is often difficult in the same way that public relations performance in general is often hard to judge.

However, in general terms, there are certain aspects of the function that realize accomplishments even though they are not always capable of being stated in terms of immediate financial reward for an organization. Some of these benefits—to the organization and to society—include:

- Becoming more aware of and responsive to the needs of society results in a better environment for a business organization
- The involvement of more citizens in the political process strengthens the democratic procedures of government
- By working toward positive socioeconomic and political goals the corporation will earn the long-term good will of its important publics
- Public affairs programs can generate considerable corporate publicity and thereby enhance the company's reputation
- Better two-way communications between business and government allow the two most dominant forces in our society to work together toward important national goals that neither can accomplish alone
- An organization that is involved in significant public affairs activities is better able to attract many capable young executives who increasingly demand such involvement as part of a meaningful career

These benefits of public affairs programs can easily be classified as valid generalities.

Specific public affairs policies and practices can enable a company to influence legislation in its favor, prevent or change punitive taxes, and influence many different kinds of local ordinances that can result in substantial corporate dollar savings. Other kinds of public affairs projects can open new marketing possibilities. Finally, public affairs decisions can prevent costly plant relocations and can avoid dangerous community antagonisms and economic boycotts and other forms of protest by one or more minority or special-interest groups.

TRENDS FOR TOMORROW

What does the future hold for the practice of public affairs? Can one forecast significant changes in direction? How will the ambitious public affairs officer make out in the organization chart rankings?

This author believes that the public affairs challenges that face the organization of tomorrow will be so complex and so serious that they would defy adequate description by most observers.

Business critics like John Kenneth Galbraith proclaim that society will have to limit the use of certain goods because of congestion or because of their adverse effects on the community. Other social critics like Ralph Nader mount vigorous campaigns to change corporate policy from within by appealing directly to corporate shareholders. Some predict that activist confrontations between employees and management will take place in company executive suites.

Today, unlike many times in the past, business seems to be looking ahead. For example, some business-supported research organizations are analyzing such potential public affairs problems as the divisions within American society; law and order; the management of change; the effects of increased automation and leisure time on employees; and the threat of the invasion of personal privacy through computerized information and data collecting and processing.

Whatever its label or niche, public affairs seems certain to be a major phase of an organization's total relations spectrum in the future.

4

Dealing with Forces for Change Through Government Action

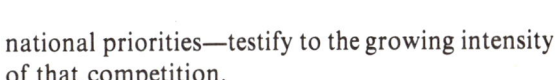

DAVID J. PHILLIPS, vice president-public relations, is head of the public relations department for the State Farm Insurance Companies.

He is a former Nebraska newspaper reporter, editor, and publisher and at one time authored a widely syndicated column carried by more than 100 newspapers in the United States and Canada. In 1947 and 1948 he was a member of the staff of the House Appropriations Committee during the 80th Congress, handling press relations for the chairman of the subcommittee on the Departments of State, Commerce, Justice, and the Federal Judiciary.

Prior to joining State Farm as public relations superintendent in 1956, Phillips was a member of the headquarters public relations staff of Union Pacific Railroad. He has three times won the Silver Anvil trophy, top award of the Public Relations Society of America, as well as the annual public relations award of the Federation for Railway Progress. He is executive director and a member of the board of the Adlai E. Stevenson Lectures on International Affairs.

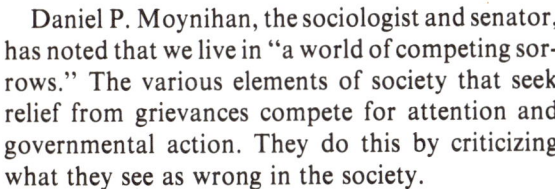

Daniel P. Moynihan, the sociologist and senator, has noted that we live in "a world of competing sorrows." The various elements of society that seek relief from grievances compete for attention and governmental action. They do this by criticizing what they see as wrong in the society.

John Kenneth Galbraith points out[1] that to win the competition for public attention, criticism must be exaggerated, dramatized, and loudly and repeatedly asserted.

As society's problems seem to multiply—or, perhaps more accurately, as social awareness of them grows—the competition becomes stiffer. The protest marches, campus demonstrations, and inner city riots of recent years—all efforts to move a particular problem to a higher ranking on the list of national priorities—testify to the growing intensity of that competition.

Others have observed that a talent for long-range planning is not an American attribute; rather, we are a crisis-oriented society, and Galbraith seems to say that our society will take no action on its problems unless they are presented as crises, real or manufactured.

CRITICISM AS A SIGNAL OF CHANGE

The lesson to be drawn from Galbraith's thesis is that rigorous, public, and frequently unfair criticism of a social institution, such as a major industry, is not the mindless, pointless malice of a few malcontents, as business sometimes views it, but signals the starting up of the process of change in the society, a process that has as its goal the passage and implementation of legislation that achieves change.

[1] *The Atlantic Monthly*, February, 1962, pp. 44-48.

Thus, the sort of criticism Galbraith describes, when perceived as part of a process, can also be accurately described as an incipient legislative problem for the institution under attack.

Just as it is dangerous to misunderstand the motives of criticism, so is it to misunderstand the role of government in the process of change. Rarely does representative government of the sort we have here initiate change; rather, it responds to the demand for it. Government acts as judge in the competition of problems for public attention. The winners go to the state and federal legislatures, and it is there that the finals are held. In other words, those "competing sorrows" that have been most successful in winning public concern are chosen in turn by the legislators for their attention, and the most compelling of these will win statutory remedies.

In dealing with government, it is necessary to understand its role of choosing the winners in the competition among problems. He who would seek government action (or seek to prevent it) should understand that he is engaged in an intensely competitive activity—a competition with few holds barred that takes place in a wide arena where reason is frequently overcome by passion and prejudice. Failure to understand the nature of the game is one reason so many businesses lose it.

Corporations are by their very nature ill-equipped to enter the lists against opponents who consciously or intuitively understand the competitive nature of social change. The businessman lives in a relatively well-ordered world of charts, graphs, computers. He is dismayed to discover that these traditional weapons of business problem-solving are pitifully ineffective in the battle for public opinion and governmental favor.

Not infrequently, truth is on the side of the embattled institution, but as Ernst Dichter and the motivation research people have discovered, public opinion reacts to problems as they are perceived, not necessarily as they are. It is the zealous reformer who manipulates that perception to achieve his own ends, which may or may not be in the long-term public interest.

DEFINING THE DIRECTION OF CHANGE

The status quo does not always deserve to be defended; but when it deserves to be, it should be defended skillfully. In this restless society, and especially among our young, change in itself is seen as a positive value, even though it sometimes fails to serve the public good the change-seekers proclaimed as their goal. Social change usually is most beneficial when it has been laboriously achieved—when an able defense has preserved what was good in established practice and reform touches only what needs to be reformed.

When ill-advised reform overtakes an institution, it can be as much the fault of incompetent defense as of too-vigorous prosecution. Too often, the challenged institution lets the reformers define the problem and set the boundaries of the debate. The institution is attacked at its weakest points, and responds within the same narrow confines, often in a negative, defensive, sometimes apologetic way.

Social problems are rarely as simple as they are portrayed by proponents of a particular solution. To debate the problem as the problem is defined by the proponents of change is to imply that the definition is accurate, when it often is not.

The point might be summarized this way:

Much of business-government relations has to do with attempts to arrest efforts for change that have been translated into legislative or administrative proposals. At that point, the process of change is well-advanced, has momentum, and is difficult to halt.

The nature of an organization's most important government relations is shaped in the public marketplace of ideas. No lobby—no matter how powerful—can forever override insistent public demand.

A successful government relations program begins where the process of change begins—with the public, and in the forums where the public mind is reached.

THE ROLE OF PUBLIC RELATIONS

As Philip Lesly points out in Chapter 1, the role of public relations includes analyzing the state of opinion toward an organization and trends that will affect that opinion; developing policies that gear to these opinions and trends while fostering the organization's purposes; and carrying out programs—largely aimed at steering opinion—that will help assure acceptance and continuation of those policies.

In the area of government's influence over business or other institutions, this adds up to sensing the course of change and carrying out programs that will accommodate society and the organization in their mutual interests.

The means of working with government and the underlying publics that move government are

DEALING WITH FORCES FOR CHANGE THROUGH GOVERNMENT ACTION

covered in Chapters 5, 6, and 7. In general, these means apply to all levels of government—federal, state, and local.

Dealing with the forces of opinion makes up the full context of this *Handbook*.

Coping with change is usually really determining what the course of change shall be, rather than trying to stop its inevitability. That is in essence what public relations needs to be in a free society.

5

Working with Federal Government

HOWARD PENN HUDSON heads Hudson Associates, public relations counseling firm with offices in Rhinebeck, New York and Washington, D.C. He has been director of Washington operations for a major counseling firm and for ten years was director of information, the National Planning Association, a public affairs organization in Washington before the term gained currency.

He is an accredited member of the Public Relations Society of America and has the unique distinction of having served as president of the Washington chapters of the American Public Relations Association and PRSA, and of the two merged chapters. He has been a director of the New York Chapter, PRSA; member of the executive committee of the PRSA Counselors' Section; and a trustee of the Foundation for Public Relations Research and Education.

He is co-editor with his wife Mary Elizabeth of "Hudson's Washington News Media Contacts Directory," editor-in-chief of "The Public Relations Quarterly," and publisher of "The Newsletter on Newsletters." He is a graduate of the University of Chicago.

If we define public relations as "organized persuasion," then the major activity in Washington, D.C. is public relations.

The federal government is the world's single biggest industry and there is little sign that it will ever get smaller. Its programs, its laws, its warehouse of information affect the present and future of all citizens, and impinge on the rights and activities of practically every organization in the country.

Every kind of special interest is represented in Washington—business, labor, agriculture, professions, health, education, welfare, city, state, and foreign governments.

The government strives to maintain its power. The nongovernment groups compete for a share of the power, to blunt the power, to change the equilibrium. This power struggle represents the "pull and push" of the American political system. The efforts are all carried out in the name of "the public interest" yet the only group not organized is the citizen.

Public opinion affects every decision of the federal government, and the federal government, more than any other organization, molds public opinion.

Relations with the federal government are less blatantly hostile than in an earlier day. There is recognition by businessmen that there are advantages to "partnership" arrangements. There is more acceptance that one can work within the framework of the government, that instead of creating hostility by seeming hostile it is wise to be friendly. There is the belief that the strategy of the indirect approach is more effective than trying to influence the government directly. And there is the recognition that although the federal government is the most powerful institution, it is not exclusively powerful.

A CHANGE IN THE CLIMATE

Still, there has been a change in the climate of Washington that is having a profound effect on the practice of public relations there. First intimations of the change began with the final years of the Vietnam war, as protests mounted against secrecy in government. A result was the Freedom of Information Act whereby citizens and organizations can now resort to the law to obtain information from the government which, while supposedly available to all, is still withheld.

With the eruption of the Watergate scandal, distrust of the government became endemic. The doubts and suspicions between government and citizens and between government and business, which intensified during the Seventies, are expected to continue. Add to this the low estate of both government and business in the eyes of the citizenry and there is a psychological climate in which efforts to create understanding are met with cynicism, hostility, or downright disbelief.

Those practitioners who work closely with the media note that previously cordial relationships have become wary. Some say that the power of the media in unraveling Watergate has given them a heady feeling. Many elements of the media feel that they are the last bastion of moral standards. Thus, every movement by a business or an association is scrutinized for "hidden meanings." When an organization approaches the media to tell its story about a current situation, it is sometimes told that there must be full disclosure. Under this procedure, the organization is asked for material it believes is irrelevant and questioned about all its operations. This does not mean that it is no longer possible to work harmoniously and successfully with the media. But it does require greater skill and patience than before.

There is also greater interest in the executive branch than in Congress. Major news bureaus have been moving to offices within a block or so of the White House. New legislative actions, such as the Occupational Safety and Health Act, created executive regulatory bodies whose rulings affect the daily affairs of business. Thus more of the media—and many specialized publications—follow these regulatory agencies closely. It behooves the public relations representatives of organizations affected to also immerse themselves in the outpouring of regulations and be prepared to advise management on steps to be taken.

The current areas of main concern in Washington are energy, environment, and consumerism. It is essential for the practitioner to anticipate what they will be tomorrow.

TOOLS AND TECHNIQUES

The tools and techniques of public relations are the major weapons in this continuing power struggle. They are the same tools and techniques used elsewhere, with the exception of some specialties such as financial public relations and product publicity. (These latter techniques are used in Washington, D.C., the city, but when we speak of Washington public relations we commonly mean relations with the federal government.)

There must also be added to the public relations approach a sense of political judgment, a realization that the subject matter is national issues, with political and policy objectives.

It is obvious that the first requirement for Washington public relations is understanding the structure of the government. People come and go, but the basic structure and the mode of operation remain relatively constant. To both neophytes and veterans, the basic guide is *The United States Government Organization Manual*.[1] This annual directory is the official organization handbook that describes the agencies of the legislative, judicial, and executive branches. It also contains brief descriptions of quasi-official agencies and selected international organizations, as well as charts of some of the more complex agencies. Since there are about 2,000 separate bureaus in the executive branch, this basic reference work must be always close at hand.

A companion piece is the *Congressional Directory*[1] with the details on the organization of the Congress, the list of senators and representatives, offices, phone numbers, staffs, and top personnel of the three branches of government, as well as news correspondents accredited to the press galleries.

More recently the *Congressional Quarterly* has produced its annual *Washington Information Directory,* which provides 5,000 information sources in Congress, the Executive Branch, and private associations—a boon to all who work in the Washington vineyard. There are other helpful guides, both governmental and private, that will be described at the end of this chapter and in Chapter 36.

[1] See Chapter 36.

ACTIVITIES OF WASHINGTON PUBLIC RELATIONS

Most public relations activities in Washington are directed toward persuading the government to take a position favorable to one's interest; anticipating the action the government will take; and executing an informational program as soon as a decision is made, which may support or oppose the government's position.

These activities can be broken down into seven parts:

1. Information gathering.
2. Interpreting government actions to management.
3. Counseling management on policies in relation to government actions.
4. Interpreting the organization's actions to government.
5. Taking an advocacy position.
6. Working with the news media.
7. Support of sales to government.

1. Information gathering. The great bulk of Washington public relations is information gathering. For whatever organization the public relations man represents, he must keep in touch with all activities of the government that may have a bearing on its particular interest. This watchdog role is one of the major differentiations between public relations in Washington and elsewhere.

The significance of the Washington watchdog role is symbolized at LaFayette Square. The White House is on one side, and looking across at it are the headquarters of the U.S. Chamber of Commerce, AFL-CIO, and the National Grange.

Morris Victor Rosenbloom, president of American Surveys in Washington, points out in "Effective Public Relations with Washington, D.C." (Public Relations Quarterly, Summer 1967) that "The Federal Government is a great ocean of facts: statistics, economic indicators, import data, opinions, decisions, research discoveries, chemical and drug reports, agricultural experimentation, patent applications and grants, copyrights, labor contracts . . . the list goes on and on, and the ocean every day gets deeper.

"Except for material classified for security considerations, almost all of this data is public property.[2] The government wants businessmen who can use them to have the facts. But often this data is not readily obtainable.

"No central computer or data-retrieval mechanism yet exists from which this information can be drawn. Much of it is still locked up in the heads of various functionaries and is not committed to paper. Some of it never will be.

"The ocean is so great that the effective distribution of appropriate facts to appropriate parties is viewed by some as the Federal Government's most insufferable dilemma. The Government Printing Office is the world's biggest book publisher, and virtually every cranny in the government issues multitudinous bulletins and distributes news releases. However, only a small fraction of government knowledge gets into public print, and much of what does may not reach the eyes of those who need it most."

Thus the information seeker taps people as well as documents. He works closely with others mining the same lode—other Washington representatives, including the press. He talks with government officials, and visits "the Hill" (Congress), international organizations, research institutions (which abound in Washington), and the embassies.

He recognizes that in dealing with a federal bureau, the top man often is not the one to see. The operations of bureaus and departments in government are so complex the top men have come to depend on certain key individuals who may not bear big titles. They are the men to see for the really sound information—and often to get an effective ear for the organization's message.

The larger counseling firms and many companies employ large staffs that are assigned to daily beats in key agencies.

In the information gathering phase, the practitioner may also be called on to report on the climate of opinion on certain issues. Close attention must be paid to the *Federal Register,* the daily publication that publishes Presidential proclamations and executive orders, and the *Congressional Record* with its 65,000 pages annually, recording every word and report of the Congress each day.

In addition, there are numerous newsletters and information services that sift through the technical details and "federalese" of government reports and evaluate their practical significance. There is so much information and some obscure new regulation may be fraught with so much significance for certain organizations that they protect themselves in depth. A large organization may subscribe to

---

[2](*Note:* In recent years some government bureaus have become less open. It may be necessary to invoke the Freedom of Information Act, mentioned above—H.P.H.)

WORKING WITH FEDERAL GOVERNMENT

numerous services, maintain its own news ticker from the AP or UPI, receive reports from associations, maintain its own staff of information gatherers, and retain a Washington public relations firm, a lobbyist, and a Washington law firm in order to feel protected.

2. Interpreting government actions to management. The Washington representative is not a serendipitist wallowing in fascinating facts. He must interpret the meaning of these facts to his organization or client, do some predicting, and suggest action.

There are two basic roles in Washington public relations, defensive and offensive. The watchdog posture is part of the defensive role. It is preparation for some government development that may be a threat or a challenge or an opportunity. The government has vast powers through its regulatory agencies and the Congress. The total reputation of an industry can collapse in an afternoon following such a government action or accusation. But if the action has been anticipated, contingent decisions can be made.

3. Counseling management on policies in relation to government actions. This is the ultimate role of Washington public relations and it is rewarded according to the competence of the judgments made. One experienced Washington counselor, Arthur G. Newmyer, Jr., estimates that 60 percent of his firm's time is spent gathering information—and 35 percent is spent interpreting and counseling. This 35 percent, he feels, is his firm's most valuable service.

This implies, then, that Washington public relations is part of an overall management public relations effort. Top management must support the function and Washington thought and action must be part of an organization's policy and planning. The Washington counselor must understand the policies and objectives of the organization he represents. Perhaps more important, top management must not think of their representative as merely "our man in Washington" to be controlled like a puppet from headquarters.

4. Interpreting the organization's actions to government. Government, too, wants to know what's going on. It wants information and it wants to know the opinion climate in various areas. The organization that makes known that it has Washington facilities will find that both the Congress and Executive branch will call on it regularly when it wants information.

The practitioner who specializes in working the

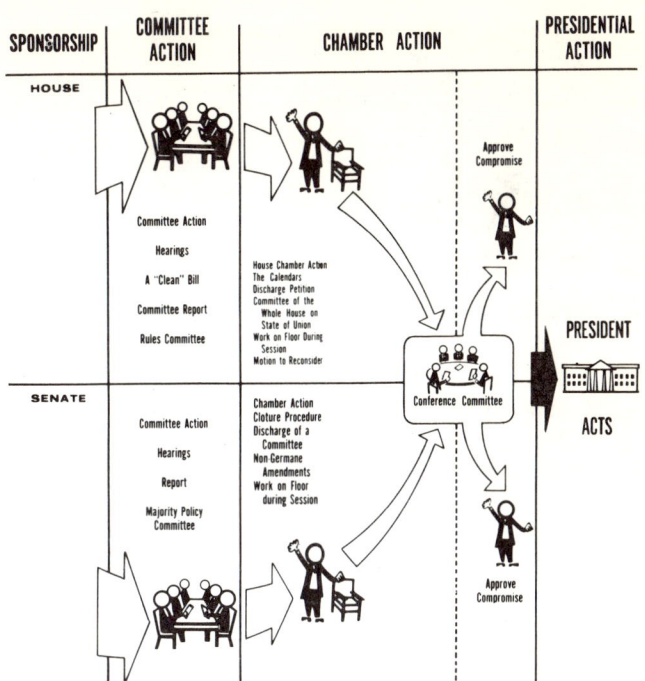

Figure 5-1. Diagram developed by the National Association of Manufacturers to show the sequence in consideration and passage of a federal law.

Hill (and Washington is so vast that there are many such specialists) uses his information gathering role as an offensive tool of public relations as well. In his regular contacts he learns the information needs of the Senators and Representatives and their all-important professional staffs. It is to these people that he constantly conveys information about his organization. He is prepared to provide special studies and technical materials bearing on public proposals.

The person working the Hill must understand timing. He learns from experience when and when not to apply efforts to a particular situation. He does not waste persuasive material until a bill has reached a point where a member of Congress will have to make up his mind. He is aware that in a typical Congress there may be 16,000 bills introduced with only 500 becoming law.[3]

The offensive role of public relations on the Executive Branch is also complicated. There are the independent agencies such as the Securities and Exchange Commission, Federal Reserve Board, Federal Trade Commission where public relations can be useful in the matter of proposed new rulings. This can be done at the hearings held by the agency.

[3]See Chapter 54.

Not only can rulings be changed or dropped, but the agencies often recognize the contribution of Washington representatives in helping them develop workable regulations.

Then there are the department agencies, such as Internal Revenue Service in the Department of the Treasury. By the time a department gets around to a public hearing on regulations, it is difficult to bring public opinion to bear. Effective action on these matters should take place at the earlier legislative level.

5. Taking an advocacy position. There are times when an organization feels that it must do more than present facts or persuade indirectly, but instead to try to influence action. Numerous public relations techniques are available in advocacy. Factual reports will be made available to legislators or agencies. A group of a Congressman's constituency may be brought in. Speeches will be prepared. Ads may be taken in Washington newspapers and on radio and television. The news media will be contacted. If it is a major situation, a national campaign may be mounted to bring grass roots pressure on the particular governmental group. Allies will be developed from associations, industries, labor organizations. Sometimes the action called for will involve having special-interest legislation enacted.

Testimony before regulatory agencies and Congressional committees is sometimes the focal point of an advocacy campaign. Here the preparation must be extremely careful. The case must be thoroughly documented and the witnesses coached well in advance. Plans must be made for getting the full story to the press and for fast rebuttal, if necessary.

We are assuming here that the organization has asked to be heard on a particular regulation or piece of legislation. What all in Washington public relations fear most is to have the initiative taken by the government—a special investigating committee of the Congress, for instance. A sudden subpoena of a company official or the bombshell of a government order affecting an industry gives the organization no choice but to testify and under adverse conditions. Many famous men have been made to look like fools in front of the whole nation by a skillful government investigation. (See Section on Investigations later in this chapter.) Which again is why effective Washington public relations emphasizes preventive action.

In regard to other efforts on behalf of an organization's position, Walter W. Belson, former Director of Public Relations and Assistant to the President of the American Trucking Associations, pointed out in the Third Edition of *Public Relations Handbook*, a predecessor to this volume:

> Efforts to arouse back-home pressure on legislators in the period between hearings on measures and their actual progress through both Houses of the Congress have been notably successful in many cases.
>
> Success in such effort is due in the majority of cases to the truly educational aspects of campaigns rather than to their intimidating effect. It would be untrue to indicate that there are no occasions in which a rousing back-home fire built under a Congressman causes him to reverse his position because of fear of non-re-election, but it would also be untrue to indicate that this factor is controlling. Properly carried out, and enlisting the support of a representative element throughout a Congressional district, such a back-home fire serves as a substitute public opinion poll so far as the Representative or Senator is concerned. Once he decides that a substantial number of non-hysterical people in his district are opposed to his thinking on pending legislation, he would be derelict in his duty if he failed to re-examine his personal position on the matter. Such re-examination carried on in the light of the additional information provided often results in a change of opinion on his part.

Working to elect Congressmen who will be open-minded to an organization's position is covered in Chapter 8.

6. Working with the news media. When the time comes to take a public stand, or in day-to-day communications, the Washington press corps offers facilities of dissemination that are unequalled. Here is the largest concentration of news correspondents in the world, 2,500 correspondents and editors representing 1,900 publications and radio-TV stations.

Whether they have offices or operate out of their homes, many correspondents spend their days at the Congressional galleries. If your client or organization is involved in a Congressional hearing, for instance, it is essential that you keep these galleries informed of statements you are issuing. However, only a portion of the Washington newsgatherers are accredited to these galleries. There are many more who are engaged in specialized activities. The chances are that whatever your area of interest, there is probably someone in the press corps who has both an interest in it and is knowledgeable. The search is well worthwhile. The Washington press is not just useful for the releasing of information; it can provide valuable information.

As the author pointed out in "Dateline Washington—The Anatomy of the Capital Press" (*Public Relations Journal,* November 1969):

> The Washington correspondent is accustomed to having access to everyone from the President on down. He knows he is in a special class and believes his is a high calling. He understands the value of public relations men, but he expects them to understand the workings of the Washington press. It is important anywhere to work selectively with the press, but it is essential in Washington. The easiest way to throw away money and gain resentment is to put the press corps on a general release list.
>
> Washington is organized for the serving of the press. AP and UPI have City Wires. Each morning they list all important engagements of officials, starting with the President, the meetings of Congressional committees, and news conferences. They also mention the meetings in town, the luncheons, and the important people staying in hotels. Even though you send special invitations, be sure to list your news conference on the City Wire.

If you want to distribute a press release, there are special services that constantly make the rounds of the major bureaus. (These services will also pick up government releases for you.) Teams of photo journalists are ready to serve you on special assignment. They are accredited, but work for a fee to give you special coverage.

The center of the press corps is the National Press Club. You can place your releases in the special racks there. The Press Club also provides one of the major forums in the country for newsmakers. Practically every world figure has addressed one of its luncheons at one time or another.

The public relations practitioner must know and can learn quickly the structure of the press corps. The starting place is the three general news services, the Associated Press (staff of 76), the United Press International (staff of 63), and Reuters (staff of 22). 475 newspapers have correspondents, some with fairly sizeable staffs, such as the *New York Times.* There are nearly 100 national syndicated columnists and specialized newspapers, ranging from *American Banker* to *Variety.* And the two daily Washington newspapers, the *Post* and *Evening Star,* consider national and international developments as the stuff that makes front pages.

In addition to the large radio-TV network news staffs, there are 130 stations represented in Washington. Metropolitan Washington has 41 TV, AM, and FM stations. With all of this representation, the physical problems of accommodating the media at a major function are staggering.

27 national magazines, familiar to all publicists, have representation. Washington is also the headquarters of the giant *U.S. News & World Report, Nation's Business,* and *National Geographic.* But when one gets to the specialized magazines, the sheer bulk of Washington journalism begins to emerge. Name any important trade publication and the chances are good that it has a Washington bureau. McGraw-Hill dominates, with 34 publications and a staff of 55. In all, there are more than 500 magazines represented in Washington, of which half are published in Washington.

Finally, the narrow, in-depth specialized character of many Washington publications is epitomized in the 300 newsletters and reporting services based there, such as the Kiplinger Washington Editors and the Bureau of National Affairs.

In stressing the national-issues aspects of Washington journalism, it should be noted that there are straight publicity opportunities as well. Government officials are always glad to cooperate with a private group if there is an appropriate angle. Congressmen have no objection to being photographed in front of the Capitol with a prominent constituent, or even introducing a new food product into the Congressional dining rooms. The White House itself lends its prestige to worthy causes, such as launching a national charity drive by showing the President with a crippled child. Good taste, skill, and timing are the obvious ingredients for such publicity.

7. Support of sales to government. The government is a major purchaser of many things, often the biggest purchaser in the country. Many companies maintain full-time sales staffs in Washington. The Washington public relations man's efforts play a strong supportive role for companies selling to the government. A public relations program that keeps key government people informed about the capacities and developments within a company can go a long way in paving the way for a favorable reaction when the sales staff moves in. Knowledge of the power structure and the thinking of key government officials can contribute to sales success.

INVESTIGATIONS AND HEARINGS

Walter W. Belson provided an insight into Washington hearings in the Third Edition of *Public Relations Handbook:*

> Representations to the Congress made before committees on more controversial measures are made orally and by brief or sometimes by letter or memorandum. Often so many witnesses wish to be heard that the limited time of the committee or sub-committee permits only the briefest personal appearance and that by a limited number of representative witnesses. Such witnesses and all others wishing to record appearances file briefs with the committee clerk and usually appear for the purpose of permitting legislators to interrogate them or to bring out with special emphasis points which the legislators feel are obscure or require emphasis.
>
> Hearings before Congressional committees or sub-committees often provide a very good opportunity for the witness to gain widespread publicity for an industry policy, problem, or viewpoint. This is especially true if the subject matter can be dramatized in testimony in such manner as to create news interest.
>
> Increasingly, over the years, the Congress has used (and in the opinion of some, has abused) its fundamental right to investigate matters affecting the public interest. Sometimes it is done by regular committees but more often by special committees or sub-committees. The target of investigations ranges over the whole area of public affairs but with considerable concentration on subversive activities, economic problems, social affairs, and labor relations. Such investigations are not comparable with committee hearings. Witnesses appear both voluntarily and under the persuasion of a subpoena.
>
> A Congressional investigation chairmanned by a skillful, publicity-conscious member of the Senate or House poses an almost unbelievably difficult problem for those handling public relations of the client or principal under investigation.
>
> A graphic description of an actual investigation from the standpoint of those being investigated can be found in comment made to a group of public relations practitioners by one who participated as an interested, involved (but non-testifying) observer at an actual hearing. Those testifying told him:
>
> "One feels almost like a laboratory specimen as the blinding kleig lights shine down on him to enable the television cameras to cover every move. On all sides sit dozens of members of the press poised to dash to the telephone with a new lead on their daily stories. And remember only sensation makes headlines. While the press waits for sensation, news cameramen crouch in front of the witness table, trying to catch an unusual shot that will depict the plight of the mighty falling.
>
> "The defendant cannot raise an objection to any statement of his accusers; he has no right of cross examination; no right to call witnesses; he has no right even to know what subjects his trial will cover. He must send his written statement to the Committee 24 to 48 hours before he appears, but the Committee has no obligation to let him know what questions it will ask. There are no rules of evidence. Insinuations are valid as testimony. The Committee calls up the 'real witnesses,' almost all of them carefully chosen hostile critics who seize the chance to acquaint the national audience with their views.
>
> "Then there is the careful timing of adverse testimony, so that the most sensational tidbit will be released just in time for the newspapers to get the story in their early editions, and just too late for the defendant to answer. The next day his careful rebuttal is drowned out by a flood of new accusations."
>
> It should be noted that although the witness files a written statement 48 hours in advance, he is warned to say nothing to the press about his testimony prior to actually testifying. The committee staff, on the other hand, may release information to the press even the night before the appearance, telling of the charges leveled at him, his company, and his industry.
>
> No one should assume that every Congressional investigation is conducted on this pattern, for this is not true. The more crusading type of investigation, however, is very likely to fall into this form—television cameras and all.
>
> How does one prepare for such an encounter? Thorough preparation involving both legal and public relations staffs is the answer offered by those who have been through the experience. Volumes of material which might be of use should be carefully cross-indexed and catalogued under numerous headings. Witnesses can thus obtain exact information quickly as the questioning moves from one area to another.
>
> Also recommended is that the witness himself, whoever it may be, should submit himself, for as long as a month before the sessions, to a complete inquisition. In the course of this preparing, he should be incessantly grilled by his lawyers and public relations staff

WORKING WITH FEDERAL GOVERNMENT

Figure 5-2. At many Congressional or federal agency hearings the media dominate the occasion. Their desire for strong news and visual materials often determines the course and result of a witness' appearance. Plans for handling the media situation are vital. (UPI photo)

with the most difficult and confusing questions they can develop.

There is no substitute for complete knowledge of the subject under investigation. Nor is there any real substitute for capacity of a witness to create headlines and stories favorable to his cause....

C. Joseph Stetler, who as president of the Pharmaceutical Manufacturers Association is a veteran of many Washington hearings, says:

Our preparation now includes a multitude of duties such as realistically pinpointing our areas of vulnerability, trying to fathom the form and substance of the attacks we can expect, roughing out the answers, and ascertaining what material we have and what further facts and figures or other information we need to support our claims.

Stetler further recommends that position papers be prepared well in advance and given to the media before they have received the investigator's charges; that witnesses go through a rehearsed hostile grilling by staff in advance; that attacks made in the hearing room be promptly and vigorously countered with accurate replies for the media; and that the organization continuously maintain good relations with the media so they will be open-minded when such a hearing occurs.

OTHER TECHNIQUES

A full spectrum of public relations tools and techniques can be employed in Washington. Despite the heavy emphasis on fact finding, research, and face-to-face contacts, the more normal methods are used frequently. These include news releases, speeches, statements and testimony before hearings, newsletters, bulletins, pamphlets, books, story placements, press relations, radio-TV placement on public affairs and interview programs, presentations with graphics and audio-visuals, news conferences, seminars, and public relations advertisements. All of these are covered in Section V, encompassing Chapters 38 through 51.

LOBBYING AND FOREIGN AGENT REGISTRATION

Many words have been written on whether public relations is lobbying, often with the implication that there are sinister connotations. The simple fact is that lobbying in Washington is a recognized activity and most Senators and Representatives find lobbyists useful in supplying facts on complicated legislative matters. If anyone, whether he is a public relations practitioner or not, actively seeks the enactment of legislation—or the defeat or amendment of legislation—he is engaged in lobbying. Then he must register under the Federal Regulation of Lobbying Act. He does this through the Clerk of the House or Senate, stipulating the name of the interest he represents and disclosing how much he spends on lobbying activities for that interest. The question of whether a public relations man should or should not register is resolved by what he is doing. And the failure to register, in borderline cases, might be more serious.

The same applies to Foreign Agent Registration where disclosure is required by registering with the Department of Justice. If the public relations man's primary function is to create favorable reactions for a foreign client, or foreign interests, it is prudent for him to register.

WHO DOES PUBLIC RELATIONS WORK IN WASHINGTON?

The congenital problem of public relations, that anyone can use the term, is maximized in Washington. The persuasive techniques of public relations are used by various kinds of persons: company, association, and union representatives; lobbyists; government sales personnel; lawyers; and retired government officials, including former cabinet officers, Congressmen, and military officers.

Thomas W. Miles, Washington public relations counselor who wrote the article, "Public Relations Practice in Washington" (*Public Relations Quarterly,* Fall 1964) has this additional comment to make on the need for a closer working relationship between the bar and public relations:

> Public relations and legal counsel have complementary roles—separate but dependent—in working with the Congress and the Federal regulatory agencies. That of the practitioner in public relations is to develop public opinion and to bring it to bear on legislative matters. That of the practitioner in the law is the nitty-gritty of method and language and especially analysis of legal implications.
>
> The differences between them are brought out strikingly at Congressional hearings. To public relations counsel these can be opportunities for clients to plead effectively not only to their Senators and Representatives but through and beyond them to the public. It must be recognized that Congressional hearings, wired to printed and electronic media, are national amplifiers of great magnitude. In certain political contexts these hearings must also be just as assiduously avoided.
>
> By contrast lawyers are inclined to regard such hearings as quasi-judicial proceedings rather than pleadings before the bar of public opinion. Their pitch is for precision if not persuasion. They rely on the cogency and completeness of the printed record more than its sales appeal. This is said not to detract from their function as much as to press for management recognition of the public relations involved in Congressional relations.

There is no accurate count of the number of persons in Washington who could be called public relations workers of a professional nature. The membership roll of the Washington Chapter of the Public Relations Society of America, approximately 350, is a start. The Yellow Pages of the telephone directory give a clue, but do not list the number of employees in the agencies listed. Then there are the public relations officers of major companies, unions, all of the various interest groups, and the trade associations.

Trade and professional associations have been moving to Washington and they are all engaged in some form of public relations activity. It is believed that Washington now has more associations than New York, which formerly led. And many non-Washington based associations maintain a Washington office or counseling firm.

But the biggest number of public relations men is in the federal government. This is general knowledge, but since they exist in fact, but not law, they cannot be counted. Under a 1913 law "publicity experts" are "not to be employed without specific appropriation, and no money appropriated by any act shall be used for the compensation of any publicity expert unless specifically appropriated for that purpose." While the law does not specifically prohibit public relations, it has that effect.

Consequently, public relations specialists in government carry out their assignments under such titles as administrators, directors and secretaries for public affairs, public or press information officers, or directors of information.

It is difficult to get reliable figures on the number of public relations persons in the federal government. It could be 4,000 or 19,000, depending on the definition, according to Alvin M. Hattal in "Washington Focus," *Public Relations Journal,* Feb. 1976. He writes:

> Just how big *is* this bureaucratic army? Bill Ragan, public affairs director for the Civil Service Commission, who should know, says there are about 4,267 jobs in public information writing and editing, including 2,375 in public information. Of the total, some 39 percent are in the Defense Dept., 38 percent in other cabinet departments, and 23 percent in other agencies. But if you include all other related job categories—e.g., technical writing and editing, illustrating, translating, audio-visual production, foreign language broadcasting, photography—the total is more than 19,000.

Hattal also quotes George Will, *Newsweek* columnist, as claiming that the government spends $400 million annually on public information, "more than the news budgets of the AP, UPI, and the three radio-TV networks combined."

By whatever name they are called, government information officers are helpful to public relations men in giving information, but can be strong competition when an organization takes an adversary position with the government. At high policy levels, public relations men function, as political appointees, in promoting their bosses, just as every Senator and Representative has someone on his staff with writing experience, often newspaper, who functions in public relations.

There is, however, one government agency that makes no pretenses about its public relations role: The U.S. Information Agency uses every device of modern communication to interpret American life and foreign policy throughout the world. It has some 8,500 employees, many of them qualified public relations professionals. Ironically, however, this agency has never been headed by a professional public relations practitioner.

During the coming decade, as the nation struggles with great social problems—unemployment, urban affairs, energy, environment—the job of the Washington public relations practitioner will intensify and will receive greater recognition. In years past, Washington public relations men have sometimes felt that their colleagues around the country did not understand the special nature of Washington. Now with the rise of public affairs as a specialty within the field, including government relations, the gap is narrowing.

One occupational hazard of public relations is accentuated in Washington. The practitioner everywhere must be close to, often a part of top management, and yet see the outside point of view. But in Washington, he deals on a friendly day-to-day basis with government officials who are potential adversaries. He becomes very much a man in the middle, sometimes suspect by the very organization he serves. Management must be educated to rely on the objectivity that brings the results that can be obtained by qualified Washington representatives.

The use of public relations by various interest groups helps insure, as in our legal system, that various points of view get a fair hearing. And if the dream of a "Citizen's Lobby" ever comes true, there will be an even bigger role for the professional Washington public relations practitioner.

SOURCES

Many sources of information important to the organization interested in Washington appear in Chapter 36 and in the Bibliography. A basic list of recommended references and tools, in addition to the important sources quoted in this chapter, includes:

Congressional Monitor and *Congressional Monitor's Bimonthly Directory of Key Congressional Aides,* Washington, D.C.

"Congress and the Media: Partners in Propaganda," Ben H. Bagdikian, *Columbia Journalism Review,* January/February 1974.

"Government Relations—The Growth Specialty," Ralph O. Baird, *Public Relations Journal,* February 1974.

"How to Explain Your Business—in Washington," Gene E. Bradley and Carl F. Hawver, *Public Relations Journal,* February 1974.

"Press Release Politics: How Congressmen Manage the News," Peter Gruenstein, *Progressive,* January 1974.

"Three Ways to Improve Government Information," Carlton E. Spitzer, *Public Relations Journal,* August 1973.

"Washington Focus" by Alvin M. Hattal, monthly column in *Public Relations Journal.*

The *Washington Influence Directory,* Ed and Amelia Zuckerman, 1975, Washington, D.C.

The Voice of Government, edited by Ray E. Hiebert and Carlton Spitzer, John Wiley & Sons, New York, 1968.

The Creative Interface, edited by Robert W. Miller, The American University School of Business Administration, Washington, 1968.

Corporate Management in a World of Politics, Harold Brayman, McGraw-Hill, New York, 1967.

"Dateline Washington; The Anatomy of the Capital Press," Howard Penn Hudson, *Public Relations Journal,* November 1969.

Politics and the Press, edited by Richard W. Lee, Acropolis Books, Washington, 1970.

The Businessman's Guide to Washington, William Ruder and Raymond Nathan, Prentice-Hall, Englewood Cliffs, N.J., 1975.

Hudson's Washington News Media Contacts Directory, edited by Howard Penn Hudson and Mary Elizabeth Hudson, Washington, D.C. (Annual compendium of Washington press corps.)

United States Government Organization Manual (Annual), Government Printing Office, Washington, D.C.

Congressional Directory (Biennial), Government Printing Office, Washington, D.C. (Annual).

Congressional Staff Directory, Charles B. Brownson, Washington, D.C. (Annual).

"Public Information in Government Policy," Carlton Spitzer, *Public Relations Journal,* February 1968.

(Note: The telephone directories of the various governmental agencies are also available through the Government Printing Office.)

6

Working with State Government

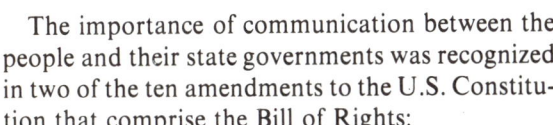

RICHARD A. ARMSTRONG is Executive Director of the Public Affairs Council, a non-profit, bipartisan professional organization of corporate public affairs executives headquartered in Washington, DC. He is recognized as one of the nation's foremost authorities on corporate public affairs.

Mr. Armstrong, who joined the Public Affairs Council (formerly The Effective Citizens Organization, Inc.) in 1957 as Field Director, was named Executive Director in 1959. Under his direction, the Public Affairs Council has become the recognized professional and clearinghouse organization for more than 500 corporate public affairs programs.

His business and professional experience includes a staff assignment with the University of Minnesota; a position with the Minneapolis Chamber of Commerce; and employment with the Mutual Benefit Life Insurance Company.

Mr. Armstrong holds a Bachelor of Arts degree from the University of Minnesota and has done graduate work at the University of Birmingham in England.

The importance of communication between the people and their state governments was recognized in two of the ten amendments to the U.S. Constitution that comprise the Bill of Rights:

ARTICLE I.

Congress shall make no law respecting an establishment of religion, or prohibiting the free exercise thereof; or abridging the freedom of speech, or of the press; or the right of the people peaceably to assemble, and to petition the Government for a redress of grievances.

ARTICLE X.

The powers not delegated to the United States by the Constitution, nor prohibited by it to the States, are reserved to the States respectively, or to the people.

THE NEED

Until recently only a few organizations had a state government relations program worthy of the name. State governments were ignored by most businesses, associations, and other private institutions. Whereas dozens of companies in the fifties and sixties opened Washington legislative relations offices or hired consultants or law firms for their "eyes and ears" on the national scene, they were virtually oblivious to legislative events in Springfield, Sacramento, or St. Paul. The "need equation" between business and state government, so apparent before the turn of the century, had been pushed out of management's consciousness by the accretion of power at the national level.

Hindered by antiquated and restrictive constitutions, malapportioned legislatures, poor use of resources, and massive public distrust or disinterest generated by earlier abuses of power, state governments had become unable or unwilling to fully exercise their residual powers. The federal government responded ahead of the states to the complex problems of modern society with an aggressive expansion of programs and services. Into the vacuum of state inaction gradually moved the subsidy programs and the administrative agency control of the Washington colossus. States became distribution agents for federal funds—a role that further eroded their legislative initiative through the overlay of federal on state priorities. In addition, controlled largely by rural interests, state legislatures were unresponsive to urban needs; cities logically turned to the federal government for help that, in turn, bypassed the state level in its response. The Depression, World War II, the growth of the cities, and the complexities of urban problems all encouraged public acceptance of the national government as the dominant force in political life.

Today, however, there is a gradual resurgence of the power of state legislatures—partly attributable to the reapportionment decisions of the Supreme Court in the mid-60's and the more recent implementations thereof, and partly due to the growing realization that the federal government is just too big and too remote to deal directly with the needs of local communities. As the Citizens Conference on State Legislatures has expressed it,

> The states determine the boundaries, the legal power and financial resources, the very existence of local government. And the states are large enough to handle the increasing array of problems that ignore all local boundary lines: pollution, transportation, education, land use and urban growth, crime, poverty, and health. States have always had the power to tackle such problems.... But the reapportionment of state legislatures has made it more likely that their membership will understand how acute these problems are and act to meet them.

To wit: in the decade following 1961, state expenditures increased by almost 200%, state employment levels jumped by nearly one million people, the volume of bills at the state level doubled.

The year 1968, however, was an even more significant turning point in the power swing within the federal system, and in the re-emergence of a viable need equation between state government and private organizations.

The election of Richard Nixon brought to the presidency a man determined to restore the power position of the states in relation to the federal government—to a degree that went beyond mere states' rights rhetoric. Nixon's "New Federalism" was designed to strengthen local and state government by giving fiscal incentive and assistance through various types of revenue sharing, and by decentralizing the administration of federal programs. Interest in the concept was intensified by the maturing of the legislatures themselves, by jurisdictional conflict between city and county as suburbs expand, and by growing public awareness that centralized institutions and national programs cannot solve all the problems. States have responded to these various challenges with a niagara of legislative activity—in executive reorganization and legislative reform, and, significantly, in expanding or protecting individual human rights in the consumer, environment, and civil rights fields.

The impact of such events is clear. The need equation between private organizations and state government has been firmly reestablished.

THE PROGNOSIS

What does the future hold? Will the need equation be sustained and strengthened? The following observations have been expressed by experienced and thoughtful public affairs executives:

• **The states will continue to move into new fields and to expand current activities of interest to the private sector.** A long-time consultant in the field estimates that the number of 'important' administrative agencies has doubled in the past five years, reflecting state interest across a wider range of issues. Of the current issues there is every reason to think that consumer protection and pollution control programs will continue to have high legislative priority. Significant related areas of growing economic concern to state legislators cover all phases of land use, as well as use of other resources supporting the extractive industries, regulation of which could have international impact.

• **Lead time for organizations' response to new issues will shorten.** According to veteran state observers, until recent years one could confidently project a three- to five-year cycle from the introduction or passage of a landmark bill in the first state until it appeared on the agenda of most of the other 49 legislatures. Now, they say, lead time on a major issue is often very short for the following interrelated reasons:

> • *The nationalization of politics and issues.* Examples: current legislative efforts to require deposits on nonreturnable containers, and to institute no-fault automobile insurance requirements;
> • *The rapid growth of activist groups* at all levels of visibility. It should be noted that these

groups are not necessarily concerned only with the passage of legislation but try to activate "customer concern" across a broad institutional spectrum, including business;
- *The facilitator of both the above factors: rapid communication.* Clearly, the extraordinary advances in media techniques have expedited public and legislative response to the issues and to their publicists.

• **There will be a continuing rationalization and sophistication of the state government apparatus.** The enhanced capability, vitality, and resources of state government will obviously affect the states' development and the elements that contribute to it. For example,

- *In the executive branch:* extensive bureaucratic reorganization, professionalization of personnel, higher salaries, widespread constitutional revision in the direction of increasing executive power;
- *In the legislative branch:* upgrading of staffing, salaries and research, vastly increased flow of information among state legislative leaders, revitalization of legislative procedures and practices;
- *In the judicial branch:* discernible trend toward unification of the court system, streamlining of judicial administration—through constitutional revision or ongoing work of the various state judicial councils.

• **The discretionary powers of state administrative departments and agencies will increase.** Legislative bodies the world over face a dilemma: as the volume, variety, and complexity of public problems increase, more and more responsibility must inevitably be delegated to the agencies administering specific programs. Enabling legislation establishes the broad policy framework; implementation is of necessity left to the bureaucrats. As a result it occasionally happens that the application or interpretation of a statute can contravene or go beyond its purpose through the arrogation of power not delegated. In such a case organizations' government relations programs having an exclusively legislative orientation would be at a total disadvantage. The executive branch obviously plays an administrative and rule-making role of considerable importance.

• **The interdependence of all levels of government relations efforts is more and more evident.** Many organizations with Washington offices coordinate all their governmental activities from there; others achieve coordination through a vice president or director of public affairs at headquarters. Whatever the system, multi-level coordination has proven necessary because:

- Governmental action at one level of government tends to stimulate pressures for parallel action at other levels. In early 1973, for instance, the Food and Drug Administration announced sweeping new labeling requirements for food products. Within days almost half of the states were considering their own labeling regulations.
- Federal law often promulgates guidelines for national policy on a problem but delegates the implementation to the states and/or local communities (e.g., air and water pollution control programs and occupational health and safety regulations).
- Interest groups seeking the passage of a bill are usually flexible, working simultaneously for action at any level—in city hall, county court house, state capitol, or halls of Congress. In 1973, for example, there were efforts at all these levels to enact land use control measures.
- Business itself is growing more pragmatic about the most desirable level for legislative remedy. Some industries (notably the automotive, canning, and detergent industries) have openly endorsed federal preemption on some issues because of the threat of contradictory and costly variations in the laws that in effect act as internal trade barriers between the states. On the other hand, the more traditional tactic of "leave it to the states" has proven sensible for an industry hard-pressed by a tough bill in Congress.
- Implementation of the New Federalism concept will activate or strengthen regional offices of major domestic agencies on one hand, and move control of spending into the hands of state and local elected officials on the other—thus creating the necessity for increased knowledge of, and access to, state and local power structures while maintaining understanding of the federal program.

• **A near-revolutionary change in the politics of state legislative affairs has occurred.** Some of the aspects are aptly described by a state lobbyist of ten years' experience:

> It's a different ball game, compared to when I first came on the scene. Things were a lot simpler then. When an offensive bill came up

you knew only a few people usually counted—often only one man, the Speaker, because he could pretty much kill a bill if he really went all out. At other times you might be worried about the committee chairman, maybe the majority and minority leaders, and probably how the labor lobbyist felt. Today you get your votes one at a time—no power brokers. It's a much more fluid situation. Not only is the power more fragmented in legislatures I cover, but there are a lot more outside groups which have their say. Even when you think you've got a situation well in hand you're never quite sure until the vote is over.

Other elements include:

- *A change in the type of legislator.* The new breed is younger, better educated, more diverse in background. "Some of these new guys," moans one corporate veteran, "think it's wrong to be seen with a lobbyist—you can't even talk to them." Turnover is also more rapid—more than 25% of the state seats up for election in 1972 were taken over by new people.
- *Institutional changes in the legislature.* Longer and more frequent sessions, pre-session committee work, and continuity of responsibility, interest, and expertise through the work of the legislative councils combine to raise the quality and increase the flow of legislation.
- *Ad hoc political groups.* The proliferation of new citizen lobbies and interest groups creates an unstable element in many legislative struggles.
- *Grass roots public affairs.* Many issues likely to surface in coming years will require public affairs programs transcending the legislative arena. For example, in recent years power companies have launched sizable information campaigns to inform the public about the intricacies of air pollution; insurance companies have undertaken public relations and advertising campaigns to generate support for their positions on disposition of gasoline tax revenues, and in these days of "energy crisis" are joining the utility companies in urging the conservation of power. The rationale for this kind of grass roots program is derived not only from the nature of the issue but from the methods of the opposition. To illustrate: on environmental matters every citizen is affected. Since activist groups are often community-based they can effectively seek understanding and support on this issue at the local level.

From the cumulative weight of these factors it seems apparent that the need equation between private organizations and state government can no longer be obscured by the Washington colossus. And whatever the reasons for the new look in state government, the ballooning impact of state government activity on the business community has impelled a wider corporate awareness. The Public Affairs Council estimates that the number of formal corporate state government relations programs more than doubled between 1970 and 1973.

STATE GOVERNMENT RELATIONS[1]

In the last decade hundreds of organizations have established broad programs to encourage better employee citizenship and to exercise their rights—and responsibilities—as corporate citizens. The terminology applied to these efforts varies—"good government," "effective citizenship," "civic affairs,"—but most generally they are thought of as "public affairs programs." The Public Affairs Council estimates that about 500 of America's largest corporations currently have fairly well developed overall programs that include at least some government relations activities. Twenty-five years ago no firms had formal employee and corporate citizenship programs.

Here are some examples of how organizations use public affairs activities to complement and reinforce state government activities:

- *Encouragement of employee political involvement.* A clear-cut policy—which encourages employees to be good citizens (register, vote, work for a candidate or party, become active in community organization) and facilitates their involvement through liberal time-off policies, leaves of absence, and promotion-evaluation standards that reward such activities—can obviously have a favorable effect on government relations.
- *Communications with employees on state issues and problems.* Many organizations use the house organ, plant newsletters, paycheck inserts, and other devices to inform employees about pending legislation.
- *Corporate efforts to facilitate good state government-business relations.* Some examples:
   - Candidates for state office may be invited in for plant tours, political rallies;

[1] Many of the principles and techniques that follow are applicable to relations with local governments—Ed.

- Companies may promote official efforts to attract industry and tourism, support needed constitutional amendments, identify with legislative reform efforts, and otherwise support "good government" issues;
- Executives may be encouraged to serve on state commissions, advisory boards.
- *Establishment of bipartisan political contributions program.* Some organizations have a two-tier system:
  - An across-the-board program to encourage voluntary employee contributions to the candidate or party of one's choice;
  - An "executive fund" that involves the collection and pooling of voluntary contributions from executives and the allocation thereof to selected candidates at the discretion of a committee or the government relations officer.

These are some of the elements of a well-rounded total state program. Most professionals in state government relations, in fact, view their function as the tip of the iceberg. The depth lies in these supportive public affairs activities.

INFLUENCING THE EXECUTIVE

In 1917 a program for state administrative reorganization enacted in Illinois set in motion a series of nationwide changes that resulted in the governorship becoming a position of increased administrative power and enhanced political prestige. In part these changes were due to declining public confidence in the state legislatures, but they also stemmed from the lessons of business experience that taught the importance of giving the chief executive control over his administrative department heads by making them directly responsible to him. Thus the movement toward legislative reform has been paralleled in the executive branch. Knowledge of the current executive structure of all states in which the organization has an interest is accordingly more and more essential to an effective state government relations program.

Influencing the executive branch, however, is often as difficult as it is necessary. Not only must the lobbyist deal with the Governor, his staff, his appointees, and other elected officials, but he must continuously cope with an increasing number of professional career administrators whose everyday actions could have a significant impact on his organization. Thus the elected and non-elected government officials are separate elements within the executive branch having quite different characteristics in their access to, or use of, power.

ELECTED OFFICIALS

The Governor heads the ticket and is the most visible of the elected officials having executive responsibility. His actual powers are of course constitutionally limited and may depend as much on his qualities of leadership (and a good staff) as on legal authority. But the range and depth of information essential to maintain this leadership is often sought from experienced lobbyists whose expertise can add perspective and practicality to his legislative policy.

In addition to the potential for contributing to the development of a legislative program, the well-prepared corporate state lobbyist, with established access to the executive offices, is able to offer advice on appointments to advisory commissions, to exercise influence on the use (or threat) of a veto on a given piece of legislation, and—in the ongoing development of rapport and respect—to contribute to a favorable political/business climate.

Two specific items to note: Today 43 states give the Governor item veto on appropriation bills; and the New Federalism revenue sharing and bloc grant program to states will give added discretionary authority to the governor.

NON-ELECTED OFFICIALS

Obviously, the goal of lobbying at this level of the administrative hierarchy is to achieve administrative personnel understanding of, and identification with, the day-to-day problems of a particular industry or interest. Influencing the professional career administrator (or regulatory commissioner/board member) is in many cases the most challenging aspect of the government relations executive's job. One such executive expressed this problem succinctly:

> Regulators in general are far tougher [than legislators] to lobby because they rarely have an elective constituency on whose good will they are dependent.

Once an agency or position is created it tends to develop a purpose and direction of its own, having as its primary goal self-perpetuation. Expertise in the program field is frequently developed well beyond the original mandate as a technique for attaining indispensability. Thus the experienced lobbyist knows that the traditional function of providing information/expertise is performed with special attention to detail and a high degree of sophistication when working with career administrators. Although their self-image can sometimes exceed their performance, these individuals consider themselves to be experts, and they usually are. Respect for the bureaucratic sense of professionalism is therefore essential. It can be demonstrated by understanding the overall complexities of the problems confronting the administrator, as well as by precise knowledge of the matter at hand. The lobbyist's credibility and access are improved by carefully researched and updated material that has been tailored to the appropriate reference.

Successful communication with non-elected officials can also arise from prior lobbying success in the legislature. For example, significant input is possible in the construction of the authorizing legislation for agencies affecting an organization's interest. Consistently providing reliable information to, and working well with, individual legislative committees and committee chairmen puts the lobbyist in a position to set the stage for future relationships with the agency—by influencing how the bill is written and the tone of its guidelines and criteria. Thus, at the regulatory stage—when the rule-making power inherent in the interpretation of the legislation is actually implemented—the lobbyist's points of view are tacitly represented and his leverage is projected through the legislative oversight function of the committee chairmen whose support he has already gained.

In sum, today's successful state government relations program necessarily includes an executive as well as a legislative lobbying effort because of the compelling potential for:

- multiplying effectiveness through the interaction between the two branches;
- creating a favorable political/business climate through rapport with elected administration officials, including the Governor;
- contributing to the development of the Governor's legislative policy;
- offering advice on appointments, and on use of the veto;
- providing essential information to non-elected government officials in the implementation of legislation affecting the organization's interests.

APPROACHES TO STATE GOVERNMENT RELATIONS

What are the components of a successful state government relations program? Technique? Type of industry? Political climate? Attitude of top management? The list includes all of these and more.

THE TECHNIQUES

"There are less than a dozen basic techniques of lobbying," according to one expert, "whether one is trying to influence the United Nations or a village Council." Accordingly, a useful way to discuss approaches to state government relations is to focus on these basic techniques.

A few—very few—organizations use all the basic approaches. The best illustrations are often found among large one-state companies with an obvious and unavoidable vested interest in effective state relations—companies whose very existence, or at least operating conditions, are dependent on state government—for example, public utilities.

The one-state company. An examination of the state government relations activities of one large utility company in an eastern state reveals the key approaches.

- The company maintains a year-around presence in the state capital. A staff of two full-time professionals monitors state legislative activities, orchestrates the company's effort to influence legislation and assists home office personnel in their relationships with the state regulatory body and other key administrative agencies.
- Managers and executives throughout the state are expected to cultivate relationships with state legislators from their localities. The manager of each local office, for example, becomes acquainted on a first-name basis with his state representatives and senators and works hard at cultivating the legislators' understanding of the company and its problems.
- Occasionally the company retains a legal firm in the state capital to help the company's professional lobbyists handle a particularly difficult legislative situation. Generally this occurs when the company is confronted with an issue in which the law firm has special competence and credibility or when a close relationship with key legislators would be especially beneficial.
- The company is also an active member of the state Chamber of Commerce and several other state

business organizations. On some issues it will coordinate its efforts closely with the association's state government relations staff, or rely on the association for the entire load.
- On relatively rare occasions and in the face of a very serious legislative problem the company may turn to satellite groups for assistance. If a proposed bill, for example, would seriously inhibit the company's growth, it might communicate its position to suppliers, customers, the company's labor union(s), and other groups that might be affected by company adversity.
- On even more infrequent occasions the company may take its case on a particular problem to the grass roots. This would occur when management concluded that "taking it to the people" is the only way to win on an important vote in the legislature.

This company makes its case with the help of six kinds of individuals or organizations:

- the professional lobbyists on staff
- the line personnel
- the consultants
- the associations
- the satellite groups
- the people

The multi-state company. Multi-state companies do the best they can to adapt and combine these techniques. However, only a minority of the Fortune 500 companies have anything worthy of being called a "program" in state government relations. Instead, the most typical approach is the "home office trouble shooter" technique. This system has worked often enough that its successes have tended to obscure the need for a longer-range view.
- The company may have a professional staff member assigned to watch the state where the company is headquartered and one or two other states critical to the company.
- Or the company's public affairs officer (who usually has other responsibilities) has had to develop some kind of mechanism to stay informed about important legislative developments in these few states.
- The company pays little attention to legislative developments in other states. In effect, it relies on trade associations or sister firms from its industry in other states to protect its legislative interests.
- Crisis: one day the company feels threatened by a proposed state law or regulation. It will put together an ad hoc operation to meet the challenge—quick contacts with trade associations, employment of high cost legal firms or government relations consultants, a number of trips to and from the state capital by the assembled team of experts—resulting in an accommodation perhaps just short of catastrophe. The learning value of the crisis often does not penetrate deeply and the company may revert to its normal degree of disinterest until the next threat arises.

At least a few of the same six groups are at work. But because of occasional success plus lack of budget, staff, and management commitment an inefficient system is perpetuated.

EMERGING TECHNIQUES

The professional staff lobbyists. Many of the organizations having investment or marketing interests in all the states, and a staff of full-time professional government affairs experts, find that a regionalized structure may offer a workable system. The country is divided into contiguous regions, each of which is assigned to an executive. Typically, a region may be composed of from six to ten states. Most companies coordinate their regional offices out of the central corporate office through the director of government relations or of public affairs—although a great diversity of organizational and operating relationships does exist. The regional representative is expected to monitor the state legislatures within his territory, to handle most of the legislative problems, and to develop strong ties with influential legislators and their staffs.

There are a variety of ways the effectiveness of a numerically limited professional staff can be expanded and supported. Here are a few:
- If it is necessary, company representation in every state capital may be accomplished through full-time employees, consultants (or a combination), with corporate executives handling the most important states.
- The company may have regional executives supplemented by use of consultants and law firms.
- The company may limit its coverage to the states in which it has the most intense interest. Legislative problems in other states are then handled on an *ad hoc* basis.
- The company may rely heavily on operating, sales, and staff personnel for much of the monitoring and contact work, with the regional executives coordinating and servicing such legislative activities.

Line Personnel. Few organizations knowledgeable in state politics ignore the potential for political effectiveness within the ranks of its employees. A trend in newer state programs is an effort to involve corporate executives at the plant or regional level more effectively in the legislative program. In the words of one public affairs officer,

> We have come to recognize that the name of the game is grass roots involvement. A plant manager acquainted with his legislator, or assisting in his campaign, or writing him a personal letter on a particular issue—these things may count more than whatever I can do. After all, he's a constituent.

Some companies have systemized what has been called a "man to man defense" whereby executives are assigned to cultivate personal relationships with designated legislators or administrators. Other companies conduct periodic inventories of middle (as well as top) management to discover "who knows who" in state government. A large number of companies occasionally request that managers, on a voluntary basis, communicate the company position on a pending issue to elected officials.

Although most experienced public affairs officers recognize the importance of such grass roots involvement, there are problems. For example, more than one company has been embarrassed by an executive's letter that overstated a problem, threatened the legislator, or was otherwise impolitic. This fact suggests that if managers are to play an effective role in the company's program, they might welcome some help with the subtleties of politics and government, some form of communication and information to keep them up to date and motivated, and some overall assistance and guidance from the public affairs department. To meet such needs, one company with a number of state government relations committees has developed the following mechanism:

- regular meetings of these state committees;
- an information newsletter to keep members posted on legislative developments and to build support on key issues;
- a "Public Affairs Manual" providing background information and guidelines for the committee members;
- annual meetings, often hosted by the company president, at which the importance of the local executive is noted and applauded;
- occasional seminars designed to build political sophistication, conducted by either the company or an outside organization.

Consultants. Almost all large companies with records of success in state government relations have used consultants on occasion. No state capital is without these experts who either have their own public affairs or government relations firms or are specialists within the public relations and legal firms that are developing a government affairs capability.

These are the usual reasons a company uses a consultant:

- the cost on an occasional basis may be less than the necessary expense for a continuing corporate program;
- the company doesn't know its way around politically in the particular state;
- the consultant happens to be a specialist in the particular field in question;
- the consultant has particular influence with legislators who have important control of the issue in question;
- outside objective expertise is called for because of internal jurisdictional conflict between the government relations, legal, or public relations departments.

On the other hand, as one highly respected consultant puts it, "Consultants are a mixed bag. It's hard for the uninitiated to sort out the doers from the talkers." And obviously, by the nature of their profession, even the best of the doers cannot be identified exclusively with the organization or have thorough knowledge of its concerns—a fact that carries the possibility of dilution of effectiveness or, at worst, an unrecognized conflict of interest. A further caution: the company should have an absolutely clear agreement as to what it expects a consultant to do, how much discretion he can exercise, and what the financial arrangements will be.

Associations. The role of business associations (multi-industry groupings such as state manufacturers' associations) and trade associations (single industry groups such as a retail merchants' association) in state government relations appears to be in transition. As a whole, these groups are devoting more resources to this task than ever before, yet many active companies are uncertain about their effectiveness. Most feel that they cannot rely exclusively on associations, but they are quick to suggest that associations can play a useful role as eyes and ears in the state capital, that they are often effective on general issues that cut broadly such as business tax legislation, and that they are undoubtedly helpful in activating apathetic elements in the business community.

Associations, because they represent diverse elements, must reach a compromise position on most issues—compatible to all constituents. This often does not square with the particular company's position. Accordingly, in general, trade associations are probably valued more highly than business associations as legislative action vehicles.

No generalization about associations can be made, however. Each association in a given state must be evaluated on its own performance. A highly regarded association under dynamic leadership can develop respect both within the business community and at the capitol. Most companies will approach the question on a state-by-state, issue-by-issue basis. They will compare the assets the association may bring into a particular situation with the accompanying liabilities.

Here are some ways affiliation with an association can be of value:

- as general contributor to a better business climate;
- as a source of intelligence and information on key legislative issues in that state;
- as a major instrument in the company's overall program. For example, a company dominant in its industry may prefer not to appear dominant and so will work principally through associations;
- as a major factor in coalescing and coordinating state legislative activity among member firms. For example, in 1972 a large association launched a comprehensive program to "assure consistent, responsible and constructive action by the industry in regard to the legislative and administrative activities of state and local government." Elements included appointment of a coordinator for each state, creation of state government relations committees, and appointment of a national director for the overall program.

Satellite groups. At least two national companies rely principally on working through suppliers, customers, and other satellite groups. This is a technique that has been used selectively by a growing number of companies.

The public affairs manager of a company that has pioneered with this technique identifies three preliminary steps:

- Mobilize the broadest possible group of satellites at the highest possible level—the executives of those servicing, or serviced by, the company (banks, unions, insurance, storage, and distribution companies, for example);
- Develop comprehensive profiles of each satellite (its ties to the company, sales, employment, potential political strengths, contact persons);
- Establish and maintain good working relationships with them on a continuing basis, so when the crunch develops the company will be able to illustrate how the proposed statute or regulation could help (or hurt), and will be in a position to offer assistance in the form of a plan of action.

The people. It can safely be predicted, for reasons noted previously, that companies will be successful in many future legislative and regulatory struggles only if they are effective in grass roots public affairs. In essence, they will have to win the support of the public before they can prevail in the legislative arena.

This probability will hold true not only for the one-state company (which often may constitute a major portion of the state's economy or provide a major portion of its services), but for the multi-state company as well—even though such a task may seem staggering for a major national organization.

NEEDS AND CHALLENGES

There are as many problems as there are companies and units of government, but two stand out as common to almost all companies considering the establishment of a state government relations program.

HOW TO MAINTAIN EFFECTIVE SURVEILLANCE

It is estimated that in 1973 140,000 bills were introduced in the various state legislatures. For a company with nationwide interests this volume appears to create an insurmountable obstacle. Furthermore, many bills are so complex or ambiguous that evaluating and analyzing even the most important would seem hopeless. There are no simple solutions, but here are ways some companies are handling the problem:

- **Private legislative information services.** While efforts have been made to establish such services, many have foundered on the immense "front end" cost of establishing an effective network in the 50 state capitals with the concomitant analytical capability. The good ones are consequently expen-

sive and scarce, and the time between bill introduction and notification of the organization is sometimes unacceptable. Value to a client is apt to be more quantitative than qualitative in terms of selectivity of information.
- **Providing a monitoring system for all capitals where the company has serious interests.** Some companies hire consultants or stringers to do this; others with a regional set-up may rely on their staff; a few train operating or staff executives to do the job.
- **Reliance on a company's own *ad hoc* system.** A sample combination: use of the industry association in some states, corporate watchdogging of the more important capitols, and use of consultants, legislative reporting services, or informal liaison in remaining locations.

HOW TO GAIN MANAGEMENT SUPPORT

A long-time consultant in government relations states flatly that the biggest single failure among companies in this field is lack of management commitment. He suggests that too many companies regard public affairs and government relations as a kind of fringe activity—underfinanced, understaffed, out of the mainstream of corporate priorities.

Significantly, he believes that the failure is not totally that of top management but rather of the government relations staff. The government affairs executive must relate his function to the "bottom line."

A number of corporations have estimated the costs saved by legislative efforts that resulted in passage or defeat of important legislation. A survey of more than 70 corporations a few years ago disclosed 54 such cases with computed corporate public affairs "savings" of more than $20 million (most of it in the legislative area). Such figures can be misleading, of course. Seldom can the government relations executive claim that his company's efforts alone killed or passed a bill. Some defeated "bad bills" may realistically have had no chance of passage anyway—with or without the company's involvement.

But even if the relationship of the state government relations program to the bottom line is measurable to a degree sufficient to make a case, the government relations executive is still likely to be more successful if his company already has the public acceptance that is generated by a strong overall public relations program.

Broadreaching public relations objectives—well-communicated by word and action, initiated and sustained by a high degree of top management commitment—are essential in dispersing adversary attitudes between the private and the public sector and in developing a climate receptive to recognizing a mutuality of interests. Thus, in the final analysis, it is the chief executive who sets the tone, and whose decisions will make the difference in business-government relations.

Oversimplified, in the long run top management interest and support will come as a result of a creative combination of the following:

- A well-prepared "selling and telling" job when the program is initiated—so the top executives clearly understand the rationale and have related it to overall corporate self-interest. Development of a corporate policy statement establishing the rationale and objectives of the government relations program can be useful.
- Education of, and communication with, management as a continuing and cumulative process.
- Use of top level policy committees to develop corporate positions on key legislation. This can be helpful in the growth of political understanding among those who develop the positions.
- A major public issue that threatens the company earnings, perhaps its very viability. Often it is only a crisis that can sensitize management on the importance of government relations. The tide of environmentally related legislation, for instance, that began running in the late sixties stimulated establishment or broadening of dozens of government relations programs in the industries affected—notably paper, chemicals, oil, and steel.
- A major public issue with high visibility that is in apparent conflict with another major issue that is causing equivalent public concern—for example, when "environment" meets "energy crisis." Such a polarity of interest can result in a temporary problem-solving truce in which top management can be encouraged to play a constructive role with government. For by responding positively in areas where business-government cooperation is necessary to overcome a problem, business can create the opportunity to increase its effectiveness on other issues touching more vitally on corporate self-interest.

WORKING WITH STATE GOVERNMENT

HOW TO GET STARTED

Following is a list of things to consider in developing a state government relations plan:

- **Profile the company from a government relations point of view.** In how many states does it have a significant interest (plant/operating, product/marketing, etc.)? Identify the legislative or regulatory areas in which operations and profits are affected, or potentially affected, by state actions.
- **Inventory the company's political resources.** What's the track record? How have things been handled and with what success? How strong is the overall public affairs program? What percentage of employees is active in political and community affairs? What is the company's public image? What business or trade associations does the company belong to?
- **Determine the components of a successful program within your industry.** Gather information from the corporate sources listed in the following section. Which method worked best? What organizations were most reliable? How was surveillance maintained? How was top management support achieved?
- **Review the political climate of the state(s) in which the company might be politically active.** (See following section.) Is the company likely to be in a vulnerable position? Are there conflicting statutes in different states? What are the voting statistics?— the party strengths?

In working up a new state government relations program, these suggestions will be helpful:

- Resist an unrealistic deadline. Insist on enough time to do the necessary homework.
- Develop a hard-nosed rationale. The case must make business sense.
- Be specific. Develop anticipated costs, outline problems and obstacles, define priorities and procedures.
- Outline options, properly analyzed as to costs, benefits, and disadvantages.
- Use the company and satellite group structure, in long-term roadmapping. Catalog things like technical division expertise, supplier interest, plant manager local contacts.

The result of your effort should see the creation of one or more new positions for state government relations work. Many companies promote from within to fill these new positions, perhaps tapping an executive who has been very active in politics or community affairs, or the person who has handled the infrequent contacts of the company with state government previously. The trend, however, is toward bringing from the outside an individual with political and legislative experience. As the manager of one of the country's most sophisticated corporate state programs puts it,

> Ideally, we need a person who knows the company through and through and is also well indoctrinated in state legislative matters. Naturally, we have few such people already as employees. Though many of my colleagues in other companies would disagree with me, I take the political experience over the company background because I think I can provide him the necessary information on the company. But I can't teach him political instincts or the subtleties of politicians. In our company, therefore, we have obtained most of our new lobbyists in recent years from among the ranks of trade association lobbyists, ex-legislators or legislative staff members, and lobbyists working for other companies or special interests.

SOURCES AND RESOURCES

CORPORATE PROGRAM INFORMATION

To develop a program tailored to its own goals the organization getting started in state level government relations needs some basic information on other programs to compare and evaluate, and from which to form guidelines. Here is a checklist of sources:

- *Other active companies,* particularly within the industry. The administrators of successful programs usually will be glad to share their perspectives and brief you fully on their activities. Write the Public Affairs Council for names and addresses (1220 16th St., N.W., Washington, D.C. 20036).
- *The industry association.* Most large associations have trained government relations specialists who are familiar with the activities of leading companies within the industry.
- *State and local Chambers of Commerce.* Many are aware of strong corporate programs within their jurisdictions and can provide leads. The Council of State Chambers of Commerce, 1028 Connecticut Avenue, N.W., Washington, D.C. 20036, can give addresses of their member Chambers. The U.S. Chamber, at 1615 H St.,

N.W., Washington, D.C. 20006, also keeps track.
- *Consultants.* There are a few public affairs firms whose specialty is advising companies on how to initiate and implement a state capability. Some companies retain a consultant on a continuing basis to furnish ongoing guidance on procedures and strategy. Write the American Association of Political Consultants, 633 Third Avenue, Suite 1330, New York, New York 10017 for general information.
- *The Public Affairs Council.* PAC's Department of Government Relations Services is available to counsel on an individual basis with companies setting up a state program, and to act as a broker of information on corporate government relations programs at all levels. In addition, the Council conducts lobbying workshops, seminars, clinics, and conferences for executives with varying degrees of experience. For example, in 1976 state level lobbying clinics and conferences were held in six different cities.

STATE GOVERNMENT INFORMATION

Once the preliminary decisions have been made about the format of the program itself, the organization must get to "know the territory" from a political standpoint—how the various state governments with which the company will be interacting are structured; the powers, duties, and responsibilities of these governments, plus something of the history and economy that bear on attitudes of the electorate and the elected. What are the issues of prime concern? What are the positions of individual officeholders apt to be? A checklist of sources:

State Government

• Most state tax commissions publish revenue and expenditure charts. • The budget and budget message can be obtained from the governor's office. • State election boards sometimes publish reports on election returns, votes on referenda, etc. • The Legislative Council or its equivalent, or the "boiler room" of either House can usually supply a directory of legislators, an outline of procedures, or a summary of proceedings.
• Reference libraries and research bureaus affiliated with the three branches of government can provide copies of bills, committee reports, or other key documents. • Regulations governing a given industry are best obtained directly from the appropriate state commission. • Individual legislators and other government officials and their staffs usually respond readily to specific requests for information.

State Organizations

• *Chamber of Commerce.* In those states where it exists, the Chamber is a good source for an overview of the economy with statistics and percentages quickly at hand. It will usually have a directory of the major state industries, the manufacturers and trade associations, and the statewide volunteer organizations and their officers.
• *Industry and trade associations.* These organizations often monitor government activities and publish periodic bulletins on significant developments. The State Chamber, or the Chambers of the larger metropolitan areas, may do this too.
• *The League of Women Voters.* In most states, the state League office publishes, and tries to keep updated, a profile of the structure and operation of the government, often including a section on the history and economy. Brief biographical material on state office-holders, as well as their position statements on selected issues, can be made available on request since Leagues usually gather this information for their pre-election voters' guides. State Leagues also monitor legislation on issues they favor or oppose and some publish legislative newsletters available by subscription. Issues vary from state to state.

National Organizations

• *National or regional trade/business associations.* On particular issues of widespread corporate impact these organizations may monitor state as well as national legislation. Write the Public Affairs Department of the Chamber of Commerce of the United States, 1615 H Street, N.W., Washington, D.C. 20006 or the National Association of Manufacturers, 1776 F St., N.W., Washington, D.C. 20006.
• *League of Women Voters of the United States,* 1730 M Street, N.W., Washington, D.C. 20036. The national office of the League serves as a clearinghouse of information about state League lobbying positions and can provide the names and addresses of state League presidents. A publications catalog is available on request.

Legislative Organizations

Generally speaking, the organizations on the following list devote themselves to facilitating the interchange of various types of state government information—through research and publication, training programs, forums, and the like. Publications of these organizations known to be particularly useful are listed.

- *Council of State Governments,* Iron Works Pike, Lexington, Kentucky 40505. An association with affiliates of state officials, their staffs, and the professional organizations of various types of state officials; seeks to strengthen and improve state government through research on the various aspects of the state's political system. Publications include: *The Book of States* (biennially) and *State Government* (quarterly).
- *The National Conference of State Legislatures,* 1405 Curtis Street, 23rd Floor, Denver, Colorado 80202. NCSL is a non-partisan public interest group—funded by the states—that works to improve the quality and effectiveness of state legislatures, to assure states a strong, cohesive voice in federal decision-making, and to foster inter-state communication and cooperation. It was established in 1975 with the merger of three previously existing legislative organizations: the *National Legislative Conference,* the *National Conference of State Legislative Leaders,* and the *National Society of State Legislators.* Publications include: *State Legislatures* (eight issues a year) and a weekly newsletter, *Dateline Washington.*
- *Legis50/The Center for Legislative Improvement,* 7503 Marin Drive, Suite 2A, Englewood, Colorado 80110. Formerly the *Citizens' Conference on State Legislatures.* This non-profit, citizen-based organization encourages reform and revitalization of state legislatures through research projects designed to educate the public on the status of state legislatures and the need for reform. Publications include: *Toward a New Decade of Legislative Reform,* 1976, and *The Sometime Governments,* an evaluation of state legislatures, 1971.

Additional sources

- *The press.* Often provides surprisingly detailed information on state government activities. At least one newspaper in every state specializes in close coverage of the legislature and state agencies.
- *U.S. Dept. of Commerce,* Bureau of Census, Washington, D.C. 20233. Publishes *Guide to Recurrent and Special Government Statistics.* Also publishes compendiums of state and local government finances for each fiscal year, available from the U.S. Government Printing office.
- *National Municipal League,* 47 East 68th Street, New York, N.Y. 10021. Monitors trends in state government, does research in areas of electoral reform; publishes periodical, *National Civic Review.*

7

Community Relations

WILBUR J. (BILL) PEAK, retired, was assistant vice president in public relations for Illinois Bell Telephone Company, Chicago.

After graduation from Knox College in 1928, he began his Bell System career with Western Electric. Shortly thereafter he joined Illinois Bell as an accountant. In 1942 he began his company career in public relations as a supervisor.

Over the years Mr. Peak has covered the broad spectrum of company public relations. Emerging functions, such as Community Relations, sprang from his responsibilities at Illinois Bell. Under his supervision the company won several national awards and public relations honors. He received the 1966 Knox College Alumni Achievement Award and the 1971 Distinguished Service Award from the Public Relations Society of America (Chicago Chapter).

He has long been involved in community relations work. He's been associated with all the Chicago chambers of commerce groups (he was president when his junior chamber was voted best in the nation), and active in community planning, taxpayer concerns, Junior Achievement, air pollution abatement, religion, education, health, zoning, Red Cross, and other areas. He is a past president of the Publicity Club of Chicago, the Chicago Chapter of the Public Relations Society of America, the Lake Shore Club of Chicago, and the Knox College Chicago Club. He is a director of The State Bank of Geneva, Ill.

Perhaps no other area of public relations has changed as much in the last few years as community relations. And perhaps no other area is having so profound an effect on the practice of public relations.

Time was when community relations was a courtesy performed aside from what was done to advance the health and welfare of the business. Today, no matter how large, small, or important an institution may be, it can be undermined if its community relationships are haphazard. Both the corporation and the people in the community have an interest in creating an atmosphere of mutual respect and understanding through a Community Relations program—a bridge between the company and the community.

Since we live in an age in which religious, educative, and governmental institutions at all levels can be shaken through the efforts of small minority groups, can any company ignore the likelihood of being similarly affected?

While this chapter looks at community relations primarily from the standpoint of the business world, not for a moment should the assumption be made that this subject is the responsibility of business alone. No institution is without responsibility or capability in this area. And no community can expect any one segment of its society to carry on without the support of its other segments.

The world of business has learned much about its role in the community. Those outside the business community, as well as those inside, can draw from these pages the inspiration and impetus to fulfill their vital community role.

WHAT COMMUNITY RELATIONS IS TODAY

The terms "ecology" and "environment" are heard today more than "community." Defining these words is useful for understanding community relations and how the concept has changed.

Ecology is a science. It once restricted itself to the

relationship of biological organisms to their environment. But business, in a social and economic sense, is also an "organism" operating in an environment. This relationship should be studied, understood, and appropriately responded to.

When speaking of environment, we refer to all the circumstances that surround a business (organism). Obviously, circumstances affect a business, are affected by a business, or affect and change themselves.

Finally, the term "community" has changed. It refers not only to a group of people living in the same locality, but to the interaction of those people. Community, in this sense, is also an organism. Individuals create or join groups; groups oppose each other, unite for a common cause, or attack problems in their own ways.

In the past, the tendency was to treat a community as a rather simple entity—a collection of people, a "home town." Today we are beginning to recognize each community as a complex dynamism of diverse, constantly changing, often powerful, and always important forces. Today, too, such forces are often skillfully organized and well-led. To learn how well-organized and effective they can be, one should read handbooks on community problem-solving techniques. One of the more explicit is "How to Get Things Changed," by Bert Strauss and Mary E. Stone (Doubleday).

Community relations, as a public relations function, is an institution's planned, active, and continuing participation with and within a community to maintain and enhance its environment to the benefit of both the institution and the community.

ITS IMPORTANCE TO BUSINESS

Business is an organism; so is its community. They can and do have profound effects on each other. And both affect and are affected by their mutual environment.

The challenges confronting America's cities and suburbs today are not simple. They require the unified commitment of both the public and private sectors of society, the combined talents and energies of both individuals and organizations.

Two important differences between a community and a business are notable: A community surrounds and permeates a business. A community is unfettered by the policies and organization that control and restrict the operations and performance of a business.

One can conceive of business as somewhat rigid, rational, orderly, protective, playing to its strengths. The community on the other hand can be said to be more flexible, emotional, unpredictable, and seeking strength and protection outside itself.

Business marries the community it settles with. It takes on inherent responsibilities with this association. The need for community relations today might be seen as a wife (community) taking a close look at the marriage vows and discovering her husband (business) owes her more than simple financial support (taxes). Ignore or refuse his marital responsibilities and the husband has the neighbors (public opinion) and the courts (local government) to contend with.

WHAT'S AT STAKE FOR BUSINESS?

From a practical standpoint, only a business' management can specifically answer this question. The relationship of each business, community, and environment is different. While some common considerations can be suggested here, later fact-gathering by you can both dramatize your company's stake in a sound community relations program and suggest the direction and form it ought to take.

You can give yourself a quick indication of this without research (at this point). Take a sheet of paper and divide it with pencil lines into quarters.

1st Block: List the things your company *provides* its community/environment aside from goods and services it is your business to provide. (Jobs? Investments? Tax support? Attractive buildings?)

2nd Block: List the things your company *gets* from its community/environment. (Employees? Transportation? Land? Police and fire protection? Water?)

3rd Block: List the things your company *needs* (but hasn't gotten or needs more of) from its community/environment. (More employees? Lower taxes? Better reputation? Zoning changes?)

4th Block: List *your* gripes about the community/environment *you* live in. (Air pollution? Poor garbage removal? Traffic snarls? Crime?)

Certain considerations should suggest themselves. First of all, the hardest list to create is probably the first one. Subconsciously, you almost have to construct it from the community's point of view.

It wouldn't be unusual if items in your second list were the same as those of your first. For example, providing jobs in a community may well benefit it. But if employees your company needs won't settle in the community, or the community itself can't provide employees, neither your company nor the community benefits.

So the second list should not only suggest the importance of the community to your firm, but may debunk, or at least modify, the idea that business somehow puts more into a community than it takes out.

The tax support argument ("We pay for what we get") bears closer scrutiny than it's generally given. The tax argument is hardly valid until someone sits down and puts dollar values on community benefits, along with the costs to a company of duplicating those services and facilities.

If the point has been made that your business needs its community as much as the reverse, this is sufficient. The third list should show that the community can do more for your company. Your community relations can help it do so.

But what of the fourth list? It speaks to *your* gripes with good reason. What perturbs you personally about your community may be viewed otherwise by your company. But what bothers you and your fellow employees directly affects your company. This list will suggest areas in which your company could play a vital community role.

No company can cure a community illness by itself (unless the company alone is the problem), but it can and should help. You have personal reasons for wanting that help.

Illustrated by your lists, the reason for company involvement is simple: A company cannot hope for a healthy economic climate in which to thrive if the community and environment are unhealthy.

Perhaps the most fatuous idea in business today is that community relations is a corporate philanthropic act, when in fact it's sound business practice. It's a function of corporate self-interest rather than just being a "good citizen."

THE COMMUNITY SPEAKS OUT

Until a few years ago, communities tended to take more passive roles toward the business world. A company coming into a community generally was considered a benefit. And the community contented itself with the same rationale businesses used. A new company meant more jobs, more tax support, more money in the community. The community needed business to survive, still does, and is loathe to jeopardize its relationships with business.

But communities today are finding they cannot remain passive. Other survival factors arise that rival the mere presence of business.

Some communities, too, have learned that most businesses are sufficiently mobile to be attracted from one community to another. So communities have learned they must compete for business. All they can offer is what the community itself can provide. One that is unattractive, problem-beset, or otherwise unhealthy can fail to attract the new business it needs and can lose the business it has.

More to the point, communities have found themselves increasingly less able to cope with the problems that have grown right along with social, economic, and technological improvements in society generally. Community pockets of neglect become pockets of force for change, mindful of their needs and wants and not impressed with the beneficence of either community or business.

The community, unable to cope with the growing magnitude of its problems, is being forced to turn to business for help. It is reluctant to do so, and each day of delay compounds the problems business ultimately will have to face, or physically desert.

For large urban communities, both the problems and their magnitude are patently evident. Businesses in smaller communities may yet have the advantage of responding to community needs before those needs get out of hand.

THE STRUCTURE OF A COMMUNITY (PEOPLE)

It was said earlier that "community" is a complex organism, a collection of diverse, changing, and potent forces. A community is much more specifically definable and has to be carefully analyzed before any reasonable community relations program can be developed.

The basic unit of a community is, of course, the individual. We start with him or her[1] because he's directly responsible for the changing nature of the community.

Man has given himself increasingly greater knowledge, affluence, and highly sophisticated means of communications and transportation. These not only give him more, but daily remind him that more is available. He not only has been able to define his needs and wants better, but he can articulate the resulting values he places on them. (This

---

[1] Wherever a masculine term is used, it applies equally to females.

COMMUNITY RELATIONS

may be one reason company presidents seem to get more and more mail from the citizenry.)

While an individual finds he can achieve certain ends by speaking out for his "rights," he also learns two other important facts. One is that if he joins with others in seeking essentially the same rights, the group voice will be louder and have greater impact. The success of many "consumer groups" points up how effective such voices can become. The other is that within the community are other individuals with common problems who collectively have common control or leverage in a vital function of that community.

Teachers, doctors, plumbers, maintenance personnel, cab drivers, policemen, firemen—these natural groupings, even when not formally unionized, become strong bargaining units in any size community. Their leverage is simply the possible withholding of their service to a community, a service the community cannot reasonably do without.

Whether a group has natural leverage or is simply formed to achieve a specific short-term goal, that group is a force in the community.

Furthermore, whatever the justification of its goals, any group can achieve at least three things: recognition, a hearing, and consideration. These things it can get with minimal effort in a free society with the means of communications the smallest community possesses.

With the first of these acquisitions—recognition—a group can gain additional sympathy and support within the community. And the force of the group grows.

Rotary, Lions, Kiwanis, PTA, Masons, Knights of Columbus, Chamber of Commerce, League of Women Voters, and the like are common community groups. Such groups generally are so ingrained, so identified with the community, and so traditional, we take them for granted. They can be potent forces working in support of sound, company-community goals. Other groups even more likely to involve themselves with company-community goals include such minority-group organizations as Urban League, NAACP, NCCJ, and Operation PUSH.

But there are still other groups that we can identify with much less certainty. These groups usually have names, but we tend to give them labels—minorities, dissidents, liberals, radicals, Yippies, left wing, and right wing groups. And, in recent years, many *new* groups have been formed to act as gadflies in such areas as public housing and job discrimination. Sometimes it's hard to find out what they really want from the community. Still others are intrinsically negative, we know it, and if they have a wholesome objective, it's lost in the unwholesome approach.

All the groups, plus perhaps a few social segments not yet organized, equal the community. All of them work for change in the community's environment.

Some groups actually may serve, or could serve, your company's best interests. Any of them could turn their force against your company, with or without good reason.

In any case, the first step in a community relations program is to know the community and its components intimately.

COMMUNITY STRENGTHS AND WEAKNESSES

Intimate knowledge of the community's components is one of three major areas of research for a sound community relations program. The second is knowledge of the community's strengths and weaknesses. (The third will involve "in house" analysis of your company in terms of its own needs, its own welfare. Does your organization properly share responsiblity for the maintenance of good environment in which its people can live and work as well as one that is conducive to successful functioning? Does it fulfill the responsibility not only in financial contributions and donations made to worthy causes but also in making available the experience and skills gained in the conduct of your business?)

No company can deal with all components of a community or take on all of a community's problems. Nor should a company try. Only some groups and individuals can serve a company's needs. Only some can harm a business if ignored or handled poorly.

Community strengths and weaknesses, advantages and problems, are circumstances (environment), some of which have no effect on your business. Others can substantially alter the course of your business and its future.

But which ones?

Business, which prides itself on careful judgment and money-management, often handles community relations investments—like financial contributions—on the merest hunch they will help the community, let alone the business.

Pure philanthropy is fine, but even it requires the kind of judgment business daily applies elsewhere. Another hospital wing for respiratory ailments, after all, is not the solution to a growing air pollution problem.

Let's look at good contribution judgment at work. The downtown area of Akron, Ohio was deteriorating. Slum conditions festered in commercial and residential property on some 400 acres around the B.F. Goodrich plant. City and company got together and B.F. Goodrich gave Akron $300,000 for a feasibility study on renewal.

The result was the start in 1967 of an urban renewal project in the company's area estimated at $37.5 million. To this the company donated $3.5 million, plus legal and public relations consultation. Called "Opportunity Park," the area is valued well in excess of $200 million. Some 12,500 jobs were saved, with 2,500 more jobs created. The psychological effect on the city and on the company's employees is incalculable.

A sound community relations program must be selective. But selection should take into consideration all the options available. These options have to be assembled.

Weighing needs and strengths. Listing all the problems of a community—crime, pollution, shortages in housing or employment, poverty, inadequate health or education facilities—is important. But so is listing community strengths, including those that account for your business being where it is.

A community needs to maintain its strong points and enhance them. The adversities of a community won't be substantially curtailed if the attractions to that community decline, or if nearby communities begin to excel in your community's strengths.

For example, if your company is in the community because of its strong purchasing power, a campaign to attract more industry to town (adding to the purchasing power) may be highly advantageous to your firm while making your community ecstatic. Promoting your community as a good place to live and work may be an important step in easing a tight labor market.

Once you know the makeup of your community and the environmental factors that affect it, a little cross-indexing can improve both research elements. Relate the wants and needs of individuals, and the causes of groups, to the community strengths and weaknesses. Note those areas that should be receiving attention but are not. Remember, too, that the most despicable individual or group you know still may be striving for an environmental change your community really needs.

SETTING PRIORITIES

It's well, at this point, to establish priorities from the standpoint of the community. What does the community need most? What does it need most to do? Establish these priorities without regard to your company's presence.

Once this is done, make the "in house" analysis of your company in terms of its own needs. What community factors best serve the interests of your company?

This is the point where the four lists suggested earlier should be pursued in earnest.

Now you can relate company priorities to community priorities. Don't attempt to pare resulting lists down. Ten areas for community relations programs, based on what activities will be required, may be simpler to coordinate than two on someone else's list.

All you have, at this point, are areas, or targets, for programs.

By inspection, some of the priorities–from both the community and business standpoints—will suggest long-range programming; some others, short-range. You may want to divide your priorities in this fashion.

YOU'VE COME A LONG WAY

What have the list of priorities and the three research analyses involving community, environment, and your business given you?

1. You have the most appropriate target areas on which your company can and should concentrate with regard to its community.

2. You have target areas with the soundest reasons for your company to take them on (why they are important to your business and the community).

3. You know who, if anyone, is presently working on these target areas. You can determine whether to support the work of individuals or groups in these areas, or work independently, and the ramifications of either approach.

4. You should have a better idea of the pertinency of the actions or lack of actions on your company by the various individuals or groups. You should know which groups are in essence helping your business and the community, and which may be causing your company trouble now or in the future.

5. You have an important list of "publics" for

COMMUNITY RELATIONS

your communications and actions in community relations activities.

Before getting into the creation and implementation of programs, three final points need be made. First, you may now be aware of one or more activities engaged in by your company that may appear wanting in terms of your present perspective. They may well be worth keeping on the grounds of good will or philanthropy. Great care is needed when dropping or easing out of such activities. Yours is not a job of creating new community relations problems for your company.

Second, some sensitivities already may be offended by the "commercial" approach to corporate community relations advocated in these pages. Our rationale is this: Your company will help the community more if a) it can see the practical benefits, b) it brings to bear its own business expertise on the solutions, and c) it stops buckshotting its efforts in a variety of causes with unstudied or unevaluated worth to the community at large.

Up to now, because charity and community relations work overlap, we've not attempted to separate them. Charity is and should be carried on by everyone, including companies. This chapter leaves charity *per se* to the dictates of conscience, and community relations (whether or not charity is involved) to the dictates of common sense.

APPLIED COMMUNITY RELATIONS

PLANNING

However target areas in community relations are stated, they need considerable refinement. The object is to set reasonable goals that can be reasonably met.

Failure to spell out specific goals kills some community relations programs before they get started. In attacking problems on too broad a front, some companies pour money, time, and talent down bottomless holes.

Lump all of a community's concerns under the heading "urban crisis" and you create at once a single, gargantuan problem and the perfect excuse for avoiding it.

Sound community relations programs should give company and community tangible results, not simply warm feelings in "doing good" by simply doing something. Certainly such programs should avoid actions that seem patronizing.

Illinois Bell Telephone, headquartered in Chicago, has two primary target areas on which it concentrates and in which it feels its years of experience give useful expertise. The areas are education and employment. The reason for them is simple: as the second largest employer in the state, the company is in constant need of new employees with adequate educational levels and skills.

These two areas, even before being reduced to specifics, suggest the corporate potential to the telephone company. Programs in these areas may mean more and better qualified employees for the company. Certainly they can mean more wage earners with better, higher-paying jobs as potential customers for the company's service. The payoffs to communities, like Chicago, are self-evident . . . not to mention the values to individuals directly affected. But what was needed by Chicago in education and employment that the company could provide?

Channeling resources. To find the answer, Illinois Bell had to not only select among apparent and hidden community needs, but to relate these to the corporate resources available for programs. These resources—common to all business—are people (time and talent), equipment, facilities, and money (aside from the fiscal value of the other three).

The company long had been providing educational aids for use at all levels of both public and private school systems. School relations people in the company continued to seek advice from, and help for, teachers in classroom needs.

While such efforts continue, the company has increasingly recognized the need to relate the learning process to life as the students will live it, to embed through student experience the practical applications of learning. It also recognizes the importance of giving students as accurate a picture of the business scene as possible.

To that end it is working with educators to develop economic education presentations for use in high school curricula. These focus on the information and informed consumer needs in a variety of everyday business situations.

In another program aimed at high schools, the company co-sponsors, together with Montgomery Ward, "Consumer Education Forums" for high school teachers. These are graduate-level courses to help educators develop innovative teaching concepts, materials, and student projects for classes in personal economics and consumer education.

At the college level, Illinois Bell has cooperated

with Northwestern University in developing a programmatic college that sponsors lecture-discussions focusing on business as an institution. The purpose is to give undergraduates an opportunity to obtain a better understanding of business and its impact on society.

The company continues developing training aids for use in the schools, but the thrust of its main education efforts is now clear.

New employment practices. One example from several in the employment field finds the company using its hiring and training skills on the problem of the so-called "unemployables." What problems are inherent in the testing and employment prerequisites for these people? New methods and new standards of testing—without lowering pertinent quality needs—are being developed. Special training is provided.

A Bell-Tel Training and Work Center now gives work to people previously considered unemployable. This Center combines adult education with production jobs—with pay. Those performing at a satisfactory level move into permanent jobs at regular going wages.

Educational relations is another area of community relations work that can generate a positive reaction in every level of society.

Information and publicity can combine to create an educational program of impressive scope. At Western Electric's regional headquarters in Aurora, Colorado, the original objective of the Technical Advisor Program was to show high school students the nature of the work in various technical-support occupations.

In a few years the program has grown from a once-a-week visit by two Western Electric "advisors" to a city-wide program using 23 advisors from 11 companies. It draws enthusiastic support from the Denver Chamber of Commerce.

Conceived to enrich the standard curriculum through demonstrations of new equipment, new films on current innovations, and individual assistance with student projects, the program was allowed to grow to include first, a deepening commitment to the career concerns of the students, and eventually more formal teacher/advisor development of ways to demonstrate the importance of career decisions and career planning. Expansion of the list of participating companies was particularly valuable since the Technical Advisor Program involved direct contact with actual jobs through visits arranged by the advisors.

The school system is pleased that industry and business people have been intimately involved in the education process. Business views the project as an opportunity to improve the community and benefit everybody. The Chamber of Commerce, although it had long been in contact with top school administrators, is pleased that input at the level of classroom instruction has yielded such a positive and rewarding response.

Having established target areas, how do you establish specific goals or program plans? Finding the specific need may sound simple. But consider the following first:

Call or visit your community's chief political officer. Give him your target area and he'll tell you the jobs that need to be done. You'll get other sets of tasks from each civic leader, the local Chamber of Commerce, and other groups. (Don't forget the lists you made for the target areas.) Newspapers and their editors often have stated community goals worth considering.

What you're collecting are *opinions*. Facts begin with opinions. They're important. But how much research sits behind the mayor's view? Does he really have the whole picture? What motivates his view?

Values of inquiries. Opinions help enlarge the field. Enough of them can give you the assurance of knowing the range of possibilities. Seeking advice has a good public relations ramification, too. It lets each community leader know your company is civic-conscious, is out to take an active part in helping the community, is applying judgment and research in the task, and has thought enough of this leader to ask his advice.

Narrowing your list of opinions to likely prospects, begin to seek out expert advice. Now you are asking about specific tasks and potential programs.

Keep careful records of who told you what in all your interviewing. Playback and recognition of individual contributions to the selected programs is both appropriate and wise. Unused opinions or facts at least deserve follow-up thanks to their providers. A channel of advice once opened needs at least this minimal maintenance toward future use.

State in writing the specific goals that seem most appropriate to your company's interests. Spell out what appears to be involved. Define the limits of the program as you see them.

Then apply the general reasoning developed for the appropriate target areas. Cite the sources that led to your recommendation.

Does the specific objective suggest what company

sources will be needed? If so, note what you think these will be should the company adopt your plan.

Previous experience may permit your outlining in detail the specific requirements of a plan, including estimated costs. Use such detail at this point with caution. You want the program, not the costs, to be weighed first.

If your program is well received, but costs appear prohibitive, you may wish to propose the involvement of others outside the firm to share in the accomplishment, benefit, and costs.

A final reason for care in spelling out resource usage and costs is the availability of others in company management who can find ways of cutting costs once the objective and plan are agreed on.

ORGANIZING

Pity the company president. In many companies, the extent of community involvement is regulated by the number of activities the president can chair. Somehow the idea has taken hold that a community function becomes a company function only if the top executive is directly involved. He may delegate work to others, but only his presence makes it official.

Community relations properly begins at the top, but it needn't stay there. Unless the top executive needs community exposure, he may welcome projects that spread the management participation.

Another tendency is to involve only the "front men"—those whose work responsibilities directly involve the public. The theory is additional community duties may produce valuable contacts for these people and at least help them become better known.

The theory may be true, but it bears looking into. Companies that involve only their contact men in community relations work have an untapped gold mine. Managers and craftsmen working in the catacombs of a business can thrive in the sunshine of the community, enlarging the corporate capability.

General Electric is a good example of personnel resources fully used in community relations work. GE's concentration of activity is problem oriented. Currently it is largely directed to the problems of the disadvantaged across the country, wherever the company's plants are. Company motivation springs from both social concern and the need to fill between 60,000 and 150,000 new jobs in a decade. The company recognizes that many people for these jobs must come from what today are central city ghettos.

Inside the ghettos are the so-called hard-core unemployed—the illiterate, the untrained, the poorly housed youth dropped or dropping out—people ready and wanting to work but already overcome by basic needs of food, clothing, housing, or medical treatment.

Within each General Electric facility are also people with skills and talents potentially helpful in solving community problems in human relations. Most are sympathetic, and—judging from the company's experience—most can be motivated through encouragement, direction, and the experience of others.

Such motivation starts at the top. Corporate commitment begins in terms of money, facilities, participation of executives in joint community-company programs to attack those problems that individual efforts alone cannot handle.

The primary programmed activity of General Electric has been directed toward improving opportunity for minorities through education. Examples are the Program to Increase Minority graduates (PIMEG) and an Expo-Tech mobile unit that was used to visit inner-city schools in major plant communities. Two years after Expo-Tech's visit to Philadelphia middle schools, some 700 minority students who showed potential and interest are participating in activities designed to increase the flow of technical graduates tenfold per year. The school systems of Philadelphia, Camden, New Jersey, and Chester, Pennsylvania are participants, and nine colleges and 24 businesses are involved. The program is not designed to make high school students engineers but is an attempt to instill in the students a sense of the kinds of skills and studies necessary to prepare for advanced studies in engineering.

Companywide involvement. At GE the community relations responsibility moves down through every level of management, including front-line supervision. Managers may have titles like engineer, statistician, materials, controller, legal counsel. Their work stations may have labels like Power Transformer Department, Mechanical Drive Turbine Department, Insulator Department. But they join together as General Electric people trying to help.

Many GE community activities are company activities, carried on by employees as part of their assigned work. But to a greater extent the efforts are clearly personal activities—employees throughout the company using their own abilities to meet community needs. In recognition of outstanding employee participation in this broad area, General Electric established the Gerald L. Phillippe Awards for Distinguished Public Service. Winners receive a medallion and can select a charity for $1,000 grants from the General Electric Foundation.

GE keeps its relationship defined in publications that report on who's helping, where, and how, such as its *Public Affairs Monitor*.

A company's community relations activities may be initiated by a community relations man, may even be coordinated by him, but properly involve as broad a spectrum of company personnel as can be reasonably committed.

Role of the community relations man. It's easy to turn a community relations man into a corporate scapegoat. He becomes the only company man the community sees. He joins all the major clubs, is seen at all the luncheon meetings. He doesn't get too involved in club projects or committees (they conflict with his many other meetings). But if you'd like anything from his company, he's the man to see (he and the president are the only employees of the firm anyone really knows).

As with other public relations activities, the community relations man can serve best behind the scenes. Requests for support or participation in community affairs properly should come to him. He should evaluate them and make recommendations as to company involvement.

Those recommendations, particularly on such matters as contributions and company-paid memberships in community organizations, should be highly selective. Employee memberships, sponsored by the company in the sense that dues, fees, and other expenses incurred by individuals are paid by the company, deserve surveillance. The company's investment here should mean active, participatory membership.

Each one holding such a membership is a potential resource center—helping keep the company, through its community relations man, apprised of circumstances in the community as gleaned from that club or organization. That man may also be the means of getting a company message distributed and understood by the community through his civic association. Otherwise, such company-paid memberships are a useless cost.

Role of volunteers. In organizing for community relations, the role of the employee volunteer must be treated with utmost care. The distinction between a company activity and an individual's activity should be kept carefully defined.

If you, for example, are active in Boy Scout leadership on your own time and expense, your company has little excuse in taking bows for your accomplishments.

It's one thing for a company to have pride in the widespread involvement of its employees in volunteer activities. But credit expressed must go to the individuals, normally with their knowledge and permission. Overt attempts to capitalize on an individual's extra-curricular activities will inevitably harm personnel relations and may do more damage than good for the company.

Company-sponsored activities in which employee volunteers participate should be distinguished by tangible evidence of the company's contribution. Even in these, work performed by volunteers should be spelled out in any promotion or discussion of the program.

The volunteer always has been an essential ingredient in community relations. The word and concept of "volunteer" deserve protection they don't get when an employee assigned to a task is publicized as a volunteer. If the old military practice of naming "volunteers" is operative in your firm, and you can't stop it, start looking for a euphemism when you actually need volunteers. A good distinction, perhaps, between a "company" position and a "volunteer" participation is seen in the policy statement of General Electric that says, in part, that the company had been, is, and will be strictly non-partisan; it neither supports nor endorses any political party or candidates. The company does contribute constructively to the *discussion* of public issues by providing information on a continuing basis (and, when appropriate, even taking a stand on certain questions that have an impact on the business). The company encourages its employees, as individuals, to participate on an active and informed basis in political campaigns. Company non-partisanship among parties and candidates in no way abridges the right of its employees, as individual citizens, to volunteer or work in politics.

Determining assignments. Your organization work, then, requires some primary determinations. If the program planned can be handled solely as a company activity:

1. Who in the company should be recommended for the task? (Play to your company's strengths: Who's best qualified? What expertise is available? Who has control of needed equipment or facilities?)

2. Who should have primary responsibility for chairing the program?

3. Will volunteer help be needed and/or desirable?

If the program planned requires outside participation:

1. Whose help should be sought?

COMMUNITY RELATIONS

2. How should that help be sought? (It may be best to work through an intermediary. For example, an education program might be coordinated through the local school board.)

The nature of the program should suggest what formal structure it requires. Generally, a committee will suffice to start. Once a program is approved and key participants selected, the community relations man should help get the program under way. Even if all details have been worked to the point where he feels his added contribution is nil, he should at least maintain *ex officio* status on the primal committee.

Under no circumstances should a community relations man turn away from a program or its committees. Even if other public relations aspects of the program are delegated, he remains the essential catalyst for the program's success (as the remainder of this chapter will show).

ACTION

It's obvious that community relations, as described in these pages, is action-oriented. That meaningful action is misunderstood is illustrated by two types of groups with whom today's community relations man is confronted. These are extremes, with many variations and degrees in between.

The first is the local community chapter of a usually well-respected, service-oriented national organization. The average age of this group seems to increase annually. It admittedly has trouble attracting new (and young) members.

Typically, this group shares its parent national's pride in accomplishment in several areas of community relations. The local itself is perplexed by its poor membership drive results and the declining attendance at meetings. "With all today's community consciousness and with all the good we're doing, one would think our ranks would grow" is the prevailing feeling.

This group certainly considers itself "active" as does the community. But inspection often shows a paucity of real involvement in the actual needs of the community. Funds are solicited, portions of dues are committed to worthy causes. The membership raises money that moves through channels to its ultimate worthwhile goal.

The work of such groups is vital; it deserves support and encouragement. But it is, by-and-large, community action by proxy. Members give money, not themselves. They don't participate directly in the action. The people this group doesn't get as members are those who want personal involvement, want to feel and see accomplishment. Neither the reputation nor experience nor publicity suggests the local chapter is so committed.

At the other end of the spectrum are the activists. These demand social change—often accurately identifying community problems with inherent inequality, injustice, or indignity. This group demands and gets the full range of publicity.

"Action" for them consists of the placard, the march, the rally, the angry shouts and slogans, sometimes physical aggression. Reasoned solutions and concrete efforts to solve anything usually are nonexistent.

Surely some groups whose activities resemble these exist because their alternatives have been exhausted. This means *is* effective in building community concern for their needs. But our society today has spawned professional dissidents with nothing to lose. Their gain is the thrill of combating "the establishment." To these latter we refer.

Between the two extremes stands the community relations man and his programs. His company's "actions" can easily resemble the results of either. On the one hand, the company's efforts can become as detached and non-involved as some groups' . . . and die from lack of interest. On the other, company committees can meet, debate, and deplore community problems, loud and long, without ever quite getting to the point of working on the ills.

Case studies. Good examples of getting action programs under way are numerous. Here are just a few samples:

The Allison Division of General Motors at Indianapolis, Indiana sought broad management support and participation to help solve that community's problems. "Operation Involvement" was created.

Planning for this program began with a review of some 50 Indianapolis area civic organizations and local government agencies. The second step was to match the names of Allison supervisory personnel with each organization on a basis of knowledge and interest. Local organizations were contacted to determine their interest in obtaining Allison support. Management personnel were appointed to selected organizations.

Shortly after the program was initiated, nearly 200 management people were involved in 81 community projects. These range from work on the mayor's task forces to school system advisory groups. Allison personnel serve on the air pollution control board, police review board, board of public works, Urban League, and others. The company's management *actively* participates, playing to its own strengths and expertise.

RCA Corporation translates "strength and expertise" as "opportunities" for company, communities, and individuals. Over the past decade RCA Service Company's educational services activity has led in providing educational programs designed to meet the needs of society's disadvantaged. Programs have been developed and carried out at federal, state, and local governmental levels. The education and training services performed range from custom-designing curricula and training materials to complete management and operation of large-scale residential centers providing prevocational, vocational, academic, and social education. In communities where the programs are centered, RCA develops public and community relations liaison to acquaint residents with goals and progress of the project and to enlist local participation wherever possible.

RCA has developed programs to help seasonal farm workers and their families in North Carolina, Choctaw Indians in Mississippi, adult prisoners and youthful offenders in Pennsylvania, handicapped youth in West Virginia, and the chronically unemployed in Chicago, Los Angeles, New York City, and Camden and Newark, New Jersey.

RCA currently operates Job Corps centers in Maryland, Oklahoma, Oregon, Pennsylvania, and Virginia, with the overall purpose of promoting human renewal through job training and instruction in preparedness for the world of work.

Criteria for activities. Action considerations are obvious and not-so-obvious. Some of the forms action (problem-solving and simply community-enhancing) can take include:

1. Creating something needed that didn't exist before
2. Eliminating something that causes a problem
3. Developing means for self-determination
4. Broadening use of something that exists to include "have-nots"
5. Sharing equipment, facilities, professional expertise
6. Tutoring, counseling, training
7. Reconstituting, repairing, dressing up
8. Promotion of a community outside its confines
9. Activating others

Preconditioning for change. In 1968 Shell Oil Company's Exploration and Production Organization wanted to do some exploratory drilling off the coast of California. Possible public sensitivity to drilling had been made clear by the previous forced cancellation of plans for an atomic energy power plant near the area of proposed drilling because of community objections.

A community relations program was created to inform various groups and organizations that might object to the drilling program and to win their acceptance of it, even before public announcement of the plans.

Shell anticipated the likely questions. Would oil rigs spoil the view from shore? What were the possibilities of aquatic pollution in the drilling process and subsequent production work? Would structures be left on the seafloor that would impede work of commercial fishermen?

The company sought to reach biologists of the University of California, land owners of shore sites, users of beaches, the Sierra Club, sports and commercial fishermen, and others. The main means of reaching these groups was to talk to them face-to-face. A Shell expert carried out this assignment and subsequently outlined the drilling program to the local press.

Following this community relations program, the only objections to the drilling that remained were those of bottom-dragging commercial fishermen. Plugged and abandoned drilling sites would leave obstructions on the seafloor that would foul their nets.

Normally, remaining obstructions sit one foot above the seafloor. Engineering studies indicated protruding pipe could be cut off and plugged below the seafloor for an extra $1,000 to $2,000 per hole. Shell agreed to the added expense and acceptance of the program was complete.

Overcoming imagined fears. With all the problems that actually beset communities, it seems incongruous that people would see problems where none in fact exist. But situations are judged not for what they are but how they appear to be. Fanned by rumor, and often faulty logic, imagined problems take on all the reality of their real counterparts.

For example, a company by virtue of being in the chemical industry can be linked with air pollution though it causes none. About all it takes is a mention in the media that a by-product of some chemical process is an air pollutant. This, through rumor, becomes "chemical companies pollute." Add the faulty logic: "The XYZ Company is a chemical company; therefore, it pollutes." The XYZ Company and its community end up with a problem they might never have dreamed of.

Denials may not be enough. But a planned action program, even though no circumstances are or should be changed, may turn such a problem into a company- and community-enhancing experience.

If people may exhibit shortcomings by imagining problems where none exist, they sometimes compensate by taking token gestures to be meaningful action. A well-conceived plan and continued surveillance of its implementation will protect against this.

A final piece of advice on action programs might best be considered basic. Before planning for action down the street, make sure the community relations problem that needs attention isn't closer to home.

What problems might your company itself be the cause of? What enhancement in your company might set a worthy example for others to follow? The poet Robert Burns wished us all the gift of seeing ourselves as others see us. He concluded: "It would from many a blunder free us, and foolish notion."

COMMUNICATING

In community relations, publicity and promotion are tools in support of an action program, not substitutes for it. A simple test for written communication used in programs is: Is the program being described one that the reader/viewer can react favorably to without additional prompting? In short, does the program stand on its own feet?

Recognition for community relations work is not only desirable for a company but for the community itself. It shows that something for the community can and is being done. It may encourage others to participate. It's up-beat news; it's progress. For example, Illinois Bell has instituted the Alexander Graham Bell Award for outstanding community service. It is presented annually to employees and retirees who volunteer their time and energies in community activities. Nominations for the award come from fellow employees, relatives, and the general public. Each year the Ford Motor Company honors employees—and wives or husbands of employees—who have performed outstanding service in their communities. Nominations for the awards come from fellow employees, relatives, and civic leaders. There's a Good Citizen citation, an Outstanding Service plaque, and the "Citizen of the Year" Town Crier bell, the program's highest award. The program is available to each company location served by a community relations committee.

The recognition of individuals for their community relations work is laudable, but the awards are backed with widespread publicity that not only salutes award recipients but reminds the community of what Ford people are doing for it. The articles become "how to do it" models for other employees and the folks in the community at large. The Prudential Insurance Company of America has a similar program in presenting its Community Service Award. All activities for which an employee is nominated must be voluntary, non-salaried, and conducted on the employee's own time. Beside news coverage in home-town newspapers, the program has been commended on several papers' editorial pages.

Inland Manufacturing Division of General Motors in Dayton, Ohio, had been recruiting more and more from that city's predominantly Black west side. Inland's public relations people met with the editor of the Black newspaper there and asked "What can we do to help you?" His answer was simple: "Just let us know what you are doing for your Black employees and for the west side community."

The upshot of that conversation was a change in basic policy at Inland. Until that time, the company had reported only personnel promotions in managerial levels. But this west side paper, like so many others, was interested in *all* promotions featuring west side people. It was interested in *all* activities that show community progress. Today, Inland and *The New Dayton Express* enjoy a cooperative relationship to their mutual benefit.

Health and safety programs. Two areas of community relations work that cross all lines to affect every level of society are health and safety.

Information and publicity can combine in a health program of impressive scope.

Allstate Insurance Company, of course, is concerned with promoting safety, and its corporate conscience has led the company into a number of health and safety activities where it feels a genuine need exists for involvement. Through the Allstate Foundation's Nursing Scholarship Program thousands of scholarships have been provided since 1957. Other community health and education activities include: involvement in day care centers, housing renovation, Opportunities Industrialization Center's body shop programs, and a drug rehabilitation program.

Leadership in national campaigns for major reform in laws and safety standards that affect all people who use streets and highways is a familiar role for Allstate. An advertising campaign and citizen action programs led the fight for drunk driver laws. Implied consent laws were passed in 13 states during 1969 alone to help protect the driving public by greatly increasing the police's ability to determine whether a driver is drunk. (Drunk drivers are involved in more than half the fatal auto accidents.)

Allstate led the effort—started in 1973—for better bumpers on today's cars. Presently, Allstate is leading a national effort to have the air bag passive restraint system made mandatory on all cars sold in the U.S. Studies show that air bags would save more than 9,000 lives per year and greatly reduce injuries.

One of the most effective ways to help the public help themselves is to get general information to the public. Allstate has created many program manuals and collateral materials for community action programs to deal with auto theft, home protection, and fire and arson prevention. Each year the company supplies millions of pamphlets and brochures to the public about auto and bicycle safety, home security, and fire safety. Also, films are available on a loan basis to schools, groups, and organizations. An extensive speakers' bureau brings important information to the consumer.

Traffic safety is of major importance to the nation's second largest auto insurer. Allstate's past and present involvements include development of driving simulation instructional materials, teacher training seminars, scholarships for driver education teachers, and active membership in local, regional, and national safety organizations.

Selecting publicity outlets. As in any other communications considerations, be imaginative and complete in selecting media in and outside the community. Cover all appropriate "publics." Avoid sameness in advertising. Meet change with change. Realize that some of your publics will judge your company by the image it projects in the media. But don't stop with these long-recognized considerations.

Where would the activists be if they limited themselves to the time-honored means of communications? Their secret is communication that affects all the senses; communication that itself conveys a sense of involvement.

There is little, if any, physical difference between students marching with placards to City Hall in protest, and the city's mayor leading a "Keep Our Town Clean" parade past the same city hall. Both may get about as much television news coverage. And whatever happens after a protest march, the parade may lead to spruced up streets and a Clean City award. Dramatization can be inspirational, participatory, and, of course, legal.

It's a shame when a carefully planned and executed community relations program is kicked off or signed off with a couple inches of copy and a posed photo in the local paper. It's a shame because virtually any action program can serve to focus a community's need for concerned attention and effort.

Publicity content. Press releases should spell out the community need and the reason your organization is involved. It's here that community leaders, with whom you've previously consulted, can help too. Their prestige (enhanced in the process) and their message relative to your program are news.

Whatever you can get others to say about the program, and whatever attention-getting dramatizations you use, play the actual news straight. Identify your company in the releases, along with any company references pertinent to the program, and let it go at that. It's hard for an editor to become a believer in a company's altruism when the releases contain product information or corporate puffery. Photos of "work in progress" with company advertisements obviously planted in the scene give editors jaundiced eyes.

On the other hand, your efforts toward keeping the mood altruistic (from the company's standpoint) can help an editor catch the spirit of your program. Your stories may run with single mentions of your firm's name. But editorials and media-initiated articles can compound those mentions with considerably more impact.

Timing communications, as always, is critical. Initial attempts at attracting publicity are a commitment to follow through with the program. Regardless of how small a mention such an announcement may draw, someone (including editors) will be looking for program action.

The world still looks for good will toward men, but with some suspicion. It wants to see the motives and the action. Once these become evident, the initial shy attention can be largely overcome.

When outside participation is involved, make sure those with you from the start share in the initial publicity. Use the entry of others into the program as pegs for continuing coverage. Where broad participation is sought, your publicity efforts should run under full steam for as long as it can continue to attract.

If your program involves physical change, don't forget those "before" photographic shots. The results of such programs are likely to depend on photographic reminders of how things were at the start.

Perhaps the most crucial timing occurs in a program with inherent special sensitivities. If your program is designed to help the community's disadvantaged to self-sufficiency, a publicity program early in your efforts may result in no recipients for your aid. The last thing the disadvantaged need is exploitation.

The general rule is, don't even inadvertently attempt to capitalize at the expense of the project. It may be months before publicity, for whatever good purpose, is advisable; and then, only with the o.k. of the participants. Again, the benefits of a community relations program should be in the program, not the publicity.

EVALUATING

Operating a community relations program without evaluation is like exploring uncharted territories and not bothering to map them. You put serious limitations on the value of your discoveries, and you stand a good chance of getting lost.

Assume your program will be a complete success, will live up to all expectations. You'll want to know what made it work and apply what success factors you can to future programs. Other people may want to know how you did it. And, if your program is to be repeated, you'll want to know what activities turned out to be extraneous, and what program parts can be improved for even greater success.

It's more likely, however, that your program will vary considerably from your plan. You'll run into crises with which you may or may not be able to cope. Factors may cause the program either to fail or to fall far short of your goals. At such times, the need for analyses becomes poignantly apparent. And how sad it is to discover your program's cure after your program has died.

For these reasons, fact-finding and record-keeping are vital. They are the basis for analysis and evaluation. If your program is built on careful research, why defend it with fabricated excuse or hyperbole? Why build succeeding programs on speculation?

We've previously stressed fact-gathering as a prelude to program formulation. Obviously there is fact-gathering and fact-refining to be done throughout the development and execution of a program. Programs tend to expand, taking in new considerations. These must be spotted and understood. For example, a new group joins the program.

Its role, motivation, and makeup are new pieces of knowledge you should have.

Keeping abreast. Facts change. Just keeping up with the turnover of community leaders is a maintenance problem.

We've talked about things as they are versus things as they appear to be. Values change. Your program efforts involve influencing others. But efforts to influence are coming from other directions, too. Community, even apart from environment, is in a constant state of flux.

So surveys are an important consideration and a tool of evaluation.[2] Surveys, before and after a program, help determine the nature and effectiveness of your program's influence. Interim surveys can help determine potential problems, the degree of effectiveness, the need for addition or change to your program.

Costs in time, effort, and money will influence your use of surveys. If you use them, make them work well for you. Use great care in assuring who and how you survey will provide the information most useful. Commit yourself to accept the results you get without forcing those results into preconceived notions of what you'd like them to be.

Keep all information in a handy form easily used and comfortable to work with. No collected fact is too minuscule to keep. But big facts can be "thrown away" simply by filing them so they can't be recalled when needed.

From the day planning starts, keep a log or diary to record details each step of the way. Such a record keeps project control in your hands. It furnishes useful ideas for publicity angles. It tips you off to otherwise missed opportunities.

A careful log of your program will keep the relationship of that program to your plans constantly apparent. Whatever the plan, whatever the program, there will be variations between them and some need for change.

Evaluation, then, is interpreting the data and records you've collected and drawing lessons, conclusions, and new courses of action from them.

It's to your advantage when reviewing a completed program to identify weak spots in it and note what changes might have strengthened them. Do this while your program is still fresh in your mind. Later reviews may give broader perspective, but important considerations by then may be forgotten.

However you report results, remain objective. Identify and use qualifiers. Unless you've comple-

[2] See Chapter 35.

ly solved a problem once and for all, don't convey that impression. You don't want to stultify future work in areas where there still is work to be done.

Assuring continuity. It's an unusual community relations program that can be completed with no need for some continued maintenance. This doesn't mean once your company takes on a program it's yours for life. But your evaluation should determine the needs for preserving the good your program has done.

This suggests at least one final action: If your company's participation must end, make sure the baton is properly passed. Find a successor, make sure he understands the maintenance task, and give him copies of the material you have that he'll need.

COMING INTO OR LEAVING A COMMUNITY

Our emphasis has been on the relationship of a business within a community. But good community relations are essential to a company *before* it moves into a community. And poor community relations in moving a business out of town can affect a company long after it leaves.

As more and more companies are learning, it's one thing to buy property upon which to build, and quite another to get acceptance for what they want to build there. Already a classic example is the attempt to bring clean power to New York City by building atomic power plants in the area. The best motivations and even the best public relations efforts may block corporate plans if community opposition is determined enough.

Community relations work prior to a move into a community is designed to gain more than passive acceptance of a company. One obviously can't build a cement factory in the heart of town and expect to receive community cooperation. But a company can prevent fears of imagined problems; it can win enthusiastic acceptance and pave the way for long-lasting, grateful community relationships.

E.I. Du Pont De Nemours & Company did that in the Fayetteville, North Carolina area. In November, 1968 Du Pont announced it was exercising options to purchase land for a plastics manufacturing facility. But rapport was already being established with the area's news media and opinion leaders. The appointed plant manager was introduced to the press and important members of the community. A luncheon, attended by some 375 people in Cumberland and Bladen counties, featured state officials and favorable remarks by the lieutenant governor. Later, a steak cookout for about 20 opinion leaders was held—devoid of formal speeches and devoted to building rapport with key people.

Activities too numerous to list were begun, and continue as this is written, to meet three main objectives: "1. Provide factual information promptly on appropriate events and various stages of the project. 2. Familiarize key groups and individuals with the Du Pont Company, its products, its policies and its people. 3. Continue to build relationships after plant startup."

Two activities were particularly noteworthy. One was the concerted effort to make key Du Pont people involved in the Fayetteville Works personally known in the community through face-to-face meetings, both formal and informal.

The other was the study of the health of the Cape Fear River (involved in the plant location) and other aspects of the environmental control program.

Dr. Ruth Patrick of the Academy of Natural Sciences of Philadelphia not only made pertinent studies for Du Pont, but her work was covered by news media. At a dinner attended by the press, she discussed her work in water management. Along with television appearances by Dr. Patrick, a booklet was distributed on Du Pont's pollution control program.

With talks by another expert on his plant life study of the area, and by Du Pont engineers on air emissions, plus follow-up talks by Dr. Patrick on her biological survey, Du Pont's plant entered production with little community fear for, and much knowledge on, its effect on environment.

Continuing familiarization. Introducing a plant continues after a plant is built. Chrysler Corporation's Toledo Machining Plant is a good example. Shortly after final work by the contractor was completed in 1968, a series of plant visits were scheduled. These included a "Government Day" for local, state, and U.S. officials representing the community, and a "Contractor Day" for principals in the firms that built the plant. "Industry Day" welcomed the leaders of business and industry in the area, and "Education Day" brought in school superintendents and other leading educators in the community.

Each program included coffee on arrival, a brief orientation on Chrysler Corporation and the Toledo plant's role in the company, a tour of the plant, a tomato juice reception, and lunch served in the office cafeteria. After lunch came a talk by a speaker, such as the Ohio Governor on "Government Day."

Each guest received a follow-up questionnaire in the mail. Chrysler not only got a high response (68%), but insight on the considerable success of such plant visits, the feelings of the community, and how future plant visits might be improved.

The General Foods Corporation has become a proven expert in careful entry community relations, as demonstrated by introductions of plants in Lafayette, Indiana and Topeka, Kansas. Thoroughness in reaching all community audiences, and using all appropriate public relations means to do so, was again the key, but other factors were also involved.

General Foods learned, as most companies are now learning, that it is almost impossible to even consider possible sites for new plants in secret. While this may seem to mean potential trouble and additional work for companies, it also means valuable opportunities for community relations personnel.

As soon as General Foods took options on available properties, brief, factual announcements were made to local media. The company carefully emphasized it was studying possible sites in a number of locations. It earnestly worked to avoid building up false hopes in any community.

With the announcement of such studies, community relations people have an opportunity to begin investigations that can be beneficial to the company's planning. The early investigations can help a company with its plant location decision, or to learn what particular conditions will have to be met to minimize problems attendant to the company's final decision. Time, that all important public relations commodity, is extended in these situations.

Once General Foods decided on their sites, they took another important community relations step. They pointed out in press releases to the "losing" communities that the places chosen simply came closer to meeting the company's particular set of requirements. They noted other companies, with different requirements, might well have reached different decisions. They avoided entering local controversies over local industrial development programs by resisting all efforts to ascertain specific reasons why a community was not chosen.

A comprehensive study of an earlier General Foods plant relocation was the subject of a book by Edmund S. Whitman and W. James Schmidt, published by the American Management Association. The book, *Plant Relocation, A Case History of a Move,* is not only a guide to opening a facility in a community but to shutting down outmoded plants in other communities.

In the book, General Foods noted its public relations program for leaving a community was based on:

- full and early disclosure of all management decisions to employees and the public in that order;
- involvement of top management through personal contacts with community leaders;
- continuing communication through bulletins from top management to the affected employees, assisting each employee to decide what was in his own best interest; and
- concern for the welfare of the affected community and the earnest attempt to ease the blow.

The creation, implementation, and follow-through described earlier apply in community relations programs for corporate arrivals and departures. If there is a difference, it is that corporate survival is a little more obviously dependent on your success.

As has been said before, business marries the community it settles with. The decision to move into a community requires a careful courtship. And the price for separating a business from a community depends most on how well the appropriateness of the break is understood and accepted.

TRENDS

No business or individual can physically exist in a community without having an effect on it or being affected by it. It's that simple and the ramifications of that point are coming to be fully understood by business.

To summarize applied community relations: *Act in regard to the community, think in terms of groups, and address yourself to the individual.*

Community relations has become the new business of business. The perils of ignoring this are becoming increasingly clear. Community needs are rapidly compounding. As business delays its response, the cost of that response goes up. It's good business sense to get a piece of the action while it's still an investment.

8

Having a Voice in Politics

MACE BROIDE is a partner in the firm of DeHart and Broide, Washington public affairs counselors.

From January 1959 to June 1968 he was Chief of Staff and top assistant to Senator Vance Hartke (D-Ind). He ran two senatorial campaigns for Hartke and had important assignments in the elections of 1960 and 1962. During the latter year he was an officer of the National Democratic Senatorial Campaign Committee.

As a newspaperman and television commentator in Indiana, Broide's forte was politics. He was political editor of "The Evansville Press," a Scripps-Howard newspaper, and covered several national campaigns and conventions as well as state campaigns and the legislature.

Broide is a graduate of Indiana University with majors in Government and Journalism. He was a combat correspondent in the Army and has done organizational public relations work.

Whatever your field, chances are there will be times when your organization will have a problem with government or a point of view to express to someone who can do something about it.

Whether it's a national, state, or local problem, you'll be better off if you know personally an elected official to whom you can talk. You will be in a better position to talk to that official, and get him to listen, if he knows that you helped him get elected. By helping him when he needs help, at election time, you get a chance to get to know him or his staff—and he or they get to know you under favorable circumstances. It's like helping any prospective business associate or customer.

Just put yourself in the official's shoes. Who is he going to show more sympathy for: The fellow he has never heard of who shows up suddenly with a problem? Or the fellow who worked in his campaign who shows up with a problem?

The more government becomes involved in business, manufacturing, advertising, professions, labor relations, and all the other fields of private enterprise, the more important it becomes for representatives of all those areas to participate in politics and campaigns.

The concert of politics and government is probably the strongest single interactive force affecting the lives of individual Americans. Every day these interactive forces shape our activities. To the extent we involve ourselves and our organizations in the political process, we can influence the direction of government. To remain aloof from politics is to minimize one's influence on government at any level.

Many political beginners think they have to be making major policy in Washington to be effective in politics. That isn't true even on a national scale. The man or organization that works effectively in the Congressman's home town is doing a mighty important piece of work—and the Congressman knows it and appreciates it. Moreover, that's how most of the big-time political leaders started.

Jimmy Carter and a small band of friends from "down home" proved the same thing can be true in a Presidential election. After they organized in Georgia and he began travelling around the

HAVING A VOICE IN POLITICS

country, a relatively small cadre of supporters began organizing at the state and local levels elsewhere. The grassroots effort was obviously effective.

The rest of this chapter is designed to explain basic party and campaign organization and to help sort out some of the ways public relations people may be helpful and attain their organizations' voice in government.

POLITICS IS CIVIC SERVICE—AND GOOD BUSINESS

In a democratic society a great deal depends on voluntary action by individual citizens. It's a civic duty to work in politics just as it is a civic duty to help forestall pollution and serve in the PTA.

Volunteer work in politics is also good business—or good labor, or good agriculture, or good medicine, or whatever your immediate economic or professional interest is. That's how our founding fathers designed it (see *The Federalist Papers*).

Time was when businessmen shunned politics, political parties, candidates, and even holders of public office. "It's bad for business" was a common tenet.

But that's not true. A food broker once reported that his business increased when he became publicly identified as a political party worker. Other examples are easy to find because volunteer work in politics can help business careers.

The president of one of America's largest appliance manufacturing firms was selected for that position after he had served a term as president of the Board of Safety in a medium-sized city.

A former roofing company head walked into a political headquarters one day to find out how he could help and immediately was drafted to address and stuff envelopes. A short time later, following success at the polls by his party, he was named to head an important board.

Literally hundreds of company executives, many of them public relations officers, today serve as volunteers in the campaigns of Congressmen, Senators, and Governors.

Volunteer work is a big business in politics. It involves menial and prosaic work like addressing envelopes. Most often it involves donating and raising money. But professional advice and skill also are avidly sought by party executives and candidates for office. Ability to write and communicate in other ways is a skill that is sought by political organizations, committees, and candidates.

More and more, larger companies and many other organizations are employing executives who have experience in political life and contacts with political leaders. This accounts for the substantial number of former public officials who become executives with this role. They are employed for their expertness, judgment, skill, and acceptability to those they will deal with—just as are executives in many other fields.

Where such an executive is available, he is likely to steer the role of that organization in the political arena and direct the proper contacts the organization makes with public officials, regulatory agencies, and other government offices. He is also likely to direct the work of the many employees or members of the organization who will work in politics as volunteers or members of candidate support committees.

VOTING, POLITICS, AND GOVERNMENT— RELATED BUT DIFFERENT

Voting itself is the most important act of participation in politics and government, an act basic and elementary.

Yet the United States rarely approaches the 70 percent mark of participation in state and national elections. So voting—informed voting—is the first basic step, but only that. Elections are one-day affairs. Politics and government go on 365 days a year.

At the outset, some elementary distinction must be made between politics and government. Politics is the process of selecting, nominating, and electing people to conduct public business. Government is the actual management of those affairs. As with most definitions, these are dangerously oversimplified. Politics and government are so intertwined in daily practice that they are often almost indistinguishable.

It's hard to be objective and say who is more concerned with public welfare and who with sheer politics.

The fact is that the public welfare often determines good politics. Thus government—good and bad—makes politics and political issues.

The point is that politics is a means to an end. That end is influence in shaping of government. Politics is organized group action, people working in concert toward common goals. Moreover, politics is local. All local elections are local, but so are all national elections. So success in politics usually means working with others, starting at the community level—with friends, neighbors, people who live in the same block or in the same part of town.

The real work of politics is accomplished by organizers who work constantly at this level. The better and harder they work, the better the chance of success on election day. Since elections are the heart of politics, success on election day is the measured goal of politics.

POLITICAL PARTY ORGANIZATION AND STRUCTURE

The purpose of organized political parties is simple. Their goals are to nominate candidates and win elections. In his booklet, *The Role of Political Parties, U.S.A.,* Joseph C. Harsch describes the American political party in terms of a corporation:

> The American party is made up primarily of those persons who choose to work in that political corporation for the benefits which continued employment in it, and service to it, can offer. Those voters who tend to support one party are its stockholders. The rest of the country consists of customers who tend to shop around for services in return for their votes.
>
> This is not a bad system. On the contrary, it is a very good system. It is just as good, and as desirable, and as useful in politics as it is in the market place. It is the system which long, and painful, experience has proved to be best adapted, by and large, to the needs and interests of the American people.

You and the Political Organization, one of a series of booklets prepared by the Chamber of Commerce of the United States for its action course in practical politics, outlines the development of political parties in America this way:

> George Washington, in his Farewell Address, deplored the danger of a party system, particularly a division along geographic lines. Yet, while Washington was still President, the Federalist party began to form under the leadership of Alexander Hamilton and the Democratic (or anti-Federalist) party took shape under Thomas Jefferson. The Federalist group wanted a strong central government. They represented most business interests and the Northeast. The Jeffersonian group favored strong state government and a limited national government. It represented agrarian interests and centered in the frontier areas and the South.
>
> Subsequent realignments of the parties took place on the basis of issues. The Federalists died as a national party following the defeat of Rufus King by James Monroe in 1816. By 1828, the Jacksonians had split off from the Democratic Republicans, principally over differences on tariff and monetary policy between propertied interest on the one hand and the agrarians and frontiersmen on the other hand. Webster, Clay and Calhoun were the founders and leaders of a new Whig Party made up of various factions of the traditional Democratic Republicans and surviving Federalists.
>
> In the 1850's, both the Whig and Democratic Parties splintered over the slavery question, leading to the formation of the Republican Party, Lincoln's victory in 1860, and the reduction of the Democratic Party to a southern regional party for many years.
>
> The parties originated and re-formed on the basis of issues, but for the past 100 years there have been two major parties with no realignment of forces successful enough to produce a new national political party.
>
> . . . The two parties no longer differ as dramatically on issues as they once did. Both parties now contain people representing a wide variety of political philosophies.
>
> Today, whether individuals are Democrats or Republicans depends to some extent on issues, but also to some degree on what party their families have traditionally belonged to—their religion, ethnic, racial and economic groups—and also on where they live.
>
> Party loyalty is determined only to a limited extent by the issues. Some people believe the two major parties take about the same position on the issues. Others indicate they don't know what position either party espouses.
>
> Comparisons of issue-orientation vs. candidate-orientation seem to show that the presidential candidates are far more important in the voter's mind than the issues.
>
> The issues tend to blur and the success or failure of the parties has come to depend more and more on the appeal of the candidates and the effectiveness of the party political organization.
>
> On the local level—the level which ultimately decides all elections—the issues tend to be played down and candidates played up. The comparable strength and effectiveness of the party organizations are principal factors in deciding who wins.

HAVING A VOICE IN POLITICS

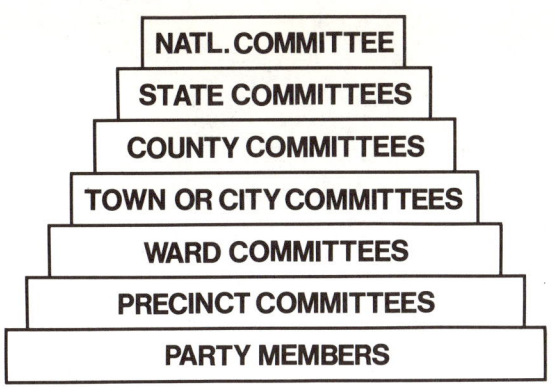

Figure 8-1. Pattern of U.S. political parties.

Political party structure, which is largely shaped by the various state election laws, generally parallels government structure. That is, a pyramiding of responsibilities from the basic election district, called a "precinct" in most states, to the party national committee at the top, in much the same way that local government is responsible to county government, county to state government, and state to federal government in many areas.

State laws and traditions largely shape political party organizations.

Precinct sizes and the whole election process, including methods for nomination and election and for voter eligibility, are products, usually, of state law. In some states the way these laws are written actually helps strengthen and tighten party organization. In others the general election laws tend to break down party organization and loyalties.

For instance, where it is possible to cross-file and enter primaries of two parties there is a tendency to break down party organization and discipline and to put a premium on individual power and personal organization. Likewise, if state laws call for primaries closed except to those who declare for one party or another, and if election board and other positions are clearly defined for representatives of party organizations, then parties are strengthened.

In some states and areas the political clubs enjoy much of the real power of local politics. But, generally speaking, it's the formal party organization—based in the precinct—that enjoys formal recognition and actual power.

Occasionally, in recent years, presidential campaigns have been organized from strong committees dedicated solely to the success of the candidate for the White House rather than to his party. In those few instances, the real power in the presidential election has remained with these special committees. That is still the exception, rather than the rule, in campaigns for other offices.

Ultimately it's the individual or group that can deliver the vote on election day that enjoys the basic power. That's usually in the precinct.

THE PRECINCT: BASIC ELECTION UNIT

While precincts differ in size, shape, and number of voters, they usually are geographically close-knit. The average precinct contains something less then 1,000 voters, but there are voting districts with only a few dozen voters in sparse, rural areas or because of quirks in laws or perhaps by design of some political leaders. One state permits as many as 15,000 per precinct. Ideally, there are few enough to allow each to vote on election day without long lines.

Key party contact in the area is the precinct leader or precinct committeeman. He's closest to the people because he lives there. If he's a good committeeman he knows his people well and marks closely the moving in and moving out of his "constituents."

He organizes and gets the vote out. That means he not only keeps track of his people, but he helps get them registered and voted.

Often in local government the precinct leader not only represents his neighborhood in higher party councils but he is their advocate before public officials of his party.

In some tightly organized communities, the fastest way to get the street fixed or a street light replaced is to call the precinct committeeman. Often he's the first one to greet a new family, faster than the "Welcome Wagon" lady.

The precinct leader who is dedicated stays in touch with "his" voters all year long. The best of them tend their "flock" as a minister would. But, good or bad, in the tradition of *The Last Hurrah* or not, the committeeman is a very important fellow. The better he does his job the better the chance of success on election day.

A well-organized precinct will have a card file of all voters with their normal party preferences entered. On election day it will be the job of the leader and his committee to get out the vote, concentrating on the people most likely to support their party and its candidates.

Often, in urban areas, the precinct leader will appoint and supervise "block captains" who will each take charge of a square block to get residents registered and voted.

POLITICAL CLUBS

In New York City the sheer mass of people and strong ethnic ties have given rise to a different kind of political organization. These are political clubs. The most famous became known as Tammany Hall.

There are other major cities, especially the old ones, where the neighborhood, or area, political club is a special force within the political party.

And there are Young Republican and Young Democratic clubs almost everywhere. In some places these are split into College Young Republicans. Others have organizations called Teen Dems.

Then there's the West Side Democratic Club and the North Township Republican Club. In many communities the club has an ethnic base, such as the Hungarian Democratic Club.

These groups function on a year-around basis. Often they have a clubhouse, but sometimes they meet at party headquarters. They are social and cultural as well as political. They may influence regular party organization in one or several precincts. More often, they'll have an important influence on county party organization and policies.

Sometimes, for ethnic or geographic balance, the party organization will look to a club to provide a candidate. Sometimes the club will make its influence felt in the party organization by insisting on "recognition" through candidates or policies.

During a political campaign auxiliary clubs often are organized. These allow participation by people who normally might not be able to join a regular club or who might be unwilling to join one of these or the regular party organization.

Candidates find that they can get work, funds, and ideas by helping supporters organize along professional, business, trade, or ethnic lines. Hence there are "Doctors for Davis" clubs as well as "Democrats for Lindsay," "Women for Jones," and "Entertainers for Nixon-Agnew."

The U.S. Chamber of Commerce has outlined the basic functions of political clubs this way:

1. Keeping party workers together all year-'round. Club activities keep workers from drifting away from the organization between campaigns.
2. Enlisting new party workers. Clubs continually recruit new members and act as a catalyst in changing politically non-active citizens into regular party workers.
3. Serving as a manpower pool to supply volunteers to the party for precinct work and campaign headquarters work.
4. Providing a political training ground for workers and leaders. The organization and operation of a political club provide basic training in political mechanics and management.

Some clubs serve two additional functions that, while not quite so basic as the four above, are also important:

1. Providing members an opportunity to study—and so better understand—issues and government organization. Such understanding and knowledge can be used in developing campaign issues and better-informed party workers.
2. Raising money. Some clubs make a point of recruiting people who are potential donors to the party war chest. Their membership causes them to identify themselves more closely with the party.

THE NOMINATING PROCESS

The beginner often overlooks the nomination as the point in the election process where hard work is most needed and where you can win or lose long before general election day.

In many states primary election day is when all candidates for the general election are nominated and precinct leaders are chosen. Some states retain the convention for nomination of statewide candidates or for endorsements to the regular primary. Since these are specialized as well as exceptions to the rule, we'll deal here with the primary.

If you and your supporters want to influence basic party organization, you have to do it at the primary, as well as by volunteering later. If you want to help choose candidates, including possible winners, you have to begin before the primary.

Out of 100 voters in a precinct, no more than 60 or 70 are likely to turn out for a general election. In years when there is no presidential election, 50 or 60 electors will turn out.

In most elections, about half of these will back the whole ticket of the majority party. About a third will back the minority party. The rest will scatter and split their tickets.

In many places, only about one-fourth to one-half of the people who will support the ticket in the fall take the trouble to vote in a primary. So seven or eight people out of 100 can determine the outcome in a precinct. It is this base that often really determines elections. It is not the mass you should focus on but these key "swing" voters.

THE POLITICAL CAMPAIGN

Product selling and promotion of services are simple compared with the political campaign. There's no second chance; no second day to offer the merchandise. A third or fourth place product can be profitable; in politics, all but the victor show a complete loss.

The political campaign is the ultimate in relating with the public.

While no two campaigns are identical, the basic organizational and procedural form does remain and it's similar to that in other campaigns for other people.

Probably the most mistaken word used in connection with a campaign is "organization." Most likely, it's disorganized.

While the organization of a campaign may be plotted and planned well in advance, daily tactics, maneuverings of the opposition, current events, and availability of time and money necessitate tactical changes.

Thus you must set up an organization with a basic plan. But you must be flexible enough to change it as needed.

The plan is geared to holding strength of supporters, pulling some support away from the opposition, and attracting those who haven't made up their minds. Thus you're in the process of confirming, convincing, and unconvincing all through the campaign.

The campaign will function through both party organization and candidate organizations. The degree of cooperation between and among these will depend on issues, geography, tradition, and a lot of other things.

In the better campaigns, professionals are enrolled increasingly. Many county candidates and political organizations use professional advertising agencies. Some retain public relations counsel.

Pollsters, photographers, copy writers, media buyers, registration experts, campaign managers all can be hired today with specific political campaign background. And that list is by no means complete.

But the skill and time of others is always sought on a volunteer basis. There simply isn't enough time and money for the candidates and the regular political organizations to do these jobs themselves or hire them out.

That's where people with skills to donate—or just plain spare time—come in.

The practice by which a business loaned an employee to a campaign while continuing to pay his or her salary never was a good idea. Nowadays, in the post-Watergate morality, it's worse. In most cases, it's probably illegal. Certainly it is by the standards of the Federal Elections Law.

Your people can try volunteering. Most likely, they'll be accepted. They'll usually start low, but with the opportunity to move up.

We've already suggested that they might volunteer to work in a precinct or to do some writing or address and lick envelopes. There are all sorts of jobs available.

They might make speeches. Or set up meetings. Or run a coffee klatsch or a cocktail party to raise funds or have people meet the candidate. Or just think about campaign ideas and speech subjects and pass them on. Or make calls for the candidate. Or organize baby-sitting services for election day or car pools to get your candidate's supporters to the polls.

There are literally hundreds of kinds of things volunteers can do to help political parties and candidates. But it's *vital* that they take directions from the campaign manager. Uncoordinated efforts can create havoc for which the transgressor will be remembered with distaste.

FINANCING CAMPAIGNS

The financial end of political campaigns is delicate and complex. Here we will provide a brief primer.

The cost of running an effective political campaign today is staggering. Candidates and political parties pay high rates for media time and space. Usually they have to pay cash on the barrel head. Because their demands for consultation, production, and other aspects of preparation are compressed into a relatively few weeks, they often have to pay a premium for these services.

It is not uncommon for expenditures on behalf of a single candidate to run 20 times his annual salary—if he's elected. Thus all candidates for office and both political parties, at every level, are in a constant scramble for sufficient funds to wage campaigns.

Anyone with expertise in raising money can get a spot in any campaign or party organization. There are other ways to help, too. Chief among them is to donate or to help organize a mechanism by which people in your company or industry or trade association or union or neighborhood can raise money for a party or candidate or group of candidates.

As with political organization, financing is structured in several ways. First there are the major political parties. At local, state, and national levels the parties are constantly seeking financial supporters. An individual or a group can donate money to the party at any level at any time, within limits set by law. Or you can participate in specific fund-raising affairs such as dinners, shows, social events, and the many events that are designed to produce needed funds.

Second, there are specific campaigns. The campaign may be at any level of government. It can be for a primary or a general election. It may encompass a group or slate of candidates. Or it may involve only one person running for Mayor or Governor or Congress or the State Legislature.

Federal election financing laws and those of many states have undergone drastic revision in recent years. There are well-defined limits to contributions to candidates, committees, and Political Action Committees. Basically, you can give up to $1,000 per election to a candidate for House or Senate and $5,000 per year to a PAC.

Candidates' committees are not required under the federal election law to keep track of contributions under $50. They must report in full each contribution in excess of $100.

The State laws covering donations to committees and candidates are varied. The candidate or the party or your organization's lawyer can guide you.[1]

Generally speaking, however, corporation and union checks may not be used as political contributions.

POLITICAL ACTION COMMITTEES

A common device employed more and more in recent years to collect and disburse money for political campaigns and candidates is the "Political Action Committee"—the PAC. Labor unions, companies, industries, and some professions have them now. On the local, state, and national scene there are such organizations as COPE (AFL-CIO Committee on Political Education), AMPAC (American Medical Political Action Committee),

Figure 8-2. Candidate support committees made up of people with similar interests, such as Teachers for Jones or Dentists for L'Hommideau, are important forces in many candidates' campaigns. Usually meeting in members' homes, they work on projects approved by the candidate's campaign manager.

AMPAC photo

and literally hundreds of lesser but similar organizations.

The United States Chamber of Commerce publishes some excellent booklets on the do's and don't's of forming PAC's.[2]

The importance of a committee of this kind—even if it's no more than a couple of dozen executives in your organization—is that together you can make meaningful contributions to the party or candidates of your choice. You can register approval or disapproval of parties and positions by your contributions.

Don't get the idea that you can buy a candidate or an official, however. Most of them can't be bought. Those who can aren't worth it.

Volunteer help at campaign time is the chief way you can let an official or a candidate know you believe in him and what he stands for. There's nothing wrong in supporting the people, positions, and parties you agree with. And there's nothing wrong in donating your skill, your time, and your money to build friendship with candidates, officials, and parties. It's common sense and it's good business.

SOME PRACTICAL IDEAS ON DONATIONS

Every candidate for office has a finance committee—even if it's the regular local organization of his party.

There are also the regular party organizations

[1] See Chapters 6 and 54.

[2] 1615 H St., N.W. Washington, D.C. 20006.

(Iowa Republican State Committee, Democratic National Committee), and congressional and senatorial campaign committees of both parties.

A donation might be made directly to one committee functioning for a candidate or group of candidates. Or it might go to the "regular" organization. Or it might go to the congressional or senatorial campaign committee.

Here are two special points to observe:

When you decide to donate to a candidate or a party, whether through direct donation or a fund-raising affair, whether individually or through your own version of a PAC, do it as early as possible. A candidate often most needs money early in the campaign. Moreover, late in the campaign a contribution can get lost in the shuffle of heavy activity.

Don't insist on making your donation directly to the candidate. He may—as many candidates do—not personally accept any funds. More than likely, he's going to be too busy anyway, especially if he's an incumbent in high office. Get it directly to his campaign manager or someone very close to the candidate himself if you hope to have your contribution recognized.

Again, don't expect that you're buying something for your contribution, no matter how large. And don't expect anyone to be 100 percent on your side. You can expect that you or your group will be more likely to get a sympathetic hearing, if and when you need one. At the least, you should get listened to. And you may even make your point, if you have a good case.

It's not much different from helping anyone else. It's very much like doing a good turn for a customer or client.

YOUR ROLE IN POLITICS

The field of politics and campaigns is vast. The jobs are manifold.

Anyone with intelligence, skill, energy, and common sense can find a way to contribute something in services at some level. Certainly anyone can contribute some money to someone or some group he believes in.

If you don't know anyone specific you want to help, but you do want to get involved and become associated with one side, the best man to see is the county chairman of the party. He's probably well equipped to advise you and he's probably the key man in the area.

Don't be surprised if he puts you or your organization right to work. Don't be hurt if he sends you out to a precinct to start.

Do be prepared to learn as well as to help. Don't try to take over the party right away. Do offer constructive suggestions on how to improve anything that you think needs improving after you've been on board a while.

Go in with your eyes wide open. Don't expect material rewards. Don't get disillusioned—at least until you find out the why of what's being done.

Chances are you'll get a lot of satisfaction out of the experience. And it might help you or your organization have a greater say in the course of events.

Watergate, the Congressman Wayne Hays affair (involving his maintaining a mistress on the public payroll), and a number of other similar happenings may have caused a wave of cynicism, or confirmed earlier cases of cynicism. Is politics too dirty to mess with?

The simple answer is "no." Besides, every dedicated, honest, decent person who becomes involved makes it less likely that an unscrupulous person will pull something.

There's a new breed of dedicated people coming into politics. They are willing to play by the rules and to abide by the new political morality.

Young people, especially women and minorities, are sought. But so are people of all ages who have something to give—time, effort, advice, money. The more who do, the better off we all are.

You'll probably find quickly that there are no more scoundrels proportionately in politics than there are outside—maybe a few less.

9

Working and Communicating with Minority Groups

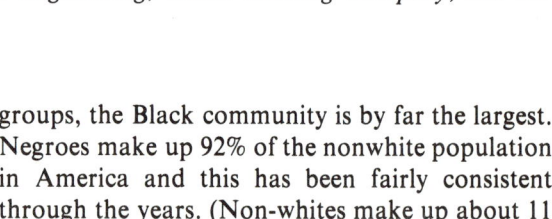

D. PARKE GIBSON is president and senior consultant of D. Parke Gibson International, Inc., a minority-owned consulting firm providing management, marketing, and public affairs counsel and services to domestic and international clients.

DPGI was founded in 1960 and is publisher of two management publications—The Gibson Report and Race Relations & Industry—that have had continuous publication since 1960 and 1966, respectively.

Gibson has been a pioneer in developing effective techniques of marketing communications to minority consumers, and of corporate and institutional race relations practices. DPGI maintains relations with heads of national Black and other minority organizations encompassing 11 million minority opinion-makers, influentials, and consumers.

Gibson is the author of The $30 Billion Negro, published in May 1969 by The Macmillan Company. It is the first book dealing with purchasing power and the shaping of attitudes and opinions in the Black community.

His firm counsels such major clients as American Airlines, Avon Products, the Government of Bermuda, Brown & Williamson Tobacco Corporation, Combustion Engineering, Miller Brewing Company, and the National Guard Bureau.

The millions of dollars spent annually by American corporations and international companies doing business in the United States to tell the public who they are, what they produce, and why they are good corporate citizens often miss their mark in America's minority communities.

The public relations efforts of many nonprofit groups and organizations serving minority groups have often failed to communicate effectively how their services benefit the minority communities.

The events of the past few years have clearly indicated minority unrest and polarization. The effects show that problem times lie ahead, particularly in the area of communication.

UNDERSTANDING MINORITY GROUP ATTITUDES

In America, there are more than 25 million minority group members. Of these minority groups, the Black community is by far the largest. Negroes make up 92% of the nonwhite population in America and this has been fairly consistent through the years. (Non-whites make up about 11 percent of total population.)

It is for this reason that the Negro has been the most vocal, most talked about minority group. The Spanish-speaking or surnamed population, particularly in the Eastern, Southwestern, and Western areas of the United States, has become more restive in the last few years.

The American Indian, though his population has dwindled, continues to be a factor.

Confrontation by minority groups is likely to increase. How well public relations men and women act and react can have a bearing on the results.

The confrontation does create awareness. For many years the majority population acted as if the minority population scarcely existed in America, because it was not pictured in communications practices or media.

The prospects of confrontation, and race relations problems that exist, call for serious study by public relations executives. Increasingly they will be called on by management to interpret what is happening in race relations, and inversely, to interpret to America's minority communities what business and industry are doing that is of particular interest to them.

How well public relations helps bridge the communications gap between business and the minority communities, and those nonprofit groups having an interest, can determine the course of race relations in the years ahead.

How well public relations executives *understand* the problems of the minority community, and *interpret* them to management, will help determine the policy and the course of action to be taken.

The attitudes of Black Americans, as well as those of the other identifiable minority groups, have to be understood. For example, it should be known that in the Black community the No. 1 Negro concern is employment, not education, housing, voting rights, or social integration. This does not mean, however, that all the concentration should be on one priority.

In the minority communities, and primarily in the Black community because it is the largest, tailored public relations practices will have to be employed.

The ideal in public relations would be to create one effort that would have equal influence among all publics. This is not possible, of course, because publics vary. As long as we have a dual society in the United States, the need to communicate separately with these publics will remain.

DETERMINING THE ORGANIZATION'S POSITION

How does one begin to work and communicate with minority groups? Following are some recommended approaches that have been used with success in learning "where you are so you can know where to go":

1. Determine what is being done in the company or organization that would be of particular interest to minority groups. (Keep in mind that what is being done for Blacks is *not* of particular interest to other minority groups, and vice versa.)
2. Ask your personnel department (if your organization has more than 22 employees) to share with you the firm's EEO Form 100, which details minority group employment, and the company's Affirmative Action Plan to increase minority-group employment. (In many cases, the personnel department has far more contact with minority groups than does the public relations department, has awareness, and can be very helpful.)
3. Conduct research to determine how the company is regarded in minority communities or among minority-group leadership in headquarters, plant, or branch cities.
4. Research through ethnic-oriented publications to determine what type of public relations material is being carried, including that of competitive firms and organizations.

This will provide a background of where your company or organization currently stands in regard to minority communities. Here is where the practice begins.

There are three basic ways in which public relations is practiced in the minority communities nationally—*press relations, community relations,* and *publicity.* Almost all successful public relations efforts in the communities have effectively used direct lines of communication to the Black and other minority communities.

At one time, perhaps, minorities could be influenced through white-oriented mass media—including daily newspapers, magazines, radio and television, and through spill-off of some general public relations efforts. It is doubtful whether this could be accomplished now. A medium that talks *about* a minority group and not *to* it can hardly be an influential factor among this group.

Ethnic media—newspapers, magazines, broadcast, and other specialized types—serve a wide audience, and can be effectively used for communicating with the audiences they serve.

These media are important today and will be increasingly, especially in the Black and Spanish-language communities of America. Communications to white-oriented media will also have to be directed to Negro-oriented and Spanish-language media for the *interpretation* necessary, for these minority groups to *understand* that the messages include them, too.

It is important for public relations people to understand that tailoring communications to minority-interest media is not *segregation-in-reverse,* but simply good communications practice.

Any public relations executive worth his salt knows when he has a good legitimate story to tell, as opposed to "horn-tooting." However, it is important to understand that what may be routine or unimportant to whites may be of significant interest to a particular minority group. Study of media can rather quickly help determine this.

TELLING THE STORY

To reach minority groups there are newspapers, magazines, radio stations, neighborhood theatres, and in some Spanish-speaking communities, television programming in Spanish.

The most important responsibility public relations people can have, as part of their responsibility to clients and organizations, is to understand that all media should be serviced, how they should be serviced, and why. These should include media geared to the interests of millions of Americans who are not white.

It is a widely accepted precept that to achieve maximum identification, communications should be oriented as closely as possible to the interests of the intended audience. It is particularly vital in the case of minority groups that information of interest to them—as consumers, voters, opinion-molders, citizens—be communicated through media geared to their interests.

Here are 15 suggestions, proved in practice, to keep in mind when servicing ethnic-oriented media:

1. Prepare material with the publications in mind. Most publications in the Black community are weeklies and monthlies. In the case of Spanish media, have material translated.
2. Publications are usually understaffed. The right material prepared with the publications' format in mind stands an excellent chance of being used.
3. Routine business announcements, unless they involve minority groups, have little chance of being used and should not be sent.
4. If product publicity is continually sent, the advertising department or the agency can expect to be solicited.
5. News releases and product publicity accompanied by photographs with Black or Spanish-surnamed subjects have a better-than-average chance of being used.
6. Keep names of editors of ethnic media up-to-date. Do not send material addressed impersonally (i.e., to Editor). Ethnic media need more-personalized attention.
7. Negro and Spanish-oriented media representatives should be invited—even if they do not attend for one reason or another—to the same press functions as other media.
8. Because of weekly deadlines, often the servicing of the Black press before a news release time does not violate good practice, can improve usage, and can lead to treatment more in keeping with the "news" angle.
9. Public relations departments should have subscriptions to national and local ethnic-oriented media to be familiar with format, editorial philosophy, and the type of publicity material used.
10. Public relations representatives should know when corporate advertising is being considered or run in Negro-oriented media (i.e., Brotherhood Week, new plant openings, recruitment ads, ads in special supplements, and/or other types of institutional ads) and, if desired, prepare editorial copy to support this effort.
11. Deal frankly and honestly with representatives of ethnic-oriented media. Do not patronize, but be understanding.
12. Understand that most ethnic-oriented radio stations carry international, national, and local news, *and* news of particular interest to minority groups. This is often an overlooked, 24-hours-a-day, direct line to these communities. It can be used effectively.
13. Newspaper supplement and magazine editors' needs should be thoroughly analyzed *before* they are approached for story consideration. The story must have a distinctly ethnic angle, or one that can be developed through graphics.
14. In using models for publicity purposes, *do not* select models that might be mistaken for white, but those who are *identifiable* to the minority group and will photograph well.
15. Remember why ethnic-oriented media exist and help fill the need that exists for tailored information and publicity.

WORKING WITH GROUPS

The second route to building good will in the minority communities, particularly the national Negro community, has been through community relations activity with Black organizations.

There are comparable organizations in the Negro community to those in the white. For example, there is the American Medical Association, which is predominantly white, *and* the National Medical Association, which is predominantly Black; The American Dental and the *National* Dental Associations; the American Bar and the *National* Bar Associations; and, of course, many more service, fraternal, and civic organizations.

At one time it was only necessary in public relations activity to build favorable opinion about a client, company, or service, to deal with what was known as the "Big Six" civil rights organizations. These were the National Association for the Advancement of Colored People, the National Urban League, the Southern Christian Leadership Conference, the Congress of Racial Equality, the Student Nonviolent Coordinating Committee, and the National Council of Negro Women.

Several of these organizations have undergone some changes themselves, but, more importantly, the "scene of the action" has shifted.

Today there are numerous organizations, particularly on the local level, that influence thinking in local communities. In New York there are hundreds of Black and Spanish-speaking organizations. There are many more on the national, regional, and local levels that can help shape what the minority community thinks of a company, its products or services, or its employment practices.

Ethnic-oriented media are an excellent means of building a list of key minority groups and organizations.

There are numerous opportunities for public relations efforts among these organizations—from having executives appear before audiences at national conventions, to exhibits and displays at convention sites and other extensions of courtesy, to undertaking special projects with these groups.

A note of caution: It is preferable that contact with these groups be made either with members of the particular group or persons who are extremely knowledgeable about the sensitivities of the group. In a Spanish-speaking situation, the individual making contact should speak the language.

TAILORING THE MATERIAL

A third channel to the minority communities is through publicity. Material should be created for ethnic media, based on the needs of the editors, and with a long-range view.

The material should also be effective when reprinted for distribution to leadership in the minority communities. This technique has worked rather well and expands the limits of the audience served by the media themselves. (A third-party endorsement is gained from the influence and prestige of the medium, as well.)

Stories on the effective utilization of minority manpower, for example, could also be used effectively in reprint form by the personnel department in compliance reviews, as well as to document the organization's affirmative action progress.

CREATING TARGET MATERIAL

In addition to the use of reprints, another successful technique to reach and influence leadership has been the creation and development of company-sponsored Negro-oriented publications and newsletters.

Here are some examples of how some companies have created target material for the Black community:

American Oil Company has distributed well over 500,000 copies of its *American Traveler's Guides to Negro History,* which lists historical sites of particular interest to Black travelers. It was written and produced by American Oil Company employees.

Pepsico has produced three long-playing records—*Adventures in Negro History; The Frederick Douglass Years;* and *The Afro-American's Quest for Education.* These records have been used with filmstrips in more than 500 school systems throughout the United States, and the consumer demand has been high.

Avon Products created integrated posters on good grooming showing well-groomed black and white teen-agers. They are distributed to schools throughout the United States on request. In addition, Avon regularly mails tailored material on good grooming with attractive Black models to the national ethnic press.

Old Taylor's "Ingenious Americans," capsule stories of Negroes who have made significant contributions to America, were the basis for an institutional advertising campaign. When put into booklet form, the response made this program a classic in filling a need for Black history.

Hamilton Watch Company annually sponsors "When They Meet," a pocket-size publication that lists most of the (some 62) national conventions of Black organizations. This is an invaluable guide to planning public relations activity at these national meetings.

R.J. Reynolds Tobacco Company through its Corporate Communications Department sponsors

Figure 9-1. Providing a needed service for a minority group while showing the organization's specific concern for its interests, American Oil's booklet tells Negro travelers where to find sites of particular interest to them. The booklet is used while driving when the owner is a primary prospect.

institutional advertisements in a number of Negro-oriented newspapers, to tell of the company's efforts in minority employment, recruitment, and contributions to higher learning.

RCA sponsors publication of *Baton,* a Black-oriented newsletter that describes RCA's employment of minorities, RCA consumer products, and information of particular interest to these communities. It has been circulated to Negro leadership for more than 25 years.

The B.F. Goodrich Company distributes a car-care column to leading Black-oriented newspapers to fill the void of such information available for automobile owners in the national Negro community.

On The Track is published in behalf of the Association of American Railroads. It has reflected over the years the changing job patterns of employment for the Negro in railroading. It also carries ads in behalf of the Association.

Columbia Pictures expanded its publicity distribution to the national Negro press for all of its motion pictures, rather than just those of particular interest to Blacks. This has increased its average of publicity being utilized.

Chrysler Corporation sponsors publication of

Volume 18, Number 7 — Third Quarter, 1969

RC/\ Baton

News of Significant Developments in Home Entertainment and Electronics

Workshop at Cape Kennedy

Aerospace contractors at Cape Kennedy have taken a big step toward bringing down barriers that exist between minority job applicants and employment interviewers. At a two-day Minority Recruiting Workshop attended by company interviewers and receptionists, participants were given some insights into developing rapport and minimizing mistrust. Discussing the program with Aerospace Contractors Equal Opportunity Committee members is W. F. "Bucky" Hatchett, RCA Staff Employment, (center) who was the guest speaker. Reviewing workshop schedule with him are John Cottingham of the Florida State Employment Service and Howard Keys, RCA employment manager and chairman of the Aerospace Contractors Equal Opportunity Committee. In his talk, Mr. Hatchett commented on the modern Black man's attitudes and behavior as they relate to his job, his family and society. He also lamented the use of such terms as hard-core and disadvantaged person, suggesting in its place, "New Work Force."

RCA Makes Deposit In Negro-Owned Bank

As part of its continuing program of assisting Negro-owned and operated banking institutions, RCA Corporation recently announced the placement of a $250,000 Tax Deposit with the Freedom National Bank of New York. Shown presenting the deposit check to the Bank's president, William Huggins, is Warren E. Hendrickson, staff Vice President, Banking and Credit Administration, as Samuel Convissor, Director, Urban Affairs and Community Relations looks on. Mr. Hendrickson reported that the National Broadcasting Corporation, a wholly-owned subsidiary of RCA, has also opened bank accounts with Freedom National Bank, the Industrial Bank of Washington, Quincy Savings and Loan Company at Cleveland, The Seaway National Bank of Chicago, and the Bank of Finance at Los Angeles, which are all Negro-owned and operated institutions.

Figure 9-2. Informing the minority group of the organization's activities for its benefit is a means of building confidence.

The Wayfarer, which concentrates on publicizing Black leadership in major American cities, as well as some of the cultural and social life of these communities. This publication also points up Chrysler's minority employment practices as well as its line of automobiles.

The Greyhound Corporation sponsors, in alternate years, a "Woman of the Year" contest in cooperation with major city Black-oriented newspapers and a "Business Opportunity Forum" for minority-group businessmen in cooperation with major city Black-oriented radio stations.

Lever Brothers Company sponsors ten-minute five-day-per-week radio programs in five plant cities, encouraging minority group youth to stay in school, and fostering career development.

United Air Lines has long used Negro-oriented media for stewardess recruitment. ("Would You Like to Become a Member of United's Traveling Public Relations Team?") This leaves little ques-

Figure 9-3. A ready teaching and reference guide to prominent Blacks in American history was prepared by Carnation Company. It is used in schools and distributed to Blacks through stores and civic organizations.

tion that United welcomes minority-group young women.

Multiple purposes. The technique of company-underwritten Negro-oriented publications, reprints of significant articles appearing in ethnic media, and tailored programs of interest to minority groups accomplishes several objectives.

The publications are sent directly, by name, to Black leadership. In addition, they appear on college campuses, in libraries, in doctors' offices, and in many other gathering places.

On college campuses they also appear in placement offices and may determine how a young man or woman feels about a particular company and whether he or she seeks employment there. The publications offer the opportunity to discuss progressive employment practices and company interest in the minority communities.

They also enable the company to associate its interest in good minority relations with its products or services.

The annual report to stockholders should also be considered for evidencing good corporate citizenship. Copies of the report should be sent to top ethnic leadership, to indicate concern for minority groups.

Negro history advertising and public relations programs, as well as those reflecting contemporary life (and this has similar appeal to other minority groups), could be important as vehicles in attempting to influence opinion or sell more products and services to these segments of the consumer market. They can be effective means of establishing identification and can help encourage initiative by providing concrete examples of accomplishment that are little noted elsewhere.

Since this technique will continue to be important, here are some guidelines in considering Black history or contemporary life among minorities in institutional advertising and public relations programs:

1. Get technical help to avoid inaccuracies or misuse of material.
2. If good, clear pictures are not available use sketches or artists' conceptions.
3. If the theme of the campaign is thought to be at all insensitive to the particular minority group, research it in the community before too much investment is made.
4. Plan how and where the campaign is to be executed—such as at conventions, colleges and universities, libraries, banks—and what supporting materials will be needed.
5. If applicable, alert dealers and distributors on the campaign and seek their cooperation to make it effective.
6. Do not attach a hard-sell to this campaign; the soft-sell can help the program gain a much higher degree of acceptance.

The public relations executive who can fix his position in the minority communities in terms of current practices and then relate his organization's efforts to these communities will go a long way toward winning friends and influencing people. Whether it is a corporation or a nonprofit service organization, tailored materials and efforts can pay dividends.

10

Winning Public Support for an Idea or Cause

HUGH C. NEWTON heads a Washington-based public affairs firm—Hugh C. Newton & Associates—that specializes in "grass-roots" public relations programs.

Before establishing his own firm he was Director of Public Relations for the Air Transport Association, the trade association representing the nation's scheduled air lines. For four years before that he was Director of Information for the National Right to Work Committee. There he received a Silver Anvil Award in 1966 from the Public Relations Society of America for the program carried out to preserve Section 14(b) of the Taft-Hartley Act. As a special public relations consultant to the Committee, he played a key role in designing the public information program that induced President Ford to veto the "Common Situs" picketing bill in 1975. He is also the recipient of a Freedoms Foundation George Washington Honor Medal for economic writing.

Before moving to Washington in 1964 Newton was Manager of Special Services and chief speech writer for Reynolds Metals Company in Richmond, Virginia, Assistant Director of Public Relations for Rockwell Manufacturing Company in Pittsburgh, Pa., an account executive for Burson-Marsteller Associates, and a staff reporter for the Danville Bee in Danville, Va.

He is a native of Dobbs Ferry, N.Y., a graduate of Washington and Lee University, Lexington, Virginia, and studied economics in graduate school at Duquesne University in Pittsburgh.

Jefferson once wrote to Madison, "The people are the only sure reliance for the preservation of our liberty." The maxim certainly does not apply if "the people" is equated with the "the mob." Otherwise the 200-year-old maxim has a great deal of meaning for those modern public relations practitioners concerned with political and philosophical issues—today's causes.

The day is past when any major issue of public policy can be formed without widespread public support. If a proposal cannot be presented in a form in which it can gain support of the general public, prospects for success are dim indeed.

For example: Meaningful gun control proposals first came up before Congressional Committees in the mid-sixties and have languished there—not because of so-called pernicious propaganda but because the public is not sufficiently convinced that strong gun control legislation would answer the crime problem; the American SST was killed because its backers could not convince the public that it was worth spending billions of tax dollars for; Section 14(b) of the Taft-Hartley Act, the Right to Work provision, could not have been retained unless the public wanted it saved and made its wishes felt; that same public expressed itself most vigorously in 1975 on the coercive "Common Situs" picketing bill, inducing President Ford to reverse himself and veto the legislation.

Jefferson was right but one cannot always rely on the people to have the necessary information with which to save themselves—and that is where constructive public relations comes into play. As Madison said, "A popular government without

GOVERNMENT AND OUR WAY OF LIFE

One of the most significant developments in American life has been the increasing interest of citizens and corporations in government. The interest, of course, stems from the spreading impact of the Federal government on every aspect of life.

For the American businessman this spreading impact had its roots with the passage of the Interstate Commerce Act in 1887. Since then a succession of federal laws has given the Federal government regulatory control over minimum wages, monopoly, restraint of trade, competition, prices, food and drugs, transportation, and communications.

As the impact and extent of government increases, the need for adequate two-way communication between public official and citizen becomes urgent. Yet, unfortunately, the growth of government is accompanied by a diffusion of responsibility tending to drive the public official and citizen farther apart. Centuries ago Aristotle put the problem this way, "The environment is complex and man's political capacity is simple. Can a bridge be built between them?"

Government today—federal, state, and local—has become far more complex and often so remote that many citizens are bewildered. How can the man on the street assert an informed opinion on whether the multi-billion dollar B1 bomber is needed for military security? Who can assert, with confidence, a solution for world problems many experts consider insolvable—such as providing enough food to feed the billions of people on this planet, the population explosion in the underdeveloped nations, the seemingly endless disputes between peoples? How can Mr. Average be expected to have an answer to such complex problems as our energy crisis when Presidents, Congresses, academicians, economists, and business experts have failed to come up with any meaningful progress toward solving the problems?

The citizen may never evolve "solutions" to these problems but he is being provided a vast amount of information—information that will allow him to develop a reasonably informed opinion. The demand for this information is the reason behind the rapid growth in political and governmental public relations.

THE CORPORATE APPROACH

Until recent years the tremendous growth in government was not matched by corporate interest and activity in politics. The seemingly unfavorable political climate in which business operated for many years was largely a consequence of its own conviction that "business and politics don't mix."

However a marked change has taken place in the viewpoint of business leaders toward government[1] and politics.[2] As Ralph J. Cordiner, former chairman of the Board of General Electric Company, said, "Government is becoming a more significant factor in business decisions with every passing year. There is a whole new field to be explored in this matter of discovering and organizing the political resources of business."

Today approximately 140 of the 200 largest manufacturers in the Unites States maintain full-time Washington representatives in Washington. While the objectives are often primarily commercial, an increasing amount of time is being spent in the area of legislative activity and in relations with the executive and administrative agencies in government.

In addition to the individual corporations, an increasing number of industrial and professional associations and various types of government relations specialists are serving special interests.

There are now more than 11,000 industrial and comercial and 500 professional associations in the United States and more than half have offices or headquarters in Washington. Some of these are horizontal in character, serving a cross-section of business, such as the United States Industrial Council, the International Franchise Association, and the Chamber of Commerce of the United States. Others are vertical groups identified with a single industry, such as the Air Transport Association and the Associated Builders and Contractors (ABC).

From a public relations standpoint, most associations are somewhat limited in their legislative effectiveness. The membership of most trade and professional associations is so large and the interests of their individual members so diverse that their legislative position on controversial questions is often weak and inflexible. The lack of aggressiveness in obtaining favorable legislative and executive decisions stems from the fact that a multi-

---
[1] See Chapters 5 and 6.
[2] See Chapter 8.

purpose association can often be compromised on any given issue.[3]

Another stumbling block to effective governmental relations is the failure by many multi-purpose trade associations to understand or accept the necessity for close liaison between the public relations and the governmental relations functions (lobbying). On a given issue success is unlikely to be attained if the association does not have a planned program utilizing the coordinated efforts of public relations and governmental relations specialists. It is rare that one is successful without the other.

What this growth in corporate and association political public relations represents is a tremendous national interest in government. Centralization and concentration of government produces a sense of remoteness in the average citizen; but this remoteness is not reflected in apathy. The increasing impact of government on every aspect of the citizen's life has actually made him more concerned than ever with what is being done to him and for him. The businessman, labor official, professional man, student and teacher, TV repairman, or clerk wants to know what is happening in Washington, why, and how it affects him. He wants his voice to be heard where it counts.

A list of topics dealt with by major consumer legislation enacted by Congress in the past decade indicates legislators' sensitivity to public dissatisfaction—automobile safety as well as automobile exhaust fumes, air and water pollution, fair packaging and labeling, coal mine safety, truth-in-lending, labeling of cigarettes as health hazards and the banning of cigarette commercials on television, the establishment of the national Commission on Product Safety, and the establishment of more menacing—to most businessmen, at least—government agencies such as the Environmental Protection Agency, the Occupational Safety and Health Administration, and the Consumer Products Safety Commission.

ORGANIZATIONS TO FOSTER A CAUSE

In addition to the rapid growth of corporate public relations representation in Washington and the increasing involvement of professional and trade associations in governmental public relations, there have arrived on the political scene many single-purpose associations.

[3]See Chapter 21.

For example, The National Right to Work Committee, Americans Against Union Control of Government, Committee for a Free China, and The National Association to Promote Voluntary Sterilization all exist to influence opinion on a single issue. Some that have come and gone, because their missions are over, include, The Citizens Committee Against the SST, the Council for a Voluntary Military, and the Coal Industry Committee on Mine Safety.

Such groups are often the most important factor in winning passage of "consumer" legislation, stirring community action, effectively opposing legislation that would have serious impact on the ability of business to function, or helping elect political candidates.

WINNING PUBLIC SUPPORT

How does one go about winning vocal public support for an idea or cause? What ethical considerations are involved? To what extent can one influence people? Can public support, once it is won, be converted into legislative action? If so, how? In other words, what are the basic principles to be followed in planning, developing, and conducting a public relations program in this sensitive area?

There are a number of guidelines that can be applied. But first let's look at a newspaper editorial that provides unusual insight into the principles involved in public relations for a cause.

On February 12, 1966 the *Fort Lauderdale News* said in an editorial by-lined by Harvey Call titled, "Right to Work Law Victory Shows Campaign Devoid of Personalities Can Win":

> There are far-reaching implications behind the success of the filibuster against the repeal of Section 14(b) of the Taft-Hartley Act.
>
> The Right to Work laws of 19 states have survived one of the best-organized, long-range attacks ever directed at a fundamental right . . .
>
> Important as the victory is, there are aspects of the success which can be more significant to America and majority interests. That will be so if those representing the majority viewpoint on major issues learn a few valuable lessons from the fight . . .
>
> The campaign was waged almost exclusively on principle—the right of an individual to work at the job of his choice without being forced to join a union against his wishes or support an organization espousing ideas with which he might not agree.

WINNING PUBLIC SUPPORT FOR AN IDEA OR CAUSE

The campaign was constructive, to the point and devoid of personalities.

Far too frequently Americans concentrate their fire on individuals through personal attacks. In doing this, sight is lost of the basic issues. Principles become lost in a welter of personality clashes.

The victory for the Right to Work principle holds the hope that intelligent discussions and a thorough disclosure of what is involved in support of principles can win public support. The message can be gotten across, and the majority interest can be sustained.

Another key to the victory was the fact that the campaign was not conducted with emphasis on benefits of the Right to Work principles to employers or any group which might be open to attack and distortion. The campaign was geared entirely to translating the principle in terms of its meaning to the individual worker.

Analyze it and it will be noted the tactics were the same as politicians have used to sell the Medicare program, poverty plans, and other welfare state ideas . . .

Summed up, a campaign conducted without selfish interest, without personality attacks and based on sound principles can win and help sustain American principles.

THE BASIC PRINCIPLES

In his analysis of one particular cause editor Call put his finger on most of the basic principles involved in carrying on what might be described, in the positive sense of the term, a propaganda program—in this case for the Right to Work, but applicable as well for other types of programs seeking public support.

These principles include:

1. *Define your problem* . . . in the simplest of terms.
2. *Focus your program on the heart of the problem.* Use every opportunity to place public attention on the principle at stake and avoid being dragged into unproductive tangential arguments.
3. *Organize a staff that believes in what it is doing.* Dedication to the cause is no substitute for professional competence, but the presence of both is essential in this type of effort.
4. *Plan. Plan. And keep on planning.* Planning determines who your allies are. (You may be surprised who your "allies" are. For example on the Supersonic Transport issue the Air Transport Association and the International Association of Machinists were allies, and on Common Situs picketing "Big Business" and the National Right to Work Committee were not.) Planning enables you to staff properly, to determine what type of outside counsel is needed. Planning, rather than reacting, will result in the effective use of research and public opinion attitude studies and on whose ground the battle will be fought. Planning does not guarantee success; but without it success is probably impossible.
5. *Find out where the public stands on the issue. The Dictionary of Mass Communications* defines public opinion as the expression of all members of a group who are giving attention in any way to a given issue. That opinion may be favorable, unfavorable, or apathetic to your cause; but before you can plan your program it is vital to know which it is. In handling a campaign for a cause it would be a serious handicap to operate without the use of opinion research data.[4] In utilizing the results of a public opinion study keep in mind:
   A. That attitude change is related to the immediacy of the issue to the individual.
   B. That events play an important part in changing attitudes and opinions. Actions do speak louder than words in influencing attitudes.
   C. That a major role in shaping public opinion is played by opinion leaders. To recognize and gain the support of opinion leaders in key economic, social, and political groups is a primary task of public relations for a cause.[5]
6. *Keep your policies simple and provide the staff with strong backing.*
7. *Keep the staff "tight."* As Philip Lesly said in an article for *Association Management,* "A small group of highly talented, knowledgeable and conscientious people will almost always outperform the largest staff of ordinary personnel."[6] But an unusually wide latitude of action is essential to the effective operation of an endeavor of this type.
8. *Keep the program honest.* Critics of public relations often refer to its practitioners as "hidden persuaders" who surreptitiously

---
[4] See Chapter 35.
[5] See Chapter 2.
[6] "The Complex Art of Public Relations," July, 1966.

mold public opinion in favor of certain products, ideals, and institutions. In a battle for public opinion the use of pernicious propaganda techniques will almost always backfire.

9. *Take your case to the people.* Arouse public opinion at the grassroots and let them demand action from government. Remember—don't rely on one communications medium. There are thousands of editors, columnists, and opinion makers who may be on your side and will help you tell your story to the public. The nation's capital IS highly insulated. While every Washington journalist professes to know exactly what Senators Kennedy, Goldwater, Proxmire, and Percy are thinking about the latest Near East crisis they are often completely out of touch with what most Americans think.

10. *Let Congress and the President know.* Set up a formal information and research program. Keep your efforts low-key. Don't try to force your cause on the Congress or members of the White House staff. But do let them know what your group is doing and what others are saying about the issue. The National Right to Work Committee's successful effort in 1966 to prevent repeal of Section 14(b) of the Taft-Hartley Act and the successful 1975 effort to defeat the coercive Common Situs picketing bill was based on the idea that they had to go *first* to the American people and *then* to members of Congress and the President.

Using direct mail. Despite rising costs of direct mail, it has been gaining as a tool in public opinion programs. Direct mail played an important role, perhaps the key role, in the program designed to motivate and mobilize millions of Americans against presidential approval of the "Common Situs" picketing bill. As the *AFL-CIO News* said after President Ford vetoed the bill, "Newspapers and opponents of the legislation shifted the debate to issues of 'individual freedom' and 'coercive unionism.' The National Right to Work Committee . . . mailed out four million pieces of propaganda to generate citizen pressure."

PLANNING A PUBLIC OPINION CAMPAIGN

"Common Situs." On August 25, 1975, President Ford reversed his long-standing position and said he would sign the "Common Situs" picketing bill. Since the bill already had been passed by the House; was actively supported by the Secretary of Labor, the AFL-CIO lobbying apparatus, and some business interests; and probably would be approved by the Senate, it appeared it would become law.

Obviously, the prospects for opponents of the bill were not bright. Intensive planning sessions were held by the executive staff of the National Right to Work Committee that showed that despite the best efforts of employers, contractors, and other opponents of monopoly union power, "Common Situs" would be approved unless, 1) the issue could be put into meaningful terms to most Americans, 2) millions of Americans could be motivated and mobilized, and 3) their efforts were channeled into enough influence on opinion leaders and politicians to either kill the bill in the Senate or make it prudent for the President to veto the legislation.

Since opinion polls consistently show that most Americans believe union membership should be voluntary, we felt we had at least a chance if we could quickly and forcefully focus public attention on the fact that by granting new coercive powers to union organizers the "situs" bill would further erode the individual freedom-of-choice of construction workers and employers, and endanger the public interest.

We knew too, that any leverage would probably have to be from the "grass roots." Key ingredients—each tailored when possible for maximum impact with a particular audience—included:

1. Briefings and coordination on the issue with key legislative supporters and opponents from both parties;
2. A national advertising campaign involving full-page ads in 49 major newspapers in 17 states and Washington, D.C.;
3. Contact with special "publics" such as minority contractors and black journalists;
4. An educational and informational direct mail program designed to motivate citizen action. During the four-month period, eight major mailings were made to more than four million individual Americans (one measure of the result was that the White House received, by official count, 646,152 letters and cards urging the President to veto "Common Situs" [versus only 7,379 letters and cards asking him to sign the legislation]. In addition, members of the Senate and House received more than a million letters and cards. The total was more mail on any issue since the Vietnam War);

5. A politically oriented direct mail appeal from Senator Paul Fannin(R-Arizona) that was produced and mailed at Right to Work expense to 200,000 key Republican contributors and leaders across the country, enlisting their help;
6. Special publicity for a new opinion poll that showed most Americans, including union members, opposed to "Situs;"
7. Personal meetings for in-depth briefings with several dozen syndicated columnists and the editorial page editors of more than 50 major newspapers; and
8. Many news bureau activities designed to gain attention and to be part of a necessary "multiplier" effect.

On December 22, 1975, President Ford announced his decision to veto the picketing bill. *The New York Times* said, "Employer spokesmen and the National Right to Work Committee marshalled their formidable resources to induce the President to veto it."

Sugar. On the consumer front, sugar, because of its universal usage and visibility, was a natural target for lay nutritionists and promoters of fad foods and diets who have appeared in recent years to capitalize on concerns generated by the consumer movement.

Early in the 1970's the industry faced a barrage of criticism in the media suggesting that public consumption of ever-increasing amounts of sugar was responsible for a far-ranging variety of health problems. As the volume of criticism increased, concern increased among the industry's primary publics: the medical community, nutritional professionals, user industries, government health officials, and the consuming public.

The Sugar Association in a short period needed to reach the medical community, nutritional professionals, sugar-using industries, the media, and government health officials with the facts concerning sugar and to enlist their aid in educating the consuming public. And it needed, over the long-run, to establish with the broadest possible audience the safety of sugar as a food.

The program involved several interesting strategies. On one hand, all association advertising was dropped, since even a nutritional message would appear to be self-serving. Also, media objectivity and balance was the prime concern, not necessarily extensive coverage. Important aspects of the program also involved surveys of public attitudes, enlistment of leading medical experts to counsel the industry, promotion of talks by qualified medical experts to speak for the industry—regardless of potential negatives, preparation of an independent survey of existing scientific data and literature, and a commitment to stand up publicly against purveyors of misinformation.

Measurement to date has been directed to the short-term objective of the program, based on the understanding the Sugar Association has developed with its key publics; the volume of publicity is a secondary consideration. *Emphasis* has been placed on the program's ability to stem the flow of negative commentary and to correct the errors of the extreme "consumer" oriented columnists and writers.

Attacks on sugar in the media have diminished sharply, and those that now appear tend to be more balanced. Announcements by the Food and Drug Administration and the National Academy of Sciences, supportive of sugar, make it less likely that sugar will be subject to legislative restrictions.

THE USE OF POLLS

Public opinion research can be effectively used in an opinion campaign in the following ways:

1. Policy and strategy guidance. Having a firm and continuous foundation of opinion research data permits attacking the problem of public education with positiveness and assurance. While much of the data may tend to confirm the instinct and feeling the professional public relation practitioner already has, having it available in scientifically supportable facts and figures helps keep educational effort on target.

If successive surveys present a consistent picture, they tend to reinforce the other. In addition, successive surveys provide a useful measure of trends and the direction in which opinions may be changing; and measure response to particular appeals by opponents and proponents.

2. Membership development. Membership appeals are strengthened by demonstrating the potential support among the majority of citizens. Factual public opinion research data demonstrate to current and potential contributors that the cause can be victorious. Most financial contributors want to be assured that they are investing in an undertaking that has at least a reasonable chance of success. And the fact that the program is based on scientific survey data inspires confidence that this is a well-thought-out program worthy of support.

3. Influencing legislation. Most elected officials

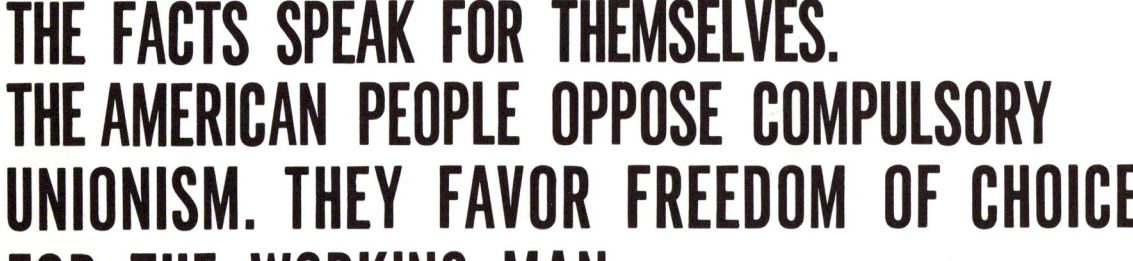

Figure 10-1. Using the results of an objective opinion survey in support of legislative proposals, this ad was aimed at members of the U.S. Senate.

are responsive to reputable and well-presented survey results. They view them as important in sensing the actual wishes of their constituencies. Together with editorials, mail from home, and other indicators, opinion surveys influence their ultimate position on some issues.

4. Influencing public opinion. Many people are influenced in their attitude toward a public issue by the fact that it is supported or disapproved by a majority of people.

TIMING AND EXECUTION

To a great extent the planning of a public relations program to promote a cause or to influence public opinion is determined by timing in the hands of others.

The campaign to preserve 14(b) is an example. In the Fall of 1964 few people in Washington gave 14(b) a serious chance of surviving to the end of 1965. Action in early 1965 was considered a foregone conclusion by all seasoned political observers. (This effort preceded by several years the effort to weaken 14(b) through the "Common Situs" legislation mentioned previously.)

Spearheading the opposition was the National Right to Work Committee, a small coalition of citizens from all walks of life—including union members—with a single purpose: Protecting the right of the individual to join or not to join a union without losing his job.

Despite the fact that the opposition would select the ground and the time for the battle the National Committee began planning a program to save 14(b).

Figure 10-2. Showing support of groups not ordinarily expected to support a cause is an effective technique. Union members picketed the AFL-CIO headquarters in support of the law restricting compulsory unionism.

1. Meetings were begun with a select group of Washington-based and allied business and trade associations to establish a framework within which all groups supporting Right to Work could coordinate their efforts.
2. In cooperation with key friendly members of Congress, work was begun to develop legislative strategy.
3. A year-long information program was outlined, based roughly on the legislative strategy and schedule. The program to be implemented included plans for forming citizen's organizations and the production and distribution of educational materials, sample speeches, editorials, and advertisements.
4. Contact was made with other key industry and trade association executives around the country requesting support.
5. Opinion Research Corporation of Princeton, N.J. was commissioned to do a nationwide study of public attitudes on 14(b) and Right to Work.
6. CENTRON, Inc. of Lawrence, Kansas, was hired to prepare a new black-and-white sound motion picture.
7. A research assistant was hired and given the go-ahead on conducting a comprehensive study to dig out all the necessary information and prepare comprehensive answers to all pro-repeal arguments; the President's complete voting record and every public statement he had made on 14(b) and Right to Work; all quotes made by union officials and administration representatives on compulsion, voluntarism, freedom, civil rights, and so on; and data to help document a strong case against providing the union hierarchy with any additional power.
8. The staff carefully analyzed the Committee's objectives, limitations, problems, publics to approach and methods to reach them, and financial requirements. Considerable time was spent in clearly "defining the issue." (The conclusion: To win, the issue had to be defined in simple terms—yes or no, right or wrong, compulsion or voluntarism.)
9. Key worker members were called in for a worker leadership conference to plan

employee activities in opposition to repeal.
10. A program was formulated to expand existing state Right to Work organizations and to organize new state citizen groups.
11. A careful study in late 1964 revealed that the nation's press—editorially speaking—were almost unanimously on the National Committee's side. This survey indicated that there was a great deal of concern outside of Washington for the individual's freedom of choice.

While every campaign must be different, dealing with the special circumstances it faces, this outline is an indication of an approach that can succeed.

11

Financial Public Relations*
I. Basic Planning and Programs

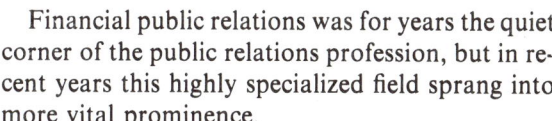

EUGENE MILLER is chairman of the Department of Business and Management at Northeastern Illinois University in Chicago. He also has his own consulting firm and is affiliated with Mel Adams and Associates.

He formerly was Senior Vice President, Marketing and Public Relations of The New York Stock Exchange and a member of its Executive Committee. He has also been Senior Vice President, Corporate Relations, CNA Financial Corporation and Vice President, Public Affairs and Communications of McGraw-Hill. Previously he was associate managing editor of Business Week in New York.

Dr. Miller has a B.S. degree from the Georgia Institute of Technology, an A.B., magna cum laude, from Bethany College, and an M.S. from the Graduate School of Journalism at Columbia University. In addition, he holds an M.B.A. from New York University and a diploma for graduate work in economics from Oxford University, England. In 1969, he received an LL.D degree from Bethany College.

He has been an Adjunct Associate Professor of Management at the Graduate School of Business Administration, New York University and an Adjunct Professor at Fordham University's Graduate School of Business. He served as a speechwriter to President Dwight Eisenhower and as a consultant to Secretary of Commerce Luther Hodges. He is the author of several books and hundreds of magazine articles. For eight years he wrote a syndicated newspaper column on business and finance.

Financial public relations was for years the quiet corner of the public relations profession, but in recent years this highly specialized field sprang into more vital prominence.

Major corporations across the country have established financial public relations or investor relations posts or have expanded existing departments to undertake the demands for better relations with shareholders, security analysts, and the financial press.

At the same time, agencies specializing in financial public relations have increased, in direct competition with the general public relations agencies that are also handling a steadily increasing share of the financial relations business.

There are several catalysts responsible for this growth, including:

(1) The increasing number of corporations selling shares to the public

(2) The increasing number of firms listed on the stock exchanges

(3) The high rate of corporate mergers and acquisitions and the desire for higher stock prices to make these transactions attractive

(4) Growing sophistication of security analysts and their increasing concentration on large companies

(5) Growing sophistication of the investing

---

*Parts of this chapter are adapted from the chapter on financial public relations by Weston Smith in the Third Edition of *Public Relations Handbook*.

public and its cynicism regarding previous claims of superior management and performance by both corporations and stockbrokers

(6) Demands for better management performance translated into higher stock prices

(7) Much tougher requirements for disclosure of information by the Securities and Exchange Commission and the New York and American Stock Exchanges. Also, policies set forth by the Financial Accounting Standards Board have established new requirements for providing accounting data to stockholders in annual and other reports

(8) Growing realization of the need for expert guidance, particularly in view of a series of court cases. There have also been several key court cases involving the work of various financial public relations practitioners that have laid down some specific guidelines in certain areas while posing many questions still unresolved.

Changes that increase need. The securities market now is far different than in the 1960's, and the work of the financial public relations expert has become much more difficult.

The paperwork crisis of the late 1960's, when financial securities firms could not cope with the volume of stock trades, signaled to the public, the SEC, and Congress that the securities industry needed a major overhaul in both systems and practices.

This back-office problem caused the consolidation and merger of a number of brokerage firms. The failures by some firms also led to formation of the Securities Investors Protection Corporation that was designed to protect customers of failing brokerage firms.

In the early 1970's the Wall Street community was forced to make several major adjustments. One resulted from the SEC's insistence on eliminating fixed commissions as well as other long-standing Wall Street practices. Elimination of fixed commissions, in turn, caused the demise or merger of a number of additional brokerage firms and reduced profitability of many of the surviving firms.

In the early 1970's the stock markets started a decline that lasted a number of years. The prices of stocks of many companies, both large and small, showed sizable declines. Price-earnings ratios that once had been ten or more declined to as low as three or four to one. That included some major "blue chip" companies. The issuance of new stock offerings almost dried up. Prices of stocks of smaller, over-the-counter companies suffered greatly. There was a sharp decline in the number of American shareholders. The total had reached more than 30 million in 1970. By mid-1975 the figure had dropped to 25.2 million, an 18 percent decline. That was the first decline in more than 20 years.

This situation created substantial problems for companies and their investor relations programs. The front-line marketers of securities are the registered representatives and the number of securities salesmen declined after 1970. Other groups that encouraged individuals to invest in the market—such as the National Association of Investment Clubs—found their membership, too, declined substantially as dropping stock prices took a toll of members and club activities.

The New York Stock Exchange, which had spearheaded much of the promotional activity to encourage stock market participation in the 1950's and 1960's, found its profits reduced and with less money for major advertising, marketing, and public relations programs than it had had in the 1960's.

The same studies that indicated a sizable drop in shareholder population also showed that the median age of the U.S. shareholders had moved up from 48 to 53 years. This, too, was a subject of concern because it indicated that the more risk-oriented younger investors were not coming into the stock market in sufficient quantities to offset normal attrition.

At the same time, some basic structural changes were taking place in the way the stock exchanges operate. One such development has been tremendous growth in the stock options business. That trend was triggered by the start of options trading in the Spring of 1973 on the new Chicago Board Options Exchange (CBOE), created by the Chicago Board of Trade. The CBOE set up a basic market in "call" options. A call option gives the option holder the right to purchase 100 shares of the underlying security at a given price during a given period. Trading volume on the CBOE on many days has exceeded the trading volume of the American Stock Exchange, the nation's second-largest market for stocks. Spurred by the success of the CBOE, a number of stock exchanges have initiated options trading.

The SEC has given some of the options exchanges the opportunity to start listing "put" options. These are the reverse transaction of call options. People buy "put" options that give them the right to sell the underlying security at a fixed price during a fixed period.

FINANCIAL PUBLIC RELATIONS

Another major development in the securities market is a composite tape showing transactions at a number of exchanges. Actually, NYSE-listed stocks have been traded on a number of stock exchanges for many years. Seven exchanges in 1973 formed a consolidated tape association to report all trading activity in NYSE-listed stocks on one composite tape. Consequently, the tape now being used in brokerage offices and the financial stock market tables that are run in daily newspapers report the composite trading activity of all seven exchanges. The financial table that used to be solely NYSE figures now reproduces the consolidated tape that lists volume and prices of NYSE-listed issues that are traded on any of the exchanges.

Search for effective programs. With all these developments taking place in the structure of the industry as well as the declining interest by investors in stocks, many listed companies have been in a quandary about the emphases of their investor relations programs. In 1974-1975 a number of companies curtailed some of their financial public relations activities because with the economy in a recession and the stock market in the doldrums they felt they could do little to overcome stockholder apathy. Cutbacks occurred in the number of communications going to analysts, the number of meetings held by company officers with security analysts, and the size and expense of annual reports.

On the other hand, a number of companies took the opposite tack and used this period to try different ways of winning recognition and interest from investors and the financial community.

Some of this new effort concentrated on getting the companies' stock listed on foreign exchanges and stepping up efforts to get foreign investors to know more about their companies. Results of these listings are still unclear but they are being monitored by companies to see if this is a worthwhile activity. Meanwhile, a number of companies have increased their visits abroad to meet with members of foreign financial communities. It has become commonplace for leading companies to have their executives regularly visit such cities as Tokyo, London, Paris, Frankfurt, Geneva, Zurich, and Brussels to meet with members of the financial community. And more and more companies publish their annual reports in a variety of foreign languages to communicate better with foreign investors and shareholders.

Still other companies have stepped up their direct communications with registered representatives in brokerage firms. The hope is that if they can interest the representatives they, in turn, can interest investors. These efforts take the form of special meetings of company officials with registered reps, special visits by reps to company headquarters, plants, and offices, and special written communications from the company to these representatives. A study by Technimetrics indicated that brokers were generally receptive to such programs, were pleased to get special literature, and liked to attend special company presentations directed to them.

Another tack taken by a number of companies was to increase advertising programs aimed at investors.[1] The value of this strategy was emphasized by a study made by two Northwestern University professors—Eugene Schonfeld and John Boyd—that indicated that such expenditures can have a positive influence on the companies' stock prices. They studied advertising expenditures over a period of time, then measured the performance of the companies' stock prices during that period. Their conclusion was that many companies could benefit by spending substantially more on corporate advertising if their objective was to achieve optimal stock prices. The study did not attempt to differentiate between corporate institutional advertising and product advertising.

In the present climate, corporations must strive as hard for investor recognition as they do for consumer recognition of their products and services. The large number of corporate name changes recently and the growing use of logotypes as identity symbols are indications of the desire for recognition.[2]

Though financial public relations is a specialized area of the field, it calls for widespread skills and involves a broad range of publics and functions.

Twelve financial publics. The public relations department or firm should act as liaison between the company's top management and the following influential financial groups:

(1) Stock exchange member firms, customers' brokers, branch office managers.
(2) Members of the security analyst societies and individual analysts.
(3) Unlisted or over-the-counter dealers.
(4) Investment bankers.
(5) Commercial bankers (trust departments).
(6) Registered investment advisory services.

[1] See Chapter 47.
[2] See Chapter 55.

(7) Insurance companies and pension funds that buy common stocks.
(8) Mutual funds and investment trusts.
(9) Investment counselors.
(10) Trustees of estates and institutions.
(11) Financial statistical organizations.
(12) Investment magazines and financial publications (semi-weekly, weekly, bi-weekly, semi-monthly, monthly, and quarterly).

REQUISITES FOR THE FINANCIAL PUBLIC RELATIONS MAN

The growth in financial public relations has been accompanied by a sharp increase in the demand for qualified personnel. This demand came suddenly and grew faster than general public relations practitioners were prepared for it, leaving a gap that has not been filled yet. Part of this gap has also been created by the attitude on the part of some that financial public relations is too complex to be handled without a specialized education or a solid financial background.

While there are many areas of common knowledge between general and financial public relations, there are a few major areas that must be mastered in order to handle financial relations effectively.

Basically, the financial public relations man must become an expert in two major areas in addition to having basic public relations skills:

(1) The regulatory guidelines for publicity in the Securities and Exchange Acts of 1933 and 1934 as well as the disclosure requirements of the national stock exchanges and court cases relating to them.
(2) The analysis and evaluation of financial statements.

The scope of responsibilities and functions of financial public relations includes:

Liaison with executive management:

(1) Board of Directors (primarily through the Board Chairman).
(2) Executive Committee.
(3) Finance Committee.
(4) Key officials (president, vice presidents, treasurer, secretary, and controller).
(5) Certain department heads (Sales, Research, Accounting, etc.)
(6) Directors of Public Relations, Industrial Relations, Employee Relations.

Financial publicity:

(1) Uncovering and developing news of interest to stockholders through liaison with key executives within the corporation.
(2) Contacting and cultivating friendships with financial editors of press services, newspapers, magazines, trade publications, radio, and TV.
(3) Directing the preparation of financial press releases (annual and interim reports, dividend declarations, management changes, operating statistics, security redemptions, financing, mergers, executives' speeches and articles, proxy fights, etc.).
(4) Interviewing newspaper financial reporters and feature writers for financial and business magazines to determine their needs.
(5) When called on to do so, supplying requested information to statistical agencies, investment services, financial analysts, investment trusts, brokerage houses, investment banking firms, and others.

Stockholder correspondence:

(1) Letters of welcome to new stockholders (signed by the company chief executive officer).
(2) Answering inquiries for financial and other appropriate information.
(3) Proper treatment of complaints from both large and small investors.
(4) Letters of thanks for mailing in signed proxies.
(5) Special form letters covering exchanges of shares in splitups, stock dividends, and scrip certificates; explaining financing, options, and changes in dividend policy (inauguration, increases, reductions, and omissions).

Conducting stockholder surveys:

(1) To determine nature of distribution of shares (geographically, average number of shares held, sexes, age levels, occupations, length of time stock is held, etc.).
(2) Readership of corporation annual reports and quarterly earnings statements (request for suggestions as to content and handling of financial statistics, criticisms, changes, additions, etc.).
(3) Other purposes (utilizing stockholder lists for opinion surveys—all names or a selected sampling—to determine majority preferences, to test new products, to select trade names, etc.).

Preparation of corporation annual report and quarterly earnings statements:

NOTE: Explained at length in accompanying text.

Other stockholder publications:

(1) Quarterly earnings statements converted into newsletters, digest booklets, and "stockholder magazines."
(2) Folders interpreting company policies, proposed changes, advertising techniques, public relations creeds, etc.
(3) Dividend "stuffers" or inserts (sent without extra postage with quarterly or semiannual dividend checks).
(4) Reprints of speeches and articles by officials of company.
(5) Biographical digests of executive officers and members of board of directors.
(6) Calendars, almanacs, diaries, product directories, recipe lists, etc.

Financial and educational advertising:

(1) Cooperation with financial executives, advertising manager, and advertising agency.
(2) Financial advertising (dividend announcements, redemption notices, annual meeting call, requests for bids on new securities, etc.).
(3) Institutional advertising (annual report and quarterly statement advertisements; announcements of mergers and acquisitions; opening of new plants, departments, and sales territories; change in corporate name; etc.).
(4) Special advertising (industrial editions of magazines, annual review numbers, souvenir programs, convention issues of publications, etc.).
(5) The press that covers the company and its industry.
(6) Foreign investors and the foreign financial community.
(7) Inclusion of press releases in the "Current Corporate Reports" section of *Barron's*.

Planning the annual meeting of stockholders:

(1) Organizing a program (schedule of routine and extra features).
(2) Selection of place of meeting.
(3) Preparations for answers to questions and criticisms.
(4) Serving refreshments at meeting, or consideration of a luncheon or dinner in company restaurant or cafeteria; club or hotel.
(5) Entertaining representatives of the press.
(6) Arranging post-meeting report to be printed and sent to absent stockholders.
(7) Consideration of closed-circuit TV coverage to reach stockholders in other parts of the country.
(8) Consideration of methods for effectively handling vocal stockholders.

Regional meetings of stockholders:

(1) Selecting cities where company has largest numbers of shareholders.
(2) Making reservations at hotels in accordance with expected audiences.
(3) Providing for slide-films or motion pictures; exhibits of products.
(4) Serving refreshments (a product of the company if in food or beverage industry).
(5) Distributing samples, booklets, calendars, or other souvenirs.

Special services to stockholders:

(1) Locating dealer nearest to stockholder for company's merchandise.
(2) Offering gift packages at special prices for Christmas.
(3) Distributing "dividend" of sample of new product when appropriate.
(4) Assisting stockholders in the sale of large blocks of shares.
(5) Arranging for visits to executive offices, factories, branches, etc.

Working with security analysts:

(1) Surveying analysts to determine the extent of their knowledge of the company and their attitudes toward the company.
(2) Arranging for individual analysts to meet the company's executives.
(3) Arranging for management to speak before various analysts' societies, including specialized and general groups.
(4) Preparing and distributing informational materials to analysts such as statistical summaries, news reports, special surveys, etc.
(5) Arranging tours of company plants and headquarters for analysts groups.
(6) Maintaining continuous liaison with analysts to insure an open channel of communications.

Activities in defense against proxy fights and tender offers (See Chapter 12)

As the extent of knowledge and professionalism required has grown, an increasing number of firms have designated an executive as a specialist in investor relations, sometimes with the status of an officer.

In 1969 the National Investor Relations Institute was formed to be the professional society embracing those doing investor relations work. Its objectives were to improve corporate investor relations through a variety of functions. By the end of 1976 NIRI membership exceeded 700 and it had chapters in a dozen major cities in the country. Numbered in its ranks are the investor relations managers or officers of many major U.S. corporations as well as general and financial public relations counseling firms.

NIRI has earned national attention by serving as a spokesman for investor relations professionals and their companies on a wide variety of topics including proposed rules and regulations on disclosure, tender offers, and the like. NIRI representatives appear before the SEC to voice the organization's position and testifies at Congressional hearings. The organization has a major Fall meeting with prominent personalities in government, business, and the securities industry as speakers. It also publishes a regular newsletter that discusses topics of special interest to its members. NIRI is headquartered at 1629 K Street, N.W., Washington, D.C. 20006.

Unlike general public relations practice, financial public relations activities are often dictated or shaped by certain legal or regulatory requirements.[3] For instance, the Securities and Exchange Commission has specific guidelines for publicity activities during the period a company has a registration statement for the sale of its shares outstanding. In another area, there are specific obligations a company listed on the New York Stock Exchange or one of the other exchanges must meet in disseminating news to stockholders and the general public.

Without the aid of a solid background in reading financial statements, a financial public relations man would find it almost impossible to communicate with two of his major publics—security analysts and institutional investors. A financial public relations man trying to discuss cash flow with a security analyst without some knowledge of accounting and corporate finance would be in somewhat the same position as a blind person trying to discuss the relative merits of the color red versus green.

[3]See Chapter 54.

The Public Relations Society of America,[4] the American Management Association,[5] New York University,[6] and several other professional organizations offer seminar courses in financial public relations. Adult education and university courses are also available in the more technical areas, such as securities analysis, accounting, and corporate finance.

The financial public relations practitioner can also launch his own self-education program easily. There are numerous easy-to-read articles available on the technical aspects. Some suggested readings are included in the Bibliography.

At a minimum, a self-education program should include a study of accounting terms and procedures and the analysis of corporate financial statements, the 1933 and 1934 Securities and Exchange Acts, a review of general corporate financial policy, and a review of stock market operations and procedures as well as a thorough study of the disclosure policies of the New York and the American Stock Exchanges.

ESTABLISHING A PROGRAM

The most effective means of gaining the necessary knowledge and, at the same time, laying a foundation for a broad program is to build a series of profiles describing the corporation's major aspects. These profiles should be as detailed and accurate as possible, rather than a mere thumbnail sketch of the corporation. They will be valuable in dealings with analysts, since it will put all of the vital facts and statistics at your fingertips.

The most important profile would be an outline of the corporation's competitive position. This should include an analysis of the company's products or services, their relative strengths and weaknesses, the company's marketing areas and methods of marketing, the company's position in comparison with other firms in the same industry, the company's past sales experience, the effects of varying economic conditions, the strengths and weaknesses of the company's research and development with particular attention to new products that may be marketed in the near future, and the company's production capabilities. Some estimate should also be made of how much products add to

[4]845 Third Ave., New York, N.Y. 10022.
[5]135 W. 50th St., New York, N.Y. 10020.
[6]PRSA-NYU Seminars, Business and Management Programs, Room 1517, 310 Madison Ave., New York, N.Y. 10017.

the public's recognition of the company as an investment vehicle. Consider how the recognition of products such as Xerox machines, Polaroid cameras, IBM computers, Dupont nylon, and Campbell's soup have helped these companies establish recognition as investment possibilities.

Financial profile. A profile of the company's financial position should also be constructed. Particular attention should be given to relating the company's history not only in terms of dollars and cents, assets and liabilities, or just sales and earnings, but also in terms of return on invested capital, profit margins, debt-equity ratio, inventory turnover, cost of sales, cost of production, and so forth.

This type of analysis should also reveal the reasons for the company's earnings figures, rather than just relate them. For instance, it is one thing to say that a corporation earned $2.50 a share and quite another to say that the company earned $2.50 a share and at the same time increased its profit margin per unit of sales because of production efficiencies. This becomes more significant when compared with other corporations. A company increasing its profit margin by more efficient operations is by far a more attractive investment than a similar company with the same sales or better, and the same price-earnings level. Similarly, there is a considerable difference between earnings gains generated internally and those generated by acquisition.

A profile should also be made of the company's securities. A financial public relations man who does not have an intimate knowledge of the market performance of his company's stock, its distribution of shareowners, including major holdings of institutions and individuals, or the performance of the stock under varying economic and market conditions is like a salesman trying to discuss a product about which he knows nothing. Here again the market performance of the stock should be compared with other companies in the same industry. An additional step in this initial phase of study would be to review security analysts' recommendations and attitudes concerning the stock over the most recent year.

Describing management. Most corporate annual reports cite the company's management and its employees as its most valuable assets, but in terms of describing a corporation these most valuable assets will often be overlooked. True, it is difficult to quantify good management or even to describe it in some cases, but administrators, like stock prices, have performances that can be charted. For instance, an electronics corporation that has as its director of research a man who has made a significant contribution to the industry, such as development of the laser, is certainly in a better competitive position from a research standpoint than others in the same field. A management profile should incorporate such vital data as experience, education, age, diversified abilities, major contributions to the corporation, and industry achievements.

A final step would be to determine the company's present image among security analysts and in the financial press. A brief survey should be made of analysts who cover the industry to get their current views of the company and to determine how well the company is getting its corporate message across. A review of press coverage would include discussions with key financial editors and a review of press clippings to determine how much attention the company has received and what aspects of its performance received the most attention. A broader evaluation of the company's image might be gained by employing a professional public opinion sampling organization.[7]

A review of the company's internal public relations policies should also be made to determine what procedures are followed in disseminating information, how confidential matters are handled, how SEC and NYSE or American Stock Exchange rules are policed, what guidelines must be followed in speaking with the press, who acts as the company's spokesman, how analyst visits and interviews are handled, and so forth. If the company has never had an active financial relations program, policies may have to be revised or new guidelines developed.

Four basic groups. The need among all publicly held companies is to cultivate confidence and build prestige among these basic publics:

(1) Present registered shareholders.
(2) The investing public, including those with shares held in brokers' names.
(3) The financial community, including bankers, brokers, investment advisers, trustees of estates, security analysts, mutual funds, insurance companies, pension funds, and others who influence opinion of securities.
(4) The general business and business-interested public whose attitudes greatly affect the acceptance of a company's securities, as well as its products.

[7]See Chapter 35.

COMMUNICATING WITH SHAREHOLDERS

Maintaining a good relationship with shareholders is not only sound public relations practice, but also sound financial management. A solid base of loyal shareholders is highly advantageous for any company. A number of corporations have managed to fend off takeover bids by appealing to this loyal shareholder base.

Stockholder communications takes a more direct approach than communications with the general public. There are many ways to communicate with stockholders—newsletters, magazines, quarterly reports, special letters, annual reports, company biographies, and booklets describing the company's products and operations.

More imaginative communications are being employed increasingly. Some corporations have produced annual reports on phonograph records and even in Braille. Dayton-Hudson has published an original pop art poster suitable for framing with the quarterly report printed on the back. A number of companies issue annual reports especially written for employees. Several, such as Wheelabrator-Frye, prepare special annual reports designed for young people.

Translations. A number of international corporations already distribute annual reports in several foreign languages. International Telephone and Telegraph has published annual reports in seven languages.

For many years annual reports were merely historical documents, consisting of a brief statement from the president summarizing the year's events, and the financial statement that was meant to be glanced at, then filed. Today's annual reports, however, have taken on the appearances of high-quality magazines and, in a growing number of cases, could be classified as promotional pieces. Many of the better annual reports employ a theme that communicates the corporation's business philosophy and goals rather than just facts and figures. These reports not only explain how the corporation earns its money, how it has met its challenges in the past year, but, more importantly, the company's business philosophy, its long-range goals, how it intends to achieve these goals, and what has been done during the year to accomplish these goals.

As the economic ignorance of the public has become more evident and alarming, many companies have been incorporating material designed to explain the incentive system of "free enterprise."[8]

Graphics are used to underscore the theme of the report and make it more attractive and easier to read.

There are three schools of thought on what level of sophistication an annual report should follow. One school believes that the report should be simple and to the point, and not confuse people with a lot of facts and figures. The other believes the annual report should merely convey the financial results for the year with no attempt to explain their meaning. A compromise is usually made between these two extremes. The complexity of financial statements can be eased considerably by working into the text an interpretation of financial statements explaining the significance of gains and losses in the various items in the statements.

Some companies publish comprehensive booklets of financial information and make them available to stockholders who request them. Nearly all companies with a substantial number of stockholders make available on request the 10-K reports they prepare for the SEC. Some incorporate these into the annual reports that go to all stockholders.

Preparing a well-balanced annual report. While the corporation annual report now is regarded as the keystone of the stockholder relations program, it is also being accepted as one of the cornerstones of a well-rounded public relations plan. Before deciding on the variety of the content or the style and character of the format, it is advisable for those who are to prepare the annual report to have some knowledge of the quality or intelligence level of the readership.

More than half of the stockholders are women, and the large majority of both sexes have had little or no training in finance, accountancy, or bookkeeping. So all materials intended for them must be clear and readily understandable by the average reader. If sophisticated and technical material is to be provided for security analysts and others, it should go into separate documents or at least be contained within separate sections of shareholder reports where it will not unduly confuse the primary recipients.

Philip Lesly's newsletter, *Managing the Human Climate* (September-October, 1975) suggests

---

[8]See "Why Economic Education Is Failing," by Philip Lesly, *Management Review,* Oct. 1976, pp. 17-23.

CHARLES FRANCIS PRESS ANNUAL REPORT TIME TABLE AND CHECK LIST

AN ANNUAL REPORT PLANNING GUIDE FOR BUSINESS EXECUTIVES PREPARED BY THE EDITORIAL DEVELOPMENT DIVISION. 461 EIGHTH AVENUE, NEW YORK

	FIRST PERIOD	SECOND PERIOD	THIRD PERIOD	FINAL PERIOD (After Receipt of Auditor's Report)
PLANNING	☐ Analysis and determination of broad Annual Report needs in accordance with current corporate problems and objectives. ☐ Selection of key personnel to serve in liaison capacity between company and Editorial Development and Production staffs of Charles Francis Press.	☐ Development of basic ideas, themes and treatments adaptable to recommended and approved Annual Report needs and objectives. ☐ Formulation and approval of basic sectional and page-by-page organization of the report.	☐ Re-planning, where necessary, of Annual Report pages presenting statistical data based on the year's corporate operations. ☐ Discussion and planning of Annual Report facts and figures in terms of their by-product use through other adaptable channels of communication.	☐ Adaptation of Annual Report copy and data to financial and institutional advertising, publicity, stockholders' meetings and other related public relations media and activities.
COPY	☐ Appraisal of previous Annual Report copy in terms of planning analysis. ☐ Development and selection of past and new copy themes adaptable to present needs.	☐ Determination of final subject list, copy style and sectional headings. ☐ Editorial research, development of final copy themes in accordance with approved planning procedures.	☐ Writing, correction and O.K. of final draft, except for portions determined by final accounting reports. ☐ Writing and correction of photo and illustration captions, chart legends and explanatory copy.	☐ Writing, correction and final O.K. of copy affected by auditor's final report of operations.
LAYOUT	☐ Study and creation of basic layout treatments in accordance with planning analysis, subject matter and established layout style. ☐ Preparation of rough layouts showing proposed treatment for cover and typical editorial, illustrative and accounting report pages.	☐ Preliminary preparation of actual page-by-page roughs based on approved themes, copy, illustration and printing production details. ☐ Discussion, correction and final approval of basic layout treatments.	☐ Refinement and adjustment of individual page layout detail in accordance with final O.K. of copy, illustration and production phases. ☐ Layout adjustment of pages dependent upon auditor's report.	☐ Final O.K. of necessary corrections on sections and pages affected by final accounting figures.
ILLUS-TRATION	☐ Recommendation, discussion and preliminary selection of photographic and illustrative treatments adaptable to the broad planning, copy and layout plans and procedures.	☐ Taking of necessary photographs, assembling of data for charts, maps and other illustrative matter. ☐ Completion and approval of final art for all major illustrative matter not affected by the auditor's report.	☐ Ordering of photo-engravings of all approved art work and illustrations. ☐ Preparation of artists' roughs for remaining charts and illustrations as based on auditor's preliminary report.	☐ Adjustment, completion and final O.K. of graphics and art as determined by final auditor's report. ☐ Ordering of all remaining photo-engravings.
PRINTING	☐ Determination of major format and mechanical requirements, delivery date, number of copies. ☐ Discussion of planning, creative and production procedures with the Production and Editorial Development staffs of Charles Francis Press.	☐ Selection of paper stock, typography and use of color; preparation of production dummy; recommendations for printing effectiveness, elimination of unnecessary and costly procedures. ☐ Preparation of production schedules and deadlines for guidance of both company and Charles Francis Press.	☐ Type composition, page make-up and final proof O.K. of copy and art unaffected by auditor's report. ☐ Printing, where possible and feasible, of cover and inside sections not dependent upon final accounting figures.	☐ Final composition, make-up correction and O.K. of remaining sections of the report. ☐ Printing, binding, delivery and distribution of completed Annual Report.

Figure 11-1. A check list and timetable for preparation of the annual report, developed by the Charles Francis Press of New York.

guidelines to help assure that the portrait of the annual report depicts the company as well as the facts justify:

A key point is that the annual report is a portrait of the character and outlook of the company's management, the portrait most people get to see. Companies that spend millions of dollars on visual identity systems, corporate advertising, and other programs all aimed at portraying the company as warm, progressive, and public-spirited often undermine other efforts in the annual report.

1. Determine objectively what is the distinctive character of the company. For example, if your company is an oil company, in what way is it different than other oil companies?

2. Determine how the traits of that distinctive character can be projected to the audience so it will be a credible reality in people's minds.

3. Plan the annual report as an entity in keeping with the distinctive character that is established. Theme, cover, writing, artwork all should be planned together to make up a consistent whole.

4. The writing especially should be done with the company's personality in mind. If the company is aggressive and imaginative, don't have the text sound dull and stodgy.

5. Be sure the artwork and the copy have the same tone. Often they shout different things about the company: For example, the art work is avante garde while the writing is conservative.

6. Be sure the graphic treatment and artwork project the character of the company and not of the photographer or artist. Avoid art for art's sake. The purpose of the report is to communicate its information.

7. Follow the other rules of good communications, including attracting the reader through his interests. Make your message interesting to him in the headlines, captions, and the way it is written.

8. It is usually best to have the final rewrite done by one person. Don't have a report read as though many people were involved, each with his or her own style of writing and approach. The final result should go through one talented individual's typewriter to give it a feeling of cohesiveness rather than of a series of articles stitched together.

The SEC has established some requirements for the format and contents of the annual report:

1. Financial statements and footnotes should be printed in type at least 10 points in size.

2. Differences in accounting principles from those used in other company documents must be explained in a footnote.

3. Audited financial statements for the past two years must be included, as well as a five-year summary of operations and a management analysis of this summary.

4. A "brief description of the business" that indicates the general nature and scope of operations must be included.

5. Breakdowns of sales and earnings for various lines of products or categories of business must be listed in the same form in which they appear in the 10-K report to the SEC.

6. All directors and officers must be named with their principal business affiliations and the nature of the organization for which they work.

7. The principal market for each class of the company's voting securities must be named, with the quarterly high and low prices for each of these securities for the past two years and the quarterly dividends paid in the past two years.

8. Copies of the 10-K report must be offered free to any stockholder in a prominent notice.

9. Companies are required to take affirmative action to make sure an annual report and proxy reaches each stockholder whose securities are held by a broker or other firm.

These do not detract from the need to use creativity and excellent communications techniques to make the report an effective document.

When the annual report brochure is humanized to a point where it will be understood by the small investor, the management finds that the same booklet will serve the needs and requirements of its employees and of many others who have an interest in the corporation's affairs, or are important as opinion-forming groups and should be given an opportunity to read the report. Some idea of the different groups to which the modernized annual report is being sent is indicated in the following tabulation:

EXTRA MAILINGS OF ANNUAL REPORTS

Distribution of the Corporation Annual Report, in Addition to Stockholders and Employees (with a separate covering letter from the president slanted to each group).

NATIONAL LEVEL

Associated groups:
Suppliers of Raw Materials, etc.
Agents and Representatives
Dealers and Jobbers
Distributors
Retailers (Chain Stores)
Customers
Trade Associations

Press and Radio:
Big City Newspapers
   Financial Editor
   Business News Editor
   Selected Financial Writers
   Editorial Writers
Press Services
Financial Publications
Journals of Commerce
Business Magazines
Selected Trade Papers
Accountancy Journals
Advertising Publications
Washington Newsletters
Public Relations Publications
Women's Magazines (if appropriate)
Feature Writers and Columnists
News Syndicates
Radio News Rooms
Selected Radio Commentators

Financial:
Big City Commercial Banks
Big City Trust Companies
Investment Bankers
Stock Exchange Member Firms
Investment Counselors
Statistical Agencies
Financial Services
Investment Trust Executives
Insurance Companies
Credit Agencies

Government Officials:
SEC, ICC, FTC, FCC, etc.
Department of Commerce
Department of Labor
Other Selected Cabinet Members
Library of Congress
U.S. Senators (All or Selected)
Representatives (All or Selected)
Governor of State Where Incorporated
Secretary of State Where Incorporated
States Where Plants Are Located

Other:
Big City Public Libraries
Leading Universities and Colleges
Schools of Business Administration
Schools of Commerce and Finance
Philanthropic Institutions

On Request—Through Paid Advertising:
Big City Newspapers

FINANCIAL PUBLIC RELATIONS 115

Financial Publications
Journals of Commerce
Business Magazines
Selected Trade Papers
Selected National Magazines
Selected Women's Publications
Labor Publications

COMMUNITY LEVEL

Associated Groups:
Suppliers of Raw Materials, etc.
Union Leaders
Employment Agencies
Transportation Services
Chamber of Commerce Members
Rotary, Kiwanis, Lions Clubs

Press and Radio:
Editors of Local Newspapers
Editors of County Weeklies
Suburban and Community Magazines
Local Broadcasting Stations
Chamber of Commerce Paper, etc.

Financial:
Local National Banks
Local Savings Banks
Savings & Loan Associations
Brokerage Office Managers
Small Loan Associations

Opinion Leaders:
Heads of Local Business Firms
Judges and Police Officers
The Clergy
Professional Physicians

Dentists
Hospital Directors
Officers of
  Fraternal Societies
  Women's Clubs
  Welfare Organizations
  Parent-Teacher Associations
Principals and Teachers of
  Grade Schools
  High Schools
  Business Schools
  Trade Schools
  Colleges and Universities
Leaders of Youth Groups
  Boy and Girl Groups
  Y.M.C.A. and Y.W.C.A.
  Junior Achievement, Inc.
  Sunday Schools

Municipal or Township Officials:
Mayor or Borough President
Members of Board of Supervisors
Department Heads

Other:
Local Libraries
Movie Theater Owners
Barber and Beauty Shop Managers
Druggists
Gas Station Operators
Chain Store Managers

On Request—Through Paid Advertising:
Local Newspapers
County Weeklies
Community Magazines
Suburban Publications
House Organs or Tabloids
Church and Fraternal Publications
Programs
Local Labor Union Publications

The physical requirements, trim size, and number of pages of the annual report will depend on these factors:

(1) The type of industry represented (manufacturing, distribution, transportation, etc.)

(2) The size of the corporation (sales volume, total assets, number of stockholders and employees)

(3) The readership to which the annual report will be sent (whether only stockholders, or if it also will be seen by employees and others)

(4) Desired life of the annual report (whether it is a year-end review to be read and discarded, or a "yearbook" to be retained for reference, and sent to new stockholders and employees throughout the year).

Generally speaking, most annual reports will vary from 16 pages and cover, to 40 pages and cover—multiples of 8 pages are the most economical to print. The most popular trim size is letter size—8½ by 11 inches, or thereabouts, which will fit in the standard filing cabinet, or fold in half to fit into the coat pocket.

About 50 to 60 percent of the contents should be devoted to editorial content and financial and statistical tabulations. The other half of the booklet should be illustrated with charts or pictorial graphics, maps, photographs, and other appropriate decorations distributed throughout the pages to lend variety to the text without giving the impression of a catalogue.

In most cases reports should be in at least two colors, and four or more colors are frequently used. In the case of larger corporations with 50,000 or more stockholders and employees, a generous supply of color in type and full-color reproductions of illustrations and photographs are warranted because the unit cost per booklet is small when the printing run is large. When only two colors (black and one primary color) are utilized, a three-color effect can be obtained by using tint blocks or reverse plates and various patterns of Ben Days for both main headings and subheads.

Lacking an anniversary or some distinctive aspect of the company to be projected, the keynote or theme might be some outstanding event of the past year that can be dramatized: a new product or service; expansion of plants, properties, or distribution facilities; establishment of a new research laboratory; achievement of management or employees recognized by an outside authority; competitive position of the company in its industry; the new philosophy of the management in serving in the public interest; introduction of a creed or code of public relations principles, and the like.

Outline and continuity of modern annual reports. The content of any corporation annual report will follow a basic pattern, but the arrangement of the material can be adjusted to suit the preferences of the management. In humanizing the report it has been found a good policy to feature in the front portion of the booklet the narrative, which lends itself to dramatization by means of photographs, pic-

PRODUCTS AND MARKETS

6

The world is struggling with an exceptional number of critical problems: widespread shortages of energy, certain basic materials and capacity to make key products, and simultaneous unsettled economic conditions. Demand is strong in those elements of the economy that meet the most urgent needs of evolving nations and living standards: the industries that must provide basic resources and those that provide machinery for their use. Since these industries produce supplies that help relieve shortages and resultant inflation, their efforts receive the highest priorities in national and international economic policymaking.

This is especially meaningful for Gardner-Denver. Our equipment is basic in meeting almost all top-priority demands. In all parts of the world, Gardner-Denver products are commonly in use in the fields receiving the most urgent attention. Gardner-Denver's role is not only the visible output of our equipment — the oil, the ore, the finished construction jobs — but the many products and services that are the end results of this output.

Figure 11-2. A theme for the annual report emphasizes an aspect of the company that it wants to get across to investors and the financial community. Gardner-Denver here and on following pages points out its growth potential as a basic supplier to most growth fields.

FINANCIAL PUBLIC RELATIONS

torial graphics, maps, and other appropriate illustrations. Key financial data are usually provided in the first two pages, with most of the statistical data appearing in the middle or latter portion of the report. Thus, the reader who will not study the comparative financial statements, because of lack of interest or inability to comprehend statistical tabulations, will gather the information he seeks in reading the text and perusing the illustrations and charts. Featuring key points in larger type in the margins also helps the skimmer get the main points. Subheads are also desirable where large copy blocks would give the appearance of a gray mass. All headings, as much as possible, should convey action, rather than just serve as labels: "Ongoing Development of Manpower" is better than "Personnel and Labor Relations."

The following outline is suitable for companies operating in almost any industry, and can be employed with applicable additions and variations:

Cover Design—Front Cover:
    Name of corporation, and title "Annual Report" or "Yearbook."
    Year of report, if calendar year—otherwise the full fiscal year ending.
    Illustration, photograph, or pattern appropriate to the corporation or the industry it represents.

Frontispiece—First Right-Hand Page or First Two Pages:
    Name of corporation, and statement "Annual Report" or "Yearbook."
    Addresses: Executive offices, General offices, or other offices to which recipient can write for further information.
    Year of the report.
    Table of Contents, Foreword, or Credo.
    Suitable decoration or illustration.

Narrative—Each page illustrated differently with photograph or chart:
    President's and/or Chairman's Letter (usually limited to two or three pages).
    Highlights—comparative round-number operating statistics.
    Departmentalized Summaries:
        Financial results interpreted on per share basis.
        Distribution of gross revenue or the "sales dollar."
        Trend of sales, earnings, and dividends.
        Simplified balance sheet—trend of net current assets.
        Prices or rates—policies or program.
        Research and technology.
        Advertising and public relations.
        Improvement of facilities.
        Employment (hours and wages).
        Management development.
        Products or services (improvements, diversification, or new).
        Competitive position.
        Industry situation.
        Taxation and cost of government.
        Legislation affecting the company.
        Government regulation.
        Raw materials and inventories.
        Utilization of productive capacity.
        Changes in capitalization—financing and refinancing.
        Trend in number of stockholders.
        Important events of the year.
        Discussion of future prospects.
        International activities.

Financial Tabulations and Other Statistics and Reference Material:
    Comparative consolidated balance sheet, indicating increase or decline, or percentage change in each item.
    Profit and Loss Statement.
    Comparative Income Accounts.
    Results breakdown by division or product line.
    Tabulation of operating statistics for ten years or more.
    Tabulations of financial position and allied statistics.
    Footnotes to Accounts.
    Independent Auditors' Report.
    Study of long-term debt, if any.
    Statistics on number of stockholders, the distribution of shares geographically, by size of holdings, classes, sexes, etc.
    Employment statistics—average number per year, total man-hours worked, annual payroll, average weekly hours and earnings.
    Management listing: board of directors, executive committee, finance committee, officers—each identified with outside connection or title of position with corporation.
    List of products, subsidiaries, branch offices, routes, etc.
    Pension costs.
    Explanation of changes in inventory policy.

Quarterly data on prices of stock and of inventories.

Management analysis of the summary of operations.

Impact of inflation on company's assets.

Number of employees in company's Employee Stock Ownership Plan.

Illustrating the modern annual report. There is an almost unlimited opportunity to interpret every phase of a corporation's operations and records by means of a pictorial graphic or line-and-bar chart. Caution must be exercised to maintain the simplicity of each chart by including in one chart only related data, and not attempting to cover too many kinds of statistics at one time. Complicated charts often defeat their purpose by confusing the reader, and there is danger of misunderstanding when trend lines or characters are not clearly identified. All captions, subheadings, and numbers must be in type large enough to see without a magnifying glass, and care should be taken in any photo reduction not to make any of the data undecipherable.

The following statistics are suitable for graphic presentation—the list is not all inclusive, but will serve as a guide and suggest other appropriate ideas:

FINANCIAL:

Operating Results—Trend of sales; distribution of sales dollar; trend of prices or rates; trend of earnings and dividends; export or foreign trade operations; trend of production by products or various services; trend of unfilled orders; etc.

Operating Expenses—Trend of cost of raw materials; trend of wages; trend of taxes; trend of advertising expenditures; trend of equipment replacement; trend of bond interest; trend of dividends; trend of earnings reinvested in business; etc.

Balance Sheet Interpretation—Pictorial balance sheet in form of scales; trend of total assets; trend of working capital (net current assets); trend of inventories; trend of net worth or book value; etc.

FACTUAL:

Products or Services—Uses; other industries served; by lines of different products; trends of distribution; per capita consumption; dates of introduction of new and improved products; etc.

Organization—Parent company in relation to subsidiaries; flow of operations in the making of primary product; flow of management authority from president through executive officers to department heads or branch managers, etc.

Employees—Trend of average number employed; trend of hourly or weekly wages by averages; accident and safety records; cost of benefits (pensions, group insurance, etc.); analysis of length of service, age groups, sexes, etc.

Stockholders—Trend of the average number; trend of average holdings by classes (individuals, fiduciaries, insurance companies, charitable and educational, brokers and others); trend of holdings by number of shares; etc.

Maps—Locating plants, branches, sales offices, distributors, stores, dealers, and consumers; indicating sources of raw materials; showing routes; geographical distribution of stockholders; export and import lines; etc.

The selection of appropriate photographs is simplified by relating the picture to the paragraph it is intended to illustrate. An accumulation of both news and commercial photographs during the year will usually build up an ample supply from which to choose. Larger corporations can well afford to hire a special photographer to take a series of views of its plants, operations, and products, and thus build a morgue that can be drawn on for several years. But such pictures should not be "head-on" shots—they should be taken with some imagination, possibly from an angle or showing action.

An annual report illustrated with carefully retouched commercial photographs of plants and products provides the appearance of a sales catalogue, and loses effectiveness. The buildings can be taken at different seasons of the year, or photographed with the employees flooding in or out. Products should be shown in actual process of manufacture or in use after they have been sold, with the worker or user in action.

Each year more annual reports illustrate the president's letter with an informal photograph of the chief executive, often at his desk or on an inspection tour around the plant. A picture of the board of directors in session provides an excellent opportunity to identify the management and executive officers. And many reports today run a series of individual photographs of the board members and executive officers with a thumbnail biographical sketch of each. On occasion, the death of a major official will call for a photograph and obituary notice with the expression of regret by the

Figure 11-3. A growing number of corporations that have a sizable number of shareholders abroad print their annual reports in more than one language. Here the code at the top of the I.T.T. annual report indicates the seven languages in which the report is printed.

president at the loss of this member of the official family.

In recent years many reports have included actual samples of products "tipped" in on the pages or inside covers—such as swatches of fabrics, carton board, and dress patterns. Other reports have utilized their products as the cover, including wallpaper, boxboard, and aluminum ink.

Accounting changes. The present trend in financial statements is to provide investors with more information and to make that information more meaningful. A few years ago, the American Institute of Certified Public Accountants ruled that, in order to make per share earnings figures more meaningful to investors, income statements should show the effect of extraordinary gains and losses and, if outstanding, the potential dilution that might occur from conversion of convertible securities.

The SEC has steadily increased the information it asks companies to include in the annual report. Other pressures on changes in accounting practices come from the Financial Standards Accounting Board, composed of certified public accountants.

Companies are expected to report profits and sales by line of business. The SEC has also insisted that companies in their reports provide greater analysis of their sales, operations, and earnings.

Data on stock prices and on dividends by quarters is now required in most annual reports. In the mid-1970s the SEC also asked companies to provide more detail on environmental problems. Also, the SEC was interested in companies providing financial forecasts. At one point the SEC was considering making such forecasts mandatory. However, the Commission backed down when companies' executives explained the wide range of problems and possible liability they might face if they made such forecasts. In 1976 the SEC also was asking companies to indicate the replacement costs of inventories and productive capacity—in other words the impact of inflation on these assets. This, too, ran into opposition from corporations on the basis of the invalidity of many such estimates and the costs involved.

In addition to providing more guidelines on what and how companies communicate with shareholders, the SEC has also set up a series of guidelines on what issues stockholders may seek to be included on the annual stockholders' meeting agenda. These new rules have served to clarify some of the uncertainty that has existed previously in this area.

OTHER STOCKHOLDER PUBLICATIONS

Although the annual report is the primary means of keeping the stockholder informed, corporations that publish quarterly earnings statements also can use a number of techniques to present information during the remainder of the year. Stereotyped quarterly reports can be converted into attractive bulletins, newsletters, or digest booklets, edited in news style and illustrated with charts or photographs.

A number of companies produce fairly lengthy, high-quality shareowner magazines three times a year as a supplement to the annual report.

Corporations paying regular quarterly dividends have the opportunity to mail a "stuffer" or insert to stockholders with the dividend check as a "free ride" on the same postage. These stuffers sometimes are combined with the quarterly earnings report, but when the dates do not coincide, they serve as an extra contact with shareholders. Such inserts have been employed to introduce new products, announce executive appointments or promotions, and to provide a return coupon requesting a sample of a product. The conventional use of dividend stuffers is to provide a form for a change of address of the stockholder.

A corporate Fact Book that is sent to security analysts and others in the financial community is used by a number of companies to consolidate in one publication many facts about the firm.

SHAREHOLDER ANNUAL MEETINGS

The annual meeting of the shareholders is the one function of the corporation during the year where the investor can meet the management face to face and hear the report of stewardship from the lips of the president. This is the shareholders' forum, but they will not or cannot attend in large numbers if the meeting requires a long and expensive journey. Hence, an increasing number of managements are bringing the meeting to the stockholders by conducting meetings in various larger cities or where there is the largest concentration of holdings. Some companies provide free transportation to meetings held at the "corporate office" when it is located in a small town that is inconvenient to reach.

The modern stockholder meeting is no longer a stuffy affair with hard seats, poor ventilation, and bad lighting. Progressive managements usually conduct both their regular and regional meetings in the ballrooms of the better hotels, and often a

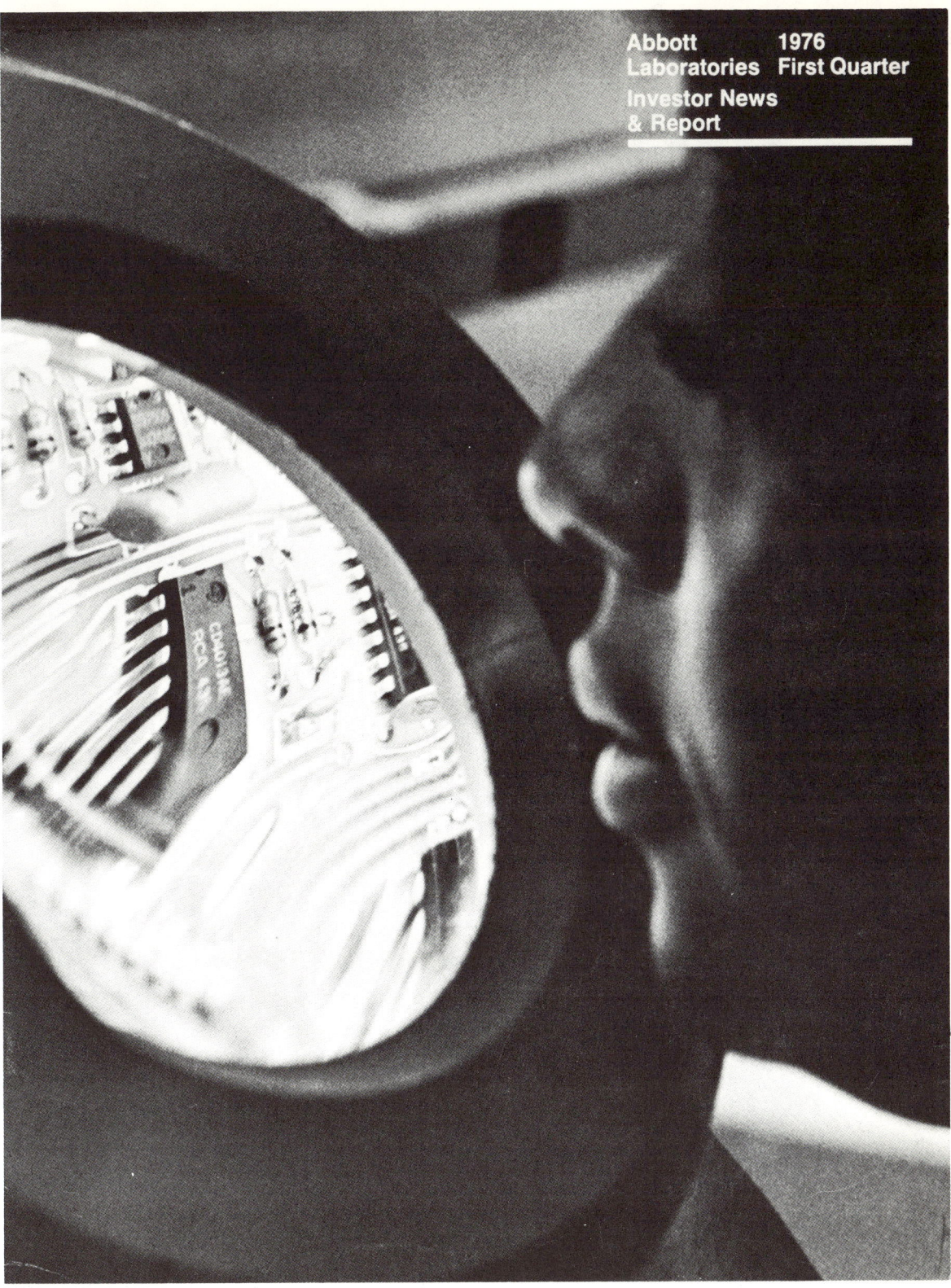

Figure 11-4. A growing number of companies issue quarterly reports in magazine format that give stockholders a great deal of material—besides financial figures—about the company and its activities.

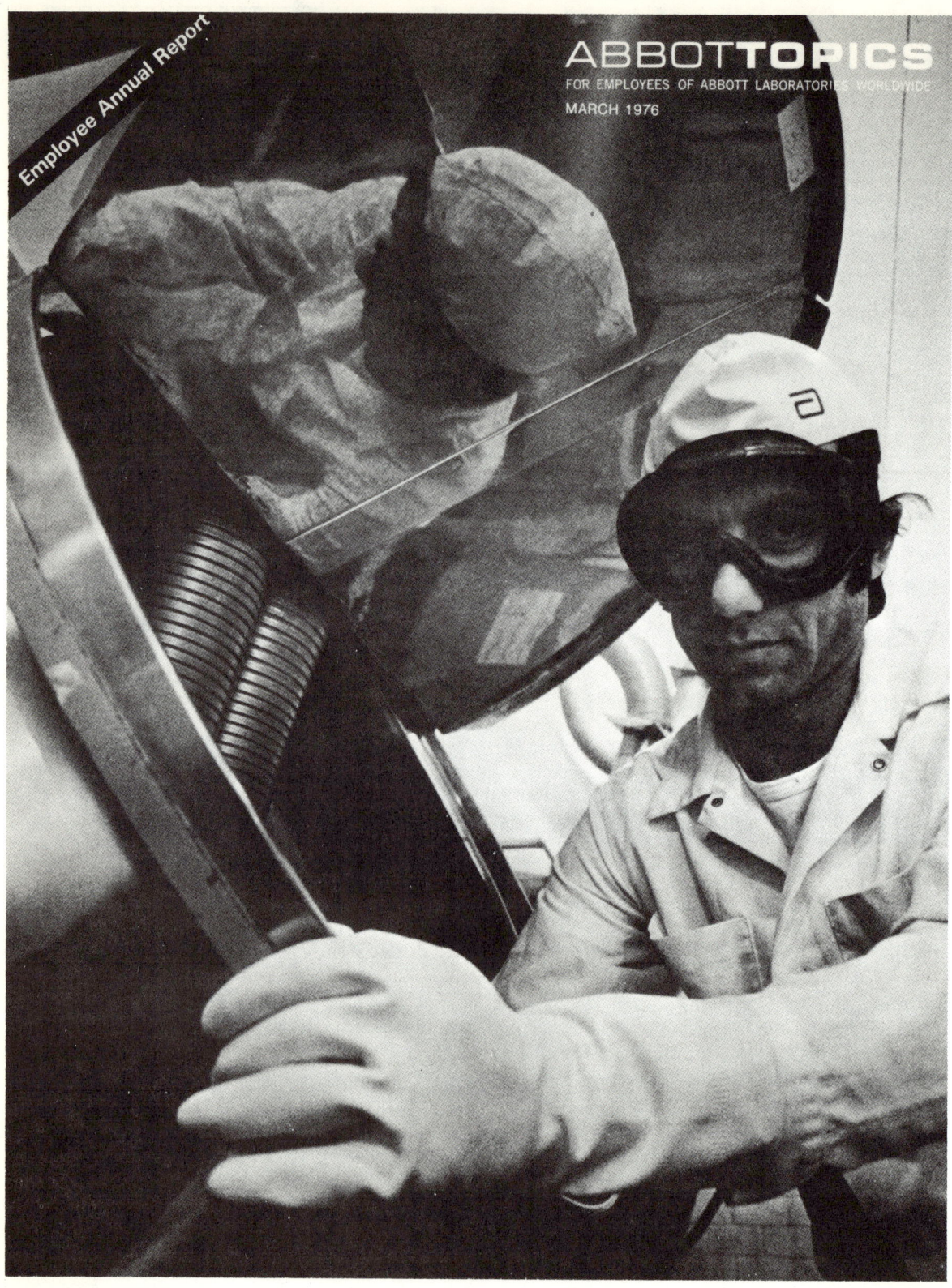

Figure 11-5. A special annual report for employees serves a double purpose: good employee relations, and extended financial communication through this vitally interested group.

Market Prices and Dividends on ITT Stock
In Dollars

	Three Months Ended			
	March 31 High Low	June 30 High Low	Sept. 30 High Low	Dec. 31 High Low

1975

Common Stock	21.63 14.63	24.75 19.38	25.13 18.63	22.75 19.13
Cumulative Preferred Stock				
$4.00 Convertible Series E (3.08)	61.50 45.00	76.88 60.00	73.50 64.25	67.25 60.00
$4.00 Convertible Series F (2.86)	62.00 42.75	68.75 61.00	68.00 55.00	60.00 58.75
$4.00 Convertible Series H (1.82)	45.00 32.75	48.00 39.50	49.50 41.75	45.50 41.00
$4.50 Convertible Series I (1.64)	47.25 34.25	49.63 44.00	51.00 43.25	47.00 43.63
$4.00 Convertible Series J (1.63)	43.00 31.88	44.75 39.00	45.00 39.00	45.00 39.25
$4.00 Convertible Series K (1.56)	43.50 32.50	44.50 39.00	44.75 38.50	43.75 38.25
$2.25 Convertible Series N (1.20)	28.50 21.00	30.50 25.25	30.88 24.00	28.88 24.75
$5.00 Convertible Series O (1.41)	53.00 37.63	52.00 47.00	52.75 47.13	47.25 45.50

1974

Common Stock	29.50 23.13	23.38 17.13	20.50 15.50	17.00 12.00
Cumulative Preferred Stock				
$4.00 Convertible Series E (3.08)	85.50 82.00	78.00 56.00	65.00 54.50	57.50 38.00
$4.00 Convertible Series F (2.86)	78.50 77.50	69.00 60.00	58.00 52.00	46.00 38.50
$4.00 Convertible Series H (1.82)	56.00 50.50	51.00 40.00	44.50 35.00	38.25 29.00
$4.50 Convertible Series I (1.64)	58.50 50.00	52.50 45.00	46.50 36.00	41.50 31.63
$4.00 Convertible Series J (1.63)	53.00 45.50	48.00 39.00	41.00 33.50	36.50 28.50
$4.00 Convertible Series K (1.56)	52.25 46.00	48.00 36.50	41.75 32.88	36.50 28.38
$2.25 Convertible Series N (1.20)	35.75 29.75	31.13 23.50	27.25 20.25	22.75 18.00
$5.00 Convertible Series O (1.41)	61.25 55.00	55.75 50.00	50.50 41.75	46.25 36.00

The above table reflects the range of market prices of ITT Common and Cumulative Preferred Stock as quoted on the New York Stock Exchange, the principal market in which such securities are traded.

During the two month period ended February 29, 1976, the high and low price of the ITT Common Stock was $30.13 and $22.25, respectively.

Dividends paid per common share were $.38 in each of the four quarters of 1975 and the last quarter of 1974, and $.35 in each of the first three quarters of 1974.

Quarterly dividends paid per share of each of the Cumulative Preferred Stock issues are equivalent to one fourth of the annual dividends indicated in the description of the issues. The number of shares of Common Stock into which each preferred issue is convertible is indicated parenthetically above.

ITT stock is listed on the following exchanges:
Common: Antwerp, Basle, Berne, Brussels, Frankfurt, Geneva, Lausanne, London, New York, Pacific, Paris, Tokyo, Toronto, Vienna, Zurich.

Preferred: All issues of ITT Preferred Stock are traded on a listed basis on the New York Stock Exchange. ITT Series N Preferred is also traded on a listed basis on the Pacific Coast Exchange, San Francisco.

Figure 11-6. The SEC now requires companies to report stock prices and dividends on the company's stock on a quarterly basis in the annual report. This is the way ITT did it for the year 1975.

luncheon is provided. Features of these meetings include demonstration of a new product, showing a motion picture or slide film, and distributing samples and appropriate literature. A discussion period is provided where any stockholder can "take the floor" and offer his or her compliments, suggestions, or criticisms. There is a genuine informality about many of these annual meetings that makes the stockholder feel at home, and an integral participant in the activities of the corporation.

With the sharp increases in numbers of stockholders, geographic broadening of ownership, and such movements as investment clubs and Employee Stock Ownership Plans, some large companies have found it useful to arrange for closed-circuit telecasting of their annual meetings into large halls in major cities across the country. In this way they permit thousands of additional stockholders to "attend" the meetings.

For a number of years there have also been regional meetings for shareholders, held on a schedule that can fit the needs of company executives. However, these are so demanding of the officials' time and often so anti-climactic, following the annual meeting at which the news and discussion were timely, that they have not proven suitable for most companies. Closed-circuit television appears to be more satisfactory for all concerned. General Electric Co. has used such a service.

Vocal stockholders. Corporations have had to handle the problem of vocal stockholders since the first publicly owned company held its first annual meeting. Regardless of how well management has performed during a particular year or how comprehensive or accurate its policies are, there will always be some point on which a stockholder will be critical, and sometimes actually belligerent.

Since stockholders are the owners of the company, they are entitled to be critical and to pass on management's actions.

However, they do not have the right to disrupt the orderly flow of business at a stockholders' meeting. This type of action deprives other stockholders of an equally valuable right.

Management's role in these situations should be to insure that all stockholders receive equal treatment. By answering stockholders' questions, and by either accepting their criticisms or showing that these criticisms are baseless, the chairman or president presiding at the meeting may be able to satisfy both sides, thereby avoiding unnecessary interruptions.

Each situation is different and requires different handling. However, there are some ground rules that can be applied:

1. Be patient—allow stockholders to state their views or ask their questions.

2. Be polite—avoid abrupt, flip, or sarcastic answers.

3. Answer all questions fully and clearly. If it appears that a point has been misunderstood or completely missed, go back and repeat it.

4. Respond to all queries from the floor. Do not attempt to avoid a stockholder who is known to be openly critical by refusing to recognize him.

5. Anticipate the criticisms that may arise and prepare to meet them, preparing slides or film clips if necessary.

6. Utilize the full executive staff in answering questions. If it is a financial matter, the chief executive officer may wish to have the vice president of finance or the treasurer supply the answer. This may also be useful if one answer is insufficient.

7. Do not allow personalities or sarcasm from the floor to dictate the content or tone of your response.

A number of corporate annual meetings have been disrupted by activist groups. Some attempts have been made to exclude these groups from annual meetings by restricting the meeting to stockholders only. However, it must be recognized that it is not difficult for activists to become stockholders and thereby gain entrance to the meeting. In fact, a number of groups have already been formed such as Proxies for People, and CAUSE (Coalition for Action, Unity and Social Equality).

Since legitimate stockholders cannot be excluded from annual meetings, management must be ready and able to use tact, diplomacy, and public relations skill to handle various activist demonstrations at annual meetings. The goal should be to answer the questions and criticisms raised and to prevent the dissident group from taking complete control of the meeting or forcing a confrontation, a situation in which management, no matter how justified, will probably come off looking unfavorable. The guidelines outlined above, while simple, can be helpful in this type of situation.

The annual meeting presents another major opportunity for stressing the company's theme. Displays, exhibits, films, slides, and speeches can all carry this common theme through to the audience. Special annual meeting literature, perhaps somewhat more promotional in nature than the annual report, can be distributed.

Some corporations have distributed sample packages of their products to stockholders at meetings. The Chesapeake & Ohio Railroad at one time offered stockholders special discounts on train tickets and at the Greenbrier Hotel, which the C & O owns.

THE POST ANNUAL MEETING REPORT

Despite geographic shifting, generally only a small fraction of shareholders are able to attend the annual meeting. Still, all shareholders have a right to know what happened at the meeting. Some companies, an estimated 10 per cent of all publicly held companies, accomplish this by means of a post-meeting report.

As a minimum, the post-meeting report should include a report of the presiding officer's remarks; any new developments; results of voting for directors, auditors, and resolutions; and any pertinent questions asked from the floor and the answers to the questions. In the latter area, management should try to be as candid as possible and include all questions and answers even though these may be embarrassing. One of the major criticisms of post-meeting reports is that significant questions are ignored. If a stockholder reads a newspaper report of an embarrassing question asked at the meeting and this question has been omitted from the post-meeting report, he may wonder whether management has omitted anything else from the report.

FINANCIAL PUBLIC RELATIONS 125

Figure 11-7. Special reports on the annual stockholders' meeting provide the remarks of the executives as well as the questions and answers at the meeting.

STOCKHOLDER LETTERS

One of the most effective means of cultivating the interest and confidence of new stockholders is a letter of welcome from the company's president as soon after the shares are registered as possible. A copy of the latest annual report and an interim earnings statement are sent, and the new owner is invited to ask questions and offer constructive criticisms. The following letter is typical of the "letter of welcome":

Dear Sir:
  It is a pleasure to welcome you as a new stockholder of our company and to express my appreciation of the confidence you have placed in our organization.

As a part owner of this business you will want to know about our products (services), our people, and our policies. A quite complete review of our operations was presented in our recent annual report, and a copy is enclosed for your information, together with the announcement of the latest quarterly earnings and dividend action.

We invite your active interest in the corporation, and are prepared to receive your comments and answer your questions. You will later be invited to attend the annual meeting of the stockholders, but if you are unable to attend a report on it will be mailed.

We trust that whenever possible you will buy the products of our company and interest your friends in doing the same. Our sales department will be happy to cooperate by providing the name of the dealer nearest you.

Cordially yours,
(Signature)
President

A number of managements also follow the practice of sending a letter of regret when it is learned that the stockholder has disposed of his shares. The purpose of these letters is to obtain a pattern of explanations for the sale of stock. The replies to such inquiries often reveal some good reasons for liquidating the investment, and the corporation can benefit by adjusting the complaints and curing the altercations. The following is typical of the "letter of regret":

Dear Sir:

We have learned with regret that you have disposed of your holdings of the shares of our company, and wish you to know that we are interested in your reason for selling your stock.

If the liquidation of your interest is a personal matter, we have no right to expect an explanation. But if you have been led to dispose of your shares because of some action on the part of the management, we will appreciate your suggestions and criticisms.

It is the policy of the management to serve equally the interests of both large and small investors in the company, and we trust you feel that you have received fair treatment while you were a member of our stockholder family.

Cordially yours,
(Signature)
President

FINANCIAL PUBLICITY

Financial publicity reaches the present and prospective shareholder and at the same time provides much of the information that must be conveyed to the professional financial community. There are five basic areas involved here:

1. News releases with copies of any document referred to, such as annual reports, quarterly reports, and other materials issued to stockholders.
2. Releases on dividend declarations, new financing, mergers and acquisitions (in progress or announced), annual, regional and special meetings of shareholders, labor relations, expansion of facilities, management changes, litigation, employment data, security redemptions, and statements on industry trends or the company's outlook.
3. Speeches on financial matters by company officials before business groups, government bodies, societies of security analysts, and other organizations.
4. Interviews with financial publications, business writers, and commentators on radio and TV.
5. Meeting requests from media.

Of course, there are many other areas not directly involved with financial matters but that have an important interest to the financial community and shareholders. These involve new products, scholarship programs, community projects and, more recently, statements on the company's contributions to suppressing environmental pollution.

Special financial news outlets. In addition to media in Chapters 40 and 41 that include business and financial news among their coverage, there are a number of media that specialize in this information. They are primary outlets for financial publicity.

FINANCIAL AND BUSINESS PUBLICATIONS

American Banker, 525 West 42nd Street, New York, N.Y. 10036

Barron's, 22 Cortlandt Street, New York, N.Y. 10007

Better Investing, P.O. Box 220, Royal Oak, Michigan 48068

Business Conditions, Federal Reserve Bank of Chicago, Publications Section, Research Dept., Box 834, Chicago, Illinois 60690

Business Week, 1221 Ave. of the Americas, New York, N.Y. 10020

Business World (business building hints for small and medium-sized businesses), 930 Clifton Avenue, Clifton, N.J. 07013

Commercial & Financial Chronicle, 120 Broadway, New York, N.Y. 10005

Corporate Communications Report, Corpcom Services Inc., 112 E. 31st Street, New York, N.Y. 10016

Corporate Reports on File, Wall Street Transcript Corp., 54 Wall Street, New York, N.Y. 10005

Dun's Review, 666 Fifth Avenue, New York, N.Y. 10019

Economic Review, Federal Reserve Bank of Cleveland, Box 6387, Cleveland, Ohio 44101

Executives' Digest, 163 Newbury Street, Boston, Mass. 02116

FINANCIAL PUBLIC RELATIONS

Financial Executive, 633 Third Avenue, New York, N.Y. 10017

Financial World, 919 Third Avenue, New York, N.Y. 10022

Forbes, 60 Fifth Avenue, New York, N.Y. 10011

Fortune, Time & Life Bldg., New York, N.Y. 10020

Gallagher Report, 230 Park Avenue, New York, N.Y. 10017

Industry Week, Penton Plaza, Cleveland, Ohio 44114

The Institutional Investor, 488 Madison Avenue, New York, N.Y. 10006

Investment Dealer's Digest, 150 Broadway, New York, N.Y. 10038

Journal of Commerce, 99 Wall Street, New York, N.Y. 10005

News Front (management news magazine), P.O. Box 380, Petaluma, Cal. 94952

The Stock Market Magazine, 16 School Street, Yonkers, N.Y. 10701

Trends in Management-Stockholder Relations, Georgeson & Co., 100 Wall Street, New York, N.Y. 10005

Trusts & Estates, 461 Eighth Avenue, New York, N.Y. 10001

Wall Street Journal, 22 Cortlandt Street, New York, N.Y. 10007

Wall Street Transcript, 120 Wall Street, New York, N.Y. 10005

SYNDICATED FINANCIAL COLUMNS

The Chicago Tribune-New York News Syndicate, 220 East 42nd Street, New York, N.Y. 10017, (212) 949-3400, Eliot Janeway

Field Newspaper Syndicate, 401 North Wabash Avenue, Chicago, Illinois 60606, (312) 321-2795, J.A. Livingston, "Business Outlook," Sylvia Porter, "Your Money's Worth"

"Greer/Kandel Report," Mike Kandel and Phil Greer, 200 W. 57th Street, New York, N.Y. 10019

King Features Syndicate, 235 East 45th Street, New York, N.Y. 10017, (212) 682-5600, Sam Shulsky, "Investor's Guide"

Los Angeles Times Syndicate, Times Mirror Square, Los Angeles, California 90053, (213) 625-2345, (800) 421-8266, David R. Sargent, "Successful Investing," Robert Rosefsky, "Speaking Dollarwise," Douglas Tuomey, "Homeowners Money Savers," Warshauer and Joselow, "Economics for the Perplexed," Roger E. Spear, "Successful Investing"

McNaught Syndicate, 60 East 42nd Street, New York, N.Y. 10017, (212) 682-8787, Louis Rukeyser, "Money"

Newhouse News Service, 1750 Pennsylvania Ave., NW, Washington, D.C. 20006, (202) 298-7080, Peter Nagan, "The Economy"

United Feature Syndicate, 220 East 42nd Street, New York, N.Y. 10017, (212) 682-3020, Don G. Campbell, "Daily Investor," "Mutual Funds," Lou Schneider, "Trade Winds," Herbert Stein, "The Economy Today"

Washington Post Writers Group, 1150 Fifteenth St. NW, Washington D.C. 20071, Hobart Rowen, "Economic Impact"

DIRECTORIES FOR MANAGEMENT CHANGES

Directory of Directors Co., Inc., 350 Madison Ave., New York, N.Y. 10016—"Directory of Directors"

Marquis Who's Who, Inc., 200 East Ohio St., Chicago, Ill. 60611

Poor's Register of Directors and Executives, 345 Hudson St., New York, N.Y. 10014

Standard Directory of Advertisers, 5201 Old Orchard Rd., Skokie, Ill. 60076

PRIMARY INVESTMENT SERVICES AND FINANCIAL STATISTICAL BUREAUS

Argus Research Corporation, 140 Broadway, New York, N.Y. 10006

Babson's Reports, 370 Washington, Wellesley Hills, Mass. 02181

Business and Financial Indicators, Federal Reserve Bank of Richmond, Research Dept., Box 27622, Richmond, Va. 23261

Commodity Chart Service, Commodity Research Bureau, Inc., One Liberty Plaza, New York, N.Y. 10006

Corporation Finance and New Issue Weekly, 54 Wall St., New York, N.Y. 10005

Dow Digest, 10 Main Center, Kansas City, Mo. 64105

Dow Theory Forecasts, 7412 Calumet Ave., Hammond, Indiana 46324

Finance Facts, National Consumer Finance Assn., Educational Services Division, 701 Solar Building, 1000 Sixteenth St. N.W., Washington, D.C. 20036

Fitch Investors Service, 12 Barclay St., New York, N.Y. 10007

Forbes Investors, 60 Fifth Ave., New York, N.Y. 10011

Kiplinger Washington Letter (also California, Florida), 1729 H. St. NW, Washington, D.C. 20006

Moody's Investors Service, 99 Church St., New York, N.Y. 10007

Standard & Poor's, 345 Hudson St., New York, N.Y. 10014

United Business Service Co., 210 Newberry St., Boston, Mass.

NOTE: Lists of brokers (market letter writers) and banks will be found in the "Membership Directory of the National Federation of Financial Analysts" and "Securities Dealers in North America." See Chapter 36.

TIPS ON DEALING WITH THE PRESS

Most dealings with the financial press will involve the handling of spot news stories. Spot news stories generally are top priority items for the financial pages of newspapers and financial publications but are even more urgent for wire services.

The competition to break a spot news story is always keen between the wire services (Associated Press, United Press International, Dow-Jones, and Reuters), and the financial public relations practitioner should always try to make simultaneous delivery to the services and carefully avoid favoring one over the other. A written copy of the press release is always preferable to a telephone call. However, simultaneous hand delivery is not always possible. The commercial newswires, such as PR Newswire and the Public Relations Newswire in New York and their counterparts in other cities, can be useful in making a simultaneous release to several points.[9]

While concentrating on the major financial publications, many corporations have overlooked the value of the smaller daily publications in other areas of the country, particularly plant areas or areas that contain high concentrations of shareholders. The corporation should attempt to service as many of these publications with spot news and feature stories as possible.

The public relations man should establish a rapport with reporters and editors and efforts should be made to have key executives become familiar with the press. Of course, establishing personal contact with a large number of editors is time-consuming and cannot be accomplished overnight.

A number of other methods can also be used to familiarize the press with the company and to meet

[9]See Chapter 40.

KOPPERS
1975 Annual Report and 10-K

What 1975 Brought:
.... The fifth consecutive year of improved earnings
.... the first $1-billion sales year
.... a rise in return on shareholders' equity.

What 1975 Demonstrated:
.... The ability to produce consistent earnings growth in a slowed economy
.... the worth of product diversification through coherent expansion as a buffer against economic vagaries.

Figure 11-8. Most companies use pictures or art work on the cover of their annual report, but some use the cover to illustrate a theme or provide key data. A growing number of companies, as in this case, also incorporate the 10-K report to the SEC in the annual report. Others offer it to any stockholder who wants to write in for it.

with key executives. These include interviews, orientation tours, plant tours, demonstrations of new products, and special press trips.

PUBLICITY DURING THE REGISTRATION PERIOD

A question that often arises is whether a company can make disclosure during the period between the time it files a registration statement with the SEC and the effective date of the registration statement. The answer is a very definite YES—for legitimate news.

The goal of the SEC requirements in this area is to avoid the issuance of any announcements, advertising, speeches, or statements that might tend to implant the idea of an optimistic future for the issuing corporation in the minds of the investing public.

Among the various types of publicity forbidden are:

- Estimates or projections of sales or earnings for the industries or product lines in which the corporation is engaged, including dollar projections, percentages, or even in broad general terms.
- Predictions of increased sales or earnings that may stem from new products or discoveries.

The company can still issue its normal press releases, provided they contain no financial projections; announce new products or developments; announce annual and quarterly earnings; announce dividends; continue normal product advertising; and present speeches, provided they contain no financial forecasts.

SECURITY ANALYSTS

Among opinion leaders in the financial community, an increasingly important group is the professional analysts of securities. Employed by brokerage houses, banks, institutional investors such as universities and pension funds, insurance companies, investment advisory services such as Standard & Poor's, mutual funds, and others who buy securities or advise others, they are specialists in acquiring and evaluating information about companies. Most of them concentrate on a given group, such as oil, transportation, chemicals, or foods. In very large brokerage houses, an analyst may concentrate on only a few companies (within a single industry).

The analyst generally issues reports to the members of his firm, who are then guided in their own purchases or in the advice they give to customers. Many analysts either write or contribute to the market letters that have a great influence on investors' practices.

Increasingly, analysts are narrowing their interest to certain companies rather than trying to cover the entire universe of publicly held companies. This means that each company needs to identify and work with those who study its industry or otherwise are interested specifically, rather than on all analysts as a group.

There are nine basic ways that public relations men communicate with these analysts:

(1) Arranging for the president or other key executive of the company to talk before one of the societies of analysts (see list below). Companies are invited to appear on the basis of their interest to the group, recency of latest appearance (generally no

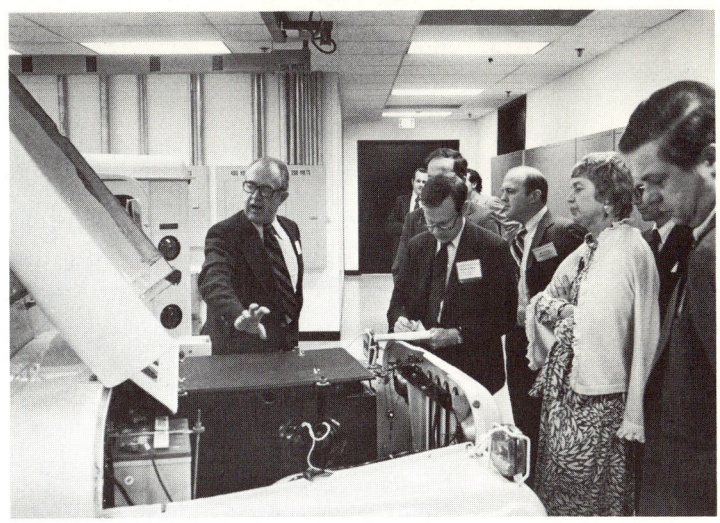

Figure 11-9. Tours for interested financial analysts are an important part of many companies' financial public relations programs. This group observes an operation at Gould, Inc.

oftener than every two years in New York), schedule available, and the interest of the company. Generally the company is expected to give detailed, unadorned information about its operations, plans, and outlook. Literature of direct interest to the analysts may be distributed. In most cases the press is invited, and the company may release information about the talk for publication not earlier than the time of the meeting.

(2) Special reports for analysts, containing detailed and technical financial information, plans that can be revealed without aiding competitors, illustrations of plants and facilities, and related material.

(3) Tours of the main plant and facilities, or a group of plants, for one analyst or a group of up to a dozen. They should be accompanied by key company officials and by specialists in the processes and operations being visited. Ample time for a question-and-answer discussion should be allowed.

(4) Dissemination of financial and corporate news to the analysts as well as to the press simultaneously.

(5) Meeting specific requests for information received from analysts, insofar as corporate security and the rules on equal disclosure permit.

(6) Personal visits with analysts at their offices or in the offices of the public relations department or counsel.

(7) Small discussion meetings with selected analysts having special interest in the company.

(8) Appearances before groups of analysts who specialize in the company's industry.

(9) Presentations at the company headquarters for large groups of analysts at intervals of two to three years. Deere and Company's meetings at its famous Saarinen-designed building in Moline, Illinois are good examples.

Following is a list of the major societies of security analysts, reflecting the growth of this field:

MAJOR MEMBER GROUPS OF THE NATIONAL FEDERATION OF FINANCIAL ANALYSTS SOCIETIES—1969-1977

	Number of members	
	1977	1969
Atlanta Society of Financial Analysts	222	153
The Austin-San Antonio Society of Financial Analysts	68	50
The Baltimore Security Analysts Society	172	86
The Boston Security Analysts Society	1,008	680
Financial Analysts Society of Central Florida	86	—
The Investment Analysts Society of Chicago	864	630
The Cincinnati Society of Financial Analysts	131	115
The Cleveland Society of Security Analysts	238	265
The Columbus Society of Financial Analysts	105	80
The Dallas Association of Investment Analysts	226	185
Denver Society of Security Analysts	127	95
Financial Analysts of Des Moines	77	55
The Financial Analysts Society of Detroit	205	235
The Hartford Society of Financial Analysts	328	310
The Houston Society of Financial Analysts	190	148
The Indianapolis Society of Financial Analysts	148	128
The Financial Analysts Society of Jacksonville	78	115
Kansas City Society of Financial Analysts	148	125
The Los Angeles Society of Financial Analysts	444	308
The Financial Analysts Society of Miami	88	—
Milwaukee Investment Analysts	182	102
Montreal Society of Financial Analysts	322	400
Nashville Society of Financial Analysts, Inc.	73	170
Financial Analysts of New Orleans	83	167
The New York Society of Security Analysts, Inc.	5,100	4,700
North Carolina Society of Financial Analysts	137	—
The Oklahoma Society of Financial Analysts	64	50
The Omaha-Lincoln Society of Financial Analysts	178	175
Financial Analysts of Philadelphia	446	480
Phoenix Society of Financial Analysts	106	90
Pittsburgh Society of Financial Analysts	136	145
The Providence Society of Financial Analysts	108	145
The Richmond Society of Financial Analysts	222	215
The Rochester Society of Investments Analysts	124	172
The St. Louis Society of Financial Analysts	179	164
Financial Analysts Society of San Diego	86	170
The Security Analysts of San Francisco	476	425
Seattle Society of Financial Analysts	101	—
Financial Analysts of Toledo	50	45
The Toronto Society of Financial Analysts	651	575
The Twin Cities Society of Security Analysts, Inc.	414	270

The Vancouver Society of Financial Analysts	68	53
The Washington Society of Investment Analysts	260	280
Western Michigan Society of Financial Analysts	56	—
Financial Analysts of Wilmington	105	95
The Winnipeg Society of Financial Analysts	62	45

Analysts' needs. The conception the investor relations person has of what is pertinent information may not coincide with that of the analyst. George Putnam, Chairman, Putnam Management Company, a large manager of investment funds, described the analyst's interest in a talk before the New York Chapter of NIRI:

> The analyst really wants to know *how* to analyze the company—what makes it tick, what the risks are, what the unknowns are, what the leverage is, how different economic conditions will impact it; its vulnerability to recession, to interest-rate shifts, to competition, to new technical discoveries, to government controls, to material shortages, to weather, to seasonality, etc. Most analysts do not want their conclusions handed to them in "packaged form," but they want to learn enough from the company to be able to examine the environment and then make judgments as to how changes will affect the company's earnings prospects.

How the analyst functions. The function of the analyst is almost similar to that of the reporter, except that the analyst must make a value judgment on the company he researches—weighing it in terms of whether it is under- or over-valued in regard to its present market price and its long-term prospects.

Just like the reporter, the analyst is faced with many deadline pressures and must use his time to the utmost value. Therefore, the analyst should be afforded the same considerations, in terms of time saving and assistance, as the financial reporter.

More importantly, the financial public relations man should appreciate the fact that the securities analyst probably already has a great deal of general information about the company. What he will need, then, is a broad picture of the company's goals and a quick synopsis of current news events. The analyst's interest in the company will be centered more on the future, including the effect of recent events, than on its past.

Generally the analyst will concentrate on how current news events will affect the company over the long term. Generally speaking, discussions with analysts will be considerably more penetrating than those with financial reporters. The analyst generally will be searching for answers to the "why" rather than the "what." This is the main reason the financial public relations man must have a good technical background and an intimate knowledge of his company.

Questions of credibility. The financial public relations profession has come under some criticism because of its handling of corporate financial information to the public and to analysts. Much of the criticism has been based on the claim that financial public relations people have been quick to boast of corporate accomplishments, often distorting the picture with misleading and sometimes inaccurate financial data, particularly in terms of earnings projections, but steadfast in withholding any negative data.

Obviously, such claims will affect the relationship between financial public relations practitioners and analysts and ultimately the investing public. And, while it is probably true that there have been instances where financial public relations people have provided misleading material, this is not true of the great majority. It is highly important that no credibility gap exist between the company and the investing public. The financial public relations man should, therefore, strive for accuracy and truthfulness.

Increasingly, actual discussions with analysts are arranged for top corporate officers, rather than by the public relations man unless he is also fully familiar with all corporate financial information and is sophisticated in finance. However, the public relations man or counsel is constantly in attendance or alert to such discussions, so that if any information should be revealed that might have a bearing on the action of the stock an immediate full distribution of the news can be made to comply with the stringent full-disclosure rules. Public relations people also maintain contacts with analysts to learn what they would like from the company and to provide a listening post of investment-community opinion to provide to the management.

A fully qualified company officer should be available to qualified analysts as freely as schedules permit.

Group Net Sales and Net Earnings
American Hospital Supply Corporation and Subsidiaries

NET SALES ($ in millions)	1975		1974		1973		1972		1971	
Group										
Hospital	$ 323.2	29%	$268.7	27%	$213.7	26%	$181.7	26%	$168.7	28%
Science Specialties	355.9	31	312.6	32	300.2	36	242.9	35	197.7	33
Medical Specialties	72.4	6	67.5	7	52.7	6	44.1	6	39.1	6
Pharmaceutical	91.1	8	74.8	8	62.0	7	54.9	8	51.0	9
Capital Goods	60.0	5	55.9	6	49.4	6	43.8	6	42.4	7
Dental	46.9	4	41.7	4	34.3	4	30.9	4	25.2	4
Dietary	43.8	4	39.6	4	30.0	4	24.0	4	21.2	4
Services	92.1	8	79.3	8	57.9	7	46.0	7	34.9	6
International	81.8	7	71.2	7	53.7	6	38.1	6	28.4	5
Unallocated eliminations and adjustments	(23.8)	(2)	(25.4)	(3)	(16.5)	(2)	(12.7)	(2)	(12.4)	(2)
Consolidated	$1143.4	100%	$985.9	100%	$837.4	100%	$693.7	100%	$596.2	100%
Total international sales	$ 202.9	18%	$168.8	17%	$125.2	15%	$ 97.4	14%	$ 81.0	14%
NET EARNINGS ($ in millions)	**1975**		**1974**		**1973**		**1972**		**1971**	
Group										
Hospital	$ 19.3	35%	$ 13.7	29%	$ 10.0	25%	$ 7.5	21%	$ 6.1	21%
Science Specialties	16.5	30	14.6	31	13.6	33	12.3	34	10.7	35
Medical Specialties	6.8	12	5.9	13	3.7	9	3.4	10	2.6	8
Pharmaceutical	6.3	12	5.0	11	4.9	12	5.1	14	5.4	18
Capital Goods	3.0	6	2.3	5	2.2	5	2.0	6	2.1	7
Dental	2.4	4	2.6	6	1.8	4	1.5	4	0.4	1
Dietary	2.3	4	1.5	3	0.8	2	0.5	1	0.1	—
Services	1.8	3	3.0	6	1.6	4	0.9	3	0.6	2
International	.2	—	2.4	5	3.1	8	1.9	5	2.3	8
Unallocated interest, eliminations and adjustments	(3.4)	(6)	(4.4)	(9)	(0.7)	(2)	0.6	2	(0.1)	—
Consolidated	$ 55.2	100%	$ 46.6	100%	$ 41.0	100%	$ 35.7	100%	$ 30.2	100%
Total international earnings	$ 10.5	19%	$ 10.9	23%	$ 7.9	19%	$ 4.9	14%	$ 3.2	10%

Group Reporting Basis

Sales and earnings for each market group include their respective export and Canadian operations. Appropriate eliminations have been made to reflect group results on a consolidated basis. Normal income tax provisions, less tax incentives and adjustments, are reflected within reported group earnings.

The International Group has responsibility for coordination of all domestic export shipments as well as direct responsibility for foreign-based operations. Total international net sales and net earnings shown as separate amounts include Canadian operations and United States exports, royalties from foreign sources, income from foreign investments, and foreign exchange gains and losses in addition to the International Group foreign-based operations.

Unallocated eliminations and adjustments reflect transactions between groups as well as corporate interest income and expense and other miscellaneous adjustments. Such unallocated interest expense after taxes amounted to $3.2 million in 1975 and $3.6 million in 1974. Other corporate office expenses have been allocated to group operations on the basis of sales and number of employees in each group.

Figure 11-10. SEC requires a breakdown of information on sales and earnings by group of products or categories. This listing is typical of the treatment given by many companies.

Analysts' meetings. Many contacts with securities analysts will be on an individual basis, but at times the company may be asked to address large groups of analysts. Some of these meetings will involve such large groups as the Analyst Societies in New York, Boston, Philadelphia, Chicago, or Los Angeles and many other cities, but may also involve smaller groups of analysts who specialize in the industry group of which the company is a member.

In handling analysts' meetings, considerations include whether the president should address the group alone or whether executives with individual expertise should be used, whether the presentation should be strictly oral or should include visual aids, what material should be distributed at the meeting, and—most important—how the company will distribute any material information that might be disclosed.

A common mistake with many analysts' meetings is to rehash the volume of information already known about the company. Sending analysts a company Fact Book, if it contains well-planned information, can provide them with most of the figures they need. It is far more profitable to spend the time telling analysts those things that are not known about the company unless, of course, the company is relatively unknown to the group.

One of the complaints often heard from analysts is that corporations spend too much time telling how they make their money and not enough time explaining why they make money. In short, they would like to know what the company's guiding philosophy is, what makes it significantly different from other companies and, most important, what will make this company unique in the future.

Inviting the press. Another consideration is whether the press should be invited to attend analyst meetings. In some analysts' societies meetings are closed to all but members, automatically excluding the press. To some extent this forces a decision on the company. However, the N.Y. Stock Exchange strongly urges companies to invite the press to analysts' meetings whenever possible. If the press cannot attend, Exchange regulations require that, if any new material is discussed during the course of the meeting, it must be promptly released to the press.

Of course, there is the other side of the coin. The analysts are not really concerned with the investing public as much as servicing their firms' clients. Their goal is to provide clients with more and higher-quality data than they can glean from the newspapers.

Obviously, both of these groups cannot be satisfied simultaneously and a middle course must be chosen. The only compatible solution seems to be to try, whenever possible, to have the press attend or provide them with the same or a similar presentation. If the press is not permitted to attend, the company must fulfill its disclosure requirements with an immediate press release covering any material developments covered in the course of the meeting.

OTHER COMMUNICATIONS OUTLETS

Additional avenues to be included in many financial communications programs include:

Investment clubs. These are groups with some similar interest—such as employment in the same company, membership in the same profession, residence in the same neighborhood, or just

FINANCIAL PUBLIC RELATIONS

Free Enterprise at Gould

The need for experimental, innovative action directed toward fundamental elements of our society is suggested by what seems to be a significant dichotomy—a division of the American mind, one part of which decries the social problems which beset us, the other part which strongly accepts the good life provided by our free enterprise system.

According to recent surveys, much of the American public is losing trust in our economy. Dependence on government to control basic aspects of business and commerce is increasing. At the same time, more people are questioning our governmental processes, possibly as a result of frustrating social and economic experiences of the past few years.

This is the negative aspect of the American viewpoint—a feeling of personal anxiety combined with criticism about unemployment, inflation, housing, taxes, environmental problems, governmental corruption, and the seeming inability of our system to deal with these conditions.

However, a closer analysis reveals a strange paradox; many Americans indicate that these problems have little effect on their personal lives. Opinion polls reveal a level of personal satisfaction that belies the supposed dissatisfaction.

Some examples:

■ In 1971, when most of the public believed our young people were discontented rebels, a Harris poll asked young people in the 15-21 year age group this question: "Has your life been happy so far?"—90% answered yes. When asked why, they credited a good home and family and the freedom to pursue their lives as they wanted. When asked about expectations for the future, 93% said that they expected to be even happier.

■ In recent years there has been a general belief that most Americans dislike their jobs—phrases such as the "blue collar blues" and the "white collar woes" are popular. Recent surveys indicate that over 80% of the people interviewed expressed satisfaction, and even happiness, with their jobs.

■ As for the alleged despair and anxiety of the American public, from 1947 through 1973 the Gallup poll conducted a survey in which they asked individuals this question: "In general, how happy would you say you are: Very happy, fairly happy, not happy, or don't know?" In all of those years the number of people who ranged from fairly happy to "very happy" never dropped below 91%. Even in a year filled with crisis and turmoil like 1973, the percentage of "fairly" or "very happy" Americans stood at 97%.

It is evident to the close observer why Americans have an affirmative judgment about their own lives. Basically, it is because most Americans have been able to realize economic and social opportunities that have exceeded their fundamental expectations. It is this element of any society that is crucial to long-term stability and personal freedom—people must be able to realize their basic expectations to remain content.

America has had as a basic proposition that people can aspire to a better life. That they can dare to dream of personal greatness and fulfillment. That they can reap personal rewards and satisfactions if they commit their talent and energy to personal goals.

Our success as a nation is unparalleled in both social and economic terms. The economic record stands uncontested over any significant time period of measurement since the founding of the nation 200 years ago. Socially, we have experienced as much turmoil and strife as any nation; including a Civil War of gigantic proportions. But we have also attempted greater social integration than any nation with a process of government (called democracy) that was alien to most of the world when we adopted it in 1776.

The settlement of wilderness frontiers, the emancipation of slaves, the industrial revolution, the great World Wars, the deep depressions of an industrial nation, the early struggles of industrial and craft unions, and our current civil rights movements involving minority groups, women and ethnic groups created problems that would have brought totalitarian governments and the abolishment of personal liberties in other nations.

Through all of these periods of hardships, Americans believed in the future. They have not been disappointed. Our combination of personal and economic freedom has resulted in economic and social progress that has benefited all elements of the society.

A free-enterprise system provides a double-edged spur to economic growth, prosperity and change. It provides oppor-

Field research indicates that today's high school students are intellectually isolated from business and know little or are misinformed about our free enterprise system. Gould has instituted a program of cooperative work/school projects that involve local summer students in daily business operations of different Gould facilities. Sherry Butvillis, the student counselor at Rolling Meadows (Illinois) High School, introduced the summer group who are now working on a half-day basis in the Corporate Offices interspersed with classroom instruction.

Figure 11-11. The annual report is being used by various companies to help fill the gap in economic education among the public.

friendship—who also are interested in investing. They form a pool by each putting specified amounts into a fund monthly. This is invested on the basis of joint decisions. Information on clubs and how to reach them is available from the National Association of Investment Clubs, 1515 E. 11 Mile Rd., Royal Oak, Mich. 48067.

Public relations news wires. Some of the teletype services that distribute press releases to media (see Chapter 40) also distribute them to brokerage offices.

PROXY FIGHTS AND TENDER OFFERS

The most stressful and crucial element of financial public relations is in forestalling and defending against efforts of outside interests to take over the company.

The public relations aspects of these problems are treated in Chapter 12.

GUIDES TO EFFECTIVE DISCLOSURE

Since the Appellate Court's decision on the Texas Gulf Sulphur case in 1968 and the NYSE's revision of its disclosure requirements, hundreds of thousands of words have been written and spoken on disclosure. The amount of information disclosed and the concern about disclosure have reached unparalleled levels in the field of financial communications.

Although this concern about adequate disclosure has been beneficial, much of it has been the result of over-anxiety about fulfilling regulatory requirements. Still, it is a tribute to American business' desire to do the right thing.

Actually, there is little reason for public relations people to be anxious about disclosure requirements, provided they follow a few simple rules. An abstract of the very thorough guidelines on disclosure prepared by the American Stock Exchange appears in Chapter 12. It covers virtually all aspects of importance to the public relations practitioner.

Also in Chapter 12 is a diagram of the reporting policies of the stock exchange and the SEC.

The New York Stock Exchange's disclosure requirements, which were developed over many years of experience in this area, are based on a few simple, common-sense policies that can be followed easily and successfully by any corporation. In brief, they are:

• Release immediately any news that might have a material effect on the price of the company's securities, including merger or acquisition negotiations past the top secret stage, imminence of a labor strike, discovery of new resources, death of a top officer, and so on.

• Maintain adequate security on confidential information until it is ready to be released, or until it goes beyond a small group of top management of the company.

• Act promptly to dispel unfounded rumors that result in unusual market activity or price variations.

• Avoid premature announcements, whenever possible, unwarranted claims, and overly optimistic forecasts.

• Avoid providing one inquirer with information that would not be given to another.

• Insure that news is handled in its proper perspective by avoiding over-optimism or unwarranted conservatism and by supplementing news releases when changing circumstances require it.

• Most important, when in doubt... DISCLOSE.

Four key sources of information in this area are the Securities and Exchange Acts of 1933 and 1934; the New York Stock Exchange's[10] booklets, "Expanded Policy on Timely Disclosure" and "The Corporate Director and The Investing Public," and the American Stock Exchange's[11] booklet on disclosure policies (abstract appears in Chapter 12).

HOME COMINGS AND OPEN HOUSES

Some companies encourage stockholders to visit the "home office," the plants, and the branches. One company makes it an annual policy to invite shareholders to visit the main plant during their summer vacation automobile tours. A special reception committee is on hand to conduct the visitors on an inspection around the property. Other companies have set aside weeks or days during the year when "open house" is held for all stockholders. Attractive invitations are sent to those who live within a reasonable distance of the property. Refreshments are served and souvenirs are often distributed to those taking the opportunity to attend.

SHAREHOLDER SURVEYS

As important as it is to determine the attitude of analysts, it is equally important to assess the attitude of shareholders. This can be done quite easily by mailing a simple questionnaire to shareholders (see sample). The questionnaire should determine:

1. Whether shareholders understand the financial section of the company's annual report as presented.
2. Whether the shareholders understand the company's operating problems and progress.
3. What shareholders think the annual report should contain.
4. What shareholders think should be added to the annual report and other reports.[12]

---

[10]11 Wall St., New York, N.Y. 10005.
[11]86 Trinity Pl., New York, N.Y. 10006.

[12]In addition, some companies find it desirable to survey their shareholders to determine how many companies they own stock in, how well-informed they are on financial matters, and the level of their understanding of financial reports. Such information can be very helpful in planning the content, tone, and sophistication of communications material. *Ed.*

STOCKHOLDER'S QUESTIONNAIRE
(No Signature Requested)

I HOW DID YOU ORIGINALLY ACQUIRE YOUR COMMON STOCK? By gift ...... By inheritance .... By purchase ......
If by purchase, did someone recommend it to you? Yes ...... No ......
(If yes) By Banker .... Broker .... Lawyer .... Friend .... Relative .... Other person ....
What is the principal reason you decided to buy this stock?
....
....

II HOW MANY SHARES OF OUR STOCK DO YOU OWN?
....

III HOW IS YOUR STOCK HELD? By an individual .... In joint tenancy .... By a corporation .... By an institution ....
In an estate or trust fund ....

IV WHY ARE YOU HOLDING THE STOCK? Primarily for income .... In the hope of selling it at a higher price ....

V WOULD YOU BUY MORE OF OUR STOCK? Yes .... No ....
(If yes) Under what conditions? ....
....
(If no) Why not? ....
....

VI DO YOU OWN OTHER STOCKS? Yes .... No ....
Several (2 or 3) .... A few (3 to 10) .... A larger number (over 10) ....
(If other companies' shares owned) Do any of these companies follow practices you would recommend? Yes .... No ....
(If yes) What company? ....
Please describe the practice ....
....
....

VII DID YOU RECEIVE THE COMPANY'S ANNUAL REPORT LAST MONTH FOR THE FISCAL YEAR?
Yes .... No ......
If you did, did you read it? Yes ...... No ......
Was it easy to understand ...... Hard to understand ......
Fully informative ...... Not fully informative ......
Should it contain pictures or illustrations? Yes ..... No ....
Should it contain graphs or charts? Yes ...... No ......
Should it be "dressed up" more? Yes ...... No ......
Did you read the President's message in the report? Yes .... No ....
If so, what was your opinion of his message? Very favorable ...... Favorable ...... Uncertain ...... Unfavorable ...... Very unfavorable ...... Why? ....
....
....

Figure 11-12. A typical stockholder questionnaire.

FINANCIAL PUBLIC RELATIONS

What should the President discuss in his message? Matters pertaining to Company operations . . . . . Matters pertaining to the over-all economy . . . . . . Both . . . . . . Other . . . .
....
....

In general, this is what I liked about the Report . . . .
....
....

In general, I did not like . . . .
....
....

VIII DO YOU THINK THE COMPANY IS GIVING ITS STOCKHOLDERS ENOUGH INFORMATION ABOUT ITS ACTIVITIES? Yes . . . . . . No . . . . . .
If not, what kind of information would you like? . . . .
....
....

IX HOW WOULD YOU EXPRESS YOUR OPINION OF THE MANAGEMENT OF YOUR COMPANY?
Very favorable . . . . Favorable . . . . Uncertain . . . . Unfavorable . . . . Very unfavorable . . . .

Why? . . . .
....

X DO YOU USE ANY OF OUR PRODUCTS? Yes . . . No . . .
If so, what do you think of them? . . . .
....

XI DID YOU NOTICE THE ADS ENCLOSED WITH THE LAST ANNUAL REPORT? Yes . . . . No . . . .
If so, what did you think of them? . . . .
....

XII THE FOLLOWING BRIEF ANSWERS ABOUT YOURSELF WILL ALSO HELP US TO KNOW MORE ABOUT OUR STOCKHOLDERS.
Male . . . . Female . . . . Married . . . . Single . . . . Widowed or Divorced . . . . Age . . . Occupation . . . .

XIII FURTHER COMMENTS OR SUGGESTIONS:
....
....
....
....
....

Figure 11-12. (Continued)

A personal letter, perhaps from the president or chairman, should accompany the questionnaire and explain its purpose and try to elicit suggestions and criticisms.

A few corporations employ professional opinion research agencies to send out personal interviewers to a selected list of stockholders to obtain direct answers to questions regarding management policies and to obtain helpful suggestions and constructive criticism. One company "checked" only its women stockholders, because they accounted for the majority of the ownership, while another approached only the employee-stockholders. In both cases, the results of the surveys revealed a high degree of misunderstanding on fundamental conceptions of the management's policies and the American enterprise system.

LONG-TERM EFFECTIVENESS

The financial public relations man is basically a communicator of information. Through his expertness in communications, he helps many people reach the decision to buy or hold his company's stock. His success can be measured in many ways but is best reflected in a realistic appraisal of his company and of its securities. To accomplish this, the public relations man must be professional and have a high regard for truthfulness and accuracy and lean on the side of conservatism in discussing future developments of his company. This does not mean that he cannot do his utmost to show that his company is a good investment, but he must at times restrain his enthusiasm in favor of a realistic appraisal that in the long term will establish or maintain his company's reputation for integrity and, at the same time, lay the basis for developing a core of loyal long-term stockholders.

Although his actions and words may fulfill today's needs by the press and public, the financial public relations man must also keep in mind that they will also be judged in light of his company's future performance.

(Full treatment of dealing with takeover efforts and disclosure regulations appears in the following chapter.)

12

Financial Public Relations
II. Takeover Efforts and Disclosure Regulations

Philip Lesly

Two areas of financial public relations that have been developing the greatest demands for expertness are dealing with efforts to take over control of publicly held companies, and the complex requirements for disclosure of "material information."

Widespread ownership of corporations and the growth of mutual funds and other institutional investors have greatly increased the potential role of the non-management stockholder.

When companies were held by a few owners, often related to each other or partners in operating the enterprise, changes of management came about through "palace revolutions" but seldom involved people outside the inner circle.

The democratization of stock ownership has made corporate control attainable through additional means.

Basic differences in takover efforts. Efforts to take over the management of a company against the wishes of its officers take two general forms: The proxy fight and the tender offer. Both involve appealing to the mass of stockholders, but they are quite different.

In a proxy fight the two sides seek to gain a majority vote of the voting stock outstanding. Each stockholder is expected to retain his (her) holdings. This means that for the stockholder, the issue is which of the contestants shall manage the company in which *he will continue to have his funds invested*. The issue in a proxy fight is usually the adequacy of the management.

On the other hand, a tender offer is designed to get the stockholder to dispose of his stock. The offer is made attractive enough to get him to sell and cease being concerned about who will manage the enterprise (except where the purchase involves securities in an enterprise that will control the one that is sought.)

In a proxy fight, the appeals to the stockholder involve loyalty, comparative confidence in the management he knows as opposed to the insurgents, concern for the future of his investment, and other considerations that will concern him in the future.

In a tender offer, money is the overriding issue. For example, a stockholder who has bought a stock at 35, finds it selling on the market at 40, and receives an offer to buy it from him at 50 is seldom inclined to consider his loyalty to the management or any other factor except that he can make a very substantial profit immediately, as compared with the previous experience he has had with the stock. (Where the stockholder has held the stock for a long time and would have to pay a substantial capital gain tax on his appreciation, he may have doubts.)

Almost all stockholders own their securities for the financial benefits they expect. A tender offer at a price substantially above the market level—especially when there is no early expectation that the stock would reach that level under other circumstances—is extremely attractive to the great majority of stockholders. This means that, other things being equal, the group making the offer has a substantial initial advantage.

Because the proxy fight is usually much more expensive for the insurgents and much more difficult to win in most cases, it has become much less common and is superseded by the tender offer as a device for takeovers.

Defenses against a proxy fight. In a proxy fight, the public relations of the defending company focuses essentially on informing the stockholder and the financial community about the merits of the present management's operation as opposed to what the insurgents represent.

To forestall takeover efforts by dissident stockholders through an effort to elect a majority of the board of directors, there are a number of basic tactics:

1. Constant development of confidence in the management through a thorough and continuous public relations program, especially in the financial areas described in Chapter 11.

2. Additional efforts to build up confidence in the management when specific issues seem to be arising that could be made the basis for a proxy fight. These are essentially the fundamental functions in a corporate public relations program, perhaps intensified.

3. Maintaining close relationships with the media, assuring that they will be inclined to come to the company first when news or rumors about it arise and that they will have a high degree of acceptance of what the company says.

4. Publicizing information that will undermine acceptance of the opposition's charges and promises. This is based on facts about the opposition group and its record, requiring as much advance research and documentation as possible.

5. Use of effectively prepared and timed communications in addition to publicity, such as advertisements, letters to stockholders, and so on.

Timing is vital in both proxy fights and tender offers. In proxy fights, the most crucial time is late in the battle, just before the stockholders' meeting at which the vote will be counted. Where stockholder votes and proxies are involved, *it is the last proxy received from each stockholder that is counted*. A campaign that climaxes too soon can bring in proxies that will later be superseded by proxies from the same stockholders who have been motivated by the opposition.

Tender offers. Since these are based almost entirely on the dollar attraction of the offer, most of the factors involved in defeating a proxy attack are not involved in protecting against a tender offer.

The stockholder is deciding whether he would rather take the money or new securities and get out, or continue to hold his stock in the company at probably a lower price. He is voting with his bank account, not his ballot.

This often presents the insurgents with a number of advantages over the management:

1. The immediate monetary attraction of the offer is difficult to offset with convincing evidence that the current management can do better in giving the stockholder a higher price in a short time. The stockholder tends to ask: If the management can assure a higher value for the stock, why hasn't the market price been higher?

2. Brokers generally have the opportunity for double or even triple commissions when they prevail on a stockholder to sell. They get a commission on the sale by the stockholder, another on the purchase by the insurgents (who immediately make known their willingness to pay such commissions), and often a third commission when the customer buys other stock with the cash he receives.

3. Arbitragers—who profit by taking advantage of the differences between the offering price and the selling price on securities—often find an opportunity to pick up stock at somewhat lower than the offering price and turn it in to the offerer.

4. What would be considered strengths of management under normal circumstances, and especially in a proxy fight, often become attractions to insurgents in a tender offer. Especially attractive are companies that have a low amount of debt, a large amount of cash, and a good reputation that will make it easier to obtain finances for buying up the stock. The higher a firm's earnings, the more attractive it is for a takeover, since insurgents often have high debt ratios and can use the earnings to pay for the company they acquire.

5. Mutual funds and other large investors sometimes find they can make a substantial profit by buying into a company they know will be subjected to a tender offer, and then selling to the insurgent. Or if they hold a stock for other reasons they may well accept the offer as a means of making a good profit.

Much will depend on the nature of the tender offer. If it is for cash, the stockholder has the simple decision of determining whether he will be better off taking that amount and then finding another investment for it or staying with his holdings in the company. Since cash tender offers are not tax free, this judgment will be affected by his tax position, the length of time he has held the stock, the condition of the market in terms of finding other investments, and other considerations. If the offer is for new securities, either with or without partial payment in cash, the stockholder's consideration is more complicated. He is faced with trying to determine the prospects for the enterprise in which he will hold new securities, how marketable they will be, and often the comparative elements of a complex structure that may involve fractional shares, subordinated debentures, and other technical matters.

The recent experience of the stock on the market will have an important influence. If the stock has been declining or failing to keep up with the trend of the market, many stockholders will welcome an opportunity to dispose of it. Also, stockholders who do not face a tax on gains are much more likely to sell than those who would have to pay a capital gain tax on the appreciation of the stock.

The nature of the company's stockholders can be important. Stockholders who have held the shares for a long time may not have done so out of loyalty, which can be readily displaced by profit, but because they are inherently conservative and slow to change. Such stockholders are less likely to jump at any attractive offer that comes along.

While some studies indicate that about 30 percent of companies sought in takeovers have succumbed in offers of securities and perhaps 50 percent when cash is offered, these figures do not account for the large number of target companies that have made mergers they otherwise would not make in order to avoid falling into the hands of insurgents. In other cases, maneuvers taken in defense—such as making acquisitions otherwise not planned—have substantially changed the target company. In total, a substantial proportion of target companies can be said to be transformed or materially changed as a result of takeover efforts.

Strategic defenses. Strategies and plans to forestall a tender offer takeover may be classified as *strategic* and *public relations.* While the strategic measures are not strictly within the public relations sphere, they are of vital importance and the public relations executive must be aware of them and, wherever possible, participate in their planning.

A good summation of rules and regulations of the Securities and Exchange Commission in regard to tender offers is *Reference Guide to Tender Offers* produced by Charles P. Young—Chicago, 320 S. Jefferson St., Chicago, Ill. 60606.

Because the rules and interpretations in this area have been changing steadily and are likely to continue to change, it is wise not only to learn what manuals such as this provide, but to keep up to date on SEC actions, court decisions, and state laws.

1. Where state laws allow, the election of the board of directors may be staggered so that only one-third are changed each year. This means that a group gaining voting control could change no more than one-third of the board in any given year.

2. Where state laws allow, the by-laws may be changed to provide that no merger action or substantial change in the control of the company may be effected with less than an 80 percent vote of the stock represented. This is some defense against control being exerted by a group that may be the largest stockholder but has less than 20 percent of the total.

3. Assets on the company's books should be fully valued. Often it has been considered good practice to leave real estate, for instance, recorded at the nominal acquisition price, even though it may have multiplied in value. This tends to keep the apparent value of the company too low and may underprice its stock.

4. Within prudent limits, have the company's pension fund acquire company stock. Usually it will be clearly in the best interests of the employees to prevent takeover by a distant and unproved insurgent company.

5. Encourage employees to become stockholders. (Keep in mind that employee-stockholders who see a loss on the stock when the market has declined are a potential source of unrest and disaffection. They may then be most likely to accept an attractive offer.)

6. A perpetual watch should be kept on the stock record lists to observe movements of holdings. A number of warning signs should be investigated, including large purchases, an unusual rate of market activity, and large blocks being picked up in "street names" that permit shielding the identity of the true purchaser. Close liaison should be maintained with the specialist in the company's stock on the floor of the stock exchange and the company's stock transfer agent.

7. The company's banks, investment banker, friendly brokerage houses, and others should be cultivated to ascertain how they would act or could be urged to use their influence in the event a takeover effort comes from any of a number of directions.

8. The transfer agent that keeps track of the changes in ownership of the company's stock can provide daily reports not only of the number of shares traded, but the names and addresses of buyers and sellers. With computerized records, it is possible to obtain detailed information on each purchaser—dates of purchases, percentages of the total shares represented by each holder, etc. Such

information can make it possible to watch the buying action of any purchaser when the name is known.

When buying is done in "street names"—that is, bought and held by brokers for the customers—the identity of the buyers is disguised. In most takeover efforts, that technique is likely of brokers' holdings in any given stock from the Depositary Trust Company in New York. A fee is charged for this service.

9. Some companies claim to have informants in the advertising departments of the *Wall Street Journal* and *The New York Times,* where most insurgent groups place their advertisements offering to buy a company's stock. That can provide an additional 24 or 48 hours of notice that the company's stock will be sought.

10. Contingency plans by the company should be kept current constantly, to be activated as soon as there is evidence a takeover effort is imminent. These may include:

- Making acquisitions that will put stock into friendly hands.
- Making an acquisition or entering a new field of activity that would put the company into competition with the would-be insurgent and create an anti-trust conflict.
- Splitting the stock (before the tender offer is publicly announced) to delay tendering through paperwork involved in issuing new stock certificates.

11. Suppliers who value the company as a customer may, in turn, be customers of the insurgent company. They can sometimes be motivated to express their disapproval to the insurgents and create concern among the stockholders of the insurgent company.

12. The active support of the communities in which the company operates should be developed, on the basis that in many cases after a takeover has been effected, plants have been shut down or operations reduced. In many cases the new owners remove management functions from the taken-over company's headquarters city, with the result that local lawyers, accountants, banks, and others lose clients.

13. Unions can sometimes be enlisted as allies of the management when they can be shown that the new owners might be a threat to the interests of the workers, to the continuation of some of the operations and therefore of many jobs, or to a good relationship between management and labor. The fear of having to deal with a hostile union can make a potential offeror back off.

14. Nearly half the states have passed legislation to hinder a takeover of a company headquartered or with operations in the state. These laws vary. In some cases a threatened company can call on the protection of these laws when only one of its operations is in a state with such legislation.

15. It is important to keep in touch with the Senators and Congressmen representing the area of the company's headquarters and other major operations. In many cases they can be helpful in stimulating anti-trust investigations, examinations by the Securities and Exchange Commission, and other governmental deterrents to the takeover.

16. If the company's finances warrant, the dividend can be increased. This is a visible stimulus to the enthusiasm of the stockholders.

17. If finances warrant, the company may want to buy its own stock for the treasury. Treasury stock cannot be voted, but since it is not actively on the market it is not available for purchase by outsiders in their efforts to gain control. The fewer the number of shares outstanding, the higher the earnings per share. Also, treasury stock is used in making acquisitions that can put that stock into voting position, generally siding with management.

18. All substantial stockholders should be cultivated consistently and kept informed about their interest in continuing to keep their investment in the company.

Public relations activities. Forestalling the tender offer takeover can involve a wide range of public relations strategies and activities. The most basic are:

1. Constant public relations efforts that maintain a high level of confidence in the company's stock and help assure that it sells at a good price-earnings multiple. Efforts to jump up the stock price will probably be self-defeating, but legitimate activities that attain a justifiable multiple are the responsibility of every company's management.

2. Keeping the public aware of the company's plans for growth, its future prospects, and its effective use of its funds.

3. When a tender offer is imminent or has developed, reporting quickly and incisively on events, statements of the management, and other developments.

4. Having addressed lists of stockholders ready, and kept fresh constantly, so at least two mailings can be made very quickly.

5. Having possible letters written in advance, leaving blanks for the name of the insurgent company and the terms of its offer. These can be reviewed, revised, and produced quickly when the time comes, instead of having to compose them un-

der stress and with inevitable delays for creativity and clearances.

6. Having proposed advertisements prepared in the same way.

7. After the offer is made, reserving space immediately in the newspapers to be used. Then make advance reservations for every two or three days thereafter for at least a week.

8. Having plans made for immediate telephone contact with all substantial stockholders, including the tentative message to be conveyed and deployment of all persons who will be assigned to make calls. That requires getting the telephone numbers—business and home—in advance and listing them on the stockholder information sheets.

9. Planning telegrams to go to other substantial stockholders. They should be night letters if some advance notice of the takeover bid is had, or 15-word immediate messages otherwise. Be sure that the Western Union office nearby can handle the volume. Otherwise you may want to apportion the list among various offices nearest the groups of recipients.

10. Having arrangements made in advance for all night services that may be needed: Producing, stuffing, and mailing letters to stockholders; producing printed material (either by company personnel or commercial 24-hour printers); layout and preparation of ads, and manning of switchboards.

11. Publicizing the negative aspects of the insurgent group, where securities are involved in the purchase package or any doubt can be cast on its ability to finance the deal—such as the disadvantages of owning securities in various types of conglomerate or diversified companies, weaknesses in the structure of the insurgent company, scandals or other vulnerabilities in its record, and so on.

12. Developing public opinion in plant communities, among suppliers and customers, and whoever else would not like to see the change. This can be aimed at bringing negative reaction to bear on the insurgent company, its customers, its bankers, and others.

It is vital to keep in mind that the *appeal* and the *warmth* of the communications are perhaps as important as the facts. Cold facts alone—especially if they sound like expostulations of the management to the stockholder—can be deadly and drive the stockholder to get out as quickly as he can. Appeals that show concern for his interests, that address him with respect and in return evoke respect for the humanity of the management, can go a long way in overcoming the sheer emotion of the dollars offered.

In no other aspect of public relations is secrecy of such great importance as in the takeover area. Extreme security measures are required within the office of the public relations staff, among mimeographing and mailing offices, with printers, and in every other area where some part of the information and strategy can be exposed. Would-be insurgents often include in their plans the suborning of employees inside any of these places. Sometimes employees who want to be in the good graces of the new management provide information that helps them achieve their goal.

There are many legal aspects on both sides of takeover fights.[1] The company's legal staff and the best available legal counsel, experienced in these matters, should be involved at all stages.

However, time is probably the most critical single factor. Unlike proxy fights, where the key time is at the end of the battle, in tender offers the critical period is immediately after the offer has been announced. Immediacy in decision-making and in carrying out all functions is urgent.

While most lawyers are by nature and training cautious and likely to advise looking at all aspects and "sleeping on it," speed can determine whether a company survives. While no violation of the law should ever be recommended, the nuances of legal interpretations often must be left for later—even at the expense of settling a lawsuit or satisfying a government agency—if it means preventing a takeover that would make all future considerations irrelevant.

DISCLOSURE POLICIES

As reported in Chapter 11, the stock exchanges require that information that may materially affect the market for a company's stock be disclosed promptly. Similar regulations should apply to securities not listed on an exchange.

The following abstract of the American Stock Exchange Disclosure Policies contains the guidelines of importance to public relations executives. While this is the major part of that document, other corporate considerations are also included. The entire document is available from The American Stock Exchange, 86 Trinity Pl., New York, N.Y. 10006.

Outline of Exchange Disclosure Policies—The Exchange considers that the conduct of a fair and orderly market requires every listed company to make available to the public information necessary

---

[1] See Chapter 54.

To Asarco Stockholders:

Pennzoil United, Inc. (Pennzoil) has made a tender offer for your American Smelting and Refining Company stock in an effort to take over your Company.

Your Officers and Directors, assisted by independent financial counsel—the investment banking firm of Kuhn, Loeb & Co.—unanimously rejected a Pennzoil proposal of merger made to your Company only two months ago. The present offer is essentially the same, except that the conversion ratio of the security offered by Pennzoil has been increased slightly (from 1.6 to 1.8). The Directors have authorized me to state that if Pennzoil were to renew its proposal to the Company with the increased conversion ratio, they would again reject the offer. You are being asked to give up solid values and to accept enormous dilution.

If you accept Pennzoil's offer:
- You lose in terms of dividend income.
- You lose in terms of per share net income.
- You lose in terms of net asset value.
- You run the risk of loss should Pennzoil's offer be found to violate the antitrust laws.
- Most important, *you would be sacrificing your present direct interest in Asarco's future growth potential.*

Asarco stockholders would contribute 66% of the earnings (average 1965-67) and 61% of the book value of the combined company in return for only 45% of the common shares of the combined company, assuming full conversion.

Your Asarco shares are worth far more than you are being offered.

There is no need for haste. You have at least until January 31 to make your decision. Tenders to Pennzoil are irrevocable. Once you tender, you cannot take advantage of any new developments or any change in market prices which would be more advantageous to you than receipt of the new Pennzoil security.

In exchange for each share of your Asarco common stock (which currently has an annual dividend rate of $3.80), Pennzoil proposes to give you one share of a new Pennzoil "cumulative preference common stock," which would pay a fixed dividend of only $3.30 annually. As long as you hold the stock, your dividends are limited to that.

9 reasons why you should <u>**reject**</u> the Pennzoil offer!

1 **This is not a cash offer.** No matter what estimates Pennzoil may make of the value of its offer, the price at which the new shares will sell is unknown. Pennzoil can give no assurance or guarantee as to how much cash you would be able to get if you wanted to sell your shares after accepting their offer. Pennzoil common stock has dropped from a high of 67¼ on November 12, 1968 to 50¾ on January 21, 1969.

2 **You lose in terms of dividends.** Asarco dividends have increased steadily over the past five years (except for the strike-affected year of 1967). The current dividend on your Asarco shares is at an annual rate of $3.80 per share. The new Pennzoil stock being offered to you has a fixed dividend of $3.30 per share, which is assured for a period of only six years after which the stock is subject to call. If you should convert the stock into 1.8 shares of Pennzoil common, you would receive only $1.44 per share at the current rate instead of $3.80 on your Asarco shares. In addition, after six years the conversion rate drops. Dividends paid by the two companies since 1963 are shown below:

Year	Pennzoil Common Stock (per 1.8 shares)	Asarco Common Stock (per share)
1963	$ .60	$1.01
1964	.66	1.58
1965	.84	2.10
1966	.84	2.48
1967	.84	2.25
1968	.99	2.63
Present Annual Rate	1.44	3.80

3 **You lose in terms of per share earnings.** For the three years, 1965 through 1967, your stake in Asarco's net earnings averaged $5.15 per share. Your stake in the earnings of the combined company would have been only $3.47 per share, assuming full conversion.

4 **You lose direct participation in Asarco's growth.** Your Asarco shares represent an investment in one of the world's great non-ferrous metal companies, with reserves of scarce mineral resources having an enormous potential. Kuhn, Loeb & Co., in its report to the Board states: "The value of the security proposed (by Pennzoil) in exchange does not, in our opinion, give adequate recognition to the earnings potential inherent in the common stock of Asarco." A total of $83 million was spent by Asarco in 1966 and 1967 to expand production facilities. In addition, Southern Peru Copper Corporation (51.5% owned by Asarco) has announced plans to bring its great Cuajone copper deposit into production at an estimated cost of $335 million. This would double the copper production of Southern Peru Copper. Further, the Granduc copper mine in British Columbia, in which Asarco has a 50% interest, is scheduled to begin production late this year at the rate of 45,000 tons per year.

5 **You lose in terms of net asset value.** Asarco's common stock had a book value of $40.04 per share on September 30, 1968. By comparison, the 1.8 shares of Pennzoil common stock you would receive on conversion of one share of the new Pennzoil stock would have had a book value of only $29.47 assuming full conversion. In addition, if Asarco's book value is adjusted to include investments in securities listed on the New York Stock Exchange at their quoted market value, net assets would increase $241.9 million or $16.63 per Asarco share. The foregoing does not reflect fully the actual market value of Asarco's interest in three great foreign mining companies—Southern Peru Copper Corporation, Mount Isa Mines Limited and Asarco Mexicana, S.A.

6 **You accept an enormous debt.** Pennzoil has an extremely heavy debt burden amounting to more than $509 million on September 30, 1968, and in October 1968 borrowed an additional $75 million through the sale of 7⅜% debentures due 1988. On the other hand, Asarco has long-term indebtedness of only $35 million. As of September 30, 1968, Pennzoil had a *net working capital deficit* of $25 million; by contrast Asarco had net working capital of $195 million. Pennzoil is obviously trying to capture Asarco's high credit standing and borrowing capacity, in order to support its huge debt.

7 **You may incur burdensome taxes.** On any reasonable assumptions, the Pennzoil exchange offer will not be tax-free. You should consider the possible income taxes you may have to pay if you accept the Pennzoil offer, as well as your loss in earnings and dividends and the effect on the rate of return on your investment.

8 **You run the risk of possible loss if Pennzoil's takeover is held to violate the antitrust laws.** Asarco has been advised by counsel that the acquisition of the Company by Pennzoil would violate the antitrust laws. Both companies are important producers of copper, a highly concentrated industry. A lawsuit has been brought by Asarco in Delaware to enjoin the Pennzoil offer and a decision on Asarco's application for preliminary relief is expected shortly. Further, the Department of Justice has requested of Pennzoil information relative to its exchange offer, and in its final prospectus, Pennzoil acknowledges that "The matter remains under review by that Department."

9 **Brokers are being paid by Pennzoil to advise you to give up your stock.** Pennzoil has agreed to pay fees which may total $19 million to dealers and brokers soliciting your acceptance of Pennzoil's offer. You should also keep in mind that it is to the financial advantage of brokers and dealers to urge you to accept the Pennzoil offer by delivering your shares through them.

You should take the time to study Pennzoil's offer most cautiously. There is no need for hasty action. If you accept the tender offer now and send in your stock to Pennzoil, you are on a one-way street. You cannot change your mind, regardless of developments. On the other hand, Pennzoil retains many options to revoke its offer.

If you have any questions, please feel free to write to me.

Sincerely,

E. McL. Tittmann
Chairman of the Board

The members of the Asarco Board of Directors are E. McL. TITTMANN, Chairman of the Board; R. D. BRADFORD, President; CHARLES F. BARBER, Executive Vice President; GEORGE CHAMPION, Chairman of the Chase Manhattan Bank N.A.; RICHARD G. CROFT, Retired Formerly Chairman of the Board of Great Northern Paper Company; CRIS DOBBINS, Chairman and President of Ideal Basic Industries, Inc.; FORREST G. HAMRICK, Vice President and Treasurer; R. L. HENNEBACH, Executive Vice President; JOHN M. KINGSLEY, President of Bessemer Securities Corporation; ROBERT S. MACFARLANE, Chairman of the Board of Northern Pacific Railway Company; J. D. MacKENZIE, Retired Formerly Chairman of the Board and President of the Company; R. F. McNEILL, JR., Chairman of the Board of Manufacturers Hanover Trust Company; C. E. NELSON, Vice President; DALE E. SHARP, Retired Formerly Vice Chairman of the Board of Morgan Guaranty Trust Company of New York; HANS STAUFFER, Chairman of the Finance Committee of Stauffer Chemical Company; SIMON D. STRAUSS, Vice President; R. WORTH VAUGHAN, Vice President and General Counsel.

AMERICAN SMELTING AND REFINING COMPANY
120 BROADWAY, NEW YORK, N.Y. 10005

Figure 12-1. Communications to stockholders in regard to tender offers for their stock must stress their interests. This ad incisively marshals the reasons the stockholder should reject the offer. Asarco defeated the takeover bid.

to informed investing and to take reasonable steps to ensure that all who invest in its securities enjoy equal access to such information. In applying this fundamental principle, the Exchange has adopted the following six specific policies concerning disclosure, each of which is discussed in fuller detail.

(1) Immediate Public Disclosure of Material Information

A listed company is required to make immediate public disclosure of all material information concerning its affairs, except in exceptional circumstances. When such disclosure is to be made during trading hours, it is essential that the company's listing representative be notified prior to the announcement.

(2) Thorough Public Dissemination

A listed company is required to release material information to the public in a manner designed to obtain its fullest possible public dissemination.

(3) Clarification or Confirmation of Rumors and Reports

Whenever a listed company becomes aware of a rumor or report, true or false, that contains information that is likely to have, or has had, an effect on the trading in the company's securities or would be likely to have a bearing on investment decisions, the company is required to publicly clarify the rumor or report as promptly as possible.

(4) Response to Unusual Market Action

Whenever unusual market action takes place in a listed company's securities, the company is expected to make inquiry to determine whether rumors or other conditions requiring corrective action exist, and, if so, to take whatever action is appropriate. If, after the company's review, the unusual market action remains unexplained, it may be appropriate for the company to announce that there has been no material development in its business and affairs not previously disclosed nor, to its knowledge, any other reason to account for the unusual market action.

(5) Unwarranted Promotional Disclosure

A listed company should refrain from promotional disclosure activity which exceeds that necessary to enable the public to make informed investment decisions. Such activity includes inappropriately worded news releases, public announcements not justified by actual developments in a company's affairs, exaggerated reports or predictions, flamboyant wording and other forms of over-stated or over-zealous disclosure activity which may mislead investors and cause unwarranted price movements and activity in a company's securities.

(6) Insider Trading

Insiders should not trade on the basis of material information which is not known to the investing public. Moreover, insiders should refrain from trading, even after material information has been released to the press and other media, for a period sufficient to permit thorough public dissemination and evaluation of the information.

Explanation of Exchange Disclosure Policies

Policy on Immediate Public Disclosure of Material Information

Immediate disclosure should be made of information about a company's affairs or about events or conditions in the market for the company's securities which meets either of the following standards:

> (a) where the information is likely to have a significant effect on the price of any of the company's securities; or
> (b) where such information (after any necessary interpretation by securities analysts or other experts) is likely to be considered important by a reasonable investor, in determining his choice of action.

Any material information of a factual nature that bears on the value of a company's securities or on decisions as to whether or not to invest or trade in such securities should be disclosed. Included is information, known to the company, concerning the company's property, business, financial condition and prospects; mergers and acquisitions; and dealings with employees, suppliers, customers and others; as well as information concerning a significant change in ownership of the company's securities owned by insiders or representing control of the company.

The Exchange does not normally consider disclosure of a company's internal estimates or projections of its earnings or of other data relating to its affairs to be necessary. If such estimates or projections are released, they should be prepared carefully, with a reasonable factual basis, and should be stated realistically, with appropriate qualifications. Moreover, if such estimates or projections subsequently appear to have been mistaken, they should be promptly and publicly corrected.

The price of a company's securities, as well as a reasonable investor's decision whether to buy or sell those securities, may be affected as much by factors directly concerning the market for the securities as by factors concerning the company's business. Factors directly concerning the market for a company's securities may include such matters as the acquisition or disposal by a company of a significant amount of its own securities, an event affecting the present or potential dilution of the rights or interests of a company's securities, or events materially affecting the size of the "public float" of its securities.

While, as is noted above, a company is expected to make appropriate disclosure about significant changes in insider ownership of its securities, the company should not indiscriminately disclose publicly any knowledge it has of the trading activities of outsiders, such as trading by mutual funds or other institutions, for such outsiders normally have a legitimate interest in preserving the confidentiality of their securities transactions.

The following events, while not comprising a complete list of all the situations which may require disclosure, are particularly likely to require prompt announcements:

(a) a joint venture, merger or acquisition;
(b) the declaration or omission of dividends or the determination of earnings;
(c) a stock split or stock dividend;
(d) the acquisition or loss of a significant contract;
(e) a significant new product or discovery;
(f) a change in control or a significant change in management;
(g) a call of securities for redemption;
(h) the borrowing of a significant amount of funds;
(i) the public or private sale of a significant amount of additional securities;
(j) significant litigation;
(k) the purchase or sale of a significant asset;
(l) a significant change in capital investment plans;
(m) a significant labor dispute or disputes with sub-contractors or suppliers;
(n) an event requiring the filing of a current report under the Securities Exchange Act;
(o) establishment of a program to make purchases of the company's own shares; and
(p) a tender offer for another company's securities.

Occasionally circumstances arise in which—provided that complete confidentiality is maintained—a company may temporarily refrain from publicly disclosing material information. The following circumstances where disclosure can be withheld are limited and constitute an infrequent exception to the normal requirement of immediate public disclosure. Thus, in cases of doubt, the presumption must always be in favor of disclosure.

(i) When immediate disclosure would prejudice the ability of the company to pursue its corporate objectives.

Although public disclosure is generally necessary to protect the interests of investors, circumstances may occasionally arise where disclosure would prejudice a corporation's ability to achieve a valid corporate objective. Public disclosure of a plan to acquire certain real estate, for example, could result in an increase in the company's cost of the desired acquisition or could prevent the company from carrying out the plan at all. In such circumstances, if the unfavorable result to the corporation outweighs the undesirable consequences of non-disclosure, disclosure may properly be deferred to a more appropriate time.

(ii) When the facts are in a state of flux and a more appropriate moment for disclosure is imminent.

Occasionally corporate developments give rise to information which, although material, is subject to rapid change. If the situation is about to stabilize or resolve itself in the near future, it may be proper to withhold public announcement until a firm announcement may be made, since successive public announcements concerning the same subject but based on changing facts may confuse or mislead the public rather than enlighten it.

In the course of a successful negotiation for the acquisition of another company, for example, the only information known to each party at the outset may be the willingness of the other to hold discussions. Shortly thereafter it may become apparent to the parties that it is likely an agreement can be reached. Finally, agreement in principle may be reached on specific terms. In such circumstances a company need not issue a public announcement at each stage of the negotiations, describing the current state of constantly changing facts, but may await agreement in principle on specific terms. If, on the other hand, progress in the negotiations should stabilize at some other point, disclosure should then be made if the information is material.

Federal securities laws may restrict the extent of permissible disclosure before or during a public offering of securities or a solicitation of proxies. In such circumstances, a company should discuss the disclosure of material information in advance with the Exchange and the Securities and Exchange Commission. It is the Exchange's experience that the requirements of both the securities laws and regulations and the Exchange's disclosure policy can be met even in those instances where their thrust appears to be different.

If rumors concerning material information should develop, immediate public disclosure becomes necessary.

Immediate public disclosure of the information in question must be effected if the company should learn that insider trading has taken or is taking place. In unusual cases, where the trading is insignificant and did not have any influence on the market and measures sufficient to halt the insider trading and prevent its recurrence are taken, exceptions might be made which should be discussed with the Exchange. The company's Exchange listing representative can provide current information regarding market activity in the company's securities with which to help assess the significance of such trading.

Whenever material information is being temporarily withheld, the strictest confidentiality must be maintained, and the company should be prepared to make an immediate public announcement if necessary. During this period, the market action of the company's securities should be closely watched, since unusual market activity frequently signifies that a "leak" may have occurred.

Information that is to be kept confidential should be confined, to the extent possible, to the highest possible echelons of management and should be disclosed to officers, employees, and others on a need-to-know basis only. Distribution of paperwork and other data should be held to a minimum. When the information must be disclosed more broadly to company personnel or others, their attention should be drawn to its confidential nature and to the restrictions that apply to its use, including the prohibition of insider trading.

It may be appropriate to require each person who gains access to confidential information to report any transaction which he effects in the company's securities to the company. If counsel, accountants, or financial or public relations advisers or other outsiders are consulted steps should be taken to ensure that they maintain similar precautions within their respective organizations to maintain confidentiality.

In general, it is recommended that a listed company remind its employees on a regular basis of its policies on confidentiality.

Policy on Thorough Public Dissemination

The steps required are as follows:

(1) Prior to Public Disclosure

Disclosure of material information can often be made after the market closes. Otherwise, when it is necessary to make disclosure of material information before or during trading hours, the Exchange expects a company to notify its listing representative in advance of such disclosure if the material is of a non-routine nature or is expected to have a substantial impact on the market for the securities of the company. The Exchange, with the benefit of all the facts provided by the company, will be able to consider whether a temporary halt in trading, pending an announcement, would be desirable. Such a temporary halt in trading is not a reflection on the company or its securities, but provides an opportunity for disseminating and evaluating the information released. Such a step frequently helps avoid rumors and market instability, as well as the unfairness to investors that may arise when material information has reached part but not yet all of the investing community.

(2) At Time of Public Disclosure

As a minimum, any public disclosure of material information should be made by an announcement released simultaneously to (A) the national business and financial news-wire services (the Dow Jones news service and Reuters Economic Services), (B) the national news-wire services (Associated Press and United Press International), (C) The New York Times and The Wall Street Journal, and (D) Moody's Investors Service and Standard & Poor's Corporation.[2] The New York telephone numbers and addresses of these media are as follows:

Name	Address	Telephone Number
Dow Jones & Company, Inc.	22 Cortlandt Street New York, N.Y.	(212) 285-5000
Reuters Economic Services	1212 Ave. of Americas New York, N.Y.	(212) 262-4000

[2] Editor's note: Companies whose stocks are not listed on New York exchanges and/or are regional in ownership should make certain the comparable media in their areas are given similar attention. Addresses of some major public relations newswires outside New York are given in Chapter 40.

Associated Press	50 Rockefeller Plaza New York, N.Y.	(212) PL7-1111, Ext. 291; after 6:30 p.m., Ext. 231
United Press International	220 E. 42nd St. New York, N.Y.	(212) MU2-0400, ask for Financial Desk
The New York Times	229 W. 43rd St. New York, N.Y.	(212) 556-1234
The Wall Street Journal	22 Cortlandt Street New York, N.Y.	(212) 285-5000
Standard & Poor's Corporation	345 Hudson St. New York, N.Y.	(212) 924-6400
Moody's Investors Service, Inc.	99 Church St. New York, N.Y.	(212) 267-8800

Two concerns that distribute press releases over private teletype networks are PR Newswire, 150 E. 58th St. New York, N.Y. (212) TE 2-9400; and PR Wire Service, 660 First Ave., New York, N.Y. (212) OR 9-8998.

Companies may also wish to broaden their distribution to other news or broadcast media, such as those in the location of the company's plants or offices, and to trade publications. The information in question should always be given to the media in such a way as to promote publication by them as promptly as possible, i.e. by telephone, or in writing by hand delivery, in both cases on an "immediate release" basis. Companies are cautioned that some of these media may refuse to publish information given by telephone until it has been confirmed in writing or may require written confirmation after its publication.

Whenever difficulty is encountered or anticipated in having an announcement about a material development published by these media, a company should contact its listing representative, who may frequently be able to provide assistance. If finally, despite all reasonable efforts, the announcement has not been published by at least (A) one of the national newswire services or one of the above-mentioned newspapers or (B) Moody's or Standard & Poor's, the company should attempt to have the announcement disseminated through other media, such as trade, industry or business publications, local newspapers (especially those in the area where the company's principal offices or plants are located or where its stockholders are concentrated), or, in cases where the announcement is of particular importance or where unusual difficulty in dissemination is encountered, by means of paid advertisements, a letter to stockholders, or both.

Six copies of all public announcements should be sent to the Securities Division of the Exchange.

The Exchange recommends that companies observe an "open door" policy in dealing with analysts, journalists, stockholders and others. However, under no circumstances should disclosure of material corporate developments be made on an individual or selective basis to analysts, stockholders or other persons unless such information has previously been fully disclosed and disseminated to the public. In the event that material information is inadvertently disclosed on the occasion of any meetings with analysts or others, it must be publicly disseminated as promptly as possible by the means described above.

The Exchange also believes that even any appearance of preference or partiality in the release or explanation of information should be avoided. Thus, at meetings with analysts or other special groups, where the procedure of the group sponsoring the meeting permits, representatives of the news-wire services, the press, and other media should be permitted to attend.

Policy on Clarification or Confirmation of Rumors and Reports

The public circulation by any means, whether by an article published in a newspaper, by a broker's market letter, or by word-of-mouth, of information, either correct or false, which has not been substantiated by the company and which is likely to have, or has had, an effect on the price of the company's securities or would be likely to have a bearing on investment decisions must be clarified or confirmed.

If a false rumor or report is circulated among only a small number of persons and has not affected and is not likely to affect the market for the company's securities, public circulation would not be deemed to have taken place and clarification would not be necessary. However, as pointed out earlier, if the rumor or report concerns material information which is correct and has not been disclosed by the company and thoroughly disseminated, clarification and confirmation is necessary regardless of the extent of the public circulation of the rumor or report.

In the case of a material rumor or report containing erroneous information which has been circulated, the company should prepare an announcement denying the rumor or report and setting forth facts sufficient to clarify any misleading aspects of the rumor. In the case of a material rumor or report containing information that is correct, an announcement setting forth the facts should be prepared for public release. In both cases, the announcement should then be publicly disseminated in accordance with the guidelines discussed above. In addition, in the case of a false rumor or report, a reasonable effort should be made to bring the announcement to the attention of the particular group that initially distributed it (in the case of an erroneous newspaper article, for example, by sending a copy of the announcement to the newspaper's financial editor, or in the case of an erroneous market letter by sending a copy to the broker responsible for the letter).

In the case of a rumor or report predicting future sales, earnings or other data, no response from the company is ordinarily required. However, if such a report is manifestly based on erroneous information, or is wrongly attributed to a company source, the company should respond promptly to the supposedly factual elements of the rumor or report in the same manner as to other false rumors and reports of a supposedly factual nature. Moreover, if a rumor or report contains a prediction that is clearly erroneous, the company should issue an announcement to the effect that the company itself has made no such prediction and currently knows of no facts that would justify making such prediction.

Policy on Response to Unusual Market Action

Where unusual market action, in price movement, trading activity, or both, occurs without any apparent publicly available information which would account for the action, it may signify trading by persons who are acting either on unannounced material information or on a rumor or report, whether true or false, about the company. Most often, of course, unusual market activity may not be traceable either to insider trading or to a rumor or report. Nevertheless, the market action itself may be misleading to investors, who are likely to assume that a sudden and appreciable change in the price of a company's stock must reflect a parallel change in its business or prospects. Similarly, unusual trading volume, even when not accompanied by a significant change in price, tends to encourage rumors and give rise to excessive speculative trading activity which may be unrelated to actual developments in the company's affairs.

The company should attempt to determine the reason for the market action, by considering in particular (a) whether any information about its affairs which would account for the action has recently been publicly disclosed, (b) whether there is any information of this type that has not been publicly disclosed (in which case the unusual market action may signify that a "leak" has occurred), and (c) whether the company is the subject of a rumor or report.

If the company determines that the market action results from material information that has already been publicly disseminated, generally no further announcement is required, although, if the market action indicates that such information may have been misinterpreted, it may be helpful, after discussion with the Exchange, to issue a clarifying announcement.

If market action results from the "leak" of previously undisclosed information, the information in question must promptly be publicly disseminated. If the market action results from a false rumor or report, the Exchange policy on correction of such rumors and reports should be complied with. Finally, if the company is unable to determine the cause of the market action, the Exchange may suggest that the company make a public announcement to the effect that there have been no undisclosed recent developments affecting the company or its affairs which would account for the unusual market activity.

Policy on Unwarranted Promotional Disclosure

"Disclosure" activity beyond that necessary to inform investors and explicable essentially as an attempt to influence securities prices is considered to be unwarranted and promotional. Although the distinction between legitimate public relations activities and such promotional activity is one that must necessarily be drawn from the facts of a particular case, the following are frequent earmarks of promotional activity:

(1) A series of public announcements unrelated in volume or frequency to the materiality of actual developments in a company's business and affairs.
(2) Premature announcement of products still in the development stage with unproven commercial prospects.
(3) Promotions and expense-paid trips, or the seeking out of meetings or interviews with

analysts and financial writers, which could have the effect of unduly influencing the market activity in the company's securities and are not justified in frequency or scope by the need to disseminate information about actual developments in the company's business and affairs.

(4) Press releases or other public announcements of a one-sided or unbalanced nature.

(5) Company or product advertisements which in effect promote the company's securities.

Policy on Insider Trading

All persons who come into possession of material inside information, before its public release, are considered insiders for the purposes of the Exchange's disclosure policies. Such persons include control stockholders, directors, officers and employees, and frequently also include outside attorneys, accountants, investment bankers, public relations advisers, advertising agencies, consultants, and other independent contractors. The husbands, wives, immediate families, and those under the control of insiders may also be regarded as insiders. Where acquisition or other negotiations are concerned, the above relationships apply to the other parties to the negotiations as well. Finally, for purposes of the Exchange's disclosure policy, insiders include "tippees" who come into possession of material inside information.

The company itself is an insider and, while in possession of material inside information, is prohibited from buying its securities from, or selling such securities to, the public in the same manner as other insiders.

"Inside information" is that which has not been publicly released and which is intended for use solely for a corporate purpose and not for any personal use and which the company withholds.

"Insider trading" refers not only to the purchase or sale of a company's securities, but also to the purchase or sale of puts, calls, or other options with respect to such securities. Such trading is deemed to be done by an insider whenever he has any beneficial interest, direct or indirect, in such securities or options, regardless of whether they are actually held in his name.

Included in the concept of "insider trading" is "tipping," or revealing inside information to outside individuals to enable such individuals to trade in the company's securities on the basis of undisclosed information.

How soon after the release of material information insiders may begin to trade depends both on how thoroughly and how quickly after its release the information is published by the news-wire services and the press. In addition, following dissemination of the information, insiders should refrain from trading until the public has had an opportunity to evaluate it thoroughly. Where the effect of the information on investment decisions is readily understandable, as in the case of earnings, the required waiting period will be shorter than where the information must be interpreted before its bearing on investment decisions can be evaluated.

Content and Preparation of Public Announcements

(a) *Exchange Requirements.* The content of a press release or other public announcement is as important as its timing. Each announcement should:

(1) Be factual, clear and succinct.
(2) Contain sufficient quantitative information to allow investors to evaluate its relative importance to the activities of the company.
(3) Be balanced and fair. Thus, the announcement should avoid:
(a) Omission of important unfavorable facts, or the slighting of such facts (e.g., by "burying" them at the end of a press release.)
(b) Presentation of favorable possibilities as certain, or as more probable than is actually the case.
(c) Presentation of projections without sufficient qualifications or without sufficient factual basis.
(d) Negative statements phrased so as to create a positive implication. E.g., "The Company cannot now predict whether the development will have a materially favorable effect on its earnings," (creating the implication that the effect will be favorable even if not materially favorable), or "The Company expects that the development will not have a materially favorable effect on earnings in the immediate future," (creating the implication that the development will eventually have a materially favorable effect).
(e) Use of promotional jargon calculated to excite rather than to inform.
(4) Avoid over-technical language, and should be expressed to the extent possible in language comprehensible to the layman.
(5) Explain, if the consequences or effects of

the information on the company's future prospects cannot be assessed, why this is so.

(6) Clarify and point out any reasonable alternatives where the public announcement undertakes to interpret information disclosed.

(b) *Securities Laws Requirements.* The requirements of the Federal securities laws must also be carefully considered in the preparation of public announcements. In particular, these laws may impose special restrictions on the extent of permissible disclosure before or during a public offering of securities or a solicitation of proxies. Generally, in such circumstances, while the restrictions of the securities laws may affect the character of disclosure, they do not prohibit the timely disclosure of material factual information. Thus, it is normally possible to effect the disclosure required by Exchange policy.

Whenever a conflict arises, the company should discuss the matter with the Securities and Exchange Commission, as well as with the Exchange, which can frequently assist in evaluating the problem.

SEC DISCLOSURE REQUIREMENTS

In addition to stipulating how and what a publicly held company must disclose as news, the Securities and Exchange Commission has established other disclosure requirements. They involve three major classifications:

1. *Financial reports.* Each company has been required for a number of years to file an annual 10-K report that is a detailed and comprehensive document describing the business, its finances, and its operations. It now calls also for briefer quarterly reports—10-Q—and monthly updated reports—8K.

In addition, annual reports (see Chapter 11) must include:

- Information, including certified financial statements, on the company's last two years.
- A summary of the company's activities for the past five years, including an analysis by management of the period.
- A layman's description of the company's business.
- A five-year breakdown of the results of the various lines of the company's business.
- Information about directors and executive officers, including their principal occupations and places of employment.
- Identification of the principal market in which the company's securities are traded.
- The price range of the stock and dividends paid for the last two fiscal years.

2. *Reports of illegal matters.* The SEC calls actions such as payment of incentives to overseas officials, beyond clearly established and what it considers reasonable commissions, to be information that must be disclosed to the company's shareholders. Bribes to domestic officials or others, or other matters that may be outside the limits of the law such as political contributions by the corporation, are also considered material and therefore require reporting.

3. *Information pertinent to tender offers.* The SEC has moved to a more aggressive position regarding disclosure of information by both the offeror and the target company.

All of these areas are evolving and they are likely to be the subject of court actions and modifications on the basis of experience. It is necessary for anyone responsible for the financial communications of a publicly held company to keep up-to-date in this area.

REPORTING REQUIREMENTS

Prepared by Robert W. Taft, Senior Vice President, Hill & Knowlton, Inc.

REPORTING REQUIRED FOR:	SECURITIES AND EXCHANGE COMMISSION	NEW YORK STOCK EXCHANGE	AMERICAN STOCK EXCHANGE	GENERALLY RECOMMENDED PUBLICITY PRACTICE ALL COMPANIES
ACCOUNTING— CHANGE IN METHOD:	10-Q. Independent public accountant must file letter indicating whether he approves of "improved method of measuring business operations."	Prompt notification to Exchange required.	8-K if filed. Notify Exchange before change is made and disclose the impact in succeeding interim and annual report.	Statement of accounting policies is required in annual report. To be consistent with 10-K, new SEC requirements, give some publicity to accounting changes, be prepared to illustrate how alternative accounting methods would affect earnings. Also, effect of alternatives, where company's accounting method differs from that prevailing in its industry, and differences in tax and financial reporting.
ACCOUNTING CHANGE IN AUDITORS:	8-K; include information on disputes over past two years and whether opinions in last two years were adverse or qualified. Departing accountant files letter as exhibit commenting on company explanation. Disclose impact of any changes made by new firm. In proxy statement, give name of current accountant and of accountant previous year, if changed, along with details of disagreements. Note whether accountant will be available at annual meeting.	Prompt notice to Exchange. 8-K when filed. The NYSE recommends that the independent audit firm be represented at annual meeting to answer questions.	Same as NYSE.	Press release desirable at time of filing 8-K if differences are major. Consider discussion of change in annual or quarterly report to shareholders. Consider clear statement in annual report or elsewhere on when and how company rotates auditing firms.
AMENDMENT OF CHARTER OR BYLAWS:	10-Q if matter subject to stockholders' approval or if change materially modifies rights of holders of any class of registered securities.	Four copies of material sent to stockholders in respect to proposed changes. Appropriately certified copy of changes when effective.	10-Q must be filed with Exchange when effective with certified copy of (a) charter amendments; (b) directors' resolution as to charter or bylaws.	Recommend immediate publicity if change alters rights or interests of shareholders.
ANNUAL MEETING (OR SPECIAL) OF STOCKHOLDERS:	10-Q following meeting when security holders' vote required except as to procedural matters, selection of auditors or uncontested election of management nominees as listed in proxy statement.	Prompt notice of calling of meeting; publicity on material actions at meeting. Ten days advance notice of record date or closing transfer books to Exchange.	Same as NYSE.	Press release at time of meeting. Competitive pressures minimize publicity opportunity except on actively contested issues; recommend wide distribution of special post-meeting report.
ANNUAL REPORT: FORM 10-K	Required by Section 13 or 15(d) of Securities Exchange Act of 1934 on Form 10-K to be filed with SEC and exchanges where listed no later than 90 days after close of fiscal year. (Some schedules may be filed 120 days after.) Certain companies must submit four copies of printed annual report with 10-K.	No specific rules.	No specific rules.	Recommend that annual report to stockholders be consistent with Form 10-K.
ANNUAL REPORT TO SHAREHOLDERS: CONTENTS	Certified financial statements for the last two years. Explanation of any differences between the financial statements in the annual report and in statements filed with the SEC. Summary of operations for the last five years and accompanying management	Recommends that: quarterly results be summarized; material 10-K information on compensating balances and other material liquidity information; line-of-business reporting indicate allocation of interest and overhead charges to extent possible; material	Requirements treat financial statements.	Check printed annual report and appropriate news releases to insure they conform to information reported on Form 10-K.

Figure 12-2. Diagram of the reporting requirements of the various stock exchanges and the SEC, from "Corporate Reporting Requirements," by Robert W. Taft, *Public Relations Journal*, April 1977.

REPORTING REQUIREMENTS (continued)

REPORTING REQUIRED FOR:	SECURITIES AND EXCHANGE COMMISSION	NEW YORK STOCK EXCHANGE	AMERICAN STOCK EXCHANGE	GENERALLY RECOMMENDED PUBLICITY PRACTICE ALL COMPANIES
	analysis. Identification of directors' principal occupations. Stock market and dividend information for past two years. Notice of Form 10-K availability. Brief description of business and line-of-business breakout similar to 10-K. Summary of quarterly results in "unaudited footnote."	differences between book and taxable income be summarized; computation of earnings per share be clarified; information on transactions with affiliated parties disclosed, also on deferred charges and material provisions of unusual items; supplementary financial data be put in a Financial Review section.		
ANNUAL REPORT TO SHAREHOLDERS: DISTRIBUTION	Annual report to shareholders must precede or accompany delivery of proxy material. Seven copies to SEC with preliminary proxy material or when given holders, whichever is later.	Published and submitted to shareholders at least 15 days before annual meeting but no later than three months after close of fiscal year. PROMPTEST POSSIBLE ISSUANCE URGED. Three copies to Exchange. Recommended release of audited figures as soon as available.	Published and submitted to shareholders at least 10 days before meeting but no later than four months after close of fiscal year. PROMPTEST POSSIBLE ISSUANCE URGED. Ten copies to Exchange, Securities Division. Recommend release of audited figures as soon as available.	Financial information should be released as soon as available; second release at time printed report is issued if report contains other material information. NYSE and Amex urge broad distribution of report to include statistical services so company information is available for "ready public reference."
ARAB BOYCOTT: PARTICIPATION IN	Where participation has a material adverse effect on income, assets (including goodwill), or profits, disclosure of the relevant facts is "mandatory." SEC policy on this topic in transition.	No requirement.	No requirement.	Publicity to meet SEC requirements.
BANKRUPTCY OR RECEIVERSHIP:	8-K immediately after apointment of receiver. Identify proceeding, court, date of event, name of receiver and date of his appointment. Same requirement on Form 10-Q.	No requirements.	No requirements.	Recommend press release at time of filing 8-K. Purpose is to tell creditors how to secure claims, not to notify stockholders of a material development.
BUSINESS PURPOSE CHANGED:	8-K or 10-Q if registrant deems change of material importance to security holders (consult counsel).	Prompt notice of any material change in general character or nature of business. Public disclosure if securities values affected.	Same as NYSE.	Timely disclosure required where change may affect market valuation of stock.
CAPITAL SURPLUS: CHARGES AGAINST	SEC has dropped this requirement from its forms. Refers to disclosure framework set out in APB Nos. 28 and 30 and in Accounting Series Releases Nos. 159 and 177.	Prior notice of any proposed substantial charge by company or by directly controlled subsidiary. Stockholder approval may be required.	Same as NYSE.	Prompt disclosure normally required if sufficiently material to warrant filing Form 8-K. (See also "Extraordinary charge or credit.")
CONTRACTS: DEFENSE AND MAJOR LONG-TERM	Progress on contracts should be disclosed in such filings as 10-K, 10-Q and registrations. Should include earnings, losses, anticipated losses and material cost overruns.	No specific rules.	No specific rules.	SEC urges that annual reports include disclosure on contract progress as complete as Commission filings. News release should be issued when any material developments affecting contracts become known. (See also "Extraordinary charge or credit.")
CONVERSION RATE—CHANGES IN:	10-Q if material change.	Prompt publicity on any change in convertible security, or termination of conversion privilege when conversions have been occurring or appear imminent. Notice by mail to holders of record. Immediate notice to Exchange.	Same as NYSE.	Publicity should be timed to the event causing the change or termination of the conversion privilege. Immediate notice to statistical services.

Figure 12-2. (Continued)

REPORTING REQUIREMENTS (continued)

REPORTING REQUIRED FOR:	SECURITIES AND EXCHANGE COMMISSION	NEW YORK STOCK EXCHANGE	AMERICAN STOCK EXCHANGE	GENERALLY RECOMMENDED PUBLICITY PRACTICE ALL COMPANIES
DEFAULT UPON SENIOR SECURITIES:	10-Q if actual material default in principal, interest, sinking or purchase fund installment, arrearage in dividends for preferred, registered or ranking securities not cured within 30 days of any stated grace period and if indebtedness exceeds five percent of total assets. Note: SEC plans unilateral publicity for companies with qualified certifications or otherwise near bankruptcy.	IMMEDIATE publicity and notice to the Exchange.	IMMEDIATE publicity and notice to the Exchange.	Immediate disclosure at time of Board action or when Board fails to act.
DIRECTORS OR OFFICERS; CHANGE IN CONTROL:	8-K if change in control of corporation. Report who acquired from whom; terms; terms of any loans involved. New directors, officers, or other insiders must personally file Form 3.	PROMPT written notice to Exchange of any change. 8-K if filed. Immediate release, if material. Recommend minimum three outside directors on Board. Recommend Audit Committee for Board—members identified in annual report.	Same as NYSE.	Recommend immediate announcement of any change in directors, officers. However, no technical requirement for publicity except where control of company changes or key man is added or lost.
DISCLOSURE POLICY STATEMENT	Not technically required by any regulatory authority. However, recent cases involving insider information have turned on whether company had developed and implemented a written statement of policy on disclosure of material non-public corporate information. SEC now frequently requires submission of such statements as part of consent decree.			
DIVIDENDS:	Over-the-counter companies must provide advance notice of record date for subsequent dissemination to investors, extending comparable stock exchange requirements to OTC market. Failure to comply places issuer in violation of Section 10(b) of the Securities Exchange Act of 1934.	Prompt notice to Exchange and IMMEDIATE publicity. "Telephone alert" to Exchange when the action is unusual and during market hours. "Immediate" means even while directors' meeting is still in progress. Ten days advance notice of record date.	Same as NYSE. Notification to Exchange by telephone or telegram with confirmation by letter.	Prepare publicity in advance and release immediately by a designated officer on word of declaration. Publicity especially important when dividend rate changes. NYSE manual implies announcement of management intention prior to formal board action may be required in case of a "leak" or rumor.
EARNINGS:	Form 10-Q for each of first three fiscal quarters. Include: unaudited income statement for current quarter, same quarter of prior year, year-to-date data for two years; balance sheet for end of latest and year ago quarters; source and application of funds for year-to-date for two years; management analysis of changes between current and prior quarter, quarter a year ago, and comparison of two years to date. Summary of quarterly results for two years in "unaudited" annual report footnote.	Quarterly. Publicity required. Shareholder mailing recommended. No set time limit but four to five weeks after close of period considered usual. NYSE urges breakout of fourth quarter results for AP and UPI P/E ratio computation. See White Paper.	Quarterly. Should be published within 45 days after end of fiscal quarter. Quarterly breakout "urged" on 3/12/73.	Immediate publicity; do not hold data until printed quarterly report is published and mailed. Release no later than 10-Q filing. Information in news release must be consistent with 10-Q. Breakout of current quarter results together with year-to-date totals desirable in 2nd, 3rd, and 4th quarter releases.
EARNINGS: FORECAST OR ESTIMATE	SEC at present "takes no position" on whether or how a company should forecast. However, SEC informally permits forecasts in filings and elsewhere when systematically developed if assumptions are stated. SEC says it is encouraging experimentation.	No specific rules.	No specific rules.	Forecasts should be either avoided altogether or widely circulated with all assumptions stated. Forecasts by others may require correction by company if wrong but widely believed.

Figure 12-2. (Continued)

REPORTING REQUIREMENTS (continued)

REPORTING REQUIRED FOR:	SECURITIES AND EXCHANGE COMMISSION	NEW YORK STOCK EXCHANGE	AMERICAN STOCK EXCHANGE	GENERALLY RECOMMENDED PUBLICITY PRACTICE ALL COMPANIES
EMPLOYEE STOCK PURCHASE AND SAVING PLANS:	Form 11-K may be required under 15(d) of '34 Act. Form S-8 may also be required.	No specific rules.	No specific rules.	Generally no publicity required or recommended.
ENERGY CRISIS:	Disclose possible impact of fuel shortages if material; also fuel cost increases.	No specific rules.	No specific rules.	Watch out for material disclosures on energy matters in speeches, interviews, other unexpected sources. Distribute in same channels as traditional material information.
ENVIRONMENTAL MATTERS:	Where material, appropriate disclosure in Forms 10, 10-K, and 10-Q under sections pertaining to description of company's business and legal proceedings. Any environmental proceeding of any size by governmental authorities is deemed material and must be reported on 10-Q. Environmental suits by others where damages claimed exceed 10% of current assets must be reported on 10-Q.	No specific provision.	No specific provision.	Immediate public disclosure, where material, or required to be reported. Subject matter may include impact that compliance with various laws would have on company's expenses, earnings, and competitive position.
EXTRAORDINARY CHARGE OR CREDIT:	See comment on "Capital Surplus, charge against" above. SEC expects discussion of nature of and reason for charge in "Management Discussion and Analysis."	White Paper recommends disclosure relative to material provisions for future losses, discontinued operations, foreign operations, future costs. Include detail on amounts reserved, subsequently used and remaining available at year-end.	No specific requirement.	Generally material. Requires immediate disclosure. Press release should precede SEC filings.
FLOAT: INCREASE OR DECREASE IN	10-Q if changed more than 5 percent of previously outstanding amount by issuance or purchase of securities or payment of indebtedness. Include this information in 10-K. If company tenders for own shares, Form 13-D must be filed.	Prompt notice when occasioned by actual or proposed deposit under voting trust agreements, etc. and brought to "official attention" of officers or directors. The NYSE requires prompt announcement of a program to purchase the company's own shares.	Prompt announcement upon establishing program to acquire the company's own shares.	Company statement on its intention to purchase stock in open market. Ads and releases where company tenders for own shares must conform with SEC filings. Publicity if change in control is involved or there is a sharp decrease in floating supply that could affect the market in the company's securities.
FOREIGN CURRENCY TRANSLATION:	No SEC requirements. FASB 8 requires report of foreign currency translation gains or losses as they occur (quarterly).	No requirements.	No requirements.	Companies are still publicly critical of this requirement and its impact on quarterly results. Recommend clear discussion of effect of translation gains or losses in quarterly earning release where applicable.
FORM, NATURE, RIGHTS, OR PRIVILEGES OF LISTED SECURITIES CHANGED:	10-Q if constituent instruments defining rights of shareholders have been materially modified or if rights are otherwise limited—including restrictions on working capital or dividend payments.	At least 20 days prior notice of change in form, nature or right of securities or certificates.	Same as NYSE.	Timely disclosure of all relevant information as soon as "outsiders" are involved in planning discussions.

Figure 12-2. (Continued)

REPORTING REQUIREMENTS (continued)

REPORTING REQUIRED FOR:	SECURITIES AND EXCHANGE COMMISSION	NEW YORK STOCK EXCHANGE	AMERICAN STOCK EXCHANGE	GENERALLY RECOMMENDED PUBLICITY PRACTICE ALL COMPANIES
LEGAL PROCEEDINGS: (SEE ALSO "ENVIRONMENTAL MATTERS.")	10-Q at start and termination of material proceedings (generally damage claims in excess of 10% of current assets); also any bankruptcy or receivership proceeding involving any part of company; also any suit against company by an officer, director, or major stockholder. Consider filing 8-K if suit is of major importance.	10-Q sufficient unless proceeding bears on ownership, dividends, interest, or principal of listed securities, or start of receivership, bankruptcy, reorganization proceedings.	Public disclosure if material. Prompt notice to Exchange.	Public disclosure recommended if outcome of legal proceeding could have material effect on company, and news of proceeding has not already become public. Company may be required to include plaintiff statement on some types of class action suits in company annual report.
LISTING: INITIALLY OR ON ANOTHER EXCHANGE	Involved and extensive legal work is required.	See listing requirements. Dual listing now permitted.	See listing requirements. Dual listing now permitted.	Bulk of routine publicity handled by exchanges. Discuss other special opportunities with legal and public relations counsel.
MERGER; ACQUISITION OR DISPOSITION OF ASSETS:	8-K, if company or majority-owned subsidiary acquires or disposes of a significant (10 percent of total assets) amount of assets or business other than in course of business or if registrant issues more than 5 percent of additional securities. Proxy soliciting material or registration statement may also be required. Check application of Rule 145(b) to any such transaction involving exchange of stock.	8-K if filed. Immediate public disclosure. Notice to Exchange.	Same as NYSE.	Current NYSE policy requires immediate announcement as soon as confidential disclosures relating to such important matters are made to "outsiders" (i.e., other than "top management" and "their individual confidential advisors"). Immediate publicity, especially when assets consist of an entire product line, division, operating unit, or a substantial part of the business.
OPTIONS GRANTED TO PURCHASE SECURITIES:	Include options granted and exercised in 10-K.	Before issuing options, unissued securities must be authorized for trading on Exchange. Stockholders' authorization is required. Summarize information on options in annual report.	Same as NYSE.	Generally no publicity.
PROSPECTUS:	Filed as part of registration statement. Copies distributed to underwriters and dealers in securities offering, and in turn to investors. Photos of management, products, maps, other visuals now permitted. Disclosure in registration statements significantly expanded in 1973.	Seven copies of final prospectus to Exchange. May be used as part of listing application if issued within past 30 days.	Copy of complete registration filing to Exchange. Recent prospectus may be used as part of listing application.	News release, if issued at time of registration, must state from whom prospectus may be obtained. It is not clear whether prospectus can accompany release at time of filing. See SEC Rule 134 for permitted content of release.
PROXY MATERIAL:	Five preliminary copies of proxy form and statement at least 10 days prior to shareholder mailing. Eight finals when sent to holders, plus three to each exchange where listed. Five preliminary copies of all soliciting material two days prior to mailing; eight finals, when mailed. Note: New rules on handling shareholder proposals adopted July '76.	Immediate newspaper publicity on controversial issues, especially when there is a contest. Four copies of definitive proxy material to Exchange. Ask for advance review in major matters.	Same as NYSE. Ten copies of all material sent to shareholders to Exchange when mailed.	Normally publicity not needed on routine matters. Press release at time proxy is mailed becoming more common. Special rules apply in contests; use caution. Corporate Responsibility Issues: no requirement to identify shareholder proposals by press release prior to meeting.

Figure 12-2. (Continued)

REPORTING REQUIREMENTS (continued)

REPORTING REQUIRED FOR:	SECURITIES AND EXCHANGE COMMISSION	NEW YORK STOCK EXCHANGE	AMERICAN STOCK EXCHANGE	GENERALLY RECOMMENDED PUBLICITY PRACTICE ALL COMPANIES
QUESTIONABLE OR ILLEGAL PAYMENTS (BRIBES):	"Voluntary" program requires filing under miscellaneous Item of Form 8-K. Guidelines for content published by SEC in May '76. Current proposals would make any management involvement directly known to shareholders.	No requirement.	No requirement.	Recommend press release conform to 8-K at time 8-K is filed. However, no technical requirement for publicity. Recommend adoption of company policy statement on ethical business practices.
REDEMPTION, CANCELLATION, RETIREMENT OF LISTED SECURITIES:	10-Q.	Immediate press publicity. Prompt notice to Exchange of any corporate or other action affecting securities in whole or part.	Fifteen-day advance notice to Exchange. Prompt notice of corporate action that will result in any of these.	Usually advertisement is required. Written notice to security holders.
REPLACEMENT COSTS (IMPACT OF INFLATION) ("CURRENT VALUE"):	Required as "unaudited" footnote in 1976 annual reports for first time, to explain impact of inflation on company's business. Quantitative data required in F 10-K but general discussion sufficient for annual report.	No requirement.	No requirement.	Publicity generally not necessary.
RIGHTS TO SUBSCRIBE:	Registration under the Securities Act of 1933. Prefiling notice covered by SEC Rule 135. Notice to NASD or exchanges 10 days before record date required under Securities Exchange Act anti-fraud provisions.	See regulations. Preliminary discussion necessary—immediate publicity. Important to work out time schedule with Exchange before any action taken. Notice to Shareholders not less than 10 days in advance of the proposed record date.	Same as NYSE.	Immediate publicity and mailing to stockholders to give all adequate time "to record their interest and to exercise their rights," according to NYSE.
SALE OF UNREGISTERED SECURITIES:	File EDP attachment with 10-Q for amounts over $100,000. Form S-8 may be required for employee stock purchase plans.	No specific rules.	No specific rules.	No publicity.
SEGMENTED REPORTING (LINE OF BUSINESS REPORTING):	10-K requires sales and pre-tax operating income for separate lines of business (amounting to 10% or more of total). Wide discretion still permitted. Starting with 1977 annual reports, FASB requires slightly expanded reporting, especially of foreign operations.	No requirement. However "recommended" by White Paper for inclusion in annual reports.	No requirement.	May be material and require immediate disclosure if there are widely disproportionate and unexpected differences in income from various operations relative to their sales.
STOCK SPLIT, STOCK DIVIDEND, OR OTHER CHANGE IN CAPITALIZATION:	10-Q required for increase or decrease if exceeds five percent of amount of securities of the class previously outstanding. IMPORTANT: Check with legal counsel. Notice to NASD or exchanges 10 days before record date under Securities Exchange Act anti-fraud provisions.	Immediate public disclosure and Exchange notification. Issuance of new shares requires prior listing approval. "Telephone Alert" procedure should be followed.	Same as NYSE.	Immediate publicity as soon as proposal becomes known to "outsiders" whether formally voted on or not.

Figure 12-2. (Continued)

REPORTING REQUIREMENTS (continued)

REPORTING REQUIRED FOR:	SECURITIES AND EXCHANGE COMMISSION	NEW YORK STOCK EXCHANGE	AMERICAN STOCK EXCHANGE	GENERALLY RECOMMENDED PUBLICITY PRACTICE ALL COMPANIES
TENDER OFFER:	Conduct and published remarks of all parties governed by Sections 13(d), 13(e) and 14(d) of the '34 Act and related forms.	Consult Exchange Stock List Department in advance. Immediate publicity and notice to Exchange.	Consult Exchange Securities Division in advance. Immediate publicity and notice to Exchange.	Massive publicity effort required; should not be attempted without thorough familiarity with current rules and constant consultation with counsel. Neither raider nor target should comment publicly until necessary SEC filings have been made.
TREASURY STOCK— INCREASE OR DECREASE:	Check Form 10-Q, Items 5 and 6 for possible application. Note: special rules apply during tender battle.	Notice within 10 days after close of fiscal quarter in which any transaction takes place. Prompt notice of any open market purchase above prevailing market price.	Same as NYSE. Recommend consulting Exchange on purchases above market price.	Normally no immediate publicity. Reason for action is normally given in annual or quarterly publications before or after event. However, see remarks under "Float," where applicable.
WITHDRAWAL OR SUBSTITUTION OF ASSETS SECURING REGISTERED SECURITIES.	10-Q unless made pursuant to terms of an indenture qualified under Trust Indenture Act of 1939.	Immediate notice to Exchange.	Immediate notice to Exchange. Timely disclosure if materially significant for investors.	Depends on terms of indenture.

Figure 12-2. (Continued)

13

Industry Relations

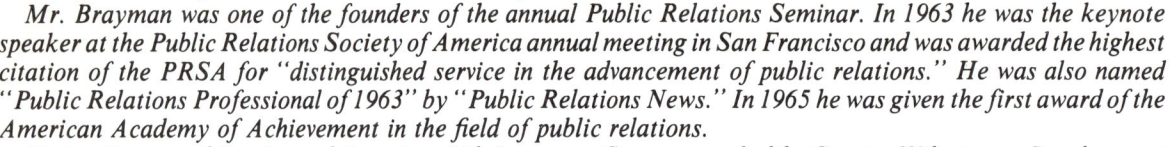

HAROLD BRAYMAN, public relations consultant, is the author of two books in this field: "Corporate Management in a World of Politics" (McGraw-Hill, 1967), and "Developing a Philosophy for Business Action," published by the Public Relations Seminar in 1969. He is also the author of "The President Speaks Off-the-Record," a book about Gridiron dinners since Grover Cleveland's administration (Dow Jones Books 1976).

For twenty-one years, to 1965, he was director of the Public Relations Department of Du Pont. Prior to that he was a newspaper correspondent for twenty years, fourteen of them spent as Washington correspondent for the New York Evening Post, when it was under Curtis ownership, and for the Philadelphia Evening Ledger. He was president of the National Press Club in 1938 and of the Gridiron Club in 1941, one of the very few Washington correspondents to have been elected president of both.

Mr. Brayman was one of the founders of the annual Public Relations Seminar. In 1963 he was the keynote speaker at the Public Relations Society of America annual meeting in San Francisco and was awarded the highest citation of the PRSA for "distinguished service in the advancement of public relations." He was also named "Public Relations Professional of 1963" by "Public Relations News." In 1965 he was given the first award of the American Academy of Achievement in the field of public relations.

He is a director of Continental American Life Insurance Company and of the Greater Wilmington Development Council, and a trustee of the Wilmington Medical Center and of Gettysburg College.

A graduate of Cornell, he has been chairman of the Cornell Council, and chairman of the Advisory Council of the Graduate School of Business and Public Administration. In 1965 he was awarded an honorary LL.D. by Gettysburg College.

THE NEED FOR COOPERATION

No business exists that does not require good relationships with other businesses for its own best performance. In developing these relationships there is no substitute for conducting one's own operations in such a way as to reflect credit on industry as a whole. This is the first essential for any good industry relations.

Technically, every business that operates in the United States does so under a charter from one of the 50 states. But in a broader sense all businesses also hold a charter from the general public, and this charter is amendable at the will of the public.

These unwritten charters are amended every time a new law lays down new procedures or ground rules for the operation of business either in a particular field or in all fields.

To be more specific, any business managed well enough to make a profit sees its broad charter amended, in effect, every time the law is changed as to what percentage of that profit the business may retain and what percentage it must turn over to the government in the form of taxes.

The general amendments that have been made to unwritten charters in the past are too numerous to list in one short chapter, and those that will be made in the future are probably equally numerous. We need only to reflect on one of them—the 82 per cent tax of several years ago on increasing earnings, which was mislabeled for political effects as the "excess profits tax."

INDUSTRY RELATIONS

The character and direction of these amendments are determined not solely by governmental needs for revenue, because there are many sources of revenue to which a government may turn; the nature of the amendments is determined to a large extent by public attitudes toward business—whether the majority of people believe business operates in the public interest or against the public interest; whether the public has good will or ill will toward specific industries or industry at large; whether people understand or do not understand to what extent their own interest is tied in with the successful operation of business organizations.

Consequently, the reflection of credit on business as a whole becomes a primary consideration for any company thinking in the long term. Hence, the basic factor in the relations of any company to others within its industry is determined largely by three things:

1. Whether the company contributes actively to aid in the constructive development of a sound and sympathetic governmental and public attitude toward its industry.

2. Whether by leadership and helpfulness to other companies, and by example in its own day-to-day relations with employees, stockholders, customers, suppliers, neighbors in its own community, and the larger public, it conducts itself in such a way as to create confidence in industry, or by its actions contributes to the destruction of such an attitude.

3. Whether it participates constructively and exercises a leadership role in contributing to the solution of industry problems through its own trade organization and through the broader business organizations, or whether it helps to create such problems.

SPECIFICS ON IMPROVING INDUSTRY RELATIONS

The company that contributes toward the easing of the public problems of business, and therefore toward a better public and governmental attitude toward its industry, almost automatically achieves the respect, the support, and in a more practical way, a preference in trade purchasing by the other companies in the industry.

Warner & Swasey. An outstanding example of how a company has greatly improved its industry relations by trying to make a contribution to public understanding is the advertising campaign that has been carried on for many years by the machine tool manufacturer Warner & Swasey.

Realizing that public opinion is a powerful influence in determining government action, Warner & Swasey, instead of advertising its products, has created a long series of advertisements designed to improve public understanding of basic economics and the incentive-enterprise system.

Because this has been a contribution to public understanding, it has built up a tremendous amount of good will among the industrial customers of Warner & Swasey, and this, the company feels, has had the very direct effect of increasing purchases of equipment from it. An illustrative example of these ads is shown here.

G. L. Hoobler, director of marketing, says that "the current value of our corporate advertising continues to be thoroughly borne out by its response, not only from our own sales and service people, but from our customers themselves."

All the 1975 profits of all corporations wouldn't pay last year's Federal deficit.

And, we then wouldn't have *any new jobs* (it takes $40,000 of *savings* to provide one job).

You'd soon have *no* jobs because our workmen would be competing with new, productive machines in competitive countries, turning out lower cost goods which would capture our markets.

So don't be too sure business profits aren't your problem (actually, they're your *job*) and don't think Federal debt and deficit are just a lot of figures (unchecked, the run-away inflation they bring will wipe out your *savings*, your life insurance, your pension, your family's future).

And another thing—remember that it now takes *all* the income taxes paid by ⅔ of all Americans just to pay the *interest* on the Federal debt.

Yes, business profits and government deficits are *very much* your worry. That's what your vote is for.

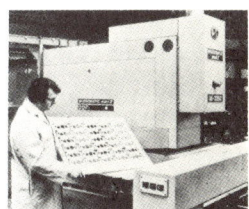

The all new MACH II CNC Wiedematic turret punch presses increase productivity and profits by their higher operating speed and wide flexibility. The MACH II is a product of Warner & Swasey's Wiedemann Division, King of Prussia, Pennsylvania.

 THE WARNER & SWASEY COMPANY
Executive Offices: 11000 Cedar Avenue, Cleveland, Ohio 44106

Productivity equipment and systems in machine tools, textile and construction machinery

Figure 13-1. By doing a job that is appreciated by most industry, Warner & Swasey gains good will and sales at the same time it carries on a long-time program of economic education.

Other systems. Numerous variations on the principle utilized by Warner & Swasey are used. Some companies regularly send out to their customers literature on various economic principles and problems. Others maintain speakers bureaus, primarily for use before organizations in the areas where they sell. (See Chapter 48.)

And in at least one instance they have gone to the extent of giving seminars for students, urging the students to write letters to editors of publications and paying the students for every letter they get published.

All these activities have tended to strengthen the corporation in its industry and increase the respect of other members of the industry for it.

Falcon Seaboard may be cited as another and somewhat different instance of a company creating respect for itself in its industry. While Falcon is only a medium-sized producer in the widely fractionated coal industry, it has handled its relations with its employees so well that almost alone among coal company employees they have refused to join the United Mine Workers or any other union.

And it was so far ahead of most other companies in the reclamation of land after strip mining that it was able to state in its 1975 annual report that "a number of the legislators and environmentalists who helped write Kentucky's surface mine law have stated that if everyone reclaimed land in the manner of Falcon, there would be no need for a law."

That this situation within its industry has been helpful to the company in many ways cannot be seriously questioned.

Every time a company conducts itself so as to win public approbation of its actions, that concern helps all other companies and makes itself an asset to the whole business community. And conversely, every time it arouses public disapproval by questionable conduct, it harms all other businesses and leads to their condemnation of the company.

For example, no one would contend, I am sure, that the industry's relations have been helped for those companies that have made illegal political contributions or illegal "payoffs" in the U.S. or abroad. To say nothing of the effects of these revelations in Japan and in Belgium, the relations of the American companies involved with others in their industry have certainly not been improved in this country. Collectively, they have done great damage to business and to business viewpoints, and have hurt all the innocent companies in their industry and out of it.

Other examples might include oil companies whose petroleum spills, such as the one in the Santa Barbara Channel several years ago, have hurt the whole oil industry because of the public reaction, deftly magnified by environmentalists.

This carries over into other industries also and does harm to them. A portion of the objection that environmentalists have been able to develop against the construction of atomic plants is related not to any accidents that have ever occurred in atomic plants, but rather to the fact that accidents do happen in other industries and conceivably could happen in atomic plants.

A further instance might be found among those companies that, on the introduction of important technological improvements, have dismissed substantial numbers of people, rather than undertaking the temporary expenditure of finding other work for them and letting the problem be taken care of over a period of time by attrition. Their shortsightedness has encouraged labor unions to fight technological advance in other companies.

Corporations that have created any of the above problems have made it more difficult for other industrial concerns to operate, and consequently have not endeared themselves either to their own industries or to the industries to which they sell.

Good conduct. On the other hand, there have been many instances of companies that have conducted themselves extremely well and consequently have attained a very high prestige within their industries because they have made it easier for others. Instances in this category are many, but perhaps among the more oustanding ones in general are IBM's handling of its labor relations, AT&T's handling of its customer relations, and Du Pont's handling of its legislative relations when it had to obtain new tax legislation permitting the distribution to its stockholders of its General Motors stock.

Furthermore, other things being equal, the industry relations will be much better of those companies that exhibit concern with the social problems in which government is involved, and that are constructive in their attitudes, instead of just sitting back and letting things drift.

Pollution. The company that continues to allow its plants to pollute either air or water compounds the problems of all others and finds its industry relations deteriorating seriously.

The public and political sensitivity that is now common on this subject has been largely brought about by some business concerns that chose to ignore the problem rather than to make an intelligent, cooperative effort to correct the situation in the communities in which they operate.

The company that continues to pour out black smoke from its smokestacks in any community is very likely to precipitate political action that makes it tough and expensive for every other company operating in the area. Such businesses inevitably build up a great deal of resentment against themselves, not only from the public but from the other industries that suffer from their neglect.

For example, a story widely printed around the country in January 1970, stating that five individuals at El Paso, Texas, had sued the American Smelting & Refining Company for one billion dollars, alleging that air pollutants from the company's El Paso plant were damaging the health of about 750,000 residents of El Paso and Juarez, Mexico, can hardly have endeared that company to others having pollution problems. Certainly the suit gave a lot of otherwise idle lawyers ideas of suing other companies with pollution problems.

However, some of the best companies in America recognized the gravity of the pollution problem a long time ago and have been doing their best to utilize every technological advance possible to operate in such a way as to be good citizens of their communities.

Du Pont is only one example—there are many others—but this company has required for more than twenty-five years that air and water pollution be engineered out of any new plant being built, before approval would be given for design of the plant. This is not quite as complete an answer as it sounds, because accidents will happen and sometimes pollution does occur, but if a company shows the proper spirit, people are usually quite tolerant of such situations.

In the present public excitement over environment, there is only one answer to the pollution problem—don't pollute, and don't wait to be forced to do the things that one ought to do anyway. Some pollution problems are very difficult and very expensive to correct, but if the proper spirit is shown, usually the time can be obtained to do the job economically.

A few years ago a United States aircraft carrier, because of an error by some individual, spread about 2,600 gallons of black fuel oil on the beach at Cannes, France. The commander of the ship ordered practically the entire crew ashore to dig trenches along the beach's edge to trap the oil and to clean up the mess, even to trucking off the oily sand and replacing it with fresh sand.

The whole thing was done within 24 hours, and public sentiment in that community gave high praise to the United States Navy. How much cheaper it might have been for the oil industry in the long run if it had acted with similar speed and resolution in the Santa Barbara channel.

Prompt and decisive corrective action by any company that causes pollution can greatly enhance its own relations with its industry and with all industry. Failure to do this can be disastrous.

Consumerism. The company in the consumer products field that ignores the rising demands of "consumerism" and continues operating just as it has in the past, cannot expect to have the same respect from other companies in its industry as does the one that makes an effort to meet these problems before they get out of hand.

The same situation is true in hiring minority members, even though employees taken on from those groups do compound the training problems of the hiring company.

Although customer relations are frequently looked on as a marketing function, rather than one of public relations, they often have a very direct effect on a company's standing in its industry.

Many manufacturing companies sell products or parts to other manufacturers in their industry. The way the salesman of another company is treated when he arrives to solicit business can have a profound effect on the visited company's standing in its industry. If he is always received with courtesy and given a fair hearing, even in cases where no order eventuates, this practice makes the company liked much better in the industry than is a company that brusquely brushes off efforts of others to sell to it.

A further example of constructive industry action that helped all industry was the embarkment a few years ago of life insurance companies on a cooperative investment program involving putting a billion dollars into investments in projects designed to improve housing in the so-called "ghetto areas."

BEING HELPFUL TO OTHERS

More than a century ago, Ralph Waldo Emerson said, "The only way to have a friend is to be one." This could well be adopted as a motto for industry relations.

No matter how bitter the competitive race between different companies in an industry, each helps all the others when it does a good job of promoting a constructive public attitude toward itself and its industry, and each harms not only itself but all the others when it does a bad job.

The forms this help can take are extremely varied, but they can be roughly classified into three categories:

(1) Help to business and trade organizations in one's own field.

(2) Help in the broader field of the national business organizations.

(3) Direct help to other individual companies.

It is vital that all companies participate actively in the programs related to trade and business organizations and contribute their proper share of support.

Sales benefits. Such evidence of cooperation has the very practical advantage of bringing business to the company. While this should not be the primary motive, it is not to be overlooked. In the complex American industrial system, a great part of trade and commerce is carried on among manufacturing companies rather than between retailers and ultimate consumers. Often this business is conducted among companies in the same industry; it is for this reason that it is sometimes said that the chemical industry is its own best customer. When the other factors such as price, quality, and service are approximately equal, the decision to choose a particular supplier may depend almost entirely on good will.

Participation in trade organizations, to be fruitful, must go much further than merely contributing dues and maintaining membership. It should include conscientious attendance at meetings and time devoted to the work of committees. It involves the obligation to give careful thought to the problems confronting the organization and the industry it represents.

Of course, wide differences exist in the effectiveness of trade organizations. Some are highly effective. There are also quite a number that are not only useless but sometimes directly harmful. Any legislator, state or federal, can provide examples.

The difference is caused almost invariably by one or both of two things: the ability of the paid executive and his staff, and the amount of thoughtful participation accorded by the members.

The influence of active members can often be brought to bear to correct personnel deficiency, but the greatest contributions can be made in thoughtful participation. Active participation and exercise of leadership will do much to vitalize the organization and will win the respect of others in the industry.

No company, however, should, because of its size or importance in the industry, seek to dominate the organization. This can be disastrous to the organization and to the reputation of the company attempting it, especially if the company happens to be the largest in the industry. The right criterion is not size or influence but the depth of thought contributed.

Such help, intelligently and constructively given, can benefit everyone in the industry and benefit the leaders in direct proportion to the success of the project.

Industry helps through careful attention to the interests of the public. For example, a few years ago, when a botulism scare threatened a product of the Campbell Soup Company, the company might have claimed it was all a scare and done nothing until it was proved to be real. If it had developed that way, it might have done great damage not only to that company but to all others in the food industry, which would certainly not have reacted to the welfare of Campbell Soup or to its long-term stature before the public.

Instead, the company acted swiftly to warn the public that there might be danger, and it sent out its representatives to recall immediately all suspect cans from 103,000 stores. The total effort cost Campbell approximately ten million dollars in sales of a product it had already manufactured.

But politically it was very astute, and it reassured everybody that Campbell was a producer of integrity whose products could be depended on. In the long-run, this swift and unhesitating action in a crisis convinced everyone of the responsibility of the company and of its determination to serve the public interest as well as its own, even at very substantial expense to itself.

There can be little doubt that this action by a major food processing company helped all other food processing companies and increased its stature and its standing with all others, as well as with the public.

Work with business groups. These principles apply equally to the broader field of national business organizations, such as the Chamber of Commerce of the United States. These organizations deal with the over-all problems of business, such as taxation, governmental relations, legislation, regulation, economic growth, and industrial statistics.

These larger national organizations are no nearer

to being perfect than is anything else in life. They have large memberships—large enough to include, inevitably, some proportion of malcontents who do nothing but pay dues and criticize. But fortunately they also include members who recognize a responsibility to contribute constructive effort.

A case in point is the continuing study of corporate taxation by the Chamber of Commerce of the U.S. By collecting and analyzing tax data, by appearing before committees of Congress, and by supplying its members with useful background information, this broadly based organization has helped clarify tax policies for the public, for political leaders, and for industry itself. By this program more and more of the citizenry is being helped to understand the serious effects of tax policies that restrict national economic growth. Cooperation by companies makes such services possible.

Such a program has been effective only because many companies with capable tax men and sophisticated political personnel encouraged these people to give their services at considerable length to the Chamber's Taxation Committee.

Helping other companies. Direct assistance to other companies on an individual basis fits the public relations concept of concentrating on one's own bailiwick—what we at Du Pont called the "precinct principle." This is defined as directing public relations efforts primarily to those audiences, such as employees, customers, and stockholders, who have a direct interest in hearing from us and hence are most likely to be influenced. It recognizes that no one company can hope to solve industry's public relations problems by working alone on a national scale, but that cooperative endeavors, with each company working in its own precinct, can accomplish much.

Aiding another company, perhaps a company engaged in a wholly different industry, might seem to be getting away from one's own precinct. However, the public relations assistance accorded to individual companies was always given on request. A company that came with such a request had demonstrated an interest in what we had to offer and thus qualified as part of our precinct.

Some businessmen feel that a company should not help a competitor. No one suggests giving out commercial or scientific information that will help a competitor take sales away; the exchange of public relations experience is far removed from any commercial consideration. When we help another to solve a problem in the area of public opinion we are also helping ourselves.

Public relations assistance. Over the last several years more than 150 companies have sought and received advice and other assistance from Du Pont on public relations problems, and several other large companies are giving similar aid. A request for public relations experience in similar situations often comes when the requesting party finds himself in actual or potential trouble. He is then not only willing but anxious to listen and to learn from the experience of others where it is applicable and helpful.

In addition to giving direct help, it becomes quite apparent that any company that conducts its own public relations in all fields well will have a much higher standing with the other companies in its industry than the one that fails in this particular field.

One might almost add that one of the first principles of developing good industry relations is to develop good company public relations. This goes above and beyond what is normally thought of as public relations.

For example, a few years ago two companies were about to get into a very nasty legal fight with suits and countersuits. It happened, however, that the public relations directors of both of these companies had been active in various public relations organizations and had come to know each other well.

The result was that both of these men recognized that such a litigation between their two companies would not only hurt each of the companies but would be harmful to their whole industry and to all industry. One of them took the initiative and made a telephone call. The two public relations directors got together, and each went to work on his own company, with the result that both delayed an overt move until the whole subject could be re-studied and re-negotiated. This led to a compromise agreement between the companies and prevented a nasty public squabble that would have done the industry considerable harm.

14

Employee Relations and Communications

JOSEPH A. VARILLA is director, corporate communications, Xerox Corporation. His responsibilities include employee and shareholder communications and the writing and coordination of position papers on legislative or social issues on which Xerox might comment.

Varilla joined Xerox in 1963. Previously he was Bureau Manager in Frankfort, Ky. for United Press International.

He has lectured on employee communications before groups of managers and business communicators.

He has a bachelor of arts degree from Lehigh University.

For many years the employees of an organization were a neglected "public" among those concerned with public relations. Internal communications tended to be one-directional—telling employees what management wanted them to know—and confined to a "house organ" or company publication that got passing attention from both those who produced it and those who received it.

Among the many changes that have occurred in relations between organizations and their publics, this has been one of the most significant. Today managements tend to recognize that their relations with the firm's employees are crucial to all their objectives. If employees understand and accept the policies and plans of the company, it is likely that those policies and plans can be carried out; if they oppose them, success is unlikely. Also, employees—having the greatest stake in what becomes of the company—are a vital communications channel themselves, with exceptional effectiveness in determining the attitudes of outsiders.

Today's employee population in most companies consists of a group that is more questioning, bright, and cynical than in previous years. Maintaining sound relations with them depends most of all on credibility—acceptance of the good faith in the management's intentions and acceptance of the veracity and accuracy of the information disseminated. That means that corporations need the judgment and skills of professional employee relations specialists and effective editors for its communications media.

The senior management of corporations is spending more time dealing with the attitudes and questions of the employees, and more effort in communicating with them.

Despite what on the surface sometimes seems to be apathy, and their identification in many cases with labor unions, employees are indeed concerned about their company's success. Their livelihood and their futures depend on it. They want to have a voice in its plans because the plans will determine their future. They want to know as much as possible about what is happening and what future conditions and problems may be. And they want to help. Though they approach the company's future from different viewpoints, both employees and management are working for the same general objectives.

Accordingly, the most important job for employee relations and communications people is to be informed about the company so they can serve as liaison between it and the employees. That calls for interpreting to management the attitudes and concerns of the employees as well as interpreting the company and its practices to the employees.

EMPLOYEE RELATIONS AND COMMUNICATIONS

To have a successful employee relations and information program, then, an organization should:

1. Hire capable, thoughtful, mature people who are sensitive to human attitudes and know how to express ideas and opinions.
2. Give them access to those who make the decisions and have the information.
3. Position them as pivots between the employees and the management, able to listen as well as to communicate in both directions.
4. Insist on honest and thorough reporting.
5. Emphasize the message, rather than the medium.

The last point is critical. The paramount concern must be the content of what is being said: What is *really* on employees' minds, rather than what seems to be the loudest among their complaints; what is really significant about the messages of the management?[1]

The actual content of the communication involved will, of course, vary from company to company and from time to time. Here we can explore the basic techniques for various aspects of the program.

INTERESTS OF EMPLOYEES

Techniques for finding out what concerns and interests employees range from full-blown surveys[2] to simple questionnaires to keeping the ears of employee-relations people tuned.

One technique that a number of companies have found useful on a continuing basis permits employees to ask questions and to question policies and procedures. Perhaps the best-known of these is the "Speak Up" program of International Business Machines that has been in existence for a number of years. Similarly effective programs are conducted by Xerox and Bank of America, among others.

There seem to be three key elements to those programs that have been successful:

1. They guarantee the anonymity of the employee.
2. They come to grips with the tough questions, not just the easy ones.
3. The questions are answered promptly.

[1] For discussions of the psychological bases of employees' attitudes toward work and organizations, see books listed under Management and Policy in Bibliography. Also, "Management Tunes in on Employee Gripes," *New York Times*, Oct. 16, 1977—Ed.

[2] See Chapter 35.

These requirements create demands on administrators, but the results indicate they are worthwhile. Such a program often provides early warning signals of problems that will develop. And it often provides feedback on employees' reactions to decisions by management.

Perhaps most important, it is a real service to employees. It affords a means for the employee to get a hearing when local communications lines are clogged or unresponsive. At its best, such a program works much like the "Hot Line" columns conducted by many metropolitan newspapers.

Indeed, a number of companies have columns in their publications that carry such questions and answers. However, having something to print in a publication is not the reason for the programs. They should be aimed at affording a channel of communication and action for the employee—a way for him or her to get around the blocks in the system. In fact, in many cases it is best not to publish some of the questions and answers but to deal with them through direct personal contact. Publication of those of general interest and not involving confidences, however, is useful in maintaining interest in the program.

Meetings with employees. Many senior managers conduct meetings with a simple question-and-answer format. The successful pattern for such meetings involves two factors:

- The manager learns as much from the questions as the employees learn from the replies, or even more.
- The answers are totally frank.

When the manager ducks a question or gives a vague hedging reply, credibility is damaged and the effectiveness of the meeting is likely to be lost. He need not answer every question or know the answer to every question. Employees will accept "I don't know, but I'll find out," or "I can't answer that question now because it's still developing," but they will not accept an evasive reply.

The principal benefit to the communicator from such sessions is better understanding of the needs of employees. He or she can analyze questions to determine those issues that require further communication.

TECHNIQUES FOR COMMUNICATING

When the communicator has identified the issues and is fairly comfortable with what needs to be communicated, he or she has a number of options for the means to be used.

Following is an outline of media, all of which could be used in a fairly large corporation. In a smaller organization a smaller number would be appropriate.[3]

Quarterly magazine. This tends to be glossy, expensive, well-written, and well-illustrated. Articles treat subjects in depth. There is considerable debate, however, about the cost effectiveness and even the communications effectiveness of such publications. To their corporate supporters they represent the ultimate in class and interpretive reporting. To their detractors they represent domination by the art director's viewpoint rather than the communicator's, a waste of money, and poor communication. Interestingly, there are probably surveys to support either point of view.

A company that feels it needs an "image" publication for its employees may use this technique. However, in today's cost-conscious environment it is wise to beware of anything that seems extravagant.

Monthly publication. This is becoming more expensive and many communicators are questioning the value of such extreme touches as five colors and glossy stock. Like the quarterly, the monthly magazine is becoming less common.

The so-called megapaper seems to be an alternative to the magazine and is growing steadily in popularity among corporations. It combines the economy of a newspaper with the freedom of design of a magazine. The models for megapapers seem to be the special sections—Travel, Arts and Leisure, Finance, Week-in-Review—of *The Sunday New York Times*.

This type of publication has grown in industry as editors realized that a monthly publication can hardly be termed a newspaper and shouldn't look like one. Instead, the publication stresses features and interpretive pieces that give the reader the necessary background on issues that confront the company. Articles are kept to no more than 500 to 600 words in many publications.

The better megapapers are almost exclusively issues-oriented. They address themselves to various aspects of the question: "How is the business doing?"

A survey at Xerox demonstrated that employees read such a corporate publication in much the same way that professionals read a professional journal. They didn't tend to read cute pieces about people, once thought to be the staple of company publications. Instead, they were looking for solid information about the business. Other publications satisfy their curiosity about personalities. In a company publication they want to know the impact of decisions.

News publications. While news is not a commodity for a monthly, there remains a need to disseminate news to the employees. For logistical reasons news is difficult to disseminate fresh within corporations, especially those that have many locations. Following are some methods that seem to work in various companies:

Newsletters. In a fairly small office environment—with up to perhaps 700 people—it's possible to have a very timely newsletter. It can be typed and run off by duplicator on a special letterhead, then delivered to every desk with the next distribution of office mail. It should be produced only when there is news to justify it. When people become familiar with the important contents of such a publication it gets an avid readership.

Bulletin boards.[4] At many factory locations these are the primary means to disseminate news. To be effective, bulletin boards must be the responsibility of someone who keeps them uncluttered, up-to-date, and effectively displayed. They must be at locations where all employees can see them.

Teletype networks. In corporations with multiple locations these are used to get news—appointments, earnings reports, acquisitions, and so on—to various locations. Usually news dissemination uses teletype circuits set up primarily for other purposes. It is important that someone be responsible at each location for having the news from the teletype processed and displayed on the bulletin boards or otherwise disseminated.

Cafeteria news. Some companies have had success with daily news bulletins that can be picked up at the cafeteria, usually at lunchtime. These often contain national as well as corporate headlines.

Dial-the-News. This system enables employees to dial a certain number to get up-to-date corporate news. To be fully effective the message should be changed a couple of times a day. The problem is getting enough news to keep interest high. It is usually effective only when confined to a single city or location.

Radio news schedules. Some companies, where they are major factors in the community, buy time at a given period on a radio station, usually when employees are likely to be driving home. They

[3]See Chapter 15.

[4]See Chapter 48.

EMPLOYEE RELATIONS AND COMMUNICATIONS

provide company news and other information of interest to the staff.

Daily newspapers. Some organizations—most notably General Electric plants—have used this technique. It is difficult to do well and requires special skills, but it is quite effective when done with finesse.

Weekly publications. The ability of modern duplicating equipment to reproduce photos well makes it economical to issue an in-house weekly. Restrictions are imposed by the equipment—page size, for instance. When done well it can be effective.

Local newspapers. Where the local media are responsible and accurate, it often is best to have them carry news about the company. The third-party identification adds credibility. It is important, however, that the employees not feel that the only way they could get the information is from an outside source; so company media should report it too.

Television. TV, although it is the most effective external medium for the delivery of news, has had little application for internal communication. Yet used well—in the form of videocassette recordings (VCR)—it can be the most effective device available.

There are many applications, dependent on the news and the resources available,[5] but a major one is the interview with the Chief Executive Officer. This helps humanize the management and provide visibility at a time when leadership of all organizations is being called on to be more accountable and more visible.

Yet TV is a most difficult medium to use effectively. The television camera tends to emphasize personality traits. It does not provide the human touch of a face-to-face meeting. No one is awed by the authority of someone on television. After all, people frequently see the President of the U. S. on television and feel free to criticize him.

Still, senior executives must learn to use television effectively. Some pointers appear in Chapter 43.

Other communications media. Beyond newsworthy material, these additional media are important:

Annual report.[6] Some companies issue a special employee edition of the regular annual report. However, interpretation of the company and its finances may be carried in the employee publication, making a special employee report unnecessary.

In-plant exhibits. These can show products, especially new ones, and illustrations of work and activities. They can also report on safety and production records, health programs, and so on.

Open houses. These offer opportunities for workers, their families, and the community at large to get acquainted with the company and its officials. Employees' families should be invited. The event should be planned so it avoids confusion and congestion in the plant or office. Trained guides should explain various operations and refreshments should be served. In many communities such an event merits publicity in the local media.

INCREASING CHALLENGES

The challenges to corporate managers of employee relations and communications are growing in many areas. For example, government is legislating that employees must receive certain information on various subjects, such as recent laws involving pension plans.

To be fully effective the communicator must have authority in areas that previously were often confined to others, such as lawyers and labor relations specialists. To be effective in dealing with employees and communicating with them, it is essential that there be sensitivity to how people develop their attitudes and skill in reaching them.

Benefits, compensation, and personnel policies are three areas in which special communications skills are essential. For the employer there probably are no more important subjects in the employee-relations field. Regulations and policies must be approached from the viewpoint of the audience and must be explained in easy-to-understand language.

In these areas the computer is becoming an important tool. It makes it possible to reach each individual with a personalized update on his or her benefits, compensation, and pension while discussing these programs as a whole. Talking directly to one person about what's most on that person's mind is real communication.

In addition, almost any activity of the company succeeds or fails on the basis of communication skill. This task is difficult and requires generalists who are equally poised while discussing benefits or production, equally at ease while working with television or print media, equally comfortable dealing with the Chief Executive Officer or the newest production worker. They must be ready to understand and use new media, new techniques, and new thinking as they emerge.

---

[5]See Chapters 43 and 46. Also, "TV That Competes with the Office Grapevine," *Business Week*, Mar. 17, 1977, pp. 49-51.

[6]See Chapter 11.

15

Company Publications

DON FABUN, now retired, was editor and director of publications for Kaiser Aluminum & Chemical Corporation for 22 years. Prior to joining that firm in 1952 as editor of its distributor publication, he had been editor-in-chief of the University of California Daily Californian, associate editor of the Kaiser Richmond (California) shipyard employee weekly, Fore'n Aft, and, after service overseas, a copy writer for McCann Erickson, Inc. at its San Francisco office, editor of the fraternal quarterly, The Masonic Star, and editor of the national dealer publication for California Packing Corporation, the Del Monte Advance News. At Kaiser he was editor of Kaiser Aluminum News, an internationally distributed "external" quarterly; was editor of two internal management publications, News/Notes and Press Summary, and assisted in planning the company's internal employee publications at various plant locations. Between 1953 and 1974, News won 21 major national and international publication awards in competitions sponsored by the American Association of Industrial Editors and the International Council of Industrial Editors. Issues of News were republished verbatim in book form by commercial publishing houses under the titles, "Dynamics of Change," "Three Roads to Awareness," and "Dimensions of Change." They are used as texts in humanities courses in many universities. Fabun is continuing an active career in writing non-fiction and television scripts, public speaking on subjects covered in News, and consulting on publication planning.

The primary function of human organizations—whether private or public—is communication. Individual human beings are brought together in one place, or assembled in a number of places, to do something that involves their joint cooperation: making a product or products, performing a service or services. As these groups grow in size, as their products or services diversify, and as they become more scattered geographically, a point is reached where oral communication between members becomes more and more difficult. At this point, these organizations may consider that an internally circulated publication will help to establish a medium for communication that will supplement oral communication, or other forms of written communication, such as letters, notes, and memoranda.

In this country, in recent years, the number of such internally generated and circulated media appears to have been increasing dramatically. Where there may have been no more than 2,000 regularly published media prior to World War II, by 1970—depending on how they are defined—there were about 8,000 to 10,000 company-sponsored publications in the United States, with a total audience of approximately 160 million persons.

Thus, in almost any organization of any size, the public relations practitioner may be called on sooner or later to establish an employee publication, to assist in its establishment by some other department, such as personnel, industrial relations, or advertising, or be asked to suggest ways an already established medium may be made more effective.

Until after World War II, a company publication was, with few exceptions, a rather simple sort of thing. It mixed chatter and gossip with some adjurations from management, and its principal purpose was to create a "family feeling" among employees. Since the mid-1940's—although there certainly are exceptions—there has been a trend toward publication of media that are more sophisticated and whose main objectives are to create the sort of informational environment in which the employee feels that his personal welfare and goals are involved with the goals and welfare of the company or organization.

The level of sophistication of the "worker" has risen. He is, typically, better educated, exposed to more communication from television, radio, magazines and newspapers; is performing a more technically exacting task and has a wider responsibility, particularly in high-speed, mass-production activities, than his pre-World War II progenitor. In general, the publications that will reach and motivate him have become, both in their graphic exposition and their content, more professional in their approach and more meaningful in their execution.

For many years, it was assumed that the purpose of an employee magazine was to provide "management" a means for reaching "employees" who could not easily be reached orally. Since about 1950, it has become more apparent that the distinction between "management" and "employees" is at best a misleading one, particularly in business firms that are owned by stockholders and where management is distinguished from "employees" only in the amount of money that it makes or the privileges that it enjoys. An employee publication may, therefore, have to take into consideration that it must appeal not only to pretty Nelly, the switchboard girl, but to an atomic physicist, a systems engineer, a market analyst, and an operations analyst. These latter are not likely to be interested in, or motivated by, bowling scores and a detailed account of the company picnic.

The public relations practitioner, then, may be called on to organize, design, and produce a regularly issued publication that can be successful only if it will attract and hold the interest of a highly diversified audience whose members have in common only that they are all on the same payroll. His problem is somewhat different than that of the editor of a general or specialty magazine, whose readers will subscribe to, or purchase on the newsstand, a publication because it appeals to some special interest—such as hobbies, sports, gardening, or homemaking. In the case of the company publication, the medium selects the audience, the audience does not select it. And the approaches that are successful with a general-interest or specialty magazine may not always be effective with an employee publication.

What we will discuss here, then, are the special problems that may be faced by a public relations person who has been asked to create, maintain, or improve an employee publication, to the extent that they differ from the general problems of any publication.

WHAT IS IT SUPPOSED TO DO?

The fundamental question that must be answered satisfactorily is quite simply, "What do we want this publication to accomplish?" It is not enough to say that management wants to communicate with employees. The distinction, as previously mentioned, is usually a misleading one and, in any event, fails to answer the questions, "What is to be communicated?" "To whom are we communicating?" and, "Assuming we have communicated, what is the response we want to evoke?"

Establishing an employee publication—or renovating an established one—begins properly by finding out why "management" feels it is not already communicating effectively; what it feels is not being communicated that should be; and an examination of whether a publication can solve, or partially solve, the problem. Magazines these days are too expensive to put out just "because everybody does it."

A clear statement of management aims, as they relate to the publication, is the foundation for a successful publication. In more advanced organizations, such a statement may well be prepared by consulting not only responsible management, but by asking the employees themselves what they feel they should know about their company in order to perform more successfully. If a publication is based on the premise that it is supposed to tell employees what "management" thinks they should know, it is not likely to achieve the aims management has set for it.

A company publication can be more successfully based on the premise that it not only helps employees gain a better understanding of management policies, purposes, and decisions, but that it also helps management understand the needs and aspirations of the employees. Communication is not a one-way street, and communications achieve their maximum effectiveness only when channels are open for "feedback" from the employees to management.

Thus, the publication begins with meaningful discussions with all sectors of responsible management and with representative employees. The policy statement that results may be a compromise between the two sets of values. Surveys of employee attitudes appear to show that an employee, of whatever level, and including management, is interested in finding the answers to these questions:

1. *What* is the company doing now?
2. *Why* is it doing it?
3. How will it affect *me*?

If these attitudes are general, the publication that just presents "the facts" without interpretation and without reducing them to the individual level of the employee, will not be as successful as one that does.

Once a publication's objectives have been decided on, they should be written as clearly as possible, widely disseminated among management for review, discussion, and ultimately, acceptance. The objectives, once agreed on, furnish a reference point both to management and the editor; they are guidelines within which the success or failure of the publication can be measured. Without clearly stated and agreed on objectives, the employee publication meanders as precariously as a ship without a rudder.

A survey of company publication editors, who listed some 27 objectives of their publications, showed that only four were considered essential by most of them. They were:

(1) To give information on company operations, policies, and problems.
(2) To draw individuals into closer contact with the company.
(3) To make employees feel they are members of a single organization.
(4) To help employees understand *each other*.

SETTING UP CLEARANCE CHANNELS

The next really important step is to establish who is going to be responsible for the publication. Curiously enough, this seems to be one of the most difficult hurdles of all. Someone, besides the editor, has to assume the responsibility for what the editor says in the publication. The editor is a technician; he may explain policy, but he does not usually make policy. Since the management group of most large companies is seldom in agreement on what the company policy is or should be, the publication editor must have some reliable and accepted official who will back him up.

There are some company publications so burdened with clearance problems that the publication is almost impossible to get out, and when it does come out, it is so watered down to satisfy conflicting opinions that it is, essentially, meaningless. It becomes an exposition in "corporatese," and thus fails to communicate. Employees are rather quick to recognize this, and the result may be that the publication antagonizes them instead of enlisting their support for company policies and objectives.

In general, the points of clearance should be as highly placed in the organization as possible: the president, an executive vice-president, or the chairman of the board. Whoever it is, he, and he alone, reviews the publication for general policy, or he appoints a subordinate to do it, but the subordinate acts, in this instance, with the full authority of the officer he represents. A second point of clearance, particularly if the publication deals with trademarked company products or processes, is the organization's legal counsel. He should not be involved in clearing matters of policy, but he should be involved in determining whether the material in any way jeopardizes the company's legal rights. A third point of clearance is the original source of the information, whether it is a technician, or a department head, or an "employee." It frequently happens that, with the best intentions, an editor may misunderstand or misinterpret what his source told him.

And that should be it. If more than three persons are involved in clearing the contents of a publication, chances are that the clearance problem will become unmanageable within the rigid time requirements of printing and distribution deadlines. What is sought is not consensus, but responsibility.

WHAT KIND OF A PUBLICATION?

In general, there are three types of company publications, defined by the audiences toward which they are principally oriented. The "employee" publication generally is restricted to people who are actually on the payroll, with some limited distribution "outside" to local newspapers or other media, to other company publications editors, and to appropriate trade magazines. Such publications are called "internal."

Some company publications may be circulated to employees, but also are sent to persons who are not on the payroll: stockholders, customers, distributors, prospects, other media, and members of local, county, state, or federal government. These have been called "combination company publications."

COMPANY PUBLICATIONS

A third type may be characterized as "external," and while it may or may not also be made available to company employees, it is oriented primarily to the business, political, and economic environment outside the company or organization. Its function is still communication, but it is not intended primarily to influence or inform people on the payroll.

The type of publication that a company decides to publish relates directly to its objectives. It frequently happens, however, that what begins as a strictly internal employee publication may become a combination publication, and ultimately an external publication. As it does, its approaches will necessarily change, and, of course, so will its objectives. Performing the transition from internal, to combination, to external may sometimes be the responsibility of a public relations man, but is more likely to evolve out of a broadening of the company's interest and to be done gradually by the editor of the publication.

WHAT SHOULD THE FORMAT BE?

For the most part, the choice of the size and type of publications is extremely limited. Paper, press, and bindery sizes are pretty standard, and the size and number of pages of a publication that they can handle economically are rigidly circumscribed.

Within these limitations, the format of the publication—whether it is to be a magazine or a newspaper type—should be dictated by the objectives. If the publication is to carry many small items about people and what they are doing, the newspaper style seems to be indicated. If the publication is to discuss and interpret in depth some of the broader activities or problems of the company, then a magazine format probably would work better.

By far the largest number of company magazines are 8½ by 11 inches overall, and are produced in multiples of four pages, with the most economical number of pages being four, eight, sixteen, or thirty-two. This is dictated by the standardization of paper sizes and printing equipment, and has nothing to do with the contents of the publication. An advantage of the 8½ by 11 size is that it fits most file drawers and binders, and it is a size that is familiar to most readers. Its disadvantage is that so many publications, memoranda, and letters are this size, it does not easily attract attention.

Some magazines are 6 inches by 9 inches. They have the advantage that they stand out from the usual run of 8½ by 11 material; they give more pages for the same amount of paper; they do not re-

Figure 15-1. Cover of an internal/external publication that deals in each issue with a broad subject, relating it to the products and services the company provides that affect that subject. This one deals with the entire range of communications between people and groups.

quire such long articles or features; and they can be carried more or less easily in a pocket or handbag. They have the disadvantage that they are more easily lost in standard-size files and it is difficult to achieve high visual impact for big stories and features.

There are "outside" magazines, 9 inches by 12 inches or larger. They have the design advantage of high visual impact, and they tend to stand out from the run-of-the-mill smaller sizes. They have the disadvantage that they usually require professional layout and art; they are more likely to get banged around and damaged in the mail; and they are almost impossible to file. They also are usually more expensive to produce because in order to be effective, they must carry large halftone areas and these cost more money than smaller ones.

A newspaper format may be indicated if the

publication is going to cover many small activities. Since the full newspaper size is rather awkward to handle, and requires a great deal of material to fill, the employee newspaper is more likely to be "tabloid" size. The tabloid format offers a great deal of flexibility in layout, can accommodate both long features and many short ones, and can be almost any number of pages. Unless very skillfully designed and edited, it seldom has the prestige appearance of a magazine. Folded in the middle, it will fit most standard file drawers, but it is expensive and awkward to bind.

LETTERPRESS OR OFFSET?

Whether a magazine or newspaper should be printed by letterpress or offset is largely dictated by the contents and by the system for clearances that has been set up. If the contents are to be largely illustrative—many photographs and artwork—it usually is more economical to produce the publication on offset presses. If the presentation is to be mostly type, there is little difference in cost. If the clearance system is complicated and there are likely to be many last minute changes in type, letterpress is usually the most economical, since making changes in the finished pasteups or film prepared for offset lithography is expensive.

With today's equipment, the quality of the finished product by either process is usually indistinguishable except to experts.

The preparation, printing, and binding costs of a publication will vary quite widely, not only between different printing firms but in the same firm, depending on its workload. It is usually economical to get competitive estimates from several firms, and to do this often.

WHAT KIND OF AN EDITOR?

Except for quite small firms or organizations, the usual procedure is to hire an editor who applies all, or most, of his working time solely to preparing and producing the publication. Many company publications are edited by one person and the one- or two-man "staff" is the rule rather than the exception. A person with professional journalistic background can quite readily learn what he needs to know about a company or an organization and then apply his experience to putting out an acceptable magazine. It is rather rare that someone who knows a great deal about a company, but nothing about journalism, can function successfully. Editing is a profession and requires a certain standard of training and ability, just as law or engineering does. A formal education in journalism may or may not be useful, depending on the quality of the journalistic department. Practical experience in writing and editing may be more important than formal training, and certainly appears to be more useful than a background in "business" or "economics." These can be acquired; writing ability seldom can.

In some large, diversified, and scattered firms or organizations, it may be necessary to organize a field reporting staff, usually made up of employees who devote some part of their time to preparing material for the publication. This is seldom easy to do, and usually proceeds along the line of trial and error. There are people who simply do not appear to be able to make deadlines, and there are people who do not seem to know what is "news" and what is not. About the only good guideline that can be established here is that it be clearly understood that the staff reporter is to perform his function on company time, and that his doing so is recognized and supported by management. The amount of company time to be used for this purpose can be established by management, but it must be made clear to the employee's immediate supervisor.

In some large companies, with facilities geographically scattered, there may be a number of employee publications, each autonomously edited by a local editor. The role of the public relations person here is to coordinate these efforts from the firm's headquarters, and to supply "general policy" information that can be used at the local editor's discretion. It sometimes also may be useful for the public relations publications editor or coordinator to supply some types of professional art and design aid, since this can be done most economically at a central location and made available regionally or locally.

HOW SHOULD THE PUBLICATION BE DESIGNED?

Magazine and newspaper design is a profession and it should not be left to amateurs. This includes both the public relations representative and/or the editor. With some exceptions, few editors have sufficient training or ability to design a publication. This usually should be assigned to a professional artist or an art service. The art service will design the masthead and permanent or standing departmental headings, determine the size and style of type for text, captions, and headlines, and prepare sample

COMPANY PUBLICATIONS

"dummies" that can serve as guidelines for solving special and recurrent problems, such as how to handle a large number of short items or small pictures, how to break up large "grey" areas of type, and how to balance art and typography.

If the budget allows, it is usually better to have an art director or an art service lay out and design each issue. If the budget does not provide for that, then it is important that a professional do a thorough job of laying out the first issue with examples of how typical layout problems can be handled. Since it normally would be assumed that the publication will have a long life, the original art "start up" costs should be amortized as a publication cost over a number of issues, and usually it will be seen that this is a very small fraction of the over-all cost of the publication.

Once the design and format of the publication have been approved by management, it is helpful to discuss with the printer how type, art, photographs, and layouts are to be marked and coded for his identification. Practices differ between printing firms, but most of them have worked out systems that are easy to follow and that will eliminate most of the causes of error. If a publication's staff consists of more than one person, some individual on the staff should be appointed to deal with the printer, and only this one person should do so. If several people are involved, errors are much more likely to occur.

"MARKET TESTING" A NEW PUBLICATION

Some organizations find it useful to enter the internal publication field on a gradual basis. This can be done by a limited production and circulation of the publication, followed by interviews with the recipients, soliciting comments, criticisms, and suggestions. Gradually, the field of distribution may be widened, starting with selected groups, until finally it goes to everyone management wants to reach.

This approach has much to recommend it: the "bugs" in the production routine can be worked out without excessive cost; errors in approach can be caught and corrected before they become widespread; and a certain feeling of participation, and therefore interest, may be generated among those management people who serve as the original board of review.

After a few issues, the editor, his printer, and management should have a smoothly running, professional publication that has—just like a company's product—been "pretested" in the area in which it will be distributed.

THE USE OF PHOTOGRAPHS

Contemporary journalism, for the most part, is becoming increasingly pictorial. This trend also affects employee publications and the choice and proper use of photographs is a major part of an editor's responsibility.

With recent improvements in both camera equipment and film, the quality of amateur photography has improved considerably. However, for magazines or newspapers of medium or large size, it is well to have a staff photographer who is a professional, or some workable and relatively inexpensive arrangement with a local photographic studio to provide for photographs of banquets, parties, new equipment or plant additions, and new products.

In addition to taking photographs on assignment, the professional photographer or staff photographer, by using his professional skills in the darkroom, often can help salvage poor-quality photographs submitted by employees. This frequently makes it possible to publish photographs that might otherwise have to be turned down, with the usual result that the employee who furnished the photograph may become antagonistic to the publication and, perhaps, the organization itself.

WHAT KIND OF MATERIAL SHOULD BE PRESENTED?

Different kinds of companies and organizations necessarily generate different kinds of news. In general it can be assumed that the news that is most likely to attract the attention and interest of an employee is that which affects him or her personally. Changes in parking lot rules may be felt by an employee to be much more important than a new plant addition, if it does not seem likely that the employee will be transferred to the new plant. Management frequently feels that the real "news" is in the amount of new capital that may be invested in plant or equipment additions, acquisitions, or developing new products. This should be presented to show how it is directly related to the personal interests of the employees.

Among the more successful company publications now, the trend seems to be to greater emphasis on giving the employee a broader view of his company, its position in its industry, the impact of research and development on the company's

Figure 15-2. An internal publication for employees of one division of a diversified corporation. This company publishes several of these—all with different format—for its divisions.

products and services, plans for the future, the relation of the company or organization to the economy as a whole, and participation by the company personnel in the affairs of the community.

WHERE DOES THE MATERIAL COME FROM?

In addition to the news items generated by the company or an organization's own activities, and the individual activities of the employees themselves, there frequently is a need for more generalized material. This may include fashion hints or tips, "how to do" articles, travel opportunities, hobbies or gardening, etc. Usually this material can be secured without charge from the public relations or publicity departments of other firms, from travel organizations, safety groups, syndicates, or feature services. Or they may be purchased, often quite economically, from free-lance writers and stock photographic firms. Usually a plentiful supply of this type of material will come in from "outside" once a publication is established, sets up "exchange" mailing lists with other company or organization publications, and lists itself and its requirements in the national directory of house magazines.

FEEDBACK MECHANISMS

One frequent criticism of the more common type of employee publication is that it provides for downward communication—i.e., management tells the employees what management thinks the employee should know about, but there is no adequate channel for "feedback" response from the employees themselves. As in any type of communication, the process cannot be considered completed unless there is a measurable response to the message. One way of providing for measurable response in an employee publication is to have a formalized channel for it. Providing such a channel can help to increase the interest in, and acceptance of, a publication that might otherwise be considered as "talking down" to employees.

Feedback mechanisms can include letters-to-the-editor, a "gripe" department, or question-and-answer columns. The degree to which these will be successful is largely dependent on how willing management is to answer questions candidly. Not all management people are willing to do this, of course. But when they are, and problems can be candidly discussed, the entire publication may take on a credibility and acceptability on the part of the employees that it might not otherwise have had.

From the standpoint of management, "feedback" from employees can serve as important warning signs of potential trouble spots that perhaps can be eliminated before real trouble occurs.

An important aspect of making the feedback mechanism effective is to make sure readers respond quickly. This naturally works best in publications with frequent publication dates—weeklies or bi-weeklies. If there is too much time-lag between question and response, the problem may be aggravated or it may lose its appeal. In some organizations it may be possible to answer questions received by the publication from employees through the use of bulletin boards.

HOW OFTEN SHOULD A PUBLICATION APPEAR?

Again, as in most other aspects of the employee magazine, the question of frequency will relate back to the written objectives. In a fast-growing or fast-changing company there not only is need for a frequently appearing publication, but there also is usually enough going on to furnish readable material for its pages. In organizations that are growing slowly, or not at all, it may be more effective to publish less frequently, but to make some greater effort toward high quality. For a quarterly to be effective, it almost always has to try to achieve a high editorial impact, since the time lag between issues is too great to sustain employee interest. Quarterly or bi-monthly frequency is more suited to "external" publications; weekly or bi-weekly to "internal" publications. Large companies may cover the whole spectrum of frequency, beginning with daily typed bulletins for supervisorial or bulletin board use; weekly summaries of important activities; monthly magazines and quarterlies that examine subjects of interest in considerable depth.

DISTRIBUTING THE EMPLOYEE MAGAZINE

Strangely enough, this seemingly simple problem may prove to be one of the most difficult of all. In organizations where the work force is relatively stable, it may not be particularly troublesome, but in organizations where there is a high rate of turnover, or where the number of employees fluctuates widely by seasons or work load, just the maintenance of lists may be difficult.

The simplest means of distribution would at first appear to be to give a copy of the publication to each person as he passes the check-in gate to report for work. This has the disadvantage that the employee may then spend some time sitting around reading it, with consequent loss of production. In a large firm, with many employees, this may represent a large hidden cost over a period of time.

If employees formally check out through guard stations or punch a time clock, it is sometimes feasible to make copies of the publication available to them as they leave work. Depending, of course, on the degree to which the publication is accepted, this method sometimes has the disadvantage that many of the copies may be thrown away in the street outside or in the parking lot, creating a litter problem. If acceptance is good, it leads to the publication's going home to be read by the family.

If the payroll system is set up that way, or personnel records are sufficiently detailed and up-to-date, mailing copies of the publication directly to the employees' homes, where their families will see it also, is a good means of distribution, but an expensive one, both in monitoring the mailing lists, and in addressing costs and mailing charges. Desk-type organizations can, of course, simply distribute through the regular internal mail channels, preferably on the last mail run of the day or the shift, since this is least disruptive of productive work time and may increase the number of copies that the employees take home.

For combination internal/externals, and for strictly external publications, it is often less expensive and more efficient in the long run to turn the distribution over entirely to firms that specialize in

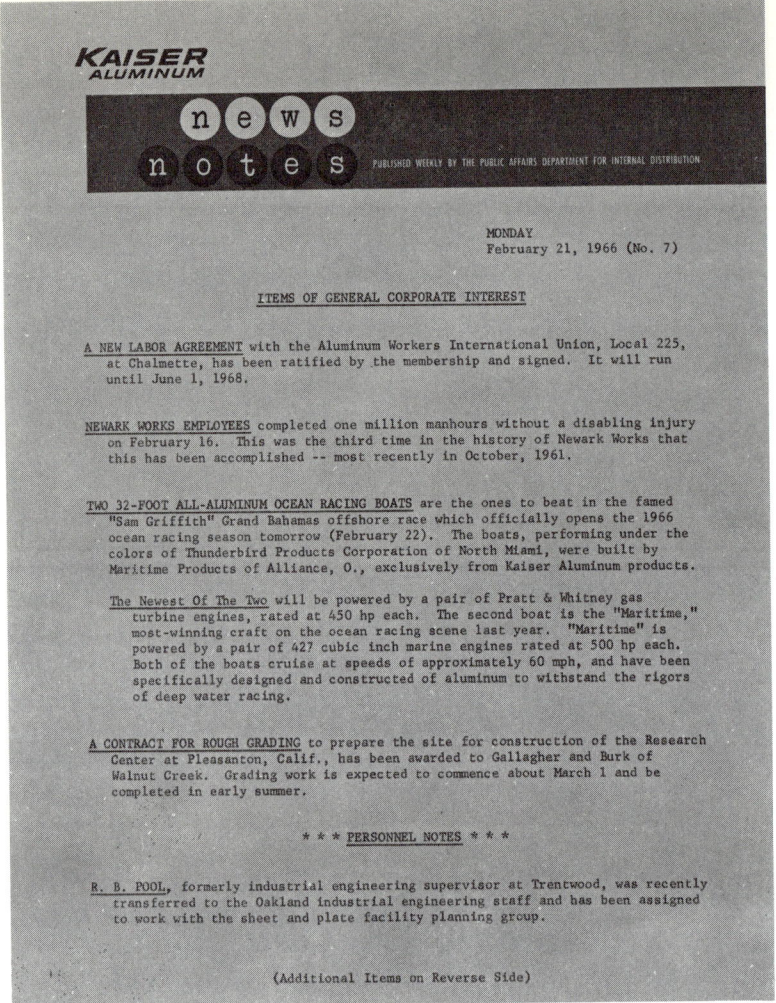

Figure 15-3. An executives' newsletter, distributed to key officials of a corporation. This supplements the general internal publications that are distributed to all employees.

keeping up mailing lists and in magazine and newspaper distribution. Their unit costs frequently may be less than the real costs of trying to have company personnel handle distribution in their "spare time."

In any event, a budget for distribution, which will include securing and imprinting envelopes, maintaining address plates, monitoring and changing address lists, addressing, stuffing, handling, shipping and mailing, should be set up separately from the actual production budget. Quite frequently the distribution cost, particularly on large circulation combinations and externals, may be larger than the cost of preparing and printing the publication itself. When the distribution costs are lumped into the production cost, the budget for the publication may appear to be larger than management feels it should be. When the distribution cost is set out as a separate charge it does not get confused with the cost of the magazine or newspaper.

WHERE TO GET PROFESSIONAL HELP

There are two organizations whose memberships are made up of practicing company publication editors. Each has local chapters in most major metropolitan areas. Membership costs are nominal. For the beginning editor, contact with other editors may frequently be a good source of help. The organizations also publish their own newsletters, and kits of helpful advice, sources of art or writing help, and useful feature sources. One organization is The American Association of Industrial Editors,

1300 Arch Street, Philadelphia, Pa. 19107 and the other is the International Council of Industrial Editors, 2108 Braewick Circle, Akron, Ohio 44313.

Every two years a directory of "House Magazines" is published by Gebbie Directory, P.O. Box 1111, Sioux City, Iowa 51102, that describes more than 4,000 company magazines of all types. The listings give the name of the publication, the sponsoring company, name and mailing address of the editor, description of the kind of material the publication normally handles, its circulation, type of audience (as between internal or external or combination) and general editorial requirements, and whether the publication purchases material from writers or photographers.

For beginning company editors it is a useful source of information, since nearly all of the publications listed are willing to send samples in response to requests, and a cross section of these can be a useful source of ideas.

CHANGING TRENDS IN EMPLOYEE PUBLICATIONS

Just as employee publications for many years were characterized chiefly by gossip and chit-chat, then began adding features with a higher informational content, and then, in turn, began developing an interpretive approach, so it may reasonably be conjectured that company publications of the future may be quite different than they are today.

This difference may express itself in two ways—in the kinds of subjects that are covered and in their graphic expression. Both are areas in which there usually can be considerable improvement.

Today, it is the rare company employee publication that will discuss those very issues that employees—particularly those who belong to organized labor—are most interested in: the effects of automation, "right to work" legislation, guaranteed annual income, labor legislation, racial integration, price and wage inflation, and a host of other topics that are freely and frequently discussed in general magazines and newspapers, on radio and television, and certainly in the employee publications put out by labor organizations. This has resulted in what has been called "The Zone of Silence"—a whole range of taboo subjects on which management does not express its opinions or points of view in the only effective medium that it has for reaching the employees.

When discussions of such subjects do appear in employee publications, they usually are so generalized, or so abstract in their expression, that employees either do not understand them, or have difficulty relating them to their own practical and specific views.

Business management has as much right to express its viewpoints clearly and specifically on economic issues as any other group. One way to do this effectively is to keep some page or department of the employee publication as an open forum in which management expresses its opinion on specific economic or political subjects and publishes alongside an equally candid expression of employees' views on the same subject.

The other general area in which employee publications may change rather radically in the future is in their graphic approaches, their basic designs. The company publication editor has some unusual freedoms that editors of subscription magazines do not have. He need not worry about news and recognition, nor about subscriber recognition, so producing the same format over and over again for "consistency" has very little point.

The company magazine editor usually need not worry about advertising pages competing with his editorial matter or about advertising approaches that can overwhelm the editorial sections. Freedom from these two restrictions has led to an innovative, attractive, and fairly free-wheeling journalistic approach.

As companies face up to the fact that each year there is more and more competition for their employees' attention, they may begin to demand that their own publications exploit the great editorial and graphic freedoms that they have. The result could be a new and exciting form of journalism.

16

Public Relations and Labor Matters

ROBERT W. HEFTY has been director of the Public Relations Office, Ford North American Automotive Operations, since July, 1976. Previously he was director of public information on Ford Motor Company's Public Relations Staff, in which capacity he was responsible for all corporate publicity and press relations including coverage of Ford's triennial contract negotiations with the powerful United Auto Workers union.

Except for Army service in World War II and the Korean war, Mr. Hefty was with United Press Associations from 1941 to 1952, lastly as Northwest news manager headquartered in Minneapolis. Prior to that he was assistant manager of the Detroit bureau where he covered the automotive and labor beats.

Mr. Hefty joined Ford's Industrial Relations Staff as supervisor of employee newspapers in January, 1952. He switched to Public Relations in 1954, and became corporate press relations manager in 1959, News Department manager in 1960, and Ford Division public relations manager in 1963. In his staff capacities, he has participated in or supervised coverage of Ford-UAW contract negotiations for almost 20 years.

Mr. Hefty is a member of Sigma Delta Chi, national journalism society, and past president of SDX's large Detroit chapter. He is an accredited member of the Public Relations Society of America and past president of PRSA's Michigan Chapter. He is president of the International Visitors Council of Metropolitan Detroit, Inc., and chairman of the Public Relations Committee of the Motor Vehicles Manufacturers Association.

Mr. Hefty is a graduate of the University of Minnesota.

For purposes of simplification, this chapter will deal with a manufacturing company and how its public relations staff handles labor matters. However, the term "company" is intended to be generic. It is expected that most of the points covered will be applicable to most other organizations also, including the labor unions with whom industry often is in an adversary position.

In the public relations of labor relations, there are two primary targets, or audiences: the customer who buys a company's products, and the employee who helps make them. They in turn—and especially the customer—are part of a larger and more amorphous amalgam called "the public."

There are special audiences, of course—stockholders, dealers, distributors, suppliers, the government, and so on. But they are incidental compared with the two main audiences—and besides they help comprise the larger consumer-public target that places them at least peripherally in one of the major spotlights.

The two principal audiences are of transcendent importance because they hold the power of life and death over the enterprise—the customer by buying or not buying, the employee by building or not building.

It therefore is necessary to communicate with both of them regularly, honestly and openly, with the objective of establishing a rapport built on mutual confidence, understanding, and respect that will see the company through whatever emergencies may arise.

With the employee, the need to communicate begins when he walks in the door and continues until he walks out. Actually, with the special type of employee who must be recruited, it begins well *before* he walks in the door.

Employee communications are particularly vital in times of crisis, though perhaps the most effective and believable communicating is done in times of calm—when the crisis often can be averted.

The public relations practitioner concerned with labor relations should understand from the outset that the employee—and particularly the unionized employee—is not the enemy. He is the heart of the organization—probably the one element without which the company cannot function.

The average employee is essentially honest—willing and usually eager to give a fair day's work for a fair day's pay. But his expectations grow with the growth of the enterprise, and his desires reflect the enormous transformation that has overtaken the land. American business—and indeed world business—are coming more and more to realize that money and security have lost some of their fascination for the modern-day worker—especially the *young* worker. He wants more than good pay and a comfortable retirement. He wants better working conditions and a more challenging job. He wants the company he works for to contribute to a better life and to be known for its good works. If these things are not forthcoming he often rebels—by quitting or striking or just taking the day off. Absenteeism, turnover, and the incidence of disciplinary cases in U.S. industry doubled during the sixties, mirroring the unrest and indiscipline so manifest in all aspects of modern life.

MAJOR CHALLENGE: THE RESTLESS EMPLOYEE

Meeting the challenge of the restless, demanding employee is a major assignment of present-day industrial public relations. Not only must the company public relations man or woman help communicate intelligently with the employee; he or she also must help persuade management to make the changes necessary to provide an on-the-job environment that motivates its work force and gives every person on the payroll—from the chairman to the janitor—a reason for pride.

Employee expectations are not always reasonable. Labor unions usually enter contract negotiations demanding more than they expect to get, eliciting predictable resistance from management. The sparring that ensues provides a continuing test of the talents and mettle of the public relations specialist assigned to labor relations.

One of the corporate communicator's primary assignments is to avoid management-employee confrontations whenever possible. A good starting point is an informed work force.

The first step in communicating with the employee, and particularly the new employee, is to tell him where he stands—what the company is prepared to do for him and what's expected of him in return. This usually is done in early interviews, but it should be implemented with written statements of personnel policies covering wages; holidays and vacations; sick, personal, and military leave; cost-of-living, separation, and transfer allowances; layoff benefits; promotional, training, and extended education opportunities; personal and employment counseling; hospital-surgical-medical protection; recreational activities, and other benefits. Separate information booklets for hourly rated and salaried employees usually are desirable, and of course they should be kept up-to-date as conditions change.

Once the employee has been initially informed of his rights, benefits, and responsibilities, every means should be taken to keep him posted on everything in the company orbit that affects his welfare—from capital investments to changes in leave time for jury duty. And he should be given the bad news along with the good; it is better he hear the former from his management than from a source claiming management is trying to "cover up." This goes back to the premise that believability and honesty are essential ingredients of an employee communications program.

The media available for communicating with employees will vary with the means and philosophies of the employers, but generally they include company magazines, plant newspapers, individual and mass meetings, newsletters, bulletin boards, suggestion programs, closed-circuit television and videotape messages, motion pictures, public-address systems, information racks, pay enclosures, open houses and plant tours for employees and their families, and direct mail.[1] The last-named—usually consisting of letters to employees from their supervisors or top corporate management—are most effective when directed to the employee's home so he has time to read them at leisure and can show them to other members of his

---

[1] See Chapters 14, 15, and 48.

family. (In many companies, employee communications actually are the responsibility of the industrial relations or personnel department rather than public relations, but the principles remain the same.)

THE IMPORTANCE OF TIMING

Timing is important in employee communications. An employee likes to hear things about his company before his neighbors and the public do. Hence, the most-appreciated communication is one that arrives at least simultaneously with a public announcement and preferably somewhat before. Where precise timing of the public disclosure is important, of course,[2] a general communication to employees considerably in advance of the public announcement would make it difficult to keep the information from "leaking" to news media.

As indicated, the labor relations function of public relations comes into play most forcefully in times of emergency, crisis, or other unusual activity—contract negotiations, strikes, plant closings, temporary layoffs and shutdowns, union organizing campaigns, representation elections, hard-core hiring, and the like. It is in times like these that the company's and management's long-term reputation for fair dealing and honest communications both stands it in good stead and faces its severest test.

Most major industrial labor contracts are for periods of two to three years, with interim negotiation permitted on reopenable issues in some cases. Generally a company can expect relative labor calm between the signing and ratification of a labor agreement and the reopening of negotiations on a new contract several years hence. Still, the interim period can be marked by authorized or unauthorized strikes, slowdowns, lockouts or threatened lockouts, and demands for contract reopenings or modifications.

Whether new-contract negotiations are approaching or just concluded, therefore, the public relations job is never done. It intensifies, however, six months to a year before the scheduled start of formal company-union talks.

PREPARING FOR NEGOTIATIONS

A logical first step in preparing for a new round of contract negotiations is formation of a communications task force consisting of key public relations, labor relations, personnel, and government-affairs representatives (the last-named because (1) government continues its close surveillance of the private collective-bargaining system and wants to be kept informed of major labor-relations developments in key industries, and (2) because growing labor unrest has increased the advocacy, by both federal and state legislators, of stricter government controls over workers, their unions, and their employers).

The task force's first assignment is to agree on what the company hopes to accomplish with information programs directed to its two principal audiences—the employees and the public. There's nothing very mysterious about this. Generally, any organization preparing to enter contract negotiations with its principal union or unions hopes to:

1. Reach a settlement that is in the economic interest of the company, the employees, the stockholders, and the customers.

2. Minimize the risks of a strike prior to conclusion of an agreement.

3. Keep employees and the public (plus of course other special audiences such as dealers, distributors, stockholders, suppliers, and so on) informed of major developments, and solicit their support for—or at least understanding of—management's positions on basic issues.

4. Discourage government involvement in the bargaining process.

It is important that both the communications goals and the media used to attain them have built-in flexibility that enables management to move quickly in the constantly changing atmosphere that characterizes modern-day labor-management relations. One unexpected union move could require a whole new set of guidelines for the company's negotiators and their communications specialists.

Once the goals are set, the public relations person assigned to labor relations must move quickly to help realize them. This means acquainting himself or herself thoroughly with every facet of the negotiations picture. It means "living" with labor relations for the duration—attending briefings on the major issues (wages, cost-of-living, pensions, profit-sharing, vacations, and so on). It means gleaning every scrap of information available on the union's likely demands and objectives—from union statements, speeches, news releases, press conferences and interviews, from speculative news stories and columns, and from conversational exchanges with colleagues in the corporate public

[2] See Chapters 11 and 12.

relations-labor relations fields. It means keeping detailed, codified records on information gathered from these sources, for ready use by both public relations and labor relations personnel. It means maintaining friendly but strictly professional and ethical relations with counterparts in the public relations departments of competitive companies and the trade unions, to the advantage of the parties most properly concerned—management, labor, and the news media.

GUARDING PROPRIETARY INFORMATION

It is important to remember that if the public relations man's or woman's relationship with labor relations colleagues is as it should be, he or she will be entrusted with much more information than he or she is expected to divulge to outside sources. Protection of proprietary data that are not available—for good business reasons—to either the union or the company's competitors, is requisite to proper working of the private collective-bargaining system. The public relations specialist therefore is the protector of some of the company's most vital operating secrets, and must screen the information accordingly.

Once the public relations specialist has done his labor relations homework, and has a specific set of objectives as determined by the communications task force, he is ready to start communicating with his major audiences.

Employees. Before and during the negotiations, the corporate communicator will make systematic use of the media already mentioned—company newspapers and magazines, letters, films, booklets, PA systems, and so on—to keep the work force informed about the company's plans, positions, and activities. News material will recapitulate and dramatize the company's already generous employee pay and benefit programs; announce the negotiating timetable and makeup of the company's bargaining team, and explain the company's economic position as it enters the negotiations. To the extent that they can be revealed without undermining management's bargaining strategy, or violating company-union agreements to refrain from public discussion of issues and positions, communications to employees further should detail company offers as they are presented to the union negotiators, and spell out company answers to specific union requests or demands. Some companies set up recorded telephone messages, updated daily or as often as developments warrant, which employees can hear by dialing designated numbers.

There are legal limitations to what can and cannot be included in company communications to employees. Section 8(c) of the Taft-Hartley Law states that the company can express an opinion or put forth its point of view, in written, graphic, or visual form, so long as the material "contains no threat of reprisal or force or promise of benefit." This clearly authorizes the company to take its case directly to the employee, but it just as clearly warns that the company message should be drafted with extreme care. It mandates that communications to employees be reviewed by attorneys familiar with both the letter and the various interpretations of the laws dealing with such communications.[3]

The public. Communicating with the public often goes in tandem with employee communications, because in many cases management can best tell its story by providing the news media with copies of letters and other materials sent to employees. However, there are numerous other means—both direct and indirect—of telling the company's story through the public media.

The most obvious *direct* routes are through written news releases, radio tapes, television film clips, motion pictures, and advertising. They have the advantage of presenting the company story in precisely the form management wants it told. In other words, they offer the greatest degree of immediate control, although of course in the case of the news release there is no way of predicting the final form in which its content will appear.

Less controllable but still direct means of telling the management story include on-the-record interviews, news conferences, and plant tours.

A GOOD TOOL: BACKGROUND "BRIEFING"

Perhaps the best *indirect* method of presenting the company's positions on actual or potential bargaining issues is off-the-record "backgrounding" of newsmen by key labor relations personnel at both the corporate and local-plant levels. Months before the actual contract negotiations are set to begin, reporters, columnists, editorial writers, and radio and television commentators can be brought in to gather from company labor relations experts material that is not to be attributed to them but that can be used to add perspective to the newsmen's own speculative stories about the forthcoming negotiations. This is a perfectly legitimate technique in labor reporting and often is preferred by the reporter, who then can write or speak

[3]See Chapter 54.

knowledgeably about his subject in print or on the air and at the same time speculate with the assurance that he is not "off base" on an important issue or position. Further, the backgrounding provides the savvy reporter with an added dimension that he can use to gauge the impact of future developments on both the management and labor sides of a dispute.

One important point: a public relations specialist should *always* sit in on the backgrounding session. Not only does he provide a needed "backstop" for both the reporter and labor relations source in the event of disagreements over interpretation, attribution, and so on, but he gains, in the course of the interview, additional experience and knowledge that—discreetly used—will make him an even more effective communicator for the company.

While we will not attempt to list specific subjects for either on-the-record or background interviews, a word of caution is offered on discussing management's ability to cope with the economic liabilities inherent in union demands. Enlisting public sympathy for such things as the corporate "profit squeeze" is difficult at best, and it is a hazardous exercise anyway since it may lead to union demands to "open the books" and a company usually does not bargain with the union on the basis of costs or ability to pay. However, this does not preclude encouraging business and labor writers from discussing, on their own, the relationship of increased labor costs to product prices and the total economy.

The question usually arises in any pre-negotiations period whether it is worthwhile to try to debate issues in the public press, or whether they are best left to the bargainers in their private sessions. At least in the past, management too often has been willing to let union charges go unanswered, on the theory that anything said would be twisted out of context by the union and used against the company. Labor thus was constantly on the offensive, and management constantly on the defensive. And with millions of readers and listeners hearing only the union side of the story, management was "guilty until proved innocent."

It is to be hoped that this time is all but past. Enlightened management now recognizes that it has an obligation to itself, to its stockholders and customers, and indeed to the very employees represented by the union it is rebutting, to present an honest and detailed account of how it stands on the issues. This again, of course, is subject to the constraints of bargaining strategy, but the fact is that more often than not, American business management now is disposed to acknowledge, explain, and when necessary refute union claims and demands. And of course it is the trained public relations practitioner who helps determine the success or failure of this effort.

PRINCIPAL RESPONSIBILITIES

Both prior to and during the contract negotiations, public relations has three principal assignments:

1. To serve management.
2. To keep employees and the public informed.
3. To help the news media do their job.

In serving management, the public relations labor specialist has these responsibilities:

1. To seek forums for effective enunciation of company positions—in speeches, interviews, news conferences, letters, public statements, and the like.
2. To research, write, and clear the necessary documents—releases, speech texts, scripts, letters, advertisements, and so on—needed to exploit these forums.
3. To help keep management minutely informed on union developments, by attending (and when possible tape-recording) union conventions and press conferences, reviewing and clipping union publications, obtaining the union's news releases, and passing along views expressed by labor reporters, union public relations men, and other experienced observers.
4. To maintain an instantaneous reporting service for management on business, labor, and government developments that might have even a slight bearing on the negotiations and the company's positions therein. This includes monitoring business and labor columns, editorials, radio and TV commentaries, wire service copy, and so on.
5. To maintain scrupulous records on all written materials pertaining to the negotiations—newspaper and magazine clippings, company and union news releases, union publications, employee communications, advertisements, company-union or union-employee correspondence, company and union speech texts, and so on.
6. To help prepare background memoranda or "white papers" on specific problems at issue in the negotiations (wages, profit-sharing, cost-of-living, fringe benefits, automation, union in-plant representation); on comments by business, government, and labor leaders on the state of the economy, the

dangers of inflation, the need for wage and price controls and the like, and settlements in other key union-company negotiations that might indicate "patterns" for the negotiations at hand.

7. To prepare quick-reference question-and-answer sheets for use in answering media inquiries—trying to anticipate questions likely to be asked by newsmen, and preparing carefully documented answers for quick use when the questions arise. This can be overdone, however; rather than try to anticipate every conceivable question (which is a futile exercise anyway) the public relations labor specialist would do better to cultivate his labor relations sources for prompt, fresh, and authoritative responses to unexpected inquiries.

Public relations' role in *serving the employee* by keeping him informed already has been covered, and its role in *serving the public* coincides with *helping the news media* do the best possible job of covering the negotiations and developments leading up to them. Prompt, accurate, balanced reporting is in the company's interest as well as the reporter's and the public's.

HOW TO HELP NEWSMEN

Following are ways in which newsmen can and should be assisted before and during contract negotiations:

• News releases—written stories, recorded and filmed statements.

• On-the-record interviews and news conferences.

• Background briefings (covered previously).

• Answers to spot questions.

• Guidance on questions that cannot be answered directly or for attribution. Discreet "steering" of a reporter groping for information with which to speculate can prevent embarrassment for both him and the company.

• A "fact book," distributed in advance of negotiations, containing historical information on past negotiations and strikes; company data on plants, employment, payrolls, products, and so on, and a list of key labor relations personnel involved in the bargaining.

• Data cards with home and office telephone numbers of public relations personnel assigned to labor relations.

• A press room equipped with typewriters, telephones, work tables and chairs, copy paper, carbon paper, and other materials. Because news coverage of contract negotiations usually involves long hours of waiting and "sweating it out," provision also should be made for lounge chairs and sofas, television and radio sets, card tables, food and soft drinks (but never alcoholic beverages), and current magazines and newspapers. There should be tables for copies of corporate *and union* news releases, fact books, annual reports and other reference materials, chronological files on key newspaper and magazine stories reporting the negotiations, and, where appropriate, transcripts of company press conferences held prior to or earlier in the negotiations. A blackboard and bulletin board should be placed for easy posting of announcements and messages. The press room should be kept neat and clean at all times. When located on company property, it should be convenient to the negotiating room and union and company caucus rooms (which are off-limits to the press), but far enough away to insure a reasonable measure of privacy for the bargainers. Union public relations representatives should be made to feel welcome in the company press room, and in fact should be encouraged to be present to answer newsmen's questions and—with appropriate security—work with corporate public relations people on joint statements, news conferences, and announcements. Similarly, as a service to reporters, spokesmen for the bargaining teams should be encouraged to drop into the press room from time to time—preferably daily—even when they have no progress to report or must spend most of their time declining comment.

• An interview area outside the main bargaining room, for newsmen and women to question the chief negotiators for both sides as they enter and leave the sessions. The area should be large enough to accommodate reporters from print media, radio and television crews, and company and union observers (including public relations staffers) but small and isolated enough to discourage unwanted kibitzers. It should provide sufficient power for television lights and cameras; ideally, a company electrician should be on hand to assist with power and lighting requirements. Drapes and carpeting should be provided to improve acoustics and a mixer system for tape recorders. Space should be provided off the main interview area for a radio-TV sound control room and equipment storage.

• Where possible, advance notices on both company and union statements and news conferences, both to newsmen in the negotiations press room and to other media representatives obviously interested in covering the events but not presently staffing. This "backstopping" of reporters and photographers not able to cover the negotiations on a continuing basis is essential to good press relations; it helps give smaller but still important media an even break with the more prosperous information outlets that can afford to staff, when desirable, on a round-the-clock basis.

• Parking space near the press room for the news "regulars."

ORGANIZING FOR THE JOB

Throughout the negotiations and pre-negotiations periods, the function of top public relations management is to work with the principal officers of the company in helping shape bargaining strategy, select the timing of various public and employee announcements, and weigh the likely public and employee reaction to the proposed settlement. Actual staffing of the negotiations and their attendant press coverage is left to trained specialists down the line.

The ideal public relations staffing arrangement involves a "Mr. Inside" and a "Mr. Outside"—or perhaps a "Mr. Inside" and/or "Mr. Outside." The "inside" staffer really is an ex-officio member of the corporate negotiating team who attends the bargaining sessions as an observer, maintains a constant liaison for the public relations staff with key company negotiators, is the principal company contact with the union public relations staff, and accompanies the chief spokesman for the corporate negotiators at all times in his contacts with newsmen and union strategists. He writes the basic news releases and policy statements, supervises preparation of "sidebar" and background materials, and maintains the official negotiations log or diary for public relations. His main function, in short, is to serve the management and specifically the company negotiating team.

"Mr. Outside" complements the work of the inside anchor man. He follows through on clearance and reproduction of releases, maintains contacts with key labor reporters, supervises the press room, and relays information from "Mr. Inside" on the start and end of bargaining sessions, scheduled news conferences, and availability of key company negotiators for interviews, clearance of public relations materials, and other purposes.

As the negotiations approach their climax, more public relations personnel—including public relations management—will help with the day-to-day news effort. Public relations executives, of course, will have worked behind the scenes, mainly on policy matters, from the beginning, but in the final days their assistance will be needed on the scene and their own interest in the proceedings will insure their being present.

Local activities. In companies with operations in a number of states, it is essential that regional public relations and employee or labor relations representatives be kept abreast of all developments from the home office on the one hand, and feed information on local negotiations *to* the home office on the other. This continuing two-way exchange is vital to the maintenance of a consistent corporate posture wherever the company does business.

As indicated, it is important that company public relations personnel maintain an effective relationship with their counterparts in the union, again on a regional as well as central basis. This insures a proper exchange of information on news releases and other public announcements, news conferences, and scheduled participation by the company and union principals in key bargaining activities. It also is of help to the news media, as well as to both parties to the negotiations, that the company and union publicists act in concert whenever such action is appropriate. From the company's standpoint, it is important that the union's concurrence be obtained in the handling of joint statements, announcements, and press arrangements.

Cooperation can be overdone, of course, and whenever possible company public relations strategists will want to time important corporate releases so as to avoid undesired "split play," in which the union has enough lead time to issue counter statements that will share billing with—and perhaps eclipse—the company's pronouncements. The union, of course, will strive for the same kind of exclusive timing for its key announcements.

One element that enters into media coverage of many key negotiations is the so-called "news blackout." This has become almost traditional, for example, in the auto industry. When the bargaining between the United Auto Workers and the so-called "target" company enters a critical stage, where one inadvertent statement by either side might impair the progress of negotiations, the two sides may agree on cessation of public comment for either a specific or indefinite period and newsmen are advised of the fact. Either party can end the blackout after serving an agreed-on notice, but in the meantime the negotiators' lips are sealed and reporters must rely on their ingenuity to keep the pot boiling. Usually they do very well.

REPORTING THE RESULTS

Contract negotiations end with a settlement that may or may not be preceded by a strike. Public relations coverage of the results is governed pretty much by the same principles and techniques that apply to coverage of the negotiations themselves.

In the case of a peaceful settlement, both the company and union want to be first to give the details—after a joint announcement that agreement has been reached. Being first requires four things: good feedback from the "inside" public relations representative of details on issues as they are agreed on; swift preparation of written releases; a well-oiled clearance machinery for the necessary reviews by financial, legal, and labor relations experts, and a first-class publicity reproduction and distribution system. Not only does superior performance in these areas enable a company to report settlement details first in its own language; it also endears the company to the eager newsmen and employees who are panting for the details and are duly grateful to the party that delivers first.

One word of caution, however: it is better to be late than to sacrifice accuracy, thoroughness, and responsiveness in a document of such vital importance to the audiences concerned.

Also, in the auto industry and others, it now is the practice to withhold details of the settlement until union members have voted either to ratify or reject it. Because the union controls the ratification process, it obviously has an advantage over the company in reporting details promptly.

The announcement of a settlement usually takes two forms—a news release, and a press conference with the captain of the bargaining team. Again, it is desirable to be first in talking to reporters, because it gives the company spokesperson an opportunity to lead with his interpretation of the settlement and also to avoid argumentative questions based on points made by the union spokesman in an earlier news conference.

Depending on the judgments of the negotiating parties as to probable interpretation by news media of the settlement terms, there often is a "gentlemen's agreement" that one or the other of the chief spokesmen will appear first to "meet the press." Such an agreement rarely if ever applies to written reports on the settlement details, however, and therein lies the competition for the ear and gratitude of the eager employee and the restless reporter.

HANDLING THE STRIKE

There are two principal types of strikes. An *authorized* strike is one that is permitted under the company-union contract, has been approved by the union membership, and has been endorsed by the parent labor organization. It can be a "national" strike, in which all union employees of a large, multi-plant company walk out at once, or a "local" strike involving a single plant. An *unauthorized* or "wildcat" strike is one staged in violation of the contract, often by a dissident minority in a local chapter of the union and usually on short notice.

The company-wide strike is of primary concern to public relations, although it should be noted that a local strike at a plant that makes parts for other plants in the company system can result in a swift shutdown of the company's total manufacturing operation.

Careful public relations planning is possible with authorized strikes, because such stoppages often are preceded by prolonged negotiations and always—under contractual mandate—by a strike "notice" and the setting of a specific strike "deadline."

Once a strike is imminent or has started, the same public relations outlets and techniques are used as in the case of negotiations—public statements of management's position through selected channels (news releases, interviews, news conferences, advertisements); letters to employees, stockholders, suppliers, dealers, distributors, and so on; statements and stories in company publications, and company communications to the union that are made public. Media fact books are needed on plants, employees, and products affected; wages and supplier outlays lost each day of the stoppage; previous strikes, and chronological events leading to the current walkout.

For a company with plants located in a number of states or communities, a strong field public relations network becomes even more essential than during the negotiations. Management and newsmen will need daily reports on local strike reaction, possible picketline incidents, and in-plant negotiations to settle local issues.

Once the strike is under way, negotiations to end it are covered closely by the news media, both because of immediate interest in the strike and because of the likely settlement "pattern" that will be established for other companies in the same industry (assuming the struck company is a major factor in the industry).

Public relations' handling of the strike and strike settlement generally tracks that of negotiations that manage to end without a walkout. Speed in relaying accurate, detailed accounts of the settlement again is paramount, for both employees and reporters.

A prime objective in communicating the results of a settlement—with or without a strike—must be to minimize the likelihood of a bad "aftertaste" in the mouths of the employees, the community, or the public. This requires a delicate, subtle representation of the settlement terms, emphasizing the balanced nature of an agreement that serves the interest of both parties and the public. Above all, there must be no "winner" or "loser."

A recent and disturbing trend in American labor is the growing tendency of union members to refuse to ratify even the most favorable-appearing settlement terms—often in defiance of contrary recommendations by their union leaders. This is a problem for labor as well as management, because it reflects a growing unrest and militancy especially among the younger workers. Helping persuade employees to approve economically sound settlements poses another demanding test of the public relations man's communications skills.

Space will not permit specific recommendations on handling of other labor-related matters such as plant closings, layoffs and temporary shutdowns, lockouts, union elections, and union organizing campaigns. However, a few general rules apply as they do to coverage of strikes and contract negotiations:

1. Tell the company's story forcefully and honestly.

2. Inform employees of impending developments at least as soon as the public is advised, and preferably somewhat beforehand.

3. *Keep* employees and the public informed for the duration of the event.

4. Help newsmen cover the event quickly, accurately, and impartially; it is in the interests of your company, its employees, and the public that this be done.

5. Keep management informed of all developments affecting the current situation and likely to influence the outcome.

6. Organize and staff properly. Establish goals, select information outlets and targets, assign competent personnel, and insure prompt and thorough feedback from local and field public relations sources.

7. Do your labor relations homework. Know your subject intimately, but know also what information should be made public and what should not.

Any public relations practitioner who applies these rules in every situation will serve his company and the public faithfully and well.

17

The Role of Public Relations in Marketing

ROBERT N. THURSTON is Senior Vice President—Corporate Affairs and a member of the Board of Directors and Executive Committee of The Quaker Oats Company, Chicago. He is a native of New Hampshire and received an A.B. from Bowdoin College, Brunswick, Maine, in 1954. He "drifted into" public relations in 1956 after military service. After 5½ years as public relations manager of a small scientific consulting firm in Boston, he joined Mead Johnson & Company in 1961. In 1963 he was promoted to Public Relations Director at Mead Johnson.

Mr. Thurston has been with The Quaker Oats Company since 1966, and was made an officer of the company in 1968. The department he heads is responsible for public policy, government relations, urban affairs and community relations, financial public relations, corporate identity, marketing publicity, employee communications, general public information and press relations, home economics, and consumer services. He is a Director of McDonald's Corporation.

The public relations business is probably more self-conscious about its stereotype image as promoter and press agent, and less successful at doing anything to change it, than any field of endeavor with an image problem. Nowhere do the ingredients of this image problem come into sharper contrast than in the role that public relations plays in marketing.

Although many public relations people might argue the point, it can be reasonably speculated that most businessmen would be able to quite quickly define the role of public relations in marketing: publicity. And a good many public relations practitioners would be satisfied with the definition as long as it was broadened sufficiently to encompass other aspects of using "public relations techniques" to promote a product or service.

This basically publicity function of public relations in marketing is important, and will be dealt with later in this chapter. It is also the function that contributes most to the rather shallow image many people have of public relations, an image that seriously inhibits the field's ability to function in a role that is more important to marketing than publicity could ever be.

This second role, and the one that will be dealt with first here because it is more important, is the steering of marketing through the maze of difficult-to-understand, volatile, and decisive public opinions that are drastically changing the requirements of marketing. This has sometimes been called the "conscience" role of public relations, and to an extent that's accurate. It is also a hard-headed business role because the marketing decision that results in public criticism or perhaps even cancellation of a product or advertising is a very bad business decision indeed. So the advice may be conceived by "conscience," but heeding it should under no circumstances be considered altruistic. Nor should conceiving the advice take place in a vacuum that ignores what is best for the business (although arguments over what is "best" are inevitable, depending on one's point of view).

THE ROLE OF PUBLIC INTEREST IN MARKETING

The history of government regulation of business in the 20th Century is one in which abuses have been identified and dramatized, legislation has been fought over (with business almost always opposed), and finally laws have been passed and regulations enforced. There is one school of thought—and perhaps a valid one—that sees continuation of this approach as the only proper method in a free-enterprise economy. By this theory, we accept that business will do *everything it can within existing law* to maximize profits. Since this approach assumes anything is okay as long as it's legal, the company professing this point of view would do well to have a large legal staff and not pay much attention to public relations' considerations in marketing. Many companies do precisely that.

Many companies feel that they cannot initiate new practices that increase their costs unless all their competitors do too. Their logic is that socially desirable actions would be self-defeating because they would penalize the firm undertaking them and make it less able to compete effectively. If one oil company discontinues a high-pressure game in promoting its products, according to this reasoning, it only loses sales volume to its competitors. If one auto maker stops promoting high power as a sales appeal, it only results in the less-safety-conscious competitors selling high-powered cars to speed-mad drivers.

In the present climate of pressure on companies to meet public expectations, this philosophy leads to giving the initiative to government. New laws and regulations that all members of an industry must comply with eliminate the likelihood of uneven cost burdens; but they abdicate still further the responsibilities for making business decisions that management wants to retain.

Each industry naturally prefers self-regulation to government controls. But where the individual practices of some members lead to most members continuing practices that arouse attacks, self-regulation breaks down.

When an industry is faced with such pressures, each company must decide whether its responsibility is to work with government agencies or Congress to help develop sound regulations that it and its competitors can accommodate to, or to oppose the injection of more governmental interference that it feels will be harmful and ineffective. When almost all proposals are opposed, however, it tends to backfire by reducing the confidence of the public and government in industry's sincerity on behalf of the public interest.

Increasingly some companies are recognizing that *the spirit of the law, and even the spirit of public opinion,* are at least as important to marketing as technical obedience to the law. In companies that have adopted this point of view, or through a mind open to sound counsel that can be persuaded to adopt it, there is a great role for the skilled and sensitive public relations practitioner. This writer thinks that public approbation is becoming so important that these companies are the only ones that will be able to grow successfully in the remainder of the 20th Century.

The changed climate is well illustrated by events taking place in Washington:

1. A *Republican* Administration was actively behind adoption of a new package of legislation aimed at protecting consumers. Such legislation a few years earlier would have been considered harshly anti-business (and still was by some businessmen). The top lobbyist of the Administration in pushing this legislation was Bryce Harlow, who previously had been Washington representative for the largest packaged goods manufacturer and advertiser in the world and who later returned to that company.

2. Organizations catering to private business competed with each other to conduct seminars and educational programs on how to ancitipate and forestall—as well as to meet—the complaints of consumers and consumerist groups.

Both of these actions were rather sharp departures from attitudes of the past. To be sure, they had been prompted by activists in the consumer protection field. But the facts were clear: the vast majority of Americans, consumers all, had lined up on the side of the consumer. Some normally very placid people—angered by unfulfilled warranties, devious promotions, malfunctioning equipment, and what they considered excessive prices for all of this—had become consumer miltants. In fact, a good many businessmen who questioned the activism of consumer militancy as it applied to their own businesses were consumer militants themselves at the auto or appliance repair shop.

A related issue, the pride of minorities, also became a factor in marketing as sensitivity to what might offend became an important ingredient in marketing decisions. Ground rules were difficult, although sensitivity was generally in proportion to past exploitation and current status of the minority group concerned.

THE NEW PUBLIC RELATIONS ROLE

The outstanding marketing people—and there are many of these—are alert to the whole spectrum of changing attitudes of the general public. It is part of their job, just as it is part of the public relations job, to be on top of this. Beyond that point, however, there is a fundamental difference between what the two functions must do: Marketing has a direct profit responsibility and cannot be expected to consider the public interest as its primary concern. Public relations, on the other hand, has no direct profit responsibility, but should have the specfic responsibility of assuring that the company is operating in a way that will avoid trouble and, in the context of the public interest, promise the best opportunity for long-term growth and prosperity. Thus the roles are quite different.

To a large extent, the way public relations fulfills its function is governed by what management expects of it. If the expectation is limited and the status of public relations is relatively low, it is unrealistic to expect much of consequence. The expectations are changing, however. One company president, addressing the Public Relations Society of America with some thoughts that are shared by many of his confreres, said:[1]

> Public relations' role has become much more than that of the "image merchant," who takes whatever situation exists and tries to project it in unblemished glory. One of the primary concerns of top management is adjusting our companies to the social, governmental, and political environments around us. Just as we expect our marketing people to anticipate changing consumer desires, we now expect our public relations staff to be sensitive to social change. We expect you to be tough enough to take what may be unpopular positions and defend them effectively, since good public relations is not always synonymous with what managers with short-term profit responsibility may propose to do. Usually, however, and fortunately, good public relations and good business are synonymous.

Given a mandate that strongly identifies public relations with the long-term welfare of the business, what are some of the specific areas in which public relations departments or counselors become involved?

1. *Long-term business development.* Some of the most enlightened companies see their long-term success closely identified with activities that a) will be attractive to young people who are increasingly socially motivated, and b) will be looked on as useful by a population increasingly concerned with meeting human needs of a nature somewhat less materialistic than those traditionally met by the private enterprise system.

Thus, while business development and acquisitions are usually functions assigned to specific departments, public relations should be involved. To cite an obvious example, it is entirely proper for the public relations director of a cosmetics, cigarette, or liquor manufacturer to counsel management on the advisability of getting into areas that are generally considered more socially useful—documenting the reasons why he thinks that is important and suggesting areas for examination.

The same principle applies to many other areas of business where certain types of products or certain marketing practices are likely to make the business unattractive to bright young people in the years ahead, or subject to restrictive government regulation or widespread consumer complaint. Heavy television advertisers, for example, will be well advised by their public relations departments to look at ways they can improve the quality of television if they want to preserve the good will they have with the public. Some companies are already taking this very seriously, and a few, such as Xerox and Hallmark, have for a long time.

2. *Advertising.* The public relations director has a particular challenge now to counsel his management on the need for better self-regulation of television advertising. The National Association of Broadcasters Code permits 9 ½ minutes of commercial interruption per hour during prime time and 16 minutes during non-prime time on network stations. On independent stations the total may be 16 minutes per hour. And frequency is only part of the problem—good taste and the effect on the audience should also be considered. The alternative to self-regulation is government regulation, and pompous statements about free enterprise will not be persuasive to critics annoyed by the quality of advertising.

3. *Truth in marketing.* Labeling, guarantees and warranties, product quality, price in relation to value, product safety assurances, ethnic sensitivities, product proliferation without significant innovation, misleading promotions, and many other current marketing problems clearly should be major concerns of public relations counsel. It is much simpler, and much more profitable, to correct a mistake before it's made.

4. *Organizing to represent the public interest in*

---

[1] Stuart, Robert D. Jr., President and Chief Executive Officer, The Quaker Oats Company. "The Business Role in Our Urban Crisis," Public Relations Society of America, Chicago, Illinois, November 20, 1968.

marketing. It is easy to chronicle some of the areas of marketing that are under criticism and state that public relations should be involved. In fact, involvement is difficult.

This is perhaps a useful analogy between the role of the legal department and that of the public relations department. The legal department, during the review that is standard with most large companies, can cite chapter and verse of the law and render a firm opinion. Thus the practice through which marketing people generally allow the lawyers to determine legal acceptability works pretty well. Lawyers are smart fellows, and even the most aggressive promoters don't get much past them.[2]

The situation is totally different in a public relations review. Legality is not the question; the attorneys have checked that. The questions are vague: Is it in the public interest? Will it create problems for us with some minority? Even though it's legal, is it misleading? Is it a fair value for the price? Is it ethical?

These are all questions that can be answered only with opinion; opinion based on experience and knowledge about what's going on, perhaps, but opinion nevertheless. And here lies the critical factor determining whether public relations can be useful: the credibility and rapport that public relations has with marketing and general management.

Some companies subject virtually everything to some form of formal public relations review, and overruling the public relations opinion is made difficult. This may well be the best answer, but it tends to take away from marketing the responsibility to consider public interest. It creates an "if public relations says it's okay, it's okay with me" philosophy, which easily extends itself to all sorts of devices for "getting things past" public relations. Because so much opinion is involved in the decisions, this writer feels that the automatic review has serious weaknesses.

In the years ahead, the public interest will have the power to make or break virtually any marketing decision. Thus the better course for public relations seems to be very close cooperation with marketing—*assuming responsibility for keeping marketing aware of the pressures and trends that are important to the business*. This requires more skill than an automatic review procedure. It requires very close working relationships; it requires periodic reviews for the marketing people on public policy matters as they relate to marketing; it requires frequent communications with marketing. It demands a total effort in which marketing and public relations work cooperatively toward an objective that ultimately they share: the maximum long-term profitability of the enterprise.

One caution: The way to be certain of offending no one is to say "no" to everything questionable. Innovation is vital to business, and a company that has traffic cops all over the place virtually guaranteeing that nothing innovative can get through is also headed toward public relations problems—with its stockholders and potential employees. The wise public relations advisor must be willing to take risks; he serves no one well by being ultra-conservative to save any possible embarrassment to himself.

In those circumstances where public relations is not recognized for its important role in coordinating the public interest and marketing, there are perhaps some opportunities to bring this about. Almost any crisis in which a product is seized, an advertising campaign stopped, the embarrassment of a congressional investigation incurred, or even a whole market destroyed is an opportunity to show how "it could have been different" if from the beginning there had been public relations involvement. This is particularly true when the crisis is felt at the top management level because it is then generally recognized that something must be done differently to avoid such a situation in the future. Responsibility for handling consumer complaints is also a potential route to more meaningful public relations involvement.

5. *Personnel*. It is obvious that the talent required to handle well a meaningful representation of the public interest in marketing is not easy to come by. Almost certainly the same people who handle product publicity should *not* be responsible for this function, although an understanding of marketing is a prerequisite for them. The skills involved are an exceptionally high degree of contemporary awareness, sophistication in government relations and public affairs, ability to use public opinion research effectively, extensive personal contacts outside the business, tough-mindedness coupled with a high degree of social consciousness, and enough intelligence to win the respect of some of the smartest people in the company, the marketing executives.

6. *Trade Associations*. Good trade associations can be important in fostering responsibility in marketing.[3] Historically, they have been defenders of the *status quo,* and as such generally a negative in-

---

[2] See Chapter 54.

[3] See Chapter 21.

I'm Cheryl. Fly me.

I'm not just another pretty face. I'm a fresh attitude towards air travel. A bright look on the outside, a personal way of thinking on the inside.

Back in the old days (last year), everyone thought airlines were pretty much alike. So we decided to change a few minds.

Part of the challenge was to tell you who we are, why we're special, and what we're doing to be even better.

Here's who we are: We're Cheryl (me), Linda, Margie, Laura and Jo. And people you never see, like Bob and Tommy and Ron and Lee. (They're not pretty faces, either.)

And here's what we're doing and why we're special. We're helping people go places. We go from all three New York airports. We'll fly you to Miami on the only 747's from New York. (And on the only 747 night coach.) This winter we'll fly you to Miami, Tampa/St. Pete, Ft. Lauderdale and the Palm Beaches on the only DC-10's, this year's airplane. And wherever we fly, we help people have fun getting there. The way we figure it, the more we like you, the more you'll like us.

So we're not just a bunch of people. We're an airline.

And you can call us by our first name: National.

(You can call us for reservations at 697-9000. Or ring up your travel agent.)

Fly Cheryl. Fly National.

National honors American Express, BankAmericard, Carte Blanche, Diners Club, Master Charge/Interbank, UATP, our own card and cash.

Figure 17.1. An advertisement may have exceptional impact on the public's awareness of the advertiser, yet have other effects as well. This one aroused great interest among men and opposition from some women. In many companies public relations executives review ads in light of their total effects on the company's stature.

fluence in terms of adapting to the public interest. Trade associations serve many masters, and it is difficult for them to take leadership stands. Many trade associations recognize their opportunities, however, and strong public relations cooperation between them and the staffs in the member companies can help them achieve their potential. There is encouraging evidence that some of the trade associations are moving sharply in more constructive directions.

7. *Consultants.* While many companies have for many years employed public relations firms to work with them on product publicity, the growing need is for counsel who provide broad experience and judgment, plus creativity, in the areas of corporate posture, policies, and programming.[4] The effective counsel will have experience in a number of industries besides that in which the company public relations staff works. He will be able to help them see the various points of view objectively. He will have a broad overview of public attitudes, social patterns, government, and other forces. He will be able to help form the company's view of its role, and help articulate it in statements, speeches, position papers, and other communications. The decision-making and administration cannot be turned over to outside specialists, but the counsel's contributions to the mixture of considerations can be valuable.

Glen Perry, former director of public relations at duPont, wrote in the *Public Relations Journal*[5]: "A jewel beyond price is the manager who says: 'Wait a minute. What effect will this have on the company's reputation?'" He went on to describe how business schools could fulfill their responsibility better by preparing future managers to factor public relations into their decision making.

Eventually, we may get far enough so that the public relations department, *per se,* won't have to be the "conscience of the business," but that prospect should not deter young men and women thinking about careers in public relations. The need will exist for a long time!

PUBLIC RELATIONS IN THE PROMOTIONAL PROCESS

It is necessary to shift gears rather sharply now to talk about the role of public relations in promotion. As noted, it is a significantly different public relations function. But anyone who has observed successes like denim clothing, the great growth of music making and tennis as leisure interests, and scores of other marketing successes can hardly ignore the capability of public relations to create a favorable climate and persuade the consumer to buy.

Actually, as mentioned in the first paragraph of this chapter, this is what most people think of as "public relations" and, in fact, this *is* what most public relations people are engaged in. The ones who are skilled, imaginative communicators and promoters command very high prices because they can move goods effectively at reasonable promotional costs.

Public relations, in this context, is primarily publicity, although here again the role has broadened from the days of P.T. Barnum and the Hollywood press agent. In fact, it becomes highly respectable when considered in certain circumstances, such as the "selling" of the new American Constitution in the *Federalist Papers* by Alexander Hamilton and James Monroe, which has been hailed by Professor Broadus Mitchell as one of the best public relations jobs in history.[6]

Product publicity is covered in Chapter 38 and elsewhere in Section V, so the emphasis here will be to cover briefly various ways in which public relations functions in promotional support of marketing.

1. *Corporate Identity.* In most companies, the Public Relations Department is a corporate department to which is delegated some or most of the responsibility for the corporate reputation. Because of this, some companies have placed their corporate identity programs under the corporate public relations department, although many others organize it elsewhere. The public relations organization for this is logical, both because of the responsibility for corporate reputation and because of public relations' traditional liaison with marketing.

In some companies—particularly industrial companies but also some consumer goods companies such as Campbell's Soup—corporate identity is a primary marketing tool, in essence the company's brand name. In others, the corporate identity serves as the visual link that holds a group of diverse operations together. In either case, the power of corporate endorsement in marketing is considerable, particularly with new products.

---

[4]See Chapter 53.
[5]Perry, Glen, "Management Sensitivity and Public Relations." *Public Relations Journal,* February 1970.

[6]Nevins, Dr. Allan, "The Constitution Makers and the Public, 1785–1790." Foundation for Public Relations Research and Education, San Francisco, California, 1962.

Corporate identity is a complex subject. It is treated in greater depth in Chapter 55. It deserves recognition in any consideration of public relations and marketing.

2. *Product Planning*. It is usually desirable to have public relations marketing specialists participate in new-product planning. There are many cases where this is unnecessary, but if public relations is to play a significant part in marketing, it should be involved at least as early as the advertising agency.

3. *Establishing a Favorable Climate*. Certain new products require a change in public attitudes, or perhaps in legislation, in order to gain acceptance. Generally these are the more innovative products. Public relations techniques are uniquely capable of creating a climate that will be favorable for the product introduction.

Magnetic recorders were first marketed in 1950. They showed steady growth, but it was not until 15 years of conditioning that the public was "over the threshold of awareness" about their uses and made them a basic desire.

4. *Third Party Endorsement*. The publicity practitioner reaches his audience almost always through a third party, the media. This has the weakness, of course, of leaving uncertainty about how the message will be conveyed—and not many people any longer think that "any publicity is good publicity just as long as the name is spelled right." Balanced against this, however, is the fact the message the consumer receives from the media has far more believability than anything the company can say in an advertisement it pays for.[7] This writer has heard several physicians comment on how closely they follow the "Medicine" section of *Time,* for example, which clearly explains why drug companies place such a high premium on news that appears in that section.

Many modern marketing men, conditioned to maximum quantification, have no idea of the impact that an article can have simply because the public places such high credibility in the source.

5. *Special Events*. Films, promotions, parties, and other events useful in marketing are covered in Chapters 38, 46, and 48.

6. *Publicity and the Salesman*. Publicity can be extremely helpful to salesmen who can use clippings and broadcast results to prove to buyers that editors, who are recognized for some discrimination about what is important, saw the importance of what they are trying to sell. They also show that many prospective customers have been preconditioned to sales efforts. Any good publicity program is likely to include the publication of big clip sheets for use by the sales force.

7. *Merchandising Publicity to Employees*. Bulletin boards and company publications (see Chapters 48 and 15) are valuable in merchandising publicity results throughout the organization.

8. *Explaining Publicity to Marketing Executives*. Management newsletters,[8] meetings of the Marketing Department, and other communications outlets afford opportunities to convey the effectiveness of both corporate respect and product publicity. Since marketing personnel are the points of contact with retailers and other sales outlets, the full usefulness of public relations results requires that they use these results to impress retailers and other sales outlets.

9. *Organization*. Traditionally, the public relations field has argued that the product publicity function belongs in the corporate public relations function, providing a staff service to operating divisions. There are three primary arguments for this: a) it provides a good and continuing public relations liaison with marketing; b) it permits flexibility in staffing to meet publicity loads that are variable; and c) the press is too important an audience to remove from the control of the corporate public relations department. The arguments are all valid.

Increasingly, however, as marketing organizations become more sophisticated about their overall public responsibilities, there will be less reason for holding the product publicists separate from the marketing line function. While overall communications policy will be set by public relations and basic questions of media relations will be in its province, it is likely that the practice of product publicity will be less often in the public relations department.

More than a few corporate leaders have pronounced: "Marketing is our business." Public relations, of course, is also their business and few company presidents are unaware of this. Corporate managements are likely to place increasing stress on the "public affairs" or "public interest" involvement of public relations in marketing. The more traditional role of direct public-relations support in promotional activities will also probably increase, but it will be less important in overall corporate priorities.

---

[7] See Chapters 2, 47, and 55.

[8] See Chapter 15.

18

Building Effective Dealer Relations*

RONALD I. GOW is Director of Marketing Communications for Whirlpool Corporation, Benton Harbor, Michigan.

He holds a bachelor of science degree from Western Michigan University where he majored in Business Administration with minors in Economics and Retailing.

A veteran of the U.S. Army, he served as a section leader in the Korean conflict. Upon release from service, he re-entered the retail business as a store manager. He began his career with Whirlpool Corporation in 1955 where he has held a variety of managerial positions in accounting, manufacturing, sales, sales training, advertising, sales promotion, public relations, and marketing.

Dealer relations is the aggregate of the many efforts employed by a supplier to build and maintain a favorable image in the minds of its dealer organization.

Primarily, the responsibility for dealer relations lies with the marketing function. However, many other supporting activities have important effects on any dealer relations program as well—finance, service, publicity—in fact, virtually every department within the average company.

THE IMPORTANCE OF DEALER RELATIONS

Suppliers of consumer products who depend on independent, multi-line retail dealers to sell their merchandise to the ultimate consumer *must* have the loyalty and support of those dealers to be successful in the marketplace. How the dealer feels

*Editor's Note: Major factors affecting dealer relations, such as the consumerism movement, safety, and government regulation of products and distribution policies, are treated also in Chapters 17 and 19.

about a company, its representatives, and its products will ultimately be the measure of that company's success. Never has this been more true than now; and consequently, never has the art of building and maintaining good dealer relations been more vital.

In most industries today, such traditional marketing advantages as superior product performance, styling, service, and pricing have all but disappeared, due to the generally high degree of similarity between competing products of like type and quality. As a result, these are being replaced by various support programs designed to help and encourage dealers to sell one brand of product in favor of another. Product quality, styling, service, and price remain important, but suppliers now must also compete on the basis of who can do the most to help the dealer sell to the ultimate consumer.

In the final analysis, a loyal dealer is one who makes a profit selling a specific brand of product; and when profitability ceases his loyalty shifts to another brand. This is as it should be in the free enterprise system.

BUILDING EFFECTIVE DEALER RELATIONS

THE ROLE OF COMMUNICATIONS

Every dealer needs to know what the manufacturer is doing to help him...a job calling for the skills of the public relations practitioner. This involves building dealer loyalty and respect; making each dealer feel he's an important part of the team; keeping him advised on new products and programs. For unless the dealer is completely familiar with his supplier and feels that he is important to him, he cannot, and usually will not, do the best job for his supplier. The dealer is an important "public" and the public relations practitioner should focus major efforts on communicating with him.

Channels available for communicating with dealers include field sales representatives, conventions, service representatives, training programs, and the like. However, the types of mass communications techniques that are among public relations skills are extremely effective. They include the application of accepted public relations techniques, such as graphics, copy, printing, and the rapid dissemination of information to communicate with a specific audience or public. The information transmitted is likely to be received exactly as sent out. Also, they are generally the most economical methods of dealer communications available.

The prime vehicle is the printed word and picture. Since in this type of communication there is no way to induce absorption of the message by the recipient, it is essential that the content be interesting and *useful* to the recipient. Though one of its merits is economy, skimping on quality in this area can be costly.

Effective dealer communications programs also encourage dealer response and provide channels through which it can be accomplished.

RESEARCHING THE AUDIENCE

In developing a dealer communications program, one must start by understanding the audience to which the communication is directed. The communicator must know what makes them tick, their problems, the nature of the market in which they operate, their customers, their venacular, the common characteristics that set them apart from other types of dealers. He must also be familiar with the different types of dealers that constitute his dealer organization: large or small, rural or urban, sophisticated or not. Of particular importance is, What do the dealers think of the supplier? There are many other questions to be answered, but the important point is that it is virtually impossible to communicate effectively unless you know your audience.

To get answers to these questions, the public relations practitioner may wish to conduct a survey.[1] A survey performed and properly interpreted by experts will not only provide the information needed to communicate effectively, but will also often yield additional insights into dealer attitudes that will aid the supplier's entire marketing efforts.

For example, a survey can be an effective means of monitoring the effectiveness of new merchandising programs or the acceptability of new products.

The public relations man can also learn a great deal about his dealer organization through association with other members of his company—particularly those who have regular and direct contact with retailers. The most effective method of all is direct, face-to-face contact with dealers. This can be done during trips for other purposes and at sales meetings and trade shows. Most suppliers conduct or participate in numerous dealer meetings, seminars, and conventions during the year, both in the field and at the home office.

Still another source of information is trade publications. By constantly monitoring them it is possible to learn a great deal about the industry and its dealers. Active participation in industry associations is also an effective way of acquiring useful knowledge of the dealer and his functions.

Knowing the organization. The public relations practitioner must know his own organization before he can effectively communicate with his dealers. He must know its products, policies, and sales and service capabilities, and understand its programs relating to such areas as finance, distribution, marketing, advertising, sales promotion, sales training, dealer education, and personnel. His major goal is to help sell the company and its products to his dealers, using his particular skills as a communicator—an impossible task if he is not thoroughly familiar with both.

Getting to know one's own company...and staying on top of what's going on...is a demanding task. It requires establishing viable working relationships with all departments within the company, since each makes important contributions to the total dealer relations program. The public relations practitioner must gain their respect and cooperation to be effective.

[1] See Chapter 35.

DEALER COMMUNICATIONS MEDIA

Though there are many media available to him, the public relations man usually finds that his options are determined by prudent use of budgets provided for dealer communication. Thus, while such communications devices as motion pictures, closed-circuit television, recorded messages, and filmstrip presentations can be very effective and definitely have their place, the major medium used to communicate with dealers will generally be the printed word and graphics, assisted by the U.S. mails.

External house publications. Perhaps the most widely used and effective printed dealer communications medium is the external house publication. Prepared in a wide assortment of formats and sizes, varying widely in quality of content and appearance, the external house publication has become "standard equipment" for thousands of U. S. companies engaged in dealer communications. The state of the art is improving rapidly, with the result that more and more good publications are reaching dealers' stores every year. Some even rival the better consumer magazines in both appearance and editorial content.

These publications, often referred to as dealer magazines, offer some distinct advantages that make them by far the most practical and effective mass medium available for dealer communications:

Flexibility. The dealer magazine lets you offer something for everybody . . . large dealers and small . . . small town and large . . . high volume and low. Just as most product lines offer a wide variety of models to meet specific market requirements, a dealer magazine can vary its content to meet specific audience requirements.

Frequency and regularity. These are important in dealer communications. Be sure they hear from you often and regularly. Not only does this confirm your company's interest but also constantly reminds them of your products and services, versus those of your competition.

Education. Today's dealer is hard pressed to make a profit, for a variety of reasons. A well-prepared publication is an ideal way to provide dealers with solutions to their marketing problems. This is an area where knowing your dealers is extremely important, because you will generally discover that the key to one dealer's success is the solution to a problem plaguing many others and all you need do is relay the information via your magazine. Ideally, the dealer communications function serves as an information clearing-house, no matter what media are used, and the dealer magazine is particularly well suited to the task.

Economy. With modern equipment and techniques now available it is possible to produce good-quality dealer magazines at a reasonable cost, particularly if yours is a large dealer organization. It is generally true that a fairly high volume is required to bring the per-unit cost down appreciably, but when compared to the cost of a salesman's call, even an expensive magazine can represent a good value.

Visual impact. The combination of good graphics and meaningful copy, using color whenever possible, is an effective way of telling your story.

Some rules to remember when planning a dealer magazine (and virtually any other type of dealer communication) include:

• Be sure your material is timely and meaningful to your audience. If your dealers can't use it, don't print it.

• Don't use it to toot the company's horn. Unless the activity under discussion will directly benefit your dealers, it will not interest them and they will stop reading the publication.

• Don't skimp on production any more than necessary. Your publication is a reflection of your company. Four good issues a year are generally better than eight poor ones. If your budget just won't permit a good-quality production, consider using less-expensive mailers or newsletters.

• Use as many good illustrations and as much color as your budget will allow. These are well-established tools for increasing readership.

• Set a schedule and keep it. Continuity and frequency are essential.

• Maintain your mailing list. Be sure you know who's receiving your publication at all times. Remember that most dealer organizations are constantly changing.

• Be sure to include something for everybody, and that your material is helpful and timely. And remember—DEALERS WANT FACTS, NOT THEORY . . . AND MOST CAN TELL ONE FROM THE OTHER.

Other printed media. Circumstances such as lack of time or cost will often dictate that you use other forms of printed media as well. Following is a partial list you might want to consider:

Monthly, bi-weekly, or weekly newsletters. Low in cost and easily prepared, informative, relevant newsletters can be an effective and expedient dealer communication device.

• *Special mailers.* These are useful for special events and as fill-ins between regular publications, but don't overdo them. Dealers get too much mail now; don't compound the problem.

• *News releases.* Sometimes your regular news releases can double as dealer mailers. If an event concerning your company is newsworthy to the press, it may also be of interest to your dealers; and all it costs is a little more press time, some paper, and postage. Furthermore, when it comes to matters that affect them, your dealers will appreciate hearing it from you first, before reading it in the press.

• *Brochures, annual reports, executive speech reprints.* Quite often, materials prepared specifically for other activities within the company can be used as a valuable adjunct to a dealer communications program. Though not specifically oriented to the dealer, they can increase his sense of involvement in the company's activities, which is an important factor in building dealer loyalty. And since the major costs of preparing such materials are generally borne by other departments or budgets within the organization, using them in dealer communications can be a real budget saver.

• *Feature articles in trade and consumer publications.* Trade and consumer publications have an insatiable appetite for good editorial material. They are generally delighted to receive and use *good* feature stories that will appeal to their readers, even when they are proprietary in nature. The time and effort required to prepare feature stories—or to assist the publication in preparing them—are well spent, for they represent an extremely effective method of communicating not only with your present dealers and the public, but with prospective dealers as well. It's also important to remember that outside sponsorship will tend to add credibility . . . and therefore value . . . to your story. And finally, don't assume that your dealers will read the magazines that use your material; have reprints made and mailed to them.

This is by no means a complete list, but it will serve as a thought starter. The important things to consider when selecting material are: Is it timely, interesting, relevant, and/or useful to the recipient?

Special situations. Though the average public relations department will, for budgetary reasons, have to rely on print materials, there are times when circumstances will call for extraordinary measures to communicate a specific message to your dealers as swiftly and dramatically as possible.

For example, a merger or the acquisition of

GOODWILL FOR DEALERS and for Whirlpool is possible when store uses "Diagnosing the Wash" booklet available from Joy Schrage, above, manager of home economics.

Help your customers help themselves

"Diagnosing the Wash" can head off laundry problems dealers don't need

How can you, the retailer, help promote good will after the sale? By supplying your automatic washer purchasers with a copy of the booklet that could save them the expense of an unnecessary service call and could have those satisfied customers coming back to you to buy additional appliances. So says Joy Schrage, manager of the customer assurance home economics department, referring to a new booklet available from Whirlpool called "Diagnosing the Wash."

Together with Tim Cuthbert, laundry products manager, technical training, Mrs. Schrage prepared the booklet that illustrates the most frequently encountered laundry problems, such as incorrect use of detergent, bleach, softeners.

Most of that laundry had been washed incorrectly over a period of weeks, after which the problem — tearing from chemical damage, greying from underuse of detergent, greasy stains from direct contact with fabric softener, etc. — was blamed on a mechanical malfunction. When a service call proved the appliance to be in perfect working condition, the laundry made its way to Joy Schrage's department for complete analysis, rewash, and return to the customer with an explanation of the problem.

"Almost 40 percent of the laundry we analyze is not clean because too little detergent was used," advises Mrs. Schrage. "Homemakers purchase large-capacity units but forget that the amount of detergent must increase in proportion to tub capacity in order to get satisfactory wash results. Diagnosing the Wash offers descriptions and illustrations to help the homemaker recognize this and other frequent laundry problems that she can solve without the assistance of a service technician."

In addition to the basic steps to good laundering, the booklet contains:
• photographs of incorrectly washed items
• detailed descriptions of damage caused by misuse of laundry aids
• diagnosis and preventive steps for the most common laundry mistakes

"Take a few extra minutes to outline the booklet to that customer who just purchased an automatic washer," Mrs. Schrage adds. "She can review it at home while waiting for delivery of the washer, and then store it in the "Bac-Pak" laundry information center — a handy storage slot featured on Whirlpool's 1976 laundry products for safekeeping of warranty letters, installation and use instructions, laundry guides, owner's manual, and other product literature.

"Diagnosing the Wash" can be a time and money saver for your customer and a valuable source of customer good will for you.

Figure 18-1. Material that dealers can benefit from, such as educational literature to make available to their customers, are prominent features of Whirlpool's dealer publication, *Dealers' Choice*.

another company, a major government action affecting distribution of the product, a major internal reorganization, an attack on the industry or the company by a consumer group, or a change in distribution might require rapid communication to minimize confusion and disruption within your dealer organization.

On the other hand, the introduction of a new line of products or the initiation of a major quality improvement program might well call for dramatic treatment to maximize impact.

In such cases, more time-consuming and costly methods of communication—such as personal contact, telephone, telegrams, dealer conventions, filmstrips and records, motion pictures, closed-circuit television, and trade advertising—are not only justified, but essential to achieve the desired results. The structure of the organization will determine the public relations function in these more costly methods of communication. If the public relations man is involved, he must weigh the cost of time and money against the desired result in determining the best communications method to employ in a given situation. In doing so, he should be knowledgeable about the method—its advantages as well as its disadvantages.

CONTENT OF DEALER COMMUNICATIONS

Up to this point, we have discussed the means of dealer communications. Content is another factor to be considered. The possibilities are almost endless, but a partial list includes:

    Government activity that affects the dealer
    Policies on warranties, repair services, etc.
    New products and features
    Industry statistics
    Research projects
    Finance programs
    Meeting schedules
    News of the industry
    Advertising schedules
    Ad reprints
    Promotion plans
    Sales training tools
    Forecasts of future business
    New markets for product
    New prints of sales material
    Company's progress
    Company's future plan
    Case studies of dealers' solutions to problems, successful ideas, etc.

HELPING DEALERS THROUGH TRAINING AND CUSTOMER SERVICE

The manufacturer is in a position to know the best techniques to use in every phase of retailing his products. He is also able to employ highly skilled training specialists in all phases of the dealer's busi-

Figure 18.2. Training dealers' personnel so they will satisfy consumers is a major phase of a dealer relations program. At a Whirlpool course for retailers' service personnel, face-to-face exchanges as well as instruction make communication effective.

ness. Making these skills available to the dealer and his personnel, of course, is an activity of great mutual benefit.

This is especially true in those areas where consumer dissatisfaction is risked—especially the condition of the product when it is delivered, and the servicing of it after it is in use.

Training programs for the personnel of dealers, then, become a vital phase of any manufacturer's effort to forestall consumer and government complaints. As products become more complex, especially, the training of retailers' personnel is an unceasing requirement. Some manufacturers include in their dealer franchise agreement the requirement that the service personnel of the dealer will attend periodic training courses offered by the manufacturer.

Satisfying consumers. To the manufacturer, any dissatisfied user of his product is not only a source of ill will and damaging word-of-mouth, but part of a potential groundswell of consumerist pressures. Also, though a given dealer may not be responsible for an individual consumer's disgruntlement because the product was bought elsewhere, he suffers from the resulting negative attitude toward the brand.

Accordingly, in addition to raising the standards of the retailers' sales and service operations, manufacturers are affording direct means of meeting the questions and complaints of consumers. In 1967 Whirlpool initiated a Cool-Line Customer Telephone Service, which lets owners of Whirlpool appliances with service needs or questions call factory specialists for help from anywhere in the continental United States, 24 hours a day, at no cost. More than 90 percent of all Cool-Line callers seek information, which trained specialists can answer immediately. The others are handled in the field by or at the direction of Whirlpool service people. The good will generated and the reduction in the number of frustrated customers have proven valuable and the program has inspired consumer help efforts by other companies.

19

Consumer Relations

RICHARD A. ASZLING is Vice President-Public Relations/Public Affairs of General Foods Corporation.

He rejoined General Foods as manager of public relations in April 1964. Earlier, he was a member of the General Foods public relations staff from 1953 through 1955. In the interim he was a general partner of Earl Newsom & Company and executive vice president of Infoplan, a public relations affiliate of Interpublic, Inc.

Mr. Aszling has been active in the public relations field since 1939, when he joined the Ohio State Medical Association in Columbus as public information director. From 1943 through 1952 he was employed by The Borden Company in Columbus, Ohio, and New York, where he served as assistant public relations director.

An Accredited Member of the Public Relations Society of America, he has also taken part for a number of years in the Public Relations Seminar and served as its Chairman in 1977. He is a graduate of Oberlin College and did graduate work in Germany. Before entering public relations he spent two years on the editorial staff of The Dayton (Ohio) Daily News.

It could be argued that the rise of the phenomenon labeled "consumerism" in the United States and the coming of age of industrial public relations were parallel occurrences. If that were true, it would be one of the great ironies of modern business history. For one of the major roles of the public relations advisor is counseling his client or employer in ways of winning the confidence, and consequently the repeat patronage, of the consumers of his products or services. Yet just as the practice of public relations became more solidly established than ever as an essential function in the machinery of the free market, the outcry of American consumers against the purveyors of goods and services and the demands for governmental protection reached new and formidable levels.

It is a fallacy to assume any kind of a causal relationship between these two developments. The spread of the consumer revolt may indeed be blamed in part on a failure of public relations to be as sensitive and effective as it should have been. But public relations cannot be held accountable for consumerism any more than marketing, production, the law, or general business management. For the movement known by the convenient misnomer of consumerism has extremely complex causes. In fact, throughout the proliferating literature on this subject one finds no really satisfactory explanation of its geometrical expansion within one decade, nor is there any really adequate definition of consumerism.

Fortune editorialized: "In some ways, consumerism is a reaction to a tension that has developed in the U.S. economy, which is geared to the mass consumption of goods by masses of people who still want to be treated as individuals." Another perceptive observer, Economist Peter Drucker, commented caustically: "We have asked ourselves where in the marketing concept consumerism fits or belongs. I have come to the conclusion that, so far, the only way one can really define it within the total marketing concept is as the shame of the total marketing concept. It is essentially a mark of the failure of the concept."

CONSUMER RELATIONS

Presidential Candidate Jimmy Carter told a group of consumer activists at the Consumers Forum in August, 1976 that one of his aims as President would be to replace Ralph Nader as the leading protector of consumers.

DEVELOPMENT OF CONSUMERISM

Some commentators simplify their explanation of consumerism. It is simply the result of a breakdown, they say, in the contractual relationship between the buyer and the manufacturer or seller of goods and services. Things bought do not measure up to expectations; when this happens often enough, buyers coalesce in their complaints and their demands for protection by the government. Political leaders sense the powerful voter appeal in this situation and promise the consumers (read: voters) full protection if elected.

Thus the Young and Rubicam advertising agency wrote to its clients: "Consumerism as a political issue and rallying point in today's America covers a multitude of widely felt grievances. Only the top of the iceberg shows in protests about product safety and packaging, lack of product information, deceptive guarantees, misleading price comparisons, poor service, refusal of refunds, and the like. Beneath the surface there are also attitudes and highly charged emotions fusing large blocks of the buying public into protest groups who march under the banners of peace, clean air and water, participatory democracy, fair housing, equal employment opportunity, the New Politics, equitable taxation, reordering of national priorities, and—a catch-all expression of mass frustration—'Power to the People.' "

This examination of the issue touches on two aspects of the phenomenon that must be understood if one is to attempt to develop constructive public relations approaches: (1) Consumerism is a mass movement, with all of the implications of crowd psychology implicit in that phrase; (2) It is inseparably related to all of the other mass manifestations of frustration or protest that characterize this era. It cannot, therefore, be dealt with by itself.

Some media, in reporting on the problem, support the simplistic approach. An article in *The Wall Street Journal* noted: "Roofs leak. Shirts shrink. Toys maim. Toasters don't toast. Mowers don't mow. Kites don't fly. Radios emit no sounds, and television sets and cameras yield no pictures. Isn't anything well made these days?"

In the same vein, *Time* examined the subject of "Inefficiency in America" in a cover article (March 23, 1970) titled "Why Nothing Seems to Work Any More." The news weekly reported in colorful detail on many of the nation's maddening frustrations, but it offered no really satisfactory explanation of why all this is taking place.

Cause of revolt. The reasons behind the apparent massive breakdown in products and services, intriguing though they are, cannot be covered in this chapter. Their combined effect, however, is central to this discussion. For the collective disappointments of 215 million American customers arising from shortcomings in the things they buy is certainly the major force, if it is not the sole factor, in the rise of consumerism. And it suggests the most effective means of attacking the problem.

Before discussing the appropriate reactions of business to consumerism—and particularly the proper public relations responses—it will be useful to review briefly the history of consumer protest in the United States and make some assessment of its present dimensions.

Legislation to protect consumers is about 100 years old in the U.S., although consumerism as such is generally considered to be a development of relatively recent times. In 1872 the Congress enacted the Criminal Fraud Statute following exposes of drastic market abuses, and in 1887 it established the Interstate Commerce Commission to curb the freewheeling railroad tycoons. These early legislative responses to the excesses of unrestricted businesses were relatively atypical in a century and a country dominated by the frontier spirit and the concepts of *laissez faire* and *caveat emptor*.

Moreover, in those early examples of consumer protection it was often a muckraking journalist or an inspired author who stirred up the support for new legislation, not a political figure with his finger on the popular pulse. Thus Upton Sinclair's novel, "The Jungle," is given credit for the establishment of federal meat inspection in 1906. Or the protective measures were enacted in response to drastic and sometimes dramatic specific developments. Deaths and illness caused by harmful foods or drugs resulted in the creation of the Food and Drug Administration in 1906; widespread charges of monopoly and unfair trade practice led to establishment of the Federal Trade Commission in 1913; the speculative stock market boom and devastating crash in the late 1920's were the immediate causes of establishment of the Securities and Exchange Commission in 1933.

Until the latter half of the 20th Century efforts to

provide consumer protection through legislation were sporadic and in response to such specific needs. President Franklin Roosevelt foresaw a trend to more general concern for the consumer, but other domestic and foreign issues kept him preoccupied. In 1959 Senator Estes Kefauver introduced the first bill to create a Federal Department of Consumers, and that measure, which was reintroduced in successive Congresses until his death in 1963, was the precursor of a number of similar bills in subsequent sessions. Kefauver was also the co-author of another important piece of consumer legislation, the 1962 amendments to the Food and Drug Law that require labeling of drugs by their generic names and pretesting of drugs for safety and efficacy.

President Kennedy's message. Major impetus to the consumer movement in the early 'sixties came from President Kennedy's message to the Congress in which he proclaimed the four "basic consumer rights": The right to safety; the right to be heard; the right to choose; and the right to be informed. That same year Kennedy appointed a 10-member Consumer Advisory Council (containing no representation from business), and his successor, President Johnson, continued the Council, expanded it to 12 members, and formalized its existence by executive order.

President Johnson initiated the practice of appointing women as Special Assistants to the President for Consumer Affairs and setting them up with offices in the White House, modest staffs, and fairly vague directives. The three incumbents up to this writing (Mrs. Esther Peterson, Miss Betty Furness, Mrs. Virginia Knauer, and Mrs. Peterson again) have been energetic and dedicated ambassadors from the executive branch to the American consumers and vice versa. Through frequent public appearances, interviews and by-lined articles, conferences with educators, and liaison with federal agencies in the consumer protection field these ladies have attempted to carry out their assignment to "encourage and assist" in the strengthening of the government's consumer protection programs. Militant consumer leaders, however, do not think a Special Assistant to the President is sufficient as a federal mechanism to protect consumers. They have attempted since 1969 to achieve passage of a bill to create an Agency for Consumer Protection (now called Consumer Advocacy) within the federal government that would have the right to intervene in the regulatory actions of other federal agencies and to force review of their decisions. It would also have other powers that business leaders fear would be disruptive and capable of abuse. This bill has passed one or the other houses of the Congress in its nine-year legislative history, and in the 94th Congress it passed both the House and the Senate but was not sent to conference committee because President Ford promised to veto it. Its proponents again sought passage in the 95th Congress, and the business community has been equally determined to defeat it.

Volume of legislation. Given the powerful political appeal implicit in "protecting" consumers, it is little wonder that legislative hoppers are choked with proposals purporting to do that. Before the 95th Congress was one month old, 50 bills aimed at consumer protection had been introduced. They ran the gamut from item pricing of foods at retail to costs of home heating. During the same period, literally hundreds of similar proposals were introduced in the state legislatures. One of them would require segregating pre-sweetened breakfast cereals in food stores and labeling them "dangerous to your health."

During the decade before 1976, some 25 major pieces of federal consumer legislation were enacted—more than in the entire 187-year history of the Republic prior to that date.

A representative list of topics covered by this massive legislative effort includes: Drug labeling and safety; packaging and labeling of consumer goods; cigarette advertising; meat inspection; product safety; flammable fabrics; licensing of clinical laboratories; consumer credit; automobile insurance; gas pipeline safety; poultry inspection; fraudulent land sales; control of radiation; freedom of information; protection of individual privacy; tire safety; warranties and guarantees; class legal actions to recover damages for groups of consumers; safety closures on drug packages; and loss or theft of credit cards.

A number of federal agencies launched studies or proposed regulations on a variety of other forms of protection that they could provide without Congressional action—nutritional advertising and selling to children via television, to name only two.

New laws and new studies were not needed, however, to make the federal government a large-scale protector of the consumer's rights and interests. Various estimates have been published as to how deeply the national government was already involved, without anything new being enacted or promulgated. One study suggested these data: More than 400 consumer-protection activities were being conducted by some 40 federal agencies that employed more than 32,000 persons and had a combined budget totaling well over a billion dollars annually. In the six years preceding the study these agencies increased their number of employees by 50 percent, and their budgets doubled.

As Casper Weinberger, former Chairman of the Federal Trade Commission, observed: "Consumer protection is an idea whose time has come.... Unless we make every effort to meet and maintain the standards demanded by the community of consumers, we may face some very undesirable changes in the free enterprise system."

State and local activity. The high level of federal activity in the field of consumer protection attracted most attention by the national news media, but in the states and cities there was action at a comparable level if somewhat less visible. In addition to the hundreds of legislative proposals, virtually every state had established some sort of consumer council in the executive branch of government by 1976, and many large cities had placed "consumer counselors" in the mayors' offices. A common characteristic among these political professionals was their skill in media manipulation, a development that has kept many an industrial public relations advisor working overtime.

With a basic political upheaval of this magnitude building up in a relatively short time, leaders of American industry—even the most perceptive of them—badly misread the signals. In the earlier years of the legislative build-up, many an American business executive who could truly claim to be a wizard in the marketplace misjudged the political potential and the implications for business in this burgeoning development. And their public relations advisors were not much more prescient, at least on the record.

A characteristic attitude was that "this movement will never amount to much because there is no broad-based public opinion in support of it." Another was that "no new laws are needed; all that is required is to enforce the laws already on the books that prohibit fraud and deception." The food industry underwrote a consumer study by the Opinion Research Corporation some time after the late Senator Philip Hart first put a serious effort behind his "truth-in-packaging" bill; the findings indicated that some 9 out of 10 housewives in the United States thought their packages and labels were quite adequate. The manufacturers took comfort from this and attempted to convince the Senate committee that it was meaningful.

One Washington resident who did not misread the signals was Ralph Nader, a young lawyer whose book, "Unsafe at Any Speed," did more than any other single event to make the automobile industry aware that consumerism is a force to be reckoned with. Nader, who has become a living symbol of the leadership of the consumer revolution, has gone on to turn the focus of his attention to other major industries and to agencies of the federal government that he has criticized for serious dereliction.

RESPONSE BY BUSINESS

If the leaders of the business community "missed the boat" during the rise of consumerism, it must be said to their credit that they have willingly reversed their position and are now facing up to what it portends. A number of quotations from prominent industrialists and other public figures will not only give evidence of this but will suggest the soundest approach to the problem for the business community:

• C.W. Cook, Chairman of General Foods Corporation–"Business failed to realize that a more knowledgeable and value-conscious, but often frustrated, consumer would readily accept government's overtures to fill the void created by business' neglect of its proper role."

• Peter Drucker–"A good many of my friends in business have been telling me over the years that consumerism is an invention of the politicians and that there is no support for it in the marketplace. ... But I've been around long enough to know that politicans don't flog dead horses—they can't afford to. They are in a much more competitive business than we are, and if there is no support for something, they go elsewhere very fast. And so I am afraid that we have to accept the fact that the politicians respond to a fairly general and fairly deep feeling on the part of the public and that they have identified here an exposed, raw, throbbing nerve."

• Former Secretary of HEW John W. Gardner (in a National Press Club speech on "entering a new decade")—"Industry should meet the rising tide of consumerism with constructive measures. Leaders in each industry should set standards of regard for the consumer and should be tough in demanding that the rest of their industry follow suit. If they don't, they will be brought under increasingly savage criticism by a bilked and frustrated public."

• W.M. Batten, Chairman of the Board, J.C. Penney Company (at a management conference on forward planning)—"What gave rise to consumerism? Modern technology certainly has helped. Today's products are wonderful indeed—when they work! Inflation has helped. It has made consumers much more conscious of what they spend and how much—or how *little*—they get for their dollars. There is a new awareness among consumers that lets a Ralph Nader, alone and without power, play Jack-the-Giant-Killer. And consumerism is a foolproof political issue. Consumerism is here to say. This is only the beginning—and our *opportunity* will grow with it."

In the light of history, perhaps one of the most noteworthy statements in this category was an essay by Thomas Murphy, the chief executive of General Motors Corp., that was published on the Op Ed Page of the *New York Times* and as the "My Turn" column in *Newsweek*. In this thoughtful and provocative piece, Mr. Murphy stated bluntly and unequivocally that American business will have to bring the quality of its products and services closer to the levels of public expectations before it can expect a restoration of confidence in business or a cessation of dependence on government protection and regulation.

These selected quotations from respected business executives and observers have two significant common elements: (1) They state or imply that business is partly at fault in allowing the movement of consumerism to reach its present ominous proportions. (2) They are unanimous that the only proper response is a constructive one and that there may be opportunity as well as difficulties for business in the consumer revolt. Both of these concepts are of major importance for people in public relations.

FOUR CHALLENGES TO PUBLIC RELATIONS

There are four broad areas of professional challenge to the public relations practitioner in helping his employer deal effectively with consumerism:[1]

1. If his client or boss is among the enlightened executives who share the views quoted above, the public relations practitioner must stay abreast of the boss in his thinking or, preferably, move a little ahead of him. This is no endorsement of radicalism (although at times it helps to be somewhat radical). It is simply a plea for intellectual flexibility where it is needed most. There is nothing more pathetic in this field than the public relations man who has to be dragged up to the level of the boss's enlightenment. The survival rate among these people is very low.

[1] See Chapter 17.

2. In discharging the more important half of his role as a two-way communicator, the public relations advisor must assist his employer in listening to consumers. He should propose and implement systems for retrieval of accurate intelligence, and he should be persistent in pushing for continuous reading of the feedback. If these systems had been working in the 1960s, some of the costly wrong assumptions would have been avoided.

3. Since the crux of the matter is the quality and performance of the things consumers buy, it behooves the public relations advisor to keep his colleagues in management—particularly in production and marketing—constantly reminded of the importance of quality and performance. This applies to packaging and advertising as well as to the goods and services themselves. This phase of the assignment will probably be the most difficult. It will test the public relations man's skills as a communicator and persuader as well as his sensitivity and judgment. He must stop short of becoming an obnoxious gadfly, but he must discharge fully the role of corporate conscience or resident ombudsman for the consumer.

4. The competent public relations practitioner will recognize a particular challenge in devising programs to counteract or offset consumer ignorance and to meet the need of consumers for information. Many of the early incidents in the consumer revolt—boycotts of supermarkets, for example—indicated broad deficiency of public understanding of the economic system. Consumers have no grasp of what lies behind the products on the grocery shelves or the department store counters. They have little knowledge of how prices are set. They seem to be unaware of quality control measures now employed by the manufacturers of consumer goods. They misunderstand the functions of advertising and marketing. In consequence of this ignorance, they mistrust business, they have misapprehensions about basic economics, and they become easy prey for political axe-grinders who need popular support for their proposals aimed at restricting business. Here, indeed, is the major challenge for public relations. And it will not be met by writing speeches or drafting news releases in defense of free enterprise.

Types of program. One cannot be precise in suggesting optimum methods of responding to these four challenges—particularly the last two. The ways the individual public relations practitioner will carry out these important assignments will depend on many variables—the nature of the product or ser-

CONSUMER RELATIONS

vice his company offers, the particular problem he is trying to cope with, the mood and temper of consumers at the moment, the nature of applicable legislative restrictions or proposed restrictions, the degree of his employer's understanding and enlightenment, and above all his own temperament and skill.

Some companies have initiated relatively successful programs along the lines suggested above. A brief examination of two of them will serve as illustration and may help provoke creative thinking.

Involving consumers. General Foods Corporation, one of the nation's largest manufacturers and distributors of packaged foods, has for a number of years conducted various programs aimed at eliciting consumer opinion and making important information available to consumers. The company bases these efforts on its conviction that consumer confidence in its products, the essential ingredient for its continued growth, is founded not only on satisfaction in use but on adequate consumer information and evidence of the company's concern for the consumer's interests.

A staff of trained women within the department known as General Foods Consumer Center reads and replies to thousands of letters consumers write to the headquarters in White Plains, N.Y. In 1976 the volume of this mail reached an annual rate of about 135,000 letters—several times the number being received at that time by the office of the Special Assistant to the President for Consumer Affairs. Each letter is answered promptly and responsively, and many of them, because of their nature, require individualized replies.

This is an expensive and time-consuming function, but General Foods considers it indispensable in winning and maintaining consumer confidence.

Figure 19-1. Tours of the packaging line at the Houston, Texas General Foods plant show community "opinion leaders" what goes into food packages and the care that is taken in preparation and handling.

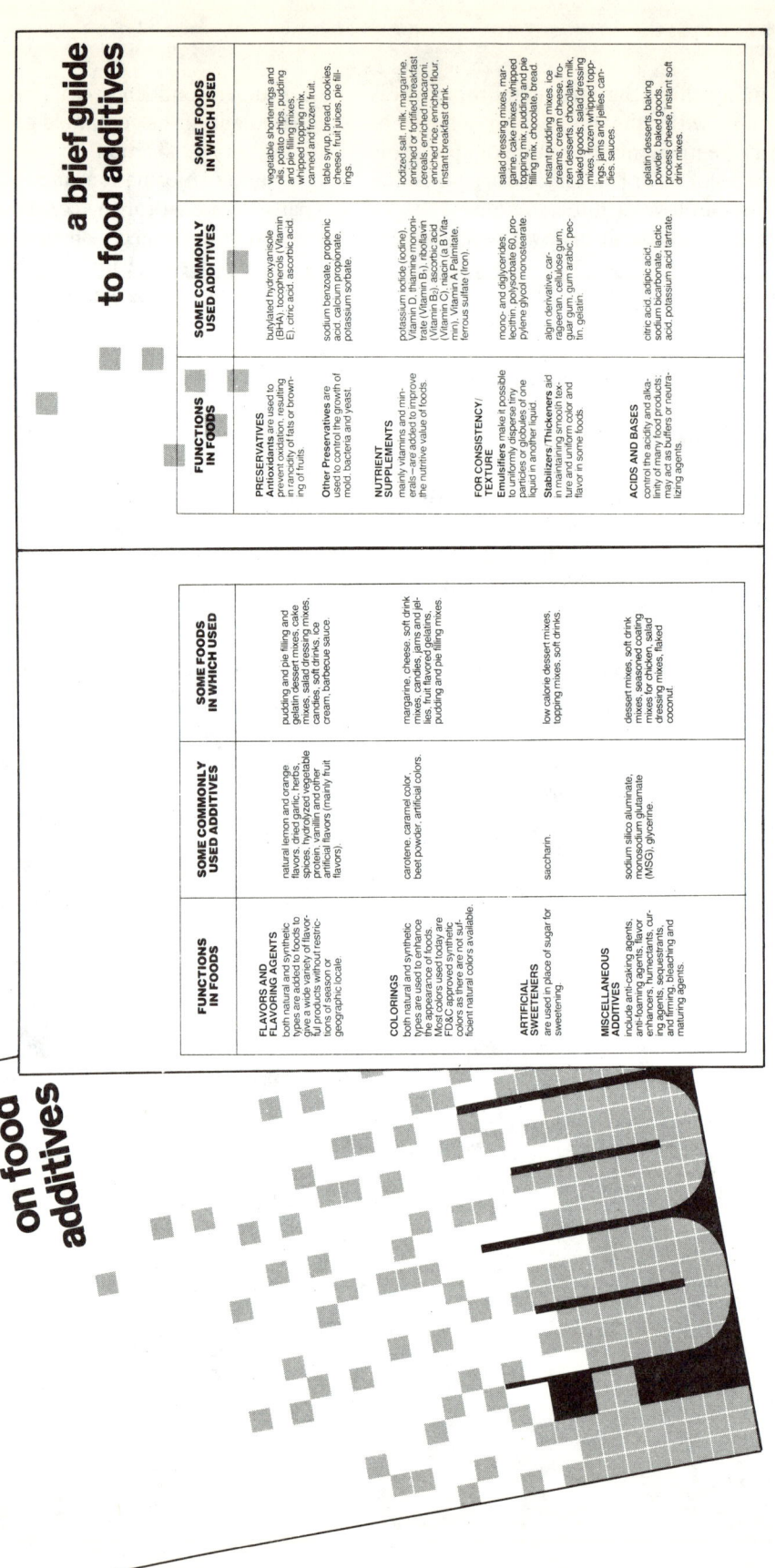

Figure 19-2. Pamphlets that explain facts about nutrition and foods are issued as a public service by General Foods Consumer Center. This diagram of major food additives explains the use of materials discussed in the text.

CONSUMER RELATIONS

One of the Presidential advisors (Mrs. Esther Peterson) was so impressed by this program that she sent members of her staff to GF headquarters to observe it in operation and to determine whether parts of it could be adapted to the White House consumer correspondence section.

Participation by community leaders. Beginning in 1966 General Foods launched another program designed to help inform consumers about the systems and the technology involved in the complex business of supplying food to the American people. This program, known as Community Leader Tours, is extremely intensive and aimed at a very small but vital segment of the consuming public. It consists of half-day educational conferences coupled with plant tours and luncheons for women leaders in the communities where the company's manufacturing facilities are located.

Groups of 50 to 100 community leaders (usually identified with the help of the local Chamber of Commerce) are invited. Prior to visiting the food plant they are given a briefing on the economics and logistics of the food industry by a corporate officer. Plant tours are then conducted in groups of no more than five guests each by trained employee guides. Following the plant tour, GF's Vice President for Consumer Affairs talks to the guests about facets of the food industry of particular interest to women. Some time later each guest is offered a kit of two talks and a set of colored slides (made during the tour) so she can offer a program to her own organization based on her firsthand experience.

Although this Community Leader Tour program, over time, will reach relatively very few consumers directly or indirectly, it is hoped that these women, as community pace-setters, will be an effective nucleus for word-of-mouth information. It is also hoped that other consumer-product manufacturers will adopt such programs and thus reach eventually a much larger group.

In another effort to close the consumer information gap General Foods is running a series of full-page advertisements in a number of consumer magazines. Each ad, framed as a letter from a consumer to "Dear General Foods," deals simply and forthrightly with a sometimes controversial and often misunderstood subject—additives in food, nutrition labeling, "new and improved" products, the need for preservatives, balanced nutrition, and the like. At the end of each ad is an invitation to write for more information to Miss Peggy Kohl, Vice President for Consumer Affairs, or to ask her to send an educational booklet specially published for readers of the advertisements. Response to the ads has exceeded pre-campaign projections, and the program has provoked considerable comment by news media and public leaders. It was backed up by extensive but non-promotional support by the Public Relations Department.

Forestalling and handling consumer complaints. One of the most widely discussed industrial programs developed to eliminate the basic causes of consumer discontent is the complex one of the Whirlpool Corporation, which was begun in 1964 and expanded and improved continually since then (see Chapter 18). Essentially it is designed to attack the major sources of annoyance among appliance buyers: Obscure warranties, service problems, lack of adequate knowledge about proper operation, and frustrating inability to get somebody interested in their difficulties. *Business Week,* commenting editorially on the respect this program has earned in Washington, said: "This adds up to an accolade that should entitle Elisha Gray II, Whirlpool Corp.'s chairman, to a medal the size of a dinner plate."

These are the principal features of the Whirlpool program:

1. A "cool line" system (begun in 1967) that permits appliance owners to call the company headquarters in Benton Harbor, Mich., free when they have questions about their appliances or service for them. Trained technicians are on the Michigan end of the line to answer the queries. In the first three years about 40,000 calls were handled.

2. The company itself makes good on warranties and does not depend on local distributors.

3. Warranties are written in clear, simple language as letters from the company to the customer.

4. Helpful literature includes a "Consumer Buy Guide" aimed at helping with purchase decisions and a "Home Care Package" designed to help consumers solve some of their own simpler problems.

5. National advertising (20% of the total budget) that tells consumers about the "cool line" and the warranty plan and encourages them to call headquarters when they need to.

6. An effective program of internal education to impress Whirlpool people with the critical importance to them and their company of assuring customer satisfaction and serviceability in their products.

Mr. Gray may not have received a dinner-plate-size medal, but he did go on to become one of the

IN CASE OF EMERGENCY, CALL (800) 253-1301

Let's say it's 95 degrees in the shade and your air conditioner is on full blast. Suddenly it conks out. Your house starts to feel like a steamroom. What do you do?

Or suppose your washing machine goes on the blink right after you move into a new town. You're miles away from the dealer you bought it from and you don't know the name of a reliable serviceman. Where can you turn for help?

Or what if your refrigerator breaks down just after you've loaded it with a week's supply of food. Where are you going to find someone to fix it in a hurry?

Well, if it's a Whirlpool appliance, your search is ended. You just call the number listed above. (Or (800) 632-2243, if you live in Michigan.) Free of charge. At any time of the day or night. From anywhere in the continental United States.

When you call, our operators will give you the name and number of the Whirlpool Tech-Care Center nearest your home. Which means that your appliance will be repaired by men trained and authorized by Whirlpool, rather than by your neighborhood jack-of-all-trades fixit man.

So if you own a Whirlpool appliance, we suggest you cut out our number and paste it somewhere on the machine. And if you don't own a Whirlpool, we suggest you save it anyway, because someday you might.

Whirlpool is the first major appliance manufacturer in the country to provide a service like this. Although, since our machines need so few repairs, we should have been the last.

Figure 19-3. Taking action to meet the most common causes of complaints among appliance buyers, Whirlpool developed a program that included clear, simply written warranties and free long-distance calls directly to the factory when service problems are encountered.

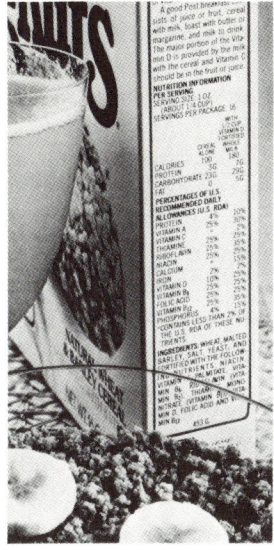

Figure 19-4. As part of its effort to forestall criticisms based on misunderstanding, General Foods has run a series of informative ads about food and nutrition. This one explains nutrition information on labels.

most effective business leaders in the effort to bridge the gap with consumers. He was instrumental in the formation, about 1970, of the Council of Better Business Bureaus, Inc. and served for several years as its Chairman. The Council was conceived by a group of national business executives as an appropriate vehicle for a positive response to consumerism. Based on a network of some 140-odd Better Business Bureaus in the United States and a respected half-century-old movement, its principal purposes include demonstrating the workability of self-regulation and persuading consumers that their best recourse is to business itself. It carries out a number of quite effective programs, including newspaper, radio, and TV information for consumers, arbitration of consumer disputes, investigation of philanthropic appeals, and consumer audits for major corporations.

The Council's National Advertising Division conducts one of its most visible and successful activities: Policing of national advertising. As the advertising industry's self-regulatory mechanism it reviews and evaluates all challenges to the truth and accuracy of national advertising brought by outside sources or initiated by its own monitoring. By 1977 it had investigated and successfully disposed of more than 1100 such challenges.

Business' response to the rise of consumerism has been institutionalized in other ways. At the 1973 Assembly of the Council of Better Business Bureaus, a new organization—The Society of Consumer Affairs Professionals in Business

(SOCAP)—was formed. It is, in effect, a new professional association for a new profession. SOCAP now has more than 700 members, many of them public relations practitioners, in the United States, Canada, and Europe, with nine active chapters in the U.S. and more in formation. Its address is Suite 301, 1430 K St., N.W., Washington, D.C. 20005.

If anything, the activist leaders of the consumer movement are considerably ahead of business in institutionalization. Whereas a decade ago the movement was a loose, disconnected assortment of charismatic consumer "spokesmen," today it is virtually a big business dedicated to attacks against Big Business. The Consumer Federation of America is by a considerable margin the giant among the institutionalized consumer protectors. Says the *New York Times:* "An organization of organizations, CFA has 225 members and an annual budget of $200,000. Among the members are 45 state and local consumer groups, 66 rural electric cooperatives, 17 credit union leagues and other cooperatives, 16 national labor unions (including the United Auto Workers, the Amalgamated Meatcutters, and the United Steelworkers of America) and about 30 other organizations, ranging from the National Education Association and the National Council of Senior Citizens to Consumers Union, publisher of *Consumers Report*."

There is even one recently formed organization that offers membership to professionals and volunteers from both camps, the consumer activist group and business. This is the Conference of Consumer Organizations (COCO). COCO held its Fourth Annual National Consumer Symposium in December 1976, which was described as an effort to "bring together representatives of consumer organizations, government, business, and industry to resolve problems of consumer concern." Its theme was "Consumerism: The Future in Perspective."

Consumer relations code. Perhaps one of the most helpful sets of guidelines for business is a 10-point consumer relations code promulgated by the Chamber of Commerce of the United States. This code epitomizes aptly the challenge facing the business community. The public relations practitioner could well adopt it as his decalogue in helping his employer cope with consumerism. The text of the Chamber's code follows:

1. Protect the health and safety of consumers in the design and manufacture of products and the provisions of consumer services. This includes action against harmful side effects on the quality of life and the environment rising from the technological progress.

2. Utilize advancing technology to produce goods that meet the highest standards of quality at the lowest reasonable price.

3. Seek out the informed views of consumers and other groups to help assure consumer satisfaction from the earliest stages of product planning.

4. Simplify, clarify, and honor product warranties and guarantees.

5. Maximize the quality of product servicing and repairs and encourage their fair pricing.

6. Eliminate frauds and deceptions from the market places, setting as our goal not strict legality but honesty in all transactions.

7. Insure that sales personnel are familiar with product capabilities and limitations and that they fully respond to consumer needs for such information.

8. Provide consumers with objective information about products, services and the workings of the marketplace by utilizing appropriate channels of communication, including programs of consumer education.

9. Facilitate sound value comparisons across the widest possible range and choice of products.

10. Provide effective channels for receiving and acting on consumer complaints and suggestions, utilizing the resources of associations, Chambers of Commerce, Better Business Bureaus, recognized consumer groups, individual companies and other appropriate bodies.

SECTION III

How an Organization Utilizes Public Relations

20

The Utility and Its Public

HOWARD A. PRAEGER before his retirement was assistant to the president of New York State Electric & Gas Corp., a utility serving one-third of the area of New York State.

He was associated with public utilities for more than twenty-five years, primarily in the field of public relations and advertising. He was a reporter on daily newspapers and had editorial and business experience in book publishing.

JAMES F. MINEHAN is manager of public information for New York State Electric & Gas Corp. He joined the public relations and advertising department in 1958 as a copywriter, specializing in employee communications and press relations. He was named to head of the department in 1971.

Mr. Minehan is former chairman of the Public Relations Committee of the New York Power Pool and former president of the Public Relations Society of the Southern Tier (N.Y.). He has served as a national officer of the American Association of Industrial Editors and has lectured on employee communications at seminars of the American Management Association. He holds both bachelor's and master's degrees in English.

Utilities, to whom the word "public" in general is virtually synonomous with the word "customers," are in an excellent position to achieve good public relations. Conversely, however, they are vulnerable to all the winds of changing public opinion that blow across the country and especially across their individual services areas.

A utility with good public relations is fundamentally one with customer-oriented objectives, sound management, and the ability not only to give customers quality service at a fair price but also to communicate favorably with them in every way. And one of the most difficult propositions for the customer to understand is that in order to give him quality service and to take care of his growing needs for energy, a utility must provide investors with a fair and reasonable return.

Most people today take their utility service for granted and think of a utility as having a simplex character; but complex operations are endemic to utilities. For, in a very real sense, a utility is a corporation that must manufacture its own consumer product (electricity) or buy from national pipeline suppliers (natural gas), and engage in all the marketing development and servicing that is generally the function of many different business organizations in marketing consumer goods.

The public relations executive within the company, often assisted by outside counsel, must be on the policy-making level and through his recommendations, leadership, and participation in policy decisions see that good public relations is the concern of everyone in the company. Just as Socrates was the gadfly to the conscience of the State, the public relations practitioner needs, on occasion, to act as a gadfly to the conscience of a corporation.

Thus the executive responsible for public relations in a utility and his key assistants keep the two-way channels of communication open between the company and the public and within the corporate organization itself. These techniques of communication may well be called the tactical side of the operation. The strategic side of public relations is understanding changing public opinion and keeping the policies of the company harmonious with the desires of the public—and in many instances showing real leadership in the communities served. On the tactical level alone, the person with assigned public relations responsibilities is merely carrying out policy that has been formulated by the organization's executive management. On the strategic level, he enters the policy-forming councils of the company and in a large measure helps to set policy. And it is only when he begins to think as a manager and understands all aspects of the business that he can help his company live in harmony with society.

THE UNIQUE NATURE OF UTILITIES

Thus the utility business is different in concept and operations from other investor-owned, business-managed corporations. In this chapter we will examine both the concerns and opportunities that utilities have in an era of heightened social awareness. Young people who are interested in public relations careers will find employment in the utility field both stimulating and rewarding. Our concern will be primarily with the operation of the investor-owned electric and gas utilities, but the concerns and opportunities that call for constant public relations judgments are often similar for airlines, railroads, and the telephone industry as well. The telephone utilities especially have community concerns that are quite comparable to electric and gas utilities and we will note these in commenting on some of the special considerations they must meet.

Public utilities today vary greatly in size, in character of the areas served, and in gross revenues received from customers. These variations naturally influence public relations programs. Utilities serving great urban centers cannot possibly have as close person-to-person relationships as those serving smaller cities and villages or predominately rural areas.

However, utilities exist by virtue of franchises to serve specific areas and from the point of view of public relations, utilities should perform as if they were re-earning the franchise to do business every day. The public utility, being "affected with a public interest," must serve all the public without discrimination as to rates, service, and employment policies. This is a proper responsibility, but one that requires constant attention and review.

An overriding obligation of utilities is meeting the growth in the use of energy. That growth may be broadly equated with the standard of living and working in America . . . or worldwide with that of civilization. Since the Arab embargo of 1973-1974, growth rates of electric consumption have diminished but have not leveled off. Interaction of a broad range of social factors, difficult to predict with certainty, determines long-range rates of energy growth. But data clearly indicate new facilities must be built to meet future needs.

The public relations challenge is compounded by the long lead times necessary to build economical and reliable production facilities. Ten or more years are needed for electric generating stations, three or more for natural gas sources. Consumers, accustomed to dealing with much shorter time spans, cannot easily reconcile their perceptions of change with the compulsion of utility managers to press on with construction programs despite a drop in overall usage rates. While consumers mistrust utility efforts to build new facilities, utilities dare not accept short-term trends, since to do so could lead to the crippling of the public's economic and social well-being.

Because of the nature of utility service and changing perceptions by consumers of their self-interest, clashes about how best to serve the overall public interest are increasingly common. One of the challenge areas involves *consumerism*. The other involves *environmental considerations*. Both of these issues have economic and social impacts on consumers and the overall economic and social systems that people accept without thought.

The resulting dialogue often escalates to widespread levels, as in the case of voting about the value of constructing nuclear electric generating stations and long-distance gas pipelines across Alaskan wilderness. Strong spokesmen of superior talent are needed to assure that the public will have enough information to make wise choices.

Relations with many publics. Although utilities do have a specific public—customers within the franchise area—they actually have many publics and through the proper consideration of all these publics, a successful public relations effort benefits from a synergistic effect.

However desirable it may seem to the orderly mind, one cannot place each person in only one of the publics (as in a pigeon hole) and deal only with one approach to an individual. Although it is true that there are special interests and associations, there are also overlapping interests. The public relations function should embrace all of the relations between an organization and its publics because all affect a company's reputation.

Customers who are, of course, the primary public that receives the company's service are classified as residential, industrial, commercial, and prospective customers of certain categories as well as municipalities. But there are other vitally important publics, too; e.g., governmental publics, the financial community, communities served, trade allies, utility industry peers, industry associations such as the Edison Electric Institute and the American Gas Association, the educational community, and the media. Employees, too, are often regarded as special members of the public as well as company workers.

Customers. In addition to quality service at a fair price, there are many services that can be provided to customers. Services that can enhance the character of the utility include information on how to get the best performance from appliances, economies that will benefit the customer, improved operations for commercial and industrial enterprises, better lighting for communities, and information regarding safe practices in the use of electricity and gas. In addition, the people must understand the reasons for safe practices in regard to transmission lines and substations.

Today there is growing customer interest in residential and commercial electric heat and that interest provides a good opportunity for public relations. Utility specialists can advise customers on the best utilization for their specific needs and make sure that contractors understand the proper installation procedures.

Regulatory agencies. The regulatory climate related to the utility's operations is extremely important. Utilities must be sure that there are effective communications with these agencies on both a state and federal level. Actually, the interests of regulators and customers are complementary and managements of utilities will not be successful in meeting their financial requirements if they ignore that fact. Regulation must protect the interest of the consumer and, at the same time, provide the investor in utility securities with a fair and reasonable return so the utility can raise the necessary capital to assure adequate and dependable supplies of energy for the growing requirements of its service area.

Considerable expertise is required from the public relations executive and counsel in preparing the informative program for a rate increase. Public acceptance is vital in regard to rate submissions. The assessment of public opinion prior to submission of a new rate schedule should be a primary responsibility of public relations. This assessment is helped by opinion surveys, by counseling with the company's managers in various communities, and by a general appraisal of economic and social conditions. Regulatory bodies, too, feel that full informative programs for the public must be carried out with every rate submission.

Financial community. This community includes company stockholders, investors and potential investors, investment banking firms, institutional investors, commercial banks, security analysts, national financial press, and state and national leaders of business and industry whose interest in the particular utility might be primarily financial. Included as well are stock exchanges and the Securities and Exchange Commission. Company relationships in this area call for considerable financial sophistication that many public relations people do not have. Consequently, these relationships are usually carried on by senior management and the company's general legal counsel through a virtually day-by-day association. The rules of full disclosure must be observed, and the public relations executive should be fully cognizant of the full disclosure requirements.[1]

Although the public relations executive and his staff may not be financial experts, they can contribute to financial relations in a significant way through the preparation of financial news releases, assistance with the annual and quarterly reports to stockholders, and sound publicity exposure for company matters on the business pages of daily papers and in financial journals.

The public relations executive may participate in the procurement of opinion surveys conducted by professional firms with analysts and in the evaluation of those surveys. In the public utility field, these surveys should include a heavy sampling of opinion from the most influential analysts. Security analysts in our largest metropolitan areas have strong influence with investors in utilities.

Communities served. Deeper community involvement than in the past in socio-economic programs of the company's service area can give the utility the kind of identity it needs and offset the idea many have that the government should be the only participant in achieving new social and economic goals. We will examine some of these opportunities later in the chapter.

Trade allies. Development and growth for utilities are closely associated with trade allies. These are manufacturers of household appliances

[1] See Chapters 11 and 12.

and commercial and industrial equipment, distributors, contractors, and the various professional associations these allies are identified with in their business. In recent years the concept of trade allies has been broadened to include insulation manufacturers and retailers, proponents of energy saving devices, architects, and others interested in energy conservation and preservation of resources.

Employee relations. It is a cardinal principle of public relations that good relations must begin within the particular organization. Employees can be the best goodwill ambassadors in the community or they can downgrade a company faster than a disgruntled customer. Management, of course, must have an enlightened approach to employee relations or there is no bedrock on which to build community relations through employees.[2] Like most other people, employees of a public utility think in terms of self-interest. However, because they are in a public service organization, they take pride in the character of their work as a public good.

What the employees think and say about the company on a people-to-people basis will carry more weight than any other single type of publicity. They all know many people in the territory served. The smaller the communities, the more effective the employee group will be. Although this need for employee enthusiasm and commitment is vitally important, many companies overlook the real asset they have in their own people. Because utilities offer great security to employees, this advantage is a strong factor toward maintaining employee stability. But a good program makes certain that security in the job does not create an unproductive employee and that the company does not allow long service and familiarity to stand in the way of employee advancement. The ways in which employees can interpret and build the company's character will be considered in more detail under the heading "Relations with Specific Groups."

SPECIFIC AREAS OF CONCERN

Consumerism. As indicated earlier, the public's interest in consumerism is growing. Perhaps the utility is less vulnerable to criticism from consumers than manufacturers of goods and service enterprises. That is, the utility should be less vulnerable if it provides good service at a fair price and has sympathetic understanding from its public about the costs of doing business.

[2]See Chapters 14 and 15.

However, the utility that is operating in the interest of the consumer in every way the company can, may nevertheless stumble into pitfalls. This situation could be brought about through poor communications with its public, through inept handling of customer complaints, through a "we are always right" attitude. Although management may be trying hard to please customers, utility employees who develop bureaucratic attitudes may, on the face-to-face customer level or over the telephone, negate company policy.

The preservation of good customer relations requires eternal vigilance. Is the point of view of the customer considered sympathetically? Can you admit that the company may be wrong in regard to a bill? If a shut-off notice is sent to the wrong person or hung on his doorknob, is there a recognizable signature on that notice that gives the customer someone he can call immediately? Does the company have a list of qualified electricians, appliance service organizations, plumbers, and contractors that can be given to the customer who is new in the community or doesn't know where he can get competent service?

Consumerism also includes being aware of the interests of such research groups as "Nader's Raiders," the groups of young investigators who probe into many fields. Regulatory commissions must consider consumerism in all commission decisions. They are committed to the protection of the consumer and their rate and service decisions will be scrutinized closely by consumer groups.

A 1975 survey by Response Analysis of Princeton, New Jersey indicated that the overall climate within which the investor-owned electric companies must operate deteriorated during the previous two years. Still, the electric light and power industry continued to be more favorably regarded than a number of other major industries. Thirty-eight percent of those interviewed felt the industry served the public well, a higher rating than was given to six other major industrial classifications. Similarly, while electricity was still considered a family item of value ranking above thirteen commonly purchased items, the trend as compared with past years was down.

Inflation and generally unfavorable economic conditions undoubtedly contributed to shifts in public opinion and influenced expectations. Fifty-two percent believed that electric rates would continue to increase at least as fast as the cost of living over the next year. Thirty-six percent expected rates would increase more than the cost of living.

The survey also demonstrated that those who are favorable toward the industry on a variety of questions are much more likely to consider rate increases justifiable. The value of good, lasting communications on basic issues is clearly demonstrated by the response.

Despite continued attacks by dedicated opponents, support for increased construction of nuclear power plants continued by a ratio of about two to one. The survey results were borne out by voter response in seven states during 1976. In all cases, ballot propositions that would have halted construction of nuclear generating stations were soundly defeated. Questions of safety and the disposal of nuclear wastes continue to be significant factors in dampening support.

Environment. Although ecologists, environmentalists, and undoubtedly philosophers have long recognized that everything on this earth has an effect on everything else, the concern in regard to environmental considerations had been limited until recently. Now it seems that everyone has discovered "environment"; everyone wants to save it, but specific ecological knowledge on how to do it has been limited.

The sweeping environmental reform movement reached a high point in the early 1970s. Once it became a target of environmental concerns, the electric utility industry committed manpower and money to achieve notable results. In 1975 alone, industry expenditures to foster clear air and water exceeded $1.5 billion. Fifty-five percent of those questioned in the 1975 public opinion survey rated their local utility favorably on the job it was doing to protect the environment and reduce pollution.

Concern about the environment has changed. In 1971 forty-one percent of the total public considered air pollution a serious problem. The number dropped to twenty-five percent by 1975. There was also a decline in concern about water pollution. But these shifts in attitude appeared to represent a recognition of the level of industry achievement rather than a loss of interest. The survey indicated a great majority, seventy-five percent, took a pro-environmental attitude and believed more should be done.

A great public relations and management challenge has emerged as a result of the disparity between people's attitudes about the need for environmental protection and their distaste for higher rates. Costs associated with environmental protection are not easily identified, particularly when they are not associated with "add on" features but rather with a state of mind that influences basic planning and simply rules out some design choices as environmentally unacceptable.

Furthermore, years can pass before environmental expenditures find their way into utility rates. The long lag between action and rate change makes it hard to keep consumer awareness focused on the cost of environmental protection. When the costs show up on utility bills it is too late to retract the order. The utility, not the public call for environmental protection, may seem to be the problem.

To date neither utility managements nor consumers have found mechanisms for determining how much money should be spent for various purposes. Environmental protection is not the only one. Others include providing poor and low-level fixed income persons with minimum amounts of energy for household purposes at rates they can afford; how major facilities, such as power stations and high voltage transmission lines, should be located; and how utility rates should be designed to best serve complex social and economic needs of consumers and investors.

A host of considerations confront the utilities in relation to environment. Many utility managements have standing committees on environment or full-time technical experts with ecological experience. There is, in addition, a new agency of the federal government. Many states, too, have established environmental departments.

William A. Lyons, Chairman and Chief Executive Officer of New York State Electric & Gas Corporation and a member of the Electric Power Council on Environment, in commenting on the responsibilities of a utility in a changing society, said: "These responsibilities are not only to provide an abundant and reliable supply of electricity and gas to meet our customers' needs at reasonable rates, but also to do so with the greatest possible protection for the environment in which we live. We share in the revitalized public interest in matters affecting our environment."

Don C. Underwood, Chairman of Underwood, Jordan Associates, public relations counselors working closely with electric utilities, has suggested that to avoid acute polarization on the issue of environment between industry and ecologists, the electric industry adopt the following type of position:

"The electric utility industry asks the rest of society to recognize that both the industry and society are beset with a dilemma. The dilemma arises from the legitimacy of two social goals: one is the continuing development of future supplies of adequate, reliable electric power; the second is the preservation and improvement of our natural environment. These social goals are not and should not be allowed to become mutually exclusive. What this means is that we must take a 'balanced approach' to these two goals. This balanced approach will have to be mapped out by all the sectors in our society which have a legitimate interest, working in close cooperation and taking into account all the factors involved. The industry is ready, willing and able to take this approach, but it requires the understanding and cooperation of society to do so."

Most people recognize that for every benefit there is a cost. Utilities are allocating substantial budgets to water resources studies aimed at pure-water objectives. They are adopting designs for transmission towers and substations that are aesthetically pleasing. Utility managements adopted anti-pollution controls for their motor vehicle fleets in advance of any legal requirements. Many years ago most utility planning was characterized by a strictly engineering approach to projects—e.g. a straight line is the shortest distance between two points—but fortunately that attitude is no longer a dominant factor in the business. Technological research will undoubtedly show the way in developing further operating procedures that will enhance the environment.

That environmental costs must be met must be recognized not only by regulatory bodies, but by the public at large, which must pay for this protection in the price of the product. Communicating that fact effectively is the responsibility of those engaged in public relations. Attaining new social goals will cost money, and this fact will revise priorities in regard to how people budget expenditures.

Environmental considerations will be all-encompassing for utilities for many years. It is such a broad subject that it cannot be treated in detail in this chapter. Expertise in this field, however, will be a must for the utilities public relations officer.

The successful utility communicator will need to adopt imaginative approaches to the public, convince customers that the company has a commitment to preserving the environment, and point out the ways, for example, that the use of electricity for automobiles and in industrial and commercial enterprises will reduce pollutants. He will need to work with management in developing a socially acceptable approach to choosing sites for new generating stations and transmission lines. He will need a thorough knowledge of the use of nuclear energy in the generation of electricity and in nuclear technology related to the development of natural gas resources.

Once a positive attitude toward environmental matters permeates an organization, that attitude will act as a catalytic agent throughout the company. Members of employee speakers' groups can do much to acquaint the public with the environmental program. Actual commitment of expenditures with accompanying publicity will put the company on record as moving in the right direction. Plant tours for the public can acquaint them with newly installed equipment that controls air quality and thermal discharges to rivers and bodies of water.

COMMUNITY INVOLVEMENT

Utilities, because of their experience in business management and because their economic well-being is dependent on the economic and social health of their communities, should consider the many ways they can participate in the advancement of their service areas.

Industrial development. Traditionally, utilities have worked with community, regional, and state industrial development groups in encouraging industries already located in the area that are expanding to build their new facilities in the service area. Utility industrial development departments also work with other agencies to attract new industries to the area. Not only do they advertise nationally and provide pertinent site and economic information to industries, but they can also, through news releases and through service-area advertising, let the public know about their efforts in behalf of developing a healthy economy for the area.

Assistance for low- and middle-income families. The necessity of utility service for lighting, heating, and cooking is well recognized. The utility industry has adopted programs that involve education, budget assistance, and cooperation with public and private agencies.

Goals of specific programs change with time as social and economic conditions shift. During the 1960s several utilities earned considerable respect for programs to develop greatly needed housing and apartment projects. Of course, these had to meet various legal and regulatory standards.

Figure 20-1. A utility's concern for the environment and public opinion can be demonstrated effectively in the design of new facilities. Virginia Electric Power Company's residential substation near Arlington, Va. is an outstanding example of utility engineering being applied to please the aesthetic interests of the community served.

During the 1970s the need shifted to issues related to pocketbook problems. Consumers found household budgets strained by inflation. Utilities, which are particularly vulnerable to inflation, found it necessary to institute a series of rate increases. Gaining public acceptance of the reasons for price changes is not enough. Farsighted managements and public relations practitioners are also seeking ways for consumers to help themselves.

Several utilities have conducted programs involving energy conservation. Insulation is an inexpensive and convenient device for producing quick results. Booklets ranging from how to purchase and install insulation to how to decide the most cost-effective areas to insulate, *e.g.*, walls vs. ceilings, are now widely available. Nearly all are distributed without charge. Most are written on behalf of local utilities and are therefore excellent guides based on local weather conditions, energy-use patterns, and energy costs. Some utilities have programs that provide their customers with financing assistance in buying insulation.

Also complex, but promising, are ways to help customers make conscious choices about when energy should be devoted to particular tasks. These take two basic forms: (1) controlling appliances so they operate only at specific times, or (2) charging different rates for energy consumption at various times. The goal is to encourage energy consumption when existing utility equipment can best meet the needs. This reduces the need to construct new facilities and avoids higher rates due to costs of financing construction.

The implications of such programs are far-

"Even with maximum energy conservation effort, we will still need nuclear power." Dr. Ann C. Birge.

"As a nation, we are going to have to face the need for stronger conservation measures to stretch our energy resources. We have to drive our cars less. We have to insulate our homes better. We have to learn to use energy wisely.

"But even with these much needed conservation steps, we must still go ahead and develop both coal and nuclear energy sources. We cannot do without either.

"Only the greater use of coal and nuclear energy can help us stop burning up our oil. With vital industries such as petrochemicals and plastics dependent on oil, our grandchildren and great grandchildren will surely be in trouble if we've burned up all the oil their generations will need.

"Compared to fossil fuels, nuclear power is cleaner—it does not pollute the air—and cheaper. It costs more to build a nuclear plant, but since the fuel costs less, nuclear power is still a net gain over fossil fuel plants.

"What about other energy alternatives? I am for exploring them all, but as a physicist and researcher I believe it will be the year 2000 before we have full-scale commercial solar power plants on line. That is not to discount the home-heating solar plants already on the market.

"So until we see what the year 2000 brings, nuclear power is buying us time: time to continue the basic research that must be done in all fields of energy.

"I don't think we can close the door on any one source of energy. We can't afford to turn off any option!"

**Edison Electric Institute
for the electric companies**
90 Park Avenue, New York, N.Y. 10016

Dr. Ann C. Birge, Professor of Physics, California State University, Hayward.

Figure 20-2. It takes a decade or more to build a new generating station. Consumers find it difficult to accept a utility's need to launch long-term construction programs when conservation appears to offer an alternative choice.

reaching and it is too soon to predict their final evolution. But it is obvious they present public relations issues of compelling proportions. Those practitioners who will do well in this area will have a thorough knowledge of utility financing, rate making, and the needs and aspirations of consumers.

Essential to the longest-range goal of better understanding is the education of young people about the relationships between energy use, environmental protection, and economic stability at household, regional, and national levels. Teachers in many states now have available to them instructional aids for all levels from elementary through college that deal with various aspects of energy issues. Those that have been most quickly adopted have been designed to fit into existing teaching syllabi. Restraint and understanding of educators require that commercial messages not be included in material for classroom use.

Minority group hiring and training. Another plus for the utility in forwarding socio-economic goals is through minority hiring and participation in essential training programs for the disadvantaged. Much progress is being made in this regard. Acceptance of this community responsibility enhances the character of the utility.

Community health, welfare, educational, and cultural interests. For many years utilities have supported the social agencies of their communities through contributions, through service on boards of directors, and through employee participation in the work of these agencies. Many employees have been engaged in volunteer work with youth groups, many serve on boards of education, and in rural areas a great many are in volunteer fire departments.

Utility managements have supported both private and public colleges and universities through contributions, and they are contributing now to community cultural programs and foundations. In many states these contributions cannot be charged against operations; consequently they must come from earnings, the equity the shareholder has in the business.

A community is an intricate collection of groups, organizations, political, economic, and religious interests and affiliations; and although all industries need to be concerned with community involvement, it is particularly rewarding for the public utility. Members of a community, especially those who are concerned about its general welfare, are quick to recognize participation in the many worthwhile programs that make a community a better place.

RELATIONS WITH SPECIFIC GROUPS

Employee relations. As indicated earlier, in a utility employees are the basic foundation for developing good community relations. They are a direct link with the customer either through the requirements of their work or through community activities or with friends and neighbors. The astute practitioner will review the status of employee relations regularly. He will check on the efficacy of the information program for employees and he will concern himself with the company's training program for those employees who are in direct contact through their jobs with customers.

Effective communication with employees and, as a matter of fact, good communication between all levels of supervision within today's corporation is one of the most difficult achievements in corporate relations. Supervisors find it difficult to communicate with those who report to them and often find it difficult to communicate with their own superiors.

Good communications within the corporation may well be more difficult to develop than good communications with the public. There is no easy road for the uneasy practitioner. He will need to try different programs and innovations and rely to some extent on periodic employee opinion surveys.

Some guidelines will help, but these will not guarantee success. We have indicated that utility employees, like others, think in terms of self-interest; they may read statements from executive management, but they are not "turned on" unless the matter touches on their self-interest.

A more detailed approach to employee communications in general is covered in Chapters 14 and 15, but we should briefly consider the methods one can use for communication within a utility.

For the new employee there is an orientation program and a handbook on his opportunities, benefits, and obligations. Perhaps he has been reached originally through a recruiting booklet that has been prepared by a collaborative effort of the public and employee relations departments. As an employee, he receives a company magazine or newspaper on a regular basis. Often this periodical goes to all the media within the service area as well.

Many utilities keep supervisors and key salaried employees acquainted with company affairs through a special management newsletter. Also, information programs prepared by the public relations department are often carried out through discussion sessions that a supervisor conducts with the group reporting to him. Electronic systems also have some distinct advantages because of the speed of transmittals. Desk-to-desk dialing systems, public address systems, and even closed-circuit television are being used with increasing frequency.

Because of the ever-increasing tempo of American business, the ideal communications program of the future (if not the present) may well be organized to do four things:

1. Send important messages within seconds.
2. Send more detailed information to the entire employee force within hours.
3. Send regular, lengthy, and complete reports on major items of interest, trends, and long-range developments to the entire employee organization. These lengthy communications may vary in form, content, and purpose, depending on what part of the employee force they are designed to reach. For example, research and development people do not have the same interests as foremen, yet both groups need information.
4. Allow easy and swift upward communication from all levels of the organization to the top.

One of the most effective ways informed employees can promote company public relations is through speakers' clubs.[3] Only a limited number of talks need to be on company subjects. Let the employee of a utility choose his own material, be sure that his presentation is sound, help him with speech techniques through training courses and see that top management keeps in touch with the program. If a company speaker has an interesting informative talk or an entertaining one, he will be well received. The very fact that he has come to speak to a group and is identified as an employee of a utility will benefit the utility's community relations.

Business and social peers. Active memberships in service clubs and other community clubs and organizations are important to utility community relations. Through these clubs a company can keep in touch with influential business and government people. Company policies can be explained in a friendly atmosphere; in critical situations people who are community leaders can be reached quickly and can hear the company's side of a controversial issue.

Government agencies and officials. Because a utility exists by reason of franchise and because it is a regulated corporation "affected by a public interest," it is imperative that relations with this special public on every level of government be the best that can be developed.

These relationships are the responsibility of both senior management and company managers in each community. In addition to the company's own relationships, public relations and public affairs officers should be in touch with overall industry relations with government. They must study proposed legislation at all levels of government and the effect such legislation may have on utility operations.

Media relations. Good media relations are extremely important to utilities. Recommended press relations policies covered in Chapter 39 and elsewhere in Section V are pertinent to utilities. However, here again the peculiar nature of the utility business means that its operations are under daily scrutiny by all media.

Viewed as a public (rather than as media), the press is influential as an opinion molder among all the other publics. Even a newspaper's selection of letters to the editor can have an effect on the character of the utility. The attitude of columnists toward a company is also extremely important.

It is especially important that editorial department news people have the names of company people to call in case of emergency or just to make queries. A good idea is to see that a map of the utility's territory is also at hand. An ideal method is to prepare a brief press background kit that can be kept up-to-date and would be quickly available to news media. In addition to the information the media have, everyone in the utility company who has relations with the press should have a brief handbook on company press policy. It is virtually impossible for the central public relations department to report on regional storms and outages, for instance. Information of that type must be handled quickly by company people in the affected area.

Media relations through advertising. Although utilities are usually not major advertisers in their areas, they may develop promotional advertising programs in support of dealers and contractors. The public relations executive has a policy responsibility in regard to this type of advertising because it reflects the character of a company.

The institutional advertising program is the special province of the public relations department. This program can be as varied as the ingenuity of the department can devise. Institutional advertising can expound the policies of a company and promote its

[3]See Chapter 48.

THE UTILITY AND ITS PUBLIC

Figure 20-3. Teaching adults and children to use and conserve energy better is a challenge to all utilities. High standards of non-commercial objectivity are required for such materials.

services and special projects. Such advertising may be particularly helpful in rate submissions because it can present the company's position exactly, whereas the news releases may be subject to the vagaries of the particular reporter who will rewrite the story in his own style and the style of the newspaper—often with disastrous results.

In many states self-styled consumer advocates have challenged the right of utilities to charge some or all advertising costs to rate payers as a legitimate business expense. These efforts are in addition to long-standing involvement by regulatory agencies in determining what type of advertising expenses are acceptable for inclusion in rates. The practitioner must remain familiar with these efforts and work closely with legal counsel and senior management to make sure consumer and business interests are protected.

SPECIAL CONSIDERATIONS FOR TELEPHONE UTILITIES

As indicated earlier, the general business character of telephone utilities is comparable to a high degree with electric and gas utilities.

The telephone industry, especially the Bell System, has been committed to extensive research programs for many years. That commitment has enabled it to achieve remarkable technological development. Meeting the accelerating demand has, of course, created some real problems. These have been primarily regional, and improvement of service in areas affected by extremely rapid growth in use is a prime concern.

One does not usually think of a great utility as being competitive but the Bell System telephone companies face increasing competition with respect to their services.

Competition is chiefly in the field of communications designed for private line services—specifically data transmission. In addition, in June 1968 the F.C.C. permitted the connection of customer-provided terminal equipment (e.g., a computer) and customer-provided communications systems. In 1977 customers were given the right to attach their own phones to telephone companies' lines.[4]

The rising thrust of consumerism is a very potent force for telephone companies to deal with, just as it is with other utilities. Here again quality service at a fair price is basic policy.

Commitment to communities served through involvement with the needs of the community is a policy that is receiving increasing emphasis. The Bell System serves the great metropolitan areas and the welfare of large cities is extremely important to the successful operation of that system. Participation in training programs, especially for the disadvantaged of the cities, is now a policy principle.

In 1969 AT&T established a Department of Environmental Affairs to study and advise management on all aspects of environmental considerations.

Just as with other utilities, there has been a drift away from the customer. The dehumanization of companies through technological advances must be counteracted by programs that rebuild employee-customer friendly relations. Employee turnover means constant attention to training.

INTRA-INDUSTRY RELATIONS

Although there is no one voice that can speak for the electric and gas utilities, trade associations and special public relations and advertising programs are open to individual utility participation. The Edison Electric Institute[5] has a broad program covering every aspect of electric utility interest. The Institute's Public Relations Committee has developed a comprehensive handbook on utility public relations and is deeply involved in setting annual goals for Institute staff. Staff carries out a broad range of functions, including publication of a magazine, press contacts, seminar planning, and distribution of educational materials for teachers. The American Gas Association[6] sponsors excellent workshops on public relations, both national and regional. Many utilities are also members of the Atomic Industrial Forum.[7]

Both the Edison Electric Institute and the American Gas Association sponsor national advertising programs that stress themes such as conditions that force prices up, the value of energy conservation, and long-range energy requirements.

Other advertisements promote the use of nuclear energy and the long-range benefits for the public in the generation of electricity. Media used in the program are television and magazines.

The Public Utilities Advertising Association[8] is one of the oldest advertising societies in America. The association is primarily a forum for the exchange of ideas in utility advertising.

Another general program supported by individual utility subscription is the Public Information Program carried on by Underwood, Jordan Associates. This is primarily an editorial and public relations informative program for electric utilities. One of its accomplishments has been the development of an Annual Youth Conference on the Atom. Utilities sponsor gifted high school students who attend this conference with their science teachers and learn about opportunities for careers in nuclear science.

Although it is not a trade association, many electric utilities subscribe to the services provided by Reddy Kilowatt, Inc. Reddy Kilowatt is a patented character who is a symbol of the investor-owned utility business worldwide.

MEETING GROWTH WITH ADEQUATE SUPPLY

Not many years ago utilities were promoting the "all you want when you want it" theme in regard to the supply of energy. Now meeting growing demand will be an accomplishment of major proportions, both for electricity and gas.

Somnolent socialists will undoubtedly awaken to challenge private operation of utilities. Their song has long been "anything you can do, government can do better." These political opportunists

---

[4]Editor's Note: Additional forms of competition are also arising. Communications satellites—both of the government-corporation type and proposed private ones—can carry both TV signals and telephone messages. New data transmission companies are arising to serve computer users, promising low rates. Facsimile (see Chapter 46), teletype, microwave relays, electronic transmission of microfilm, and other techniques all potentially may develop systems competitive with existing telephone companies.

[5]90 Park Ave., New York, N.Y. 10016.

[6]1515 Wilson Blvd., Arlington, Va. 22209

[7]475 Park Ave. South, New York, N.Y. 10016.

[8]Les Bierbaum, International Gas Co., 555 S. Cole Rd., Boise, Idaho 83707.

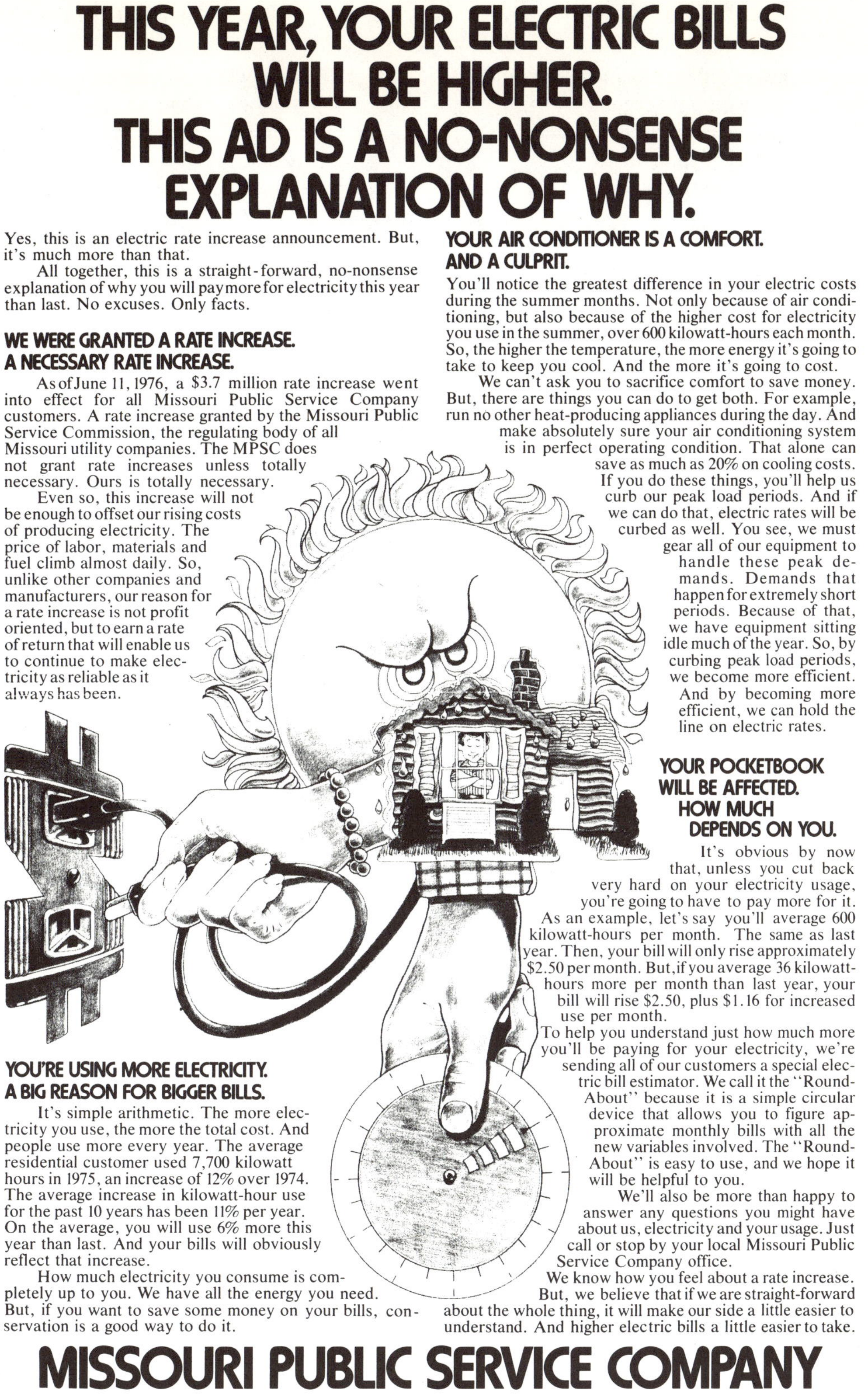

THIS YEAR, YOUR ELECTRIC BILLS WILL BE HIGHER. THIS AD IS A NO-NONSENSE EXPLANATION OF WHY.

Yes, this is an electric rate increase announcement. But, it's much more than that.

All together, this is a straight-forward, no-nonsense explanation of why you will pay more for electricity this year than last. No excuses. Only facts.

WE WERE GRANTED A RATE INCREASE. A NECESSARY RATE INCREASE.

As of June 11, 1976, a $3.7 million rate increase went into effect for all Missouri Public Service Company customers. A rate increase granted by the Missouri Public Service Commission, the regulating body of all Missouri utility companies. The MPSC does not grant rate increases unless totally necessary. Ours is totally necessary.

Even so, this increase will not be enough to offset our rising costs of producing electricity. The price of labor, materials and fuel climb almost daily. So, unlike other companies and manufacturers, our reason for a rate increase is not profit oriented, but to earn a rate of return that will enable us to continue to make electricity as reliable as it always has been.

YOU'RE USING MORE ELECTRICITY. A BIG REASON FOR BIGGER BILLS.

It's simple arithmetic. The more electricity you use, the more the total cost. And people use more every year. The average residential customer used 7,700 kilowatt hours in 1975, an increase of 12% over 1974. The average increase in kilowatt-hour use for the past 10 years has been 11% per year. On the average, you will use 6% more this year than last. And your bills will obviously reflect that increase.

How much electricity you consume is completely up to you. We have all the energy you need. But, if you want to save some money on your bills, conservation is a good way to do it.

YOUR AIR CONDITIONER IS A COMFORT. AND A CULPRIT.

You'll notice the greatest difference in your electric costs during the summer months. Not only because of air conditioning, but also because of the higher cost for electricity you use in the summer, over 600 kilowatt-hours each month. So, the higher the temperature, the more energy it's going to take to keep you cool. And the more it's going to cost.

We can't ask you to sacrifice comfort to save money. But, there are things you can do to get both. For example, run no other heat-producing appliances during the day. And make absolutely sure your air conditioning system is in perfect operating condition. That alone can save as much as 20% on cooling costs. If you do these things, you'll help us curb our peak load periods. And if we can do that, electric rates will be curbed as well. You see, we must gear all of our equipment to handle these peak demands. Demands that happen for extremely short periods. Because of that, we have equipment sitting idle much of the year. So, by curbing peak load periods, we become more efficient. And by becoming more efficient, we can hold the line on electric rates.

YOUR POCKETBOOK WILL BE AFFECTED. HOW MUCH DEPENDS ON YOU.

It's obvious by now that, unless you cut back very hard on your electricity usage, you're going to have to pay more for it. As an example, let's say you'll average 600 kilowatt-hours per month. The same as last year. Then, your bill will only rise approximately $2.50 per month. But, if you average 36 kilowatt-hours more per month than last year, your bill will rise $2.50, plus $1.16 for increased use per month.

To help you understand just how much more you'll be paying for your electricity, we're sending all of our customers a special electric bill estimator. We call it the "Round-About" because it is a simple circular device that allows you to figure approximate monthly bills with all the new variables involved. The "Round-About" is easy to use, and we hope it will be helpful to you.

We'll also be more than happy to answer any questions you might have about us, electricity and your usage. Just call or stop by your local Missouri Public Service Company office.

We know how you feel about a rate increase. But, we believe that if we are straight-forward about the whole thing, it will make our side a little easier to understand. And higher electric bills a little easier to take.

MISSOURI PUBLIC SERVICE COMPANY

Figure 20-4. Helping consumers understand the causes and effects of rate changes is vital to utilities' well-being. This ad offers a simple calculator to help customers estimate monthly electric bills.

generally ignore the tax differential in the operating costs for private utilities and the regulatory controls that govern investor-owned utilities.

Meeting projected growth is clearly one of the major tasks for utilities. Despite a break in the rapid rate of increasing energy consumption, the nation's energy needs are still growing. There is unease within the utility industry about whether demand for electricity will stabilize within the more modest growth rates now used in planning.

In 1975, national survey data showed a large majority, 70 percent, believed we should try to conserve electricity; people should not be allowed to use all they want. Seventy-nine percent reported having already cut down on usage. However, by mid-1976 the U.S. peak electrical demand reached a new all-time high. There were regional indications that within some groups of customers electric usage was growing at rates nearly mirroring those of the mid-1960s.

As the Edison Electric Institute has pointed out in national advertising, today we are in the midst of a great transitional storm between two energy epochs—the fossil fuel age and a future energy era, as yet not fully defined. To many, it appears that conversion of basic energy sources to electricity may increase as the transition continues. Since it takes ten or more years to build generating stations, some doubt that all needs could be met if increased consumer demand were to accelerate.

The nature of the public relations challenge is highlighted by the public's widespread acceptance of generalities but its failure to accept the personal responsibilities required. The disparity between views on conservation and actual consumption levels is a case in point. Another is the widespread general endorsement of nuclear generating stations and the strong local opposition when sites are chosen.

The utility industry is devoting increased time and talent to dispel personal and local-level resistance to matters that are widely endorsed as generally desirable. One of its most difficult tactical challenges is finding ways to summarize complex issues in 20- 40-second messages suitable for the needs of local reporters.

STRATEGY AND TECHNIQUES

In this overview of the utility and its public only the highlights in regard to public relations strategies, techniques, and public concerns endemic to utilities can be covered.

Overall strategy in utility public relations should embrace both short-range and long-range plans. Such a program gives direction and stability to all the programs and the proper emphasis and attention to long-range objectives. Although some public relations departments operate without outside counsel, the merits of such assistance should be given great weight. Outside public relations counsel not only brings a more independent perspective to planning and executing public relations programs, but it also can free company people for creative research and planning that will have a beneficial effect on a corporation's community relations.

Virtually nothing in public relations today is locked in concrete. That means possibilities for innovations for the practitioners—innovations that relate more effectively to a society of social change. Innovations that are unconventional today may well be routine practice tomorrow.

Public participation in planning. One such change could be involvement of the public in company decisions affecting public relations through the technique of *negotiation.* Today's economic "lifestyle" is more and more the result of negotiated compromises . . . even in areas, for example, where it has heretofore been illegal to strike.

It is possible that information programs alone will be inadequate in dealing with the "new" public. Effective public relations in some situations may be primarily a matter of give and take. When a company takes a controversial course, it must be prepared to face criticism and, literally, *deal* with its critics. This type of approach calls for more candid information to the public long in advance of the resolution of plans for a new project such as a generating plant. This new approach, in a sense, is in recognition of the fact that the objectives of the conservationist and the environmentalist have changed and a company must negotiate with them and the public in regard to future plans.

Since the early 1970s, regulatory control of the siting and construction process has increased. This has brought utility and critic together in a judicial-type atmosphere as well as in the public forum so commonly used to resolve local issues in America. Public relations is closely involved in these activities.

Corporate identity systems. Another relatively new proposition for utilities is the formal "corporate identity system." In the past, according to conventional theory, a corporation achieved an identity with its public or publics through the sum of all of its public relations efforts. There were,

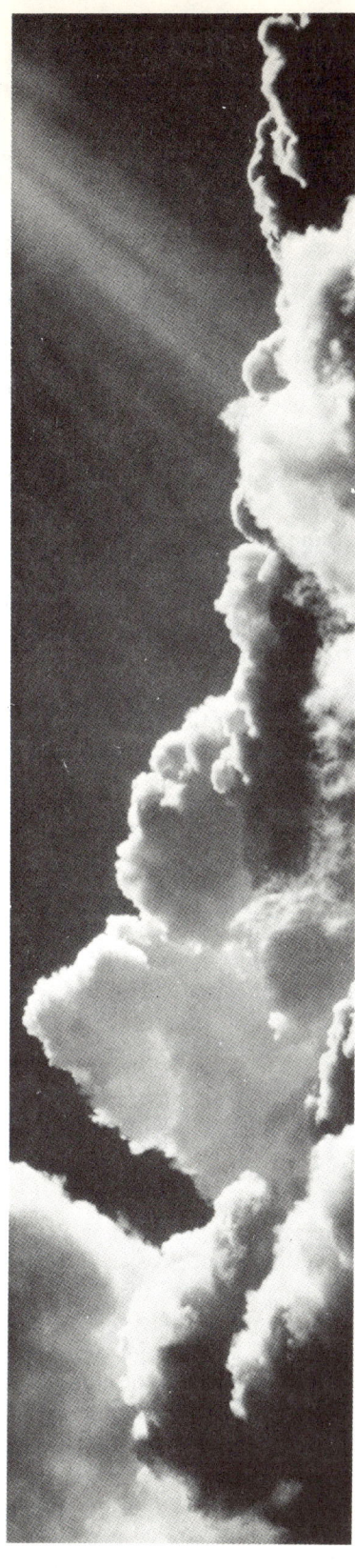

THE TRANSITIONAL STORM.
PART I. AN EXPLANATION.

HOW CRITICAL IS THE ENERGY "CRISIS"?

The energy situation in America today is serious. On the other hand, it is not the end of the world.

It is true there is an energy crisis in the sense that there is an increasing scarcity of certain *fuels*. But there is no scarcity of *energy*.

There never *has* been.

There never *will* be.

There never *could* be. Energy is inexhaustible. Edward Teller puts it this way: "...*unlimited* energy exists. What is missing is the practical way to use this energy efficiently."

No — there is no energy "shortage." There is an energy "crisis" because we have reached a critical juncture in the availability of means to provide our energy.

THE TRANSITIONAL GAP

The end of the fossil-fuel age is clearly discernible. The beginnings of a *future*-energy age are not yet clearly established.

But that is not an earthshaking situation for us to be in. The phasing in and phasing out of fuel epochs is nothing new.

Roughly a hundred thousand years ago, man learned how to burn wood. This gave him a primary fuel for the production of energy when and as he needed it — in this case, energy in the form of heat.

By 1400 AD, man was capturing energy through windmills and through the flow of water over water-wheels. But even more important, he had learned how to burn coal. And with that, the fossil-fuel age had begun.

Finally, in the last century, man discovered natural gas and petroleum. The fossil-fuel age was fully launched, and the advanced industrial society we know today was made possible, including the generation of electricity.

FOSSIL FUELS DISAPPEARING

Yet now we find the industrial society's appetite for energy is so prodigious that some of our fossil fuels — natural gas and oil — are already fast disappearing, and coal is by no means inexhaustible. In hindsight, it is clear that from the first, man expected too much of the fossil-fuel epoch. Everyone alive today was born years after it began. We were born into it as we were born into the constants of rain, sunshine and the tides. It is understandable, therefore, that without giving it much thought, we more or less expected fossil fuels to go on forever.

As Dr. M. K. Hubbert of the U.S. Geological Survey has said: "It is difficult for people who are living now...to realize how transitory the fossil-fuel epoch will eventually prove to be when viewed over the significant span of human history."

In a period of only 1300 years from beginning to end, Dr. Hubbert estimates, man will have consumed the world's entire available supply of fossil fuels. Further, he estimates that 80 percent of that supply — all but the first and last ten percents — will have been consumed in the incredibly short period of 300 years.

Clearly, in historic perspective, this is a rather insignificant though at times troublesome period, and it is important that we adjust our thinking to accept this insignificance lest we fall victim to the despairing notion that the world will go out of business when the last barrel of oil is pumped.

It won't. The fossil-fuel epoch may be passing, but energy itself remains permanently with us. The challenge of the moment is for us to do everything possible to find ways of capturing that energy.

THE IMPERATIVES

The imperatives we face are these:

First, we must stretch the fossil-fuel epoch to its absolute limit. Conservation of *all* energy is a must — and especially conservation of petroleum resources. And we must substitute coal and uranium for other fuels wherever possible.

Second, we must speed the development of other sources of energy so that we can move into the future-energy epoch as soon as possible.

That sounds simple, but what makes it more difficult than it needs to be is the lack of public consensus — the notion promoted by some that there are other options, including a halt to growth.

But the fact is — given a growing population and a continuing desire by everyone for a satisfying life-style — no other options exist. Increased supplies of energy are essential.

OUR SEPARATE ROLES

It is also essential for all the players in this enormous drama to have a clear understanding of their separate roles.

The utility industry's part is to meet consumer demand and at the lowest possible cost and with acceptable environmental impact. It must press ahead on research and development on new sources of electric power. It must share in the task of seeing that people learn how to use electricity more efficiently.

Given today's complexity of environmental and energy regulations and the huge investment required for energy research and development, government, commerce and industry all have a vital role in the energy drama. They must join the utility industry in encouraging consumers to use energy wisely.

The consumers' role is in many ways the most important. Since they are the users of electricity, they are the ones that can make "wise use of energy" mean something. They must make it a way of life. They must encourage their neighbors to do the same. They must also support research and development that will lead to new sources of electricity. And they must face the reality that dwindling fossil fuels, staggering investments for research and development, and equipment for the protection of the environment are inevitably influencing electric rates.

Perhaps most important of all, consumers must give serious, practical, realistic thought to public decisions to be made regarding energy sources and environmental concerns.

None of these roles will be easy to perform. What makes the drama worth the playing, however, is the promise at its end: the discovery that satisfying lives need not come to a grinding halt and that a new, more abundant epoch will follow the old.

And in the final analysis, there is no alternative to our playing our roles conscientiously. As Dr. Glenn Seaborg, former Chairman of the Atomic Energy Commission, said: "...the future of energy is the future of man. Without it we become nothing. With it, we become whatever we wish."

Edison Electric Institute
for the electric companies
90 Park Avenue, New York, N.Y. 10016

Figure 20-5. Effective communication with the public is perhaps the only way to resolve the dilemma that many utilities face—providing energy on an ever-increasing scale while maintaining the quality of the environment. As this advertisement says, "... the future of energy is the future of man. Without it we become nothing. With it, we become whatever we wish."

however, general objectives. Undoubtedly this practice had considerable success, but the kind of identity the corporation established was arrived at informally. There was no concerted effort within a company to determine just what opinion it wanted the public to have of it as long as the company had reasonably good relations with the public. Today's theory dictates a different and much more formal approach to establishing a corporate identity.

Consequently, intensive research and survey programs related to establishing a more formal corporate identity are receiving considerable attention from utilities today.

One cannot fault a program that seeks to establish a more viable corporate identity as long as the time and effort devoted to this relatively long-range project do not interfere with the day-to-day stewardship of the public relations program. There is always the danger, however, that an obsession with a long-range objective may damage or even defeat short-range operational needs. A bankrupt firm doesn't need a new enchanting symbol. A new corporate symbol, which usually is one of the products of an intensive identity research program, has no magical message for the consumer if the firm's overall performance in the market is bad.

However, in defense of the corporate identity objective as a public relations system, it may well give everyone a better perspective on the company, involve all levels of management more intensely in promoting the corporate character and goals, and even eliminate bad corporate performance.

On balance then it could well be a good discipline for the public relations department and others in the company to do all of the research and study necessary to set up a formal corporate identity system. This type of study that would not neglect on-going public relations programs and short-range objectives could have long-range benefits.

UTILITY PUBLIC RELATIONS CHECKLIST

In looking to activities and programs that should be considered, the following suggestions from "The Electric Industry and the Public in the Early 1970's" by Underwood, Jordan Associates are pertinent.

I *Community Relations*
Public relations should be responsible for:
1. Encouraging participation by executives and key employees in civic affairs.
2. Providing executive leadership and individual financial support to worthwhile causes—Community Chest and Red Cross campaigns, etc.
3. Giving generously in both money and manpower to health and welfare, education, professional and civic fund-raising drives of a community-building nature, in accordance with company policy administered on a uniform basis.
4. Arranging periodic surveys of public opinion, conducted for the company by independent sampling organizations.
5. Maintaining a system of routine daily calls on residential customers by trained employee-interviewers.
6. Conducting periodic reviews of customer service and accounting policies and procedures to make sure that they are adequate, understandable and friendly.
7. Determining the particular "social" needs of the community and then developing specific company-led or company-sponsored programs designed to help meet those needs.
8. Advertising and otherwise publicizing the company as "a good place to work," not only to attract job applicants but also to humanize the corporate image.
9. Taking a position of genuine leadership in area development by means of industrial expansion efforts.
10. Conducting tours of company facilities for organized local groups—and occasional "open houses" for the general public.
11. Maintaining (and vigorously promoting) a company speakers' bureau.
12. Keeping ahead of technological developments affecting the electric industry, and making sure that the public is aware of the company's investment in time, energy, and money in research and development.
13. Planning, organizing, and staging special events, anniversaries, and other company observances in a manner that emphasizes, above all, the identity of interest between the company and the communities and people they serve.

14. Making sure that company properties are so designed, landscaped, and maintained as to provide an example of responsible industrial concern for the environments in the communities in which the company has facilities.
15. Installing and properly maintaining attractive and uniform identification signs at appropriate company properties.
16. Participating broadly in local exhibitions and fairs of general public interest, thus achieving further identification of the company with the community.

II *Public Information*

Public relations should be responsible for:

1. Planning, preparing, and distributing news releases concerning company and electric industry developments of public interest or concern.
2. Arranging and conducting individual interviews and collective press conferences between company executives and representatives of press, radio, and television.
3. Maintaining a prompt, efficient, uninterrupted press information service that operates around the clock, 365 days a year, to answer inquiries from press and radio-TV people relative to service interruptions and the like as soon as they are received, at any hour of the day or night.
4. Publishing institutional advertisements regularly in daily and weekly newspapers and important regional magazines throughout the company's service area.
5. Planning and processing personalized mass mailings, made over the chief executive officer's signature, to newspaper editors, radio and television executives, educators, clergymen, public officials, and other local opinion leaders calling to their attention current developments on the local or national scene that importantly affect the company, the industry, their area, and the public interest.
6. Promptly and fully satisfying requests from public and school libraries throughout the company's service area for factual material concerning the policies, practices, and accomplishments of the company and the industry.
7. Organizing series of "Editorial Roundtables" between the company's top management and the editors and publishers of area and regional newspapers, magazines, and radio-TV stations and networks. These "Editorial Roundtables" are not conceived as meetings for the working press. What the company should be looking for at them is knowledge and understanding from the *policy-makers* of the news media of the company's position on issues of public concern.
8. Developing and distributing widely (via television, speakers' bureau, and/or commercial theater showings) motion pictures portraying the company's operations and highlighting the economic advantages of the company's service areas.

III *Customer Information*

Public relations should be responsible for:

1. Sending "welcome" letters signed by the chief executive officer to customers new to the company's service area, including helpful or desirable information concerning rates, procedures, and service facilities.
2. Preparing an attractive booklet summarizing "what every customer ought to know" about the company, its rates, and facilities.
3. Developing a periodical customer publication to be mailed as an enclosure with each bill or timed for delivery to each customer's home with his bill.
4. Giving the company's "contact" employees special public relations training for general guidance in meeting customers and the public.
5. Periodically reviewing the company's collection letters, correspondence forms, and the like, to make sure that

they promote a friendly understanding of company policies.
6. Developing brochures and other informative material directed to specific customer segments—women, farm groups, small business proprietors, etc.
7. Preparing special mailings on company and industry problems for transmission over the chief executive officer's signature to customer-stockholders.

IV *Employee Information*
Public relations should be responsible for:

1. Making sure that the employee publication regularly reviews and reports on major *industry* developments, accomplishments, and problems of critical importance to the company and therefore to its employees.
2. Providing company supervisors with special public relations training to improve their human relations with their employees and to inform them about economic and political issues affecting the industry locally and nationally.
3. Preparing material on major company and industry developments for use at employee meetings or conferences and in conducting the question periods that follow.
4. Mailing to employees' homes (and therefore to their families as well) occasional letters from the company's chief executive officer concerning important changes in personnel policies or administration, or directing attention to major local or national developments that are likely to excite comment or controversy regarding the affairs of the company or the industry.
5. Using bulletin boards in well-lighted employee traffic centers to focus employee attention on current public relations approaches and on current problems of the company and the industry.
6. Developing for use in conjunction with the indoctrination program for new employees, informational materials that properly stress the company's history, business, and problems, an employee manual covering the aims and policies of the company and the industry, as well as the rules and regulations of employment.
7. Providing a sound public relations approach for the company's booklets on safety, medical care, pensions, and other matters of special employee interest.
8. Distributing carefully selected information pieces concerning the company and the industry with employees' pay envelopes or salary checks.
9. Making applicable items among the suggested activities listed above in this section available to retired as well as active employees.

V *Stockholder Information*
Public relations should be responsible for:

1. Explaining public relations problems and objectives of the company and the industry, in terms of special current developments, in the company's quarterly dividend folders and other stockholder communications.
2. Preparing and sending to all stockholders a transcript or highlights of the chief executive officer's remarks at the company's annual meeting.
3. Giving special attention to the routine daily informational needs of security analysts and financial editors, and encouraging free interchange of information with investor organizations.
4. Conducting special tours of company properties for security analysts and financial editors.
5. Preparing an attractive booklet summarizing the company's history, organization, present status, and future prospects, to be mailed to all current stockholders and sent to new ones with an initial letter of welcome.
6. Making sure that each stockholder inquiry receives a prompt, per-

sonalized response, signed by the chief executive officer, the secretary of the company, or the officer to whom the inquiry was directed.
7. Distributing to all stockholders occasional reprints dealing with developments vital to the company and the industry and making other reprints available to interested stockholders on request (the offer normally being made through the quarterly dividend folder).
8. Arranging periodic surveys to ascertain the characteristics and preferences of the company's stockholders and their basic reasons for investing in the company.

21

Public Relations for the Business and Professional Association

J. CARROLL BATEMAN became president of the Insurance Information Institute on January 19, 1967, after serving as general manager of the organization from February 1, 1960. The Institute is a public information and education organization supported by several hundred insurance companies in the property and liability field. The Institute has its headquarters in New York City and branch offices in nine other cities.

From 1934 until 1942 Mr. Bateman was a reporter and feature writer for the Baltimore (Md.) Evening Sun. He became associated with the Baltimore and Ohio Railroad in Baltimore in 1942 as assistant editor of the B & O Magazine, later was named public relations representative, and in 1951 was promoted to assistant director of public relations.

He joined the Eastern Railroad Presidents Conference in New York in 1953 as assistant chairman for public relations and advertising. In 1955, he was appointed public relations director of the Milk Industry Foundation in Washington, D.C., which he left in 1960 to assume his post with the I.I.I.

Mr. Bateman holds a Bachelor of Science degree from Johns Hopkins University, Baltimore, and a Master of Arts degree from the School of Education at New York University. He has been an instructor in public relations at Johns Hopkins University and the Bernard Baruch School of Business Administration at the College of the City of New York, and a guest lecturer at numerous other universities. Since 1968 he has served on the American Council for Education in Journalism, the official accreditating agency for colleges and departments of journalism.

Mr. Bateman was the 1967 national president of the Public Relations Society of America. He served in 1964 as chairman of the Business and Professional Association Section of PRSA, and in 1966 as national vice-president. He has been a member of the Board of Trustees of the Foundation for Public Relations Education and Research and a contributing editor to the Public Relations Journal. In 1976, he was General Chairman for the VII Public Relations World Congress, held in Boston and attended by 1,500 public relations practitioners from 48 countries.

When the youthful Frenchman, Alexis de Tocqueville, wrote his penetrating analysis of the American system, *Democracy in America,* following his visit to the United States early in the nineteenth century, he made particular note of the propensity of Americans to form associations for almost every purpose. It is a national trait that has, with the passage of time, become even more pronounced. There are so many associations and societies that it is diffi- cult to obtain an accurate count. The Internal Revenue Service (which grants tax exemptions to non-profit organizations) estimates there are 42,370 non-profiit trade and business associations and professional societies in the United States. The American Society of Association Executives estimates there are 17,000 national and international associations and societies headquartered in the United States, and close to 25,000 other associations at the state, local, or regional levels. All these figures may include small or inconsequential groups. A more likely figure, for the purposes of this chapter, is provided in a monograph on Association Public Relations by the Public Relations Society of America[1], which gives a figure of 18,000 business associations and professional societies. These are the organizations likely to be involved in public relations activities.

The American Society of Association Executives defines three distinct types of membership associations in the nonprofit field (as distinguished, for example, from a profit-making business service that may use the word "association" as part of its name). These three are described as "professional societies or associations," whose membership is made up of individuals (such as doctors, dentists, engineers, and so on); "trade or business associations," whose membership is companies in the same business, and "federations," which are organizations having other associations as their members.[2]

Among these three types, the trade association or business-sponsored organization seems to be most common.

The first trade associations in this country date back to the late eighteenth century—before de Tocqueville's visit, of course—but impetus was given to the proliferation of business associations by World War I, the Great Depression of the Thirties, and World War II.[3]

The "countervailing forces" character of American democracy also has encouraged the development of various kinds of individual membership associations in great numbers in recent decades. In addition to the professional societies representing doctors, dentists, engineers, lawyers, etc., recent years have seen the creation of "activist" organizations representing consumers, environmental protectionists, highway safety advocates, and others. These activist groups have shown aptitude in public relations, especially with reference to gaining widespread attention on television.

When an individual seeks social, economic, or legislative goals that he feels he cannot accomplish alone, he looks naturally to an association that can work to such ends—and if the appropriate association does not already exist, he sometimes seeks to form a new one.

Thus, each association is made up of individuals or corporate entities that have a mutual interest that draws them together. Almost inevitably, in attempting to achieve their common goals, they utilize—formally or haphazardly, as the case may be—the concepts, the functions, and the tools of public relations.

As this is being written, the American scene is boiling with new challenges both to business organizations and to individuals. The "activist" movements are in high gear; and even though the speeches and the slogans may die away with the passage of time, these movements will leave behind a plethora of new laws and regulations affecting business, as well as a number of new government agencies designed to watch over business activities.

Some such agencies already are exerting widespread influence. Among them are the Occupational Safety and Health Administration, the Equal Employment Opportunities Commission, and the Commission on Consumer Product Safety. Other traditional governmental agencies, such as the Securities and Exchange Commission, the Justice Department, and other federal regulatory bodies are multiplying their rules and regulations for added protection to investors, consumers, and citizens. There is also a proliferation of consumer protection agencies at the state and local levels. And all of these initiatives by government are placing greater burdens on the associations and societies representing the businesses or professional people involved. The association or society is looked to as the mechanism for dealing with the governmental agency in developing regulation that will be "liveable," in disseminating necessary explanations and instructions to its members, and in speaking out to influence public opinion if and when the hand of government becomes too heavy, deadening opportunities for initiative and enterprise.

The social problems faced by our country seem almost insurmountable: the rehabilitation of deteriorated urban centers; the renovation of our educational system; the integration of our society; the salvaging of our environment, and the general improvement of the quality of life. All of these chal-

---

[1]"Association Public Relations," published by The Business and Professional Association Section, PRSA. New York. (1965).

[2]See "Policies and Procedures of Associations." Published by the American Society of Association Executives. Washington, D.C. (1968).

[3]For more information about the history and development of trade associations in the U.S. see Chapter 1 of "Association Management," edited by Kenneth G. Hance and published by the Chamber of Commerce of the United States, Washington, D.C. (1958).

lenges call for new efforts from businesses, from professional groups, and from other kinds of individuals, and associations are being looked to by their members as appropriate mechanisms for dealing with some of these problems.

While the ultimate patterns of association activity in this area are not yet crystallized, the recognition of these problems has led to an increased emphasis on public affairs, governmental relations, and programs of social responsibility in many associations, and it has resulted in the establishment of some new organizations for the special purpose of grappling with certain of these problems.

In this area, it is worth noting that the Chamber of Commerce of the United States, reacting to the consumer movement early in the 1970s, adopted as its official policy a "Basic Business-Consumer Relations Code" that reads as follows:

We reaffirm the responsibility of American Business to:

1. Protect the health and safety of consumers in the design and manufacture of products and the provision of consumer services. This includes action against harmful side effects on the quality of life and the environment arising from technological progress.
2. Utilize advancing technology to produce goods that meet high standards of quality at the lowest reasonable price.
3. Seek out the informed views of consumers and other groups to help assure customer satisfaction from the earliest stages of product planning.
4. Simplify, clarify, and honor product warranties and guarantees.
5. Maximize the quality of product servicing and repairs and encourage their fair pricing.
6. Eliminate frauds and deceptions from the marketplace, setting as our goal not strict legality but honesty in all transactions.
7. Ensure that sales personnel are familiar with product capabilities and limitations and that they fully respond to consumer needs for such information.
8. Provide consumers with objective information about products, services, and the workings of the marketplace by utilizing appropriate channels of communication, including programs of consumer education.
9. Facilitate sound value comparisons across the widest possible range and choice of products.
10. Provide effective channels for receiving and acting on consumer complaints and suggestions, utilizing the resources of associations, chambers of commerce, better business bureaus, recognized consumer groups, individual companies, and other appropriate bodies.

It is especially interesting to note that article 10 of this code looks specifically to associations as a mechanism for dealing with consumer relations. Also, articles 3, 4, 7, 8, 9, and 10 call for the assistance of public relations and communications specialists, if they are to be properly implemented.

One of the unusual responses to the public's demand for greater social responsibility by business is the Clearinghouse on Corporate Social Responsibility, initially sponsored by four associations representing 500 life and health insurance companies. The Clearinghouse is designed to encourage, advise, and assist its members in their social-responsibility programs. The concept grew out of the effort in social responsibility by insurers when they allocated $2 billion of their investments to urban redevelopment over the years 1967-1972. In 1975 alone, 154 insurance companies reported to the Clearinghouse that they had committed $788 million in investments "which would not otherwise have been made under the companies' customary lending standards, in which social considerations played a substantial part in the investment decision." Stanley G. Karson, director of the Clearinghouse, claims that "the life and health insurance business has been the most consistently involved of major businesses in corporate social responsibility programs."

It should be observed that this program grew out of the actions of four trade associations and required the establishment of a new organization for its implementation.

One thing seems certain: the role of associations will not be lessened by consumer relations and social problems, or by new government initiatives. Indeed, the likelihood is that the role of associations will be expanded, and their significance will grow in the decades immediately ahead.

ORGANIZING FOR PUBLIC RELATIONS IN THE ASSOCIATION

Public relations is a significant function of most associations. Many of them have individuals or complete staffs that specialize in public relations activities. Even where professional public relations

Figure 21-1. As the consumer movement has grown, more and more associations have increased their activities in consumer education. Food editors of major consumer magazines attend a special conference conducted by the Public Relations Department of the American Meat Institute in New York. Initiated in 1962 and repeated annually, this day-long conference has proved to be an effective vehicle for disseminating information to consumers. Participants include leading consumer specialists of the U.S. Department of Agriculture.

people are not employed as staff members, public information and public education activities frequently are conducted under the direction of other staff members or with the assistance of external public relations counsel.

The activities of the trade and professional associations generally are broad in nature, encompassing government relations, technical research, membership education, public relations, sales promotion, and the establishment of codes of ethics and industry standards, to name only a few. Some associations are formed expressly to conduct public relations activities on behalf of a particular industry or business. Whatever the program of a particular association may be, public information and public education efforts are more likely than not to be one of the principal activities.

The public relations staff. The public relations staff in an association may range numerically from one person to more than a hundred. Where staffs are large, naturally there will be departmentalization within the staff itself. Generally this departmentalization occurs on a functional basis—that is, there may be a department for press relations, another for publications, another for school and college relations, another for motion picture development and production, and so on. More frequently, however, the public relations staff of the association is not large enough to justify departmentalization. In such cases, the staff professional may be well advised to utilize to the maximum possible extent external service agencies that can provide specialists in various fields. Where the public relations staff specialist himself attempts to

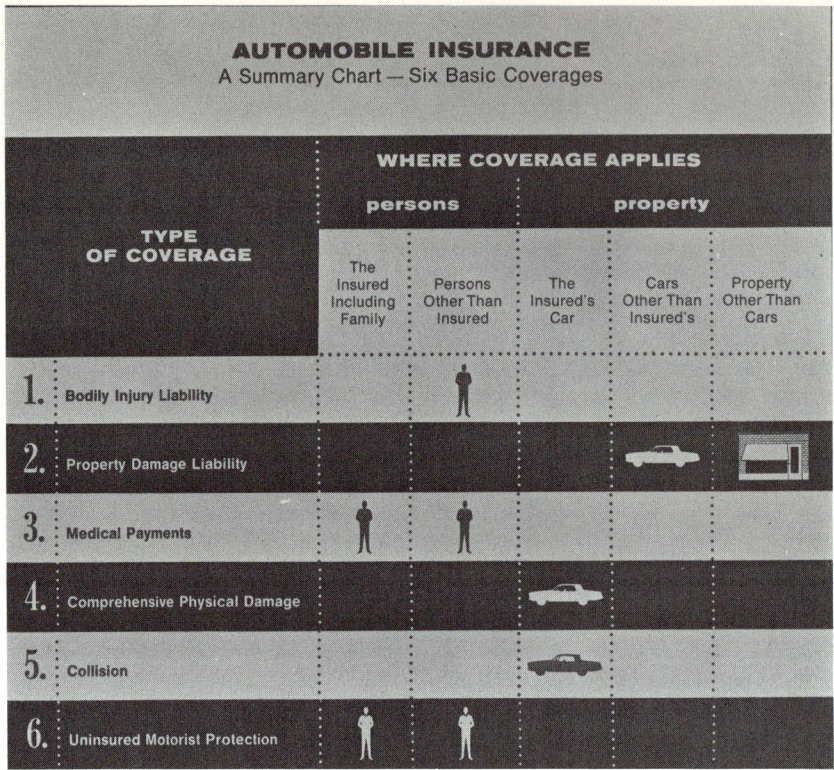

Figure 21-2. Making information about an industry understandable is a challenge to many trade associations. This chart from the Insurance Information Institute—designed for use by driver education instructors at the high school level—explains graphically what is included in various forms of automobile insurance coverage.

be a jack-of-all-trades, his output in some areas is bound to be mediocre.

Employment of counsel. Whether the internal public relations staff is large or small, it may be desirable to employ also an external public relations counselor or counseling firm. Such an arrangement will be most useful where the need for an objective outside viewpoint is important. Sometimes the "outside expert" is in a position to aid the public relations staff executive in winning board approval for worthwhile special projects that might otherwise be lost. A public relations firm also may be able to provide important contacts with media people outside the normal contact range of the association staff. Finally, the external counseling firm may be equipped to provide experts in certain areas where the internal staff may be weak.

The external public relations counseling firm may be hired either on a continuing or temporary basis, depending on the situation.[4] Temporary employment of external public relations help may be advisable to meet certain contingencies that require a large-scale effort beyond the capacity of the permanent staff—such as the celebration of a major industry anniversary or a major fight on a legislative matter.

With or without external help, however, the interests of the membership are best served when there is a professional, full-time public relations practitioner on the staff of the association. Especially is this the case when the status of the public relations executive within the organization is sufficient to permit him to deal at first hand not only with the executive director or executive vice-president, who heads the staff, but also with board members and officers and other industry leaders.

The public relations organization of the association often includes a committee of individual members or member company representatives that serves as an advisory group to the professional public relations staff.

Financing the association program. The financing of an association public relations program may be accomplished in several ways. More commonly, the public relations budget is financed from the general income of the association, which in most cases is

[4]See Chapter 53.

comprised mainly of dues, assessments, or membership fees.

Where some portion of the membership may object to this method (as may happen when some members of the association feel that, for special reasons, they may not benefit as much from the proposed program as certain other members will) a special fund may be set up for the public relations effort. This fund may be based on voluntary assessments, paid by those members of the association who are persuaded of the value of the effort to them. This compromise enables a program to be initiated without the support of all members, the expectation being that eventually more member companies will become convinced of its value and render support to it.

In some instances, a public relations program for an association may be financed by revenues not coming from members. For example, an association with a magazine that accepts paid advertising may use some of the advertising revenues for public relations purposes. Other associations that sponsor periodic exhibits or trade shows may utilize income from these for financing public relations activities. However, in view of the interest of the Internal Revenue Service in the nature of association income, there may be tax problems in such cases. In still other cases, a public relations program for an industry may be supported by levies on related industry trade associations. (For example, over the years, the National Dairy Council's efforts in nutrition education and research have been paid for in part by related organizations of dairy farmers, dairy food processors, and dairy equipment manufacturers.)

Whatever the method of financing, the public relations executive of an association should have an annual budget so he can plan his activities intelligently. He is seriously handicapped when each project has to be submitted for board approval and for a special appropriation before he can proceed with it.

Purposes of association programs. The purposes of association public relations programs cover a very wide range. Some typical purposes include:

1. Promoting sales through product publicity.
2. Creating consumer understanding of how to use the industry's services or products effectively and safely, and of the benefits resulting from their use.
3. Overcoming inequities or other problems in the competitive situation in which the industry finds itself, such as may be caused by imports of foreign goods.
4. Creating public understanding of the effects of regulation of an industry by government, in order to assure equitable regulation.
5. Combatting government interference in or competition with an industry or profession.
6. Creating public support for legislative proposals that the association favors or public opposition to legislation it opposes. (This can be done effectively only by stressing the public interest in the matter, but this point is often overlooked.)
7. Obtaining public recognition for the social and economic contributions that an industry or profession makes to the nation.
8. Seeing that an industry or profession is properly represented in the curricula of schools and colleges, and assisting educators in teaching about the industry.
9. Recruiting qualified people (especially from among college graduates) for careers in an industry or profession.
10. Creating public understanding of an industry's equal employment opportunities policies and of its labor union relations.

Although many association public relations programs originate in response to attacks on an industry and the initial purpose is to a large extent defensive, a long-range public relations effort must be positive in its approach and its objectives should be positively stated. A program devoted exclusively to answering attacks on a business is futile over the long term. After years of defensive efforts in public relations, an industry may find itself exactly where it began—or even in a poorer position.

SEVEN BASIC STEPS IN DEVELOPING A PROGRAM

Establishing an association public relations program on behalf of a business or industry, or a professional group, involves a series of steps that, although subject to some variation in differing situations, generally will include:

1. Analysis of the situation.
2. Definition of problem areas.
3. Identification of pertinent publics.
4. Establishment of specific objectives.
5. Planning of program.
6. Implementation of program.
7. Periodic evaluations of progress.

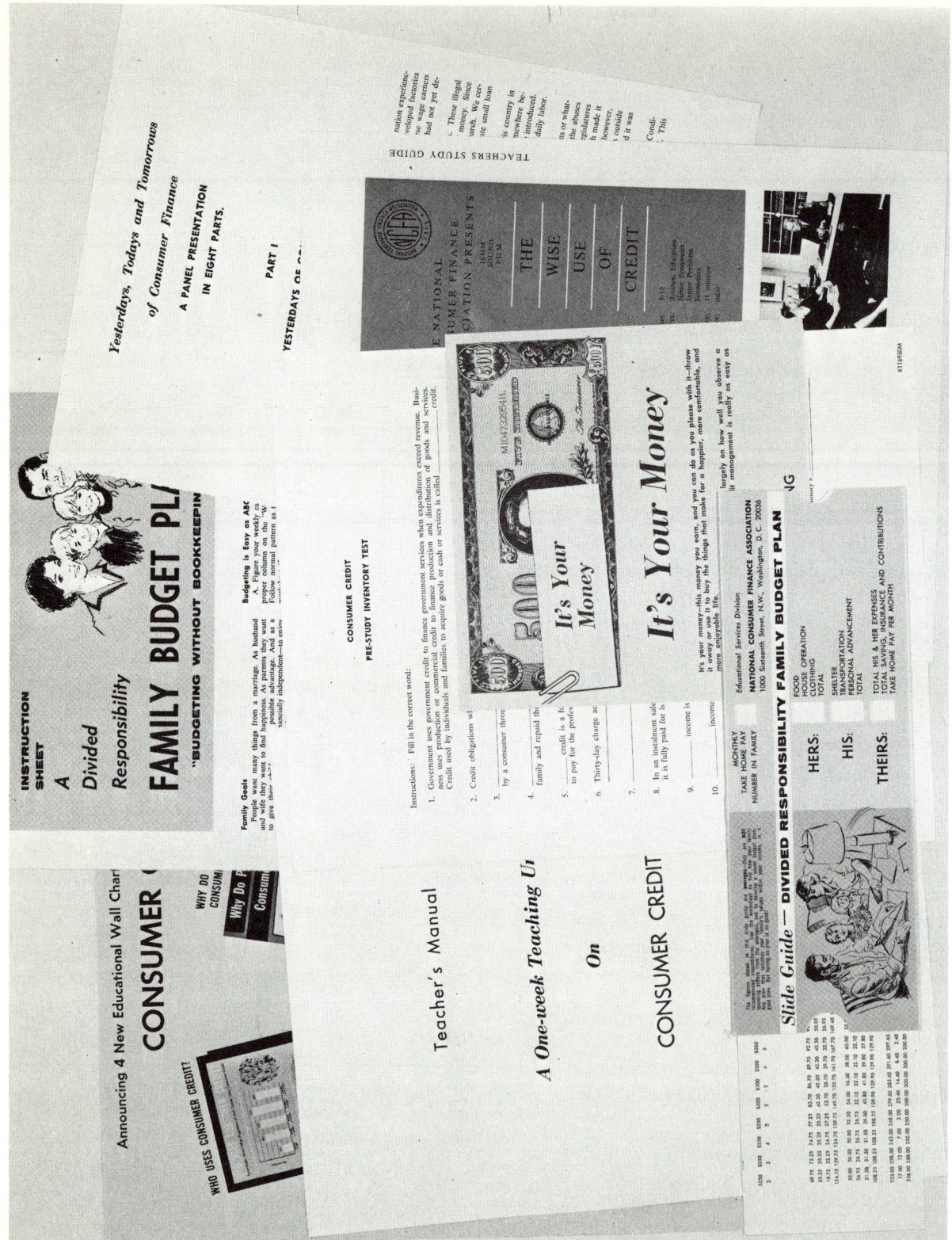

Figure 21-3. To help home economics teachers in the nation's high schools deal with the subject of family finance, the National Consumer Finance Association puts out a kit of teacher's and classroom materials, provided free of charge to all interested educators. These are some of the items included.

Analysis of the situation calls for broad study of all aspects of the business that affect the public. The starting point will be the people in the business or industry (particularly those who are active in the association, such as board members, appropriate committee chairmen and members, and so on) who appear to have awareness of the public relations situation. The public relations executive newly arrived in an association will begin by interviewing such people; from them he will go to people outside the business but in a position to observe it more closely than the average layman (these may include editors of trade publications, officials of chambers of commerce and better business bureaus, government officials concerned with the regulation of business or profession—if there are any—and others). Finally, this basic study may approach the general public for additional views. This may be done through an opinion or attitude research study, or market research, conducted by a recognized research firm. Sometimes, this may be done on a more informal basis where the budget will not permit formal research. Such an approach to the general public will be designed to provide a profile of the business as it appears in the public mind. Opinion research is discussed later in this chapter.[5]

Definition of problem areas will follow naturally from these interview and research activities. Comparisons among the views of the public, of people in the business, and of those who are close observers of the business may reveal some interesting parallels as well as differences and may indicate some cause-and-effect relationships. It should be noted, also, that ignorance and misconception will not always or necessarily be found only in the public mind. Industry people more often than not will be found to have some misconceptions about the public's viewpoint, too. In such an event, correction of industry thinking will be called for. Sound public relations practice may require changing the attitudes of the client (diplomatically, of course) as much as it involves endeavoring to change the attitudes of certain publics. As a matter of fact, although the public relations man is usually hired to change public attitudes, he sometimes performs his most important task in changing the attitude of his client or employer.

(In today's climate, the role of the public relations practitioner is enlarging. He should be capable of observing and analyzing the social, economic, and political trends and helping his management or client become aware of their significance to the institution they represent. Through such expanded awareness, the manager or client comes to view his business or institution in a new and different perspective.)

Identification of publics. A public is a group of people bound together by a specialized interest with reference to a focal point. Thus, employees in the steel mills may constitute one of the publics of a steel industry association's public relations effort; dairy farmers may be a special public of the association representing the milk processing industry; automobile dealers a special public of the association representing automobile manufacturers, and so on. Customers of a particular business always are a primary public, along with employees, suppliers, dealers, community neighbors, and stockholders.

For an industry association, executives of member companies will be a primary public; for a professional society, the individual members will also be one. Indeed, the association's members should not be overlooked in any public relations effort; their understanding and support are necessary.

Establishing objectives. Once the problem areas are defined, long-range objectives should be established. Usually, these will be outlined in terms of the respective publics involved.

Objectives should be drawn with perspective in order to serve as guides over the long range. If they are drawn only in respect to immediate, short-term problems, they will not serve to provide continuity of direction and they will need constant revision. For example, it would be unwise to draw an objective in reference to a specific piece of current legislation that is to be opposed or supported, for once the legislature has adjourned, the objective is meaningless. Instead, a long-range objective might describe in general terms the nature of legislation that an industry favors, viz.:

> To support, in the respective states, legislative efforts that will enable our business to serve the public on a competitive basis in accord with the traditions of a free-market economy, and to oppose legislation that would deny this opportunity.

Any association public relations program must be flexible; obviously it should be modified as time and circumstances may require. But if it is drawn with sufficient perspective, the changing day-to-day and month-to-month problems will be found to fit within the framework of its general objectives. And,

[5] See also Chapter 35.

of course, short-range objectives will be developed from time to time. In addition, if sound communications networks have been developed to implement long-range objectives, these networks will facilitate the solution of the passing and temporary problems. But common sense demands a long-range plan with specific objectives against which results may be measured.

Some typical objectives from varying fields may be given as examples. Among its objectives the Insurance Information Institute, representing companies in the property and casualty insurance field, includes the following:

> To serve as a strong voice of the property-casualty insurance business through identification of and emphasis upon areas of industry agreement and consensus; and to broaden the public's understanding of principles of property and liability insurance, of the many ways in which the industry as a whole serves the public, and of the industry's role in the economy of the nation and the security program of the family.
> To cooperate to the fullest extent with other industry organizations sharing in the responsibility for insurance public relations.
> To inform the public about developments and trends in the business of property and liability insurance.
> To provide and maintain channels of discourse and information on public relations matters among those who earn their livelihood in the business of property and liability insurance.
> To assist educators in teaching the principles of property and liability insurance and in transmitting to students an awareness of the business as a provider of essential services, as a contributor to the economy, and as a field that provides important career opportunities.
> To study short- and long-range trends of the social and physical environment and provide evaluations and recommendations to management; and to gather information of a nature that will enhance the total communications program of the property and liability insurance industry, provide the basis for decision-making in the context of the industry's public relations activities, and assist management in adjusting to society's interests and needs.
> To examine the needs and interests of publics with special problems related to insurance, and reflect to management the need to implement appropriate programs for the alleviation of such problems; and to establish and maintain channels of discourse between consumer organizations and insurance management.
> To establish and maintain working liaison with branches of the federal and state governments, monitor governmental activities and trends, report significant developments to insurance management, and provide governmental decision-makers with information designed to assist them on matters related to insurance, while refraining absolutely from lobbying for or against specific items of legislation.

The public relations goals of the American Meat Institute, an association of meat processors and packers, include these:

> To promote and enhance public understanding and acceptance of meat packing and processing as an essential industry performing a vital public service.
> To maintain and enlarge a favorable operating environment within which the industry can succeed economically in performing its essential public service.
> To promote and foster a growing consumer acceptance of meat and meat products as highly nutritive, highly desirable food.

Program planning involves laying out in detail the various activities and communications that will be employed with reference to the key publics that have been pinpointed in the objectives.

Let us assume, for example, a situation in which an association of home appliance manufacturers finds that the industry has lost standing in the public mind because a substantial number of consumers are dissatisfied with the repair and maintenance services. The industry association identifies, as one of its publics, the retail appliance dealers who are responsible for servicing. The objective with respect to this public is to indoctrinate the dealers on the necessity for providing quality repair services and to provide information to them on the methods by which high quality servicing may be established.

The program plan will outline the activities to be directed toward gaining the support of dealers for this mutually beneficial purpose. It may, for example, call for the preparation of a "code of good service" and of a manual describing the service functions the dealer is expected to perform. Further, this part of the plan may call specifically for a series of dealer meetings in various communities; for special articles to be prepared for trade publications that are circulated among dealers; for a special periodical to be published by the association especially for the dealer-audience; for paid advertisements in industry publications, addressed to dealers; for the conduct of special training schools for the service people employed by the dealers; or for any combination of these and other techniques, some of which may lie outside the field of public relations, strictly defined. But good public relations must, inevitably, be based on good performance, and it should be noted that all of these measures would be designed to improve performance in repair and maintenance.

Implementing the program involves carrying out these steps. It calls primarily for hard work by the association's public relations staff or the external counsel. In association work, however, the implementation of a public relations program frequently requires the active participation of people in the profession or industry. Indeed, in respect to many objectives, the only path to success is to enroll the people in the business or profession who are located at many points across the country.

No association staff, however large, has sufficient people to perform the grass roots indoctrination task all by itself. Frequently, therefore, means will be devised for recruiting people who are working in the business, but who are not themselves public relations people, to assist in the public relations efforts of the association. For example, for some years the Eastern Railroad Presidents' Conference, a regional association of railroads, sponsored "Railroad Community Committees" in major cities throughout its territory. These committees consisted of local representatives from each of the railroads serving a particular city. They maintained speakers' bureaus, engaged in public-service projects, participated in business-education days and in career days at local high schools, and in other ways demonstrated the interest of the railroad industry in the community's welfare.

For any grass roots efforts by a national, regional, or even a state association, reliance on local representatives of the business, industry, or profession is essential. This is especially important when an attempt is being made to influence legislators, who will be more inclined to listen to their own constituents. Implementation of objectives that focus on relations with individual communities generally involves recruitment, indoctrination, and motivation of volunteers from the profession's or industry's ranks.

Periodic evaluations of progress are necessary. Such evaluations should be made on a continuing basis, of course, by the professional public relations staff or public relations counselor of the association. Progress reports should be made regularly also to the membership and to interested committees and boards of the association.

In many associations, the public relations advisory committee, broadly representative of the association's membership, makes a periodic review of the program and suggests improvements or changes in the effort. To assure continuing top-level support of an association public relations program, it is also wise for the public relations executive or counselor to make a periodic presentation of results to the board of directors. Certainly such a presentation is vital at the time when approval is sought for the succeeding year's public-relations budget.

TECHNIQUES OF ASSOCIATION PUBLIC RELATIONS

The techniques utilized by association public relations people are basically the same as those utilized in other public relations fields, and thus most of them need not be discussed in detail here. However, certain techniques perhaps are more pertinent to the association public relations effort. These include:

1. Research on:
   (a) Public opinion[6]
   (b) Industry gain (as a basis for communications about the industry's progress, problems, and developments)
2. Publicity and personal contacts with media people[7]
3. Institutional advertising[8]
4. Motion pictures and slide films[9]
5. Speakers' bureaus and speakers' kits[10]
6. Periodical publications for special audiences[10]
7. Pamphlets (especially statistical yearbooks and handbooks with general background information and consumer-education materials)[10]

The industry association is in a fortunate position as the creator of publicity because its news releases need not contain trade names that often lend an air of commercialism to company publicity. Also, the

---

[6] See Chapter 35.
[7] See Chapters 38-45.
[8] See Chapter 47.
[9] See Chapter 46.
[10] See Chapter 48.

Figure 21-4. The motion picture can take a complete and graphic demonstration of a principle, a method, a process or a cause directly to large numbers of people. This is a scene from "Keyboard Experiences in Classroom Music," produced by Teachers College, Columbia University, in conjunction with the American Music Conference, to demonstrate methods to teachers. While the audience sought for this film is in the thousands, many association-sponsored pictures reach millions at meetings, on TV, and in theaters.

association frequently will be looked to by the press as a more objective and authoritative source of news about the industry as a whole.

Two kinds of research. Sound public relations planning—in the trade association or anywhere else—begins with two kinds of knowledge:

1. Self-knowledge—the understanding that people in a business or profession should have of themselves and their respective fields of endeavor.
2. Knowledge of how the business or profession appears to others with whom it has relationships.

In collecting and disseminating such knowledge for a segment of the business or professional world, the association provides a service of major value for its members. The biggest single achievement of a public relations program can be the enlightenment that dawns with this new knowledge. When business executives begin to see themselves and their enterprise in an objective light, they are subtly moved in directions that will tend to improve their public relations. George Eliot once wrote that our deeds tyrannize over us; so also does our knowledge. Truth is the knowledge that makes us better human beings. This kind of knowledge is the basis for sound public relations.

Industry data. To a great extent, the public relations effort revolves around communication in one form or another—communication of facts and ideas to specified audiences in the form of the printed word, the spoken word, or the graphic presentation. Unless it is based on facts, such communication is empty and aimless—and generally not credible. For an association program, such communication must be based on facts even though emotional questions are involved.

Hence one of the first major steps in developing an industry or professional program must be the accumulation of facts, on an industrywide basis, about the activity. It is surprising how little most industries know about themselves. Of course, each company knows what its figures are for such things as employment, payrolls, taxes, gross income, profit, expenditures for materials and supplies, and so on. But frequently, before the beginning of an industry public relations program, no one has bothered to collect and consolidate these figures into national aggregates, unless government regulatory authorities have required it. For some business or professional programs, of course, it may be desirable to have aggregates for various states and major communities, as well.

In many cases the public relations staff must initiate this type of research. Unless such information is available from another authoritative source, the public relations staff of the association has no alternative but to try to compile it.

Opinion research. Opinion research as a public relations tool is perhaps more widely utilized in association public relations than in other areas of public relations practice. However, the probing of public attitudes is not so widely understood and not so broadly utilized as conscientious public relations practice would require it to be.

Opinion research may be described as the attempt to measure, both quantitatively and qualitatively, public attitudes toward a company, industry, profession, or other organization and toward its policies, personnel, services, or products. Where services or products are involved, such research may overlap the area of "Marketing Research."

There are at least four general reasons for the use of opinion research in association public relations:

1. To provide guidance in establishing and developing a public relations program or a specific project. On such occasions, opinion research serves to help crystallize the public relations problem or problems; to help define the crucial issues, to identify significant publics, and to establish objectives. It is, in effect, a navigational tool of the kind that Abraham Lincoln—an expert in public relations long before it became an organized field of effort—may have had in mind when he said: "If we could first know where we are and whither we are tending, we could better judge what to do and how to do it."

2. A second reason is to facilitate membership agreement on public relations objectives and courses of action. If, as is so often the case in trade and professional association work (and may be true in corporate life as well), a public relations program is subject to the jurisdiction of a committee or board of directors representing diverse elements, the area of common agreement may be limited. Each member of the group may have his own pet ideas as to what ought to be done; arguing these to a conclusion can be a futile and never-ending process. An opinion survey enables the public relations executive to sell his program on the basis of facts that only the most negative and resistant persons should have the temerity to dispute.

3. Where opinion research constitutes a continuing function in the public relations operation, it can uncover incipient problems before they become crises. Thus some major headaches may be forestalled.

4. Opinion research may be utilized to determine the results of public relations efforts—progress toward stated goals. The pitfalls inherent in this utilization are great; hence the reluctance of many public relations practitioners to consider research in this connection. Certainly, changing basic attitudes is a long-range process, and the degree of change, even over a period of several years, may be hardly measurable. Nevertheless, in certain cases such measurement of progress toward goals can be valuable.

In the railroad industry, for example, such measurements were carried out over a period of years to evaluate the proportion of public opinion favoring government ownership of the railroad industry. This was a crucial problem as evidenced by the fact that at the beginning of World War II 50 percent of the U.S. adult population favored government ownership and operation of the railroads. Effective wartime performance under private ownership and effective reporting to the public on railroad achievements during the war resulted in reducing this sentiment to only 13 percent by 1946, as demonstrated by a continuing public opinion audit.

Aim toward action. Opinion research should be developed on an actionable basis. It does little good to ask questions about people's attitudes if the answers do not provide a basis for action—practical, concrete action within the framework of your public relations potential. Sherwood Dodge, former marketing vice president for Foote, Cone and Belding, has written:

> Make an estimate of the possible outcome of a key question or point. Then ask yourself how this outcome would influence your decision if it proved correct, and how differently you would

act if it were incorrect. This is the test of 'actionability'... The more the questions take on the form of a hypothesis, related to alternative courses of action, the more research will operate in the field of maximum utility.

An illustration may be found in the Milk Industry Foundation's experience with a nationwide consumer survey designed to provide the basis for its public relations program. There had been considerable pressure from industry representatives for a communications effort to convince people that the price of milk was low. "Actionable-type" questions in the survey showed that 55 percent of the public thought that the price of milk was "reasonable"—and only 33 percent thought it was "too high." Of the 33 percent, only eight percent said they had reduced their consumption of milk because of the price. Another question showed that milk ranked above six other important foods, in the public's opinion, as giving the consumer "most value for his money." In view of these responses, it was decided not to give great emphasis to price in the public relations communications for fear of creating a major problem where only a minor one existed.

Marketing values of research. In trade association work it may be easier to sell the idea of a joint marketing and public relations survey than to sell a public relations study alone. Member companies in a trade association are inclined to see more dollars-and-cents value in a study that will give them information they can use in their marketing efforts than in a study that deals with the intangibles of public relations problems only. Combining the two areas of study into one project frequently may be possible, and it may facilitate the appropriation of necessary funds.

Finally, in trade or professional association public relations, it is essential to have a plan for disseminating the results of opinion research to members. In corporate public relations, it may be necessary only for the public relations department and top management to know the results. In an association, judgment dictates that research results also should be widely reported to the membership both to demonstrate the value of the study and to encourage the individual members to take appropriate actions of their own.

Bringing together allied forces. Rare is the industry association that does not have a number of allies or potential allies. These allies frequently have their own associations, with related interests. Some successful association public relations programs bring together as many forces as possible to bear on a particular problem. Thus, for example, railroad associations may seek the help of the associations of manufacturers who provide supplies and equipment for the railroad industry; the industry associations representing insurance managements may seek the help of the associations of insurance agents or brokers; associations representing the processors of dairy products may seek the aid of associations representing the dairy farmers, and vice versa.

Despite the inevitable differences that occur on some matters between such groups, there are always grounds for cooperation in specified areas. It is unwise to allow admitted differences in limited areas to prevent useful cooperation in other areas. The practical solution, when such a problem exists, is by common agreement to build a fence around the areas of dispute and declare them off-limits insofar as the cooperative effort is concerned. In any event, the mutual benefits from cooperation among associations with allied interests usually will be found to over-balance the advantages (if any) of conflict.

The trade press editor as a friend. In too many instances, the association staff people in the industry profession are inclined to take the trade press editors for granted. The association public relations staff has no greater ally, generally speaking, than a trade press editor who is convinced of the value and effectiveness of the industry public relations effort.

From his objective perch, the trade press editor can be a powerful force in showing the industry's leaders how the program is progressing. He can say things about the program and the industry or profession that the public relations executive can never say for himself. It is important that every association public relations program include continuing efforts to keep trade press editors informed about the progress of the program. Association public relations executives rarely have suffered from taking a trade press editor into their confidence. To the contrary, frequently they gain a great deal.

DIFFERENCES FROM CORPORATE PUBLIC RELATIONS

For the association, the principles and techniques of public relations generally are the same as for the individual corporation. But implementing public relations in the association field has certain marked differences from the corporate practice of public relations.

A major difference involves establishment of

public relations policy for the association. In corporate practice policy may be agreed on by a few members of top management; once established, such policy may be promulgated and enforced through a directive by the chief executive officer of the company. Although much consideration may be devoted to developing the tenets of such a corporate policy, the process of policy establishment, promulgation, and enforcement is relatively simple.

In the association, the situation is different. For one thing, the association staff is not usually in a position to issue directives to the industry. Hence, developing association public relations policy may involve crystallizing and codifying unwritten policies that already exist. This may be accomplished through informal consultation with individual industry leaders, then reducing the resultant knowledge to a simplified statement and submitting this statement for approval to the association's board of directors or to appropriate committees of the association.

Once approved, such policy may be promulgated throughout the industry in a manner designed to encourage its implementation—but it cannot be imposed on association members. Its acceptance must, of course, be a voluntary act on the part of each member. Obviously, in developing policy the public relations executive of the association is in a position to nudge the membership here and there to correct certain defects or omissions in public policy—but success in this respect demands a degree of diplomatic skill rather than a dictatorial posture.

As Reuel Elton, at one time the General Manager of The American Trade Association Executives (now the American Society of Association Executives), once said:

> The Trade Association does not order, it advises. It does not coerce, it persuades. It does not issue mandates, or even instructions. It uses only the moving eloquence of a reasoned appeal to the self-interest of its members. It does not tell its members what they must do. It tells them what, if influenced by a decent regard for their own interests, they will be glad to do. It assumes that its members are intelligent men, that they can think about the problems of their business and that if the facts out of which these problems arise are placed fairly before them, and if the significance of the facts is pointed out, a proper and profitable line of action will result.

Relationship to purposes. Association public relations policy necessarily must equate with the broad

Figure 21-5. An exhibit, arranged by the public relations department of an association, can give viewers firsthand information about an industry's products in use. This outdoor toy show, sponsored by the Toy Manufacturers of the U.S.A., in conjunction with the Children's Aid Society, illustrates the wide variety of educational and recreational playthings specifically intended for outdoor use.

general objectives of the association (which usually are developed at the time of its establishment and frequently may be found in the association's constitution). But public relations objectives and the general purposes of the organization, except in a few instances, are not necessarily identical.

Although many associations do not have a written public relations policy or written objectives, having them in writing serves to provide steady guidance and continuity to a program that may be buffeted off course and led down unprofitable alleys when officers, directors, and committees made up of membership representatives undergo their perennial rotations and changes. Indeed, this is one of the greatest hazards to association programming. As the elected officers change from year to year, there is an inclination on their part to shoot off in new directions, to drop old programs and start new ones, without much evaluation. In the face of this, the public relations executive must endeavor to keep a steady hand on the helm.

Gaining support. Another characteristic that distinguishes association public relations from corporate public relations relates to enlisting and mobilizing the aid of others.

Again, in the corporation this is relatively simple to do. Once the public relations executive has gained approval of top management for a program of action, generally he can rely on it to issue instructions to subordinates that will assure cooperation with the public relations plan.

But in the association any attempt to mobilize its professional members or employees of many companies into an effective task force for association public relations purposes must rest on persuasion and voluntary action. Thus, the public relations executive of a trade association needs continuously to woo voluntary help and cooperation. For this reason, he should find ways to enable many people to participate in the development of his program—for others will tend to support and assist in implementing a program they feel is at least in part their own. This participation often may be accomplished through the mechanism of committees.

Reports to members. A further necessity in association public relations is a system of reporting—with regularity and frequency—to the membership. The association public relations executive can never assume that his members know what he is doing, and why, unless he makes a conscious and continuing effort to let them know.

Communication to the membership thus is the sine-qua-non of success in association public relations, as indeed it is the key to success for any aspect of association administration.

It is, of course, always desirable for the association public relations executive to be in close liaison not only with the executive secretary or executive director (the principal staff officer of his organization) but also with the elected officers and directors. In the ideal situation, he will report periodically and in person to the board, and he personally will present his proposed program and budget. Where this is not possible because of the attitude of the executive director, the effectiveness of the public relations executive—and of his whole program—may suffer.

In addition to reporting to the officers and board members, however, means should be established for reporting to the membership at large on the progress of the public relations effort. This might be done through the association's magazine or newsletter, or with an audio-visual presentation at the annual convention of the association.

Personal qualities of the association public relations executive. The association public relations executive needs all the professional abilities and attributes of his peers in corporate public relations and counseling—and yet more. He must have the diplomatic talents to satisfy the demands of not one executive or several clients, but of scores or hundreds—and sometimes thousands—of corporate officers or individual members of his association. Among countless diverse points of view, the association public relations executive must search out the common ground, establish mutually acceptable objectives, and produce generally satisfactory results. His tasks, in these ways, often are far more demanding than those of the corporate public relations practitioner.

22

Public Relations for Financial Organizations

Philip Lesly

Since all financial institutions deal with the same "product"—the dollar—they compete largely on the basis of how people feel about them: their convenience, their character, their services, their people, their helpfulness.

These are qualities that are difficult to convey. Most financial institutions must base their "image" on a composite of such intangibles.

In an era when the *visibility* of an organization is the major factor behind its recognition and standing (see Chapters 2 and 55), this dependence on the *invisible* aspects of their character presents great challenges to financial institutions.

Most executives in financial organizations are exceptionally fact-minded—oriented to measurable figures and balanced evaluations—and therefore trained to emphasize tangibles. Their orientation is at one pole and the nature of their institutions' growing problems is at the other. This means that perhaps no group of businessmen has a greater need for guidance and assistance in public relations. And perhaps no group has a greater need for having this guidance asserted forcefully enough to overcome natural resistance and be heard.

Although there are many differences in the requirements of various types of financial institution, in these main areas they have the same needs and problems. The fact that they deal in the same dollar bills and are differentiated from each other mostly in their intangible qualities is characteristic of banks, savings and loan associations, insurance companies, brokerage houses, investment companies, consumer finance companies, and other types of financial institution.

BASIC PRINCIPLES AND DIFFERENCES

Most of the fundamental considerations in the public relations of a financial organization are similar to those for any other type of corporation and are covered elsewhere in this *Handbook*. They include:

1. The seven steps in the cycle of public relations functions (Chapter 1):

   (1) Analyzing the general climate of attitudes;
   (2) Determining the attitude of any group toward the company;
   (3) Analyzing the state of opinion;
   (4) Formulating policy;
   (5) Planning means of improving the attitude of the group;
   (6) Carrying out the planned activities;
   (7) Feedback, evaluation, and adjustments.

2. Developing emergency plans (see Chapter 39) for occurrences outside the normal scope of planning and activity.

3. Use of appropriate communications techniques (see Section V).

Particular needs. We shall concentrate here on the specific differences that affect the financial institution. These include:

1. The essentiality of developing and projecting a sharply *distinctive* image for the institution. Since it cannot stand out as a result of branded products, it will inevitably seem to be just one indistinct entity in its field unless it concentrates on attaining such distinctiveness. If it goes on being an undefined unit in a nebulous mass, its fate is relegated to whatever

happens to the industry it is in and to such uncontrollable factors as location and the changes in the market it serves.

This is an age of visibility, yet businesses that deal in intangibles are the least visible. What they do to achieve visibility is thus more crucial than it is for firms that deal in products.

Major areas in which such *distinctiveness* and *visibility* are sought include:

(1) *Buildings* (see Chapter 55). Banks have been notably progressive in this area. Some of the most distinctive and handsome structures built in recent years bear the names of banks. Since it needs primarily to make its impression in a narrow geographic area (unlike multinational manufacturers, insurance companies, chain retailers, and others) a bank's building can achieve a high degree of impact on its publics.

(2) *Graphics* (see Chapters 51 and 55). Visual symbols, type style, color, and other graphic factors can convey the impression of the institution as distinctive from all others.

(3) *Services.* Besides achieving marketing purposes, some services focus distinctive attention on the institution. These may include banking services, such as assistance with tax matters, or good will services, such as making the auditorium available for meetings of civic groups.

(4) *Respected personalities.* Fewer businessmen are individualistically identified in the public mind than there were in the days of the self-made tycoon. The opportunity is open for the bank officer to become respected as the statesman of the community. This calls for taking thought-leadership positions on the issues that matter locally and helping to inspire the thinking of the community. It goes beyond commentary on interest rates or inflation; it probably will include issues that are controversial—schools, pollution, housing patterns, and so on. The 1970 study of public attitudes toward banks made by Louis Harris showed that bankers are respected as important figures but more is expected of them in taking leadership in their communities.

(5) *Advertising.* It is probably in this area that financial institutions have made the most progress in achieving distinctiveness and reflecting their actual personalities. Determining the distinctive concept of how the institution should be thought of by its publics comes first. Art style, typography, themes, and the rest should fit this concept, while consistently pursuing the marketing goals. "You have a friend at the Chase Manhattan" seeks to bring the huge bank into view as the aide of the typical customer. Wells Fargo takes advantage of its romantic beginnings in the stagecoach days to convey the impression of its modernity in the computer age. The Continental Illinois uses distinctive, stylized line drawings to depict modern ideas and diversity of services.

(6) *Publications.* Just as with advertising, the message is not all there is to the medium. The stolid-looking folder that is all type except for a chart or two and a couple of subheads depicts conservatism, which may be desirable for the trust department but may not be for consumer loans or international trade.

(7) *Forums.* The financial institution is a focal point of the economic system. It is a logical sponsor of forums that bring together experts in various industries to discuss legislative proposals such as new tax laws, or the outlook for the economy. Semiannual forums on industrial expectations have been effective for The First National Bank of Chicago in focusing attention on its catalytic role and its knowledgeability.

2. Identifying the institution with the publics' interests, rather than its own predominantly. This includes not only handling communications from the audience's point of view—a fundamental of good communications—but making the recognized thrust of the organization the serving of public needs, rather than one of primarily promoting services the institution would like to make profitable.

The Continental Illinois developed a program to combat "economic illiteracy" in the schools. It worked closely with school systems in refining the materials and helping integrate them into course outlines. Then it developed a modified version for adults. It was successful enough to attract other banks to take on the program on a franchise basis. That bank lists more than 40 activities unrelated to profitability that it conducts, including services and funds to foster education, minority business, urban advancement, public health, and assistance to the aged.

To help college students meet the growing cost of education a number of banks developed special loan programs at lower than the going interest rates, in cooperation with foundations and government. This has the special advantage of demonstrating their dedication to service to college students, who not only can be customers for another half-century, but tend to be most critical of the financial system.

Participation by bank officers in civic activities is

the most common—and therefore the least distinctive—form of public-service identification. While it is expected that the local financial institutions will have chairmen of charities and members of commissions, it is not adequate to settle for this type of participation in building respect for their public leadership.

3. Reaching the publics that are decisive in the future of financial institutions but are outside their normal range of exposure and statements: the academic community, government, and many of the media. In many respects, these groups are least likely to deal with any individual institution in normal commerce. The attitudes developed by college faculties, legislators and regulators, and reporters for national media set the climate in which decisions will be formed about what the institutions can do.

4. Anticipating and staying ahead of the trends in public and governmental pressures so the institution is not constantly reacting to the initiatives and criticisms of others. The limitations of trade associations in these fields have generally prevented imaginative, forceful efforts that meet this need for their members. This presents a greater need, and a greater opportunity, for the individual institution to meet the need.

SPECIAL CONSIDERATIONS

While the fundamental public relations considerations of all financial institutions are similar, the history and development of the various types have been different and make the problems of some the opportunities of others.

The vast and rapid changes in living patterns have multiplied the number of families who are in the market for financial services. This has meant broad expansion of the total market, but has changed the competitive pattern among the various types of financial institution. The longest-established group, the banks, are faced with inroads of the newer ones, such as mutual funds.

Banks in the United States traditionally were repositories for excess funds of businesses and individuals; sources of loans to finance worthy business and government ventures; and trust companies affording advice and management of estates and other funds.

They were tied closely to their communities. Their depositors and customers mostly were residents of the area within easy reach. While the banks made it known they welcomed good new clients, most of their business walked in the door and asked to be served.

The first major shift from this pattern followed the success of the economic system they helped nurture. Many more people and businesses had resources and thereby become potential bank customers. So the banks gradually moved into "retail" service to help many modest customers, as well as continuing the "wholesale" services for bigger businesses and wealthy individuals.

This created healthy competition with loan companies, mortgage companies, and other services. In turn, there has been a rapid increase in the competition being faced by the banks. Now many people put their savings into mutual funds, stocks, bonds, annuities, real estate syndicates, and other investments once limited to the few. The lending field involves insurance companies, direct placements, credit unions, small loan companies, small business investment companies, and others. Trust services of banks face competition from institutional investors, professional fund managers, and insurance companies. Consumer credit is increasingly offered by mass merchandisers, non-bank credit cards, and finance companies.

Most of these competitors face less regulation than banks and are not restricted geographically.

At the same time, the patterns of the cities in which large banks function have been changing dramatically. Not long ago each metropolis had a business center surrounded by rings of industry and then residential areas and suburbs. Now the outlying areas attract industry and business as well as residents. The older central core tends to become blighted. Transportation is congested, time-consuming, and increasingly expensive. As a result, businesses and services of all kinds tend to look outward for personnel and services. Yet in many areas banks are restricted by branch banking laws from following the spread of population and business.

The explosion of demand. At the same time, explosive change and growth have hit the operation of banks like a sonic boom. With millions of new bank customers and multiplication of services, the masses of paperwork threatened to paralyze the system.

The great increase in the number of women who work and the accompanying emphasis on conveniences meant not only a vast increase in checks and transactions, but an expansion of customers' expectations.

Almost every family has become a nest of

financial record keeping. With very little preparation in schools for this role, it can be said that family bookkeeping in 50 million American households is the greatest area of unskilled labor in the Western world.

The maturing of the computer as a means of coping with the volumes of transactions, and of the credit card as a means of funneling many of these transactions into the system, fortunately coincided with the upsurge in demands.

With the growth of centralized record-keeping for more and more families, there will probably be demand for central financial bookkeeping, bill paying, and credit revolving around the identification card and the computer.

The combination of growing public demand and electronic technology has created the greatest ferment of change involving financial institutions in many years. Savings and loan associations, credit unions, and mutual savings banks have been moving to broaden the services they provide, making incursions into areas that the banks had had to themselves. By broadening the type of loans they can provide and offering what amounts to checking services, they can appeal to many in the broad public base of the banks. The electronic revolution has moved rapidly to make available various types of electronic fund transfer systems. They enable customers to make most of their financial transactions at any hour of any day at a bank or other institution office, and there is strong pressure to break down the chaotic array of legal restrictions on setting up electronic stations wherever they can be helpful to people. The pattern that finds some areas providing these services almost without restriction while laws prevent them from being provided in other areas is likely to be resolved in the courts. When it is, the instantaneous and inexpensive electronic tools for conducting financial business over vast distances will create new questions of consumer education on a broad scale. The entire pattern of competition in financial services is likely to be restructured.

As a result of these developments, and to cope with the "department store of finance" appeals being made by newer financial institutions with fewer restrictions, banks have been considering becoming "department stores of finance" themselves, where the depositor can not only have all his financial transactions centered and recorded, but can buy such services as insurance, travel, tax reporting, and so on.

Changes in social patterns. These cross currents of demand, operating problems, and competition are further complicated by the changing social climate in which financial institutions operate. Our society shows signs of becoming both more and less materialistic: At the same time there is demand for credit cards and new financial services, there are pressures to reduce the emphasis on material purchases and the levels of conspicuous consumption.

The pressures for services among those without money to deposit or credit with which to borrow are increasing as political forces. Pressures to put the incentive system into reverse—such as by giving credit to those who lack money and by insuring property of those with a record of destroying property—change the rationale that until now has made the economy work. And in the face of the growing need for bigness that can cope with the explosion of demands and need for facilities, there is a recurrence of opposition to bigness in financial institutions as well as in other aspects of society.

In the 1930's banks were prime targets of attacks by government and the public on the economic structure that was blamed for the Depression. They then had a remarkable restoration of prestige and confidence that lasted a full generation. Until recently, they have had a benign image—so benign, in fact, that the banking profession was concerned about how "unexciting" it appeared to the best young people it sought to attract.

Now, as visible symbols of concentrated money, the banks are becoming the focus of political and public concern about inflation, great concentration of economic resources, and a keystone of the "establishment."

It seems clear from these trends and the problems they bring that a bank should now assume an *active* posture—it should reach outward and innovate, rather than passively affording services as a depository, a lending source, a trust instrument, a vault, and a money recording resource. It can no longer dominate finance through only location, contacts, and service to those who call.

To assume an active posture, a bank should first clearly define what it is that distinguishes it from all others; what it seeks to be, and how it seeks to have its publics think of it. It should then carry out programs and functions that will indeed make it that kind of an institution—followed by functions that will make its publics fully aware of its new character, purposes, and thrust.

It should become an active, adaptable institution. It should articulate to its own people its new purposes and character. It should function so it will have widespread respect, understanding, and acceptance.

Then it can have its antennae out in readiness to sense whatever desirable new services it can provide and to transmit what it has to offer to any elements of the public.

Its ability to do this depends on how restrictive government regulations on a bank's functions may be. This, in turn, will be largely determined by the failure or success of the banking industry through the years in developing a climate of understanding of its problems and the public's needs.

IMPLICATIONS FOR OTHER INSTITUTIONS

Financial organizations are perhaps the most regulated of all American enterprise. This reflects the financial consequence of the great importance of money in the structure of society; the great attraction for abuse because of the great rewards possible; and the severe abuses that have marked virtually every period of financial panic and depression.

However, the nature and the restrictiveness of the regulation on each type of institution is different. Banks and savings and loan associations, for instance, face severe geographic limitations. Insurance companies, investment companies, and brokerage houses, while they have few geographic limitations, face a network of regulations at the federal level, in every state, and in many municipalities they choose to function in.

In all of these, a favorable climate of opinion when they seek consideration for modifications and innovation is important. For them, as well as for banks, the fundamental determinant of the future may well be the perceptiveness and effectiveness of their public relations planning and programs, as groups and as individual institutions.

23

Public Relations for Retailers

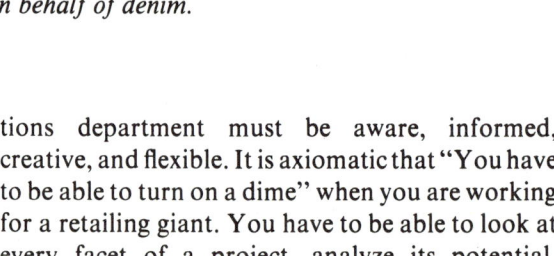

TERRY MAYER has had a diversified career in publicity and public relations for retailers. A native New Yorker and graduate of Long Island University, she began in publicity at Macy's, New York. She then served at Gimbel Brothers, New York, with Bernice Fitz-Gibbon. Later she became Publicity and Advertising Director for David Crystal, Inc.; Fashion Director for Amos Parrish, the advisor on fashion merchandising for retailers, and Fashion Coordinator to J.C. Penney's stores. She established her own publicity firm in New York in 1964.

For eleven years she selected and presented the National Retail Merchants Association's "Top Fashion Promotions of the Year," and for five years the "Top Home Furnishings Promotions."

Miss Mayer has been President of the Publicity Club of New York and headed the Public Relations Committee for New York City's 300th Anniversary. She is on the Board of Directors of the Pan American Society of the U.S. and PRSA-NY Chapter, and was a board member of the World Trade Club of N.Y.

She is perhaps best known for her publicity program on behalf of denim.

There are specific characteristics of the retail business that make it especially in need of public relations.

All the aspects of public relations covered in this book apply to retail stores, but retailing public relations has one major aim. That is to give the store *visibility* and *identity*.

The store that loses out is the one that is lost in the crowd. Retailers who are regarded as "outstanding citizens" are the ones whose stores never stop making a mark on the community, the employees, the manufacturers, and on the national scene as well.

A store may not be human, but it is composed of thinking humans. It *does* have a personality. The man at the top is reflected in the people who work for him. If he is knowledgeable about communications, he will see that they mirror him for everyone's gain.

To obtain visibility and identity, a store must plan ahead for the unknown. To capitalize on the assets a store has, the public relations department must relay its story to the community. The public relations department must be aware, informed, creative, and flexible. It is axiomatic that "You have to be able to turn on a dime" when you are working for a retailing giant. You have to be able to look at every facet of a project, analyze its potential, develop its possibility.

This chapter will describe how some stores arrange to be forever in the public eye with their distinctive personalities, and describe methods that can be used or adapted to assure more visibility for any store.

SPECIFIC CHARACTERISTICS OF RETAILING

The people of a store, the advertisements of a store, the merchandise of a store all bring management into direct contact with the public. To sell merchandise or services, one must know the pulse of the consumer, understand her pocketbook and where she is apt to apply it, know her family, and the man of the family. It is necessary to really know the store's customers.

PUBLIC RELATIONS FOR RETAILERS

The community's attitude toward the store must be analyzed constantly. When a new boutique for the young set opens a block away, will your customers be loyal? Will advance merchandising techniques, sales promotion, special events that make news hold them?

The charm of a freshly sprung boutique is its "personality," which reflects the perspicacity and the taste of the owner, and his knowledge of what the community wants.

The community's attitude toward a store is dependent on the attitude of its management toward the community. The personal magnetism of the man at the top, or of the publicized authority, like the Fashion Coordinator or Home Furnishings Coordinator; the respect they are held in; the knowledge the community has about them; how they participate in the community—all contribute to the regard people have for the store.

Changes in style and public desires affect the retailer more quickly and more acutely than most businesses. Retailers caught with too many of a couturier's styles at the end of a season, or after a reasonable period of no-sale, mark them down. Computers that keep track of product movement and inventories help keep the action fluid. Trade periodicals like *Women's Wear Daily, HFD Retailing Home Furnishings, Clothes Magazine, Menswear,* and *Daily News Record,* help keep the merchant and retail publicist alert to public opinion and demand. The Sunday *New York Times* often shows how things will be in the U.S.A. shortly.

Communication between management and personnel is vital. Large stores have learned the importance of weekly staff meetings and in-department meetings. For instance, in a fashion department the buyer shows the newest styles to her sales people, with the group getting pointers on fiber, fabric, cut of the garment, and care of the garment. The store's fashion coordinator informs the staff at fashion shows for employees, passing on all the news they can use. The publicity department follows the publications that set consumer tastes and provides analyses for the sales people so they will talk the customer's language.

VARIOUS TYPES OF PROGRAMS

Distinction between various types of retail companies in regard to public relations needs are not so clearly marked as in other fields.

The national chain. The giant operation has its executives working as a team. Each person supports the abilities of others and their composite skills are passed on in training programs for the whole organization.

Sears has a public relations manual for store executives, who may not have had any public relations training at all. The Sears Manual is indexed so a man can get a fairly ready response to almost any problem that may come up.

Sears' public relations department is regionalized. There are public relations directors in various large cities with men under them. This is a network of professionals whom store managers can turn to for quick advice and help on public relations problems.

Sears believes that the store manager should become involved in the community. The manual discusses general policy, membership, donations, high school programs, garden club programs, women's club programs, legislative activities, and so on. The national chain's public relations program is highly developed in community participation. Sears, Penney's, and Wards are all involved in programs with the high schools; with some form of in-store Charm School, for both girls and boys; with on-the-job training for teenagers; with national organizations like the 4-H group and the Boy Scouts, and so on.

J.C. Penney supplies store managers with a booklet called *Publicity, How to Get It* that was produced by the company's Media Relations Department.

Penney's advises that publicity can do several things for the store: "Create Interest, Build Good Will, and Attract Customers." The booklet outlines a series of events that can form a basis for publicity and make news. They are: Fashions, store events, style shows, community projects, personnel promotions, new construction, contest winners, important visitors, personal events, big or unusual sales, exhibits, speeches, trips, conventions, humorous incidents.

A page on "Establishing Press Relations" could be a guide to any publicist. It says:

> Sometimes there is fear connected with the idea of approaching the editor of a newspaper. This fear usually is felt only by those who haven't approached an editor.
>
> Most editors are businessmen like yourself and will consider any straightforward proposition just as you would. There is one problem, though, that store managers have that others seeking publicity may not have—you are an advertiser. Because of this it is imperative that

as thorough an understanding as possible of the newspaper editorial policies should be obtained before meeting with an editor. Some newspapers have firm policies regarding publicity for advertisers, but mention of these policies should be left strictly to the discretion of the editor.

Usually editors will evaluate your story on the basis of its merits alone and if it is a good one, and accepted, he will thank you warmly for bringing it to his attention.

Once you are well acquainted with the newspaper you and the paper will find it expedient to contact the appropriate editor for the story involved. If it's a business page story, see the business editor; see the women's page or fashion editor when you have a story of interest to women.

Many Penney managers, some near you, can give case histories of their excellent relations with the press. Some have established relations to the degree that the editors now ask them for story ideas!

Through help like this Penney's store manager becomes conscious of publicity and its benefits. He learns the basics of publicity techniques for store openings and modernizations; special event publicity; what makes a good news picture, and how to write a press release.[1]

Penney's has various public service programs geared to provide information at the stores. These respond to current events and the needs of their potential customers. Booklets about protection of the home from theft and fire educate the reader while tying in merchandise available in the hardware areas. Some of the Penney stores have special events called Home Security Workshops and give out booklets. The activities are recognized as public service while they feature merchandise.

The local department store. The local department store is often built on the acceptance of the brand names it carries and how it merchandises those names and labels. Having nationally advertised brands is a tradition and has consumer acceptance. But it is how the store stage manages what it has to sell that brings in more customers.

The local department store should be the focal point of the community in meeting most of its shopping needs. Macy's in New York is the largest store in the world, yet it is dependent on the community for its business. Therefore it is in its own self interest to benefit the community. More than most stores, it

[1] See Chapters 38 to 41.

Figure 23-1. Ads that feature merchandise but are primarily aimed at projecting the store's distinctiveness are used by Marshall Field & Company.

has done a series of "salute" advertisements for cultural organizations. It has helped the city, for instance, with its salute to the New York Summer Festival. Macy's knows it is a leader, and it acts as a leader.

According to Harold F. Haener, former Senior Vice President of Sales Promotion and Public Relations, "You must select the things that you do that will be most important to the betterment of the total community. You try to find things with broad appeal and broad benefit. A department store is also a showplace. People come to a store for an idea."

Knowing that people are tremendously interested in their physical well-being, Macy's featured merchandise that was new in health and beauty products, which made news. Another area that city people are interested in is the crowded housing situation. Macy's put together merchandise ideas, mini-dryers, mini-washers, wall units, all under the heading of "Space Exploration." This was of interest to the public, and a new way of inviting them to see a collection of merchandise. It provided a "peg" for coverage by the media.

Where Macy's has always served a broad range of customers, other stores can focus on a single type of customer.

The department store must determine what it has to offer that competition doesn't. What unique characteristic can it develop?

To know this, the public relations director must involve himself with the merchandise as well as the store, its personnel, and its public. He must plan both institutional and product publicity.

At the start the public relations department must set out total objectives for a season to achieve a well-balanced program. There must be continual review of the success of the program. At Macy's, each head of a department analyzes his part in it, questions what has been done, is alert to responses to a promotion, and watches the figures daily to see how sales are progressing.

Dayton's, Minneapolis, from a public relations standpoint, seeks to strike a balance and appeal to all age groups. The store wants to project an image of fashion, excitement, and innovation; and at the same time, to uphold the store's tradition of quality, integrity, and good citizenship.

In establishing its identity and setting objectives, Dayton's wants people to think of the store in the following terms:

- A responsible "good citizen" in the community.
- Concerned about the individual customer, and providing courteous, helpful service.
- Offering a wide variety of quality merchandise at fair prices.
- The fashion leader, featuring the newest looks in apparel and home furnishings.
- Progressive, exciting, innovative in merchandise presentation and events.
- A well-operated business, with efficient executives and offering favorable working conditions and benefits for employees.

Dayton's theory on how to acquire good will for the store, internally and externally, is that it is necessary to communicate with:

- Employees and managers (current and potential)
- Customers
- Residents in communities where stores are located
- Visitors from out-of-town
- Vendors
- "VIP" groups such as government and community leaders, the academic community, and members of the news media
- Corporation shareholders, the financial community, and management personnel of the Corporation and other operating companies (handled mostly by Corporate Information office).

Dayton's over-all public relations program is a model that can guide many retailers:

Research

Including in-depth consumer surveys to pinpoint current attitudes about the store.

Community Relations

The store works with many civic organizations in staging benefit fashion shows and other events such as an "Orphan Animal Sale" in the store's auditorium for the benefit of the Animal Humane Society.

Flower show preview for the benefit of the University of Minnesota Arboretum.

Annual ball of People to People, Inc., held each summer in the store's auditorium.

Institutional Advertising

Including ads emphasizing courtesy, service, and so on; salutes to major league baseball and football teams.

Storewide and Department Events

Planned for various age groups, to bring traffic into the store and to create good will. Dayton's has the largest department store auditorium in the country, and this space is utilized throughout the year for events such as bridal shows, flower shows, import fairs, art exhibits, speakers and entertainers, and so on.

Internal Communications

Monthly publication, the *Daytonian,* published by Employee Publications Office, with cooperation of Public Relations Department. Also a weekly newsletter "This Week at Dayton's."

Other public relations efforts directed toward employees include: audio-visual presentations by Training Department; special programs geared to helping employees advance into better positions ("Operation Upgrade" and a Tuition Refund Program); suggestion program, special "courtesy"

```
               SCHEDULE OF ENTERTAINMENT AND DEMONSTRATIONS                                    - 2 -

               DAYTON'S "NOT-SO-FAR EAST"     SEPT. 19 - 27           CHINA PAINTING   (6th Floor)

MATSUMOTO DANCE TROUPE                                                Friday and Saturday, Sept. 19 and 20:  Store hours.

Daily performances:       10 a.m.------6th Floor                      BONSAI GARDENING   (7th Floor)
                          12 Noon------Main Floor
                           2 p.m.------Auditorium Teahouse            Monday and Thursday:  7 to 8 p.m.
                           4 p.m.------Main Floor                     All other days:  12:30 to 1:30 p.m.
Additional performances
Monday and Thursday:       6 p.m.------Auditorium Teahouse            ORIGAMI   (8th Floor)
                           8 p.m.------Main Floor
                                                                      Both Fridays and Wednesday:  11 a.m. to 3 p.m.
ROKUSHU MIZUFUNE, WOODCUT PRINTMAKER   (6th Floor)                    Both Saturdays:  10 a.m. to 4:30 p.m.
                                                                      Monday:  11 a.m. to 3 p.m., and 6 p.m. to 8:30 p.m.
Monday and Thursday:  10 a.m. to 8 p.m.                               Tuesday:  10 a.m. to 5 p.m.
All other days:  9:30 a.m. to 5:30 p.m.                               Thursday:  10 a.m. to 5 p.m., and 6 p.m. to 8:30 p.m.

JAPANESE "BUN RAKU" PUPPET THEATER   (5th Floor)                      ORIENTAL COOKING DEMONSTRATIONS   (8th Floor)

Monday and Thursday:  6:30 and 7:30 p.m.                              Daily:  11 a.m. and 2 p.m.
Both Saturdays:       11:00 a.m., 12 Noon, 1 p.m. and 2 p.m.

JUDO DEMONSTRATIONS   (2nd Floor)

Friday, Tuesday, Wednesday and Friday:  11:30 a.m. and 12:30 p.m.
Monday and Thursday:  11:30 a.m., 12:30, 2:30 and 4:30 p.m.
Both Saturdays:       11:30 a.m., 12:30, 5:30 and 7:30 p.m.           JAPANESE GARDEN   (8th Floor Auditorium) will be open during all store hours.

CALLIGRAPHY   (5th Floor)                                             TEAHOUSE will serve meals from 11 a.m. to 5 p.m. Tuesday, Wednesday, Fridays
                                                                               and Saturdays ... 11 a.m. to 7 p.m. Monday and Thursday.
Daily demonstrations:  11 a.m. to 2 p.m.                                       Sake, tea and other beverages available during all store hours.

TEA CEREMONY   (5th Floor)
                                                                                                             ###
Every day:  2 p.m. and 3:30 p.m.

PAPER CUTTING AND ORIENTAL BRUSH PAINTING   (6th Floor)

Tuesday, both Fridays and Saturdays:  10 a.m. to 5 p.m.
Monday and Thursday:  11 a.m. to 8 p.m.

JAPANESE FLOWER ARRANGING   (6th Floor)

Monday and Thursday:  12:30 to 8 p.m.
All other days:       12:30 to 5:30 p.m.
```

Figure 23-2. A store-wide promotion based on a Japanese theme at Dayton's, Minneapolis, motivates customers to visit many departments and come to the store on various days.

awards, service awards, and so on. Employees are invited to preview major auditorium events.

Sales-support Publicity and Promotion

Newspaper, magazine, trade paper, radio and TV coverage obtained to publicize events, new store openings, new shops and services, other business news, and editorial coverage on merchandise.

Dayton's and other Associated Merchandising Corporation stores have sponsored a "Children's Movie of the Month" program, which is a series of wholesome, quality movies for children, with tickets available in the store.

Dayton's has a wide variety of special events. Many are of a public service nature like a "Fireworks Spectacular" on New Year's Eve, at one of the city's lakes; a make-up party and fashion show for blind girls; an annual flower show, and an "Empty Nest" symposium for the mature woman.

Under the Community Resource Volunteers program, Dayton's provides speakers to the public schools. School tours are also arranged for events of special interest to children.

Each month Dayton's sends an "Events Calendar" to their complete local and trade media lists. This is a listing of all events scheduled for the month, with a brief description of each. Many of these do not warrant a complete news release, but the calendar keeps the press aware of what is going on at Dayton's, and results in many inquiries and subsequent news coverage.

Television and radio are used extensively for publicity. Dayton's offers appropriate guests to women's shows, children's shows, radio talk shows, and others.

Dayton's generally has several major press parties each year, to preview major auditorium events. Smaller press parties are occasionally held with an imaginative invitation and theme, for opening of special shops or other special occasions.

Although customer complaints are generally handled by the Customer Service Department, the Public Relations Department answers complaints of a general nature, and works with Customer Service, the Credit Department, and other areas of the store in handling special customer problems.

The specialty shop. The specialty shop arouses interest because of its character and personality. They must make *visual* what they have to sell. Abracadabra, a boutique in New York City, displays its clothes on pipe racks, with dazzling lights beamed on them. The environment of the store sells it. A fur boutique in the midwest has "carpeted," "walled" and "ceilinged" its store in fur. Since it is different and curious, people come in to see, and to touch, and to try on.

In seeking the new and refreshing, specialty stores are turning to plastics in their displays. They give distinctiveness to the appearance of the store.

Bergdorf Goodman in New York expanded its Bigi floor. Bigi (Bee-gee) stands for the initials of Bergdorf Goodman, and is a device for giving the younger set its own "place." With a press preview and release, the store opened "Bigi's Bite," a counter and stand-up place to eat. The L-shaped counter faces a zany seven-foot malted milk mixer. The menu, chosen by a panel of 100 teenagers and *Seventeen* Magazine, includes Salad-On-A-Stick.

Also launched with a press release and press preview, Bigi's Cutaway, a fast-paced haircutting place, is minus tipping and appointments. It is a mini-salon on the Bigi floor. The young customer-to-be writes her name on a huge slab of glass with a Vis-a-Vis marker. No appointments are necessary; it is first-come, first-served. A loudspeaker pages the youngster as she shops when it is her turn.

It is ideas and selling the distinctive "Signature" that feature good public relations in the specialty store. Attention to detail, interesting packaging, color, concentration on the new theme all are plusses. Adding this to basic public relations techniques makes for a good program. A store has many assets that can make it unique. The task is to find them, and then tell.

The discounter. The discounter competes with the luxury of the specialty store by convincing the middle class it can match it at a lower cost. Each discounter, of course, also competes with other discounters. He must lure the public with special events and showmanship; services to the family, like a place to park the children; contests, and community get-togethers.

GEARING TO CURRENT EVENTS

The retailer must assess the national climate every day. Both community and world events affect his business. For instance, a parade, once a joy because it brought traffic, is now often feared, because of activists who have appeared in the community. Stores are considered landmarks and places to make news. They are often singled out by militant groups. In some towns, store owners now lock their doors during the day and admit people on recognizance. A Protection Department should be well briefed in dealing with difficulties and cooperating with the police department.

The store is often a mirror of the community. The people of the store are the ones who make it work. Their willingness to participate makes the store a better place.

One such store is Abraham & Straus in Brooklyn. It has made itself into a community center. A typical program saluted the "Brooklyn Renaissance." Gerda Clark, A.I.D., A&S Home Fashions Coordinator, designed appropriate fashion rooms as highlights of a mid-winter home furnishings show. A room inspired by the Brownstone Renovation Movement evoked favorable comment, and A&S formed a "renovator's information exchange" to be manned on Monday and Thursday nights by a number of Brooklyn residents who live in brownstone houses.

This community action at A&S brings potential brownstoners to the information desk. They speak to the advisory group of the evening, and are given names of glaziers and mold makers, real estate brokers, banks providing mortgage money, engineers to check out houses before purchase.

A&S is serving the community's young public, who will no doubt purchase housing interiors there.

DEFINING THE STORE'S DISTINCTIVENESS

Stores are constantly analyzing themselves and looking at the type of image they are projecting. Some stores have never found the image to put them across. People can't recall where they are located in a city full of stores. Others are an experience to be talked about. This is the aim of every sophisticated store today.

The aim of many is to have a national image like Bergdorf Goodman, Neiman-Marcus, I. Magnin, Marshall Field, Saks Fifth Avenue. There are many contenders for that role because the country and the world are becoming smaller as people become more mobile. Also, if a store is well known and has a unique mailing catalog, it will get business from all over, and proudly point to its customers in the 49 other states. And vendors will love it and service it first.

A successful store in projecting an image uses repetition in its advertising style. The concept, the tone, the layout are immediately recognized. Horne's of Pittsburgh impressed its customers with a large series of ads quoting designers talking to its own fashion coordinator. The ads were believable and gave added prestige to the store. Each ad carried a sketch illustrating a possible fashion trend by a name designer, whose ideas were in the copy. This was followed by a benefit luncheon and fashion show for which 1900 tickets were sold. Tea was served afterward, giving the audience and several hundred students a chance to mingle with leading designers, and even get autographs. Horne's advanced its position as a fashion leader in the community.

Packaging and visible symbols. Consumer tastes are constantly changing. To win the customer, you must give her "the new."

You also have to give her the "status bag" if you want her to carry it. Bergdorf Goodman is known for its mauve-colored paper boxes carrying the history of fashion silhouetted across them. At Christmas, it is a mark of status to receive the silver-foil-covered gift box topped with a red rose. Tiffany's box is a pale turquoise, and Cartier's is brilliant red with the impressive signature.

Bloomingdale's discovered a few years ago that they could provide an artistic, colorful bag and leave its name off, and everyone would know that it came from "Bloomies," as they have been nicknamed. Burdine's of Florida has a shopping bag that gayly says: "Burdine's: We sell everything but the sun tan." On a bus in New York City, many recognize the brown and white striped Henri Bendel packaging, and the brown and white Saks Fifth Avenue plaid.

Specialty stores around the country often work with popular artists and paper product producers to participate in chain purchase of shopping bags and cartons. The printer changes the store logo for each order. By working together, the price of the bags and boxes is lower, and a smart look is achieved for all participating stores.

Just as the letterhead is important, since it suggests the attitude of the store, so are the color and quality of the stationery. It is important to review the impression being made and determine the one the individual store should have.

WINDOWS AS IMAGE BUILDERS

Store windows have long ceased being merely display space for merchandise. But in just the past few years many leading retailers have recognized their power in establishing a distinctive character for the store. Retailers such as Bloomingdale's and Henri Bendel in New York, Marshall Field's and Carson Pirie Scott in Chicago, and Neiman-Marcus in Dallas have become venturesome in their window display.

Bloomingdale's attracted national attention by injecting sexual overtones into the choice and positioning of mannequins. Bendel used humor, suspense, and unusual props to make the store stand out from the many in midtown Manhattan. Field's—whose windows have always been noted for their distinctiveness and good taste—adds humor and whimsy without sacrificing taste. Carson's uses windows in sequences to tell a story. In one called "Out on the town," the first window featured several beautifully dressed women before a chrome-and-glass background. The second window showed them at a theater ticket booth. The next had one man and two of the women at a cocktail lounge. The fourth showed them at the theater; the fifth at dinner; the sixth at a discotheque; the seventh outdoors in the moonlight; and the last focused on one of the women at home with an antacid and an ice bag.

The window is the opening of the store to the world, so it says at least as much about the personality as does the eye of the person about him.

APPEALING TO YOUTH

Reaching the young buyer and future employees requires special techniques. *Seventeen* Magazine often works with store promotion directors, giving them ideas, and helps to put on a fine program.

May D&F made news in Denver with its "Great Put On." *Seventeen* Magazine and *Glamour* participated.

May D&F substituted a seven-hour marathon television show for the usual fashion shows in the store. It worked fashion for boys and girls into TV variety. It was backed by a high-impact series of newspaper ads. This promotion replaced the usual high school and college fashion shows and boards of

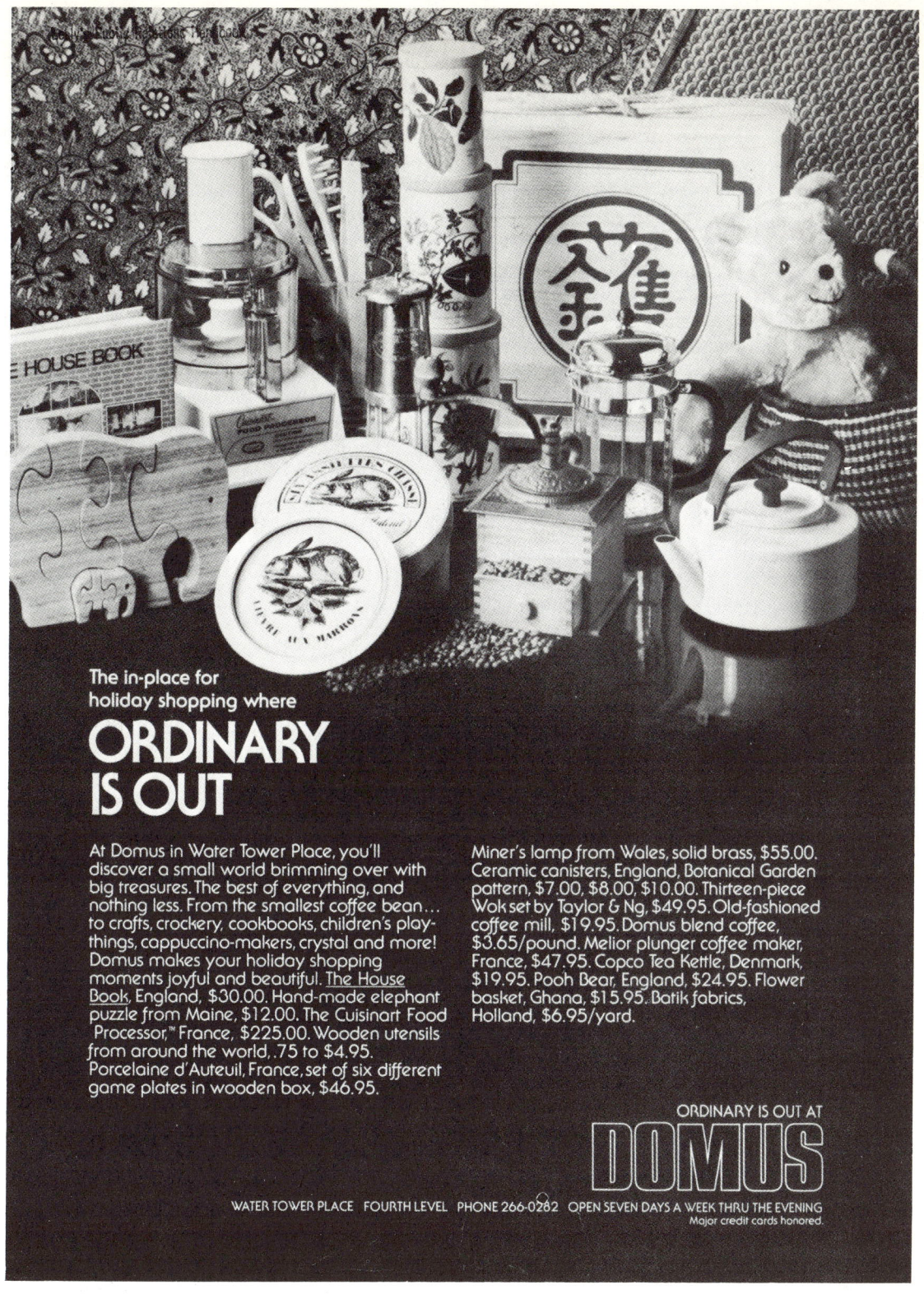

Figure 23-3. Establishing a distinctive identity is vital for a retailer. Domus lifts itself out of the ordinary by demonstrating it carries no ordinary merchandise.

college students acting as temporary fashion experts.

Produced on a local television station from Friday at 9:30 p.m. until 5 a.m. Saturday, this seven-hour telethon combined fashions, "camp" movies, rock bands, and a teen telephone board seated in bleacher rows on a stage, each with her own telephone.

Hundreds of prizes were given during the evening and early morning to those who called in. To qualify for a prize, and the grand prize, TV viewers telephoned the station to register their names. The TV screen showed the telephone number, which led to 20 telephones serviced by pretty co-eds. The phone number had been carefully kept secret during the advance publicity for the show—an element of staged suspense. A *Seventeen* Magazine fashion sequence, taped in advance, was part of the show, as were five "camp" movies. Eleven thousand calls jammed the lines. At 4:30 a.m. the name was drawn for the grand prize, but it was not announced. Instead it was locked in a canvas bag and put into a guarded armored truck that was parked for the rest of the night in front of May D&F's downtown store. At 2:45 p.m. Saturday a guard unlocked the car and carried the winning name to the Junior World where the crowd waited. There were rock groups entertaining and soft drinks were served. It was a traffic builder, and an original and different way to make news.

Some stores participate in ventures like The Boys Clubs of America, the Police Athletic League, the 4-H, and other youth groups. Imaginative ideas bring new customers into the stores and at the same time serve the community by providing constructive activities for young people.

The Higbee Co. of Cleveland, Ohio has a baseball oriented Dugout Club and a football-geared Mascot Club that has thousands of 7- to 15-year-old boys as members.

Dayton's has a profitable ski club for 9- to 17-year-old boys and girls who take to the slopes together, often taking Dayton's apparel and equipment along.

More than 50 prominent retail firms sponsor and counsel Junior Achievement companies made up of high-school-age youngsters.

J.L. Hudson of Detroit has had a car paint-in and a co-ed fashion show, tied in with *Seventeen* Magazine as part of a Teen "Out of Sight Week." They staged festivities in their auditorium, and included a snappy boutique at one end of it. Four co-ed discotheque fashion shows were staged, each running 15 minutes without commentary. A snappy formal fashion show was held and a big-name band and disc jockey performed.

There was a Psychic Corner of colorful tents, built by the store display department, which housed a guest handwriting analyst, a tarot card reader, an ESP reader, and a horoscope analyst. A Demonstration Corner housed special booths featuring wig demonstrations, make-up demonstrations, men's barber shop, and A Make Your Own Sundae Booth. A Pull Your Own String Thing for a nickel gave participants a chance at a grab-bag prize. Visitors were marked on the forearm, arm, and hand for the duration of their stay by an Op Dot they got at the entry door. Admission was free and there were free soft drinks and chips and free samples. About 20,000 boys and girls were attracted.

Many stores have school programs, and many have part-time school employees to give the students a taste of retailing.

EMPLOYEE COMMUNICATIONS

Though management policies and the store's posture should be revealed in the pages of the company publication, it should not be completely "managed" by management.[2] It is better to have a saleswoman tell her story of the "hardest sale I ever made" to inspire other employees.

Effective use of a publication for employees is demonstrated in the *Daytonian*. A typical issue carried a message from the President who called attention to a company-wide program called "It's Friendly Time at Dayton's." Courtesy awards to Daytonians who gave outstanding service to customers were cited. An article commending an employee for curbing fraud by calling Protection carried photographs of her on the job. A section called "New Faces in New Places" featured photos of new employees and of job changes among employees.

STORE-WIDE PROMOTIONS AND EVENTS

Since 1957 Neiman-Marcus in Dallas has been known for its Fortnights, celebrating the arts and crafts and products of a particular nation. They involve intricate planning, cooperation of officials and dignitaries, and obtaining investment of money by interest outside the store.

Twenty buyers went to France for merchandise for the event. Dallas leaders were invited to lunch

---

[2] See Chapter 15.

nine months before the event to get their cooperation. French paintings were exhibited at the Dallas Museum of Fine Arts. French tapestries were shown at the Memorial Auditorium. French films were shown at local theatres, French entertainers were booked into Dallas night clubs, civic clubs heard French speakers. Both *Vogue* and the Dallas *Times-Herald* had advertising supplements. The Ambassador from France to the United States and the Mayor of Dallas officiated, attending the gala balls and festivities. Air France arranged a charter flight for 200 French visitors.

This first Fortnight was so successful that before it was over, British interests invited the store to do a Fortnight for Great Britain the next year. This custom has continued. As a result Neiman-Marcus has greatly increased its prominence in the community and the world.

In a similar Texas-like fashion, Sakowitz of Houston arranged a Festival of Folkways. Sakowitz adapted the history of Texas to its storewide promotion.

Since patchwork quilted fashions were in fashion, this fact was exploited. The way America was "stitched together" out of diverse peoples, customs, and countries was demonstrated. A symbol was developed of a patchwork in the shape of a star, and it was colorfully put on posters, shopping bags, program covers, invitations, and other materials. The "world's largest patchwork quilt" became the festival banner over Sakowitz's front door.

In the store, a large group of old patchwork quilts was on display, and a rare historical collection of clothes and accessories of early America was on view. An American history slide show drew crowds to the first floor; the second floor featured 1,000 famous American toys and games; there was a cavalcade of comics and a history-spanning horde of political campaign buttons. The third floor included a roundup of early American farm relics and an exhibit of ethnic confluences in Old New Orleans. Jazz and other music was featured. The fourth floor had an old-fashioned facsimile of America's first drug store, furniture of the folkways, the valentine-strewn history of greeting cards, and a history of American slang. The fifth floor had a Texas-size history of the Lone Star State, a Sky Terrace menu of foods of the folkways, and an old-fashioned American apple-ducking barrel.

It was a store-wide celebration, topped with the launching of Houston's fall social season at a benefit at a hotel with a "Fashions of the Folkways" fashion show. Well-known designers appeared.

Cartier, the high-fashion New York jeweler, joined with the Denim Council to develop an $1,850 denim cape lined in white Tibetan lamb fur. The contrast of the luxury items with the once-humble—now used in fashionable circles—was featured in many newspapers.

These events win publicity because they make news. Newspapers and radio and television stations will cover a happening in which a large part of the community is engaged. The public relations department can set up photographs, arrange interviews, and suggest features coasting on the momentum. Releases, biographies, and speeches can be based on the event. When a store is imaginative enough to attract all age groups it generates publicity in many media.

COMMUNICATION BY MAIL

Most stores mail to their charge customers monthly. Some also enclose chatty newsletters, printed on attractive stationery. Elizabeth Arden beauty salons once sent a letter with the salutation, "Dear, dear Customer" to be just a little friendlier than the stock mailing piece.[3]

Special effort to be original while consistent with the character of the store is called for to make mail communication fully effective.

INVESTOR RELATIONS

Information on Investor Relations in Chapters 11 and 12 is applicable to any publicly owned retailer. It is wise to treat this as though the company were a blue chip company on the stock exchange, for any financial statements made must be highly professional. Many stores retain consultants to help them handle this very important and specialized area.

COMMUNITY RELATIONS

Information on community relations is in Chapter 7. This subject is threaded through this chapter, for it is one of the most important and changing areas of public relations for a merchant in daily contact with the public.

Community affairs cannot be predicted, and the ability to adapt to new situations is essential.

MINORITY GROUP RELATIONS

Minority group relations are treated in depth in Chapter 9.

[3]See Chapter 48.

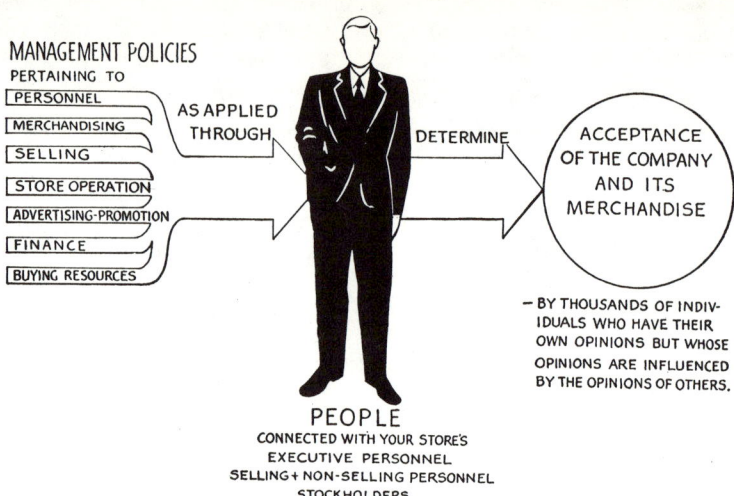

Figure 23-4. A diagram to explain the function of public relations to a store's employees. (Adapted from "A Case Example in Public Relations" by Paul Garrett, formerly Vice-President, General Motors Corporation.)

Carson Pirie Scott, Chicago, pioneered in the 1950s employing Blacks in visible jobs. But Carson's managers recognized that they had to be more responsive to urban problems after a series of six internal fires broke out in their famous landmark store, which was designed by Louis Sullivan, in 1968.

The management decided to start with a conference on "Urban Racial Crises" for executives. It was later repeated for two additional groups.

Norbert F. Armour, Carson's president, arranged for the first conferences with the Chicago Business Industrial Project, a non-profit agency serving as a liaison center among competing groups within and outside Chicago's power structure.

A series of meetings and three-day workshops on race and human relations were held for branch store managers and assistant managers, personnel managers, and first-line supervisors. Topics included a study of preconceived notions about people from other social and ethnic groups, individual attitudes, attitudes of minority groups, and techniques in applying good management and human relations principles.

Carson's had an employee opinion survey and organization development program conducted for the 8,500 associates in the retail division by the Industrial Relations Center, University of Chicago, using the Associated Merchandising Corporation Employee Opinion Survey Program. Both feedback and report-back techniques provided information that was relayed to the store's staff. Task forces established programs and projects to help Carson's reach a more adequate ratio of minority-group associates at middle and top-level jobs. Posting of jobs at the State Street store lists job openings. Store tours are conducted for inner-city students to broaden their knowledge of job opportunities in retailing.

Communication is made easier with the Urban League retained as consultant. Carson executives also act as consultants to Black entrepreneurs, providing retail expertness to vendors and suppliers.

Carson Pirie Scott has received the Personnel Division Merit Award from the National Retail Merchants Association in recognition of its responsiveness to the social condition of its community.

In another area, Dayton's Employment Opportunity Program provides special training and help for the disadvantaged and minority groups.

EMERGENCY SITUATIONS

A store's ability to deal with difficulty protects its character in the community.

Emergency procedures for retail stores are often standardized and similar to those of other businesses. See Chapter 38 for basic information. Often, though, a store will be original in handling an un-

PUBLIC RELATIONS FOR RETAILERS

Figure 23-5. Imagination and showmanship create distinctiveness for a retailer while fostering what it has to sell. Sakowitz in Houston used this 20′ x 44′ "flag" of DuPont quilting fabrics to depict the Americana theme of its product promotion.

foreseen difficulty and win admiration for its efforts. When New York City had a mail strike, Bergdorf Goodman executives quickly developed a plan. Six people wearing blue sweatshirts lettered in white, saying on the front Bergdorf Goodman and on the back Special Mail Delivery, took to bicycles. They carried 400 special invitations originally meant for the mails, addressed to the press and invited guests for an event to be held 10 days later. They were bicycled and delivered in five hours. The event, a preview of a new Bergdorf antique shop at headquarters, received additional attention because of the original concept of forwarding invitations.

Dayton's have procedures for dealing with many types of emergency situations or possible negative events. For example, there is a clear-cut procedure to be followed in the event the store has to be closed for severe weather conditions.

Most stores have learned by experience the need for a master book of emergency procedures. The pages are constantly added to, as history is overtaken by current events.

Among the more basic, necessary examples is one developed by Sakowitz of Houston called a Fire Drill and Evacuation Procedure. This is an 11-page outline of general instructions, including having periodic fire drills in which all employees are required to participate. Fire drills are conducted prior to store opening. A special fire alarm bell has been installed in the downtown store to be used for emergencies only. At the sound of the fire alarm bell, all personnel follow instructions given by the floor captains responsible for their respective floors. The procedures are:

1. Walk to the appropriate stairway and line up two abreast at the stairway entrance doors.
2. Act promptly—Walk briskly—Do Not Run!
3. Be calm.

An added precaution! There is NO SMOKING anywhere in the building during an evacuation drill.

The instructions also say that the elevators and escalators will not be used to evacuate personnel. Special instructions indicate that a fire should be reported immediately to the store operator "by dialing O." (Nothing is left to chance, for in an emergency one is apt to forget simple procedures.) "Give the operator the location and a brief description of the situation," the procedure manual says.

Instructions are then spelled out for the operator:

1. Call the superintendent's office and report the situation.
2. Call the City Fire Alarm Building, CA 7-2323, and report the fire.
3. For other emergencies, call the Police Department, CA 2-9351, ask for the "Police Dispatcher," and report the emergency.
4. The chief operator will dial the code emergency number or closing bell, 6-555.
5. The operator will then ring the fire emergency bell, with three long blasts with a pause after each blast.

The Sakowitz procedure goes on to indicate how each floor should handle the emergency, down to the smallest detail.

Because of militant and violent groups, retailers are having their executives and staff meet with the public relations people of the police departments to learn the basics of handling emergencies of various kinds.

Though each community has its own problems,

many are similar. For instance, in Palm Beach the Worth Avenue Merchants' Association has meetings to discuss such mutual problems. Local chambers of commerce welcome participation of this nature. The National Retail Merchant's Association, 100 West 31st Street, New York, N.Y. 10001, has procedures that can be of help in many situations. Its newsletter, *Promotion Exchange,* has a file of examples of how stores have handled emergencies.

Remodeling. Even remodeling can be handled with minimum friction and maximum finesse when a plan is developed. Gimbel Bros., New York, had to meet customer annoyance at hammering and noise and obstruction and determined to help their customers look forward to the new facilities. Framed boards 4½ feet high and 10 feet long were placed on partitions. Copy was written to get interest and enthusiasm for the new Gimbels. Words on the signs were: "Behind these walls will soon be America's thriftiest and most beautiful street floor . . . price tags by 108-year old Gimbels." And "We look a perfect fright now . . . but wait till you see us when Raymond Loewy is through! If we're not the sleekest, modernest, most beautiful street floor in New York, we'll eat this partition."

Remodeling or any inconvenience in a store is disturbing. Clear explanations make people more understanding.

MAGAZINE TIE-INS AND EDITORIAL CREDITS

An area of store exposure that impresses the customer is the magazine editorial credit. Whether it be home furnishings or fashion (men's, women's, children's) the merchandise that the store has bought that is in a magazine is likely to bring in added business. The store has the opportunity to be acknowledged as headquarters for this new merchandise, so the publicity department is effective when it gets this coverage for the store.

To become listed, an amicable relationship must be established with the suppliers. Buyers should take the publicity personnel on visits to the leading manufacturers they buy from.

For instance, a company like David Crystal, Inc., manufacturers of women's, men's, and children's fashions, works closely with magazine editors. When they show a new line to buyers, the commentator often announces that a certain style will be seen in a certain magazine; the month it will appear is announced.

Over the past 20 years magazines have enlarged their store promotion and merchandising staffs. Magazines like *Vogue, Harper's Bazaar, Glamour, Mademoiselle, Seventeen, House & Garden, House Beautiful,* and others have invitations extended to "tie-in" stores to visit their headquarters so they can learn their plans.

The route of the magazine tie-in has become the track the wise merchant can take. Those who attend the magazines' semi-annual seminars get pace-setting promotion ideas, often supplemented by handsome kits that include newspaper ads, radio scripts, news releases, display themes, and other materials. The tie-in stores have learned to be performers when the issue hits the subscription list and newsstands.

Good vendor relations help a store get into this program. Because magazines merchandise editorials to get the most distribution of a product so readers can find it at a store, their merchandise editors ask the manufacturer for a list of stores where the product may be obtainable, in large and small cities. Some of these lists have been known to appear in single or double columns. The double column usually ties in with a manufacturer's or fiber company's advertisement in the magazine.

There are subscribers in each city who might be delighted to rush to the mentioned store to purchase a dress that's on the cover of a well-known magazine. If no store is listed in the city, they may order it by mail from a nationally known store.

To show the store's interest to the manufacturer, when an ad or editorial appears, it should be mounted on a display card next to the merchandise. A window display can be designed around it. Take a picture. Send it to the manufacturer and to the magazine editor.

If you visit the city where the magazine is edited, ask for an appointment. See the photos they show of store "tie-ins." Listen to their future plans.

This can be done in special-interest markets, too. *Bride's* Magazine has a thorough promotion program that helps a store sell more by promoting an issue of *Bride's.*

See Chapters 39, 40, and 41 for futher information on working in this area.

24

Public Relations for the Nonprofit Organization

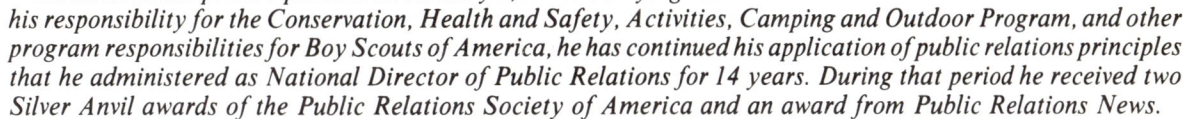

REBEL L. ROBERTSON, now Director of Program Support for Boy Scouts of America, previously served as the movement's Director of Public Relations. He started his professional Scouting career as a district Scout executive in Houston, Texas; served in the United States Navy during World War II; and continued his Scouting career in Tyler, Texas, Los Angeles, California, and San Mateo, California before joining the national staff in 1956.

During his naval service he took part in the landing at Iwo Jima and did youth work in naval military government on Tinian Island in the Pacific. He was honored by the Boy Scouts Association of Japan in 1951 for his work with Japanese youth.

He assumed his present position on January 1, 1971. Carrying out his responsibility for the Conservation, Health and Safety, Activities, Camping and Outdoor Program, and other program responsibilities for Boy Scouts of America, he has continued his application of public relations principles that he administered as National Director of Public Relations for 14 years. During that period he received two Silver Anvil awards of the Public Relations Society of America and an award from Public Relations News.

While there may not be a direct *profit* motive in public relations of nonprofit organizations and institutions, the need, nevertheless, is a prime one.

There may have been a time when good works spoke for themselves, but that day is far gone. The complexity of our highly competitive society demands attention to building concern among different publics. This has created a great need for planning and building public relations programs to interpret those "good works."

The approach to nonprofit public relations is not greatly different from commercial or industrial enterprises. It has certain special publics and needs related to interpreting the work of the agency. The particular needs applicable to a nonprofit operation can be easily recognized.

Members of the organization must be motivated first to join, then to continue and carry out the work outlined for that membership to accomplish. With highly competitive demands for use of a rapidly increasing amount of leisure time, it is important that the agency vigorously advocate its relevant worth. That takes public relations, planned and executed in a highly professional manner.

There is not a nonprofit organization among the thousands existing today that does not need volunteers. The scope of such volunteer participation may vary, but the very word "nonprofit" indicates that all or much of the work of related agencies must depend on volunteered time, effort, and money to reach their objectives.

These volunteered efforts take many forms.

Often the work of the agency itself is done by volunteer "employees" with only a handful of professional staff members available for guidance, training, and inspiration of the volunteer corps.

A broad goal of public relations in the volunteer nonprofit agency is to make people *want* to do those things on which the agency is dependent. People must *want* to join that cause; must *want* to serve as volunteer board members or line workers; must *want* to provide the financial resources needed to carry on the work.

Most nonprofit organizations depend on volunteered dollars to meet required budgets, whether by public solicitation or by financing through various means of federated giving, or—in an increasing number of cases—through dollars "volunteered" through legislatively appropriated funds.

Nonprofit organizations and agencies financed through public allocations of funds must maintain a climate of high acceptance so that as increased needs require increased budgets legislators will want to provide needed funds.

In addition to legislation for financial support, nonprofit agencies and organizations have become increasingly affected by many other types of legislation, as well as inquiries, hearings, and decrees by legislative committees, and state, federal, and local regulatory agencies. Specific attention to legislative and government publics is highly important.

PRIME PUBLICS OF NONPROFIT AGENCIES

Let us review, in general, the publics or audiences related to the average nonprofit organization or agency:

Board of directors. Every nonprofit organization or agency has a board of directors. They vary in size. They vary in makeup. They are responsible for administering the work of the agency and usually answer to some larger body or "council" of wide representativeness that elects them on an annual or some other periodic basis.

Generally they make up a cross section of the part of the so-called "general public" that is related to the work of that particular agency. They are named because of their ability to influence others, and because of their particular interest in the work of the agency.

Their acquaintance, their *knowledge,* of the work of the agency is all-important. It is through their person-to-person contact that many things can be caused to happen in favor of the agency's program: more volunteers recruited, more members reached, clientele better served, more funds raised, and so on. Their ability to influence others is in direct proportion to the extent of their knowledge. The public relations program of any agency starts with the board of directors.

Training board members is an art in itself. Useful booklets on this subject are available from most national volunteer agencies.

In addition to the formal training given new board members on their induction as members, to informal training conversations conducted during their tenure, and to periodic re-training meetings held by the board, a specific tool should be developed for use when board members need to interpret the agency's work.

This may be a "Board Member's Manual," simple in makeup but including basic information on the agency, lists of other board members, key staff, key volunteers in line operation, and so on. It can also include the current budget, historical information, and "official" replies to questions frequently asked by the public.

Board members should become intimately involved with the public relations programs of the agency. They should know what is available through national service organizations related to the local affiliate of which they are a member, the agency's own public relations program, and current emphases of the local agency. This calls for planned public relations involvement at all board meetings, and at periodic meetings devoted to informational backgrounding.

Staff. An often-overlooked emphasis must be placed on public relations training of the staff. Much reliance, in larger agencies, is often placed on the staff person or persons related to the public relations function, with the feeling "it's his (or her) job to do our public relations." Nothing could be further from realism. Every member of the staff must be a public relations person in his or her own right, and be equipped to do the best possible job.

Office staff members and nonprofessionals often have almost as much public contact, particularly with internal publics, as board members or professional staff members.

Regular sharing of all information—pro and con—related to agency operation should be standard operating procedure. Every staff meeting should devote some time to the public relations impact of those matters being discussed by the staff. After the professional staff discussion they should be shared with the office and nonprofessional group.

Members. These can be a vital, effective extension of a public relations program if they are properly informed and motivated. Communications with membership cannot be left to chance. Careful planning and execution are required. While good meetings are in themselves strong communications devices, these should not be the sole means. Regular meetings should be highly informative and designed to build motivation. Emphasis should be continually placed on the need for members to reflect positively the work of the agency in their own spheres of influence. Written communications in the form of well-developed, informative, and strongly motivational publications such as newsletters and magazines should be developed.

Clientele. In many nonprofit agencies, the "client" . . . the recipient of the agency's service . . . is a major public that may be overlooked. In recent years many nonprofit agencies have received unfavorable publicity as a result of a lack of understanding and support of the agency's "clients." Health and welfare agencies dealing with disadvantaged groups have been attacked in print and public demonstrations for their policies, programs, and operations that were not fully explained to the public. There are special problems in communicating with the disadvantaged, the handicapped, the foreign-born, and so on. Local publicity councils and many national service organizations offer guidance and assistance in this area.

Among clientele, as well as other publics, the word "why" is a good catalyst, and more of the "why" should be communicated as clients are assisted by the agency. This is particularly important among privately financed organizations that depend on people talking about the work of the united fund or other federated financing agency. If an employee's family, in a major plant, is assisted through one of the united fund agencies, word of that help—properly communicated—becomes instant news via the plant grapevine. If, on the other hand, something went amiss, and the "why" was missing, it can have a highly negative reaction.

Volunteers. Voluntarism is the strength of a democratic nation, and nowhere is it more evident than in the work of volunteer agencies. The American Red Cross, the Girl Scouts of the U.S.A., the Boy Scouts of America, the Camp Fire Girls, and hosts of others would be out of business without the dedicated work of thousands of men and women who voluntarily devote their talents and energy.

Volunteers are much like any employee in an industrial or business organization, and techniques applicable to communicating with such employees are readily adaptable to the volunteer. They need to be *involved*. They need to know they are important; they need to know the *what* and the *why* of the job they are performing. They are, without doubt, the most important audience of the nonprofit organization.

Volunteers expect to be held accountable for their performance. They have the right to demand excellence in staff assistance, a well-spelled-out task to do with some terminal point of measurement to prove their effectiveness, and the right to be kept informed on organizational or agency policies on a regular basis.

Communications is the key. Good meetings, regular staff service, and well-written meaningful newsletters are essential. These people *do not have to* do anything asked of them. They perform as they are motivated to, and as communications of all sorts deliver the reasons for their service.

Related organizations. An organization cannot be a world unto itself. In today's society the interworking of agencies, governmental and nonprofit, demand that public relations programs account for intercommunication. Spelling out the publics for a given nonprofit organization includes all other agencies interrelated to its work and a formal system of communication to keep them advised of the aims, purposes, and operations of the initiating agency.

Contributors. In most nonprofit organizations one of the basic reasons for good public relations is to build the climate that will facilitate fund raising—dollars secured from volunteer contributors.

This makes the contributor public a very key one, and plans need be formulated to keep them advised of results and successes of their investment.

Community organizations. The makeup of our system is one of interlocking relationships in the opinion-making process, and most of these opinion-makers are members and officers of community organizations (religious institutions, service clubs, school boards, and so on). The understanding sought through a sound public relations program demands that these leaders be informed of the interested organization's work and accomplishments.

Government and legislators. Government is coming more and more into areas previously considered part of the private sector. One never knows when good will, held on the part of key legislators, can be an asset to the operation of a nonprofit organization. Other chapters of this book have covered this subject for the profit-making company.[1] The same principles apply to the nonprofit field.

---

[1] See Chapters 3-8.

PUBLIC RELATIONS AND POLICY MAKING

The boards of directors of nonprofit organizations are policy-making bodies, so public relations needs are high in those circles. The public relations impact of any policy decision must be carefully weighed in the light of its implications to the many publics of the agency.

This gives a high priority to manning the public relations committee.

Its personnel should be of board-level timber and should afford communications know-how and resources that can communicate with related publics. Most nonprofit organizations have excellent manuals on this subject available through their national offices. Smaller local organizations can get help from the National Communications Council for Human Services, c/o Public Relations Society of America, 845 3d Ave., New York, N.Y. 10022. It has a variety of literature available, either produced by its staff or recommended by them. NCCHS also publishes a periodical that carries new information for the public relations people of nonprofit organizations, entitled *Channels*. For its members it has an extensive lending library and reference service.

NCCHS also makes available on a purchase basis a number of cassettes. Topics include:

> Building Media Relations: Radio-TV Accountability and Credibility
> What Opinion Polls Say About Public Attitudes Toward Nonprofit Health and Social Welfare Organizations
> What Newspapers and Magazines Want to Know About What We Do
> How Television Helps People
> How Television Can Do More to Help People
> Essentials of Nonprofit Relations
> Publicity/Media Relations
> Print/Audio Visual Materials Production
> (Videotape) Building Public Relationships to Help People

The public relations function should also be staffed. In larger organizations this may be a major and singular responsibility. In smaller ones it may be the function of the executive director or a key staff member. Regardless of size, the responsibility for staff needs to be carefully fixed with specifics of accountability. This calls for a written job description, written performance standards, and regular review against objectives and performance standards.

A recommended staff position description developed for a local council of the Boy Scouts of America follows.

STAFF POSITION DESCRIPTION
TITLE: Director of Public Relations

1. *POSITION CONCEPT*

Responsible for planning, developing, and administering through key volunteer leaders, experts in the communications field, a comprehensive program of Public Relations.

2. *PRINCIPAL RESPONSIBILITIES*

   a. Give leadership to the development of a complete and comprehensive program of public relations and publicity that will enhance the image of the Boy Scouts of America.
   b. Coordinate public relations activities among mass media covering the major market area with neighboring councils, in line with agreed upon programs developed with the regional office.
   c. Guide and direct public relations activities in the districts of the councils, aiding and assisting by training and service of material and manpower.
   d. Work closely with all communications media (newspapers, industrial publications, magazines, television, radio, outdoor advertising companies, transit display companies, etc.), regularly cultivating all management and key operating personnel, and serving them with material needed to enable broadest possible public relations coverage.
   e. Perform staff work essential to building, training, and operating a public relations committee, staffed by the best men in the communications fields, serving as secretary and giving leadership to maximum lay involvement in PR support of council functions, activities, and operations.
   f. Maintain liaison with advertising and public relations associations, firms, and groups to better secure their lay support of Scouting.
   g. Work with selected advertising or public relations firms who are named as volunteer agencies for the councils or for projects affecting the market area, serving as resource person for information and material needed by them in carrying out duties for Scouting.
   h. Be sensitive to the various audiences of Scouting represented in the council area and be familiar with means of reaching and communicating with these publics.
   i. Give leadership to surveys or studies reflecting public attitudes on Scouting, recruiting volunteer help to accomplish such studies.
   j. Advise and counsel with other functions of

the council to see that public relations priorities are considered in planning phases of activities, programs, and projects.

k. Maintain such reports, clip books etc. as may be required in measuring quantitative and qualitative progress of the function.

3. *SPECIAL RESPONSIBILITIES*

a. Maintain newsroom operations at all major council events.

b. Cooperate with regional and national public relations operations conducted in the council territory (regional annual meetings, national annual meetings, major Explorer events, etc.).

c. Work closely with national public relations representatives in maintaining relationships with national media headquartering in the council territory.

4. *POSITION QUALIFICATIONS*

a. One alternate: A graduate of an accredited school of Journalism or Public Relations, preferably with Master's Degree, backed by experience in school related to public relations, and with a volunteer or boy experience in Scouting. Must have excellent public approach, strong imagination, enthusiasm, and willingness to match odd hours with desire to perform at maximum capacity.

b. Second alternate: Strong educational background in communications skills, with civilian or military experience in the public relations field, coupled with lay experience in Scouting. Must have excellent public approach, strong imagination, enthusiasm, and willingness to match odd hours with desire to perform at maximum capacity.

c. Third alternate: Strong educational background in communications skills, backed by one or more successful experiences in a council having a public relations director, with a wide background of experience in working with public relations media and personnel. Must have excellent public approach, strong imagination, enthusiasm, and willingness to match odd hours with desire to perform at maximum capacity.

MAKING THE PUBLIC RELATIONS OPERATION SUCCESSFUL

A thorough study of the principles and procedures outlined in other chapters of this *Handbook* is the guide for successful operation of a public relations function. One need only read into those pages the need for nonprofit organizational understanding (with its resultant payoffs) in lieu of the profit motive.

Public relations programs must be based on policies and conduct, and be planned to reach specific objectives. A well-known blueprint for planning a public relations program is the "Public Relations Problem Solving Sequence" devised by Robert A. Kelly, Assistant to the Vice President, Texaco, Inc. His sequence is:

1. Who are we talking to? Careful identification of our publics. What do they think? Determination of their existing attitudes and opinions.

2. What is the difference between what they think and what we need to have them think? Here we define our public relations and communication problems.

3. What degree of opinion-shift do we want to achieve? From this we establish our communications or PR goals; what is desired is a shift in attitude to the betterment of the agency.

4. How to build specific messages designed to guide thinking of a specific public toward our desired communications goal? We now build or create the "action messages."

5. What methods can we use to help our message influence opinions and attitudes toward our communications goal? This is action. This is programming.
It is done through activities *and* through publicity. It is done through utilizing those techniques best applicable to the publics who are our prime targets. Visibility can be gained through planned activities that will convey the "action message." Publicity resources can be utilized to further deliver that "message."

6. Finally: Did we achieve our goal? Did we miss it? By how much? Which of the other steps in the problem-solving sequence must be reviewed and adjusted to achieve our goals? That's evaluation of our efforts.

Surveys. The best way to determine facts is through professional opinion-finding surveys, done by professionals in the field.[2]

It is recognized, however, that this is not always possible, chiefly due to resources available for fact-finding. In this event, simple techniques can be used that, while not as definitive as a thorough professional survey, can provide guidelines in communications programming.

These are principles in do-it-yourself surveys:

1. Be alert to misinformation being spread about the agency, to critical comment being aired.

[2] See Chapter 35.

2. Listen carefully to comments of members, clients, or constituents. They have their own opinions; they reflect those of others with whom they come in contact.
3. Familiarize yourself with opinion surveys done about similar agencies in the same community, or surveys of opinions made in other communities about the same agency.
4. Establish a "marketing panel" of community participants.
5. Dare to ask questions about what other leaders in the community think of your agency or organization.
6. Record the questions that come in to the information desk. Do they reveal areas of obvious misunderstanding?
7. Remember, too, that in most communities there *are* resources for doing surveys on a rather inexpensive level—by college classes for instance, or by training board members or volunteers in interview techniques.

Management by objective. This is a topic much discussed in executive and management circles, and it has direct implications for public relations practitioners. Simply stated, it is the determination of certain basic organizational objectives, with all elements of the organization gearing in to those objectives and making each action count toward meeting the overall objective. Nowhere is this more important than in the public relations function.

Once organizational objectives are spelled out, the problem-solving sequence should be applied, from which are built the specific objectives for public relations. This comes down to the detail of actually work-scheduling and planning each public relations event or project, and it is most important these be carefully done. Too often, public relations practitioners overlook the amount of detail essential. This should be done with pencil and paper and drawing board and with careful attention to work calendars.

On the next page is a type of planning sheet used by a non-profit organization.

Involvement as a principle of operation. The heavy involvement of people in the programming and execution of the nonprofit organization's operation is a key to wide understanding on the part of its own people. This understanding speedily spreads much broad "public" understanding.

The success of such programs as the American Red Cross, the United Way of America, Boy Scouts of America, American Cancer Society, the Girl Scouts of the U.S.A., and hosts of others show the validity of this principle. Their programs are planned with people in mind, people doing things that they must talk about to those with whom they come in contact in daily living.

Media analysis. Much is said about this in other chapters of the book (38 through 49). It is of vital importance to nonprofit organizations. A complete analysis of all media of communications should be kept updated.

Use of volunteer agencies. The Advertising Council[3] has done a tremendous job in building public understanding for causes of prime importance. It deals only with national campaigns, is advertising oriented, and has certain steps that it follows:

1. A campaign is proposed to the council by a sponsoring agency.
2. The council, through the board of directors, accepts (or rejects) the proposal.
3. A volunteer coordinator is selected by the Association of National Advertisers.
4. An advertising agency is chosen, through the American Association of Advertising Agencies, and offers its voluntary services.
5. The campaign is created by the agency and made available to various media through the Advertising Council.
6. Advertising space and time are contributed by magazines, newspapers, television and radio stations and networks, business papers, company publications, outdoor and transit media, and direct mail media—some or all of these—without charge.

Only campaigns of national scope can be considered, but for local agencies much volunteer help is available on the same basis on a local level, provided the cause is right and justifies volunteer advertising or public relations firms in giving their time and effort. In any such effort, however, volunteered firms are not expected to cover out-of-pocket costs for the campaign. People working in the communications field are very public-service minded, and as volunteers make invaluable contributions.

The agency has a heavy responsibility should it secure the cooperation of a local advertising or public relations firm. It must make its case, giving specific objectives sought, and provide adequate staff backup and support to see that the efforts made by the firm do not just "remain on paper." The advertising agency or public relations firm volunteers its expertise, and that expertise should

[3] 825 Third Ave., New York, N.Y. 10022

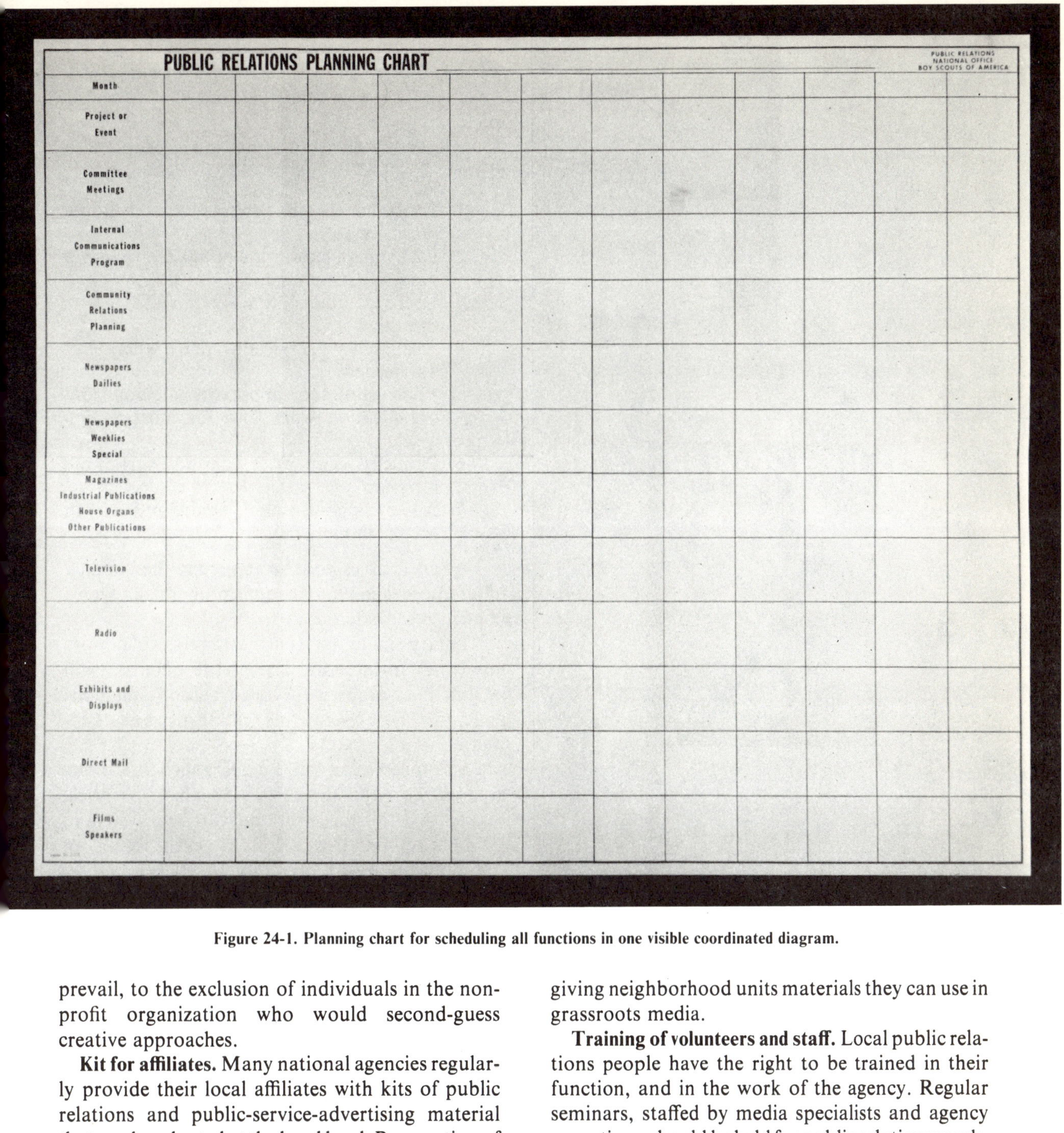

Figure 24-1. Planning chart for scheduling all functions in one visible coordinated diagram.

prevail, to the exclusion of individuals in the nonprofit organization who would second-guess creative approaches.

Kit for affiliates. Many national agencies regularly provide their local affiliates with kits of public relations and public-service-advertising material that can be adapted at the local level. Preparation of such kits demands constant review of what the local affiliate can best and most wisely use, tailoring contents to the needs of the current public relations emphases and to media acceptability.

Local organizations having many units such as a Boy Scout or Girl Scout council have further applied this technique to the next level of organization, giving neighborhood units materials they can use in grassroots media.

Training of volunteers and staff. Local public relations people have the right to be trained in their function, and in the work of the agency. Regular seminars, staffed by media specialists and agency executives, should be held for public relations working members, for public relations people working with lower-echelon organization components, and for board members and others in the organization for whom public relations is important.

National organizations have suggested outlines for these training experiences, and the National Communications Council for Human Services can

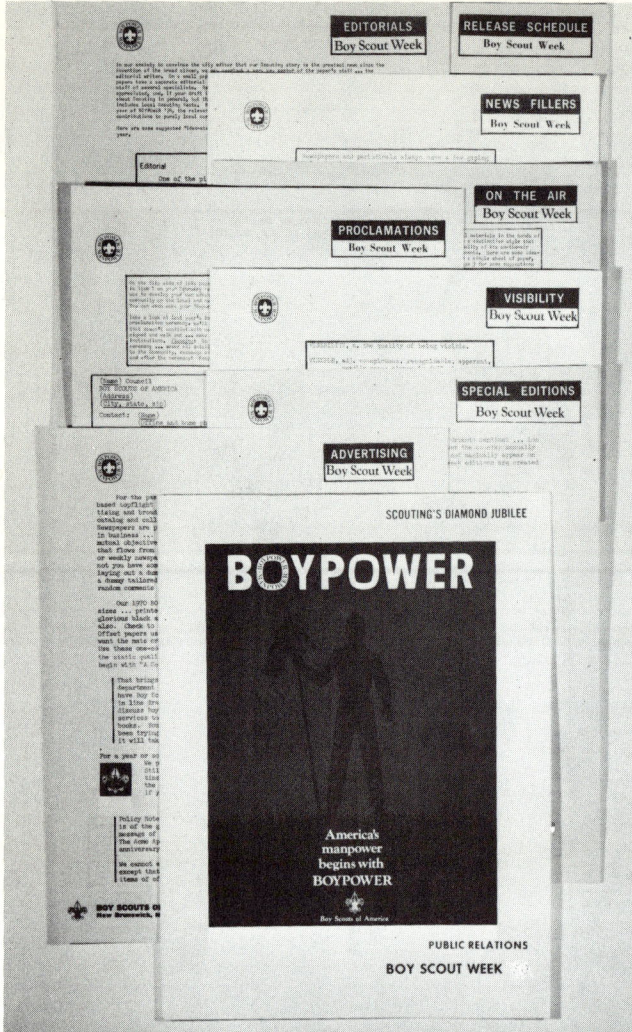

Figure 24-2. Press kit for a major nonprofit organization event, with types of material included featured in boxed headings.

provide outlines for nonaffiliated organizations choosing to affiliate with it.

Internal public relations. Broad internal understanding is imperative for nonprofit success. Our own people are our best spokesmen. Too often in spite of good public communications some well-intentioned but poorly informed constituent disavows the message by saying: "Now just a minute, let me set you straight, I'm on the inside." It's "Mr. Inside" with whom we should be especially concerned.

How do we get our people to act for *any* cause?

People go into action through phases that may be entitled:

UNAWARE—AWARE—COMPREHENSION
CONVICTION—ACTION

This is a continuing process of communication and education. The keys that stimulate the process are *what, how,* and *why;* what it is, how it works, why it works as it does, what it does, and what it does for me.

There are seven factors that move people into action:

1. Performance—the program will result in a *repeat* sale.
2. Packaging—how it looks; will the program have a first-time sale?
3. User recommendation—*MR. INSIDE* carries the word.
4. Availability—services available where they are needed.
5. Price—not too important in nonprofit organization work, but for most a high asset.
6. Publicity—important as a total part of the program.
7. Advertising—closely related to publicity in nonprofit work.

These principles need be applied to the building of an internal communications program, and have import to the external as well.

A good point to start is with an analysis of how we now communicate with these internal publics. It will be seen that we must go beyond traditional methods and analyze the operation of the agency and its activities.

From this we can build a chart such as the one used by local affiliates of Boy Scouts of America, Figure 24-3. We then work out our own system of rating how well we are using each means of communication with each target audience.

This shows how to correct internal communications programs.

Newsletters and bulletins. Much has been written on this, in this book[4] and in other excellent publications. It must be emphasized that these must be well done, with careful attention to communications objectives and with distribution planned to carry the message to those who should receive it.

The complaint system. In no other field is it more important to give special attention to complaints. None should be overlooked. Each may well affect the understanding of key people. There are no "unimportant" complaints. Many agencies feel that this area is important enough to involve top management, with careful follow-through on each complaint to see that the complainant is satisfied. A

[4]See Chapters 15, 48, and 51.

careful recording of complaints can also give good guidance to future communications planning.

Speakers' bureau. Every nonprofit organization, no matter how small, should have a formalized speakers' bureau. Details on the organization of such a bureau will be found in Chapter 48. Emphasis is placed on the need for constantly and consistently informing speakers of aims and purposes, and especially the communications objectives, of the agency.

BUDGETING

If it is to be a meaningful operation for the agency, public relations should have adequate operating funds. The budget will depend on the program developed, but will certainly cover the out-of-pocket costs for all functions involved. We can often "promote" the larger things, the talent, and the time and effort of volunteers. We should be in position to support them with the material things that require relatively little outlay of dollars.

The larger agency will need to weigh carefully the need for staff and staff assistance and to include those expenses in the public relations budget.

SPECIAL CONSIDERATIONS OF MEDIA AND NONPROFIT PUBLIC RELATIONS

A thorough treatment of media relationships and service appears in Chapters 38 through 45. A few special comments are offered as they relate directly to nonprofit public relations:

Broadcast. Both television and radio provide special opportunities for the nonprofit organization, since local stations, as well as networks, budget part of their advertising time for public service. There are many competitive organizations seeking the limited amount of time available, so materials—both program and spot announcements—provided to stations must be of the highest quality, professionally done with an eye to holding audiences.

A developing opportunity for nonprofit public relations is community antenna television (cable TV), known as CATV. Many different systems are being used, and it is recommended that local agencies check with facilities available in their own territories.

Newspapers. These continue to be a major outlet for news of the activities of nonprofit agencies as well as editorial support and recognition for worthwhile community projects. They insist they are not in the business of handing out free space and that nonprofit organization releases and events will

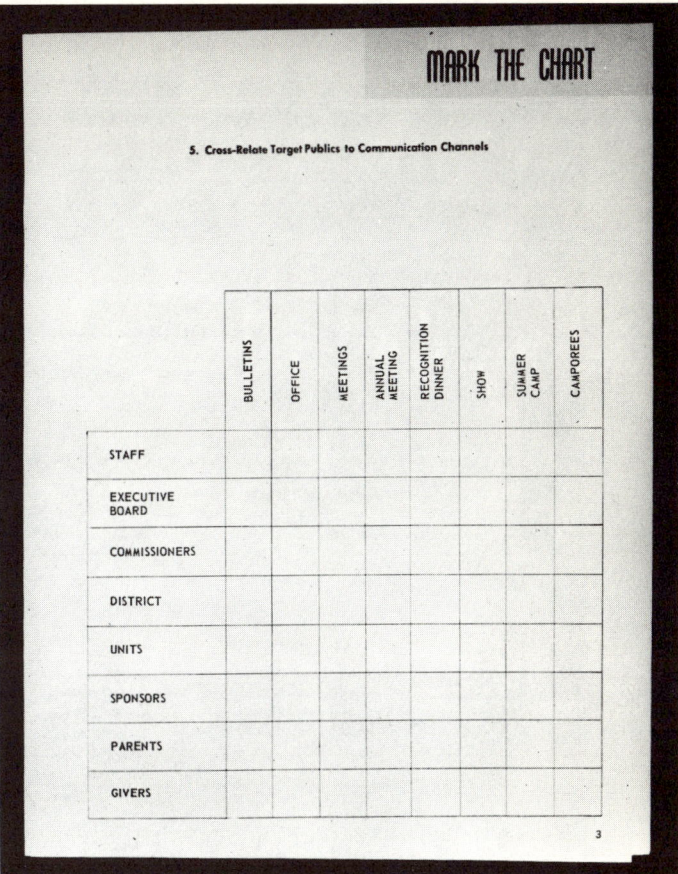

Figure 24-3. Cross-reference chart relating type of function to the publics involved.

be judged on their *news* value alone. This attitude decreases with the size of the paper. Major metropolitan dailies have more rigid requirements and less space, while small city dailies and suburban weeklies can be more generous. Nonprofit organizations have many opportunities to create news by using the devices employed by profit making organizations. These are treated in greater detail in Section V. Some of the more commonly used are: Stage a special event, form a committee, recognize volunteers, make special awards, hitchhike along with another news event, issue a statement on a public issue, announce a change in program or policy, use a celebrity.

Magazines. There are many locally printed magazines that may be utilized to explain the work of an agency on the local level. (See Chapter 41.)

Industrial publications. The more than 12,000 company publications provide rich opportunities for both the sponsoring firm and the nonprofit agency. Firms like to recognize the involvement of their people in worthwhile community events. Personal acquaintance with local industrial editors

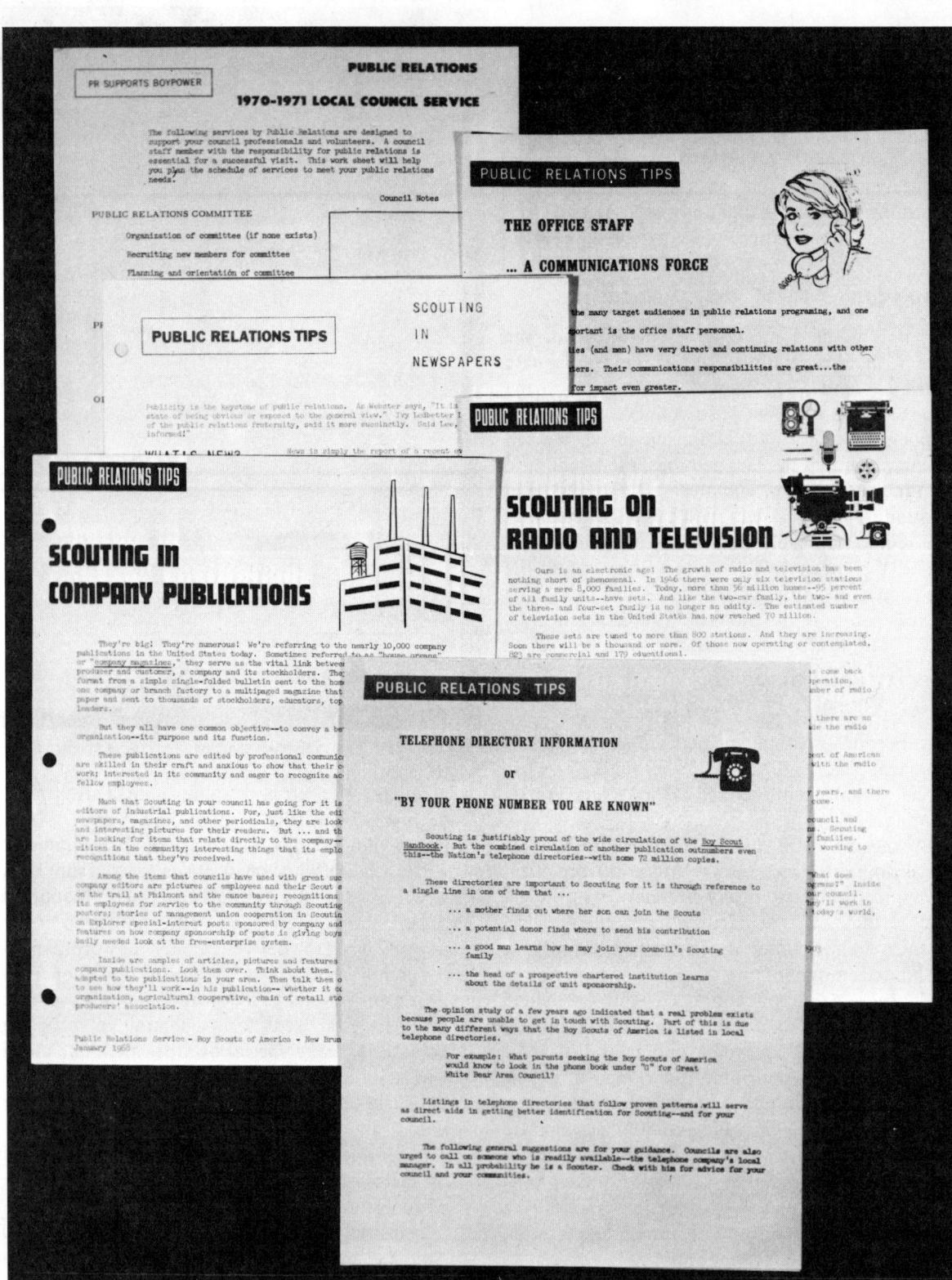

Figure 24-4. Examples of bulletins and pointers for local units.

will provide the guidance needed on the types of material they can use.

Billboards. Many local agencies use billboards to help carry their annual campaign message. They should cover costs of posting the paper on billboards. This is a recent development and should be considered in building a public-service advertising and public relations program.

Media check sheet. Figure 24-5 shows such a check sheet prepared for easily and thoroughly selecting and keeping track of all possible avenues.

Making media material work overtime. An excellent editorial in support of the agency's work can be made to work long after it has run in the daily paper. Good reprints, tied to a report on current organizational achievements, can be distributed to opinion leaders and others. A good news story, reflecting work of the agency, can be handled in the same way (See Chapter 38).

If a television station has reported the work of the agency on a news show, the film or videotape may be made available for further showing.

SPECIAL EVENTS AND THEIR PUBLIC RELATIONS VALUE

Almost any special event scheduled by the organization can be given publicity effect, if planned that way. A key to this is involvement of public relations in the actual planning of the event, so that newsworthy events do occur in its execution and maximum publicity values are suggested.

Open houses and come-and-see tours. These have special impact for personally showing opinion leaders and constituents the work of the organization. Carefully organized, with special attention to invitations and hosting, they can do a communications job done through no other means. Guidelines set up for industrial open houses apply, in principles of organization, to such a special event (See Chapters 38 and 48, and Bibliography).

METROPOLITAN COORDINATION

Care should be taken, in the case of several affiliates of nonprofit agencies existing in a single communications watershed, to effect careful coordination of public relations programming, so that the work of one does not convey something not applicable to others. More and more there is close coordination being built among affiliates so that one basic story goes to those mass communications media that blanket the trade territory, with more local

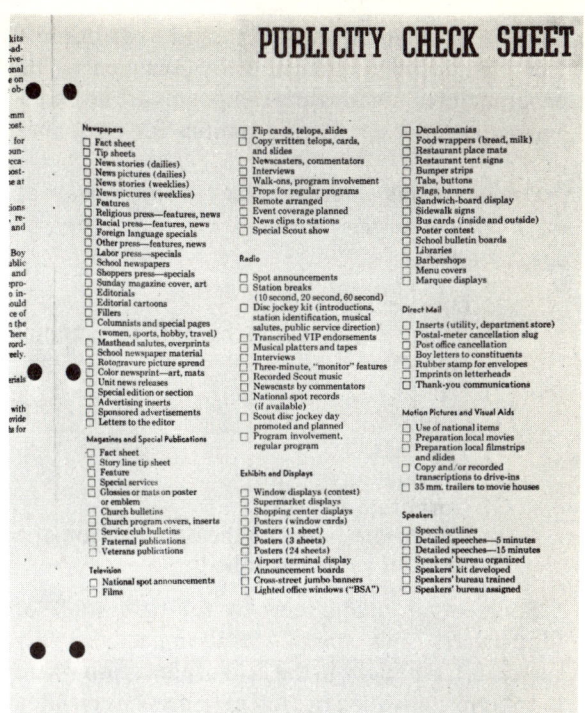

Figure 24-5. Check sheet listing all potential publicity functions, to be marked for each program or campaign when plans and budgets are made.

media carrying specific identification of the affiliate at the grass-roots level.

HOW TO RAISE MONEY

The principles and techniques of fund-raising for the nonprofit organization were ably presented in the *Public Relations Handbook,* edited by Philip Lesly, that preceded this volume. Following is the treatment by Raymond Rich and Charles M. Swart:

Many nonprofit organizations develop their public relations programs because they need to raise money or increase membership. But the public relations program should be considered as an over-all part of operation and policy. It should not be restricted to a publicity program at campaign time for the sake of promoting public good will and cooperation, because if it is so restricted it inevitably becomes less and less effective in supporting the fund-raising effort.

Rather, fund-raising should be considered as one of the opportunities resulting from a sustained public relations program. And in turn, a fund-raising campaign is an opportunity to focus and expand the program of public relations. For example, if participation is the best method of promoting good public relations among those who can become identified with the organization by taking part in its program, then fund-raising campaigns are an excellent means to extend opportunities for participation.

Organizing the campaign. There are many ways of organizing fund-raising campaigns. There are, to suggest a few:

(1) Direct mail appeals;
(2) Benefits, such as balls, bazaars, testimonial dinners;
(3) Rallies;
(4) Contests;
(5) Tag days;
(6) Foundation appeals;
(7) Corporate appeals;
(8) Campaigns based on the organization of a corps of volunteer solicitors.

Some organizations employ full-time staffs of fund-raisers. This type of operation has been very successful, especially in the field of education where long-term cultivation by staff members has resulted in accumulating large sums in memorials, legacies, foundation grants, and so on.

But the most satisfactory fund-raising method for most organizations is by use of volunteer solicitors. Volunteer fund-raising has the advantage of broadly extending individual participation, and for that reason increases the opportunities for promoting good public relations.

The paid staff and campaign expense required for such an effort is small compared with the large number of individuals involved as volunteers, the possibility for extending coverage of the community, and the amount of money raised. Although this form of campaigning has been highly successful even when the appeal is limited to a few hundred prospects for large gifts, or to certain types of business and industry, it is especially indicated when a broad appeal is to be made to the general public.

One of the most important factors in the organization of such a campaign is leadership. The most prominent and influential man or woman who can be found should be selected to head the campaign, and the general chairman should surround himself with the most representative group of leaders he can find.

These leaders should be thoroughly indoctrinated with the policies, objectives, and needs of the campaign at the time they are enrolled and should in turn pass on this indoctrination to those whom they select to aid them. Probably one of the most important keys to success is to transmit understanding, conviction, and enthusiasm for the campaign's goals throughout the entire organization.

This process advances the public relations of the organization for which funds are being raised by multiplying the number of people in all segments of the public who have knowledge and understanding of its policies and problems, and sympathy for and identification with its objectives.

Organization structure. The type of campaign organization required in any given instance will vary in accordance with the nature of the cause, the number and types of people to be solicited, and the amount of money to be raised. A typical organization structure, however, might be:

(1) *General Campaign Chairman:* A prominent leader who will give enough time to enrolling other leaders for various jobs in the campaign to assure thorough advance organization. He will take responsibility for general administration of the campaign.

(2) *Vice-Chairmen or Associate Chairmen:* A sufficient number of leaders to represent all important elements of the public. They will share direct responsibility, under the general chairman's guidance, for supervising the work of the fund-raising and public relations sections of the campaign.

(3) *Special Gifts Chairman:* Heads the committee on special gifts, which is responsible for selecting possible sources of large contributions and donors who require special cultivation or approach. This committee should be composed of men and women who know financial resources. Volunteer solicitors should have access to those sources.

(4) *Industrial Chairman:* Heads the industrial division, responsible for obtaining corporation gifts from industry, and for soliciting executives and employees. It should include leadership from management and labor, and a sufficient number of volunteer workers in each company to contact all prospective givers.

(5) *Commercial Chairman:* Heads the commercial division, responsible for obtaining corporation, executive, and employee gifts of the nonindustrial firms such as department stores, chain stores, theaters, and the like.

(6) *Government Chairman:* The Government division conducts the campaign among office holders and Government employees. Sometimes public schools are included in this division. But because of the educational nature of fund-raising for most organizations, the schools often are set up

as a special division including not only public but parochial school children and teachers.

(7) *Neighborhood Chairman:* Heads the geographically organized division of the campaign, which is responsible for door-to-door coverage of the homes and all small businesses, offices, and so on, not included in other sections of the campaign.

(8) *Public Relations Chairman:* His section of the organization does no direct solicitation of funds. It is responsible, however, for preparing materials to be used in publicizing the campaign, instructing volunteer workers, and reporting progress. Usually it includes special representatives or committees for newspaper, TV, radio, company publication, and other publicity as well as persons skilled in producing posters and pamphlets, salesmanship instruction, speakers' bureau operation, writing suggested speeches, and so on. Also in this section come special committees for arrangement of report meetings, rallies, special events.

If our campaign is organized along these lines, we will need a minimum staff of personnel experienced in fund-raising and public relations techniques. They can guide and help the volunteer chairmen and workers, and follow through and give continuity to the campaign effort. They will more than pay for themselves in public relations values and actual funds raised.

EMERGENCY PUBLIC RELATIONS

These principles are quoted from a public relations directive of the Boy Scouts of America. With minor adaptations they may apply to any nonprofit organization.[5]

1. *We, the professional leaders, must be the news source.* The newsmen must quickly learn that we have all the information, that we will keep them fully informed, and that we trust them to handle the story sensibly. The real trouble comes when we assume a "no comment" or "keep it out of the papers" attitude, forcing the newsman to piece together his own story from rumor, half-truths, and emotional exaggeration. Later "corrections" seldom get read or heard.

2. *Facts and accuracy.* These are our basis for building mutual trust.

3. *Fairness and keeping faith.* There can be no "exclusives." And we help an editor keep his deadline schedule. If an editor needs the latest facts "by 3 p.m.," be sure to call him by 3 p.m.—even if there are no new developments. In return, editors will keep faith with us by not overplaying a story and by not releasing names or other details until notification of relatives or for other legitimate reasons that apply to that particular case.

4. *Have a plan.* Have one spelled out on paper, have someone designated to handle the news, and be sure everyone knows what the plan is.

5. *Have a positive approach.* An emergency story is also an excellent opportunity to tell of Scouting's outstanding safety record and about our pacesetting health and safety procedures.

If your council has an emergency news handling procedure, it's a good time to review it and see that it's current and usable. If not, get a plan outlined and operational. Emergencies won't be forecast on your work schedule.

Steps. Some steps to preparedness:

1. *Make a plan.* Build it around your regular emergency-handling plan. Get help from public relations committeemen. Get samples from airline managers, public utility managers, or nearby industries. Check it out with key local newsmen. Keep it at hand.

2. *Pinpoint the man responsible for news.* Be sure other staff members know who it is. In an emergency, he, and only he, becomes our spokesman to media.

3. *Develop complete media lists.* Have names, addresses, and phone numbers of not only print and broadcast media in the council but of media covering out-of-council camps. Be sure to locate the part-timers or "stringers"—especially those serving Associated Press, United Press International, and broadcast networks. Their information will reach the most, the fastest. We must be sure it's accurate. Keep the lists handy.

4. *Cultivate those on the lists.* See that they know that they're welcome to come cover our feature-filled program any time and that they can count on our cooperation in any emergency. See that they all have file cards on "BOY SCOUTS OF AMERICA—For Emergency Use" with key staff names and phone numbers where they can reach us at any hour to check out an accident rumor or report. (Sometimes it's the first way we hear about it.)

5. *Follow through.* After the handling of an emergency story, call or drop by those on the list to

[5]See also Chapters 23 and 39.

see if we can be of any further help and to thank them for their objective, accurate reporting.

6. *Health and safety standards.* Be sure all health and safety standards are understood and that proper practices are strictly followed by all leaders and staff to keep accident possibilities to an absolute minimum. May you never have one to handle!

7. *Immediate notification to national office.* News services use telegraph wires—so must we! Send telegraph notification of all emergencies to the national director of the Health and Safety Service at the home office and call or wire your regional office.

Good press relations are just like good human relations. They should be continual. Editors, when treated honestly and told fully the implications of emergency publicity, bend over backward to be fair to Scouting and to kids and their families.

And the editors who didn't "get the runaround" in an emergency will be mighty helpful in telling of Scouting's purpose, operations, and needs in the future.

PERSPECTIVE

Worked into the warp and woof of the nonprofit agency, public relations can bring levels of understanding that will definitely ensure its success.

The principles of sound opinion building must be rigidly adhered to with determination of valid and reachable objectives, the development of a meaningful and receivable message, and the projection of that message on an intelligent level through all means of communication.

There are differences between public relations programming for a profit-making venture and the nonprofit organization, but the same general principles apply to both. The ultimate aims are different, with outcomes of profit not being one of the nonprofit group's objectives. Care must be taken in interpreting public relations practices applicable to business, but in general it takes only good judgment to interpolate and make workable almost any technique to be found in the other pages of this book.

25

Public Relations for Religion and Religious Groups

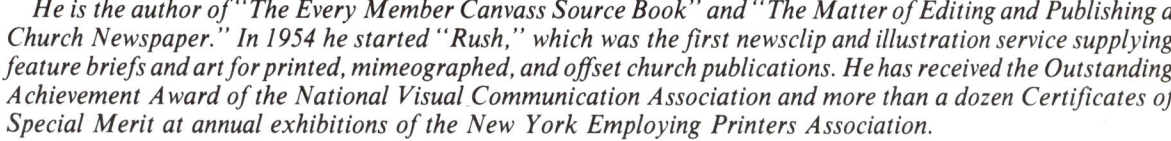

MARVIN C. WILBUR is Assistant Director of the United Presbyterian Foundation, and since 1959 has been the Executive Secretary of The Religious Public Relations Council, Inc. An ordained minister, Dr. Wilbur has been in communication and public relations activities with the United Presbyterian Church since 1951.

Previously he was Director of Public Information at Union Theological Seminary (New York) from which he was graduated in 1943.

A native of the State of Washington, Dr. Wilbur took his journalism work at Oregon State University where he was editor-in-chief in his senior year of the student newspaper, "The Oregon State Daily Barometer." After graduation he served as assistant director of public information for the Oregon State System of Higher Education. He also did graduate work at George Washington University, Washington, D.C. Alma College conferred a Doctor of Divinity degree on him in 1956.

In World War II, Dr. Wilbur was a chaplain in the United States Navy. He then was Presbyterian Chaplain to students at Yale University for three years.

He is the author of "The Every Member Canvass Source Book" and "The Matter of Editing and Publishing a Church Newspaper." In 1954 he started "Rush," which was the first newsclip and illustration service supplying feature briefs and art for printed, mimeographed, and offset church publications. He has received the Outstanding Achievement Award of the National Visual Communication Association and more than a dozen Certificates of Special Merit at annual exhibitions of the New York Employing Printers Association.

Johann Gutenberg, the 15th Century inventor of printing from movable type, took five years to set and print the Bible. Today, the new Linotron high speed typesetter in use by the Government Printing Office can set the entire Bible in type in 77 minutes, with copies becoming available very quickly thereafter.

Today, all 1,245 pages of the Bible can be recorded on a film negative no larger than a postage stamp, and every one of those pages can be instantly retrieved, blown up, and printed on 8 ½ x 11 paper.

Change has always been part of the religious scene, but the speed up of change in the present generations becomes one of religious public relations' major challenges. This is easily seen in the technical fields.

Thirty years ago every man, woman, and child in the United States made an average of one telephone call every day of the year. Now they make two per day. The mails have increased more than 300 per cent. Seventy-five per cent of all the books ever published have been produced in the last ten years.

But greater than the technological changes in communication are the sociological changes. Man has proved that he can tolerate change—at least when it is as relatively slow as it has been in past centuries. But ideas today are exchanged more rapidly than ever before. People now must accept or adapt to more changes in one month than they did in one year 30 years ago.

Today we have more means of communicating, but we have more necessity. We go through a whole series of changing cultures in one lifetime. The public relations problems of the churches today are alienation, war, poverty, mutiny, moral decay, riots, reparations, polarization, generation gap, brutality, segregation, conflict—and these are not words that gladden the heart.

Community, a newsletter for Methodist communication leaders, had a special issue on "A Look Toward the Year 2000." It said:

> Despite technology and preoccupations with 'things,' ideas will still be the primary agents of change.
> Despite the probe of technology into all the unknowns, people in the year 2000 will still be asking the age-old questions:
> "Who am I?"
> "What is my purpose?"
> "What does it all mean?"
>
> And in that X factor within man, which prompts those searching questions, lies the only mandate any religion has for existence. Either a religion earns the right of survival by helping man ask ever better questions and discover his own truth, or a religion fails to help man and becomes simply a lingering monument to the past.

Religion has always been in need of public relations, but has not always recognized this need. Some years ago, Arthur Krock, the famed *New York Times* columnist, wrote:

> Among the anomalies of the American scene is the persistent fact that "public relations" is an art that often is least comprehended by those who must depend on its sound practice. On numerous occasions there have been amazing demonstrations that the ablest personages in industry and government fail to comprehend the simplest principles for establishing a favorable public psychology toward their activities.

Religious institutions, whether headquarters or local church, are not exempt even today from this indictment, but most of them have come a long way in recognizing that they have public relations whether they want them or not. Not long ago, religious public relations was known more for its technique than its policy. There was a time when the Department of Public Relations was in actuality the publicity office, the promotion division, a radio program. As is indicated elsewhere in this *Handbook,* good public relations may be all of this, but it is something more.

Developing standards. Certainly religion has tooled itself for public relations and communication as never before. After five years of planning, a Religious Communication Congress was held in Chicago in 1970 with an attendance of more than 450 religious communicators. Interfaith in character, the Congress was sponsored by more than 40 organizations, and included professionals in public relations, journalism, communications, radio, television, film, research, and publishing. The second is scheduled for 1978.

A group of religion public relations professionals from all faiths and denominations together produced in 1976 the second edition of a handbook, *Religious Public Relations Handbook,* that has been widely used. The table of contents gives an inkling of the wide field of religious public relations today.[1]

> Public Relations
> Media for Your Message
> Press Relations
> Broadcasting
> Advertising
> Congregational Publications
> AudioVisual Aids
> Photography
> Displays and Signs
> Overlooked PR Opportunities
> Community Relations
> Direct Mail
> Organizing for PR
> Other Resources Available

Every public relations man is familiar with a listing of this type. However, they are included here to indicate that what's good for general public relations is good for religious public relations. Yet many churches feel that they are exempt from following the basic public relations rules and understanding the effective use of all media. They feel that religion is one of the mightiest forces on earth and people will understand. Nothing could be further from the truth. A lie repeated often enough over a period of years will be accepted sooner or later as "truth" by a large percentage of hearers. Possession of truth does not guarantee understanding or acceptance. Ideas are competing on every hand. If the church and synagogue are to remain vital forces, they must know how to interpret their messages convincingly to the community.

Of course most of the Table of Contents listed

---

[1] *Religious Public Relations Handbook,* edited by Wilmer C. Fields, Religious Public Relations Council, Inc., Room 1031, 475 Riverside Drive, New York, N.Y. 10027. $2.

PUBLIC RELATIONS FOR RELIGION AND RELIGIOUS GROUPS

Figure 25-1. Serving various religious denominations and groups, the Religious Public Relations Council helps churches with materials like this 58-page guide to techniques.

above is what other chapters in *Lesly's Public Relations Handbook* are all about. Detailed chapters cover most of the subjects as well as many other areas. These chapters are commended to all religious public relations professionals and are integral auxiliaries to this chapter.

Special attention, however, is due three aspects of religion public relations. These are:

1. Organizing an effective religion public relations program.
2. Financing the religion public relations program.
3. Setting up a workable communication center.

ORGANIZING AN EFFECTIVE RELIGION PUBLIC RELATIONS PROGRAM

Since public relations is a coin with the two sides of policy and technique, it must be represented in the top policy-making group of each religious institution. One of the greatest hindrances to effective religious public relations today is the widespread ignoring of its policy-making function.

This often results because there is no clear-cut organizational structure. The responsibility for the public relations program should lie with the top policy-making body in any religious institution. This body should establish the public relations committee with a well-defined purpose and authority. The chairman of this committee should be a member—or at least a corresponding member—of the top policy making body.

Many churches take it for granted that the pastor will be the public relations chairman. He often edits the newspaper, greets the Sunday morning visitors, sends stories to the local press. There is no doubt as to the image the pastor or rabbi holds in relation to his institution, but he should not be expected to take over the duties of the public relations committee. These duties can be done effectively by lay people. He should, however, participate in the meetings of the committee, and at all times be kept well informed. On his part, he should see that the public relations committee knows of his actions, contacts, speeches, and the like.

Gathering the facts. One of the major duties of the public relations committee will be to set up a research or fact-finding program. This will include the determination of the "publics" within the congregation and within the community. This would include how each "public" might react to theological, sociological, or ethical interpretation.

Jim Suggs, in his chapter on "Organizing for Public Relations" in the *Handbook on Church Public Relations,* says that the public relations committee should know or be seeking the answers to such questions as these:

- What do people of the community think of our congregation: Do some segments of the population ("publics") have a better understanding of the church's purposes than others?
- Do members of the congregation think the church's program is balanced and has the right priorities? Do they have a clear understanding of the purposes of the church?
- Where do church members get their information about the plans and activities of the congregation?
- In the minds of various publics—within and outside the church—does the program of the church live up to what it says about itself, or to what it preaches to the world?

The public relations committee should have free access to information, and authority to have representation on all boards and committees that need assistance. It is often as important to know what not to say as to know what to say.

Finally, in organizing for an effective religion public relations program, a competent staff must be brought together. This is a problem both in national headquarters where for the most part budgets are inadequate, and at the local institution where volunteer help is the norm.

These are factors that should be taken into consideration:

- A book on how to recruit volunteer help should be read.
- Few things can be edited well by a committee.
- Establish guidelines, and then give your editor a free hand.
- Expect to pay for most of the services you use.
- Do not take advantage of the talents of your members from which they must make their living.
- Establish a system of cultivating members in the public relations field.
- Get rid of the incompetent volunteer, but don't make any enemy.

FINANCING THE PROGRAM

There's an old adage that says you have to spend money to make money. Public relations in the church will cost money, and should be budgeted. The public relations committee should project its budget in accordance with the budgetary practices of its religious institution. And without apology! Even in lean years!

Remember that in presenting your budget to the Joint Budget Committee you should use the best public relations techniques you know. It should go without saying that "overkill" is not a good technique. You may not get everything you asked for, but remember that you have informed a lot of key people about your program.

SETTING UP A COMMUNICATION CENTER

Timing is one of the most important elements in public relations. The techniques of public relations take space, equipment, storage, servicing, repair, books. Much of this material may seem expensive. However, if amortized over a number of years the cost can be shown to be reasonable.

A special office should be set up as the communication center with duplicating machines, addressing and folding equipment, postage meter, and the like. It should have locked closets for storing projection equipment and screens, easels, tape recorders, display equipment, turnover charts and portable blackboards, stereo phonographs, and perhaps even videotape equipment. There could also be many fonts of different size adhesive type for offset printing or posters as well as other graphic arts equipment. If you are lucky enough to have someone who is a hobbyist in silk screening, equipment for making attractive and inexpensive display posters will be desirable.

And, of course, the communication center should have a highly selective library including the directives and past minutes and history of your local church, yearbooks of the national church, the National and World Councils as well as the faith you represent, Bible dictionaries, commentaries and concordances, gazetteers, almanacs, and the like. Also selected photographs present and past—all well identified.

ORGANIZATIONS THAT CAN HELP

There is much assistance available for all groups interested in developing religious public relations. All the major faiths, including most Protestant denominations, have public relations and communication organizations. There are also specialized professional societies and associations whose publications can be excellent sources of assistance. Some of the major areas of assistance are listed here.

Professional Associations

The Religious Public Relations Council, Inc., Room 1031, 475 Riverside Dr., New York, N.Y. 10027. Marvin C. Wilbur, Executive Secretary. An interfaith, professional society with a membership of 600, located in 11 chapters across the country as well as members-at-large in 30 states. Publications include MEDIAKIT, a kit of ideas in communication designed to keep membership informed about what's going on in public relations, a quarterly newsletter, *Counselor,* a *Directory,* the *Religious Public Relations Handbook,* and the filmstrip "The Church at Jackrabbit Junction." Conducts annual convention and monthly chapter meetings, publishes biennial directory.

Associated Church Press, 1978 Union Ave., Memphis, Tenn. 38104. C. Ray Dobbins, President. An organization consisting of some 200 religious publications, fostering helpfulness among editors and publishers and higher standards of religious journalism. Conducts annual convention, prints biennial directory and quarterly trade publication.

World Association for Christian Communication, 7 St. James St., Byron House, London SW 1, England. Dr. Hans Florin, Executive Director. A voluntary organization of Christian communicators that gives aid to communication enterprises in many parts of the world. Membership is both personal and corporate.

Fellowship of Christians in the Arts, Media and Entertainment, P. O. Box 9323, Seattle, Wash. 98109. Phill Butler, Executive Secretary. A professional society of Christians in the arts, media, and entertainment from both the "secular" world and church-related organizations. Publishes a newsletter and plans to produce a directory of Christians in these fields.

Religion in American Life, Inc., 475 Fifth Avenue, New York, N.Y. 10017. David W. Gockley, Executive Vice President. RIAL is not a membership organization but a public relations resource for American churches and synagogues. It utilizes millions of dollars worth of free space and time in the mass media made available through the Advertising Council, including television, radio, newspapers, consumer magazines, business magazines, outdoor posters, transportation posters, and car cards. Materials available include newspaper advertisements, media kits, and resource guides.

National Association of Church Business Administrators, P. O. Box 7181, Kansas City, Mo. 64113. Floy Barnes, Executive Director. An international interfaith association with a membership of approximately 550 religious institutional administrators, meeting in 22 active local chapters and an annual National Conference. Publications include the *NACBA Ledger,* a tri-annual journal containing articles and reports in support of the profession; *NACBA-Gram,* a monthly report on activities within the association; annual *Conference Proceedings;* and an annual *Membership Directory.*

Interfaith Organizations

Catholic Press Association, with offices at 119 N. Park Ave., Rockville Center, N.Y. 11570, which publishes bi-monthly *The Catholic Journalist* and annually *The Catholic Press Directory* ($8.00). James A. Doyle, Executive Director.

American Jewish Public Relations Society, United Hias Service, 200 Park Avenue, S., New York, N.Y. 10003. Hyman Brickman, President.

Evangelical Press Association, P.O. Box 707, La Canada, Calif. 91011. Norman Rohrer, Executive Director.

Baptist Public Relations Association, 460 James Robertson Parkway, Nashville, Tenn. 37219. Wilmer C. Fields, Contact Person.

United Methodist Communications, 601 W. Riverview Ave., Dayton, Ohio 45406. Curtis A. Chambers, General Secretary.

Public Relations Department, General Conference of Seventh-day Adventists, 6840 Eastern Ave., N.W., Washington, D.C. 20012. W.R.L. Scragg, Director.

Communications Commission, National Council of Churches, Room 856, 475 Riverside Dr., New York, N.Y. 10027. William F. Fore, Assistant General Secretary for Communication. A co-operating agency of eighteen member denominations and groups who have come together to develop programs and policies of mutual value. Provides news and information services for the Council, including a quaterly publication, *Chronicles,* and the electronic Ecumedia News Service. Coordinates a specification sheet service describing all available broadcast programs from member groups. Works closely with all networks and distributes films from NBC's religious specials, CBS's "Look Up and Live" series, and ABC's

"Directions" series. Edits "Film Information," a monthly appraisal and review of all theater films ($7.00 yearly).

Broadcasting and Films

A number of organizations participate in the broadcasting and films areas including the following:

National Religious Broadcasters, Box 2254-R, Morristown, N.J. 07960. Benjamin Armstrong, Executive Director.

Association of Regional Religious Communicators, 1100 W. 42nd Street, Indianapolis, Ind. 46208. Rev. Fred Erickson, President.

Office for Films and Broadcasting, U. S. Catholic Conference, Suite 1300, 1011 First Avenue, New York, N.Y. 10022. Rev. Patrick J. Sullivan, S.J., Director.

Religious Periodicals

Every person handling public relations for his religious institution, be it local, state, national, or worldwide, should be familiar not only with his denominational or diocesan papers but also at least one or two interdenominational or interfaith periodicals. Some 175 of these periodicals are listed in the *Yearbook of American and Canadian Churches,* edited by Constant H. Jacquet, Jr. (Abingdon Press, 201 Eighth Avenue, S., Nashville, Tenn., 37202. Issued annually $10.95.)

The Catholic Press Directory lists 450 Catholic publications. (See Catholic Press Association listing earlier.)

Every public relations library should have these indispensable references with their up-to-date statistics and facts on America's major faiths, Protestant, Catholic, Greek Orthodox, and Jewish, and their related organizations.

If a more inclusive listing of religious periodicals is needed, it can be found in the *Ayer Directory of Publications,* Ayer Press, 210 W. Washington Square, Philadelphia, Pa. 19106.

Religion Editors of the Secular Media

One of the great allies of religion public relations and communication personnel is the interest of secular journalism, both print and broadcasting, in religion today. Few are the churches that could not get some story, or at least announcement, in the local press. Denominations and faith groups set up excellent professional press rooms to accommodate the religion journalists appointed to cover special assemblies and conventions. All of the major news services and dailies have religion editors or an assigned religion beat.

Religion writers of the major news services are:

> David Anderson, Religion Editor, United Press International, 315 National Press Building, Washington, D.C. 20004.
> George W. Cornell, Religion Writer, Associated Press, Rockefeller Plaza, New York, N.Y. 10020.

Religion editors of the secular press are organized as the Religion Newswriters Association, and have as their objectives "to advance the standards of religious journalism in the secular press." They hold an annual convention and publish a *News Letter.* (Editorial address: Lester F. Heins, Apt. 1408B, 19 S. First Street, Minneapolis, Minn. 55401.) Many of the religion editors today are theologically trained as well as being journalists. A few of these editors of the daily press are:

> Kenneth Briggs, Religion Editor, *The New York Times,* 229 W. 43rd Street, New York, N.Y. 10036.
> Richard Ostling, *Time,* Time and Life Building, Rockefeller Center, New York, N.Y. 10020.
> Marjorie Hyer, Religion Reporter, *Washington Post,* Washington, D.C. 20005.
> Ben L. Kaufman, Religion Editor, *The Cincinnati Enquirer,* Cincinnati, Ohio 45201.
> Susan Cowley, *Newsweek,* 444 Madison Avenue, New York, N.Y. 10022.
> Roy Larson, Religion Writer, *Chicago Sun-Times,* 401 N. Wabash Ave., Chicago, Ill. 60611.
> Willmar L. Thorkelson, Religion Editor, *Minneapolis Star,* 425 Portland Ave., Minneapolis, Minn. 55415.
> John Dart and Russell Chandler, Religion Editors, *The Los Angeles Times,* First and Spring Streets, Los Angeles, Calif. 90035.

One of the most comprehensive sources (and outlets) of religious copy and photos is Religious News Service, 43 W. 57th Street, New York, N.Y. 10019, Lillian Block, managing editor and director. RNS is an independently managed organization within the National Conference of Christians and Jews.

The major supplier of news to Catholic publications is the NC News Service, 1312 Massachusetts Avenue, N.W., Washington, D.C. 20005.

A number of radio and/or television stations as well as all major networks have religion editors. These include:

> Doris Ann, Manager, Religious Programs, NBC News, National Broadcasting Company, 30 Rockefeller Plaza, New York, N.Y. 10020.
>
> Pamela Ilott, Vice President for Cultural and Religious Programs, CBS News, CBS, Inc., 524 W. 57th Street, New York, N.Y. 10019.
>
> Sid Darion, Manager, Cultural Affairs, ABC News, 1926 Broadway, New York, N.Y. 10019.
>
> Brian Bastien, Group W Religion Editor, 6419 Hollywood Boulevard, Los Angeles, Calif. 90028.

A publication of value to all religion communicators who work in the broadcast media is "If You Want Air Time," a handbook for publicity chairmen, prepared by the Public Relations Service of the National Association of Broadcasters, 1771 N St., N.W., Washington, D.C. 20036.

A complete and detailed listing of all religion editors (they have assorted titles) for newspapers, magazines, wire services, radio, and television appears in the five companion volumes of *The Working Press of the Nation,* published by The National Research Bureau, Inc., 424 N. Third Street, Burlington, Iowa 52601.

The Editor & Publisher International Yearbook, 850 Third Ave., New York, N.Y. 10022 lists religion editors among staff people of daily newspapers in the U.S. and Canada. Its annual Syndicate Directory lists the religion columns of press services and syndicates.

26

Public Relations for Educational Institutions

MICHAEL RADOCK is vice president for university relations and development and professor of journalism at The University of Michigan. A past president of the American College Public Relations Association, he has had a career combining the academic, business, and professional fields in journalism and public relations.

Radock was on the faculties of four institutions, one private and three public, and rose from instructor to professor of journalism. He has had broad experience in newspaper work and radio and television news. He was chairman of the campaign steering committee for Michigan's three-year $55 Million Capital Fund program that raised $72.8 million, the largest amount ever raised by a public university in a capital campaign.

Before joining Michigan in 1961, Radock was a member of the Ford Motor Company public relations staff for nine years. He was manager of educational affairs, with responsibility for company-wide educational relations activities. He also served as manager of the public relations department and of the graphic and information services department.

He is a graduate of Westminster College and the Medill School of Journalism at Northwestern University and did post-graduate study at Western Reserve University. An accredited member of the Public Relations Society of America, he has served on national advisory groups for the United States Information Agency, The Urban Coalition, National Science Foundation, the Office for the Advancement of Public Negro Colleges, and the Interlochen Center for the Arts. He is a White House appointee to the Board of Foreign Scholarships, which supervises the Fulbright Scholarship Program and educational exchange under the Mutual Educational and Cultural Exchange Act for the U.S. State Department.

Several major trends have made a significant impact on the role of the public relations officer of the American college and university. In the past few years the public relations officer has literally moved from the boiler room to the board room. The scope of his responsibilities in the management area has broadened considerably, both internally and externally. The stature of the major national professional organization in the field has increased substantially with the merger in 1974 of the American College Public Relations Association and the American Alumni Council into the Council for Advancement and Support of Education (One Dupont Circle, Washington, D.C. 20036). Some 2,000 colleges, universities, two-year colleges, and independent schools, represented by more than 7,500 individuals, are members of CASE.

Recent developments in higher education have caused great pressures on our schools and colleges and have brought significant changes in both the character and structure of education in America.

Declining enrollments, after a period of spectacular growth and expansion, have been the source of major concern. Continuing financial crises have raised the question of survival for many marginal institutions. The increasing involvement of the federal government in higher education through government-mandated programs has troubled members of governing boards, educational administrators, and faculty. The impact of inflation has severely limited the college or university's freedom to operate. Other problems have arisen in the inability of many graduates to find appropriate employment. Tensions have developed as a result of internal competition for scarce funds.

Changing attitudes. The president of the University of California, David S. Saxon, examining the future of public universities, contrasts the change in public attitudes:

"Scarcely over a decade ago, higher education was surrounded by an aura of confidence, esteem, and optimism. Today that aura has changed to one of foreboding and worry, and not without reason. We have heard earlier some of the hard demographic facts about future growth. And we are all aware of other similarly unpleasant and threatening facts—financial deficits, Ph.D. gluts, cutbacks for basic research, and more. The concerns being generated by these developments are giving rise to some symptomatic questions: Are universities worth saving? Do they have a future?"

"The truth," Dr. Saxon adds, "is that universities are both tough and delicate institutions. They are sensitive to changes taking place within and around them, easily damaged in important ways, but also surprisingly tenacious and resilient in the long run. In this they are like humanity itself. And, like humanity, universities *will* survive. They do have a future."

The former education editor of *The New York Times,* Fred Hechinger, observes: "America is in headlong retreat from its commitment to education."

A leading American intellectual, Prof. Kenneth E. Boulding of the University of Colorado, predicts "the management of decline."

He adds: "The greatest problem which is facing the whole education system in the next twenty years is the high probability of declining enrollments. This decline has already hit the grade schools; it will move into the high schools very shortly and into the colleges in the 1980s. We are ill-equipped, however, for the management of decline... The implications of all this for education, and especially for higher education, is profound. Education is likely to be the first major segment of the economy to suffer a relative decline, and management of decline may very well set the tone for the management of general slowdown."

The president of the American Council on Education, Roger W. Heyns, noting such tensions, observed:

"Universities have emerged from obscurity to prominence in the last 20 years. Now the members of the academic community are involved with the society in many ways. The tensions of the society find expression in the behavior of campus communities and in the reaction of the society to that behavior. It is a matter of the greatest moment, not that we cease being sources of discomfort, but that we be uncomfortable for the proper reasons—those that derive naturally from our educational tasks and not those that arise from other characteristics—among them our inability to solve our problems in an orderly way."

Formula for survival. Recognizing the widespread anxiety over survival of colleges and universities, the Carnegie Foundation for the Advancement of Teaching has listed various ingredients for survival:

- Attract all ages rather than only 18 to 21
- Provide for part-time students
- Have public state support
- Be of an effective size
- Be located in an urban area
- Be an older institution
- Have comparatively low tuition
- Have a national reputation
- Have a stabilized undergraduate enrollment
- Be related to the health professions

The biggest problem in American higher education—as well as in society at large—is learning to accommodate to change.

Editorially, the *Public Relations Journal* noted:

"No sector of American society has enjoyed a more sheltered position than higher education. Up to the present, it has been taken for granted by the public as a somewhat esoteric business that is nevertheless good and necessary. An Ivy Curtain has shielded the campus, and few have moved to penetrate it." But, it added, "the higher education industry is in for major public relations troubles."

Forces for change. Dr. Donald N. Frey, chairman and chief operating officer of Bell & Howell Company, sees forces for change as market changes that will drastically affect higher education. He notes that growth in enrollment of traditional students is down and therefore the demand for teachers also is down. He also observes that "people are getting off the educational treadmill that carries them non-stop from kindergarten through college." Other factors he cites are rising educational costs, the reduced job market for graduates, a seeming lack of interest in hiring liberal arts graduates, and a probable drop in the perceived value of traditional education.

In 1966 a national poll on confidence in higher education showed that 60 per cent of the American people expressed a great deal of confidence in higher education; in 1972 the figure dropped to 33 percent. On many fronts institutions of higher learning are devoting attention to improving the emotional and social health of the world, and while a wide array of college and university efforts are "relevant" the public is often unaware of potential impact of the efforts.

Because the structure of higher education is changing, as well as the status and role of both students and faculty members, the problems of managing university communities approach and, in some instances, surpass those of managing cities and corporations. These are different organisms with peculiar traditions.

From education comes the manpower, the ideas, the basic research, the innovation, the necessary heresies for a dynamic society. All of this spells change. Almost by definition, change is unsettling, whether it is a new way of doing things, a new way of thinking, or a new demand on resources.

How to explain change. Fundamentally, the assignment of the educational public relations man is to explain change occurring in and coming from the college or university.

Gone is Joe College. Gone is dear old prexy. Gone is the good old absent-minded professor. Gone are the unquestioning alumni. Gone are the indifferent and apathetic students. Gone is the ivory tower. Gone is *in loco parentis*. Gone are the sharp distinctions between the public and the private institutions, the church-related and the secular institutions, the men's and women's colleges.

Look at the growth of enrollment in higher education in America (degree-credit enrollment):

1950—2 million
1960—3½ million
1965—6 million
1970—7.9 million
1975—9.7 million
1980—11.1 million (projected)

Consider another factor—the proportion of college students attending public and private institutions. Traditionally, in the period between 1910 and 1950, the division was about 50/50, public and private. The new trend started about 1952. In 1955 about 56 per cent of college students attended public institutions. This figure rose to 59 per cent in 1960; then up to 67 per cent in 1965. In 1970 about 73 per cent attended public institutions. By 1975 the students at public colleges and universities reached 76 per cent, with a projected increase to more than 78 per cent by 1980. Higher education, it seems, is becoming a public endeavor in the main.

Another change is the emergence of new types of institutions, including the community and junior college and the regional university. The phenomenal success of the junior college movement is seen in the growth from 500 community colleges in 1950 to 1,230 in 1975. Likewise, enrollment growth has been from a mere 250,000 in 1950 to 4,500,000 in 1975.

Identity crisis. While the community and junior colleges appear to have survived a growth period and found their identity, this is not true for the regional universities, including many former state teachers colleges and state colleges. These rapidly developing institutions are now suffering an acute identity crisis, seeking to find their proper niche in the educational spectrum.

Meanwhile, the nation has seen the virtual disappearance of the municipally supported senior institution and the spectacular growth of the large public university, the so-called multiversity or comprehensive university.

Accompanying the growth in numbers of the past two decades has been a trend toward greater coordination and centralized control of public institutions by state boards, super-boards, and similar agencies, and a greater emphasis on planning functions. Meanwhile, private colleges have moved to join in consortia, regional groups, or "cluster college" arrangements.

The nature of a university. A major responsibility of the public relations officer is to convey to the public or publics the nature of the institution so it is not undermined because of ignorance, so it is supported because of understanding. A university, to continue to meet its responsibilities for education, research, and service must have resources and freedom.

The public relations departments must try to help educate the public to understand, to appreciate, to tolerate, and to defend the vital necessity of freedom for the student to learn and for the scholar to search for the truth without restriction.

The public must be adequately informed of the true function of a university so it will learn to cherish free inquiry and reckon with pressures, particularly in times of hysteria and tension.

In the public spotlight. It is the business of the public relations counselor to be aware of the vulnerability and the opportunity of the university in the circumstances of the time. More public attention is being focused on education for a number of reasons, among them the age composition of the nation's population, the large percentage of youth seeking college and graduate education, and the consequent demands of education on financial resources.

What is happening in and about and because of, or lack of, education is now more important to more people, whether the issue is activism, admission standards, efficiency, financial needs, inter-institutional cooperation, teaching and/vs. research, and the many tangential responsibilities of higher education.

At the policy level. The public relations officer plays a policy-making role. How large a role depends not so much on his clearly defined responsibilities as on his colleagues' appreciation of public relations and their willingness to seek and consider professional counsel.

The basic function of public relations as a part of university administration is to help the school's people do their job and to make sure the climate is as conducive as possible for them.

THE CHANGING WORLD OF UNIVERSITY RELATIONS

Recent studies of public relations programs and activities in American colleges and universities provide substantial evidence of the acceptance of the public relations professional as an integral member of the educational management team in many institutions.

However, the academic community still harbors a deep suspicion of "public relations" and relates it to "press agentry" or "propaganda."

"Why should we spend so much money for public relations?" asks the economy-minded administrator.

"Is this an activity that belongs in an educational institution?" asks a faculty member.

"Could not the dollars spent on public relations be used more effectively for faculty salaries and laboratory and other instructional needs? Who needs public relations?" These and other pointed questions trouble college presidents and administrators.

Because of this climate of distrust and suspicion in the academic environment, and because the results of public relations expenditures most often are intangible, the college public relations department is a target for investigations, audits, and criticism.

Changing faculty attitudes. A Chancellor of a large eastern university explained to a national conference of educational public relations officers the reasons for academia's "instinctive reaction" against public relations:

". . . the atmosphere of public relations is uncongenial to the typical academic person, and for some very fundamental reasons: In the first place, academic people are accustomed to having people come to them, not going to people. The student comes to us, the problem comes to us. Ours is not an outgoing kind of reaction to take the product, to take the story, to take the service to the people, to the public. In this sense public relations people are almost diametrically opposed to us, and we're inclined to be analysts and inclined to be concerned about detail. You're concerned about broad impacts. You see things in general terms, as you should; we tend to see them in highly particularistic terms, as indeed we should. Again, we look on things—every problem, every subject—with reservation; you look at it with enthusiasm and from a positive point of view. So once again in discharging your function in a positive sort of way, it's almost inevitable that the academic people feel a little uncomfortable.

"Again, we're not comfortable with the media of public relations. The press conference is not in our blood. It's something that the typical academic person shies away from. Promotional literature seems a little unscholarly, and the biographical sketch in a national magazine suggests something less than appropriate academic humility."[1]

Semantic problems. As a result of these circumstances and attitudes, functions broadly categorized under the vaguely suspect term "public relations," being as necessary in schools and colleges as in business and industry, must be performed under a more acceptable name. Hence, "university relations" has tended to become the academic facade for public relations at many institutions, including The University of Michigan, which as early as 1931 created the position of vice president for university relations.

Other semantic variations include "public affairs," "information services," "planning and

---

[1] Edward H. Litchfield, Chancellor, University of Pittsburgh, American College Public Relations Association National Conference, Cincinnati, Ohio, July, 1965.

development," "community relations," "assistant to the president," "news and publications services," "public information," and similar labels.

The Greenbrier Report. The most significant development in the recognition of public relations took place through the efforts of a study committee of the American College Public Relations Association and the American Alumni Council. These efforts resulted in a conference on organizational principles and patterns of college and university relations at The Greenbrier in White Sulphur Springs, W. Va., in 1958. The major recommendation was a unified organizational approach with a major coordinating officer, reporting directly to the college or university president, responsible for the direction of public relations, alumni relations, and fund-raising.

The practice of effective public relations in colleges and universities, participants in the Greenbrier meetings agreed, required certain basic conditions:

1. A clear statement of institutional purposes.
2. A "sound product."
3. An adequate budget.
4. Adequate personnel.

For educational public relations, the Greenbrier study set forth these basic conclusions that are applicable to a wide variety of institutions:

1. The administrative functions of public relations, alumni relations, and fund-raising exist on each college campus.
2. Each of these major functions is an essential part of a broadly conceived program of institutional advancement.
3. There must be organizational and administrative coordination of these and other related functions in order to serve the institution's best interests.
4. No single "ideal" organizational pattern can achieve the necessary coordination.
5. Each institution should determine the most effective organizational structure to serve its special needs and characteristics.

Commitment and cooperation. The key administrators should be fundamentally agreed on the purposes of a program of internal public relations. And they ought to be realistic about expectations. They should understand what is involved in terms of allocation of financial and personnel resources and be willing to make the commitment over an extended period. To agreement on purposes and realism about possible accomplishments and com-

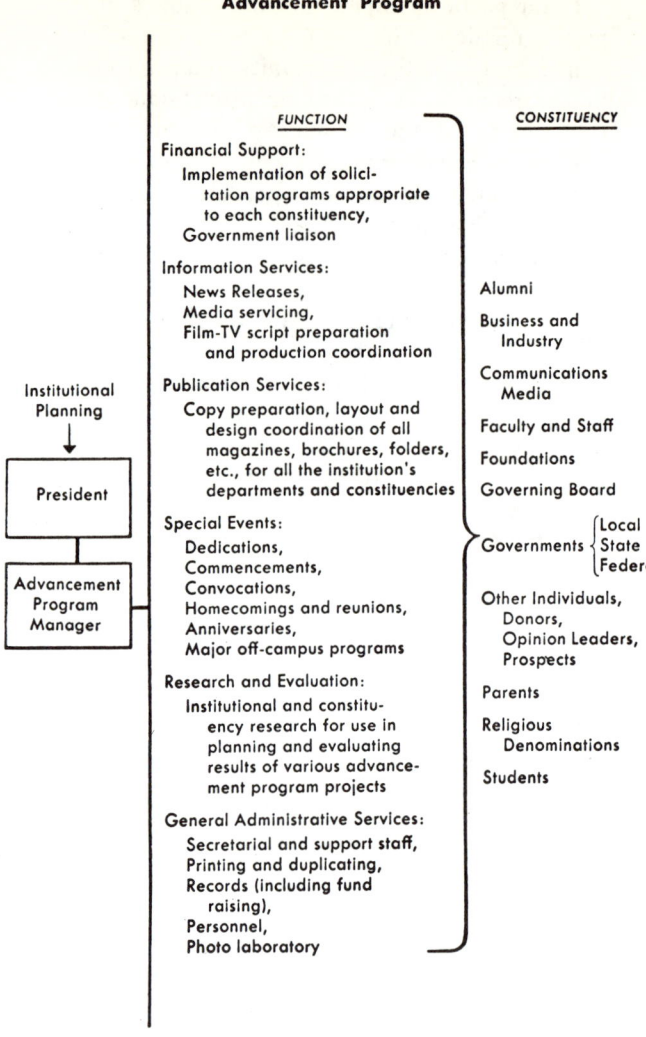

Figure 26-1. Outline of a typical "Advancement Program" for an educational institution.

mitment of resources another ingredient must be added: cooperation. While the public relations unit may have the job of carrying out the program, the public relations department cannot do it without the continuing cooperation of key administrators. This should be clear before you embark on a program.

Basic organizational structures. A basic principle is that no single organizational structure or pattern applies equally well at all colleges or universities.

A definitive study published in 1969 by the ACPRA showed that certain patterns of organizational structure were best suited to private colleges and universities, and a variation of those structures for public universities.

In this study the term "advancement program" is

used to designate the total program devoted to information services, alumni relations, publications, and fund-raising.

Two basic patterns are suggested. A common structure in a state university has a central coordinating officer, usually a vice president reporting directly to the president. In some institutions the chief coordinating officer is a director or assistant to the president.

For smaller institutions a common pattern is to have three major functions reporting directly to the president. A frequent variation has two major officers, one for public relations and one for fund-raising, reporting directly to the head of the institution.

Inventory of resources. The standard public relations process of fact-gathering, planning, communication, and evaluation are as essential in educational institutions as in any other area or activity.

A number of the larger institutions have created an Office of Institutional Advancement, combining the functions of public relations and development or fund-raising. Typically, the umbrella concept is used to refer to public relations (including information services, publications, community relations, and governmental relations), alumni relations and programs, fund-raising, student recruitment, federal relations, university press, and printing activities.

One of the leading proponents of the institutional advancement concept, Dr. A. Westley Rowland, vice president for university relations at the State University of New York at Buffalo, stresses the importance of establishing goals for the advancement program:

"Goals are important because they set directions; they provide a target toward which institutional relations efforts and resources will be directed; they indicate priorities; and they give a real sense of what the institutional relations program is all about, where the program is going, and what, through institutional relations, the college or university wishes to achieve. Thus goals become important operationally because they determine the level of budget needed, the number and type of staff, and the nature of program and activities."

Broadened responsibilities. The principal public affairs responsibility of the central administration office of the 64-campus State University of New York rests with the Office of the Vice Chancellor for University Affairs. The term as used in the SUNY System is defined as covering "the service functions of communicating and relating with the internal and external constituencies of the University for their understanding of what the University is, what it's becoming; more specifically, for example, what educational opportunities it offers and will offer, how it views its progress at the moment and for the next decade." The vice chancellor is given the responsibility "to ensure that every citizen, as a kind of stockholder in this multi-billion dollar enterprise, is kept fully aware of the University's performance for the purpose of making intelligent judgments, not only as to participation but also to provision of more or less support."

The following activities are assigned to the Office: Communication, Development, Alumni Affairs, Community Relations, Liaison with the Association of Council Members and College Trustees, and Special Events.

A basic step in any in-depth analysis of the potential for a public relations program is a careful inventory or audit of resources. Here are some of the questions that the public relations director and associates should try to answer:

1. What are the characteristics of your institution? Multiversity? Church-related college? Community college: Urban? Small-Town? Activist and liberal? Passive and conservative?
2. What does the administration or governing board believe are your purposes and responsibilities? Are they the same responsibilities you believe you have accepted?
3. What kind of public relations department do you have? Is it basically a news and information service or a comprehensive, multi-faceted operation? Are fund-raising considerations more important than student and faculty support?
4. What are the basic operating policies and guidelines that serve as constraints in your daily operation? Must the president, dean, or some other official approve every statement that is issued? At what level of policy-making in management do you exist?
5. How is the institution or the department organized?
6. What is the total environment in which you live and work? Reference to environment means it must be described totally: politically, socially, economically, physically, and geographically. Study of these factors helps the public relations officer recognize that the climate in which the institution exists may be favorable, neutral, unfavorable, or downright hostile.

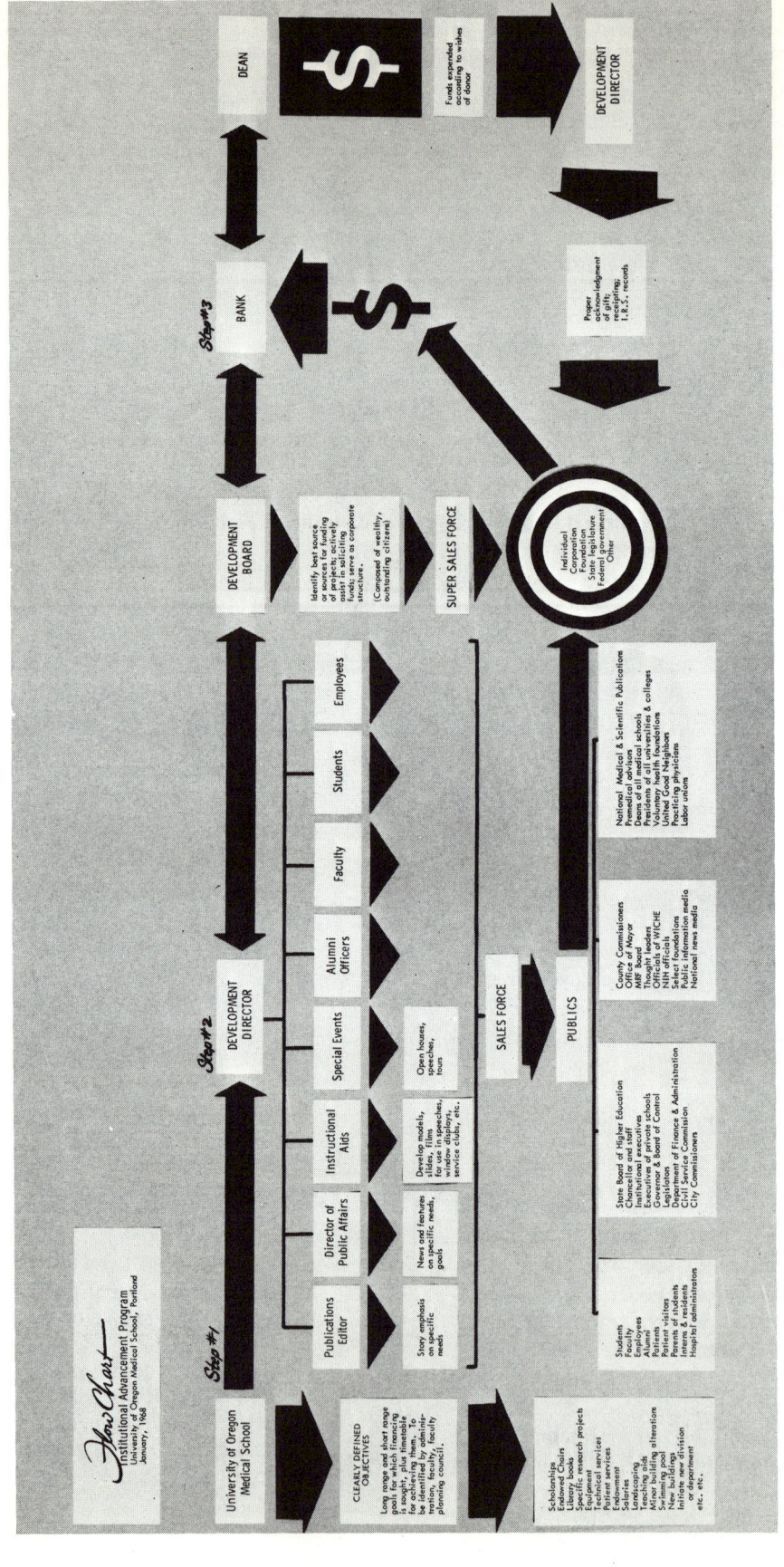

Figure 26-2. Full organization and workflow chart of the development program of the University of Oregon Medical School.

PUBLIC RELATIONS FOR EDUCATIONAL INSTITUTIONS

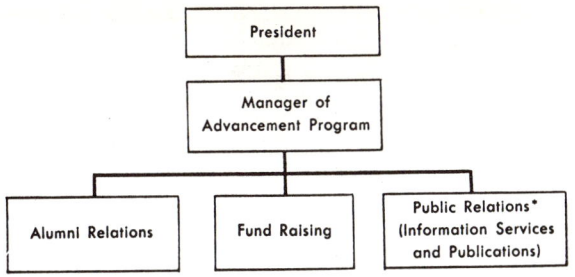

Figure 26-3. Organization structure for a large institution.

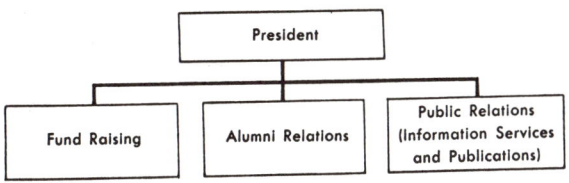

Figure 26-4. Organization for a smaller institution.

(Figures 26-3 and 26-4 reprinted from *Focus on Understanding and Support: A Study in College Management*, by John W. Leslie, American College Public Relations Association, Washington, D.C., 1969.)

7. What are the strengths and weaknesses of the department and the institution? Is the public relations department under-staffed and under-budgeted? Is it strong in the print media and not in the electronic media? Is there any know-how in community relations, or special events, or communication? Does the public relations staff spend all its time on external publics and ignore the faculty, students, and staff?

8. Is the public relations department adapting itself to the changing nature of the institution and the demands of its constituencies? Are there periodic evaluations of its practices and policies?

QUALIFICATIONS FOR THE HIGHER EDUCATION PUBLIC RELATIONS MAN

Professor or professional—which is most important? Both the colleague relationship with the faculty and the talent and skills for the public relations function are desirable, of course. And particular institutional circumstances make a general rule inappropriate. But if a choice must be made, most colleges choose the professional. Professional trappings do not protect from establishment coloration the teacher who "reluctantly" takes on the administrative task— even if the reluctance is sincere. It is better to have a dedicated professional than a disjointed professor.

What kind of professional? Is he a journalism man by education and/or experience? Is he an administrator? What about industry and association public relations background? How useful is government background—either administrative or legislative? How important is an understanding of fund-raising? What priority goes to knowledge of alumni relations and acquaintance with the particular institution, region, or state? Is he a graduate or non-graduate of the particular institution? These and other considerations need to be weighed against the specific institution's requirements.

THE INTERNAL PUBLICS

By design or by accident, a good share of the job of relating with the internal publics of an educational institution may fall to the public relations unit.

Beyond the fact of skill availability, there is another good reason for linking organizationally internal and external public relations: one affects the other. Attitudes inside affect actions outside. High morale and enthusiasm developed within an organization radiate beyond the organization. In the same way, low morale and dissatisfaction seep to the outside.

Complex communication. Internal communication in an institution of higher education is more complicated than it may appear to the outsider. The reasons are that: (1) the university is not a homogeneous unit, and (2) the university is unlike any other organization.

While it may appear to the outsider (and even a few narrow-visioned insiders) that a college or a university is composed of students and faculty and a few clerks, and that they are similar human types held together by old school ties, that is at best old mythology. Even assuming a similarity between a nuclear physicist and a classical scholar, the clerks and assorted other non-academic types outnumber the teachers on most campuses. Furthermore, ranging from architect to salad girl on the cafeteria line, they may have less in common than the physical scientist and classicist of the faculty. The modern institution of higher education is composed of a great variety of people—more different types, ranging further to the extremes, probably, than any other organization of comparable size. This complicates the communication job.

Another complication is the nature of the organization—its peculiar structure, relationships, and traditions. A college or university has some attributes of, but is different from a civil government, a corporation, an army, a church, and an anarchy. For example, faculty members are not employees; bright students are not orderly soldiers; academic freedom is essential, but so is legislative appropriation and/or private contribution; profit-making is not a purpose, but business methods are necessary; institutional loyalty is traditional, but the society is mobile and the educational institution is geographically constrained; stability is expected, but so are social and scientific innovation; a college can be at once a citadel of conservatism and a provenance of radicalism.

Channels of communication. You may be able to influence such formal means of internal communication as staff meetings. You may be able to influence such informal communication channels as conversational exchanges between people about their work situations. You may be able to work with existing faculty or student publications. But your control is marginal at best.

Expectations of accomplishment and the general plan for internal public relations must take into consideration what already exists. In some cases you can work with existing channels of communication, providing material and recommendations. Sometimes you may have to work around the existing channels. And occasionally you may find it necessary to run counter to existing channels. Also to be considered are public news media that reach your internal publics.

Before you develop a plan, determine what you want to accomplish. There are many examples of internal communication programs—some quite elaborate and costly—that have no specific objectives.

Establishing a program of internal communication because it's the thing to do, or because some advisory committee has decried the inadequacy of internal communication, or because the union organizer is signing up members, is not likely to result in a successful effort. There must be objectives and then a plan for reaching them.

Internal communications program. Some purposes for a program of internal communication—not an inclusive list and not necessarily applicable to all institutions—include:

1. Communication of work-related information.
2. Development of morale.
3. Enlistment of support for and participation in specific institutional objectives.
4. Counter-communication.

Under No. 1 may be included things so functional as a faculty and staff directory, or course time and class schedules, or a new employee handbook, or wage and salary regulations, or promotion of safety and efficiency on the job, or the availability of new services, and so on.

No. 2 encompasses a broad area. You may want to promote insitutional pride or unit loyalty, perhaps competition. You may wish to encourage a "family" spirit. Perhaps you want to develop the status of and trust in "management," to use an industrial relations term; at the university level it may be a new president or dean or members of the governing board. You may want to promote satisfaction with employment conditions and/or compensation. Simply providing information about "what's going on" so staff members feel more intimately a part of the institution or unit may be a significant contribution to morale. A formal opportunity for feedback or for two-way communication also may be important for morale purposes.

No. 3, in some respects, overlaps the purpose of development of staff morale. If you have good morale it is much easier to enlist support for and participation in specific institutional objectives; and such involvement itself promotes morale. Examples are alumni relations, fund-raising campaigns, community relations, legislative "lobbying." Faculty and staff support might be enlisted in a broad public relations campaign to publicize the institution's cultural contribution or its economic value or its research impact or its academic status or its faculty prestige. The goal could be as direct as high participation in the community chest.

Communications in crises. No. 4, counter-communication, is by all measures the most delicate and difficult and often the reason that a formal program of internal public relations is initiated. Some problem becomes so pointed, some situation becomes so uncomfortable, some crisis appears so imminent, that a program of internal communication seems the answer—or at least, part of the answer.

A formal program of internal public relations, born of crisis, is not likely to suddenly set things right. Crisis communication is most effective as a part of a larger and well-established and credible program of internal public relations. This is treated more fully later in this chapter.

How to combat rumors. Rumor mills operating on

or off campus may include a hostile union or business or political group, an unfriendly newspaper or broadcast station, an irresponsible student publication, or an "underground" periodical.

Counter-communication is most delicate and difficult, because you are in a defensive, reactive posture and because you run the risk of sounding like a cry baby or a white-washer. You are in some danger of being forced into an unwise response because of internal pressures to answer some aspersion. On balance, though, the danger of being pushed into a response is less likely than the danger of missing an opportunity to correct or clarify because of executive reluctance and delay.

Counter-communication, by its very nature, places you in opposition. You may find yourself in opposition to an organization or group of considerable credibility. Your counter-communication, if it is to be effective, also must have credibility. This credibility must be earned, and earned over a period of time.

Education's internal publics. In developing the plan for a program of internal public relations, the internal publics generally may be categorized as faculty, staff, and students.

It is true that diversity exists within these three categories, and these interests ought to be served. But for a formal program of internal public relations some major groupings must be assumed. The problem is not usually too-precise categorization but over-generalization—assuming too much community of interest, trying to make one approach broad enough to reach all the audience. Except for very simple, unsophisticated communication—say, bulletin board posters about the blood bank—the all-encompassing approach is not likely to be very effective.

Matching the audience and the message. For more sophisticated messages you need to use styles and methods designed for the audience. A faculty newsletter, if it is effective and useful to the faculty, is not likely to serve the purpose of communication with the maintenance crew. Information about hourly rates and overtime pay, although of considerable interest to some members of the work force, will not be of much concern to faculty except as supervisors of hourly rated personnel. And those with supervisory responsibilities should be receiving communications from the personnel office. These, too, you may be designing and writing, but they are specialized for special purposes.

An argument may be made for trying to design one communication program for teaching faculty and non-teaching personnel. Of course the financial outlay tends to be smaller. But the major tenet of the argument is that a single approach tends to unify the work force. Conversely, separate programs set up class distinctions. This is a danger. But with as broad a spectrum as the university paid staff represents, it seems better to design separate programs if your purposes are more than communication of the most elementary messages.

You may find that an even more fragmented approach is useful. A highly autonomous unit of the institution, with its own distinct working conditions, may be most effectively served by a separate communications program that augments the larger design. You also may find that a concentrated effort to communicate a particular message to a segment of the work force cannot be carried out effectively through the more general communication vehicles. Again, a supplementary program may be needed, although perhaps only temporarily.

Employee communication, in the industrial sense, has become a part of the internal public relations program at some institutions. Chances are this will occur in more and more institutions as unionization of public employees spreads and as these organizations adopt industrial union patterns.

Blue collar personnel are usually the most likely prospects for unionization. Teaching fellows may organize on some campuses. Those institutions with large research complexes separate from the instructional program of the university may see attempts to organize the technical personnel. Office workers also are targets for unionization. University faculty may be the least likely to join a union.

It is not anti-union to say that if the institution is treating its staff fairly and as adequately as resources will permit, a labor union is unnecessary. But the facts must be communicated so an informed judgment may be made about whether unionization would be useful or unnecessary.

The cloistered academic institution is no longer protected from the rigors of what amounts to labor-management relations.[2] Those charged with internal public relations must be prepared to serve the institution in this realm of communication.

COMMUNICATION WITH STUDENTS

Students have interests in common with other members of the university community. But students, as a body, also have needs and concerns that require a communication program designed

[2]See Chapter 16.

Internal Communications at The University of Michigan

Objective	Vehicle	Audience	Frequency	Quantity
Communicate items of faculty interest, problems of faculty concern, inform campus community of forthcoming, significant events on campus.	University Record	All academic, some related non-academic	Weekly, Sept. through April; bi-weekly, May through August	23,000
Inform non-academic staff of University activities, programs; and to correlate individual staff members' welfare with institutional welfare of the University.	UM News	All non-academic staff	Monthly	13,500
Immediate communication of facts and background relating to a crisis situation.	Report to the University Community	Faculty, academic and non-academic staff, students, community	As needed	8,100 to 23,000
Immediate communication of facts, highlights, campus developments.	News Briefs phone lines (audiotape)	Campus community (Available for radio taping and general public call-in)	Twice daily or more often as needed	(does not apply)
Inform academic community of current issues in collective bargaining between the University and employee unions.	At The Table	Academic, non-academic staff and management	Bi-weekly during negotiations and as needed	5,000 to 7,500
To inform managers of University policies and procedures, serve as personnel teaching and training aid.	Management Intercom	Supervisory staff and management	Monthly and as needed	3,500

---

specifically for them. Students are the members of the university community most easily categorized; they are transitory, of a relatively limited age span, and so on.

A recent development in higher education has been widespread student participation in decision-making and policy matters. Schools and colleges have made special efforts to open new channels of communication between students, faculty, and administrators and to enable students, particularly, to participate in and contribute to institutional governance.

Students have been named to governing boards, university-wide administrative councils, faculty senates, and standing committees on curriculum, course evaluation, tenure and promotion, planning, discipline, student affairs, and other areas. Some institutions have given students full voting privileges similar to faculty members' and administrators'.

Communication and consultation with students have been greatly increased through additional devices such as student advisory committees for administrative officers, student membership on presidential-selection committees, president's or regents' "Round Table" groups, alumni boards, special study commissions, and other consultative agencies.

Both students and faculty members have been selected to serve as college or university "ombudsman," a new official position as "people's man," adapted from a similar public watchdog idea common in Sweden. The campus ombudsman receives and investigates complaints and grievances against acts of university officials and faculty and staff members.

Under pressure from students who sought a more responsible role in decisions affecting their lives, many colleges and universities have opened meetings of faculty and administrative groups and governing boards to the public, and encouraged student participation and dialogue.

Communications devices. The devices and techniques of internal public relations are standard but are enhanced with imagination. The important aspect is judgment in when and how to use them in the environment and with the special as well as more common internal publics.

The most familiar devices probably are the printed media: newspapers, newsletters, magazines, pamphlets, annuals, annual reports, financial reports, pocket guides, speech reprints, brochures, news releases, special publications, and mass-produced letters and memoranda.

Printed material is more than a published record of what one needs to say. Any printed item reflects the competence, professionalism, and stature of the institutional unit that produces it.

What to publish. Any publication should be planned on the basis of answers to four questions:

1. What is the audience for the publication?
2. What do you wish to tell that audience; i.e., what purpose will the publication serve?
3. What action do you wish that audience to take after having read the publication?
4. When must the publication be ready for distribution?

Planning a publication around the answers to these questions will insure that it achieves an impact and effect that justifies the cost in time and money.

Importance of design. The design of a publication is the first thing that strikes the reader. Well-designed booklets invite readership and predispose your audience to attend to your message. A professional designer develops his design in terms of the audience, content, planned distribution methods, and tone of the publication. The subsequent layout then provides a blueprint that enables all parties—author, editor, designer, and printer—to visualize the finished publication.

One device among the printed media that is not unique, but that can be used in different ways, is the clipping collection. If you are trying to show internally what great productivity is achieved by the public relations department externally, the clipping collection will be of all the stories published in all the papers that make your place look good. A more useful service is to collect also items that are critical of the institution—columns and editorial content in particular. Or you may want to clip, reproduce, and distribute articles of concern and interest to the people of your institution, regardless of specific mention of the institution. These methods may be combined.

Other familiar devices include posters, displays, exhibits, buttons, and bumper stickers.

Exploiting the ordinary. Another broad category includes variations of the conference and mass meeting, oral annual reports, welcomes and commencements, open houses, and so on. The important thing to remember here, beyond the needs for content and staging, is full exploitation. For instance, a president's annual address to the faculty on the state of the university ought to be a position paper for quotation and extrapolation the rest of the year. It should be exploited immediately for news release and broadcast, taped for delayed broadcast in full, published in some campus organ, perhaps reprinted in pamphlet form.

NEW TECHNIQUES FOR EDUCATION

An area not quite so familiar in educational as in industrial circles is formalized upward communication. With increased size and complexity, educational institutions are experiencing some of the same problems of business and industry.

The suggestion box may even be appropriate in some parts of the institution. A variation is the advisory committee. Another is a letters column in an internal publication. Fairly closely related is the ombudsman, who provides an outlet for frustrations. The suggestion survey is another device. You must be careful when you solicit suggestions or advice or complaints or attitudes that you make some response—the more promptly the better. If you conduct a survey, do not fail to let those surveyed know the results and what action is intended.

Audio-visuals. The use of audio-visual devices for internal communication depends somewhat on what facilities are available. Where the university dominates the community and is heavily covered in the local news media, the community broadcasting facilities become outlets for internal as well as external public relations. Some institutions have their own radio-TV facilities; some also have student-run campus stations.

Slides and motion pictures can be used effectively for student and new staff orientation. A message you convey to external publics through, say, a motion picture, may be the same message you would like to reinforce internally. Preview your presentation for the campus.

Changing technology. Tubes, scanners, and computers continue to change the daily operations of the mass media. You should examine implications of these developments for your particular operation. Hundreds of newspapers have switched to optical character readers (OCRs), video display terminals (VDTs), computers, and on-line phototypesetters, reducing the number of personnel employed in punching and correcting news copy. Just as news media have saved dollars by "capturing original key strokes," you may be able to achieve financial savings by a central keyboard. Some campuses have set up Word Processing Centers, with dial dictation equipment designed to accommodate the needs of faculty and administrators. For several years a number of college news offices have taken advantage of modern technology by sending out computerized hometown news. (See Chapter 40.) You may also find the computer helpful for direct mail, directories, labels, and management reports.

New uses for telephone. The telephone line has become a means of formal internal public relations. Religious and political groups have used the telephone message for propaganda. It also is being used as a communication tool in industry. The telephone message is particularly useful for emergency communication. Without going into such technicalities as how multiple lines are provided on the same number, fundamentally the system gives a recorded message to the person who calls. The message can be a rewrite of the day's top story from your university news bureau, announcements of events on campus, a message from the president, or the latest word on legislative action concerning the institution. It has the advantages of novelty, immediacy, accuracy, and accessibility.

Attainable goals. In planning a program of internal public relations you must take into account the existing channels of both informal and formal communication. You must be clear about what you hope to achieve and realistic in your expectations. The clarity and realism should be shared by your administrative colleagues. You must have a long-term commitment of adequate resources and cooperation. You must build credibility.

Carefully analyze your internal publics. Design your program to reach the particular audience. Remember that the more sophisticated your message the more elaborate must be your plan, probably involving separate approaches to different segments of the university community.

The generation gap. Recognize, too, that the contemporary institution of higher education is a different place than it was a generation ago and that the positive side of this story needs not only to be told outside but understood inside. The student body—the largest internal public—is different. *In loco parentis* is passe. A bureaucratic attitude is not a good substitute. A professional service-to-client relationship may be the best approach.

EXTERNAL PUBLICS

A modern major college or university requires the services and support of a great variety of people. While its publics are generally above average in intelligence and somewhat parochial in interest, the range is broad and diverse—from discipline-oriented scholar to assembly-line worker, from major donor to a rural legislator, from corporate personnel director to local union president, from the fourth generation alumni family to the culturally disadvantaged student.

Not only are these audiences numerous; they are prone to "participate" in the operation of the institution. Thus the college public relations man must be deft in balancing a broad spectrum of interests, alert to rapidly changing concerns among his publics, and imaginative and agile in meeting the demands of these special publics.

A continuing program of information and communication is essential to any public relations program. However, broadside communications approaches do not work with all external constituencies of any educational institutions.

Recognizing that a survey of public attitudes can be helpful in determining the direction of public relations activities, a group of state colleges and universities commissioned a survey research group to study attitudes and interests of a cross section of the adult population in the state.

The survey experts found that they could divide the adult population of the state into five broad classifications, with respect to their knowledge of the institutions and their degree of interest in their educational programs. They are:

1. *The Isolated.* This group, comprising about 20 per cent of the population, had less than eight years of education, had never seen a college or actually met anyone they considered to be a college graduate. About half could name one or two of the public institutions in the state.
2. *The Uninterested.* This group, made up of about 30 per cent of the adult population,

had between 7 and 12 years of education, with some minimum contact with colleges or college-educated people. This group showed more negative attitudes toward colleges and college professors, concluding that, for most of them, the sense of involvement was low, but the job-security threat was real.

3. *The Hopefuls.* This group, about 30 per cent of the adult population, had slightly more formal education than the previous group, but still averaged less than 12 years. Most actually could give names of four or five state institutions, but many were familiar with some aspects of a university's program, particularly medical research and extension courses. This group could be classified as having more favorable attitudes toward higher education, and almost all had high hopes that their sons and daughters would attend college.

4. *The Disaffected.* This group included about 15 per cent of the adult population; all had gone to college but about one-half were what one would term "drop-outs." Most of the noncontributors to college and university development programs were in this group.

5. *The Influentials.* This group comprised only 5 per cent of the total population but in the study would be classed as most important. They had the most favorable attitudes about the importance of higher education and had considerable knowledge of teaching and service activities of the educational institutions. As a group, these persons wanted more emphasis on the fundamentals of education and favored higher rather than lower admissions standards. These respondents also were very active in civic, educational, and community groups.

The significance of this study is that different means of communication are necessary to reach and appeal to groups with such widely divergent characteristics.

Changing constituencies. Educational public relations and communications officers are developing programs to improve relationships with the "new constituencies" of higher education.

Included in various new clienteles are:

- High school students who have advanced beyond the high school level in one or more subject areas.
- High school students who have completed all requirements for their diplomas by the end of the 11th grade.
- Transfer students, stop-outs, drop-outs, cop-outs, flunk-outs who can be retreaded.
- Adults making mid-life career changes.
- Service personnel and persons in occupations that cause them to move around the country.
- Veterans.
- Professionals in need of continuing education and updating.
- Persons in business and industry requiring special training programs.
- Women interested in resuming educational programs.
- Senior citizens interested in continuing their learning.

Another important trend in changing constituencies is the emergence of a new breed of consumer. *U.S. News and World Report* characterized this group as younger, more middle class, articulate, mobile, creative, suspicious, impatient, educated, environmentally conscious, and casual.

HANDLING CRISES

As a key member of the educational management team, the public relations officer, in a crisis situation, often is the key communicator, the interpreter of events, the institutional spokesman, and frequently one of the administrative strategists. The effectiveness of the public relations officer and his staff most often will be measured in terms of the impact of a crisis on a school or college and the relationships of that institution to its diverse publics. Experienced public relations practitioners recognize that the major method of avoiding panic in crises is through intelligent advance planning.[3]

Here are some basic steps to avoid panic-button crisis management:

1. *Premeditate.* Develop plans, understand plans, and revise and update plans. Ask yourself: "Are you prepared to meet an unexpected crisis on your campus?"
2. *Coordinate.* In the event of an emergency or other crisis, does your staff know and understand its assignments? Do you have a special task force for comprehensive news coverge in a crisis situation? Everyone should know who is doing what and when. A simple crisis plan makes provision for several assigned duty officers who cover assignments, notify key officials, and handle inquiries under a preplanned arrangement.
3. *Communicate.* Beware of that "com-

[3]See Chapter 38.

munications gap" that shows up so often during the campus crisis. Demonstrators, student militants, and other activists quickly publicize their demands. A common complaint among the working press is that educational administrators fail to communicate during times of trouble, or delay their responses. This results in an emphasis on the dissidents' point of view. The university community, too, often is ignored in crisis communications and must rely on student newspaper reports that often are highly biased accounts that are issue-oriented. More and more colleges and universities are taking steps to see that views of the administration are quickly made available to students, faculty, staff, community, alumni, and friends, as well as to mass media.

4. *Mediate*. The public relations officer must serve as the mediator between the administrator or trustee or other officials who are reluctant or unwilling to talk, and the reporter or television newsman who insists on getting a statement.

5. *Evaluate*. Planning to avoid panic suggests that one should learn from his or others' mistakes. What did you do wrong the last time? What should College X or University Y have done under the circumstances? Did all the letters the institution received from parents, alumni, taxpayers, or others indicate some constituencies had not been informed? Tomorrow's plans mean an evaluation of yesterday's actions and programs and a revision of today's practices and procedures.

PROGRAM EVALUATION

Close scrutiny is a key part of accountability. It is not surprising that evaluation is in demand. First came student evaluation and teacher evaluation; now program evaluation has moved to practically every section of the university. For people in public relations, program evaluation can be an effective management tool. It is most valuable if it is considered not as a one-time project but a process to to be used on a regular basis rather than just in crisis. If you conduct periodic program evaluation and build an operational base of information, you have at hand a set of indicators that you can use as background for decisions and for better projections about the future.

One of the most ambitious evaluations of public relations and development operations in higher education was that developed in 1974 by COPE (Committee On Program Evaluation) at The University of Michigan. Dr. Harvey Jacobson, who directed the study of operations involving eight units and 150 persons, maintains that regardless of the size of the institution, the evaluation process tends to embody the same basic characteristics. The manager who wishes to conduct systematic evaluation should consider at least seven steps:

(1) *Select the rationale*. What is the guiding philosophy or model? Is the evaluation conducted by internal or external evaluators? Who is the major client?

(2) *Specify objectives*. Define and state objectives of the evaluation itself, the objectives of the overall public relations program, and the objectives of the specific units or elements of the program.

(3) *Develop measures*. Develop and maintain measures of resources, finances, beneficiary groups, target groups, activities, and outcomes.

(4) *Administer the measures and collect the data*. Data can be collected by observation, questionnaire, monthly reports, interview, and other techniques.

(5) *Analyze the data*. Allot sufficient time to assure synthesis and interpretation.

(6) *Report the results*. Findings should be translated into recommendations and shared with others.

(7) *Apply the results to decisions*. If recommendations are expressed in terms of operational statements they are more likely to assure follow-through so the report does not gather dust.

27

Public Relations for Newspapers

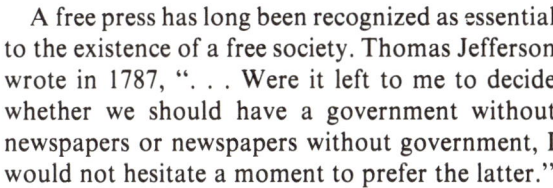

VIRGINIA BUTTS is Vice President of Public Relations and Public Affairs for Field Enterprises, Inc., a national and international corporation involved in communications, educational publishing, life and health insurance, papermaking, real estate, and the energy field. The company, with headquarters in Chicago, publishes the Chicago "Sun-Times."

The Chicago "Tribune" included Miss Butts in its 1976 series, "Chicago's Most Powerful Women," for being "the only woman high in the corporate structure of the major daily newspapers." The same year she was named Businesswoman of the Year by Lewis University (Lockport, Ill.) School of Business.

From 1956 to 1963, Miss Butts was Midwest public relations director for "Time," "Life," "Sports Illustrated," and "Fortune" magazines. She had been the writer for David Garroway's NBC network radio program from New York. Later she became a television producer, writer, and talent for WBKB-TV (Chicago) and then for the CBS Chicago outlet.

An accredited member of the Public Relations Society of America, she serves on the board of the Chicago chapter. She is past chairman and member of the accreditation committee and a national assembly delegate. She has held similar posts in the Publicity Club of Chicago.

A graduate of the University of Chicago, she is a member of the Visiting Committee to the College.

A free press has long been recognized as essential to the existence of a free society. Thomas Jefferson wrote in 1787, ". . . Were it left to me to decide whether we should have a government without newspapers or newspapers without government, I would not hesitate a moment to prefer the latter."

Criticism of the media. In the last 15 years both print and broadcast media have been criticized for their aggressive investigation and reporting of failings in the governmental, business, and social sectors of our society. Often the solutions offered on the newspapers' editorial pages are unpopular with readers.

As newspapers continue to expand the use of investigative reporting, a pressing problem demands more attention and thoughtful consideration: what is the role of the press in reporting on the political process, controversy, terrorist groups, trials, secret grand juries? Is its role one of advocacy or solely objectivity? Is it possible for reporters and photographers to be totally objective and candid while working in tense, emotional, and often dangerous situations?

Psychiatrists and behaviorial scientists question the possibility of complete objectivity at such times. Reporters and photograpers frequently become involved in the events they cover. They have a strong opinion, a social consciousness, or a built-in prejudice and report the scene as they "see it."

The media have been severely criticized for overemphasizing problems in government. Former Senator J. William Fulbright has called the press "excessively mistrustful and even hostile. If once the press was excessively orthodox and unquestioning of government policy," Fulbright said, "it has now become sweepingly iconoclastic."

The question of subpoenas for photographers' film and reporters' notebooks has brought some public relations practitioners into consultation with corporation lawyers. In the instances of court cases, the public relations person should seek the advice of company counsel when servicing news releases. Legal public relations, like financial public relations, is becoming a specialized field.[1] Certainly anyone working in public relations for a newspaper becomes involved in these areas.

A strong and continuing dialog between the communications media and their critics has been engaged in on a number of levels, ranging from the White House, before and during the Vietnam War and Watergate, to local citizens. Organized groups have marched on newspaper plants to express their intense dissatisfaction with the news coverage of specific issues. In short, the media are no longer sacrosanct.

Often the severest criticism of the media has come from the media themselves. Print media attack electronic media and TV commentators castigate newspaper columnists.

Many newspapers have instituted a code of professional standards, a statement of principle for their own newspapers that is used as a bench mark by which their readers can judge their performance. Prompt corrections and clarifications are being made in newspapers throughout the United States under such headings as "Bureau of Fairness and Accuracy."

Analyzing the problem. A study group of the National Commission on the Causes and Prevention of Violence declared in the early '70s that the news media can help reduce violence not by ignoring conflict when it occurs, but by accurately reporting its causes. The report represents the views of a task force staff directed by former Justice Department attorney Robert K. Baker and sociologist Dr. Sandra J. Ball. It recommended the creation of an independent national center for media study to evaluate the performance of print and broadcast journalism.

The report advises that what is needed is a "new kind of journalism" that begins with an objective description of events but then moves to "a fair portrayal of alternative solutions."

Public service reporting. Investigative reporting and in-depth "think" pieces are appearing more frequently and more widely in the press. Seymour Hersh, an award-winning investigative reporter for the *New York Times,* calls this the "age of the great exaltation of the investigative reporter."

Newspapers have been delving into areas that previously would be discussed only in specialty periodicals: abortion, homosexuality, sex reassignment, environmental problems are being reported clearly and concisely and are receiving a large share of the available space. Newspapers are concerned and their columnists, editorial cartoonists, and editors' notebooks reflect thoughtful, if not always popular, views.

Newspapers' public relations role changing. Consequently, the role of public relations for a newspaper has become much more sophisticated, challenging, and demanding. It is imperative that those in public relations for the press be informed and involved in the broad field of communications. As the role of the newspaper in society changes and becomes more complex, so does the role of public relations.

As serious publishers state the problems facing newspapers in the last portion of this century, the primary one is the need to maintain a newspaper's integrity. Without believability the press cannot function with its readers, advertisers, or the community.

Management may come to rely on public relations. The head of the public relations department in long-range planning must anticipate and be responsive to changes and be prepared to assist management in meeting the inherent problems, while continuing to strengthen the image of today's newspaper.

As management recognizes the importance and value of a sound public relations program and the ability of the public relations department to deliver such a program, management will more and more seek its advice in developing overall goals for the newspaper.

In this role the public relations director is in a position to provide all the services in public relations covered in this *Handbook*. All aspects—analysis, research, counseling, and so on—are as necessary for the newspaper as for other organizations and can be adapted to the newspaper's special character. In this chapter emphasis is placed on the distinct nature of functions especially suitable for the newspaper.

A growing number of public relations vice presi-

---

[1] See Chapter 54.

dents and directors are acting as liaison between the publisher's office and the editorial staff, as well as between the publisher's office and the newspaper's long-acknowledged publics: readers, advertisers, and the community.

In some instances, personnel and employee relations are also part of the public relations department's overall responsibilities.[2]

Publicity as part of public relations. Publicity is a significant part of any public relations program.[3] Results can be seen and measured, success or failure evaluated.

To conduct a successful public relations program requires a staff with certain skills, the most important of which is facile writing. Working for a newspaper demands that news releases be clear and concise. Accuracy is imperative and requires thorough research.

News releases not only provide stories but are representative of the department's professionalism. Editors, often critical of "handouts," are especially sensitive to news releases they receive from their own public relations department. A standard of excellence on the part of the department usually results in editorial acceptance. If this performance is maintained, and if the public relations department is kept informed by management, editors come to rely on the public relations department and to consult its head on stories about the newspaper enterprise.

The placement of news releases about a newspaper in other newspapers, magazines, trade publications, and on television is much more difficult than placing a release on a corporation or company not competitive with the newspaper industry. With 1,756 daily newspapers competing for readers and advertisers, a story has to have strong value to see print.

Photos serviced with news releases must be of high quality, in addition to being imaginative unless, of course, they are head shots of personnel whose promotions are announced for the financial pages. The captions that go along with the pictures should be handled with the same care that goes into news releases. A confusing or poorly written photo caption can doom the entire news story.

Electronics in the publicity program. Contacts in the radio and television media must be cultivated and maintained.[4] It is necessary to have material used on the air), to know how news producers work and how program producers operate. Television and radio news programs have deadlines just as do newspapers, and where and how to service a breaking news story can make the difference between a news release being used or ignored in an unopened envelope.

It is important to know as much as possible about the show before you contact the producer. Know the type of guest and talent the producers are likely to use; the length of the show; if there are several or just one guest; if the show is taped or live. The producer will be much more receptive to your ideas if you can talk intelligently about his program.

Reporters, columnists, photographers, cartoonists, and publishers are welcome guests on interview shows, particularly when such arrangements are made to tie-in with a current story. The public relations department should follow up with memos to TV editors of newspapers and should alert management to upcoming shows.

Wire services. Speed is important in working with wire services, and here the hour of release is a matter of precise timing, for it must be compatible with one's own newspaper's deadlines. The ever-present problem is to prevent your own paper from being "beat" by the wire service, but still to get the story moved on the wire. An innate or developed sense of timing based on knowledge of how the local wire services operate and a rapport with the sources to be serviced produces the best results.

Language and good taste. In writing releases quoting exclusive stories the public relations department can be faced with a problem of language and good taste, a problem becoming prevalent among newspapers today. One metropolitan newspaper offers this guidance in its stylebook: "Newspapers communicate with their readers in the way their readers communicate with one another. On occasion this means using language, including profanity, which in the past may have been considered taboo. If the language is not appropriate or obviously intended to shock, rather than inform, it should be deleted, whatever its nature or how innocuous it might be. If the language is appropriate in its particular context, it should be allowed to stand. Finally, it should be remembered that no guidelines can substitute for good writing and forceful expression."

When profanity is used in news stories, the public relations department can expect to answer readers' letters of protest. Such a policy requires sophisticated and delicate judgment.

[2]See Chapters 14 and 15.
[3]See Chapters 38-46.
[4]See Chapters 43 and 44.

PUBLIC RELATIONS FOR NEWSPAPERS

Figure 27-1. The publisher's civic activities often contribute to the public relations program of a newspaper. Marshall Field (second from right), publisher of *The Chicago Sun-Times*, is chairman of Chicago's Lincoln Park Zoological Society capital fund drive. Field and (from left) Chicago's Deputy Mayor Kenneth Sain; Chicago Park District President Patrick O'Malley; Diane Penar, zoo keeper; and Dr. Lester Fisher, zoo director, show Henry, a chimpanzee, a model of the Great Ape House, the chimp's future home.

Other functions in the newspaper's public relations include:

Public service bureau. A public service bureau or readers' service bureau is usually an integral part of a newspaper's public relations department. The bureau engages in day-to-day contact with the public. It is highly visible and therefore subject to criticism from the public and employees. Readers call newspapers for information on travel, weather, traffic, election results, accidents, and catastrophes. Usually these calls go directly to the public service bureau, relieving the hectic city desk. In times of natural disasters or civil disturbances, public relations departments set up rumor central telephone services to allay fear, help keep citizens calm, and dispense information.

In election years an all-night election central has created much good will, especially among those wanting local results not available on television or radio.

Back copies. Back copies of the newspaper are available in the public service bureau, and, in some cases, classified ads are received in the bureau too.

Plant tours. Tours of the newpaper's plant are scheduled for school children, foreign visitors, tourists, club groups, and others. With the use of electronic editing systems on the rise and the increase of computerization in the composing rooms and press rooms of many newspapers, the training of tour guides has become a challenging problem for public relations practitioners because the things to be seen are more technical and complex.

If a film is shown before the tour, the public relations department may have produced it or at least supervised it. The film is a device for letting visitors see restricted areas and restating what is emphasized on the tour.

Many papers at the conclusion of the tour give pamphlets or brochures telling how a newspaper works. Sometimes the visitors are also given complimentary copies of the latest edition of the paper.

Permissions. Reprint permissions for both text and graphic materials require the knowledge of Newspaper Guild contracts. The public relations practitioner also must acquaint himself with copyright laws governing the use and re-use of printed material. Proper credit must be given and material must be quoted in context. Permission requests from national news magazines must be handled with expediency to meet deadlines. The re-use of a paper's text, pictures, or cartoons in national magazines is extremely desirable publicity.

Special events. Special events or projects staged by newspapers are varied in scale and in kind. *The New York Times'* "100 Neediest Cases of the Year" at Christmastime has long been an outstanding fund

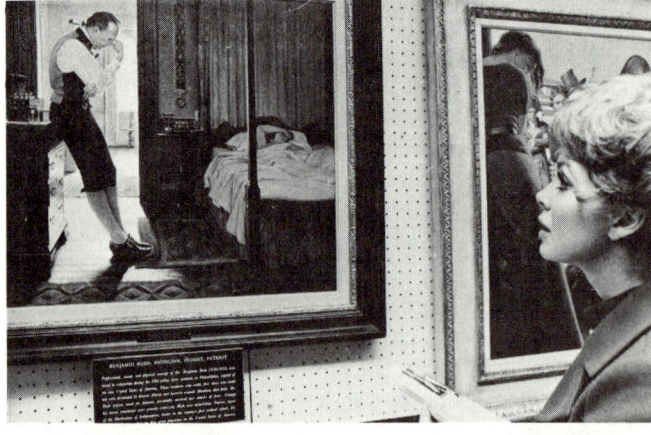

Figure 27-2. Lobby displays are especially effective for newspapers, whose offices usually are centrally located in the area they serve. Actress Barbara Rush (right) looks at a painting of her famous ancestor, Dr. Benjamin Rush (1745-1813), in a display on the "History of Medicine" in the lobby of the Chicago *Sun-Times* building.

PUBLIC RELATIONS FOR NEWSPAPERS

Figure 27-3. Public-service programs are effective in building community good will for newspapers. *The New York Times'* annual "100 Neediest Cases" campaign was originated in 1912.

raiser for eight of the city's charities. *The Los Angeles Times'* Women of the Year promotion honors individual achievement and is supported heavily by editorial promotion.

A number of newspapers stage sports events, athletic contests for youths, fashion shows, or mother or father of the year contests. Some papers sponsor art competitions, best letter contests, or civic projects. All are aimed at involving the reader and enhancing the newspaper's image.

Figure 27-4. Sponsorship of a popular event is used by newspapers to focus community interest and build support with influential groups. San Francisco *Chronicle* annually sponsors the Opening Day Yacht Parade at beginning of Spring.
© Chronicle Publishing Co., 1975.

A distinction must be made between circulation promotion, the objective of which is to sell newspapers, and public relations activities that seek to build and develop a good image for the newspaper.

Range of responsibility. The broad spectrum of at least one large daily metropolitan newspaper includes planning and supervision of a kitchen staff to serve the executive dining room. In addition, the department plans all VIP entertaining in the newspaper building: luncheons and cocktail parties. This includes planning the menus, table settings, and decor. The president or publisher acts as host for government, civic, industry, arts, and communications leaders.

As newspapers entertain more both at the plant and at clubs and hotels, many public relations departments design invitations, handle guest lists, and plan food and beverages.

Withholding bad news. All efforts to create an impression of a strong, honest, aggressive newspaper can be seriously impaired if, in times of crisis or a situation unfavorable to the paper or one of its executives, the public relations department tries to "cover up" or "stonewall." If the truth can't be told to inquiring media, no story should be given. Almost inevitably it is better to tell the story of the circulation drop, the realignment of key personnel, or the accident than try to hide it.

Acquisitions. In the case of acquisitions or mergers, the Securities and Exchange Commission has set forth a clear and rigid policy to follow on disclosure of information.[5] This applies to publicly held newspapers on the same basis as other corporations.

The press' sensitivity. One truth the public relations department soon learns is that no one is more hypersensitive to a "bad press" than the press itself. The press-section editor of a national news magazine readily admits that his section of the magazine never writes a story that completely pleases the subject. "Editors and reporters rank just above politicians in their supersensitivity to what is said about them in print," he points out. The newspaper's public relations staff must be prepared for this sensitivity whenever publicity is involved.

Standard of excellence. To carry out an excellent public relations program for a newspaper enterprise demands a staff of professionals in the field who are sensitive, flexible, intelligent, healthy, and have a sense of humor. Perhaps in no other industry does the department have to be as well-read and well-informed as in the newspaper business.

---

[5]See Chapters 11 and 12.

28

Public Relations for Broadcasters

JOHN M. COURIC has spent more than 20 years as a Washington association executive. He is Director of Interprofessional Affairs for the American Podiatry Association and previously was Vice President for Public Relations of the National Association of Broadcasters where he directed that organization's public relations program for 14 years.

Before entering association work he was a reporter and wire service executive. He began his journalism career on the Dublin (Ga.) "Courier-Herald" and later was employed by The Macon (Ga.) "Telegraph," The Macon "News," and The Atlanta "Constitution" before working for United Press in its Atlanta, Tallahassee, and Washington bureaus.

Mr. Couric is active in the National Voluntary Organizations for Independent Living for the Aging. He is a former member of the Executive Committee of the President's Committee on Employment of the Handicapped and of the Boards of Directors of the American Heart Association and the National Easter Seal Society for Crippled Children and Adults.

He is a lecturer at the University of Maryland and an adjunct professor at The American University, Washington, D.C., where he received his M.A. degree. He received his B.A. degree from Mercer University in Macon, Ga.

The American broadcaster can claim—with considerable justification—to be a "licensed" public relations practitioner. The Communications Act of 1934 requires a broadcasting station to be operated in "the public interest, convenience and necessity" and a licensee must submit his past performance to the official scrutiny of the Federal Communications Commission every three years when he applies for renewal of this license.

Operation in the public interest, convenience, and necessity involves three basic public relations elements for the broadcaster:

First, finding out what a broadcaster's public wishes, needs, and expects from his station.

Second, guiding his policies to fulfill these needs and desires.

Third, communicating and interpreting a station's policies and actions so that the broadcast licensee's public will know he is acting in the interests of that public.

These, of course, are classic descriptions of public relations practice.

Public relations also is of special importance in day-to-day broadcasting operations because the only thing a broadcaster has to sell is the relationship between his station and his listening or viewing public. Public acceptance determines the number of listeners and viewers who tune in his programs—and their response to what they see or hear. This—in turn—affects sales to advertisers, or the station's ability to make money.

In broadcasting, then, public relations is not just

one of many management tools. It is the be-all and end-all because—by law and by business necessity—a broadcaster must practice good public relations to continue to merit his license, his most valuable asset, and to attract and hold his audience and his sponsors.

Because he is in the business of communicating with the public, just about everything a broadcaster does makes an impression on the public. Every minute of air time is an opportunity to express a station's personality and to evoke a favorable response. But his relationship—and that of his colleagues, employees, or associates—is no less a challenge off-the-air. Every time a telephone is answered, a letter is written, a sign is erected, a speech is delivered, personal leadership is displayed on a civic committee, or an open house is held a broadcaster has the opportunity to make a good—or bad—impression.

But, of course, a good public relations program calls for more than good intentions coupled with recognition of basic principles. Planning and execution are vital. A public relations plan should be founded on a bedrock of background information about a station's strengths and weaknesses. The situation should be surveyed to determine:

1. Types of present audience.
2. Audience potential.
3. Signal coverage.
4. Specialized interests of present and potential audiences.
5. Station programming as it relates to the community of license.
6. Opportunities for public service.

Developing the plan. With this information a station public relations plan can be developed as follows:

First, establish an institutional personality. Such a personality not only breathes life into a station; it helps distinguish it from a cold, impersonal business unit. Institutional personality also is valuable because it is not transient. It is with a station when that station's prize disc jockey, news commentator, or panel show moderator has left the community or switched his allegiance to a competing station.

Second, identify the station *off the air* as well as on with leadership in—not just support of—a variety of community activities. Becoming an *integral* part of community life is the key here.

Third, stress the station's vital role in keeping the people informed. Radio and television are vital as news media. It is basic to have a good news operation and then never let the public forget or take for granted this contribution to their lives.

Fourth, assign public relations responsibility. This should be a full-time job in larger stations. It can encompass promotion and advertising, but it cannot be a collateral duty of the employee or employees responsible for these two functions. Since a station manager has ultimate responsibility he may wish to assume this executive responsibility himself, particularly in a smaller station.

Fifth, encourage staff participation in station public relations activities. Explain to station employees what their station is trying to accomplish. Put the outline of the station's public relations plan in writing for them as well as for the executives responsible. Generate the enthusiastic support of employees by letting them know that successful execution of the plan means a better place to work, greater individual recognition, higher income, and the satisfaction of superior performance.

AMBASSADORS TO THE COMMUNITY

Every member of the station staff is vital to a successful public relations effort. A surly telephone operator or a discourteous employee can undo much that a careful public relations program has accomplished. Make station employees aware that they are ambassadors to the community and acquaint them with these nine simple rules:

1. *Be interested.* Play an active role in your station's public relations. Find out what is being done and what needs to be done. Offer your help whenever you can, wherever you can. Our station's future, and your own livelihood, depend in large measure on community acceptance, support, and good will.

2. *Be active.* Lend a helping hand in community affairs. Let management know the organizations to which you belong, the civic programs in which you are interested. Offer to represent the station as its good will ambassador. You'll help make your community a better place in which to live and help improve relations between the station and local groups.

3. *Be visible and vocal.* Make your presence known and speak up for our interests. At meetings, let others present know that you also are there, ready and willing to help. Offer your services. Avoid a tendency to be blatant and boastful. Strive for a reputation of quiet, dependable efficiency.

4. *Be sensitive.* Look on station public relations as a key part of your job. Your manner in answering

the telephone, in greeting visitors, in discussing your job with strangers, vitally affects the station. What you say, what you do, even how you look, can give us a good name or a bad one.

5. *Be friendly.* Work hard at your job as an ambassador of good will. A warm handshake, a sunny smile, and a genuine interest in what people do will win friends for you and the station. Be courteous, understanding, helpful. A scowl, an irritable disposition, a curt reply make more enemies than friends.

6. *Be informed.* Keep posted on late developments. Whether making a speech, answering the phone, or talking with a visitor, be ready with the answers. If stumped, don't hedge. Check and find out. Misinformation can be more damaging than no information at all. Offer to look up the facts or refer the inquirer to someone who has them.

7. *Be straightforward.* Stick to the truth. Colored, slanted, or distorted information can backfire against all of us. If a mistake is made, don't try to cover up. Tell what happened, why it happened, and why it won't happen again. Fudging might avoid embarrassment for the moment, but a reputation for forthrightness and fairness is much more important.

8. *Be alert.* Keep in close touch with the changing needs of the community, of advertisers, of others with whom you have contact. Remain mobile enough and flexible enough to change pace and shift programs to meet those changing needs. Don't bog down in a we've-always-done-it-this-way rut. Keep tuned to a new frequency.

9. *Be understood.* Use simple language in speeches, letters, and telephone conversations. You want to get your message across without misunderstanding or misinterpretation. Avoid tangled and dangling clauses. Scratch "utilize" from your vocabulary. Try "use" instead. Substitute "excuse" for "exculpation," "variety" for "multiformity."

CHARTING THE COURSE

Much of the information a station needs for the foundation of a public relations plan already is available in initial or renewal applications for license. These application forms generally are prepared by a lawyer to guarantee observance of bureaucratic jots and tittles and to assure maximum protection for this most valued asset. However, this legal filing can be a bonanza of information for use in less esoteric public relations plans. In turn, the accomplishment of the plan provides the attorney with facts and actions needed to justify the renewal application.

There is a wide diversity in the way stations obtain survey information, not only for FCC requirements but for their own business and public relations needs. Some design and conduct their own surveys and studies; others depend on professional firms working under contract. Information on research practices, methods, and sources of this service can be obtained by writing Research Department, National Association of Broadcasters, 1771 N Street, N.W., Washington, D.C. 20036, and Advertising Research Foundation, 3 East 54th Street, New York, N.Y. 10022.

Complete knowledge of a community not only helps station management program better for its audience; if properly interpreted this knowledge can help management remind people of its service, explain why certain actions were or were not taken, and obtain sympathetic feedback for mutually desirable goals. For example, the manager of a station in a bedroom community with few active luncheon clubs would do well to design his speakers' bureau for other types of organizations. Stations serving ethnic populations will find that thorough knowledge of these groups not only provides the ability to program meaningfully for them but gives insight into these groups' own, off-air channels of communications.

Non-commercial radio and television stations[1] are licensed by the Federal Communications Commission as are their commercial counterparts. While they do not sell advertising or seek to make a profit, they also are dependent on public acceptance for their success. Their financial support comes from the public in varying ways—contributions, foundation grants, and governmental appropriations. If such a station does not seek to serve the public—and make the public aware of this service—its audience will desert it or never develop, and its financial sources will diminish or cease to exist. Therefore, everything in this chapter, other than comments relating directly to commercial practices, apply to this special category of American broadcasting stations.

SCOPE OF STATION PLANS

It is obvious that no station can use all the public relations techniques and that the execution of all public relations plans must be limited by size of

---

[1] See Chapter 44.

staff, income of the station, and similar practical factors. However, there are many routes to reach a station's public relations objective so all of them need not be used. Having decided on goals, a broadcaster next must decide on methods. Can he afford to advertise or must he rely entirely on publicity? What promotional means should he use to gain widespread recognition and identification for his station's call letters? How much can he cooperate with competitive media?

Advertising. Almost all successful station operators use some form of competitive advertising media for specific promotional purposes without feeling they are derogating the effectiveness of their medium. Billboards are an excellent way to inform travelers of the dial location of a radio station. Matchbooks are similarly used in many localities. Radio and television stations frequently are owned by newspapers and, even where they are not, many stations use newspaper advertising, particularly when such advertising can be purchased, or "traded out," contiguous to broadcast program listings. Trade press advertising also is very important to any station seeking national advertising business because these ads serve to remind time buyers for agencies, advertisers, and station representatives of certain unique qualifications of individual stations—pinpointed geographical coverage, special programming, and local recognition of award-winning service that tends to heighten a station's credibility, to name a few.

Publicity. Because of competitive aspects, many broadcasters feel that they frequently cannot obtain news space in newspapers and other periodicals. Broadcasters should attempt to ameliorate this situation wherever possible and should never refuse to carry legitimate news about the print media in retaliation. After all, both newspapers and the broadcast news media must realize that they are depriving the public when news is arbitrarily rejected. Broadcasters also should not be reticent to broadcast news of their own professional, business, or public service accomplishments. Radio and television are the most pervasive communications media ever devised and the public has both a stake and an interest in them. In addition, the personnel of a station are residents of the community in which they live and their friends, neighbors, and fellow residents are interested in them.

Promotion. Promotional activities can result in newsworthy events, but promotion is not, in itself, publicity. Since it does not involve the use of space or time it also is not advertising. It does consist of all other attention-getting devices and activities that a station uses. Stations use promotions to build audiences, sell advertising, tie-in with sponsors. Promotional activities occur both on and off the air waves. The kinds of promotion are almost limitless. Here are but a few examples, some of them applicable to both radio and television, others pertinent to only one:

• Use checks to promote broadcasting. Imprint across the top portion in bold type: **"THE POWER OF BROADCASTING TO MOVE GOODS AND SERVICES MADE THIS CHECK POSSIBLE."**

• Use a port-a-panel, a billboard on wheels, to promote the station's personalities and programs. The panel can be pulled behind a vehicle through shopping centers and along main streets.

• To give citizens a quick means for summoning aid in an emergency, provide wallet-size cards with telephone numbers of the police and fire departments and ambulance service, and space for their physician's number. Call letters and other station information can be printed on the other side.

• When planning a station birthday obervance, consider presenting a fashion show as one of the highlights. If station facilities are large enough, hold the event in the station lobby, or in a hotel ballroom or local department store. A fashion show can be a logical tie-in with the anniversary theme because many are symbolized by paper, cotton, wool, silk, or other fabrics.

• Give listeners and/or viewers, school children, civic, religious, and social groups a chance to see TV or radio in action and to meet your on-air personalities by holding an open house.

• Many advertisers will be glad to cooperate with promotion of a station on their delivery trucks. The signs can point out that the advertiser offers up-to-the-minute notices of sales and new products on the broadcasting station.

• Radio stations can tie in with automobile dealers to sell car radios. Retail dealers of portable and plug-in radio and television receivers also are eager to participate in promotions that help sell their products.

• Enclose promotion reminders with mailings, advertising, and bills. Many advertisers also will be happy to help build their broadcast audiences.

• Arrange a parade in the downtown area in the community. Use floats, school bands, and pretty girls. Radio station operators should not forget to include a unit on which everyone carries transistor radios—tuned to martial music being played over the station.

- Stage a series of stunts at main intersections during the day, preferably during the lunch hour. For example, in the spring and summer have girls in picnic outfits carrying signs reminding people that radio is a necessary ingredient for any picnic... "Radio Adds Fun to Outdoor Sun"; "Radio's Fun for Any Outing... Anywhere"; and, for an FM station, "FM... Sounds as Big as All Outdoors." Of course, have the girls carry good-quality portables that do justice to the sound of the station. With television becoming more and more portable, these stunts can be adapted to that medium.
- Shut-ins make up a loyal broadcast audience. Send them at home and in hospitals special greeting cards or small boxes of candy as a remembrance from their favorite station. Blind citizens depend heavily on radio. Consider a greeting in braille for them.
- To demonstrate the flexibility and mobility of TV and radio, conduct a series of broadcasts from unusual places—from an airplane, city bus, boat, historical site, or vacation spot.
- If the weekly public school menu is not printed in the local newspaper, consider incorporating this in a newspaper advertisement for the station. Mothers are interested in what their children will be having for lunch so they won't prepare the same thing for dinner. Many will clip the ad and post it in the kitchen to help them plan their weekly menu. The station's call letters will be right there, too.

INVOLVING THE COMMUNITY

Community relations. The National Association of Broadcasters, the overall trade association for the broadcasting industry, maintains close liaison with dozens of national organizations, including professional, vocational, charitable, fraternal, civic, and religious. Many of them work cooperatively with NAB in establishing organizational campaigns. For example, Kiwanis International has been a long-time supporter of National Radio Month, which the NAB sponsors each May. Kiwanis headquarters offers its local clubs a special Radio Month kit to enable them to cooperate specifically with their local radio stations during the May celebration. Other organizations provide their local groups with special on-air materials that thank the local stations for their support and tell the public how helpful broadcasting has been in the fight to conquer heart disease. The General Federation of Women's Clubs has established cooperative programs with NAB. Local broadcasters should avail themselves of all such opportunities for close cooperation with local units, not only because of the over-all public relations value but for the more specific benefit of showing licensee responsibility and community participation.

Many of these non-profit groups want public service time, the donation that usually redounds to the benefit of the broadcaster as well as the organization. To avoid misunderstanding about the responsibility and role of broadcasting, as well as to assist the station in preparing on-air material, organizations should have a superficial knowledge, at the least, of the techniques of on-air publicity. To meet this need the National Association of Broadcasters' Public Relations Department first published in 1961 the booklet "If You Want Air Time." Since then more than 600,000 copies have been distributed by NAB and its member stations. Individuals may receive the booklet free on request to Public Relations Department, NAB.

Speakers' Bureaus. An excellent way of conducting a community relations program is through a speakers' bureau.[2] Both management and on-air staff should participate in the bureau and the public can be told of its existence through direct mail or by broadcast announcements. Broadcast announcements may bring in more requests than the staff can handle and thus create ill will unless it is clearly spelled out that audiences must be of a specified size to obtain such a speaker. Station personalities will, of course, be greatly in demand because they are entertainers. It is the responsibility of management and the person assigned to the station public relations function to assure that the performer is apprised of station policy and industry situations, is mentally equipped to deal logically with constructive criticism, and knows how to rebut unwarranted or destructive comments or charges.

Such appearances, of course, spotlight the activities of a specific station, but the speaker also should discuss industry problems, such as artificial limitations on broadcast news coverage, the role of private enterprise in a government-licensed medium, and what broadcasting, supported by advertising as opposed to the foreign systems of government sponsorship, means to the average American. The Television Information Office, 745 Fifth Avenue, New York, N.Y. 10022, semi-autonomous arm of NAB, provides its member sta-

[2]See Chapter 48.

tions with speakers' guides, suggested speech drafts, and visual and audio presentations that outline general industry positions. General material on these subjects also can be requested by members of the public. NAB offers its members a means to exchange speeches that the members have written and delivered.

Contests. Everyone enjoys the excitement of a game or contest; broadcasters recognize this device as a useful way to attract attention and build audiences. The variety of contests is as limitless as the imagination. However, broadcasters must be careful to avoid running afoul of lottery laws. Wherever there is any doubt about contests, either those of the station or of an advertiser on the station, legal counsel should be consulted.

Direct mail. A properly executed mail campaign will enable the station operator to reach selected groups of people, but considerable effort is required to maintain current mailing lists. Lackadaisical maintenance of such lists can result in bad public relations when mail is addressed to individuals who have died, changed jobs, or perhaps, changed names because of marriage. Direct mail is effective in informing viewers and listeners of special programs, in assisting in sales promotion, and in countering criticism that may be widely circulated in competitive media. Mailing lists can be purchased from firms specializing in them, but stations generally prefer to tailor their own.

Awards and citations. Stations should be on the lookout for opportunities to have their activities recognized tangibly by others. Each year dozens of organizations give awards for creativity, public service, and other exceptional contributions. Some of the awards include cash stipends to individuals. Winning such an award helps remind viewers and listeners of a station's worth and should be publicized widely. NAB has compiled such a listing for broadcasting.

Exhibits. Broadcasters can use both static and moving exhibits to tell the story of their community involvement and service. Retail store windows, the lobbies of banks and utility companies, and the station's own headquarters are good possibilities for exhibits. Store windows lend themselves to the display of antique equipment, posters, and signs, while lobbies can be used for exhibits that onlookers can activate by push button. The use of station personalities in connection with exhibits at state and county fairs also is effective, as are remote broadcasts from these sites.

RELATIONS WITH GOVERNMENTS

Public servants compose an important special public for broadcasters. Every individual has a stake in government and a responsibility for participation in the election and governing processes; for broadcasters this is crucially true because they operate their stations as private enterprises but with close government regulations. Therefore the broadcaster must be active politically in his community, state, and nation.

Political activity begins at the grass roots, and it is here that the broadcaster also can be most effective.[3] Broadcasters should make it their business to know their representatives in the state legislature and the Congress. One effective way to do this is by providing technical guidance on the use of the electronic media for campaign purposes. Some broadcasters prefer to prepare their outlines or guides for candidates while others use "Is Your Hat in the Ring?" and "Campaigning on TV," two pamphlets provided to stations belonging to the NAB. In addition, broadcasters can provide even more specific guidance on a personal basis. A broadcaster also should consider political activity on behalf of the party or candidates of his choice; leadership does not encompass neutrality.

When engaging in political activity the broadcaster may act as any other citizen off the air, but on the air he must abide by certain restrictions. Section 315 of the Communications Act requires equal opportunity for candidates, which means that if one candidate is given time on the air, all other candidates for that same office are entitled to the same opportunity. If a candidate is sold time, the same conditions must be available to other candidates.

Section 315 means that if a station newsman, disc jockey, commentator, or other on-air performer announces for public office he must stop appearing on the air or else the station is subject to providing opposing candidates with the same broadcast opportunities. Another limitation, the Fairness Doctrine of the Federal Communications Commission, requires broadcasters to be able to make a showing that they have presented both sides of controversial issues of public importance. When in doubt about these restrictions, broadcasters should seek the advice of legal counsel.

But even with these limitations, broadcasters can be of great public service in illuminating issues and helping to crystallize opinion. Broadcasters who

[3]See Chapter 4, 5, 6, 7, 8.

editorialize on the air find that cogent, carefully researched, temperate editorials enhance station prestige as well as broaden the dialogue between the elected and the electorate.

PROFESSIONAL STANDARDS

A profession, according to the classic definition, must consist of three elements: research, or a body of knowledge; standards of practice or a code of conduct, and standards for admission to practice. Broadcast research is developing rapidly and there already is a considerable body of knowledge about the art. There are no individual standards for general admission to practice but station licensees must demonstrate good character, citizenship, and financial responsibility in their license applications. Certain station personnel also receive individual licenses attesting to engineering competence in specific areas.

It is with their voluntary Radio and Television Codes that Broadcasters have come closest to classic professionalism. Stations subscribing to the codes observe standards for programming and for advertising in recognition of the public interest.

Subscribing stations are monitored by the Code Authority of the National Association of Broadcasters for compliance. When deviations or violations are noted, they either are corrected or a station's right to use the seal is withdrawn. While to some this does not appear to be a stringent sanction, it deprives the station of a credential that is growing in importance with advertisers and with the general public. In themselves, the codes are not "public relations gimmicks." They do nudge broadcasters to maintain high standards of program and commercial content and thus help achieve superior performance, the bedrock of good public relations.

Career training. Training and recruiting of people for radio and television are supported by the Broadcast Education Association, 1771 N Street, N.W., Washington, D.C. 20036. The Association is composed of more than 200 colleges and universities offering major sequences in radio and television courses and some 60 junior or community colleges offering broadcasting courses. It receives additional financial and staff support from NAB. BEA publishes a scholarly quarterly, the *Journal of Broadcasting. Television Quarterly,* the journal of the National Academy of Television Arts and Sciences, 291 South La Cienega Boulevard, Beverly Hills, Calif., also provides useful information to those interested in a career in broadcasting.

Many stations offer college scholarships, sometimes in cooperation with other groups or organizations. Others provide summer internships. State and national broadcaster associations have similar scholarship programs. A listing is available from the NAB Public Relations Department.

NAB also operates the Employment Clearing House that promotes minority hiring by putting NAB stations in touch with minority groups or individuals seeking careers in broadcasting. In addition, Employment Clearing House gives minority individuals information on the availability of jobs in the broadcasting industry.

BUILDING BROADCASTING WITH BROADCASTING

A good public relations program for broadcasting stations and networks should include the use of the electronic media for publicity, as aids to promotion, and for general public relations. Audio and video spots containing jingles, celebrity endorsements, promotional announcements, or simple voice-over announcer copy can provide consistent reminders of broadcasting's service. Such copy can also build audiences for specific programs by reminding viewers or listeners of coming shows, but good public relations practice does not limit this activity to program promotion. The general story of broadcasting's service also should be told.

Mike Shapiro, general manager of WFAA radio and television, Dallas, Tex., for example, reaches WFAA TV's audience in prime time with a program called "Meet the Manager." Mr. Shapiro reads questions sent to him from listeners and, never ducking issues, explains why his station does or does not do certain things. He also has guests with him to discuss industry matters and to explain the why's and wherefore's of television operations. Other stations have similar programs, some of them call-in telephone shows.

Civic leaders can be invited to serve on panels that discuss broadcasting on the air, or a group of school teachers at a county or state education meeting can be asked to hold a forum on broadcasting with parts filmed, taped, or recorded for later airing.

In an overcommunicative society, broadcasters must use every appropriate public relations technique to make sure that the two-way communications process remains effective.

29

The Public Relations of Government

CARL F. HAWVER, Ph.D., has been active in the public relations field on the Washington scene since 1950. He has served as administrative assistant to a member of Congress, as a member of the public relations staff of the National Republican Congressional Committee, as "program liaison" and member of the top policy council of the U.S. Department of Agriculture, and as the public relations officer and chief executive of the National Consumer Finance Association, a large national association based in Washington.

Professional recognition has included presidency of the Public Relations Society of America (PRSA) and its Washington Chapter, national chairmanship of the PRSA Business and Professional Association Section, and of several PRSA committees. He is PRSA accredited (by examination) and has won the National Key Man Award given by the American Society of Association Executives for outstanding association work, several Freedoms Foundation awards for outstanding communications efforts in speeches, columns, and films, and several film festival awards; and in 1976 he won the National Louis M. Linxwiler Award for outstanding contribution to consumer education.

Dr. Hawver is author of the book, "The Congressman's Conception of His Role," and co-author of "Money and Your Marriage" and of a special supplement published by the U.S. Chamber of Commerce entitled "Dialogue with the Hill."

"All the world's troubles can be traced to semantics," Barbara Ward[1] said some years ago, and this may describe the problems of establishing sound, professional public relations practices in and for government in the United States, at all levels. The term "public relations" itself is the center of the semantic battle. The fact that the term has no generally accepted definition lends a certain mystical quality to the practice of public relations, and results in some mistrust. We are wary of those who might attempt to manipulate our minds and influence our decisions. Add to this a degree of distrust of government historically held by those governed, and some admitted secrecy and news management by government, and you compound the problem.

Max Weber, in his classic analysis of bureaucracy, holds that a preoccupation with secrecy is an inherent characteristic of administrative institutions[2]. Such secrecy, however, leads to distrust not only between the government and the governed, but also between the various segments and levels of government. Clark Mollenhoff[3] reports that an Indian uprising along the Indiana-

---

[1] Sligh, Charles R., Jr. "Public Relations Aspects of Government-industry Relations." *News from National Association of Manufacturers,* Reprinted from an address given to the New York Chapter of the Public Relations Society of America, New York City, October 17, 1962, pp. 1-7.

[2] Gerth, H.H. and Mills, C. Wright (eds.). *From Max Weber: Essays in Sociology.* New York: Oxford University Press, 1946, p. 233.

[3] Mollenhoff, Clark R. *Washington Cover-Up.* Garden City New York: Doubleday and Company, Inc., 1962, p. 21.

Ohio border in 1791 set the stage for the first investigations by Congress of decisions in the executive branch. A 1913 law[4], still in effect, states that "No money appropriated by any Act of Congress shall be used for the compensation of any publicity expert, unless specifically appropriated for that purpose." It is not surprising, therefore, that no government employee carries a title that would suggest he is a "publicity expert."

Even the attempt to survey the opinions of the people has been met with distrust. In 1935 the 74th Congress proposed H.R.2729[5] to stop the "vicious practice" by prohibiting the use of the U.S. mails for taking public opinion polls. As late as 1956 a Congressional Committee took the Post Office Department sternly to task for a $11,653 contract to get measurement of public opinion of postal service. The Committee noted five objections, the last (and probably most damaging) of which was that "the report was really used to attempt to influence Congress in the matter of postal rate increases."[5]

FREEDOM OF INFORMATION

"... A democracy works best when the people have all the information that the security of the Nation permits. No one should be able to pull curtains of secrecy around decisions which can be revealed without injury to the public interest." These were the words of President Lyndon B. Johnson when he signed the Freedom of Information Act into law on July 4, 1966.

The new law followed eleven years of study of the extent to which the "executive bureaucracy" was withholding information.

The 1972 report by the House Committee on Government Operations on the Administration of Freedom of Information Act (FOI) complained that when a department received a request for information under FOI, the expert advice of its chief public information officers was not always sought, with the request going instead to the chief legal officer. That meant the decision would be based on whether the law *required* the release of the information instead of whether it would be in the best interest of the department and the public to have it released.

During the 1972 hearings, Harold R. Lewis,

[4]Archibald, Samuel. "Public Relations, Politics and Government." *Public Relations Journal* (June, 1967), pp. 38-40.

[5]Hawver, Carl F. *The Congressman's Conception of His Role.* (Washington, D.C.: Hennage, 1963), p. 26.

former Director of Information for the Department of Agriculture, pointed out: "Information people are by nature of their training and in the performance of their job, more sensitive, I think, to the general needs of the public than are technical and administrative people. They work every day with media people, and know better the impact of what is going to happen, either good or bad, based on how an information situation develops."

The committee report concluded that "a more clearly defined role for public information personnel in the Federal Government and a general uplifting of their status within the bureaucracy are long overdue. Not only could such steps have significant impact on more conscientious administration of the Freedom of Information Act—both the letter and spirit of the law—but it would also give proper recognition to the legitimate and increasingly necessary role of public information officers as a bridge between faceless government and its citizens.

"This committee recognizes the increasing dangers of impersonal government by computers and the adverse effect it can have as a dehumanizing force in our increasingly complex and interdependent society. It also recognizes that Federal programs have been expanded into virtually every facet of human endeavor and their administration has been greatly decentralized to the community level. There is, therefore, an even greater need to relate such programs to individual citizens and groups through efficient, skilled, non-partisan public information specialists. Otherwise, it will be difficult for many Americans to benefit fully from the programs created and funded by the Federal Government."

The Freedom of Information Act with its 1974 Amendments brought new emphasis on public relations in government, though it relates only to a part of that total activity. As usual, improvement is made more difficult because there is no clear definition of the role of public relations in government. Indeed, there is no agreement on the term by which any communication function may be identified. Congress can require (sec. 3107, title 5, U.S. code) that appropriated funds may not be used to pay a publicity expert unless specifically appropriated for that purpose, and at the same time require that these same agencies use appropriated funds to provide information under the FOI.

It is not likely that one will find any job descriptions in the government information services that define the incumbent as a "publicity expert" or "public relations" person. People with such functions tend to be disguised under other titles.

James C. Hagerty, who was press secretary to President Eisenhower, reminded the committee during the 1972 Freedom of Information hearings that there must be a "workable balance" between the citizen's "right to know" and his right to keep private what he has confided to his government. He warned that the government must conduct part of its operations privately if it is to formulate policies successfully and reach decisions in both foreign and domestic affairs.

Robert O. Beatty of the Department of Health, Education and Welfare gave some guidelines for change to the House Committee on Government Operations. He recommended that the ancient (1913) provision contained in section 3107 be superseded so as to "legitimatize public affairs as a valid function of Government, clearly defining its functions and responsibilities across the board." He also suggested other ways to upgrade the status of Government public information:

"In summary, what this country needs is more information about its Government—and more resources allocated to the task, not less. One way to achieve this would be to:

- Establish an assistant secretary for public affairs in every executive department;
- Supersede the 1913 law that places the role of public affairs personnel in Government in doubt;
- Require accountability to the Cabinet level and to Congress for public affairs planning, performance, and budgeting;
- Investigate, with a view of legislative or administrative action to correct, the morass of bureaucratic constraints on effective governmental communication.

Another step would be to quit making public affairs offices dumping grounds for political patronage. The complex task of communications requires skills every bit as specialized as law or accounting, or the other service professions."

The impact of Watergate. Government attitudes toward public information and public relations programs fluctuate sharply in reaction to other events. "Watergate" drove the term "public relations" temporarily undercover in government since President Nixon was charged with using "public relations" to cover up information. Actually Nixon had no public relations persons on his staff. His communications people were from the media and from advertising.

THE ROLE OF PUBLIC RELATIONS IN GOVERNMENT

The function or role of the government public relations officer, by whatever title he is known, has been variously defined. President Jefferson defended his post road program on the grounds that it is "a matter of the highest importance to furnish the citizens with full and correct information."[6] Patrick Henry worried that government must be prevented from "covering with the veil of secrecy the common routine of business, for the liberties of the people never were, or never will be, secure when transactions of their rulers may be concealed from them."[7] Henry admitted that some secrecy was necessary in "such transactions as relate to military operations or affairs of great consequence, the immediate promulgation of which might defeat the interests of the community."

Most qualified observers agree that within these limits one of the primary roles of public relations in government is to tell the citizens what it is doing. In 1953 Rep. John Moss, Jr. (D-Calif.) was denied information from the Civil Service Commission and started a campaign to end such secrecy. In July 1966, by a roll call vote of 307 to 0, the House passed a bill ensuring the citizen's right to know what his Federal government is doing.[8] From this grew the "Freedom of Information" law.

Bernard Rubin expands this with the suggestion that government also has a responsibility for "advertising"—conducting a reporting program that attempts to describe the public's government.[9] There is one other aspect of the "telling" role that should be considered. Morris Rosenbloom reminds us that the Federal government is a great ocean of facts, much of which could be of great value to its citizens—if they knew it existed, and where and how to get it. Much of it has simply never been made

[6]Rourke, Francis E. *Secrecy and Publicity*. Baltimore: The Johns Hopkins Press, 1961, pp. 7-9.

[7]Cohen, Wilbur J. "Communication in a Democratic Society." *The Voice of Government*, Ray Eldon Hiebert and Carlton E. Spitzer (eds.) (New York: John Wiley and Sons, 1968), p. 13.

[8]"Bureaucracy Unbound." *Time*, Vol 88, #1, (July 1, 1966), p. 14.

[9]Rubin, Bernard. *Public Relations and the Empire State*. New Jersey: Rutgers University Press, 1958, p. 57.

available at all.[10] The public's right to know and the government's obligation to tell may include this area as well.

A second role of public relations in government is that of salesman or persuader. Dimock, in 1934, complained that "the most neglected aspect of public administration is salesmanship."[9] Rubin spoke of the two primary roles as reporting and persuading. "Certain administrative measures will not succeed . . ." without such activity, he said.[9] Aristotle, in his *Politics,* speaks of the importance of information to the citizen "who shares in governing and being governed," and Plato, in his *Laws,* suggests "we ought to have some institution . . . to tell us what is the aim of the state, and . . . to inform in how we are to attain this."[9] In short, government may need to tell its citizens "why" as well as "what," and sometimes one branch of government may feel it must persuade the citizenry to bring pressures on another branch to accomplish its own objectives. This persuasive role, in a sense, attempts to force the citizen into a full, active partnership in government.

Needs for restraint. Government persuasion, however, could also be used to mislead the public in the hands of power-hungry officials. Francis E. Rourke cites the public apprehension over this role of government and the fear it will be employed to "sell" the public official policy.[6] "But manipulation of official information is by no means the only danger that governmental use of publicity today presents. It has become increasingly clear that the weapon of publicity can be used not only for the purpose of engineering consent on the part of the community but also to punish individuals when the government chooses to do so."[6]

A third role grows out of increasing demand for a two-way communications program between government and its publics. Telling and selling are both one-way techniques; there is also a need to learn what those governed want, and need, and like. Rubin lists publicity, advertising, propaganda, promotion, and public opinion research as the major necessary public relations functions of modern democratic government.[9] While the dividing lines between the first four may be hazy, the last stands clearly apart as a different sort of a role.

The two-way communication role is described by William Ruder as the "second half of the public relations function in government."[11] One-way communication encourages a proprietary point of view, a tendency toward secrecy, and a temptation to manipulate public support, he says, and adds that none of this is healthy. Two-way programs involve the establishment of techniques for stimulating and receiving messages from government's publics. It is not enough just to listen. A situational climate must be developed in which such communications will flow. Government has developed ways to communicate with its publics when *it* wants to talk; now it must help the citizen find a way to communicate when *he* has something to say to government. When government receives and reacts to this communication from its publics, the information, judgments, frustrations, and attitudes received affect programming and change the substance of government.

Building the public image. It seems necessary to introduce a fourth role that is in a large degree a product of the first three. This is the role of public relations in government in image building for a political administration in power and for those who occupy positions of power within it. In December 1968 *Time* magazine described Herbert Klein's responsibilities in the new Nixon Administration and added that Klein admitted that the object of his new job, unprecedented in the Federal Government, would also be "to develop a better image" for the Nixon Administration.[12] The public positions taken by Vice President Spiro Agnew in 1969 and 1970 seemed to indicate a conviction that the government has a right, and perhaps an obligation, to answer its critics—to talk back to its backtalkers in defense of its public image.[13] Ford's Vice President, Nelson Rockefeller, seemed uncomfortable in that role.

Image-building, however, is not necessarily a self-serving activity. It is important that we build public confidence in our government and its leaders. Sensitivity to the public image often results in programs that are more carefully designed to meet the needs of the people, and in programs calculated to lessen the risk of things happening in government that could damage its image.

---

[10] Rosenbloom, Morris Victor. "Public Relations in Washington Today: Its Expanding Functions and Importance." *Tips and Tactics—Public Relations Reporter* (a special weekly supplement for subscribers), Vol. 5, Number 33, October 2, 1967, Part 1, pp. 1-2.

[11] Ruder, William. "Information As Two-Way Communication." *The Voice of Government,* Ray Eldon Hiebert and Carlton E. Spitzer (eds.) (New York: John Wiley and Sons, 1968), p. 78.

[12] "Superchief of Information." *Time,* Vol. 92, #23 (December 6, 1968), pp. 30-31.

[13] Lerner, Max. "The Need for a Two-Way Dialogue." *Current,* (January, 1970), pp. 46-47.

A case in point is the employment of Clark Mollenhoff by President Nixon. Mollenhoff was a crusading newspaper man and author of *Washington Cover-Up*, a book on secrecy and misdeeds in government. Apparently his responsibility was to seek out such problems in the Nixon Administration and take steps to correct them before they could erupt into public scandals to damage the Nixon image.

Unfortunately the palace guard seemed to feel threatened by his presence because some of the problem areas he brought to their attention related to their activities and to those of highly placed officials. Ultimately they succeeded in cutting off his access to Nixon and he resigned in disgust. History might have been changed if Nixon had provided Mollenhoff the open door he was promised.

Basically, as George Reedy points out, the most useful function that can be filled by a White House press secretary is to be believable.[14] This is equally true of all those public information officers who are involved in image-building for government at any level. Naturally, most of the image-building effort is aimed at the communications media and this provides a natural background, for, as Pierre Salinger (President Kennedy's press secretary) said, "No two institutions in the country have a more important relationship than the government of the United States and the press . . . The basic reason for the controversy between the press and the President is the fact that the objectives of the two institutions collide. The press, rooted in American history and a tradition of freedom, attempts to find and report every single piece of information. The government naturally wishes to present its programs and positions in the best possible light. It therefore resists . . . the pressures brought on it by the press."[15] This brings charges of "managed news," at cabinet levels as well as at the White House. Some of the interesting techniques used in White House news managing from the time of George Washington to 1963 are outlined by J. Carroll Bateman in the August, 1963 issue of *Public Relations Journal*.[16]

News management. Managed news, or the practice of releasing information on a timetable calculated to be most favorable to the releaser, is generally said to have become a widespread practice under President Franklin Delano Roosevelt. He used this technique to bring hope to a nation lost in a depression-born despair, by the careful timing of new Federal aid programs and fireside chats.

The economic recovery program introduced a new government role—that of spending billions of dollars to seek social and economic security. With these new responsibilities it was essential that the people be given maximum information about the government's programs for two reasons: first, so they would know how to take advantage of the new programs available to them; and second, so they would remember FDR and his administration as the source of this help when they went to the polls.

The practice, however, dates at least as far back as President Lincoln, who waited two months to find the right time to release the Emancipation Proclamation. Later he wrote, "Finally came the week of the Battle of Antietam. I determined to wait no longer. The news came on Wednesday that the advantage was on our side. The Proclamation was published the following Monday."[17]

THE PUBLICS OF GOVERNMENT

Having compartmentalized the public relations roles of government into: telling, selling, two-way communicating, and image-building, we examine next the publics of government—the targets for all this activity. Primary publics may be divided into four classifications: the individual voter-citizen, the special interest groups, the business community, and the government community. The basic means for reaching these publics is through the mass communications media.

It is sometimes considered significant that the Founding Fathers of our nation carefully refrained from creating an official information system for government. Instead, the function of keeping people informed was left to the press. By the middle of the 20th Century, however, informing the public about the activities of government could no longer be handled by the press alone and a growing army of information officers had appeared. In James McCamey's words, "The glut of occurrences each day in the vast chaotic web of Federal administration simply could not be followed by newspaper staffs unless they were enlarged many times their present size."[17]

---

[14] Reedy, George E. "Speaking for the President." *The Voice of Government*, Ray Eldon Hiebert and Carlton E. Spitzer (eds.) (New York: John Wiley and Sons, 1968), p. 108.

[15] Ladd, Bruce. *Crisis in Credibility*. New York: The New American Library Press, 1968, p. 9.

[16] Bateman, J. Carroll. "Techniques of Managing The News (Practiced by the White House from George Washington's Time to the Present)." *Public Relations Journal,* 19:6-9 (Aug. 1963).

[17] Cohen, Wilbur J. "Public Information in a Democratic Society." *Public Relations Journal,* (December, 1967), pp. 6-8.

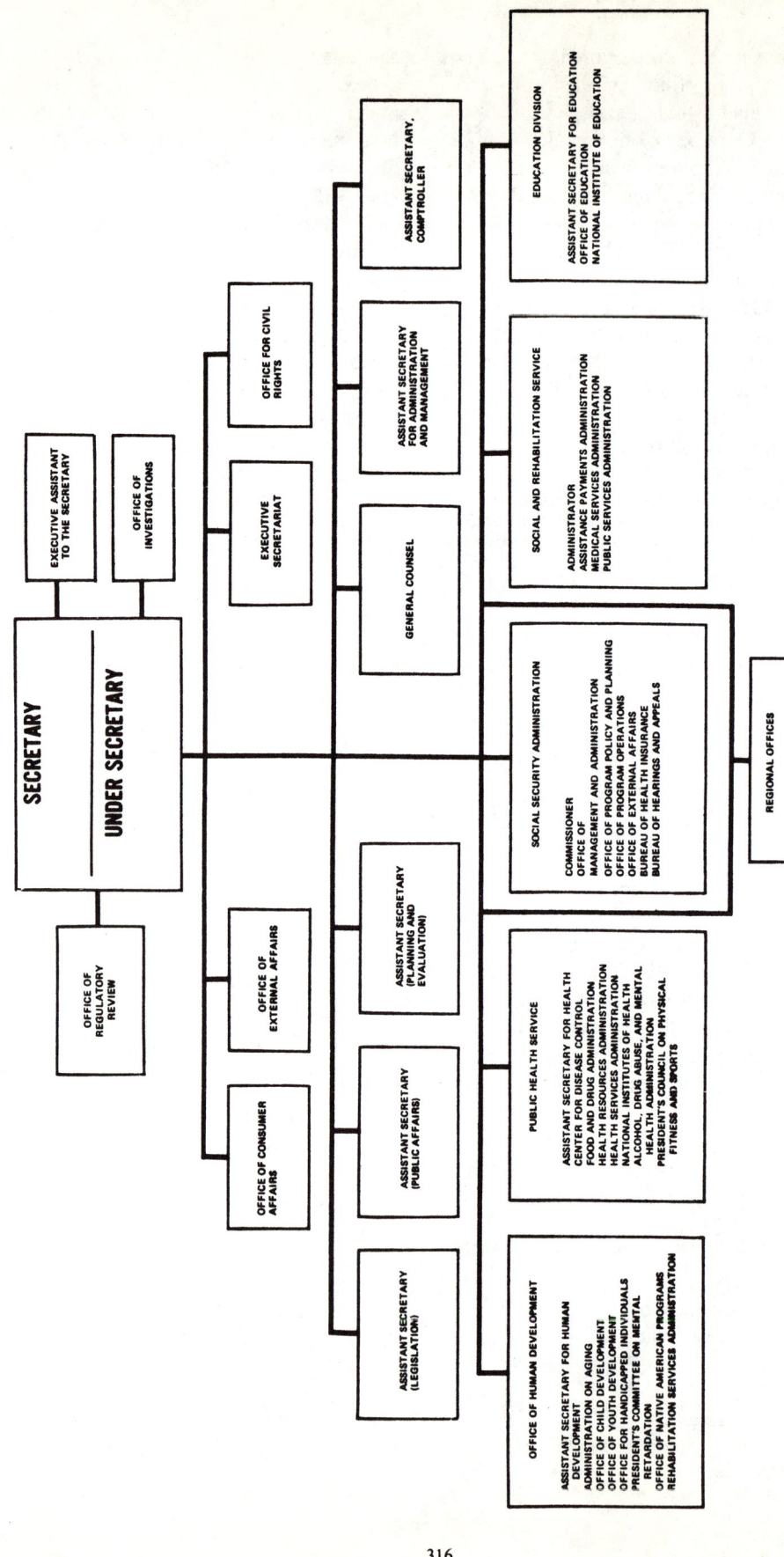

Figure 29-1. Although the term "public relations" cannot be used in Federal government offices, the function is high in many organization charts. It is the "Office of External Affairs" in the Department of Health, Education and Welfare and the "Office of Public Information" in the Federal Trade Commission.

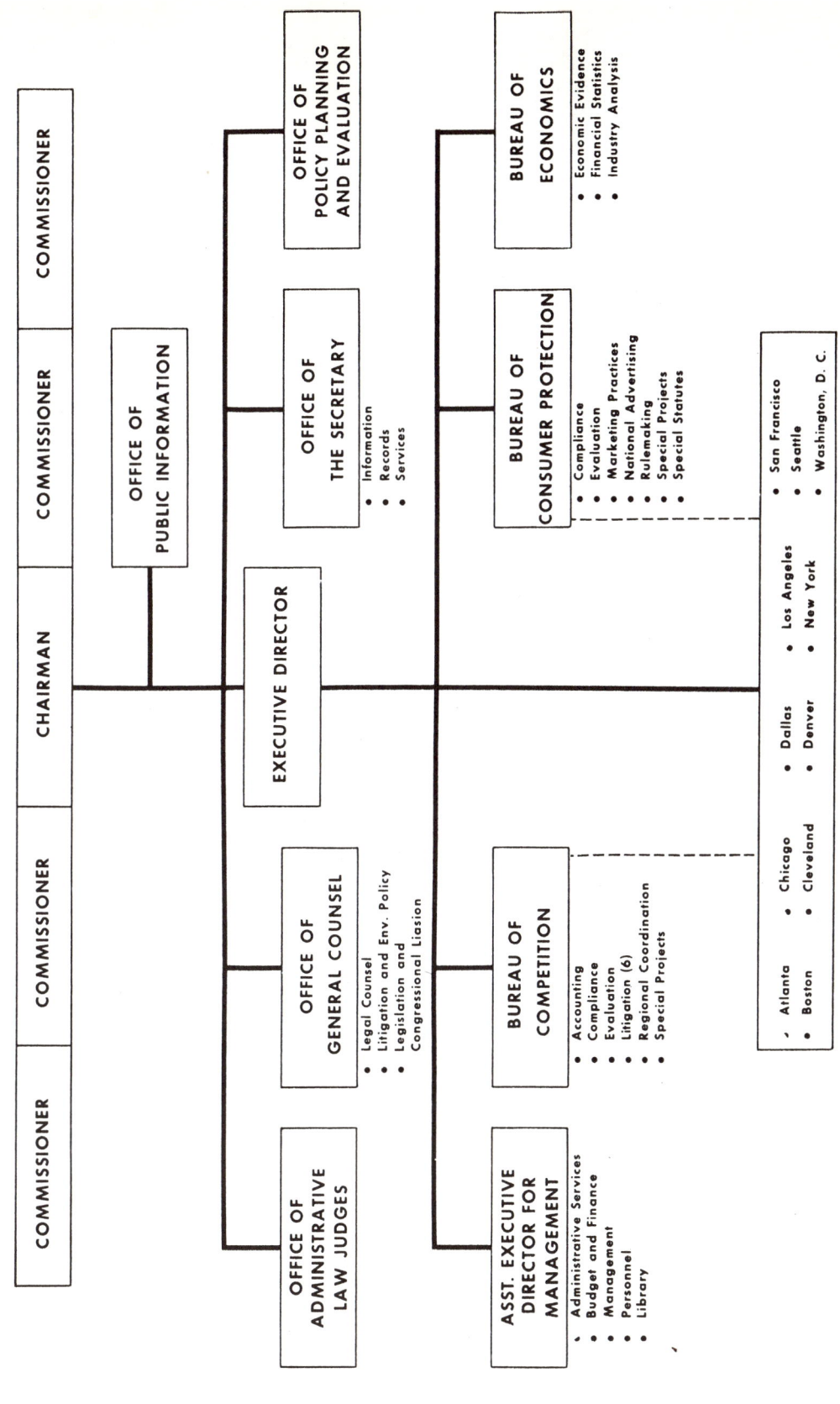

Figure 29-1 (continued)

As government information officers (PIO's) began mass producing press releases, media reporters began to badger them to get something special for their readers—some facts not included in the stock releases. This has not always resulted in a good working relationship between the PIO's and the media representatives. Spitzer suggests that "most government officials are inclined to hide when trouble strikes and reporters call. As a result, stories that might have appeared only once, stating both sides of the question, are strung out for days, usually with one side, the side willing to talk with the media, making its point time after time in the public mind."[18]

For their part, PIO's complain that the media are more interested in what is wrong than in what is right and refuse to carry stories on the sound operations of government programs, because this isn't exciting enough. Government scandals, however, no matter how small, get full treatment—for days. This emphasis on the negative creates an unfair bias that contributes to the difficulty of the PIO's job. Media representatives, however, say that information officers are too often guilty of propagandizing and of withholding news, and that their "facts" are frequently successfully challenged by the press and by business. In response to the challenge, government information specialists are finding new non-media ways to communicate with their publics. These include special conferences, seminars, advisory bodies, audio-visual presentations, and so on.

The individual citizen-voter is a prime public for government public relations efforts because this is the key to continuation in power. Government officials feel that the individual must be "told" what his government is doing, "sold" on its objectives, "listened to" through its two-way communications program, and "impressed" by the image-building efforts that convince him that these are his kind of people and he should support them at the polls. Government information officers, however, sometimes let their anxiety to impress this key public become their undoing. In the words of Harold Brayman, "... frequently governmental agencies, in their desire to protect the public interest, or their eagerness to make a record, put out information that is highly damaging to the people concerned."[19] An example is the unfortunate cranberry scare of 1961, or perhaps the birth control pill scare of the early 1970's.

Negative reactions. Sometimes, however, the individual citizens react so negatively to a communication from government that the entire program is changed. Phillip Rothchild, Acting Director of Information, The Internal Revenue Service, told an interviewer in March 1970 of one such case. The IRS had developed a gun control information program, carefully working out the message and translating it to a 30-minute film. The film commented only on the straight points of the law, but the audiences reacted with such an emotional force that the agency was finally forced to withdraw the film.

The individual citizen-voter is more likely to get emotionally involved in the dramatic expose of a government misdeed than in an account of solid agency achievement. He may, therefore, be over-impressed with the accounts of misdeeds emblazoned in the media and may tend, as a result, to vote "against" rather than to vote "for." This has led some political observers to note that bad weather and a light turnout at the polls is a favorable sign for the incumbents.

Government, however, needs more than the citizen's votes. President Nixon in his 1969 Inaugural address said, "We are approaching the limits of what government alone can do. It is time now to reach beyond government, to enlist the legions of the concerned and the committed." Without public confidence, law enforcement cannot succeed, social programs cannot succeed, and our educational system cannot succeed. Much of our floundering today is due to the fact that the government has not been able to develop that confidence.[20]

Other publics. A second important public for the government's public relations effort is the special interest group. This category includes labor unions, consumer organizations, educational associations, and so on. A part of the problem is that special-interest group leaders feel under some pressure from their members to make strong—and sometimes unreasonable—demands. Government retaliates by making its representatives less available and its statements less illuminating.

A third public is the business community. Much of the misunderstanding here results from a lack of

---

[18]Spitzer, Carlton E. "Public Information in Government Policy." *Public Relations Journal,* (February, 1968), pp. 24-26.

[19]Brayman, Harold. "Accuracy and Fairness in Government Releases." *Public Relations Journal,* (September, 1968), p. 27.

[20]Hawver, Carl F. "The Need for Change in the Public Relations Approach of Government, Particularly in Law Enforcement." (A published address presented at the 19th Annual Social Science Seminar in Palo Alto, California, February 13, 1969), pp. 11-15.

personal dialogue. Martin Powers pointed out that the businessman is baffled by the diffusion of tasks among government departments, agencies, bureaus, divisions, sections, and offices. He never seems able to take his problem to the right place.[21] (See Chapter 5.) Government employees seem unwilling or unable to help, and personal atnagonisms develop. However, as Leo Rostin wrote, "we must learn that those we like are not always right and those we don't like are not always wrong . . ."[22] All of this has created a general distrust of government by businesses.

Ted Sorensen, President Kennedy's top aide, assures us that Government "is just as suspicious of business as business is suspicious of Washington . . . They do not have the time, the information or the resources to take into consideration the business point of view or what business might have to offer on a particular project."[23]

Fenn points out that "when a businessman is looking out for the best interests of his company or his industry, he is not being selfish but is doing what he is being paid for. The government official, likewise, is doing what he is being paid for when he looks out for the public interest as he and the current administration perceive it."[24]

This makes neither of them anti-business or anti-government. This lack of rapport between business and government has, however, had a negative and limiting effect on the formation of public policy. In an effort to find solutions to the problem the Chamber of Commerce of the United States created a special task force of heads of national trade associations to study means of creating a better business-government dialogue. The guidelines developed as a result of these studies were published and distributed by associations to help their members develop better relations with government at all levels.[25]

---

[21] Powers, Martin C. "Cooperation for Common Advantage." *Public Relations Journal,* October, 1966), pp. 75-76.—taken from American University Business-Government Conference, "Business-Government Communication: A Symposium."

[22] Spitzer, Carlton E. "Dialogue: Best Hope for Business-Government Rapport." *Public Relations Journal,* (August, 1966), pp. 10-13.

[23] Sorensen, Theodore C. "Corporate Leadership in the Public Arena." *Public Relations Journal,* (January, 1968), pp. 27-29.

[24] Fenn, Dan H. "How to Talk with Government," *Public Relations Journal,* (November, 1967), pp. 33-35.

[25] "Dialogue With The 'Hill' " (a monograph) William Story, James Adduci, Alfred Ercoland, Carl Hawver, William Mott (eds.) (Washington, D.C.: U.S. Chamber of Commerce, 1969), p. 2.

The arena of businessgovernment relations is not, however, without some successes. James McCrory, Vice President of Management Communications, Inc., in March 1970 commended the efforts of government practitioners who have brought business and government together in institutional advertising and public education programs. In the same month Emil Michael Aun, Associate Editor for *Manpower* magazine, U.S. Department of Labor, told an interviewer that the industry-government partnership had been growing steadily since President Johnson's Jobs Program started in 1963.

The last major public of government relations is government itself. There is a constant struggle within government to find ways to let related agencies and offices know what is going on. A considerable amount of duplication of effort and resulting confusion and inefficiency are the price of failure in this effort. Even when they are informed, it is often difficult and frequently impossible to get two government agencies to mobilize their resources to meet an overlapping problem.

The problem is serious enough within a simple department where two agencies may duplicate efforts because of poor internal communications. It gets more serious when we consider inter-departmental communications problems, and is most severe when we consider the lack of effective communications between the three major branches of government: legislative, executive, and judicial. It is in this area that the government public relations officer may face his greatest challenge.

THE SIZE AND COST OF GOVERNMENT INFORMATION PROGRAMS

It is claimed that the first information program of a federal government office was initiated by the U.S. Patent Office in the 1830's to inform farmers of new technical aids available. The program was at first carried out at the personal expense of Patent's Commissioner Henry L. Ellsworth. It was not until 1910, however, that the idea of employing an information specialist (a newspaper man, in this case) to handle the press and public relations of a government agency was favorably considered.[17] In 1941, World War II made it necessary to hire more such specialists to explain spending on national defense.

By the end of the Truman Administration there were 3,632 government employees classified by Civil Service as "Information Specialists" or "editors." In addition, numerous public affairs officers were working under titles of special assistants to cabinet officers and even as Assistant Secretaries. In the first four years of the Eisenhower Administration the number of information specialists in government nearly doubled. In 1963 the Moss committee study (not published) reported "5,192 federal administrative and secretarial employees spend a 'substantial part' of their time in 'public relations work.' Total cost of these operations was about $47.5 million in fiscal 1963." Top salaries went as high as $35,000. The Defense Department alone reported 2,302 persons engaged in such activity.[4]

In 1967 an Associated Press survey reported 6,858 government information specialists with direct costs of about $225 million annually, and another $125 million spent by the Government Printing Office in producing publications for the information programs.[17] Estimates of expenditures in 1970 topped $500 million, but no substantiating figures were available since much of the effort is still hidden under different job titles.

No one knows the current number of "public affairs" people who work in the Executive Branch of the Federal Government. In 1975 the Defense Department alone had a $24.5 million world-wide public relations operation utilizing 1,518 people, while HEW had more than 1,000. David Brown, writing in the *Public Relations Review* in 1976, reported that the Civil Service Commission officially classified over 6,000 Federal employees in the two major public relations/information categories. However, he estimated that there may be as many as three times that number who perform public relations tasks under other job titles, and this is only the federal count.[26]

There were in the United States in 1976 "about 1,950 daily newspapers; 50,000 house organs; 10,609 periodicals; 8,184 radio stations; 962 TV stations; two major press associations; three major radio-television networks; tens of thousands of newsletters, trade journals; and a miscellany of other media of information, serving an exploding population that exceeds 200 million persons."

The government information officer must be able to plug into this vast communications network and use it effectively. In addition, there is an increasing emphasis on direct communication efforts that include speeches, films, handouts, how-to-do-it manuals, and seminars and other meetings.

The outlook for public relations in government is unusually bright. In 1963, 69 percent of government agencies reported that their public information officers "participated" in discussions of policy matters. That percentage has been rising steadily since that date, with most top officers serving as regular members of policy boards and not merely invited as "observers."

Growing acceptance of public relations. Government administrators are losing their fear of using public funds for public relations purposes in the fullest sense. They have found the information lag, and the resultant danger of an uninformed or a misinformed citizenry, a much greater risk. Most agree it is time to dispense with the semantic nonsense about calling public relations activities by some other name. It may be expected that budgets will soon contain allocations for public relations personnel and activities—by that name. Government, at all levels, finds it must make a greater effort to reach recipients of economic, social, and medical programs, and to make sure that the great majority of Americans who are living in relative comfort feel that they are getting their money's worth from their government. To do this government will need the finest public relations practitioners available. To get them it will need to be more competitive in salary and in program.

Congress, too, must face its responsibility to provide the necessary support for the kind of a public relations program government needs to fulfill its full obligation to its constituency. When Congress attempts to trim the budget by hacking at communication items it not only seriously curtails these programs, but also has an adverse effect on the morale of the professionals who escape the cut but who are forced to cover the work with depleted staffs. This resulting insecurity drives many fine professional practitioners out of government service and brings unnecessary hardships to those who stay because of their personal dedication to the work they are doing.

Government public relations, however, offers some special opportunities for the younger practitioner. In the words of veteran government information officer Mel White, when he was Deputy Director of Information, Bureau of Health and Manpower, "For the young man or woman with a passion to get into public relations where the action is, government service, it seems to me, is the place. With our meager budgets and staffing patterns, we

---

[26]David H. Brown, "Information Officers and Reporters: Friends or Faces?," *Public Relations Review* (Vol. 2, No. 2, 1976), pp. 29-31.

just cannot afford to waste talent on pencil-sharpening and news-clipping jobs. The recruit will very quickly get his chance at every job in the shop . . . and will be given responsibility just as quickly as he shows he is ready for it."

It is no longer enough for government to crank out an ocean of press releases and hope that John Q. Public will thereby get the word. New public relations techniques are already being used. More will be developed. These include conferences, seminars, advisory groups, films, speeches, and upgraded techniques applied to the more traditional communications methods. Government will also use these improved techniques in internal communications and in relating to state and local governments as well as to other federal departments and branches, as more jointly sponsored social programs are developed. All of the techniques and principles in this book are being adopted—with varying degrees of effectiveness—by government at all levels.

30

Public Relations for the Professional Organization

RICHARD R. (DICK) CONARROE is the author of Public Relations for Professional Organizations (Cahners, 1978), the first book on that subject, which has separate editions for various types of professional organizations.

Since 1961 he has headed Walden Public Relations, Westport, Connecticut, which specializes in providing counsel and service to professional firms. He has served more than 50 such organizations.

He was previously Editor and Vice President of "Business Management" magazine, a member of the public relations staff of Scott Paper Company, and Editor and Staff Director of Public Relations for the Administrative Management Society.

His other books include "Bravely, Bravely in Business" (American Management Associations, 1972) and "Executive Search: A Guide to Recruiting Outstanding Executives" (Van Nostrand Reinhold, 1976). He is a contributor to two other handbooks, both published by McGraw-Hill: "The Industrial Engineering Handbook" and "Top Management Handbook." He is the author of numerous articles on management, personal success, health, and public relations.

Conarroe is a graduate of the New York University School of Commerce.

Professional organizations need the judgment and techniques of public relations just as much as any industrial or commercial enterprise. In fact, in many ways the judgment, experience, and skills of public relations are more important and more effective for a professional organization than for other kinds of institutions. Law firms, CPA firms, architects, management consultants, engineering firms, designers, executive recruiting firms, health organizations, veterinary hospitals—professionals in these and other service areas have found that a well-conceived and well-executed public relations program can be vital in building a practice that is strong and healthy, profitable, and growing. For example, one young firm whose service is counsel on tax-sheltered investments acknowledges that the firm's present position of leadership in its field could not have been achieved—certainly not in such a short period—had it not been for a reputation for professional excellence the firm built in its infancy through a well-planned public relations program.

All the aspects of professional public relations that are dealt with in this *Handbook* apply to some degree to professional organizations. Such organizations also increasingly need skill in judging the trends of public attitudes that may affect their fields as well as the individual firm—pressures for government control, social responsibility, hiring of minority and female personnel, environmental impact, and so on. And they need knowledge and skill in dealing with these problems and their implications for the firm's reputation and the ability to function.

For the professional, both accenting good works and avoiding negative impressions are probably even more important than for corporations, associations, and other organizations. That is why so many lawyers, doctors, architects, accountants, and others actively provide their skills to public service organizations; and why they are especially concerned about avoiding charges of malfeasance or other improper practice.

Accordingly, material elsewhere in this book that applies to these and other aspects of public relations for other organizations applies equally to professional organizations. Here we will focus on their special needs—particularly gaining the benefits of prominence and good reputation.

MARKETING STRATEGY NEEDED

To be successful, every business—whether it is a giant conglomerate selling products or a one-man professional firm selling services—needs a marketing strategy. Increasing numbers of professional firms are discovering that public relations, when used as part of their marketing strategy, is relatively low in cost and high in effectiveness—not necessarily through instantaneous results, although that sometimes happens, but more commonly over the longer pull. One management consulting firm, for example, has been conducting an active public relations program for the past 15 years, almost from the day the firm was founded. The firm now has an international reputation and is generally recognized as one of the leaders in the management consulting profession. While the chairman, who founded the firm, says he knows of only two or three clients that have been signed up as a direct result solely of the public relations program, he gives it a significant share of credit for the firm's success. The program has not only reinforced this firm's position with its existing clients, but has put it in a favorable light with prospective clients who, as a result of the publicity, already know the firm by reputation before any overt sales contact is made.

The best way to build a favorable reputation, of course, is to have satisfied clients recommend the firm to their friends. But building that kind of reputation in a vacuum is slow and hit-or-miss. A public relations program can spread the favorable reputation faster and more broadly, on a more controlled and managed basis.

As the economy becomes increasingly service-oriented, with more and more people devoted to providing professional services rather than producing and selling tangible products or commodities, the competition in virtually every field of professional service is intensifying. Today it is only the exceptional professional field that enjoys a true seller's market, where the customers press to seek out the professional service. The number of professionals is growing faster than the markets they serve. It has become essential for a high-quality professional services firm to set itself apart from the crowd, to think in terms of influencing markets, to gain not only visibility but credibility and the implied endorsement of publications and other media.

Ethical considerations. In professional fields, of course, there are legal and ethical considerations. Overt marketing, such as through advertising or direct solicitation, may be frowned on. However, no one can frown on the fact that a third party—a respected professional journal, for example—discusses the results of good work done by an organization or individuals in a professional group. Yet such third-party endorsement, especially if it is in print or broadcast, may have far stronger value than the direct sales efforts that are proscribed.

In some professional fields—law and management consulting, for example—some of the old barriers are being dropped. Advertising is becoming acceptable now in professional fields where it was unacceptable before, provided it is done with restraint and dignity. Direct mail is growing in importance in fields where it was not considered good practice. These liberalizing changes in traditional restrictions represent challenges for the professional service organization. If restrictions are being liberalized, it is likely that some professional firms will be taking full advantage of these changes to strengthen and broaden their strategies for visibility.

A major ethical consideration involves the interest of the firm's clients. All professional organizations, from medical offices to advertising agencies, are bound to retain as confidential everything they know about a client, as well as everything they do on his behalf, unless the client clearly authorizes exposure of information. For many years management consultants, accountants, and other professionals avoided public discussion of knowledge that even by inference might have been derived from their service to clients. The result was that professionals leaned back so far to avoid possible criticism that they sentenced themselves to virtual anonymity except through activity in professional societies.

The need to maintain the confidentiality of any client's interests remains paramount. However, many clients now agree to have information about their activities reported on, so long as it does not provide undue help to competitors or reveal their weaknesses. And many professionals report on work they do in general terms, without possible identification of the clients involved, when the clients do not want their names used. Just as doctors have for generations been able to report in journals on their findings from serving unnamed patients, now consultants and others often report the knowledge they have derived from solving problems or developing programs for unnamed clients.

There is yet another point to consider. Every professional services organization faces the critical need to identify its specific service niche in the minds of potential clients. (For the remainder of this chapter, the word "clients" will be used in referring to buyers of professional services, even though in some professional fields the "customer" may be known as a patient or by some other specific designation.) Proliferation of competition in a field, and the likelihood of a cacophony of competitive messages heard by clients, probably causes vagueness in their minds concerning any one firm's service specialty and areas of expertness. Public relations can be helpful in solving this problem, too.

THE VALUES OF PUBLIC RELATIONS

The benefits an active public relations program can offer a professional firm include:

Visibility. Public relations—or more specifically, an ethically carried out publicity program—makes the professional organization known to those organizations and individuals who may need or want its services.

Credibility. A book or a play may be excellent, but if those responsible for selling it to readers or audiences don't seek and get reviews and other mentions in the media, the book or play may die in infancy. No matter how good the firm's work is, the word-of-mouth process is too slow and undependable. Using existing communications media—newspapers, magazines, radio, TV, or other appropriate media—the firm can get its story across to far more interested people, and do it in a fraction of the time. Getting endorsement of the media establishes credibility, authority in the field, leadership, and success.

Prestige by association. Just as there is guilt by association, there is prestige by association. Buyers of professional services certainly know this; often someone will use the services of a physician, an attorney, or an architect, for example, because of the professional's reputation and the prestige that's associated with his name. In the client's mind, some of this prestige of the professional rubs off onto the client himself.

The prestige-by-association phenomenon works both ways. If a firm has prestigious clients and takes proper and ethical steps to see that its name is associated with these clients, some of their prestige rubs off on the organization.

Cost effectiveness. It would be difficult to find a lower-cost way to communicate positively with clients and prospective clients than through the techniques of publicity. The instruments of communication are there, waiting to be used. Somebody else pays all the costs and handles all the work and problems involved in running the professional journals, newspapers, newsletters, and other available publicity media. The principles of effective publicity in Section V can be adapted readily by the professional organization. If conducted effectively, the media will welcome the publicity material, using it to their own advantage but building the organization's reputation in the process. A well-run publicity program for a professional organization creates a situation in which everybody wins: the professional firm, the media that carry the firm's messages, and the audiences who receive the messages.

Attracting top-caliber personnel. The quality of a professional organization is determined, of course, by the quality of the professionals in it. There will always be too few top-caliber professionals to go around. Sometimes one of the most important—but most overlooked—values of public relations is that it helps an organization attract the best people. Star players like to be associated with teams that are recognized as champions.

START WITH A PLAN

Probably the most important four words in this chapter are: Start with a plan. Without a thoughtfully conceived plan, one will probably waste time and money, get paltry results, and decide that using publicity was a bad idea because it doesn't work. Conversely, with a plan one will most likely get meaningful results, economy of time and dollars, and experience that will make the program increasingly effective.

The plan need not be inspirationally creative or complex. In fact, particularly in the beginning, the simpler the better.

The plan should be committed to writing before action is begun. Although there will probably not be unanimity, it's important to get as much support as possible for the plan from all the key people in the organization.

Preparing a sound public relations plan cannot be done in a vacuum, or on a theoretical basis.[1] It will require an analytical look at the entire organization, its present position, its strengths and weaknesses, and its needs for the future. The planning job will probably require researching the public relations plans of others, as well as the unique opportunities available to this organization, the barriers that stand in its way, the distinctive features that give it special personality and uniqueness, the best sources of publicity raw material in the organization, and so on. It's also necessary to determine who has the talent to carry out the program and what time to allot—or which outside services to employ.

The publicity plan should include these six ingredients:

Goals. What specifically is it that the program should accomplish? The tighter and sharper and finer the goals are defined, the more effective the program is likely to be. For example, it would be difficult to hang a meaningful program on a goal like this—"to make the principals of our organization better known in the community we serve." A more specific and therefore better goal would be: "During the next 12 months, to attract new clients to our organization that will represent a 15 percent increase in our dollar volume."

It may be decided to aim at only one goal or objective. More typically, there will be two to five specific but closely related goals.

Audiences or markets. The next step is to determine specifically who it is that should be reached to attain your goals. Typically, a key audience consists of the best prospective clients. Are they high-income homeowners? Are they presidents or other senior executives of giant corporations? If your market (audience) consists of companies, you may want to identify them in terms of size, type of business, geographic location, who in the company should be your initial contact, who will make the final buying decision, and so on. If your audience consists of individuals, they may be identified in terms of sex, age, geographic location, income level, occupation, and so on.

Secondary audiences may be influential people who are in a position to indirectly endorse the organization, or recommend it to potential clients. In this category might be bankers, professors, attorneys, heads of professional societies, and so on.

Media. It's a relatively easy matter to indentify the media that reach the audiences selected. For example, if the public is insurance executives, obviously all the worthwhile professional and trade publications in the insurance field should be on the media list. It's a good idea to divide your list into at least primary and secondary targets. Primary media targets will be those enjoying the greatest respect and/or with the highest circulation (commonly the two go hand-in-hand). For example, if your audience is business executives throughout the U.S., *Fortune, Wall Street Journal,* and *Business Week* will probably be among the media targets. If the market for services is national, cost effectiveness can be attained by aiming efforts at national magazines and network TV programs, for example, rather than local newspapers or local radio stations.

Messages. Now a decision is needed on what information to offer—in terms of news, ideas, or other messages—that will appeal to the media selected (and in turn to their audiences) and will at the same time help accomplish the goals. By looking at the organization as if through the eyes of a journalist or feature writer, it is possible to examine the organization as such a reporter might and to write down all the ideas that would probably appeal to him or her. This can provide a "feature ideas inventory" that will serve as excellent raw material.

Each possibility must meet all of these needs: the interests of the organization, the requirements of the media, and the interest of the ultimate audiences.

Special projects. In addition to communicating information that already exists in the organization, it may be wise to create news or other publicity material by special projects. For example, giving a speech or conducting a seminar in one's field of expertness can be a legitimate news event worthy of coverage with photographs in newspapers or appropriate journals. Conducting a survey or other research can serve the same purpose.

One of the common problems of professional organizations is that they don't usually generate much news. However, with a little imagination they can often use special projects to create news where it didn't exist.

Measuring results. The final section of the written plan should specify what will constitute success. For example, after the first year, what should have happened as a result of this effort? Because of the nature of public relations activity and results, it is

---

[1]See Chapter 37.

sometimes difficult to relate results directly to predetermined goals, but this should be done whenever possible and to the degree possible. If no basis is established for measuring the success of the program, there will be little to keep the program on track and there's a far greater chance the program will splinter into a number of meaningless segments. With predetermined standards for measuring success—even if it's only in terms of the quantity and quality of publicity sought—the organization is more likely to keep the program focused, narrowed down, disciplined, and aimed at its objectives.

THE PERIODIC AUDIT

There is another critical requirement: Actual performance should be measured against goals and the other aspects of the plan at regular intervals. This should be done at least every six months, and probably at shorter intervals during the start-up year. Such a formal review will be invaluable in helping determine which parts of the program are working and which are not, and thus to revise the program—and perhaps even the goals—to achieve the greatest possible cost effectiveness.

TWELVE BASIC TOOLS

At this point serious consideration should be given to the available techniques.

Long experience and trial-and-error have shown that of all of the dozens of techniques available, 12 basic techniques work best for professional organizations. It is not necessary to use all of them and they can be combined in many ways, but if the program is confined to these 12 techniques, avoiding the temptation to experiment with more esoteric and perhaps even more interesting methods, there is the best chance of accomplishing the objectives and getting the maximum return for the time and money invested.

News releases. The workhorse of almost every publicity or public relations effort is the news release. Discussions of news releases and how to use them appear in Chapter 40. Since professional services firms do not tend to generate much hard news, news releases will probably be used sparingly. There are exceptions, of course. A research organization may be doing work for its various clients that produces potential news almost every day. If this information is not totally proprietary or confidential, it may be turned into favorable publicity material either jointly with the client or without mentioning the client. Of course, use of any such material must have the client's approval.

A news release should have some real news to report or have a truly fresh and interesting idea to express. Expression of an idea without news should be considered only as a substitute.

Quotes, mentions, and short items. A look at newspapers, magazines, and other media of interest to a professional organization's clients will show that most of the material used deals with people—what they are doing and what they have to say. Editors know that their readers' interest can be captured best by stories about people. Stories about tangible things come in second and stories about concepts or theories are a distant third. Professionals can take advantage of this "people interest" of the media by having themselves or other people in the organization quoted in various stories and articles, or mentioned for what they are doing in their professional work. Short written items about the organization and its people can be published—with the advantage that short items in a professional journal, for example, often get far more readership than do longer articles and features.

The way to penetrate into a person's consciousness is through spaced repetition. By being mentioned continually and often quoted, a firm's awareness builds up in the minds of its prospective clients.

The easiest way to get these quotes, mentions, and short items published and broadcast is to set up an open, two-way channel of communication between the organization and the media of primary importance to it. For example, opportunities should be created to meet the editors of important publications personally—in their offices, at lunch, at meetings. They should come to know the organization is available as an authoritative source of information in its field. They should be asked what projects they are working on for which helpful information can be provided. Such meetings should be followed with a letter and fact sheet or press kit (see below and Chapters 39 and 40).

Chances are such editors will call back from time to time when they want opinions or specialized information. But it's not necessary to wait to be called. Once you have met the editor, if you have an idea or something you think is worthy of editorial attention you can simply call him or her.

In many successful publicity programs, a major proportion of the coverage results from making the organization a respected source that media people turn to often.

Endorsement articles (or case histories). Since one of the underlying values of a good program is third-party endorsement of the professional firm, endorsement or case history articles are an ideal technique. They provide a double endorsement—from both the publication that carries the article and from the client who serves as the author or subject of the article. For example, one architectural engineering firm specialized in designing school buildings. After one of the firm's projects was completed, with highly favorable reactions from all concerned, the firm asked the chairman of the local school board if he would by-line an article in a national education publication, discussing some of the new design ideas used and why they worked so well. The school board chairman agreed, and the firm worked closely with him in getting a favorable article written and placed in a prestigious education publication, where it appeared with attractive photos of the school showing its unique design features. This was a typical situation where everybody benefited. The editor who accepted the article was delighted since it was by-lined by the school board chairman and thus could not be construed as merely a puff piece for the architectural firm. The school board chairman and his community were happy because the article turned the spotlight of favorable publicity on them. And the firm, which was prominently (but not blatantly) mentioned in the article, gained the indirect but strong endorsement that resulted in inquiries from other school boards. Such endorsement articles have the added advantage that they also benefit the clients.

Reprints, brochures, and other direct mail. Certain people are obviously more important to the professional organization than others. No matter how much publicity a firm may get, many of the people in its primary audience will probably miss it. It frequently pays to take the extra step of making reprints of the best publicity material and sending it directly to a mailing list consisting of present clients, prospective clients, business feeders, and others.

The easiest way is simply to photo-reproduce the publicity exactly as it appears, by low-cost offset. The reprints can then be used as enclosures with letters or other material going out of the office. Alternately, they can be sent specifically to a mailing list with a brief covering letter. The covering note might say simply, "Recently some of the work of our firm was discussed in the XYZ publication. Perhaps you saw the article, but in case you didn't, I'm taking the liberty of sending you this reprint. Incidentally, if our services mentioned here might be of interest to you, I would welcome hearing from you."

Some professional firms make their reprints more elaborate and attractive. There are many ways to do this; adding color and some form of attractive design is perhaps the most obvious. One research company had a feature story about its services in the *New York Times*. Instead of making an unadorned reprint, they printed an attractive two-color folder, with the feature story reprinted inside and the cover prominently featuring the logotype of the *New York Times*. Although first printed many years ago, this reprint folder continues to be used year after year as a mailing piece and handout of the firm.

Direct mail is an important aspect of any public relations program since it permits you to rifle shot your message to the people you want most to reach. But as with all mail operations, it is essential to devote attention to keeping mailing lists up-to-date (see Chapter 48).

By-lined articles and features. For the professional firm, articles in technical and professional journals, trade publications, and other appropriate periodicals represent one of the most effective ways to obtain valuable publicity. If someone in the firm writes an article dealing with a timely aspect of the field and has the article published in a respected publication, prospective clients are given a visible demonstration of the firm's expert knowledge, experience, and skill.

Before investing time and work in writing by-lined articles, check with the editor of the target publication to make sure the article is something he wants and will match his current editorial requirements. It's not uncommon for an author to write an article and submit it for publication only to be told by the editor that although the article is good, a similar article on the same subject has just been accepted. The author then may have to try to place his work in a secondary publication.

Of equal or perhaps even greater importance is a feature article about the firm. Here the publication itself may assign its own writer to come in, research the interesting and timely aspects of the work the organization is doing and the personalities involved, and then write a story, probably with photographs and other illustrations. Such articles, of course, put the firm directly in the spotlight and have the advantage of someone else writing what amounts to a review of its work. Presumably, if the writer attempts to produce a balanced story (the best kind from everyone's point of view) everything the article says about the firm will not be totally favorable, but if it is handled carefully it is probable that the feature will be generally favorable. Some publications will permit the subject to see the story before it is published, in order to verify accuracy of all the facts, but others refuse to do this to prevent efforts to alter other content.

To increase your chances of a strongly favorable feature article it is wise to prepare as much material for the writer as possible in advance and then give him or her as much cooperation as possible.

For more information on working with the media, see Chapters 39, 40, 41, 43, and 44.

Research projects. Because professional firms don't generate a great deal of news on their own, they often create news by conducting research, the findings of which will be of timely interest to prospective clients and others important to the firm. The research findings are issued in the form of news releases, by-lined or feature articles, speeches, literature, and so on, and clearly identify the firm as the source. It usually helps to include a professional analysis or interpretation of the findings, which further helps establish the firm as an authoritative spokesman in its field.

Sometimes research being done on behalf of clients can be used for publicity purposes as well, if the clients approve. Sometimes, however, it is advisable or necessary to create special research projects, the sole purpose of which is publicity for the firm.

It is wise to keep publicity research projects simple, quick, and low-cost. Otherwise the time and money required may outweigh the publicity value. But often such research can be based on a simple survey questionnaire—or even can include library research, where information is pulled together that already exists, and that shows some trends or other interesting insights that might not otherwise be seen.

For example, one management consulting firm was interested in building its credibility in the eyes of corporation presidents. It did a research study on the backgrounds of presidents of major corporations. The findings showed that over the years, during different phases of the economic cycle, corporations tended to choose their presidents with different kinds of backgrounds and experience. This simple study produced a bonanza of nationwide publicity for the management consulting firm in many of the leading business and management periodicals—so much, in fact, that the "Origin of Presidents" study has become a continuing part of the firm's public relations efforts.

```
                            Consolidated Research Consultants
                            711 Park Avenue West
                            Boston, Massachusetts 01613
                            Telephone:  617/222-3939

What They Do:

Consolidated Research Consultants is a research and consulting
firm specializing in the design, organization and implementation
of pre-retirement counseling and assistance programs for employees
of corporations and institutions.  The firm serves clients through
four offices in the U.S. and one in Canada.

What Makes Them Unique:

.   Founded in 1957, Consolidated Research is the largest firm
    in its field of specialization
.   The firm has the most extensive automated information bank
    on pre-retirement and post-retirement U.S. workers (ages
    55 through 70)
.   At two of its offices, the firm operates "pre-retirement"
    indoctrination schools and courses, run by professional
    psychologists, to help those approaching retirement make
    the transition with a minimum of trauma

Areas of Special Knowledge:

.   Financial planning for retirement
.   Building a new life in retirement
.   Utilizing skills to supplement retirement income
.   Planning and managing geographical relocation
.   Early retirement vs. running the course--pros and cons
    based on computerized experience data
.   Health and therapeutic aspects of work vs. leisure

Key People:

C. Homer Grant, managing director
Dr. Ralph Esterline, chief psychologist
Harold Kirkpatrick, senior financial consultant

For More Information:

Contact:  Edward Parks
Acme Public Relations
1 Broad Street
Waltham, Massachusetts 02173
Telephone:  617/754-1515
```

Figure 30-1. A typical fact sheet for a (hypothetical) professional organization. Besides answering editors' questions about the makeup and functions of the firm, it identifies subjects on which it can be consulted as a spokesman.

Fact sheets and press kits. The quick, easy, low-cost action of preparing a fact sheet about the firm and its services, and putting copies of the fact sheet in the hands of all appropriate editors and other media contacts, has substantial value for a professional services firm. The fact sheet alerts editors to the firm's existence, its areas of expert knowledge, and its availability to provide authoritative material in its field. The result may be telephone calls, for example, from editors who want comments on subjects that the firm is able to provide insights on. Or they may ask for by-lined articles, or to come in and do a feature on the firm. In many cases, editors will file the fact sheet so they will have the firm as a regular source of information when they need it, or so they can contact it in the future.

The fact sheet may take a variety of forms. One of the best is a single 8 ½ x 11 sheet consisting of the following information: name, address, and telephone number of the firm; a brief description of what it is and what it does; a brief description of what makes the firm unique or special; a listing of its areas of expertness; and the names and titles of the key people who can be contacted for more information. Figure 30-1 illustrates a fact sheet that follows this format. It's a good idea to mail an updated copy of the fact sheet with a brief note to the entire media list every six months or year.

As the program develops it may be desirable to prepare a more elaborate information package, commonly known as a press kit. Usually a press kit consists of a folder with pockets containing the fact sheet, a brochure on the firm or other such literature, photos of key people and other appropriate subjects, perhaps the history of the firm briefly presented, reprints of articles or other publicity about it, perhaps a list of subjects on which it is prepared to write by-lined articles on request, and so on. In other words, the press kit should contain all the pertinent information about the firm that might be of interest or value to editors and other press representatives. It is usually distributed with a covering letter suggesting that the editor may find some immediate use for some of the material in the press kit, but that you recommend he file the material for possible future use or reference. As with fact sheets, press kits should be revised and redistributed at appropriate intervals (see Chapter 40).

Newsletters and brochures. In addition to working with existing publications and other media to carry your publicity material, there are advantages to producing a firm's own publication. For example, a feature article about the firm appearing in a professional journal has the advantages of endorsement of the press and wide distribution on an economical basis. On the other hand, this approach is unlikely to control what the article says and how it is written. Furthermore, the publication may not reach all of the desired audience. On the other hand, the advantages and disadvantages of publishing one's own newsletter, for example, are probably just the reverse. The organization probably can't get the same kind of broad distribution, since it must carry all the publishing and distribution costs itself, but it can have total control over what the publication says and how it says it, and it can target its newsletter directly at the primary audience.

Many professional services firms use newsletters as communications tools. Details on the use of newsletters appear in Chapter 48.

Publication of each issue of a newsletter is in itself an event worth publicizing. Some firms merchandise their newsletters to the press by sending out news releases on the contents of each new edition. At least, copies of the newsletter should be sent to the editors of appropriate publications and other media.

In many professional fields, descriptive brochures about the firm and its services are considered essential, and clients and prospective clients expect such brochures to be available. Many professional firms make the mistake of publishing brochures that talk about what interests them rather than what interests their clients and prospective clients. Another mistake is publishing a brochure that looks and sounds like the brochures of other firms in the field. Too many brochures are long-winded, written in professional jargon, poorly designed, and bland. Such brochures usually end up in the wastebasket, unread.

It is good to prepare a brochure about a firm for the non-reader. The recipient is likely to look at the pictures, skim the headlines, read the short blocks of copy, and perhaps the photo captions. It's vital to stress the physical appearance of the brochure and the first impression it makes. Often the biggest value of a brochure is that it establishes the style or personality of the firm—high prestige, down-to-earth, highly technical, expensive, or whatever. Therefore, the design should reflect the true personality of the organization.

Books. The public relations values of writing and publishing a book on the firm's special knowledge are great. Information packaged between the hard covers of a book somehow exudes a special high level of authority. A book gives third-party endorsement of the publisher, who obviously has found the content worthy. A book has long life; whereas a magazine article, for example, may have a lifespan of only a week or a month, a book's life can extend for years or, with revised editions, even decades. The first editon of this *Handbook's* predecessor was published in 1950. And a book gives the author the distinction of being not only a professional in his field but an authority as well. This distinction usually attracts other publicity opportunities, such as speech invitations and invitations to write more articles and books. The author of a book published by a respected publisher has one of the chief credentials of a bona fide expert in his or her field.

Books, however, are difficult and time consuming to write, and because of the competition difficult to have published. Most professionals who have succeeded in having good books published find the effort well worth it, from a public relations point of view, especially since a successful book will produce royalty income, and thus may represent a self-liquidating publicity effort and may even produce more income than was lost by the time and expenses involved in writing it.

For other information about books in public relations see Chapter 42.

Speeches. The special value of speech-making is that it puts one in direct, face-to-face contact with prospective clients or others important to the firm. Another advantage is that the material prepared for a speech can usually be used for other publicity purposes—news releases, by-lined articles, book chapters, and so on—if it is planned properly (see Chapter 48). Furthermore, unlike a published article for example, a speech, once prepared, can be reused repeatedly before different audiences unless it is reprinted fully where the audience was likely to see it.

The best way to get speaking invitations is to give one outstanding speech and let the word get around that you are a good person to have on programs. A more direct approach can also be used: simply writing letters to program chairmen of appropriate organizations indicating that members of your organization are available to speak. It helps, of course, if a member of the firm is a member of the organizations approached.

Seminars, round tables, and other sponsored meetings. In many ways seminars, round tables, and other meetings the firm sponsors and conducts itself are even better than speeches. The firm has total control over the program, the kind of audience invited, and so on. This does not mean that a seminar, for example, can be made a blatant sales pitch for the organization's services. A successful seminar or other sponsored meeting gives the audience worthwhile, practical, and timely information and knowledge; the effectiveness of the meeting is diminished by making the program self-serving.

Conducting seminars, round tables, and other meetings requires a lot of work. However, properly planned and organized a seminar program can be a highly effective technique. It may be possible to charge participants a fee, making the project self-liquidating or even profitable. And once the program has been perfected through a few sessions, it becomes easier to do and probably more and more effective.

Regular columns. A doctor at a medical center writes a weekly health column for his local newspaper. A financial consultant writes a regular column on investment strategy in a financial magazine. The head of an advertising agency writes a column on effective advertising techniques in a marketing publication. All of these, and many like them, are examples of a proven publicity technique that has many special advantages. First of all, if you sell an editor on publishing a by-lined article, for example, you've made only one sale. But if you sell him on running a column regularly, with the same sales effort you get an ongoing flow of regular publicity.

Furthermore, being a regular columnist on subjects related to one's services affords an extra level of prestige and credibility.

Despite these advantages, it is sometimes relatively easy to get a column-writing assignment from a good publication. It may be as easy as preparing three or four sample columns, sending them or taking them to the editor, and asking if he would like to have such a feature regularly. Preparing sound material in your sample columns, you have a good chance of succeeding with your objective. And in some cases—but certainly not all—there may even be a token writing fee for the author.

GETTING THE JOB DONE

Almost all of these 12 basic techniques involve dealing with editors, program directors, or others in a position to accept or reject ideas or material. Many people who are not experienced in public relations techniques are awed by this seemingly high hurdle. "Why should an important, busy editor be willing to talk to me?" they ask themselves. "I'm handicapped because I don't have any special 'in' with the editor."

The fact is that you don't need an "in" and you don't need to feel self-conscious about approaching editors directly, even the most important. All editors are constantly seeking to upgrade the quality and value of the material they use. If you have material that will help them accomplish that, and if you present it to them in a clear, concise, understandable way, you will be welcomed, not fended off. For some editors it's best to make contact in writing, by letter. For others it makes sense to pick up the phone, introduce yourself, and present your idea. Circumstances and a little trial and effort will determine the best approach to use in each case.

Don't hesitate to make personal contact with appropriate editors, visit them in their offices, take them to lunch, invite them to see the firm's facilities. When you make such introductory contacts, it is best to have some specific ideas that the editor may be interested in immediately, but your underlying purpose can be to establish a good, continuing personal relationship that will work to your mutual interests.

The firm may find that the public relations job is too big to be handled as a supplementary, when-time-permits function by someone in the firm. It may be wise to appoint someone to pursue this function full-time. If the function is to be handled internally, it should be handled by someone with stature and influence in the organization.

Often there are value and economy in calling on outside public relations experts and services. Just as the organization can conduct its professional services for its clients better than they can do it themselves, a public relations expert can often handle a public relations program better than the firm can do it itself. It's important that the public relations firm selected understand the subtleties involved in professional services and is aware of the taboos and ethical standards involved, as well as the judgment, experience, and skills detailed here.

31

Publicity for Travel and Tourism*

KENNETH KOYEN is a public relations consultant and free lance writer in New York. As public relations counsel he has served many clients in the travel field including the United States Travel Service, the 1968 World's Fair, P & O-Orient Lines, and the Government of Curacao. Mr. Koyen was for four years director of public relations of the British Travel Association in the United States and was in Washington, D.C. for two years as the public relations representative of The General Dynamics Corporation. He is a former assistant public relations director of United Aircraft Corporation. Before entering public relations he was a reporter and feature writer for the New York "Herald Tribune" in New York and in Paris, where he was on the staff of the European edition for two years. He has written for major newspapers and magazines.

During World War II he was a captain in the armored force of the Army of the United States, and served as the public relations officer of the Fourth Armored Division of General Patton's Third Army in Europe. He is the author of "From the Beach to Bavaria," a history of his division. He received on behalf of a public relations firm a Silver Anvil award in 1962 from the Public Relations Society of America. He is a native of Fremont, Nebraska and received his A.B from the University of Minnesota.

The modern-day tourist is one of the most sought after men in the world. Now he is a hero to the proprietor of the summer hotel in Maine, the casino manager in Nice, and the director of the new hotel in Hawaii. The tourist says his motives are simple. He just wants to "get away, have a change of scene, see how other people live, do some sight-seeing." But the results of his seemingly casual decisions can start a boom in one state, bring resorts to the edge of bankruptcy in another, deplete the national treasury of one country, and heap dollars into the exchequer of another.

For these reasons the tourist has become the target of one of the most rapidly increasing phases of persuasion ever developed through publicity and advertising.

*This chapter is adapted from an article in *The Public Relations Quarterly*, Summer, 1962, with additions and modifications.

Almost everyone is in the market for travel these days. In 1975 more than 213 million international tourist arrivals were recorded by the World Tourism Organization. In the United States leisure travel is expected to soar to $127 billion in 1980.

Widespread general prosperity, despite recession setbacks, the increase in real incomes, the shorter work-week, the spread of paid vacation periods, and early retirement have put people in the mood for a holiday away from home.

The competition for the tourists has increased at about the same velocity as the speed of transportation. With big jets now skimming the world, the old rivalry between Florida and Southern California has lost its point. They both compete with Jamaica, Hawaii, Tahiti, and the Greek Islands. In the United States alone, the total expenditure for tourist promotion and advertising by the state governments and domestic areas has rocketed.

The travel stakes are high in the United States. More than 660 million persons took at least one trip during 1975. Americans spend more than $72 billion annually on domestic travel. In 1975 a total of 23 million U.S. tourists spent $18.8 billion on foreign travel. The way these travel dollars are spent can be influenced by travel promotion. The popularity of "this year's" country or "this season's" resort can, to an important degree, be a result of publicity and advertising. Travel trends do change, and this flexibility provides the opportunities as well as the headaches.

The tourist wants assurances, especially on the first trip into those rather mysterious realms over the seas, that this course is a resonably well-tried and tested one. If he can read and hear that his destination is especially popular with fellow-Americans, so much the better.

Broad currents of international politics and economics affect the tourist's choice. Student riots in France, the Soviet occupation of Czechoslovakia, and the activities of Palestinian terrorists have at one time or another depressed American travel to parts of Europe and the Middle East and probably contributed to an upsurge of traffic to the Caribbean, South America, and the Pacific. Advertising and publicity create other currents that affect the tourist's course. One European country or Caribbean island moves up in popularity over several others; an airline captures a larger share of the market than its next competitor; the majority of overseas travelers turn from ships to airlines. These are indications of the flexibility of the travel market.

The foreign oil embargo in late 1973 and early 1974, accompanied by a shortage of gasoline and a sharp increase in prices, for a time depressed all travel—both foreign and domestic. The possibility of such disruptions is a factor to be considered in the planning of all tourism-related organizations and countries.

Of course, public relations cannot by itself overcome major problems without appropriate action. Some disasters seem too tough to beat. A case in point is the closing of Philadelphia's premier tourist and convention hotel, the Bellevue-Stratford. The hotel and promotion groups in Philadelphia struggled valiantly to stimulate business for the hotel in the aftermath of the death of 29 persons and the illness of some 150 others. A so-called Legionnaire disease, the cause of which was not determined, struck members of the Pennsylvania American Legion who had attended its convention in the hotel in July 1976.

Positive action in another type of situation can achieve results. When El Al, the Israeli airline, was first made the target of terrorists, it was thought that the line's traffic might suffer permanently. But when the airline tightened its security to the point where it became known as one of the safest to fly in that respect, traffic responded favorably. One unusual effect of terrorist actions in Israel itself was to increase travel from the United States to that country, according to Israeli travel sources.

El Al launched a new, positive travel promotion campaign called "O Jerusalem!" It consists of an unusual tour of the city and is offered the year around. Included in the tour are invitations to dine in the homes of local families.

Budgeting to attract tourists. To win the high stakes in this market, as well as in the development of commerce and industry, areas seeking more tourists must invest in publicity and advertising. Many tourists would travel even if there were no four-color advertisements or no travel feature stories. But the traffic would not be so heavy, and the area that has no significant tourist industry cannot develop it without telling the world about its attractions.

How much should the promotion program cost? It has been suggested that one-half of one per cent of the total income derived from tourism would be a reasonable sum to plow back. If little or no tourist traffic exists, an arbitrary figure must be developed. The budget should be based on the potential market and the communications media to be employed.

If a budget cannot provide adequate national advertising, it should be weighed in favor of publicity that can reach the largest audience most effectively. Larger budgets should allot an important percentage to publicity, because the two communications techniques together multiply their effectiveness. The two campaigns should be coordinated.

Not to be forgotten is an evaluation of the number of tourists that can be accommodated in the area at peak seasons. An all-out campaign successful in bringing swarms of tourists to a newly discovered spot will backfire if the travelers have to spend their nights as well as their days on the beaches for lack of hotel rooms.

Who should do travel publicity? Areas seeking to launch or expand such programs need expert assistance. In the United States they may find it in public relations firms, a few of which specialize in travel. Such organizations have the personnel and the knowledge to carry out these programs effectively in cooperation with the staffs of the client areas.

Selecting a theme. Budget in hand, the campaign should begin with selection of a theme that expresses the area and illuminates the features potential visitors will find most appealing. This can be a symbol, a phrase, a sentence, or a description. These aspects are not necessarily the same things that the natives believe to be their strongest charms. Australians deem the kangaroo a pest, for example, but Americans would be disappointed if the beasts were not part of the tourist scene.

National and regional pride is a sensitive point that must be held in account in planning a campaign. Travel promotion cannot give first place to the modern industrial achievements of a city or nation. The average American tourist is unmoved by this facet of the place he may visit, although he may note it once he is on the spot and be favorably impressed. The unique, the historic, the beautiful—these qualities fascinate the tourist. Tourism and industrial development can be combined and coordinated in the same office by the same persons, but it should be recognized that there are two jobs rather than one.

Tourists' interest vary according to the ages as well as the backgrounds of visitors. Young travelers are more intent on sports and night life than their seniors. Hiking, bicycle trips, and overnight stays in youth hostels appeal to the student set. Their elders want to be assured of comfortable hotel rooms and easy transportation while seeing much the same sights as the youngsters. The fundamental or basic appeal of a country is the primary magnet to tourists. This pull can be increased by presenting it in the most attractive fashion by emphasizing its brightest aspects, by distilling its essence.

Within these fundamental characteristics of an area are a wide range of appeals and facilities that can be developed to attract special-interest groups. Does the area have unique wild life, unusual fishing, excellent golf, good skiing, beautiful gardens, picturesque but docile aborigines? Does it have scheduled festivals or unscheduled volcanoes? Is its architecture outstanding and its museums unmatched? Are the music and the night life moving and exciting? All these qualities and many more are themes for development of newspaper and magazine articles, films, and photographs. From year to year these subordinate themes may take precedence over the main theme as new events of worldwide interest occur and transitions take place. Extension of the travel season into slack months may become a major objective as peak months are crammed beyond capacity.

Figure 31-1. Making certain that tourists' accommodations will be comfortable and pleasant is a vital part of travel public relations. The U.S. Travel Service presents this plaque to hotels that have staffs able to speak English, Spanish, French, and German.

Scheduling. Having determined the main theme of the publicity campaign and its objectives, the plan for putting it into effect should be carefully laid out over a long period, at least a year in advance. A complete program will embrace press, radio, television, films, and photographs. Magazines, newspapers, radio and television broadcasts, theaters, and group cinema showings are used to reach the public that buys the tickets.

Working with travel organizations. Another public, smaller but essential, is the travel trade—which includes travel agencies, the tour operators, the carriers. Without the support of the travel trade the campaign to develop tourist travel is severely handicapped. Most long-distance travel is bought through travel agents. Well-informed travel agents, enthusiastic about a particular area, can add strength to travel promotion. Standard "package tours" are devised for wide sale in the trade, and an area will be included only if the agents have sufficient information about transportation, hotels, restaurants, rates, seasons, and commissions. The American Society of Travel Agents is the largest group in this field. A national organization, it includes some 5,000 travel agencies in the United States and Canada. Its roster of members and associates numbers 15,000 and includes all facets of

Figure 31-2. Travel posters have wide appeal. U.S. travel is promoted abroad with full-color posters in several languages.

travel and tourism in 120 countries. The roster is a convenient reference for direct mail lists. (711 Fifth Ave., New York, N.Y. 10022.)

Several major organizations promoting tourism work primarily or closely with travel agents. The United States Travel Service, created in 1961 as an arm of the U.S. Department of Commerce, is such an agency. The offical tourist office of the United States, the USTS promotes inbound group and individual travel from foreign countries. The agency works with travel trade and tourism groups abroad and in the United States to develop more package tours into this country. The USTS also works with trade and state groups for support of the Visit USA program.

Foreign travel wholesalers are encouraged to develop Visit USA package tours for groups. Retail travel agents abroad are enlisted in promoting U.S. tour destinations. USTS regional offices provide foreign travel agents with sales literature translated into the language of the area. Seminars and familiarization tours are also arranged by the USTS offices. A network of Visit USA travel planning centers has been created in six nations. Newsletters are published regularly in a major travel trade publication in each of most of the various countries. In 1975, for the first time, USTS was also granted authority for domestic tourism.

Discover America Travel Organizations, Inc. is a national organization of the U.S. travel industry that promotes travel within and to the United States. The nonprofit association provides government with a source of private interests to assist in working on programs to motivate travel. Members are businesses and associations in the travel field and state government travel departments. DATO cooperates with USTS in staging an annual Discover America International Pow-Wow and a Discover America Travel Mart.

One aspect of DATO's "Take a Spin—Discover America" campaign is the creation of 100 "Perfect Vacations"—two for each state—with literature and display material provided to travel agents on commissionable sales.

The Pacific Area Travel Association, with headquarters in San Francisco, has as its objective the building of tourism in the vast Pacific region and in Asian areas. PATA emphasizes programs designed to inform travel agents and carriers' sales representatives about destinations and services and the constant changes accompanying the region's rapid growth in tourism. Thirty-one governments are members of PATA. There are more than 25 chapters, including a European office in London and an East Asian office in Manila. The chapters have been established in key cities to assist in carrying out the programs. A *Pacific Travel News* magazine is distributed to the travel trade. Film strip and slide presentations are made to sellers of travel. Literature is provided to agents. PATA publishes an annual Pacific Area Destination Handbook.

The mission of the New York Convention and Visitors Bureau public relations program is to tell the traveling public about New York City's advantages as a vacation and convention center. In accomplishing this, the bureau is involved with all aspects of the travel industry. Brochures are made available in bulk to travel agents. The Bureau's "New York Is a Summer Festival!" campaign, designed to turn the city's old off-season summer into a period packed with special events, each year brings the city to the attention of the public and travel agents. The Summer Festival Queen visits cities in this country and abroad as official ambassadress of the mayor for the visitor industry. Coverage by all media is extensive. Representatives of the Bureau meet with travel industry officials throughout the United States and abroad.

To combat erosion of the city's attraction due to economic, political, and social problems, the Bureau in the early 1970s launched a "Big Apple" campaign. The term—derived from the jargon of jazz, entertainment, and sports—is intended to denote that New York is still "the Big Time."

Planning press coverage. Just as a telling theme is essential for a campaign, so planning for the press service is fundamental to any publicity effort. A press release schedule of major stories and features should be laid out with mailings timed every two or three weeks. Too frequent mailings, for the sake of sheer volume, defeat their purpose. Editors would much rather get a well-written story, tailored to their own needs, now and then than a flood of releases they cannot possibly use.

The year's release calendar is based both on the needs of the travel page and the story material available in the area being publicized. Seasonal round-up stories of spring, summer, fall, and winter events are staples that are always welcome. The calendar of events enables readers to plan their trips well in advance and shape their itineraries to take in specific festivals, theater performances, sporting events, displays, or fairs.

The different deadlines of travel and Sunday editors on newspapers, and magazine travel writers and editors must be kept in mind. The travel editor should have copy for his newspaper page at least a week in advance of publication. The Sunday editor, who at many newspapers handles travel features, would also like his stories on hand at least a week or more ahead of publication. If the stories are aimed for local supplements with color or special printing, the editor should be given at least eight weeks to handle the article. Nationally distributed newspaper supplements such as *Parade* should be given material at least three months in advance, especially if the stories are pegged to a specific date or season.

Magazine editors work further ahead than any of the newspaper writers, and the magazine people need story leads six to nine months in advance. In planning a special issue devoted to an area or a country, magazine editors may schedule their story and photographic assignments as far as a year in advance. An entire issue on winter sports in a particular area, for example, calls for pictures taken on the spot in the midst of the activities of the winter before publication. When new areas, out-of-the-way spots, hotels, and special events are to receive well-timed magazine attention, personal notes to the editors outlining article ideas and suggesting that they be noted in the editors' "future" books can be productive. The ideas are on hand when the editors begin scratching for story ideas, and the suggestions may lead to centering entire issues about the proposals.

Publicity content. The quality of a story is important. Editors lament the cliche-ridden travel story with overworked adjectives sprinkled here and there. One exasperated magazine editor maintains that she can take most travel releases, strike out identifying names, and have stories that sound as if they all describe the same place. A fresh, sharp story stands out and is most likely to be used.

Unscheduled and even unexpected events that provide a favorable news peg for area travel promotion can be mined for publicity. Perth flashed into the news when the Australian city turned on its lights and was seen by Astronaut John Glenn. The event provided an opportunity to offer the wire services a short feature about the city and its tourist attractions. Travel editors could have been interested in a news-pegged feature with more details and photographs about the city.

In addition to the stories aimed directly at the traveler, special stories must be provided to the travel trade press giving current information that will be of use to the travel agents and the carriers. New facilities, new rates, commissions, detailed description of major events with accommodations and promotions are of interest. This material serves to supplement the basic information that should be available yearly in booklet form to agents. Colorful brochures on different subjects should be developed for distribution to the travel trade and for direct information of travelers. Posters and display materials are also necessary.

Travel pictures. Photographs are as important a part of the press service as stories. Despite the hundreds of thousands of pictures taken each year of almost every inch of the globe that contains a tourist attraction, very few are of a quality that will survive an editor's scrutiny. One national magazine discards 99 out of 100 shots taken by its own expert photographers. A head-on shot of a new hotel, lifeless as an architect's drawing, may qualify for a real estate story but not the travel page of a newspaper or the cover of a magazine.

A good travel picture must have more than clarity, composition, and a beautiful scene. It should give a sense of action and participation. People are one of the most appealing ingredients of travel. Where it is appropriate to show the residents

Figure 31-3. Festivals and events with historic backgrounds provide colorful material for travel pictures. This scene is of the Joust of the Saracens, which takes place each year at the town of Acerra, near Naples.

of the area in the photographs, by all means do so. If the natives dress and appear different from tourists, the photographs will carry the color and conviction of the place.

The tourists themselves should not be forgotten. When appealing to Americans, the photographs should include tourists who are unmistakably American. A couple in continental dress is quickly identified as somehow not American. Different hairstyles—the man's haircut is often a give-away—and the tailoring of a suit, or a dress, or even the eyeglass style, show that this is not the typical American couple.

Once the photographs covering the features of an area have been taken, the photo service cannot sit back and relax. Last year's picture will not always do this year. Women's fashions, for example, quickly date a photograph. The tourist attractions or their surroundings change. Westminster Abbey was scrubbed for its 900th birthday. Photojournalism techniques and styles evolve. The *National Geographic's* pictures of 1945 are completely different from the big, vivid, color shots the magazine now prints. Color shots of the major landmarks are a necessary part of the photo file. Good transparencies lead the way to magazine color spreads, covers, and newspaper features using ROP (run of press) color—now used by most leading newspapers.

How does one get these good photographs that are so essential a part of the publicity coverage of a tourist area? Look first to staff photographers of newspapers and magazines, if any, serving the tourist area. They may be commissioned to cover specific areas or events. The agreed price should include the negatives, which should become the property of the publicity office. Commercial photographers offer another source, either for commissioned shooting or purchase of photographs from their files. Pictures should be purchased outright with no restrictions on reproduction. If a fee is demanded for each use, the picture is valueless as a publicity item. Experience will soon show which photographers can deliver the goods and which cannot.

An alternative, but an expensive one, is to commission a photographer of national reputation to photograph the tourist highlights of an area. If the section or the country is large, it will be impossible to do more than develop a story theme or two, but this could be a worthwhile investment. Outstanding photographs, first offered on an exclusive basis, could score in one of the top magazines. Other prints could later be distributed on a national basis.

Photographs of visitors at tourist sites can be mailed to their hometown newspapers. This involves use of a photographer on a permanent or part-time schedule, depending on the volume of tourist pictures that are desirable and available. With a brief story or detailed caption appended, the hometown picture will usually be well-received and printed, often on the local society page.

A photograph should be sent with every major news release unless the editor indicates he is not in the market for pictures. A good picture need not be accompanied by a story. If the photograph tells a dramatic story or presents an unusually attractive scene, a caption is all the text required.

Figure 31-4. This picture of the Heerenstraat, one of the main shopping areas of Willemstad, capital of Curacao in the Netherlands Antilles, shows the activity on the Caribbean Island when shoppers from cruise ships visit the port city. The palm in the foreground establishes the Caribbean atmosphere, and the arcades of the buildings provide the flavor of the old Dutch architecture. The scene is natural, believeable, and unposed.

Other services to the press. Press service also includes checking manuscripts and providing writers and editors with information, on request, for stories and background. Writing special stories to order for writers or publications, no matter how desirable a goal, is not always possible. A large staff of writers could easily be kept busy doing nothing but filling specific orders for some tourist areas of wide popularity. Requests for special stories must be weighed carefully and budgeted according to the importance accorded to the publication or the person.

The expense accounts for transportation, accommodations, and meals for travel writers and photographers on several long trips a year can stagger a newspaper business manager. How is a travel editor to cover travel adequately and not punch a sizable hole in his publication's budget? To be valid, by-lined travel stories should relate the personal on-the-spot experiences and impressions of the writer. A travel publicity program can tackle the problem in several ways. Special trips for a number of journalists traveling together can be arranged. This often can be done cooperatively with some of the carriers if it marks an inaugural flight service in the case of the airlines. Government and airline regulations permit allotment of seats to publicize a new service. The cost of hotels, meals, and transportation at the destination is considered the concern of the host when a group of writers come on invitation.

Arrangements for visits of individual writers are a matter of negotiation. If an area wants first-person stories in magazines and newspapers it must be prepared to select individual writers and issue invitations. More than the invitation is usually required. Definite story ideas and leads are necessary to "sell" trips, especially to better-known writers. Once the invitation is accepted, the host is usually expected to defray all or part of the cost of the trip. Some of the best travel writers are free-lancers who regularly sell to outstanding publications. Working with free-lancers of this caliber can be as productive as working directly with the publications. Many of the established travel writers are members of The Society of American Travel Writers. Hosts should not expect that stories resulting from such trips will be completely without critical notes. A writer owes it to his publication and his readers to give a rounded description of his experiences.

Refusals must be given to some writers with newspaper and magazine connections, and others with none that can be discerned. Writers doing a piece on speculation warrant all the help they can get on information, but realistic budgets do not permit assisting all of them with transportation and accommodations. Many a fledgling writer has a happy inspiration that by calling on a tourist office, an airline, or a steamship line, he can walk away with a holiday trip with little expense to himself. No sound publicity program can meet such requests.

Broadcast media. Radio and television, along with press, are effective tools for travel promotion. Short scripts on travel features are presented for use on feature programs. With a seasonal tie-in, the material may be used on women's feature and interview programs. Taped interviews, made on the spot in the tourist area, are widely used on local radio stations throughout the country. The interviewers may be with an unusual personality or someone doing an unusual job connected with a tourist event or place. Interviews such as these must, of course, be made by a skilled interviewer familiar with radio techniques and the operation of a tape recorder. The final interview can be edited to two or three minutes and distributed on a record or a tape to the some 500 local stations in the country that regularly broadcast this type of material. This type of service is available commercially, but since the interviewer usually must travel to the area being promoted and spend considerable time getting the interviews, the cost quickly mounts. Good interview tapes, however done, should first be offered to radio network programs.

Perhaps an interesting personality from the tourist area may be made available for live interviews in the United States, Program directors should be queried about scheduling the visitor. Network television as well as radio is a possibility for the interview or participation show.

Films, from a 28- or 13-minute feature down to a one- or two-minute spot, will be accepted by television stations. Quality again is the criterion; films will not be used unless they are interesting and informative and without a blatant commercial. Since most travel films accomplish their purpose by providing a setting, the acceptance of such films can be high. Special mailings should be made to the stations to offer the films. This can be done with letters, folders, and catalogues, which include reply cards. Placing and distributing films on a regular basis is a time-consuming job. Staff must be assigned, or the work placed with one of the several commercial firms handling placement on a commission basis.[1]

Motion pictures. Travel films for showing in motion-picture theaters are another means of reaching the public. A color film in a first-run or an art movie house reaches travel prospects with an impact that cannot be achieved on a television screen or through a 16-millimeter showing before a club or a local group. A well-made short travel film, about ten minutes long, will find a place on the theater screens throughout the country as a fill-in "short subject." Print costs are especially important here, because scores of prints are needed to service several hundred theaters within a year or two-year period. Distribution can sometimes be arranged through a theater chain on an exclusive basis. The cost of production and prints for 35-millimeter films, necessary for theatrical showings, is much higher than for 16-millimeter films.

A 35-millimeter film is an ambitious project and can be considered only if the budget is geared to it after providing complete service in other fields. Only professionals, bound by a strict price contract, should be entrusted with a 35-millimeter film project.

A practical alternative in developing 35-millimeter coverage is to offer help to film producers in the form of information and assistance on location. Feature films in color with striking scenes as background accomplish a great deal in spreading wanderlust.

The impulse to travel lies very close to the surface in most of us, and skillful public relations can make tourists of us all.

[1] See Chapter 46.

32

Public Relations for Political Candidates

JOHN F. KRAFT, as president of John F. Kraft, Inc., of New York and Washington, was a major factor in hundreds of election campaigns. Some 30 United States Senators were among the office holders who drew on Kraft research and advice in their campaigns.

In addition to political polling and counsel, for which he was most widely known, he conducted other types of opinion polling. His urban studies produced Senate reports and television documentaries.

MORRIS VICTOR ROSENBLOOM, who provided material on recent legislation dealing with elections, is president of American Surveys, which he founded in 1939 as a public relations, opinion survey, publishing, and economic research firm serving international, national, and local clients.

During emergency mobilization periods, he has been an executive with the War Production Board, the National Security Resources Board, the Defense Production Administration, and the Office of Defense Mobilization. In 1951-52 he organized and served as Executive Director of the Institute on Economics of Defense Mobilization, co-sponsored by the American University and the Office of Defense Mobilization.

Public relations is an across-the-board term that is applied—or misapplied—to a variety of activities covered by this book. In talking about public relations as it applies to a political campaign, however, we have no semantic problem at all: A good political campaign *is* public relations. The relations between a candidate, or a political party, and the electorate are measured irrevocably as of a particular moment when the relationship is made final through a counting of the votes.

In this measurable competition between one winner and one or more losers, only the public decides. So on that basis—that the public is the jury and that all appeals from party or candidate are to the public—whatever helps the candidate win, or causes him to lose, is a matter of public relations.

The problem becomes, too simply stated, how you win with what you have.

There are guidelines, and some of them will be given here. But that's all they are: guidelines. There are no formulae that can be that broadly applied, no sure-fire answers for all the questions. The watchword for the public relations counsel in a political campaign is the one beloved by the late Thomas Watson of IBM: THINK. For example:

- Design a beautiful billboard in yellow and black because the colors are visible. But, don't do it against a Western autumn background, where it gets lost with the golden fields and back earth.
- Come up with a slogan that says it for your candidate: "In your heart you know he's right." But you'd better think first of the opponent's possible counter that says "Yes, he's very *far* right."

Good politicians, whether they be candidates or the people who know how to help elect them, are all public relations practitioners. It is not necessary that they have PRSA confirmation of the role. We are talking here about people who either can, or think they can, measure public reaction to a specific political action.

The public relations practitioner involved for the first time in a political campaign must therefore reconcile himself to a fact of life: However expert he is in public relations, he is dealing with people who consider themselves expert, too, and in the very sensitive area of politics.

Actually, much political or public relations sense is acquired by soaking up every experience, be it written, visual, spoken, or overheard from the old pros or fledglings. Anyone whose vocation or avocation is politics will glean as much information from as many different sources about it as possible. This means that the public relations firm or staff must be sharp to stay ahead of the campaign team.

The political team's wisdom can be put to a speedy test by noting the date it first checks in with a public relations firm or advertising agency.

The wise politicians retain firms early enough to jump the gun on the opposition. Even if it turns out that it isn't needed for six months—or needed at all—the foresighted politician is not left searching for a firm at the last minute. And the smart candidate will give the retainer contract to the firm that can prove that regardless of his office, he will get special care and not get lost beneath bigger accounts.

In ideal circumstances, the candidate or manager should decide at least a year ahead of election day who they want as their public relations advisors, and inform them. Even if there is no immediate need for counsel (or inability to pay, because funds won't really roll in until the last months), the advisors will consciously or unconsciously begin thinking and reading about "their man," and the value of subsequent counsel will inevitably be increased. The same argument for early selection applies in many cases to the advertising agency. And it can be important for the public relations firm to know and establish early rapport with the research firm to be employed.

The campaign organization. Part of the perspective for the public relations consultant is understanding the campaign structure. The accompanying chart presents what is commonly regarded as the ideal organization, though variations will exist from one campaign to another.

The reason for such advance planning is that the candidate and his team must gear up for the final three hectic months of campaigning and they want no last minute extraneity interfering with the intensity of their efforts.

Particularly during the last three months before the one-day sale of the political product, the candidate—be he[1] aspiring mayor or U.S. Senator—must vie intensively for the attention of

---

[1]The pronoun "he" is used according to style. This is in no way meant to discount or discredit the increasing number of female candidates and managers, whom I feel have too long been lacking from the visible political spectrum.

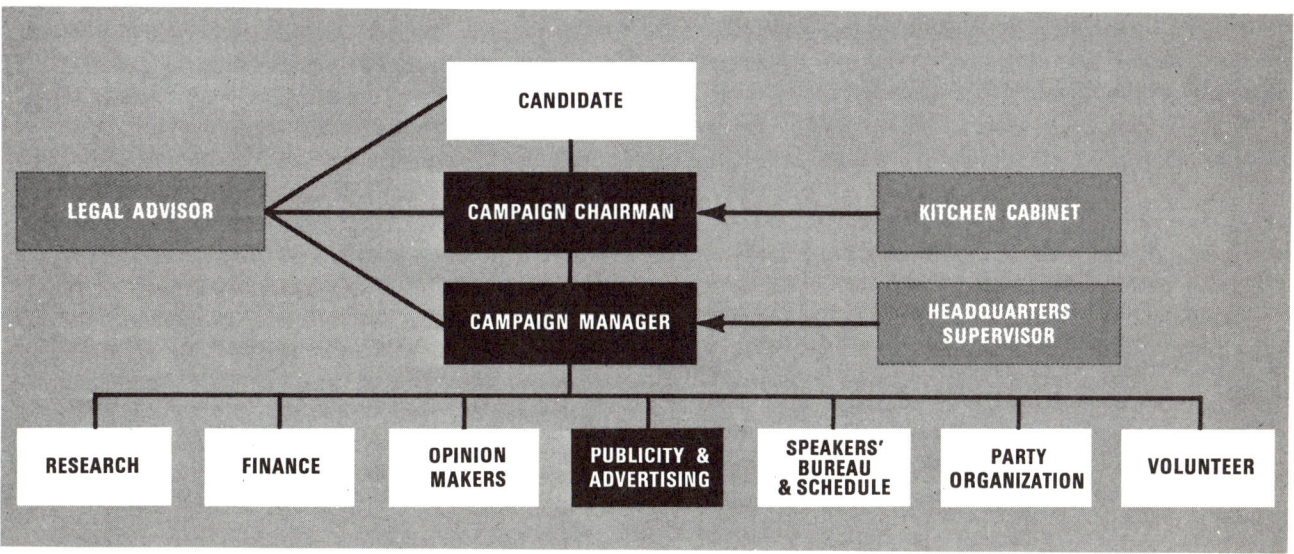

Figure 32-1. Organization chart for a typical political campaign, as developed by the American Medical Political Action Committee.

the voter. And he will be in blood-and-guts competition for that attention with every other politician of the season.

Focusing interest on the candidate. The major question becomes, how do you get the voter's attention to *your* candidate rather than to the dozen others? Of course, while the political competition for attention is in progress, there will also be competition from campus disorders or axe murders prominently featured in the news, the demands on the consumer-voter to buy, the suggestions that he subscribe, that he read this or that, and that he listen to the requests of his family.

The competitive situation calls for raising the candidate's voice effectively enough to be heard by a sufficient number of people by election day. This means in those last three months of concentrated effort, the candidate must be seen, heard, and listened to by the majority of voters. And the message he espouses must appeal to them to support him. For the reason generally given when asked why a vote was cast a certain way, is that the voter was encouraged to do so by one of three sources: the candidate, a party worker, or a friend. It might be said that *the whole business of a political campaign is to ask people to vote for you.*

Reaching the voter. The ways are numerous: speeches and rallies by candidates and supporters; party organization workers ringing doorbells and asking for support of the slate, and the candidate's personal organization asking workers to go out in the candidate's behalf. The candidate can reinforce these efforts by personal letters, advertising, radio spots, and television time.

In any of these ways the candidate is basically asking for the vote. To persuade people to be his followers, he must appeal to all sorts of them. There's no right or wrong way to go about this. However, certain factors apply to making the decision about the way the candidate states his appeal. For example:

- *Television* is undoubtedly an excellent tool if the candidate is running for Mayor in Salt Lake, Atlanta, or Boston. But in Jersey City? Virtually all of the audience votes in New York City and its suburbs.
- *Radio* is a good buy—particularly at 4:30 in the morning in North Dakota when the farmers begin the milking by turning on the radio in the barn. But who would buy the same time in San Francisco?

Appeals for the voter's attention should be tailored as nearly as possible to the kind of voter and person he is. *The voter can only be reached in a way that interests him.* Is it best to communicate on the voter's way to work or home from work by car radio or is it better for him to receive the word via a car card, from a friend, at the shopping center, or at a union meeting? A reprint of a magazine article, brochures or buttons, balloons or girls in sashes, sound trucks or banners, endorsements or debates? In certain areas, voter appeals must be specialized by using the telephone, direct mail, or personal visits.

For instance, direct mail sent to residents of New York's Silk Stocking 17th Congressional District stands to have much less impact than direct mail to poor white families in Appalachia. The 17th District is deluged with mail—so much that often letters get thrown away after a glance at the envelopes.

At campaign time voters are swamped with political-type mail. So unless it's exceptional, political mail is often thrown out and forgotten.

The trick of sending mail personalized with individual address labels via computer is losing its charm, but this is much better than shotgun efforts addressed to "Occupant."

However, if computer programs are available and can be afforded, it is possible to send out more than one message to many different groups of voters or different messages to houses on opposite sides of the street. A series of letters can be sent to persons of different levels of education, occupation, and income.

The techniques a candidate uses in asking for the vote will vary from place to place depending on circumstances. There should be consideration of the cost and numbers involved, quality, and the possible effect on the recipient. Common sense will determine how the appeal is made in light of *the four major components of each political campaign: money, the candidate, the political organization, and the issues.* Public relations plays a keen part in fulfilling each of these components.

EFFECTS OF FUNDING LAWS

The rules for raising funds by the major national parties and candidates for President, Vice President, and Congress have been changed drastically in recent years. The effect has been to change the entire nature of national party politics and the campaigns for the top offices of the nation.

However, these rules do not yet apply to the thousands of other political campaigns at the state and local levels.

PUBLIC RELATIONS FOR POLITICAL CANDIDATES

Figure 32-2. A vital part of the election process for every incumbent is keeping the voters informed between elections. This is a page from a mailer sent to his constituents by Senator Charles Percy of Illinois.

Major provisions of new laws affecting the national races include:

Disclosure. Detailed records of a campaign's financial dealings must be kept and reported to Washington. The name and address of every person giving in excess of $100 (in the aggregate) within a year must be reported.

Limits. Individuals (except candidates contributing to their own campaigns) may give no more than $1,000 per election to one candidate. Individuals may give no more than $25,000 in total per year. Multi-candidate committees, such as House and Senate campaign committees, may give up to $5,000 per candidate per election.

Independent outlays. Individuals may make expenditures (such as for advertising) to a candidate, without these amounts being counted toward contribution limits, if the outlay is an independent one—not made in collaboration with the candidate or his committee or agents. But if such an outlay exceeds $100, it must be reported to the Federal Election Commission.

Federal money for Presidential races. Presidential candidates in a primary who raise enough money to qualify for federal matching funds must agree to a spending limit in the primary election. In 1976 that was approximately $13 million each. In the general election of 1976, each major candidate received about $21.8 million that the federal government had collected through voluntary payments of taxpayers. By accepting public funds for the general election, however, the candidates had to give up the right to accept private donations.

Federal money for national conventions. The major political parties receive taxpayers' funds to conduct their nominating conventions. In 1976 the Democratic and Republican Parties each got about $2 million for this purpose.

As a result of these changes, the small (say, $25 or less) contributor has been made the paramount force. The large contributor has been largely neutralized. The former ability of the well-to-do to balance the masses of manpower thrown into campaigns by labor unions and other special-interest groups has thus been largely vitiated. That makes the importance of using communications techniques to reach the voters more important than ever for business, professions, educational institutions, and other organizations.

Accompanying these developments has been a proliferation of firms that specialize in fund raising through massive direct-mail solicitation.

The growth of Political Action Committees (PAC's) has also been very rapid. The law is theoretically even-handed in giving both business and labor the right to organization committees to support candidates. In practice, it is doubtful whether the PAC's of business, the professions, and industry can ever approach the efforts and impact of the AFL-CIO.

One effect of new funding laws for national offices has been a shift in the media used. With funds limited, such things as buttons and bumper stickers have faded and more emphasis has been placed on the major medium of television.

Efforts are likely to be made to extend the principle of federal financing, as well as limits on size and nature of contributions, to House and Senate races.

Effects on dealing with politicians. Office seekers are likely to deal more cautiously with potential campaign contributors than ever before. To fail to comply with some provision of the complex new laws—however inadvertently—can bring swift accusation from an opponent, with serious damage to the chances for election.

Even in non-election years and even among incumbents secure in office, lobbyists, trade associations, and constituents may encounter increased caution and a tendency to put "everything on the record." In part, this can be attributed to scandals under the loose heading of "Watergate." However, there is also pressure on Congress to open up its own proceedings—to permit televising floor action, to make the *Congressional Record* more truly reflect what actually was said in Congress, and to further publicize government payrolls, among other things.

Effort to reform lobbying is a continuing process that calls for close attention to what is permissible. A former chairman of the House Judiciary Committee defined lobbying as the

> "... 'total of all communicated influences upon legislators,' pointing out that the distinction between good and bad lobbying is 'not whether the objectives of persuasion are selfish or altruistic, liberal or conservative, pro-labor or pro-business, but solely and simply whether the message conveyed is intelligible, accurate, and informative, or cryptic, deceptive, and obscure.'"

Pressure for elections and lobbying "reforms" are placed on Congress continuously. In view of changing developments in political operations and opportunities, candidates will lean heavily on their attorneys and their campaign treasurers. Public relations advisors assisting candidates (whether as staff members or under contract) must follow every development in the field of campaign law and ethics.[2]

FUND RAISING AND MONEY MAKING

In all other campaigns the importance of raising money remains crucial.

People do not want to throw away their money; they want to go with the winner. The finance committee's success is dependent on its convincing people that the candidate has a chance of winning. If the candidate says things the people want to hear, it can be an additional boost to fund raising, but the candidate's words must be publicized or no one will reach for his checkbook.

While contributors must be convinced that the candidate is on top, they also need reassurance that each contribution is vital for the candidate to win.

In actuality, it is not so important what the contributor gives just as long as he gives something. Anyone who gives $1 or $5 has a vested interest and will probably talk about and vote for the candidate.

Money is the name of the game. Regardless of money's abundance or absence, the most effective campaign involves developing a budget well in advance and deciding on an advertising and public relations plan that is feasible enough to stick to. Careful advance planning will save shredded shirts during the heat of the political battle when time can be spent better than on debates over postcard purchases. A smoothly running campaign headquarters presents a solid impression, whereas one where people are haggling over prices and expenditures presents a picture of obvious lack of organization.

Some people think it's best to ask the big givers first for help to set a high collection pace or average gift for the campaign. Others think big gifts should be paced to keep morale levels high throughout the campaign.

No matter what money-raising theory is followed, the quickest way to lose or lower the size of a gift is not to know the answers to people's questions about where the money is going. Canvassers should be schooled in how to answer the most frequently asked questions and how to handle objections. They should have a direct answer ready when people ask how the money will be used.

Of course, if time and money are available, professional fund raisers can advertise the money drive effectively and give the public relations chairman pointers that few amateurs are aware of. Regardless of the degree of professionalism, it will take organization, a timetable, and training.

THE CANDIDATE

Part of the public relations of dealing with any candidate is an appraisal of that candidate. Is he free of serious flaws that can be used to attack him? Will he stand up under pressure?

No matter how you have to find the answers to these questions, do it. If you don't know the candidate's weaknesses, you don't know and won't be

[2]See Chapters 5, 6, 8, and 54.

prepared for what the opposition might come up with. You also have to know how your candidate and his opposition behaved if ever in office previous to the present election.

Victory depends on the most effective projection of the candidate and the issues—and avoiding unfavorable exposures.

Is the candidate healthy? Can he stand the pace of a strenuous schedule the last three imperative months? Does he have the stamina to complete a 16-hour day, day after day after day? How avidly does he want to win? Does he have the drive? Can he communicate his desire and drive to the voter?

The candidate should be measured by appraising his assets and his deficits in hard reality. Is the candidate attractive and articulate? He may be intelligent, but what does his voice sound like when he talks? What are his wife and children like? Is he from a segment of the community where he stands strong *vis a vis* the power structure? Is he happy in a crowd? Is he good with women or more popular with men? These are some of the many things involved in an appraisal of the candidate. In some way or another, each element of the appraisal determines the methods the candidate will use to get the attention of the voter.

Deciding the candidate's approach. It must be determined whether the candidate can benefit from high visibility or if he should be prevented from surfacing. If the candidate is not effective on television, keep him off camera; if his voice is poor, keep him off the air. If someone else's voice can tell the candidate's story better than the candidate, use it. Or if a touched-up still photo behaves better on television than the candidate, but voice is no problem, use the still and the candidate's voice. Your appraisal of the candidate will indicate the right combination and determine whether he should be exposed to public view over a long period of time. Remember, how well he will do as a public servant is not closely related to the charisma he shows or lacks in running for office.

By maximizing the candidate's strength through insights provided by analysis, he stands a better chance of winning. However, he must be advised not to overstep his natural bounds or territory if he is to maintain a campaign strong on the offense rather than being put on the defensive.

Of course analysis works two ways. The candidate will no doubt ask similar questions and make similar decisions about the background of the manager and the public relations executive. So in either case, when sizing up the personal traits that indicate ability and character of the would-be clients, check these items:

Trustworthiness—through reputation or association.
Compatability—to hold up between the candidate and staff executives during the strain and closeness of the campaign.
Experience—the more, the better.
Objectivity—ability to face reality.
Administrative ability—ease in delegating, supervising, following up, and relating.
Energy—stamina.
Good judgment—thorough thinking.
Unflappability—remaining cool under pressure.

The virtues of either the campaign manager or candidate may be much the same, but the degree of trait development may differ. For instance, it's more important for the manager than the candidate to possess the highest degree of administrative ability.

Categories of candidate. It's imperative to examine the candidate's potential in realistic terms of where he sits in the political arena. For the sake of simplification, there are two categories of candidates.

Category One is the incumbent—sitting behind the office holder's desk with full staff, a robot machine, privileges, and status—and the man who should have moved into gear for the next campaign the day after his last election.

Category Two is the non-incumbent—most often the novice, the loser, or the rising candidate—fighting for identity or seeking a new look that will make this campaign a winner, or trying to get ahead by convincing people that he's man enough for a heftier job. In any case, he is faced with a different type of problems and circumstances than the incumbent. (Old pros sometimes come out of retirement and back into this category as strong but nevertheless Number Two category candidates.)

Knowledgeability is the weapon that can most readily close the gap between the incumbent with a record of active service to constituents and materials and facilities, and the Category Two candidate clamoring for volunteers, a budget, a record, and some prestige.

PARTY STRUCTURE

The importance of the party structure varies a great deal. If it is weak, or fractionated, or there is no party structure at all, the candidate and his manager may have to go it alone.

Where an organized party actually exists it is important to work on the basis that party structure or organization is imperfect at best. But that's not enough reason to ignore or slight it. If you do, the party machinery—well-oiled or not—will slice the candidate to bits. It's important to get along with the party and to show that you want to.

The candidate and the campaign manager should check with the organization leaders on a regular basis at least once a week. A developing and continuing liaison of this kind prevents any misunderstanding that the candidate is running his own show. Similar efforts must be taken to keep the candidate in good graces with other members of the ticket, the political offices, and the workers. This doesn't mean a lot of yes-mamming and cow-towing, but just simple party etiquette or preventive medicine for a fatal disease known as political back-stabbing.

Working with the party organization. Regardless of the structure, the party or following must be more than acknowledged because it can be helpful to the candidate—and in some cases can decide the election. Party organization can help the candidate educate the voter as to registration and how to vote using a machine, and in distribution of other candidate-selling information.

Established organizations most often have files of community leaders, good speakers, and community information that can provide great insight when shared with the candidate trying to build up lists of workers, fund raisers, friends, and even foes. Coordination of plans means strength, but watch out for any signs that someone or some group may be trying to use another politically.

Motivating supporters. The organization can be helpful, but because of natural party structures the candidate must develop his own organization auxiliary to the party's. He will need Candidate Support Committees, such as Teachers for Jones, Doctors for Jones, and so on, as well as his own personal group of supporters. He must deal with his auxiliaries on a personal level because most of the volunteers he enlists will be working out of love. How does he keep them happy?

One way is to thank them a lot. This means meeting with key volunteer leaders *at least* once a week to tell them what a good job they are doing and will do. If they add names and addresses to the computerized mailing list, make them feel that they are the key to whether a letter reaches its destination.

In return for showing personal interest, the candidate and manager will generate an alert following that will demand as much as it receives. It will of course demand that all meetings be worth attending. Otherwise volunteers, party organization members, and other followers will consider meetings a waste of time or feel their absence won't really matter.

Another way to keep the followers happy is through a special newsletter marked "Confidential" that goes on a regular basis to each volunteer. By getting personal political tidbits from the candidate the volunteer feels like the insider that he is, but more importantly like a member of the team.

To keep his team members happiest the candidate should never be put in the position of saying "no" to their requests. The candidate must be protected from requests for a job or demands on his time by referring them to his secretary or manager—after acknowledging his interest in the request. It's passing the buck, but it keeps the money in circulation longer and the candidate concentrating his time and energy where the campaign plan requires.

THE ISSUES: HOW TO FIND THEM

Communicating with the right voters at the right time, in the right place, with the right message is the essence of the campaign. And they must all be tied together. Without this kind of expertness the candidate and his manager are flying blind.

It used to be enough for the candidate to know his district or state by extensive travel through it, and by listening to counsel of friends who felt they knew what this group or that group of voters were concerned about. But changes have occurred and are continuing to occur. Twenty percent of the population now moves each year, the average voting age is younger, and more and more people who were previously unregistered are getting onto the election rolls.

Use of surveys. This is why since 1955 there has been a steady, if not remarkable, growth in the use of "voter attitude studies," or "surveys" or "polls," depending on one's choice of definitions, that are designed to find out what messages a candidate should be attempting to convey to his various voting publics.[3] Other studies develop precinct profiles and other sophisticated guides developed with the aid of computers.

The breakthrough year for the use of private

---
[3]See Chapter 35.

political surveys by candidates was 1958. Of the 34 seats contested in the U.S. Senate, 19 were held by Republicans and 15 by Democrats. After the election, 26 were held by Democrats and just 8 by Republicans. The Democrats gained 11 seats—an extremely impressive accomplishment.

In each of the elections where a Democrat unseated a Republican incumbent, one or more election surveys—six in some cases—had been done for the Democrat. It is safe to say that in no more than one of those same 11 elections did the Republican candidate have a "poll" as part of his campaign strategy.

A well-done survey, used widely by clever campaign management, should add two or three percent to a candidate's strength—at a very conservative minimum. In 1968, 28 House seats were decided by a margin of less than three percent.

A candidate who has had no prior exposure to surveys wants to know what he's buying, and usually begins with two basic questions:

1. "How is a survey done?"
2. "What do I get out of it, or what can I learn?"

A succinct answer to the first question from a professional pollster would be something like this:

"First, we try to learn as much as we can about you, your assets and liabilities, and those of your opponent, and what you feel the issues may be. We then construct a questionnaire that will be used by professional interviewers who will conduct in-person interviews in the homes of the voters. The people who are interviewed will be pre-designated by a plan drawn up by our statistician in such a fashion as to insure that it will represent a cross-section, or microcosm, of your entire electorate. The interviews are returned, processed, and the computer print-out is analyzed, resulting in a written analysis of the results. Discussion should follow to permit us to offer suggestions and recommendations. The end-product of the research should be thought of as a campaign tool to guide strategy and campaign tactics."

The benefits of research. This leads into, and anticipates, the answer to the second question. In 1964 National Democratic Committee Chairman Lawrence O'Brien made these comments about the value of poll-taking. Here is quoted from his *Democratic Congressional Campaign Manual:*

What can be learned:
- The issues people are concerned about, and how they feel about those issues.
- Voter reaction toward specific proposals or programs advanced or under consideration by a candidate.
- Voter attitudes toward a candidate and his opponent.
- Areas of strength and weakness for a candidate and his opponent. (These may be classified by race, religion, income, amount of schooling, sex, age, national ancestry, region, or any other pertinent factor.)
- Voter evaluation of various office-holders and the job they are doing.
- Priority ratings which exist in the minds of voters on various issues or proposals.
- Relative standing of the candidates at the time the poll was taken.

There are other uses of this same kind of research, of course. In a Midwestern state a few years ago the incumbent was considered unbeatable, and his opponent's fund-raising efforts were producing negligible results. Then a survey showed that he had an excellent chance of unseating the incumbent and the money started flowing. That opponent is now a Senator.

In an Eastern state a survey analysis demonstrated that the gubernatorial candidate could win if only the voters could be persuaded the election really was important. The lassitude on the part of the voters was overcome, just enough, when the President was persuaded by the survey results to make a special trip to the state and stress the importance of the election of that candidate. It has been suggested that the Presidential endorsement may have resulted in getting another 100,000 voters to the polls. The candidate won by a few tenths of one percent of the total vote.

Aside from the basic purpose for conducting surveys, they have been used to:

1. Raise funds, or discourage fund-raising.
2. Buoy up the spirits of the campaign workers, or discourage the workers for the opposition.
3. Get important support from people in higher office, even if it means no more than one percent of the vote.

But these are ancillary uses of research. The use of opinion research is on the rise for many reasons. Research efforts in a sensibly conducted campaign should be guided by these "do's and don'ts":

Do:
Start research early. Some gubernatorial and senatorial candidates conduct voter attitude research all through their terms of

office. Many others, if not most incumbents, start pulse-taking two years or more prior to election day. The trend in this direction of earlier, more-intensive use is on the rise.

Investigate the background of your research firm. What do its former clients think of it?

Ask who the candidate will be dealing with in the firm.

Confine the reporting of research results to no more than one or two key campaign decision makers.

Give the researcher a thorough backgrounding regarding the needs, candidates, and issues.

Expect a full discussion of the written research results. Insist on complete interpretation.

Don't:

Haggle with the research firm about price, once you've established that the firm is respected and to be trusted.

Buy a bunch of tabulations and statistics without explanation.

Buy research on the assumption that it is a prediction of whether your candidate will win. The real value of research is not to predict the election results, but to help you affect the outcome.

Keep the researchers in the dark. Hiding information prevents the firm from full interpretation of the data produced.

THE TOOLS TO BE USED

After culling all of this information, it takes public relations tools to make the knowledge work for the candidate. The obvious tools are advertising, television, radio, newspapers, magazines, direct mail, billboards, car cards, posters, bumper stickers, and gimmicks like personalized pot holders, combs, or other items.[4]

Each of the tools must be considered carefully. For instance, when it comes to advertising, for the most part it is usually best done by an agency. It can buy time, book space, lay out ads, and so forth. It should help decide *how* and *when* things should be said, but not *what* should be said. If this decision is left up to the agency, there is risk that the messages will reflect the professional ad man and not the candidate's sense of his constituency.

One more caution: The agency, not surprisingly, tends to be somewhat heavy in advocating use of commissionable media. It's likely to be less than enthusiastic about using anything else. Take advice from the baseball shortstop by being sure you play the ball and not let the ball play you.

Choice of an advertising agency. Selecting an agency involves much of the same appraisal as is involved in sizing up the candidate. What is the agency's background? Has it worked for political candidates before? If it hasn't, the candidate may stand to lose in the hottest of all campaign moments. There's a good deal of difference between marketing the political product and a bar of soap, and the agency without perspective concerning that difference might try to wrap the candidate in too fancy a foil for the voters.

Other determinants include the agency's ability to work quickly, and on-call, and its talent for delivering good art and layout.

The agency, like everything else the candidate touches, must be respected and accepted by the media it deals with. Again, much of the decision should be based on how high a priority the agency will give the candidate's account.

Of course, the advertising must be closely supervised by the campaign manager. He should do the directing, implementing all efforts of the advertising agency and publicity director. With his coordination, the efforts come together into sharp focus, making direct appeal to the populace.

Public relations in the campaign. The public relations substance for a campaign comes in from a variety of sources: research, finance, opinion makers, publicity and advertising, speakers' bureau and scheduling, party organization, and volunteers.

These sources must all be under the command of the manager. It cannot be stressed too strongly that *everything* must be cleared through him. Otherwise the most important campaign element—theme—will be forgotten and there will be a lot of loose ends and a lot of lost votes on election day.

Importance of the theme. Theme gives unity to the entire campaign. It is the central idea that binds all the single chords into a solid rope. It must be clear enough to describe the campaign in less than 20 words.

Eisenhower took "Peace, Progress and Prosperity" and from it came up with the combined slogan "Time for a change—I like Ike." Every issue brought the theme and the slogan home to the voter.

The next candidate, John Kennedy, couldn't argue with peace and prosperity, so he took progress and had the theme, "Let's get the country moving again!"

---

[4]See Section V.

In picking a theme, it is important to use a broad brush and to paint the words in bright poster colors instead of pastels. To do this, every aspect of the campaign, from direct mail to where the candidate will speak, must add up to saying the same thing. It must be the focal point. Otherwise the voter sees a blurred kaleidoscope. The point of "theme" is to magnify and focus. And the theme is needed before the first fund raiser.

Avoiding shackles. Staying fluid is sometimes difficult to do—particularly when a candidate gets locked into the notion that he must have certain things in the public relations aspects of his campaign. The certain things may be anything from a half-hour documentary to billboarditis. Candidates or their managers tend to get locked in much the same way they pick up good plans: from their own vanities or from someone who stands to make a buck off the placement of the half-hour documentary. Needless to say, neither source is completely objective.

Another way to get locked in or bogged down is by the friend. The candidate usually has some friend who runs a local advertising agency or who is a printer, or who purports to be a designer, or whatever, but there is only occasionally any evidence of this friend's professionalism in the production of the brochures, or even bumper stickers.

Perhaps the most landlocked of all is the candidate whose campaign strategists consist of relatives—his administrative assistant and an appointment secretary. These people immediately become self-appointed experts in the fields of advertising, media research, precinct organization, public relations, and many other vital areas.

A candidate is often better than his campaign, and, as has been well-established, the campaign is sometimes much better than the candidate. Those who make the decision to get involved in a campaign, to be honest with themselves and the candidate, will commit themselves to the fact that the idea is to win, and that Judgment Day comes when the voter pulls the lever down.

Unlike the commercial world, the only "share of market" a political candidate can care about is "50 percent-plus-one."

33

International Public Relations: I. The Developing Need

Philip Lesly

The rapid changes in international economic affairs are marked by a great interchange of techniques. Countries are borrowing methods and ideas from each other with increasing speed. This has been occurring especially in communications, selling, and persuasion techniques.

As is so often the case, commerce has been most ready to develop these new trends. But easy communication and transportation have made nations aware that the insularity of the past is impossible. Governments, finding that their options are often determined by the climate of public attitude in many other countries, now are unanimously adopting variations of modern public relations.

MULTINATIONAL BUSINESS COMMUNICATION

A few years ago there were great and noticeable differences between America and the rest of the world in both social customs and conduct of business. Most other countries had social structures solidified over centuries of tradition. Comparatively few people were well-to-do and in the market for any goods beyond subsistence. Political systems were designed to perpetuate that structure. Communications media reflected this system and tended to speak for the status quo, often through direct influence from governmental and industrial leaders. As a result, there was little change in market opportunities, so there was little incentive for industrialists to develop new products, work out new marketing techniques, give any attention to winning the good will of the public, or be concerned about the likely effects of political change on business. The tendency was to perpetuate things as they were. Almost everywhere, the old ways were honored as "traditional" and new methods resisted as vulgar. The gap between the top and the common level of society was so great—and the opportunities to rise so limited—that businessmen who had achieved some stature were reluctant to take risks; their first thought was to hold on to what they had. Cartels, limited production, and protection of markets were widespread.

Several factors combined to change this old pattern: Industrialization in Europe and Asia accelerated by World War II; emergence of demand for better life by the ordinary people everywhere; and exposure to Americans and their way of life resulting from the war and postwar conditions. The "multinational" company has arisen in response to opportunities in a rapidly industrializing world. Though they include some sophisticated and advanced enterprises headquartered elsewhere—Unilever, Shell, Volkswagen, Philips, Sony—they have been mostly American. Country after country has been propelled into an industrialized speedup of progress. In many places—France, Germany, Japan, Italy—the leaders and industrialists have managed to adjust fast enough to guide the trend and benefit from it. In many other countries—particularly the "emerging countries" of Asia, Africa, and South America—failure of the established groups to recognize the pace of change has led to their own expulsion. In many places they have been replaced by nationalized industries or private-government combinations that operate as monopolies.

Being projected from a low level of economic vitality into efforts to compete with America has created for foreign businessmen—whether private entrepreneurs or government appointees—a problem of sensing, understanding, and adopting American outlooks and methods in the field of intangibles—marketing, design, advertising, public relations. People who for generations had in effect stifled imagination and innovative thinking now were faced with imaginative concepts largely alien to them. As a result, there have been few cases in which progress in these areas has been anywhere near as rapid as technological progress.

Successful appeals to U.S. market. There have, of course, been a few notable exceptions: European auto manufacturers—notably Volkswagen—sensed the changing temper in America and introduced reliable small cars at a propitious time. They have taken up American thought on how to appeal to the peculiarities and unique traits of the American consumer.

• Olivetti introduced to America its design-award-winning Lettera 22 portable at a time when American portable typewriters were virtually unchanged, except for face-lifting, for a generation. The dramatic advancement in utility, appearance, and service that Olivetti provided quickly captured a large share of the American market. A small price advantage helped, but it was primarily the image Olivetti projected of the quality of its product that made this possible. The entire typewriter industry was stimulated, with the result that American, German, and Japanese manufacturers developed new design and marketing methods. The result was a boon to consumers in many countries.

• Before World War II there was a clearcut public image of Japanese goods: shoddy, shady copies of American products, or cheap items no American firm could make. Then the still cameras of the Japanese gained an enviable reputation for quality, reliability, and innovation, achieving a remarkable turn-around of public image in a short time and were followed by other types of precision products, such as watches. Japanese electronic products and autos next benefited from this improved image.

• Other examples, while not so dramatic, include Danish bleu cheese, Dansk housewares, Austrian sweaters, Scandinavian tableware, Italian shoes.

On the other hand, hundreds of other foreign products and companies have not had the benefit of American thinking and technique and so have not made a real dent on the American market.

Understanding differing attitudes. As in most cases, this is a two-way matter. Hundreds of American companies and industries still have not learned the lesson that every country is distinctive and must be approached in its own way. In the same way as many Europeans assume that generations-old marketing methods of their homelands are all that are needed to sell here, many Americans try to export American images, appeals, and messages. The Italian auto worker is not a distant counterpart of his Detroit competitor—his heritage, his interests, his tastes, his mores, his aspirations, his prejudices, and his desires are all different.

Even in Canada, the country whose people are most like those in the U.S., the importance of approach through Canadian eyes and minds has been made amply evident with the growth of Canadian sensitivity to American influence in Canadian industry.

This is multiplied when companies or industries try to sell in many nations. Not only must each American company work out a different approach and plan than that used in the United States, but usually a different one is required for each country, though broad basic principles may be applied to all.

Knowing the temper of each country can avoid serious errors, such as using sex to sell in Italy, pressing for fast action in countries where speed is still considered unseemly, failing to go through proper political channels in countries where nothing happens without politicians and their relatives.

Coordination, of course, is vital. This is a task for skilled professionals who not only are experts in U.S. matters but have judgment and knowledge of the needs for operating in foreign lands.

Lessening of price as a factor. The Japanese, Germans, Italians, Belgians, and others for years found their toehold into American markets eased by substantial price advantages due to low wage rates. However, people and economics, being part of nature, abhor vacuums. Pressures from labor to increase the workers' share of the rising income are growing in most industrialized nations. If American unions show restraint in their own demands, the wage gap is likely to continue to narrow and decrease the price advantage of imports to the U.S. over American-made goods. In the same way, of course, the price advantage of foreign-made goods in competing for world markets is being narrowed, paving the way for better results for American export marketing efforts.

If price gradually ceases to afford European and Asian companies an automatic advantage over American goods, these foreign producers will need to learn more of America's skill in the intangibles of marketing, merchandising, advertising, and public relations. The successful ones mentioned earlier—plus industries like the Scotch distillers, the British woolen weavers, the French perfume blenders—have learned how to do this. But most have not.

Increase in importance of foreign trade. The United States is the most industrialized nation in the world, with productive output in thousands of products that awes the world—yet it has had the lowest percentage of international trade, in relation to gross national product, of any major nation in the free world. While more foreign manufacturers learn to make and sell what Americans want, Americans have been slower to find the ways to appeal to foreign consumers.

Not only are foreign firms increasing their sales to America faster than Americans to them, but they have increased their share of other foreign markets because Americans have been slow to learn how to sell against them. Japan, West Germany, and other nations have become great exporters in recent years and compete aggressively against the U.S. everywhere.

Through all the erupting changes moves another violent force—the Communist bloc. Russia and China know that true world dominance must come from dominance of trade. They are working hard to upset the careful plans of free peoples for orderly trade operations. They are aggressive, hard-hitting, and ruthless in their economic practices as in their politics. Ingenuity and knowledge of how to work best with people and to win their patronage have always been strong assets of free people. The greatest battleground of trade rivalry will be the minds of men. The skills of the American public relations person will be vital in competing for foreign markets—by analyzing and adjusting to the distinctive mold of each people's psyche.

In the same way, producers in other countries need the skills and talents of Americans to appeal to Americans. As Volkswagen and Chanel learned that when in Chicago they must think as Chicagoans do, so will many other European, Asian, and Latin American industries.

GOVERNMENTS' ACTIVITIES

Virtually all nations now conduct international public relations programs. Sophistication varies greatly, depending on awareness among the nation's leaders of the effect on their goals of attitudes abroad. In general, there is now little recognition of the advisory function of public relations people in helping to guide policies and international relations. But in the areas of assessing attitudes and carrying out information programs, the pace of growth has probably matched that in commerce since the early 1960s.

Programs among smaller nations tend to be directed toward tangible goals, such as tourism (see Chapter 31), investment in local industry, and marketing of local products.

Large nations, on the other hand, are finding it vital to have active programs in many countries, as well as activities originating at home that are beamed abroad. Gaining understanding of the country's policies and actions is increasingly vital to its ability to carry them out.

In some instances—notably, Red China—what may be called "guerrilla propaganda" is predominant. This includes intrigue, proselyting, subversion, and other devices that are effective to the degree they are hidden from view. Among Western countries, such functions are the assignments of separate agencies such as the Central Intelligence Agency of the United States, and have little place in the public relations role of the country.

Information and persuasion are the primary functions of British, West German, American, and other government-operated programs in many countries.

Of the 8,830 employees of the United States Information Agency, for example, 4,230 are foreign employees in countries outside the United States. USIA operates the Voice of America radio network that broadcasts nearly 800 program-hours a week in more than 36 languages. Films and television programs—produced by both its own staff and private producers—are shown to audiences in more than 100 countries. Publications are produced for various foreign audiences. A radio-teletype service dispatches news, background, and statements to all USIA offices and to many publications. Its information centers operate libraries, design and manage exhibits, and oversee translations of books.

Questions about what USIA's role should be—whether it should make a contribution to policy considerations, whether it should merely disseminate information or try to stimulate favorable attitudes toward the U.S.—have been rife since it was formed in 1953. However, the occasional suggestion that it be dropped entirely gets very little consideration. At least as a pipeline for communicating with the world at large, the international information service appears to be an indispensable part of every country's public relations function.

34

International Public Relations: II. Functioning Abroad

WILLIS PLAYER is Senior Vice President-Assistant to the Chairman of Pan American World Airways. He has been a Pan Am official since 1964.

Mr. Player had been Vice President, Public Relations, for American Airlines from 1957 to 1964 and previously had been Vice President in charge of public relations for the Air Transport Association of America, an industry group representing scheduled airlines in the United States.

He served with the "Wall Street Journal" before his graduation with honors from the University of Michigan in 1937. He also was a reporter for a time for the Chicago "Daily News," and later was a special writer for Booth Newspapers, Inc.

During World War II he was an officer in the Navy, assigned to Air Combat Intelligence. He served on the staff of the Air Force Commander, Pacific Fleet, on the staff of the Commander-in-Chief, U.S. Pacific Fleet and Pacific Ocean areas, and in the aviation information section of the Office of the Secretary of the Navy, in Washington.

He is a member of three scholastic honor societies—Phi Beta Kappa, Phi Beta Phi, and Phi Eta Signa.

The activities of the International Public Relations Association give ample testimony to the existence, the vitality, and the growth of public relations as an international discipline, practice, or profession.

In refuting Rudyard Kipling's line, "East is East, and West is West and never the twain shall meet," a recent President of IPRA, Ivy Lee, Jr., said, "East and West have met, and live in one world . . . . we in public relations have a major role to play . . . in urging representatives of the various nations to understand the other person's viewpoint . . . ."

True. But it remains also true that there is no such thing as international public relations, because it is not generally possible for a public relations expert from any one country to drop into any second country and be equally expert there.

There are business enterprises that conduct their own public relations activities in several or in many foreign countries. There are public relations firms that have branches or affiliates abroad. But as a discipline, an art, or a practice there is no such thing as international public relations.

The best, the most practical, and the most realistic counsel that can be given to someone who has a public relations need or business opportunity in a foreign land is to seek expert advice on that country.

There is, of course, another avenue—provided you have the time. This other alternative is to become an expert on the foreign country. This involves much research, including study of the country's literature, and interviews with representatives of the national leadership—the real leadership, not just the leadership titled as such.

Thus, you would need to talk to executives and officials, to academicians and to labor leaders, to churchmen and politicians, to students and to traders. And when you had finished there would be a good chance that differences in idiom would have misled you.

The method of self-education was, of course, the method used by the American business pioneers abroad: People like W.R. Grace & Co., who went abroad not just to visit and to trade but to remain. Today in most countries it is possible to find an expert and save yourself the time and the errors of self-education.

UNIVERSAL DIFFERENCES

You probably have seen some such statement as:

> The world consists of individuals who basically all share the same personal hopes, fears, motivations, and desires.

If this statement were true the practice of international public relations would exist. But it is not true, except—maybe—in a very limited sense. Not even in America is it true. There are variations in values between California and New England or between Harlem and Queens. The variations between countries are far greater—even between countries that have some similarity of background, such as Canada, the United Kingdom, and the United States.

If there were citizens of the world, you could begin to visualize an international public relations. But wisdom in the practice of what is called international public relations begins with the knowledge that there are, as yet, few citizens of the world, only citizens of nations or regions, and that habits and values differ between them.

Differing outlooks. In conversations with acquaintances from Marxist countries, it becomes clear that there is no such thing as objective truth, as Americans understand the phrase. Americans tend to believe truth can be established by objective facts; the Marxists define truth relatively, that is, by conformance to doctrine.

Yet, the Marxists believe, at least some of them, that their doctrine is objectively true. Thus, you have confusion not only of terms but of concept.

Many Americans value efficiency and hard work. Many Frenchmen and Italians regard the American version of those "virtues" as uncivilized vice. Even some Englishmen and Germans insist that the passion of the American executive for work is a form of madness.

And then, of course, there is a famous and quite true cliche about being on time in Latin America.

Almost all North Americans believe there is merit to being on time. Latins who have not been conditioned by North American managements frequently seem not even to be aware of the concept of being on time.

Those examples are a few illustrations of how values can differ. They suggest why it is wise to seek the counsel of someone who is an expert on the value systems and communications systems of a foreign country in which you intend to do business.[1]

MAJOR CONSIDERATIONS

You can, however, list certain subjects on which you may wish to seek counsel. Here are some of them: your local identity; local values/ethics; specific publics of special importance; communications media; local language and idiom;[1] allies; national interests.

If you are going to do business in the hypothetical Republic of Maldon, would you hold yourself forth as an American citizen or as a Maldonian citizen? In Maldon, as elsewhere, the answer to that question depends on the nature of your business and the circumstances and values within Maldon.

If you are an American-flag international airline, you will probably hold yourself forth as American when it comes to flying, because American airmanship has an appeal to a great many persons; and if Maldonians have a passionate, over-riding devotion to their own airline, no pretense of being Maldonian will do any good.

However, your Maldonian counsel probably will advise you to maintain a staff composed largely of local nationals.

If you are a hotel company, you will have a different choice.

On the one hand, you can hold yourself forth everywhere, including Maldon, as the same hotel. Thus, the international traveler finds you identical in Britain and in Maldon. Many customers like the security of visible sameness. Or you can hold

---

[1] Editor's note: Tedd Joseph cites the importance of language idiom and translations. He cites this item in a prominent French newspaper:

> "CORRECTION"
> In our issue of May 24, we published a press service dispatch reporting that at Seoul the military junta, which has recently taken power, had shot a dozen functionaries and officers who had not reported for work at the regular time.
> In fact, the functionaries and officers in question had only been dismissed (in English: "fired"). A bad translation is obviously the origin of the inexact text published by the press service whose dispatch we used.

yourself forth as a Maldonian hotel, with distinctive Maldonian decor and style. In that case, you will emphasize to your clientele that wherever they go, Maldon or Britain, they will find the same American standards of efficiency behind the scenes.

In either case—whatever facade your hotel puts forward to the world—your counsel probably will advise emphasizing to the Maldonian business community, labor leaders, religious leaders, and government officials that you as an individual hotel are Maldonian in intent and in function.

Your counsel may suggest that your local company have Maldonians as majority partners, that you employ and train Maldonian help, and purchase Maldonian supplies. He may even ask you to consult with the local astrologers, if any, and accept their advice—as when the date of the official opening of the Hotel Siam Inter-Continental in Bangkok was determined by the Royal Astrologers.

Determining local posture. Even if your primary concern is publicity for a specific product, you probably will need local counsel on what your posture should be. Has the space program given American technology such a good reputation in Maldon that Maldonians want to be able to boast that they own a radio "Made in U.S.A."? Or, whether radio or toothpaste, are Maldonians more impressed with a product that has a wholly Maldonian national identity?

Values/Ethics. These may indeed differ from country to country. An attitude that is acceptable in the U.S. may be offensive in Maldon. Business practice that is customary in Maldon may be unacceptable in the U.S. Authoritative local counsel with respect to such subjects can enhance your effectiveness as an enterprise and minimize your exposure to embarrassment.

Major publics. The Maldonian publics who are important to you can broadly be classified into two groups, and they may overlap. One consists of the people who will or who can buy your product or your services. These people are frequently depersonalized and referred to as your market. The other group consists of those who will control your destinies as an enterprise.

Time and money will be wasted if you do not make accurate identification of each group. For example, if a small group of people determine Maldon's opinion and values, your counsel may urge you not to over-use mass media. He might even say that *The Economist* of London is one of your best avenues to reach the top Maldonian leadership.

In general, the selection of media to use is directly influenced by the publics you wish to reach, but evaluations based on knowledge of one country are not necessarily true of another. For example, the news programs produced by the three major networks in the U.S. are notable for both their extensive coverage and high credibility. However, some countries do not even have television as a mass medium—but in some of those that do not, there may be comprehensive radio coverage.

And whether you are using broadcast or print media, you must educate yourself to be skeptical of your own expertise in the matter of translating your message into foreign languages. To be certain you will not appear obtuse or foolish or even vulgar, you must rely on the advice of persons who are expert in the foreign languages you propose to use. It is necessary, for example, to remember that Spanish is not a uniform language. One of the more enlightening exercises for anyone who wishes to devleop public relations programs in Latin America is to listen to public relations executives from each of several different Latin American countries discuss how an idiom that is quite acceptable in one country is equally unacceptable in another.

Allies can be extremely important. To cite just one example, almost a *reductio ad absurdum,* any hotel company that intends to build or operate a hotel in a Marxist country must have as an ally the government department that is responsible for hotels. And if that department is convinced that its programs can be served and its problems best solved by your hotel company, a mutually beneficial relationship can be formed.

The United States is itself a good example of the value of domestic allies for foreign businessmen. Importers of German or Japanese goods often develop and protect a domestic market in the United States for German and Japanese businessmen.

Identifying with local interests. The question of whether your business needs to demonstrate that an important national interest is served is a question that your local counsel or representative would help you answer. The airline industry, perhaps more than most, frequently has had to prove its value to a country in order to begin, maintain, or expand air service.

The Philippines provide an example. For some years the Philippine government vigorously restricted the rights of foreign-flag airlines to serve the islands. This was essentially a protectionist measure favoring the country's own flag carrier, Philippine Air Lines. One result of these travel restrictions and the consequent slackening of promotional efforts by the affected airlines was stagnation of the tourist industry in the Philippines.

The various tourist and travel agencies with interests in the Philippine market mounted a campaign to sell the benefits of increased travel and increased tourism to all sectors of the islands' economy. This was a straight-line presentation of facts and figures, for tourism is one of the most productive and profitable industries any economy can enjoy. It was also pointed out that as tourism grew all the participating air carriers (including the islands' protected airline) would benefit from the increased business.

The target areas for this mutually beneficial campaign of persuasion were decision-makers in government, in local tourism and travel activities, in business and banking, and in the labor pool at various levels—for more tourism meant more jobs of all sorts in a revitalized industry.

The intermediary agencies were, for the most part, Philippine publications—newspapers and magazines. A certain amount of direct conversation and persuasion was involved, but here extreme caution had to be observed—for this was, after all, a purely domestic decision.

The Philippine media became interested in the problem. Stories were published. Editorials and columns both pro and con appeared. The subject of Philippine tourism became, to a degree, a public issue.

During the several years that followed, the government Tourist Commissioner, the prestigious Philippines Association, the Philippines Chamber of Tourism, and various hotel and restaurant associations all officially endorsed the policy of additional air service for the islands as being in the nation's interest.

The foreign airlines serving the Philippines obviously had a special interest in bringing about an easing of restrictions on their operations. But it was the self-interest of Filipinos, not of foreigners, that brought about the easing of restrictions. As a foreigner, whether in the United States or elsewhere, you have a better chance of serving your own objectives if they are genuinely linked to the interests of the host country, and an important mission of a public relations program abroad can be to establish and demonstrate such linkages.

Similar episodes have occurred elsewhere. Take the situation not many years ago when the U.S. Government proposed a ceiling on the expenditures of Americans traveling abroad. In effect, this would have radically reduced the number of Americans traveling abroad. Since Americans form the bulk of the overseas travel market, this would have adversely affected many foreign economies.

As Congress debated the matter, U.S. segments of the travel and tourism industries marshalled and presented facts and figures. American dollars spent abroad, they said, came home to buy American goods and pay American workers. And in any event, the way to narrow the travel gap was not to restrict American travel abroad but to stimulate more travel and tourism from other countries to the United States.

That was the theme told by the American segments of the industry. Foreign enterprises also made an appeal to American self-interest. In particular, SAS—the Scandinavian Airlines System—took a vigorous position that its services benefited the American economy. For example, SAS advertised that it spent more in the U.S. than it took out of the country in fares from Americans traveling abroad.

The effective educational effort made by the alliance of American and foreign economic interests was instrumental, probably crucial, in preventing the restrictions from being adopted.

STAFF AND COUNSEL ABROAD

With respect to representation abroad, the question is frequently asked: Do you keep the same person or the same group in the same country for the rest of their lives? Or do you, like the U.S. State Department, shift your representation periodically?

Experience suggests that there is no single comprehensive answer. Pan Am has simultaneously used both systems. It has kept representatives at the same foreign post for a number of years. It has shifted others when circumstances seemed to require.

Each system has its advantages. Each has its disadvantages. The decision you make rests on judgment as to the specific persons and the specific circumstances.

How do you find a foreign representative or advisor for your company? Sometimes you find him through mutual friends. Or you can ask the embassy, or other American firms doing business in the country. Frequently officials or businessmen of the country concerned can give you good advice. A good way is to seek the counsel of a public relations firm that has affiliates or experience abroad. Or you can rely on the membership roster of the International Public Relations Association.[2]

But no matter how you find foreign public relations expertise, the point is: Find it. It is a good general rule that your own expertise will be deficient in a foreign context. That the profession of public relations continues to grow, in skill as in scope, in many countries does not yet mean that today you have a better chance of finding good foreign counsel or good foreign representation than you would have had even five years ago.

---

[2] U.S. Chapter, 74 Trinity Pl., New York, N.Y. 10006.

SECTION IV

Analysis and Preparation

35

The Role of Research in Public Relations: I. Purposes and Types *

ROBERT O. CARLSON is Dean of the School of Business Administration at Adelphi University. Previously he served for eighteen years as an executive with Standard Oil Company of New Jersey (now Exxon) working on management problems of the parent company in the U.S. and those of its operating affiliates in the Middle East, Africa, the Far East, Australia, and Europe.

He received his A.B. from the University of Pittsburgh and his Ph.D. in Social Psychology from Columbia University. He has served as President of both the Public Relations Society of America and the American Association for Public Opinion Research as well as having been the Executive Officer of the American Sociological Society. For many years he was Chairman of the Editorial Board of the Public Opinion Quarterly and still is a member of that Board.

His doctoral research at Columbia was an evaluation of the effectiveness of public health information programs among Blacks in the South. He then directed the Columbia University Bureau of Applied Social Research's study of communications patterns in the Middle East; data from that field work comprises Daniel Lerner's book, The Passing of Traditional Society. He has taught at Columbia University, served as a consultant to the Rand Corporation, and is a member of the Market Research Council and the Advisory Board, Graduate School of Communication, Fairfield University. Dean Carlson has contributed articles to many professional journals, including an article on "Public Relations" in the International Encyclopedia of the Social Sciences, and edited the book, Communications and Public Opinion—a Public Opinion Quarterly Reader published by Praeger in 1975.

Typically, public relations research serves three functions. Most frequently, it may simply *confirm* assumptions and hunches about the state of public opinion on an issue, a product, or a company. Although hardly world-shaking, this is a highly useful kind of back-up function, in many ways analogous to the use of quality control systems in the manufacturing end of a business.

*Adapted and updated from "Public Relations Research—Problems and Prospects," by Robert O. Carlson; *Public Relations Journal,* May 1970, pp. 6-9.

A second role of research is to *clarify* questions on which limited information is available or on which apparently contradictory data are to be found. For example, such studies can help determine if expressed attitudes are related to actual behavior, whether in the supermarket, the voting booth, or a fund-raising campaign. Research can help sort out what people really mean when they say they like or dislike an organization—the reasons they cite for these feelings, and even the origin of the feelings.

Finally, research occasionally *reorients* our thinking and conceptualization on a public relations problem. One assumes that such was the case a few years ago when the banking industry discovered that it was frightening potential small customers away by its austere, no-nonsense image. Whatever the reason, the change in the public posture of banks has been profound and I would not be surprised if advertisements were soon to appear inviting me to stop by my friendly neighborhood bank for a social drink with one of its vice-presidents.

There is an unintended bonus in conducting research. The process of defining its design and assigning priorities to areas of investigation forces various individuals and departments in an organization to make explicit their beliefs as to which publics and which problems are most serious. Such an exercise frequently generates an internal dialogue that turns up surprising differences in opinion as to the exact nature and degree of importance which different people and departments attach to various problems.

MANY TECHNIQUES AVAILABLE

Those who have had little first-hand acquaintance with formal research can not fully appreciate the variety of techniques and study designs available. A very old and still useful method is to carry out a *content analysis* of how a topic or an organization or a problem is treated in the press, textbooks, radio, or television. Such research gives a pretty fair measure of the saliency of the problem and often useful hints as to which aspects of it seem to be arousing greatest public interest. Several caveats must be observed with respect to content analysis studies—what weights, if any, should be assigned to the length of coverage, position on the page, the page number itself, and so on. Used with intelligence and a clear recognition of its limitations as a research instrument, content analysis can be a useful tool.

Public relations programs that have as their chief objective the raising of money for some cause, or the election of a particular candidate to public office, can profit from *secondary analysis* of past giving records or previous voting profiles. Census data, on a district by district basis, provide data in terms of age, sex, level of income, and education that can then be juxtaposed against past giving or voting records.

For many people, the term research is synonymous with *public opinion surveys* and their various survey techniques, each of which has its merits and its limitations. Properly used, these different techniques can complement one another and produce a mosaic of data giving new insights into long-standing problems.

If an organization is embarking on a public relations program for the first time, or if some new or relatively unknown factor becomes relevant for an on-going program, the *profile survey* can be useful. It is a one-time snapshot (or perhaps X ray) of public reactions to a particular company, issue, or program. Correctly used, it can help identify sub-groups who are most favorable or most hostile with respect to the issue in question. It can give a general idea of the saliency of an issue and the extent to which people are getting information about the issue from the several media or from their friends, family, or fellow workers and the context in which they view it. The danger of using a profile type survey is that it is static. Its findings may become perishable or biased by reason of some unique political or economic event. Properly employed, it can provide valuable heuristic labels for describing sub-groups in the public at a given moment in time.

When a profile survey is repeated, retaining the basic sample design and interview guide but employing a new sample of respondents, a *trend survey* is taking shape. Trend surveys are a double-edge sword, particularly if they are employed as *effectiveness studies* of an information program. Properly used, they can provide critically important clues as to which facets of a message are getting through to the audience and which are not. But when misused and wrongly interpreted, they can create no end of mischief. Some first-class programs have actually been sabotaged because poorly designed and poorly interpreted effectiveness surveys have suggested that the message was not getting through.

Before-and-after reading. By definition, effectiveness surveys must have a before-and-after reading where data are typically gathered on such matters as how informed people are about a topic or a particular company and whether their feelings are generally favorable, unfavorable, or apathetic. The general public, it should be noted, has very limited information or interest in the major business corporations of the country. They have difficulty correctly identifying a product with the company that manufactures it. They have only the dimmest idea of who constitutes the management of these companies and what the "corporate philosophy" of these firms may be. Under these circumstances, it is not surprising that surveys turn up a great deal of "no opinion" or "don't know" responses. In recent years, perhaps out of frustration at finding a low level of public awareness and interest in the institutional message of large companies, opinion researchers have developed elaborate scales that are said to discern delicate shifts in the public feelings toward our major corporations. While the aim of these fancy scales is laudable, the research results are of questionable validity and use. Slight movements in a more favorable direction on these rating scales are seized upon with delight by over-anxious practitioners concerned about justifying a large outlay of money. In many cases these "favorable research findings" result from the sampling procedures and in other instances they are the artifact of the random answers to questions that have a low level of interest or relevance to the respondent.

It is both amusing and dismaying to observe the excitement generated by "findings" from an effectiveness survey that show an increase in favorable attitude of three, four, or even five percentage points. By themselves, such data mean very little, especially if they do not look for the canceling-out effect that takes place in public opinions. For example, a survey may show little or no change in the general public's attitudes on civil rights. Closer analysis, however, would show that during the period under study, upper-class, professional people were becoming more sympathetic to this cause, but that this shift was being canceled out on an over-all basis by the fact that middle-class, white-collar workers were growing less sympathetic to the civil rights movement. Even when a survey spots this canceling phenomenon, it usually can provide only limited information as to its causes.

Only when the time, trouble, and expense are taken to permit the same respondents to be re-interviewed on another occasion can these trend surveys be converted into a *panel survey*. These panel surveys permit the dynamics of opinion change to be more fully studied. By re-interviewing the same respondents on one or more occasions, it is possible to indentify the context for individual shifts in attitudes from one time period to another and to probe for specific reasons that might account for these changes.

Other tools for public relations. Two other forms of opinion research are useful tools for the public relations profession. One is the *depth survey* which is nothing more than an effort to let the public tell the researcher, in its own words, how it views a company, a public issue, or a particular individual. In these surveys the researcher carefully avoids imposing his point of view on the respondent. Rather, he encourages the person being interviewed to freely associate and ramble on in his own words in describing his perception of the matter under study. Depth studies are useful in the early stages of a program in giving clues to the perimeters of a problem. They also can provide some really valuable themes that copywriters and creative departments may incorporate into a campaign.

Finally, a stepchild of the research field is the *pretest*. While pre-tests are rather extensively used in product advertising campaigns, they tend to be less used in developing storyboard treatment of films or in sharpening a print advertisement campaign or testing reader interest in proposed pamphlets and executive speeches. This is a pity, for while effectiveness studies can tell us whether a program struck out or not, this information is a bit academic inasmuch as money has already been spent on films and advertisements. Apparently, pre-tests are viewed with alarm by some creative people who see in them a threat to their prerogatives. This is unfortunate, for properly used, they can give powerful support to creative people in developing better, more effective copy.

How to use the tools. It is not realistic to expect formal research studies to be part and parcel of the everyday routine in a department or counseling firm. There is simply not enough money to support such studies, nor enough wisdom latent in the archives of the social sciences or our profession to recommend them as a constant diet. But they can be helpful tools when employed at the right time by practitioners who make reasonable demands on them.

Research in public relations is not primarily a product to be bought or sold as our whims or anxieties may dictate. It is preeminently a point of view, a way of looking at problems, a predisposition for organizing past and present experiences. In this sense, research is not detached from the on-going activities of a public relations program, but is at the heart of it. Research is the educated counsel and experience that are brought to bear on the design of a new program based on the cumulative experience of all the public relations people who discuss, dissect, and define it. It is the knowledge of the success and failures of others in the past who dealt with similar problems. It is the feelings in the air of professional meetings and luncheons, and the prevalence of small talk with colleagues, that alerts us to some new concept or development in our field.

Good research takes time—management often needs answers in a hurry. Management frequently feels it must have research results immediately if they are to be of any value in planning action programs. This sense of urgency runs smack into the irksome fact that good research requires a reasonable time to organize, pre-test, execute, analyze, and write up.

Good research, unlike good wine, need not age and, in fact, it usually goes sour with time. There are few problems on which at least some significant preliminary data cannot be collected within a few weeks. Subsequent analysis and refinement of these data will actually benefit from the early comments and questions management addresses to these initial findings.

There is no need to doggedly pursue to the bitter end every research study simply because it seemed like a good idea at the time it was O.K.'d and money has been authorized for it. Public relations problems are frequently elusive and may occasionally defy systematic research study. There is still plenty of room for the educated, intuitive guess in situations where events are moving fast, and there are critical variables influencing these events.

Still other problems are so general and all inclusive as to almost certainly result in banal research findings that contribute nothing to the planning of an action program.

EVALUATING RESEARCH

There are no clear-cut criteria by which management may evaluate the worth of a public relations research study. In actual life, the most widely accepted criterion of the success or failure of a study is whether or not our boss says he likes the finished job. But his first reaction has only limited validity and longevity. He cannot know whether a particular study meets his needs until he has had a chance to translate some of the findings into action. In fact, initial reactions to a research study may change—growing more or less favorable as the relevance of the findings is tested out in day-to-day operations.

Under the heading of bad or useless research one must certainly place those studies that are commissioned solely in the hope they will support a particular point of view that may be under challenge by others in the organization. Research cannot afford to be the tool of special pleading by any person or faction in an organization.

Unfortunately, research is often regarded as a kind of report card on the performance of an individual, a department, an advertising or consulting agency, or on a particular program. This view is unfortunate for it does not take into account the many variables that have an important bearing on performance at any given time. These variables include changing political and economic conditions or competing events, which may detract from, or give heightened attention to the program or problem under study. Very likely, practitioners themselves are ambivalent regarding the desirability of research. While they might gain a better understanding from research data, they fear these data may also measure their performance unfavorably.

Evaluation of a research study is a complicated business. It would be very wrong to assume that top management has the training or resources for translating research findings into public relations programs. It is likely that more than one boss has decided that a particular piece of research was bad when, in fact, his real problem was that he did not have the staff or the personal ability to translate research findings into successful programs.

Public relations research often deals with those frail and invisible entities—attitudes and information. Such data are by their very nature intangible and far more elusive than, for example, findings from advertising research studies whose data can be validated by comparison with subsequent sales figures, share of market data and so on, or employee relations research findings that can be measured at some later date against manpower turnover figures, rates of absenteeism, rates of productivity, and other factors.

NEW DIRECTIONS

In the past, corporate public relations programs concentrated their time and money on reaching certain predictable audiences thought to be of greatest importance to the corporation—shareholders, employees and their families, customers, key government officials, the financial community, and other opinion leaders. In turn, these sub-groups were the subjects studied in corporate public relations research programs. It is easy to understand why management elected to use this method of classifying its publics. The system has the merit of being neat and quickly understood by top corporate executives. Moreover, delivery systems for reaching these static publics are relatively simple. Mailing lists can be compiled for each of these groups, speeches directed to them, and print advertisements and television commercials tailored to their special interests.

But political and social forces that emerged in the late Sixties and early Seventies have changed this simple and safe way of categorizing the corporation's critical publics; and these forces, in turn, have redefined the focus of public relations research. During the Sixties and early Seventies three massive social and political movements had profound impact on the corporate world and appeared for the first time on the agendas in board rooms where policy is shaped. These three issues were:

1) a concern with protecting and improving our physical environment;
2) consumerism (including concern about protecting investors); and
3) demands for upgrading the career opportunities for women and disadvantaged ethnic and racial groups.

These political and social movements, and the resulting legislation that they generated, caused corporate public relations programs to become more "issue" oriented and less "public" oriented.

Today, public relations researchers recognize that criteria previously thought to be sound for studying their publics—place of residence, level of education and income, sex, and race—are no longer reliable indicators of an individual's lifestyle and his or her social and political, intellectual, and emotional orientation. The design of a public relations research study cannot make any firm assumptions about the attitudes of a particular sample based solely on their census characteristics. For example, in the area of attitudes on environmental issues, the long-haired activist on a college campus may well be a co-worker with a conservative suburban housewife in campaigns to protect the environment and prevent companies from building new plants and facilities in a particular community. The conservative small-town banker may find himself joining with the politically more liberal professors of economics in bringing pressure to insure that financial reporting by major corporations is more explicit and reliable. In still another area of public concern, black middle-class urban dwellers may be as outraged as their white suburban counterparts when abuses are found in urban relief, unemployment, and welfare programs.

The labels "politically conservative" or "liberal" no longer belong to particular sub-groups in our population. And this complicates enormously the job of the public relations researcher in trying to identify key target groups whose attitudes might affect the well-being of his or her organization. Corporate institutional advertising is increasingly being directed at particular issues rather than to specialized publics. Better research techniques are needed for measuring the effectiveness of these new "issue" oriented corporate messages carried in the op editorial pages of leading newspapers or in magazine and professional journals favored by politically militant groups.

Perhaps the single greatest challenge facing public relations researchers today is devising better early-warning networks for their management. These networks help identify the still small and inarticulate public-interest movements that may one day impact on the company's future well-being. Some companies are employing an in-house early-warning network to gather data on public attitudes toward them. They are looking to the observations and experiences of key employees as a source of their information. These employees often provide timely early warnings regarding new problems on public relations issues that are only beginning to yeast in the public's mind.

A program for systematically debriefing these employees several times a year represents a form of public relations research that is inexpensive yet holds significant findings. Among employees who are likely candidates for such debriefing sessions are salesmen, retailers, those working in employee relations departments interviewing applicants for jobs, and those who recruit professional staff personnel on college campuses.

CONCLUSIONS

The importance of sound and significant public relations research to management of all organizations is greater today than it has been in the past. Top executives in the petroleum, automobile, paper, and drug industries (to cite a few examples) are spending many hours each week worrying about how public attitudes toward their industries may translate into unfavorable legislation affecting their future operations.

The focus of public relations research has been changing from the study of traditional publics to a greater attention to the study of "issues" and how best to modify public attitudes on them. For the most part, the tools of public relations research have changed little in the past decade. There is reason to believe that the successful use of marketing models in the market research field will slowly be adopted by public relations researchers. The development of public relations research models, based on the sophisticated use of electronic data processing techniques, holds breathtaking promise for bringing timely and actionable data into the hands of decision makers in a matter of days, rather than weeks or months.

35

The Role of Research in Public Relations: II. Guidelines and Techniques

GEORGE GALLUP, Jr. is President of the Gallup Poll, Princeton, N.J., with which he has been associated since graduating from Princeton University in 1953. He has also studied at Oxford University in England.

He has made thorough studies of the voting behavior of various groups in the population, and has published reports on voting patterns among farmers, young voters, intellectuals, Blacks, and members of labor unions.

He is a member of the Board of Directors of the Roper Opinion Center at Williams College, and is a member of the American Association of Public Opinion Research and of the World Association of Public Opinion Research.

The assistance is gratefully acknowledged of ALEC GALLUP, Vice-President of The Gallup Organization, Inc., and Coordinator of Gallup International, Inc.

With survey research fast becoming an indispensable part of public relations programs, it behooves persons engaged in the field of public relations to have at least a general knowledge of research techniques and capabilities.

First questions to ask. The public relations man must first decide what his survey objectives are. A survey that starts without well-defined objectives often produces a mass of extraneous data.

He should next determine his target groups—that is, the specific groups whose attitudes and beliefs are of significance with respect to his problems. These groups might consist of consumers of a given product, dealers, purchasing agents, business leaders, financial analysts, bankers, employees—or the general public.

He must then determine what degree of accuracy is required for his purposes. Does he need only a general overview? If so, perhaps a 500-case sample or less is suitable.

On the other hand, if he is interested in determining the division of opinion with a high degree of accuracy, or "reliability," or wants to analyze the findings by subgroups within the sample, he should consider samples of 1000 cases or more.

In interpreting survey results, it should be borne in mind that all sample surveys are subject to sampling error—that is, the extent to which the results may differ from what would be obtained if the whole population surveyed had been interviewed. The size of such sampling errors depends largely on the number of interviews.

Accuracy in all sampling operations tends to increase with the addition of cases. However, it is important to keep in mind that the addition of many thousands of persons has very little effect on the survey result after the first few hundred.

FOUR ESSENTIAL INGREDIENTS OF SURVEYS

These are:

(1) *The Sample:* This should be expertly designed to be representative of the population being studied.

(2) *The Questionnaire:* This should be carefully

366

tested to insure that the required information will be obtained.

(3) *The Interviewers:* These should be trained and experienced in the art of asking questions.

(4) *The Analysis:* This should be carefully done so as to provide a reliable basis for reaching decisions.

The sample. Once the survey takers have identified the large group called the "universe" that the sample is to represent, the sample can be drawn. Selecting the sample may be carried out according to two basic methods—*quota* sampling or *probability* sampling.

Quota sampling divides the population into subgroups and assigns each subgroup a proportion in the final sample. Normally, the subgroups are selected on the basis of (1) geographic location, (2) community size, (3) economic level, (4) sex, and (5) age. The final sample in a survey of the total adult population must have the right proportion of persons who live in large cities, suburbs, small towns, and rural areas. It must have the right proportion of men and women, and of older and younger adults. The resulting sample will be representative in terms of these five controls, but the sample may not be representative in other important respects. This is the problem will all quota samples.

Probability sampling overcomes this defect in the quota method by selecting the sample so that all units of the population have a known probability of being selected. If the sample is drawn in this manner, all subgroups in the population will be represented in approximately correct proportions, provided the sample is large enough and the completion rate is sufficiently high.

The questionnaire. Before the questionnaire is formulated, it is an important first step for the researcher and the public relations man to talk informally to the types of people the survey is designed to reach. These conversations will provide important insights into the thinking of the target groups.

A wealth of information can emerge from discussion groups in which an unstructured questioning technique is used in the preliminary stages of a survey. Respondents can be encouraged to express frankly and openly their views about a company, a product, an institution—or a major social or political issue.

The next step is to formulate the questionnaire, paying particular attention to the wording of the questions.

Designing the Questionnaire. Formulating the questions is a delicate task. The questions must be worded so that everyone in the sample can understand exactly what is being asked. They should contain no unfamiliar words, or words with ambiguous meanings.

The questions should be unbiased, using no pejorative or emotionally charged words. They should seek one answer at a time.

The form of the question is as important as its wording, and depends on the nature of the subject, how widely it has been discussed, how clear the issues may be, and other factors. Some questions ask simply for a "yes" or "no" answer. In others, the person is asked to pick from several statements the one that comes closest to expressing his own view. Or the person may be asked for his general opinion in an open or free-answer question.

Dealing with Complex Issues. In any given survey the researcher inevitably must deal with complicated issues where it is difficult to state both sides clearly and fairly.

In such cases it is often wise to use what is termed an open-end or free-response question, such as: "What do you think of this plan?"

On some issues it is important to separate informed persons from the uninformed, and to measure opinion in more than one dimension. This can be done by a simple question design devised by the Gallup Poll. It is a series of questions that begins: "Have you heard or read about 'X' issue?" The respondent can answer "yes" or "no."

If the answer is "yes," the respondent is asked: "Please tell me in your own words what you consider the chief issue to be?" This question determines the extent or level of knowledge possessed on the subject. The interviewer then records the respondent's exact words.

The next question asks: "How do you think this issue should be resolved?" or, depending on the nature of the controversy, a variation of this question. The respondent is permitted to explain his views with as many qualifications as he wishes.

The fourth in this series of questions poses specific issues that can be answered "yes" or "no." Often it is possible to explain the issues in a few sentences; in effect, to inform the person being interviewed, and then to record his opinions. Individuals who said they had not heard or read about the issue are eligible at this point to answer both this and the last question.

The fifth and last question attempts to establish the "intensity" with which the respondent holds his views. How strongly does he feel that he is right? What steps would he be willing to take to implement his opinions?

Intensity of Opinion. Measurement of the intensity of opinion is obviously of key importance. Whether people feel keenly about an issue can make a difference in what they do about it. Similarly, it is important to those who have the responsibility of interpreting the views of the group interviewed.

One key development in public opinion research has been the invention of rating scales to measure the intensity of opinion in a form suitable for use in typical interviewing situations. Two such scales were devised by Jan Stapel of the Netherlands Institute of Public Opinion and by the late Dr. Hadley Cantril, former chairman of the Institute for International Social Research and former chairman of the psychology department of Princeton University.

The Stapel Scalometer was the first of its type. Basically, it is a column of ten answer boxes. The top five boxes are white, the bottom five, black. The boxes usually are numbered from "minus five" at the bottom to "plus five" at the top.

The interviewer hands the respondent a reproduction of the scale and explains its use in these or similar words: "You will notice that the boxes on this card go from the highest position of plus five—for something you like very much—all the way down to the lowest position—for something you dislike very much. Now how far up or down the scale would you rate the following?"

The interviewer then asks the respondent to rate the person, company, or proposal with which he is concerned. The scale can be used to measure intensity of feeling by asking the person interviewed how strongly he feels about the issue, how certain he is that he is right, how much he hopes that his view will prevail, how hard he is willing to work to see that his view is adopted, and so on.

Researchers have found the extreme positions on the scale are the most indicative and the most sensitive to change. These are the positions "plus five" and "plus four" on the favorable side, and "minus five" and "minus four" on the unfavorable or negative end of the scale. Frequently in reporting, these two positions are combined to produce a "highly favorable" or a "highly unfavorable" rating.

Getting at the "why." Persons who are asked to give their opinions in a survey usually are asked to tell why they hold the opinion they do. But often the "why" behind the opinion comes out more clearly from a careful analysis of the findings by different groups in the population, and by cross-tabulations with other questions these persons have been asked.

Every survey result can be analyzed from the viewpoint of the education of the respondents, their religion, age, sex, economic status, section of the country in which they reside, and occupation. From such analyses it is possible to shed light on the "why" behind the public's views.

Motivation research—employing psychological techniques to gain insights into behavior and attitudes—can be an important part of a research program. However, unless this research (typically undertaken with a small number of people) is coupled with quantitative research (a full sample), the findings should not be projected to the universe being sampled.

Interviewing. There are two basic methods of obtaining interviews—by *independent samples,* where different respondents are interviewed each time; or by *panels,* where the same people are interviewed a number of times.

In independent samples, interviewing is normally conducted in four ways: (1) with personal interviews; (2) with telephone interviews; (3) with mail interviews; and (4) with personal drop-off.

Personal interviewing is generally considered the most reliable. It has obvious advantages because it is possible to obtain a more representative sample then by other methods and because greater interviewing *in depth* is permitted.

Telephone interviewing is less expensive, but there are disadvantages in this method. One is that the refusal rate is higher normally than with personal interviewing. Another disadvantage is that there is a bias in favor of upper income people, since those who do not have telephones are found chiefly in the lower income levels.

Mail interviewing is also relatively inexpensive. The great disadvantage is the problem of return. Low-income and poorly educated persons are less likely to return the questionnaire than are others in the sample.

One way to minimize this problem is to send out a second request to persons not replying to the initial contact, urging their participation in the survey. The characteristics of this latter group can then be compared with the group that initially responded. If there is little or no difference, the assumption may be made that you have a reasonably good sample. Another approach is to sample the non-respondents either by telephone or in personal interviews, and weigh the results accordingly.

Personal drop-off is a combination of personal and mail interviewing and has advantages of both methods. First of all, response rate is high because the interviewer who "drops-off" the questionnaire at a particular household has already established rapport with the respondent (often through a personal interview). Secondly, the dropped-off questionnaire (or portion of it) is self-administered (filled in by the respondent himself), thus providing fuller and franker responses than can sometimes be obtained in personal interviews. The dropped-off questionnaire is either mailed to the headquarters of the survey research organization or is picked up by an interviewer for this organization, usually the one who made the initial contact.

Panels are used less frequently than independent samples for public opinion research, although they are used extensively in marketing research. Panels have the advantage of enabling the researcher to measure changes in attitudes exactly, since the same person is interviewed on successive occasions. The disadvantage, particularly in the case of surveys measuring awareness or knowledge, is that the panel being interviewed tends to become super-informed and thus atypical.

IMPORTANCE OF RESEARCH KNOW-HOW

The problems discussed in the preceding paragraphs point up the need for public relations practitioners to have at least some background or experience in survey research. The need for research know-how is apparent when decisions must be made about survey methods and costs.

In addition, the research-oriented public relations man should work closely with the researcher in each phase of a survey—in defining the objectives of the survey, in question formulation, and in interpretation and analysis.

The researcher is in a good position to give valuable advice on how to translate the survey results into an effective public relations program. He has lived closely with the survey and is likely to have insights that might escape the public relations man who is not experienced in analyzing survey data. He is also typically more familiar with the limitations of the sampling procedure.

It is often in the sponsor's interest to have the survey conducted by an independent organization, since otherwise findings may be viewed with suspicion.

WHAT SHOULD A SURVEY COST?

A well-directed and properly conducted survey will usually yield valuable returns for a relatively small financial investment.

The cost of survey research depends on many factors, including the size of the sample, length of interview, the type of questions, and whether the survey is "syndicated," i.e., is shared by other clients, or is specifically designed for one client.

To provide a general idea of costs, it may be helpful to bear in mind that many research companies set a total price for a survey that is roughly four to six times the total cost of interviewing—typically the single most costly item in the survey.

A high price quotation for a survey is not necessarily an indication of a competent job—some research organizations must ask for high prices because they have high operating costs. On the other hand, if the price quoted is extremely low, it may be an indication of shoddy work, of cutting corners.

Survey research has reached a high level of sophistication. Aided by the computer, it is destined to play an even greater role in our lives. Not the least beneficiary will be the public relations man.

36

Fact-Finding for Public Relations

WILLIAM W. COOK, retired Director-Public Communications Services, United States Steel Corporation, has been a public relations man, newspaperman, and magazine editor since his graduation from college in 1935.

He joined United States Steel in 1959 after six years as a partner in the New York City public relations counseling firm of Pendray & Cook. Before that he was an account executive in Cincinnati and New York for Hill and Knowlton, a copy editor on "The New York Times," and Executive Editor of "Motor Magazine."

He received a Bachelor of Arts degree from the University of Michigan in 1935, and a Master of Science degree from the Graduate School of Journalism, Columbia University, in 1938.

He was a Public Relations Officer with the Eastern Defense Command in New York during World War II.

He has taught journalism courses at Columbia University and a course in public relations at the College of the City of New York. Mr. Cook served two terms as national treasurer and a member of the Board of Directors of the Public Relations Society of America in 1963-64, and was President of the Society's New York Chapter in 1959-60. He is a trustee and past president of the Foundation for Public Relations Research and Education, and a member of the Public Relations Advisory Committees of Pace College, New York, and Fairfield University, Fairfield, Conn.

Facts, and their implications, are the bricks and mortar of public relations. No matter how skilled he or she may be with the tools of the calling—the publicity, films, speeches, and other means of transmitting information designed to build public understanding and support for his organization—the success of the public relations person's efforts depends primarily on his materials, i.e., the facts about the organization. Only secondarily does it depend on his mastery of public relations tools and techniques.

Few outsiders appreciate the degree to which the practice of public relations is based on painstakingly documented facts. It distresses practitioners that the harshest criticism leveled at them stems from the fact that much of what the average layman mistakenly thinks of as public relations is based not so much on the documentation and presentation of facts, as it is on their distortion or suppression.

While the conscientious public relations man often may wish he had more palatable facts to work with, he does his best with what he has and stands or falls by the results. It is an axiom of good public relations (as it is of good business practice generally, and the two are usually synonymous) that people like to do business with companies they trust. Thus, whenever he prepares a public statement such as a news release or a speech, the public relations man is aware that its accuracy will have a direct effect on his organization's reputation.

To present his case effectively in the court of public opinion the experienced public relations man knows that he must marshal all the pertinent facts, both pleasant and unpleasant, that he can lay his hands on. He must assemble his case with the diligence with which a skilled lawyer digs into an issue to be tried in a court of law. Like the lawyer, the public relations man is an advocate for his company or client. He must be constantly alert to make sure that the pressures of advocacy do not cloud his judgment, to see that his assessment of a situation is not based on incorrect or inadequate information, or colored by his own or management's preconceptions. He can never afford the fleeting comforts of self-deception, for his usefulness is directly proportional to his capacity to get at the truth, analyze it correctly, and lay the results on the line.

Public relations can never be static even under the most serene conditions. People and their opinions change constantly. In our turbulent times, new situations of crisis or opportunity arise at a breathtaking rate. For an organization in business or industry, there rarely comes a moment when those charged with its public relations can relax with any feeling more reassuring than one of allayed apprehension. Thus the ability to stay abreast of changing situations and keep kaleidoscopic facts in perspective is essential.

REDUCING THE ELEMENT OF CHANCE

The service that fact-finding performs in public relations has been likened to the function of radar in guarding air and sea lanes by warning of approaching hazards. The more information we can gather to assess the nature and scope of a public relations problem, the better able we are to approach it with some assurance that we have minimized uncertainty.

The burden this places on research is clear. Those responsible for an organization's public relations find themselves needing to be skilled fact-finders in an awesome variety of disciplines. Obviously, the well-rounded practitioner today must have a thorough knowledge of his organization and the field in which it operates. Increasingly, however, he finds himself also expected to have an up-to-date knowledge of fast-changing conditions in business and finance generally, the political arena, education, international affairs, and the social sciences, with growing emphasis on sub-disciplines such as socio-economics and ethnology, let alone such arcane natural sciences as ecology and agrobiology.

Much of the information a public relations man needs to serve his company or his client lends itself to systematized storage and retrieval. Literature such as reports, news clippings, and statistics are examples. But some of the most useful information does not lend itself to a mechanical or electronic retrieval system. How, for example, can one store in a filing cabinet or on tape the knowledge of how to deal with sensitive racial issues accumulated from a lifetime of study, discussion, and personal experience?

But while the busy public relations executive can never delegate all the functions of what is generally regarded as research, he finds himself needing to call on others increasingly to help him with various aspects of it. To see what parts of the job he can or cannot delegate, let us examine what we mean by "public relations research."

The term "research" itself presents a semantic problem, since it tends to conjure up visions of owlish Ph.D's in white smocks hunched over vaporous beakers. In fact, research for public relations, while always an exacting and often an arduous job, is simple enough in concept. The term "public relations research" is commonly used to mean:

- Public *opinion* research for public relations purposes.
- The series of functions involved in:
    1. Keeping close watch on the social, political, and economic scene in a "radar scanning" operation to detect early signs of problems and developing trends that are likely to affect an organization's public relations.
    2. Deciding what research activities, including public opinion research (see Chapter 35), are needed to determine the nature and scope of developing problems or trends and obtain the information required to deal with them.
    3. Gathering the information.
    4. Analyzing the data in terms of the organization's public relations needs and the specialized interests of individuals and departments.
    5. Getting the appropriate information into the right hands.
    6. Filing the information for ready retrieval.
    7. Retrieving information bearing on a particular subject or project as needed.
    8. Analyzing this information, as well as data from other sources, in terms of a specific public relations problem and using it in a public relations project or program.
    9. Evaluating the results by means such as public opinion research, analysis of press and radio-TV news coverage and commentaries, and field reports from all available sources. At this point our series comes full circle, and we find ourselves back watching our radar screen for signs of significant trends and shifts in opinions and attitudes.

Since public opinion research is dealt with in Chapter 35, we shall focus our attention here on the other aspects of finding and using facts for public relations purposes.

QUALITATIVE DISTINCTIONS IN FACT-FINDING

First, we should recognize certain qualitative distinctions among various steps in the series.

The first step, scanning the horizon to detect signs of public relations problems and trends, calls for broad knowledge of the current scene outside the organization, as well as a thorough grounding in the organization's history, structure, policies, products and people, its operations and its aspirations, and an awareness of its public relations objectives and activities.

Steps 2-5, deciding what research activities are needed, gathering information, analyzing it in terms of public relations needs, and getting it into the right hands, call not only for knowledge of the organization and the social, political, and economic scene, but also for the special skills of a researcher who is familiar with the tools and techniques of fact-finding and versed in the behavioral sciences.

Steps 6 and 7, filing the information and retrieving it as needed, call for experience found in a variety of specialists, including file clerks, secretaries, librarians, research librarians, and increasingly, computer programmers.

Step 8, analyzing the information in terms of an organization's public relations needs and using it in a public relations project or program, calls for an architect of ideas. It is best handled by someone who can recognize the scattered bits and pieces that apply to a particular situation and adapt them to it. Our idea architect should have the experience and the vision to see how an article in *Fortune* can be turned to account in a situation developing in a plant community; how a statement by an 18th Century Prime Minister clarifies a point that the Chairman wants to make in a speech to stockholders; how the failure of a public relations project attempted a decade ago by another company points the way to success today.

The final step, evaluating the results, calls again for the researcher who is skilled in the methods and techniques of fact-finding, versed in the social sciences, and keenly attuned to subtle changes in opinions and attitudes.

While the distinctions among the various steps seem clear enough when we consider the differing skills they require, they are distinctions that sometimes escape not only top management, but an occasional Public Relations Director as well. At times the person who is skilled at storing and retrieving facts is expected to perform as an idea architect too. This often leads to the disillusioning discovery that the qualities that make him excel at processing information are not necessarily the ones that enable him to interpret the information wisely in terms of public relations needs.

The point, then, is that while all these functions are essential to get maximum mileage out of the fact-finding operation, the talents needed to handle them are not always found in the same individual. Thus such questions as who will do the fact-finding and analyzing, who will file and retrieve facts, and who will apply them to the practice of public relations, are by no means academic in setting up the mechanism to handle these functions.

Often these questions answer themselves in simple terms of manpower. In public relations' earlier days, the practitioner usually did his own research, often aided by his secretary. This still holds true in smaller departments and firms where personnel limitations make versatility not just a virtue, but a necessity. However, as public relations firms have expanded, and corporations, banks, associations, and other organizations have come to rely more and more on inside and outside assistance, there has been a growing tendency to set up some special facility to handle the functions involved in gathering and processing facts.

Such standard repositories as filing cabinets, desk drawers, and library shelves and stacks are customarily used for information storage and retrieval. Increasingly, however, computers are being called on to take over the chores of storing, retrieving, transmitting, and to a limited extent, analyzing information used in public relations work. Terminals that provide access through phone circuits to a central time-sharing computer enable different units of the same company, such as district public relations offices, to share a single data bank. Each terminal may be used to feed into the bank such data as names, dates, and statistics, and documents such as news releases, executive speeches, and policy statements, and to retrieve these and similar materials fed in from other terminals. A system of this sort enables a company to transmit news releases or other copy without delay from one terminal to any others on the network, and simultaneously to store it in the data bank where it is on call at a moment's notice from all points. It also makes possible the analysis of press coverage of an important news story across the country from data supplied from all terminals. As in other cases where a latter-day Aladdin summons an electronic genie to help him, though, it is well to keep in mind the dictum, "garbage in, garbage out."

KNOWLEDGE OF SOURCES IS ESSENTIAL

No matter who—or what—handles various parts of the fact-processing operation, certain sources of information are uniform for virtually any public relations operation. A working knowledge of these sources, together with a handy reference shelf in one's own office, eliminates the need for a great deal of original investigation. It helps to keep us from "inventing the wheel" all over again when we undertake a new project, and anyone engaged in public relations should become thoroughly familiar with these sources.

Certain standard works are so useful to public relations practitioners in every field that they are virtual "musts" for the office bookshelf. These include such staples as a dictionary (preferably two: a desk edition within arm's reach and an unabridged close by); *Roget's Thesaurus, World Almanac, Information Please Almanac,* a good world atlas with adequate maps of the United States and individual states, the *Congressional Directory,* statistical and fact books of special interest to the organization, and public relations reference works and case studies. Other volumes, such as the *Statistical Abstract of the United States* and *United States Government Organization Manual,* may be used often enough to warrant keeping them close at hand.

The procedures for gathering and arranging facts so they can be applied to the solution of public relations problems are fairly uniform. The late Dr. Karl E. Ettinger, a New York public relations and research counselor who contributed the chapter on fact-finding for predecessors of this *Handbook,* and to whom the present writer is indebted for much of the material that follows, set forth certain requirements for a basic fact file for each project or client. Dr. Ettinger visualized this file as a ready source of facts and figures to inform both the practitioner and the public. Such a file must be updated constantly in a continuing intelligence activity that helps adjust policies and actions to the changing scene and recognizes trends that are likely to affect an organization and its plans. Here are some of the things recommended for such a file:

1. Statistical figures concerning the organization.
2. Charters and bylaws of the organization.
3. The organization's publications, news releases, advertisements, speeches, background statements, and the like.
4. Color and black-and-white photographs of plants and other facilities, products, activities.
5. Biographies and pictures of key personnel.
6. Pertinent clippings from newspapers, magazines, trade publications.
7. Radio and television monitoring reports.
8. Basic reference books dealing with the activities and problems of the organization.
9. Trade association and trade union literature of organizations concerned with our own or similar problems.
10. Lists of key individuals interested in our organization and its problems (Board of Directors, trade association officers and members, public officials, opinion leaders, others).
11. Lists of related or interested organizations.
12. Mailing lists of selected groups.
13. Lists of all government agencies and officials (federal, state, county, municipal) concerned with the organization.
14. Pertinent legislation and pending bills; important legal decisions.
15. Reports on government and legislative hearings.
16. Findings of public opinion studies concerning the organization or matters related to its interests.
17. Lists of editors, reporters, and commentators in all media covering the organization's news.
18. Literature of competitors and antagonists.
19. Information about individuals and institutions from which an adverse influence on public opinion may be expected.
20. Biographical data on individuals with whom contacts are desirable.
21. Calendar and timetable indicating occasions for publicity (anniversaries, memorial days, plant dedications, conventions, national weeks and days) and occasions when publicity or events should not be planned because of holidays, conflicting or competing events.
22. Lists of possible publicity tie-ins with other organizations, products, or events.

By subscribing to the services of clipping bureaus and radio-TV monitoring services,[1] some of the material needed for continuous compilation of the file may be obtained. Most of the remaining material will accumulate from a systematic reading of publications and reports, subscription services, and other literature that normally flows across the practitioner's desk.

Many free materials available. It is useful to make sure that those who are responsible for gathering facts are placed on lists to receive the many free materials available from industry, government, and other sources as research tools. These include speeches, annual reports, fact booklets, news releases, company publications, and research reports of similar organizations, as well as a variety of government publications that are available free or at a nominal charge. Another source not to be overlooked, of course, is regular contacts with people performing similar functions in other organizations who can provide leads on research techniques, reports, and surveys, and offer guidance on contemplated projects.

Gathering information about a company or client and seeing that maximum use is made of it is important. Equally useful, at times, is collecting adverse criticism and analyzing it objectively to keep a running account of where the organization stands in public opinion. The public relations person is paid to know what is going on and to counsel management on what to do about it. Any time he finds he is being paid to tell management what it wants to hear, rather than what he thinks management should know, he is well advised to take his talents elsewhere.

In approaching a public relations problem, the following procedure is useful:

• *Determine in writing what the problem is.* Formulating it in this manner is advisable even where you are conducting the study alone, for it helps to clarify your thinking and supplies your organization with a record. Where more than one person works on a problem, a written record is indispensable to avoid misunderstanding and duplication of effort.

• *Write down the questions you want to answer by collecting pertinent facts, figures, and opinions.* Public relations problems tend to be complex, and a single fact rarely supplies all the information needed to solve one.

• *Look for precedents.* Compare your organization's situation with those of others in similar circumstances. You need to learn as much as you can about the technical conditions and social forces that have played a role in comparable situations in the past.

• *Make a list of all available sources you intend to use.* Preparing such a list at the beginning of a fact-finding operation helps you organize it quickly and efficiently. The list will include a bibliography, and the names, addresses, and phone numbers of all potential sources of useful information. In preparing the bibliography, consult the catalogs of libraries, reference books, a volume such as *Guide to Reference Books* (American Library Association) and the bibliography services offered by the Library of Congress. For sources other than printed ones, list all persons with experience in the field in which you are interested. These may include association executives, government employees, and trade journal writers and editors. Your roster of sources may then look like this:

SOURCES OF INFORMATION

Printed material	People	Others
Reference books and reference periodicals	Own organization and staff	Public registers
Other books and periodicals	Own observation	Correspondence
Newspapers & clippings	Customers	Pictures
Government publications	Government officers	Foreign sources
Company & association literature	Governmental information depts.	U.S. Patent Office
Competitors' publications	Librarian, public library	Monitorings and recordings of radio & TV broadcasts
Newsletters	Librarians, special libraries	Documentary and other motion pictures
Directories	Newspaper and trade paper editors	Detective services
Newspaper morgues	Association executives	Experiments
Library catalogs	Technical and other experts	Price lists
Trade lists	Legislators	Samples
"Who's Who"	Lawyers	
Chronologies	Witnesses	
Maps	Other public relations people	
Census reports and other statistics	Public opinion researchers	

• *Examine the sources that look most promising.* You will soon find which ones are likely to provide the most useful information and be able to judge the relative weight and bias of the material available. Often it will not be necessary to consult all the sources listed, since you will arrive at a satisfactory answer after studying the most productive ones. In assembling facts and figures, a standard form of collecting such materials is useful. Short notes may be

---

[1] See Chapter 38.

FACT-FINDING FOR PUBLIC RELATIONS

typed or written on file cards. More voluminous material may be copied, photocopied, or microfilmed for future use and reference. A tape recorder or other recording device may be helpful. Whatever method you use in collecting your material, the following requirements should be met:

1. Indicate the source of every fact so it can be checked.
2. Make a record that is readily understandable to others who may work with you or carry on the project.
3. Date your notes so you can reconstruct the sequence of the study.
4. When you quote others, use quotation marks to separate your statements and conclusions from theirs.
5. Order reproductions such as photocopies in the standard 8 ½ x 11" size so they will fit into your reports, and indicate sources of photocopies and pictures.
6. File your material in accordance with a standard system so you and others can locate portions of it as needed.

• *Prepare progress reports at intervals* giving your findings and indicating sources that have been consulted without results. In some situations, negative findings are as useful as positive ones.

• At the end of your investigation, *prepare a comprehensive report of your findings*. This may include summaries of progress reports drawn up in the course of the project, as well as updated findings and conclusions from previous studies in the same area.

• As a final step, *prepare and submit your recommendations for public relations actions based on your findings*.

The following updated bibliography will help locate various kinds of information that is useful for public relations purposes. While the lists are not complete, they are ample for most public relations needs.

INFORMATION SERVICES

A number of commercial organizations have developed files of information or devised means of getting information from various data banks. Some of those active for public relations offices are:

Editec, 53 W. Jackson Blvd., Chicago, Ill. (312) 427-6760. Provides computer readouts on literature available on almost any subject. Charges on a contract basis or by project.

FIND/SVP—The Information Clearing House, 500 Fifth Ave., New York, N. Y. 10036. (212) 354-2424. Has monthly contracts providing for immediate replies to questions by telephone, or promptly if a search is required. Undertakes research projects on an hourly charge basis.

Information for Business, 730 Third Ave., New York, N. Y. 10017. (212) 867-7030. Specializes in economic and sociological research projects. Charges per project.

The Information Source, 1800 W. Magnolia Blvd., P. O. Box 7733, Burbank, Cal. 91510. (213) 849-1441. Conducts information searches on an hourly basis, with discounts when blocks of time are purchased in advance.

Packaged Facts, 274 Madison Ave., New York, N. Y. 10016. (212) 532-5533. Specializes in gathering information on a specific subject, such as background and source material for a feature article.

This list has been compiled by The Philip Lesly Company.

Following are major sources, with addresses, for information cited. Libraries can be checked for information about availability of any of these materials, updated editions, and other information.

American Library Assn., 50 E. Huron, Chicago, Ill. 60611

R. H. Bacon Co., 14 E. Jackson Blvd., Chicago, Ill. 60604

R. R. Bowker Co., 1180 Avenue of the Americas, New York, N.Y. 10036

Commerce Clearing House, 4025 West Peterson, Chicago, Ill. 60646

Dun & Bradstreet, 99 Church St., New York, N.Y. 10007

Editor & Publisher, 850 Third Avenue, New York, N.Y. 10022

Gale Research Company, Book Tower, Detroit, Michigan 48226

Gebbie Press, Box 1000, New Paltz, N.Y. 12561

Harper & Row, Publishers, Inc., 10 E. 53rd St., New York, N.Y. 10022

Marquis Who's Who Inc., 200 E. Ohio St., Chicago, Ill. 60611

National Register Publishing Co., 5201 Old Orchard Rd., Skokie, Ill. 60076

Prentice-Hall, Inc., Englewood Cliffs, N.J. 07632

Rand McNally, & Company, 8255 N. Central Park, Skokie, Ill. 60076

Standard & Poor's Corp., 345 Hudson St., New York, N.Y. 10014

Superintendent of Documents, U.S. Government Printing Office, Washington, D.C. 20402

U.S. Bureau of the Census, Washington, D.C. 20233

U.S. Department of Commerce, 14th Street between Constitution Ave. and E. St. NW, Washington, D.C. 20230

H.W. Wilson Co., 950 University Ave., Bronx, N.Y. 10452

HOW TO DO RESEARCH

Fundamental Reference Sources. Frances Neel Cheney. Amer. Library Assn., Chicago. Used as a textbook for beginning and intermediate courses in research.

The Modern Researcher. Rev. ed. Harcourt, New York. (1977).

Public Relations and Survey Research. Edward J. Robinson. Appleton-Century-Crofts, New York; 1969.

Research Centers Directory. Edited by Archie M. Palmer. Gale Research, Detroit. Also companion volume: *New Research Centers*—periodical updating service. Basic information concerning virtually all university-related and other non-profit research centers throughout the United States and Canada.

ENCYCLOPEDIAS AND REFERENCE BOOKS

Americana Annual. Americana Corporation, New York. (Annual.) A supplement to the *Encyclopedia Americana* and a record of progress in given subjects.

Awards, Honors and Prizes. Edited by Paul Wasserman. Gale Research, Detroit. An international directory of awards and their donors.

Biographical Dictionaries. Edited by Robert B. Slocum. Gale Research, Detroit.

Britannica Book of the Year. Encyclopaedia Britannica, Chicago. Annual record of progress in given subjects. Includes bibliographies.

Collier's Encyclopaedia. Collier Publishing Company, New York. 24 volumes. General encyclopedia with emphasis on atomic-age scientific material. Volume 20 is a separate bibliography to complete set.

Commercial Atlas and Marketing Guide. Rand McNally & Company, Chicago. (Annual.) Detailed listings and statistical material for about 117,000 cities, towns, communities, and other locations in U.S.; indexes additional thousands of foreign cities.

Consultants and Consulting Organizations Directory. Edited by Paul Wasserman and Janice McLean. Gale Research, Detroit, 5,314 entries.

Consumer Sourcebook. Edited by Paul Wasserman and Jean Morgan. Gale Research, Detroit. Consumer information sources.

Countries of the World and Their Leaders. Gale Research, Detroit. Latest reports on 164 nations and territories.

Dictionaries, Encyclopedias, and Other Word-Related Books. Edited by Annie M. Brewer. Gale Research, Detroit.

Encyclopedia Americana. Americana Corporation, New York. 30 volumes. Emphasizes American subjects, and gives special attention to science, technology, and biography.

Encyclopaedia Britannica. Encyclopaedia Britannica, Chicago. 30 volumes.

Encyclopedia of Associations. Gale Research, Detroit. Listing of trade, professional, and voluntary associations provides sources for specific information on an industry or subject.

Encyclopedia of Information Systems and Services. Edited by Anthony T. Kruzas. Gale Research, Detroit. Descriptions of 1,750 organizations concerned with information products and services.

Ethnic Information Sources of the United States. Edited by Paul Wasserman and Jean Morgan. Gale Research, Detroit. A guide to organizations, agencies, foundations, institutions, media, commercial and trade bodies, government programs, research institutions, etc. on specific ethnic groups.

Harper Encyclopedia of the Modern World. Richard B. Morris and Graham W. Irwin. Harper & Row, New York and Evanston, 1970.

International Who's Who. Gale Research, Detroit. About 17,000 listings.

List of Management and Small Business Aids. Small Business Administration, Chicago.

The New Columbia Encyclopedia. Columbia University Press, New York. Alphabetical arrangement of all material. Compact.

Rand McNally Green Guide. Chicago. All U.S. cities, towns, and villages with a population of 100 or more listed alphabetically by state with their zip codes. More than 44,000 places.

Rand McNally Zip Code Atlas. Chicago. Also lists vital statistics such as population, number of households, retail sales, and passenger car registrations.

Random House Encyclopedia. New York. Heavy emphasis on illustrations and easy-to-read treatment of subjects.

Webster's Guide to American History. Merriam. Springfield, Mass., 1971.

ALMANACS AND CHRONOLOGIES

American Almanac. Grosset & Dunlap, New York. (Annual.) Statistical Abstract of the United States.

Anniversaries and Holidays. Mary E. Hazeltine, Amer. Library Assn., Chicago. Lists holidays, holy days, special observances, seasonal dates, historical anniversaries, important events, birthdays of notable men and women, and other significant dates, and Register of Important Events.

CBS News Almanac. Maplewood, N.J. (Annual.)

Days and Customs of All Faiths. Howard V. Harper. Fleet Publishing Corporation, New York. Arranged by month and day.

Encyclopedia of American Facts and Dates. Crowell, New York. Chronologically arranged.

Facts on File. Person's Index, Facts on File, New York. (Weekly.) Digest of world news from newspapers, periodicals, Government announcements. "Statistics indexed under the name of the agency issuing them and of the subject or field affected such as Agriculture, Aviation, Business, Labor, etc." Cumulative index bi-weekly, monthly, quarterly, and annually.

Gallup Political Almanac. American Institute of Public Opinion, Princeton. State-by-state, group and sectional voting, political, and related information.

Information Please Almanac. Simon & Schuster, New York. (Annual.) Handbook on wide variety of topics: population figures, state voting figures, income per capita, homes with telephones, etc.

Municipal Yearbook. International City Managers' Association, Washington, D.C. (Annual.) Activities and statistical data about American cities. Discusses current problems, analyzes trends, lists major officials and their salaries.

New York Times Index. New York Times, New York. (Semi-monthly.) Annual cumulative volume. Reference guide to all articles that have appeared in its columns.

Reader's Digest Almanac and Yearbook. Pleasantville, N.Y. (Annual.)

Stateman's Yearbook. St. Martin's Press, New York. (Annual.) Brief historical, statistical, and governmental information about all countries of the world.

Whitaker's Almanack. Whitaker, London. (Annual.) Almanac for British Isles. Lists events of the year, members of Parliament, royalty, nobility, clergy, etc.

World Almanac and Book of Facts. World Almanac, New York. (Annual.) Quick reference to a wide variety of information.

Yearbook of American Churches. Federal Council of the Churches of Christ in America, New York. (Annual.) Information about Catholic and Protestant churches. Lists different denominational headquarters.

BIBLIOGRAPHICAL PUBLICATIONS

American Library Association Catalog. Amer. Library Assn., Chicago. (Supplements every five years; kept current by annual *Booklist Books.* Now twice monthly.) Lists outstanding books.

Applied Science and Technology Index. Wilson, New York. (Formerly *Industrial Arts Index.*) Monthly with quarterly and annual cumulations. Indexes periodicals mainly in the technical and industrial fields. Annual volume lists technical societies and trade associations.

Bibliographic Index: A Cumulative Bibliography of Bibliographies. Wilson, New York. Subject list of books, with annual issue containing all material listed in previous issues of that year.

Bibliography. Information Center, Public Relations Society of America, New York.

Bibliography of Corporate Social Responsibility: Programs and Policies. (Annual.) Bank of America, San Francisco.

Biological and Agricultural Index. Wilson, New York. (Monthly supplements.) Indexes agricultural periodicals, books, pamphlets. (Formerly *Agricultural Index.*)

Biographical Dictionaries Master Index. Edited by Dennis La Beau and Gary C. Tarbert. Gale Research, Detroit. Issued at 2-year intervals. Guide to more than 800,000 listings in more than 50 current *Who's Who* and other works of collective biography. 3 volumes.

Books in Print. R.R. Bowker Co., New York. Indexes to the available books on a subject. Lists over 450,000 books.

Bulletin of the P.A.I.S. (Public Affairs Information Service), New York. (Annual cumulation.) P.A.I.S. is an association of public, university, and special libraries that publishes current bibliographies of materials in English relating to economic, social, and political affairs.

Business Periodicals Index. Wilson, New York. Contains index of business subjects from periodicals formerly indexed in *Industrial Arts Index.*

Business Service Check List. U.S. Department of Commerce, Washington, D.C. (Weekly.) Free. Contains complete list of available publications, statements, and reports, printed and mimeographed.

Canadian Periodical Index. Canadian Library Assn., Ottawa. (Monthly, with annual and quinquennial cumulations.)

Census Publications. U.S. Government Printing Office, Washington, D.C. (Quarterly, annual cumulations.)

Cumulative Book Index. Wilson, New York. (Monthly.) *A World List of Books in the English Language.* Supplementary to the *United States Catalog,* published by Wilson. Author-title-subject index.

Directory Information Service. Gale Research, Detroit. Three times a year, lists new sources of information for public relations and other personnel.

Encyclopedia of Business Information Sources. Edited by Paul Wasserman. Gale Research, Detroit.

F & S Index—Domestic. Predicasts, Inc., Cleveland. Citations of articles appearing in major business publications indexed by company and by product code.

Guide to American Directories. Edited by Bernard Klein. Gale Research, Detroit. More than 5,200 directories listed; more than 300 subject classifications.

Guide to Reference Books (and supplements). Amer. Library Assn., Chicago. (Updated editions of the Mudge *Guide to Reference Books.*) Supplements irregularly.

Humanities Index. Wilson, New York. (Quarterly, with annual cumulations.)

Irregular Serials and Annuals; an international directory. R.R. Bowker Co., New York. (Biennial—beginning 1972.) A companion to *Ulrich's International Periodicals Directory.* The two publications are issued in alternate years.

Library Bibliographies and Indexes. Edited by Paul Wasserman and Esther Herman. Gale Research, Detroit. Organized primarily by subject. More than 1,500 subjects; more than 40 entries.

Monthly Catalog of U.S. Government Publications. Superintendent of Documents, Washington, D.C. (Monthly.) Lists new publications; valuable source of up-to-date information. Lists arranged by agencies.

Political Handbook and Atlas of the World. Edited by Walter H. Mallory (for Council on Foreign Relations), Harper, New York. (Annual.) Political information about all countries of the world, parties, party leaders etc. Editors of leading newspapers and publications.

Publishers' Trade List Annual. R.R. Bowker Co., New York. Bound volume of publishers' catalogs with books published during the year.

Readers' Guide to Periodical Literature. Wilson, New York. Monthly and cumulative index covering most of the general and better-known magazines.

Selected Publications to Aid Domestic Business and Industry. (Pamphlet.) Department of Commerce, Washington, D.C.

Subject Directory of Special Libraries and Information Centers. Gale Research, Detroit. 5 volumes. Presents every entry contained in the basic Directory, but in a convenient subject arrangement.

Subject Guide to Books in Print. R.R. Bowker Co., New York. (Annual.) An index to the Publishers Trade List Annual.

Survey of Current Business. Government Printing Office, Washington, D.C. (Monthly, with weekly supplements.) Descriptive and statistical material on basic income and trade developments in the U.S.

Technical Book Review Index (TBRI). Special Libraries Assn., New York. (Monthly except July and August.)

United States Catalog. Wilson, New York. Published every five years, and kept up-to-date by *Cumulative Book Index,* published monthly with annual cumulation. A world list of books in print in the English language.

Vertical File Index. Wilson, New York. (Monthly, with annual cumulation.) Lists pamphlets, booklets, leaflets, mimeographed material.

SOURCES OF BUSINESS INFORMATION

Business Books in Print. R.R Bowker, New York. Complete, current bibliographic information on virtually every inprint business book available in the United States.

Concise Desk Book of Business Finance. Donald W. Moffat. Prentice-Hall, Englewood Cliffs, N.J.

Directory of Business and Financial Services. Edited by Mary McNierney Grant and Norma Cote. Special Libraries Assn., New York.

Directory of Special Libraries and Information Centers. Gale Research, Detroit. 3 volumes. Key to the holdings, services, and personnel of 13,078 special libraries, information centers, documentation centers, and similar units.

FACT-FINDING FOR PUBLIC RELATIONS

Directory of National Trade and Professional Associations of the United States. Edited by Craig Colgate, Jr., Columbia Books, Washington, D.C.

Dun & Bradstreet Million Dollar Directory and *Dun & Bradstreet Middle Market Directory.* New York. Addresses, telephone numbers, names of key personnel, principal industries, and estimate of size for companies responsible for about 80% of the business in the U.S. Also listings by location and industry.

Dun & Bradstreet Reference Book. Dun and Bradstreet, New York. (Bi-monthly.) Capital and credit ratings of commercial corporations. Not available in public libraries. Sold only to private subscribers, but sometimes accessible in special libraries or individual firms.

Editor and Publisher Market Guide. Editor and Publisher Co., New York. (Annual.) Surveys United States and Canadian newspaper centers—population, schools, stores, bank deposits, automobile registrations, etc.

Poor's Register of Corporations, Directors and Executives. Standard & Poor's, New York. (Annual; cumulative supplements issued April, July, and October.)

Predicasts. Predicasts, Inc., Cleveland. Abstracts of forecasts and estimates that have appeared in major business publications, indexed by product and code.

Securities and Exchange Commission Files. Survey of American listed corporations. Registration statements and other public documents filed with the Commission available for inspection at the home office in Washington, D.C. or at regional offices in New York and Chicago.

Standard & Poor's Industry Surveys. New York. Gives trends, projections, and current analyses of the major U.S. industries.

Thomas' Register of American Manufacturers. Thomas' Register, New York. (Annual.) Lists manufacturers, trade names, commercial organizations, and trade papers.

GOVERNMENT

Almanac of American Politics, by Michael Barone, Grant Ujifusa, and Douglas Matthews. Gambit, Boston. (Biennial.) Profiles of each Senator and Representative including votes on key issues; political and economic analysis of every state and Congressional District.

Bimonthly Directory of Key Congressional Aides. Congressional Monitor, Washington, D.C. Lists key aides to members of Congress, key aides on committee and subcommittee staffs, with their names, titles, room and phone numbers, and their subject-matter specialties. Loose-leaf. Updatings every other month.

Capitol Services, Inc. (CSI) Report. Washington, D.C. Completely individualized daily legislative information, containing relevant data in specified area of interest from list of topics covered daily in *Congressional Record.*

Congressional Directory. Government Printing Office, Washington, D.C. (Annual, for each session, March in odd years, January in even.) Complete listing of federal, legislative, and executive offices, Congressmen and Senators (with bios), high ranking staff personnel, independent agencies, diplomatic corps, international organizations, press, District of Columbia offices, maps of Capitol Building, voting statistics.

Congressional Index. Commerce Clearing House, Chicago. (Weekly.) Contains list of all congressional bills, current reports on legislative developments, data on Congressmen, and committees.

Congressional Quarterly. Washington, D.C. Weekly reports of Congressional and political activity for the current week. Includes texts of Presidential press conferences and statements, summaries of floor action, analyses of bills, voting records, etc.; the cumulative quarterly index; the *Almanac* published yearly which reorganizes and cross-indexes the full year of political decisions.

Congressional Record. Government Printing Office, Washington, D.C. (Daily when Congress is in session.) Contains official report of the debates and other proceedings of the open sessions of Congress. Index issued twice a month. Daily digest includes summary of action in each Chamber, committee meetings, bills signed, and committee meetings scheduled following day.

Congressional Staff Directory. Mt. Vernon, Virginia. (Annual, April, with biennial election index and annual advance locator published in January.) Comprehensive listing of personnel on Congressional staffs and committees, key personnel of executive offices, cabinet, and independent agencies; 1,800 staff biographies; includes list of all state Congressional delegations by district with population statistics and cities/towns of more than 1,500 population and counties in each District.

Digest of Public Bills and Resolutions. Washington,

D.C. (Published periodically.) Contains complete listing and description of all bills introduced in Congress at time of publication.

Encyclopedia of Governmental Advisory Organizations. Edited by Linda D. Sullivan and Anthony T. Kruzas. Gale Research, Detroit. Lists 2,678 groups.

Federal Register. Government Printing Office, Washington, D.C. Daily supplement of the *Code of Federal Regulations.* Notices to the public of proposed issuance of rules and regulations, full text of regulatory documents, executive orders, status of regulations, deadlines for compliance, etc.

Federal State Reports. Arlington, Virginia. Copies of all the bills in a specific legislative field. Individualized "clipping service" consisting of photocopies of press releases and pertinent material from the *Congressional Record* and *Federal Register* within the field specified by the client.

National Journal Reports. Washington, D.C. Three-part information system includes 52 issues of the *Journal* analyzing changes in federal policy through the actions of Congress, the White House, Courts, and interest groups; and the *National Issues/Outlook,* a monthly report each of which gives one-page summaries of twelve policy areas selected on the basis of important recent, or probable future, developments.

Official Register of the United States. Government Printing Office, Washington, D.C. (Annual.) Lists persons in administrative and supervisory positions of the federal government, inside and outside Washington. Gives title and the State or Congressional District from which they come.

United States Congressional Record. U.S. Congress, Washington, D.C.

United States Government Organization Manual. Government Printing Office, Washington, D.C. (Annual.) " . . . the official handbook of the Federal Government . . . contains sections dealing with every agency of the Government in the legislative, executive, and judicial branches. Each of these sections is an official statement covering the organization and functions . . . " Provides excellent overall view of governmental activities, what kind of information emanates from the different agencies, and a guide to their publications and how to order them.

Washington Potomac Books. Washington, D.C. Issued every two to four years, listing key personnel in government, the press, organizations, cultural institutions, colleges and universities, associations, R & D firms, clubs, unions, and businesses in the Washington metropolitan area.

PEOPLE, INSTITUTIONS, AND MEDIA

American Jewish Yearbook. Jewish Publication Society of America, Philadelphia. (Annual.) Directory of Jewish national and local organizations in the United States.

American Universities and Colleges. American Council on Education, Washington, D.C.

Annual State Directories and Government Manuals. Published by most state legislatures or state governments in state capitals.

Annual Syndicate Directory. Editor and Publisher, New York. All types of syndicated newspaper features.

Ayer's Directory. (See Directory of Newspapers and Periodicals.)

Bacon's International Publicity Checker—European Edition. R.H. Bacon Co., Chicago. Lists of trade, technical, and business publications in Western Europe that accept publicity releases.

Bacon's Newspaper Directory. R.H. Bacon Co., Chicago. (Annual.) Lists of daily, weekly, semi-weekly, and Black newspapers.

Bacon's Publicity Checker. R.H. Bacon Co., Chicago. List of periodicals, syndicates, major newspapers; revised and published annually in October.

Book of the States. The Council of State Governments, Chicago. (Biennial.) Information about state governments: personnel, revenue, services, agriculture and conservation, public works, health and welfare, education, business, veterans' offices. Bibliographies.

Broadcasting Yearbook. Broadcasting Publications, Washington, D.C. (Revised annually.) Audience analyses, radio-TV reference sources, associations, awards, regional networks, FCC rules, station representatives, billings.

Dictionary of American Scholars. R.R. Bowker, New York.

Directory of National and International Labor Unions in United States. Department of Labor, Washington, D.C. (Annual.) Lists state, national, and international labor unions.

Directory of Newspapers and Periodicals, Ayer's. N.W. Ayer and Son, Philadelphia. (Annual.) Guide to publications in the United States and Canada. Other information—population of states, cities, towns in which publications appear, frequency and type of publication; lists trade, technical, farm, and foreign language publications. Maps, statistics.

FACT-FINDING FOR PUBLIC RELATIONS

Directory of Professional Writers. American Society of Journalists and Authors, New York. Names, addresses, and areas of interest of writers available on an assignment or contract basis.

Editor and Publisher International Yearbook. Editor and Publisher, New York. (Annual.) Directory of newspapers—daily newspapers of the United States, Canada, Great Britain, Latin and Central America, and other foreign countries; foreign language papers in the U.S., Black newspapers, newspaper and advertising associations, clubs, organizations, etc. Gives radio and television stations affiliated with newspapers; personnel, advertisng rates, circulation of daily papers in the U.S.; schools and departments of journalism.

Editorial Offices in the West. Simon/Public Relations, Los Angeles.

Educational Directory. Government Printing Office, Washington, D.C. (Annual.) Federal and State education officers, county and city school officers, colleges and universities, educational associations, parent associations, directors of educational research, etc.

Encyclopedia of American Associations. Gale Research, Detroit.

Foundation Directory. Russell Sage Foundation, New York. Lists foundations, with background, history, activities, and publications of the larger foundations.

Gebbie Press All-in-One Directory. Gebbie, New York. Lists of most outlets for publicity in the U.S.

Gebbie Press House Magazine Directory. National Research Bureau, Burlington, Ia.

Hudson's Washington News Media Contacts Directory. Edited by Howard Penn Hudson and Mary Elizabeth Hudson. Hudson's Directory, Arlington, Va. (Annual.) Revisions issued quarterly to subscribers.

International Motion Picture Almanac. Quigley, New York. (Annual.) Includes associations, theater circuits, film exchanges, radio stations, non-theatrical companies, reviewing and censorship organizations, publications, etc. Biographical sketches of actors, directors, and others prominent in the industry.

International Yearbook and Statesmen's Who's Who. Burke's Peerage, London. (Annual.)

Media. (Midwest). Midwest Newsclip, Chicago. Lists of newspapers, periodicals, and broadcast media in Illinois.

Membership Directory of National Federation of Financial Analysts. New York. (Annual.) Lists analysts' societies and members of each.

News Bureaus in the U.S. Richard Weiner, New York. Addresses and personnel of wire services' and syndicates' offices in various cities.

New York Publicity Outlets 1976. Washington Depot, Conn. Listings for all consumer media in Metro New York Area: 14 TV stations, 110 radio stations, 85 TV and 95 radio interview shows, 300 magazines, 49 daily and 464 weekly newspapers.

O'Dwyer's Directory of Corporate Communications. J.R. O'Dwyer Co., New York, 1975.

O'Dwyer's Directory of Public Relations Firms. (Annual.) New York.

The Official Museum Directory: United States and Canada. American Assoc. of Museums and Crowell-Collier, Education Corp., New York. Lists 6,657 museums of art, history, and science.

Patterson's American Education. Educational Directories, Inc. Mt. Prospect, Ill. (Annual.) Lists, with descriptions, public, private, endowed schools, colleges, and other institutions of learning; school officials, Boards of Education, education associations and societies, college colors.

Securities Dealers in North America. Standard & Poor's, New York. (Annual.)

Social Register. Social Register Association, New York. (Annual.) Lists families active in social life, with addresses.

Standard Directory of Advertisers. National Register Publishing Company, New York. (Daily, monthly.) Directory of advertisers in the U.S. using national media, advertising budgets, agencies, account executives.

Standard Directory of Advertising Agencies. National Register Publishing Company, New York. (Three times a year.) Lists advertising agencies of the United States, including accounts and personnel.

Standard and Poor's Corporation Directory. Standard and Poor's, New York. (Annual.) Standard corporation description. Contains records of all American corporations listed on stock exchanges.

Standard Periodical Directory (Fifth Edition). Oxbridge Communications, New York. Lists 62,500 periodicals in the U.S. and Canada.

Standard Rate and Data Service. Standard Rate and Data Service, Skokie, Ill. (Monthly.) Advertising rates. Has separate sections: business papers, general magazines, newspapers.

Syndicated Columnists. Richard Weiner, Inc., New York, 1975.

TV Publicity Outlets Nationwide. Box 327, Washington Depot, Conn. 06794. More than 1,250 listings. Programs listed in geographical order with call letters and channel numbers.

Updated directory every 3 months.

Ulrich's International Periodicals Directory. R.R. Bowker, New York. (Biennial; supplement issued alternate years.) Lists in-depth information on 57,000 periodicals from all over the world, alphabetically arranged according to 250 subject headings.

Who's Who in the World; Who's Who in America; Who's Who in Finance and Industry; Who's Who in the East; Who's Who in the Midwest; Who's Who in the South and Southwest; Who's Who in the West. A.N. Marquis Company, Chicago. (Biennial.) Brief biographical information about prominent living persons.

Who's Who in American Education. Robert C. Cook Company, New York. (Biennial.) Biographical directory of American educators, giving names, ages, titles, activities, publications, etc.

Who's Who in Public Relations. PR Publishing Co., Exeter, N.H., 1976.

Who's Who of American Women with World Notables. A.N. Marquis Company, Chicago.

Working Press of the Nation. National Research Bureau, Burlington, Ia. (Annual.) Four volumes list personnel of newspapers, radio and television stations, news magazines, newsreels, syndicates, columnists, feature writers, etc.

Writer's Market. Writer's Digest Publishing Company, Cincinnati. (Annual.) Contains name, address, rate of payment, and editorial requirements of publications and publishers.

STATISTICS

Agricultural Statistics. U.S. Department of Agriculture. Government Printing Office, Washington, D.C. (Annual.) Farms—number, acreage, value, housing, population, employment, wage rates. Statistical data.

Annual Survey of Manufactures. U.S. Bureau of the Census. Government Printing Office, Washington, D.C.

Catalog of United States Census Publications. U.S. Bureau of the Census. Government Printing Office, Washington, D.C. Census publications cover "statistics of population, agriculture, manufactures, retail and wholesale distribution, occupations, and religious bodies."

Census of Manufactures. U.S. Bureau of the Census. Government Printing Office, Washington, D.C. Statistics of manufactured commodities, by industry and for states and cities.

Congressional District Data Book. U.S. Bureau of the Census. Government Printing Office, Washington, D.C. (Biennial.) Arranges census data by Congressional Districts.

Editor and Publisher Market Guide. Editor and Publisher Company, New York. (Annual.) Surveys United States and Canadian newspaper centers—population, schools, stores, bank deposits, automobile registrations, etc. Compiled from information sources such as Bureau of Census, Chamber of Commerce, Boards of Education, business associations, individual business executives, and newspapers.

Handbook of Labor Statistics. U.S. Bureau of Labor Statistics. Government Printing Office, Washington, D.C.

Historical Statistics of the United States. U.S. Bureau of the Census. Government Printing Office, Washington, D.C.

Marketing Information Guide. U.S. Department of Commerce, Washington, D.C. (Monthly.) Provides a guide to information on domestic marketing. Lists studies by various departments of the federal government, state and municipal governments, foundations, colleges, and commercial organizations.

Population Index. School of Public and International Affairs, Princeton University, N.J.; Population Association of America, Inc. Washington, D.C. (Quarterly.)

Statistical Abstract of the United States. U.S. Bureau of the Census. Government Printing Office, Washington, D.C. (Annual.) Statistics in condensed form of all government agencies, and some state and private agencies. Gives sources that show what type of statistics are gathered by the various agencies and where fuller information is published.

Statistics Sources. Edited by Paul Wasserman and Joanne Paskar. Gale Research, Detroit. More than 21,000 citations on 11,800 subjects.

Survey of Current Business. U.S. Office of Business Economics. Government Printing Office. Washington, D.C. (Monthly.) Disseminates significant economic indicators for business use, including analytical findings of the Office of Business Economics, as well as statistical series originating from both public and private sources. Monthly data supplemented by weekly release, *Business Statistics.*

Vital Statistics of the United States. U.S. National Vital Statistics Division. Government Printing Office, Washington, D.C. (Annual.) Reports on birth and death registrations, causes of death, incidence of specified diseases, etc.

Yearbook of International Trade Statistics. United Nations Statistical Office, New York. (Annual.)

37

Analysis, Planning, and Programming

Philip Lesly

As in statecraft, politics, and military affairs, the overwhelming majority of participants in public relations deal with day-to-day execution of *techniques*. A smaller percentage is responsible for the *tactics* that set the pattern for technicians. And a few broad-gauged individuals assess the whole cosmos involved and develop the *strategy* that gives meaning and direction to it all—and determines whether anything meaningful will be accomplished.

In limited areas and with limited goals, carrying out specific activities without such an overall strategy can have its values. This may be the case where product publicity is desired to augment the other exposures of the product and its uses. It may be helpful to a politician or an entertainer who needs to become known to the public. To some extent it is of value to a company whose stock is offered to the public or that needs to be known to prospective employees.

In most cases, however, the entire value of the public relations operation will depend on the caliber and thoroughness of the analysis and thinking that precede the execution of techniques.

Characteristics required. Providing this caliber of intelligence calls for:

- Breadth of scope capable of seeing the whole of the organization's "universe" together and understanding how the various elements affect each other.
- Judgment capable of evaluating the significance of various symptoms, and of the soundness of suggestions for action or inaction in any given situation.
- Diversity of experience and education, with as much training as possible in all the tactics and techniques of public relations.

- Creativity, both in bringing forth ideas and recommendations, and in expressing them so they will persuade others.
- Objectivity—being far enough removed from the intricacies of the organization to see it as others do, and forthright enough to express the viewpoint of these outsiders to the management.

This is a formidable combination of attributes. It is at this critical level, therefore, that the highest caliber of counsel or internal executive makes the great difference between various organizations' public relations efforts. Where the internal executive does not have all of these traits, he and his stature benefit from combining with a counsel who augments him.

ESTABLISHING THE ESSENTIALS

Before any notes are made on possible programs or activities, several aspects should be thought through:

1. *What are the objectives?* Are there a few clear, vital goals for the public relations function to achieve or contribute to, or has there been just an accumulation of mostly unrelated tasks? Following is a paraphrased excerpt from a confidential analysis made for a large association:

> Events and trends in this field and in our social system have rushed on, while the members and the Association have been absorbed in keeping up with their own affairs on the basis of training received a generation ago. Trends and circumstances have thus outrun the member's usual pattern of concentrating on here-and-now affairs and developments. As a

result, *there is too little relationship between the climate of attitudes that now engulfs the field and the priorities of the Association in dealing with this climate.* It appears that to a considerable extent, functions in the Association have *accumulated,* rather than been planned. Much of this accumulation has been through projects and functions that have been imposed by individuals, committees, or others, rather than been planned as an integral and coordinated part of a whole.

2. *What are the present climate of attitudes and the underlying forces* that affect whatever the organization will do or say? This calls for assessing the entire cosmos in which the organization functions: internal conditions and plans; the industry it is in; the social trends in the locality, nationally, and internationally; the attitudes and practices of the media to be dealt with, and so on.

In an analysis and program made for a large fraternal organization, the following factors were pinpointed as having a bearing on the group's planning and what it needed to do in public relations:

(1) The rapidly increasing level of education, which greatly broadens people's sophistication and independence of thought.
(2) Urbanization and suburbanization, which break down the importance of fraternal organizations in men's lives.
(3) The multiplication of interests for people to pursue. When there was little to do outside working hours, the lodge was very attractive. It now must compete with travel, books, music, education, television, sports, hobbies, boating, art.
(4) An increased number of organizations and functions that attract potential members' interests, including many urged on them by their employers.
(5) The trend in population toward a younger average age, while lodge membership traditionally has attracted older men.
(6) Independent interests of young men, with many assuming major responsibilities early.
(7) The "anti-Establishment" attitude of many young men, in which fraternal organizations are identified with the Establishment.
(8) The problem of momentum. It is extremely difficult to reverse a downtrend in interest, such as has faced this group in recent years.

The planning and program were devised in keeping with these factors, and periodic evaluations of the program were related to the changes in these patterns.

This analysis of the human climate should include judgment on where the trends are leading and what the climate will be when the organization's efforts have had time to take effect. A large proportion of public opinion programs attack problems as they existed two years ago.

3. *Has an objective analysis been made of the organization?* It is especially important to define how it is different from all other organizations. No organization can succeed in trying to be all things to everyone, and few organizations can succeed in modeling themselves after some other organization they would like to duplicate.

4. *Have the audiences to be reached been carefully defined and described?* No matter how compact an organization is, today it must think in terms of multiple audiences. On almost any subject, whatever an organization does is certain to be unpopular with some segments of its publics. There are many antithetical groups, even within what would normally be considered a given public. For instance, "women" include millions of dedicated homemakers and mothers, and millions of women who consider a career and complete autonomy to be the essentials of a fulfilled life.

There are great variations in sophistication among segments of every organization's audiences. Great variations exist in the extent of knowledge and the degree of suspicion. The sources of influence on them vary greatly. They are likely to be dispersed geographically. They have varying degrees of receptivity and they look to completely different sources for their leadership.

5. *What are the specific obstacles?* Is there a political barrier, such as solid entrenchment of opposition in a strong bloc of Congress? Is there a prejudice against the organization that logic and information will not dispel? Planning may have to work around these, rather than attempt to beat them down.

6. *What are the special opportunities?* When the American Music Conference was being formed in 1946, it was pointed out that postwar America was fed up with austerity; people were hungry for individuality and self-expression; parents and educators were concerned about creative outlets for children's energies. These and other factors in the social climate were played on to create the boom in music making that marked the next 20-odd years.

7. *What are present activities* and how do they measure up against these criteria and conditions?

8. *What are others doing:* allies, opponents, others not directly related but whose functions will compete for attention or affect what may happen?

9. *Is emphasis being placed on leading the target*–on establishing the climate of attitudes in the future, rather than responding to what has happened to date? Hundreds of companies began to communicate about their efforts in curbing pollution and improving their products after massive attacks on them had already been launched. Inoculation against the virulence of criticism is much more healthful than attempting to cure the rampant disease after it has struck. In general, the climate of opinion about issues should be worked on two years or more before it is likely that an audible criticism will be felt.

10. *Is there an overview of the entire system* that logically considers the chain reaction of various activities? As in chess, an amateur considers one move at a time; a master considers the chain of consequences many moves ahead.

11. *Have allowances been made for the specific personalities, politics, and peculiarities of the situation?* For instance, a professional society such as the American Dental Association is not only an association, in which control is diffuse and diverse, but a political organization, in which the leaders are elected and must be responsive to the nuances of the grass roots. Plans and activities that do not account for the politics in such a situation are likely to fail. In one company the chief executive may be outgoing articulate, eager for respect; in another he may inherently resent anything that puts him into the limelight.

12. *Has your case been carefully developed? Have the ideas and facts that need to be conveyed been selected and identified? Have the most effective appeals been worked out, in terms of the interests of the audiences?* A remarkable number of organizations never take these essential steps. They have no tightly reasoned case, their concepts are not highly refined, the basis for seeking the interest of the audience is vague.

13. *Have the media and other channels of communication that are available been assessed?* What is their present posture in regard to the organization and the field it is in? How accessible are they? What is the organization's stature and credibility with each of them? What are their prejudices that must be recognized and dealt with? What are their relationships with the publics that the organization has identified as the universe it must work with?

14. *What are the resources available*—budgets, manpower, allies? If new needs are demonstrated, can new resources be obtained? If not, can priorities be shifted so some "sacred cows" will be eliminated?

Clarifying these factors is often the most crucial aspect of all. As Donald W. MacKinnon of the Institute of Personality Assessment and Research at the University of California, Berkeley, has said:

"When a problem is properly conceived, the very statement of the problem carries within it hints or suggestions as to how it is to be solved . . . The first task . . . is to make a sufficient analysis of the situation, narrowing down and simplifying the complex situation until the crucial difficulty in the task is isolated."

ELEMENTS OF PLANNING

Every analysis will be different. So will every plan. It is tempting for the experienced executive or the public relations firm to draw on experience to the extent of building on familiar frameworks. Some firms even use a "basic presentation" that is changed just enough for each prospect or client to make it look original. But the primary value of good public relations judgment is its capacity for studying the uniqueness of each situation and coming up with original thinking, even while drawing on reservoirs of experience.

With this need in mind to avoid predetermined outlines, the following are some general functions that are likely to be involved in any plan:

1. Spell out objectives incisively. Don't have more than a few major ones so they will definitely be focused on.

2. Determine the functions, again being selective so the vital ones will get enough attention.

3. Establish the budgets.

4. Recruit, train, and assign the personnel—and block in how the principals of the organization will be involved.

5. Retain the outside help that will be needed—counsel, a range of services, specialists such as artists and photographers, and so on. Except where necessary, do not be confined to internal specialists in any area, who then must be used for that function whether or not they are suitable for each task that comes along. One artist may be excellent for an annual report but impossible for a cartoon book or a display for an open house. One photographer may be good for industrial shots but mediocre on portraits or action events. The best available choice

can be made in every case when all talents in the field are available; and the specialists are not on the payroll all year long, finding things to do (with expenses) to keep busy.

6. Set up a flow chart of the functions, with lead time, relationships, responsibilities clearly defined.

7. Set up feedback and research points to measure progress or assess trends.

8. Arrange for periodic review of plans and functions, to assure flexibility. It is usually best not to do this at 12-month intervals; the very regularity of such a period is out of keeping with how things happen, and therefore deceptively artificial. Sometimes a new look might be wise in a few months; some things should not be expected to be assessed in less than two to three years. While organizations may require annual budget approvals, this should not require that the period for fresh looking be the same.

9. Build in procedures for keeping the principals informed and involved.

In more limited planning for campaigns and specific programs, the procedures in Chapter 38 will provide a more specific and detailed guide.

Following is a representative outline of priorities for a hypothetical corporation. It serves as a guide on which any organization can pattern its own such outline.

TYPICAL CORPORATE PRIORITY SCHEDULE

Basic Functions—Initiative

Financial
Stockholder publications, including the annual report
Financial announcements
Security analyst communications
Feedback from financial community
Annual meeting

Corporate
Developing and proposing programs for meeting problems and developing good will
Providing information and assessments on public attitudes and trends, for the knowledge and consideration of management
Contacting and cultivating the media—business publications, newspapers, broadcasters, key trade publications
Special events—new plant openings, groundbreakings
Corporate announcements—new officers and directors, etc.
Producing external and internal publications

Employee Recruitment
Literature
Career conference

Product Publicity
New-product introductions
Continuous publicity on products on basis of budget allocations
Handling media requests for loans and purchases at a discount

Government relations
Liaison with Congress
Liaison with federal regulatory agencies
Liaison with state and municipal government bodies

Basic Functions—Passive

Financial
Handling inquiries from media
Handling inquiries from security analysts
Screening and assessing correspondence from stockholders
Maintaining lists for mailing of reports, etc.
Periodic studies of stockholder and analyst attitudes

Corporate
Handling inquiries from media
Keeping biographies, photos, facts up-to-date
Preparing backgrounders and fact sheets on divisions and operations
Representing the company in various associations, on boards and committees, etc.
Participation in intra-company groups—Policy Committee, inter-plant liaison and communication, etc.
Bulletin board and reading rack programs

Community relations
Contributions program
Periodic research on corporate "image," public attitudes

Possible Unanticipated Needs

Financial
Merger or acquisition—strategy discussions, announcements

Corporate
Change in name and identification program
Emergencies—disaster, attack by militants, problem with a product in the market, etc.

Government Relations
      Appearance before Congressional committee
      Dispute with regulatory agency

Secondary or Optional

   Financial
      Seeking and arranging additional security analyst meetings
      Setting up circulation of displays for brokerage offices and bank windows
   Corporate
      Plant open houses
      Scholarship program
      Communications seminar for junior executives and trainees

Obviously, this is not complete for any company, and the pattern for any firm will vary greatly.

Allocations of effort. It is important that sufficient flexibility be built into such a priority outline. Many of the most important needs for public relations help will be unpredictable; the proportion of time and resources left uncommitted should be great enough to assure ample attention to them. Giving in to the temptation to provide a tight, neat packaged program months or a year in advance can result in a sterile, routine operation that will be unprepared for the great challenges and opportunities that cannot be anticipated.

In the hypothetical outline above, the Basic—Initiative portion might be allocated about 45 percent of the effort, the Basic—Passive about 25 percent, Possible Unanticipated Needs 25 percent, and Secondary and Optional (and therefore expendable if something has to give) 5 percent.

SECTION V

The Techniques of Communication

38

Preparations for Communicating

Herbert M. Baus*
Philip Lesly

While the communications function is just a part of the total spectrum that makes up public relations, it is often the point at which the whole operation brings about a desired result. It is toward the end of the spectrum—after research and analysis, policy formation, planning, and programming. It is followed, usually, by assessment of what is done and feedback of the publics' reactions to the organization. But it is the most visible part of the spectrum, the area where the organization's officials can see tangible evidence of public relations efforts, and where the effect on the publics can sometimes be observed.

For these reasons, the communications functions that largely gave rise to this field still are its most prominent aspects. Though the conception of public relations as only communicating is fading, the communications role employs most of the field's personnel, consumes most of the budgets, and gets the most attention.

While some public relations executives have only rare dealings with them, knowledge and judgment of these functions are vital to the ability of the executive to advise his principals, plan his operations, employ and direct his staff, and assess what is accomplished.

The next 14 chapters deal with the techniques and principles of communicating. Eight of these deal with various aspects of publicity, and seven with other communications techniques.

Role different in various countries. Communications techniques probably vary the most of all aspects of public relations in various countries. In the United States publicity is dominant because of the diversity of media, their openness to all sources of information, and the receptivity of the people to all the information media.

In many other countries, even among democracies, the media are restricted either by political affiliation or traditional suspicions between the press and other aspects of society. Many newspapers and magazines expect payment for editorial coverage, either directly or in advertising. In most countries television and radio are limited to government-operated outlets and either no others or limited private sources. In these areas there is a natural emphasis on communications that the source can control, such as printed materials, meetings, posters, and sponsored films.

PLANNING THE PUBLICITY PROGRAM

The job of publicity is to tell the story.

In a broad sense, all techniques employed by an organization to convey its messages are phases of publicity.

Almost everything printed in a newspaper or a magazine, or broadcast by television or radio, is publicity for some person or some thing. It is the job of the publicity man to find the news, interesting information, and ideas in the organization he represents, or to develop it, and to present it in such form as will qualify it for publication, broadcast, or other dissemination.

"Promotion" is a word that covers the field between publicity and advertising, and in application includes them both. It connotes tie-ins, special

*Mr. Baus is a public relations counsel and author residing in Los Angeles.

events, and stunts to get attention, whereas publicity is more often regarded in the sense of getting something printed or broadcast. Publicity is slanted more from the straight news side, promotion more from the advertising and commercial side.

Publicity work boils down to analyzing the vast store of human interest and news material that is inherent in any organization of human beings, selecting a portion of it, dressing it up properly, and making it available to media of information. In other words: a nose for news, a technique for production, and the energy to do the work.

NEWS AND PUBLICITY

News is something that interests *many people* today. From the point of view of the New York *Times,* that means many people in New York and many of the national readers of the *Times.* From the point of view of the Pittsburgh *Courier,* it means many Blacks. To the editor of a house magazine, news is something that interests many employees of the plant served.

Every medium has a news standard of its own, and this is the criterion the publicist goes by in attempting to address publicity to the public through that medium. This standard is, "News is something that interests *many of our audience* today."

The basic factors of publicity are people, time, and place. What are the people doing, and how does what they are doing affect other people? At what time are they doing it? Something a group of people do for publicity interest may command liberal newspaper attention on Tuesday, but on Wednesday it may be shaded if not obliterated by a flood, a murder, or an outbreak of war. What is news in Port Angeles, Washington may be of no interest in Miami Beach, Florida.

From the publicity man's point of view there are three classifications of news: *spot news,* or any news not planned or developed by the publicist; *feature news,* which has broader interest and usually less critical timing than spot news; and *created news,* which he controls and/or helps to create.

Spot news. Spot news consists of a spontaneous outburst of nature or of mankind, such as a flood, earthquake, typhoon, war, revolution, fire, or accident.

Spot news concerning his organization is often unfavorable to the publicist, although his proper handling of it can to a major degree relieve the harmful impact. For example, a railroad accident is news unfavorable to the railroad. The railroad's publicity director can win a sympathetic news handling by making himself and his staff of maximum assistance in reporting all the facts quickly, accurately, and fully.

Suppose the railroad publicist is notified at 3 a.m. that a calamitous accident has wrecked one of his company's trains on the desert. He immediately notifies the news media and takes a carload of reporters and photographers by fast train to the scene of the accident. The media appreciate his courtesy in helping to cover a necessary story. The story treatment is more likely to be sympathetic to the railroad. It emphasizes the railroad's efficiency in clearing the wreckage, accentuates the heroism of the train crews, indicates that the railroad was not at fault, desensationalizes the details, and gives the railroad the benefit of every doubt. The publicity is temperate because the newspapers have confidence that they are getting all the facts and that the railroad is doing its best.

On the contrary, suppose the publicist attempts to censor the accident. He endeavors to belittle the scope of the disaster and strives to keep the newsmen from locating and reaching the scene. This forces the media to undergo considerable expense to ferret out the details of the catastrophe. Perhaps they charter a special plane, scour the desert, and eventually locate the wreckage. By this time their tempers are up at the unnecessary suppression, and they are pressed for time on their deadlines. The tone of the stories castigates the company for its recalcitrance. The newsmen are suspicious that the noncooperation indicates unsavory circumstances, which the railroad is attempting to hide from the public. To justify their expenditures in getting the story, the editors spread the subject sensationally and make all they can of it. Bad public relations in handling of spot news has severely penalized the company.

Ways to make news. Here are some of the most effective legitimate ways to create news. There are many ways, but these are the basic ones:

- Tie in with the news events of the day.
- Tie in with another publicity man.
- Tie in with newspaper or other medium on a mutual project.
- Conduct a poll or survey.
- Issue a report.
- Arrange an interview with a celebrity.

PREPARATIONS FOR COMMUNICATING

- Take part in a controversy.
- Arrange for a testimonial.
- Make an analysis or prediction.
- Arrange for, write, project, cover a speech.
- Form and announce the names of a committee.
- Hold an election.
- Announce an appointment.
- Celebrate an anniversary.
- Issue a summary of facts.
- Tie in with a holiday.
- Adopt a program of work.
- Make a statement on a subject of interest.
- Make a trip.
- Bring a celebrity from elsewhere.
- Make an award.
- Hold a contest.
- Pass a resolution.
- Appear before public bodies.
- Stage a special event.
- Write a letter.
- Release a letter you have received.
- Adapt national reports and surveys locally.
- Entertain.
- Stage a debate.
- Organize a trade promotion.
- Tie into a well-known "week" or "day."
- Fete an institution, such as the Bill of Rights.
- Inspect a project.
- Organize a tour.
- Develop a community calendar or program.
- Issue a protest.
- Issue praise.
- Issue and diagnose statistics.
- Stage a demonstration.
- Stage a "gag."
- Make a picture (this may accompany many of the foregoing).

When is it news? It is news when it contains one or more of the major ingredients of human interest, namely:

- When it is new; e.g., launching a man into space.
- When it is novel; e.g., identical twins suffer identical injuries.
- When it relates to famous persons; e.g., any entertainment column.
- When it is directly important to great numbers of people; e.g., information about the income tax.
- When it involves conflict; e.g., battles, divorces, athletic contests.
- When it involves mystery; e.g., most crimes.
- When it is considered confidential; e.g., the revelations of columnists.
- When it pertains to the future; e.g., plans for improving a city.
- When it is funny; e.g., a group of Young Pathfinders gets lost on a hike.
- When it is romantic or sexy; e.g., check what catches the eye scrutinizing the "cheesecake" of any newspaper or magazine.

PLANNING PUBLICITY

Publicity is not merely a process of getting stories and pictures into the newspapers. It is a major-scale operation requiring planned and ordered execution of thousands of small details. Effective publicity is being achieved when Mr. Citizen sees the subject being publicized in his morning paper, in his afternoon paper, in some technical publications, in two trade journals, in his neighborhood free-circulation newspaper, in a national magazine, on a ticket, on a couple of direct mail pieces, in his church leaflet, on labels and lapel buttons, on automobile bumper strips, on outdoor billboards; when he hears about it on his radio and sees it on TV; when he gets a telephone call about it and discusses it with his friends at lunch. This is the kind of planned publicity that brings in a volume of sales, or votes, or results of whatever kind may be sought.

All of this costs money, requires manpower and experience, consumes time and resources. It can either be done in an ordered manner like a well-planned military campaign geared to encounter every problem of enemy ingenuity, adverse weather, and sudden circumstance; or it can be done in a slipshod manner with hit-or-miss efforts that may or may not muddle through.

The steps in planning a publicity operation that gets results are these:

Research. Analyze the history and existing facts of the subject to be publicized. Examine the records and fine-comb the scrapbooks. Meet the key people and as many as possible of the little people, obtaining the benefit of their ideas and experience and giving them the psychological lift of feeling that they are called upon to make contributions to the publicity. (See also Chapter 36.)

Pry into the basic statistics and facts. Study the profit-and-loss record. Analyze past and present policies. Go over the calendar and pick out the anniversaries, historic dates, elections, and traditional special events. Make a complete file of the names and pedigrees of the officers. Make a record of such statistics as the number of members and employees and stockholders. Make an inventory of resources. Some publicity offices maintain a complete library or "morgue" including all this information with such details as pictures and complete biographies of all principals for immediate reference in case of death, promotion, or other sudden news developments.

Set the objective. The publicist may desire to sell products for a company. Does he aim at a local, regional, national, or international market? The Pasadena Tournament of Roses has a double objective—to attract hundreds of thousands of people to see one of America's most colorful winter pageants, and to create national news that will publicize the fact that Southern California's climate is so balmy as to attract 1,500,000 people to come out in their shirt sleeves to see dozens of floats spectacularly bedecked with flowers. A big trade show might have one or all of these objectives: attract a large paying audience; publicize widely the concentration of products and a market in the given area; win perennial confidence of exhibitors so they will purchase display space in future years. A small community may present a festival with the dual objective of attracting cash customers and informing people in 49 other states and 100 nations of the charms and advantages of the community.

The Republican Party has a broad national objective and a number of more limited local objectives. A Lions Club may wish no more than a notice to its own members to get them out to the Thursday luncheon. Hitler had a series of objectives, from international publicity as a concomitant to his most expansive dreams, down to local publicity in Germany to maintain the stranglehold of his Nazi Party on the life of the nation.

Most events, and indeed most news, magazine, and broadcast features, are planned with an objective. The publicist must analyze the subject he is handling because the scope of his efforts will influence the tools he will use, the direction in which he will aim, the money he will spend. Every bit of effort plunged into national publicity, for example, may detract from the intensity of local publicity.

Local publicity aims at local newspapers, radio stations, television stations, house magazines, trade publications, and direct mail. *Sectional publicity,* aimed at a part of the state, expands on the local technique with an additional effort to send copy and illustrations to a wide number of community newspapers. *Regional publicity,* going statewide or to several states, introduces news and photo syndicates. If an intensive effort is contemplated, it requires a greater staff to produce localized news for aiming at specific publications in local areas. *National publicity* brings into heavy play the news and photo syndicates, plus newsreels, national magazines, and network television. (For international publicity, see Chapters 33, 34.)

Direct coverage is likely to be limited to a mailing list of from one hundred to two hundred major newspapers and perhaps additional pin-point efforts such as, "Mr. John Citizen of Our Organization, who graduated from high school in Walla Walla, Wash., today did thus and so . . ."

Plan work with individual media. While considerable emphasis is placed here on mass distributions and lists, often the most important publicity is the result of work with individual publications or broadcasters. In fact, mass distribution is less desirable than carefully selected placements with major media. For instance, placement of a story with Associated Press, United Press International, or one of the major press syndicates will reach many newspapers under the aegis of a service they subscribe to and respect. This is clearly more effective—and much less expensive—than mass mailing the story to many newspapers from a source they consider to be an outsider. "Over the transom" mail is heavy in all publications' offices, and each piece has an uphill fight to get attention and acceptance, while the wire service or press service story gets priority attention and prime acceptance.

In the same way, placement of an exclusive article in an important national magazine will reach many people in the area where a locally placed story would appear. Being in a national publication tends to give it greater stature in the mind of the reader.

A network television program, or widespread showing of a film or videotape show, also multiplies the impact of the television showing both numerically and in influence.

Working to arrange individual placements requires the time of capable people and has many complications, such as arranging to see the proper editor, waiting for a response to the inquiry, meeting further requests for added information and service, and the like. For this reason, many publicity people prefer to take the easier route of mass mailing releases, photos, films, and tapes. Once they

PREPARATIONS FOR COMMUNICATING

have the material prepared, it can be turned over to the mailing department and be done with.

It is far more profitable for the publicist to spend the client's money on production and mailing than his own staff time on working with editors. For this reason, the organization should review the wisdom of a program in which the preponderance of effort and expense budget is devoted to mass distributions. Also, a volume of mailings *look* like more work is done than the invisible work with editors and producers, so officials often mistake the volume for effectiveness. Local programs or others with special circumstances may justify the mass approach, and there are often merits in individual mailings when mass impact placements are not attainable. But this should not be assumed to be the case.

Factors involved in working individually with the various media are covered in the following seven chapters.

Make the lists. Lists to govern distribution of news material require irksome detail work. Difficult enough to get at the outset, they invariably react to the migratory neuroticism of humanity by becoming dated before one can finish them. However distressing, these annoying compilations constitute perhaps the most vital single detail of successful publicity.

There is not only a great diversity of media to be considered, but a wide range of services available to reach many of the media or to help with the production tasks. An invaluable guide to many of these is *Professional's Guide to Public Relations Services*, Third Edition, by Richard Weiner, 888 7th Ave., New York, N.Y. 10019. Since changes occur rapidly in this field, however, it is wise to check the facts about any service before using it, or to recheck if it has not been used for a few weeks. Prices should be obtained for each project or assignment, or ordering done with purchase orders that indicate the charge that is authorized.

In recent years, with the growing sophistication of the publicity field, a number of organizations have set up services to meet many of the publicist's needs. Among these are firms that maintain mailing lists and will produce and distribute releases on order. By spreading the task and cost of maintaining lists, production equipment, and staffs among many customers, they are in a position to do the job more expeditiously, more inexpensively, and more quickly than many individual publicity offices. It is important, however, to evaluate the quality of the service, the speed, and the costs in comparison with what would be involved internally.

Also, safeguards must be set up to assure secrecy, since personnel in these offices do work for many publicists, including some who compete with each other or who represent competitive clients.

Another factor to be weighed is the time required to reach the distribution service with the material to be processed. If it must go out-of-town, the unpredictability of mail service—from one day to several days between any two points in the United States, including intracity—can foil mailing schedules. Copy may be sent by teletype to some of these services. Locally it should always be delivered so timing can be accurate.

Each service should be individually investigated and cost quotations received. Many of the services provide forms that can be readily checked to indicate which media are to be serviced, which are to receive photos, which are to be delivered or sent air mail, and other determinations.

Among the services in this field are:

Ad Systems, Inc.
723 S. Wells
Chicago, Ill. 60607
  (Branch in New York)

Associated Release Service
2 N. Riverside Plaza
Chicago, Ill. 60606

Bacon's Publicity Distribution Service
14 East Jackson Blvd.
Chicago, Ill. 60604

Chase Direct Mail Service Corporation
228 E. 45th St.
New York, N.Y. 10017

Derus Media Service
8 W. Hubbard St.
Chicago, Ill. 60610
  (Branches in Detroit, New York, Miami, Los Angeles)

Media Distribution Services
260 W. 41st St.
New York, N.Y. 10036

Public Relations Aids
221 Park Ave., South
New York, N.Y. 10003

Even if such an outside service is used, it is necessary to be fully familiar with all lists and to keep up-to-date on the needs and preferences of the media.

BUSINESS B1

A — DAILY MEDIA WITH HEAVY COVERAGE OF BUSINESS
xrf C11-A business eds of local gen dailies

Choose type(s) of media:
- WIRE SERVICES (eg AP, UPI, Reuters) — natnl — 4 AAB$ — XXB*27:T
  - xrf B2-A financial ticker services
- SERIOUS NATL GEN DAILIES (eg NY Times) — natnl — 1 AAD$ — XXB*28:T
- NATL BUSINESS DAILIES (eg WSJ, J of C) — natnl — 3 AAF$ — XXA$35:1

Choose an editor:
- Auto business editor (some dup in C7-A) — 27:T
- Electrical equipment editor — 27:E
- Electronic equipment editor — 27:ø
- Industrial machinery/equipment editor — 27:1
- Iron/steel/metal-prods mfg editor — 27:8
- Non-ferrous metals editor — 27:9
- Aircraft/missile mfg editor — 28:T
  (some dup in C1-A aerospace eds)
- Air transport editor (some dup in C1-A) — 28:E
- Marine editor — 28:ø
- Railroads editor — 28:1
- Trucking editor — 28:8
- Atomic energy editor — 28:9
- Utilities editor — 29:T
- Building materials editor — 29:E
- Real-estate/construction editor — 29:ø
- Hotels editor — 29:1
- Chemicals/chemical-products editor — 29:8
- Coal editor — 29:9
- Petroleum/petroleum-products editor — 30:T
- Plastics editor — 30:E
- Pulp/paper editor — 30:ø
- Rubber editor — 30:1
- Textiles editor — 30:8
- Drugs/health-industry editor — 30:9
  xrf C1-A medical eds
- Farm-business editor (some dup in C1-A) — 31:T
- Commodities editor — 31:E
- Food/beverages editor — 31:ø
- Tobacco editor — 31:1
- Apparel editor — 31:8
- Franchising/rental editor — 31:9
- Home-furnishings/housewares editor — 32:T
- Leisure products/services editor — 32:E
- Sporting-goods editor — 32:ø
- Retailing editor — 32:1
- Shoes editor — 32:8
- Trading stamps editor — 32:9
- Cameras/film business editor — 33:T
  xrf C7-A photography editors
- Advertising editor — 33:E
- Publishing/printing editor — 33:ø
- Broadcasting business editor — 33:1
  xrf C4-A TV-radio entertainment eds
- Business-management methodology editor — 33:8
- Defense contracts editor (some dup in C1-A) — 33:9
- Foreign trade editor — 34:T
- Indus-science/eng editor (some dup in C1-A) — 34:E
- Intl-business-operations editor — 34:ø
  xrf C1-A gen foreign-affairs eds
- Banking editor — 34:1
- Bonds editor — 34:8
- Brokerage-house/stock-exchange mgmt editor — 34:9
- Corporation-earnings-statements editor — 35:T
- Credit editor — 35:E
- Insurance editor — 35:ø
- Investment-banking/new-finance editor — 35:1
- Mergers/acquisitions editor — 35:8
- Mutual funds editor — 35:9
- Stock-market roundup editor — 36:E
- Wall Street gossip columnist (if any) — 36:ø
- Business economics editor — 36:ø
  xrf C1-A natl-govt economics eds, C9-A personal-business eds
- Gen business columnist (if any) — 36:1
- Business/financial editor-in-chief — 36:8
- Miscellaneous (business news desk) — 36:9

B — OTHER GENERAL BUSINESS MEDIA

GEN BUSINESS NEWS PUBS (except natl dlys) — natnl 5 / regnl 7 / state 20 / local 25 — XXA$35:ø AAJ$ AAK$ AAL$ AAM$
(eg Business Week, Dun's Rvw)
Choose an editor:
- Company-profile editor — 27:T
- Foreign-company editor — 27:ø
- International-business editor — 27:8
- Technology editor — 28:T
- Marketing editor — 28:ø
- Basic-research editor — 28:8
- Management-methodology editor — 29:T
- Personnel-mgmt/labor-relations editor — 29:ø
- Transportation-industry editor — 29:8
- Mining/oil editor — 30:T
- Real-estate/construction editor — 30:ø
- Business-outlook editor — 30:8
- Stock-market-trends editor — 31:T
- Finance (money market &c) news editor — 31:ø
- Economics editor — 31:8
- Miscellaneous (general) editor — 32:8
  xrf C1-A public-affairs eds

NOTE: Regnl/state/local media above use natl business-outlook & mgmt-methodology matl, but only localized business news

LEGAL NEWSPAPERS USING SOME BUSINESS NEWS — local 16 AAP*27:9
(use some natl business-outlook & mgmt-methodology matl, but only localized business news)(dup in B24-G)

GEN BUSINESS FEATURE PUBS (eg Fortune) — natnl 5 / state 10 / local 26 — XXB$29:ø AAR* AAT* AAU*
Choose an editor:
- Architecture editor — 27:T
- Economic outlook editor — 27:ø
- Intl-business editor — 27:8
- Science editor — 28:T
- Miscellaneous (general) editor — 28:ø
  xrf B13-A mgmt methodology media, C1-A general local magazines

GEN BUSINESS-OUTLOOK PUBS — natnl 8 AAW*27:T
(no news of co's as such)(also cover mgmt methodology)(eg Nation's Business)

BUSINESS ECONOMIC OUTLOOK MEDIA — natnl 4 / state 21 / local 1 — ABB*27:T ABD ABE
(no company news) xrf B21-C academic economics

BANK EXTERNAL HOUSE-ORGANS COVERING BUSINESS ECONOMIC OUTLOOK — natnl 6 / state 2 — ABG*27:T ABJ

BUSINESS FEATURE PUBS FOR YOUNG-BUSINESS-MEN/COLLEGE-GRADS — natnl 2 AAR*28:1
xrf B13-G career/job-improvement media

GEN NEW-PRODUCT NEWS FOR BUSINESSMEN — natnl 3 ABN*27:T
(incl indus/commercial/personal prods)
xrf B3-A indus new-product media, C9-A consumer new-product eds

AD-AGENCY EXTERNAL HOUSE-ORGANS COVERING GEN NEW-PRODUCT NEWS FOR BUSINESSMEN — natnl 2 ABP*27:T

C — OTHER CONSUMER MEDIA COVERING BUSINESS
xrf C1 all gen consumer media

LIGHT NATL GEN DAILIES (eg NY News, Post) — natnl 2 ABS*
Choose an editor:
- Real estate editor — 27:T
- Business editor — 27:ø

SERIOUS FEATURE NEWSPAPERS—BUSINESS EDS — natnl 2 ABU
(eg Chr Sci Monitor, National Observer)

GEN NEWS MAGAZINES — natnl 6 / regnl 1 — XXB$29:T ABW* ABX*
(eg Time, Newsweek, US News)
Choose an editor:
- Foreign business editor — 27:T
- Business editor — 27:ø

GEN MASS MAGAZINES—BUSINESS EDS — natnl 3 XXB$29:E ABZ

Figure 38-1. Sample order form used with one distribution service to designate media that are to receive publicity releases. A wide range of choices is provided while reducing the time needed to make up lists.

192-OHIO

D 23 CONNEAUT NEWS-HERALD
182-184 Broad St.
Conneaut, OH 44030

Phone: (216) 593-1166
(e) 5,000

1.
2.
3.
4.
5.
6. Address All News Releases
7. and Photos to the Specific
8. Editorial Department by
9. Title.
10.
11.
12.
13.
14.
15.
16.

A) Thomas Cooley
B)
C)

D 25 (Dayton)
JOURNAL HERALD
37 S. Ludlow St.
Dayton, OH 45402

Phone: (513) 223-1111
(m) 110,000

1. Brainard Platt
2. Alvin Sanoff
3. Brainard Platt
4. Harold Piety
5. Jane Littleton
6. James Babcock
7.
8. Virginia Hunt
9. Virginia Hunt
10. Clara Weisenborn
11. P. J. Bednarski
12. Brainard Platt
13. James Babcock
14. Ritter Collett
15. James Robey
16. Virginia Hunt

A) Dennis Shere
B) William E. worth
C) Catherine Martindale

D 27 DEFIANCE CRESCENT-NEWS
Second and Perry Sts., Box 249
Defiance, OH 43512

Phone: (419) 784-5441
(d) 18,000

1. Frank Craig
2. Mary Shock
3. Frank Craig
4. Mary Shock
5. Make Cummins
6. Roger Buehrer
7. Mary Shock
8. Kathy Punches
9. Kathy Punches
10. Kathy Punches
11. Mary Shock
12. Frank Craig
13.
14. Al Smith & Bob Stearns
15. Roger Buehrer
16. Kathy Punches

A) Mike Cummins
B)
C) Roger Buehrer

D 24 COSHOCTON TRIBUNE
115 N. 6th St.
Coshocton, OH 43812

Phone: (614) 622-1122
(e) 9,000 (S) 10,000

1. Gary Anderson
2.
3. Gary Anderson
4. Vic Pytko
5. Kathy Fox
6.
7. Debbie Endsley
8. Luanna Sowers
9. Luanna Sowers
10. Jerry Gouldsberry
11.
12. Gary Anderson
13. Ken Melton
14. Frank Shepherd
15.
16. Luanna Sowers

A) Vic Pytko
B)
C)

D 26 DAYTON DAILY NEWS
4th & Ludlow Sts.
Dayton, OH 45401

Phone: (513) 223-2112
(e) 155,000 (S) 225,000

1. Darwin Sator
2. Betty Dietz Krebs
3. Jim Good
4. Thomas Teepen
5. Larry Kinneer
6. James Bland
7. Douglas Elliott
8. Linda Heffley
9. Linda Heffley
10. Linda Heffley
11. Thomas Hopkins
12. Darwin Sator
13. Jack Jones
14. Si Burick
15. Jack Osler
16. Linda Heffley

A) Jim Fain
B) Arnold Rosenfeld
C) Jim Dygert

D 28 DELAWARE GAZETTE
18 E. William
Delaware, OH 43015

Phone: (614) 363-1161
(e) 9,000

1. Harold C. Reed
2.
3.
4. Harold C. Reed
5. Virginia Knisely
6. Karen Radde
7. Karen Radde
8. Ruth Bachtel
9.
10.
11. Virginia Knisely
12.
13.
14. Gary Henery
15.
16. Ruth Bachtel

A) H. C. Thomson
B) H. C. Reed
C)

1. Automotive 2. Book Review 3. Business & Financial 4. Editorial Page 5. Education 6. Environmental & Ecology 7. Farm 8. Fashion 9. Food 10. Home & Garden 11. Radio & Television 12. Real Estate 13. Science 14. Sports 15. Travel 16. Women's A) Editor B) Managing Editor C) City Editor

Figure 38-2. Sample page from *Bacon's Newspaper Directory*. It can be used to make one's own mailings or to designate editors and papers to be serviced by Bacon's distribution service.

249

Metal Trade (51)—continued

51-12 IRON AND STEEL ENGINEER, 3 Gateway Center, Suite 2350, Pittsburgh, Pa. 15222. John A. Kotsch, Ed. Mo. 10th. 15,200. Assn. of Iron & Steel Engineers. Phone: (412) 281-6323. 1-2-3-4-5-6-7-11-12 ★

51-13 JOURNAL OF METALS, 345 E. 47th St., New York, N. Y. 10017. Dr. Konrad J. A. Kundig, Ed. Mo. 15th. 16,000. The Metallurgical Soc. of AIME. Phone: (212) PL 2-6800. 1-3-4-5-6-7-9-11 ★

51-13B LEAD, 292 Madison Ave., New York, N. Y. 10017. Jerome F. Smith, Editor. 2 ti. yr. 90,000. Lead Industries Assn., Inc. Phone: (212) 679-6020.

51-14 LIGHT METAL AGE, 693 Mission St. - Penthouse, San Francisco, Calif. 94105. Mr. Roy Fellom, Jr., Ed. E.O.M. 10th. 5,600. Fellom Publications. Phone: (415) 781-1431. 1-6-11 ●

Manufacturing Engineering (See listing in Industrial-41.)

51-14B METAL/CENTER NEWS, 7 East 12th St., New York, N. Y. 10003. Mr. Donald McGill, Ed. Mo. 3rd. Fri. Prec. 11,744. Fairchild Publications Inc. Phone: (212) 741-4419. 1-2-3-4-5-6-7-10-13

51-14C METAL FABRICATING NEWS, 724 Forbes Street, Rockford, Ill. 61101. Ronald L. Fowler, Ed. E.O.M. 15th. 70,000. Metal Fabricating Institute, Inc. Phone: (815) 965-4031. 1-2-3-4-5-6-7-9-11-13 ★

51-14D METAL FABRICATOR, 97 Columbia St., Peace Dale, RI 02883. D. R. Frost, Ed. 6 ti. yr. Walter B. Frost & Co. 1-2-3-4-5-6-7-9-11 ★

51-15 METAL FINISHING, One University Plaza, Hackensack, N. J. 07601. Palmer H. Langdon, Ed. Mo. 1st wk. 13,600. Metal and Plastics Publns., Inc. Phone: (201) 487-3700. 1-2-3-4-5-6-7-10

51-17 METAL PROGRESS, Metals Park, Ohio 44073. Harry E. Chandler, Ed. Mo. 29th prec. 52,000. Amer. Soc. for Metals. Phone: (216) 338-5151. 1-2-4-5-6-7-9-11 ▲

51-18 METAL STAMPING, 27027 Chardon Road, Richmond Hts., Ohio 44143. Attn: Editor. Mo. 1st wk. 15,000. American Metal Stamping Assn. Phone: (216) 585-8800. 1-2-3-4-6-7 ★

51-19 METAL TREATING, 19 Church St., (Berea) Cleveland, OH 44017. Jim Toedtman, Publ. E.O.M. 10th. 16,000. Temple Publ. Inc. Phone: (216) 243-8250. 1-2-3-4-5-6-7 ★

51-20D METALS ENGINEERING QUARTERLY, Metals Park, Ohio 44073. Carl R. Weymueller, Editor. Qrtly. 3 100. American Soc. for Metals. Phone: (216) 338-5151. 6 ▲

51-21B METALS SOURCEBOOK, 1221 Ave. of the Americas, New York, N. Y. 10020. Dorothy Fabian, Ed. 24 ti. yr. Mon. 600. McGraw-Hill, Inc. Phone: (212) 997-2823. 1-3-7 ▲ ★ **Newsletter**

51-21D METALS WEEK, 1221 Avenue of the Americas, New York, N. Y. 10020. Gary Reibsamen, Ed. Wkly. Mon. McGraw-Hill, Inc. Phone: (212) 997-2823. 1-2-3-7-8-11 **Newsletter**

51-22C METALWORKING DIGEST, 20 Community Place, Morristown, N. J. 07960. George Littlewood, Ed./Publ. E.O.M. 25th. 101,000. Gordon Publ., Inc. Phone: (201) 267-6040. 1-2

51-23 METLFAX MAGAZINE, 5821 Harper Road, Solon, Ohio 44139. Thomas H. Dreher, Ed. Mo. 15th prec. 102,000. Huebner Publns., Inc. Phone: (216) 248-1125. 1-2-3-4-5-7-11 ★

1. New Prod. 2. Trade Lit. 3. Gen. News 4. Personnel 5. Events 6. Articles—By-Lined 7. Articles—Staff 8. Financial 9. Letters 10. Ques. & Ans. 11. Books 12. Contracts 13. Films 14. Entertainment
★ Change from previous edition. ● Charges for cuts. ▲ Does not use publicity photos.

Figure 38-3. Sample page from *Bacon's Publicity Checker*, which features trade publications and magazines. Information is provided to facilitate selecting a distribution list for each mailing.

Even in designating what the service is to do, this knowledge is essential.

The first principle in using any list is: *update the list every time it is to be used in a campaign.*

The following are reliable sources of lists:

(1) *Editor and Publisher International Yearbook*[1] includes every daily newspaper published in the United States and Canada, and many published in Latin America and Europe. It lists the major editorial executives of each newspaper. It also gives separate lists of syndicates, feature services, advertising agencies, sports editors, women's editors, other department editors, foreign-language dailies of the United States, and leading Black publications. *Editor and Publisher International Yearbook* is the most valuable reference work on newspapers in the United States and many other countries.

(2) *Bacon's Publicity Checker*[2] (annual) is an indispensable guide to all major magazines and newspapers published in the United States and Canada. It classifies them by subject interest and cites circulation, frequency of publication, name of editor, address, and telephone number; and it has a code that indicates the types of publicity material each is interested in receiving. Periodic correction sheets, scored for easy pasting into the directory, help keep the listings up-to-date.

(3) *Ayer's Directory of Newspapers and Periodicals*[3] lists most of the public publications of

[1]850 Third Ave., New York, N.Y. 10022

[2]14 E. Jackson Blvd., Chicago, Ill. 60604

[3]West Washington Square, Philadelphia, Pa. 19106

America, with address and name of publisher. They are listed by cities, alphabetized under state headings, with an alphabetized index of the entire group at the end of the directory. It is published annually.

(4) *Membership List of American Society of Journalists and Authors*[4] includes names, addresses, areas of interest, and publications served regularly of many of the most successful non-fiction writers in America. Many of these writers, in addition to preparing articles on assignment for the magazines or on their own speculation, will accept writing assignments from publicity people. In this case, however, it is clearly understood that the writer is working for the publicity office, and editors to whom his manuscript is submitted are informed of the sponsor's interest.

(5) *Standard Rate and Data Service,*[5] the *Directory of Professional Photography,*[6] *Broadcasting Yearbook,*[7] *Television Factbook,*[8] and many writers' publications publish valuable lists and tips for publicists.

(6) *The Gebbie Press House Magazine Directory,*[9] which lists more than 4,000 of the nation's leading house magazines; *Ulrich's Periodicals Directory,*[10] a listing of all major periodicals in the world by categories; *Directory of Newspaper and Magazine Personnel and Data,*[11] a list of British Commonwealth media plus correspondents from all over the world based in England; *Foreign Language Press of America;*[12] *The Working Press of the Nation,*[13] a directory of key personnel under more than 100 different news classifications for newspapers, magazines, radio and television stations; *The Standard Periodical Directory*[14] and the *National Directory of Newsletters and Reporting Services*[15] are all useful sources of lists for distribution of publicity material.

(7) Very helpful, too, are *America's Education Press,*[16] a classified list of educational periodicals issued in the U.S. and Canada; the *U.S. Government Organizations Manual,*[17] which includes names of public information people in all divisions of government and their adresses; and the *Catholic Press Directory,*[18] which lists Catholic publications and their publication dates.

(8) The Department of Commerce publishes state-by-state lists of trade associations, with separate lists for New York City and Chicago. In addition, it has a special list of national trade associations. *The Encyclopedia of Associations*[19] is another source.

(9) The United States Chamber of Commerce[20] has a list of chambers of commerce.

(10) Other good source references for lists include newspaper publishers' associations, radio and TV broadcasters' associations, various trade groups, competent publicity clubs and public-relations groups, classified telephone directories, advertising agencies, many individual organizations, direct-mail houses, clipping services, and, in some cases, list brokers.

(11) Annually in July *Editor and Publisher* issues a *Syndicate Directory* carrying listings of syndicates and names of features handled and their authors.

(12) A guide to the press services is *News Bureaus in the U.S.,* Richard Weiner, Inc., 888 7th Ave., New York, N.Y. 10019.

(13) A list of special editions of publications that are suitable for specific types of publicity is offered in *The Mediamatic Calendar of Special Editorial Issues* (423 W. 55th St., New York, N.Y. 10019). For example, editions of trade publications dealing with specific types of products or a specific trade show are listed with their deadlines and the type of information sought.

Different clients, organizations, and campaigns require different lists. One large regional trade

---

[4]123 W. 43rd St., New York, N.Y. 10036

[5]5201 Old Orchard Rd., Skokie, Ill. 60076

[6]Professional Photographers of America, Inc., 1090 Executive Way, Oak Leaf Commons, Des Plaines, Ill. 60018

[7]Broadcasting Publications, Inc., 1735 De Sales, N.W., Washington, D.C. 20036

[8]Television Digest, 1836 Jefferson Pl., N.W., Washington, D.C. 20036

[9]The Gebbie Press, Box 1000, New Paltz, N.Y. 12561

[10]R.R. Bowker Co., 1180 Ave. of the Americas, New York, N.Y. 10036

[11]World's Press News Publishing Co., Ltd., 9-10 Old Bailey, London E.C. 4, England

[12]Waxelbaum Advertising Co., 79-09 37th Ave., Jackson Hts., N.Y. 11372

[13]National Research Bureau, Inc., 424 N. 3rd St., Burlington, Ia. 52601

[14]Oxbridge Publishing Co., 150 E. 52nd St., New York, N.Y. 10022

[15]Gale Research Co., Book Tower, Detroit, Mich. 48226

[16]Glassboro State Colleges, Glassboro, N.J. 08028

[17]Superintendent of Documents, Government Printing Office, Washington, D.C. 20402

[18]Catholic Press Association, 432 Park Ave., South, New York, N.Y. 10016

[19]Gale Research Co., Book Tower, Detroit, Mich., 48226

[20]U.S. Chamber of Commerce, 1615 H. St., NW, Washington, D.C. 20062

PREPARATIONS FOR COMMUNICATING

association, for example, requires a list including five metropolitan newspapers with separate lists of the city editors, financial editors, general columnists, editorial editors, and society editors; ninety selected home-town papers; forty controlled-circulation papers; thirty trade publications; sixteen radio stations; eleven TV stations; and fifteen nationally syndicated columnists.

A properly selected and serviced list becomes a tool of publicity production and distribution that grows more productive with time, as the individual editors become acquainted with the publicist and learn from experience that they may rely on him.

To develop the best possible list or series of lists, the publicity person will take these steps:

- Obtain the basic lists described above.
- Seek, compare, and analyze all available existing lists.
- Select from the classified section of the telephone directory all classifications to be included.
- Obtain as many lists as possible from such sources as large corporations, railroads, advertising agencies, trade associations, and other organizations that may have them.
- If you do not have access to a computer for lists and mailings, note each of the publications and names on a 3 x 5 card, including publication name, address, telephone number, date and frequency of publication, publisher's name, editor's name, name of any other key personnel for publicity purposes, deadline date and time, field covered, circulation, and classification (for example, architecture, medicine, association, employees' publication, radio station, special group, or whatever). Use of 3 x 5 cards in master lists overcomes duplication and facilitates quick assembly of special lists. "Working" lists can be transferred from the cards to paper, after which the individual cards are returned to their position in the master file. Where computer facilities are available, the list can be programmed and readily corrected and updated. This can replace the 3 x 5 card file, since a printout can be had of the up-to-date list or any category in it whenever it is needed.
- The distribution services mentioned earlier maintain many lists. Some use computers, whose efficiency is made available to each client.
- With important lists it is a wise precaution if the time is available to verify each item by telephone. Publications come and go; editors and addresses change.

It is *imperative* to revise each list at least once a year and to revise it before using it in a new campaign.

Make the budget. A basic problem in any publicity campaign, or in planning a permanent publicity program, is formulating the budget. Ideally, the publicist should determine his objective, the geographical limits, the media he desires to use and set his budget up accordingly. Often, however, he will be arbitrarily limited at the outset by a maximum figure and be required to adjust his efforts to the limitations of that figure.

The following elements figure in a well-balanced publicity budget:

Fee: In the case of a publicist who is the employee of an organization on a permanent basis, the salary can be anything from one hundred dollars a week to more than $50,000 a year. There is also a wide range in fees for serving an organization on a client or campaign basis. In general, it is a more satisfactory basis to stipulate a fee as the contractor's personal reimbursement and charge all expenses in addition. A package arrangement, in which a contractor undertakes to meet the expenses himself for an overall fee, will make the fee seem much larger than it actually is to a client and tends to lead to suspicions by the client that the contractor is skimping on expenses.

The simplest way to arrive at an equitable fee is for the publicist to figure how much he wishes to make for an hour of work, figure how many hours the particular contract will require, multiply the two figures, add his overhead and a small margin of safety, and set the fee at the total.

Expenses, in addition to fee, that will be encountered in publicity work include:

Photographs: Photographs will usually cost not less than twelve dollars a negative plus $1.00 or more for each 8 x 10 inch print in addition to the first one. Many photographers quote by the day rather than by the negative. Typical rates are quoted for a half-day (often the minimum time available) or by the job (plus extra for prints). Prices in New York are considerably higher than in other parts of the country. The publicist should make his arrangements with a photographer, on the basis of how many pictures he will desire to produce, and stipulate the total amount on the budget. Some photographers are willing to work on a basis of so much for their time plus all expenses, including travel and supplies.

For a local campaign one different picture will be

needed for each local daily with about two extra to allow for a choice by every editor. For a national campaign one different negative will be required for each photo syndicate plus some extras to allow for choice.

Suppose the photographer charges fifteen dollars per negative plus one dollar per extra print. The publicist desires to produce six picture stories. A picture story to him includes six versions of a single subject, each one sufficiently different to justify simultaneous publication by different editors. Six stories times six pictures is thirty-six, which multiplied by fifteen dollars would entail a total cost of $540. However, at this volume, a quantity rate often can be arranged. Allowing for emergency calls for other pictures, extra prints to take care of trade publications and contingencies, a budget figure of $650 would be in order.

A list of photographers available to publicists appears in the annual *Feature Writer and Syndicate Directory,* a volume in the *Working Press of the Nation* series published by *National Research Bureau,* 424 N. 3rd St., Burlington, Iowa 52601. Names, addresses, and phone numbers of qualified photographers in various areas are available from the National Association of Free Lance Photographers, 4 E. State St., Doylestown, Pa. 18901. Other sources are the commercial divisions of Associated Press and United Press International.

Film Footage: In smaller cities the television stations sometimes will accept film from a publicist to use on news programs or in local documentaries. This filming should be done in color by a professional motion-picture or television cameraman. Prices should be obtained for each assignment.

Mats: Smaller newspapers will not undergo the expense of engraving most publicity pictures, but many of the community papers like interesting photographs if sent to them in matrix form instead of mats. Many newspapers now use glossy proofs for offset printing. The same photographs that are produced for the metropolitan dailies offer a selection from which a photo can be chosen for reproduction into a mat or glossy proof.

Basic prices for mats and glossy proofs vary in different places. Price quotations should be obtained, including the halftone, composition, and proofs to accompany mats and show editors what the picture looks like. With this information, the publicist can figure his budgetary requirements on the basis of how many small papers are to be served, how many releases are to be distributed, and what size mats and proofs he will use. The total represents his budgetary figure for mats and proofs.

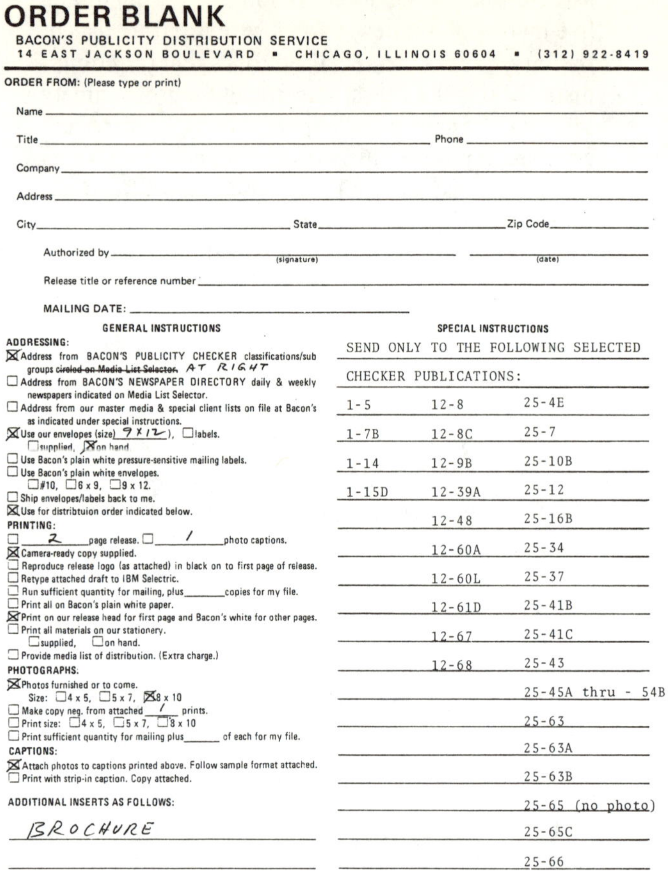

ORDER BLANK

BACON'S PUBLICITY DISTRIBUTION SERVICE
14 EAST JACKSON BOULEVARD ▪ CHICAGO, ILLINOIS 60604 ▪ (312) 922-8419

ORDER FROM: (Please type or print)

Name ______

Title ______ Phone ______

Company ______

Address ______

City ______ State ______ Zip Code ______

Authorized by ______ (signature) ______ (date)

Release title or reference number ______

MAILING DATE: ______

GENERAL INSTRUCTIONS

ADDRESSING:

☒ Address from BACON'S PUBLICITY CHECKER classifications/sub groups ~~circled on Media List Selector.~~ AT RIGHT

☐ Address from BACON'S NEWSPAPER DIRECTORY daily & weekly newspapers indicated on Media List Selector.

☐ Address from our master media & special client lists on file at Bacon's as indicated under special instructions.

☒ Use our envelopes (size) 9 X 12), ☐ labels. ☐ supplied, ☒ on hand

☐ Use Bacon's plain white pressure-sensitive mailing labels.

☐ Use Bacon's plain white envelopes. ☐ #10, ☐ 6 x 9, ☐ 9 x 12.

☐ Ship envelopes/labels back to me.

☒ Use for distribtuion order indicated below.

PRINTING:

☐ 2 page release. ☐ 1 photo captions.

☒ Camera-ready copy supplied.

☐ Reproduce release logo (as attached) in black on to first page of release.

☐ Retype attached draft to IBM Selectric.

☐ Run sufficient quantity for mailing, plus ______ copies for my file.

☐ Print all on Bacon's plain white paper.

☒ Print on our release head for first page and Bacon's white for other pages.

☐ Print all materials on our stationery. ☐ supplied, ☐ on hand.

☐ Provide media list of distribution. (Extra charge.)

PHOTOGRAPHS:

☒ Photos furnished or to come. Size: ☐ 4 x 5, ☐ 5 x 7, ☒ 8 x 10

☐ Make copy neg. from attached 1 prints.

☐ Print size: ☐ 4 x 5, ☐ 5 x 7, ☐ 8 x 10

☐ Print sufficient quantity for mailing plus ______ of each for my file.

CAPTIONS:

☒ Attach photos to captions printed above. Follow sample format attached.

☐ Print with strip-in caption. Copy attached.

ADDITIONAL INSERTS AS FOLLOWS:

BROCHURE

SPECIAL INSTRUCTIONS

SEND ONLY TO THE FOLLOWING SELECTED CHECKER PUBLICATIONS:

1-5	12-8	25-4E
1-7B	12-8C	25-7
1-14	12-9B	25-10B
1-15D	12-39A	25-12
	12-48	25-16B
	12-60A	25-34
	12-60L	25-37
	12-61D	25-41B
	12-67	25-41C
	12-68	25-43
		25-45A thru - 54B
		25-63
		25-63A
		25-63B
		25-65 (no photo)
		25-65C
		25-66

Figure 38-4. A distribution order based on Bacon's Publicity Checker. The first number in each column designates a section devoted to one category of trade publications.

Distribution to Smaller Newspapers: The press associations of several states offer added service in the form of publicity release mailing service. Often, for a nominal fee, the association handles all of the details of mimeographing, mat making, and mailing. The story and art copy with instructions as to what coverage is desired are all the publicity representative needs to supply.

If, as is necessary in some cases, the mats are made by someone outside the regular matrix service offered by the association, the only additional cost is a slight handling fee and the additional postage costs.

This system has many advantages to the publicity representative. The material is mailed to an up-to-date list on stationery from the newspaper's own

PREPARATIONS FOR COMMUNICATING

organization and is therefore given priority attention almost without exception.

In addition to the state newspaper publishers' associations, other organizations are set up to perform a similar service. (See Chapter 40.) The publicist should contact the available service, get its rates, figure out the volume of his work and analyze his budget figure accordingly.

Of course, many publicity offices handle the distribution themselves. It then becomes a simple matter of figuring postage, cost of mats and proofs, cost of supplies, and totaling.

Mailing: If a volume of mailing is to be done, the publicist should get in touch with the nearest postal station and inquire about pertinent details from the superintendent or his assistant in charge. It is advisable when inquiring about rates for printed matter to submit a copy to the post office rather than to ask for a telephone ruling.

The publicist should watch carefully all rules of proper addressing and packaging. He should be careful of colors used so they will show up well and not fade out.

Because postal rates and regulations are changed frequently, it is wise to query the post office before any large or unusual mailing, and to keep in touch with regulations.

There are many services that will handle large mailings of stuffers and literature for rates from twenty-five dollars per thousand up, including folding, stuffing, addressing, and actual mailing. Postage, of course, is extra. Where the campaign, such as a political campaign, will require a heavy volume of such mailing, it may be advisable to engage such a service.

Production of Copy: Large volumes of copy can be produced by mimeographing, multigraphing, offset, letterpress printing, or other processes.[21] Many different organizations offer these services, but each job presents an entirely separate problem. General rates are almost impossible to quote, each contract depending on such facts as which process will be used, size and grade of paper, fold, manner of stamping, current labor rates, and other factors.

Important new technology makes it possible to increase the use of material sent to newspapers that set their type by computer, whose numbers are increasing. They use "scanner ready" copy, whereby material is transposed directly from the copy to type ready for publication. Copy submitted on an IBM

[21]See Chapter 51.

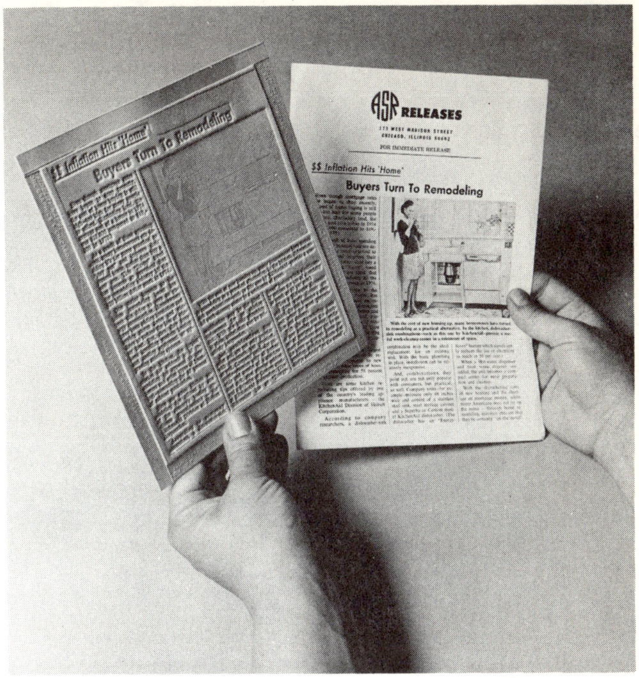

Figure 38-5. Publicity mat (left) and proof of the story and illustration it contains. The mat and proof are sent to small newspapers that print by letterpress. The proof shows the editor what the story contains. The proof—known as a Litho Repro—is sent alone to papers that reproduce by offset. They can reproduce it or edit and reset.

Courier 12 Delta typewriter is most likely to be accepted. This has the added advantage of often reducing the amount of changing done by the editors.

Messenger: Messenger service is important to deliver and pick up items in a hurry, deliver copy to city desks and broadcast stations, and many other spontaneous duties in a publicity campaign. Rates vary in different cities.

Mileage: Most publicity campaigns involve a certain amount of driving. Costs should be figured on a mileage basis, with allowance for likely increases in costs.

Entertainment: Many publicity campaigns involve and justify a certain amount for purchasing dinners and luncheons, and other entertainment expenses. In some instances this item may include one or more planned dinners or cocktail parties with many persons to be present. This item can be figured out for a certain allowance and budgeted accordingly.

Models: In some publicity campaigns it may be feasible to engage models rather than to rely on volunteer models to contribute their time. In such a

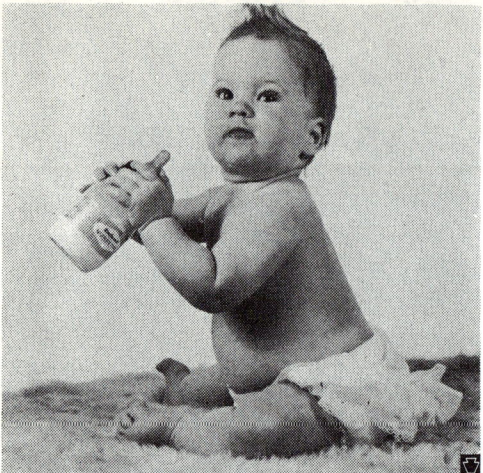

Figure 38-6. A proof of a mat, showing how material is sent to small newspapers.

case, it is desirable for the publicist to inquire as to fees and make the indicated provisions. In cities where there are no model agencies, college girls and girls appearing in local night club shows will take free-lance modeling assignments.

Clipping Service: Some clipping services charge a minimum of fifty dollars a month or more and thirty cents for every clipping. The charges vary. The publicist can figure how many months he wishes to carry the service and allow an override for the big volume of clippings that may be expected to come in at the end. In a publicity campaign of any size, it is impossible to compute how big the bill might grow to be for the clipping service. The advisable thing to do, if this cost must be limited, is to make a flat sum arrangement with the clipping service, ordering all clippings that can be purchased up to the sum stipulated. (See later section.)

In various campaigns there are other charges that may be involved. Sometimes the publicity director will handle an advertising campaign, in which case the amount should be figured and broken down appropriately between the media to be used. Perhaps if a broadcast is to be arranged for a special event, several hundred to more than a thousand dollars will be required to pay the charges of installing wires, microphone, engineers' charges, light rentals, transportation, and other items. The campaign may involve such items as automobile bumper strips, posters, outdoor advertising sheets of various sizes, display materials, props for pictures, such as costumes and special lighting, and many other details.

The *steps* in planning a budget will include:

(1) Determine the over-all figure to be allowed, or monthly allotment, if it can be set.

(2) If the figure has not been set, determine the desirable figure on the basis of total budget of the enterprise, objective, amount of work to be done.

(3) List the *items* to be used in the program, including those analyzed above and any others to be employed.

(4) Telephone or contact the suppliers in *each* instance to get the exact up-to-the-minute rates, including local taxes and other details.

(5) Weigh the relative value of the different items in light of the total figure and with respect to their potential weight in solving the particular problem involved.

(6) Total each item on the basis of the volume of it to be used.

(7) Total the entire amount.

(8) Allow a sum of at least 10 per cent of the expense budget for miscellaneous and contingency, because in every program there will be unforeseen requirements, changes, sudden charges for important new ideas, price increases, and similar factors.

In *billing* the client, properly support each item with bills or receipts substantiating the amount claimed. Be precise and detailed. This eliminates misunderstanding.

Miscellaneous: It is well to have a fixed amount budgeted for miscellaneous expenditures, which can include such items as odd postage, supplies, petty cash items, long distance telephone, telegraph, cab fare, purchase of and subscriptions to publications, making copies of clippings or documents, and others.

Schedule the activity. In a regular, year-around publicity assignment the schedule will fit into the calendar of the organization. Publicity will be timed with the annual election, annual banquet, new products, special events of the organization, appointments and personnel changes, annual report, new construction, and subsidiary campaigns when called for by activities of the organization.

In scheduling a specific short-term campaign, either as part of a continuing program or an isolated one, the first step is to research the situation and accumulate as many ideas as possible. Sit down in solitude and make an unrestrained list of ideas, stories, pictures, supporting events, personalities, special media promotions, tie-ins. Let the list cool off for a few days. Redigest it. Weed it out. Revise. Review it with a photographer, a friend, an assistant. Trim it. Eliminate ideas, add others. Then begin reorganizing the pieces, adapting them to other factors such as budget, list of media, timing, objectives.

Three separate lists are then in order. If the event is to be a pageant of national importance, for instance, the highlight event of the advance build-up may be the choice of a queen. Her selection may be the nucleus of an *event list* something like this:

- Announcement of the queen contest.
- Selection of district candidates.
- Narrowing of the contest to forty or so girls.
- Close-up stories of the different contenders.
- Choice of the seven or so finalists.
- Picking the winner, putting the other six in her court.
- Stories on the queen's activities, private life, aspirations.
- Costuming the queen and her court.
- Several events for the queen's appearance and participation.
- Advance preparations for floats in the pageant.
- Preview of the beautiful queen and her court riding the floats.
- Other participants in the floats.
- Actual float-building, with flowers and details.

Now will come a *list of stories*. Each event on the event list is the possible nucleus of several stories. Suppose the elimination of queen candidates to seven finalists takes place at a society tea. The tea is on the beautiful lawn of some society matron. Advance stories of this semifinal elimination go to all the local papers. One day it is presented as a straight story in the general news section. Another day it is formed into material for the society pages.

Little items are offered to the columnists. Then comes The Day. The queen is named with fanfare. Cameras are clicking. The big story goes out to the papers, with negatives to place with the syndicates. Possibly some radio or TV station will dignify the event with a spot broadcast or a taping for rebroadcast that night. Maybe a TV station or local show will have a star present to confer a crown of flowers on the lucky queen, in which event their publicists and cameras will be present. The story list has anticipated this barrage of individual "breaks" built around one feature on the event list.

Closely geared in with the list of stories will be a *list of visuals*. The three lists are threaded into a master list, a "script" or "shooting schedule," which includes the timetable and assignment sheet. During the campaign, the plan may be revised daily, with substantial chunks of it torn out to make room for better ideas. Progress of a campaign and effect of outside ideas may frequently stimulate new ideas and new opportunities.

Some publicity planners overlook no detail in their advance calculations and listings. They make a cross list of publicity materials (events, copy, visuals) and days. They set down each ingredient of publicity to be used. Under each head are listed the steps to be taken, in chronological order. Under each step are listed the items necessary to complete it, and opposite each item is the date by which it should be accomplished. After counterchecking, a datebook or flow chart is then filled in, with the details to be disposed of on each date enumerated under that day on the calendar. After such a blueprint has been perfected, execution is the only remaining required step in the campaign. (See illustration in Chapter 24.)

Many new things will come up, but the more smoothly the campaign is planned, the more smoothly things will run. A big backlog of material is stabilized and ready. No matter what emergencies develop, the fundamentals are organized and the machinery is purring. Crises, last-minute switches, disruptions of nature and human temperament do not seriously retard an organized publicity machine.

It is better to overplan than to underplan. The more of a "stockpile" of pictures and stories the publicist can build up in advance, the surer he is of impact and volume in the closing rush. It is better to throw away some of his material than to miss major opportunities because needed materials are not available.

ARRANGING FOR APPROVALS

All materials prepared in a communications program should receive the approval of an authorized executive of the organization on whose behalf they are to be issued. The process for obtaining approval varies greatly between organizations and depends on the nature of the material.

Material originating within the organization is usually submitted for approval and verification to the executive in charge of the function involved. For instance, a press release about a company's quarterly earnings is likely to be approved by the treasurer, who may also submit it to the chief executive officer or other executive. Photographs and captions on a new product are likely to be approved by the head of marketing for the division responsible for that product, who may also call for the approval of the division's top executive.

Approval involves making certain that the facts, quotations, and other content are accurate and have the support of the management. It also alerts those who see the material to what is to be released so they can handle inquiries from the media properly.

Material originating with an outside firm is usually submitted for approval to the public relations liaison person within the client organization. He then approves it if he has the authority or submits it to the executives who would receive it if it had been prepared internally.

In most organizations the approver is asked to initial the copy he has seen and return it. This is a way to make certain any changes are made as the approver has indicated, and that the initialed record of the approval process is in the file in case any questions should arise.

When the final version of the material—press release, photographs and captions, literature, speeches—is produced, copies are sent to those who approved it and to others in the organization who need to know what is involved. In the case of films, videotapes, and other materials requiring special handling, the executives are usually invited to a screening or told that the material is available for their review on request.

ORGANIZING THE FILES

Materials to be filed tend to become voluminous. Both for efficiency in keeping track of information and activities, and to assure accurate records for verification and reports, files should be set up carefully.

Included in a basic filing system are:

1. Background information on the organization and its activities, source materials, reference materials, information on opposition groups or competitors, and so on.

2. All manuscripts prepared in the program—press releases, backgrounders, speeches, TV and film scripts, and others. Each should include at least one copy of the final manuscript, corrected copies of the manuscript as received from approvers, source materials used, references to sources contacted, and a copy of the distribution order.

3. Photographs and other illustrative material. (See Chapter 40.)

4. Correspondence, memos, and other materials exchanged with executives, sources, or others.

5. Legal records, such as model releases, lawyers' approvals, and documents to and from government agencies.

6. Copies of reports about the program.

7. Copies of finished materials—copies of booklets and financial reports, newspaper and magazine clippings, transcripts or reports on television and radio coverage achieved.

8. Bills, purchase orders, and other records of payments and expenses.

SPECIAL EVENTS

Special events are acts of *news development*. The ingredients are time, place, people, activities, drama, showmanship. One special event may have many subsidiary events, such as luncheons, banquets, contests, speeches, and many others, as part of the build-up.

The special event is the *coup de maitre* of publicity, propaganda, and public relations. From the launching of a man into space to prove a nation's prowess in science to the yearly Oscar Awards presentation in California, from a state band competition in Chicago to a scout jamboree in Maine, the special event is a publicity splash. Done on a major scale, it includes and involves all of the tools and techniques of publicity.

A special event involves a mass of details skillfully blueprinted, presented, dramatized, and reported.

An entire book is not big enough to include a fully detailed check list for special events. They follow certain elements of a formula. The prime rule is to check details with precedent, with each other, and with the world about, in order to avoid conflict, to assure acceptability, and to synchronize so that the end product is integrated and will function.

The elements of a special event are the basic "news questions" with which all newspapermen are familiar:

• *What?* Name of event, its scope, necessary build-up, budget, elements of program.

PREPARATIONS FOR COMMUNICATING

- *Why?* Purpose and objective.
- *When?* Full schedule of timing, with deadlines for each preliminary, all worked out as to dates and hours.
- *Where?* Geographic locale, facilities, including ample facilities for every detail necessary to complete functioning.
- *Who?* Who will engineer, star, be invited, attend, follow up?
- *How?* How will all these things be done?

Publicity arrangements for an event include:

- Advance planning for full coverage.
- Announcements by press, TV, radio, magazines, direct mail, outdoor advertising, and other media.
- Stockpile of stories, pictures, features.
- Mechanical arrangements for coverage—press room, typewriters, telephones, accommodations for press, provisions for photography, wiring for radio and TV, quiet room for interviews.
- Information arrangements—advance copies of speeches and reports, programs, interviews, press conferences.
- Checking coverage—stenographer to check details, photographer to get pictures for distribution afterward to publications not taking their own pictures.
- Follow-up—thank-you notes, scrapbook, final report.

The most important detail of publicity and special events is staffing. People with the know-how and sense of responsibility to follow through are the keys to any planned human activity.

Special events of every description are created to tell a public relations story and influence public opinion. They serve as media in themselves and as focal points for other media. A major special event will merit coverage by press, radio, television, and magazines to further the impact beyond the actual on-the-spot audience.

Major forms of special events are:

- *Shows, displays,* and *exhibits* ranging in magnitude from world fairs to local trade shows limited to commercial audiences.
- *Road shows* packed and put on the road for reshowing in numerous locations.
- *Fairs,* of which more than 2,200 are annually presented in the United States before combined audiences of some sixty million.
- *Parades, pageants,* and *processions,* such as the Tournament of Roses.
- *Mass demonstrations* and entertainment events, ranging from the mammoth Communist party rallies in Iron Curtain countries that attract hundreds of thousands of people, to local demonstrations against segregation.
- *Athletic competition* with sideline effects of showmanship.
- *Commercial displays* in store windows, inside of stores, and on thoroughfares. These may be tied in with fiestas as is done in Santa Barbara and other Southern California communities to commemorate the region's early Spanish traditions. Christmas decoration of a commercial center constitutes another example.
- *Stunts,* such as minature parades, *gags* like marching an elephant down the street, and such devices as massed flights of airplanes and a massed review of ships.
- *Banquets and luncheons,* attracting a large number of people and providing a sounding board for the expression of certain ideas by certain leaders.
- *Meetings,* both with and without food and drink, ranging from small and confidential affairs not designed for publicity to elaborate convocations that every medium in town will want to cover.
- *Conferences and conventions* usually offer productive publicity possibilities because of the large number of people attracted from distances, and the substantial number of leaders who come to address such an audience. "An expert is a man away from home," it has been said, and a fellow who may be quite ordinary or at best only human at home in Chicago or New York or Seattle is sometimes made into a one-day minor prophet by his performances and utterances while traveling in a distant section.

With proper coverage, the covention is a sure springboard of man-made news covering as many localities as may be represented by delegates. The formula for covering a convention, properly adapted, is an effective blueprint for covering most special events:

(1) *Press Room:* Set up near headquarters with plenty of telephones, typewriters, tables, and supplies, such as paper and carbon paper. At big conventions, a copying machine and a photocopier may be most helpful. Remember to have special wiring that may be needed for TV lighting; a tape recorder or two; a bulletin board to post messages for reporters; a display of speech manuscripts, releases, photos, and other materials for the visitors to choose from. Often neglected is a quiet room where TV and radio interviews can be held without

background noises interfering. Often there is also need for another small room where an official and one reporter can have a private discussion.

(2) *Personnel:* This press room should be manned at all times by at least one informed person capable of answering questions, rendering service, and getting information. Frequently a local business college or school of journalism will furnish such helpers—who sometimes are glad to serve for the experience.

(3) *Advance Copies:* More than anything else, reporters will welcome and appreciate advance copies of speeches and reports. Advance copies are the hardest of props to obtain, because many speakers prefer to speak from notes or extemporaneously and will not undertake to make copies; and other speakers do not get the copies in on time. Such copies will greatly facilitate the work of both reporters and publicists and will invariably multiply the results obtained. Advance film footage helps TV coverage.

(4) *Press Memos:* Daily or even more frequent last-minute round-up memos of what will happen during the day to come assist in the coverage. When possible, it is well to furnish city desks, syndicates, and broadcasting news rooms before the convention opens with a complete agenda of the proceedings, and copies of printed programs, if any.

(5) *Badges and Tickets:* Plenty of badges and tickets for every session, luncheon, banquet, and party will be appreciated by press representatives.

(6) *Committee Helpers:* Local members "in the know" can be helpful by cooperating in helping reporters make connections. A major convention is bound to be too big for a single reporter or publicist to handle, and indeed some of them have squadrons of publicists and several details of reporters and photographers from major metropolitan dailies and news services.

(7) *Messengers:* It is a helpful service to make messengers available to deliver telephone messages from city desks of the newspapers to working reporters, to deliver rush stories and art from reporters and photographers to their editors, and to perform other duties that require quick action.

(8) *Liaison:* The publicity department may serve the media by remaining in constant touch with all departments of the convention so that any sudden newsworthy event or last-minute change will be reported reliably and rapidly to the media. Frequently spot news, elections, resolutions, and similar features will require instant action.

(9) *Celebrities:* Provision should be made for setting up press interviews with celebrities, speakers, and other dignitaries who may attend the convention.

Special events. In addition to the type of event described above, many publicists build stories or features around special "days" and "weeks," such as Law Day or Music Week.

Such a "day" or "week" is made the climax for numerous subsidiary events. Committees develop phases of the observance. Meetings, luncheons, banquets, speeches, queens, picture ideas, and special "propaganda" stories are part of the technique.

These special "days" and "weeks" are excellent springboards for the so-called "propaganda" type of publicity—legitimate publicity planned to instill an idea with the public for general observance throughout the year.

The formula for this publicity is the established general publicity formula: create news. Develop events that attract names and manufacture news *ipso facto.*

Another form of special event is the *observance,* such as laying cornerstones for new buildings, placing tablets on completed buildings, presenting awards, and unveiling statues and sundials. Observances are constantly built into events for stimulating popular interest and publicity coverage.

Observances of this type are symbolic events betokening accomplished facts. The technique is to build a program around the symbolic event, assemble prominent personages, and have one or more speeches delivered to convey thoughts appropriate to the occasion. The necessary element of drama is provided by the prominence of the leading participants and by showmanship in the decorations and music.

Typical observances, with important publicity effect in their respective locales, are America's hundreds of graduation ceremonies.

A peculiar and colorful form of special event is the *"stunt"* created strictly as a feature vehicle of sufficient human interest to qualify picture and story material for widespread publication and broadcast.

Special events tell the story of the sponsoring organization and/or area while they furnish a setting for the presentation of features by many individual sponsors who join the over-all events as a medium for telling their individual stories. For example, a major industrial exposition may be sponsored by several cooperating trade associations. Each sponsoring organization will benefit from this opportunity to dramatize its story to the public. Hundreds of exhibitors will benefit from the opportunity of presenting their particular story and product. All of the sponsors and exhibitors will pool their efforts and money to produce an over-all show and an over-all publicity campaign that attracts strong public interest.

The public relations effect is extended not only by news coverage through established media, but through tie-ups of all kinds, such as travel advertising to bring in people from elsewhere, inserts in mailing, marking on auto license plates, stickers, bumper strips, soap wrappers, and many other devices for projecting the story to more people. A network TV program may be imported in its entirety to the show for a run of several days, providing substantial exploitation benefits to the event, TV network, and sponsor. Half-price tickets to the show may be distributed to hundreds of thousands of people, enclosed with monthly statements through arrangement with a major utility or department store.

The special event may be a tour, such as the numerous tours of editors and writers conducted by the National Aeronautics and Space Agency as pilgrimages to its facilities at Houston. Major airlines also sponsor such traveling "junkets" to demonstrate the wonders of new planes. Many tours are sponsored by hotels interested in publicizing new resort sites.

An effective type of special event is the trade tour, in which a group of businessmen travel in a body, sometimes with itinerant exhibits and displays, visiting business groups in various other cities and localities. Such an event stirs up good will, generates new business, and creates news that stimulates publicity wherever the tour travels.

Chambers of Commerce often conduct tours throughout various states. On one such tour, the participating business men dressed in railroad overalls, wearing trainmen's caps and carrying railroad lanterns to dramatize the spirit of their travels.

PRODUCT PUBLICITY

Most publicity activity on behalf of a firm's products or services follows the patterns of publicity generally. There are a few principles, however, that are distinctive in product publicity.

Most important is basing the approach on the status of the product when the plans are being made. There are basically three conditions:

1. The product starts a whole new field; it performs a function not performed by anything else. In this case, the primary objectives should be (a) to pre-empt the concept of that product for the manufacturer and (b) to stir potential purchasers' desire for what it will do.

When Bell & Howell was introducing the first "Seeing Eye" movie camera, the entire marketing strategy was built around these two objectives. Publicity efforts were intensive and preceded any advertising by several months. This assured that the media and the dealers would know about the product and Bell & Howell as its producer long before any competitor could have a similar product to talk about. In the first few weeks after the introduction announcement, orders came in for the full production several months ahead. Advertising and sales promotion were then geared to picking up this momentum and the position of Bell & Howell as the innovator.

At the same time, the publicity featured the camera's ability to enable any user to take excellent movies with very little training or error.

2. If the product is an advance in an established field, the publicity should focus sharply on the new features.

3. If the product has nothing particularly new or unique—if it is mature and established—it should be associated with characteristics the public is interested in. Ceramic tile for years was publicized in stories about keeping bathrooms and kitchens clean to protect health, or enabling the housewife to do the cleaning with a minimum of work. Maytag developed plans for many types of "model laundry rooms" because it found few homes had sensible provision for this second-most-demanding task. And, of course, cosmetics, deodorants, fashions, and jewelry base their publicity on desire for social acceptability.

The importance of product publicity in marketing consumer goods is shown in a study by *Merchandising Magazine* (October, 1976). It found that respondents get the information about products that determines their interest in buying from (1) friends and relatives, 44 percent; (2) newspaper and magazine articles, 25 percent; (3) advertisements and commercials, 24 percent; and (4) salespeople, 2 percent.

Samples and giveaways. There is a fine line between graciousness to the media and implied attempts at bribery. When a new product is being introduced to the press, samples are usually in order when they are modest in value and especially when using them for a while is important in evaluating the product. Thus it may be appropriate in introducing a new hair spray to give a container of it to each editor or writer contacted. But it would be inappropriate to give out samples of a new television set.

There are pitfalls in product sampling, as well as ethical questions. When Milton Reynolds introduced the first ballpoint pens in the United States, at a retail price of $15, he gave them out to media people all over the country as if they cost a few cents to make (which they did). This helped generate a vast amount of publicity—partly because the new writing instruments intrigued hundreds of people who write for a living; but also because a large proportion of them failed to write.

Giving away products in return for publicity is another technique with both ethical and practical considerations. Working with television and radio giveaway shows is a special field (see Chapter 43) with established rules and avenues to pursue. Some newspapers and individual broadcasting stations occasionally will run "auctions" in which they turn over the proceeds to charities or their own public-service projects. They auction off products they obtain free from manufacturers who seek both product publicity and a slight aura of service from cooperating. So long as these arrangements are open and generally known, no onus attaches to them. They can be judged on their merits as publicity vehicles.

Some professionals feel that having a product frequently identified as giveaways demeans the product in public esteem. Something that is so often seen being given away may not seem attractive enough to pay substantial amounts for.

MEDIA OF PUBLICITY

Media are the tools by which an organization tells its story to the public. Just as different weapons are needed to fight a war, different media are needed to solve different problems—to fight a political campaign, support a sales program, win a community's good will, or explain the client's viewpoint in a dispute.

As the weapons of war have advanced from the spears and swords of the old days to the missiles and H-bombs of today, so have media advanced from letters and signs and speeches to include radio, telephoto, television, and facsimile.

But just as the slogging foot soldier carrying a sharp dagger is still important in our Army, speeches, pronouncements, and signs are still fundamentals of modern public relations. New media will command attention and offer variations of attack, but the old and basic media of word-of-mouth and man-to-man communication remain necessary to attainment of the public relations objective.

Detailed reviews of the various publicity media are given in following chapters.

CONTROLLING RUMORS

Any organization or individual that gains public attention is likely to encounter rumors that at least can be annoying and at worst can be severely damaging. Coping with them is the most nebulous aspect of the communications operation.

Particularly when a publicity program is about to increase an organization's visibility, or when it is about to enter a controversial area, it is wise to take precautionary steps to cope with rumors. These include:

1. *Establish a rumor center.* Someone should be assigned to this responsibility on a constant basis. All members or staff people should be alerted to report any rumors they hear, and to enlist their friends to call their attention to reports that may be true or false.

2. *Send out the facts.* When a rumor develops that is erroneous, even if it may not be harmful in its original form, consider disseminating correct information. That may forestall the spreading and accumulative distorting of the rumor.

3. *Consider holding a news conference.* If the rumor is important and the consequences are serious, it may justify calling the media together to get the facts, ask questions, and clear up the situation. The exposure of reporters to this exposition of the information will also help forestall the circulation of other rumors of a similar type.

4. *Get a third-party spokesman to comment.* If the rumor deals with a matter that puts the organization's own credibility in doubt, ask a respected person who is not directly associated with the organization to scotch the rumor.

5. *Give the facts and demonstrate the truth.* Don't

PREPARATIONS FOR COMMUNICATING

just issue a denial or repeat previous statements. Present the facts fully. If possible, *show* that the reports are false. Many a politician has disproved rumors about estrangement from his wife by having her prominently with him on a long trip or a vacation.

PRESS CLIPPING BUREAUS

The most helpful tool in arranging a report of publicity results is the press clipping bureau, which will furnish clippings from newspapers and publications over a given area, whether international, national, or local, for fees based on the nature of the service contracted for.

Clipping bureaus may be divided into four classes: national, sectional, state, and specialized. In the United States, there are about 65 such companies. In other countries around the world, there are about 90 others.

The **national bureaus,** which endeavor to read the newspapers and magazines of the entire country, are:

Bacon's Clipping Bureau
14 E. Jackson Blvd.
Chicago, IL 60604

Burrelle's Press Clipping Bureau
75 E. Northfield Ave.
Livingston, NJ 07039

Luce Press Clipping Bureau
42 S. Center St.
Mesa, AZ 85202

Press Intelligence, Inc.
734 15th St., N.W.
Washington, DC 20005

A service that specializes in trade publications is:

American Trade Press Clipping Bureau
5 Beekman St.
New York, NY 10038

Regional, State and Local Clipping Bureaus

Listed alphabetically by state

Alabama Press Clipping Bureau
1925 Queen City Ave.
Tuscaloosa, AL 35401

Alaska Clipping Service
2209 McKinley Ave.
Anchorage, AK 99503

Allen's Press Clipping Bureau
657 Mission St.
San Francisco, CA 94105

Pacific Clippings
P.O. Box 11789
Santa Ana, CA 92711

Colorado Press Clipping Bureau
1336 Glenarm Place
Denver, CO 80204

Western Press Clipping Bureau
P.O. Box 653
Loveland, CO 80437

Congressional Record Clippings
1868 Columbia Rd., N.W.
Washington, D.C. 20009

Home Economics Reading Service
1341 "G" St., N.W.
Washington, DC 20005

Pan American Press Clipping Bureau
P.O. Box 785
Miami, FL 33144

Florida Press Clipping Service
3008 Palmira
P.O. Box 10278
Tampa, FL 33609

Charles A. Rawson & Associates
Suite 114—Beta Bldg.
Atlanta, GA 30318

Hawaiian Clipping Bureau
P.O. Box 2033
Honolulu, HI 96805

Idaho Press Clipping Service
P.O. Box 1067
Boise, ID 83701

Midwest Newsclip
P.O. Box 1359
Chicago, IL 60690

Indiana Newsclip
2575 E. 55th Place
Indianapolis, IN 46220

Iowa Press Clipping Bureau
511 Shops Bldg.
Des Moines, IA 50309

Kansas Press Clipping Service
P.O. Box 1773
Topeka, KS 66601

Kentucky Newsclip, Inc.
400 Sherburn Lane, Suite 150
Louisville, KY 40207

Metropolitan Press Clipping Bureau
P.O. Box 66061
Baton Rouge, LA 70806

Michigan Press/Reading Service
126 S. Putnam St.
Williamston, MI 48895

Western Press Clipping Bureau
15 South Ninth St.—Suite 420
Minneapolis, MN 55402

Capitol Newspaper Clipping Bureau
  P.O. Box 9306
  Jackson, MS 39206
Magnolia State Clipping Bureau
  1491 Canton Mart Rd.
  Jackson, MS 39211
Missouri Press Clipping Bureau
  8th and Locust
  Columbia, MO 65201
Superior Clipping Service
  P.O. Box 398
  Superior, MT 59872
Universal Press Clipping Bureau
  Suite 1027, Redick Tower
  1504 Harney St.
  Omaha, NE 68102
Nevada Press Clipping Bureau
  P.O. Box 6088
  Reno, NV 89503
New Jersey Clipping Service
  99 East Northfield Ave.
  Livingston, NJ 07039
New Mexico Press Clipping Bureau
  P.O. Box 11278
  Albuquerque, NM 97112
American Press Clipping Service
  119 Nassau St.
  New York, NY 10038
New York State Clipping Service
  Box 7
  Livingston, NJ 07039
Pressclips, Inc.
  47 Lawrence St.
  New Hyde Park, NY 11040
Empire State Press Clipping Service
  205 Hill Side Place
  Eastchester, NY 10709
Carolina Clipping Service
  2911 Essex Circle
  Raleigh, NC 27608
Ohio News Bureau Company
  1900 Euclid Ave.
  Cleveland, OH 44115
Oklahoma Press Clipping Bureau
  3601 N. Lincoln
  Oklahoma City, OK 73105
Mid-Atlantic Newspaper Services, Inc.
  2707 North Front St.
  Harrisburg, PA 17110
Mutual Press Clipping Service
  220 South 16th St.
  Philadelphia, PA 19102
Tennessee Press Clipping Bureau
  P.O. Box 8123
  Knoxville, TN 37916
Texas Press Clipping Bureau
  1604 Main St. Bldg.—Suite 505
  Dallas, TX 75201
Utah Press Clipping Bureau
  467 East Third, South
  P.O. Box 1327
  Salt Lake City, UT 84110
Virginia Press Services
  410 Virginia Bldg.
  Richmond, VA 23219
West Virginia Press Service
  Room 2, Martin Hall
  Morgantown, W. VA 26505
Wisconsin Press Clipping Bureau
  Washington Square
  33 N. Dicksinson St.
  Madison, WI 53703
Wyoming Press Clipping Service
  1015 Garfield
  Laramie, WY 82070

Foreign Bureaus
(members of International Federation of Press Clipping Bureaus):

  AUSTRIA
    Observer GMBH
    Wollzeile—11
    Vienne 1010
  BELGIUM
    Auxiliarire de la Presse S.A.
    18, Quai du Commerce
    Brussels 1000
  BRAZIL
    Lux-Journal Recortes Ltda
    Rua Buenos Aires 176
    Rio de Janeiro
  BULGARIA
    Agentur Sofia-Press
    Levskistr.,
    Sofia
  CANADA
    Bowden's Information Services Ltd.
    220 Richmond Street W.
    Toronto, Ont. M5V 1VG
  CZECHOSLOVAKIA
    Prazska Informacni Sluzba
    Betlemske namesti 2
    Prague 1
  DENMARK
    Journalistforbundets Avisudklips
    Bureau
    Ravnsborggade 2-4
    Copenhagen 2200
  ENGLAND
    Durrant's Press-Cuttings, Ltd.
    8, Herbal Hill
    London ECIR SEL

    International Press-Cutting Bureau
    1 Knightsbridge Green
    London SWIX 7Q6

Newsclip (U.K.) Ltd.
69 Fleet Street
London EC4Y INS

Romeike and Curtice Ltd.
Hale House
290-296 Green Lanes
London, N13 5TP

FINLAND
Sanomalehtien Ilmoitustoimisto
Kasarmikatu 44 (S.I.T.A.)
Helsinki CO130

FRANCE
Agence Francaise d'Extraits de Presse
1 Avenue de l'Opera
Paris 75001

Argus de la Presse
21 Bd. Montmartre
Paris 75002

Nouveau Courrier de la Presse—
"Lit Tout"
15 Rue du Colonel Driant
Paris 75001

Presse-Clearing
1 Rue Mirabeau
Paris 75016

GERMANY
Argus Pressebureau und Verlag
Kniebisstrasse 24
Stuttgart 7000

Der Ausschnitt
Konigsbergerstrasse 37
1—Berlin—45

Hermes Zeitungsausschnittburo
Weberstrasse 92
Bonn D53

Metropol-Gesellschaft
Uhlandstrasse 184
1—Berlin—12

Presse-Archiv
9-11 Jahnstrasse
6101. Eschollbruecken/Darmstadt

HOLLAND
Antal Persknipseldienst
Waalsdor perweg 122
Den Haag

Persbureau Vaz Dias N.V.
Singel 91, Postfach 491
Amsterdam 1001

HUNGARY
Magyar Hirdeto-Sajtofigyelo
Ulloi Ut 51, H1450—PO Box 76
Budapest 9

INDIA
Indian Press Service
16-A, Friends Colony
New Delhi 110014

IRELAND
Irish Press Cutting Ltd.
10 Mountjoy Street
Dublin 1

ITALY
L'Eco Della Stampa
Via Giuseppe Compagnoni 28
Milano 20129

JAPAN
Universal Information Service
2-8 Kyobashi, Chuo-ku
Tokyo 104

NEW ZEALAND
The Press Research Bureau
106, Courtenay Place
Wellington

NORWAY
Norske Argus
Pilestredet 7
Oslo 1

POLAND
Biuro Wycinkow Prasowych Glob
Plac Starynkiewizca 7
Warsaw 02015

PORTUGAL
Recorte
Av. Almirante Reis 19-20
Lisbonne

SPAIN
Agencia Interacional Camarasa
Reyes Magos 22
Madrid 7

SWEDEN
AB Pressurklipp
St Goransgatan 84
10220 Stockholm 12

SWITZERLAND
Argus International de la Presse SA
Streulistrasse 19
8030 Zurich

USA
International Press Clipping Bureau Inc.
5 Beekman Street
New York, NY 10038

YUGOSLAVIA
Novinsko Izdavacko Preduzece
Post fah. 95, Knez Mihailova 2/1X
11000 Beograd

Uses of Clippings. There are literally hundreds of uses that can be made of a clipping service. It can provide any information appearing in the press, and it can be adapted to almost any need.

A director of public relations of a business or enterprise that is subject to legislative attacks, or that, for any reason, must be sensitive to public opinion, will find the clipping service an invaluable

412   PREPARATIONS FOR COMMUNICATING

Figure 38-7. A clipping as it is sent to the subscriber by a clipping service. Note how the subject ordered (in this case, the name of the company) is marked by the bureau's reader. The date of publication is also shown.

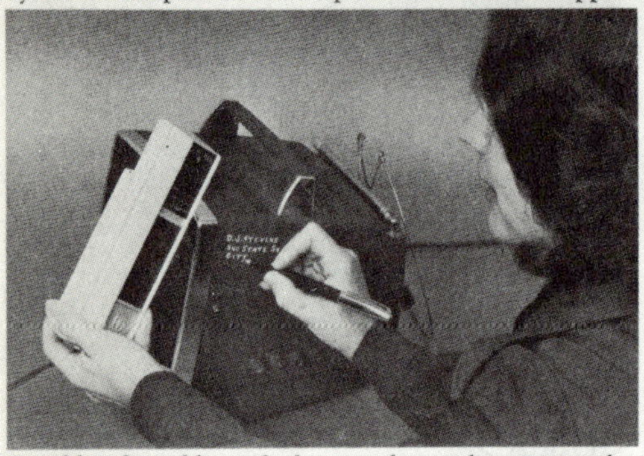

tool to help him keep his ear to the ground for all rumors that may lead to the type of action against which he is entrusted to safeguard. A clipping service acts as his watch dog in detecting the sources of such rumors, or the beginnings of such agitation. For example, a clipping of a report of a resolution passed at a local club meeting may reveal a move that has serious possibilities, and that may be adjusted to or stopped in the beginning by prompt and diplomatic action.

Publicity should be carefully planned to accomplish a specific objective. Clippings and broadcast reports are a measure of the degree of its success. If the objective is to reach a given public or constituency, the clippings will show whether the stories have been published in the papers of the area where the constituents reside, and which they read. For example, a West Coast industry that has numerous heavy stockholders in the New England states may desire, through financial news in the papers of that area, to keep the stockholders informed about their investments. Clippings indicate the extent to which the released material is reaching the desired audience.

If the subject featured is of a controversial nature and of wide interest, clippings of editorial comment and letters to the editors provide an index of public opinion as well as indicating the points of misunderstanding. This information will help determine the nature of future releases.

Publicity that endeavors to keep a certain name before the public in the best light and as constantly as possible should, obviously, be directed toward the greatest circulation. The success of publicity cannot be gauged entirely by the number of clippings. The summary must include the types and circulation figures of the papers from which the clippings are taken. Some clipping services show circulation figures on the tab that identify each clipping. (The final and vital determinant of what effect the publicity has on the readers depends on still further factors. These require assessment of the psychological response. See Chapters 2, 35, and 55.)

If publicity is designed to create interest in a coming event, a required volume of stories and pictures about the event may be scheduled well in advance of the opening date. An actual ratio is sometimes established between the volume of good publicity attained at a given point on the calendar, and the

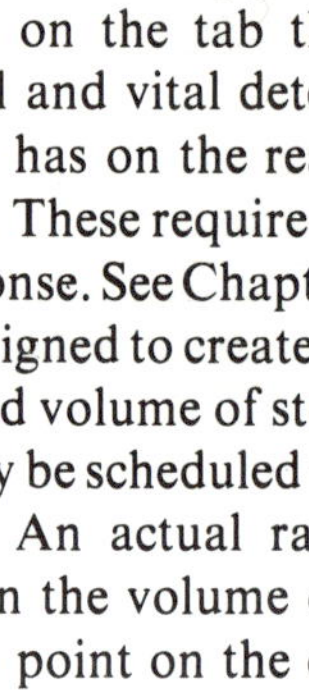

Figure 38-8. Publicity on a general concept (here, artificial turfs for athletic fields) is an important form of coverage for a leading company in the field, as well as for an industry association. Concept publicity keeps subjects newsworthy after announcement of the item.

PREPARATIONS FOR COMMUNICATING

volume in gate receipts when the event opens. For example, a large annual event such as a county fair may, after maintaining clipping records for a number of years, determine the volume of publicity necessary a month prior to the opening to assure the desired volume in gate receipts.

Assuming that a clipping service is reasonably complete, even the absence of clippings on a given story can be a means to a worth-while saving. The results may indicate that the story is not properly written, and that considerable time, materials, and postage are being wasted in sending out such stories. Careful study may show that a different slant, more brevity, better photography, or other improvements get better results.

Anyone contemplating use of a clipping service must be cautioned that, at best, they are seldom more than 35 percent efficient. On national coverage, they frequently find no more than 25 percent of all stories appearing on a given subject.

Scott Radio and TV Results During Chicago Boat Show

1.
March 23
The Tony Weitzel Show
WBBM radio
8:30 p.m.
Interview time: 30 minutes
Estimated audience: 250,000

Dave Beach was a guest on this program. He gave a clear description of the Flying Scott . . . even to listing component parts, price, etc. Then he and Jim Wynne of Volvo discussed boating in general.

2.
March 24
The Art Mercier Show
WBBM radio
9:45 p.m.
Interview time: 15 minutes
Estimated audience: 63,000
    homes

Art Mercier interviewed Norm Owen. A 15-minute discussion of Scott and its products. They talked about the Flying Scott, the Chicago Boat Show, other Scott motors, how the company is designing motors specifically for fishermen. He also noted that next fall Scott will have a complete line of combination units.

3.
March 24
The Jack Eigen Show
WMAQ radio
12:45 a.m.
Interview time: 5 minutes
Estimated audience: 23,000
    homes

Dave Beach was introduced as Scott's marine architect and described the Flying Scott on exhibition at the boat show. He discussed the principles behind the boat-motor-trailer integration.

4.
March 28
The Lee Vogel Show
WTAQ-AM and WEAW-FM
10:15 p.m.—10:45 p.m.
Interview time: 30 minutes
No audience estimate available

Dave Beach and Bill Holland appeared. Discussed the Flying Scott, advantages of outboard motors over inboards, the boat show, industry marine safety programs, various other Scott products.

5.
March 29
The Sig Sakowicz Show
WTAQ radio
12:45 p.m.
Interview time: 10 minutes
No audience estimate available

Gordon Barron discussed specifics of Flying Scott, the boat show in general, prospects for the industry, marine safety. Various Scott mentions.

Figure 38-9. Example of a report on radio and television publicity obtained for a client. Essential information is given in brief form.

Figure 38-10. Sample of a display of clippings included in a report. This one, on the program of the American Music Conference, cites examples of nationally distributed articles that convey positive messages about the advantages of amateur musical activity.

For this reason, if the budget permits, it is wise to employ two or more services. The duplication of clippings will not be great.

BROADCAST AND COMPOSITE REPORTS

Broadcasts, unlike press material, leave no ready record to be gathered in. The broadcast signal goes out into the air and is lost forever unless special effort is made to retain it—either in the form of a tape or videotape of the original, or in an audited report from a listener or viewer.

Where the publicist knows in advance that a broadcast will use his material, he can often arrange to order a tape, film, or videotape for his file.

Periodic or terminal reports on a publicity operation are important. Creation of a scrapbook, a report, or a summary of results, plus recommendations for the future help assure clear understanding of the program by management, and serve as guides for continued efforts. Things to do may include:

(1) Prepare a scrapbook of all clippings, TV reports, radio scripts, and photos of exhibits, displays, and signs.

(2) Prepare a written report of results and ac-

complishments. The results should be neither interpreted nor reported in terms of column inches, total pages, and other quantity standards. The results of publicity and its quality, what it says and not how much, are what count. Above all, reference should never be made to whatever dollar volume the publicity might be thought to approximate. This represents a conception of publicity as "free advertising," which is completely false. Publicity is news of interest to many people, and should be so regarded. A report that "so-and-so many inches were obtained, or an equivalent of so-and-so many dollars in paid advertising" is meaningless and misleading. There is no money value to publicity space. Money could not buy it under any circumstances. It is beyond premium. Such a measure of publicity results is misleading to the client and insulting to the media that cooperated by offering a vehicle to carry the material to the public.

(3) Organize and winnow the "morgue" of information, notes, and papers for future guidance.

(4) Organize and winnow the "morgue" of photographs, many of which will be useful in the future.

(5) Draw an outlined plan and schedule for future activities, including suggestions of things to be avoided and suggestions for new approaches or themes to be adopted.

39

Relations with Publicity Media

Philip Lesly

The publicist is a liaison between the organization that employs him and the media. His effectiveness in the long run depends on his ability to represent one to its satisfaction, while meeting the needs of the other. In this way he is somewhat like a catalyst that changes both of the elements it deals with while remaining unadulterated by either.

That requires maintaining sound journalistic judgment and standards in dealing with the client— including strong advocacy of the fullest disclosure feasible, availability of officials, and promptness in responding to the media. It also requires being fair and frank, as well as accommodating and conscientious, with the media.

This can be accomplished only through absolute integrity with all concerned, combined with sound judgment and experience. The person who makes a practice of compromising these principles is likely to run out of either employers or media acceptance.

The good publicist or publicity staff combines these characteristics:

- Sound editorial judgment, diverse and versatile enough to apply to a great variety of media.
- Creativity, capable of finding and defining the interesting, the novel, the significant in any subject that arises.
- Writing skill, a sense for graphic communications, and an ear for vocal communication.
- High productivity and motivation.
- A thorough knowledge of all the types of communications media covered in this book, including how they work, their needs, their specialties, and their standards.
- Initiative in working within the organization and in approaching the media.

- Acceptance by the media on the basis of respect and confidence. The warmer the relationship, the better—but social acquaintance is no substitute for skill and integrity.
- The physical resources and the basic budget to do the job—directories, lists, access to sources and services, handbooks, equipment, telephone and sometimes teletype service, and funds for necessary travel.

Sovereignty of the media. In a free society, the independent communications medium is closer to having absolute sovereignty than any other element. Presidents rail at their impotence with Congress, bureaucracies, and the media. Industrial tycoons are restricted by many government agencies, the courts, and labor unions. But an individual newspaper, magazine, broadcasting station, or trade publication often can reign in Olympian independence. Especially in the case of those media with little or no direct competition, an occasional loss of a subscriber or an advertiser is little felt.

For this reason, as well as because of the power of media, they sometimes feel almost exempt from the give-and-take accommodations that are required of individuals and institutions in our society.

It is axiomatic, therefore, that the relationship between a source of information and the medium is not an equal two-way pattern. The medium decides absolutely, in most cases, what it will use, when, and in what form. The editorial judgment or attitudes of the editors, however they may differ from those of the publicist and his organization, are the only determinants.

While all responsible media have a policy of being accurate and fair, and will often correct (in an inconspicuous way) proved errors, there is little other recourse from the medium's judgment or treatment. The publicist and his employer must recognize that the media have this sovereignty and that no one can argue with a printing press or a broadcast tower.

Though this presents problems, it is part of the pattern of a free press. The media must have as much independence as possible from all sources of pressure, and inevitably they sometimes convert independence into what in other areas would be considered arrogance.

The occasional exceptions of media that badly distort their content, by omission or commission, or that bow to the pressures of major advertisers, are greatly outnumbered by those who do not. People sense those that they can most respect and generally make them most successful. The great need is for as much diversity and competition among media as possible, to assure that everyone has choices for his information and that no medium can be entirely sanguine about its omnipotence.

PATTERNS OF WORKING WITH MEDIA

There are generally three forms of publicity work:

1. Responding to the requests of the communications media. This is a passive, service function. It calls for having information and sources organized, then conscientiously responding to the initiatives of those to be served.

2. Arranging for media coverage and dissemination of information on events and the routine output of the organization. This calls for constant awareness of the news-making functions within the organization and routine channels of contact with the media, but it is essentially a passive function.

3. Using initiative in stimulating the media to carry the information and viewpoint of the organization. This calls for creative development of ideas and concepts; maintaining and nurturing respected liaison with hundreds of media people and writers; and constant initiative in making them receptive to the organization's ideas and materials.

All of these are important, but only a minority of publicity staffs do an effective job on all three. No. 3, in particular, usually marks the exceptionally effective operation.

NEWS CONFERENCES, BRIEFINGS, AND INTRODUCTIONS

Calling media representatives together is one of a number of means of disseminating information. As the most publicized publicity activity—well-known to the public because it is utilized by heads of state and is reported as such by the media—this technique is often the first one thought of by executives or publicity people when they feel they have something to report. As a result, it is overused.

The press meeting should be considered from the viewpoint of the media people first. To call a news conference or briefing that 10 or more press people will attend means a composite of many hours of expensive staff time, transportation, and shifting of schedules. Accordingly, the first rule in regard to such meetings is:

1. Call a press meeting only if it will be of real service to the media and provide them with something they could not get in simpler ways. They should find it beneficial by getting more information or illustrations than they could get in releases and advance photos; by being able to probe an important subject by getting substantive answers to their questions; by meeting really important people who are likely to be newsworthy in the future; by being able to explore important plans; or by seeing a new building or product that must be seen to be fully understood.

Other rules on *news conferences* include:

2. A news conference should be called in the case of a major news event, such as a violent disruption, a major accident, the sudden death of a top official, or some other emergency. It should help make sure that rumors and confusion are forestalled by presenting the facts, affording an opportunity to have questions answered, and clarifying rumors.

3. In general, the location should be wherever it is best for the media people. The organization's office—board room, conference room, auditorium—is good if it is convenient to those who are invited, or if it is necessary because of availability of materials that cannot readily be moved. Otherwise it is best to hold it in a central place. The city in which the organization is located is generally best, because the local media are the most concerned and most often deal with it. However, New York, Chicago, Washington, or another metropolitan center with heavy media representation may be desirable if the news is of major importance and the home city is not suitable for the media who will want to cover it. (Always be sure the evaluation of the news is *objective* and not colored by internal wishes or hopes.)

Sometimes it is wise to consider simultaneous news conferences in two or more places. For instance, some organizations will have some executives meet the local media in their home town at the same time national media are meeting other executives in New York.

This has been carried further by using closed-circuit television to hold simultaneous meetings in several cities. Firms that arrange for such events are:

General Television Network
13225 Capital Avenue
Oak Park, Michigan 48237
(313) 548-2500

Videoconference Networks, Inc.
Time & Life Building
Rockefeller Center
New York, New York 10020
(212) 541-5950

A good hotel that has quiet meeting rooms and can provide good service is a logical choice, if the meeting is to be held away from headquarters. A club is suitable if it has no rules against women or minority-group members, who now make up a substantial portion of media staffs.

4. Facilities should be planned to meet the needs of both print and broadcast media. It may be desirable to have two separate rooms, so the broadcast people can have quiet surroundings and access to authorized spokesmen while the print people are hearing others. Or, if urgency is not overriding, there should be two sessions, with the print media usually first. In either case, these arrangements should be explained in the invitations and at the start of the conference.

There should be ample room for all who come to have seats within good hearing and seeing range. Coffee, tea, and soft drinks should be available, with rolls if the conference is in the morning. It is usually best not to serve lunch at a news conference unless it is something of a socializing event, or the urgency of it coincides with lunchtime. In that case, it will probably be best to have a variety of sandwiches and salads, rather than a leisurely meal.

Cocktails should be served, usually, only if socializing is part of the occasion or (as explained later) the event is a briefing or introduction.

A convenient coatroom should be near the entrance and well staffed so the guests will have a minimum wait either arriving or leaving. Be sure there is no tipping permitted and that there is a large sign to this effect clearly visible.

If transportation is needed by any of the guests, arrange to have it available and explain it in the invitation. For instance, out-of-town press people sometimes will not have ready transportation available to and from the airport. If the organization's office is in a suburb or small town, transportation may be needed from the nearby transportation center.

An ample number of telephones should be nearby and the switchboard should be prepared for a sudden heavy load.

If possible, teletype service should be available to those who want to transmit their stories to their offices.

It is often desirable to make a tape recording of the session. It can be referred to later by media people who want to check exact quotations or statements; it can provide a record of what the management said for review when memories are fuzzy or commitments are being checked; and it affords a record in case the Securities and Exchange Commission, the Anti-Trust Division, the National Labor Relations Board, or other government body questions what occurred.

5. Developing the invitation list calls for balancing various judgments and considerations. Everyone who regularly reports on the organization, or who has a regular interest in the subject of the conference, should be invited. This will include specialists in the organization's field, local media, trade press in fields the organization serves, and so on. No one should be omitted because of hard feelings, personal quirks, or arbitrary numbers.

If the news is strong enough to go beyond this group, all categories of media should be sifted: news magazines, other magazines of various types, television and radio news departments, foreign-language and other minority media. A list should be made up especially for the occasion, since each news event has its own characteristics.

In the case of newspapers in the area, the invitation should go to the city editor. A backup invitation may go to a staff man who regularly covers the organization, with indication that the city desk has also received an invitation. Out-of-town newspaper outlets and magazines should be addressed via the managing editor, with backup invitations to specific individuals where desirable.

6. Invitations may be sent in various ways, depending on the time needed, the extent of the list, and other factors:

• *A letter* from the president of the organization or the public relations director. It should contain all information about the meeting and give enough information about what will be covered to enable the recipient to judge its importance. The letter calls for individual typing and personal signature.

- *A memo* to editors, which may be mass produced and can consist of the essential information.
- *A telegram.* This should be faster and receive greater attention from the recipient, but delivery schedules are uncertain and cannot be relied on if speed is vital.
- *Public relations newswires.* (See Chapter 40). These can reach most of the media in major cities in a short time. Those not on the wires' lists can then be covered in separate teletype or telephone contacts.
- *Telephone.* If time is vital, if manpower is available to disperse the number of calls, if the content of the invitation can be covered easily without laborious spelling out of details, and if most media people can be reached at convenient times, this is the surest means.

The invitations to the print and broadcast media should set different times if two sessions are to be held.

If it is important to know approximately how many will attend, it is permissible to ask for a reply. In invitations that are mailed, a return postcard or form may be enclosed.

A prudent and gentle follow-up by telephone the day before the event to those not yet heard from is usually acceptable.

Invitations that try to be cute or to command attention through novelty are like humor in other forms: helpful if very good but chilling if they are not.

7. Timing the news conference involves a number of considerations. If spot news is involved, it should be called immediately—even in the evening in the case of a real emergency. Otherwise, there is some advantage to alternating news conferences between morning—about 10 a.m.—and afternoon—about 3 p.m. This follows the traditional concern about afternoon and morning newspapers, going back to the days when newspapers and press services were the only news media of importance. It is now unwise to follow this practice rigidly when television, radio, newsmagazines, and other publications are involved.

In general, the morning tends to be better for news coverage by the press services, television and radio, magazines, and trade publications. This allows time for the writer to get back to the office, prepare the story, and have it processed the same day.

Tuesday, Wednesday, and Thursday are generally the best days of the week, with Monday slightly behind. Friday is a less-desirable day because the weekend media generally have less room for news.

However, it is important to consider what competition there will be for news. If others are likely to be scheduling events or announcements for these prime times, it is likely that news in the other periods will do better than if in a head-on competition.

This means that one of the first things to be done when any press event or release is planned—except spot news—is to check on what other news may be in competition on the contemplated day. That can be done by checking chambers of commerce, hotels and clubs, some of the media most likely to be invited, and so on.

8. The news conference should be geared to conveying the essential information and meeting the needs of the media. That means there should be a tight format and no frills.

The highest official available should be the focal point. Supporting him should be the specialists who can provide expert knowledge in answering questions. The principal should be at the head table, with the others preferably in an informal arrangement nearby rather than as a phalanx facing the press. If the crowd will be large, microphones should be provided for all who will participate and for those who will ask questions.

The meeting should start promptly—no more than five minutes after the time designated, in the case of hard news, or ten minutes if there is less urgency.

The public relations man may introduce the principal and then let him conduct the session. If desired, the public relations man rather than the principal can direct the questions to the proper authority, but he should say as little as possible. This avoids any impression that it is a public relations meeting rather than a session for the benefit of the media.

It should be explained how the print media and the broadcast media will be served—either in separate rooms or in succeeding meetings.

Photographers should be permitted, with the understanding they will not flash bulbs directly into the faces of the speakers or get in the way of others.

The principal should make a concise statement of the news or the position of the organization on the issue involved. He should explain what materials are available, so reporters will not take needless notes. Then the meeting should be thrown open to questions from the visitors.

9. Whenever possible the executives who will participate in the conference should go through a briefing session in advance. This should attempt to anticipate the trend of the conference, with special emphasis on the toughest questions and even "nasty" ones. While few media people will deliberately try to embarrass someone, some use this technique as part of their reportorial approach. Often inadvertent information or reactions resulting from probing questions will provide more meaningful material than other methods. It is important that the executives expect this and maintain their poise.

Participants should be cautioned to say, "I'm sorry, but I can't comment on that," if a question would call for information that is highly confidential, improper because of law suits pending, or otherwise unanswerable. They should *not* ask that anything be "off the record." The media people were invited to get material for their use, not to hear what they cannot use. And it is assumed that nothing can be truly secret if a substantial number of people has been called together to hear it.

10. Prepared materials might include:

- A background article on the subject involved
- Printed materials that are directly pertinent
- Pictures of the subject; and, for requests only, of the principal spokesman
- A news release, if it can be prepared in time
- Visual materials for television on-camera use, if suitable materials are available.

11. Follow-up activities involve those who are not able to attend the conference, as well as those who do.

Requests by guests for specific materials or photos should be met as expeditiously as possible. If a private interview is requested it should be arranged if the spokesman is available and if the number of requests is not excessive.

The news release and other pertinent material should be sent to those invited who could not attend. Those who took the trouble to come should not be penalized; but they will have had the news soonest, will have had the opportunity to ask questions and to hear the answers to questions asked by others, and will have had a broader backgrounding. With limited staffs and many news events, media cannot cover all the things they would be interested in reporting.

Briefings for the media. Sessions intended to provide background to interested media people, rather than hard news, can be more relaxed and informal. They may involve a lunch or dinner, or be held at the cocktail hour with drinks, tea, soft drinks, and canapes served.

Invitations should point out that the meeting will be a briefing and will not involve hard news. That will make certain that no one who comes will feel misled, and that no one will fear he would be missing something essential if he does not come.

A press kit (see Chapter 40) may be prepared for distribution.

Briefings may be held for such purposes as a year-end review of the organization's operations or outlook; a discussion of forthcoming labor negotiations; an airing of a dispute with a dissident group; or a periodic updating of the media because considerable time has elapsed since the last one.

Except for the physical arrangements needed, the rules are generally the same as for the news conference.

Press showings. When a new product is to be introduced, a striking new building announced, or some other news involves showing or demonstrating something, the characteristics of the news conference and the briefing may be combined. If urgency is not involved, the occasion may be more social than a news conference. For instance, a model of a new building may be unveiled at a lunch or dinner at which the mayor is a guest.

If the product is small and inexpensive, samples may be made available to the media people.

Greater attention is usually given to photos, and a press kit may be called for.

THE EXCLUSIVE STORY

Determining whether a given story should be an exclusive for one medium or offered to all who might be interested calls for as much judgment as any area of publicity. Individual conditions will have important bearing—the nature of the organization, the locale and its media pattern, the nature of the story, the responsibilities to law or specific groups such as stockholders, previous relations with the media involved, and others.

Here are basic guides in reaching decisions:

1. A reporter is generally entitled to an exclusive on a story he discovers or develops. For instance, if he calls to say he is doing a feature story about an organization's work with underprivileged children

he is entitled to protection in keeping his secret until his story runs. This is true even if the organization was in the process of developing publicity on that subject. It is also true if the story is likely to be unfavorable, unless there is strong reason to feel that it will be biased (*actually* biased, and not just seeming to be in the partisan eyes of the organization).

However, if a reporter calls about a story with broad legal or other requirements—such as a major new product not yet announced by a company whose stock is publicly traded—other considerations must come to bear. In this example, it would be wise to consult the stock exchange where the company's shares are traded, to avoid possible accusation of failing to make full disclosure.

If the news is of great importance not only to the organization but to the community, as in the case of decisions in a strike or relocation of a plant, the judgment must be made whether the medium involved would provide sufficiently broad announcement. If it is AP or UPI, or one of the broadcasting networks, its exclusive treatment would usually means wide dissemination. If it's a trade paper or one modest-sized local medium, however, the consequences might be more serious.

Even in the rare case where an exclusive cannot be permitted, however, the reporter who originated the story must never be beaten on it. He should be told the circumstances demand the organization make its announcement to coincide with his publication or broadcast.

2. When a major feature (not news of general importance) is being placed, it is usually necessary to offer it exclusively to one medium in each classification, or even to one only regardless of classifications. An editor is unlikely to accept a feature article if he feels one much like it may appear in a competitive outlet.

If a story is offered on an exclusive basis, it must not be offered elsewhere until a decision has been reached by the first outlet not to use it. This entails problems when the editor is slow in responding, or when no word can be received. If time drags on and it is necessary to try elsewhere, the first editor should be informed that because time has run out the offer of the story has to be withdrawn. This is preferable to the severe irritation of having two media, both thinking they had exclusives offered, coming out with the same story.

In some cases it is feasible to develop one for newspapers, a variation for magazines, a third for TV, and a fourth for a trade paper. This requires strong story judgment and a sense of the viewpoint of the media. If in doubt, fewer versions should be attempted.

General news or matters of strong public or financial importance should never be offered on an exclusive basis. This is the material that all interested media consider themselves entitled to receive, and that the people affected have a right to expect to find in whatever suitable media they read or view.

3. Some publicity materials are of limited interest and might not be run by any medium if the editor feels that all have received it. Yet as a modest offbeat story, it may appeal to one if he knows he has exclusive use of it. This is true, for example, of the "human interest" story, such as discovery that a grand-niece of a former Vice-President of the United States is working as a computer programmer in XYZ Company's inventory department.

4. The confidences of any reporter must be honored at all times. For instance, if a writer should call to get information for a general roundup story, which may or may not mention the publicist's organization at all, it is a gross violation to tell any other medium that such a story is being developed. Publicists' reputation for trustworthiness or lack of it spreads widely and rapidly.

HANDLING INQUIRIES FROM MEDIA

A publicity staff may spend more than half of its time and energies on matters it does not initiate or plan.

It is a mark of a successful publicity program when writers, editors, broadcasters, and others come to the staff with requests for information, opportunities to interview officials, or suggestions for broadcasts. The more effectively the total publicity job is done, the more the appetites of the media grow for such service. Often two organizations in the same field—such as two life insurance companies—may have a vast difference in the frequency of their inquiries from the media. In this type of situation, the organization contacted most can expect to have far more publicity than the other.

It is desirable, then, to create a climate in which media people will think of the organization whenever it might be part of a story.

Some of things that create this climate are:

1. The verities of publicity practice—absolute reliability, accuracy, promptness, fairness, objectivity.

2. A good batting average in meeting the difficult or unattractive requests, such as interviews with an official when a controversy or unfavorable story is

developing; providing background information on matters that may have no apparent publicity value to the organization; verifying or correcting controversial material or rumors.

The publicist is in the middle between the client or employer on one hand, and the media on the other. In satisfying both, a good part of the time he will not seem entirely accommodating to either. He must press his advocacy of good media relations with the client to prevail over its objections as often as possible; and he must press his representation of the client with the media to modify their expectations or demands.

3. Establishing the best and most readily available source for a body of information can make the publicity staff a focal point for the media. For many years the American Music Conference's public relations firm was the storehouse of information and photos on amateur musical activity in the United States. Editors and broadcasters knew that this was the one place to turn whenever they were dealing with that subject. At times fully half of the publicity about musical activity was the result of media coming to the firm for help on stories and broadcasts they thought of. In most cases the resulting publicity carried some of the flavor of what the AMC was interested in conveying to the public.

4. Helping the media reach information sources is a valuable means of building acceptance. This means more than prompt, courteous, reliable response to contacts made at the office. The after-hours and emergency contact is most appreciated. Many publicity offices provide large lists of media with file cards listing the names of members of the staff, their special fields of expertness, and their home and vacation telephone numbers. These should be replaced with updated cards whenever changes occur.

Often a publicist can build good will by helping a medium locate or identify an authority or source not associated with his own organization.

5. Convenience of the media is most marked in connection with locale. Being human, reporters tend—other things being equal—to contact someone close by whenever they seek information. Since most media people are in New York, for instance, this results in New York organizations or their publicity firms being most often contacted. A consequence is the often-discussed myopia of much press and broadcast coverage, reflecting conditions and attitudes within five miles of Rockefeller Center rather than in the rest of the world.

Aside from being located as close as possible to the media offices, or having a publicity firm there, these things can be done to heighten accessibility:

• Make it just as easy for a reporter to reach the publicity office by phone as if it were four blocks away. If the organization has WATS (wide area telephone service) lines, let the media know that their calls will be accepted on the recipient's WATS line without cost. If not, or if the WATS line is busy, acceptance of all collect calls from media can be authorized. Let the media know what arrangements are available for their calls, including direct-call numbers for each person in the publicity office. Similar arrangements for receiving collect calls and direct-dial calls should be made for the home phones of all staff members.

• Make a suitable spokesman available for an interview by phone or a fast trip to New York, Chicago, or elsewhere. Except in emergencies, it is seldom possible for a writer to arrange an interview with a New York executive on less than a day or two notice. An executive can fly in from Beloit or Knoxville just as promptly. This calls for the publicity office having up-to-date travel schedules for all officials at all times, so the regularly scheduled trips can be utilized to set dates or a man can be rerouted for the purpose.

6. Press kits and background articles or "white papers" serve the added purpose of providing file material for the media. When the material is referred to later, it reminds the editor of its source and stimulates calling to get new information.

7. Occasionally media personnel dealing with advertising sales will contact the publicist. This may or may not be an effort to use implied influence with the editor to have the medium considered as an advertising outlet. That is rarely the case with important media. Such calls should always be referred to either the advertising department or the advertising agency. Every effort should be made to keep editorial and advertising relations entirely separate. Editorial people resent any indication that their own advertising staff or any publicist feels they can be bought through advertising pressure.

HANDLING EMERGENCIES[1]

Relations with the media are most critical in stressful, unexpected situations. It is the purpose of the media to get the most spectacular news, which a

[1] See also Chapters 23 and 24.

disaster or crisis usually represents. At the same time, the organization involved is disrupted by the unexpected event; and its personnel have a natural tendency to protect it that can become a barrier to the media.

In dealing with the media in the course of an emergency, the way it is handled will determine not only how the organization is made to appear to the public in the news reports, but the coolness or warmth of its rapport with the media for years ahead.

Robert L. Barbour, the late editor of PR Reporter,[2] cited the two major types of critical situations that have historically faced organizations:

1. Non-catastrophic situations, which are usually of local concern. For example, a hospital is suddenly deprived of water when a main breaks. Or an area-wide commuter train delay occurs that may last for hours due to flood conditions or a power outage.

2. Sudden catastrophes of national or regional, as well as local, concern, involving heavy and increasing pressures exerted by the news media and the public and with such initially unknown factors as the originating cause, the extent of loss, and legal entailments. For example, an explosion traps miners underground; a chemical plant explodes, with a number of casualties; or a plane crashes.

To these types of emergency there now must be added:

3. The attack. A militant group disrupts a convention, a bomb destroys the company's offices, or a mob turns over and sets afire the company's trucks.

Guidelines for emergencies and disasters. In the case of the localized emergency, Barbour pointed out, the greatest need is likely to be communicating with relatives and friends in the community to avert panic and assure them that things will be restored to normal soon. Much of this is internal: telephone calls to staff people who can inform all employees and occupants of the building; in the case of a hospital or school, calling relatives. Releases might be needed for the local radio and TV stations and the newspapers. Inquiries from the media should be answered promptly and with a frank explanation.

In the event of an occurrence such as a fire or a serious accident, the fundamental principle in dealing with the media is to recognize that it is a legitimate news event to which they and their public are entitled to have the facts.

Additionally, since widespread attention to the disaster is inevitable, effectiveness of the public relations handling will be in attaining coverage as factual and unemotional as possible, with a minimum of criticism of the organization. If the facts are freely available quickly to the media, the chances of their exaggerating the seriousness of the event or of criticizing the organization for efforts to cover up or mislead will be lessened.

Making up an advance "disaster plan," then, starts with the assumption that the role of public relations will be to expedite the orderly and accurate handling of information in cooperation with the media, excepting only such matters as classified government contracts and research operations.

For disaster plans, the guidelines cited by Barbour are:

1) Make a list of all the things that conceivably could happen to your organization (thought starters: Explosion, collapse, fire, riot, plague, food or chemical poisoning, flood, mass electrocution, crash or collision, hurricane, power outage, water cutoff). Don't rely just on your imagination in compiling the list; talk with those who know what could happen. Try to divide the list into Emergency and Disaster situations as explained previously. Remember that your concern is with on-premises, unforeseen physical events of an emergency nature affecting *groups* of people rather than an individual.

2) Try to develop Plans that include techniques & procedures applicable to all your potential Emergency or Disaster situations. But don't try to cover every detail of every situation under every conceivable circumstance, or you'll never get your Plans off the ground. Include instructions to improvise, where indicated, as common sense and imagination dictate.

3) Spell out exactly—by name, title, extension, and home telephone number—the sequence of notification to be followed the moment an emergency or disaster occurs. This is generally a chain procedure (each person notified notifies others) and usually starts with calls to the chief operating officer, the director of public relations, and the head of the department involved, if any. Make it clear who starts the ball rolling.

---

[2]PR Reporter *Tips and Tactics* section, Vol. 8, Numbers 9 and 10, March 30 and April 20, 1970.

4) Remember that in time of crisis, instant internal & external communication channels *must* be kept open and clear. Unless you make arrangements for the necessary physical equipment and personnel ahead of time, an emergency will clog your lines of communication and frustration will heighten confusion all around. So use this checklist to determine what arrangements you can make *now:*

A. *Press Room.* Needed instantly in disasters and graver emergencies. Determine where it shall be (easily accessible to newsmen, preferably near public relations department; plenty of telephones, desks, chairs quickly available; typewriters, copy paper, pencils to be brought in; supply coffee (urn available?) & sandwiches if long duration is probable).

B. *Telephone Switchboard.* Discuss with head operator—and with telephone company, if indicated—how best to assure that the extra load of in & out calls will be handled without delay (extra or specially-assigned trunk lines? call-back on purely business calls? minimum conversation request? embargo on personal calls not emergency-connected?). Arrange for switchboard operators to be on call, and for switchboard to stay open on your request with full complement of regular or special operators.

C. *Short-wave Radio.* If telephone lines are knocked out, a short-wave hookup with the police & fire departments—and possibly also with a friendly company headquarters or plant nearby—will keep you in two-way touch with the outside world.

D. *Electronic Bull Horns.* Keep at least one in your office (you'll find them useful during special events, too). If a communication emergency occurs, your voice will carry up to around 1500 feet. But practice using it, first.

E. *Personal Check-in.* Have a member of the Public Relations Department check with you at regular intervals for errands & assignments and report to you when completed (in person or by walkie-talkie). You'll need to know what's happening in areas you can't reach in any other way.

5) After having outlined your Public Relations Emergency & Disaster Plans and made the necessary arrangements to assure free-flowing crisis communication, include the assignment of specific responsibilities. For example:

A. If your staff is large enough to cover all critical fronts, *you stay in your office!* As public relations director, you're the key man in linking your organization to the outside world. There'll be 1001 matters of information, coordination and judgment you'll have to handle personally, and no time must be wasted finding you. If you cannot remain at your post, have your secretary cover the telephone and keep her informed every time you move from one location to another (or tell the switchboard operator).

B. Station someone—anyone—at the building entrance to direct newsmen to the press room and relatives & friends to the board room or some other quiet segregated area. *Keep press, visitors, and victims apart.* All questions by newsmen & visitors should be referred to person in charge of each room.

C. Assign your assistant or press relations head to the press room with authority to answer questions fully & frankly within predetermined limitations and to make on-the-spot decisions & arrangements necessary to proper news coverage. Also post a competent, calm-natured PR man or woman in the room to which visitors have been directed, with instructions to answer questions briefly, as positively as possible, and with discretion. Supply coffee.

D. Assign a "floater" from public relations to tour all public relations posts and other vital areas on the property rotationally, to check on how things are being handled and report to you regularly with comments & suggestions.

E. *If you're a one-man Public Relations Department:* Your office should be the press room. Brief your secretary on how to handle press & telephone inquiries, then give her authority to do so if you're on another line or out of the office. Set up a room for relatives & friends of victims nearby, and post a corporate officer's secretary there with instructions (see "C" above). Do your own "floating," but as you make the rounds recruit whoever you can for errands, assignments and liaison. *And* go over all suggestions in Parts 1 & 2 of this article to determine how you can best adapt them to the limitations of your one-man office.

Guidelines on handling attacks. The activist assault on an organization creates a number of additional challenges not present in either the emergency or the disaster. In the latter cases, there is no intent to make the organization look bad; there is no opposing intelligence mapping strategy that must be anticipated and coped with; and there is no possible predilection on the part of the media to side with the source of the trouble. As unpredictable and stressful as handling media coverage of a disaster may be, these additional complicating factors make the handling of an attack much more difficult and potentially more damaging to the organization.

There are a number of factors to be included in planning and coping with this type of problem:

1. Keep alert to all of the organizations and groups that are likely to become activist in your area or in connection with the industry you are in. Study in each case the group's nature, tactics, and especially the objective it might seek to attain in attacking your organization. Management should be prepared to deal with the legitimate requests or complaints; but the plan should be drawn up to prevent the attacking group from attaining its other objectives by using your organization as a symbol, to gain widespread publicity for itself, or otherwise to exploit the situation.[3]

2. Assess objectively what the response of the media is likely to be. Have they shown a penchant for featuring the spectacle of any attack rather than the merits of the situation? Are they likely to make every effort to make the organization look good, or might they take advantage of the opportunity to make the militants look good? In many cases, the organization that has been attacked and whose buildings have been bombed or burned down has seemed to be the villain in the media treatment.

3. It is important to recognize that in the arena of present "attitude management," not the facts but the *impression* people get of a situation is the real reality.

What the public thinks is "real" will probably determine the result, and not the merits or the actual conditions. This is the distillation of Marshall McLuhan's "The medium is the message."

You cannot be sure that if the facts are on your side you will prevail. In countless cases, the dramatic visibility of a contrived situation has prevailed.

What really happens at a demonstration or a confrontation is not crucial, but what gets out to the public is.

4. In this climate companies, institutions, industries, and individuals are all "inbounds" to activist critics. The right to privacy is being eroded for individuals but blasted away for organizations. Few functions now retain true confidentiality. The new posture of activism is a "smart bomb" that seeks out any organization it seeks to attack.

5. It is important to note that impersonal organizations are most vulnerable to attack, because their size makes them visible and they seem to be inhuman monoliths instead of human institutions. Every effort should be made to personalize and humanize the organization.

6. It is also important to consider that a "low profile" indicates secretiveness; in today's human climate the impression of secretiveness breeds distrust. (For information on combatting rumors, see Chapter 38.)

7. It is vital to recognize that communication in our society is in revolution. The standard processes whereby information and ideas seep through the populace, from the top down or horizontally, cannot compete with the visible, dramatic, easy-to-sensationalize communication that results from activism. (See Chapter 2). Accordingly, the standard word-oriented transmission-process communication is no match for the spectacular imagery of the activist attacks.

8. It must also be recognized that dissidents have little to lose and can afford to be irresponsible. They can act as wildly as necessary to capture attention, they can focus the attention of the media and the public on untrue assertions, they can create the movement and the action that are the raw material of communications media today. That means, of course, that responsible institutions operate at a disadvantage, and strategy for coping with such events must take this into account.

9. *Objectively assess the climate your institution has among the media and the public.* In the event of a breakout of hostility, would they be likely to give you the benefit of the doubt?

10. *Assess the climate of the dissidents.* Do they have the advantage of the underdog role? Have they been wearing patience thin with an accumulation of abrasive actions or irresponsible accusations?

11. *Assess the timing and the current circumstances.* When the Weathermen faction of SDS ran amuck in Chicago in October, 1969, the temper of media and public was entirely different from that at

---

[3]Parts of this section are adapted from "Survival in an Age of Activism," by Philip Lesly, *Public Relations Journal,* December, 1969, pp. 6-10.

the Democratic convention a year before when media treatment strongly favored the attackers.

12. *Weigh the political realities within your organization.* Are there limitations resulting from the make-up of your stockholder group or membership that have to be weighed along with the other factors that determine what you do, what you say, who your spokesman is, etc.?

13. *Weigh any other factors that may be involved.* Do you have legislation pending or on-going negotiations with civic organizations or labor unions that could be materially affected by what happens in the confrontation? However, concern about immediate consequences should not obviate consideration of overall long-range matters.

14. *Determine what can be done to reconcile the situation related to the activism.* An activist thrust may represent those who feel the need for change and have been unable or unwilling to wait for "normal processes." Many institutions have lost their independence because they held firmly to their "principles" (based on the old and the entrenched) against efforts to get them to accommodate to the new.

15. *Determine what visible action can be taken.* Don't settle for a statement, appointment of a student group, or other non-dramatic steps. What can your institution *do* in connection with what the dissidents are driving at? How can you make a *visible impact?*

16. *Be sure to include an objective broadly experienced participant in all your organization's considerations.* There is no situation in which the outside, questioning, widely experienced viewpoint is as essential as it is here. A group, no matter how capable, who all see things from the same axis point are unlikely to make a proper reading of either the dissidents or the public.

17. *Be sure you have a clear understanding of the actual workings of all the communications media involved*—especially how activist groups time their actions to make certain TV shows and press deadlines, to create the headlines with the greatest impact, and to create situations embarrassing to you.

18. *Anticipate and prepare in advance.* Set up "war games" plans on the basis of each foreseeable circumstance. Have all the facts ready and in clear form. Prepare statements and have them in readiness. Have the spokesmen and other officials ready and briefed. Know where they can be reached at all times. Put them through the kind of grilling they will get in a confrontation, in a hostile press conference, before a Congressional committee, or whatever other circumstances might be involved. Have your staff briefed and constantly available. This means literally a 24-hour-a-day basis so they all can be on hand when needed. Be sure you have access to copying and photo departments, and have arrangements lined up with all-night outside services. Set up plans to deploy all of your people to make phone calls to those they know, so that everyone important can be contacted as quickly as possible, preferably by someone he knows and trusts.

19. *Consider the attitudes and possible reactions of the non-militant crowds on the periphery of the action.* Curiosity seekers and others may be neutral or sympathetic to the organization, but be panicked or "radicalized" by the impression they get of what occurs, or through lack of calm explanation. Plans for an outdoor public address system or a powerful bullhorn to be manned by an executive who will be fully posted on the situation should be an integral part of the preparations.

20. *Be sure that all personnel who might become involved are briefed.* Panic by factory workers, office girls, or others can have serious consequences on the public reaction. This should be done in a matter-of-fact way, indicating that no such development is expected but that the organization feels everyone should be prepared for any eventuality. At the same time, it should not be so detailed that a leak would tip off would-be activists to what the organization's responses would be.

21. If it's possible to anticipate which group might attack and what its accusations will be, *advertisements should be prepared in advance* and ready for immediate placement in the newspapers and, possibly, on radio and television. These should succinctly and factually explain the entire situation, putting it into proper and unhysterical context.

22. *Keep your constituents fully informed immediately of the issue and your position.* This includes employees, stockholders or members, suppliers, and others. Properly informed and sympathetic, they can serve as a backwater against automatic acceptance of what the dissidents may charge or do.

OTHER PRINCIPLES

There is a lot of hocus-pocus about "contacts" and "knowing the right people." It is much more important to produce sound material and service for the media than it is to have a big entertainment budget and know a lot of media people by their first names.

Other things being equal, a publicist can do a better job if he knows a given editor or reporter or photographer than if he does not. A friend in the newspaper business can give the publicist the benefit of the doubts, tip him off on stories, sometimes advise on advance planning. But these friendships almost always result from being dependable, effective, expeditious aides to the media. Friendships based on other factors are ephemeral when experiences turn sour, or when inevitable shifts in jobs replace a friend with a new man in his position.

Media have antennae that will bring in information. They are psychologically more disposed to play up concealed information than information that is revealed with frank reasons for not releasing it at the time. The author rarely has had a professional journalist violate a confidence.

Foolishness can reach extremes in the matter of gifts to newspaper people. A *"gift"* is given in a spirit of generosity with nothing expected in return. In that spirit, a gift to anybody is a fine thing. A publicist who considers his effectiveness to be measured in any way by his gifts is a living insult to the media.

A dangerous tendency of some publicity men is to develop a patronizing attitude toward journalists. They should not try to control everything the reporters find out about their clients. What is planned for the media should be guided by policy and effectiveness; but when the client talks with the media, he should not be restricted so that he loses the integrity of his own personality and sincerity.

Keys to media relationships. The sound public relations worker follows these points in media relationships:

News Editors and Reporters:
- He loses no opportunity to give them service.
- He answers all questions fully, honestly, promptly.
- He treats a newsman as he would treat a customer.
- He knows his own organization, its details, its spellings.
- He is never a barrier or obstruction; the public relations man is *not* a "suppress" agent.
- He honors a legitimate "exclusive," however much he is tempted to balloon it into a more general break.
- He is impartial between one medium and another.
- He does not bluff, misrepresent, exaggerate, or pad.
- He makes every effort to provide a story for a newsman who desires one.
- However much provoked, he is not abrupt with a newsman.
- He is as energetic in helping the media cover an *adverse* story as any other kind.

The Cameraman or Photographer: The man with a camera has the toughest job in journalism. The reporter can usually get a story without putting himself in the spotlight, but a photographer is identified and slowed down by a cumbersome camera and is sometimes considered fair game by ruffians who desire to obstruct the work of the media.

- The skilled publicist extends himself to help the news photographer or TV cameraman.
- He knows what constitutes good graphic material and helps the photographer line up pictures, set up props, pose subjects, and write captions.
- He lets cameramen photograph what they are assigned to "shoot," whether or not the client desires the picture to be used. It is a major error to hamper a photographer at work.
- He always has accommodations—tickets, meals, a place to "shoot" from—for photographers. He treats a photographer as he would treat a managing editor.

The experienced publicity man is careful, whenever possible, to deal with the editor who actually will handle the type of copy being moved.

Most important is to observe all deadlines. The early publicist gets the play, because all editors need time to process their material and what can be done unhurriedly and scheduled early will get preference.

The thoughtful publicist avoids taking too much of an editor's time. He does not persistently check up on the fate of a story once it has been delivered.

He is careful to avoid "double planting"—placing two or more stories on the same subject with two shows on a TV station or in different sections of a newspaper of the same edition. If he sends duplicates of a release to more than one department, he marks each to show who is receiving copies.

40

Publicity in Newspapers

Herbert M. Baus
Philip Lesly

Though broadcast media have become the predominant influence in our society, the newspaper retains a powerful position. There is good reason that the popular impression of many people is that publicity is getting something into the newspapers.

There is a psychological reason for this, and there are a number of physical reasons. The psychological reason is that most families in the Western world have one or more newspapers that they consider "their newspaper." Each person will praise and defend it. It will influence him; perhaps more than any other medium it has the power to help him articulate and shape his opinions. Often it is most capable of motivating him to action.

Much of the psychological power of the newspaper is due to its nature as a medium.

Because almost every literate American reads at least one newspaper a day, the newspaper becomes a habit. The citizen becomes addicted to certain features. The newspaper is a local thing, a lifeline between the citizen and the world about him. Television, abdicating its opportunity to become this lifeline by concentrating on money-making mass entertainment in its shows rather than on material meaningful to the daily life of its viewers, has left the way open for newspapers to hold their position.

The newspaper, too, is read whenever the reader is ready for it. The printed word waits for his convenience, while the electronic message is tyrannically demanding—he must grasp it while it's there.

Being a regular medium, the newspaper lends itself to the cumulative build-up. It can be referred to repeatedly. The reader is alert when perusing the newspaper—in contrast to his relative relaxation when listening to the radio, watching television, or gliding by the billboard. The message becomes important because it is arrayed with the kaleidoscope of life as revealed by the newspaper.

Most newspapers are presumed by the reader to be impartial in the news columns. (There is notably, however, a trend toward "interpretive" reporting. Background detail supplied by the publicist may be reflected in news as well as feature coverage. This trend on one hand broadens the potential motivating power, while on the other hand it brings into question the paper's impartiality and may weaken its credibility.)

Newspapers have drawbacks, of course. Each issue's period of effectiveness is short. Advertising in newspapers cannot be so spectacular or so attractive as it can be in slick paper magazines where fine engraving and lavish colors set the stage for drama in print. The newspaper cannot bring the living, pulsing, vital essence as do radio, television, and the motion picture.

DAILY AND SUNDAY NEWSPAPERS

The circulation of daily newspapers in the United States is 60,655,000, according to the *Editor & Publisher Yearbook*. There are 1,819 daily papers, plus about 9,400 weekly, semi-weekly, and tri-weekly newspapers, according to the *Ayer's Directory of Publications*. The number of Sunday newspapers is 642. In *The Newspaper as an Advertising Medium,* published by the American Newspaper Publishers Association, it is estimated that each copy of a newspaper reaches 2.5 adult readers, or about 153,242,500 readers of daily newspapers alone.

The able public relations person understands the many separate departments of a daily newspaper and knows the techniques of preparing and processing news for use in the different sections.

Most publicity matter is designed for the *city desk,* which supervises the general news department. Here is the clearinghouse for the great volume of general news about events on the state and local scene, and on many newspapers, on international and national matters as well. Any publicity material not directly suitable for one of the other departments, each of which is designed to cover a limited field, may best be presented to the city side. If there is a question as to this, the recommended procedure is to discuss the designation of the story material with the departmental editor, who will be glad to advise and to use the material if it is appropriate to his columns.

Because content of the *editorial page* is determined by the policy of the paper, it is usually well to present material for this department in the form of a letter to the publisher or managing editor, a procedure that the chief of the editorial page is likely to follow in any event. There are cases in which the editorial page chief has a large measure of leeway in deciding what he will publish, and other cases where for personal reasons the publicist may prefer to deal directly with the editor or publisher.

Producing editorials is a matter of persuading editorial editors to write in favor or against a given event or subject.

The easiest and most direct way is to send all editorial editors a letter detailing the information to be editorialized. Who will sign such letters, the publicist or an appropriate official, depends on the press relationships and other factors involved.

Another method is to make a personal call on the editors to discuss the subject. Sometimes it pays to have officials of the cause being publicized contact the editors or make arrangements with publishers.

If editorialists are put on general lists to receive news releases, they will often pick up items to write about.

Remember that editorials reflect the policy of a newspaper. If the paper's policy is opposed to the cause being publicized, favorable editorials will not result. If the paper's policy is on the fence, it may be appropriate to make efforts to convince the newspaper publishers involved to back the policy at issue.

The *cartoon* of most newspapers is an editorial-page feature and is subject to the same control as the choice of editorial matter. In suggesting editorial treatment, the publicist will generally find it well to include his cartoon suggestions in the same package. Because there is usually only one cartoon a day, they are in the main devoted to international and national events, although in certain local connections such as Community Chest drives, the cartoonist will often be invited by the paper's management to make a local subject.

Letter to the Editor has an appeal to the discriminating newspaper reader who may seek in this column an index to public opinion. Some newspapers on certain days devote the editorial page very largely to this form of public forum. Where a matter of serious public interest is at stake, it will frequently justify a publicist's efforts to encourage a client or a private individual to express a view in a letter to the editor. In most metropolitan newspapers a better effect will be obtained if the letter comes from a private citizen rather than from a publicity man because it is generally an editorial policy to judge letters absolutely on their merits as interesting documents treating vital public issues, rather than to be influenced at any time by the identity of the letter writer.

Many newspapers now have "op ed" pages on which they carry material written by people not on the paper's or a press service's staff.

If the public relations person serves an organization that has activities of interest in the world of *sports,* or in *society,* or in *women's activities, science, agriculture,* and other such fields, specific treatment can be applied to qualify the material for one of these departments. Frequently, applied creative imagination will make possible the expansion of an activity into some of these spheres to increase public interest.

For example, a special preview of an entertainment event for a social or charitable purpose can secure society page publicity as well as entertainment page publicity. Combining a new line of sports equipment with new sports clothes is one way to produce a woman's page or sports page feature. The story of a furniture maker can be expanded into a feature story for a decorating or home-building editor.

In dealing with these specialized sections of a metropolitan daily newspaper, these principles obtain:

(1) The subject matter and the people involved must be pertinent. For example, women's page

material must be about women's activities, women's clubs and organizations, and women's leaders. Some newspapers have limited space. Others, such as the Milwaukee *Journal,* St. Louis *Post-Dispatch,* and Chicago *Tribune,* devote considerable coverage to women's interest now often titled "family interest" or "lifestyle."

(2) On many occasions, stories and art must be arranged for weeks or months ahead of time. In few cases does the material have the time and news urgency that prevails in the general news section. Many stories and pictures offered with a time element are nevertheless held and published at a later time, suiting the exigencies of make-up and editorial discretion.

(3) Pictures are judged less from the point of view of news impact than from the point of view of the pertinence and importance of the persons in the photographs. In spite of this, almost all editors lean to pictures of attractive people for the simple reason that such pictures make up a more effective newspaper page.

(4) Usually the specialized sections have specific policies of their own on what is news, what may and may not be mentioned, timing, and other specifics. Intensive publicity work on a specialized subject justifies great pains to learn these points and apply them.

Columnists by the thousands in the newspapers of America are constantly seeking material. They are grateful for exclusive bits that fit the style of their columns. Some publicity people, particularly in the New York theatrical and Hollywood TV and motion picture firmaments, make a living entirely by feeding items to columnists. Many New York show publicists seek items of no particular concern to their own clients but of interest to the entertainment columnists. They hope only to be repaid by a concession now and then in the form of a plug for one of their clients as a return favor.

Every columnist has his own unique field and individual style. It behooves the interested publicist to provide appropriate items and make them exclusive, for it is part of the stock in trade of the columnist to present precious bits offered by none of his competitors. The material can be offered by telephone, by letter, or in person.

It is well to put columnists on mailing lists to receive general publications, brochures, programs, and releases. Sometimes from this material the columnist may find an "angle" that pleases him, or be motivated to follow through and develop an aspect of the subject.

Every columnist has a following, and some have substantial followings. The individual columnist's treatment of a given subject has value to the publicist and his client to the extent of the columnist's particular following.

State page or state edition covers the news of the state outside of the paper's own metropolitan area. Often papers will maintain "string men," or correspondents, paid by the column inch. In some important towns, salaried bureaus are maintained. The state page or edition will be interested in news of a small community festival, fair, pageant, or show, and will desire coverage when something newsworthy happens to a client or a client's official in an outlying town.

Comics sometimes constitute a publicity medium when a subject of broad general interest is treated in them. For example, many of them cooperate with the Boy Scouts of America during national Boy Scout Week. Gift-giving holidays, sports, science, motion pictures, and many other broad commercial features of American life are featured in the comics.

A study by the South Bend *Tribune* (reported in *Public Relations News*) showed that at least one comic strip or cartoon in each issue is read by 95.8 percent of the men, 95.5 percent of the women, 98 percent of the boys, and 98.9 percent of the girls.

Every metropolitan daily has a number of *"beats,"* such as *court, police, political,* and *hotel.*

Beats are segments of the city's life that require special coverage; they get it from staff members who are assigned to get all the news they have to offer. Sometimes the beat is a sort of branch office. For example, the police beat is in the pressroom at police headquarters. The hotel beat is an office with typewriters and telephones in some central hotel, from which reporters dash about town to other hotels.

Many publicists constitute "beats" for newspapers. An airline publicity person covers his line as a beat. He reports important arrivals, covers the details of accidents, and reports new equipment and many other specific facts of news value to the papers and of publicity value to his line. The publicity person for an association covers his organization as a beat and keeps the city desks posted on all happenings of news interest. Publicity people for all other organizations likewise become regular sources of news for the papers.

The relations of publicists with newspaper beats are a special problem in each instance. Every newspaper in a city may have a different setup.

The publicist who does not know the particular beat man and is in doubt should work through the city desk.

The publicist who has regular dealings with a beat is urged to consult beat men and operate through them. They prefer this and are properly indignant when routine matters appear to be routed past them. They will promptly refer a matter to the city desk if that's where it belongs.

Any reporter who generates a good story not assigned by his editor enhances his position. The publicist who gives a good story directly to any beat man or reporter is helping raise his prestige. The reporter welcomes such material and is grateful for it.

Political beats. Political beat reporters cover the city hall, county courthouse, and state capitol. Today most large newspapers have a Washington correspondent or staff. Political beat men usually are assigned to edit and cover, and in many cases make decisions regarding, political campaigns and issues. Hence any public relations man whose work includes political action in any form will find it imperative to know and work with the political editors and writers of the metropolitan daily newspapers.

Court beats. Court reporters cover federal, state, county, and city courts. They have power of decision on whether to use or ignore a particular attorney's name, whether to pose him in a picture, whether to mention him to his advantage or omit his name.

Other beats. Newspapers tend to develop special beats to cover specific interests in their area. For example, most maritime cities have a marine department. The water-front reporters cover arrivals and departures of ships, important figures coming in, and waterfront labor problems, naval news, interesting cargoes.

Towns in agricultural areas have farmers' sections. Mining towns, factory towns, river towns, and lumber towns develop beats to cover their industries. Many papers have labor experts.

Rising newspaper specialists in new fields are eager for any news they can get. For instance, in recent years many papers have added science and medical editors, and papers in some centers of aircraft manufacture have developed "aviation editors." Publicists can profit by understanding and helping the growth of these new newspaper sections.

General Sunday section. The big Sunday edition of a metropolitan daily newspaper includes many sections, usually compiled under the direction of a Sunday editor. On other Sunday papers each section editor is responsible directly to the managing editor.

General Sunday papers often include television, book, entertainment, travel, and magazine sections and enlarged departments for such daily features as society, sports, and comics.

Often newspapers with no Sunday issue bring out these special sections on other days.

The general news section usually has a special Sunday make-up editor who begins assembling Sunday copy on Tuesday or Wednesday afternoon. Most of the Sunday paper is compiled and sent to press on Thursday or Friday, with many of the early editions mailed to suburbs and resorts for Sunday sale. The flow of spot news slows down on Saturday, with the courts and other sources of news closed. Since it is usually also larger, the Sunday paper is more open to publicity than the daily editions.

Publicists have debated the relative effectiveness of material in the Sunday paper. Those favoring it cite its greater circulation, its more leisurely reading, and the tendency of the entire family to absorb it. Those preferring the daily editions say the Sunday paper is so full that any one item is likely to be lost. However, surveys of readership indicate the Sunday papers are well read, and the large volume of advertising they carry demonstrates that advertisers have found this to be true, also.

The intelligent course is to route material to the papers as it comes up, being careful mainly to avoid days on which the papers are especially thin or overcrowded.

Religious publicity. Afternoon papers often give religion a page on Saturday, with past-tense stories on Monday. Daily papers that also have Sunday editions tend to run religious copy Saturday, Sunday, and Monday.

The religious editor will be interested in festivals with religious implications or in civic or charity projects of interest to church people. Occasionally the publicist may circularize a list of ministers with the suggestion that they mention a certain subject. This has interest for the religious editor.

Financial page. Of particular importance to the public relations worker for a business or industry is the financial page, much more widely read and understood today than a few years ago. Business news has gained so much in interest that some material that formerly appeared on the financial page now frequently appears in the general news section. One metropolitan daily newspaper's managing editor recently said, "The tremendous growth of trade publications is one index of the increasing popularity of news about business. The newspapers look to public relations men to help them cover this business news."

In a check with some of the leading financial writers of New York City, *Editor and Publisher* found expressions for such improvements in handling of financial releases as:

(1) Elimination of numerous items that interest only financial experts;

(2) More interpretive writing for the mass of new investors; and

(3) A broadening of the base of the financial page to provide an economic interpretation of day-to-day finance in the average home, and to aid in such transactions as buying a house or planning for a "rainy day."

Sylvia Porter, widely syndicated financial columnist, has said she would like to see financial sections have a stocks section, a bond section, and a commodity section; cartoons, personality stories, industry stories; improved make-up with intelligent use of "boxes"; much more abbreviated writing; writing aimed at explaining the technical facts, not just reporting.

Television-Radio section. Newspaper TV-radio sections have value to publicists of the broadcasting companies and of entertainers and programs, as well as to publicists using television and radio publicity media and desiring to mention that fact in the newspaper TV-radio section in order to increase listenership and over-all publicity effectiveness.

Drama and movie sections. Appearing prominently in every day's issue of the metropolitan newspapers, this section carries news about motion picture theaters, legitimate theaters, outdoor pageants, and various shows and festivals.

Although dominated by Hollywood and Broadway material, these sections are open to appropriate releases from publicity men having dealings with these media in connection with other activities or when handling publicity for a local dramatic production.

Home and garden sections. Sometimes this department is integrated with the real estate section. Sometimes it comprises a special magazine in the Sunday paper. It is primarily an advertising medium for contractors, seed companies, fence builders, furniture manufacturers, and other makers and distributors of materials that improve the home.

A publicist for a women's club or a civic organization's clean-up campaign can often prepare material for the home and garden section.

Automobile sections. In addition to automobile publicity and advertising, the automobile page covers accessory industries such as the tire, gas, and oil industries.

Travel sections. Travel sections of newspapers usually comprise canned stories and stock pictures about the glories of certain localities. They are a valuable medium for the travel and community publicist drumming up travel to his section of the world. The travel department is read by many persons seeking ideas for vacations and trips.

Real estate sections. The real estate section appeals chiefly to realtors and home builders and their associations. It is used as a clearinghouse for their news and advertising.

Many real estate sections include home and garden material. Some are expanded into business and industrial fields and constitute a weekly summary of the entire business picture.

Books. Limited to book reviews, news about books, and advertisements, this section is of increasing general interest.

Special editions. Special editions of metropolitan newspapers furnish an excellent publicity medium for organizations that carry advertising space and for community organizations and associations. Types of special editions include:

Annual Editions: Many large papers bring them out on New Year's Day, Labor Day, and other anniversaries.

Periodic Editions: These are issued when a city has a world's fair, a Mardi Gras or other pageant, or a huge convention.

Educational Editions: Before each school term, educational sections usually come out with stories and ads from private schools.

Special Business Editions: Some papers put out special financial editions around New Year's Day. Many put out special Automobile Show editions with the beginning of a new automobile year. Often when a new store or business institution opens, a small business edition is published.

A masterpiece of special-edition work occurs when the publicist can build his subject sufficiently to see special editions wrapped around it. Such an achievement provides a whole section, supports the client with advertisements paid for by many others, and bends the publicity efforts and budgets of numerous copy writers and photographers and photo suppliers to the advantage of the special edition and the subject it honors. Many such sections, however, are contingent on providing a specified volume of supporting advertising.

HOME-TOWN PRESS

America has more than 9,400 weekly, semiweekly, and triweekly newspapers.

Where the metropolitan mammoth reaches tens and hundreds of thousands of readers, the small-town paper reaches thousands or only hundreds. But it *reaches* them. It reaches their hearts.

A majority of the readers of a small-town paper know its editor or some staff member. The hometown paper is a member of the family, hence it *can* tell the reader. Because it carries the names of many people the reader knows, it is read thoroughly. When a publicist has a story in a small-town paper, he may rely on a good audience from most of its readers. For this reason, aiming material at the small-town newspaper is more important than the circulation of the paper might indicate.

For years publicity people have dumped avalanches of general mimeographed articles in the mails. Estimates are that editors of small-town papers have dumped as much as 95 percent of this material into wastebaskets.

The formula for success with the home-town press is simple, but the application is difficult because there are so many community newspapers. Local news plus local contacts will do the job.

If an organization has a local branch, representative, official, dealer, or other person who can deliver the story material by hand, its chances for publication are increased greatly. If the trouble is taken to mention a local name or place or some local "angle," it will probably mean the difference between the editor's use and discarding of the story.

The armed forces make particular use of a device often employed by hotels, schools, and other organizations. They send specific stories to hometown papers about the activities of servicemen from those towns. If Mr. John Doe is from Dearborn, Indiana and he engages in some activity elsewhere—gets promoted, gets married, wins an award, is graduated, or whatever—it will make a good story for any small-town newspapers serving Dearborn, Indiana.

The local contact method of national coverage involves effort by a central headquarters to organize the contacts. The most efficient method is a form of publicity kit, copies of which are made available to each local publicity man, chairman, or contact. The kits include general instructions for efficient publicity in the community. Usually there is a calendar with suggestions for stories at different times of the year. There are a number of prepared stories with blanks for filling in local names. In many cases a new kit is sent out each month. Vital elements of news are *names* and *locations*. The central office cannot furnish these through mass mimeographed mailings. But a kit furnishes the skeleton, conforming with national policy. The local contact can fill in the all-important local news facts, names, and angles, and deliver the completed story to local editors.

Motion picture publicity approaches the community newspaper often through the local theaters, not directly from the studio mailing departments. The local theater manager advertises in his own name, not in the name of the studio that produced the picture he is releasing. He eats at the Rotary Club with the newspaper editor. The copy coming from him is local copy. Of course the substance was generated in Hollywood, but it was planted with a local angle supplied by the local theater manager.

One publicist for a big city company with many small branches made it a point personally to cover the rural front. He knew the newspaper boys by their first names, took them to lunch occasionally. One of the editors told him, "If the President of the United States was assassinated just at press time, I'd still say, 'Let the presses roll.' But if Jim Jones of the local high school got an attack of appendicitis, I'd say, 'Hold the presses and include the story.'"

There came the time when the publicist's corporation was switching branch managers, promoting one who had worked in that editor's town and moving in another one. Although he regularly limited his stories to a single page of copy, the publicist in this case stretched the story to two pages because he had a strong local angle. He also sent a picture of the new man. The editor phoned him.

"Say, that's a big story. Send down a picture of your building here. Include a picture of the man's wife and children. If he has a dog, send a picture of the dog too."

Increasingly, computerized lists and systems are being used to simplify and speed localized releases. They make it more practical to make large mailings of localized releases from a central point. *Publicist* offers these tips that are especially helpful in localizing mailings when computerized systems are used:

• Include the name and telephone number of a local or regional contact in the heading if they are available. These are merely two more blank spaces to be filled in by the computer.

• Write a model release text, leaving blank spaces for local information.

• Prepare an itemization of the material to be inserted into the various versions of the release. Label each with a part key, such as AA, AB, AC etc.

• List the geographic localities to which releases are to go. Each locality should be keyed to an entry in the list of fill-ins.

• Select the types of media for which the releases are suitable.

The computerized mailing services (such as Public Relations Aids, 221 Park Ave. South, N.Y. 10003 and 173 W. Madison St., Chicago 60602; PR Data Systems, 149 Rowayton Av., Rowayton, Conn. 06853) will select all media of the types indicated that serve the localities listed and produce the number of releases required for each locality by filling the local information into the model text. Each release will appear individually typed, with no evidence of the fill-ins. The localized releases will be inserted mechanically into the appropriate envelopes and mailed.

The cost of making computerized mailings of localized releases will usually run between 50 percent and 100 percent more than the cost for the same number of releases that are not individualized.

In addition to lists of weekly newspapers in directories mentioned in Chapter 38, a *National Directory of Weekly Newspapers* is published by National Newspaper Association, 491 National Press Building, Washington, D.C. 20045.

The home-town press is a soapbox or cracker barrel for industry. Because the editors, like farmers, are free enterprisers themselves, they are natural champions of private initiative in business. Because these newspapers are small and intimate, they have more influence with their readers than do metropolitan daily newspapers. Of course, the publicity man can make a bigger splash in the New York *News,* but often the man-to-man effort to put a message across in the home-town press will accomplish sufficient results to justify undertaking the difficult task involved.

SPECIAL NEWSPAPER CLASSIFICATIONS

Publicity workers will find the many foreign-language dailies and hundreds of weeklies worthwhile media for reaching specific racial and national groups, especially on controversial matters, such as politics. Sometimes these papers are rather thin and verge on being advertising rackets; they should be studied and understood before they are used.

Financial and business newspapers, such as the *Wall Street Journal* and the *Journals of Commerce* published separately in New York, Los Angeles, and Seattle, are excellent media for all kinds of business, professional, technical, and financial news.

Of the 500 U.S. labor publications, newspapers and magazines, more than 400 are members of the International Labor Press Association, an affiliate of the AFL-CIO.[1]

[1] 815 16th St., N.W., Washington, D.C. 20006.

Labor papers generally carry news about social as well as economic problems, gossip, and news on amusements, industry news, legislation, and negotiations affecting wages and working conditions.

In most cases, labor papers are mailed to the homes of union members.

Since circulation figures are considered important, ILPA maintains information on this and other matters about its members in a printed directory that is updated and republished annually.

This vast labor press medium is attracting the eye of national advertisers, and it merits as well the study of public relations planners seeking new effective outlets for legitimate publicity copy.

There are about 75 major foreign-language newspapers in the United States, both daily and weekly. Many of these have a strong influence on their readership. Their interest is predominantly in ethnic and neighborhood matters of direct concern to their readers. For effective treatment, material should be provided in the language of the newspaper, whenever possible. Lists are available in the *Editor & Publisher Yearbook* and *Ayer's Directory*.

There are about 150 newspapers with Black interest. Most of these carry only material of direct concern to their readers, though some function as the primary newspapers of their audiences. It is important to know the viewpoint of each paper, since some are oriented to helping their readers succeed in American society while others are strongly militant.

NEWS SYNDICATES

For spreading news over a wide area from regional to international in scope, the publicity worker will find that syndicates of various kinds bring much better results than direct servicing by mail. The material must be especially good to be accepted and distributed by a syndicate, but if a syndicate picks it up, tremendous circulation is obtained with no further trouble and expense to the publicist.

Major U. S. news networks or "wire services" are:

Associated Press, 50 Rockefeller Plaza, New York, N.Y., 10020

Reuters, 1700 Broadway, New York, N.Y. 10019

United Press International, 220 E. 42 St., New York, N.Y., 10017

Each has local offices in important cities.

PUBLICITY IN NEWSPAPERS

These news syndicates welcome news from publicity sources. Often they pick up news of a publicity origin from newspapers and other local media. Where a publicist's material has potential interest to these networks, a copy of the story should go to the wire services at the same time it goes to the newspapers and broadcasting news rooms. This not only speeds coverage and gives the story full attention, but also makes it easy for the syndicate editors to telephone the source and further develop the story.

If national publicity is a prime objective, the publicist should prepare special stories for these services in the specific styles they prefer, and so mark them. Frequently the services will work with a publicist to develop a story.

Special attention is required for timing, specifications of the syndicates, the pattern of regional services and relay points that limit geographical coverage of story material, deadlines, and other details. Every publicist will build a different pattern depending on the requirements of his clients; if he serves more than one client, he will develop a different pattern of syndication for each client.

There are many types of syndicates that can help public relations organizations in specific ways. For example, the National Catholic News Service, 1312 Massachusetts Avenue, N.W., Washington, D.C., 20005, is an excellent medium for reaching the Catholic readers of America because it directly serves the diocesan press. Reuters and the Department of State, as well as AP and UPI, are among services for distributing news internationally. The Associated Press, Reuters, and UPI financial wires and the Dow Jones News Service, headquartered at 22 Cortlandt St., New York, N.Y., 10007, handle business news. In many metropolitan areas a local "city news service" is subsidized either by a group of local papers or by a national news service to service local news to many client papers within the metropolitan region.

FEATURE SYNDICATES

Some 400 feature associations of varying sizes buy, promote, and distribute comic strips, mat releases, news features, columns, cartoons, and other services. Washington and Hollywood are centers for many such organizations specializing in national affairs and the entertainment industry, respectively. Frequently these services will include publicity material if it is appropriate.

Among the leading feature syndicates are:

AP Newsfeatures, 50 Rockefeller Plaza, New York, N.Y. 10020

Associated Press, 50 Rockefeller Plaza, New York, N.Y. 10020

Chicago Tribune-New York News Syndicate, Inc., 220 E. 42nd St., New York, N.Y. 10017

Chicago Tribune-New York News Syndicate, Inc., Tribune Tower, Chicago, Ill. 60611

Chronicle Features Syndicate, 870 Market St., San Francisco, Calif. 94102

Columbia Features, Inc., 36 W. 44th St., New York, N.Y. 10036

Copley News Service, 350 Camino DelaReina P.O. Box 190, San Diego, Calif., 92041

Doubleday Syndicate, 245 Park Ave., New York, N.Y. 10017

Editors Press Service, 60 E. 42nd St., New York, N.Y. 10017

Enterprise Features, 230 Park Ave., New York, N.Y. 10017

Fairchild Syndication Service, 7 E. 12th St., New York, N.Y. 10003

Field Newspaper Syndicate, 401 N. Wabash Ave., Chicago, Ill. 60611

Gannett News Service, 55 Exchange St., Rochester, N.Y. 14614

Dorothy H. Jenkins News Service, P.O. Box 908, Norwalk, Conn. 06852

King Features Syndicate, 235 E. 45th St., New York, N.Y. 10017

Knight News Wire, 321 W. Lafayette, Detroit, Mich. 48231

Los Angeles Times Syndicate, Times Mirror Square, Los Angeles, Calif. 90053

McNaught Syndicate, Inc., 60 E. 42nd St., New York, N.Y. 10017

Newhouse News Service, Suite 1320, 1750 Pennsylvania Ave., NW, Washington, D.C. 20006

Newspaper Enterprise Association, 230 Park Ave., New York, N.Y. 10017

New York Times Special Features, 229 W. 43rd St., New York, N.Y. 10036

North American Newspaper Alliance, Inc., 220 E. 42nd St., New York, N.Y. 10017

Register and Tribune Syndicate, 715 Locust St., Des Moines, Iowa 50304

Religious News Service, 43 W. 57th St., New York, N.Y. 10019

BP Singer Features, 3164 W. Tyler Ave., Anaheim, Calif. 92801

United Feature Syndicate, Inc., 220 E. 42nd St., New York, N.Y. 10017

United Press International, 220 E. 42nd St., New York, N.Y. 10017

Washington Post Writers Group, 1150 Fifteenth St., NW, Washington, D.C. 20071

Washington Star Syndicate, 444 Madison Ave., New York, N.Y. 10022

Women's News Service, 220 E. 42nd St., New York, N.Y. 10017

PHOTOGRAPH SYNDICATES

One of the most important national publicity outlets of the publicity worker is the photo syndicate. When a photo syndicate accepts a picture, prints are mailed or wirephotoed to newspapers and magazines constituting the service's clientele. Because so many publications use syndicate photos, the results when a photo syndicate distributes a picture are great.

Figure 40-1. A nearly perfect news photograph, requiring no caption. This was arranged to call attention to the fact that the city could accommodate no more in-migrants. (Photo: Eyre Powell, Powell Press Service.)

Photo services constitute one of the most formidable challenges of publicity. For a combination of reasons, photo syndicate men and TV cameramen are the most exacting craftsmen in the news profession. Their standards necessarily are high because the photograph is a permanent record and a form of art, although often made under difficult, fast-moving circumstances. Photographers must coordinate composition, angles, lighting, and shutter speed with the action they are photographing.

These challenges of their trade make the photo syndicate personnel fast and sharp. They dislike amateurism and are annoyed by the many examples of it shown by publicity photographs submitted to them.

Here are a few principles to remember when serving the national photo syndicate:

• Whenever possible, submit a negative rather than a print.

• The picture must stand alone. In local publicity the picture often accompanies a story that amplifies and helps carry it. In national syndicate publicity, the picture and caption must measure up without a story. Hence:

• The picture must tell a story. It must be so framed that with its caption, it will be completely self-explanatory.

• The picture must have universal interest. What is universal interest in a picture?

(1) Beauty of scene or limb.

(2) Imagination and contrast, like the New Year's publicity gag showing Father Time coming out of the sea accompanied by four nymphs in bathing suits, to convey the idea that it's warm in dead of winter in the specified resort area.

(3) The ingenuity of mankind, as shown, for example, in a picture of dozens of newly manufactured airplanes symmetrically poised to take off.

(4) Colorful events, like a parade of floats with flowers and beautiful girls.

"Universal interest" in a picture will command the attention of any reader anywhere.

• The picture must be mechanically right. The composition must be good. The background must be suitable. No unnecessary objects may be shown. Everything in the picture must have a reason, and must explain itself or work logically into the caption. The focus must be exact, with lighting, exposure, and techniques combining to consummate a perfect picture. Good mechanics implies also economy in size. The more compact the picture, the more easily the editors can use it. The best picture is so flexible that an editor can run it in full for a three- or four-column cut, or can crop it to a one- or two-column cut without damaging it.

Photo syndicates have thousands of pictures submitted daily and select only a few in a stringent competition.

- The picture must be well captioned. Captions have "sold" many pictures to editors and readers. The publicist must inject the message he is paid to put over and explain everything not manifest in the picture in a very few words. All persons must be named. The place and the occasion must be described.
- A series of negatives should be made. Shoot four identically similar negatives on each setup, one for each major syndicate. Newspapers do not like to get the identical pictures supplied to their rivals, but syndicates do not object. They frequently cover towns not supplied by their rivals. The New York office of one syndicate expects its local representative to get a negative similar to one put in service by a competitor.

The major picture syndicates and their addresses are:

> Associated Press News Photo, 50 Rockefeller Plaza, New York, N.Y. 10017
> UPI Newspictures, 220 E. 42nd St., New York, N.Y. 10017
> Wide World Photos Inc., 50 Rockefeller Plaza, New York, N.Y. 10020
> Globe Photos Inc., 404 Park Ave., South, New York, N.Y. 10016

Others are:

> Black Star, 450 Park Ave. South, New York, N.Y. 10016
> Newspaper Enterprise Association, 230 Park Ave., New York, N.Y. 10017
> PIP Photos, 404 Park Ave., South, New York, N.Y. 10016
> Underwood & Underwood News Photos, 3 W. 46 St., New York, N.Y. 10036
> Wagner-International Photos, 1271 Avenue of the Americas, New York, N.Y. 10020

Some of these organizations have offices in the major cities. If they are not stationed in a given area, negatives may be mailed to their nearest editors. Photo-service men are always looking for good pictures and will gladly consider them.

When moving negatives to the syndicates, the publicist can often simultaneously offer prints to the local papers and get the always desirable local break in addition to national coverage.

DISTRIBUTION SERVICES

Certain national and regional mat, editorial, photo feature, and cartoon services distribute publicity material commercially as a service to public relations people. In many cases such a service is more effective and more economical than direct distribution.

To distribute publicity material to hundreds or thousands of newspapers, the element of expense frequently requires that copy be mimeographed, multigraphed, or otherwise produced in numbers, although having it individually produced is more personal and, therefore, more effective. Major newspapers prefer to make their own engravings, but smaller papers cannot afford this process and usually will not use art unless it is supplied in the form of matrices or reproduction proofs. Mats are more effective if accompanied by proofs showing what they look like. If the caption is cast with the cut in the mat, it guarantees against loss of caption and insures the desired credits. Type already cast into plates—called boiler plates—is excellent for smaller papers. Some syndicates and services get out full pages or sections in boiler plate or mat form, or glossy proofs for offset printing.

Some of the publicity distribution services feature one or more of the above processes. Some of them offer a choice of processes.

These services keep their lists up to date. Many of them have especially good standing with editors because they handle only material of acceptable quality. The cost is moderate. Well-known services include:

> Associated Release Service, Inc., (Mat, radio, television, and feature distribution), 173 W. Madison St., Chicago, Ill. 60602
> Communications Channels, 118 S. Clinton St., Chicago, Ill. 60606
> Continental Features, Inc., 507 Fifth Ave., New York, N.Y. 10017 (Black newspapers)
> Derus Media Service, 8 W. Hubbard St., Chicago, Ill. 60610 (Mat, radio, television, and feature distribution)
> Family Features, P.O. Box 8398, Shawnee Mission, Kan. 66208 (Color pages distributed to newspapers using ROP color)
> Industrial News Review, 4443 N.E. Airport Rd., Hillsboro, Ore. 97123
> King Features Syndicate, 235 E. 45th St., New York, N.Y. 10017 (Feature service)
> Metro Associated Services, Inc., 80 Madison Ave., New York, N.Y. 10016 (Mats and features)

National Press Service, 35 W. 53rd St., New York, N.Y. 10019

Newspaper Enterprise Association, 230 Park Ave., New York, N.Y. 10017 (Feature service)

Planned Communication Services, Inc., 12 E. 46th St., New York, N.Y. 10017

PR Data Systems, 149 Rowayton Ave., Rowayton, Conn. 06853

Public Relations Aids, Inc., 221 Park Ave., South, New York, N.Y. 10003

R.O.P. Color Service, 812 W. Van Buren St., Chicago, Ill. 60607 (Syndicates to a list of color-using newspapers, publicity material for reproduction in full color)

Special Correspondents, 723 S. Wells St., Chicago, Ill. 60607 (Mat, radio, and television service)

SCW, Inc., 20433 Nordhoff St., Chatsworth, Calif. 91311

Sta-Hi Color Service, P.O. Box 2810, Newport Beach, Calif. 92663 (Distributes color mats and publicity material to list of newspapers with ROP color facilities)

In general color is used for food, decorating, or travel pages or for special sections or Sunday magazine sections of the paper. Publicity budgets favor food on an all-year basis. In order to cover the cost of photography and distribution, use by many papers should be assured if the project is to be worthwhile. A color service provides lists of U.S. and Canadian dailies with color facilities, handles mailings, and analyzes returns on the numbers of papers using the supplied material in various forms.

Often a color placement is offered exclusively to one editor in a city, in the major cities where papers have facilities to run color.

PUBLIC RELATIONS NEWSWIRES

Public relations newswires now operate in many major cities of the United States and Canada. These frequently make available direct teletype connections with the offices of public relations firms and other subscribers to the service. They accept news stories by wire, phone, or mail and re-transmit them over teletype machines into the news rooms of daily newspapers, magazines, and radio and television stations.

Speed and simultaneous coverage are the obvious advantages of this service. For example, an action taken by a company's board of directors that may affect stockholders, employees, and customers can be relayed to all interested media within a few minutes. Through conference connections of the teletype machines, a story can be transmitted simultaneously to the public relations newswires in all the cities that have them and can also be relayed by teletype to similar public relations newswires serving the major cities of Canada and England. These wires now make it possible to reach more than 200 daily media and 75 magazines and trade publications in 70 cities, plus a large number of financial institutions.

Several of the U.S. operations also are set up to handle fast distribution of photographs and speeches or background material that is too lengthy for wire transmission.

The U.S. and Canadian public relations newswire services include:

New York
PR Newswire
150 E. 58th St.
212/832-9400
Branches:
Miami, Florida
3892 Biscayne Blvd.
305/576-8020
Los Angeles
205 S. Broadway
213/683-0218
San Franciso
145 Montgomery St.
415/781-7210

Chicago
Public Relations News Service (City News Bureau)
188 W. Randolph St.
312/782-8100

San Francisco
Business Wire
235 Montgomery St.
415/986-4422
Branches:
Los Angeles
3600 Wilshire Blvd.
213/380-8383
Seattle
905 Tower Bldg.
206/622-1632

Washington, D.C.
Press Relations Wire of Washington
979 National Press Bldg.
202/347-5155

Detroit

Press Relations Newswire
24500 Southfield Rd., Southfield, Mich.
313/557-7474

Minneapolis-St. Paul

Newswire Central
224 Franklin Ave. West, Minneapolis
612/871-7201

Atlanta

Southeastern Press Relations Newswire
161 Peachtree St.
404/523-3030

Dallas-Houston

Southwest Press Relations Newswire
1355 Mercantile Dallas Bldg.
1807 Commerce St., Dallas
214/748-1943
Branch:
1303 Fannin Bank Bldg.
1020 Holcombe Blvd., Houston
713/795-0631

Canada

Canada News Wire
Suite 1025, 1350 Sherbrooke St. West
Montreal 109, Que.

CLIPSHEETS, PRESS BOOKS, AND PRESS KITS

Clipsheets are sometimes a valuable form of mail coverage for national publicity. Clipsheets consist of material, arranged in column widths, from which selections of news can be made by the editor. With a clipsheet the editor can see how the story will actually appear and what size space it will fill. The clipsheet is neater than mimeographed reproduction.

The editor has a choice of several stories of various lengths and on various phases of the sender's subject. Some clipsheets include a selection of photos and cartoons for which mats or glossy prints may be obtained on request. Editors often hold them for use when a hole of a certain size is available in a page about to go to press.

Clipsheets are an admirable conveyance for "filler copy," that is, little one- and two-paragraph squibs that can be dug up and offered to newspapers for quick insertion in blank spaces that occur in make-up. Such fillers are particularly helpful to country editors and editors of smaller newspapers. Squibs can be prepared concerning unique facts, and then inserted in obscure corners of newspapers and magazines or run into business letters and organization publications.

Clipsheets are also excellent vehicles for jokes adapted for directing favorable attention to a subject.

The name of the issuing organization, its officers, and the clipsheet's purpose are clearly stated, for the benefit of all concerned. The efficiency of good clipsheets is signified by the prestige and acceptance they have in the important field of small-town and rural journalism—the "grass-roots," too often underestimated in value.

Although its service is free, a clipsheet of the National Association of Manufacturers is subscribed to by more than 3,500 weekly newspapers which, at their specific order, receive the clipsheet of news and features, and its two-column editorial cartoons in mat form, each issue. These cartoons enable the weekly newspaper to dress its front or editorial page with the topical work of outstanding cartoonists. NAM also supplies mats of one- and two-column standing heads of regular features dealing with economics and Washington trends as they affect the reader in small town and farm areas, and with short, bright news and features that, because they are written in the idiom of the smaller newspapers, fit desirably into their columns. Additionally, a monthly service for company publications goes to 1,600 company publications, and thus gains additional readership.

The fact that this particular clipsheet—as should be the case with any service of this type—is prepared especially with the needs, tastes, limitations, and highly prized independence and individuality of country editors constantly in mind, undoubtedly accounts for its wide use. Actually it functions as a welcome special service to country journalism. In addition, a well-prepared clipsheet is frequently used by bigger newspapers to provide standing type that can be used at any time, as needed.

Closely related to the clipsheet is the press book or kit. A press book is a mine of source material distributed to provide large numbers of editors with a steady flow of stories and pictures throughout a sustained publicity campaign. The press book is the journalistic equivalent of what a speakers' manual is to a speakers' bureau campaign. Press books fit such campaigns as a motion picture's publicity campaign or a season of publicity for the United Fund or a world science fair.

NEWS on FAMILY LIVING

Vol. 1, No. 1   Issued by the American Home Economics Association, 1600 Twentieth St., N.W., Washington 9, D.C. Full permission given for reprinting in context.   MAY, 1960

Women's News Covers Life and Living

Washington, 00 — One of the most challenging careers in the field of home economics is women's news reporting. A highly specialized type of communication, women's news reporting demands a well rounded knowledge of both news reporting and home economics.

The technical and administrative techniques of newspaper work must be mastered. They include typography, photography, layout and how to work with models, artists, copyreaders, fashion writers, food editors and child specialists.

According to Dorothy Roe, Women's Editor for Associated Press, mastering these fundamentals is only half the battle. The women's news field, says Miss Roe in *Editor and Publisher,* "requires not only basic training in news reporting, but a knowledge of home economics, business, etiquette, dress, family relations, children, food, home management, travel and the general business of living."

Women with this full background are hard to find. One reason for their scarcity is that only 20 years ago newspapers started to realize the importance of their women readers. It wasn't enough to run a few recipes or put together a society page the night before publication. The newspapers had to do better to hold the attention of their new-found readers.

Now, women's reporters and editors are very much in demand. Newspapers are continually searching for the calibre of women who not only have a nose for news, but who also have administrative ability, and a thorough working knowledge of the broad field of home economics.

It is true that there are more competent women's reporters and editors than ever before, but as they have increased in number, so has the demand.

As Miss Roe stresses, "Today's women's news reporter has the world in her hands. She can select her field, train for it, and the sky's the limit."

Mind Over Money

Washington, 00 — Money management, rather than the amount of money available, often determines a family's solvency. With this fact of life in mind, an increasing number of schools throughout the country are offering courses in money management for America's future homemakers.

The American Home Economics Association points out that today's homemaker — in addition to her traditional role as wife and mother — assumes, in most families, the important task of managing family funds. Therefore, says the AHEA, early training in money management will greatly simplify the problems a high school girl can expect to meet when she becomes "family treasurer and controller."

Dr. Alice Thorpe, head of the Department of Home Management and Child Development at Michigan State University, explains why this is so. "The girl who has had high school home economics courses in financial management has a much better idea of the wide range of items which must be provided for out of current income. She also has some idea of what constitutes reasonable expenditures for these items."

Women In Business

The 3,500 home economists pursuing careers in the business world are playing an increasingly important role in our economy. Although their top assignment is usually consumer education, they also aid in product testing, design and development; sales training and methods;

The field of home economics includes the full use of scientific methods in the study of all phases of homemaking. Here, tests by the U. S. Department of Agriculture, using a portable respirometer, help determine the most efficient and convenient placement of a modern oven. The portable respirometer is the latest type of equipment used to measure energy expended while performing household tasks.

Home Economics Study Offers Triple Benefits

Washington, 00 — Today's professional home economists have more career opportunities available to them than their counterparts of 50 years ago even envisioned.

In 1909, the year the American Home Economics Association was founded, most professional home economists became teachers, either in secondary schools or in the very few colleges and universities that offered so-called "household arts" courses.

Today, home economics career opportunities are virtually unlimited. Design, textiles, family relationships, child development, sales promotion, consumer education and relations, home management and general education are only a few of the many areas now open to home economics graduates. Opportunities — and salaries — for teachers of home economics in high school and college, as well as in research, continue to increase — yet, says the AHEA, the supply of trained home economists never meets the demand for their services. In business and industry, especially, there is a constantly increasing demand for professional home economists to fill positions of growing importance and responsibility.

According to Olga P. Brucher, president of the American Home Economics Association, "Modern schooling has had to adapt programs to meet the expanding needs of home economics education. Varied and extensive programs must equip the potential professional to meet the challenge of the scope and diversity of home economics. Programs must also include courses in associated fields, such as business methods, creative writing and human relations, just to mention a few.

"The progress of the education aspect of the profession is illustrated by the many master's degrees and doctorates now available in special home economics fields, something that was not fully envisioned in 1909 by AHEA's 700 charter members.

At present, there are approximately 8,000 home economics majors graduating from colleges and universities every year. Yet the demand for trained home economists constantly exceeds the supply.

Miss Brucher comments on this increased interest: "Home economics in most institutions of higher learning offers multiple benefits: education for personal development, for family living and for professional specialization."

and often act as communicators between manufacturers and consumers. Home economists are found in manufacturing and distributing firms, trade associations, public utilities, newspapers, magazines, radio and television. Because a home economist is trained to relate products and services directly to family living, she is uniquely valuable to business and industry.

Home Economics Boom

In 1909, the year the American Home Economics Association received its charter, there were approximately 8,000 women in all colleges and universities in the United States. Today, 50 years later, more than 8,000 women graduate each year with college degrees in home economics alone. But, despite this number, the supply of trained home economists never meets the demand.

The American Home Economics Association was founded in 1909. It had 700 charter members. Today it has more than 25,000 members, plus 450 affiliated college clubs with approximately 20,000 members.

Today's Teen-Agers Set Citizenship Goals

Washington, 00 — A half-million students in America's high schools are setting their elders a challenging example of organized good citizenship.

In more than 10,000 chapters, these enthusiastic teen-agers — the Future Homemakers of America — work together for the improvement of personal, family and community life.

The FHA — nationwide in membership and effort — is co-sponsored by the American Home Economics Association and the Home Economics Education Branch of the U. S. Office of Education. This July 1,000 representatives of these high school home economics students from the United States, Puerto Rico, and the Virgin Islands will stress the *Home as the Hub of Good Citizenship* at their National Meeting in Washington, D.C.

Through general sessions and special events the youth delegates will carry out four objectives in line with this theme:

- To help members develop a better understanding of their responsibilities as citizens.
- To appreciate the contributions the home makes to training for good citizenship.
- To promote good citizenship by developing potential abilities.
- To gain a keener appreciation for their American heritage.

Variety Is Spice of Life, Home Economists Prove

Washington, 00 — What do these people have in common — a director of consumer services for a nationwide trade organization, a consultant to a national moving van firm, and the founder of a newspaper clipping service?

They are all home economists. The variety of careers in home economics makes it the most influential profession of the many concerned with every-day living. As stated by Miss Olga Brucher, president of the American Home Economics Association, "There are several professions that deal with more than one of the aspects of living, but home economics is the only one concerned with them all."

Mrs. Ellen Semrow, graduate home economist, is Director of Consumer Services for The American Institute of Baking.

United Van Lines, Inc. of Missouri conducted a survey and discovered that in 70 per cent of all moving, women did most of the work. It was not the struggle with the sofa or the packing of dishes, but it was the mental work involved — the plans and decisions of what to take, what to leave behind as well as the questions about the new location. For instance, what transportation, school, church, shopping and home service facilities will be available? With 40 million people moving every year, United Van Lines thought these women could use some help. So, home economist Bette Malone (Mrs. Charlotte Will) was hired as a consultant for the company.

Another career started because of the tremendous growth of the home economics profession. Miss Alice Brueck of Washington, D.C., started a newspaper clipping service for home economics groups and advertising-public relations organizations involved in publicity directed at women. There was a need for such a service in the field and Miss Brueck credits her varied experience in home economics for the successful start of the Home Economics Reading Service.

There are other good examples of the variety of home economics careers — fashion designers, school lunch program directors, public relations consultants, dietitians, authors and so on. There are approximately 5,000 home economists in the Extension Service of the U. S. Department of Agriculture and in 4-H Club work who provide needed counsel for families and communities. Add 46,000 more who are teaching in secondary schools, colleges, universities and adult education programs and the total number of professional home economists approaches the 60,000 mark.

But in spite of the fact that more than 500 colleges and universities offer courses leading to degrees in home economics, the supply of professional home economists is still well below the demand. According to Miss Brucher, "The number of professional home economists could triple and there would be ample opportunities for everyone."

Child development is an important phase of home economics study. Here, home economics students at the University of Chattanooga, Tenn., conduct a nursery class as part of their training.

Figure 40-2. A good example of a clipsheet for the American Home Economics Association. Variety in stories, lengths, and pictures makes the material most useful to editors.

PUBLICITY IN NEWSPAPERS

Press books are mimeographed, multigraphed, or printed. They contain stories, pictures, cartoons, graphs, editorials, and arrays of facts. These features can be arranged by topics that fit the campaign's subsidiary events; they can be arranged by dates; or they can be presented *en masse* and in no particular order. The pictures and cartoons shown can be numbered so that the individual editor can 'phone or write to the publicity office requesting the specific photos or mats he desires.

Press books obviate the necessity for repeated contacts or weekly and daily mailings; hence, obviously, a press book must be backed by a stiff advertising budget or strong public interest in the campaign subject. If the campaign is strong enough to warrant a press book, the device is an economical way to develop a large amount of publicity.

A variation of the press book is the press kit. This is a sort of loose-leaf publicity blueprint prepared by national headquarters to be adapted by local publicity representatives. The cover usually includes a publicity calendar with printed suggestions and space for the local chairman to write in other suggestions. Boldface suggestions are printed urging the local chapter to save clippings, photos, programs, and other publicity material. National or regional addresses are given with the request that local material be forwarded. The national office uses this material as the basis for national publicity releases and as part of its record.

Usually enclosed in the press kit are suggestions for local publicity and some mimeographed publicity stories with blanks for insertion of local names, places, and dates. Local chairmen are urged to convert this canned copy by injecting all local names and facts, and then to place the material personally with local newspapers and other media.

Press kits or publicity kits may include such enclosures as the following:

- "Publicity code" or formula for acquiring local publicity.
- Brief on rules and mechanics of publicity.
- Brief on press relations.
- National matter for pickup and local "planting."
- Prompting for local participation in national moves, such as anniversaries, national conventions, contests, and others.
- Photos and mats for local "planting."
- Features.
- Clipsheets.
- Canned editorials.
- Shorts and fillers.
- Stimuli for each local unit to contribute its resources and information to the national headquarters and to other local units.
- Calendar to be followed locally.
- National features, announcements, events, and other details for local adoption.
- Guidance for local participation in and extension of national events.
- Cartoons for local use.
- Monthly suggestions to keep the speakers' bureau active.
- Monthly suggestions to stimulate local committees to new activity.
- Suggestions for stimulating local activity by generating competition with other local units.

Press kits are also developed for national use or for a local program, rather than to be used as source material by a grass roots unit. A bank about to move into an impressive new building, for instance, might have a press kit containing releases, feature stories, photos, historical and statistical background, and so on. Press kits are also often developed for introductions of new products (See Chapter 38).

MECHANICS OF PRESS PUBLICITY

Copy is the backbone of publicity production. Copy is the text of a story, a picture, a broadcast, a letter, a publication. For copy there is a basic rule: Put in all that is needed to tell the story, in the right order, in the most direct and simple language possible—that, and no more. There is a general rule: Conform as closely as possible to the style requirements of the particular medium for which placement is planned.

Following are rules to be followed in preparing copy:

(1) When using names, the first name, middle initial, and last name should be given, and the person's title, if any. In stories to out-of-town papers using a name to establish a local angle, the person's home address should be given, both for its local interest and to facilitate matters if the newspaper desires to contact him or his family for additional information.

(2) Good newspaper copy is written in a simple, straightforward, objective style with sentences neither too long nor too short. It is important to avoid editorial comment, personal opinions, colored words, or conclusions. Where material of this kind seems desirable, it must be presented as the

direct quotation of an important individual whose name is used to "carry" the story.

(3) The most acceptable copy paper is 8 ½ X 11 inches in size and good clear stock. To facilitate any urge by the editor to check details or seek more story material, source of the story is usually given in the upper left-hand corner. Information desired includes name of the client and name, address, and telephone number of the publicist. If the source is an agency handling several accounts, including the name of the client not only identifies the object of the story at a glance but preserves mention of the client's name in the story.

(4) Release instructions should go in the upper right-hand corner. If the news is to be released when issued, the instruction should read "FOR IMMEDIATE RELEASE." If the copy is issued somewhat in advance of release date, release instructions should read "for Thursday *Times*" or "release Saturday, June 22, 2 p.m." By setting the release date ahead, the item can be handled by the editors and set into type during slack time. A release date or time should be used only when it is required or justified, as in the case of an actually scheduled meeting or announcement.

(5) If the release is more than one page long, pages should be numbered and the word "more" should be at the end of each page except the last. The story should be closed by an end mark such as "30" or "###" or "*****." Whenever possible each page should end on the end of a paragraph.

(6) The staff of an afternoon paper is at work before 7:30 a.m. Copy should be placed in the editor's hands during the middle of the preceding

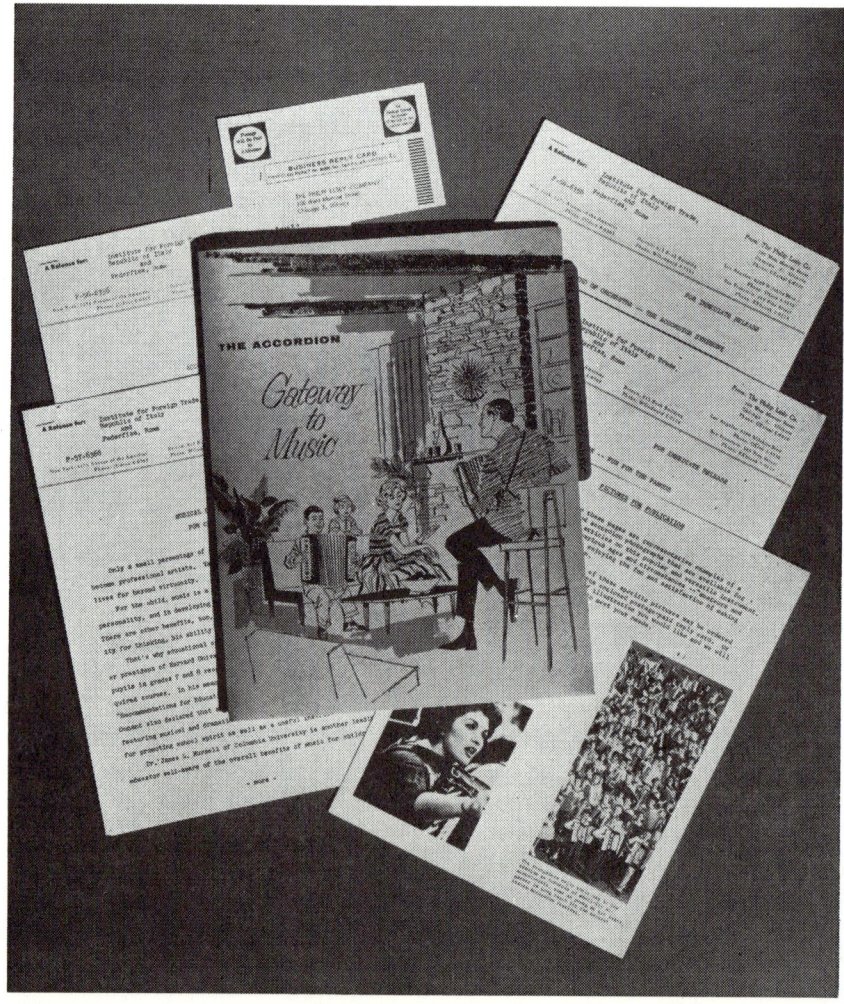

Figure 40-3. A press kit, containing articles for publication, background information, a portfolio of illustrations that are available on request, and a postcard for making requests for pictures and other material. The cover has pockets on the inside for grouping the materials, and a tab on the right edge that will identify the kit when it is filed in a publication's reference drawers.

afternoon if possible. In few instances will a story get full attention if submitted later than 11 a.m. of the same day. Morning papers should receive publicity releases between 10 a.m. and noon of the preceding day. Stories submitted before 3 p.m. are likely to make all editions, and important stories usually can be placed with morning papers as late as 10 p.m.

(7) Sunday copy should reach the city desk before Friday noon, or before Thursday noon if the paper has advance "bulldog" editions for country circulation. Spot news can be submitted as late as 4 p.m. Saturday.

(8) When a story is short, skip a third of the page to allow room for copy-desk marking. Type all stories with double or triple spacing. Leave ample margins on both sides. Type on one side of the paper only. In almost all cases, use one page only. Sometimes a well-written headline three spaces across the top of the "lead" or in upper right-hand corner helps to "sell" a story to the editorial desk.

(9) Always have the date on a release. It can be in the dateline (Des Moines, Feb. 7 —) or at the beginning or end of the story. Editors want to know whether the material is timely when they get it. Also, when copy is filed and then referred to later, there is no way of telling when it originated unless it is dated.

(10) The newspaper lead—that is, the opening—answers these questions: Who? What? When? Where? Why? How? The expertly written news or publicity story can be cut from the bottom up and still be complete. It is severely accurate. Where possible, copy conforms to the style of the publication to which it is issued. The name of the client or the publicity point of the story is woven into the lead or as high into the story as possible in such a way that it cannot easily be deleted without destroying the core of the story.

(11) Every editor's interpretation of news is different.

Whether or not a story is news depends primarily on three points:

- The actual, universal news interest involved
- The individual newspaper's policy
- The local angle—local names, organizations, interests.

An important publicity problem sometimes requiring simultaneously the judgment of a Solomon and the tact of a Talleyrand is concerned with exclusives, special breaks, whether to offer a story to morning or to evening papers, and rotation of such breaks. See Chapter 39.

When a release is broken in the morning papers, it should be reslanted or given a new lead in the p.m. papers if possible. One evening paper picture editor who has dealt with hundreds of publicists never fails to mutter when offered a picture on a subject that the morning papers will run ahead of him. But he is enraged when a publicist offers him a picture without *telling him* that the morning papers will use it first. He sometimes consents to run the same picture after the a.m. papers, but he likes to know in advance that he is doing it. This attitude emphasizes a point of human nature in dealing with editors: be perfectly candid and straightforward in dealing with them, and they will respond with good will. They justifiably resent evasiveness or any tactics that may be interpreted as pulling wool over their eyes.

Only the rarest publicity stories will involve a high ingredient of universal news interest. Inadequacy of news interest and neglect of policy and local angle account for estimates that more than 90 per cent of the publicity written and distributed goes into the wastebasket.

PHOTOGRAPHS AND ILLUSTRATIONS

Photographs have many advantages to the publicist. A good photo may be syndicated to hundreds of newspapers and magazines. Where the hurried or lazy reader may not see a news story, he can hardly miss the pictures. Seeing a picture, he will absorb the message at a glance. A big advantage of the photo is that it can seldom be altered by editing. It is either used or it isn't; if it is, it tells the story, providing it was properly conceived.

The photographic program begins with planning the pictures, synchronizing them with the story schedule. The photographer is carefully briefed so that he will know what the publicist desires to achieve.

Good publicity pictures are framed to fill as small a space as possible, because an editor who can't use a large picture may have space for a small one; if he likes the small one, he can always blow it up. The best pictures are those that can either be used in full or cropped—with part of the picture cut off without hurting the remainder.

A news picture in itself tells the story. It may be good enough to tell the story without even a caption but it will never be printed if submitted without a caption.

The best pictures convey action or a candid view. Models who look into the lens usually are looking the picture out of the newspapers. "Poster" or "billboard" pictures, in which models are displayed holding signs that tell the story, constitute an evasion of orginality and creativeness that usually gets no farther than the editor's wastebasket.

The caption identifies all persons in the picture with full name and initials, in order left to right, with sufficient background information so that there is no question in the editor's mind. It is better to tell too much than too little. The caption is best pasted under the print or stripped into the print (see Fig. 40-5) so the editor can look at picture and caption without shifting. It is never wise to write on the reverse side of the print.

Most publicity art is printed on glossy 8 X 10 inch paper. With some newspapers, matte (dull finish) will do. If the photo is exceptionally good, it may pay to present it in the more spectacular 11 X 14 inch or 20 X 24 inch sizes. Portraits may be 5 X 7 inches.

In working with Sunday magazine sections, color may be used. A transparency is preferable to a print. For the most part in placing color publicity on a widespread basis it is preferable to work through a service set up to make national contacts (as discussed previously).

When mailing or dispatching photo copy, a manila envelope with cardboard inserts to prevent cracking is suitable. The image side is best pointed toward the back of the envelope so that the post

---

A Release for: State Farm Insurance Companies
Bloomington, Illinois 61701

SF-270

FOR IMMEDIATE RELEASE

Bloomington, Ill., Jan. 25 -- State Farm, the nation's largest casualty insurer, is moving into the health insurance field.

The company today said its "Medi-Ca$h" policy, which pays $15 for every day that a family member is hospitalized, has been tested in seven Midwestern states and will be expanded nationally. It is expected to be in 22 states by the end of tne year and will be sold by the same agents who sell State Farm's auto, fire and life insurance.

Premiums may be paid every six months, or as part of a monthly payment that can include State Farm auto, fire and life insurance as well.

More than 1,000 policies have been sold since the program was introduced experimentally in August.

"Premium volume for 'Medi-Ca$h' may reach the $5 million mark by 1970 and climb to $25 million by 1975," predicted Robert D. Bischoff, assistant vice-president.

- more -

Figure 40-4. A good example of a news release.

Figure 40-5. Two ways to attach captions to publicity photos. At left the caption was typed and stripped into the negative before the photo was printed. At right is the more common tipped-on caption, which is pasted to the bottom edge of the photo. (PR Aids photo).

office stamp won't damage the print. It is well to mark plainly: "Photographs, Do Not Bend."

Advance cost understanding with the photographer is good budget insurance. The photographer can be paid on a so-much-a-print basis or on a time-plus-expenses basis. Best results are obtained if the photographer is hired for his excellence, not his economy; there is no saving in pictures that editors will not use.

It usually pays to send a publicity man out to help the photographer. Often two men may be needed to arrange props, handle lights, record names for captions, and take care of other details.

The publicist's job is to make all arrangements, line up the place, see to it that the models and others involved are there on time, and have all necessary props on hand. Most publicists make suggestions to the photographer but find it profitable to heed the photographer's judgment.

For legal safety, it is wise to have everyone appearing in a picture sign a simple form to the effect: "Permission to use my name and/or photograph for publicity purposes is hereby given.———————
————————————(signed)." A more complete legal release form is shown in Figure 40-6.

There are several types of publicity pictures:

(1) Straight news shots are photos of such news events as train wrecks, or combat shots of troops and/or equipment in action.

(2) "Mug art" is the trade name for straight portrait pictures, easy to have done, economical, and attractive to editors because such shots require only one column by three inches of space, or can even be run in the same column beside type.

(3) "Leg art," known in the trade as

PHOTOGRAPH & TESTIMONIAL RELEASE

FOR VALUE RECEIVED $\frac{I}{WE}$ hereby give The John J. Jones Company, its clients, agents and assigns, full permission to use, publish and copyright photographic prints or other reproductions from all negatives made of me and/or my property, or any part thereof, either in conjunction with or without using my name, and to make changes or alterations therein and/or additions thereto for publication, for advertising, in connection with testimonial copy with fictitious name or otherwise, and for any and all commercial purposes whatsoever.

Date ——————— 19—

——————————— (SEAL)
(If minor, Parent or Guardian signs below.)
I, the parent or guardian of the above minor child, do hereby consent to the above release.
——————————— (SEAL)

Witness ———————————

Figure 40-6. A form to be signed by models to release the publicist from any liability in using the pictures taken.

Figure 40-7. A product publicity photograph. Emphasis is on the idea Maytag identifies with its products—proper planning of laundry room facilities around proper selection of equipment.

"cheesecake," will be popular as long as beautiful women hold their place in the minds, hearts, and imaginations of men.

(4) Action shots show the subject doing something, such as a mechanic working on an engine or an athlete performing.

(5) Pattern shots—or inanimate object shots—show views of objects usually arranged in patterns to attain a striking arrangement, symmetry, and perspective. These are excellent for industrial publicity.

(6) Product shots are designed primarily to show off a product. Good taste is a paramount element in photographs. Because the editor, like any other man, has an eye for a pretty girl is no cause to overdo cheesecake. Corny gags may make the papers, but create a laugh *at* the client instead of *with* him. Better no picture than one that reflects on the subject. "I don't care what you say about me just so you use my name" is an axiom of the pre-public relations era of publicity. It is unsound today.

For many purposes, stock or special photographs may be needed. In most cities there are shops that can provide such pictures for local use. For national use, good sources include:

Advertising Age, 740 N. Rush St., Chicago, Ill. 60611

Bachrach, 48 E. 50th St., New York, N.Y. 10022

Bettman Archive, 136 E. 57th St., New York, N.Y. 10022

Culver Pictures, 660 1st Ave., New York, N.Y. 10016

Ewing Galloway, 420 Lexington Ave., New York, N.Y. 10017

Globe Photos, 404 Park Ave., S., New York, N.Y. 10016

Historical Pictures Service, 17 N. State St., Chicago, Ill. 60602

Kaufman & Fabry, 180 N. Wabash Ave., Chicago, Ill. 60603

Photo Researchers, Inc., 60 E. 56th St., New York, N.Y. 10022

Three Lions, Inc., 150 Fifth Ave., New York, N.Y. 10011

Underwood & Underwood, 3 W. 46th St., New York, N.Y. 10036

United Press International, 220 E. 42nd St., New York, N.Y. 10017

Wide World Photos (Associated Press), 50 Rockefeller Plaza, New York, N.Y. 10020

The picture syndicates, listed elsewhere, are excellent sources from which to purchase pictures on a variety of subjects.

Stock photograph sources are also listed in the classified pages of telephone directories in many major cities.

Other types of illustrations include cartoons, maps, drawings, graphs, architects' plans, and architects' drawings. If the subject has enough news interest, frequently a newspaper's artist will cooperate in preparing an illustration sufficiently different from the usual photographs to be a good attention-getter.

PHOTOGRAPHY FILES

It is essential that systematic and complete files be kept of all photographic materials. There are a number of filing systems, but the essentials of all good ones are:

1. A central file containing a file copy of each photo, in whatever form it may have been taken—black-and-white, color transparency, color print, slide, or overhead projector transparency. This copy should be marked "DO NOT REMOVE." With it should be information on the photographer, date taken, negative number, location, and other pertinent information. Model releases covering persons shown either should be filed with the photo or a note should be enclosed indicating where the model release is filed. If the photo has been purchased, information should be filed on the price paid, to whom, and for what rights.

2. A record of where each photo has been submitted. It is especially important to indicate when a photo has been offered exclusively to one medium, with what story, for what period. If a photo has been mass produced and distributed widely, either a summary of the distribution or a copy of the distribution order should be kept with it.

3. A record of publication, broadcast, or other use of the photo. This is to avoid embarrassment in the future from using a photo that has been seen previously, if the editor or broadcast outlet wants one not previously exposed to public view.

4. Cross references indicating other versions of the photo. For instance, one shot may have been used for newspaper publicity, in a slidefilm, in a booklet, in an annual report, and in an advertisement. Both color and black-and-white versions may exist. It is essential that whoever encounters it in any file knows that other versions exist and should be checked.

41

Publicity in Magazines

Herbert M. Baus

The magazine may be considered as a combination of newspapers, designed to be read on the run, and books, designed to be digested at leisure. The magazine is an elaborator and interpreter of matters of current interest.

Many magazines are excellent vehicles for the explanation of a client's policy because their stories often allow for personal opinion on the part of the writer. An effective article also tends to make a strong impression on the reader, and to be especially useful in reprint form for direct-mail and other secondary distribution.

Although magazines are good for spectacular single publicity "breaks," a single magazine "break" alone is likely to be a monolith on a desert of silence. The big advantages of newspapers and broadcast publicity media are their greater constant and frequent intimacy with the individual, because of the frequency and the local angle, plus the fact that newspapers, radio, and television lend themselves to the day-in-day-out persistent treatment that is most effective in molding public opinion.

The United States has about 400 monthly magazines, many other weeklies, and several thousand trade magazines and company publications—sometimes called "house organs."

The best general references to magazines are *Bacon's Publicity Checker*,[1] *The Standard Periodical Directory*,[2] *Ayer's Directory of Newspapers and Periodicals*,[3] *Standard Rate and Data Service*,[4] the *Working Press of the Nation*,[5] and the *Writers' Market*,[6] which classify magazines by types and reveal what they publish.

Consumer magazines can be classified into three major groups: general magazines, news and illustrated magazines, and specialized magazines. Each of the three types has a different approach, has a different effect on its readership, and must be approached by different publicity techniques.

Unlike newspapers, magazines tend to be quite distinctive from each other, even within general categories. It is wise to study two or three consecutive issues of a publication before approaching its editor with story ideas or material.

HOW TO DEAL WITH MAGAZINE EDITORS

Major national magazines—as rated in terms of circulation and staff strength—prepare or buy their own material. They rarely, if ever, use publicist-written text intact. They do, however, use the services of publicists. What is required from the publicist is news judgment, intuitive or lucky timing, sure feature sense, reliable research, and a sense for good illustrations—in short, editorial ability.

While the top-circulation general magazine has long been averse to using trade-names or credits in its editorial material, recent changes in format help the publicist. In general publicity on a product treated generically is much more acceptable than material about one brand of product. However, product credits are also attainable under certain circumstances.

For example, a publicist for the diamond industry

[1] 14 E. Jackson Blvd., Chicago, Ill. 60604
[2] 150 E. 52nd St., New York, N.Y. 10022
[3] West Washington Square, Philadelphia, Penn. 19106
[4] 5201 Old Orchard Rd., Skokie, Ill, 60076

[5] 424 N. 3d St., Burlington, Ia. 52601
[6] 9933 Alliance Rd., Cincinnati, Oh. 45242

may readily place a number of feature ideas dealing with the great gems of the world, favorite gems of well-dressed women, and so on, in all cases offering research and anecdotal material, and aiding the editor in crystallizing a feature about the appeal of gems. In the same way, a publicist who represents an association—say, florists or fishing tackle manufacturers—can place a feature favorable to all by supplying factual material, suggesting interview possibilities, helping set up photo arrangements, and performing similar functions to meet the editor's needs.

The large magazine is bombarded with thousands of publicity releases a day, scores of visitors bent on publicity missions, and constantly ringing phones. How then do you reach an editor?

Almost every editor relies on a list of known experts when information is required, keeps a file of those who are well-placed and well-known as suppliers of usable news and ideas, and avoids those who "follow up" too frequently to check on the status of their offerings.

Rewarding primary contacts with an editor are made in a number of ways and can lead to productive cooperation over the years.

There are several effective ways to approach these important national media:

Visits to the editor. The editor who knows and respects the publicist may extend himself by letting the publicist submit a story about a client, by assigning an ace staff writer to the subject, or by accepting a batch of material and having it rewritten for the magazine. He will be more receptive to personal letters than will an editor who does not know the writer of the letter. Major magazines are targets of bales of letters, manuscripts, and communications of all kinds; it goes without saying that an approach from someone known to the editor and who has earned his confidence will have better results than the random shot. However, the welcome of the editors can easily be outworn by overuse. Request an appointment from the editor or his secretary. Don't drop in unexpectedly.

Writing to the editor. Often a well-written letter or memorandum will spark the interest of an editor and lead him to request more material to determine whether he will want a story.

Queries. When a feature idea requires extensive research, it is best to query the editor in advance with a brief outline. If he feels it may be a good possibility, he will suggest you develop it for serious consideration.

Contacting local magazine outlets. Many national magazines have local editors and correspondents in many areas, to serve the local free-lance writers and to assure full national coverage of story possibilities. These local magazine representatives are looking for good ideas. Proper contact with them will sometimes enlist them as energetic proponents of the proposed article. Some publicists find it worth while to keep a large file of pictures for these local magazine writers and representatives, while others circularize them regularly. One large chamber of commerce, charged with publicizing its area, sponsors and helps finance a "Professional Writers' Association" and presents periodic dinners to maintain the contacts and stimulate the activity.

Press conferences or showings. Meetings with the organization's officials or dramatic displays of new products can be a meeting ground for the publicist and for many magazine editors. It is important that the new product justify the editors' time. Frequently a breakfast, a luncheon, or other entertainment is associated with the press conference. Editors prefer clear invitations and time-tables. An invitation that specifies *Cocktails: 12:30, Luncheon: 1:00* saves the time of a teetotaling or heavily booked editor. A press conference not associated with entertainment can also be held effectively when the occasion warrants—at a company plant, in a hotel ballroom, at an exhibit hall, or elsewhere. Any press conference should begin on time, be concisely planned, and allow for early exit. (See Chapter 39.)

Hospitality suites. In connection with a convention, a trade show, a symposium, a junket, or similar event, hospitality suites can be maintained for the working press including newspaper and magazine editors. A suite in a leading hotel or on the premises—at a housewares show, builders' show, furniture show, or elsewhere—can be opened to provide comfort and sociability and can be staffed by the publicist Some hospitality suites offer morning coffee, extra typewriters, carrying cases for trade literature, coat checking, or champagne. Depending on the occasion and the facilities, the publicist serves as would any host or hostess. Press kits are made available for visitors, and company officials are encouraged to be on hand for informal introductions and interviews. Notice of the hospitality suite is provided well in advance to editors.

Product demonstrations and special entertainments. The chance to use a new product or see it demonstrated is often most persuasive in forming editors' judgments. New cars may be demonstrated and tried out by automotive or other news editors.

```
                United States Steel Corporation
                        525 William Penn Place
MILTON J. WURZBACH         Pittsburgh, Pa. 15230
  STAFF DIRECTOR
PRODUCT INFORMATION
ROBERT H. MARQUARDT
ASSISTANT STAFF DIRECTOR
PUBLIC RELATIONS DEPARTMENT
       391-2345

    Dear (Name of Editor)

         You are cordially invited to attend a press preview introducing
    United States Steel's Residential Tech Center at our Research Labora-
    tory in Monroeville, near Pittsburgh.

         The program, which will include remarks by ranking United States
    Steel research and commercial executives, will begin at 1:50 p.m.,
    Wednesday, August 4, in D Auditorium at the Research Laboratory in
    Monroeville.

         Transportation by bus will be provided from the United States
    Steel Building at 525 William Penn Place.  The bus will leave from the
    United States Steel Building for the Research Center at 1:15 p.m.,
    Wednesday, August 4.  If you wish to go by bus, please be in the lobby
    of 525 at 1:00 p.m.

         Our program for August 4 includes a slide presentation on new
    materials and coatings as they apply to the residential construction
    industry; a visit to one of the research facilities housing laboratory-
    size basic steelmaking equipment; demonstration of new systems and
    applications of steel for home and light building construction; and
    examination of the Tech Center headquarters facility where many of these
    new ideas have been installed for testing.

         Following the program at the Tech Center, which is expected to
    last approximately 2½ hours, we plan dinner and refreshments at the
    Penn-Sheraton Hotel in Pittsburgh.

         Would you kindly return the enclosed reply card to let us know
    whether you or one of your associates will attend.

                                              Sincerely,

    WJW/Wjab
    Enclosure                                 (signed)
```

Figure 41-1. A memorandum to editors and writers about a newsworthy development and demonstration. Essential information is presented concisely. Such memoranda may be followed up by telephone among invitees who do not return postcards.

Snowmobile rides can be arranged in a public park (usually by securing a city permit in advance) for sports editors and other guests. Meals planned around a new food product may be sampled by food editors at a company luncheon. A separate showing of an industrial "musical" can entertain the press and allow subsequent sampling of new products such as foods or sports equipment. The use of consumer panelists on stage may encourage editors to ask questions and secure typical case histories of product use. Filmed presentations can add a dramatic backdrop to product introductions. The techniques can be as unlimited as the publicist's creativity. Often events of this type offer a welcome change of pace. Some events are scheduled annually, such as award lunches, trend-setting fashion shows, manufacturers' presentations.

Tours. Editors may be invited to view an interesting site—vineyard, spa, factory, research center, recreation area, resort hotel, striking new building, planned community, design center. A tour of this kind adds to the editor's background data and strengthens his professional relationship with the publicist and organization.

Releases and photographs. Often the dissemination of news is confined to the standard release and captioned photograph. These are the year-in-year-out foundation for keeping editors informed. All too often incoming publicity material is discarded because of journalistic lapses. For instance, all material should include the date—undated material is a bane of editors; and all material should be factually complete—full names and titles, specifics on quantities and locations.

Major magazines will generally take their own photographs or use press service pictures unless there is a truly distinctive and excellent photo available on an exclusive basis.

Work with established writers. Sometimes a writer whose material is often used by a magazine can be interested in doing a story. If he queries the editor in his effective style and with the assurance that it will get a receptive review by the editor, the chances of its being accepted are greater than from a direct query by the publicist. The writer must be free to treat the story as his judgment indicates, of course. He need not check it with the publicist or have any obligation to treat it as the publicist desires. Also, the writer should let the editor know he is working with the source. Payment should be by the magazine or by the publicist with the editor's full knowledge—so he can be aware of the self-interest that may underlie it—not from both.

A partial list of free-lance writers and the types of things they write appears in the annual *Feature Writer and Syndicate Directory of the Working Press of the Nation.* (See Chapter 38.) An additional list can be found in *Directory of Professional Writers,* published by the American Society of Journalists and Authors, 123 W. 43rd St., New York, N.Y. 10036.

Try a free lance article. The biggest magazines will buy articles from unknowns—if they make a hit. If the subject has possibilities, it may pay to try this. These articles should be submitted free to the magazines, since it is not ethical to be paid both by the magazine and by the client. The research necessary to write the story undoubtedly will have other useful applications.

Few editors consider it part of their work to supply clippings or progress reports. The publicist should follow each issue of a publication or—more economical from a time standpoint—rely on a clipping bureau. (Clipping bureaus are discussed in Chapter 38.) The clipping bureau should be supplied with a copy of material sent to the magazine or should be alerted to watch for specific mentions.

MAGAZINES' TIMING

Many of the large-circulation national monthlies work three to four months ahead or more. An April feature is completed and is in proof in January. Christmas features are well wrapped up for the printer by August or September.

Although department editors plan their own pages, regular staff meetings are scheduled to balance the "book" as a whole. The monthly magazine editor thus needs a good running start to germinate an idea, get it scheduled for a specific issue, produce text and photographs, and provide the printer with final material months ahead of the newsstand distribution date. The publicist should thus plan his contacts a couple of months before the magazine's deadline, or about six months before publication.

News magazines, weekly magazines, illustrated magazines, and trade magazines work on shorter deadlines. A news weekly, as the name implies, calls for rapid production of material and requires the publicist to have all preparation done in advance to supply statistics, stock photographs, or other material immediately.

Trade magazines are more leisurely than consumer monthlies in their requirements, and often close the main editorial section a month before distribution date.

It is naturally helpful to know which magazines may be planning to do stories on given subjects. Though there is considerable secrecy within editorial offices on most stories, they often must contact what they consider good sources for material they need. So being recognized as a good source—for instance, for having excellent files on musical activity in the United States, or boating, or research being done on mental health—is an excellent way to increase the volume of magazine coverage.

Sometimes editors or writers will let it be known that they are seeking certain types of material. For instance, *PR Aids' Party Line,*[7] and *Contacts,*[8] both weekly newsletters, convey notes of this type and changes in staffs.

CLASSIFICATIONS OF MAGAZINES

While the directories mentioned contain full lists and information, it is helpful to cite key publications in the major categories that will be of interest to publicists, with guides on working with them.

GENERAL MAGAZINES

Leading magazines in this field are:

Changing Times, 1729 H St., NW, Washington, D.C. 20006

---

[7] 221 Park Ave. South, New York, N.Y. 10003
[8] Larimi Communications Associates, 151 E. 50th St., New York, N.Y. 10022

```
A Release for:   American Music Conference
                 332 South Michigan Avenue
                 Chicago, Illinois  60604


MEMO TO EDITOR:

     More than 39,300,000 people in the United States now play
musical instruments.  The rate of growth continues to increase
and many people want to know

                   HOW TO START MAKING MUSIC

     Here are some background facts for an article that will
answer the basic questions.

   . Which instrument to choose?

     Musical instruments require different degrees of interest,
physical and mental coordination, and physical attributes --
although most limitations can be overcome if the desire is
strong enough.

     Woodwind players generally progress faster if they have a
good set of teeth.  Long fingers are helpful to harpists,
guitarists and pianists.  A person with a "life-of-the-party"
outlook will probably find the guitar or accordion best suited
to his personality.  Serious-minded people might choose any of
the four major stringed instruments.

   . What should you pay for an instrument?

     Prices vary according to the instrument.  Pianos can cost
$5,000 -- or $50 (for a very second-hand purchase).  A ukulele
can cost $4 or $100.  The general rule for amateur musicians,
especially beginners, is to avoid the bargain-priced and the
expensive instruments.  A "bargain" instrument, that even a
"pro" would have difficulty playing, might discourage a begin-
ner and could be a complete waste of money.  On the other hand,
a violin costing $4,000 is hardly the instrument to hand to a
beginner who stands one chance in a million of becoming a con-
cert artist.


                             - more -
```

Figure 41-2. First page of a short memorandum to an editor offering a suggestion for an article, and indicating the nature of material that can be provided.

Coronet, 7950 Deering Ave., Canoga Park, Calif. 91304

Family Health, 149 Fifth Ave., New York, N.Y. 10010

Grit, 208 W. Third St., Williamsport, Pa. 17701

Holiday Magazine, 1100 Waterway Blvd., Indianapolis, Ind. 46202

Human Behavior, 12031 Wilshire Blvd., Los Angeles, Calif. 90025

Money, Time & Life Bldg., 1271 Ave. of the Americas, New York, N.Y. 10020

Moneysworth, 251 W. 57th St., New York, N.Y. 10019

National Enquirer, 600 S.E. Coast Ave., Lantana, Fl. 33464

National Geographic Magazine, 17th & M Sts., NW, Washington, D.C. 20036

New York, 755 Second Ave., New York, N.Y. 10017

The New Yorker, 25 W. 43rd St., New York, N.Y. 10036

Pageant, 21 Elm St., P.O. Box 704, Rouses Point, New York, N.Y. 12979

People, Time & Life Bldg., 1271 Ave. of the Americas, New York, N.Y. 10020

Psychology Today, One Park Ave., New York, N.Y. 10016

The Saturday Evening Post, 1100 Waterway Blvd., Indianapolis, Ind. 46202

US, 488 Madison Ave., New York, N.Y. 10022

Canadian:

MacLean's Magazine, 481 University Ave., Toronto, Ont. M5W 1A7, Canada

WEEKLY NEWSPAPER MAGAZINES

A variation of the general magazine is the newspaper magazine, edited and produced nationally and distributed as a weekend feature of a number of different newspapers. The three major nationally distributed newspaper magazines are:

Family Weekly, 641 Lexington Ave., New York, New York 10022

Parade, 733 Third Ave., New York, New York 10017

Tuesday, 10 E. 40th St., New York, New York 10016 (Black interest monthly)

Many Sunday newspapers publish their own magazines as separate sections. They should be checked separately.

Each has its own type of material. As with all magazines, it is always wise to be familiar with the style and content of each publication before seeking to place any article.

NEWS AND ILLUSTRATED MAGAZINES

The major news and picture magazines are as follows:

News Magazines

Jet, 820 S. Michigan Ave., Chicago, Ill. 60605 (Black interest)

Newsweek, 444 Madison Ave., New York, N.Y. 10022

New Times, 1 Park Ave., New York, N.Y. 10016

Time, Time & Life Bldg., 1271 Ave. of the Americas, New York, N.Y. 10020

U.S. News & World Report, 2300 N St., NW, Washington, D.C. 20037

Illustrated General Magazines

Ebony, 820 S. Michigan Ave., Chicago, Ill. 60605 (Black interest)

Life, Time & Life Bldg., 1271 Ave. of the Americas, New York, N.Y. 10020 (Special issues only)

Outgrowths of modern journalism, news magazines attempt to summarize the news highlights of the entire world. They confront the publicist with a unique problem. His chances of getting his story into them by individual effort are more limited than with newspapers, although it is done frequently. News magazines boil down volumes of news material into a limited space.

These magazines get their material from four sources:

(1) Wire, photo, and feature syndicates.
(2) Field editors and "string men."
(3) Clippings from newspapers and other publications.
(4) Reliable sources such as publicists who provide them with leads and source materials.

Efforts to place material in news magazines should be directed *first,* to building up material in syndicates, an important source of news to the news magazine; *second,* to cultivating field editors and "string men" who may establish a good story from the publicist's locality; *third,* to achieving heavy results with regular newspapers and trade magazines, because news magazines frequently pick up material from these sources; and *fourth,* to approaching directly the appropriate department editor because he is always seeking good material for his pages.

String men are of all types. Some are competent men whose judgment is respected at headquarters; others are less able. The paid bureau managers are trusted and capable, but sometimes too busy to respond. If the local man is busy, ask him to let you work up some material and send it in to the main office with a note, "Correspondent suggested I send this to you." Also send a copy to the correspondent.

SPECIAL MAGAZINES

In recent years the trend has been toward growth of special-interest magazines and a decrease in the number and comparative dominance of magazines reaching vast audiences. This is due to the ascendency of television as the medium that has the greatest appeal to large audiences; the advanced educational levels and other factors that have made millions of people seek individual interests that set them off from the crowd; and increased affluence and leisure time that give millions the means and opportunity to pursue their special interests.

Accordingly, more of the publicist's work in the magazine field is being devoted to specialized magazines. Often this type of "rifle shot" placement is more effective than a comparable article in a mass magazine, since the audience may be precisely the one that will take a strong interest. For instance, an article about an idea in *Harper's*—reaching opinion leaders in government, education, and the media—may have more consequence in fostering it than an article of the same size in *Reader's Digest*.

Approach to the "special" magazines—those reaching specialized groups, but not trade publications—depends on several things. When they are national, the same processes can be applied that are used in reaching the large general magazines. When they are local, the technique is much the same as it would be in the case of a local newspaper.

The special magazines—there are many types—are frequently available by indirect penetration through an influential member of the group to which the magazine circulates. The "class" magazines might be effectively reached through the intervention of a respected socialite. A sports figure might be a better advance runner than the publicist himself for a sports magazine. Institutional magazines are often more accessible by the indirect method of using an important figure in the institution.

It is sometimes effective to have the intermediary who is to be the liaison with the particular publication place the story and/or use his by-line, although the story may actually be ghost-written by the publicist. This kind of personal handling will usually please the editor and frequently make the story of greater value to the publication and of greater interest to its readers.

Developing the campaign. To cover special magazines on a significant scale will require extra manpower. To do a magazine publicity campaign, first draw up a list of the publications to be used. Because many magazines and magazine editors come and go rapidly, be diligent in keeping the list up to date. Check the magazines carefully and list them in a chart, including the name of the magazine, the editor, the address, and telephone number. Leave blank spaces for other information to be filled in after a personal approach has been made.

Approach each editor, preferably in person or by telephone. Discuss with him the suggested subject. Sell the editor on using the story you have in mind. Learn how long a story he will take, what his deadline is, how much of what kind of art he will accept, and any angles he would like to have stressed.

After the preliminary survey, a complete work chart will include a column on deadlines, which tells the dates by which the material is due. Another column notifies at a glance how many and what kind of pictures are desired. The job then is to research for information and write the copy to fill the specifications. After mailing the copy and pictures to the editors, or sending them by messenger, it sometimes pays to follow up with a discreet telephone call to ascertain whether the material satisfies the editor's standards.

There are several other techniques for reaching many magazines simultaneously. In some cases mass copies of a memo or story will get good results with a large group of trade or technical publications interested in the general subject being covered. Editors may use the mimeographed releases as they are or revise and slant them to fit the particular publication's requirements and interests. Frequently such releases lead to negotiations resulting in special stories.

Another technique for servicing a large group of magazines simultaneously is to arrange a group tour for editors and writers. Some tours may consist of a planned afternoon in a plant. Others may be a long trip covering a big installation or series of installations.

Class magazines. The "upper bracket" periodicals deal chiefly with expensive recreations, quality clothes, fashions, styles, and elegant living. They are potential media chiefly to publicists whose clients deal in such things. Leading class magazines are:

> *Gentlemen's Quarterly,* 488 Madison Ave., New York, N.Y. 10022
> *Harper's Bazaar,* 717—5th Ave., New York, N.Y. 10022
> *Promenade,* 45 E. 45th St., New York, N.Y. 10017
> *Town and Country,* 717—5th Ave., New York, N.Y. 10022
> *Vogue,* 350 Madison Ave., New York, N.Y. 10017

Women's and home magazines. Excellent media to reach women, because they are read so thoroughly by them, is the group of magazines that deals with the planning, building, furnishing, and landscaping of the home; with clothes and fashions; with children; with the needs of career women; and with other subjects important specifically to women. Leading magazines in this category include:

> *American Baby,* 575 Lexington Ave., New York, N.Y. 10022
> *American Home,* 641 Lexington Ave., New York, N.Y. 10022
> *Apartment Life,* 1716 Locust St., Des Moines, Iowa 50336
> *Baby Care,* 52 Vanderbilt Ave., New York, N.Y. 10017
> *Baby Talk,* 66 E. 34th St., New York, N.Y. 10016

Better Homes and Gardens, 1716 Locust St., Des Moines, Iowa 50336
Bride's Magazine, 350 Madison Ave., New York, N.Y. 10017
Cosmopolitan, 224 W. 57th St., New York, N.Y. 10019
Essence Magazine, 1500 Broadway, New York, N.Y. 10036
Family Circle, 488 Madison Ave., New York, N.Y. 10022
Family Safety, 425 N. Michigan Ave., Chicago, Ill. 60611
Flower and Garden Magazine, 4251 Pennsylvania Ave., Kansas City, Mo. 64111
Glamour, 350 Madison Ave., New York, N.Y. 10017
Good Housekeeping, 959 Eighth Ave., New York, N.Y. 10019
Gourmet, 777 Third Ave., New York, N.Y. 10017
House Beautiful, 717 Fifth Ave., New York, N.Y. 10022
House & Garden, 350 Madison Ave., New York, N.Y. 10017
Ladies' Home Journal, 641 Lexington Ave., New York, N.Y. 10022
Ladycom, 520 N. Michigan Ave., Chicago, Ill. 60611
Lady's Circle, 21 West 26th St., New York, N.Y. 10010
Mademoiselle, 350 Madison Ave., New York, N.Y. 10017
McCall's Magazine, 230 Park Ave., New York, N.Y. 10017
Modern Bride, 1 Park Ave., New York, N.Y. 10016
Mothers' Manual, 420 Lexington Ave., New York, N.Y. 10017
Ms., 370 Lexington Ave., New York, N.Y. 10017
National Business Woman, 2012 Massachusetts Ave., NW, Washington, D.C. 20036
New Dawn, 99 Park Ave., New York, N.Y. 10016
New Woman, 2900 N.E. 12th Terrace, Ft. Lauderdale, Fla. 33307
Parents' Magazine, 52 Vanderbilt Ave., New York, N.Y. 10017
Playgirl, 1801 Century Park East Ste. 2300, Los Angeles, Calif. 90067
Redbook, 230 Park Ave., New York, N.Y. 10017
Seventeen, 850 Third Ave., New York, N.Y. 10022
Sphere, 500 N. Michigan Ave., Chicago, Ill. 60611
Sunset Magazine, Menlo Park, Calif. 94025
Tan Pride, 2514 N. 24th St., Omaha, Neb. 68111
Viva, 909 Third Ave., New York, N.Y. 10022
"W", 7 E. 12th St., New York, N.Y. 10003
Woman's Day, 1515 Broadway, New York, N.Y. 10036
Women Today, Suite 2102, 261 Fifth Ave., New York, N.Y. 10016
Workbasket, 4251 Pennsylvania, Kansas City, Mo. 64111
Working Woman, 110 E. 59th St., New York, N.Y. 10022

Canadian:

Chatelaine, 481 University Ave., Toronto, Ont. M5W 1A7, Can.
Homemaker's Magazine, Yonge Eglinton Centre, 2300 Yonge St., Toronto, Ont. M4P 1E4, Can.
Young Family, 37 Hanna Ave., Box 8, Station C, Toronto, Ont. M5W 1A7, Can.

Men's magazines. Counterpart to the women's and home magazines, the men's group includes:

Argosy, 420 Lexington Ave., Suite 2540, New York, N.Y. 10017
Esquire, 488 Madison Ave., New York, N.Y. 10022
Gallery, 99 Park Ave., New York, N.Y. 10016
Hustler, 36 W. Gay St., Columbus, Ohio 43215
Oui, 919 N. Michigan Ave., Chicago, Ill. 60611
Penthouse, 909 Third Ave., New York, N.Y. 10022
Playboy, 919 N. Michigan Ave., Chicago, Ill. 60611
Stag, 575 Madison Ave., New York, N.Y. 10022

Juvenile magazines. Dealing largely with matters of appeal to children, the juvenile magazines are of interest chiefly to publicists with long-range programs designed to reach today's youth with the objective of influencing the adults of tomorrow. Chief juvenile magazines include:

American Girl, 830 Third Ave., New York, N.Y. 10022
Boys' Life, Route #130, North Brunswick, N.J. 08902
Children's Playmate Magazine, 1100 Waterway Blvd., P.O. Box 567B Indianapolis, Ind. 46206
CO-ED, 50 W. 44th St., New York, N.Y. 10036
Trails, Pioneer Girls, Inc. P.O. Box 788, Wheaton, Ill. 60187
My Weekly Reader, 245 Long Hill Rd., Middletown, Conn. 06457

Scholastic Magazines, 50 W. 44th St., New York, N.Y. 10036

Teen, 8490 Sunset Blvd., Los Angeles, Calif. 90069

Intellectual magazines. This chiefly unillustrated group is valuable mostly for disseminating ideas. They reach those who lead the thought and often the actions of others. Chief intellectual magazines are:

The American Mercury, P.O. Box 1306, Torrance, Calif. 90505

American Scholar, 1811 Q St., NW, Washington, D.C. 20009

The Antioch Review, P.O. Box 148, Yellow Springs, Ohio 45387

The Atlantic Monthly, 8 Arlington St., Boston, Mass. 02116

Atlas World Press Review, 1180 Ave. of the Americas, New York, N.Y. 10036

Commentary, 165 E. 56th St., New York, N.Y. 10022

Commonweal, 232 Madison Ave., New York, N.Y. 10016

The Critic, 180 N. Wabash Ave., Chicago, Ill. 60601

Foreign Affairs, 58 E. 68th St., New York, N.Y. 10021

Harper's Magazine, 2 Park Ave., Room 1809, New York, N.Y. 10016

Hudson Review, 65 E. 55th St., New York, N.Y. 10022

Midstream, 515 Park Ave., New York, N.Y. 10022

The Nation, 333 Sixth Ave., New York, N.Y. 10014

The New Republic, 1220—19th St., NW, Washington, D.C. 20036

Quote, The Weekly Digest, P.O. Box 4073, Station B, Anderson, S.C. 29621

Saturday Review, 488 Madison Ave., New York, N.Y. 10022

Sewanee Review, University of the South, Sewanee, Tenn. 37375

Smithsonian, 900 Jefferson Dr., Washington, D.C. 20560

South Atlantic Quarterly, Duke University Press, Box 6697, Durham, N.C. 27708

Virginia Quarterly Review, 1 W. Range, Charlottesville, Va. 22903

Vital Speeches of the Day, Box 606, Southold, N.Y. 11971

Yale Review, 399 Temple St. 1902A Yale Stn., New Haven, Conn. 06520

Digests. Reader's Digest is the dean, in point of age and size, of the digests, which reprint most of their material from other magazines, newspapers, books, and various publications. Their material is in the main of general interest. Because so much of their material is reprinted, they offer a less susceptible field for a direct approach than most publications. Some of them do use original material. Leading periodicals in the digest group include:

Catholic Digest, P.O. Box 3090, St. Paul, Minn. 55101

Farmer's Digest, Box 363, Brookfield, Wis. 53005

Reader's Digest, Pleasantville, N.Y. 10570

Science Digest, 224 W. 57th St., New York, N.Y. 10019

Newsletters. Not magazines in the strict sense of the word, newsletters are usually four-page leaflets approximately 8½ X 11 inches in size, reproduced by offset, multigraph, or mimeograph, and purporting to present news and information of a confidential or semi-confidential nature about a given subject. Like the digest, the newsletter has become a large family of imitators with a small nucleus of well-established sucesses enjoying substantial circulation. The newsletter is a worth-while medium for a publicist covering a subject in its particular field, because it is likely to enjoy an intense, concentrated audience.

Many newsletters are listed in the National Directory of Newsletters and Reporting Services, Gale Research Co., Book Tower, Detroit, Mich. 48226.

Sport and hobby magazines. Some sports magazines cover specific sports like football, baseball, golf, and bowling; others cover the whole realm of sports. They are excellent media for sports publicists and for publicists plugging geographical localities through seasonal sports. Leading magazines include:

American Field, 222 W. Adams St., Chicago, Ill. 60606

American Rifleman, 1600 Rhode Island Ave., NW, Washington, D.C. 20036

Boating, 1 Park Ave., New York, N.Y. 10016

Bowling Magazine, 5301 S. 76th St., Greendale, Wis. 53129

Car Craft, 8490 Sunset Blvd., Los Angeles, Calif. 90069

Field and Stream, 383 Madison Ave., New York, N.Y. 10017

Flying Magazine, 1 Park Ave., New York, N.Y. 10016

Fur-Fish-Game, 2878 E. Main St., Columbus, O. 43209

Golf Magazine, 380 Madison Ave., New York, N.Y. 10017

Golf Digest, 475 Westport Ave., Norwalk, Conn. 06856

Guns & Ammo, 8490 Sunset Blvd., Los Angeles, Calif. 90069

Modern Photography, 130 E. 59th St., New York, N.Y. 10022

Motor Boating & Sailing, 224 W. 57th St., New York, N.Y. 10019

Motor Trend, 8490 Sunset Blvd., Los Angeles, Calif. 90069

Outdoor Life, 380 Madison Ave., New York, N.Y. 10017

Popular Photography, 1 Park Ave., New York, N.Y. 10016

Road & Track, 1499 Monrovia Ave., Newport Beach, Calif. 92663

Rudder, 1515 Broadway, New York, N.Y. 10036

Ski Magazine, 380 Madison Ave., New York, N.Y. 10017

Skiing, One Park Ave., New York, N.Y. 10016

Sport Magazine, 641 Lexington Ave., New York, N.Y. 10022

The Sporting News, P.O. Box 56, St. Louis, Mo. 63166

Sports Afield Magazine, 250 W. 55th St., New York, N.Y. 10019

Sports Car, P.O. Box 344, West Nyack, N.Y. 10994

Sports Illustrated, Time & Life Bldg., 1271 Ave. of the Americas, New York, N.Y. 10020

Travel, 51 Atlantic Ave., Floral Park, N.Y. 11001

Travel & Leisure, 61 W. 51st St., New York, N.Y. 10019

World Tennis, 383 Madison Ave., New York, N.Y. 10017

Yachting, 50 W. 44th St., New York, N.Y. 10036

Institutional magazines. An institutional magazine is the official organ of some specific organization of people united in their interests, occupations, ideas, religion, or social life. Institutional magazines include religious, fraternal, university, lodge, and organization publications.

An official organ is must reading for the devoted members of a movement, and in addition it is usually scanned by the casual members. With material in an institutional publication, the publicist is certain of an attentive readership in a specific stratum of society; here he can slant his material to register definite ideas to fit a known pattern of thought.

Many institutional magazines fall also into other classifications. *Boys' Life,* for example, is both a juvenile magazine and the official organ of the Boy Scout movement. Leading magazines in the institutional field are:

The American Legion, 1608 "K" St., NW, Washington, D.C. 20006

Columbia (Knights of Columbus), P.O. Drawer 1670, New Haven, Conn. 06507

Eagle Magazine, 2401 W. Wisconsin Ave., Milwaukee, Wis. 53233

The Elks Magazine, 425 W. Diversey Pkwy, Chicago, Ill. 60614

Future (Junior Chamber of Commerce), P.O. Box 7, Boulder Park, Tulsa, Okla. 74102

Kiwanis Magazine, 101 E. Erie St., Chicago, Ill. 60611

Leatherneck Magazine, P.O. Box 1918, Quantico, Va. 22134

The Lion, York and 22nd Sts., Oak Brook, Ill. 60521

Moose Magazine, 100 E. Ohio St., Chicago, Ill. 60611

The Rotarian, 1600 Ridge Ave., Evanston, Ill. 60201

Scouting Magazine, North Brunswick, N.J. 08902

V.F.W. Magazine, Broadway at 34th St., Kansas City, Mo. 64111

The publicist can expand this list in the particular field he desires to cover, by research into the various organizations connected with the particular institutional field.

CITY AND STATE MAGAZINES

A field that is becoming important and that offers many opportunities for publicity programs in their areas are the magazines dealing with interests of individual cities and states. These include:

Boston, 38 Newbury St., Boston, Mass. 02116

Charlotte Magazine, 12211 Westinghouse Blvd., P.O. Box 15843, Charlotte, N.C. 28210

Chicago, 500 N. Michigan Ave., Chicago, Ill. 60611

Cincinnati, 120 W. Fifth St., Cincinnati, O. 45202

Cleveland, Keith Building, 1621 Euclid Ave., Cleveland, O. 44115

Colorado, 7190 W. 14th Ave., Denver, Col. 80215

Connecticut, 831 Black Rock Turnpike, Fairfield, Conn. 06430

The Magazine of Dallas, 2902 Carlisle St., Dallas, Tex. 75204

Denver, 8000 E. Girard, Suite 210, Denver, Colo. 80231

Hudson Valley, P.O. Box 265, Pleasant Valley, N.Y. 12569

Kansas City, Box 2298, Shawnee Mission, Kan. 66201

Los Angeles Magazine, 1888 Century Park East, Los Angeles, Cal. 90067

Miami Magazine, 3361 SW 3rd Ave., Miami, Fla. 33145

New Mexico Magazine, 113 Washington Ave., Santa Fe, New Mexico, 87503

Palm Beach Life, 265 Royal Poinciana Way, Palm Beach, Fla. 33480

Palm Springs Life Magazine, 250 E. Palm Canyon Dr., Palm Springs, Cal. 92262

Philadelphia Magazine, 1500 Walnut St., Philadelphia, Pa. 19102

Phoenix, 4707 N. 12th St., Phoenix, Ariz. 85014

Sacramento Valley Magazine, 3609 Marconi Ave., Sacramento, Cal. 95821

San Diego Magazine, P.O. Box 81809, San Diego, Cal. 92138

St. Louisan, 7110 Oakland Ave., St. Louis, Mo. 63117

The Washingtonian, 1828 L St., N.W., Washington, D.C. 20036

Yankee, Dublin, N.H. 03444

BUSINESS MAGAZINES

Business publications range from nationally known outlets, such as *Nation's Business* and *Business Week,* to local business reviews with a limited circulation. General business magazines are news and feature publications covering the immense field of business for the business executive.

Fortune devotes detailed articles to major business organizations and developments. *Business Week* covers the field of business as comprehensively as a news magazine covers general news. It has field editors in American sectional business capitals such as San Francisco, Chicago, Detroit, and Washington. Backing up this organization is an array of "string men" who, on a commission basis, cover other important business centers by correspondence. Any of these field editors or string men are glad to receive acceptable business news from publicists in their territories.

Leading business magazines and periodicals are listed in Chapter 11.

Agricultural magazines. A number of important magazines circulate exclusively or chiefly to farmers and constitute effective media for conveying a message to them. A list of widely circulated farm papers includes:

Farm Journal, 230 W. Washington Sq., Philadelphia, Pa. 19105

Prairie Farmer, 2001 Spring Rd., Oak Brook, Ill. 60521

The Progressive Farmer, 820 Shades Creek Parkway, Birmingham, Ala. 35209

Successful Farming, 1716 Locust St., Des Moines, Ia. 50336

Wallaces Farmer, 1912 Grand Ave., Des Moines, Ia. 50305

Trade publications. Trade publications are craft magazines circulating to specific industrial groups or trades and to members of trade organizations. *Iron Age* is a trade publication that reports the metal industry to businessmen interested in the metal trades. *Editor and Publisher* is a trade publication that circulates news about their business to editors, publishers, publicists, and advertisers.

In this category for our purposes may be included technical and professional magazines and, sometimes, agricultural publications—although the latter category is sufficiently distinctive to justify a separate classification.

Designed for doctors, lawyers, architects, and other professional men, the technical and professional publications are limited in their appeal. Their content, usually highly technical, is restricted to the particular group's professional mysteries. Only when the publicist has a subject of obvious interest to a professional group will its journals be eligible vehicles for publicity messages.

Usually the public relations worker will find it desirable to build his own list of trade publications to fit the particular organization, client, or campaign he is serving. For example, to publicize the annual Home Show of Southern California, a list of more than one hundred publications was built up from such sources as the fifteen sponsoring trade associations, publicity men in the construction field, classified telephone directories, *Ayer's, Bacon's Publicity Checker,* and *Standard Rate and Data.* As a campaign develops, editors not on the list will hear about it and ask to be included, which adds to the scope of the coverage.

Included among trade publications are those limited to a specific trade, such as the bakers, and those limited to a certain organization, such as the journals of the American Medical Association and similar organizations, national and local.

Also included are more general scientific and

technical magazines such as *Popular Science, Scientific American,* and *Popular Mechanics,* which are of interest to a great many trades. Another type is the publication such as *Television,* which in general covers an entire industry. These magazines are frequently outlets for product publicity and other business publicity.

In almost every category there are dozens of trade and specialty magazines. Here, too, a list will crisscross many categories.

For example, in directing publicity for a major manufacturer of heavy machinery there are more than 50 metal trade publications, 60 petroleum publications, 50 municipal and county publications, 25 civil engineering and construction publications, 25 aviation and aerospace publications, 15 building publications, 15 business and commercial publications, 25 electrical and electronics publications, and many others to consider. Among these, the publicist may prefer to work exclusively with one magazine in each field, or he may use a saturation approach as in the case of an announcement for an important new product.

In working with the trade and professional press, the publicist can often rely heavily on the standard news release and the captioned photograph. Frequently his material will be used approximately as presented, provided it meets all the usual journalistic standards. Sometimes it will be edited or rewritten or included partially in round-up stories and survey articles. Trade names and other product data including model numbers are included in many trade releases.

Trade editors are as eager for fresh material as their consumer counterparts, and will often work receptively with a publicist on an exclusive feature of benefit to their readers.

In developing and using lists of trade publications, constant reference to *Ayer's, Standard Rate and Data, Bacon's Publicity Checker,* or *The Working Press of the Nation* is essential. (See Chapter 38.) The number, variety, and scope of these publications demands careful analysis and selection in each case.

Internal house magazines. These publications, sometimes called employee or company publications, are published for and about employees by business organizations. They constitute one of the most effective resources of modern public relations. For most outside publicity subjects, house magazines are generally inaccessible. Their subject matter is confined in the main to treatment of the company that publishes it and its people.

Some extraneous matter of interest to all employees is sometimes admitted, such as publicity about the Community Chest, public welfare activities, and general public information. If the company is participating in an outside event—for example, a sponsor of The Miss America Contest—the activity may be publicized in the company publication.

Company publications sometimes furnish excellent outlets for publicists representing firms that use the company's products. Such publicity, explaining the end use of the products, by helping to educate employees of contracting firms constitutes good supplier relations and tends to expedite production.

Although there were a few house magazines as far back as the 1880's, today the *Gebbie House Magazine Directory,*[9] lists more than 4,000 company publications of all types. Their readership probably exceeds fifty million.

External company publications. Of greater value to the publicist than a company's internal publication is its external publication. Generally, this magazine is mailed free to stockholders and customers (present or potential) and to community leaders and business executives whom the company would like to familiarize with its story.

These external house publications today number 10,000 as compared with about 8,000 in 1966, according to directory officials.

Original artwork, graphic design, and informative articles that sell "softly" if they sell at all characterize the best of external house magazines. Many of these publications compare favorably with general consumer magazines in terms of circulation, writing, artistic talent, and originality of ideas. Deere & Company's *Furrow,* Ford Motor Co.'s *Ford Times,* and *DuPont Context* are examples.

Most external house publications utilize a magazine-type format, and most of them carry articles on a wide variety of subjects in each issue. Travel, fashion, art, international problems, social problems, and space exploration are typical external magazine fare.

Publicists wanting to use the medium of company publications—either internal or external—may most quickly develop a list pertinent to the need by using the *Gebbie House Magazine Directory.*

[9] 424 N. 3d St., Burlington, Iowa 52601

42

Books and Other Publications

Herbert M. Baus
Philip Lesly

Books are being used increasingly as public relations media. They are employed in several ways.

Efforts may be made to have suitable information included in books published by others, particularly textbooks. There has been a tendency for American textbooks to stress the "robber baron" side of business rather than its contributions as the source of America's standard of living and its comparative international strength. To some extent this tendency is the result of neglect by business, which in many instances has failed to make its story and facts available to the scholars who write textbooks. Consequently authors have been left to other sources, which often feature such documents as the records of legislative investigations and other atypical situations.

Increasing effort has been made by businesses and their trade associations to tell the constructive business story in textbooks.

Many books in themselves constituted tremendous propaganda campaigns, such as *Das Kapital* by Karl Marx, *Mein Kampf* by Adolph Hitler, the works of Voltaire, Harriet Beecher Stowe's *Uncle Tom's Cabin,* Wendell Willkie's *One World,* and Gunnar Myrdal's *An American Dilemma.*

Other books written by authors for a profit may have a publicity value to certain sources, such as travel volumes like Pan American Airways' *Passports and Profits* and the series of travel guides published by Mobil Oil Company. Some books of this sort are stimulated or subsidized by the potential users, rather than published as their own by the companies.

Sometimes an organization has its own book written, as a company history or a service to the field it functions in. Such a public relations book is more solid and more personal than space or radio advertising, more permanent, but more limited in range. A clothbound book has one major advantage—it is seldom thrown away. In many cases, it is also seldom read. Judgment requires that the book be of vital interest or use to the audience, rather than written from the viewpoint of the sponsor.

Constructive books about business portray the spirit and personality of an organization, particularly when it performs a useful function for the recipient.

A clothbound book is a handsome gift that includes appreciation and carries with it an implied obligation to read and preserve it. It makes the recipient feel that he has been singled out for a distinction. The drawbacks to books as media are the comparatively high cost of the individual unit, the difficulties of widespread distribution, and the uncertainty that the entire message will be read.

Arranging for publication. A sponsored book may be privately printed and issued by the sponsor; but if it has true merit as a book, and real likelihood of being read, it can probably be issued by an established publishing house as part of its regular book list. There are three common methods of arranging this with any one of a number of well-known publishers:

(1) *Underwriting*. The sponsor agrees to cover any costs (plus a reasonable margin of profit) not recovered by the publisher from sale of the book. Costs to the sponsor can ultimately range from nothing to virtually 100 per cent of the cost of

editing, printing, binding, handling, and distributing the work.

(2) *Purchase of copies.* The sponsor agrees to buy for his use and distribution a quantity of copies at an agreed-on price. The total is usually enough to insure the publisher a profit, no matter how few copies may be sold through regular channels.

(3) *Subsidy.* The sponsor makes an outright payment to the publisher, sufficient to insure profitability of the venture.

In all cases, of course, the publisher insists that the book meet standards of quality and integrity in keeping with his reputation in the publishing business. Even after sponsorship has been agreed on, the publisher may refuse to put his imprint on it if it is likely to be criticized by respected critics for puffery, distortion, or other abuses. The more honored and valued the colophon of the publisher, the better the book must be—and the more effective it is likely to be as a spokesman for its sponsor.

Some excellent books have been issued through sponsorship. *Everything and the Kitchen Sink*, sponsored as a service to industry by Crane Co. during its Centennial in 1955, was widely lauded by critics, government officials, educators, and businessmen. More than 5,000 copies were distributed by the U.S. Department of State to its libraries all over the world as an excellent means of clearly and simply depicting the human benefits that have resulted from American industrial enterprise.

A three-volume history of the Ford Motor Company by Allan Nevins and Frank E. Hill was written by these distinguished historians with the full cooperation, but not the review, of the company. It was widely praised by reviewers, historians, and educators for its thoroughly objective treatment. Though it contains material the present members of the Ford family probably would prefer be forgotten, it has raised the general esteem of the company among opinion leaders.

Some other books that have been subsidized or written with the "supervision" of the subjects, however, have drawn scorn from the intended audiences. They have been prose versions of the romantically flattering portrait that is admired only by the subject or his descendents and usually can hange with honor nowhere but in the company's board room.

A few "vanity" publishers are in the business primarily of issuing books for payment by the authors. These rarely receive any attention, but copies are as useful as books printed for the sponsor with no colophon.

PAPERBACK BOOKS AND MINIBOOKS

The paperback book became a medium of public relations a few years after the burst of popularity of these low-cost volumes in the 1940s. Their use has been accelerated by the rise in price of newsstand paperbacks from their original 25 cents to a range between $1.75 and $3.50. The cost of the books when ordered in large quantities by a commercial sponsor makes it possible to sell them at the attractive rate of about 50 cents and thereby liquidate their cost. The Maytag Company recouped the full cost of producing its *Encyclopedia of Home Laundry* in less than three years. It has put 500,000 copies into use among home economics teachers, public utility home economists, dealers, and consumers. In

Figure 42-1. Since there was no book available that contained all information about laundering needed by a housewife, Maytag prepared this paperback and underwrote its publication. It has been sold to schools, utilities, and dealers.

addition, several thousand copies were sold through regular book outlets.

There are two basic arrangements for publication of a paperback by a commercial organization:

1. Commitment for a specified number of copies to be produced by a regular publisher of paperbacks. This calls for a volume that the publisher agrees meets desired standards for its imprint and sale. In this arrangement, the sponsor gains the prestige and acceptance of the publisher's imprint among the public, and some sales through normal book channels, handled by the publisher for whatever return it will bring. It is rare, however, for a sponsored book to get much display space, and therefore sales are well below what would be required to make an unsponsored publication worthwhile to the publisher.

2. Having the book produced for the sponsor's distribution only. This may or may not carry the imprint of the publisher. This procedure permits being more direct in fostering the sponsor, and can be targeted to a precise audience.

Examples of the first type, aside from the *Maytag Encyclopedia*, include the *Home Comfort Handbook* (sponsored by the National Fuel Oil Institute); the *Weyerhaueser Building and Remodeling Book* and *Home Decorating Made Easy; Top Form Book of Horse Care* (Merck & Company); and *Westinghouse Cook Book*.

Examples of the second type include *Feel of the Road* (Ford); *Elementary Fishing* (Garcia Corporation); and *Vision—The Story of Boeing*.

Another growing practice is syndication of books. The Benjamin Company produced *How to Manage Your Money* and arranged for production, with different covers, for various banks in the United States. *Consumer's Buying Guide* was produced for various Better Business Bureaus, and then sold for public-relations use to various manufacturers, utilities, and savings institutions. A shorter version may be produced of a book developed for another sponsor, where a nonexclusive arrangement has been made by Benjamin.

Firms active in the paperback book field are:

The Benjamin Company, 485 Madison Ave., New York, N.Y. 10017

Dell Distributing, Inc., 1 Dag Hammarskjold Plaza, New York, N.Y. 10017

Popular Library, Inc., 600 3rd Ave., New York, N.Y. 10016

The Snibbe Company, 140-1 Overbrook Blvd., Belleair Bluffs, Fla. 33540

Costs will vary depending on the number of pages, the number of illustrations, quality of paper, and how much color is used. For art and production—exclusive of editorial costs and internal illustrations—an order of 500,000 copies will range from about 20 cents to 70 cents a copy.

A later development is the minibook. While the typical paperback measures about 4 ¼ x 7 ¼ inches and about 150 to 200 pages, the minibook measures 3 ½ x 5 inches and contains about 64 pages.

While most minibooks are produced for use as premiums and in sales promotion, some have public relations purposes. Examples include *Questions and Answers about Contact Lenses*, produced for Barnes-Hinds Ophthalmic Products, and *A Complete House Plant Guide*, for Plantabbs Corporation.

Minibooks—or "purse books"—are a prominent service of Dell Distributing, Snibbe, and The Benjamin Company. Cost, exclusive of preparation of the contents, range from about 3 ½ cents in quantities of 5,000,000 to about 22 cents at the 100,000 level.

PUBLICITY THROUGH CARTOON BOOKLETS

The cartoon booklet medium, once considered for children alone, is now doing a man-size public relations and promotion job. No longer are cartoon books pure entertainment. They are being used to sell products subtly, to win votes, raise money, organize workers, educate, and put over messages. Some of the better ones are directed at a well-educated level.

Principal commercial users of cartoon booklets are large corporations and trade associations that employ them as public-relations or sales-promotion tools, most notably the electric and gas utilities.

Several branches of the U.S. Government, too, have made widespread use of such booklets. Church, labor, and political movements also use this medium as do more than 2,000 schools that supplement classroom teaching in specific courses of study with cartoon books.

Some users employ made-to-order cartoon books. Others find stock commercial cartoon books for imprinting serve their purpose. In many cases, sponsors of cartoon booklets are able to check results carefully.

Consumers Power Company, Jackson, Michigan, first offered two cartoon books in its catalogue on resources available for teaching use. Modest requests were received. When a third

BOOKS AND OTHER PUBLICATIONS

Figure 42-2. A page from a cartoon booklet, prepared for electric companies to distribute to school children. It tells the story of the development of nuclear energy to generate electricity, with emphasis on the safety of such use of atomic power.

booklet was published samples were mailed to teachers. Large orders came in for the new one, and for the first two as well. In the first nine months of this procedure more than 128,000 booklets were provided for school use in the company's service area.

The company began to use cartoon books with reservation because it felt teachers might have a negative reaction to this form of literature. According to Romney Wheeler, former Director of Public Relations:

> We suspected teachers might tend to associate any cartoon books with non-educational publications like *Batman* and *Superman*. Yet, cartoons have been used to convey information ever since the first cave drawings. Michelangelo used cartoons as the preliminary drawings on which he based his masterpieces. Hogarth used cartoons for savage satire. Indeed, it has been only in the last 50 years that cartoons have become identified with comic books and comic strips.

When the teaching value of this form of material was pointed out to the teachers, they agreed. Content of the booklets is heavily informative and nonpropagandistic.

Prices of cartoon books vary. A made-to-order booklet will involve preparation of a script, artwork, engravings, and printing in color on newsprint stock. A 16-page booklet, 7" x 10", self-cover will cost from about 3 to 4 cents a copy in lots of a million or more.

Today there are about a dozen cartoon book publishers. Some are newsstand publishers who handle every phase of the commercial job, from story line to printing and drop shipment. Some use creative studios that handle the entire job, subcontracting for the printing. Some specialize in miniature books used for package inserts, premiums, and giveaways. Some specialize in books with coloring pictures, quizzes, and games.

Leading suppliers of cartoon books for public relations use are:

Custom Comics, Inc., 10 W. 19th St., New York, N.Y. 10011

Dell Distributing, Inc., 1 Dag Hammarskjold Plaza, New York, N.Y. 10017

SPECIAL PUBLICATIONS

The literature of an organization—the reports, histories, surveys, pamphlets, brochures, directories, books—can range from unpretentious mimeographed leaflets to expensive tomes done in velour with plastic covers.

Of vital importance is skilled technical assistance on art, layout, typography, and composition. Frequently a public relations man who is not himself a specialist on such publications will find it wise to consult with a specialist who will supervise the production. In such an event it is standard practice to allow the specialist a fixed fee in advance to produce a complete dummy for approval before final arrangements are made. That will make possible a cost analysis of the over-all job and will produce a clear picture to the client of what kind of a publication is being developed.

The publication should be planned on the basis of: budget; objective; length; amount of art; amount of type; sectional breakdown; and general style.

The experienced public relations man will guard against too elaborate a production, to avoid seeming extravagant. At the same time he will guard against falling below proper quality standards. In public relations work this rule is a sound one—DO IT WELL OR NOT AT ALL.

For information about types and production of printed materials, see Chapter 51.

READING RACK BOOKLETS

Many factories and offices offer small booklets on helpful subjects that are displayed in racks. Employees are encouraged to take them. The companies that produce these and sell them to the employers sometimes accept suggestions for topics and material to be used in them. They include National Research Bureau, Burlington, Iowa 52601. Copies of these booklets may be purchased in quantity for secondary distribution to an organization's members or supporters, employees, stockholders, or others.

Figure 42-3. An employee reading rack, placed near the time clock where all employees will see it and have time to make a selection.

43

Television and Radio Publicity

Philip Lesly

Television is now the most pervasive and most influential medium of mass communication. Combining sight, the spoken word, and immediacy, it brings a multitude of impressions and bits of information into almost all homes in North America and to many in other countries. To millions of people today, the selected segments of programming that show on their picture tubes are more "real" than other aspects of their lives.

Radio, at the same time, continues to bring immediate impact to millions. In less-developed countries where TV is not yet predominant, radio is the invisible cord of communication that holds societies together or spreads dissension.

While humanity had hundreds of thousands of years to accommodate to speech, thousands of years to adjust to writing, and 500 years to spread the impact of printing, it has had scarcely one generation to absorb the broadcast media. Millions of active people are alive who were educated before even radios were common in homes.

To the publicist this presents a number of challenges. Much of the population is still oriented toward print media for their information, their ideas, and their motivations. Millions of others are predominantly affected by the broadcast media and by motion pictures. Clearly, no program that uses one form exclusively is likely to reach the full audience. And no publicist who is oriented primarily toward one form is likely to be fully effective.

The "media gap" is a hard reality among the circumstances under which communications functions are planned and carried out.

The broadcast media continue to evolve rapidly. They are structured and operated quite differently in various countries. Even the Canadian system—in which the government-operated Canadian Broadcasting Company is prominent[1]—is markedly different from that in the United States.

In the U.S broadcasting stations are licensed by the federal government, unlike print media, because of the limited number of broadcast channels that can be used without chaos. The authority for licensing is administered by the Federal Communications Commission. Stations are granted licenses to serve the public interest, convenience, and necessity. These licenses are subject to renewal, though for years the renewal was automatic and the license often can be sold for millions of dollars.

Changes in social patterns, such as the desire among minority groups for a greater voice, have made the licensing of stations a public issue.

Other developments that have a bearing on the pattern of broadcasting in the U.S. include:

• *Community Antenna Television (CATV)* that transmits many types of programs into homes, offices, and schools by cables that do not affect the limited span of the broadcasting band. This can multiply the number of stations, the variety of programming, and the source of financing. Besides providing potential outlets for films, news, and interviews in competition with broadcast TV, CATV is capable of helping the viewer shop by exhibiting available products, showing stock tickers, electronically transmitting newspapers, sending mail, carrying police and fire communications,

---

[1]The CBC operates television networks in English and French; two AM radio networks, two FM networks, and a Northern Service in six languages—Innuit (Eskimo) and native peoples' languages as well as English and French; an International Service in 11 languages; and a service for Canadian Armed Forces abroad. An independent television service—CTV Television Network Ltd.—operates nationally. In addition, a number of publicly owned independent stations provide their own programming.

connecting each outlet with centralized libraries and data banks, delivering telegrams, and providing two-way banking transactions and information.

- *Pay-TV*, involving the individual's selection of programs he chooses to see at a specified charge.
- *Space satellites* that not only transmit live programs immediately over vast distances but may bypass the network and perhaps even the local station and carry programs directly to the receiving set from almost anywhere in the world.
- *Videotapes* that can capsule programs, much like home movies, to be shown at any time on any properly equipped receiver. These can permit delayed viewing of regular telecasts or selection from a vast variety of recorded cartridges with educational, hobby, cultural, or other programming.
- Utilization of the TV receiver in conjunction with *information banks, computers,* and *facsimile systems.* This will enable the individual to call on the resources of the central bank for any information, news, feature material, entertainment, or other material—and in many cases make a paper copy of what he wants.

In a field where developments have been so rapid, it is vital that the publicist keep ahead of changes in order to know what the facilities are and how to use them.

WORKING WITH BROADCAST MEDIA

The electronic media differ from print media for the publicist in these key ways:

1. Development of broadcasting put predominant emphasis on entertainment—music, humor, adventure, drama. There is comparatively little room for information and persuasion.

2. The broadcast signal is ephemeral. Until recording and storage practices advance, the shows reach tuned-in audiences only and seldom are repeatable to those audiences or to those who missed them.

3. The broadcasts are much less susceptible to promotional use than magazine and newspaper articles, which can easily be reprinted and distributed.

4. While the impact of a broadcast is great when it occurs, its intangibility leaves the publicist less able to demonstrate his results to his client if they were not tuned in at the time.

The publicist should consider the distinct features of the two major types of broadcast media.

Television

The major characteristics of television that are important to the publicist are:

- The immediacy and personal identification with personalities and ideas that television brings directly into the home.
- The effectiveness of television as a means of persuasion—combining sight, sound, motion, and immediacy with personal involvement of the audience.
- The great flexibility in showing timely events whenever the audience is available, aided by the development of magnetic videotape.
- The opportunities through closed-circuit television to inform large audiences at a single showing about new products and services, events at a meeting of shareholders, new techniques in surgery, and many other subjects for widely scattered but specialized audiences.
- The growth of public information programming. Numbers of large corporations now sponsor or initiate public service features. Safety quizzes, panel shows, and debates are all used for public information purposes.

Radio

The principal characteristics of radio that are important to the publicity person are:

- The strong listener identification created by enlisting the listener's imagination to complete an impression.
- Radio's ability to reach people outside the home—driving on expressways, sunbathing at the beach, etc.
- People can pursue other activities—eating, housework, do-it-yourself projects—and listen to radio at the same time.
- The around-the-clock news coverage that is provided by many stations has accustomed people to rely on radio for news and weather. More of the total broadcast schedule is based on conveying information and comment on radio than on television.
- The "open mike" or audience telephone programs give listeners a sense of participation and active interest in the events under discussion.
- The excellent sound reproduction available on good stereo and FM receivers attracts many discerning and well-educated people who now spend little time with commercial TV or AM radio.

BROADCASTERS AND ACTIVISM

Sensing both the impact of television and the penchant of broadcasters to feature action and excitement, various groups of activists have shaped their entire existence to get TV coverage. Often issues are selected and events are planned solely with television in mind. If the TV stations cover it, it is considered successful. If TV ignores it, no matter what the merits of the "issue" or the "event," the activist group knows it has failed.

The organization that may be subject to such activist efforts is at a great disadvantage in this situation. It usually cannot know where or how the attack will come, and it is restrained by a need to be responsible that often is not felt by the attackers.

The impact of action and controversy as exhibited on television screens is so great, every organization must try to overcome these disadvantages.

This calls for the following functions:

1. Constant alertness to which groups may be singling out the organization for attacks, what their issues may be, and how they generally operate.

2. "Inoculating" the broadcasting news staffs against unquestioned acceptance of the legitimacy of what may be attempted or charged, by providing them in advance with background on the matters involved. They should also be provided with film footage, stills, names and contact points of spokesmen, and other materials that will help them get balanced coverage should something occur.

3. Briefing officials on how to handle themselves in various types of situation—demonstrations, riots, shouted insulting accusations, provocative questioning by reporters, and so forth.

4. Keeping the print media informed in advance and given full cooperation in anticipation of various events. Balanced treatment in one type of medium helps to deter other media from going overboard for a sensationalized effort to manipulate the news. All media are increasingly sensitive to being proved unsound in their treatment.

STRUCTURE OF BROADCAST MEDIA

The origin of programs varies greatly. Network shows usually come from New York or Los Angeles. Networks also pick up "remotes" from member stations, relaying the shows in turn to other outlets. A national network broadcasts to as many as 300 stations.

Independent stations originate their own programming. Other stations are either owned by a network or affiliated with a network. If network-owned and -operated, the station normally carries much of the programming originated by the network. If affiliated, a station exercises a wider choice in its programming. Stations associated primarily with one network sometimes broadcast programs from other networks. In one-outlet cities, a station may carry programming originated by all three major networks.

Syndicates produce and distribute programs to local stations as well as to networks, selling the right to use programs they produce. These independent contractors are also known as packagers.

For audience-participation shows that give merchandise prizes, some independent contractors serve as brokers in obtaining the products to be awarded. Many such programs are completely produced by independent packagers.

Other syndicators distribute news feature and institutional films, but most syndicated material is in the quasi-entertainment category.

TYPES OF PROGRAMMING

Programs on radio and television fall into two basic categories: *information* or *entertainment*.

Information includes news, special events, and public information shows.

Entertainment includes audience-participation programs, panel or game shows, interviews, and show business formats—dramatic programs of all kinds, variety programs, and the like.

Personnel. These people are responsible for radio and television programs:

- *Program managers* supervise all programming at an individual station.
- *News managers* supervise all news-type programs, directing cameramen and reporters.
- *Producers* are in charge of overall presentation and supervision of a program: timing, content, casting, technical requirements. Producers are often responsible for originating show ideas. At individual stations, the producer may write material and act as interviewer or star as well.
- *Writers* research and write a comprehensive script, ready for broadcast.
- *Directors* put the various elements of a show together and develop it into a smooth unit.
- *Announcers* read or present copy prepared by writers.

Broadcasting personnel and programs change frequently. When the size of the audience falls or fails to meet expectations, program personnel are sometimes replaced. New personnel are added as shows expand or modify formats.

The publicist must keep up-to-date on changes in both programming and personnel.

ARRANGING FOR BROADCASTS

In working with various levels of broadcasting, the publicist finds many similarities. Networks, syndicates, and individual stations all produce news, public-service, and entertainment programs.

In general, *information* and *public-service* shows offer greatest potential outlets for publicity materials. However, *entertainment* programs are also receptive to good ideas and content.

Information programs. Information shows—which include news, public-service, and special-events programs—offer a wide range of opportunities. There are three basic types of shows:

(1) *News shows* are the most common single type of program on radio and television, national or local.

Gaining acceptance on a network news show is a challenging assignment. The story must have major significance and the publicist must adhere to good journalistic standards: copy must be accurate, objective, factual, terse.

Radio and television newsrooms almost always subscribe to one or more of the news wire services. A large percentage of broadcast news comes from these sources. Therefore, material accepted by news services often gets on the air.

Along with a news release aimed at television the publicist may include a still photograph (mat finish) for reproduction "on camera." Pertinent motion-picture footage is even more welcome.

Newsroom staffs are small. News directors welcome imaginative and professional outside material. Once the publicity man proves himself a reliable source, he can hope to get consistent coverage.

(2) *Public-service shows.* By Federal Communications Commission policies, a percentage of broadcast hours should be educational or cultural. The public-service program helps meet this requirement.

Included are shows that interpret and explain historical significance of news, explain worthy causes, offer practical advice, or explain scientific and technical developments.

The publicist often finds an effective vehicle in the *documentary,* a program designed to interpret history and current events or to explore economic, philosophic, religious, or cultural subjects.

Documentary techniques on radio and television are basically journalistic. The material could also be used to write a series of feature stories in a magazine or newspaper. The producer works from interviews and other information to form an overall profile.

A radio documentary is composed of taped interviews, commentary, and sound impressions. Television adds the picture, movement, and color.

Facts and statistics, locations suggested for filming, possibilities for interviews, suggestions for subjects—all are welcomed by documentary researchers, writers, and producers. Material covering vital social, economic, political, and governmental issues is particularly well received.

Producers of special commentary, discussion, and so-called *think* programs will consider suggestions on topics and authoritative guests. The publicist sometimes suggests a team of guests who present parts of an overall theme, one of whom is the publicist's spokesman. In some cases, producers demand controversy. In this event, the publicist would be wise to point out the controversial aspect of the subject and, perhaps, suggest a guest who would take the opposing viewpoint from his spokesman.

Suggestions are submitted to producers of public affairs programs at the network. Since many documentaries are produced by news divisions, contact with the news staff is also appropriate.

Public-affairs shows at individual stations are

Figure 43-1. An articulate spokesman on a topic of listener or viewer interest is welcome at many local radio and TV stations. Along with talks before women's clubs and at retail outlets, Mrs. Mary Lou Rooney of 3M Company (left) makes many such appearances.

similar to the network formats, with the appeal more localized.

At a local station, the newsroom is usually the hub of public-service activities. Material can be directed to the program director, as well. Local issues frequently suggest documentary themes: how one state lowered its highway death rate with a sound sign program; how one community organized an amateur symphony orchestra.

Panel discussions or authoritative interviews on local issues are often welcome.

(3) *Special-events shows* include roundtable and panel discussions, individual interviews apart from regular programs, talks, monologues, and scientific or other demonstrations. Programs may comprise several elements—for instance, a monologue followed by an interview, a debate followed by a demonstration.

Also included are live or taped coverage of sports events, religious and educational services and ceremonies, presentations, groundbreaking ceremonies, open houses, ribbon cuttings, dedications, activist rallies, political speeches, parades, and other events not covered on regular programs.

A special event often does not exist until someone suggests it. Therefore, the publicist is free to conceive of an entire program.

Entertainment programs. There are five basic types of entertainment programs:

(1) *Audience-participation shows* in which products or services are often given away as prizes to winners. Prominent and favorable on-the-air exposure of the product is given in exchange for prizes donated. Game shows, both local and national in origin, are found more on television than radio. The publicist makes his arrangements with the syndicator or station producing the show.

(2) *Panel shows,* which provide opportunities for personal appearance of prominent representatives of a client, spokesman for a point of view, or authority on a product.

Formats of panel shows vary. Some use guests with occupations, identities, or other characteristics that must be uncovered by a panel of participants. Producers welcome suitable suggestions. Requirements for gaining acceptance of a suggestion are often specific, such as an amusing occupation, an unusual documented biography, a unique product demonstration, a *first* of some sort.

(3) *Magazine-format programs* may include a variety of elements—music, interviews, monologues, exhibitions, filmed features. Usually an established host serves as master of ceremonies.

Magazine programs on local stations are especially receptive to suggested materials. At an individual station, contact with the program director or station manager is called for.

Magazine programs, although included in the *entertainment* grouping, are often partially *informational*. This is particularly true of women's-interest and farm-interest shows.

In many areas, farm and women's commentators are influential personalities in the community. Inclusion on one of their shows, implying endorsement, often offers valuable exposure of a subject.

(4) *Talk programs,* whether the conversation variety on television or the "open mike" type on radio, fit into both the *informational* and the *entertainment* categories. Producers of these shows are very receptive to suggestions from the publicist, whether the suggestions be topics for discussion or possible guests.

The radio audience-participation program, in which listeners are invited to telephone the station to participate in a discussion or to ask questions of a guest, is a common type of radio program. Used originally by small-town radio stations, this format was adopted by a St. Louis station, and before long stations all over the country were using it.

Some of the television conversation programs, telecast by local stations, also invite audience participation via telephone to give opinions, ask questions, etc.

(5) *Show business formats—variety and dramatic programs*—offer the least opportunity for the publicist. One approach is lending products as props for television programs. Another is arranging for a product or service to be included in the action of a dramatic script.

However, these techniques are comparatively unpredictable and time consuming. Most of the time they are comparatively expensive.

HOW TO APPROACH BROADCASTING PEOPLE

Professionals are conscious of these day-to-day techniques in dealing with broadcasting people:

• In the first talk or letter, state clearly what client, firm, or service is represented. Be specific in your suggestion of an idea, story, guest, or prop. Instead of asking a producer how an idea might fit into his show, show through your suggestion that you understand what the program uses.

• Contact the person responsible for making the decision. On network programs, associate producers often handle the various aspects of the same program. Only one is assigned to your interest. Find

```
MEMO TO BROADCASTERS:

In spite of all our modern laundry appliances, it sometimes seems as though
Grandma had it easier on washday.  At least she didn't have as many decisions
to make.  She had only cotton and linen to wash ... and only soap, bluing
and lye to get the laundry clean.

Today's homemaker is confronted with an almost countless number of finishes,
fabrics and blends, plus innumerable laundry aids.  No wonder washing can be
so confusing.

But it needn't be.

"THIS IS THE WAY WE WASH OUR CLOTHES," a 13½-minute educational film produced
by the Maytag company in cooperation with the University of Illinois audio-
visual department, demonstrates a simplified approach that has been developed
for laundering with today's automatic equipment.  Now the homemaker needs to
know just six basic laundering procedures, no matter how many kinds of fabrics
she has in her washbasket.

Available in black-and-white or color, "THIS IS THE WAY WE WASH OUR CLOTHES"
is offered to you exclusive in your television area.  If you would like to
receive a print for screening and possible use on your station, please fill
in and return the attached postcard.



Consumer Information Center

Attachment
```

THE MAYTAG COMPANY / *Newton, Iowa 50208* / *Telephone 515-792-7000*

Figure 43-2. Memorandum to television program directors, offering an informational film for use. The nature of the film is described in detail, and the non-commercial nature of the content is indicated.

him. Others may be willing to listen but are unable to make a decision.

• The broadcasting publicity specialist is meticulous about detail. He rehearses guests well in advance of interviews. He briefs the producer about the guest. He assembles product photographs and artwork for television flip cards. He submits biographies of guests. He suggests discussion questions. Above all, he delivers what he promises—on time.

• Broadcasters usually prefer a brief memo or letter following the telephone call, outlining the program ideas. Detail what has been agreed, and confirm a scheduled recording, broadcast, or rehearsal.

HOW TO BE EFFECTIVE IN TV INTERVIEWS

Perhaps the most common opportunities for an organization to reach a television audience are through interviews of its spokespersons, or their participation in panels. This is a distinctive type of communication, different from all others that the individual may have experienced. Here are some tips to the interviewee for assuring effectiveness and forestalling a negative effect:

1. Remember that television is show business. Everything from heart disease to a distant war is treated in terms of dramatic effect. Broadcasters know from experience that their best efforts to really educate the audience by providing substantial background and detail result in poor ratings.

2. As much as possible, give answers and dramatize dangers; do not just explain or give reasons. Television dramas, documentaries, and commercials always wrap the subject up neatly. The audience has been trained to expect pithy points and tied-up ends, and so do television interviewers.

3. Visualize yourself in the average person's living room, not with your peers at the University Club. But do not talk down. The audience is not sophisticated or knowledgeable, but it is not stupid.

4. Don't express an opinion if you can cite a fact. But if you are an expert in the field being discussed, you may cite your views as being based on the study that has made you an expert.

5. Study the style of the interviewer in advance. Does he help the interviewee by leading his comments, or does he try to show up the guest? Does he talk much or leave most of the exposition to the interviewee?

6. Prepare in advance three or four cogent, terse sentences that make your key points. These are most likely to survive editing and to get on the air; and they are the hardest to edit into conveying another meaning. Watch for the chance to use these, even if you have to answer a question only obliquely. Then you need not be dependent on the interviewer to ask the questions that will enable you to make your points.

SYNDICATING SELF-PRODUCED PROGRAMMING

The publicist may produce and syndicate his own material. Types of activity that may be included:

• A *recorded interview* for radio on tape can be mailed to stations that request it after receiving a call or letter about its availability.

• *Scripts* can be mailed directly to stations, suggested for inclusion on existing programs.

• *News and feature stories* can be written for broadcasting, directed at existing news shows.

• *Film for television* can be produced and circulated to stations. News films are usually 30 seconds to 60 seconds in length; feature films can run four to five minutes; institutional films fit 15- and 30-minute time slots. Color film is usually required.

Success in self-syndication requires professional material with a minimum of overt commercial mention. The publicist must understand the medium's needs, produce quality material, and be meticulous in servicing it. Skilled personnel in close proximity to the major broadcast centers are also valuable.

Particularly recommended are brief instructional materials available from the National Association of Broadcasters, 1771 N Street, NW, Washington, D.C. 20036. The booklet, "If You Want Air Time," for example, suggests preparation of filmed or taped materials in professional form and includes examples of public service announcements.

SOURCE FILE ON BROADCASTING

National radio and television networks.

American Broadcasting Company, 1330 Avenue of the Americas, New York, N.Y. 10019

Columbia Broadcasting System, 51 West 52nd Street, New York, N.Y. 10019

National Broadcasting Company, 30 Rockefeller Plaza, New York, N.Y. 10020

Radio only.

Mutual Broadcasting System, 1755 Jefferson Davis Hwy., Arlington, Va. 22202 and 60 E. 42nd St., New York, N.Y. 10017

Regional networks.

Regional radio and television networks offer little benefit to publicity people. Some groups of stations band together to sell commercial time but do not interchange programming.

However, others broadcast programming simultaneously when a major news event is involved, and some originate programs and syndicate them to other stations. Publicity arrangements are best made with individual stations or with networks. Any additional coverage from regional groups is a bonus.

Special networks.

Voice of America, division of U.S. Information Agency, Health Education & Welfare Building, 330 Independence Ave., S.W., Washington, D.C. 20547

More than 100 separate VOA programs are broadcast via shortwave daily in 37 languages. VOA guests are frequently interviewed in a foreign language, although extensive fluency is not required. Feature interviews usually concern aspects of American business, industry, and life.

Figure 43-3. Recording footage for television showing with portable video tape equipment. Instant replay permits the participants to judge what they have done and to edit or replace any portion. L.C. Michelon of Republic Steel Corporation is the speaker.

Armed Forces Radio Service, 1117 N. 19th St., Arlington, Va. 22209.

Programs reach American servicemen and their families stationed outside the continental limits of the U.S. Broadcast coverage includes news, features, and interviews in a wide range of categories. The sound portions of some network television programs are also broadcast on this service.

Programming service for public and university radio stations.

Educational Broadcasting Corporation, 304 W. 58th St., New York, N.Y. 10019.
Major source of programming distributed nationally to 250 public television stations by the Public Broadcasting Service.[2]

[2]See Chapter 44.

National Public Radio, 2025 M St., N.W., Washington, D.C. 20036.[2]

Individual radio and television stations.

Sources for information on individual radio and television stations:

Radio and TV Directory, The Working Press of the Nation, The National Research Bureau, Inc., 424 N. 3rd St., Burlington, Iowa 52602.

This directory lists major radio and TV stations throughout the U.S., Canada, and territorial possessions, including categorized sections on kinds of programming, supervisory and creative personnel.

International Television Almanac, Quigley Publishing Company, Inc., 1270 Avenue of the Americas, New York, N.Y. 10020.

TV Publicity Outlets Nationwide, Box 327, Washington Depot, Conn. 06794.

This publication includes national, local, and regional TV and radio stations, personnel, broadcasting celebrities, special services for film production, recording, foreign and special programming facilities.

Television Contacts, Larimi Communications Associates, 151 E. 50th St., New York, N.Y. 10022.

U.S. Publicity Directory, 353 Nassau St., Princeton, N.J. 08540.

These directories list specific shows available to publicity people.

Broadcasting Yearbook, Broadcasting Publications, Inc., 1735 De Sales St., N.W., Washington, D.C. 20036.

This yearbook lists national and local stations, supervisory and creative personnel, government regulation information, background information, technical and historical information.

Television Factbook, Television Digest, 1836 Jefferson Pl., N.W., Washington, D.C. 20036.

This directory lists all television stations in the United States and Canada and their technical facilities and production personnel.

TV Film Producers include:

Avco Embassy Pictures Corp/TV, 1301 Ave. of the Americas, New York, N.Y. 10019. Also Memphis and Los Angeles.

Columbia Pictures Television, Colgems Sq., Burbank, Cal. 91505.

Crawley Films Ltd., Box 3040, Ottawa K1Y 3B5, Canada. Also Montreal and Toronto.

Bing Crosby Productions, 780 N. Gower St., Hollywood, Cal. 90038.

Walt Disney Productions, 500 S. Buena Vista St., Burbank, Cal. 91505.

Don Fedderson Productions, 1626 Vine, Hollywood, Cal. 90028.

Filmways Inc., 1800 Century Park East, Suite 300, Los Angeles, Cal. 90067. Also New York.

Alan M. Fishburn Productions, 333 N. Michigan Ave., Chicago, Ill. 60601.

Goodson-Todman Productions, 375 Park Ave., New York, N.Y. 10022. Also Hollywood, Cal.

Hearst Metrotone News, 235 E. 45th St., New York, N.Y. 10017. Also Washington, D.C.

MCA TV, 445 Park Ave., New York, N.Y. 10022. Also Cleveland, Universal City, Cal., Chicago, Dallas, Atlanta, Minneapolis-St. Paul, Philadelphia, St. Louis.

National Telefilm Associates, 12636 Beatrice St., Los Angeles, Cal. 90066. Also New York, Toronto, London, Paris, Athens, Mexico City, Rio de Janeiro, Buenos Aires, Sydney.

Fred A. Niles Communications Centers, 1058 W. Washington Blvd., Chicago 60607. Also New York and Los Angeles.

Paramount Television, 5451 Marathon St., Los Angeles, Cal. 90038. Also New York, St. Louis, Chicago, Marietta, Ga., London, Sydney, Toronto.

Rose-Magwood Productions, 1414 Ave. of the Americas, New York, N.Y. 10019. Also Hollywood, Cal., Toronto, Chicago, New York.

20th Century-Fox Television, 10201 W. Pico Blvd., Los Angeles 90035.

United Artists Television, 729 Seventh Ave., New York, N.Y. 10019. Also Chicago, Culver City, Cal., Toronto, Cincinnati.

Warner Bros. Television, 4000 Warner Blvd., Burbank, Cal. 91505. Also New York.

WGN Continental Productions, 2501 W. Bradley Pl., Chicago, Ill. 60618.

TV Film Distributors include:

Association-Sterling Films, 866 3rd Ave., New York, N.Y. 10022. Also Dallas, Atlanta, LaGrange, Ill., Sun Valley, Cal., Ridgefield, N.J.

Modern Talking Picture Service, 2323 New Hyde Park Rd., New York, N.Y. 11040. Also Atlanta, Chicago, Cincinnati, Dallas, San Francisco, Summit, N.J., Don Mills, Ont., Canada.

A DIVERSIFIED BROADCASTING EFFORT

An illustration of how broadcast publicity can be integrated into a total publicity program is the activity of the 3M Company. Aside from its corporate information and advertising activities on TV and radio, the company conducts five product-related functions:

1. Packages of material on a given product, including a script and samples of the materials involved. For instance, for a Christmas theme the package included adhesive, wrapping materials, and ribbon, plus a script for use by the TV station's announcer.

2. A traveling home economist who is interviewed by TV and radio stations in major cities, which she visits for this purpose and to promote the

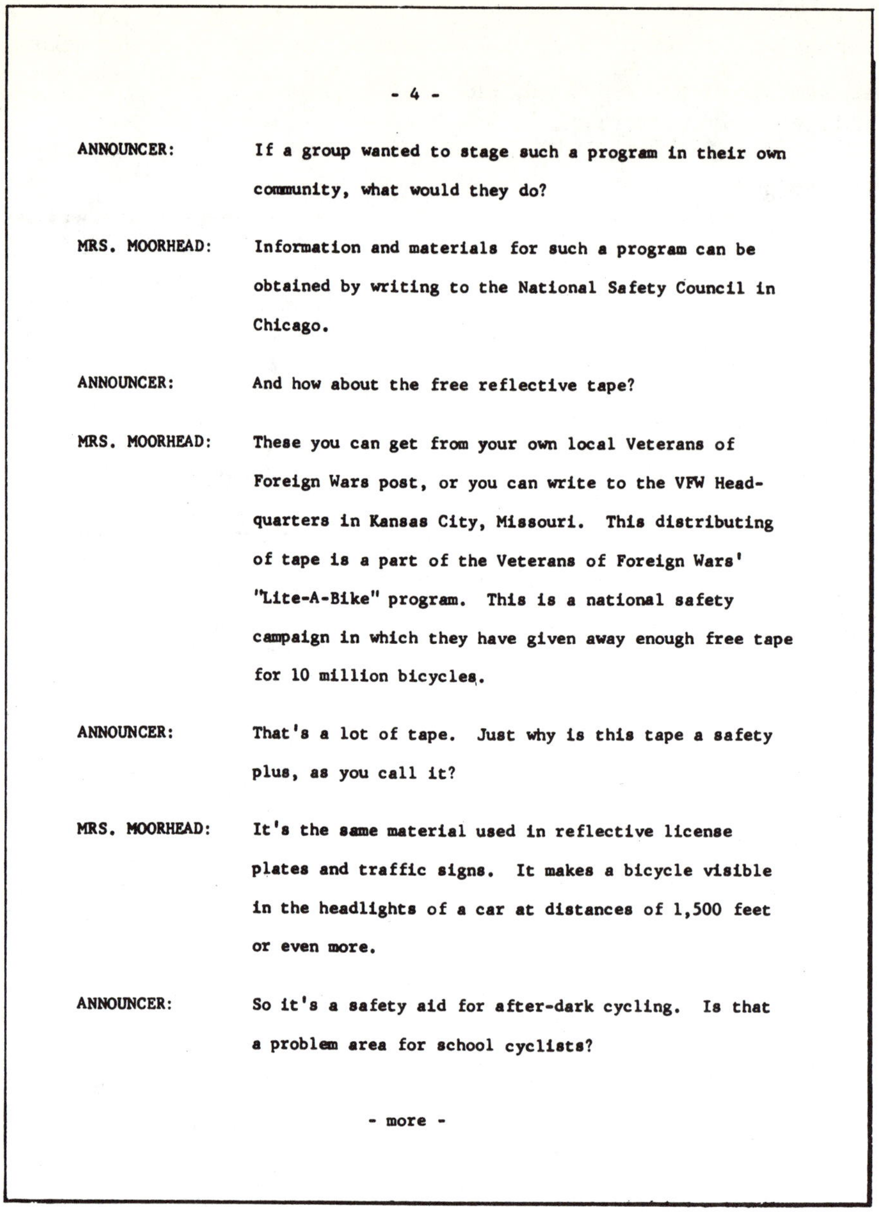

```
                - 4 -

ANNOUNCER:      If a group wanted to stage such a program in their own
                community, what would they do?

MRS. MOORHEAD:  Information and materials for such a program can be
                obtained by writing to the National Safety Council in
                Chicago.

ANNOUNCER:      And how about the free reflective tape?

MRS. MOORHEAD:  These you can get from your own local Veterans of
                Foreign Wars post, or you can write to the VFW Head-
                quarters in Kansas City, Missouri.  This distributing
                of tape is a part of the Veterans of Foreign Wars'
                "Lite-A-Bike" program.  This is a national safety
                campaign in which they have given away enough free tape
                for 10 million bicycles.

ANNOUNCER:      That's a lot of tape.  Just why is this tape a safety
                plus, as you call it?

MRS. MOORHEAD:  It's the same material used in reflective license
                plates and traffic signs.  It makes a bicycle visible
                in the headlights of a car at distances of 1,500 feet
                or even more.

ANNOUNCER:      So it's a safety aid for after-dark cycling.  Is that
                a problem area for school cyclists?

                              - more -
```

Figure 43-4. A page from a script for a radio interview show. The interviewer directs the course of the discussion with his questions but leaves most of the comment to the guest, who is usually an expert in the field involved.

products before women's clubs, retailer organizations, and others.

3. Institutional films for TV, such as a 70-second sequence on the company's power unit in the signaling equipment left on the moon by Apollo 11. This was accompanied by a script, and was timed to reach the stations a day before the launch of the moon rocket.

4. Movie footage and scripts designed to help the sales of the company's customers (such as fabric producers who use its soil repellent).

5. Scripts designed for radio use only, sent to selected lists of stations that use this type of service material.

CAPITALIZING ON BROADCAST COVERAGE

Favorable exposure on radio or television is a worthwhile accomplishment in itself. However, to get full benefit from the broadcast the publicist must:

• Report the event completely and clearly to the personnel of his organization or client.

- Promote interest in the program through other media.
- Examine the broadcast material for secondary uses.

Reporting on results. Newspaper and magazine coverage can be reported through clippings and tear sheets from the publication, or through reproductions. Similarly, moderate-priced equipment is available for making off-the-air videotapes of programs. The Sony Betamax is in use in many public relations offices. Videotapes made this way may not be rebroadcast because of copyright regulations.

Ideally, of course, the publicist will alert concerned officials before the show is broadcast so they can tune in the actual program. However, broadcasting is most unpredictable, so caution should be voiced that while a show is *scheduled* at such-and-such a time, last-minute changes may interfere.

Further, alerting everyone is not always advisable or economic. Therefore, publicity people generally seek other reporting methods. A number of ways are available when videotapes cannot be made off the air because the broadcast time is not known or because equipment is not available:

(1) *Scripts* reporting verbatim on the show. If the publicity aspect of the show is short, it can be recorded by personal monitoring.

(2) *Videotapes* can sometimes be purchased from the television network or station.

(3) Still photographs of a guest at a broadcasting studio—sometimes with the show's master of ceremonies—illustrate coverage effectively. Pictures are worthwhile adjuncts to tapes or scripts.

Publicizing the broadcast. When a person or product is featured on a broadcast, this event itself can be handled as news. Alert publicists get additional benefit from radio and television coverage through magazines, newspapers, and trade publications.

An announcement story preceding the broadcast is often appropriate. This offers another opportunity to talk about the organization, service, product, or idea. Publicity about a show also helps increase its audience.

Advance stories timed for release to coincide with the broadcast are particularly appropriate when a speech or discussion can be reported as news, quoting the program as the source.

After the broadcast, stories can be distributed to newspapers, business, and specialized publications. Pictures taken at the studio are often well received, particularly by trade publications in the field of the organization involved. Publicity about the show should follow news standards, quoting the guest or broadcaster briefly and significantly.

Publicity staffs at networks and larger stations are often helpful. By supplying the station's publicity people with advance material about a guest or product, the publicist may get additional coverage at little cost.

Secondary uses for broadcast material. After arranging broadcast coverage and promoting it internally and externally, the publicity man should examine the broadcast material for other uses.

Scripts, broadcast reports, tapes, and films—at one time or another—can be pressed into additional service:

- Reports and scripts make effective mailing pieces to dealers and field representatives.
- Tapes and films are valuable aids for sales meetings, showing coverage that backs up the efforts of the selling force.
- Pictures and reports can be used as editorial material for the organization's publications.
- Live audiences—stockholders, schools, clubs, civic groups—are frequently eager to view films produced for television.
- Rebroadcasts are often possible. When a film or tape has been used in one city, the publicist can often arrange additional broadcasts on other stations. Broadcast film clips are often held and resubmitted for use in a documentary program.

44

Public Television and Radio

JEANE RIDGE YOUNG has been engaged in public relations for public broadcasting since 1967 when she became Community Relations Director for the public television and radio stations in Memphis, Tenn., where she was also on the faculty of the Memphis State University Journalism Department, teaching courses in public relations. Previously she had served on the journalism faculty of the University of Evansville (Ind.) and the public relations staff of the University of Wisconsin Extension Division. She was a member of the first national public information advisory committee for public television, becoming its chairman in 1973. In December, 1973 she joined the Public Broadcasting Service (PBS) as Public Information Director.

Mrs. Young holds a B.S. degree from Memphis State University and took graduate study at the University of Wisconsin. She is the mother of two adult children.

Public television in the United States is the largest television network in the world with 265 stations dotting the nation from Maine to American Samoa and other noncontiguous points in Alaska, Guam, Hawaii, Puerto Rico, and the Virgin Islands. Because of its geographic spread, its growing audience numbers, the relative affluence and influence of its audience, and its reputation for quality television, public television offers unique public relations opportunities for business, industry, and non-profit organizations.

LOCAL AND NATIONAL OPPORTUNITIES

Public relations opportunities with public television exist mainly at two levels. One is with the local station for local community impact. (Unlike the major commercial networks, the public "network" is not fully interconnected but operates primarily through interchange of films and tapes.) The other is at the national or "network" level. Both levels provide opportunities that vary considerably from those of commercial television.

The stations. At this writing, more than 150 organizations are licensed to operate the more than 265 public television stations in existence.

All stations are responsible to their local communities and have complete freedom and responsibility to select and schedule programs for their own broadcast in response to the needs and interests of their local communities. Most stations produce and air local community-interest programs and many produce and air programs specifically designed for school and other educational uses. Public relations directors of business, industry, and non-profit organizations should stay in touch with local stations. Many opportunities exist to place experts on discussion shows, gain access to public-service time, and participate in stations' community activities. Station policies differ throughout the system.

Many stations produce programs for national

distribution (nearly all national programming comes directly from the stations themselves) with stations in New York, Boston, Washington, Pittsburgh, Chicago, and Los Angeles providing most of the major productions. Opportunities to underwrite national programming are available through producing stations.

The Public Broadcasting Service. The Public Broadcasting Service (PBS) is the national organization of the public television stations. It is responsible for the selection, scheduling, promotion, and distribution of the national program service, for the coordination of numerous station services, and for representation of the stations' interests on the national level. It is located at 475 L'Enfant Plaza, S.W., Washington, D.C. 20024, (202) 488-5000.

The Corporation for Public Broadcasting. The Corporation for Public Broadcasting (CPB) is a private, non-profit corporation established pursuant to the Public Broadcasting Act of 1967 to foster the development of the nation's noncommercial television and radio stations. It receives and distributes federal funds for radio and television and assists in a variety of system activities including audience research, professional training, and technological development. CPB is located at 1111 16th Street, N.W. Washington, D.C. 20006, (202) 293-6160.

Audience. The public television audience has been increasing steadily as the result of more households being able to receive a good public television signal, improved program quality, and increased availability of money for promotion, publicity, and advertising. More than 35 million homes were viewing PBS-distributed programs in March 1976, representing 50.4% of the nation's TV households, according to an A.C. Nielsen survey.

While audience figures are small compared with commercial broadcasting the audience "quality" is significant to organizations considering program underwriting as part of their public relations programs. The public television audience tends to be:

- From households headed by a professional or white collar worker
- In middle- to upper-income brackets
- Among the better educated, with heads of households having attended one or more years of college

Public television also tends to reach audiences with their special, rather than general, interests—music, drama, analysis of news and public affairs,

(Courtesy WTTW/Chicago)

Figure 44-1. Intelligent discussions of ideas are a basic part of public television. Here Robert Cromie interviews Saul Bellow, Nobel Prize winner, on "Book Beat," which originates in Chicago and is carried on many public TV stations.

health and consumer information, quality children's programming.

National program underwriting. National program underwriting by corporations and associations grew from barely a dozen in 1972 to nearly 50 by 1977. These organizations contributed nearly $14 million in 1976, more than 23 percent of the total funding for national programs that year.

Organizations' reasons for making underwriting grants to public television are as different as the organizations, but seem to have one major purpose in common—the opportunity to be identified with what is considered a quality public service that reaches an audience selective in its viewing habits and often influential.

When Prudential Insurance made its first public television program grant in 1976, its chairman and chief executive officer Donald S. MacNaughton said, "Business may be the life-blood of the body politic, but culture is its soul. Each needs the other. . . . The public expects business to go beyond the production of goods and services and to make additional contributions to the general quality of American life." Measuring the value of those contributions is not easy but tangible evidence is available. That first Prudential venture—a one-time-only special—netted 18 known stories in major publications in addition to 17 television appearances and 20 radio appearances by stars of the show. Prudential was credited in much of the print and in every radio and TV interview except two.

In 1976 three Silver Anvil Awards were made by the Public Relations Society of America for programs involving public television. Gulf Oil Corporation and its agency received two of them for the PBS National Geographic Special "The Incredible Machine." This program presented a unique view of the human body from the inside.

While non-commercial underwriting guidelines limit on-air recognition to a simple underwriter credit at the beginning and end of a program, the public relations opportunity came from the television program serving as a peg for major off-air publicity and promotion. Gulf, which saw its involvement with National Geographic and public television as an opportunity to improve the public's perception of the company as a public-minded corporation, undertook a campaign to reach national magazines, dailies, weeklies, wire services, syndicates, and freelance writers covering regions with PBS stations; its own customers, employees, and shareholders; and the educational and professional community.

Gulf distributed more than 3,000 press kits. One thousand formal announcement cards went to a prestige group including its own senior management, members of affiliated Boards of Directors, and selected media.

Gulf used its own channels of communication by providing four-color posters to its dealers; including a feature article in *Gulf Dealer News;* providing 3.5 million flyers in mailings of bills to credit customers; and including a special feature in its own *Orange Disc* employee publication.

Access to other information/promotion channels was effected with nearly three-quarters of a million reprints of the *Orange Disc* article included as inserts in public television stations' program guides; on-air television spots aired in every public television market; and the National Geographic Society carrying special articles in *National Geographic* and *World Magazine* with a combined circulation of more than 10 million.

The educational community was also a prime target, with scholastic poster-teleguides going to more than a half-million teachers; Prime-Time School Television poster/guides also to teachers; and the entire issue of *World Traveler,* a magazine distributed to 28,000 schools, homes, clinics, hospitals, and correctional institutions, devoted to the special.

E.G. Marshall, host of the National Geographic Society series, made a nine-city promotion tour that resulted in wide press coverage.

The program was viewed in nearly 12 million households, the largest audience in public television's history, with a national audience share of 18 percent, double the previous public television audience record. Post-show studies showed significant improvements in attitudes toward Gulf among those who were reached by the campaign or the show.

REACHING THE COMMUNITY

Another reason for underwriting national programs is the potential for local impact through programs that afford opportunities to reach communities. A process unique to public television, this extends the value of a nationally telecast program into local communities. When Bristol-Myers underwrote "The Killers," a series of documentaries on the major causes of death in the United States, more than 100 communities carried local follow-up programs that ranged from phone-ins to full-fledged documentaries. Medical professionals and representatives of the local chapters of the American Heart Association and the American Cancer Society manned telephones, often for hours after the broadcasts, to provide viewers with expert information.

Because it feels public television makes a unique impact at the community level, 3M Company has specialized in supporting programs dealing with social and medical concerns that have the community aspect. When 3M underwrote "VD Blues" in 1972, the program and the underwriter were widely praised in publications throughout the country.

Most programs underwritten by 3M have involved controversy. Subjects have included alcoholism, problems of the elderly, and breast cancer. All included community activities that involved thousands of volunteers and dozens of major national organizations. In 1976 it underwrote "The Puzzle Children," a documentary about learning disabilities. Months before the program was to be aired, representatives of WQED, Pittsburgh (the producing station) and 3M were in Seattle urging the national convention of the Association for Children with Learning Disabilities to participate at national and chapter levels. Later similar presentations were made to the U.S. Department of Education, the American Medical Association, National Congress of PTA's, Kiwanis, National Education Association, and about 10 other organizations with an expressed interest in the project. 3M usually offers a small seed grant (around $300) to each station that broadcasts the program to

Figure 44-2. Underwriters of public television programs build both audience and recognition for their public-service role by advertising programs they fund. IBM ran this ad to support one of its underwritten programs.

stimulate follow-up telecasts. Station staff handles all the local coordination with chapters of the national organizations and other volunteers.

Promotion. Although underwriters receive on-air audio and video credit at the beginning and end of each program or hourly if the program runs longer than 60 minutes (a requirement of the Federal Communications Commission), the public relations opportunities come in the publicity and promotion campaigns that are cooperatively planned by the underwriter and/or its agency, the producing station, and the PBS staff (if the program is national) or the local station publicity staff, if the program is local. These campaigns usually consist of traditional audience-building activities such as program advertising and development of press kits, credit card statement stuffers, and special mailings.

Most underwriters find that corporate identification in press coverage of public television programs they support is considerably higher than for programs they sponsor on commercial television.

Reaching educators. An increasing number of underwriters have added another dimension by developing ancillary materials for school and other educational uses. Educational material relating to "The National Geographic Specials," "Theater in America," and "Nova," among others, has been made widely available to schools through local public television stations. "The Adams Chronicles" and "The Ascent of Man" were used as the basis for college credit courses at more than 200 colleges and universities. Underwriters and program producers work closely with the PBS Educative Services department to coordinate all parts of the public television system.

UNDERWRITING COSTS AND PRACTICES

While television production or acquisition can be expensive, not all underwriting grants are large. National program underwriting grants can range from as low as a few thousand dollars for a one-time special to several million for a major 13-week series. Increasingly, more than one underwriter—usually a corporation and a foundation—join to fund a program or series in which they have a mutual interest.

Opportunities for local underwriting exist in many public television markets and can be inexpensive while offering excellent local public relations opportunities.

To protect its non-commercial character and the public's perception of it, PBS has developed national program underwriting guidelines designed to assure that there is no editorial control by program funders; to guard against any perception of program control by funders; and to assure its non-commercial status. Local station guidelines vary but generally conform to the national ones.

LOCAL STATIONS

Several public television station activities lend themselves to public relations opportunities for local businesses, industry, and non-profit organizations:

1) *Locally produced community programs*— Most stations produce one or more programs with a local focus and look to community business and organizations as sources of expert information and program guests. Opportunities vary considerably station by station.

2) *Public service announcements*—Policies vary from those stations that will accept no public service announcements to community-minded stations highly responsive to requests. Who holds the station license—school board, college or university, state authority, or community foundation—is often the determining factor.
3) *Pledge nights and auctions*—These are an important part of the fund-raising activities of more than half the nation's public television stations. Local companies and organizations can gain on-air recognition and identification for their community involvement by having a company executive assist as an on-air performer or by donating goods or services to the auction. Auction donations have ranged from automobiles and fur coats to college tuition, apartment leases, and dry-cleaning certificates. The more imaginative the donation, the better its chances for generating newspaper recognition as well as an on-air credit.
4) *Local underwriting*—Many stations accept—and seek—underwriting for locally produced programs and to defray some of the local costs of acquiring national programs. Underwriting differs from sponsorship on commercial television in that it provides credit only on-air for the corporation, foundation, or organization and can not provide product information.

Organizations interested in underwriting national public television programs should contact the PBS Development Department at 75 Rockefeller Plaza, New York, N.Y. 10019, (212) 489-0945 or the development office of a producing station.

For discussion of programs or cooperative activities locally, the program director of the local public station should be contacted.

Public radio. National Public Ratio (NPR) is the networking organization for more than 200 public radio stations. Incorporated in 1970, it began broadcasting on May 3, 1971 with the first edition of "All Things Considered," an award-winning public affairs magazine-of-the-air. NPR offers about 45 hours of network programs each week to stations serving communities in 47 states, the District of Columbia, and Puerto Rico.

Since 1974, NPR has been accepting underwriting for radio broadcasts from foundations and corporations. Its most important national programming funded by a corporation has been "National Town Meeting," which features national leaders in responsive discussion and originates in Washington, D.C. NPR is located at 2025 M Street, N.W., Washington, D.C., 20036, (202) 785-5400.

There are about 35 AM and 900 FM stations that are either sponsored by educational institutions or operate as public broadcasters. They are located in most metropolitan areas. Their programming policies and broadcast content vary greatly, so it is necessary to study each one to determine what it may be interested in and to contact the program directors with suggestions on program materials.

45

Publicity in the Movies[1]

MARTIN M. COOPER, vice president, Harshe-Rotman & Druck, Inc., a public relations firm, has been associated with the motion picture field since 1962. His firm has represented the film industry's honorary professional association, the Academy of Motion Picture Arts and Sciences, for more than 20 years. Cooper supervises public relations activities for the Academy and its internationally telecast Oscar Program. He was previously associated with two major motion picture producing companies, Universal City Studios and Walt Disney Productions.

Whether projected on a 50-foot screen in a darkened theater or on the small TV tube, in the family den, film is one of the most powerful tools available to a communicator.

The influences of movies on the general public are well-known. The results of Clark Gable revealing only a muscled torso beneath his shirt led to a large drop in sales for the undershirt industry when "It Happened One Night" was released. On the other hand, the wardrobe of the characters in "Bonnie and Clyde" started a whole new fashion trend.

But these unanticipated movie-generated trends are the exception, not the rule. More typically, film depictions of products or locations are the result of hard work and close corporation between the publicity person and individuals involved in film production.

NEW PATTERN OF FILM AS A MEDIUM

In the early 1950's public relations professionals realized that there was a vast audience viewing films, an audience of more than 50 million Americans each week who were ready to be influenced by their products or services as depicted on the silver screen.

For the next two decades products were given to film executives to influence their choices. The same model of automobile that raced across the screen would occupy the producer's garage, the same brand of dishwashing detergent that appeared in a domestic scene would be found on the sink of the property master's kitchen, and the star's wardrobe would hang in his or her personal closet when production was completed.

An actor would take a drink from a readily identifiable bottle of Scotch . . . and would receive a case of the liquor each month for years. Legend still has it that one well-known film comedian has a warehouse filled with "gifts" from firms whose products he mentioned or displayed in his films.

Such activities were the exception, of course. Professional filmmakers expected products used in films to be supplied free since their depiction on the screen could boost the product's sales. Such activity was legal, common, and in the interest of the publicist.

Another promotional vehicle that proved to be mutually beneficial was the post-production tie-in. Whether initiated by a manufacturer or the studio publicity department, the results were mutually beneficial. The star of the film would pose with the product—such as a refrigerator—for full-page advertisements in major women's magazines. The advertising would also mention that the star was now appearing in such-and-such a film. Such ac-

---

[1] The author acknowledges the help of Sol Dolgin, whose chapter on this subject appeared in the first edition of *Lesly's Public Relations Handbook*.

tivities, which did not depend on the use of the refrigerator in the film, would stretch the advertising exposure the film received without adding to the studio's budget, while gaining the manufacturer a glamorous star to help sell his product. Today's independent top film stars are rarely likely to engage in such activities.

But the days of such close cooperation and mutual benefit became less frequent. Motion pictures have changed greatly in recent years, and so has the potential for using them as a publicity vehicle. The emphasis now is on tie-ins, rather than in-film use of product, although the latter still exists, particularly for such specialized subjects as automobiles, airplanes, and locations. Several factors brought this change about:

1. Television is the single largest factor. When TV first appeared, Hollywood's leaders scoffed at the "little box." Their scorn turned to panic, however, as theatergoers by the millions discovered they could enjoy film entertainment in the comfort of their own living rooms . . . and free. The star system faded, huge studio overhead could no longer be supported, and Hollywood appeared destined for ghost-town status.

Television programming executives soon realized, however, that the highest ratings were to be snared by using Hollywood films which had been stored in film vaults, and by providing movies-made-for-television.

So television became the savior of the industry it almost destroyed. But it altered the motion picture business so greatly that no longer could three or four major studios control most of the total production. Today studios supply as much film product to television as to theaters, and many films made for American television are released theatrically abroad. Conversely, many films distributed theatrically do not turn a profit until sold to a network or television syndicator a year or two after initial release.

2. Television has also complicated the situation because of product interchangeability. A film made for theatrical release might later be sold to television. Strict Federal Communications Commission (the FCC regulates TV) guidelines prohibit "plugs" within editorial programming. Also, potential sponsors of a television program will not buy into a film that has a competitor's product displayed prominently within it.

3. The "studio system" is greatly reduced. At one time the film industry supported five or six major studios and several secondary ones; now production companies produce the bulk of American film product. Many production companies work out of tasteful Beverly Hills offices rather than on sprawling movie lots, and hire technical, artistic, and theatrical people only as they need them. Today a publicist must work with dozens of prop men, assistant producers, and writers—not just a handful as in the past.

4. Exhibitors came to resent what they considered to be over-commercialism on the big screen. One studio publicity director recalls that in a few cases blatant film plugs caused theater owners to object so strenuously that initial prints had to be withdrawn and deletions made.

5. Fewer pictures are being made today than in past years. Almost from the inception of motion pictures shortly after 1900 to the early 1950's, going to the movies was a major outlet for the nation's leisure time. It was a family event, usually occurring one night a week, and on Saturdays for the children. The studios had to turn out hundreds of films a year to satisfy a seemingly insatiable demand. A major studio that once made 60 pictures annually now produces fewer than 20. And the fewer movies released, the fewer opportunities there are for publicity in films or promotion related to them.

6. Not only the numbers but the type of films being made has changed. The "small film," once the staple of Hollywood, has become the made-for-TV movie. Today's theatrical trend is toward the "big picture"—big in scope, big in budget, big in promotion.

7. The cost of attending a first-run movie has escalated. Recently tickets have jumped from $2.00 for a double-feature bill to $4.00 for a single-feature first-run film. While these increases have not been out of line with other general inflationary costs, they are competing with the free television programs.

As these factors have reshaped the movie business, they have altered the opportunities for the publicist. While most of the following points relate to theatrical motion pictures, the basic concepts are almost equally applicable to television dramatic programs.

PUBLICITY OPPORTUNITIES TODAY

Despite the gloom that one hears about the movie industry today, there are still excellent opportunities for the creative publicist to use motion pictures as a medium. Although the scope and type of such use varies greatly, publicity in the movies can be divided into three major areas: use of locations, in-film promotion, and tie-ins.

Locations. One of the most basic elements of any film is the location. Historically, Western films have been shot in undeveloped areas of the West, films shot in urban locations have been photographed on city streets, and interiors have been recreated within giant Hollywood sound stages. Since the advent of talkies in the late Twenties, sound stages have provided the setting for most films. Interruptions caused by airplanes, passing motorists, and other distractions are eliminated, and the cinematographer need not plan his shooting around the weather.

But today's films are making greater use of specialized locations, and a publicist can take advantage of that trend. Such locales as amusement parks, airports, cruise ships, and skyscrapers are hard to fit into a sound stage. Publicity personnel should be aware of the possibilities of motion picture filming in, on, or around locations they represent.

By maintaining liaison with the major producing companies and reading the Hollywood trade papers, one can learn which scripts have been sold to what producers. A telephone call or letter offering your location can often bring an interested response. One firm that operates several amusement parks carries on an active program of having movies and television shows emanate from their properties.

On a broader scale, cities, states, and even foreign nations are aware that movies or television programs can be a positive force. States such as New Mexico, Arizona, Washington, and New York actively seek to have films produced within their borders, and many have "film councils" whose job it is to attract production companies.

Municipalities such as New York City are also well aware of the dual advantage of filming within their city limits: tourists and those with investment projects are reminded of the advantages of such a location, and the economic benefit realized by the expenditures of the production company for products and services are valuable to the local economy.

In-film promotion. Even with decreased opportunities for depicting products in films, this does have potential. Each film presents its own problems for the property master. Hundreds of household items, automobiles, and all the trappings necessary to create an environment are needed for each film. While much of the material is either stored by the studio or constructed specifically for the film, many opportunities for providing products do exist. Today's directors are seeking realism, and realism means using real products.

There is no guarantee, of course, that the director or cinematographer will use a provided product to the degree the publicist might wish, unless a major promotion timed around the film's release has been pre-arranged. Keeping an eye on the Hollywood trade papers for announced film projects that may logically have need for a specific product or offering your product to a prop master can be helpful. But the real key to in-film use of products is box office-promoting tie-ins. Producers seek every avenue to increase their return on investment, so they are much more likely to become involved with an outside firm if part of the arrangement includes advertising or promotion that will help achieve that goal.

A good example of the combination of in-film promotion and release-time tie-ups was Warner Bros.' "Gumball Rally." That was a realistic automobile racing film, so the producers wanted to use real products. Such items as Castrol (motor oil), Cibie (high-performance driving lights), Hy-Gain (radios), Goodyear (tires), and many more were logically depicted in the picture. Many of the firms whose products were shown engaged in promotions at the time of the film's release, utilizing counter cards, in-store promotions, contests, and other activities combining mentions of the product with mention of the film. The Goodyear blimp showed the film's title in lights as it cruised over populous areas.

Release-related tie-ins. Even more than in-picture promotions that may result in promotion at the time of release, producers look for tie-ins that will help market *their* product—the movie.

While promotional tie-ins have been used for years, the variety of outlets is more diverse than ever. A few examples:

— A Chicago confectionary company distributed its regular summer supply of two billion gumballs, imprinted with the words "Gumball Rally" at no cost to the film's producer.

— Popsicle built a $750,000 advertising, promotion, and publicity campaign around United Artists' "Huckleberry Finn."

— A major dairy chain in the Northeast based a three-picture ("The Bad News Bears," "Won Ton

Figure 45-1. For Dino De Laurentiis' remake of "King Kong" the film's distributors arranged an impressive array of promotions and tie-ins, even though the picture did not lend itself to depicting products within the film. The large ape is shown here straddling the top of the twin towers of New York's World Trade Center.

Ton, the Dog Who Saved Hollywood," and "The Big Bus") tie-in with Paramount Pictures, based on milk carton panels with artwork from the films.

— A bakery chain in New York sold a pie named after Columbia's "The Black Bird," with promotion and publicity to match.

T-shirts, bumper stickers, paperback books based on the screenplay, posters, sound track music albums, and many other items—some traditional and some zany—have been used to promote box-office sales. At the same time, the popularity of a film can be used to sell the publicist's product.

Dino De Laurentiis' remake of the classic "King Kong" is a good example of opportunities for tie-in activity. Paramount Pictures, which distributed the film, boasted to a convention of exhibitors and film buyers before its release that the studio had arranged more than $9 million worth of advertising, publicity, and promotion that "will be paid for by someone else." The cooperating firms included:

— Jim Beam distillery, which used "King Kong" in advertising and promotion and put out a limited edition "King Kong" bottle as well as a new drink it concocted—the "King Kong";

— Schrafft's Candy Co., which marketed a "King Kong" peanut butter cup candy bar;

— GAF Corp., which offered "King Kong" View-Master stereo picture packets; and

— Sedgefield Sportswear, which promoted a key chain supposedly containing a hair from the giant ape.

In addition, an extensive number of licensed items using the "King Kong" name were created, and such firms as Ajax, Burger Chef, and 7-Eleven Stores conducted tie-in promotions.

Most promotional tie-ins last for the theater life of the picture, ranging from a few weeks to a year or more.

TAKING ADVANTAGE OF PUBLICITY OPPORTUNITIES

The best way for the publicist to take advantage of the continuing stream of motion pictures is to create ideas that will help sell both his or her product and the picture, and to convince the appropriate people at the studios of the mutual benefit to be gained.

The basic rules for success in using motion pictures as publicity vehicles are similar to other areas of publicity;

1. *Know the Product.* The publicist should have a rudimentary knowledge of motion pictures and how they are produced, distributed, and promoted. A few books that can be helpful are: *The Movie Business: American Film Industry Practice,* by William A. Bluem and Jason E. Squires, New York, Hastings House, 1972; *The New Hollywood: American Movies in the '70's,* by Axel Madsen, New York, Crowell, 1975; and *Movies and Society,* New York, Basic Books, 1970. Periodicals are also important in keeping up with this fast-changing field.

2. *Know the Potential.* Obviously, some films lend themselves better to publicity opportunities than do others. Reading the motion picture trade journals, particularly *Daily Variety* and *Hollywood Reporter,* will provide good information on which producer has announced what project, which studio (or promotion company) will film it, who will write the screenplay, etc. These publications provide the best "early warning system" regarding upcoming films and are a source of ideas. One of the 'trades,' *Boxoffice,* runs a "Showmandiser" section that details promotions being arranged and reports on the results of previous efforts.

3. *Know the People.* The successful publicist establishes good relationships with professionals in the field. Producers, wardrobe masters, property masters, screenwriters, advertising and publicity directors, and others are able to make decisions related to the use of products, places, situations, and marketing activities.

4. *Know the Timing.* One grocery chain executive approached the location finder of a studio with an offer to allow the production company free use of one of his supermarkets—two weeks after the scene had been filmed! Be sure to contact the right people . . . at the right time.

46

Sponsored Motion Pictures and Other Audio/Visual Media

LOREN J. KALLSEN is president of Vibrant Films, Inc., Minneapolis-based producer of sponsored motion pictures. His company has made public relations, marketing, and motivational films for such clients as AT&T, 3M Company, and ITT.

He has produced, written, and directed throughout the United States and Western Europe, in the Caribbean, and in South America.

Over a 12-year period his films have won Gold Awards at such leading competitions as the annual CINE Festival in Washington, D.C. and the International Film & TV Festival of New York.

Prior to forming Vibrant Films in 1973, Mr. Kallsen was for eight years Executive Producer, Films & Broadcasting, on the headquarters Corporate Relations and Advertising staff of International Telephone and Telegraph Corporation in New York City. In that capacity he had responsibility for the creation, production, and administration of ITT's public relations films worldwide. He also handled public relations contact with the TV networks and major stations.

Before his assignment at ITT, Mr. Kallsen was a free-lance film writer in New York City and, for five years, a reporter, writer, and producer at WCCO Radio and KSTP-TV in Minneapolis.

He is the editor and/or modernizer of two books of Americana—The Kentucky Tragedy, A Problem in Romantic Attitudes and The Explorations of Pierre Esprit Radisson. He is a graduate of the University of Minnesota.

The highest degree of impact and the greatest retention of meaning are achieved through mass communications that combine sight and sound: audio/visual communications.

This assumes, of course, that the audience is reasonably sight-and-sound oriented (as are most people born since television became universal), rather than primarily word-oriented. It also assumes that the given subject matter is amenable to audio/visual handling.

Because of the potency of audio/visual techniques when they are applied to receptive material, they are being used increasingly in situations ranging from small meetings to audiences of millions through theaters and/or television. (See Chapters 43, 44, and 45.)

SPONSORED MOTION PICTURES*

The motion picture, whether produced on film or videotape and whether shown in direct projection or via TV, is the most effective audio/visual medium. To the elements of sight and sound it adds the crucial dimension of motion, with all the excitement, drama, and impact that motion imparts. It attains a high degree of audience involvement.

Public relations people use sponsored motion pictures because they present most stories more quickly, accurately, and memorably than can be

---

*For the purposes of this chapter, video tape is included in the broad "motion picture" category. Unless otherwise indicated, either specifically or by context, the terms "motion picture," "film," "picture," and "video tape" are used interchangeably.

done by speech or the printed word alone. It is estimated that in the United States between 17,000 and 20,000 sponsored motion pictures are produced annually. These include not only public relations films but also those used for marketing to and education of the sponsors' many internal and external audiences.

In making motion pictures there are at least as many exceptions as rules, for both the buyer and seller of the film. But it is possible to set down certain guidelines that will help assure the effectiveness of the final product... that will help keep all concerned out of The Graveyard of Floundered Films.

It is essential that everyone involved realize that making a successful public relations film is a complex aesthetic, technical, and political undertaking. It follows that the basis of any serious project is *professionalism* on the part of both the sponsor (or agency) and the producer of the picture.

How to begin. The place to start is for the sponsor to analyze and write down the objectives and audiences for the potential film. These may change as the project is further defined, but for the time being all will at least have a common reference point.

Before going further, the first-time sponsor may wish to gain some general background by reading a reference book such as *The Technique of Documentary Film Production* by W. Hugh Baddeley (N.Y.: Hastings House).

Selecting the producer. The next step is to bring in a fully professional producer. How do you find him? Word of mouth may be the best way; talk to some satisfied clients. The Yellow Pages phone directory can provide leads. A number of production directories can give you pointers: not all the producers listed are good; not all the good ones are listed; but it's a place to start:

- *Broadcasting Yearbook,* published by Broadcasting Publications, Inc., 1735 De Sales St. N.W., Wasington, D.C. 20036
- *CINE Golden Eagle Film Awards,* published annually by the Council on International Nontheatrical Events, 1201 16th Street N.W., Washington, D.C. 20036
- Film/Tape Production Source Book, published annually by *Television/Radio Age* magazine, 666 Fifth Avenue, New York, N.Y. 10019
- *Motion Picture, TV & Theatre Directory,* published semi-annually by Motion Picture Enterprises, Inc., Box 276, Tarrytown, New York 10591
- TV/Industrial Film & Tape Directory, published annually by Back Stage Publications, Inc., 165 West 46th Street, New York, N.Y. 10036

Regardless of how you locate your producer, it is important to learn his capabilities and reputation first-hand. Screen his recent work. Talk to him straightforwardly, and insist that he do the same to you. (Do not, however, demand a firm quotation during your initial conversation; usually the producer can respond meaningfully only after tighter specifications have been developed.) Match the producer to the job. This does not mean that he has to be an expert in your subject, or that he must have already made a film just like the one you think you want; that may or may not be helpful. Rather, it means that you should be able to infer from the work he has shown you, and from his long-term record, that you can expect to get the desired result.

Contracting, budgeting, paying. Having made your commitment to the motion picture medium, and having selected the producer, the next step is to set up a mutually useful working relationship. For a project of any complexity, this relationship should be carried out under a formal client-producer contract that clearly spells out the obligations of each party. Properly drawn, this document is to everyone's advantage. It will save a lot of misunderstanding as the project progresses.

Normally there are separate contracts for the script and for the production. This practice has two virtues: (1) The script, which is a separate cost, provides meaningful specifications on which to base the production contract and price. (2) If the script fails to meet the client's requirements, he can escape from the project without further obligation except to pay the script fee.

Typically, whether it is a script or a production, payment is made on a step basis. Though arrangements may vary, there normally is a substantial advance payment upon signing of the contract: anywhere from 33 percent to 50 percent, depending on circumstances. There will be one or two progress payments at specified points and a final payment on delivery.

What is an appropriate budget for a motion picture? There is no blanket answer. A film can properly cost only a few thousand dollars or it can cost hundreds of thousands, depending on many variables: where it is shot, over what period of time, the number of locations, the size of sets, types of costumes, the quality, the style, the amount and kind of animation and opticals, the kind of music, the kind of cast, and so on.

Length is, of course, an element of cost, but it is generally not a meaningful index. Cost per minute is a seductive way of evaluating the price of a picture (it's neat, like buying a pound of this or a foot of that), but it is usually misleading. The true indices of cost are the variables that go into each minute.

The sum of this, perhaps, is that there is no such thing as a cheap picture; there are only films that do the job for you or fail to do the job. Good pictures can be made on lean budgets, but they cannot be made on inadequate budgets. A $25,000 film that fails to give value is far more expensive than a $50,000 picture that does what it is intended to do.

The client's best protection is to "learn the territory" and deal with a trustworthy competent producer, whether that producer is from a client's in-house unit or is a commercial independent.

Developing the script. With the working relationship defined, the next step is to develop the script, which is the basis for all that follows. If you don't have a good script, the rest of the project may degenerate into nothing more than a salvage operation.

Research is part of the creative process and precedes serious writing. It is important that the client open necessary doors and supply essential information; that he give the producer or the producer's writer any reasonable assistance.

Once subject research has been completed, the script usually is developed in either two or three stages, depending on the complexity of the project, the exigencies of schedule, the client's internal approval procedures, and so on.

First comes a brief *concept,* which should deal with the broad story line and the production approach. Will professional actors be used? Shot on location or on a stage? Original or library score? On-screen or off-screen narrator? Animation, and what kind? 16mm or 35mm film? Videotape? (As a practical matter, a tenative oral concept frequently precedes research, thereby helping guide the research and keeping the researcher from constantly going over old ground.)

Next is the *treatment,* a longer document that is not yet a script but that will give the reader a good idea of what the picture will look and sound like. It will not have complete description of action and sound. (If the *concept* has been quite detailed, or if time presses, the *treatment* in some cases may be bypassed.)

Finally comes the *script,* which will contain scene-by-scene action and sound descriptions and the approved narration and/or dialog.

The client has the right of approval throughout. Before giving approval at any particular stage of scripting he should satisfy himself that he has what he wants. Changing specifications later may be costly.

Production. Under the word "production" we include the three aspects of picture making that follow scripting: pre-production, production itself, and post-production.

Pre-production covers the plans made and actions taken after script approval but before shooting begins. Pre-production includes such things as defining the production contract, location scouting and clearances, casting, selection and assigning of production personnel, scheduling, and the hundreds of details that must be handled before the cameras turn. While the burden of pre-production falls on the producer, the client also needs to contribute. On a corporate image film, for example, he will have to make any necessary arrangements within his own company. Many times the client will be asked to gain the cooperation of, say, other businesses or government agencies. The client will also be responsible for setting up his own approval procedures and making sure that his designated representatives actually have the authority to make decisions as they are needed. Like scripting, pre-production requires close collaboration between producer and client. Good pre-production leads toward an effective conclusion. Its absence leads to chaos.

Production is the actual shooting of the picture and the recording of all synchronous and non-synchronous sound connected with the shooting. The client should be present during the shooting of those scenes that require on-the-spot technical or political approvals. His presence during the rest of shooting is a matter of his own interest and the strength of his legs. Many people quickly discover that watching a film crew at work can become a boring and exhausting experience.

Once production is under way it is wise to follow the producer's recommendations in film-making matters. To meet his obligations he must maintain consistency of creative viewpoint and technical procedure. Surprises forced on him by the client will tend to deteriorate the quality of the picture and raise its costs.

Post-production covers the many steps necessary to complete the film. It includes picture and sound editing, recording studio sound, creation of music and sound effects, opticals and titles, final script polish, and laboratory work.

During post-production, the client evaluates the picture and gives approvals at least four times: (1) At rough cut. (2) At fine cut. (3) At interlock, when the fine cut workprint is projected with the full but probably unmixed sound track. (4) At answer print, when the completed film is presented with all its optical effects, titles, mixed sound track, and color corrections.

The role of careful planning and control throughout the project will be reaffirmed to both client and producer during post-production. If major changes must be made because, as it turns out, the approved script is inadequate, or because the client has new ideas not in the script, the picture will be more expensive for the client. If major changes must be made because the producer did not fulfill the specifications of the script, he will have additional expense. If no serious changes must be made, both parties are winners.

Distribution. Distribution is frequently the most overlooked aspect of the public relations use of motion pictures. A film or videotape is of no use unless it is seen by its target audience. Yet that is the fate of many productions; they sit on the shelf for lack of foresight in planning or funding.

A distribution strategy should be developed, and its costs foreseen, during the conception of the project. Sometimes the sponsor may wish to handle his own distribution, but the planning and funding must nonetheless be provided. Under some circumstances the producer may be set up to distribute. Generally, if it is intended to reach a large and dispersed audience, a picture receives its most effective handling through a full-scale distributor.

Distributors are prepared to build audiences according to the type of message and the sponsor's objective. They will promote the picture; schedule, ship, and maintain the prints; prepare collateral material. They will turn in accurate reports of showings, including such information as number and makeup of audience, date, location, name of organization. If the picture appears on public service TV, the report will give the station call letters and affiiliation, estimated number of viewers, time slot, and a figure on what would have been the air cost of the telecast had it been purchased rather than shown on free time.

Leading distributors of sponsored non-theatrical motion pictures, with offices and film exchanges in major cities, include:

Association-Sterling Films, 866 Third Avenue, New York, New York 10022

Modern Talking Pictures Service, 2323 New Hyde Park Road, New Hyde Park, New York 11040

Sponsored pictures can be distributed to service clubs, professional meetings, civil and social organizations, consumer groups, trade fairs, resorts, and other bodies and audiences of many kinds.

Figure 46-1. Whether the medium is film or videotape, post-production work requires professional skill and equipment. This is a typical professional videotape editing operation (3M photo).

Schools welcome good films that are factual without being too commercial. School films must be open and fair and clearly indicate the sponsor. For best effect they should be colorful and entertaining as well as educational. Those are traits of all good sponsored films.

Movie theaters throughout the country frequently will accept sponsored films in the form of theatrical short subjects. To warrant theater exposure a sponsored film must have high production qualitiy, be entertaining or otherwise intensely interesting, have minimal and unobtrusive commercial content, and be the right length for the given theater's programming needs. About ten minutes of screen time is usually the preferred length—certainly not more than 20 minutes.

The sponsored film distributors can develop theatrical strategies that are tailored to geography and demographics.

Sometimes the sponsor or producer arranges directly with a major theatrical distributor such as Paramount, United Artists, or Universal, among others, to distribute the sponsored short exclusively. In exceptional cases, a major theatrical distributor will pair a sponsored short with a top entertainment release at no charge, the handling and screening being given free in exchange for the program material.

As with production, it is meaningless to generalize much about the cost of distribution. There are too many variables in terms of saturation, schedule, objectives, and acceptable ratios of cost effectiveness. (Talk with the distributors; the reputable ones all have price lists and descriptive literature they will supply without obligation.) It can be said that with good planning and a large long-term distribution program the right kind of public relations film can reach millions of people at a cost per viewer that compares favorably with the cost of advertising exposure through national TV or national magazines.

The life span of a public relations picture varies with the subject and its handling, the sponsor's commitment to the medium, and the dating factors in the story. For most films an excellent run might be four to seven years, at which time a judicious updating might provide rebirth. One of the earliest industrial films made in color, "Steel—Man's Servant," was used for 22 years before it was retired. At more than 104,000 screenings it had been viewed by nearly ten million persons, mainly school children.

TV RELEASES AND OTHER FILMS[1]

The growth of television, with its daily coverage of the news, led to the demise of newsreels in theaters.

From the public relations viewpoint, the newsreel has been translated into the TV newsfilm release. This is a film of, generally, one to two minutes in length that is distributed free of charge—and without obligation—to the news or public service departments of individual stations and networks. To be considered for airing, handouts must look and sound like newsfilm and must have, within the standards of the evaluating organization, bona fide news or public service interest. As a practical matter they also contain information or a viewpoint that benefits the sponsor. Their commercial content should be minimal or they will not be used.

Handout TV newsfilm usually falls within one of two broad categories: hard spot news, which is produced against a deadline and must hit the air quickly to be valid, and the feature "evergreen" story, which is not tied tightly to a specific event or date and is airable any time for weeks or even months after it is produced.

From a technical viewpoint, newsfilm can be turned out by any competent producer. However, the client is more likely to be well served if, for this somewhat specialized medium, he engages a producer who has had working TV news experience. Generally he will have the better grasp of news format and content, and he will be able to contribute an intangible judgment that will enhance the acceptability of the handout.

The great disadvantage of handout newsfilm is that the sponsor cannot absolutely control his message; the news organization may rewrite or edit the picture in such a way that the message is deleted. On the other hand, if the sponsor's viewpoint gains the air, the handout newsfilm takes on credibility that a TV commercial can never have; the message has squared with the considered news judgment of the broadcaster.

Most TV stations, groups, and networks in the United States (and throughout the world, for that matter) utilize handout newsfilm at one time or another. So does the U.S. Information Agency in the reels it ships overseas. At each place there usually is a single best person to receive a film. This may be the news director, or the assignment editor, or a producer, or a syndication editor. It is important

[1]See Chapter 43.

that the distributor of the film—whether it be the client, or the producer, or the commercial distributor—know to whom to send it. Again, past experience in the TV news business is valuable. In the absence of personal acquaintance with key individuals at key stations, *Broadcasting Yearbook* is a good place to start to build a mailing list; it identifies the news directors at stations throughout the country. *Broadcasting Yearbook* also lists many, though not all, commercial producers who have newsfilm expertise.

Though the classic newsreel is dead in the United States, and increasingly moribund throughout the world as TV news comes to dominate, some newsreel derivatives are alive and healthy. Association-Sterling produces and distributes "Theater Cavalcade" as a theatrical short subject. It is made up of several brief news feature films (often modified handouts) that have been melded into a single package. Hearst Metrotone, 235 E. 45th St., New York City, has used its vast library of historical newsreel footage in creating "Screen News Digest." This series of documentary films is distributed to schools, with the public service sponsor of the pictures receiving screen credit in specified cities or regions.

SLIDEFILMS AND SLIDES

Although normally less impressive and dramatic than motion pictures, slidefilms and slides can be successful communications vehicles. When the budget cannot stand the cost of a motion picture, or when the subject requires audio/visual treatment but would not be enhanced by motion *per se,* the answer may be a slidefilm or slide show.

The slidefilm is a continuous strip of film on which the frames are presented statically in a fixed sequence. Individual slides, on the other hand, may be varied easily in sequence or easily substituted. Projection can be controlled manually or automatically, depending on the equipment used and the function of the show.

A slidefilm (sometimes called a filmstrip) or a slide show may be presented with or without a recorded sound track on disk or magnetic tape. When recorded sound is not used, the cost of production is cut. Also, the human element is injected into the pre-

Figure 46-2. A multi-media multi-screen production integrates tape recorders, slide projectors, movie projectors, and other media through systems designed for the purpose, such as the Wollensak "Digi-Cue" programmer at lower right.

sentation by the person making it, and he or she can expand or minimize any particular information at will. The disadvantage of using a live presenter is that the message may not be conveyed equally well at each show, not to mention the likelihood of flubs: the human element works both ways.

A recorded sound track, which can be as simple or elaborate as desired, is necessary when exact reproduction of the message is needed.

Usually slidefilms and slide shows cost from one-fourth to one-half as much as motion pictures, though it is dangerous to generalize because they can become extremely complex, with costs that equal or exceed those of a film.

For example, large multi-image shows of the kind that became popular in the late 1960s (and remain popular today) are expensive. Yet they are essentially slide shows. But the standard single screen has been increased to, say, 2, 3, 4, 5, 6, or more screens; and the projectors have been increased from one to anywhere from 2 to 20, and their control is complicated. And the sound track contains not just one unadorned narrative voice but a whole cast of voices, with original music. When this happens, generalizations about relatively lower costs break down. Such a "slide show" can be an excellent value if there is a need for a show-stopper in a setting that calls for multi-image: at expositions, theme parks, one-shot extravaganzas, etc.

Volumes of material are available on the various types and uses of slidefilms and slides. But the only true way to explore these possibilities is through experience. Thus, as with motion pictures, it is wise in the search for the proper audio/visual medium to be guided by a professional.

SOME VISUAL AND/OR AUDIO AIDS

Tests made on oral communications by the University of Minnesota have shown that, on average, 75 percent of the things we say escape the listener's mind. With only 25 percent being retained, it is important to consider the use of visuals with an oral presentation.

Overhead and front projectors permit projecting onto a screen the contents of a transparency, which can be made from a printed page, a chart, a photograph, etc. A pointer can pick out specific items while the image is on the screen, and erasable ink markings can be written on the transparency by the speaker.

Rear projectors are a convenience that permits material at a lecture or in a display booth to be projected from in back of a screen while it is read from the front.

Opaque projectors. Materials in their solid form—rocks, pieces of machinery, a page from a bound book, etc.—can be shown on a large screen. This is often effective at a quick press conference when a new device or mineral find is being shown to a large group, where other ways of showing it might be confusing or time consuming. Also it is useful when materials that should be handled only by experts, such as very delicate crockery or sections of tissue, are to be shown.

Charts are by far the most-used visual aid. A chart may be painted, printed, or drawn. It must be large enough and simple enoguh to be seen and comprehended in the presentation setting.

Flannel boards consist of board covered with felt. Sticky-backed visuals are placed on the surface, allowing a speaker to put some movement and flexibility into an otherwise static presentation.

Magnetic boards are much like flannel boards, except that magnets permit the use of heavier three-dimensional visuals.

Video cassette, audio cassette, and disk recordings are useful in overcoming some of the difficulties of

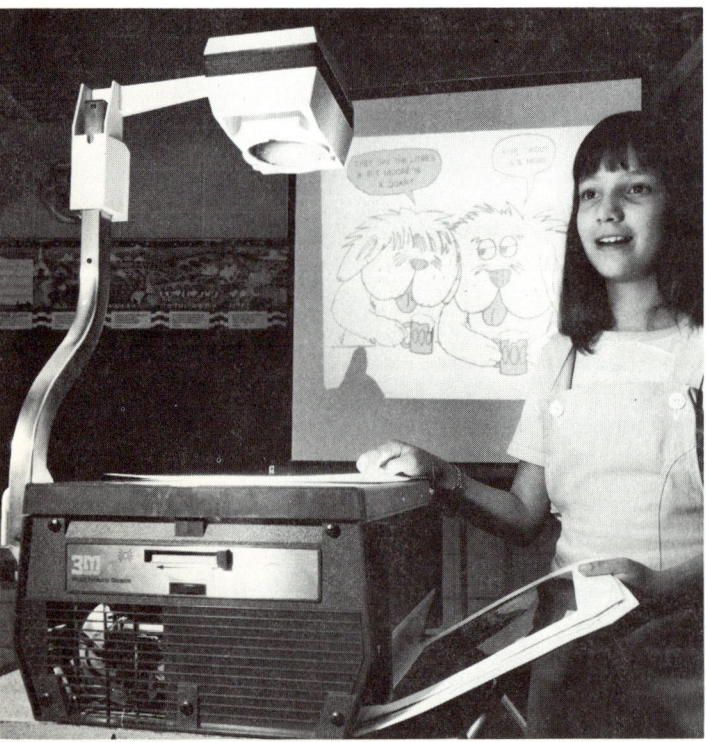

Figure 46-3. The overhead projector permits showing enlargements of graphic or written materials. Transparencies made from individual sheets are projected upward and behind the speaker.

working with a diffuse and loose-knit organization. They assure that all concerned get exactly the same message with the desired visual and/or audio emphasis. For example, monthly picture and voice memoranda from the director of public relations at a company's headquarters may go out to plant and branch personnel, commenting on surveys, new programs, problems being explored, ideas submitted from the field, and other matters. Field people may respond in the same media. Generally, these video cassette, audio cassette, or disk communications, though carefully prepared, are modest in their techniques. They intentionally do not have the ambitions—or costs—associated with full-scale productions.

Electrowriters. An executive or demonstrator can write his "blackboard" notes across a long distance through a transmitter unit hooked up by telephone lines with a projector unit and screen.

Tele-lectures. A useful technique for making an audio/visual presentation at a distance. With the help of the telephone company there is a hookup from a speaker's office to a meeting or classroom, where visuals can be shown while the speaker is heard. Members of the audience can question the speaker through a two-way hookup. This permits the speaker to "appear" at many locations without the full time or expense of going there; and it permits remote groups to engage speakers they otherwise would not attract.

Facsimile sends between distant cities, via telephone lines, exact copies of blueprints, layouts, and other visual materials. It is now used increasingly to transmit copy between the offices of agency and client or between an organization and a communications medium.

47

Using Advertising for Public Relations Communications

Philip Lesly

For many years Americans have considered advertising the predominant form of communication available to business and other organizations. Though it is but one of many techniques for reaching the public (with its own sub-techniques such as printed advertisments, radio commercials, television commercials, billboards, and others) it has overshadowed the indirect means of communication for several reasons:

(1) It developed into an important technique long before most of the others matured.

(2) Because it financially supports so many of the media of communication, it is naturally very important to both the media and the public that are exposed to the advertising.

(3) Because it is always immediately apparent to be a communication from an interested party seeking to reach the public, it achieves conscious prominence that is absent from the indirect communications techniques.

(4) Because advertising is essential to the sale of vast quantities of goods produced by our advanced productive system, it attracts many times the amount of investment of other forms of communication.

(5) Because it is always clearly visible and often measurable to the sponsor, it readily gains understanding and support from the practical executive.

As a result, there is wide misunderstanding about the relative position and utilization of advertising in an organization's projection of its image, in its total communications practices, and in its planning of public-relations functions.

SPECIAL NATURE OF ADS AS COMMUNICATION

Since public relations encompasses all functions that project to large groups the character of a company and its messages, it is apparent that advertising is one of the techniques involved in public relations. However, the basic function of the great majority of advertising is to sell a company's product or service. This is a highly specialized form of communication and one that usually requires intensive impact, controlled forms of communication, controlled choice of medium, selection of timing, and other factors.

The nature of the selling message is sufficiently different from other forms of communication that many of the principles applied to publicity, literature, films, meetings, and other techniques do not directly apply. A company can, of course, create enemies and a bad image through product advertising that insults the intelligence of its audience, depicts the company as a group of sharpies attempting to put things over on people, and annoys the sensibilities with brash and repetitive exhortations. However, a bold and direct pleading of the company's selling purpose in a sound and tasteful way is clearly acceptable, whereas such aggressiveness could not be acceptable in other techniques.

Accordingly, there is a great difference between the types of mentality and abilities needed in directing effective advertising for a company's products and in conducting an effective opinion-developing program involving other means. Advertising to sell products or services is a selling function and therefore a subordinate phase of the marketing operation of the company. Consideration of its other effects on public attitudes involves public relations judgment, but effectiveness as advertising calls for the direction of hard-hitting sales-minded people. On the other hand, persuasive communication through indirect means calls for sensitivity to public attitudes, sensibilities, and tastes; restraint in beating the drums for the product, the cause, or the organization; and a judgment covering the whole range of human psychology and attitudes.

For these reasons, there are few instances of an effective advertising man or organization that is equally capable of performing in the broad public relations field. And, for the same reasons, the fully effective public relations person or organization is seldom capable of performing at full effectiveness in the product advertising area. The fields are as different as a carpenter and a jewel cutter: both deal with hammers, but the force and deftness with which they use them are at opposite poles.

Yet a knowledge of advertising and how to employ it is vital to the public relations practitioner. He will be involved in its effects on the organization's total posture,[1] and he may use it for specific needs in communicating.

John Orr Young, a co-founder of the Young & Rubicam advertising agency and later a consultant to management on public relations, said:[2]

"The public relations practitioner ... must, at some time or other, use every known medium of communication and enlightenment to execute programs that will achieve the desired results ... A public relations practitioner who does not understand the history, the uses, the techniques, and the value of advertising is simply not equipped to perform all of his job. Technically, advertising used for public relations purposes must be *good* advertising; but to be good public relations, it also must be the *right* advertising. Advertising so used does not lose its identity, but its voice and the message it speaks become the legitimate child of public relations. It is a clear-cut case of advertising helping public relations to help management."

EFFECTIVE USES OF ADVERTISING

As a result of the more prominent knowledge of advertising than of public relations techniques, there has continued to be broad confusion regarding the utilization of advertising as a public relations technique *per se,* aside from the sale of products or services. There have been many instances in which organizations, seeking to establish understanding with their publics, have turned to broad advertising programs on the basis that the way to reach many people in this country is to conduct an advertising program that "gets the story across." Being duly impressed with what advertising has done in helping to establish the mass production and mass distribution systems in America, the assumption has been made that it can just as readily "sell" ideas.

An analysis of what advertising can and cannot be expected to accomplish in a public relations program is preliminary to the planning of any broad communications effort that might include the purchase of space in publications, broadcast time, and other forms of advertising.

Functions it can be expected to accomplish if properly planned and executed include:

Conveying information, such as:

(1) Announcing to a community that a company is planning to establish a plant there, what its purposes will be, the personnel it will be interested in employing, the economic and social effects of having the company's plant as a new neighbor.

(2) Notifying personnel of changes in work schedules, layoffs, or recalls, and similar information that must reach employees when they are not in touch with company facilities.

(3) Explanation of the reasons for interruptions in service and what the public should do—such as a power-line failure of an electric utility, or the effects of a wreck on a railroad's services.

(4) A report on changes in the company name and the reasons. For instance, an extensive advertising campaign was conducted by Exxon when its name was changed from Standard Oil Company of New Jersey and by IC Industries when its name was changed from Illinois Central Industries.

(5) Explanation of the issues in a strike or work stoppage *if* care is taken to present the facts impassively, objectively, and fairly.

(6) Reports on the company's activities. Some companies run an ad when a major new product is introduced, or when a space achievement is aided by one of their components. Some run ads from time to time to report on progress—a year-end look at growth, an acquisition, entry into a promising new technological field—to assure publication of the complete story when and where they seek to reach the desired publics.

---

[1] See Chapter 17.
[2] *Public Relations Handbook,* edited by Philip Lesly. Prentice-Hall, Englewood Cliffs, N.J., 1967, pp. 684-5.

Figure 47-1. Storyboard of sequences in a television commercial for United Technologies that ties together the various elements of the company to identify them with the corporate name.

(7) Contributing to the image of the organization in the public mind, along with the product ads, when the advertisement is oriented from the viewpoint of the audience and not from that of the company. For example, ads that say in effect: "This is what we want you to know about X Company" are efforts to impose themselves on the reader, rather than to provide information or service to the reader. Such ads are interpreted as calling: "Please spend five minutes of your time listening to what I have to say about myself, because I've spent good money on it." On the other hand, the advertisement for one of the companies making a contribution to an American achievement in the space age, relating what its role has been, is interesting and significant to the reader and conveys the image of the company as a by-product.

Performing a needed public service and establishing the interest of the advertiser in the welfare of the community, such as:

(1) The New Year's Eve advertisements by a whiskey company urging that "the one for the road" be coffee, for safety.

(2) Ads informing the public about the importance of local causes or projects, such as the Community Fund or the local job-training program.

Alerting the public to an issue it may not be aware of, where the interest of the company and of the public may be closely allied. Ads by various utilities about the need to develop coal resources, solar power, and other sources of energy are this type. Ads urging support for the fund-raising efforts of colleges are others.

General Electric provided a new offer in line with employee concerns, union demands and the needs of the nation's economy.

What the unions don't say about prices, profits & pay.

There's nothing new about inaccurate or misleading information from union officials during a strike. Invariably, the most serious distortions of fact involve three main issues: prices, profits and pay.

Electrical industry prices up only 9.5% since 1965.

Since the strike against General Electric began, union officials repeatedly have cited price increases in the electrical industry as feeding inflation and justifying heavy wage demands.

What is the full story?

Since 1965, while prices in so many other areas have soared, wholesale prices of electrical equipment and machinery have risen only 9.5%, as shown by Bureau of Labor Statistics data. And wholesale prices of electrical household appliances have risen only 4.9%.

Union officials seem to forget that *competition* limits any company's ability to raise prices – and the electrical industry is highly competitive.

General Electric profits down nearly 30% since 1965.

Union officials are also quick to point to General Electric's 1968 profits of $357 million. They call this "excessive" and use this figure as supposed proof that General Electric can meet the unions' heavy pay demands.

By no stretch of the imagination can this level of profits be considered excessive when you look at all the facts. *General Electric profits in 1968 work out to only 4.3 cents per dollar of sales.* For the first three quarters of 1969, profits fell to about 4 cents on the sales dollar. In fact, since 1965 General Electric profit per dollar of sales has dropped nearly 30%.

Union demands can't ignore the need for adequate profit to attract necessary capital and keep a business and jobs going.

General Electric offer keeps employee pay ahead of cost of living.

Union officials claim that General Electric wages are "falling far behind the cost of living, far behind the levels in other big American manufacturing industries."

This is simply not true. Estimates of the increase in the Consumer Price Index in 1970 by leading U.S. economists are averaging between 4 and 5%. *General Electric's new offer amounts to an average wage increase of nearly 7.5% in the first year of the contract – at least 2.5% over the CPI forecast.*

Further, the new offer provides basic wage increases plus cost-of-living adjustments in the second and third years of the contract.

In addition, General Electric's Insurance Plan substantially protects employees and their families from one of the fastest-rising elements in the cost of living: soaring medical costs.

As to the comparison with other manufacturing industries, the General Electric offer is fully competitive with other settlements in manufacturing in 1969.

These are some of the things unions don't say about prices, profits and pay. However, only a realistic look by responsible union officials at these key economic issues can lead to the constructive negotiations necessary to end this strike.

We want a sound settlement so we can all get back to work soon.

GENERAL ⓖⓔ ELECTRIC

Figure 47-2. In fighting a nationwide strike, General Electric used incisive factual advertising to reach the company's employees, as well as the public, communities, and government. Headlines and subheads convey the essence of the message, for those who do not read it all.

Figure 47-3. With diversification and complex technologies making many companies hard for the public to know, this type of advertising seeks to convey the company's character through use of striking examples.

BROADCAST MEDIA

With the growing dominance of television as the medium that reaches most people, many organizations have developed means of using television for public relations advertising.

This is aside from the use of TV as an advertising medium to sell products or services; the use of TV as an unpaid outlet for publicity material (see Chapter 43); or the sponsorship of non-commercial TV shows as a public service (see Chapter 44).

There are three basic forms of public relations utilization of commercial TV:

1. Sponsorship of programs that perform a public service, with commercials absent or confined to the beginning and end, or strictly institutional in character. This projects the company's name and character with no apparent commercial ax to grind. A notable example was sponsorship by a division of what is now Exxon of a series of British-produced plays of Shakespeare. The series was about to be abandoned when the company came to the rescue, gaining not only the usual good will but a great deal of extra attention and public commendation. Though the series originated on a non-commercial station, it was carried on commercial channels in some cities.

2. Sponsorship of an informative program on such matters as science, education, or natural resources—with the tone and nature of the commercials adapted to the character of the show. Though the commercials deal with products, they are more subtle than usual, and often have a relationship to the program's theme.

In one notable example, the 3M Company devoted a commercial on its documentary shows to its policy of allowing research people to pursue their own ideas. It told how one researcher found a liquid that wouldn't do anything to anything—and how that "useless" substance gave rise to many possible product applications. Mail was heavy both from industries wanting samples of the inert liquid to try out applications, and from young people—especially in college and high school—expressing interest in 3M as a place to work. Though the sequence was a paid portion of a commercial TV show, it had significant public relations benefits.

3. Paid announcements, utilizing television in the same way announcement ads have been utilized in newspapers for many years.

Local radio is also employed in these ways. Radio affords a means of reaching desired segments of the total audience, at a much lower cost than buying time on an area-wide TV station. Illinois Tool Works, for instance, has bought spots in a daily morning newscast on a major Chicago station, timed to reach many businessmen who drive to their offices. The commercials have been geared to the theme: "You're never more than a few feet away from a product of ITW," to convey the firm's broad diversification, rather than to promoting individual products.

The question of whether an advertiser can buy "idea" commercials on regular television and radio stations has been hotly contested for a number of years. Until the early 1970s, the Federal Communications Commission took the position that broadcast stations, as government licensees, could take no stand on controversial issues and could not make their wavelengths available to others to take stands. That policy was modified to permit broadcasters to editorialize so long as they made time available for rebuttals of dissenters. However, the broadcasters for the most part continued to deny others access on over-the-air stations (as contrasted with closed-channel stations) even when the intended advertiser offered to pay for the time of the opposition.

It is likely that this situation will be fluid and will vary from network to network and from individual station to station. Accordingly, public relations people who want to consider using broadcasting to express viewpoints should check on the current situation.

INEFFECTIVE USES OF ADVERTISING

Advertising, on the other hand, has been notably unsuccessful in most efforts to overcome a prejudice or an attitude of indifference that is deep-seated. The psychological reasons for this are well established. Pierre Martineau in his book *Motivation in Advertising* pointed out:

> Almost all adults . . . resent direct suggestion. All of us have had the experience of seeing an idea of ours violently rejected by another only to find that some time later the person had adopted our idea as if it had come from his own thinking. When he can feel that the idea came from his own thinking, he is far more likely to follow it.[3]

Dr. Rex F. Harlow in his *Social Science in Public Relations* points out:

> People distrust a person or an organization with an obvious ax to grind. They resist messages that smack of selfish propaganda . . . In most situations an indirect content and an indirect approach tend to win more acceptance and support of an idea or a cause than a hard-hitting content and a direct-attack approach.[4]

There are many examples of advertising campaign failures to illustrate this: the effort of several years and several million dollars by the Men's and Boy's Wear Institute to shame the American male into spending more money for clothes by telling him to "Dress Right—You Can't Afford Not To," followed by the signature indicating that the money for this exhortation came from the people who sell

[3]*Motivation in Advertising,* New York: McGraw-Hill, 1957. Pp. 128-9.

[4]*Social Science in Public Relations,* New York: Harper, 1957. P. 46.

Figure 47-4. This ad, dealing with the elementary need for profits to provide tax revenues, appeared in *Dun's Review,* a magazine for management executives, as well as other publications.

clothes; the extensive efforts to convince people that the benefits of whole oranges are substantial enough to overcome the extreme conveniences of frozen and prepared orange juice; the series of advertising campaigns by the Better Home Furnishings Council of Greater Chicago to shame the householder into refurnishing his home rather than spending his money on other things; and the many ineffective campaigns directed toward the labor movement, tax levels, and other social and economic concepts, in each case exhibiting the self-interest of the sponsor and thereby notifying the reader that someone with a selfish interest is paying substantial money to try to force him to change his viewpoint.

Efforts to force the image of a company on an uninterested public are at best very ineffective in relation to their cost. The type of ad referred to earlier in

The need to be understood

It's vital in business, too.

A new craving, born of the pace and impersonality of the times, is welling up in the land.

It is <u>the need to be understood</u>. On a personal basis. On a business basis.

How is Nekoosa involved?

The business communication papers from Nekoosa are your raw materials for transmitting ideas and information. Whether it's for sophisticated business machines, for simple office equipment, for designing or for printing, Nekoosa makes the papers that help you communicate quickly, accurately and dramatically.

<u>Nekoosa helps you to be understood.</u> And that's a lot.

Nekoosa-Edwards Paper Company • Port Edwards, Wisconsin

The link of understanding between man and machine...

Figure 47-5. The fine line between corporate advertising and product advertising marks this ad, which is an example of using one medium to convey the character of a company and to communicate what it has to offer.

Figure 47-6. An advertisement intended to motivate people to exert influence on Congress. The architects seek to combine benefit to the public and to their profession.

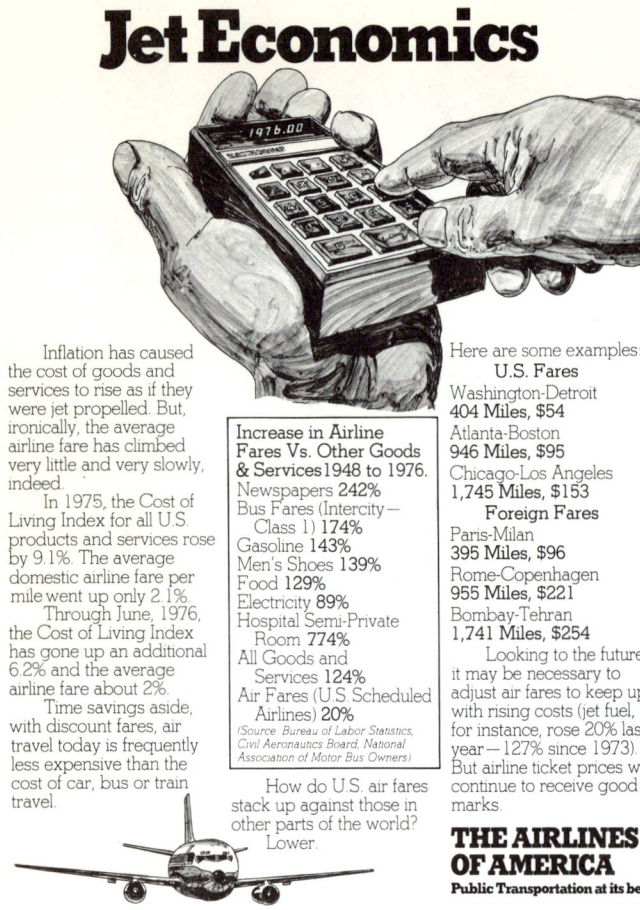

Figure 47-7. Persuasion is combined with sales effort in this advertisement for the airline industry. The emphasis is on the comparative economy of air travel, but the point is made that regulatory officials should be amenable to higher fares.

Figure 47-8. Insensitivity to the orientation and feelings of the audience is typified in this ad. It tried to develop empathy for President Ford among ethnic groups—but was signed by two men with distinctively WASPish names. President Ford seemed to have drawn ahead in the race when this ad ran. He lost in the ethnic communities.

which a company seeks to command attention to a description of itself is typical.

Pleading a selfish cause when the reason is apparent is equally ineffective. The company that signs advertisements urging that necessary new tax revenue be raised through a sales tax rather than an increase in corporation taxes is likely to solidify the resentment of its original opponents and to sway the undecided person toward the opposite viewpoint.

Also dubious is the practice of running ads in publications reaching those already convinced of the advertiser's viewpoint, such as an exposition of the merits of free enterprise in the *Harvard Business Review*.

Frequently a complex case for a viewpoint cannot be made through advertising unless it is simplified to create one key opinion in the public's mind. For example, an extensive series of ads was run by the steel industry during the strike of 1959-60. These attempted to cover so much ground in such a complex way that later studies indicated readership was largely confined to people who already strongly sympathized with the steel companies.

Advertising is an exceptionally alluring medium because it enables the advertiser to say exactly what he wants, exactly when he wants, to exactly the audience he seeks to reach. For these very reasons it is probably often the most ineffective and wasteful form of mass communications for public relations purposes. The fact that it permits the advertiser to control the conditions and direct his messages at the audience makes it a one-sided form of communication. It is likely to be ignored, to be discounted, or even to create a resentful backlash because it is a visible effort to impose others' ideas on the audience.

Accordingly, the use of idea advertising requires even greater sensitivity to the viewpoint and self-interest of the audiences than other media. Unless it is conceived and carried out with exceptional finesse, it may be an expensive means of aggravating the advertiser's relationship with his public.

Finally, a barrage of advertising is unlikely to overcome many years of neglect of proper public relations. Efforts by the railroads to gain public support for releasing them from government supervision and the problems of "featherbedding" in employment met great resistance because for many years the railroads had been ignoring the importance of public good will. Similarly, the heavy barrage of advertising run by the oil industry after it was blamed for the effects of the Arab oil embargo had far less beneficial effect than the companies expected. Their long-term neglect of the principles of sound public relations made the sudden loud pleas for understanding—especially since many were oriented to the advertisers rather than to the interest of the audience—seem opportunistic. Since opportunism was one of the charges made against them, the effect was to some extent counterproductive.

48

Direct Communications Methods

Herbert M. Baus

Philip Lesly

SPEAKERS' BUREAUS

The speakers' bureau is perhaps the most troublesome of media in relation to the number of people reached. There is a tremendous volume of detail work to getting the speakers, arranging the meetings, preparing the speakers to tell the right story, and orienting them sufficiently to handle questions and answers and to avoid embarrassing if not dangerous errors. There are such uncontrollable dangers as that of the speaker being late or missing his appointment.

Yet speakers are very valuable as a medium of communication. They project the public relations story before live audiences that concentrate their attention on the subject matter during the speech. This is an effective mass publicity method if the speech and its delivery have the power of motivation.

The speakers' bureau can take advantage of the numerous meetings, forums, lectures, panels, symposiums, round-table discussions, and similar occasions that are constantly being held by all kinds of organizations.

One well-known and most successful speakers' bureau is that of The National Academy of TV Arts and Sciences. Its bureau provides volunteer lecturers and advisers to colleges and civic and service organizations from the academy's 6,000 members.

A number of large corporations and associations—the American Medical Association, for example—prepare speech kit material for members, enabling them to make polished public appearances. The typical kit outlines the basic structure of a good speech and advises on persuasive ways to gain and hold attention.

Each such speech has the attendant publicity value of prior announcements and subsequent coverage in the press, publications of the audience organization, and direct mail.

The speakers' bureau is a sensitive device of public relations in that after the speaker is chosen and dispatched everything is up to him and the public relations director has lost control of his planning, objectives, and presentation of ideas.

The technique of building a speakers' bureau includes the following steps:

(1) Develop a file of research data, perhaps a "speaker's manual" summarizing the information about the subject being publicized.

(2) Prepare material in advance to send out with speakers for distribution at meetings.

(3) Develop a list of speakers and subjects. Choose men and women who speak well, are well received, know the subject. List all pertinent data about speakers, including information necessary for proper authority and publicity.

(4) Set up training programs for speakers who have not had such instruction. Cover subject matter, styles of delivery, how to handle question-and-answer periods. (See Bibliography for reference and instruction books.)

(5) Select a few titles—preferably active and catchy, aimed at the interest of the audience. "Where Has All Your Money Gone?" is better than "The Problem of Inflation."

(6) Formulate a list of organizations to which

Figure 48-1. The speaker's platform provides an effective form of public relations communication, for it enables an organization to present specific information to many audiences. To help its members convey factual and positive messages about the advantages of dairy products, the American Dairy Association furnishes industry spokesmen with do's-and-don't's on speaking, pertinent subjects for discussion, and information for answering questions.

speakers will be offered. Contact them by direct mail or other means. Promptly fill all requests.

(7) Follow through with advance and spot coverage publicity to all local newspapers and radio stations, "house" papers or trade publications, and so on.

(8) Get maximum publicity from the speech itself. Often the impact will be greater from the stories about what is said, appearing in mass-circulation newspapers or other media, than from the effect on the audience. Though a speech should not be written "around" the audience, it should have as much newsworthiness and as many sharp quotations as possible, to catch the media's interest as well as that of those present.

(9) Follow through afterward for audience reaction, dropping poor speakers and moving the good ones up on the list for more frequent use.

A public relations man will often be called on to talk. He will be required to direct committees. Without necessarily being an orator, the skilled public relations worker knows how to say enough and not too much in simple language. If he cannot get up and say his piece and leave a message squarely in the laps of his audience, he may be well advised to take speech courses and learn how to do so.

Although it is much better to speak spontaneously or to use notes, if a speaker must read his talk, either because of limited ability as a speaker or

Figure 48-2. As part of speech training of personnel, video tape recordings are made of rehearsals. Here the Carborundum Company tapes a speaker's performance for his review.

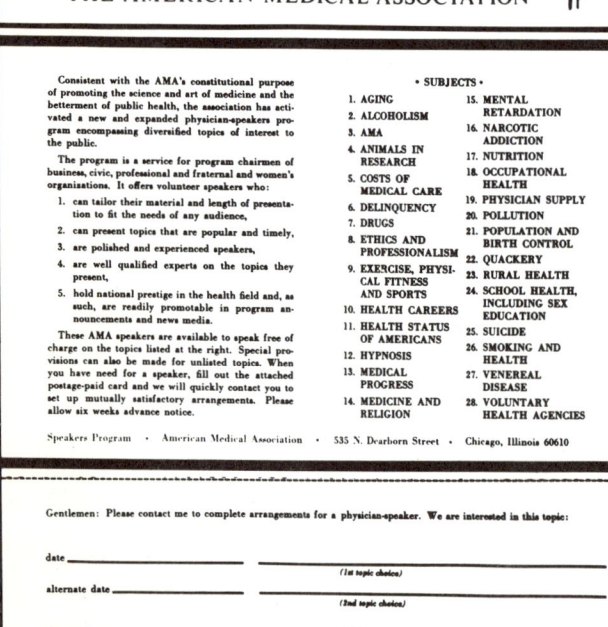

Figure 48-3. A folder sent out to solicit invitations for speaking opportunities. A postage-paid addressed card is detachable.

```
                                                                    12.
    It is symptomatic of our confusion that
so many people say, "If we can put a man on
the moon, we can solve our problems on earth
by putting our minds to it and committing the
necessary funds."  But the moon is a fixed
target.  Our scientists could predict exactly
in 1960 where it would be on July 20, 1969.
No other circumstances would change the
nature or the scope of the challenge.
    Unfortunately, each of the problem areas
on earth is constantly changing.  Other cir-
cumstances develop that alter every social
target we set.  Secondly, the moon program
was a triumph for the very "systems approach"
we neglect here at home.  All conceivable
elements were considered together, and the
interplay between them was accounted for in
calculations, in planning and in patient
trial before the historic Apollo event.
```

Figure 48-4. Page from a speech manuscript typed on a bulletin typewriter. Actual type is about twice this size. Large type face makes delivery easier without undue attention to the manuscript. Each page always ends on a complete sentence.

because of the danger of being misquoted on a delicate subject, the following points will make the reading better received:

(1) Do not apologize for reading.
(2) Read slowly and loudly, avoiding monotone, and pause from time to time for variation.
(3) Sometimes relief devices are helpful, such as looking away from the speech and repeating an important point in spontaneous words or asking a question as if the audience were expected to answer.

The point is to inject vitality into the talk, not to make it a perfunctory reading.

If possible, a video prompter should be used. It enables the speaker to read without seeming to. Q-Tv Prompting Services and Video-Cue, Inc., both of New York, make them.

When a public relations man is playing host to a speaker, he is obliged to pay him every courtesy. What are the speaker's travel preferences, ticket and reservation needs? Have arrangements been made to meet him and take him to his hotel room? Is someone following up with a letter thanking the speaker? Have precautions been taken to avoid cluttering up the speaker's time with overlong announcements, committee reports, and trivial speeches, and to avoid the equally disagreeable bad timing of introducing the afterdinner speaker so soon that he must compete with waiters' juggling of dishes?

Speeches are often sent to a press distribution list, with highlights marked or verbatim. A major speech can receive extensive exposure in this manner.

THE TELEPHONE AS A PUBLIC RELATIONS DEVICE

A telephone call is more effective than a letter as a last-minute reminder or an incitement to action. The telephone is good for getting a person to do something he should do although he might prefer not to, such as attending a meeting. He can dodge a letter more easily than the personal commitment of a telephone conversation. But for a technical or monetary commitment both parties will find it advisable to put it in writing to seal the telephone agreement.

The secret of success in a large-scale telephone campaign is to obtain reliable telephoners—people with pleasing telephone personalities and the persistence to keep after each number until they actually reach the proper party and drive the message home.

Maximum effectiveness is obtained in a telephone drive when every prospect is reached over the 'phone by a personal acquaintance.

During all election campaigns, workers for all parties make extensive use of the telephone as a vehicle in lining up votes for their candidates.

The Bell Telephone System has published several booklets about telephone courtesy that will be helpful to anyone using the 'phone as a contact device. The telephone being an instrument of human contact, courtesy and tact in its use are important in winning the understanding and good will of the person on the receiving end. The telephone personality of an organization and its employees is a vital aspect of its relations with the entire community, with many different publics, and with every individual contacted by 'phone.

Employees may be trained to answer promptly and clearly and arrange for the 'phone to be answered in the absence of the party who usually responds. Thoughtful employees will leave word of approximately when they will return. If they are out for a great deal of the time, they will check in as often as feasible to pick up and return their calls.

It is courteous to let the other party hang up first.

Telephone transfers are irritating and it is good policy to avoid them if the party originally called can possibly take care of the caller.

People in business can win good will by answering their own telephones if possible. It is the worst kind of telephone manners to have a secretary ask every caller, "Who's this?" "Who are you with?" "What is the call about?" "Couldn't I have someone else help you?" President Kennedy made it a point to answer his own telephone whenever he could.

The story is told of a trade association executive whose salary was raised because of the spectacular success of his public relations program. The boost sufficiently impressed the executive that he instructed his secretary to constitute herself as a barrier to people trying to reach him over the telephone. One of the nation's most important trade associations decided to hire a permanent president and sent a committee that tried for some time to get by the executive's secretary. She refused to let them reach her boss without explaining their business. Because they declined to explain to her that they were offering him $75,000 to take a new job, they searched elsewhere to make their appointment.

A glaring telephone discourtesy is to have a secretary put a call through and then hold up the party being telephoned because the caller has become tied up with something else. It is better for people in business to make their own calls.

The president of a major corporation fired his public relations man because the president was made to wait while being telephoned. The president said, "He obviously is a poor public relations man if he treats *anybody* that way on the telephone."

COMMUNICATING THROUGH ACTIVISM

Activism as a means of gaining public interest probably antedates widespread literacy. Activist tactics were a force behind the rise of Christianity, and the split in Christianity was accelerated by such activism as Luther's nailing his 95 theses to the church door.[1]

However, the rise of television as a primary force led to a strong movement toward visualization and

---

[1] "Survival in an Age of Activism," by Philip Lesly, *Public Relations Journal*, December, 1969. Vol. XXV, No. 12, pp. 6-10.

action. This, in turn, magnified the role of activism in various ways:

• By showing activism vividly in full motion, sound, and color, affording "instant involvement";

• By feeding the appetite of the media for sensation and controversy;

• By multiplying the number of activist forces exerting pressures at the same time;

• By accelerating their growth and aggravating their impact; and

• By motivating others to agitate for their causes.

In the late '60s the tide of activism in the United States seemed to be superseding all other aspects of mass communication. Demonstrations, occupation of college buildings and public parks, provocation of the police, and heckling of public figures all gained widespread attention. However, it became apparent that using this technique was increasingly dangerous. It was often like letting loose a force that could as readily turn on the originator as achieve his ends.

In 1968, for instance, the activism of the forces for Senator Eugene McCarthy attained extreme visibility and public attention. But studies after the Presidential election by the University of Michigan showed that more votes had been swung to the Nixon position than had been voted for the extreme position of immediate withdrawal from Viet Nam that McCarthy had espoused. The reaction of resentment and fear against the multiple activist groups was expressed by millions of voters when they responded to Nixon's appeal to "lower our voices." They rejected those who aggressively sought to force drastic change.

To understand the tenor of the public to be influenced and predict how it will respond to any form of communication, its heritage and character must be assessed. The American social and political system has throughout its history been a flexible one, able to absorb many variations, but thereby almost always diverting all extremes into the midstream that represents the great majority.

Activism often is an extreme form of press agentry—a form that is often embraced by media that would scorn other types of press agentry. But like press agentry of other types, it may succeed in getting attention while failing to achieve its purpose, or even backfiring against its source.

In general, public attitudes often follow laws of physics: the greater the potential potency of a given influence, the greater the potential reaction against it. Careful, low-key, gradual communications may take a long time and be drowned out, but they are not likely to create a negative backlash. Aggressive methods may bring fast, dramatic results, but the chance they will lead to setbacks is great.

WORD OF MOUTH

Word of mouth can spread like a prairie fire. If the subject and content are right, it can burst into spontaneous combustion as an entire forest may suddenly be overrun by a conflagration. Through word of mouth, rumor and innuendo may spread with extreme speed and spontaneity if the subject is close to the emotions of people. Feelings and not thoughts most quickly take wing on word of mouth. In stimulating a word-of-mouth campaign, the important thing is to present subject matter of such interest as to cause people to repeat it to others.

Word of mouth is perhaps the most subtle of publicity tools. It is the hardest to control. At times it is the most negative and destructive, taking the form of gossip and slander. Its manipulation is not subject to cut-and-dried mechanics, as is the case with so many publicity media and instruments. The things that contribute to word-of-mouth circulation are:

(1) A spectacular and successful event or product.

(2) A spectacular publicity or advertising campaign.

Figure 48-5. Having made sure the television cameras were there, protesters picket a convention of the American Medical Association in New York (AMA photo).

(3) A good catchword or slogan.
(4) Capitalizing on a mass trend or catchword.

When Daniel P. Moynihan ran for the Senate from New York in 1976, his greatest handicap was that word of mouth about him was negative among the large Black electorate. He had advised, a few years earlier, that a policy of "benign neglect" be pursued in regard to Blacks and one of his best-known studies reported on the dispersal of Black families. He overcame the problem by disseminating literature and stimulating word-of-mouth communication on how strongly he supported having the rest of the country help New York City and New York State out of their financial crises. He emphasized that his opponent, Senator James Buckley, advocated fiscal responsibility for New York governments, which would mean temporary reductions in welfare and other payments.

Also in the 1976 elections, Jimmy Carter faced the problems of being little known and having an undistinguished record in his one term as Governor of Georgia. His campaign used word of mouth and other means to exploit the public's dissatisfaction with the professional government establishment.

In both cases, they countered the negative word of mouth and fed the stream with what they wanted. (See Chapter 38.)

LETTERS

Letters, which enable one person to reach out to another despite the limitations of time that cut down on personal visits and telephoning, are among the most ancient and perhaps still the most important of all media of communications. It has been said that letters are the only selling medium that, if taken away, would disrupt the entire modern business structure. At the present time only 15 percent of the total mail load is attributable to personal correspondence. All else is commercial.

Letters for every conceivable purpose—to sell products, put over ideas, win votes, incite to action of all kinds—are sent out as individual letters, form letters individually addressed, and form letters addressed something like "Dear Friend."

They are sent out with every kind of enclosure: pamphlets and leaflets, order blanks, samples, pictures, return post cards, and many others.

The well-written letter has a major advantage over all other media—it is directed *personally* to an individual. If it is designed to please and flatter him rather than to irritate him as an invasion of his privacy, it commands his attention for a little while—perhaps just long enough to motivate him to do what the writer wants him to do.

One trouble with letters is that almost everybody writes them. There is too much competition. It is true that people like to receive mail. But mail is a personal thing. The citizen likes to get a letter written *for* him as well as addressed to him. He likes it to express regard for him, offer him a better job, make a promise, or contain a check. When a publicist sends out a letter written for the client's benefit instead of for the recipient's, the recipient's privacy is being presumed upon. The recipient may resent it. He may throw the letter away without reading it, or read it only to turn against the writer.

One survey showed that 58 percent of those in the advertising and related fields think that less than 15 percent of the direct mail pieces are effective. Only 5 per cent think that more than half of the direct mail pieces are effective.

If direct mail is too *cheap,* it can be the most expensive publicity available. On the other hand, when well done it has extensive possibilities. Both quality and selectivity of mailing are factors to be weighed. A maker of automatic controls picked up $2 million in orders as a result of a mailing to 110 key executives.

Direct mail at its best is direct mail that is or appears to be *direct* mail, namely shooting with a rifle and not shooting with a shotgun.

These elements will help attain the maximum in results:

Lists. Lists constitute the aiming of direct mail. Their importance cannot be overemphasized. A misspelled name or a slovenly address means the cost of processing a good direct mail letter has been wasted. Lists can be grouped according to interests. Ways to get direct mail lists include: Members of organizations, house-to-house canvass, precinct lists, telephone books, "coupon" advertisements, list brokers, directories, publication subscription lists. Lists can be kept up to date by filing on 3 x 5-inch cards and by noting address changes as they come in. Lists are available from many brokers at a cost of a few cents a name or a rough average of $35 a thousand depending on the type of list desired. A central source of information is the Direct Mail Marketing Association, 230 Park Ave., New York, N.Y. 10017.

Approach. Letters can be personalized in physical appearance and content. Most tests show that first-class mail more than pays for the extra cost in increased results over second-class. Fill-in letters are more effective when the name, address, and salutation are indistinguishable from body type. Electronic methods of letter preparation make it possible to repeat the family name or make other individual references in the body of the letter to personalize a mass-produced presentation. These are available through large mailing houses and through IBM service offices.

It is important who signs the letter. It is well for the signature to be by the person with most influence on the addressee, and signed personally rather than processed, if possible.

Contents. Appeal, specific application, instructions for action are vital ingredients. Make-up can be made concrete, sincere, persuasive, and vivid. It is worth the trouble to make the contents timely and based on confluence of interest between the writer and the addressee. Recommended is a simple writing style that seems in character with the writer. Attention, interest, desire, action, in that order, have been found to furnish the most effective sequence.

Outward form and appearance. Paper, letterhead, envelope may be planned to be of appealing color, style, size, and quality. Typography is advocated that looks distinctive as well as dignified. Readership is increased if each envelope is individually addressed or addressed to look almost exactly like original handling. It is cut down by a printed postage permit used in place of the stamp. Even the style of folding is important. The standard twice-horizontal folding is best in most cases.

Enclosures. Copy and layout can be designed to attract attention and tell the story effectively. The use of too many different enclosures annoys and bewilders the recipient.

Continuity. It has been estimated by a trade spokesman that continuity in mailing is next in importance to a correct mailing list:

> On the basis of 100 percent for the success of a direct mail campaign, one mailing will be worth about 5 percent; two mailings 15 percent; three mailings 40 percent; four mailings 60 percent; five mailings 75 percent, and six to eight mailings 100 percent.

With repeated mailings, intervals not exceeding two weeks best sustain the effect of preceding mail. In a series, earlier letters may best concentrate on information, later ones more on appeal to action.

Timing. Letters mailed Monday or Tuesday hit the target in midweek, the best time. Letters mailed late in the week hit the offices on Monday, when his desk is piled with the weekend accumulation.

Testing. Especially in a large mailing, it may be good insurance to try out a letter on a random portion of a group. A test of reasonable size can usually be depended on to indicate the percentage of return to be expected from a mailing to the entire group.

Etiquette of letters. Concise letters, written with sincerity and restraint, will make the writer's voice heard by elected legislative and executive officials of the national or state Government. The proper manner of addressing these officials is:

> To the President of the United States:
> The President
> The White House
>   or
>
> The President
> Washington, D.C. 20500
> Salutation is:
>   Sir: or To the President: or, My dear Mr. President:
> Complimentary close is:
>   Respectfully submitted—or, Yours respectfully—or, Faithfully yours (informal)
>
> To a Cabinet Member:
>   The Honorable _____
>   Secretary of State
>   The Department of State
>   Washington, D.C. 20520
>
> To a Senator:
>   The Honorable _____
>   The United States Senate
>   Washington, D.C. 20510
> Salutation is:
>   Dear Sir: My dear Senator: or, My dear _____: (informal)
> Complimentary close is:
>   Very truly yours.
>
> To a Representative:
>   The Honorable _____
>   The House of Representatives
>   Washington, D.C. 20515
> Saluation is:
>   Sir: or, Dear Sir: or, My dear Mr. _____: (informal)
> Complimentary close is:
>   Very truly yours.

Style in writing to state and local officials will follow these models.

There are elements of courtesy by mail that pay off in cumulative dividends. It is well to answer personal mail within twenty-four hours. When that is impossible, the secretary can write a polite

DIRECT COMMUNICATIONS METHODS

explanation, promising a full reply at the earliest opportunity.

To put as much individuality as possible into every letter, an executive will find it best to sign his own mail. Use of a form letter to answer a personally addressed letter is an insult and will be so interpreted by the recipient. It is well to salute and sign with first names if the degree of acquaintance warrants.

In any business matter where there is the slightest possibility of subsequent misunderstanding, it is advisable to put the matter on record with a letter to avoid future misunderstandings and to supplement the memories of all concerned.

Every letter an organization mails is a little public relations worker. Its work will be good or bad, according to the quality of the worker. An organization that mails thousands of letters daily has, in that fact, a public relations opportunity. Recognizing this, many firms make letter writing courses available to their employees.

POST CARDS

Post cards—quick and easy to prepare, quick and easy for the recipient to absorb, economical to mail—constitute an effective adaptation of direct mail to reach large numbers of people with a message that can be punched home in a paragraph.

In many campaigns, large numbers of individuals can be stimulated to sign and then send post cards to their own friends and contacts. This personal touch has more influence with the recipient than would a communique from a stranger.

The picture post card on one side publicizes an attraction and on the other provides space for mailing and a personal message. Many restaurants, hotels, and resorts provide free mailings to encourage the dispatch of more of these cards. A real advantage of post cards is that, because they are so easy to prepare, they are a convenient method to enlist patrons to do personal advertising for an organization—giving it a personal touch with their individual endorsements.

NEWSLETTERS

Another form of direct-mail communication that is increasing in use is the newsletter. Despite the term, many of these do not deal with news and they are not letters. Any publication of a few pages, usually written in concise form and generally appearing at regular intervals, is called a newsletter.

Managing the Human Climate
Guidelines on Public Relations and Public Affairs
by Philip Lesly

No. 34

Corporate Portrait: The Annual Report

In thousands of corporate headquarters and public relations firms the groaning time of the year is near: planning and preparation of the annual report. Seldom do so many strain so hard for so little as in the gestation of this one document.

The annual report is many things: a legal requirement, the chief executives' visible show of their stewardship, an outlet for pride or apologies on the year, a communications tool with the financial community, the most tangible regular exhibit of the company as a corporate entity, a concise composite of the company for thought leaders and others.

But it is also one thing more...something that seems to be lost sight of in the preparation of most reports: It is a portrait of the character and outlook of the company's management. And behind much of the postured posing and polishing on the surface there often can be seen the candid reality of what kind of personality fills those executive suites when the posing is over.

Many reports show either flabby or rigid personalities in the front offices. And even untrained readers sense that when they review the reports.

Companies that spend millions on visual identity systems, corporate advertising, public service programs or motion picture series -- all aimed at portraying the firm as warm, progressive and public-spirited -- undermine other efforts in the comparatively modest-priced annual report.

Now new SEC requirements for content of these reports have led to further stifling of the personality that many reports project.

There are eight guidelines to help assure that the "portrait" of the annual report depicts the company as well as the facts justify:

1. Determine objectively what is the distinctive character of the company. For example, among all oil companies, what is different about this oil company? What emphases, traits, practices set it off from the crowd? Just as no one sees himself as others

Figure 48-6. First page of a newsletter. This one features helpful information and commentary. Others emphasize concise news.

The newsletter originated as a commercial publication, providing hard-to-get and up-to-date information on a specific subject for an annual subscription price. *The Kiplinger Washington Letter,* for instance, reports weekly on developments and expectations in the capital that may be useful or interesting to the subscribers. Many others deal with limited subjects, such as the petroleum market, demand for gold, or grain trading.

The public relations newsletter is usually provided free to a selected list of customers or clients, prospects, media, and others who can be helpful to the issuer. In some cases, the subscription method and free distribution are combined. Philip Lesly's *Managing the Human Climate,* for instance, goes to clients, prospective clients, and media without charge; it is sent on a paid subscription basis to others. This publication, like many others, does not deal with news but with other material that is expected to be helpful or impressive to the recipients.

Many newsletters are highly graphic and are printed in more than one color. Others are usually all-type and in one color.

There are a number of points to be considered before undertaking a newsletter. Once started it is intended to be a long-term commitment, so advance planning will have significance for a long time.

1. Does the organization have something to offer in a newsletter that meets an unmet need and that will make the desired impression for the issuer? It is unwise to issue a newsletter just because others do or if it will be one of a number on the same subject, without distinctive value.

2. Will it convey to the audience what is unique about the organization or why the recipients should give special attention to the source?

3. Is a distribution list readily available or can it be assembled and maintained with reasonable effort and cost?

4. Is there someone available with the knowledge, skill, time, and access to sources that are necessary to do an excellent job with every issue? Many newsletters are poor and damage the reputation of the issuer.

5. How often should it be issued? Is immediate news a major factor, so weekly or even more frequent dissemination may be called for? What can the budget provide for? In any case, it should be issued no less than once every two months. It is unlikely that recognition can be maintained if the intervals are longer.

6. What should the format be: four pages, more, or variable with each issue depending on how much material there is? Should enclosures be made from time to time, such as reprints of speeches or articles? Should it be black-and-white or multicolored? Should it regularly contain illustrations or be essentially all-type?

7. With all these considerations and others peculiar to the organization, are you sure this is the best means to accomplish the objective? Other media may not require so much staff time, or such a long-term commitment. Is it worth the cost when budgets are prepared with a liberal allowance for increases in postage rates and other growing costs?

A source of information is *Newsletter on Newsletters,* 44 W. Market St., Rhinebeck, N.Y. 12572.

EXTENSION HOME ECONOMISTS

There are about 3,000 offices of extension home economists scattered throughout the United States. They are operated by federal, state, and local governments to educate consumers on matters such as food, money management, health care, home remodeling and repair, education, home decoration, safety, clothing, toys, gardening, housekeeping, and community problems.

Some of the EHEs write regular newspaper columns. Others have television and radio shows, or write monthly newsletters, or speak before various audiences.

As a group the EHEs represent an influential audience that in turn reaches many individuals. Lists of the offices and services for reaching them are available from Associated Release Service, 2 N. Riverside Plaza, Chicago, Ill. 60606.

Figure 48-7. Stickers and labels can be effective in driving messages home. These are offered by the National Safety Council: top, a sticker for an auto dashboard; below, a typical label for chemical containers.

Figure 48-8. Sample postage-meter imprints.

OTHER DIRECT MEDIA

(1) Mailgrams command attention but at a higher price per person reached than letters. They reach people quickly. Sometimes a batch of them sent to people in the same city at a special rate will command precise, immediate interest.

(2) An economical reminder medium is stickers to be glued on letters, post cards, envelopes, newsletters, bills, windshields, windows, doors, and other convenient places.

(3) Inserts are frequently designed to accompany letters, bills, and other mailings. Pocket calendars are an excellent form of insert; they are handy for the recipient to have around and are kept for use, whereas the ordinary insert is usually thrown away, sometimes without more than a cursory glance.

(4) Many organizations use their regular bank checks to carry messages. Several national associations have promoted this plan by sending sample checks to members illustrating the use that can be made of this medium. The technical space of the check is reduced to provide a greater margin, which usually carries a sketch in color to put across a message.

(5) Lapel buttons make emissaries out of human beings, label a person as a supporter, stir up questions and curiosity. When many adherents wear them, it creates a feeling of power and mass endorsement.

(6) Thousands of persons can be reached at little or no extra cost by stamping mass mailings with postage meters using for special messages the boxed space ordinarily taken by post office cancelling machines. The problem is to prevail on organizations using postage meter machines to use a cut putting over the message being publicized. For drives in the public interest, such as for Red Cross, Community Fund, Easter Seals, and the like, a poster meter manufacturer[2] will usually make available a list of clients. For example, the Red Cross may work up a letter to go to all clients, address Red Cross envelopes from the postage meter company's list, and send out the letters. The letters urge the individual client to buy from the postage meter machine company a cut publicizing the Red Cross. For mass use of this medium in such drives, the desirable first step is to contact the postage meter company, which will outline the steps to be followed.

(7) A rubber stamp can be created, carrying a message sometimes including a drawing, and used to stamp the message by the thousands on envelopes or letterheads.

(8) Jokes are themselves a medium. They can be devised or revised, and adapted, for directing favorable attention to a subject when related before meetings, printed in publications, embodied in comic strips, or broadcast.

(9) Often a catchy slogan, adopted for a campaign or an organization, can be worked into posters and signs, referred to in talks, and made a catch line for editorials and story mentions.

Slogans and catchwords have decisive impact in political publicity. "He kept us out of war" helped elect Wilson for his second term. McKinley rode in on the slogan, "The full dinner-pail." President Lyndon B. Johnson campaigned on "All the way with LBJ."

The form of the slogan can be, among others:

- Statement of character—"Good to the last drop."
- Imperative—"Send me a man who *reads!*"
- Admonition—"Don't look if you can't stand the sight of courage."
- Endorsement—"Me? I'd pick Schick . . . for myself."
- Claim of superiority—"Pure elegance . . . with a two-year/24,000 miles pledge of excellence."
- Reason why—"From contented cows."
- Promise of results—"Daydreams come true with Evening in Paris."
- Play on words—"Does she . . . or doesn't she?"
- Summary of features—"Sure, safe, and simple."
- Prediction—"Good things begin to happen when you start a meal with soup."
- Prestige—"The soap for people who like people!"
- Suggestion—"Enjoy life more with music."

(10) Symbols—objects that carry instantaneous meaning—are effective tools in mass impulse and propaganda. A flag, a national anthem, a great man are all symbols. The caduceus is a symbol of the healing professions. The swastika was the symbol of the German Nazis; the hammer and sickle is the symbols of the Communists. John Bull for England and Uncle Sam for the United States are symbols. These accepted tokens convey immediate meaning. They are eloquent tools of expression and are used repeatedly as shafts of publicity and propaganda.

(11) Bumper stickers are another publicity medium, often used by advocates of a public policy, a political candidate, or a fund-raising organiza-

---

[2]Pitney-Bowes, Inc., 69 Walnut St., Stamford, Conn. 06904.

tion. Preferably these should be presented to the car owners, rather than applied without permission, to maintain good will. Many people will refuse to mark their cars with public stands on issues or a memento of a resort, even though they support them.

SIGNS

Probably the oldest advertising medium in history, outdoor advertising dates at least as far back as ancient Egypt and even now is a large, successful business in areas like China where other media of modern advertising are largely undeveloped. Pasted posters on building walls are part of the decor of Rome.

Outdoor advertising features the following types of posters:

(1) *"Poster panels,"* in which the poster is pasted up for a given period of time, accounting for about 66 percent of the printed outdoor advertising industry's revenue;

(2) *"Painted bulletins"* that go up on walls or specially erected *signboards,* a more elaborate and expensive form, accounting for about 33 percent of the revenue from printed types;

(3) Electric *"spectacular displays"* and semi-electric painted bulletins, the most dramatic—and expensive—of all types, jointly accounting for a small proportion of the total outdoor advertising revenue.

(These computations of sales volume include only the members of the OAAA, the Outdoor Advertising Association of America, 625 Madison Ave., New York, N.Y. 10022.)

In addition, store signs are a basic form of outdoor publicity.

Reputable outdoor advertising concerns make every effort to maintain attractive signs, landscaped and decorated to contribute to rather than to deteriorate the surrounding area. By their endeavor to protect scenic sections of rural roadsides from inappropriate commercial use and to preserve areas with recreational or historical value, outdoor advertising companies have followed a public relations policy that makes their medium of greater value to their clients.

For public relations purposes, outdoor advertising has a strong reminder value. It helps spur to direct action. To get the best results, it is necessary to present outdoor advertising in few words and distinct outlines so the story will be told at a glance, because the passing motorist or pedestrian for

Figure 48-9. Posters reach passing crowds in schools, theaters, and other public places. Small ones go onto bulletin boards, large ones into poster frames.

whom it is prepared will have only a passing instant to absorb the message.

A variation of sign media is the bulletin board, used by organizations for display of posters and messages in meeting places. Bulletin boards have a strong "habit value" when located at places where employees or other constant audiences gather regularly. They are a good medium for reminders, special messages, and official announcements.

Posters of all kinds for display from counters, in store windows, in meeting halls, in schools and offices, in lobbies and in many other places constitute a sign medium widely used in special promotions.

Skywriting and plane-drawn streamers are among the most spectacular forms of advertising and publicity, and are useful in establishing a name or idea.

Advertising signs suspended from or dragged from behind by airplanes and blimps constitute a somewhat more effective use of the sky, particularly at night when colored lights are shown. This kind of publicity is often used by the entertainment industry at crowded places that provide a large audience for such a display. Also, they do not add to pollution of

DIRECT COMMUNICATIONS METHODS

the air. These signs are sometimes accompanied by sound effects to intensify their impact. A variation on this medium is the illuminated mobile blimp.

FAIRS AND EXHIBITS

One of the most spectacular special events and at the same time most tangible media of publicity takes form in the fairs and exhibits that enrich the life of America with dynamic showmanship plus salesmanship.

Every year the United States has approximately 2,200 fairs viewed by some 75,000,000 people. And, beginning with our first overseas venture in Bangkok, Thailand, in 1954, American exhibits have been seen by millions of people in countries thoughout most of the free world. Hundreds of millions of dollars are invested in various fair properties. Some individual establishments are worth more than $30,000,000. Considerably more than 10,000 people are employed yearly by these fairs, with wages running into uncomputed millions.

Fairs constitute both a merchandising medium and a publicity medium. As a merchandising instrument they can have good effect if exhibitors plan their displays cleverly.

Except when the publicity is tied in with direct merchandising of specific products, as in the case of store displays in the windows of stores, exhibits at fairs, conventions, trade shows, and elsewhere sometimes tend to cost more money and trouble than they are worth for publicity alone.

The function of the fair is changing with the sudden broadening of communications and attractions for the public. Where as recently as 1939, a fair could assemble many wonders that were not otherwise available to the public, by 1964 television, full-color magazines and books, foreign travel, audiovisual techniques in education, and other factors had brought wonders within easier reach of the population. It is no longer necessary for people to travel hundreds of miles, go to great expense, and walk for miles to see any exhibit except the extraordinary.

It is unlikely that the spectacular World's Fair will be a continuing attraction. While the Century of Progress in Chicago during 1933 and 1934 made money during the Depression, the 1964-65 World's Fair in New York—even though it used some of the same sites and facilities as the 1939-40 Fair—lost a great deal of money for the sponsors and many of the exhibitors.

Special-interest fairs, such as trade exhibits and agricultural fairs, continue to have a strong attraction because they serve functions not otherwise met.

This trend emphasizes the importance of keeping abreast of social and cultural trends in planning any public relations activity.

When considering publicizing a client with a fair exhibit, weigh all the angles: timeliness, dramatic possibilities of the display, competition from other displays, publicity possibilities, tie-ups available, etc.

DISPLAYS

Important considerations with respect to acquiring, planning, and arranging window displays to influence the public were outlined in a booklet entitled *Displays,* published by the public relations department of the American Red Cross:

> The merchant's window is his most valuable stock in trade, and he there features the merchandise by which he wishes to be judged.
>
> The window display is set up to motivate the onlooker to action—to come in and buy.
>
> Window displays are gauged to focus public attention sharply on a certain point, and each display should be used to drive home a single idea.
>
> Window displays should be carefully timed, and launched simultaneously to capitalize on press and radio work to incite to action.
>
> A sufficient number of window displays creates an atmosphere of urgency abetted by the feeling that the entire community is behind the project.
>
> A window display should not be crowded with details, should offer a simple idea that can be grasped at a glance.
>
> The best displays lure the eye with a device that helps to tell the story, has the unity of a good poster. Its purpose is the same as a poster's, to excite, not to instruct.
>
> The display should fit the character of other displays in the same store.
>
> Color harmony is important, and a safe rule is to combine one predominant with two offsetting colors.
>
> Preparing a window display schedule requires knowledge of how many stores of each type exist in a community. The more that is known about stores in relation to economic and social areas and traffic movements, the more efficiently a publicist can place his displays properly to accomplish a specific purpose.
>
> Displays should be planned and arranged well in advance, because stores tend to tie them

up with merchandising drives far ahead of time.

Types of stores include drug, grocery, barber and beauty shops, hotels, banks, jewelry stores, women's and men's clothiers, variety stores, utility offices, and department stores. Usually department stores prepare their own exhibits, but the publicist must be prepared in the other cases to furnish all or much of the exhibit material, and possibly even to install it himself. Leading types of display are:

(1) The simplest window display is a poster. The most desirable window location for a poster alone is adjoining the doorway.

(2) Photographic prints, 11 x 14 inches, or larger blowups, make eye-catching displays, alone or with other materials.

(3) Displays of models, cutouts, figures, and materials with captions and perhaps with posters furnish dramatic exhibits.

(4) The outdoor display has the same problem as the outdoor advertisement—to catch the eye of a public on the move. "Tell it. Tell it simply. Tell it briefly," is the formula. The types of outdoor display are:

(a) The fixed display, which must have familiarity of symbol to register quickly, unexpectedness to catch the eye, impact to hold the attention and leave an impression.

(b) The moving display, an affair of floats and costumed figures.

(c) The exhibit, which must possess lure, originality, color combined in forms and figures that will halt the steps of the roving spectator. The exhibit should be manned by personnel able to meet the public, explain the booth, and sell the merchandise. The exhibit must combine showmanship with salesmanship.

PUBLIC ADDRESS SYSTEMS

Public address systems at meetings, shows, gatherings of employees, or mass audiences of any kind make it possible mechanically to project the human voice before large numbers of people.

Mounted on a truck, the PA system can be transported from place to place, presenting speakers and programs as it goes, and reaching a widely distributed audience. Sound trucks can also be rigged up at stationary locations, providing facilities for meetings and special programs in lieu of a permanently installed PA system. In Texas, six sound trucks were used to reach three million people in an election campaign. Portable bullhorns afford great mobility wherever amplified sound is needed. It is bad public relations to use sound amplifiers where the noise will annoy local residents.

Recordings make it possible to "capture" a speech or radio program and replay it by radio, before an audience, or over a PA system anywhere. Some recordings are made on the spot at special events. In other cases, special programs are deliberately produced at a recording studio.

49

Working with Influential Groups

Herbert M. Baus

An influential group may consist simply of the "leaders" of a community, or it may be any one or combination of organizations.

Thought leaders are not necessarily the people who hold the titles in organizations, although usually the title-holders are among the thought leaders. An articulate barber, a serious-minded citizen, a labor union member without portfolio, a person who is a member of many groups but an officer of none, may be a thought leader by reason of his vitality, personality, intellect, ability at self-expression, gregariousness, or range of interests.

Every service club, women's group, political party, labor union, religious unit, association, civic organization, welfare body, veteran's organization, or organization of any kind can constitute an influential group.

These groups can be reached by direct mail, speaking to their membership, interviewing their leaders, telephoning, publicizing through their publications, and other means (See Chapter 48.)

They become useful media when they officially endorse a cause or align themselves with it.

Each of these groups represents a segment of the community. Each overflows into other groups through members who belong to other units, relatives, friends, and other human ties. The official action of any such group influences other groups and the attitude of members of such a group reaches other people. Every time such a group is won over, the victory is a stroke in the task of winning public opinion as a whole.

The power of these groups is tremendous. In a political system designed to reflect the popular will through representative rule, we sometimes virtually have a government of organized minorities. Influential groups have often been able to control large blocs of votes in Congress and state legislatures. These groups often define the policies and personnel of government. Some of the groups have at times been referred to as "The Third House" of Congress, or "The Invisible Government."

It is a strategy of sound public relations, particularly in openly controversial matters such as political campaigns with an underdog start, to attack the problem with a "wedge and kessel" or "divide and conquer" policy. The procedure is to win over one group or group of groups at a time, taking on small, easy-to-handle groups in succession. As each group is won over the cause grows stronger and gains adherents and allies.

Indeed it is basic in public campaigns to create a group with an attractive name, as a "Greater New York Committee" might be set up to support a campaign to pass bonds for the improvement of the City of New York. The "Committee for Tolerance" was set up to fight a misnamed "Fair Employment Practices Act" in California and was a strong factor in defeating a measure represented by its backer as a provision for the economic betterment of minorities.

When such an organization is set up as a campaign weapon, the first step will be to name prominent citizens—"thought leaders"—as members of the committee. The very presence of their names on the committee's letterhead wins powerful support for the cause. Because many of these figurehead committees are not what they seem—for example, American Youth for Democracy, a pretty name for what was formerly more honestly labeled the Young Communist League—prominent citizens are well advised to study carefully every such organization

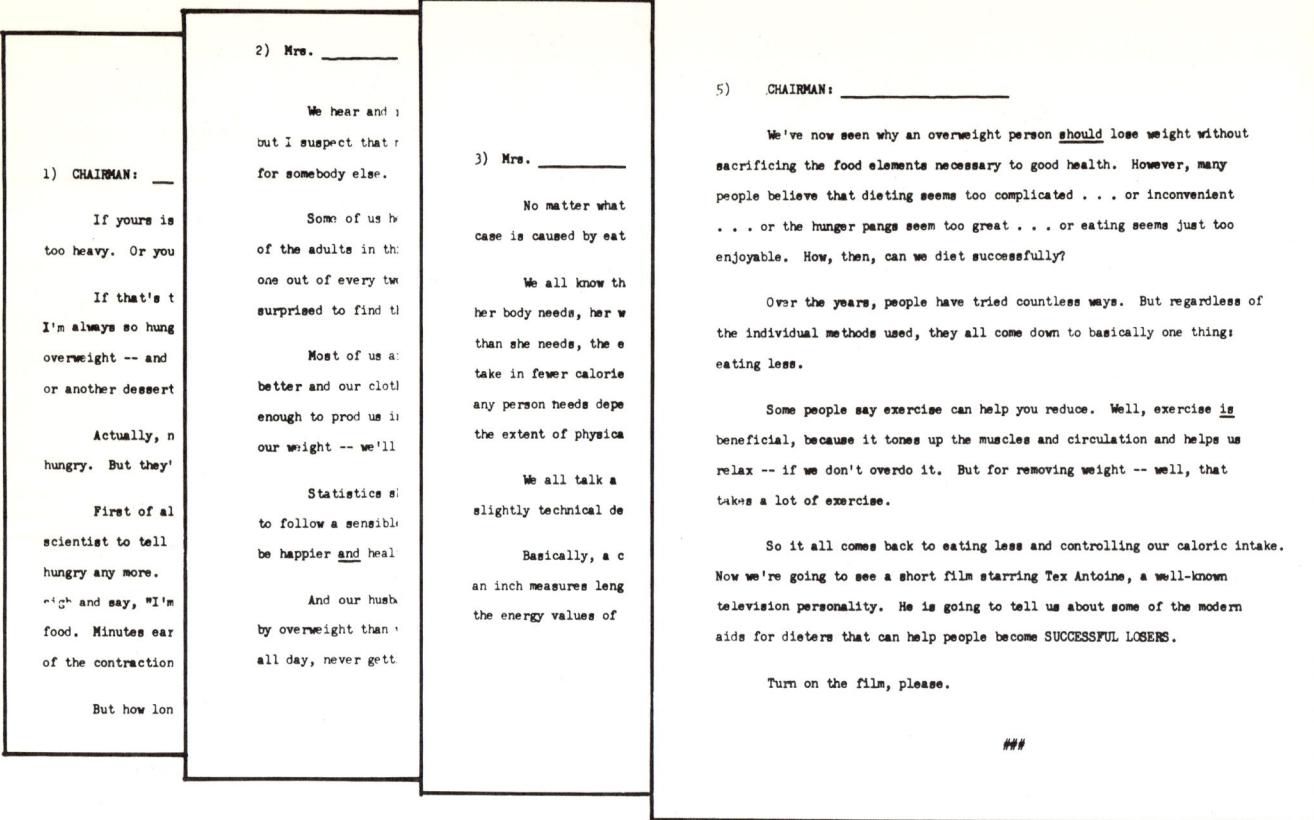

Figure 49-1. Elements of a meeting kit for women's or service clubs. A manuscript is prepared for each participant's part of each phase of the program.

and make sure of its *real* backers and its *real* motives before lending it the use of their names. In establishing such a group it is important to have all facts open and available for study.

Influential groups are most desirable allies in any public relations operation. Regarding one of them, women's organizations, James W. Irwin wrote:

> American business ... has been lax in cultivating the friendship of the women of America. They influence almost everything a man does—and buys! The truly farsighted company soon will have a woman officer or counsellor whose responsibility will be the development of acquaintanceships with the leaders of women's national organizations, and an interpretation for her associates in management of the woman's view of the company's activities, products and services.

Women's groups. The "women's liberation movement" has focused attention on the anomaly of women as potent forces in our society: On one hand women's groups are powerful organizations; on the other hand, women increasingly dislike being treated as a separate "public."

While the women's rights movement takes shape, the interests of women as women are important considerations; and the women's club is a readily identifiable focal point of women's interests.

Writing that "to ignore the importance of women's clubs and their tremendous influence in swaying public sentiment is sheer folly," Winifred Jordan said that some industries have done a good job with this biggest of all groups, including the food, airline, motion picture, broadcasting, and life insurance industries. Until recently, the automotive and petroleum industries catered almost exclusively to men.

Realizing that people can best be influenced through the organizations to which they belong, industry has become increasingly aware of the "women's club market." The market contains a heavy proportion of those leaders who influence other women.

With purchased mailing lists likely to be few and

incomplete, and with state and national federations jealously guarding their lists for fear of exploitation, the women's group has been hard to reach.

Illustrating the technique by which a group may be reached, some manufacturers have hired speakers and listed them with speakers' bureaus. (Refer to chapter on Direct Communication Methods for more information on arranging speaking engagements.) Others buy advertising space in magazines published by state and national federations of women's clubs. Still others retain skilled specialists to prepare a "program package" for its use, mail it to a list of clubs, and handle requests for other clubs that hear about the literature and want it. The "program package" appeals to leaders of women's clubs who must not only plan a year's schedule of meetings for their groups, but must also help member-speakers to state their respective programs.

Typical of packaged programs is the "Good Grooming Portfolio," which the Women's Club Service Bureau prepared and distributed for Bristol-Myers Company. It included detailed instructions for planning and conducting meetings, outlines of talks on grooming, wall charts, suggested questions for the chairman to plant in the audience, a printed quiz by which the individual member could check up on her personal grooming, a form on which the chairman could report the results of her meeting to the bureau—a form of cooperation that is given by many of the women—and sample leaflets together with return post cards by which the program chairmen could order enough copies of the leaflets to make one available for each member.

Among leading national women's organizations that may be of interest to public relations workers are:

> American Association of University Women, 2401 Virginia Ave., NW, Washington, D.C. 20037
> General Federation of Women's Clubs, 1734 N St., NW, Washington, D.C. 20006
> League of Women Voters of the U.S., 1730 M St., NW, Washington, D.C. 20036
> National Council of Catholic Women, C/O United States Catholic Conference, 1312 Massachusetts Ave., NW, Washington, D.C. 20005
> National Council of Jewish Women, 1 W. 47 St., New York, N.Y. 10036
> National Council of Women of the U.S., 345 E. 46 St., New York, N.Y. 10017
> National Federation of Business and Professional Women's Clubs, 2012 Massachusetts Ave., NW, Washington, D.C. 20036
> National Organization for Women, 5 S. Wabash Ave., Suite 1615, Chicago, Ill. 60603
> Young Women's Christian Association, 600 Lexington Ave., New York, N.Y. 10022

Farm groups. Leading national farm organizations include:

> American Farm Bureau Federation, 225 Touhy Ave., Park Ridge, Ill. 60068
> Farmers' Educational & Cooperative Union of America, P.O. Box 2251, Denver, Colo. 80201
> National 4-H Service Comm., 150 N. Wacker Dr., Chicago, Ill. 60606
> National Grange, 1616 H St., NW, Washington, D.C. 20006

Veterans' organizations. Another major influential group consists of war veterans. They express themselves through powerful organizations such as the American Legion, Veterans of Foreign Wars, and others, listed here with their national headquarters. Also listed are related patriotic organizations.

> American Legion, 700 N. Pennsylvania Ave., Indianapolis, Ind. 46206
> American Veterans Committee, 1333 Connecticut Ave., NW, Washington, D.C. 20036
> AMVETS, 1710 Rhode Island Ave., NW, Washington, D.C. 20036
> Catholic War Veterans of the U.S.A., 2 Massachusetts Ave., NW, Washington, D.C. 20001
> Disabled American Veterans, 3725 Alexandria Pike, Cold Springs, Ky. 41076
> Jewish War Veterans of the United States of America, 1712 New Hampshire Ave., NW, Washington, D.C. 20009
> Marine Corps League, 933 N. Kenmore St., Suite 317, Arlington, Va. 22201
> National Society, Daughters of the American Revolution, 1776 D St., NW, Washington, D.C. 20006
> National Society, Sons of the American Revolution, 2412 Massachusetts Ave., NW, Washington, D.C. 20008
> Veterans of Foreign Wars of the United States of America, V.F.W. Building, Kansas City, Mo. 64111

Church groups. The thousands of churches of America and their millions of followers constitute another major influential group of the United States. They can be approached through denominational magazines and newspapers, through national headquarters, through local ministerial associations, and by means of direct mail and individual approach to the individual minister. The publicist representing a cause that enjoys or can obtain church approval can project his story with the help of the church groups by the following techniques:

(1) Sending direct mail to ministers.

(2) Obtaining endorsement of ministerial associations and similar clerical organizations.

(3) Putting the story over through church press and publications.

(4) Sending speakers to special events, forums, meetings, and other church events that will receive outside speakers on appropriate subjects.

(5) Tying in with issues and causes that have church backing.

(6) Making prominent church personages officials of or participants in the organization, association, or cause being publicized.

(7) Working through such church-affiliated organizations as the Knights of Columbus.

(8) Developing special events jointly sponsored by church groups.

Leading religious publications and news services of America are given here. Other religious publications of local or regional character can be obtained from the Ayer directory, mentioned previously.

Baptist:
  Baptist Standard, P.O. Box 6330, Dallas, Tex. 75222
  Christian Index, 2939 Flowers Rd., S., Atlanta, Ga. 30341
Catholic:
  America, 106 W. 56th St., New York, N.Y. 10019
  Catholic Standard, 1711 N St., NW, Washington, D.C. 20036
  Commonweal, 232 Madison Ave., New York, N.Y. 10016
Christian Science:
  Christian Science Monitor, 1 Norway St., Boston, Mass. 02115
Jewish:
  Jewish Observer, 5 Beekman St., New York, N.Y. 10038
  Jewish Spectator, 250 W. 57 St., New York, N.Y. 10019
  National Jewish Monthly, 315 Lexington Ave., New York, N.Y. 10016

Lutheran:
  The Lutheran, 2900 Queen Lane, Philadelphia, Pa. 19129
  Lutheran Standard, 426 S. 5th St., Minneapolis, Minn. 55415
  Lutheran Witness, 3558 S. Jefferson Ave., St. Louis, Mo. 63118
Methodist:
  Methodist Christian Advocate, 1100 Campus Circle, Birmingham, Al. 35204
Presbyterian:
  Christian Observer, 412 S. Third St., Louisville, Ky. 40202
  The Presbyterian, P.O. Box 901, Denton, Tex. 76201
  Presbyterian Journal, P.O. Box 3108, Asheville, N.C. 28802
  Presbyterian Outlook, 512 E. Main St., Richmond, Va. 23219
  Presbyterian Survey, 341 Ponce De Leon Ave., NE, Atlanta, Ga. 30308
Protestant:
  The Christian Century, 407 S. Dearborn St., Chicago, Ill. 60605
  The Christian Herald, 10 W. Main St., Chateaugay, N.Y. 12920
  Guideposts, Carmel, N.Y. 10512
Protestant Episcopal:
  High Church: *Living Church,* 407 E. Michigan St., Milwaukee, Wis. 53202
  Low Church: *The Churchman,* 1074 23rd Ave., North St., St. Petersburg, Fla. 33704
Society of Friends:
  Friends Journal, 152-A No. 15th St., Philadelphia, Pa. 19102
  Quaker Life, 101 Quaker Hill Dr., Richmond, Ind. 47374
United Church of Christ:
  Firm Foundation, Box 610, Austin, Tex. 78767
  Restoration Herald, 5665 Cheviot Rd., Cincinnati, Ohio 45239

Other influential groups with their national headquarters include:

Business:

Business Council, 888 17th Ave., NW, Washington, D.C. 20006
Business Roundtable, 71 Broadway—15th Floor, New York, N.Y. 10006
Chamber of Commerce of the United States, 1615 H St., NW, Washington, D.C. 20006

Committee for Economic Development, 477 Madison Ave., New York, N.Y. 10022

Conference Board, Inc., 845 Third Ave., New York, N.Y. 10022

Council of Better Business Bureaus, 1150 17th St., NW, Washington, D.C. 20036

Council of State Chambers of Commerce, 1028 Connecticut Ave., Rm. 1018, Washington, D.C. 20036

National Association of Manufacturers, 1776 F St., Washington, D.C. 20006

United States Jaycees, 4 W. 21st St., P.O. Box 7, Tulsa, Ok. 74102

Education:

Adult Education Association of the USA, 810 18th St., NW, Washington, D.C. 20006

American Association of Colleges for Teacher Education, One Dupont Circle, Washington, D.C. 20036

American Association of School Administrators, 1801 N. Moore St., Arlington, Va. 22209

American Association of University Professors, One Dupont Circle, Washington, D.C. 20036

American Council on Education, One Dupont Circle, Washington, D.C. 20036

Association of American Universities, One Dupont Circle, Washington, D.C. 20036

National Congress of Parents and Teachers, 700 N. Rush St., Chicago, Ill. 60611

National Education Association, 1201 16th St., NW, Washington, D.C. 20036

World Confederation of Organizations of the Teaching Profession, 5 Chemin Du Moulin, 1110 Morges, Vd., Switzerland

Fraternal and Service:

Benevolent and Protective Order of Elks, 2750 Lake View Ave., Chicago, Ill. 60614

B'nai B'rith, 1640 Rhode Island Ave., NW, Washington, D.C. 20036

Civitan International, 115 N. 21st St., Birmingham, Ala. 35203

General Grand Chapter, Order of the Eastern Star, 1618 New Hampshire Ave., NW, Washington, D.C. 20009

Great Council of U.S. Improved Order of Red Men, Box 683, Waco, Texas 76703

Imperial Council of the Ancient Arabic Order of the Nobles of the Mystic Shrine for North America, 323 N. Michigan Ave., Chicago, Ill. 60601

Independent Order of Odd Fellows, 16 West Chase St., Baltimore, Md. 21201

Kiwanis International, 101 E. Erie St., Chicago, Ill. 60611

Knights of Columbus, Columbus Plaza, New Haven, Conn. 06507

Knights of Pythias, Pythias Bldg., Room 201, 47 N. Grant, Stockton, Ca. 95202

Lions International, York and Cermak Rds., Oak Brook, Ill. 60521

Loyal Order of Moose, Mooseheart, Ill. 60539

National Exchange Club, 3050 Central Ave., Toledo, Ohio 43606

Optimist International, 4494 Lindell Blvd., St. Louis, Mo. 63108

Rotary International, 1600 Ridge Ave., Evanston, Ill. 60201

Supreme Council, Ancient Accepted Scottish Rite of Freemasonry, (Northern Jurisdiction), 33 Marrett Rd., Lexington, Ma. 02173

Supreme Council 33rd Degree, Ancient and Accepted Scottish Rite of Freemasonry (Southern Jurisdiction), 1733-16th St., NW, Washington, D.C. 20009

Labor:

American Federation of Labor and Congress of Industrial Organizations, 815 16th St., NW, Washington, D.C. 20006

International Association of Machinists and Aerospace Workers, 1300 Connecticut Ave., NW, Washington, D.C. 20036

International Union, United Automobile, Aerospace & Agricultural Implement Workers of America, 8000 E. Jefferson, Detroit, Mich. 48214

International Union, United Mine Workers of America, 900 15th St., NW, Washington, D.C. 20005

Minority Groups and Allies:

American Civil Liberties Union, 22 E. 40th St., New York, N.Y. 10016

Anti-Defamation League of B'nai B'rith, 315 Lexington Ave., New York, N.Y. 10016

Congress of Racial Equality, 200 W. 135th St., New York, N.Y. 10030

Indian Rights Association, 1505 Race St., Philadelphia, Pa. 19102

National Association for the Advancement of Colored People, 1790 Broadway, New York, N.Y. 10019

National Congress of American Indians, 1346 Connecticut Ave., NW, Washington, D.C. 20036

National Urban League, 55 E. 52nd St., New York, N.Y. 10022

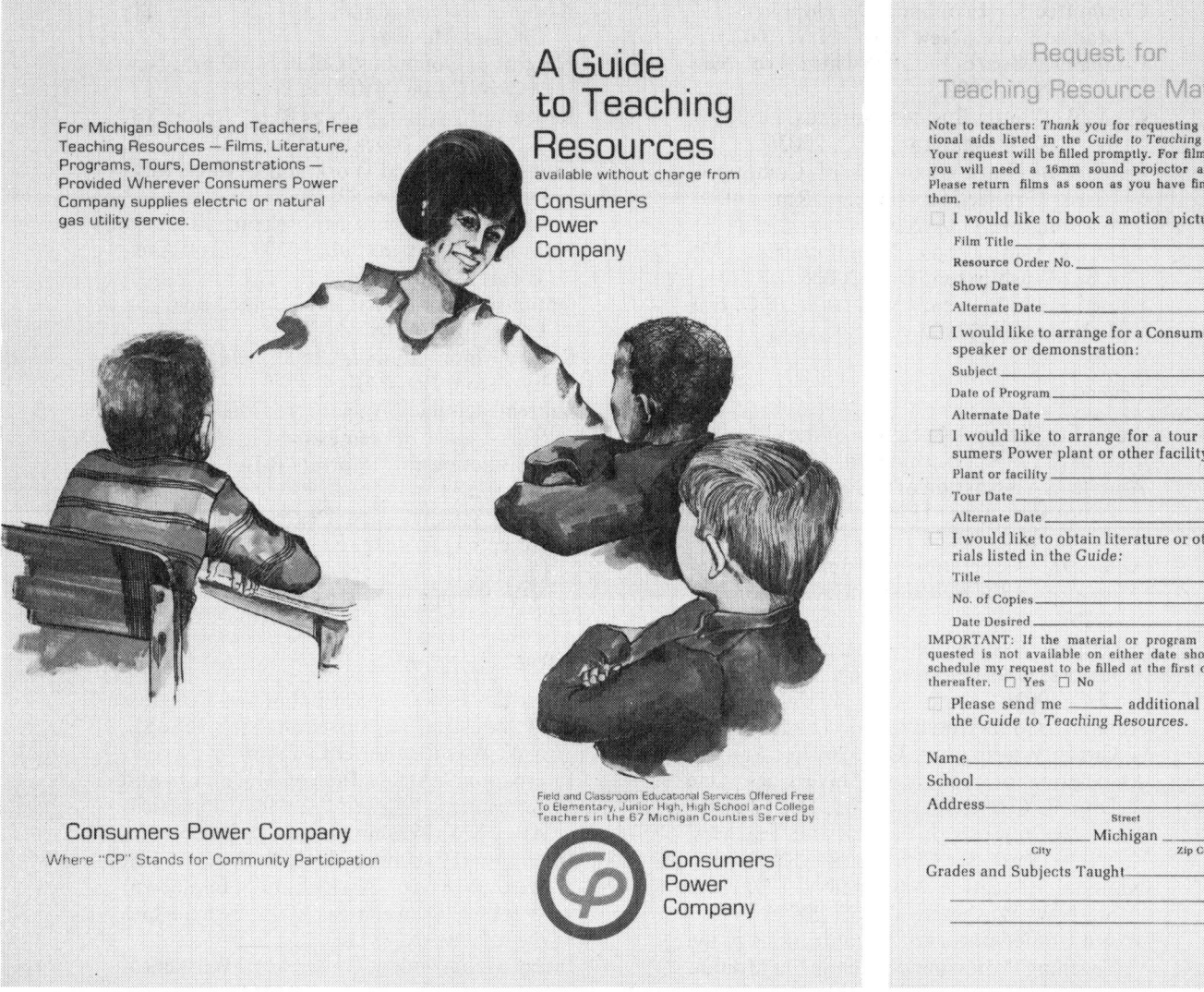

Figure 49-2. Request form from a booklet for teachers listing educational materials available from Consumers Power Company, Jackson, Michigan.

Welfare:

American Friends Service Committee, 160 N. 15th St., Philadelphia, Pa. 19102

Association of the Junior Leagues of America, 825 Third Ave., New York, N.Y. 10022

Child Welfare League of America, 67 Irving Place, New York, N.Y. 10003

Goodwill Industries of America, 9200 Wisconsin Ave., Washington, D.C. 20014

National Conference on Social Welfare, 22 W. Gay St., Columbus, Ohio 43215

National Information Bureau, Inc., 305 E. 45th St., New York, N.Y. 10017

National Jewish Welfare Board, 15 E. 26th St., New York, N.Y. 10010

National Legal Aid and Defender Assn., 1155 E. 60th St., Chicago, Ill. 60637

Salvation Army, 120 W. 14th St., New York, N.Y. 10011

United Way of America, 801 N. Fairfax St., Alexandria, Va. 22314

Volunteers of America, 340 W. 85th St., New York, N.Y. 10024

These lists are useful for national campaigns and nationwide public relations work. For local or regional campaigns, corresponding lists of more localized organizations, or regional and local headquarters of the national groups, may be obtained from the usual sources such as chambers of commerce, classified telephone directories, associations, and other public service groups.

In addition to these major influence groups, or publics, there are many others ranging in size from a few people to millions.

The members of an individual's fraternity or service club form a specific group. Women form an independent public. Children form another public. Each age group of children constitutes an independent public of its own. Labor is a public. White collar workers are a public. Farmers constitute a public. Every minority group is a public. Every religious sect is a public. Opinion leaders are a public, ranging from an estimated few thousand to 20 per cent of the adult population and including editors, ministers, writers, financiers, teachers, heads of associations, and other people in a position to shape the public opinion in their communities. Each of these publics is a potential group of considerable influence.

An early step in any public relations operation is to make a list of all the publics important to achieve the goal and to map a campaign to produce the desired impact on each of these publics and, cumulatively, on the total public.

Interlocking effect. While the best results might be obtained from dealing with individuals as such, there is seldom enough time or resources for such an exhaustive task. Handling the problem on the basis of the general public without effort to concentrate on specific publics would usually be the easiest way but is too often tantamount to spreading ammunition shotgun fashion. Effective campaigns aimed at specific publics will contribute to the impact on the general public. The important thing is to choose the most important specific groups or publics as targets, and do the best possible job with them.

The employees of a company constitute one public. Many of them will be members of other publics that affect the company's destiny. As citizens they may bring pressure for or against the company in the sphere of its government relations. The creditors, suppliers, stockholders, dealers, or any other public of a company will include many persons who may be influential in causing some other public to which they belong to go either for or against a company.

A basic public relations problem of a company or other organization is to make these publics allies rather than enemies. They can be enemies even though the company does business with them. If an entire public, or most of it, feels animosity toward a

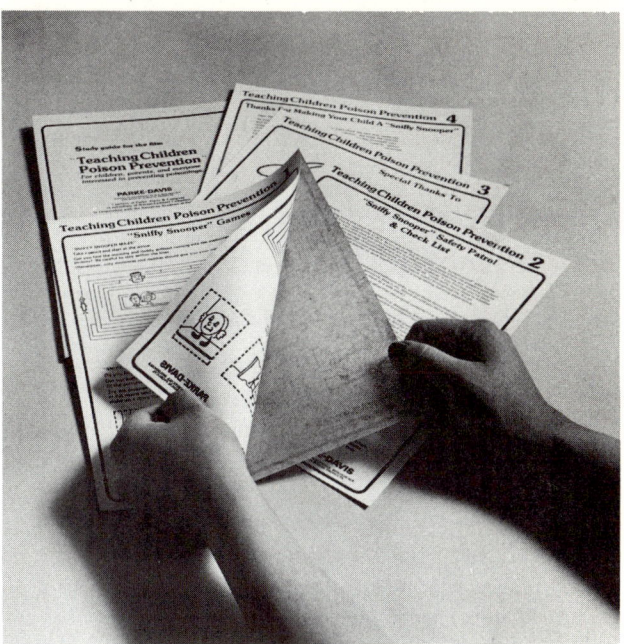

Figure 49-3. Spirit masters are provided by Parke Davis & Company to teachers so they can make reproductions to send home with children. These accompany a film provided free to the schools on how to prevent poisoning (PR Aids photo).

company this unfavorable opinion will automatically, through the processes of human relations, be contagious and spread into other publics. Good will is similarly contagious.

A vast campaign ground for publicity workers is the national capital, or any state capital. A floodtide of communication pours out daily from federal, state, and local government bureaus; federal, state, and local legislatures; propaganda agencies, both domestic and foreign; and from trade associations, the armed services, and private newsletters such as Kiplinger and Whaley-Eaton.

All of these are potential media of expression by a public relations operation. They are concentrated in the national capital because in Washington is the nation's strongest concentration of influential groups' headquarters. Others are in state capitals. Many operatives are stationed in Washington and lesser political centers to be close to them. The government sources in particular have a profound influence on people and frequently offer direct access to the first-line media. (See Chapters 5 and 6.)

One of the quickest ways to get national publicity is by arranging to have the client's messages conveyed through one of the above channels. To stage an event in Washington that will put the message to be publicized into the news by causing it to be projected from the floor of Congress, or from a federal investigation of some kind, it is to enlist the powerful and numerous Washington press gallery in the cause of publicizing the particular subject. Many publicists send a batch of copies of their releases to the National Press Club, National Press Building, Washington, to reach the Washington representatives of hundreds of newspapers.

SCHOOLS AS A MEDIUM OF COMMUNICATION

As a particularly good long-range medium, adaptable to programs having a five-, ten- or twenty-year point of view, the schools are strategic. Schools include an immense network of present and future purchasers and voters including students, teachers, and administrators.

There are many ways to work effectively with schools when the material is presented in an educational and generic way. A film, for example—"How a Newspaper Is Published," "How Shoes Are Made"—will often be acceptable for assembly programs. Booklets—"How to Use the Telephone," "How to Read a Map"—will be usable by teachers on the elementary school level. Demonstration charts—"How to Cook Frozen Vegetables"—are suitable for the high school home-economics teacher.

Many visual devices can be adapted for educational purposes. Frequently local teachers, principals, and Parent-Teacher Associations will provide opinion on acceptability or usefulness for various levels.

Materials may be publicized through personal visits to administrators, through educational magazines, through booths at teachers' conventions, or through informative mailings to school faculties.

The importance of tours in arranging programs with schools should not be overlooked. Field trips may be arranged with some teachers to visit industrial or cultural sites—a trip to a major baking plant, for example, or a tour of a new building will attract student groups.

Forums and presentations. Forums or other presentations can often be arranged at department stores with auditorium facilities or at local halls and community organizations with meeting areas. Exhibits, safety discussions, good-grooming demonstrations, and other presentations with a public service aspect can often be presented in this way when school assembly halls are unavailable or otherwise engaged.

Cooperation with school Career Days often yields excellent results. Speakers from the company or industry, brochures about the business, films, visual aids, posters, and other tools aid the guidance counselor who is instructing students in preparation for various fields.

Projects for schools—to be launched only after getting acceptance of the plan from qualified educators or consultants—include art competitions, sewing contests, essay awards, athletic prizes, or other tokens of merit that inspire student effort and cooperation.

Examples of organizations providing effective materials for schools include Johnson & Johnson (offering first aid materials, course materials in baby care for home-economics students, dental care instructional material, and other study aids); Eli Lilly and Company (offering educational material about the proper use of drugs); Parke Davis & Company (providing material on poison prevention (see Fig. 49-3)); Aetna Life & Casualty (issuing material on home safety); and Bausch & Lomb (supplying material on recommended eye care).

One major corporation publishes a number of illustrated science booklets for free distribution to schools. The corporation also makes available elaborate scientific charts and posters. It provides motion pictures and gives away a number of small scholarships. The company's policy is that the education program is primarily a constructive contribution to the community and the country, with the added advantage that it results in favorable publicity among members of a group—school students — who will for many years spread the resulting good will.

Companies have provided such educational aids as a handbook on *How to Organize a Teen-age Night Club,* a calendar featuring the work of leading artists, and books on family income management and "better buymanship."

A means of reaching many school children is the editorial-type insert offered by Scholastic Magazines (50 W. 44th St., New York, N.Y. 10036). A typical instructional insert, bound into a regular issue of *Scholastic* and called "Managing Your Money," was prepared by CUNA Mutual Insurance Society in cooperation with *Scholastic*. Other inserts of an educational nature have been sponsored by American Iron & Steel Institute and Encyclopaedia Britannica.

Westinghouse Electric has conducted a Science Talent Search since 1940. The Search annually evaluates the science potential of about 25,000 high school seniors. This group is sifted down to the 40 with the most promise. These youngsters are awarded trips to the Science Talent Institute in Washington, where they compete for $67,500 in scholarships and awards. Ten receive scholarships of $4,000 to $10,000. The others get $250 each and are recommended for scholarships to leading colleges and universities.

Films. Filmed material to reach schools is often effective, but costs dissuade some sponsoring organizations. In some cases a portion of the cost of a film for school use can be recouped through sale of prints, when the film is considered by schools to be truly educational. For example, Sandler Institutional Films, 1001 N. Poinsettia Place, Hollywood, California 90046, estimates that $12,500 can be regained by a sponsor if 500 prints are sold to schools over a five- to ten-year period, with the average print priced at $150 and a portion of the income going to the sponsor. The cost of making an 8- to 12-minute film runs from $12,000 to $20,000. Frequently films can be made in several versions, for school or other uses.

Among the firms sponsoring such school films have been a bank (on credit), a container company (on lunchroom etiquette), and a cosmetic company (on grooming).

It is often advisable to set up a panel of educational consultants or a special board of advisors made up of nationally known persons in the educational field when launching a special project or educational resource program.

Basic principles of dealing with schools as a publicity medium require that the publicizing organization:

(1) Refrain from being too commercial.

(2) Hold the educational needs and interests of students as the paramount consideration.

(3) Avoid activities that may interfere with studies or unbalance the daily schedule.

(4) Remember that schools must never be used to promote any activities except those conducted for public welfare.

(5) Remember that school activities and materials must always conform to standards of educational value, factual accuracy, and good taste.

College students can be reached with information of direct interest to them through colleges, newspapers, and magazines. Nearly 500 such publications are listed in the *Directory of College Student Press in America,* Oxbridge Communications, 1345 Avenue of the Americas, New York, N.Y. 10019; and through the College News Bureau, 141 E. 33rd St., New York, N.Y. 10054.

50

How to Write for Readership

JAMES M. LAMBIE, JR., Assistant Executive Director of CARE and formerly Executive Assistant to the President of Town Hall, New York, is a graduate of Washington and Jefferson College. Mr. Lambie studied law at the University of Michigan and ceramic engineering at Penn State before entering his father's clay products plant.

He served three and a half years in the Navy air combat force, assigned to intelligence and public relations, and became intensely interested in the readability of communications.

He became a member of the staff of Town Hall in 1948. In the 1952 presidential campaign, Mr. Lambie joined a new crusade, the Eisenhower movement, and served in Washington on the White House staff.

As used in the heading of this chapter "readership" is thought of as meaning two things: (1) high incidence of reading; (2) high incidence of understanding. The two go hand-in-hand; there is a high correlation between them; but they are not the same.

"Readership" is most closely associated with advertising endeavors. People spend a lot of money adding to their techniques of gaining "readership"; more still to discover whether or to what extent they get it.

Up to a point, people can be induced to read a piece of copy without knowing much about what it says. For example, one will read—even commit to memory—Lewis Carroll's "Jabberwocky," but he hasn't the vaguest notion what, if anything, it means.

WHY DO WE NEED GOOD READERSHIP?

Public relations communication has two aspects. One is philosophic. It is concerned with the answers to such questions as: what should be our attitude or point of view about something; what attitude do we want to encourage in other people; and so on. The other aspect is technical: what devices best serve our purposes? The technical aspect involves many problems of media; it also involves the question of the language to be used in whatever media may be chosen. The purpose of this chapter, then, is the narrow one of suggesting some of the considerations in using language for communication purposes.

HOW CAN WE ACHIEVE IT?

If you want to tell somebody something, communicate an idea or concept to him, you have only two problems. You have to be sure he has the ability to grasp the idea. And you have to be sure that you put the idea into words in a way that gives him the chance he needs to grasp it. If the idea is too complicated, or your man is simply not intelligent enough to understand it, there is not much you can do except, perhaps, to educate him. But that is not the usual difficulty in communication efforts. People, by and large, have intelligence adequate to comprehend most ideas. They do not have the language *experience* to comprehend an idea if it is presented to them in complicated language.

You seldom have trouble in conveying your

meaning to somebody in conversation. When you are talking to a man, you can see whether he understands what you are saying. By rephrasing, by repeating, by gestures, you can make pretty certain that he gets your idea. When you write to him, however, you don't have the advantage of face-to-face conversation. One would think, then, that a written message would have to be even simpler than a spoken one. It should, as a matter of fact, be so; but it seldom is.

What happens in our minds when we want to put our thoughts on paper? Something queer; we are now concerned with the sacred written word. We can't just say what we mean; we've got to dress it up. Do we forget that the important thing is to be understood?

A manufacturer wants to tell a few hundred thousand stockholders about their business. He wants to say: "Raw materials are still hard to get." That is the way he would say it if he were talking to a stockholder. But on paper—in his report—it comes out like this: "Raw materials are not yet generally available in normal supply."

What is the difference? Just this: the reader has to translate what he reads into language he understands. If he has enough language *experience,* he can do it all right. He has only wasted a little time. If he does not have this word-and-sentence experience, he cannot make this translation; the meaning is lost on him. Failure or success of communication is a matter of language.

You ask your fifteen-year-old son: "Did you like the movie you saw last night?" He replies: "Sure did, Pop." But suppose you ask: "Was the cinematographic exhibition witnessed by my adolescent offspring as the culmination of yesterday's activities productive of a critical appraisal which may be considered as satisfactory?"

You are likely to be asked to repeat or translate. ("Huh?" or "I beg your pardon?")

Your language failed to do its job: communication. The language of public relations (news releases, financial statements, employee statements, company publications, and so on) often fails the same way. These pieces of writing should be simple exposition.

Consider the corporate report, for instance. Its potential audience is, let us say, some part of the vast number of people who have life insurance policies and thus indirectly have ownership interest in American corporations. These people on the average have the language experience—the capacity to get meaning from words and sentences—of your sixteen-year-old son. (The average schooling of the American adult is about 12.1 years, and it is from formal schooling we get most of our language experience.)

Here is the gist of the communication difficulty. Language conveys meaning to other people who "speak" it, but to varying extents. You cannot just "speak English" to someone else who "speaks English" and necessarily convey your thoughts to him; you have got to speak the kind of English he knows. You have got to reach his *language level.*

There is nothing new about this concept, but it is now beginning to get the attention it deserves. Some of the credit for that goes to Rudolf Flesch.[1] Dr. Flesch has clearly shown the correlation between a man's capacity to get meaning from words and the amount of his formal schooling. He has also worked out a yardstick by which to measure your writing to see how many people understand you easily. It is not the whole answer. But it is a handy tool.

As a mouthpiece for and interpreter of his organization, the public relations person *must* study his language, his tool of communication.

Forty-five per cent of Americans think most companies "make more" than they say they do. More than half the people in this country think most companies do not make their corporate reports easy to understand—"use too many big words."[2]

Is the public becoming conscious of the importance to its own welfare of the results of corporate operations? Does it sense a lack of clear and reliable information about business profits?

That is a reasonable conclusion; people don't understand very well what businessmen try to tell them, and they want to know. Their failure to understand leads them to a suspicion of motives, a general attitude of distrust.

If business is failing to get its story across, it is not for want of trying. It is rather a failure in the telling. This failure is due in large part to writing that readers can't understand. Not only are annual reports too complicated; press releases, institutional advertisements, and all other corporate communications tend to be too turgid, too high flown. The responsibility for correcting the situation falls largely on the public relations man. He can and must help management talk in terms that mean something to people.

[1]Whose book, *The Art of Readable Writing* (New York: Harper & Row, 1974), almost anybody who reads and writes may profit from reading.

[2]Findings of a survey by Opinion Research Corporation for the Controllership Foundation, Inc.

Management, by definition, understands business language. But it is apparent that much of the public does not. So the public relations man must do his business reporting in terms so simple and clear that everybody can understand. Business effectiveness depends on understanding of its facts and problems. The same kind of thing applies to all other kinds of organization, from church and charity organization to labor union and government.

Examples. Before going into an analysis of writing faults and their correction, a few more examples may give the feel of it. The late President Roosevelt had the knack of making himself clear—when he wanted to be clear. When he made a speech (spoken writing) you knew what he was talking about without having to translate. Here's an amusing example of his feeling for the way people talk.

When James Landis was Director of Civilian Defense, he wrote a letter for FDR's signature on blacking out federal buildings. As reported in The New York *Times,* it started with this (thirty-eight-word) sentence:

> Such preparations shall be made as will completely obscure all . . . buildings . . . from visibility by reason of internal or external illumination.

It went on:

> Such obscuration may be obtained either by blackout construction or by *termination of the illumination.* This will require that in . . . areas in which production must continue during blackout, construction must be provided that internal illumination may continue.

Roosevelt, when he quit laughing, said:

> Tell them that in buildings where they have to keep the work going to put something across the window. In buildings where they can afford to let the work stop for a while, turn out the lights. Stop there.

The Government is notorious for what Maury Maverick called "gobbledygook." We put it down to "the legal mind at work." It certainly makes the reader work hard. Do the Government and lawyers in general *have* to be so *un*readable? No, but there's this about Government writing: nobody cares whether it's readable or not; the burden is on the reader; either he figures it out—or gets somebody to explain it—or he can go climb a tree.

But what about people who are interested in being understood? What about businessmen, who want a *lot* of people to get what they say? If they talk in language like the *Yale Review's,* they'll reach only the relatively few people who can read and understand that journal.

Yet that's the language a lot of businessmen use: in brochures, press releases, directives to personnel, manuals, dozens of other media. They want to reach people whose capacity to read and understand is at *The Reader's Digest* level; but they write at the level of difficulty of scholarly journals. That's where the public relations man, the communicator, comes in; he must keep them from "terminating the illumination" when they mean "putting out the lights."

Here's a manufacturer talking to his foremen:

> The utmost care must be exercised in the packing of this product as it is frangible and will be irreparably damaged if dropped or struck by a hard object.

Why not this:

> Be very careful in packing this product. It will break if anybody drops it or . . .

How about advertisers—on a mass medium like radio? A few years ago I heard a "reporter" on an automobile manufacturer's program. He has just visited one of the sponsor's plants, talked with the plant engineer; air conditioning for cars was coming. This "will obviate the necessity of rolling the window up or down . . . Bill emphasized that this . . . would be *evolutionary* rather than *revolutionary*"! Fine. Twenty-five per cent of our population knows the word "obviate." How many people do you suppose catch the distinction between "evolutionary" and "revolutionary"—accent the first syllables as you will?

Again on radio: here is the opening sentence of an "address in the public interest" by a radio network:

> The terrible sacrifices made by the men and women of the world who cherish freedom will have been made in vain if we allow ourselves to ignore the shades of totalitarianism that still linger in the corridors and lobbies of victory and which perhaps await only the raucous commands of some new leader to take substance and replunge the world in a war of utter destruction.

In the "public interest"? The public may be interested; but not much of it knows what this man is talking about. You don't need any rules, any measurement, to imagine how well this breathless prose will get across.

A number of banks and similar institutions put

out business letters. These are full of valuable facts. They are well reasoned. They are also often unnecessarily tough going for the reader. The typical reader is a highly educated man. He can usually make sense of it, no doubt. But he would make more sense more easily and faster if an able public relations person were allowed to lower the language level. Here is an example:

> Probably the present attempts of the administration and the strikers to get wage increases which will be absorbed by the managements, and so not operate to raise prices, will prove to be ineffective. The whole record of the Census figures indicates that the share of the customer's dollar that the factory worker can get is a nearly constant forty per cent. Professor Blank of Middlewestern University discussing this relationship wrote recently that the factory worker's share of the customer's dollar remains almost constant year after year, decade after decade, in good times and bad, in Republican and Democratic administrations, under Old Deal and the New, and whether labor is unorganized or welded into powerful unions.

It takes a language experience of at least a college graduate to handle that kind of thing. Here it is set up for the average American:

> The administration and the strikers are now trying to get wage increases and have management absorb them, so as not to raise prices. That attempt will probably fail. We can see from the Census figures that the share of the customer's dollar the factory worker can get is a nearly constant forty per cent. Professor Blank of Middlewestern University studied this relationship. He wrote recently that the factory worker's share of the customer's dollar stays almost constant year after year, decade after decade. The figure stays the same no matter what the conditions: good times or bad; Republican or Democratic adminstration; Old Deal or New; labor organized or not.

The sonorous phrases of the corporate executive are not only stuffy; they lack punch; they lack the human quality. For instance, this is not an especially good tribute to employee-veterans:

> It is appropriate that the Company express its pride in the distinguished military and naval services of its employees whose number in the armed forces exceeded two-thirds of the permanent pre-war corporate personnel. Exceptional credit must be accorded the entire organization for its skill and diligence in endeavoring, under difficult circumstances, to meet the global wartime demand for ... from both military and civilian sources at home and abroad.

Would not something like the following sound perhaps a little more felt, a little more sincere:

> Two-thirds of our permanent prewar personnel were in the Armed Forces. I should like to express the pride we all feel in their war records. Great credit, too, goes to all our people—the whole organization—for their skill and diligence in trying to meet demand under difficult circumstances. The wartime demand for ... was, of course, exceptional; it came from military and civilian sources at home and abroad; it could not be fully met.

You might be called on to report to the public on business-tax news. Nobody with a sense of communication, I think, worked over this copy:

> Recently, representatives of twelve local taxpayer groups attended a regional conference at Middleville. The delegates urged an all-out economy program at all levels of government, and asked that no increased state-aids or other taxes be imposed at the forthcoming legislative session. They also demanded that the federal budget be balanced for fiscal 1979, and called for lower taxes from local government units when levies are set later this year.

A public relations person concerned with the above would probably have done at least as well as this in lowering the language level:

> At a recent regional conference in Middleville, representatives of twelve local taxpayers' groups made their aims clear. They urged an all-out saving program at all levels of government. They asked for no increase in state aids. They want no new taxes from the legislature in its next session. They want to balance the federal budget for 1979; lower local government taxes when they are set this year.

The atrocious material that appeared during World War II as orders of one or another executive board is full of horrid examples. The one below is not so much "Governmentese" as just the usual legal jargon. The particular selection has some interest because it was the official resolution of an intramural difference.

> The Chairman of the War Production Board may perform the functions and duties, and ex-

ercise the powers, authority, and discretion conferred upon him by this or any other order through such officials or agencies, including the Office of Price Administration (created by the Act of Jan. 30, 1942, Pub. Law 421, 77th Cong. 2nd Sess.) and in such manner as he may determine. In such and all cases the decision of the Chairman of the War Production Board shall be final.

This to me is a clearer way of saying it:

This and other orders give the Chairman of the War Production Board certain duties and powers. This order is to make clear how he may act under those powers; he may act through other agencies, including the Office of Price Adminstration; he may work in any way he sees fit. When acting under his powers as Chairman of the WPB, his decisions shall be final.

The employees' manual is a prime opportunity for human relations. Here's the kind of thing that muffs the chance, that sounds like a journal of applied social science:

The expense of maintaining retirement benefits for our people who entered the service, normally shared by the individual and the Company, has been completely absorbed by the Company for those periods during which they were in military service. For all benefit purposes no interruption in the veteran's record of employment with the Company results from his absence due to service in connection with the war.

Now try this:

Normally, the Company and the individual employee share the cost of retirement benefits. But when any of our people went into the service, your Company took over the whole share while they were there. We try to see that nobody suffers in his relations with the Company from having gone into military service; for all benefit purposes, we consider that this service does not interrupt the veteran's employment record.

Technical manuals give us, to be sure, a special problem. There are technical words we can't help using. But, again, we don't need to plant those words in a mesh of language that is hard in its own right. Here is the kind of thing I mean:

To prevent interference where very high frequency radios are employed in airplanes equipped with subject engines, it has been found necessary to give special attention to the bonding of the ignition system. The following procedure is recommended in this connection.

Remove the paint from the upper surface of magneto mounting flange under each hold down nut. This should be accomplished by removing one hold down nut at a time, scraping the paint from the flange and replacing the nut, in order that the timing of the magneto will not be disturbed. After this operation is completed and all nuts have been replaced, cover all exposed areas with some suitable corrosion preventative.[3]

Clean the matting surfaces of magneto oil covers. Other covers on the magneto are insulated with gaskets and this operation will not be required.

Remove all covers from the magneto and spotface each recessed washer seat just enough to remove all paint and present a clean and smooth surface. After the covers have been replaced, apply a corrosion preventative around each screw head.

Remove the distributor covers, and the four flathead screws that secure the distributor block to the housing, then loosen the fillister head screw under the tension lead, *using a protected screwdriver to prevent injury to the ignition wires and high-tension lead*. Loosen the gland nuts on each side of the distributor housing with a PWA-1217 wrench.

It is a little uncomfortable writing about something you don't understand anyway. But we can improve on the above:

You may find radio intereference in VHF radios in planes that use these engines. If you do, the trouble is probably in the bonding of the ignition system. Therefore, give special attention to this bonding. We recommend this procedure:

(1) Take the paint off the upper surface of the magneto mounting flange under each hold-down nut. To do this, take off one hold-down nut at a time, so as not to disturb the magneto timing; scrape the paint from the flange and put the nut back. After all nuts are back, cover all exposed areas with a corrosion preventive.

(2) Clean the matting surfaces of magneto oil covers. (But not other covers on the magneto; they are insulated with gaskets, so you don't need to.)

(3) Take all magneto covers off. Spotface each recessed washer seat just enough to take off all paint and make a clean, smooth surface.

[3]This word is a form of "preventive" not recommended by dictionaries.

Put the covers back. Put corrosion preventive around each screw head.

(4) Take off the distributor covers. Take out the four flat-head screws that hold the distributor block to the housing. Then loosen the fillister-head screw under the high-tension lead. To do this *use a protected screwdriver so you won't injure the ignition wires and high-tension lead.* Loosen the gland nuts on each side of the distributor housing with a PWA-1217 wrench.

Here is another case in a technical field: stainless steel plate instead of electrical connections. Here we are trying to advertise the benefits of a particular product:

"Properties at Elevated Temperatures"
Some have felt that appreciable internal stresses would be set up within clad plates at elevated temperatures due to the difference in the co-efficients of expansion of the components; as a result, stainless-clad has been used in the past chiefly for unfired pressure vessels or for vessels not subject to temperatures above 250 degrees F. and pressures of 100 pounds per square inch. Results of experiments and reports on actual operating vessels, however, prove that Brand Stainless-Clad Steel can be safely used for much more severe service. Various grades and thicknesses have been tested at various temperatures ranging as high as 1,700 degrees F. with no failures resulting in either of the components or in the diffusion-weld zone. Vessels are now in operation wherein the temperatures vary from room temperature to 1,200 degrees F., alternating several times a day; one of these has been operating since June 1959, and is reported to be in A-1 condition with no evidence whatsoever of any failure in the diffusion-weld zone or of the component metals.

A possible rewrite that would make the "properties" a little clearer, even to a nonsteel man:

"Properties at High Temperatures"
Some people have felt that you can't subject clad plates to high temperatures; they've felt that the difference in coefficients of expansion of the components would set up too great internal stresses. As a result, in the past, people used stainless-clad chiefly for low-temperature pressure vessels: for either (a) those unfired, or (b) those below conditions of heat and pressure of 250° F. and one hundred pounds per square inch.
Now you don't have to be that careful. We prove from experiments and reports from actual operating vessels that you can use Brand Stainless-Clad safely for much more severe service. We tested them at various temperatures—as high as 1,700° F.; there were no failures in either of the components or in the diffusion-weld zone. People are now operating vessels of our clad at temperatures that vary from 70° F. to 1,200° F., alternating several times a day. One firm tells us of one of these vessels in operation since June, 1959, still in A-1 condition; they see no evidence of any failure in the diffusion-weld zone or of the component metals.

Suppose you are telling the public or employees about your company's plan for the future. This is the way it shouldn't be done:

The Company plans extensive modernization and enlargement of existing stores and development of many properties acquired for expansion. Because current commercial construction costs are extremely high, the major portion of this program is being postponed temporarily. However, work is in process on a number of stores, including one which will be larger in sales area than any now operated. It is hoped that the remainder of the program can be undertaken without undue delay.
The Fiftieth Anniversary of the Company's founding will occur during 1978. It is believed that the year should be a very satisfactory one from a sales and profits standpoint. Although currently, the Company is severely handicapped by inability to obtain its customers' requirements in adequate quantities, it is anticipated that the supply situation will steadily improve as the year progresses, and as import restrictions are modified or eliminated.

Rather, it should be something like this:

Your Company plans some expansion. We want to modernize and enlarge existing stores. We want to develop many properties we bought with the 1980's era in view.
As you know, the cost of financing construction is very high right now; so we will have to postpone for the moment a large part of our building program. But the picture is not all dark. We have already begun on a number of stores; one of them will be larger in sales area than any we now operate. We hope we can go ahead with the rest of the program without too much delay.
In 1978 our Company will have the Fiftieth Anniversary of its founding. We are severely handicapped by not being able to get all the things our customers want—or in the quan-

tities they want them in. But we think the supply situation will steadily improve as the year goes on. Import restrictions will be going out, and that will help. All in all, we believe the coming year should be a very satisfactory one from a sales and profits standpoint.

If your field is life insurance and you want to help your colleagues prepare reports for the public and policyholders, you *can* express your ideas as this statement does:

> It is possible to develop graphically and with quick impact on the reader the story of where the income of a life insurance company comes from and how it is used. The point of such a chart is, of course, to emphasize the relatively small part of income that goes to expenses and the large proportion of income that is applied to policyholder benefits. A secondary point is to show the substantial contribution of investment earnings to total income. For charting purposes there is an advantage in simplifying the story by presenting it in terms of the average income dollar rather than using detailed figures.

But you might better say something like this:

> There are a lot of stories you can tell graphically, with quick impact on your reader. One is: where the income of your company comes from and where it goes. In such a chart you can emphasize the relatively small part of income that goes to expenses, the large part that goes to policyholder benefits. Another, if secondary, point: you can show how investment earnings contribute to total income. In charts of this sort, you may find you can simplify your story this way: show income and its use in terms of per cents or fractions of the average income dollar. This is clearer than using detailed figures.

Even a life insurance policy can be written to be read—and still be legal. But the life insurance people must first get over this kind of overpowering thing in their public relations thinking:

> One of the greatest obstacles that all business, including the life insurance business, faces in developing to full usefulness the annual report as a public relations medium consists of presenting the story in terms which people will understand. Every business, every profession has a language peculiar to itself, and because of its familiarity with that language, too often takes for granted that the people it is addressing will share its understanding of the terms used.

> In the preparation of an annual report the difficulty is multiplied because here is encountered not merely the special language of the business but of the accountants and of the lawyers it employs, whose cooperation in the preparation of the report is indispensable. Beyond this there are variations in the terminology used in the professions as they apply to different fields. As an example of this, the man who is able to comprehend the annual financial statements of a manufacturing corporation may have difficulty in grasping the significance of the statement of a life insurance company.

This should get more cooperation "in developing to full usefulness the annual report as a public relations medium":

> One of the tough problems in getting the most out of our annual report as a public relations medium is this: the problem of telling our story in terms people will understand. Every business, every profession has a language of its own. Its language is familiar to its own people. They too often take it for granted that people outside are as familiar with their language as they are.

> In the case of an annual report, the situation is especially bad. Here we have not only a special business language. We have also the language of the lawyers and accountants who inevitably help get our report out.

> Another thing: professional language varies as it applies to different fields. For example, a man may understand the financial statement of a manufacturing company; the same man may have trouble grasping the significance of the statement of a life insurance company.

Banks face the same problem. Here is the way to make the people even more confused than they are already:

> Because of the immense rise in deposit liabilities during the wartime period, the banks of this country have followed a conservative course by retaining a substantial proportion of earnings to build up their capital funds in order to provide fuller protection to depositors and to continue the best possible banking service to the nation as a whole.

> The quality of bank assets now is high and bankers will do their utmost to maintain that condition. But commercial banking involves taking some risks on loans if banks are to continue to meet their responsibilities to our American system of private enterprise. No one can foresee what economic changes may occur

in the forthcoming decade, nor can banks avoid incurring some losses on loans if business conditions become widely depressed.

Viewing the banking system as a whole, the conservative policies followed by the banks with reference to investments, earnings, dividends, and augmentation of capital accounts are wise from the standpoint of the owners of the banks, their depositors, and the public interest in maintaining a sound banking structure.

Here is a way to confuse them perhaps a little less:

When bank deposits go up a lot, the wise course for a bank is this:

(1) Build up your capital funds: if you do, you protect your depositors better and can continue to serve everybody best; (2) be conservative in your handling of investments, earnings, and dividends. This is the wise course from all standpoints. The owners of the bank benefit; the public interest in keeping a sound banking structure is served.

That is what happened during the war: bank deposits rose immensely; and the banks of this country took the sound, conservative course.

The quality of bank assets now is high, and bankers will do their best to keep things that way. But the very idea of our American system of private enterprise means that commercial banks must take some risks on loans. Nobody knows what economic changes may come in the next few years. Banks cannot avoid some losses on loans if we should have a recession.

From the examples so far, the reader may have drawn some conclusions about some of the things that made the rewrites more readable. In general, the sentences are shorter; there are fewer modifying phrases or clauses; there are more common words, fewer uncommon words. There are more references to people; there is more active voice, as opposed to passive voice. These are things that make writing simpler. Compare these two ways of saying the same thing:

(1) In the great depression era, impoverished by the heavy delinquency in property taxes and urgently in need of additional revenue, state governments sought new revenue sources, and a tax on income appealed to some as a solution to this burdensome exigency. During adverse economic times, however, the proceeds yielded by the income tax are observed to decline to a proportionately greater extent than individual incomes, in consequence of which, states which converted to heavy dependence upon income taxes as a source of revenue discovered that such taxes could not be relied upon as a stable source of revenue during a recession period.

(2) During the depression a lot of people didn't pay their property taxes. This, of course, meant less money for the state. So states had to find other ways of getting money. Some of them turned to the income tax. But there is this bad feature about income tax as a way for a state to get money: when times are bad, people's income goes down; but the yield from the tax on their income goes down at a faster rate. So states find this tax isn't a stable source of revenue.

Most college graduates can understand the first way—though few will want to try. Most other people neither can nor will. If the man with those ideas about income taxes wants to transfer them to any large number of people, he would do well to try the second way. About 85 per cent of American adults will understand him. About 10 per cent understood him the first time.

Is this language barrier, then, a matter of vocabulary—of terminology? That is an element, to be sure. People's lack of knowledge of specific terms used naturally impedes communication with them. In one study, the Gallup Poll found that only three out of every ten Americans had a clear idea what "free enterprise" means. (Some responses: "The ability of industry to exploit labor without Government interference"; "Freedom to exploit other people who know less than you do"; "I heard about it all my life, but I never seen it, and it never did anything for me, free or otherwise.")

A less extensive survey four years later indicated not much improvement: people still did not understand "free enterprise." (One response: "Free enterprise is where the Government sets a veteran up in business.") But people do understand "private property."[4] The moral: if to you the two terms are equivalent ones for describing an economic system, use "private property" to be widely understood.

The difficulty of making ourselves understood isn't *just* a matter of terminology. Granted there are certain "hard" words in any given field; some of them you can throw out, find substitutes for. Do that where you can. Some of them you have to use. But be consoled by the fact: "hard" words are not the biggest deterrent to communication. Rather it is the words *around* the "hard" words that make

---

[4]The probable difference is in the abstractness of the two terms: "property" is more tangible that "enterprise."

writing hard to read: the framework of language that carries those words—the sentence structure.

It's here that Dr. Flesch's research has made its biggest contribution. He doesn't say anything that editors haven't been telling their writers for years: use short sentences; avoid dependent clauses; prefer short, common, simple words to longer, less familiar, complex ones; prefer concreteness to abstraction; use as many references to people as possible (proper names, personal pronouns).

To demonstrate the *relatively* small hazard of the "hard" word, let's try an example. Take the word "expoliant." That's a "hard word"—just made up for the purpose of this discussion. Now you are told:

"You must file an expoliant."

Almost everybody gets the idea; all he has to find out is what it is he has to file. The hard word doesn't interfere with understanding the meaning of the sentence. But try this:

> Congressional legislation relative to the filing of an expoliant comprehends the requirement for filing of the same by all persons not considered by any preponderant majority of their acquaintances to be in possession of heads in excess of one.

Practically nobody gets the idea; the hard word is a lesser hazard than the structure that contains it.

So far, we have defined the problem as one of failure of communication: language not doing its job. We have suggested two approaches to a solution: (1) find out what terms in your professional vocabulary are not widely understood; discard or explain them; (2) gauge the rest of your expository language to the level of your readers.

We have just barely indicated what is being done. The fact is, there is a growing consciousness of the need for more "plain talk." Better communication—with ensuing understanding—can cut down differences of opinion. Difference of opinion has a vital place in horse racing; exacerbated (sic) it is not a good thing when you want concerted action.

In short, we can stand a little more *rapprochement* (hard word) among various groups of people.

There is increasing report to public polling. That is well; we are finding out more about what people think, what they know and don't know. For instance, the American Economic Foundation knows that "free enterprise" is not alone in failure to convey meaning. It knows a lot of other economic terms are not understood by a large fraction of the people, and have equivocal meanings to many of the rest. It is trying to clear up that misunderstanding by suggesting substitute terms; it feels that "profit" is not "something left over," as one large business lobby is wont to put it; rather is "profit" a "payment for the use of *tools*."

Several professional analysts of writing effectiveness ("readability") now offer a service based on Flesch's research. They undertake to rate the readability of written matter, recommend changes where needed. Thus if the audience has a language level of the pulp magazines, an *Atlantic Monthly* level can be avoided.

There also are firms that undertake the whole operation of clearing away the misunderstanding that comes from faulty communication. One such organization completed a quite remarkable service to a New England manufacturer. The means were simply the use of plain language to effect labor-management concord. To illustrate by one interesting particular of the case:

The firm's labor contract was up for renewal. One of the points in dispute was a company-sponsored retirement plan. In fact, a retirement plan had been in effect for two or three years. But a quick survey of the workers showed hardly any of them knew it or knew how it worked. The management people had not neglected to announce the plan; they had put out a little booklet on it. But the booklet just did not make sense to the workers. An almost complete failure of communication!

In the field of financial reporting, the *Financial World* has for some years been having a good influence. It advocates simpler, clearer, better-presented reports. It offers annual prizes for best reports and improved reports. And there is a growing response from business to this competition. Still, in their scramble for "Oscars of industry," some businesses miss the point; they are content with dressing up for the occasion. Glossy paper, four-color illustrations, pretty type, fancy covers are all good; they gain reader interest. But it takes clear language to gain reader understanding.

Some companies have merely prettied up their old usual form. Others have done a good job with purely financial data but have forgotten something: the financial statement is usually a part of a year-end "report of operations" by the president. If his message, interpreting, predicting (yes, and back-patting) doesn't make a clear impression, it detracts from the value of the report as a communications medium.

Here is a good example of that kind: half good, half bad. In the back of the report is a normal "comparative consolidated income accounts" statement (1976 and 1977); a "consolidated balance sheet"; a "consolidated surplus account" statement. *But* in the middle of the report is a "balance sheet in simplified and explanatory form." It is headed: "How the company stood financially at the end of 1977—compared with 1976." The left side of this form is headed: "The company owned"; the right side: "The company owed"—and "Remaining for stockholders."

After each of the in-themselves illuminating entry terms, there is a short explanation. Thus after "Amount Set Aside for Unforeseen Possible Losses," the explanation is: "Even though management is careful and prudent, there are always some possible losses which cannot be insured against."

That is one good way to make a balance sheet clearer.

This company also had a statement of profits in simplified form.

In this report, however, the president's language does not stand up well against the exemplary handling of the financial data. His very third paragraph:

> It has been impossible on a short-term basis to reflect properly the operating results of a business where well over a year's time has been required in constructing, delivering, and obtaining payment for a single unit of the major product.

That is not the *kind* of language that will be understood by people of average language-experience. This president seems to recognize his problem, in these words:

> The orthodox, stereotyped, financial report is almost unanimously condemned by the present-day stockholder as being too technical, uninteresting, confusing or insufficient.

But it is questionable whether he finds the solution:

> ... Information sufficient to provide a basis for an intelligent appraisal of equity values is readily available....
>
> ... It was therefore the company's policy to disburse, out of earned surplus, cash dividends which bore a moderate relationship to the annual current net income....
>
> ... This triumph displayed a gigantic panoply of power, the creation of which should be carefully pondered by those who may be intrigued with the utopian unrealities of a planned economy in substitute for our American doctrines of free enterprise....

THE EVILS OF FANCY TALK

It is clear that the tendency of such double talk is to detract from an otherwise good job. If the corporation president wants to say—as he apparently does—not that foremen do a good job but that they "turn in a creditable performance" . . . not that things get done fast but that they are "accomplished expeditiously" . . . not that sales drop off but that "there is a curtailment of consumer activity" . . . if, to him, an end must be a termination, a use a consumption, a need a requirement, and so on . . . then he needs public relations counsel.

The executive or counsel responsible for public relations can help management tell its story understandably. Given the chance, he can point this out to management: if writing is turgid, round-about, if expressions are abstract, if thoughts (sentences) are compounded, it isn't readable—not easily understandable.

(And, using your prerogative, you can say with truth that such language wastes money. Enough of those stuffy words and phrases, strung together in forty-word sentences as they usually are, make tough going; even the minority of our population who are college graduates begin to have trouble reading them. For the rest, the money invested goes down the drain.)

SUMMARY

In our relations with people in general, we must keep in mind two tendencies we have: (1) to *overestimate* the amount of information people have; (2) to *underestimate* their native intelligence. Language facility is a matter of information. In other words, people tend to be pretty intelligent and tend to lack information in large quantities. They have the capacity to grasp most concepts (intelligence); they may not have the language-experience they need to know what the writer is trying to say.

So, write as you would talk:

• Use short sentences (an average of not over nineteen words).
• Avoid complex sentences.
• Avoid figures of speech.
• Prefer the common word to the uncommon, the familiar to the unusual.
• Prefer active voice to passive.
• Avoid the abstraction; prefer concreteness.
• Include as many personal references as possible.

In applying these rules, prefer the short word to the long; prefer Anglo-Saxon words to Latin-root words; prefer the single word to the circumlocution. In observing these cautions in combination, written matter will have fewer "affix-words" and will be more easily understood.

meaning from words. The success anybody has (in getting meaning) depends, as we have noted, on his language experience—something he gets largely through formal education.

To "measure" roughly the readability of written material, here are three tests Dr. Flesch offers.[5]

Description of Style	Words in Average Sentence	Affixes Per 100 Words	Personal References Per 100 Words	Potential Audience (% of U.S. Adults)*
Very easy	8 or less	22 or less	19 or more	90
Easy	11	26	14	86
Fairly easy	14	31	10	80
Standard	17	37	6	75
Fairly difficult	21	42	4	40
Difficult	25	46	3	24
Very difficult	29 or more	54 or more	2 or less	4½

* Typical audience is one step below the "potential."

A note about affixes. Affixes are the prefixes and suffixes that modify the nature of a root word. To take just one example: a root verb is "serv(e)." One affix makes it a noun: service; another makes the noun into an adjective: serviceable; another makes a negative: unserviceable; still another makes another noun: unserviceability. Confronted with "unserviceability," your mind has to remove the affixes one by one to get at the meaning of the root; then it has to build the word up again with the changes each affix makes in the meaning. It takes you only a split second to go through this process; but it does take a measurable amount of time and effort. The more affixes, therefore, the harder and slower it is to get

The reader who has learned something from reading this chapter will restrain himself from writing, professionally:

> Scintillate, scintillate, Globule Vivific
> Fain would I fathom thy nature specific
> Loftily poised in the ether capacious
> Strongly resembling the gem carbonaceous.

He will be satisfied with the less intellectual but more communicative "Twinkle, twinkle, little star...."

[5] *Op. cit.*

51

How to Use Graphics and Printing

PAUL R. NELSON, President of Flagler & Nelson, Inc., Buffalo, has had broad experience in public relations and in graphic arts for more than 35 years. A former vice-president and director of public relations for The Birge Company of Buffalo, he also has been account executive with Selvage & Lee, public relations counsel. He is a past chairman of the Advertising Agency Council of the Buffalo Area Chamber of Commerce.

A graduate of the University of Illinois School of Journalism, he has been a typography salesman, printing estimator, and assistant sales manager of a printing plant. As advertising manager and assistant advertising manager for Chicago concerns, he handled production of a wide variety of printed matter. He was a member of the editorial staff of the St. Louis "Post-Dispatch" and has edited a number of internal and external company publications.

During World War II, while serving as a Naval Air Combat Intelligence officer on the staff of the Commander, Air Forces, Pacific Fleet, he set up a printing press and trained men in its operation in the performance of his duties as publications officer. He also served as a public relations officer and an assistant operational intelligence officer on the staff of Fleet Admiral Chester W. Nimitz.

WHY PRINTING IS IMPORTANT IN PUBLIC RELATIONS

Printing is the principal medium for disseminating information, a primary function of public relations.

The most successful people in public relations understand thoroughly every phase of printing and know how to work with printers so that the information to be presented appears in the most interesting and readable manner.

If the public relations person is to do his work quickly, economically, and satisfactorily, he must know printing and its affiliates—art, typography, photography, and engraving. This knowledge will enable him to instruct properly those preparing the printed matter, thus preventing delays and costly errors. And he will be able to suit the type of printing to the job at hand.

There are many types of printing and many types of printers and each has its use for someone in public relations. In printing, as in almost any trade or business, you usually get what you pay for. Since labor costs in a given locality are about the same and material costs usually are identical, price differences almost always are due to the difference in quality. Most printers can give constructive counsel in the preparation of printed matter. The more a public relations person tells the printer, the more he understands the printer's problems, the better results will be from cost, quality, and service standpoints. Therefore, it is desirable for the public relations person to know as much as possible about printing, and it is particularly important that he become familiar with these fundamentals:

- The principles of layout and graphic design
- Types and uses of printed material in public relations

- Methods of distributing public relations printed matter
- Printing processes and techniques
- Preparing copy for printing
- Typography
- Engraving

WHAT TO USE WHEN

Basically, there are three forms of printed matter:

(1) The flat piece called a *sheet* or *leaf;*
(2) The folded sheet, or folder;
(3) The *book* made up of a collection of leaves.

These basic forms, used in varying sizes and shapes, are utilized frequently by the public relations person in his work.

Announcements. In addition to news releases, there are many occasions when public relations people will be called on to prepare formal announcements of consolidations, purchases, new products, new offices, changes in officers or directors. Such announcements may be engraved on debossed cards or may be colorfully illustrated brochures.

Annual report. The yearly summation of a firm's financial activities for the information of stockholders and employees is presented in the annual report.[1] It is designed by public relations men to give a lucid portrayal of a firm's financial results and accomplishments over a year of operation. Usually, annual reports are prepared in book form with paper cover, generally known as a booklet or brochure, although some firms are able to tell their stories in folders. For special occasions, such as a company's centennial, annual reports may be more elaborately prepared in book form, sewed, and bound in boards.

Judicious use of graphs, charts, and illustrations; headlines in pleasing type variations; and large, readable type well leaded will make the essential statistical details more interesting and understandable to readers not highly skilled in the intricacies of corporate accounting practices.

Answer set. Response to inquiries stimulated by product publicity should be carefully planned. Too often this phase is overlooked or left to someone not concerned with a company's public image. Materials included in such an answer, such as a form letter, brochures, and samples, are called "Answer Sets." Answer Sets should go out as soon after receipt of an inquiry as possible. Answer Sets will vary with the reader audiences, which may be the general public, dealers, or industrial or commercial users.

Award. Sometimes takes the form of a hand-lettered and framed citation or a printed certificate, much like a diploma. The art of hand lettering or engrossing is fast disappearing but may still be found in major metropolitan areas. With the proliferation of script and cursive faces now available in phototypesetting, they are used increasingly.

Book. The book form is used infrequently in public relations work because few business messages require so many pages that board bindings are necessary. Special occasions do arise, however, that may warrant printing a book, either to increase the life of the printed matter or to increase the appreciation of its contents.

In addition to annual reports on special occasions, public relations men may use the book form for a special testimonial when a highly esteemed person retires from active business; for text books used in employee training; and, rarely, for a biography or historical sketch, where the life of an individual or organization is particularly interesting to the public. (See Chapter 42.)

When publications of such proportions are planned it is generally advisable to obtain the counsel of experienced book designers.

Bleed. When an illustration goes all the way to an edge of a page, it is said to "bleed." To allow for slight variations in trimming, an additional one-eighth inch in size on any side having a bleed should be allowed.

Booklet. A stitched pamphlet of eight or more pages, usually with a cover, the booklet ordinarily is small enough to be carried in a pocket. This form frequently is used for employee manuals, union agreements, group insurance, and profit sharing or pension programs.

Broadside. A single sheet of paper with at least two folds, a broadside usually opens up to a large display (see "Bulletin" and "Clipsheet"). It is economical because it requires no binding. Sometimes it is used as a self-mailer.

Brochure. Larger, more impressive booklets, such as anniversary books or histories, are called brochures. Generally, they are distinguished from books and catalogs by their binding, which usually is saddlewire stitching. Catalogs and books normally are casebound, side stitched, or have looseleaf or mechanical binding.

Brownlines. There are a number of terms for the final proof one receives when a black-and-white job is printed by offset. In addition to "brownlines,"

[1] See Chapter 11.

HOW TO USE GRAPHICS AND PRINTING

these proofs may be called "bluelines," "silver prints," or "Van Dykes." Some may have the copy appear brown and some blue, depending on the printer. These are reproductions from the film before the offset plate is made.

Bulletin. The bulletin may be an official notice posted on a company's bulletin boards, a factual report sent to technical men in an industry, or informative material sent to salesmen, distributors, or dealers. Bulletins are issued at irregular intervals when information becomes available. They may be used, for example, to encourage employee participation in a suggestion program, or to advise distributors or dealers of opportunities to capitalize on something newsworthy.

The bulletin may be prepared on any of the three basic forms of printed matter, and may be either printed, or reproduced by some process such as facsimile, mimeograph, or multigraph.

"C" prints. Type "C" color prints are becoming increasingly popular for reproduction purposes. An advantage of the Type "C" print over color transparencies is the ease with which such prints may be retouched. With the increasing use of ROP color by metropolitan newspapers, editors are increasingly interested in color photography. Many magazines also are interested in color photography to illustrate articles.

Camera ready copy. Type has been set and positioned on a mechanical with photo areas indicated and crop marks made on accompanying illustration. In other words all copy is ready to be photographed to make offset plates.

Catalog. Essentially a booklet, but larger, with more pages. Generally case-bound or loose-leaf. Devoted to information about products. Some catalogs are "perfect bound," best illustrated by large telephone directories, a process of gluing the pages to the backbone of the cover, permitting pages to open fully.

Chromalin. This is one of several ways to prove color separations before printing. The old method of pulling progressive proofs, standard procedure in letterpress plates, is fast disappearing with the letterpress process, as more and more printing is offset. In offset, progressive proofs require the making of proving plates, a costly and time consuming process. Other fast, economical methods are "Color-Key" and "Transfer Keys." Often printers may refer to "Color-Keys" just as "3M's." A "Gravure Key," similar to the "Color-Key" has been developed by 3M for gravure.

Circular. An announcement of an activity, event, or product prepared in any of the three printing forms, a circular may be used, for example, to announce the opening of a store, to describe an organization launching a fund-raising campaign, to announce a contest, to describe a new product.

Clipsheet. A sheet or bulletin containing a variety of stories, filler material, illustrations, and charts prepared in newspaper style and mailed to editors is called a clipsheet. Clipsheets may be accompanied by mats of certain material, particularly illustrations and charts, to encourage use by publications that otherwise might find reproduction costs prohibitive. Clipsheets enable overworked editors to see at a glance how the stories would appear in their publications.

Color separations. With the greater use of offset printing for magazines, extra uses may be obtained for color separations used in preparation of brochures and other printed matter, particularly in trade publications. Many trade publication editors are grateful to be able to avoid the cost of color separations, while improving the appearance of their publication with four-color illustrations.

Comic book. An effective means of mass dissemination of a message, the production of a comic book story is best handled if put in the hands of one of the large organizations specializing in this work.[2]

Computer cards. The increasing use of computer cards for contacts with various publics points to the need for making these cards as attractive as possible.

Computer letters. It is now possible to individualize form letters printed by computer, inserting names and addresses in the body of the letter. Such individualized computer letters, while more costly to produce than printed letters, can be done for much larger lists at a much greater speed and for less cost than individually typed letters.

Computer typesetting. Increasingly, newspapers of all sizes and commercial printers are using computer typesetting. Typed copy can be fed into the computer and it will produce perfect justified lines of typeset material. In addition, the computer will punch a tape that can be used over and over again for resetting the copy when necessary.

Cold type. Another name for phototype and other substitutions for hand- and machine-set composition. Cold type is being used increasingly, because of its versatility and economy spurred on by the growing use of offset printing.

Consumer house organ. (See "House organ.")
Counter booklet. (See "Welcome booklet.")

[2]See Chapter 42.

Dealer house organ. (See "House organ.")

Employee manual. This is an informative handbook or guide explaining company policies, shop practices, employee benefits, obligations, and privileges—an excellent opportunity to build good will among employees. It is usually prepared in booklet form.

Facsimile. Rapid reproduction of a limited number of copies of an original document or record now is readily available through a variety of simple office machines, such as the Xerox and 3M copiers. While not so attractive as true photographic reproductions, or photostats, most facsimile reproductions are much faster and more economical.

Fact sheet. Detailed background information and data which may be included in a Press Kit with a news release, captioned photographs, and samples.

Financial report. (See "Annual report.")

Flip cards. Generally reproduced in small quantities, frequently by silk screen process, flip cards are effective aids in oral presentations of corporate messages to community, family groups, customers, and stockholders.

House organ.[3] The house organ is a periodical publication in booklet form, designed either as a magazine or newspaper, which explains the philosophy of a firm's management to customers, dealers, or employees, and promotes good will. Often it is referred to as a company paper. House organs must be well edited with a variety of subjects and interesting appearance, or much of their value will be lost. Greatest danger in house organs for employees and dealers is an overbalance of lengthy, preaching copy. Consumer house organs should avoid too much "sell" in the copy. Many concerns limit selling in consumer house organs to advertisements.

Illustrated letter. This is usually a four-page folder 8 ½ X 11 inches with the front page resembling a letterhead and designed to carry a typed, signed message. The other pages may carry pertinent illustrations and printed matter.

Insert. A folder or leaflet enclosed in pay envelopes or accompanying correspondence with dealers or customers is called an insert. It may be used effectively to further understanding of a firm's policies. Or it may serve as a constant reminder of facts about an organization appearing less frequently in other types of printed matter.

Instruction book. The instruction book is a booklet or manual, occasionally a book, used to teach the proper usage of equipment or materials.

Invitations. Invitations to press parties, open houses, and other important functions vary from the severely simple, formal engraved invitations to very colorful printed pieces, which may include specially designed envelopes, to attract attention and to pique the interest of editors and writers regularly bombarded with requests to attend press parties or special affairs.

Key numbers. Long used by mail order advertisers to trace the effectiveness of advertising appeals and media, key numbers or keyed addresses may be used in other areas of public relations to determine the effectiveness of various means of communication.

Labels. Usually, the public relations man will be concerned only with the preparation of address labels. Occasionally, however, he may be called upon to help in redesigning labels for containers. Labels are a specialized form of printed matter. They may be gummed or ungummed. There are specific Government regulations concerning the information to appear on labels and the manner in which it is to appear. It is advisable to consult specialists in label printing.

Leaflet. A thin printed booklet. Often a single sheet folded once. Used for carrying a specific message, for wide distribution, envelope enclosure, and so on.

Manual. (See "Employee manual.")

Mechanical. Camera ready copy in position with overlays, where necessary, indicating tint blocks and percentage of color to be used. This is final copy preparation before going to the printer or engraver when plates are to be made.

Memorandum. Usually a booklet, a memorandum is used to inform legislators of an organization's views on a matter of public interest such as pending legislation.

Negatives. The film used for producing offset plates with the image in reverse. Some publications request negatives and some positives, emulsion side down.

Newsletter. A publication usually 8 ½ X 11 inches that goes periodically to a specific audience to convey news, opinion, or other information. It usually consists of four pages, but can be more or only two.

News release.[4] Release forms are sheets bearing the name, address, and phone number of the

---

[3] See Chapter 15.

[4] See Chapter 38.

organization issuing the release. The information for release generally is prepared by some inexpensive process such as mimeographing. Many firms now use the offset process with paper plates because of its better reproduction, either with in-house printing units or through letter shops. The vast improvement of facsimile processes has also made that method of reproduction popular.

Pamphlet. Similar to leaflet, though often containing more pages.

Paper backs. Associations and corporations are turning increasingly to the producers of paper back books to tell their industry or corporation stories to the public. Generally the industry or corporation will find that in addition to the books purchased for distribution through industry or corporation channels, paper back producers will place quantities of such books on sale at bookstands, through their regular book distribution channels.[5]

Personalized letters. (See also Computer Letters.) Personalized letters are an effective means of getting a message to any special public. Such letters are being used increasingly by charitable and fund-raising organizations. They may be used just as effectively to reach stockholders and other special-interest groups.

Photostats. Photostating is a fast, economical, easy method of showing an illustration reduced to the correct size in a layout. Recently photostats in color have become available. These may be an economic way to show a blow-up at an exhibit, rather than the more costly color photograph Color-Keys.

Posters. There will be times when posters, single leaves of paper or card, should be posted in public places to announce a public meeting, an open house, or some other event of general interest. Poster messages should be brief and exceptionally legible.

Press kit. Package of material generally containing one or more news releases, photographs, fact sheets and, occasionally, samples provided for those attending a press party or conference.

Press release. (See "News release.")

Press type. Press type is being used increasingly in place of expensive hand- or machine-set type for the occasional line or two of display. Art stores have virtually unlimited styles and sizes of press type available on transfer sheets in black, white, red, and blue. It is easy and economical to use.

Questionnaire. Usually questionnaires are sheets or folders containing questions with space provided for answers. They should be designed for ease in answering and returning.

Release. (See "News release.")

Release (on a photograph).[6] A release in this sense is a sheet containing authorization to use a photograph or a statement, signed by a person or persons appearing in the photograph or quoted. Guardians must sign for minors. A simple, inexpensive type form is all that is necessary. Many organizations use mimeographed or multigraphed forms. (See Chapter 40.)

Reports. Reports of special findings or surveys that require wide dissemination may be printed in book form. Many firms make special reports of progress to their employees on their business at the time financial or annual reports are made to stockholders. Such reports are of great value in building understanding and cooperation between management and employees. They may be in booklet or newspaper style.

Reproduction proofs. The use of publicity ad mats is declining with the increase of offset-printed newspapers. Instead of mats, more and more publications need good reproduction proofs, sometimes referred to as "slicks."

Retouch. Both color and black-and-white photographs frequently may be improved through retouching, to remove extraneous matter, improve definition of the subject matter in the photograph, or correct objects photographed. The photographer, advertising department, or advertising agency can help locate a good retoucher.

Return card. A return card is enclosed in a mailing for the convenience of readers who may wish to make some response to the message contained in the mailing.

The once popular post-paid (permit) return postcard or envelope is being used less frequently. Where once the required permit was free for the asking, there is now an annual fee charged by the postal service. Postal rates and the additional charges levied for each returned card or envelope are now high. Tests of the effectiveness of the postage required card or envelope versus the permit form have convinced mail order firms that, while fewer responses may be received by requiring the respondent to apply the postage, the responses prove to be of higher quality.

Run-of-press. Increasingly, metropolitan newspapers are using ROP, four-color reproduction, which opens new opportunities for use of four-color

---

[5] See Chapter 42.

[6] See Chapters 40 and 54.

photography for public relations purposes. Many captions on black-and-white photographs sent to newspapers now inform the editors that the photographs also are available in color.

Scanners. The old method of making color separations using the intermediate step of a continuous-tone separation and the more recent direct separation, going directly from the copy to the halftone separation negative by use of filters and masks for the four halftone negatives—Cyan, magenta, yellow, and black—is being replaced by the swifter process of scanning. This may be compared with the method used to obtain an image in television. The latest improvements in scanning utilize laser beams for faster, finer images.

Self-mailer. This is a direct-mail folder, booklet, or book that can be mailed without an envelope or wrapper. Some house organs are mailed in this manner.

"Slicks." (See Reproduction Proofs)

Transparencies. The increasing use of color in magazines and newspapers calls for greater availability of transparencies or Type "C" prints in public relations. Many publications prefer transparencies to color prints, but is is very difficult to retouch or correct transparencies. Frequently a transparency used in the preparation of an annual report or a brochure may be used for extra mileage in magazines or newspapers. Color photographs prepared for special use by magazines may later be used for newspaper reproduction.

Welcome booklet. This is an informative booklet on a company and its products, for distribution to visitors at a firm's reception desk. It is an excellent means of making a visitor's lasting first impression of an organization a good one.

HOW AND WHEN TO DISTRIBUTE PRINTED MATTER

Time and *appropriateness* are of primary importance in distributing public relations literature. Postage economy is of secondary importance, but it should be unnecessary to point out that it is inappropriate for a public relations person to use postage needlessly.

Items of a very timely nature, such as releases, annual reports, clipsheets, and questionnaires, generally are mailed at first-class rates to assure prompt delivery. Of primary importance in expediting the delivery of news releases, company publications, or any other matter sent through the mail is the use of postal zip code numbers. The local postmaster can provide zip code information.

Without the zip code, at the very best there is risk of delay in delivery and there may well be risk that the delivery will not be made. Very often, to overcome a natural tendency on the part of recipients to discount the importance of printed matter dispatched by third- or fourth-class mail, the public relations person will send other printed matter such as booklets, bulletins, circulars, and illustrated letters at first-class rates.

Occasionally house organs may be mailed first class. More often, they will be mailed as second-, third- or fourth-class matter at lower rates.

Your postmaster will be glad to work with you in handling a mailing, for the rating of his post office is largely determined by the amount of mail it handles. Ask him about current postal rates and regulations. By consulting him on mailings you will facilitate the handling of your printed matter and avoid costly errors and delays.

Anyone engaged in frequent and varied use of the mails is well advised to obtain from the U.S. Postal Service Department Chapters 1 and 2 of the Postal Manual, which contain regulations and procedures for public use. To enable purchasers of the Manual to keep up to date with current information and changes as they occur, a loose-leaf supplementary service is included. The basic material and supplementary service is sold on a subscription basis only, at a price of $6 a subscription.

Since the Postal Service is now trying to at least break even, larger cities now have post office account executives whose job it is to help large mail users. They are helpful in suggesting methods to reduce costs and move mailings faster.

First-class matter includes that sealed against inspection, post cards, letters enclosed in business reply envelopes, letters wholly or partly in writing (including typewriting and carbon copies) and business reply cards. Nothing larger than 70 pounds or exceeding 100 inches in length and width combined may be sent first class. The minimum size is 3 by 4 ¼ inches. To avoid being confused with slower class rates, large First Class envelopes, such as a 6 ½ in. × 9 ½ in. or a 9 × 12 inch envelope, should be printed on white envelope stock with green triangles printed as a border.

Express Mail, at premium rates, is usually guaranteed for delivery the next day.

Priority Mail is air parcel post.

Second-class matter includes newspapers and periodicals that bear notice of entry as second-class matter, such as house organs, when sent unsealed. There is no weight limit. If fourth-class rates are found to be lower, printed matter in the second-class rate may be sent fourth-class.

Third-class matter includes booklets, brochures, circulars, form letters, and bulletins weighing up to but not including 16 ounces, excepting letters for the blind. Envelopes and cards that measure less than 3 by 4¼ inches in either dimension are non-mailable. There are no other size restrictions. Envelopes may be sealed when stamped "third class."

When printed matter is sent by bulk third-class mail and pre-cancelled stamps are used, the words "Bulk Rate" must be printed or hand-stamped in the upper right-hand corner of the address side. It is necessary to get a permit from the post office to use this method.

Bulk third-class printed matter in quantities of 200 pieces or more or weighing 50 pounds or more may be mailed at a bulk rate under the following conditions:

(1) A permit from the postmaster must be obtained.

(2) The mailings for each state must be tied together, all addresses faced one way, the top address covered with a label bearing the name of the state. Where there are 10 or more pieces addressed to one post office, these should be tied together, all addresses faced one way except the last which must be reversed to expose its address on the outside of the package.

If there are less than 10 pieces per state, all addresses should be faced one way and the pieces tied into a package. The top address should be covered with a label bearing the words, "Mixed States."

(3) The mailing must be delivered to the proper department at the post office.

(4) A "Statement of Mailing" (which may be obtained from the post office) must be filled out. One such statement must be submitted with each mailing.

Such printed material may be sealed provided the sender's name and address and the following words are printed or stamped on the face of the package: "Third Class."

The words "Bulk Rate" must be printed or stamped above or below the position of the postage, which may be either precancelled stamps, printed nonmetered indicia, or metered indicia.

Fourth-class matter must weigh 16 ounces and no more than 70 pounds. Included in this classification are books, bulletins, circulars, house organs, and other wholly printed matter. Rates are by pound and mailing zones.

Booklets having 24 or more pages, including the cover, at least 22 of which are printed and containing no advertising other than incidental announcements of books, may be mailed at a special rate. Check your post office. Such matter must be marked "Special Fourth Class Rate—Books," to distinguish it from other fourth-class mail. Publications that are sold, directories, and calendars will not be accepted at these rates.

PRINTING PROCESSES AND TECHNIQUES

The printing industry, said to be the fifth largest industry in the nation, has been undergoing immense change. Today the computer, video screen, and laser are taking over many functions, while the typesetter as he was once known, the electrotyper, and the mat maker are becoming extinct.

The four most commonly used printing processes in public relations work are letterpress, offset lithography, intaglio, and silk screen.

Letterpress, printing from raised surfaces, is most frequently used for printed matter that is primarily type; for printing on low-grade machine-finish stock; for printing that demands short production time or frequent copy changes, either during a run or at each reprinting; for printing on high-gloss enamel stock; and for printed matter that requires sharp definition in illustrations and clean, sharp, black type. Typography relying on fine serifs and thin elements for character and beauty are reproduced best by letterpress.

The major kinds of letterpress presses are:

(1) The flat-bed cylinder, which consists basically of a flat, iron bed on which the forms are placed and which moves back and forth under a revolving cylinder that presses the paper sheets against the inked forms. The Miehle Vertical is a variation of the flat-bed having a vertical rather than a horizontal bed. This form of printing is being replaced by other faster, more versatile, and more economical methods for most items used in public relations.

(2) The web press, which prints both sides of a continuous sheet fed from a roll. It differs essentially from the flat-bed in that the forms are placed on a stationary rather than a moving bed and the revolving cylinder moves across the bed instead.

(3) The rotary press, which differs from the above presses in that a cylinder, on which curved stereotype reproductions of the matter to be printed are bolted, is used rather than a flat surface for carrying the printing forms. The paper is fed from a roll

Figure 51-1. Continuous rolls or "webs" of paper are lithographed in color on both sides by this Harris web offset press. Higher speeds and automatic folding make web printing more economical than sheet-fed.

to the cylinder and is pressed against the stereotype plates by an impression roller.

Flat-bed presses are used for fine, close-register printing where speed is not the main requirement. Web presses have greater speed than flat-bed and are commonly used for printing house organs and smalltown newspapers. The rotary press, which can print at high speed in one continuous operation an almost unlimited number of pages merely by adding cylinders, is used principally for printing metropolitan newspapers, books, and magazines.

While letterpress continues to be the primary method of printing newspapers and magazines, with which public relations activities are primarily concerned, high production costs are forcing many changes. In increasing numbers, newspapers and magazines are converting to the offset process as amortization of expensive presses is completed and web offset presses become available for larger newspapers and magazines.

There is increasing use of phototypesetting, and computers now are being used to speed up the production of justified tape for the operation of typesetting machines. The computer is particularly helpful for automatic line spacing and hyphenation. Among the recent developments in the preparation of printing plates is the photopolymer material Dycril, which has a press life comparable with nickel electrotypes, will withstand hot or cold electrotype molding, and is being used successfully as a wrap-around letterpress plate.

Offset lithography has become increasingly popular for printing public relations material as its many attributes have become known. It differs from direct lithography in that the ink impression is transferred from the plate to a rubber "blanket" (roller or cylinder with rubber surface) which in turn prints on the paper, whereas in direct lithography the image is transferred directly from the plate to the paper.

The increasing number of newspapers and magazines converting to offset is of importance to public relations people because it changes the nature of the material to be supplied. The mats with coarse-screen halftones frequently supplied for letterpress newspapers are not desirable for offset newspapers. Glossies or reproduction proofs as fine as 100-line screen are preferable. Many magazines printed offset are eager to use four-color illustrations where the color separations are readily available. The Cronar process, which converts type forms and letterpress plates to film for making offset plates, is one of the latest in a series of conversion processes for use when dealing with offset publications. The use of electronic color scanners for the preparation of separated continuous-tone transparencies has increased greatly. These separations may be used to make plates for any printing process.

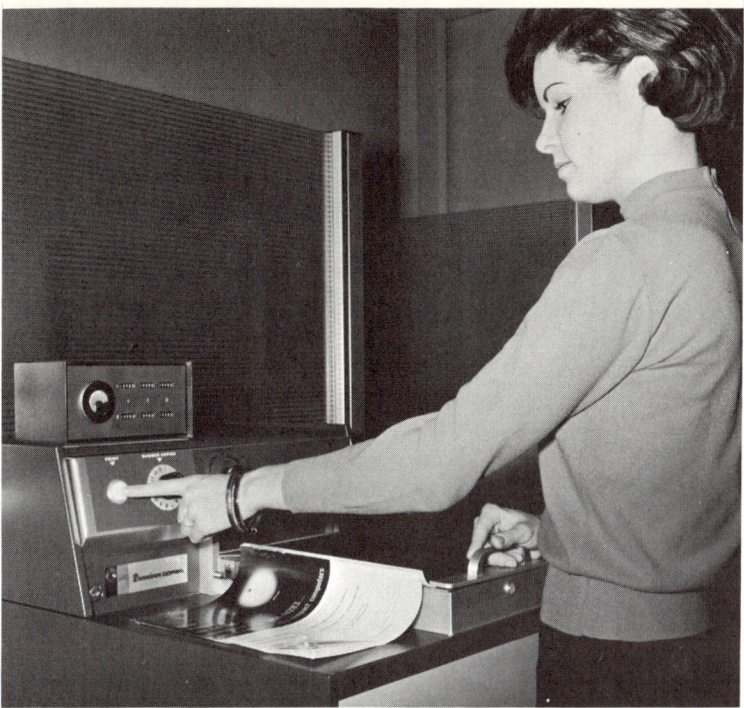

Figure 51-2. An office copier that reproduces pages from bound volumes such as books, magazines, or scrapbooks as well as all other written or printed materials has many uses in a public relations office.

Printed matter entailing complex artwork, which would require expensive engravings and electrotypes if produced by letterpress, is most economically handled by offset.

Economy of storage space is another advantage of offset printing. Offset plates take up little space and are generally held for a relatively short time, for the negatives from which the plates are made can be used if another printing is required.

The spectacular growth of microfilm emphasizes the space economies of offset. Gone is the need for storing large quantities of type and electros. Today one may select from a file that may number in the thousands the form that is to be reproduced, make a plate, and have it running on an offset press in a matter of minutes. Economies are so great even limited copies of less than 100 can be printed economically from paper plates.

Offset plates do not wear out so quickly as do letterpress forms because the plane surfaces that transfer the image to a rubber blanket do not receive the pounding that raised surfaces do in letterpress. Offset plates may be used repeatedly for different jobs by wiping off the images with chemicals and placing a new image on the plate by the photographic process.

Offset printing permits many economies in typography. Frequently, type composition is replaced by Varitype, photo-composition, and the photographic reproduction of ordinary typewriting.

Offset permits the use of special paper stocks that are not practical in letterpress printing due to their irregular surfaces. The rubber blanket used to transfer the image to paper in offset printing can print in the low surfaces of the paper without mashing the paper, whereas in letterpress the texture may be destroyed at the point of actual contact with the raised printing surface because of the great pressure needed to touch the low surfaces of the paper.

Offset permits soft gradations in tones not possible in letterpress.

Planography is an inexpensive form of offset printing in which many different jobs are printed at one time in a combination run. In planography paper negatives may be used for type matter.

The development of simplified offset equipment that can be operated by secretarial personnel has caused many firms to convert to this form of printing from mimeographing.

Intaglio printing is printing from depressed surfaces. The ink in the depressed surfaces is piled onto the paper to make the impression. Familiar uses of intaglio printing include engraved stationery and gravure.

Rotogravure is gravure printing from rolls of paper, usually of low grade, such as that commonly found in pictorial supplements to Sunday newspapers. This process has been perfected in recent years to the point where some magazines now are using it for full-color reproduction with considerable success. Some persons, however, object to the oily feel of surfaces printed in gravure. Reading matter, particularly under 10-points in size, has a fuzzy characteristic that may be tiring on the eyes. Rotogravure's value rests principally in its excellence for photographic reproduction. It is not economical for short runs.

Sheet-fed gravure, which permits greater control of the printing than does rotogravure, produces beautiful tone values. It permits the use of finer paper stock than does rotogravure. Shorter runs are more practical from a price standpoint in sheet-fed gravure than in rotogravure. Gravure is a slower process than letterpress.

Silk Screen. One of the oldest forms of printing, silk screen printing until recently was too slow and too costly for public relations men to use except on rare occasions. Now that screens can be prepared photographically, rather than hand-cut, and screening is mechanical, rather than by hand, the use of this process may be expected to increase.

One of the most commonly recognized uses of silk screen is for materials that glow in the dark. Silk screen is excellent for posters and for printing book covers.

Silk screen printing uses a transfer of ink through the mesh of a silk (or other material) screen stencil by use of a squeegee. The ink is pressed directly onto the paper, cloth, or other surface. The inks, either opaque or transparent, usually are deposited in layers.

Copiers. The office copying industry became important in 1955 when the Thermo-Fax office copier was perfected, and came of age in 1960 with the development of the electrostatic process, pioneered by Xerox. Today there are many companies in this field offering "wet" and "dry" process machines with about as many differing capabilities.

Advances in copying systems are so frequent it is difficult to keep pace with them. Now even color can be reproduced by copiers and some printers suggest that the day may come when all printing will be done "dry" rather than with ink.

With so much to choose from, the public relations executive must constantly bear in mind the end product desired—the copy. He should weigh cost per copy, quantities desired, quality, speed and ease of operation, and space required when considering the lease or purchase of such equipment. He also should be aware of the nearby service centers in his community and their production capabilities.

Copying devices now compete with such established duplicating processes as Mimeograph and Ditto, turning out copies at rates as high as 2400 an hour for as little as ½¢ a copy on ordinary bond paper—and the companies in this field are investing heavily in research that will bring about continuing advances. Already being put in use are high-speed, high-quality electrostatic long-distance copying systems that may further revolutionize the handling of much printed and written matter.

Other. So-called "office duplicator" equipment, including the simplified offset mentioned above, has made such great strides in recent years it must not be overlooked. For example, at the press of a button, anything microfilmed can be blown up to 18 X 24 inches and copies made on a microfilm reader-printer. This type of equipment and various photo and facsimile producing equipment are in great demand for what the Navy terms "compulsory" reading: essentially, short-run jobs that must be produced quickly and economically to provide important information helpful to executives in making decisions.

PREPARING COPY FOR PRINTING

Typesetters, engravers, and printers are skilled in handling copy and exert every effort to turn out work that will reflect to their credit. Unfortunately, they are not mind readers—although they do become expert cryptogrammatists. Their skill and zeal in correcting errors in copy may be partly responsible for the flood of unintelligible copy that comes to them. It is axiomatic that clean copy properly marked, correctly cropped and scaled artwork, and an accurate and detailed layout are your best assurances of a good job. Don't expect printers to think for you. Their responsibility is to follow copy.

Equally disconcerting as messy copy is copy that is improperly scaled for the space it is to occupy, and improperly marked for type faces and type sizes. Furthermore, it is costly for the public relations man, for it may involve serious delays in production and costly alteration charges. A familiar complaint from the printer is, "Type isn't made of rubber. You can't squeeze that type into the space indicated."

HOW TO USE GRAPHICS AND PRINTING

Copy tips.

- Copy should be typewritten with the lines double- or triple-spaced.
- At least one inch should be allowed for margins on left and right sides.
- Don't carry a paragraph over from one page to another.
- Place the word "more" at the bottom of a page if copy continues to the next page.
- Type on only one side of a sheet of paper.
- Number pages and place an identifying word or phrase at the top of each page.
- Clearly indicate end of copy.
- Show where copy is to go in layout by markings such as "Copy A" or "Caption 1," duplicating such markings in the layout.

Artwork. Photographs, drawings, tint blocks, and other decorative matter should be marked for size and position in the finished job.

Never mark on the back or face of a photograph with a hard pencil or pen, for it is very likely the impression will be picked up by the engraver's camera. It is best to mark photographs with a Vis-a-Vis marker or Expresso pen.

Mark dimensions plainly on the edges of the photograph and indicate the screen desired.

Most photographs are improved for halftone reproduction by judicious retouching to strengthen contrast which might otherwise be lost in screening.

When ordering black-and-white working drawings, inform the artist of the printing process contemplated so he may prepare the artwork according to the special requirements of the various processes. This precaution will prevent needless extra work in preparing plates.

Among the types of artwork used in public relations work are line, scratch board, ross board, drybrush, and wash drawings; water colors, oil paintings, and hand lettering. Tints may be added to line drawings by laying Ben Day or similar artificial tints.

Your advertising department or advertising agency probably deals with art studios and freelance artists having special talents. One may be a retoucher, another may do excellent line art, another wash drawings, and one may be a cartoonist. When in need of specific art talent, get a specialist to do the work for you. It will save your time and money and will result in a better job.

Layout. In determining the layout or format of a printed piece—the binding or folding, colors, illustrations, paper, shape, and size—it is advisable to consult someone fully experienced in printing matters until you become familiar enough with printing processes to avoid costly mistakes.

In addition to advertising agency art departments, there are art studios that specialize in preparing layouts and in completing mechanicals so they are camera-ready for the engraver or printer.

The design of printed matter is an art comparable to architecture; in fact, many of the basic concepts of printing design are based on architectural symmetry. As in architecture, printing avoids the use of the perfect square in illustrations, blocks of copy, and sheet dimensions as being monotonous. Preferable dimensions approximate the "Golden Oblong" of architecture, a three-to-five or five-to-eight proportion.

Standard practice in determining margins in book work is to begin with a narrow inside margin or gutter, increase the measure progressively, moving first to the top, then the outside margin, and finally to the bottom of the page.

When placing illustrations in a layout, attention should be given to balancing one illustration with another or with a block of copy. The balance of a page revolves around the optical center, which is equidistant from left- to right-hand sides and slightly above the center of the page from top to bottom.

A solid page of text matter is dull and repelling, except in books of fiction to which readers have become accustomed to accepting such a format. Even in books of fiction, an attempt is made to break up solid masses of type with frequent paragraphing. Without a doubt, book publishers could increase their sales by making their formats more attractive, for it is well-established that most persons are picture-minded, as demonstrated by the growth of visual education. An old saw well worth repeating here is, "One picture is worth a thousand words."

In selecting type variations for a layout, select type that will reflect the message you wish to convey. Select type variations that will harmonize, and avoid too many type variations.

For the beginner, the simplest and safest means of obtaining an attractive printed piece is to confine selections to the variations within one type family—variations such as boldface, condensed, italic, all capital letters, capitals and small capital letters—and changes in type sizes.

When making layouts in which illustrations are to bleed, be certain to indicate the bleed plainly, both on the illustration and the layout, providing at least

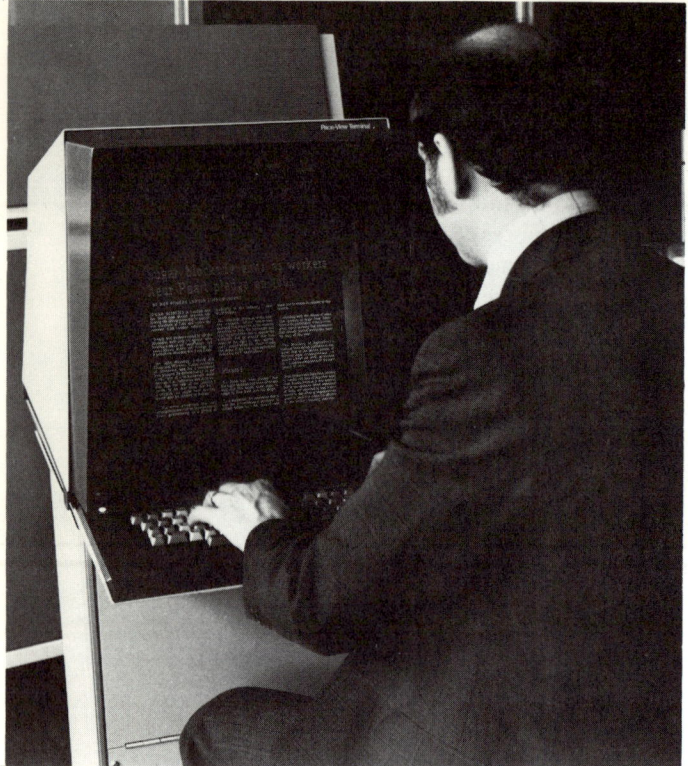

Figure 51-3. A new Mergenthaler full-page graphics display terminal system, called the Page View Terminal, enables newspapers and commercial typographers to construct, modify, and display up to a full newspaper page exactly as it will appear as an end product.

one-eighth of an inch additional area to assure a clean trim.

When possible, the head and foot of a page should be squared off. It is bad to end a page or start a new one with a "widow"—a short line of reading matter.

Type runarounds, half-column lines of type around cuts, usually head-and-shoulder pictures of persons, are space wasters and are to be avoided as unattractive.

When cropping pictures, watch for keystone effects that may occur at the left and right sides. The head of a beautiful woman or any object of beauty appearing in an illustration is enhanced by allowing "head space" at the top of the picture.

Pictures should face into the copy they illustrate, or in the direction the designer wishes the reader's eye to follow, wherever possible.

Long blocks of copy should be broken with subheads to relieve the monotony and encourage the reader to continue.

TYPOGRAPHY

Once type used in printing was principally hand set, foundry type, or machine-set "hot metal."

Today more and more newspapers are going to "cold type," which is essentially photocomposition, largely because of the escalating expense of the older methods.

Computers are now the standard for direct-entry phototypesetting and we probably have seen the last of the craftsmen who once painstakingly set type by hand.

Today's "composing room" is based on a systems structure with three basic components: Keyboard units produce the input; video terminals display and correct the type ordered by the keyboard tape; and phototypesetting units convert the corrected tape into the type used for printing.

It is predicted the next step will permit a laser-oriented digital scanner to transmit art and the typewritten manuscript. Already, in the newspaper realm, a group of newspapers has joined forces with International Business Machines and others to perfect a full-page composition system referred to as "pagination." Mergenthaler provides a full-page graphics display terminal, enabling newspapers and commercial typographers to construct, modify, and display up to a full newspaper page exactly as it will appear as an end product.

Old style machine-set, slug-cast, or individual pieces of type still will be found in small shops and rural newspapers, but even here the change is rapid with increasing use of electric typewriters having different type fonts and a variety of low-cost reproduction systems available. Automation is rapidly changing all stages of printing so it is difficult to keep up with the advances. The public relations professional who may not be in constant touch with the printing industry would be well-advised to use the services of an advertising department production manager, where available, or the company's advertising agency for most of his printing needs.

Firms in the printing equipment industry are combining electronic video typewriters, editing terminals, and computerized phototypesetting equipment into word-processing systems. Computers store hundreds of fonts of type in their memory banks, available at the touch of a button.

Teletypesetting, a method whereby the same copy may be set in type simultaneously in widely separated printing establishments, is of importance to public relations men principally in dealing with newspaper chains using such facilities. It emphasizes the importance of sending information to the main office. The increase of multi-plant commercial printing operations would indicate that this method of composition might prove helpful in handling the dissemination of large-scale, bulky printing.

Photo composition, also referred to as "cold type," phototypography, and phototypesetting, is a relatively new process that gives sharper reproduction of type. Individual type characters on film are assembled in lines by keyboard action, then automatically projected on a new sheet of clear film or paper for reproduction.

The growth of "captive" or private printing departments has been stimulated by the development of equipment such as the Varitype machine. The old Varitype machine, operated like a typewriter with a range of type faces and sizes, has been replaced by a direct entry phototypesetter with video screen. Other firms also make comprehensive lines of direct-input phototypesetters. They are being used increasingly for house organs, texts of speeches, and news releases.

Handlettering can be used for special appeal and effectiveness. Because offset does not require the expense of zinc originals and electros, handlettering may be used more frequently. Because of the scarcity of expert handlettering artists, handlettering is largely being replaced by photocomposition and its vast selection of type faces.

Electric typewriters, with uniform appearance of each character and with improved faces and letter-spacing, have stimulated reproduction of typewriting in printing, particularly in offset, where characters may be typed directly onto paper plates. Many electric typewriters now offer a variety of type faces and sizes and are able to justify lines. Interchangeable ribbons permit the use of one ribbon for typing letters and a carbon ribbon for typing copy to be used in printing.

Press type is a transfer type available in a wide range of styles and sizes through art supply stores.

PRINTING TYPES

There are five main kinds of type: Text, Script, Gothic, Italic, and Roman. New type faces are being issued with great frequency. Some catch on while others do not. For that reason representative faces are shown in this book. The printer or typesetter will provide a book showing type he has available and will bring the type book up to date as he adds new type faces. With the plethora of new type faces, the type faces shown here are merely to indicate basic differences. It is advisable to consult with your printer, advertising manager, or agency on the type faces available to you.

Text type, the oldest kind, is patterned after the handwriting of the copyists in monasteries. It is very black, has ornate serifs, and is difficult to read. A line or two used in connection with the Christmas season may be very appropriate.

This Line Is Set in Old English

Script type looks like handwriting. It has a lighter appearance than other kinds of type. It is graceful and sensitive and hence is useful in creating an atmosphere of beauty or intimacy. It is useful in treating articles having a feminine appeal.

This Line Is Set in Trafton Script

Gothic type is very plain, having no serifs. It is a bold, black, strong type commonly found in banner headlines, for example. Gothic body type has a clean simplicity excellent for use in offset reproduction where fine serifs might be lost. Gothic has been cheapened somewhat by its frequent use for bargain-sale advertising.

This Line Is Set in Franklin Gothic

Sans serif describes a number of type faces that have no serifs and are recognized as "modern." Microgramma, Optima, and Venus are popular examples.

This Line of Type Is Set in Optima

Italic type originally was designed as a space saver but today is only the name for the sloping variation of any Roman type face. The principal uses for italic today are to *emphasize* words or phrases; indicate *foreign words or phrases;* show the *title of a book, play,* or *periodical;* indicate an *individual letter* when referred to in copy; and provide *variety in headlines.*

Roman type is the most commonly used type in this country. There are many variations of Roman type, but all Roman types have one thing in common—serifs—and it is the variations in the serifs that largely account for the differences in Roman type. All Roman type falls into two major classifications, old-style or modern. Old-style types, such as Caslon, Kennerley, and Garamond, do not have such pronounced differences in the weight of elements as do the modern, among which are included Bodoni, Century, and Scotch. Roman types are used for all types of public relations printing.

This Line Is Caslon, an Old-Style Face

This Line Is Bodoni, a Modern Face

Type families. A type family includes all of the sizes and variations of a type face such as italic, boldface, boldface italic, condensed, expanded, extra condensed, inline, outline, extended, and so on.

Most type families are made in all the commonly used sizes from 6-point to 72-point. Each size of each type face is called a *font*. All the fonts of one type face constitute a *series*. All the series of one type face compose a *family*.

Type is measured in "points," each of which equals 1/72 of an inch. "Body type"—the type-set material of the main portion of books, magazines, newspapers, leaflets, and other printed materials—generally ranges from 7-point to 12-point. Sizes smaller than 7-point are commonly used only for tabular material, "small type" in legal forms and other text that is not intended for regular reading. Sizes larger than 12-point are generally headlines, section headings, and other display material. On the next page is a display of various type sizes.

Selecting a type face. There is a seemingly endless number of type faces and their variations. Foundry type for a certain face, for example, differs slightly from the type made for Linotype, Intertype, or Ludlow type-casting machines. When selecting type faces, it is well to know what families your printer or typographer may have, for the wide selection makes it virtually impossible for him to have all available faces. Most printers and typographers have specimen books to give to their customers. Following are a few examples of commonly used faces. Each face is set in two sizes: 24-point and 12-point leaded 2 points. Some of their characteristics are described.

In most type faces, the public relations person may obtain additional interesting contrasts in the same face and size by using capitals, capitals and small capitals, small capitals, bold face, and so on.

This type is CASLON

THIS PARAGRAPH IS SET IN CASLON. An old proverb of typography is, "When in doubt, use Caslon." Caslon is warm and sympathetic, yet impersonal. It is one of the most serviceable of all types, one of the most easily read, and one of the most widely used. There are a number of varieties of Caslon; this is Caslon Old Style. *Caslon Old Style italic is illustrated by this sentence.*

Proofreading. The commercial proofreaders—the typographer and printer—are responsible only for deviations from copy, although most proofreaders also will correct obvious mistakes and question others. It is the responsibility of the public relations man, therefore, to check carefully the proofs returned from the printer.

There are two systems for marking proofs, the *book* system and the *guide line* system. The guide line system simply circles the section in the text that needs correcting and draws a line to the nearest margin where the proper proof marks are made. The guide line is used primarily on newspapers.

The book system is the better system for public relations people to use, for there is less likelihood of confusion, particularly when it is necessary to make many corrections. Figures 51-6 and 51-7 show the standard proofreader's marks and their application.

Type measuring and calculating. The system in use today by all American typographers, the point system, was originated in France early in the eighteenth century. At one time, every point size had a name, but today only two, *agate* and *pica,* are commonly used. A point is 0.01384 of an inch or about 1/72 of an inch. Standard measurements in use are: 72 points equal 1 inch; 12 points equal 1 pica; 6 picas equal 1 inch; 5½ points equal an agate line; 14 agate lines equal an inch. The length of type lines and the depth of a block of copy are based on picas. Type composition is computed in *ems* of the type being used. The em of a piece of type is its square. The em of any size measures the same on all sides. In the point system the type face is not measured, but the body on which it rests is measured. Thus, in type-casting it is possible to set an 8-point face on a 10-point body, commonly referred to as "8 on 10." This is the equivalent of *leading* a line. Leading is the spacing between lines. A lead is a thin strip of metal normally 2 points, but it is advisable to specify points. When copy is not leaded (pronounced ledded), it is said to be "set solid." Leading increases legibility and the general appearance of copy. *Slugs* are leads thicker than 4 points. Figure 51-8 illustrates the difference in appearance and legibility between a block of copy set solid, one leaded 1 point, and one leaded 3 points (the type used is Times Roman [10-point]). For further comparison, note that the body type of this book is leaded 2 points.

In general, the amount of leading used depends on the size of the type, the length of the line, and the blackness of the face. Short lines need less than long lines; small sizes, less than large, and light faces less than bold. Following is a table showing the amount

THE SIZE of	48 point
THE SIZE of ty	42 point
THE SIZE of type	36 point
THE SIZE of type	30 point
THE SIZE of type	24 point
THE SIZE of type	18 point
THE SIZE of type	14 point
THE SIZE of type	12 point
THE SIZE of type	10 point
THE SIZE of type	8 point
THE SIZE of type	6 point

Figure 51-5. Common type sizes (**Bodoni Book**).

A FAMILY OF TYPE	Caslon Old Style
A FAMILY OF TYPE	*Caslon Old Style italic*
A FAMILY OF TYPE	**Caslon Bold**
A FAMILY OF TYPE	***Caslon Bold italic***
A FAMILY OF TYPE	Caslon Condensed
A FAMILY OF TYPE	Caslon Shaded
a family of type	Caslon Old Style
a family of type	*Caslon Old Style italic*
a family of type	**Caslon Bold**
a family of type	***Caslon Bold italic***
a family of type	Caslon Condensed
a family of type	Caslon Shaded

Figure 51-4.

551

This type is MELIOR

THIS PARAGRAPH IS SET IN MELIOR. One of the newer type faces, Melior has a high degree of legibility as well as a very pleasing appearance. There is considerable strength to this type face that may account in part for its rapid growth in popularity, not only as a display face, but also as body copy. *Melior italic is illustrated by this sentence.*

This type is PALATINO

THIS PARAGRAPH IS SET IN PALATINO. Considered by many as one of the most beautiful type faces, the Palatino series by Herman Zapf is named for the Italian artist, Giambattisto Palatino, one of the most famous 16th Century calligraphers and a contemporary of the great French designer, Claude Garamond. *Palatino italic is illustrated by this sentence.*

This type is STYMIE

THIS PARAGRAPH IS SET IN STYMIE. Somewhere between Modern Roman and Sans Serif we find the range of "flat" or "square" serif type faces, which includes Stymie, Memphis, Karnak, Beton, Girder, Cairo, and Tower. Lacking the beauty of the Roman faces and the simplicity of the Sans Serifs, these faces do appear neat, clean, and readable. **Stymie Medium italic is illustrated by this sentence.**

This type is BODONI

THIS PARAGRAPH IS SET IN BODONI. Of the types previously illustrated, Caslon, Garamond and Palatino are so-called Old Style faces. Bodoni and Melior are so-called Modern faces. Old Style types can be distinguished by their slanting serifs (serifs are the little bars or finishing strokes at the tops and bottoms of letters) and by their slight contrast between light and heavy strokes. Modern type faces have greater contrast between light and heavy strokes, and have precise but graceful lines. Bodoni comes in a number of varieties; this is Bodoni Book. The headline is set in Bodoni Bold. *Bodoni italic is illustrated by this sentence.*

This type is CENTURY

THIS PARAGRAPH IS SET IN CENTURY. Century, like Bodoni, is a Modern type face. It is not an especially good looking face, particularly in the larger sizes, but its legibility in the smaller sizes is to be recommended. Where it is necessary to fit a large message into a comparatively small space, Century is a good choice. *Century italic is illustrated by this sentence.*

This type is OPTIMA

THIS PARAGRAPH IS SET IN OPTIMA. A simple yet elegant Sans Serif with subtle balance, Optima has been designed in the 20th Century idiom. It blends well with the major type faces used today. It has character as well as style. While most Sans Serifs should be used sparingly, Optima, with more visual appeal, may be used more freely. *Optima italic is illustrated by this sentence.*

This type is STANDARD

THIS PARAGRAPH IS SET IN STANDARD There are a great many Sans Serif type faces, identified by their straight lines, lack of contrasting light and heavy elements, and absence of serifs. Few, however, can equal Standard, designed by the Berthold Foundry in West Germany. Its graceful, unpretentious lines actually have their root in the last years of the 19th Century, though it has achieved contemporary popularity because of its "modern" appearance. *Standard italic is illustrated by this sentence.*

This type is SCOTCH

THIS PARAGRAPH IS SET IN SCOTCH ROMAN. Scotch Roman may be considered a Modern face, although it has certain of the characteristics of Old Style faces. While it is not especially beautiful, Scotch Roman is a very legible, useful face for both display and text purposes. Its appearance in display may be judged from the line set in 24 point. *Scotch Roman italic is illustrated by this sentence.*

This type is FUTURA

THIS PARAGRAPH IS SET IN FUTURA. Futura is an example of a so-called Sans Serif face. Sans Serif faces have straight lines, with no contrast between light and heavy strokes, and they have no serifs. Sans Serif faces are popular because they strike a modern note. Futura may be used as either a body or a display type. However, although it is a good looking type, it is not very easily read, and hence should not be used except where only a few lines have to be set. Futura comes in a number of weights; this is Futura Medium. *Futura italic is illustrated by this sentence.*

of leading normally recommended for use with various sizes of body type:

AMOUNT OF LEAD USED BETWEEN LINES OF BODY TYPE FOR EASY READING

Size of Type	Minimum Lead	Maximum Lead
6	Solid	1 pt.
7	Solid	1 pt.
8	Solid	2 pts.
9	1 pt.	2 pts.
10	1 pt.	4 pts.
11	1 pt.	4 pts.
12	2 pts.	6 pts.
14	3 pts.	8 pts.
18	4 pts.	8 pts.

When determining the length of a line of type, the size of the type to be used must be considered for legibility and appearance. A simple rule of thumb is that a line should be no shorter than a pica for each point in the type size (*i.e.*, 6 picas for 6-point type) and no longer than double the number of picas for the number of points (*i.e.*, 12 picas for 6-point type).

CALCULATING SPACE AND COPY FITTING

When planning a printed piece, it is necessary to compute the space the copy will occupy, or to fit the copy to the space available. Very often, knowing how to compute type composition will save time and money.

Copy fitting by word count. Given a certain amount of space and the size of type that is to be used, the approximate number of words can be found by the following method:

(1) Reduce the dimensions of the space to points by multiplying the number of inches by 72 or the

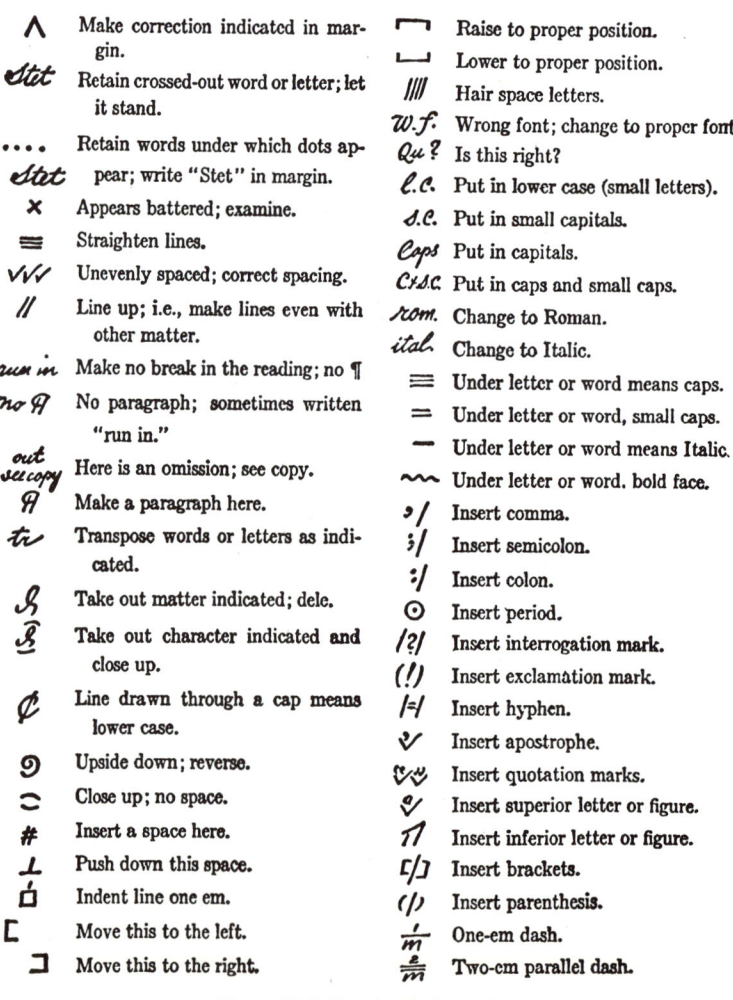

Figure 51-6. Proofreader's marks.

It does not appear that the earliest printers had any method of correcting errors before the form was on the press The learned The learned correctors of the first two centuries of printing were not proofreaders in our sense they where rather what we should ferm office editors. Their labors were chiefly to see that the proof corre sponded to the copy, but that the printed page was correct in its latinity that the words were there, and that the sense was right. They cared but little about orthography, bad letters or purely printers errors, and when the text seemed to them wrong they consulted fresh authorities or altered it on their own responsibility. Good proofs in the modern sense, were impossible until professional readers were employed men who had first a printer's education, and then spent many years in the correcton of proof. The orthography of English, which for the past century has undergone little change, was very fluctuting until after the publication of Johnson's Dictionary, and capitals, which have been used with considerable regularity for the past 80 years, were previously used on the miss or hit plan. The approach to regularity, so far as we have may be attributed to the growth of a class of professional proof readers, and it is to them that we owe the correctness of modern printing. More errors have been found in the Bible than in any other one work. For many generations it was frequently the case that Bibles were brought out stealthily, from fear of governmental interference. They were frequently printed from imperfect texts, and were often modified to meet the views of those who publised them. The story is related that a certain woman in Germany, who was the wife of a Printer, and had become disgusted with the continual assertions of the superiority of man over woman which she had heard, hurried into the composing room while her husband was at supper and altered a sentence in the Bible, which he was printing, so that it read Narr instead of Herr, thus making the verse read "And he shall be thy fool" instead of "and he shall be thy lord." The word not was omitted by Barker, the king's printer in England in 1632, in printing the seventh commandment He was fined £3000 on this account.

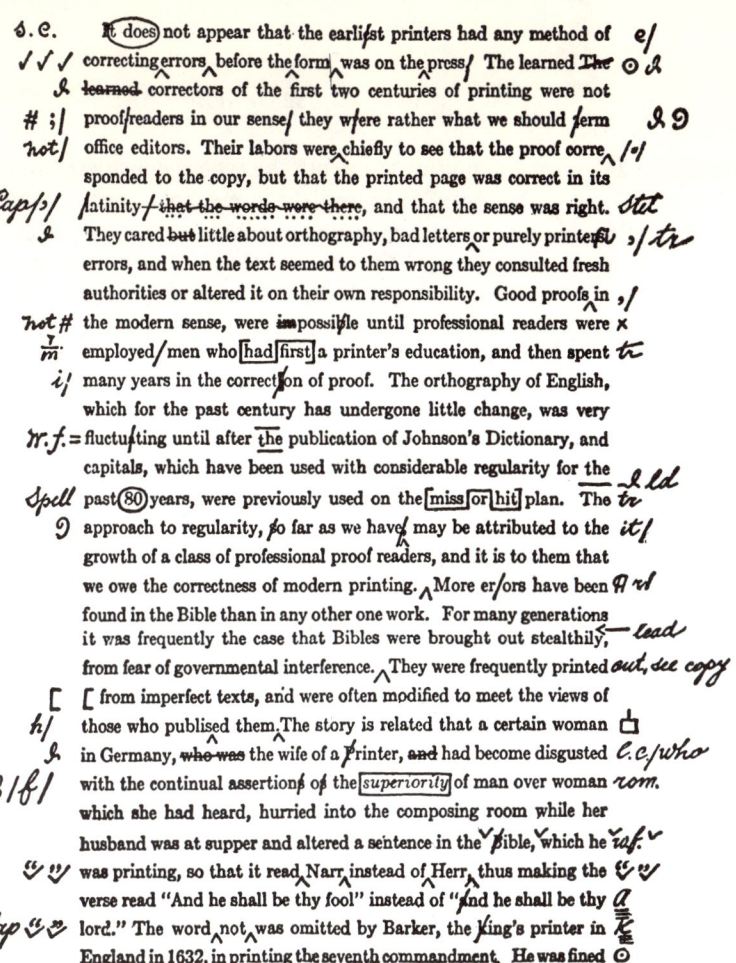

Figure 51-7. A piece of corrected proof.

Set solid.

The citizen is inevitably nation-conscious nowadays, inevitably conscious too of the reaction of foreign and international events upon his purse and his larder, his home and his employment. Man is more and more identified with his country and its fortunes. Is there then a philosophy of international life in which patriotism—this identification of the man with his country—has its part? For that surely is the new patriotism which we must seek. I believe there is.

Leaded 1 point:

The citizen is inevitably nation-conscious nowadays, inevitably conscious too of the reaction of foreign and international events upon his purse and his larder, his home and his employment. Man is more and more identified with his country and its fortunes. Is there then a philosophy of international life in which patriotism—this identification of the man with his country—has its part? For that surely is the new patriotism which we must seek. I believe there is.

Leaded 3 points:

The citizen is inevitably nation-conscious nowadays, inevitably conscious too of the reaction of foreign and international events upon his purse and his larder, his home and his employment. Man is more and more identified with his country and its fortunes. Is there then a philosophy of international life in which patriotism—this identification of the man with his country—has its part? For that surely is the new patriotism which we must seek. I believe there is.

Figure 51-8. A piece of copy set solid, leaded 1 point, and leaded 3 points.

number of picas by 12. Thus, a space 4 inches, or 24 picas, wide is 288 points in width (4 x 72 = 288, or 24 x 12 = 288.) If the depth of the space is 6 inches, or 36 picas, the space is 432 points deep (6 x 72 = 432, or 36 x 12 = 432).

(2) The next step is to calculate the number of ems[7] of type in the space, which in step (1) was determined to be 288 points wide and 432 points deep. This is done by dividing the number of ems in the width by the size of the type in points, dividing the number of ems in the depth by the size of the type in points, and then multiplying the two figures obtained; the result is the number of ems of type in the space. Thus:

If the type to be used is 10-point:
   288 ÷ 10 = 28.8, length
   432 ÷ 10 = 43.2, depth
   28.8 x 43.2 = 1244.16, ems of type
If the type to be used is 11-point:
   288 ÷ 11 = 26.1, length
   432 ÷ 11 = 39.2, depth
   26.1 x 39.2 = 1023.12, ems of type
If the type to be used is 12-point:
   288 ÷ 12 = 24, length
   432 ÷ 12 = 36, depth
   24 x 36 = 864, ems of type
If the type to be used is 14-point:
   288 ÷ 14 = 20.5, length
   432 ÷ 14 = 30.8, depth
   20.5 x 30.8 = 631.40, ems of type

(3) For convenient figuring, the average word is taken to be 3 ems in length. To complete the computation and find the number of words that will fill the given space, divide the number of ems in the space by 3:

In 10-point, 1244.16 ÷ 3 = 414.72 words will fill the space
11-point, 1023.12 ÷ 3 = 341 words will fill the space
12-point, 864 ÷ 3 = 288 words will fill the space
14-point, 631.4 ÷ 3 = 210.4 words will fill the space

These computations are for type that is set *solid*—that is, without any extra space between the lines of type. When type is leaded, the space computation must take the leading into consideration. The leading has the effect of increasing the depth of the lines of type, but does not increase the width. Thus, if the type to be used is 12-point, and it is to be leaded 2 points, for the width the 12-point computation is

[7]The *em* is approximately the space occupied by the capital M in the type used.

used, but for the depth the type is considered to be 14-point. For example, assume that a space 4 inches (or 24 picas) wide, and 6 inches (or 36 picas) deep, is to be set in 12-point type leaded 2 points; then the number of words in the space is calculated as follows:

4 inches (or 24 picas) = 288 points
288 ÷ 12 = 24, width
6 inches (or 36 picas) = 432 points
432 ÷ 14 = 30.8, depth
24 x 30.8 = 739.2 ems of type
739.2 ÷ 3 = 246.4, words in space

For the convenience of their customers, many printers prepare tables showing the number of words of type per square inch. Such a table is illustrated below. The figures are, of course, only approximate, and apply to the average type face.

NUMBER OF WORDS OF TYPE PER SQUARE INCH

Size of Type	*Set Solid*	*Leaded Two Points*
5	69	49
5½	55	45
6	48	37
7	36	27
8	30	23
9	25	20
10	20	15
11	15	12
12	12	11
14	10	9

To illustrate the use of the table, assume that a space 4 inches by 6 inches is to be set in 12-point type, solid. In this space there are 4 x 6 = 24 square inches. According to the table, there are 12 words to the square inch in 12-point type set solid; then the number of words that will fit the space is 24 x 12 = 288. According to the table, there are 11 words to the square inch in 12-point type leaded 2 points; hence, if the space 4 inches by 6 inches were to be set in 12-point type leaded 2 points, there would be 24 x 11 = 264 words.

Some printers go further, and, when preparing tables for the use of their customers, take into consideration the fact that the number of words per square inch varies with different type faces. The table given on this page is a portion of a table used by one printer to show the number of words per square inch for some of the more commonly used type faces.

NUMBER OF WORDS PER SQUARE INCH FOR VARIOUS TYPES

Type Face	6 Point	8 Point	10 Point	12 Point	14 Point
Bodoni	52	29	19	15	11
Bodoni Bold	48	26	17	13	10
Bookman	43	27	17	12	9
Caslon No. 471	53	36	23	15	11
Caslon No. 540	58	32	21	14	10
Cloister Old Style	53	32	22	15	13
Cloister Bold	45	30	20	14	11
Futura Light	..	32	22	15	12
Futura Medium	..	31	19	14	12
Futura Bold	..	28	17	11	8
Garamond Old Style	50	32	21	16	12
Garamond Bold	44	28	18	14	10

Copy fitting by character count. Word-count methods of copy fitting are not always accurate enough for careful work. Where exactness is necessary, the character-count method is preferable. As an illustration of the character-count method, assume that a space 3 inches by 4 inches is to be set in 11-point Caslon No. 540, leaded 1 point. How many lines of typewritten copy will be required to fill the space? The calculation is made as follows:

(1) The printer will supply the customer with specimens of type faces, and, after the face to be used has been chosen, the customer can determine the average number of characters to an inch by counting the characters per inch in the specimen of the type chosen. The number of characters per linear inch for 11-point Caslon No. 540 is found to be 15; the number of characters in a line 3 inches long is, therefore, 15 x 3 = 45.

(2) The next step is to find the number of lines in the depth. Since the type is 11-point leaded 1, there will be 24 lines in the space 3 inches by 4 inches (6 x 4 = 24).

(3) The number of characters in the space 3 inches by 4 inches is now found by multiplying the number of characters per line by the number of lines: 45 x 24 = 1080.

(4) A typewriter with pica type produces 10 characters to an inch; a typewriter with elite type types 12 characters to an inch. Suppose that the typewriter has elite type, and that it is set to type lines 5 inches in length. Then the number of typewriter characters per line is 12 x 5 = 60.

(5) The number of characters of 11-point Caslon No. 540 leaded 1 in the space 3 inches by 4 inches was found to be 1080. The number of typewritten characters per line was found to be 60. The number of typewriter lines, each 5 inches in length, that will be required to fill the space 3 inches by 4 inches is found by dividing 1080 by 60 (1080 ÷ 60 = 18). Hence the copywriter should write 18 lines of copy, 5 inches in length, to fill the space.

Many printers provide their customers with character-count tables, showing the number of characters per linear inch for various type faces. The following is a portion of a table of this kind.

CHARACTERS PER LINEAR INCH

Type Face	Size of Type				
	10	11	12	14	18
Bodoni	16	15	14	13	10
Caslon No. 540	16	15	13	10	9
Scotch Roman	17	16	13	11	8
Century	14	13	12	11	10
Cloister	20	18	17	16	12
Garamond	18	17	16	14	11

Always use the tables provided by the printer who is to do the work. If your printer has no such tables, reliable tables can be obtained from the Mergenthaler Linotype Company, Brooklyn, New York; the Intertype Corporation, Brooklyn, New York; or the Lanston Monotype Machine Company, Philadelphia, Pennsylvania.

The Haberule Visual Copy-Caster method of copy fitting has become increasingly popular with those who must do a great deal of very accurate copy fitting.

The International Typographic Composition Association also provides a copy-fitting system being used by persons who must regularly be involved in accurate copy fitting of varying type faces.

It is important to avoid "author's alterations" in copy that has been set, for each new set of proofs becomes increasingly expensive. The more accurately the copy has been scaled, the less likely changes will be necessary.

ENGRAVINGS

In offset printing, instead of providing a mounted or unmounted etched plate, the photoengraver provides negatives or positive film for the printer. Otherwise, the following information applies equally to all printing processes.

There are two basic kinds of engraving, *halftone* and *line*. Halftones are used to reproduce photographs, paintings, wash drawings, and other illustrations in which variations of shading are

Figure 51-9. Line Plate. The line plate (or line cut, as it is frequently called) is the simplest form of photo-engraving. Note that there are no gradations of tone between black and white; shading can be suggested only by lines of various weights and by areas of solid black. A line plate cannot be made from a photograph, a painting, or a wash drawing; it can be made only from a drawing that consists of lines and of areas of solid black. The drawing from which this line plate was made was a pen-and-ink sketch. A line plate is the least expensive form of photo-engraving and can be printed on even the roughest papers with good results.

Figure 51-10. Line Plate With Ben Day. The Ben Day process, named after the man who perfected it, adds life and sparkle to a line plate, and gives it some of the gradations of shading found in a halftone. Ben Day is available in various "screens"; a pattern book may be obtained from your engraver. In the line plate shown in Figure 51-10 five screens have been used; close study of the picture will reveal where the different screens were "laid on." Ben Day is a hand operation, and hence is expensive. Compare the line plate with Ben Day with the line plate illustrated in Figure 51-9 and with the square-finish halftone illustrated in Figure 51-11.

essential, and to produce flat tones, or tint blocks, of less intensity than a solid.

A halftone is created by photographing the original copy through a fine screen placed between the camera lens and the film or plate that is to become the negative. The image transmitted through the screen appears on the negative as a pattern of broken or dotted lines. Dark areas in the copy are reproduced in the negative as heavy dotted lines. Lighter areas are recorded as rows of smaller dots. The surface of the paper to be used in a printed job determines the screen to be used in making a halftone. The most commonly used halftone screens are 55, 65, 85, 100, 110, 120, 133, and 150 lines. The designations indicate the number of dotted lines in a linear inch.

For low-grade paper stock such as newsprint, the coarser screens are used, the 55-, 65-, or 85-line screen. For English finish and supercalendered papers, 100-, 110- and 120-line screens are used. For enamel- or smooth-coated stock, 133- and 150-line screens may be used. The finer the screen, the greater the amount of detail retained by the process. Generally, finer screens can be used for offset than for letterpress. Check with your printer.

Line engravings are straight reproductions of solid tones produced in much the same manner as halftones without using a screen. Line engravings reproduce well on virtually any type of stock. An appearance of shading may be obtained in line work by varying the thickness of lines, by varying the space between lines, and by applying some process such as Ben Day, which superimposes halftone-line dotted areas. Most line engravings are etched on zinc and are referred to as *zinc* etchings. Artwork containing fine lines should be etched on harder metal than zinc, generally copper.

With all signs pointing toward increasing emphasis in every area on color, it will be important for public relations men to follow process improvements in color photography, electrostatic plate making, and electronic color separations for both letterpress and offset lithography. A continuous series of improvements is bringing rotogravure sections nearer to magazines in quality of color reproduction. A new process developed by the Graphic Arts Research Department of the Rochester Institute of Technology provides vast improvement in the use of color on newsprint. Increasingly the public relations person will be

HOW TO USE GRAPHICS AND PRINTING

Figure 51-11. Square-Finish Halftone. There are various kinds of halftones. The simplest is the so-called square-finish halftone. The term "square finish" does not refer to the shape of the picture or to the shape of the plate, for a picture which is oval or circular may be reproduced as a square-finish halftone. The term refers to any halftone on which the screen covers the entire area. A square-finish halftone is the least expensive type. Comparison of Figure 51-11 with Figure 51-9 shows the obvious difference between a halftone and a line plate. The halftone has subtle gradations of shading between the black and white areas.

Figure 51-12. Halftone Showing Screens. The term "screen" refers to the fact that when the picture is being photographed, a screen is placed in the camera in front of the plate. Screens are known by numbers; those most commonly used are 55, 60, 65, 85, 100, 110, 120, 133, 150. In Figure 51-12 three screens are illustrated; namely, 85, 55, and 110. The fineness of the screen affects the fidelity of the results obtained. The proper screen to use depends upon the quality of the paper on which the halftone is to be printed. Smooth-finish paper can "take" a fine-screen halftone; the coarser grades of paper require coarse-screened halftones.

called on to use color to obtain maximum impact for his message.

Sizing or scaling an illustration. When possible finer reproduction will be obtained by straight copying or by reduction. When a halftone is larger than the copy from which it is reproduced, the delineation and shading in the illustration tend to break down.

Persons who know how to use a slide rule or one of the many devices available for sizing illustrations may readily determine the proportions required for a printed piece. If the area available for an illustration has been determined in the layout, they need merely to set their scales at the required dimensions and arrive at the comparative lengths in the artwork by considering which area must appear in the illustration, measuring one dimension, and reading the corresponding dimension on their device.

Without a calculating device, the easiest method is to place a tissue overlay on top of the artwork, mark the rectangle to be reproduced, draw a diagonal line on the rectangle, determine one dimension desired in the reproduction, mark off that dimension beginning at one of the starting points of the diagonal, and draw a line perpendicular to the known dimension at its termination. Measure the length of the line thus drawn from the end point to the intersection of the diagonal and the other dimension will be found. (See Figures 51-17 to 51-19.)

Another way to scale the size of an illustration in print from the original artwork or photograph is to use a proportional scale, such as shown in Figure 51-20. These scales are available in graphic arts stores and are provided to customers by some printers or reproduction houses.

Cropping. Selecting the most effective portion of a photograph or artwork calls for training and a keen eye for effect. Few photos are ideal for reproduction to the full extent of their coverage. A simple means of going over a photo to determine how it will reproduce most effectively is shown in Figure 51-21. Two L-shaped pieces of cardboard are moved about the surface to see how the photo will look with various cropping positions. When the ideal cropping is determined, marks can be made with a Vis-a-Vis marker or Expresso pen on the margins *outside* the photo content so when imaginary lines are drawn across the photo they will encompass the part to be printed.

Figure 51-13. Vignette Halftone. The so-called vignette halftone, illustrated in Figure 51-13, shows the object against a background that fades away with soft, cloudlike effect. Vignette halftones can be used very effectively in public relations brochures and booklets, but paper of good quality, and firstclass presswork, are required. On paper of the coarser grades, a vignette halftone tends to smudge rather than to fade. Thus, a vignette halftone can seldom be used in a house organ printed on newsprint. It can be used, however, in house organs printed on good paper stock. A vignette halftone costs approximately 50 per cent more than a square-finish halftone.

Figure 51-14. Silhouette Halftone. In the square-finish halftone illustrated in Figure 51-11, the screen covers the entire area of the picture. There are times, however, when a screen over the background is not desired. When all that is wanted is the object, a silhouette halftone (sometimes called an outline-finish halftone) may be ordered. In Figure 51-14, everything but the subject is cut away, and hence the background is pure white. A silhouette half-tone has more character than a square-finish halftone; the objects silhouetted stand out clearly on the page. A silhouette halftone costs about 50 per cent more than a square-finish halftone.

Figure 51-15. Highlight Halftone. A highlight halftone (also sometimes called a drop-out halftone) is one in which certain areas of the picture are highlighted or cut away. In the highlight halftone illustrated in Figure 51-15, the area around the fish is highlighted; so also is the fisherman's white shirt and a part of the sky in the background. When the halftone is made, the white areas in the original illustration are covered by the screen; the screen covering the areas that are to be highlighted is then tooled out by hand, and the areas so tooled are pure white. A highlight halftone is approximately three times as expensive as a square-finish halftone.

Figure 51-16. Surprint. It may be desired to combine a halftone and a line plate in a single engraving. This can be done in either of two ways. In a surprint, the line plate material (Fishing in Canada) is made to appear superimposed upon the halftone picture. In a so-called combination plate the line plate and the halftone adjoin each other. These figures could have been made square halftones, but the screen would then have covered the entire area, and the printed material would have been less legible. There is a slight extra charge for a surprint; a combination plate costs about twice as much as a square-finish halftone.

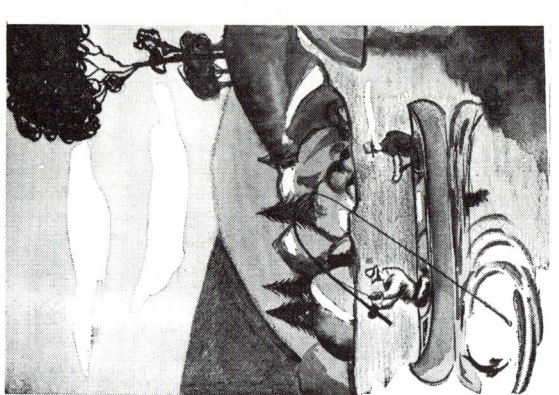

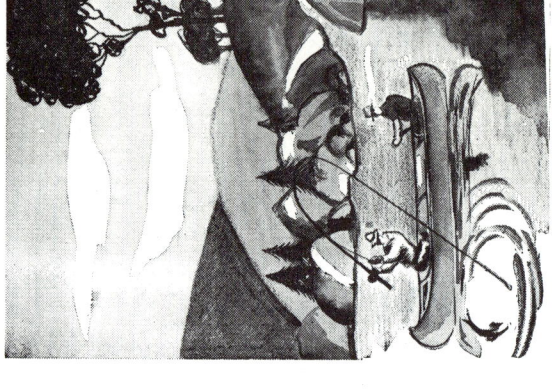

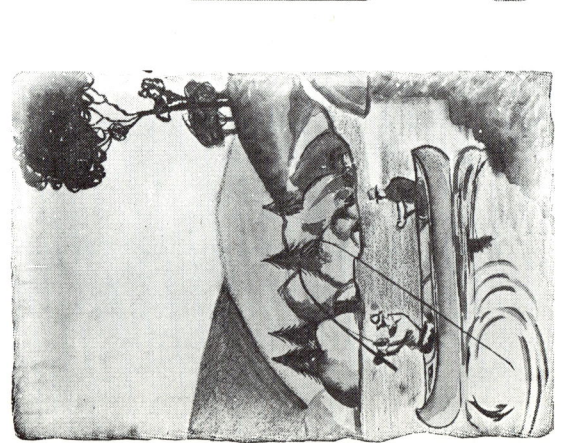

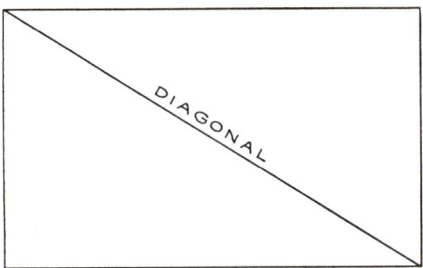

Figure 51-17. Area of artwork to be used with diagonal.

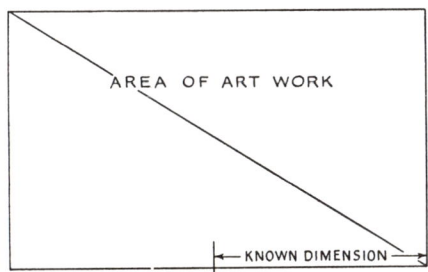

Figure 51-18. Known dimension marked for reproduction.

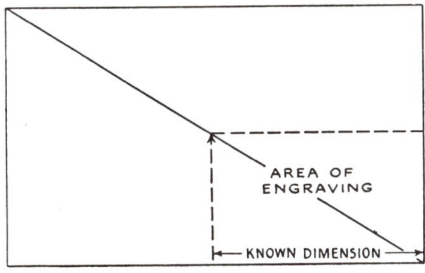

Figure 51-19. By drawing dotted line perpendicular to known dimension, other dimension is obtained.

Figure 51-20. A scaling wheel used to proportion artwork to the size desired in printed form.

Figure 51-21. Simple cardboard L-shaped guides make it easy to try various croppings for a photo or artwork.

561

RECOMMENDED PAPER SIZES
FOR BOOKLETS AND CATALOGUES

This Page Size	In the Following Number of Pages	Cuts Economically Out of These Sheet Sizes
3 × 6	4, 8, 16, 24, 48	25 × 38—38 × 50
4 × 9	4, 6, 8, 16, 24, 48	25 × 38—38 × 50
4 ½ × 6	4, 8, 16, 32, 64	25 × 38—38 × 50
6 × 9 ⅛	4, 8, 16, 32	25 × 38—38 × 50
9 ¼ × 12 ⅛	4, 8, 16, 32	25 × 38—38 × 50
3 ½ × 6 ⅜	4, 8, 16, 24, 48	30 ½ × 41—41 × 61
5 × 7 ¼	4, 8, 16, 32, 64	30 ½ × 41—41 × 61
7 ⅜ × 9 ⅞	4, 8, 16, 32	30 ½ × 41—41 × 61
10 × 14 ⅞	4, 8, 16	30 ½ × 41—41 × 61
3 ¾ × 5 ⅛	4, 8, 16, 32, 64	32 × 44—44 × 64
3 ¾ × 6 ⅞	4, 8, 16, 24, 48	32 × 44—44 × 64
5 ¼ × 7 ⅝	4, 8, 16, 32, 64	32 × 44—44 × 64
7 ½ × 10 ⅝	4, 8, 16, 32	32 × 44—44 × 64
10 ¾ × 15 ⅝	4, 8, 16	32 × 44—44 × 64

RECOMMENDED PAPER SIZES
FOR UNSTITCHED CIRCULARS

This Page Size	In the Following Number of Pages	Cuts Economically Out of These Sheet Sizes
3 ⅛ × 6 ¼	4, 6, 8, 12, 16, 24	25 × 38—38 × 50
4 ⅛ × 9 ½	4, 6, 12, 16, 24	25 × 38—38 × 50
4 ¾ × 6 ¼	4, 8, 16, 32	25 × 38—38 × 50
6 ¼ × 9 ½	4, 8, 16, 32	25 × 38—38 × 50
9 ½ × 12 ½	4, 8, 16, 32	25 × 38—38 × 50
3 ¾ × 6 ¾	4, 6, 8, 12, 16, 24	30 ½ × 41—41 × 61
5 ⅛ × 7 ⅝	4, 8, 16, 32	30 ½ × 41—41 × 61
7 ⅝ × 10 ¼	4, 8, 16, 32	30 ½ × 41—41 × 61
10 ¼ × 15 ¼	4, 8, 16,	30 ½ × 41—41 × 61
4 × 5 ½	4, 8, 16,	32 × 44—44 × 64
4 × 7 ¼	4, 8, 16, 24	32 × 44—44 × 64
5 ½ × 8	4, 8, 16, 32	32 × 44—44 × 64
8 × 11	4, 8, 16, 32	32 × 44—44 × 64
11 × 16	4, 8, 16,	32 × 44—44 × 64

Figure 51-22.

COMPARISON CHART OF PAPER STOCKS
including only the better known writing, book, and cover papers

PAPER	SPECIFICATION	DESCRIPTION	PHOTO-ENGRAVING RECOMMENDED	COMMENTS
WRITING	Flat Writing.	This is the paper used in the making of inexpensive school writing tablets and notebooks. Better grades of it are used in correspondence stationery.	A. Line plates.	I. Not used extensively for public relations advertising purposes. II. As the quality of a Flat Writing stock becomes better, it moves into the class of Bonds.
	Bonds.	Most letters received in the business office are on this stock. Its grades vary from that in which wood pulp and sulphite are used, to the better qualities made of linen rags. The weight in most common use is 20 lbs.	A. Line plates. B. 100-screen halftones. C. Highlight halftones.	I. Bonds provide a large variety of tints. II. Some come in finishes such as "crash" simulating the cloth; also glazed. Most bonds come in a plain unglazed finish. III. Engraving plates for use on bonds should be etched deep.
	Ledger.	A very high-class sheet of writing paper, used mostly for documents and accounting work. Has a tough, sturdy body, and a surface finish which has been plated (compressed between sheets of metal). This sheet is heavier, as a class, than bonds; also more expensive. In its lighter weights it is also used for executive stationery.	A. Line plates. B. 100-screen halftones.	I. Comes mostly in white and buff.

PAPER	SPECIFICATION	DESCRIPTION	PHOTO-ENGRAVING RECOMMENDED	COMMENTS
BOOK	Newstock.	Received its name from its use for newspapers. The least expensive of book papers and sometimes considered as a class by itself. Has a thin, porous body and a rough surface.	A. Line plates. B. 65-screen halftones, tooled well. When printed offset, finer screens up to 100-line may be used. C. Quartertones.	I. Comes mostly in white (which varies in its tones). II. Qualities vary. Finish does not have to be specified.
	Antique.	A book paper whose body is of higher quality and heavier weight than that of news, but which likewise has a rough, uneven surface.	A. Line plates only.	I. Limited range of colors. II. Has a number of different finishes, as *eggshell, antique wove, antique laid.*
	Machine Finish. (M.F.)	The least expensive of the book papers which can take half-tones dependably well. Represents an additional process through which antique paper goes. The stock is "sized," or submersed in chemicals, which fill up the pores, making the paper less absorbent. It is then "calendered" or ironed, the surface obtaining the smooth finish which permits the use of halftone. Sometimes known as "S.&C." (Sized and Calendered.)	A. 120-screen halftones.	I. Moderate range of colors. II. A very utilitarian paper. Permits reproduction of wash drawings and photographs. Creases well. Especially good for booklets and catalogues to be issued in quantity.

(Cont.)

Figure 51-23.

COMPARISON CHART OF PAPER STOCKS (*Cont.*)
including only the better known writing, book, and cover papers

PAPER	SPECIFICATION	DESCRIPTION	PHOTO-ENGRAVING RECOMMENDED	COMMENTS
BOOK *(Cont.)*	English Finish.	A grade smoother than Machine Finish, but not as high as the one next described. For most purposes in which a halftone is to be used, this offers a serviceable, attractive stock.	A. 120-screen halftones.	I. Moderate range of colors. II. Folds well. Can withstand fingering and usage. Good for leaflets and booklets, house organs, and moderately high-class catalogues.
	Sized and Super Calendered ("S.&S.C.").	This is a machine-finished paper which has been "sized," like Machine Finish and English Finish, but which has been given an additional ironing. The surface is consequently glossy.	A. 133-screen halftones.	I. Moderate range of colors. II. Folds well. Suited for uses similar to those of English Finish, when a more attractive effect is sought.
	Enamel Coated ("Coated").	The smoothest of book papers. This is a machine-finish paper which has been given a coating of clay and glue, then passed through the calender rolls at high speed. The result is a hard surface, dull, or glossy. Is brittle. Does not fold well. Otherwise shows reproductions to very best advantage.	A. 133, 150-screen halftones. Can take vignette finish.	I. Most expensive of the book papers. Looks good. Good for extra fine work. Cannot stand much fingering and usage.
COVER	Antique.	Refers to the rough-surfaced finish. Antique cover is usually rougher than antique book.	A. Line plates.	I. Broad range of finishes, including *ripple linen, crash* and many fancy-finish patterns. II. Good for folders, and for booklet covers.
	Plated.	The surface has been pressed, as in ledgers.	A. 120-screen halftones.	I. Good for booklet covers.
	Enamel Coated ("Coated").	A cover stock which has been given a treatment similar to book cover stock.	A. 133, 150, 175-screen halftones.	I. The acme of cover stocks in appearance.

From Kleppner, "Advertising Procedure." Englewood Cliffs, N.J.: Prentice-Hall

Figure 51-23 (**Cont.**)

SECTION VI

The Practice of Public Relations

52

Organization and Function of the Corporate Public Relations Department

CHARLES H. PROUT has organized and headed the public relations functions at two major American companies and is a well-known writer on public relations.

He is Vice President Corporate Relations and Secretary for Culter-Hammer, Inc., electrical/electronics manufacturing. He has full responsibility for the public relations function, and serves as Chairman of the Company's Public Policy Committee and President of the Culter-Hammer Foundation. In addition he is corporate secretary. Prior to joining Cutler-Hammer in 1963 he had been for nine years Director of Public Relations at Mead Johnson & Company, pharmaceutical and nutritional products manufacturer. As a corporate public relations executive he has dealt with all facets of public relations discussed in this chapter.

As the founder and for two years (1958-1960) editor and publisher of "PR Reporter," a professional newsletter, Mr. Prout has studied, analyzed, and written about the full range of public relations programs and problems. "PR Reporter" gained prompt acceptance and became one of the leading professional periodicals in the public relations field.

Prior to his association with Mead Johnson, he was with Richardson-Merrell, Inc. and with the Associated Press. He is a journalism graduate of Rutgers University. During World War II he was a public relations officer in the U.S. Army, entering service as a private in 1942 and leaving as a major in 1946. In addition to his professional public relations writing, he has had his free-lance articles published in a number of the country's leading general circulation magazines.

Although business was not the first field of American socio-economic endeavor to discover the need for organized public relations effort nor the opportunities provided by it, business now has taken the profession firmly to its bosom. (Results of a survey conducted in 1976 by *O'Dwyer's Directory of Corporate Communications* indicated that 1,187 (82.5%) of the 1,458 companies ranking in the "biggest" lists of industrial firms published by *Fortune* and *Forbes* magazines had formal public relations or communications functions.)

This partially results from the post World War II emergence of so many industries and corporations from the relative obscurity of smallness to the bright spotlight that goes hand-in-hand with bigness, bringing with it many urgent public pressures in today's fermenting society. It also is a result of growing recognition by corporate management of the positive contributions that public relations can make to corporate growth and progress.

Role of public relations in a corporation. The principles of public relations in a business organization are treated in the first 18 chapters. We may summarize here that it is the function responsible for corporate good will—protecting that which the company has, building additional stores of it for the future.

Public relations, in essence, builds acceptance for the corporation as a whole much as the marketing departments build acceptance for individual products.

To accomplish its role public relations often has to take two different postures: defensive in the face of attack, positive in the effort to enhance good will. But in all cases it must be based on coordinating corporate performance with the public interest while simultaneously assuring public awareness and understanding of that performance. As has often been stated in public relations circles, "No organization can be made to look better than it actually is." Public relations cannot be fancy window dressing for a company whose policies and actions are unworthy of public scrutiny and acclaim. So, essentially, good corporate public relations begins at the top management level with establishment of company policies and practices that are ethical, honest, and in keeping with the public interest. Then the public relations staff function can take those policies and practices to the public for acclaim, understanding and, if need be, for use as defense against attack.

Two things corporate public relations should not be—but often is misinterpreted as—is a willy-nilly "do gooder" function or a purely publicity operation.

Publicity is a tool of public relations and is widely and effectively used. But publicity does not constitute a public relations program any more than an employment office represents a personnel program or a bookkeeper represents a financial division. Only insofar as a management recognizes this difference can it hope to make effective use of public relations.

"Doing good" is a logical part of a sound public relations program, because such action helps keep corporate actions aligned with the public interest. But public relations cannot be an effective part of the management team if it is not contributing toward corporate progress. Tangential, inconsequential activities designed to do good with no discernible benefit to the corporation can become wasteful and noncontributory.

T.J. Ross, one of the early leaders of the profession, lent emphasis to the point when he said:

> A public relations man is not worth his salt if he succumbs to "pie-in-the-sky" thinking divorced from the realities of his business. And he will not stay long on the management team if he does. In his zeal to place his corporation in the most favorable public light, he must not forget that a business is first and foremost a profit-making enterprise, not an eleemosynary institution. In the relationships he seeks to create between the corporation and its publics he may be softhearted but he must not be softheaded.

SCOPE OF PUBLIC RELATIONS FUNCTION

In actual practice the role of public relations in corporations varies widely with the type and size of company, the understanding management has of the proper uses of public relations, and the caliber of the internal public relations staff and/or external public relations counsel.

This is not surprising since public relations is still such a new facet of business life—concepts for its proper use have not fully permeated the business community. And, in truth, even many long-established business functions such as advertising, personnel, and finance still tend to vary considerably in their application in different companies.

However, the preferred and most productive role for public relations in the modern corporation has been clearly defined and demonstrated in many companies that have had long experience in the field.

Public relations properly practiced at the corporate level should be an integral part of the top management team, serving alongside such other staff functions as finance, personnel, legal, and long range planning, to provide guidance and counsel on the corporation's basic decision processes. At the same time, it must be geared to provide professional communications planning and service to both the corporation as a whole and the various operating units on a broad range of subjects from management communications to financial disclosure to product promotion publicity.

In order to achieve these objectives, the public relations staff must be prepared to function in four basic service areas:

(1) Advice and counsel
(2) Communications service
(3) Public relations research and analysis
(4) Public relations promotion

Advice and counsel on public relations-connected subjects is provided to both corporate management and the management of other departments and divisions. Since public relations is a staff function, it customarily does not establish policies or make basic operating decisions. But it bears a direct responsibility to look for, identify, and recommend to management appropriate corporate decisions and policies in order to assure maintenance of an even public relations keel for the company.

Ideally, the top corporate public relations executive does this by sitting as a member of the corporate management committee and in personal discussion with line management executives. However, lacking such a position in the organization, he still has the responsibility to make his recommendations known through whatever oral or written channels are available to him in the structure of his particular company.

These recommendations may range all the way from advising on the best way a public announcement of a corporate action might be made, to recommending a change in a basic corporate policy or proposed activity to bring it closer into line with the public interest; analyzing and interpreting the impact on the company of pending governmental policies or regulations, to producing a corporate public relations program designed to help the company advance toward its goals or to cope with problems.

Communications service is the role most frequently associated with public relations. It includes the outward communication of information about the company and its activities to all of the various publics of interest to the company via whatever communications media are deemed appropriate.

It is far broader than mere issuance of news releases. Communications service encompasses the total process of projecting the corporate image, whether via news media, setting a corporate citizenship example, or disseminating information about the company's actions and motives in the form of booklets, speeches, or institutional advertisements. It includes assuring compliance with requirements for appropriate public disclosure of financial, environmental protection, and product safety information. It also includes communicating the company's views on pending legislative and regulatory issues to leaders of government, as well as to employees, shareholders, and other interested publics. In essence, it is the function of "letting the public know" by whatever means are appropriate to the individual situation.

Public relations research is a less widely recognized activity, but nonetheless valuable. While communications service implies outward dissemination of information, public relations research means the identification, evaluation, and communication inward to the company of information of the outside world that may be of value to the company in managing its affairs—the business equivalent of military intelligence.

While deeply engaged in the day-to-day operations of a business, management often has neither the opportunity nor the inclination to stay fully abreast of outside developments of interest to the company. Through close association with public agencies and publications and through the use of professional journals, clipping services, and opinion surveys, often the public relations department can detect trends or anticipate events of pertinence to the company. Or it may seek out and measure tides of public opinion that may affect the company's operations. This is particularly true in the case of government regulation and legislation, but also applies, on occasion, to many other forms of socio-political pressure and/or expectation. When broad or specific evaluation of a climate of opinion is desired, an opinion survey may be called for.[1]

Public relations promotion encompasses a variety of programs designed specifically to build acceptance for the company among its various publics—customers, plant communities, stockholders, and so on. While all public relations activities are intended to produce good will to one degree or another, some of them are neutral or defensive in nature—designed to maintain good will or protect it against attack. On the other hand, public relations promotion programs are usually more comprehensive, more positive, and most creative. They are designed to generate new good will or enhance that which already exists—to increase company acceptance with customers as a means of indirectly stimulating sales,[2] with government agencies to avert restrictive rulings,[3] with the local community[4] as a means of reducing friction over industrial annoyances and as a means of attracting more and better employees.

In some instances corporate public relations promotion activities may encompass noncommercial services provided to customers or other publics. By thus helping the publics with some of their own problems, acceptance and good will are engendered for the sponsor that presumably may be converted to increased sales or cooperation at a later date when the company's need is great.

In another area, public relations promotion may be provided as product publicity to marketing divi-

---

[1] See Chap. 35.
[2] See Chaps. 17-19, 38.
[3] See Chaps. 4-6
[4] See Chap. 7.

sions. Often through other programs, encompassing the use of publicity in the editorial channels of the public and trade press, plus other means of exposure in influence-molding locations and situations, a degree of acceptance for a company or product can be achieved that would be almost impossible to achieve through direct advertising and promotion alone.

Such acceptance often takes the form of a ground swell of public awareness and use of a product or adoption of a corporate concept. As a consequence, such promotion is most effective when the product or concept is new, although promotional publicity can be used successfully to support continuing programs.

Because it usually is quite difficult to fully separate product publicity and corporate publicity, this type of promotion is centered in the central public relations department, even while other purely product promotion is concentrated within the separate marketing units. Of equal importance is the fact that product publicity involves specialized personnel and techniques that are most economically provided on a service basis to all marketing divisions from a central department, as needed.

FUNCTIONS OF THE PUBLIC RELATIONS DEPARTMENT

The list of functions performed by corporate public relations departments to accomplish the role just described varies from company to company, but certain standard functions have emerged as common in most balanced departments. They are listed below in approximate order of prevalence.

• *Public Relations Policy*—Develop and recommend corporate public relations policies; contribute public relations viewpoint in formulation of corporate decisions. Provided mainly to top management but also to other departments and divisions.

• *Corporate Publicity*—Development and issuance of announcements of company activities to external communications media; handling inquiries from the press; development and placement of promotional publicity about the corporation as a whole or any of its units.

• *Product Publicity*—Announcement of new products through editorial channels of communications media; development and execution of promotional product publicity campaigns.

• *Government Relations*—Maintain liaison with appropriate governmental units at local, state, and national level; report trends in government affecting the company; advise action as needed; help prepare for and direct corporate appearances before investigating bodies or legislative hearings; direct programs designed to promote the company's point of view in legislative or regulatory matters.

• *Community Relations*—Plant community contacts . . . performance and/or coordination of corporate "good neighbor" activities, including compliance with environmental protection standards, fostering equal employment opportunity, and cooperating in urban improvement programs; development of community understanding of company's problems and needs.

• *Stockholder Relations*—Communications between company and shareowners; also between company and the investment community in general; development of acceptance of company among investors via broadening exposure of company's policies and financial results in the investment community; preparation of annual report, quarterly reports, dividend check inserts, etc.; planning and staging of annual meetings of stockholders and appearances before meetings of security analysts.

• *Public Relations Promotion Programs*—Institutional promotion programs designed to build corporate acceptance among key publics; institutional advertising; public relations literature; special events.

• *Corporate Donations*—Develop policy for company contributions; process donations requests; administer company's foundation; conduct of employee solicitations for approved drives.

• *Employee Publications*—Prepare and publish employee magazine, newspaper, bulletins, management communications, etc.

• *Guest Relations*—Plant tours; new plant and/or building dedications; guest reception activities.

• *Miscellaneous*—Speakers' bureau; education relations.

PUBLIC RELATIONS IN THE CORPORATE ORGANIZATION

To operate effectively, the function must fit into the corporate organization structure directly under top management. This reporting relationship to top management has emerged strongly over the years, as experience has demonstrated its necessity. It now applies in all major corporations that have significant public relations programs.

This is easy to understand in light of our outline of the role and functions of the public relations department. Most of the functions listed are of direct concern to top management—and are of only indirect or partial concern to any one of the operating divisions or departments of a company.

The specific person to whom public relations reports in top management varies with the company's overall organizational structure. The president is the most frequent person. Others may include the chairman of the board, the board of directors itself, or an executive vice-president. However, the most common arrangement has the public relations officer reporting to the chief executive officer, whatever his title.

It may be appropriate to note the most common misalignment and why it usually is unsatisfactory.

Sometimes public relations is assigned to report to the marketing function. However, since any successful marketing executive must maintain a rather narrow view on "how to sell products—now," it is rare that a public relations function aligned organizationally under marketing is anything more than a product publicity operation. By the mere parochial focus he must maintain on immediate sales results, the marketing head usually does not concern himself to any significant extent with broader corporate problems reflected in a total public relations program. Hence, he normally demands and expects equally narrow attention to sales from his product publicity man, who is considered an adjunct to the advertising function even though he may be labeled with the more prestigious title of public relations.

ORGANIZATION OF THE DEPARTMENT

The designation under which the public relations department or its top executive is known is most often "public relations." However, in recent years there has been a tendency in a number of companies to move to other designations deemed to more fully encompass the range of responsibilities or to avoid negative connotations that have become attached to the term "public relations" in some people's minds.

The choice of alternate designation seems to vary with the size of the company. In the Conference Board's study of 141 medium- and large-sized corporations, the split was almost even between "public relations" and "public affairs," with such names as "corporate communications" and "corporate relations" following as distant seconds. Other assorted designations trailed even further behind.

Meanwhile, *O'Dwyer's Directory of Corporate Communications* found that "public relations" dominated in its broader sample of 1,187 companies, being favored by 30.8 percent, with "public affairs" occurring in only 8.5 percent of cases. "Communications" was in second place at 18.4 percent and "advertising/public relations" followed "public affairs" at 8.2 percent. Various other designations made up the balance of the responses.

Since "public relations" is by all standards the most commonly accepted designation—and as this book indicates, "public affairs" is encompassed within it—it is used throughout this chapter to encompass all of the aforementioned titles. The reader may make such mental substitutions in the semantics of nomenclature as he finds desirable—the substance will remain the same.

The size and organization of the public relations department naturally varies with the size of the company and the scope of the public relations program. Departments range from one-man operations in smaller corporations to organizations of more than 200 persons in some giant companies.

Recent surveys by *PR Reporter,* a leading professional newsletter, and by the Conference Board have determined that among many large corporations in the United States, the average public relations department was 5-20 professional staff members. By contrast, smaller organizations (including businesses, associations, and institutions) usually have public relations staffs of 3 to 10 persons.

In addition, of course, many of these companies also retained public relations firms or counsel.

The corporate public relations department usually is headed by a person bearing the title of Vice President or Director of Public Relations. However, designations such as Senior Vice President or Executive Vice President also are used in some larger companies as the breadth of the public relations function grows. In some smaller firms or in those where public relations has not achieved full management recognition and confidence, Public Relations Manager is the title applied.

The vice-presidential designation is growing in use rapidly both because management has recognized the significance of the contribution to corporate affairs made by the public relations function and because the title facilitates the public relations department's dealings with other departments and divisions of the company, as well as with outside groups.

Obviously, the allocation of functions among

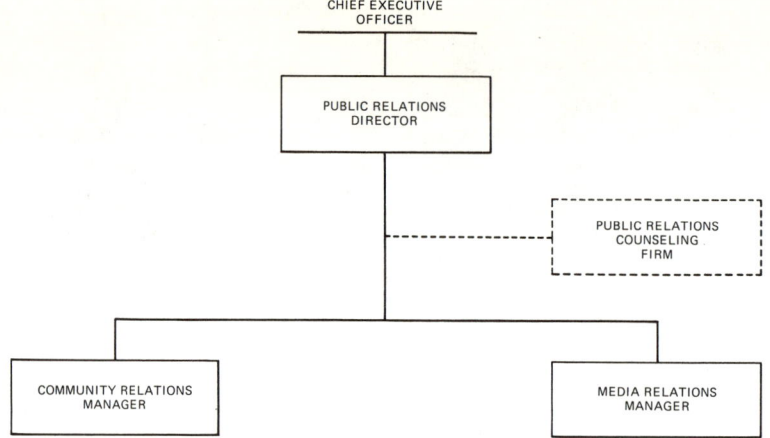

Figure 52-1. Typical small public relations department.

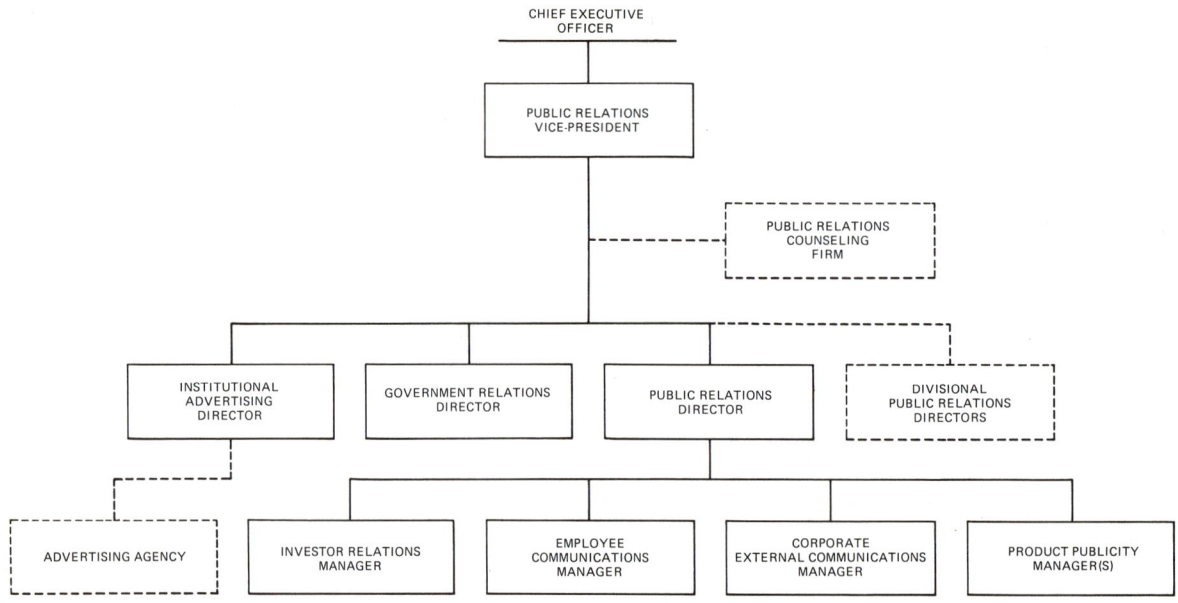

Figure 52-2. Typical medium-sized public relations department.

staff members of the public relations department varies widely from company to company, according to the needs of the organization and the abilities of the individuals. There is no absolutely right or wrong. The first staff member to be added usually is assigned responsibility for press relations and publicity, since that is the single heaviest area of work load. The department head personally handles all other duties. Later staff additions normally are assigned such responsibilities as community relations, stockholder relations, institutional promotion, government relations, employee communications, and so on, according to the needs of the particular company.

In larger, multi-plant companies members of the public relations department often are assigned to detached service at various plant locations, dealing primarily with plant-community relations. In such instances the staff member has a dual reporting relationship: a direct staff responsibility to the plant manager and a dotted-line policy relationship to the central public relations department.

Similarly, in larger, multi-division corporations with independent divisional marketing functions

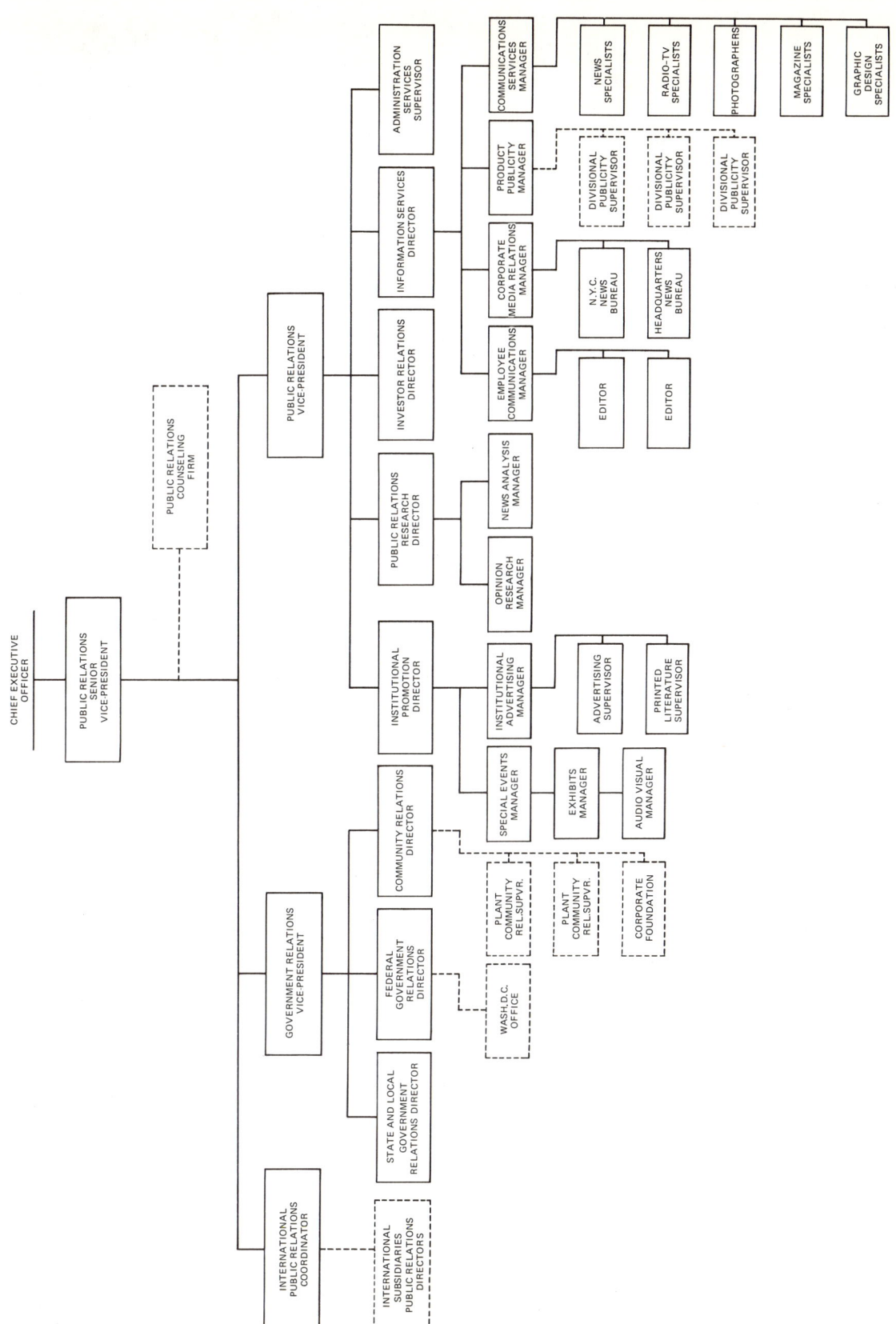

Figure 52-3. Typical large public relations department.

often members of the central public relations department are assigned on detached service with each division, or at least to all that are large enough to require such service. These persons normally devote most of their time to promotional product publicity for the divisions concerned, while the central public relations department carries on all other corporate public relations functions and also provides product publicity service to those divisions not large enough to support a full-time staff member. In particularly large and decentralized companies, each divisional public relation office takes on a more autonomous role and performs a complete range of public relations functions. As in the case of the public relations staff on plant duty, these divisional public relations personnel usually report directly to the division head but maintain a dotted line responsibility to the central public relations department for corporate coordination and policy compliance. They also draw on the central department for advice and staff support in times of heavy work load.

On the accompanying pages are three representative organization charts for typical small, medium, and large public relations departments.

PUBLIC RELATIONS SALARIES

Corporate public relations budgets are determined mainly by three factors:

(1) The scope of the public relations function.
(2) How much of the cost of public relations programs is charged to the public relations budget and how much is charged to the operating divisions being benefited.
(3) The size of the company.

Thus it is difficult to give meaningful comparisons or suggestions, other than to indicate that it would be difficult to have a significant program in a small- to medium-sized company for less than $150,000 to $200,000 a year. In larger firms, budgets ranging from $1 million to $10 million are becoming increasingly common.

However, salaries can be compared in a meaningful way and provide a good insight into budgets,

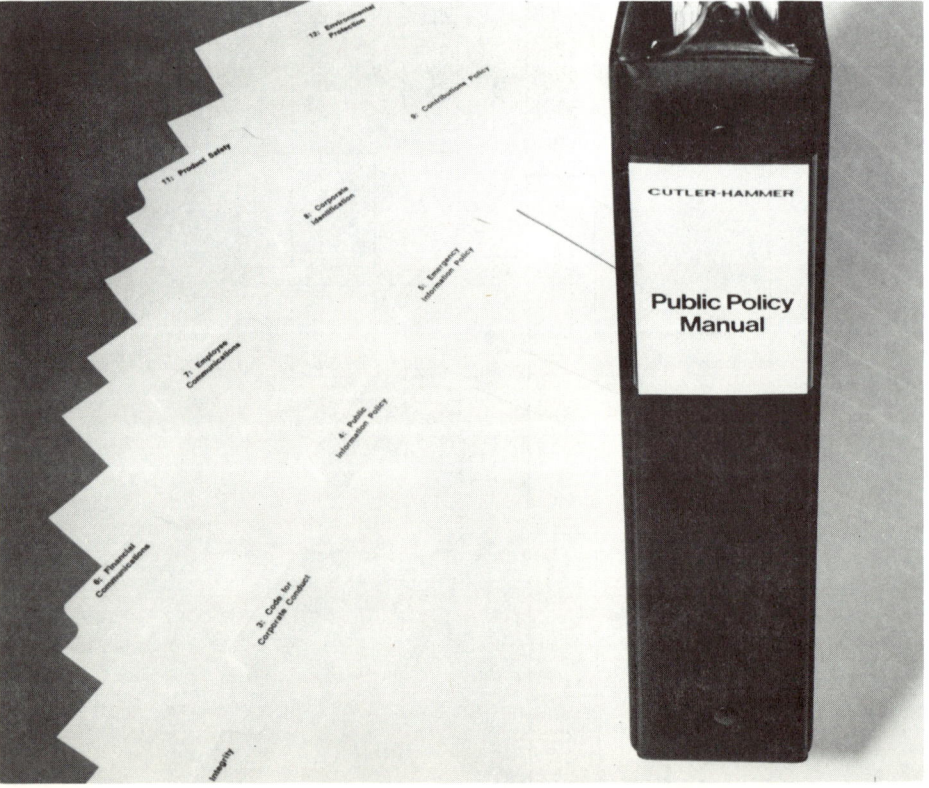

Figure 52-4. Multi-sectioned Public Policy Manual issued by Cutler-Hammer, Inc. for guidance for all facilities managers and other key executives is representative of frequently used technique in multi-plant companies to assure consistent understanding of corporate policies and practices in public relations.

since salaries are the major factor in the expenses of most public relations departments.

Salaries in corporate public relations tend to follow fairly consistent patterns and have been clearly defined in salary surveys over the years.

Corporate salaries and those in public relations counseling firms tend to run rather parallel to each other, with a slight edge enjoyed by the counseling firms. Other types of organizations (colleges, universities, trade associations, and so on) lag significantly on salary levels.

The 1976 *PR Reporter* survey found that the top public relations executives in the companies surveyed were paid median salaries of $25,000 to $32,000 per year depending on geographic area and size of company. However, most larger corporations paid salaries in the $50,000 and up range to their top public relations executive, with some individual instances running into the $100,000 to $135,000 bracket. This reflects the growing importance of the public relations function in business life and the broad range of capabilities and experience that are required in the public relations executive.

BOARD OF DIRECTORS PARTICIPATION

In recent years, as public demands and expectations for closer Board of Directors attention to the ethical, moral, and legal conduct of business have grown, board involvement in the public relations function has increased. This is a welcome development for the public relations staff, since it evidences top corporate attention to public relations as well as assuring serious and attentive consideration of public policy issues throughout all levels of the organization.

Since the directors cannot and should not become involved in the day-to-day public relations activities of the company any more than they can or should be involved in other day-to-day operating functions, their principal public relations involvement usually comes through an overview—audits of corporate ethical practice and/or establishment of policy standards for the guidance of management.

Most frequently a public policy committee of the board is established to perform these functions. Participation may be solely by directors or by a combination of directors and non-director officers representing operating management. The top public relations officer is a key member in the latter instance, or a close staff associate in the former.

ROLE OF THE PUBLIC RELATIONS FIRM

Outside public relations counsel plays an essential role in corporate public relations, whether or not an internal department exists. This is amply evidenced by the fact that one-third of the corporations participating in the broadly based 1976 survey of *O'Dwyer's Directory of Corporate Communications* reported using outside consultants, although they also had inside public relations departments. The Conference Board's survey of medium- and large-size companies found that most of the corporations used one or several consulting firms, often retaining one full-time and bringing in additional ones from time to time for special assignments.

In the case where no internal public relations function operates, outside counsel usually is retained by management to do one of two things:

• Advise the company on public relations problems and act as the public relations service function.

• Assist the company in establishing an internal public relations department, including the formulation of policy and recruitment of personnel.

In companies where internal public relations departments already exist, the role of the outside firm is usually a combination of advising and counseling the internal staff on basic problems and serving as a staff extension of the internal department in handling peak work loads or specialized projects, and in providing creative services and facilities.

Since public relations is a diverse field with a variety of facets, new and unexpected problems frequently present themselves. In such instances the public relations staff, as well as top management, can benefit from the cumulative experience and wide range of contacts of the outside counsel as gained from working with a good many other clients.

By the same token, an outside counseling firm with its multiple clients can maintain a staff of creative specialists that it is not economically feasible to maintain in an internal public relations department, where only sporadic use would create an undesirable overhead problem. Hence, the outside agency serves as a ready pool of extra talent to be called on for specialized tasks as needed by the internal department.

53

The Place and Function of the Public Relations Counsel

Philip Lesly

The executive responsible for an organization's public relations must know the functions, benefits, and practices of the specialists he may call on. Any consideration of the part played by the professional counsel in public relations must begin with an analysis of what the term "public relations counsel" means, in its broad and strict senses.

WHO IS A PUBLIC RELATIONS COUNSEL?

Because this business is becoming a profession without standards for acceptance, the title is conveniently adopted by a wide variety of practitioners in any activity that involves contact with people—obviously, an extensive area. Men who are essentially press agents, lobbyists, "fixers," publicity representatives, union negotiators, personnel specialists, and ghost writers call themselves "public relations counsel." Although in a very limited sense each counsels on relations with the public, they are not "public relations counsel" as the term is generally accepted today, and will not be considered as such in this study.

The true public relations counsel is a professional who functions independently on a fee or retainer basis for one or more clients. His advice and service cover virtually all of the aspects of public relations that have been considered in this book. And he functions on the executive level of the client's management, rather than with subordinates, in most cases.

Actually, there are few people who are strictly public relations counsel in North America today, compared with the large number of workers in the various phases of public relations, such as publicity, labor relations, government relations, financial community relations, and company publications.

The public relations counsel is often the face an organization puts before its most important publics: the press and broadcasters, important organizations, schools, communities, all of whom the counsel deals with on behalf of the client. For this reason, the counsel an organization chooses is important to its own "image." The organization frequently can rise no higher in esteem than the caliber of counsel it retains, no matter how good a program may be conceived and executed. For this reason, the caliber of a counsel's clientele is one of the most important measures to be applied by a prospective client. A client concerned about its esteem and prestige is more likely to advance it with a counsel who is esteemed than with one known for lesser characteristics.

In a real sense, clients and counsel tend to find each other on the basis of characteristics they have in common.

The counsel's background. Because of the broad scope of his or her activities, the counsel must necessarily be a person who has had extensive training in many fields, as well as the abilities called for in serving the clients:

- Judgment;
- Ability to think in sharp, logical patterns;
- Ability to express oneself clearly, both orally and in writing;
- Ability to plan on a broad scale—going below the surface, far beyond the immediate horizon;

- Executive ability, to direct extensive operations involving much detail and many abstract elements;
- Sales ability, to know how to put over an idea, a product, or a cause;
- Constant objectivity—keeping himself in the background, able to evaluate any situation from the outsider's viewpoint;
- Open-mindedness—even after *almost* all the facts seem to lead to one conclusion;
- Humility, to be able to acknowledge that his judgment may be wrong;
- Courage, to be willing to lose a client if continuing could require compromising his convictions and judgment;
- Ability to put just as much stress on details as on vast plans;
- Interest in people, in their ideas, in why they do things;
- Lively imagination, tempered by good judgment.

In almost all cases, the professional public relations counsel is a principal or an executive in a firm of counselors, or in an advertising agency. This makes him a business man who deals with problems of rent, personnel, taxes, overhead, and other matters that do not directly involve his clients, but are essential to his ability to serve the clients effectively. We shall consider these business aspects later. The counsel's functions on behalf of his clients receive first attention.

HOW HE WORKS WITH A CLIENT

A counsel or a public relations firm as a whole is retained by a corporation, trade association, nonprofit organization, individual, institution, or other group on any of several bases:

(1) He is retained only for counseling the management and public relations personnel of the client organization on matters that will affect public opinion toward the client.

(2) He is retained to provide all of the public relations services utilized by the client—counsel, research, planning, publicity, preparation of institutional literature, and other functions—either with or without direction by a public relations executive.

(3) He and his staff provide the counsel and services, with a Director of Public Relations acting as a liaison and agent of the management within the organization.

(4) He counsels the management and guides the public relations activities, which are carried out by the Director of Public Relations and his staff.

(5) He and his staff provide counsel and conduct specified public relations activities, while the Director of Public Relations and his staff coordinate on behalf of management and conduct other specified activities.

(6) He may be called in by a firm that has its own staff, when his advice is sought or when his special abilities, experience, and facilities may be required. Sometimes this type of assignment is a publicity project, such as an anniversary observance. More often it is a continuing relationship of indefinite duration.

(7) He is called on to study the client's situation, to make recommendations, and perhaps to supervise installation of what he recommends. This may involve any or all of these:

- Analyzing the conditions in which the client is likely to have to function
- Assessing its present policies and personnel in light of anticipated needs
- Developing a proposed program and timetable
- Specifying personnel needed or reassignments of present personnel, general compensation patterns, and organization
- Finding candidates for new positions
- Making recommendations on outside services to be employed
- Helping guide the staff and management through the transition stage
- Providing judgment and ideas as the program proceeds.

The trend in recent years has been toward combining the services of the counseling firm and the internal staff. Most frequently the counseling firm affords specific services, as well as advice and creativity, while the public relations department carries out most activities. In a few cases, the counsel selects the man who is placed on the organization's staff as its public relations director. Not only is the counsel's knowledge of public relations invaluable in judging the person's fitness for the job and in creating the setup in which he will function, but he is able to select the person for qualities that will enable him to coordinate effectively with the counsel's operations.

WHAT THE COUNSEL HAS TO OFFER

With this wide variety of patterns in which the counsel may be employed, it is important to evaluate what he affords the client that cannot be obtained any other way. The advantages that a counsel affords include:

(1) Because there is always a shortage of exceptionally capable people in the field, a counsel serving a number of clients can make his talents available to all of them. Since there is a tendency for exceptional people to function as professional counsel because of the greater income and other advantages, it is difficult for any organization to employ an entire staff of unusual ability. The good counsel, then, often makes available the highest degree of skill the client can retain to augment his public relations aide.

(2) Similarly, the counsel's staff can be made up of people with more than average ability, since the flexibility of the counsel's agency—serving a number of clients—permits them to use their skills intensively and thereby increase their earning power.

(3) In serving a number of clients, the counsel's organization can be made up of a number of capable people who are experienced in many phases of public relations. To get the same variety of skills, any single organization's staff will have to employ full-time the same number of people, at far greater cost.

(4) The counseling firm is flexible. When one client has an emergency, a seasonal need, or an important event, a number of people can be assigned to it until the need has been met. The organization with its own set staff has no such flexibility—the personnel available for emergencies are the same as are on hand during routine periods.

(5) Similarly, the facilities of the counsel's firm are available to all the clients. The mailing lists, for instance, are maintained constantly and are accessible for use on the work of every client. If each client maintained its own staff operation, each would have to keep up its mailing lists, its addressing plates, its mailing staff, and so on.

(6) By carrying on a great variety of public relations activities, the counsel develops a wide range of experience, broad judgment, and extensive contacts. The employed staff of an organization, on the other hand, works year after year on one subject, in one area.

Ideally, the counsel provides the strong trunk of the client organization with an instant transplant of wide knowledge and years of diverse experience. As in other forms of transplanting, the resultant organism becomes far more than if it grew strictly on its own.

(7) The counsel's reputation accrues to the client. When an agency has been issuing publicity releases for a number of organizations, for instance, the firm becomes recognized among the media. If its work is good and reliable, the press and broadcast editors come to accept it. This immediate acceptance is available to each new client of the counsel, whereas if the client organization sent out its own material it would have to develop its own acceptance—often after a period of ineffectiveness or harmful mistakes.

(8) The counsel is more independent. First, he is a professional, able to meet top executives on their own level. Second, he has a number of sources of income and is not wholly dependent on any one client. Third, when his contact within the client organization is established, he is reasonably free of the internal political problems that beset the paid employee. Independence in a public relations man is essential if he is to provide the proper guidance in policy and the most effective handling of activities.

(9) In the same way, the counsel is objective. He is not involved directly in the operations and machinations of the client organization. He does not spend all of his time dealing with a particular cause. He is able to retain the point of view of the outsider, the type of person who is the object of the public relations program. The fact that he is also representing a number of other organizations, in different fields, also gives him a broader perspective.

Donald W. MacKinnon of the Institute of Personality Assessment and Research at the University of California, Berkeley, reported to a PRSA conference that studies in the field brought this judgment:

> If, as compared with the public relations officer in a company, the public relations counselor is at a disadvantage as regards the manner in which problems are presented to him, he has the distinct advantage of being able to look at them with a fresh eye unclouded by long and intimate association with the firm. He is thus in the fortunate position, if he has any creative potential at all, of more easily restructuring and reformulating the problem, reconciling his general expertise in the field of public relations with a fresh, unhampered perception of the specific situation which now confronts him.

He added:

> One must have the relevant and necessary information if the problem is to be solved.

But... too much information can interfere with the attainment of a creative solution... Most of the major inventions have been made by persons who have not been experts in the field of their innovation.

(10) In many cases, the counsel's services are more economical. The centralized facilities, the flexibility of manpower, the opportunity for the counsel to serve more than one client when he makes business trips and in other ways, all provide economies. And, of course, nowhere is it more true than in public relations that no service is worth what it costs except good service—"cheap" service is often extremely expensive, whereas excellent service always more than repays the cost.

(11) There are frequent occasions when the counsel can benefit several clients at one time. For instance, when a publication is developing a complete story on business conditions, he may provide the point of view of several of his industrial clients.

(12) The organization of the counsel's business often affords the client the service he needs wherever and whenever he may want it. Large public relations organizations have branch offices in cities throughout the United States, on whom they can call for help in these localities on an instant's notice.

(13) By handling a variety of public relations assignments, the counsel and his organization gain experience that is valuable to each client. The know-how, the groundwork, and the techniques involved in each given situation can most effectively be applied by those who have themselves applied them effectively in other cases.

(14) The counsel can be a focal point on whom the diverse and sometimes conflicting elements in an organization—the members of an association, the department heads in a corporation—can agree and turn to for advice.

LIMITATIONS OF PROFESSIONAL COUNSEL

At the same time, it must be recognized that in some cases the counseling firm, serving alone, has limitations. These drawbacks are among the reasons for the trend toward a combination of internal departments and outside counsel. Some of the limitations that have been cited are:

(1) Because he is not spending all of his time and concentration on the one organization's problems, the counsel cannot become so familiar with all aspects of its operations. In providing objectivity and a great variety of experience, he sacrifices having a complete knowledge of any client.

(2) Because he sometimes deals with top-management executives, the counsel is sometimes exposed to the jealousy of lower officials who would be superior to the public relations director if he were a staff employee. The desirability of policy-level consideration of public relations thus has its disadvantage. This occasionally creates friction within the organization, sometimes resulting in lack of cooperation on public relations matters.

(3) On the surface, it is sometimes more economical to carry on public relations activities within the client organization. Existing office space, telephone service, mimeographing and mailing facilities, and stenographic personnel can be used, instead of having to pay for these when they are used by the counsel. Actually, of course, on a strict accounting basis these functions must be charged to public relations anyway, and seldom represent a true saving.

(4) Internal public relations executives sometimes are negative to outside counsel. Some counselors have been known to undermine the status of the staff executive for their own aggrandizement, though this is rare. Seeking to gain the acceptance of management, staff executives sometimes see the outsider who has this acceptance as a barrier rather than an aid to their progress. In some cases, where the counsel is selected by management, internal executives resist cooperating in the hope they will discredit the counsel by forestalling his ability to function. The more inexperienced and insecure the internal executive, the more likely he is to prefer an outside firm he is sure he can dominate, rather than one best able to provide professional skill and judgment. Thus, the more respected the outside counsel, the more likely it is that the public relations director is a sound and conscientious executive. There are many instances in which strong public relations officers and strong counselors work harmoniously together, with the result that the status of both is greatly enhanced with the managements.

(5) In medium- and large-sized counseling firms, the caliber of judgment and skills will vary greatly, depending on which personnel happen to be assigned to the account. Often the principals devote their main efforts to obtaining new clients and to administering the business, rather than to serving clients. Though the organization is large, staff people often work in virtual isolation from each other. It thus is necessary to the success of the relationship for the client to ascertain at the start which personnel will provide counsel, skills, production of

materials, and other services; and how the firm plans to service the client—to what extent its full resources will be provided or whether the account will be "pigeonholed" with limited personnel.

PAYMENTS: WHEN AND HOW MUCH

Because public relations is still a new profession, and because it involves such a wide variety of possible functions for clients, there is a wide range in methods of charging for services. There is also a wide variance in the rates charged, just as there is in other professions. Rates generally depend on the reputation and caliber of the counsel's organization, but do not necessarily reflect the quality of the service to be provided. It is important for every prospective client of a public relations organization to analyze the operating methods of the various firms and the components included in various budget items at the same time that he evaluates the prices quoted. Otherwise, he may find that public relations service is a "blind" item.

The most common systems of charges are these:

(1) A retainer fee for counseling only. This method applies whenever the counsel's guidance and attention are all that are desired, and is similar to the retainer of an attorney on an annual basis. This fee may be a fixed annual amount, or may vary with the rate of activity, as in (6) or (9).

(2) Sometimes a counsel is retained to analyze an organization's public relations operations, problems, and needs, and make a report and recommendation. This is charged for either on a *per diem* basis, or at a flat fee, with expenses added.

(3) Some counseling firms establish a breakdown of charges to apply to every client, regardless of the size of the project involved, or the scope of the services required:

(a) A set fee for the counsel.
(b) The total cost of all personnel required, on an hourly basis that allows for all costs of the counsel's firm and allows for a profit.
(c) A proportionate share of the firm's total overhead, including rent, light, telephone, depreciation on equipment, taxes, supplies.
(d) All expenses entailed in serving the client—so-called "mechanical expenses," such as travel, photography, mailing costs, clippings, stationery, long-distance telephone and telegraph, mats, and so on.
(e) A fixed percentage of override on items b, c, and d—usually 15 per cent.

(4) The most common system breaks the budget down into two items:

(a) Fee, covering the entire services of the counsel's organization, including personnel, overhead, his own services.
(b) Mechanical expenses.

As in all the methods discussed here, some firms charge the mechanical expenses at actual cost, while others add a percentage to cover "cost of handling." This relieves the firm of the incentive to hold down expenses (and, in fact, often rewards swollen expenditures). If the client is fully aware of these factors in advance and exerts control over them, it seems to make little difference which method is used; but, since this "cost of handling" charge is absorbed in the fee of firms that do not bill the client for it, its presence or absence has an important determination on any comparison of fees.

(5) Another common method breaks the charges down into three categories:

(a) Fee, covering all the firm's costs except the salaries of personnel required on the account.
(b) Personnel costs—either charged at a specific hourly rate for each caliber of employee, or at the actual weekly or monthly salary, when all or almost all the employees' time is spent on the account.
(c) Mechanical expenses.

(6) Where the demand on the counsel's services is irregular or unpredictable, charges are sometimes made on an hourly basis for the firm as a whole. The counsel sets the rate per hour to suit his own needs and the requirements of the account. Since this system makes it very difficult for the counsel to plan his staff schedule or predict his own costs, it is rarely accepted by an established firm unless there is also a retainer fee, as in (3) or a monthly minimum, as in (9).

(7) Where a client wants to retain the counsel for a specific assignment—such as meeting a problem that arises suddenly, or augmenting his own staff to plan observance of an anniversary—a flat-charge arrangement, plus expenses, is usually made. The counsel estimates the costs of personnel, overhead, his own time, a margin of safety, and his profit, and sets a fee for the assignment. Mechanical expenses are billed either at cost or with an "override," as agreed with the client.

(8) Sometimes the retainer fee and the assignment budget are combined. The counsel may accept an annual fee for normal service, and quote a

EMPLOYEE_____																	
TIME SHEET	(FIRST) (SECOND) HALF OF _____, 19__															APPROVED_____	
CLIENT TIME	1/16	2/17	3/18	4/19	5/20	6/21	7/22	8/23	9/24	10/25	11/26	12/27	13/28	14/29	15/30	31	Total	Leave Blank
CLIENT OVERTIME																		
TOTAL CHARGEABLE																		
COMPANY																		
Co. Promotion																		
New Business																		
Administration																		
Office Matters																		
COMPANY OVERTIME																		
PERSONAL																		
Off Duty																		
Sickness																		
GRAND TOTAL																		

Figure 53-1. Example of a time record sheet for executive and creative personnel in a public relations firm. All business time, including overtime, is accounted for.

figure for each special project that may come up during the year. These special budgets are agreed on before the project planning begins.

(9) Where there is to be continuing service, but the level of needs will vary considerably, a minimum guaranteed fee may be set. Thus there may be basic payment of perhaps $2,000 a month. In those months when time charges exceed $2,000, the total accrued is billed. This permits assigning the attention of skilled executives and staff, and adjusting payments to needs as basic levels are exceeded.

In most cases where the counsel is on a continuous basis, the budget is set annually and the agreement runs for one-year periods. Sometimes the agreement is bound in a strictly legal contract; more often there is a covering letter citing the terms of the agreement, accepted by both parties; frequently there is merely a gentleman's agreement. Because of the confidential and intimate nature of this profession, disagreements over terms or payments are incompatible with good service, and it is widely considered that a gentleman's agreement is really the basis for every arrangement, whether there is a legal contract or not.

The annual budget is usually broken down into monthly installments. If the fee is $24,000 and the estimated expenses are $18,000, for instance, the budget would call for $2,000 and $1,500 a month, respectively. Though the monthly budget for expenses should be watched as a guide to the pace of activity and the balance of the program, it is not wise to set it so rigidly that it prevents exceeding it when necessary. Monthly expense costs vary widely in many cases, and in the example, the $1,500 should be taken as an average. Where the billing method also varies costs for personnel and other things from month to month, it is more difficult to make the annual budget come out even and the possibility of its being spent too soon is greater; but careful management by the counsel and supervision by the client will control it.

Variations in charges. Even aside from this variety of billing methods, there are other differences that affect the cost to the client.

As in every human activity, the demand for the counsel's services—as reflected in the compensation he receives—inevitably affects the fees he charges. This explains why, when several counsel are asked to submit bids for an account, their charges may differ by 300 to 400 per cent. By setting a price on their services that they feel is justified, successful public relations counsel automatically are being selective of prospective clients; they are eliminating those that cannot or will not pay this standard. It is possible by looking at a counsel's lists of clients to evaluate the comparative selectiveness (by fees) of different counsel.

Aside from the counsel's own compensation, there are variations in all other factors of his charges:

(1) *Personnel:* The salaries he pays usually reflect the caliber of the men and women he employs. It is important to remember, however, that charges made on an hourly basis (and sometimes on a monthly salary basis) do not necessarily reflect the salaries actually paid to the employees. They may be a working scale devised on a theoretical system, or they may be developed on the basis of what the traffic will bear.

(2) *Overhead:* Some firms believe that distinguished-looking offices in the finest available building are necessary for their prestige and standing. Others prefer to settle for utilitarian working space that is as inexpensive as possible. Most are moderately between these extremes. Sales efforts, stationery, equipment, and other items are also variable. It is up to the client to decide whether he benefits from the cost of the counsel's overhead, or whether it is important enough to make any difference to him.

(3) *Billing methods:* Some firms prepare bills in minute detail—listing every single item, wherever possible, and attaching invoices for all billed items. Others give only a broad outline of expenses incurred. The first system involves much more bookkeeping expense than does the second. Indirectly or directly, the client pays for the cost of the system. Usually the carefully detailed billing system is preferred because it can be demonstrated to be authentic.

ORGANIZING TO SERVE A CLIENT

Before an effective working plan can be established, there are several steps the counsel should take:

1. Be sure there is a clear-cut definition of the goals and purposes of his function. Fundamental as this may seem, it can prevent serious difficulties due to the client and the counsel coming to the relationship with entirely different backgrounds about public relations and having different impressions of what the function is to be.

This is not taken care of by vague generalities such as: "Improve the company's image," or "help increase effectiveness of the entire marketing mix," or "make certain the financial community fully appreciates the merits of the company and its stock."

The definitions should be incisive:

- "Establish the changing character of the company—from a specialized industrial producer to a research-oriented, diversified, highly technical firm in the forefront of fast-growing industrial and consumer markets."
- "Convince the public by demonstration that the company is a good citizen of its plant communities: supporting desirable community efforts, unrestricted in its employment policies except on the basis of merit."
- "Convey the 'difference' behind the company's products from those of its competitors by conveying the exceptional character of its management and principles."

2. Management executives should be involved in public relations up to the highest level at which it realistically may be a factor in that organization. This will usually be the president or the executive vice-president, and should include the chairman of the board. Their thinking should be obtained at the start on what they see the public relations needs of the organization to be and their reasons for having the function. The counsel should determine—on the basis of what they say and his judgment based on experience with various other management executives—how far they will go to participate in the functions of public relations. He should assess how conservative they are, so he can know how far and how soon to propose innovations and how to call attention to policy questions. He should also assess how they will do in dealing with the press, security analysts, or other publics, as well as how they project in a public meeting. What may be unsound for one organization's top executive may be ideal for another.

3. Interview editors of publications in the client's field of interest, others in that field, staff personnel, and former employees or members—with the client's permission in advance—to get an objective analysis of the organization's characteristics, how it functions, and what can realistically be expected in response to innovative suggestions or to unexpected developments.

4. Analyze the organization's public relations staff personnel to assure the best possible rapport with them. Some staff people, by experience and personality, are more aggressive or venturesome

than others; some lean to traditionalism more than others.

5. If the role for which the counsel has been retained is not clearly defined, determine where he will be needed most: providing ideas; guiding internal staff; creative work; contacts with various publicity media, security analysts, or other outlets for communication; setting up and handling events; getting out publications; producing literature or films; acting as a listening post to feed back information about the client derived from various sources.

EDUCATING THE CLIENT

In many ways, the most difficult phase of any public relations account is developing full understanding among the client's executives and personnel about the nature, scope, and functions of public relations; the techniques, problems, ethics, and standards of the counsel; and the means of using and judging the counsel's services.

Difficulties that most often arise include:

(1) The client misunderstands practices of the profession. He wants to use advertising pressure on newspapers to print stories. He thinks every news release should be printed verbatim in every newspaper to which it is sent. He thinks the management's point of view should be forced on the employees and that the only measure of success is how well this point of view is accepted. He wants to withhold some facts from the public, and blames the counsel when the watered-down story is not accepted, or the full story comes out with an unfavorable slant. These are just a few examples.

(2) He has a narrow knowledge of public relations. He may recognize that the counsel is involved in publicity functions, but neglect to call on him in employee relations matters, or stockholder relations, or any other phase of the problem.

(3) He may try to restrict the counsel's part in functions that are necessary. He may ask that the president's statement be written for the annual report, but refuse or neglect to have the counsel guide the planning of the report itself, or its distribution.

(4) Most commonly, he may misevaluate results. He may put great emphasis upon newspaper clippings and fail to see the intangible benefits in improved employee morale, prevention of customer complaints, and other successes. Because most executives are accustomed to dealing with tangibles and "black and white," they have difficulty in appreciating the value of intangibles.

(5) He may by-pass the counsel, inadvertently or by failing to consider him an integral cog in his own operation. This reflects itself in formation of policies having great influence on attitudes toward the company, without consulting the counsel; or dealing directly with the press, without the counsel's knowledge and sometimes opposite to the counsel's own commitments and plans.

These are problems of the counsel that he must meet by educating the client. The client, in turn, is wise to seek a clear understanding on such matters as soon as possible in his relationship with the counsel.

Establishing a working pattern. At the beginning of his relationship with the client, the counsel must set up a plan of procedure. This plan should include:

(1) Arranging for him to be called upon as soon as anything involving public notice—particularly publicity and press relations—occurs.

(2) Arranging for his participation in all meetings that affect the organization's policy—with the possible exception of board of directors' meetings, but ideally including these.

(3) Arranging for periodic (preferably monthly) meetings between officials of the client organization who guide the public relations program and the staff members of the counsel's firm who carry out the program. At these meetings the events, accomplishments, and problems encountered since the previous meeting should be discussed; all matters affecting public relations should be evaluated and worked into the program; and plans for future activity should be made.

(4) Setting methods for judging the results of the work. If periodic reports are to be made to the client, what form should they be in, how often should they be made, what aspects of the effort should be emphasized? If clippings and broadcast time are to be important, the methods of obtaining and evaluating them should be agreed on.

(5) Setting up channels for getting information before any activity is begun. Someone within the client organization should be specified as the liaison for information, or one person should be named as source of information on each phase of the organization's operation.

(6) Establishing clear understanding that all material and stories must be approved before publication, use, or release. It must be established that once an item has been approved by the authorized person, it has the official blessing of the client, and except where a crisis is involved must be backed up by the client.

(7) Arranging for periodic checking by the counsel of all pertinent phases of the client's operations.

(8) Establishing communication between the counsel and the client. Should the counsel send the client carbon copies of all correspondence he handles on the account, or only on specified subjects or in specified connections? Should the counsel prepare a written report on each meeting with client personnel, for circulation to all concerned within the client organization and the counseling firm?

THE WORK IS CONFIDENTIAL

It is always assumed that everything the counsel knows about each client and everything he does for him is held in strict confidence, unless it is issued as public information or the client agrees to have it revealed. This not only applies to what the counsel says to the press or to competitors, but also to his other clients. A leak is serious whether it occurs in an interview with a reporter for the Associated Press or across the desk from the president of a company in an entirely different line of business. Corporation presidents are human enough to pass on what they hear.

This requirement of secretiveness is the basis for many counsel's opinion that it is permissible to represent two organizations which may in whole or in part be competitors. Since there is no transfer of information or conflict of interests, they feel there is nothing to prevent their doing an objectively honest job for both. In this respect, they say, they differ from advertising agencies, which because of the nature of their operations cannot establish such objectivity between accounts, and therefore generally will not represent competitors. In general, however, most counsel will not represent organizations that compete broadly with each other.

Open-book policy. While keeping the affairs of clients confidential, the counsel should maintain the most open policy about his own affairs. In this respect, it is practicing what he preaches to let interested parties know the truth about his own firm. There has always been a strong tendency in the profession either to refuse information about the number of accounts represented and the number of persons in the firm, or to distort these figures grossly. Lack of a central ethical society to which reports on these matters must be made has permitted falsification to go unchallenged.

Accordingly, it is wise for the prospective client to ask for detailed and verified information about any

---

STRICTLY CONFIDENTIAL

Maintenance of absolute confidence is an inherent necessity for effective public relations. Information regarding any of our accounts; any prospective accounts on which we may be working; and any company activities, techniques, or policies should not be mentioned outside the office even when with our own staff members. Such mention can lead to very serious consequences in relations with clients or in our ability to obtain new clients, thereby being harmful to all of us. It is all right to talk enthusiastically about how well we do on certain situations, but we should give no information on specifics.

It is also a good policy for individual staff members to maintain confidence concerning their salaries, bonuses, and fees. Executives working on an account may have information about its budget, but this must not be disseminated to others. This is important in protecting us from efforts of competitors to determine our fees.

CONTRACTS AND RELEASES

Each member of the executive and creative staff is asked, as a condition of employment, to sign a contract agreeing to maintain the company's standards of practice and to forego employment or other association with any client of this firm for a reasonable period after he may leave its employ.

Model releases should be signed immediately on shooting of photos in which one or more persons are identifiable. A release is necessary for each individual.

Photographs that contain an identifiable likeness of an individual should not be used in connection with public relations material you may prepare and distribute unless the written consent of such individual is obtained.

All contracts or commitments should be made subject to approval of the account supervisor to whom you report.

OUTSIDE ACTIVITIES

Outside activity that might in any way reflect on the company or affect anything the company does should be checked with the president. This might include volunteer publicity service for a non-profit organization; participation in group activities that might identify the person with the company in print or otherwise; writing on subjects that directly or indirectly might affect our connection with a client or a publication or other medium—in other words, those things which good judgment would indicate ought to be reviewed because they can have an effect on the company's position, reputation, or activities. This is especially true if in any way the work involved might require contact at the office or activities in conjunction with office activities.

Figure 53-2. Page from a manual of policies and procedures of a public relations firm.

firm it is interested in retaining, and to check the information given.

Frankness in dealing with clients, the press, and everyone else is also a necessity for the counsel. He must acknowledge his errors or failures immediately, to be certain that the client has the facts necessary to guide his judgment on everything affecting his public relations. Of course, there should never be any attempt to distort information to the press, to mislead a reporter, to withhold information desired in favor of other media, or to do anything else that will cause any representative of the press or broadcasters to feel he has not been treated with complete fairness.

THE COUNSEL IS A BUSINESSMAN

Organizing the staff. In the well-rounded public relations firm, regardless of size, certain basic abilities and talents are required:

(1) Writing skill—versatile, prolific, distinctive, clear.

(2) Broad knowledge of business affairs, and good judgment.

(3) Ability to make intangibles and abstractions attractive to great numbers of people—to "sell ideas."

(4) Sensitivity to the mass mind, or the feelings and reactions of people.

(5) Knowledge of the production processes involved in printing, photography, and other techniques employed in public relations.

(6) Knowledge of media—newspapers, magazines, radio, television, movies, books, speeches, special events, and the like.

(7) Organizing and planning ability—to develop broad, long-term operations as well as organize masses of details.

(8) Intimate knowledge of the specialties involved in the firm's accounts—technical information, women's interests, financial affairs, and so on.

The firm combines these qualities in its personnel; and at the same time, it has the right kind and the right amount of manpower available to meet the needs of its clients at any time.

This almost inevitably demands great versatility in the persons employed. The only alternatives are departmentalization that is almost certain to be wasteful, and therefore expensive; or specialization, whereby the counsel or the firm limits the scope of what it offers to provide to clients.

For this reason, most public relations organizations are largely nondepartmentalized. Although persons with special experience and skill are called on when needed, most persons are also called on to fill other needs.

Branch operations. Public relations firms have three methods of carrying on their activities in cities outside their headquarters city:

(1) *Branch Offices:* These require either one very large account that can support the cost of an office to augment the headquarters' services, several accounts needing consistent service there, or several accounts in the region.

(2) *Reciprocal Arrangements:* For example, one counsel in New York will agree to handle assignments from another in Washington, in return for similar consideration when needed. Either each charges the other at a specified rate, or an effort is made to keep mutual favors balanced without exchange of money.

(3) *Correspondents:* A firm in Chicago may assign a man or a firm in Houston to carry out a project, at a mutually satisfactory rate. This may involve the one assignment, or may be a permanent arrangement. The so-called "field networks" that for a time attracted attention in this field are essentially made up of lists of such correspondents.

Specializing. Because the scope of public relations is so broad, and the needs of various clients vary so greatly, there is a tendency for some counsel to specialize. Some represent only nonprofit organizations; others handle only industrial relations matters; still others have a clientele composed entirely of trade associations. Major areas of specialization are financial relations, public affairs, and product publicity.

At the other pole from specialists is the counsel who has developed a very broad scope of experience, judgment, and creativity. All these traits are scarce, and such a counsel can benefit almost any organization without attempting to provide services that are readily available through staff personnel or standard outside firms.

Specialization seems to have merits and weaknesses. Because public relations is such a broad field, the counsel who narrows his interest and activities is cutting off wide areas of experience and contact that are helpful in serving any client. Also, the specialist has an inflexible type of business and is more vulnerable to changes in economic and social conditions.

At the same time, it is true that a specialist in such fields as financial public relations, non-profit corporations, and industrial relations is able to learn these fields thoroughly, which a general counsel might not be able to do.

This seems to be one question in the profession that shows no signs of being resolved soon. While some counsel are turning toward specialization, others are very successful in handling a wide variety of accounts, and are sought out by all types of clients because they have proved their over-all ability in public relations.

The size of the organization. Another question on which there are divergent views is the limitation of the counseling organization's clientele. Some claim that it is primarily the ability of the head of the firm that is employed by clients, and that he is able to serve only a few accounts effectively by devoting his personal attention to them. Whether "few" means six accounts or nine often depends on whether the counsel advocating this policy has six accounts or nine. At the same time, where a firm is established to provide chiefly the benefits of one mind, it is undoubtedly true that a low limit must be set on the clientele.

Few men can know all of the aspects of public relations, can embody all the necessary skills, or can provide the many types of thinking that are called for in public relations work. But the thoroughly experienced counsel is versatile and has had opportunity to work in all important areas. Also, his broad judgment enables him to select those special skills needed and to find sources of special information.

On the other hand, much can be said for large firms. No one any longer questions the ability of a large advertising agency, for example, to do an excellent job even though its principals do not write all the copy, plan all the campaigns, devise all the themes, or make all the layouts.

It is the practice in good public relations organizations in which there is more than one trained executive to hold conferences about major matters involving any client. The ability, skill, and imagination of everyone is brought into play for each problem. The interplay of minds sometimes comes up with a result beyond the capacity of any one of the minds.

The conclusion seems to be that, for a client who prefers constant personal attention from one man in whom it has great faith, there is need for the counsel with a limited number of clients. For other counsel, the size of the clientele depends on their ability to build a sound, efficient, and intelligent organization that works together as a unit.

Related to this question is the problem of whether a firm should concentrate full authority and last judgment in one man, or should have two or more principals who are equally fitted to represent the firm with clients, the press, or others.

In instances where the firm has been built up by one man, and his reputation has become the cornerstone of the business, it is probable that he will always be looked upon as the one head of the firm.

Where the founder of the company is not such an outstanding figure, partners who work compatibly together can help each other. In either case, it is essential for the client that one man be in a position to make definite decisions and take direct action without delay.

Sales activities. Whether public relations is a business or a profession, it is faced with the business necessity of attracting clients. Because it tends toward being a profession, the means of gaining a clientele are limited by propriety and good taste. It is generally considered unethical to sell judgment and counsel through salesmen, pressure promotion, or other devices used to push merchandise. At the same time, the need for public relations is not yet so well established in the minds of the public that many counsel can afford to wait for businessmen to seek them out, as patients seek out doctors. It is necessary to find a middle ground between hopeful waiting and brazen chasing.

In general, firms in this field tend to be either "selling oriented" or "service oriented." The first type concentrates primarily on seeking new clients, devoting a major share of the principals' time and talents, as well as resources, to this function. Serving the clients then becomes a follow-up requirement.

The firm that is oriented to serving its clients, on the other hand, counts on the caliber of its service to build its reputation and help attract clients. Seeking new clients is confined to available time and attention.

The marks of the "selling oriented" firm include frequent mass sales contacts or broad mailings soliciting business and, usually, a high turnover rate of clients.

For counsel who are established and have built a good reputation, new accounts usually come through recommendations of present clients, word of mouth in business circles, or tips from friends. This, of course, is the ideal way to get new business. Because of its irregularity and unpredictability, however, it usually cannot be the only source of accounts. When a counsel has resigned an account, for instance, or has completed an assignment, he may find it necessary to add business to keep his margin of profit.

These are methods of selling that are generally accepted as ethical within the profession:

(1) Personal inquiries made of prospects at clubs, business meetings, or conventions.

(2) Letters or calls prompted by reports that the recipient is contemplating employing counsel.

(3) Mediation of mutual acquaintances who feel that the counsel and the prospect can benefit each other.

(4) Distribution of institutional literature on public relations or phases of it, in which low-key description of the counsel's organization and services may be included.

(5) Mailings containing specific information about a specific type of business, with distribution confined to that business (such as newsletters, folders on activities conducted in that field, and the like).

(6) Third parties who inform the counsel of "tips" to follow. It is considered ethical to pay "finder's fees" or commissions, not to be added to the fee charged the client, for such leads.

The following are considered acceptable by most practitioners:

(1) Institutional advertising, including mailing of information about the firm, inviting inquiries.

(2) Brochures about the counseling firm itself or about its principals openly intended to be sales devices.

(3) Offering commissions to advertising agencies, management consulting firms, and others who can direct public relations accounts.

These are generally considered improper:

(1) Employed salesmen who make the rounds of possible clients, and are paid out of fees received from the accounts brought in.

(2) "Cold calls" in letters, in person, or by telephone.

(3) Solicitation of accounts already held by other counsel when sales methods involve criticizing the services, undercutting the fees, or offering favors.

Presentations and proposals. Public relations is not yet well enough understood among businessmen, and the means of measuring counsel are not well enough defined, to enable most organizations to choose a counsel on reputation only, as doctors and lawyers are chosen. It is usually necessary for the counsel to demonstrate what he feels he can do for the prospective client, and in many cases he must also define the ways in which public relations itself will function.

This means that counsel are faced with the necessity of preparing a presentation or proposal before being retained. The term "presentation" generally means a rather elaborate accumulation of facts, ideas, graphic devices, sales talk, and budget. A "proposal" may consist only of a brief analysis of the services required and the terms of the counsel for performing them.

Because of the variety of public relations problems and techniques, it is hardly possible to develop one presentation that can be adapted for almost every prospect, as many advertising agency presentations can be. They must be made to order, and as a result their preparation can become a major problem for the counsel. There has been a trend for organizations, particularly trade associations, to invite eight to twelve counsel to make presentations for an account. To compete favorably, each must go to considerable trouble and expense for what is, at best, a long-shot possibility. As a result, there has been discussion within the field of an agreement to limit the type of presentation that a counsel may be called on to prepare for such a process of selection.

Another suggested remedy is that the prospective client agree to pay the costs of a presentation. Rather than making this a financial burden, it is expected to discourage wholesale interviewing and lead the prospect to narrow his field to two counsel before calling for presentations.

How much to put into a presentation or proposal is also a matter for debate. Many counsel say that since the chief stock in trade of a public relations man is his ideas, it is a mistake to fill the presentation with the ideas that are to be the basis for the fees he expects to receive. Although they are rare, there have been instances of organizations culling ideas from a number of counsel's presentations and utilizing them without compensation.

Until the time when public relations counsel will be retained on their reputation only, it will probably be the problem of each one individually to determine how he must proceed in dealing with each prospective client's demand for proof of competence and what can be accomplished.

Resigning an account. The value of a public relations counsel to a client is based on common understanding and respect, complete cooperation and confidence, and mutual willingness to help the other in the common cause. When any of these elements is lacking, the ability of the counsel to perform the function for which he is retained is decreased. And when he feels that this ability is so much affected that he is not serving effectively, he should feel justified in resigning the account. It has become a common saying in the field that the true public relations counsel must be continually prepared to lose his job or his client. No stigma is attached today to such resignations.

The counsel is equally justified in breaking off relations with a client when demands for service make the account unprofitable, or when the client's policies would force the counsel to put his name on releases or reports he cannot believe in.

It is difficult to give up an account, especially

when it is profitable. But it is often wise to protect one's reputation and feeling of integrity, even at the cost of momentary financial profit.

Internal functions of the firm. In general, operation of the counsel's office is similar to the functioning of any general business office. Bookkeeping, for example, follows normal patterns and the specific techniques depend largely on the methods of billing discussed earlier in this chapter.

There are a few procedures, however, that are peculiar to the business:

(1) *Mailing Lists:* The discussion of lists in Chapters 36 and 38 makes clear how important and extensive is the job of building and maintaining lists. Since almost all the contacts the counsel's clients have with their publics depend on the use of these lists, they are a cornerstone of the firm's procedure.

(2) *Clippings:* Recording, sorting, collecting, analyzing, and preparing clippings and other reports of results for presentation to the client frequently require major consideration, particularly during publicity campaigns for a client.

(3) *Contacts with the Client:* Usually all meetings and discussions with a client that are more than routine checks or seeking of information are handled by a principal of the firm or an executive assigned to the account. The contact between the client and the firm not only establishes policies and sets plans, but is the crucial point at which the counsel and his associates serve as liaison between the client and his publics. Because it is so important, it demands the best skills and experience of the firm.

(4) *Reports:* Where monthly round-table meetings are held with the client, a progress report and an outline of proposed new activities are required as the agenda for the meeting. In other cases, periodic reports are desirable even where the client does not request them. They serve to keep before him what is being done and the up-to-date status of the program. Memories of busy men are short unless they are prompted.

54

Considerations of Law in Public Relations

MORTON J. SIMON is a practicing attorney in Philadelphia who is active in representing many practitioners and organizations in the communications field. He is author of "Public Relations Law," "Advertising Truth Book," and "The Law of Advertising and Marketing." He is instructor of a course on "Legal and Ethical Problems of Advertising and Communications" at the Charles Morris Price School of Advertising and Journalism of the Poor Richard Club and lectures at the University of Pennsylvania and Temple University.

Mr. Simon is a graduate of Brown University and the Harvard Law School.

Until recently literature about public relations gave little attention to "Considerations of Law in Public Relations." But now the picture has changed so drastically that we may anticipate an ever-increasing flow of legal/public relations materials. Public relations has come of age, legally speaking. Its legal burdens seem to be increasing on a seemingly geometric basis. More than that, they are expanding into legally affected areas that not long ago would have seemed remote from the activities of the public relations practitioner—whether the affairs of large or small organizations were involved.

Our purpose here is to direct the mind of the public relations practitioner toward the relatively new sector of his field: *public relations law*. It is also to help organize his or her thinking about the manifold problems—and their solutions—involved in this area. The purpose is not to make lawyers of public relations practitioners.

Broad Basic Premises. These are several of the basic and broadly applicable premises that should be kept in mind when considering the potential legal pitfalls of public relations:

(1) The public relations practitioner must develop a continuing and prophylactic understanding with both his lawyer and the law.

(2) The more the public relations man or woman knows of the nature and incidence of his legal exposures, the simpler and less cumbersome will be their solution.

(3) Public relations' legal involvements are here to stay and will increase as time passes.

(4) The public relations practitioner who does not recognize this will be doing less than an adequate job for his company or client.

(5) The increasing legal involvements deal with both the quantity and quality of public relations activities.

(6) The public relations practitioner's "legal boo-boos" can sometimes be disastrous and/or extremely expensive to company or client.

(7) Public relations people *themselves* can become civilly or criminally involved—quite apart from client or company.

INCREASING PUBLIC RELATIONS INTEREST IN THE LAW

Both the individual practitioner and his trade associations are showing an ever-increasing awareness of the need for understanding the public relations/legal interrelationship. More than that, they have been doing something about it.

As part of its continuing program, the Foundation for Public Relations Research and Education made a substantial grant to the author of this chapter that resulted in the publication in 1969 of *Public Relations Law*.

The *Public Relations Journal* has been carrying more and more articles having either a legal concentration or thrust. Its Washington Reports plus scattered articles explain various judicial, statutory, and administrative agency legal mandates.

Similar interest is evident in other publications in the field.

Beginning in 1968 PRSA has sponsored a series of seminars and conferences dealing with the law in general as applicable to public relations and with certain specific legal elements such as labor law, financial communications, government relations, and regulation. Individual PRSA chapters in 1969 and 1970 began to present similar programs to their own membership and their local business communities. "Legal speakers" appear more frequently on such programs from month to month.

The interest in public relations law is not limited to the public relations community. Similar seminars have been held by the Federal Bar Association, Federal Bar Building, Washington, D.C. 20006, and The Practicing Law Institute, 20 Vesey St., New York, N.Y. 10007.

From its inception the PRSA accreditation program has examined applicants on legal areas related to public relations and the program's required reading list currently includes *Public Relations Law*.

Reasons for increased legal involvement.

(1) Government and the law are having a greater overall impact on and control over our lives and activities generally.

(2) Relatively speaking, the increased governmental attention to the various phases and channels of communications is greater than to most other activities of organizations.

(3) Public relations has itself increased so tremendously in sweep and impact—and in public and governmental awareness of it—that it has come to "merit" greater legal, judicial, and legislative thrust.

(4) Public relations is becoming more and more a tool and function of management—at the very top—so it is becoming integrated into almost every legal exposure of the organization.

(5) As the public relations practitioner extends his techniques beyond verbalism (publicity) and participates in corporate activism, the legal perimeters expand.

(6) The average member of the public is becoming far more sophisticated and well-informed—particularly as to his "rights."

For these reasons, the practitioner must understand and accept the rules of the legal game he must play.

Law as a genetic force in public relations. The foregoing premises are part of a larger concept. Insofar as public relations is concerned, the law is now becoming more and more a formative and creative force or prod as well as an inhibitory leash. This has been true for some time in regard to our lives and activities generally. It is now a fact in public relations.

This is as might have been expected. To a considerable degree, public relations deals with intangibles—despite the tangible nature of its tools. The law and government are now turning their attention to these intangibles.

Current concerns of the public deal much with the "quality of life." This refers to the "climate" of our country and people, having in mind both the material progress and the intangible values—the particular emphasis being on the latter. Public relations has long dealt with such things—whether we call it the climate, the atmosphere, or the surroundings—in which we live and do business. The relationship is clear.

Government movements such as the consumer protection program—called by some one of the greatest challenges to communicators—and the burgeoning anti-pollution campaign are, for example, creating new public relations functions and areas.

No longer does the law consist merely of a series of "shalt nots." In many ways it now genetically and dramatically directs a goodly fraction of the public relations endeavor.

A public relations person may once have been concerned only about libel laws or obtaining a release for use of a picture in a company publication. Today he is required—as Ernest Little, Public Relations Manager of Texaco Canada, says—"to keep on top of . . . legislative developments which can affect his company and his industry."

But it goes beyond this. Philip Lesly (Editor of this *Handbook*) has reminded *Public Relations Journal* readers that the government is "filing lawsuits charging pollution, unjustifiable noise and other abuses"; that the Kefauver-refined technique of one-sided hearings is "now widely used in Congress" and regulatory agencies are commonly "making an allegation or announcing a product seizure before the company can react."[1]

It constantly becomes clearer that the law and government are taking the initiative in many areas in which public relations is much concerned.

GOVERNMENT ATTITUDES

Over the years, one of the most important supervening "legal developments" in public relations has been the government attitude toward the function. This has become more and more important because that attitude colors the increasing interest of government in business generally.

The attitude may be generally described as hostile. As far back as 1913 public relations became a dirty word in the federal lexicon. It was then that Congress forbade the use of appropriated funds "for the compensation of any publicity expert, unless specifically appropriated for that purpose." The attitude has continued over the years and explains why Uncle Sam's public relations and publicity nephews are called Public Information Officers.

Early in 1970 Senator J. William Fulbright fulminated against public relations again when introducing legislation against the millions being spent by the Department of Defense, the Army, the Navy, and the Air Force for publicity. He charged that much of the money was being used for "public relations" and, in effect, propaganda, making it clear that he had no objection to use of the money for "informational" purposes.

Regardless of the Senator's views on the Viet Nam war, this attitude—or at least the wording of his criticism—made it clear that his anger was merely part of the continuing anti-public relations and -publicity attitude of many legislators.

Any public relations executive concerned either with government relations or government controls must always recognize this basic legislative antagonism. This is particularly true in view of the *quantum* of governmental intervention in the communicatory function of business and in the defensive activities of the industry.

MAJOR CLASSIFICATIONS OF LEGAL EXPOSURES

A working understanding of the legal areas of concern can be simplified by first breaking them down into a few major elements—described from the practical public relations point-of-view.

(1) *Day-to-day operational public relations activities* are probably most common. Also, they require the most rapid resolution and frequently permit little extended consideration by legal counsel. They should, therefore, receive the most forehanded attention by both public relations man and lawyer.

(2) *Administrative public relations matters* are usually much less frequent but, in the long run, may be of very great importance. They are likely to arise more often with the independent public relations counselor than the inside public relations director or staff. They pertain to such matters as counsel-client relations and contracts; employment relationships within the company or the public relations firm; long-range antitrust stances, and so on. Normally their frequency of incidence will vary inversely with their importance.

(3) *Government relations* should be considered separately because of its increasing importance in the legal arena. Actually, many operational problems are government-oriented: the Securities and Exchange Commission with financial public relations[2] or the Federal Trade Commission and Food and Drug Administration with product publicity.[3]

However, the term is used here in the context of company relations such as government contracts, corporate reaction to proposed legislation, involvement in administrative agency rule-making, lobbying, and so on. It is to be distinguished from government regulation.

(4) *Government regulation* covers policing and control of industry practices by government. Internal corporate responsibility in such matters will vary from company to company. It frequently falls to the public relations arm—usually, but not always, in conjunction with legal counsel.

More commonly—whether or not it be of an adversary nature—it will fall to legal counsel, the company's "Washington man," or specialists such as rate experts, food and drug technicians, and others. The public relations executive must still be acutely aware of their handling even though he is not charged directly or primarily with the government contacts.

[1] *Public Relations Journal,* December 1969, Pp. 6-10.

[2] See Chapters 11 and 12.
[3] See Chapters 17, 19, 23, 38.

TABULATION OF SPECIFIC LEGAL AREAS

The following tabulation specifies the areas or activities of the public relations and publicity functions that carry potential legal exposure. Each such activity has been cross-referenced to the author's 1969 work *Public Relations Law*.[4]

The cross-references point to the principal treatment of the subject in question. Further recourse should be had to the detailed index in *Public Relations Law*. The work also contains in its footnotes and bibliography many further references, both legal and otherwise. These include many "public relations materials" that are available in many public relations libraries and at the office of PRSA, 845 Third Ave., New York, N.Y. 10022.

Specific Public Relations Activities and Functions Involving Legal Exposures	Cross-References to Simon, Public Relations Law
Artwork	295-332
Athletic program sponsorship	472-479
Awards and their exploitation	428-432
Broadcasting	644-649
Censorship of business communications	99-142
Certifications and Seals of Approval	428-432
Client-Public Relations Counsel contracts	45-62
Codes of ethics in public relations and communications	667-696
Community relations	467-493
Company books	595-598
Company legal manuals, etc.	19-24
Company mail	479-481
Contests and lotteries	437-463
Contract rights and liabilities of public relations counsel	35-41, 45-62
Consumer relations	638-644
Copyright	145-175
(The new Copyright Act of 1977 changes many provisions. See "The New Copyright Law," by Frank Walsh, *Public Relations Journal,* August 1977, pp. 6-7.)	307-312 587-590
Cultural program sponsorship	482-486
Deception in public relations and publicity	381-408
Defamation	209-238
Employees of public relations counsel	65-94
Employee relations	699-729
Financial public relations and publicity	541-543 733-799
Foreign Agent activity	825-841
Government information	526-531
Government publicity and public relations	607-626
Government regulation	632-638 passim
Government relations	601-665
Graphics	295-332
House organs and employee publications	575-595
Ideas and their protection	177-207
Industrial espionage	543-573
International public relations	653-655, 825-841
Labor relations	714-729
Legal status of public relations counsel	29-35
Libel	209-238, 326-328
Litigation and public relations activities	16-19
Lobbying	799-822
Loss of materials	328-330
Marketing intelligence	551-554
New product introduction	523-546
Newsman's privilege	655-657
Non-contract rights, liabilities of public relations counsel	41-45
Obscenity	128-136
Open houses	472-479
Photographs	295-332
Privacy, right of	239-281, 316-326
Product tests, exploitation of	426-428, 536-538, passim
Proxy solicitation publicity	773-776
PRSA codes and standards	677-680, 745-747
Publicity, right of	281-286
Refusal by media of releases and advertising	122-128
Relations with legal counsel	3-15
Releases of liability	239-286, 316-326
Research	495-521, 646-649
Restrictive covenants	74-94
Self-regulation of public relations industry	667-696
Slander	209-238
Surveys and studies, exploitation of	426-428
Testimonials and endorsements	409-433
Timely disclosure	748-773
Trademarks	333-380, 585-587
Trade secrets	547-573
Unfair trade practices	381-408

[4](EDITOR'S NOTE: This form has been followed at the suggestion of the Editor. *Public Relations Law* is the most complete and authoritative single legal sourcebook for the public relations practitioner and the lawyer venturing into a "public relations case.")

RELATIVE DEGREE OF LEGAL DANGER

Even a cursory reading of the foregoing tabulation suggests a considerable variation in the possible "cost" of legal mistakes. In financial public relations, the "legalities" must override everything else because improper handling may even put a company out of business or subject it to very severe penalties, financial or otherwise. At the other extreme is a routine use of a photograph in a release about a corporate staff promotion.

By and large, however, only experience can lead to "safe" working decisions by the public relations executive because the great bulk of the public relations/legal situations fall into an intermediate gray area where snap judgments can be costly. Normally only *ad hoc* and well-informed advice by legal counsel should be relied on.

This is good advice for any department but is particularly relevant for the public relations director because of the "egg on the face" concern that is always present in his mind. To the well-indoctrinated public relations executive even seemingly routine releases should be checked out by counsel. For example, one company public relations man had been issuing releases for years about product price changes and always without having them screened. Then one was the root of long antitrust litigation that subjected the company to triple-damages payments in seven figures.

THE DANGERS OF DECEPTION

One of the most important, broadly applicable legal traps for the company communicator is the deceptive message. A wide variety of government (federal and state) administrative agencies—together with the courts—react vigorously against commercial deception. Included are the FTC, Federal Communications Commission, FDA, SEC, Federal Power Commission, Civil Aeronautics Board, and others proceeding under a wide variety of statutes.

In recent years the FTC has also been applying what we might call its "unfairness doctrine" as a basis for action—either in the form of adversary proceedings or under its rule-making function, the latter having been broadly expanded under the 1975 Magnuson-Moss Act. At one time, the businessman and his public relations or publicity people could rely on "The truth shall make you free." No longer is this true.

Advertising as well as news releases and other business or trade practices, no matter what their degree of verity, may be subject to attack if the Commission and/or the courts consider them to be "unfair" to the consumer. The danger lies in trying to define that word "unfair."

The best approach in attempting to screen an activity or program on the basis of its possible unfairness is to "let your conscience be your guide" and/or "if in doubt, don't." Each practitioner, each manager, is usually as qualified as a company lawyer to make decisions in this legal area.

The one precept that is definite is this: The increased application of the doctrine of "unfair trade practices" is definitely a potential trap for any company statement or activity.

Over the years there has developed in some public relations minds the belief that public relations and publicity are *not* subject to the same rules as paid advertising when it comes to deception and unfair trade practices. This is not correct. In fact, some of the earliest FTC actions involved the "false front" organization and deceptive use of magazine article reprints. The SEC frequently takes action against misleading financial releases or other communications.

In other words, the news release can be as deadly a weapon as the paid advertisement. This is true not only with product publicity but with the president's speech, stories in a company publication, civil rights activities, announcements at press parties or on paid junkets, and so on.

Therefore the public relations or publicity language must be screened with the same care as the copy and layout in a paid advertisement.

PUBLIC ISSUE ADVERTISING

The public relations man or woman has long been concerned with what has been called corporate advertising, image advertising, identity advertising, or institutional advertising.

Such involvement probably is increasing. New legal exposures are becoming important as such advertising leans more toward what has come to be called "public issue advertising." This is paid advertising explaining a company's or entire industry's posture on some public, often vital, issue. Two things seem certain: The volume and variety of such public issue advertising is increasing, and by its very nature—public and not-infrequently controversial—it is likely to generate a variety of attacks from a variety of sources.

It is difficult to define "public issue advertising" or at least to pinpoint its perimeters. This becomes clear merely from mentioning a few of the public issues with which such advertising is involved: The environment, current energy problems, civil rights activities, and all the corporate relationships that fall under that large umbrella, "consumerism." Although technologically speaking such company or client matters may be considered as "internal," nevertheless every experienced public relations practitioner recognizes they are truly "public" factors—recognition that has almost been forced upon both practitioner and company by the government and various activists. This is true regardless of the degree of social responsibility by the company or client.

With the expansion—both in kind and degree—

of the legal questions involved, it is almost impossible to anticipate the locations of the legal horizons.

Thus far the Federal Trade Commission has held its fire in situations such as this, pointing to the First Amendment as a shield for advertising in such instances. On the other hand, the FTC has made it clear that it will consider each case on an *ad hoc* basis, applying a "rule of balance"—whether the principal purpose of the advertising in question is oriented toward an issue or toward product promotion.

The FTC continues to be extremely interested in this form of corporate advertising. It also continues to be under great pressure from Congress and activists to take steps on the ground of deception or unfairness.

Furthermore, in the realm of broadcasting we have the "Fairness Doctrine" of the Federal Communications Commission. Any broadcast programming or even paid commercials should be preliminarily scanned as presenting possible springboards—under this "Fairness Doctrine"—for demands for equalizing exposure by opponents.

LOBBYING

An active public relations practitioner is likely to find himself—knowingly or otherwise—engaged in "lobbying" or other activities close to it.[5] By training and experience, many public relations people seem well-qualified for lobbying. It is important to realize that lobbying is a legitimate form of approach to government and is constitutionally protected. President Kennedy loosely defined lobbying as "efforts by which various groups or individuals attempt to secure the passage or defeat of legislation." Many legislators have called it "an honorable profession."

On the federal level, the present statute is the 1946 Federal Regulation of Lobbying Act. The law does not restrict lobbying but requires that lobbyists register with the Secretary of the Senate and the Clerk of the House and file quarterly financial reports. The law has been criticized over the years as ineffective and too limited.

Both the House and Senate have been working on "lobbying reform" bills but they differ materially. Yet these two bills do have certain common characteristics:

• They broaden the definition of lobbying and adopt the concept of a "threshold level" at which an organization must register as a lobbyist.

• Only an organization could become a lobbyist. It is thereby hoped to avoid conflicts with First Amendment rights of petition, assembly, and free speech.

• For the first time they cover to a varying degree persons who lobby the executive branch of government—not merely members of Congress.

• They cover also, to varying extent, "grass roots" lobbying.

All the states have long had lobbying or "corrupt practices" laws, varying in approach and content.

THE PRACTITIONER IN POLITICS[6]

In recent years company public relations people and public relations firms—innocently or otherwise—have been sometimes misused in politics. Illegal corporate political campaign contributions have been carried on company books as payments for public relations or publicity. An outside public relations firm may or may not have been implicated as a conduit for such contributions.

Sometimes the individual owner of the public relations firm has made a seemingly legal political contribution in his own name, later conniving with the corporate client to pad his firm's otherwise legitimate bills. The legal exposure of the public relations person depends on the existence or nature of the personal involvement as it would with any other person.

Similar "under the table" relationships have been exposed in connection with some of the multimillion dollar international bribes paid by certain multinational companies. Again, the liability of the public relations people allegedly involved is essentially the same as that of any corporate officer or other "courier."

The variety of techniques used in such less-than-legal relationships may also be analogized to the Supreme Court's warning about lotteries and contests, when the Court commented on "the seemingly inexhaustible ingenuity . . . to circumvent the law."

TREATMENT AND USE OF RESEARCH MATERIALS

Elsewhere in this *Handbook* is discussed the use of various kinds of research as a part of, or contributory to, public relations practice and activity. (See Chapter 35.) We are here concerned with another aspect of research—the legal aspects of its use.

---

[5]See Chapters 5 and 32.

[6]See Chapter 8.

Essentially we are again in the field of deception—specifically, deceptive or other unfair business practices in the *presentation* of the research results to the public. Even the most valid research can be misused. As the FTC and other agencies enlarge their reliance on allegations of "unfair" practices, there is a potentially expanding exposure resulting from such things as unjustified extrapolation, improper interpretation, failure to disclose limiting factors, and other practices.

INTERNATIONAL PUBLIC RELATIONS OPERATIONS[7]

The public relations firm that "operates internationally" encounters many special legal problems, whether it serves a multinational client from the home office or operates through its own branch offices in one or more foreign countries.

Public relations people—advertising people also—have long encountered built-in problems in relying on literal translations from English into a foreign language. That has led to a variety of results, ranging from simple embarrassment (based perhaps on unintended humor) through various gradations of bad taste to legal breaches under foreign law.

Our concern here is not with language and translation but with the legal requirements or restrictions of the foreign country involved. Among them may be licensing requirements, minority-ownership limitations, substantive and procedural rules relative to operation on behalf of clients, and so on. A top executive of an American-headquartered public relations firm with a number of foreign branches and "affiliations" has said: "Operating outside of the United States isn't merely working in a jungle. It is a whole series of jungles, with each one having practically its own legal flora and fauna."

The reverse is also true. An American public relations firm may have to register *in this country* as a "foreign agent" if it serves certain foreign interests in the United States. That term "foreign agent" should not conjure up cloak-and-dagger images. Such registration as a foreign agent may mean nothing more than the firm is representing the tourist bureau of some friendly foreign country or a respected international trade association.

PUBLIC RELATIONS AND LITIGATION

The business world is becoming more litigious, not only internally but as a result of activist-instigated actions—usually with business on the defensive. This trend seems almost certain to continue. New "rights" and "duties" are being created and existing ones extended by legislatures and agencies (federal and state) and by the courts. Every company should look to its PR people for help in such litigation.

Whenever a case is tried there are really two "trials": one inside the courtroom or hearing room and the other outside, in public opinion. The latter may be more important in both the short and long run. The classic example is probably the government case against DuPont, eventually requiring divestiture of its massive holding of General Motors stock. The case was lost but the "outside" or "public relations trial" was apparently won. Congress later enacted legislation that resulted in favorable tax treatment when the GM stock was divested pursuant to the court order.[8]

There are essentially three categories of company litigation and the public relations person's responsibilities and contribution vary with each.

1. The "big case"—litigation upon which the entire future of a company may depend or that may result in great financial loss. It is most likely to occur in the fields of antitrust, labor relations, securities and stockholder matters, product safety cases, and so on.

2. The "human interest" case—an action in which little money or even basic principle may be involved but that has newsworthy appeal for some reason. Perhaps a "glamour name" is involved or some community interest seems to be at stake.

3. The routine case—litigation that every company must face with more or less frequency. This would include contract litigation, tax refund claims, automobile/truck negligence matters, and the like.

The public relations involvement is likely to be greatest in the first two categories. As to the *relative* imputs of the legal/public relations team, the lawyer's posture should prevail in the first and third but the public relations practitioner's decisions should probably control in the second.

Of course, public relations people may themselves be called as witnesses if they participated in or contributed to the matter being litigated. In such instances, their rights and obligations are the same as those of any other witness.

Also, they may have the responsibility for shaping the releases describing the case from the company's point of view. Here the basic rule is factual reporting—no double-talk or deception. *Misguided activities in this area have themselves led to further ac-*

---

[7]See Chapters 33 and 34.

[8]See Chapter 13.

tions against the company—either by private parties or government agencies such as the FTC.

A single example—the *Imdrim* case—will serve as a warning. The FTC had sought an injunction against allegedly false advertising of Imdrim, an arthritis remedy. The lower court refused the injunction. While an appeal was pending, the company issued releases alleged by the FTC to be deceptively descriptive of the lower court decision. The FTC brought a *second* action—based on misrepresentations concerning the lower court action—quite apart from any charges (as in the first case) about the product advertising. This second action ended with a fine under the FTC Act.

Beyond these fundamentals, we are facing a broad-based development of overriding significance.

Recently there has been "a radical transformation" in the function and methods of our judicial system. This is, of course, very meaningful to the bar, the courts, and the legislatures. It should also be recognized as extremely important to the public relations practitioner whose client or company is, or may become, involved in litigation.

At the risk of oversimplification, the "traditional model" of a law suit involved the prosecution of a *private* right by one party against another party before a tribunal that merely applied precedents ("existing law") to a factual relationship existing between the parties. The public relations role in such litigation was relatively simple and limited.

This judicial transformation must now be understood and implemented by the public relations function. From that perspective probably the greatest shifts are: the increased judicial concern with *public* rights as against *private*; the impact of a decision on vary large numbers of persons who may not even be aware of the litigation; the retention of judicial jurisdiction and supervision even after the apparent "final decision" and determination of relief by a court; the shift from the purely decisional or interpretive to the "legislative" as an important judicial function, based perhaps on perceived political needs or public concerns requiring correction. As to the latter, it has been suggested that courts are more and more becoming catalysts of public and social change, the judges sometimes becoming even detailed managers of large sectors of public relationships.

Perhaps these generalities fall into better perspective by reference to this sampling of broad-based public concerns with which courts are becoming more and more involved: civil rights and all of their *sequelae* such as school desegregation, a company's personnel policy and activities, etc.; the broad spectrum of environmental and ecological matters ranging over such practicalities as the construction of a new atomic power plant, off-shore oil-well drilling, land use and zoning law changes; consumer protection in all its ramifications; practices of small loans companies and credit-card use; the federal Freedom of Information Act and a variety of other "sunshine laws"; the implications of an advertisement or other corporate statement as an enforceable product warranty; product safety and resultant product liability and recalls; the treatment of the many new rules concerning individual "privacy"; the scope of First Amendment rights, individual or corporate, including the constitutional posture of corporate statements of various kinds, and so forth.

One clear-cut result of this transformation must be the increased significance of public relations in the minds of management. In view of the expanded incidence and impact of the judicial process on business, management must be more alert to avoid litigation.

Assuming such increased managerial recognition and reliance, it follows that public relations must justify its contribution long before the onset of litigation; it must identify and forestall. Public relations people must recognize long in advance the issues likely to be involved, the increased number and variety of publics to be considered and addressed, and the continued need for addressing such publics over extended periods during and after litigation.

LIABILITY OF PUBLIC RELATIONS PEOPLE

Important to all public relations practitioners is their increasing personal legal liability for their activities on behalf of their companies or clients—quite apart from the liability of the company or client. In financial public relations, especially, public relations people have been joined as defendants or respondents by government agencies or in other litigation.

The same has been true—going back many years, in fact—in antitrust cases. In one such case, the public relations firm was called the "alter ego" of the culpable corporate client.

So far as we know, government agencies—such as the FTC, Food and Drug Administration, and the Environmental Protection Agency—have not yet joined a public relations firm as a party in an action. However, this may be anticipated in the future, especially as public relations seeks with increasing success to become "a part of management."

We may say generally that the PR practitioner will probably be joined if he originated, contributed to, knew, or should have known of the impropriety.

An exception to this overall rule appeared in the Supreme Court's 1976 *Ernst & Ernst* decision concerning the alleged liability of an accounting firm under Sec. 10(b) of the SEC Act. The court absolved the accountants in the "absence of ... *scienter*, i.e. intent to deceive, manipulate or defraud..." This doctrine—refusing to "impose liability for negligent conduct alone"—would quite probably be applied in favor of financial public relations operations also.

However, this "scienter approach" should not be taken as protecting general (non-financial) public relations activities, since the Court stressed that the word "manipulative" is "virtually a term of art used in connection with securities markets (connoting) intentional or willful conduct designed to deceive or defraud..."

More and more, this potential exposure is coming to be appreciated by public relations people. Certain public relations firms have undertaken what we might call a "protective program." This is being done in connection with public relations and publicity generally—not just in the more "touchy" field of financial public relations.

Under such a program the firm or practitioner does not supinely accept information from the client or management. In cases where judgment indicates the need, they make their own independent investigation of the facts given them—questioning information received from the client—not merely from third-party sources such as independent research organizations.

THE LAWYER/LAW DICHOTOMY

It is important to distinguish conceptually between "the law" and "lawyers." Some of the antagonism in the minds of the public relations man or woman is undoubtedly due to some unhappy personal experience with a particular lawyer.

More than this, however, some public relations executives take a dim view of lawyers generally. They have called them "deterrents" and "hobbles on creativity." Lawyers are said "not to understand the importance of public attitudes." They are said to be "too rigid in their thinking" and some have been accused of "thinking they know public relations when they don't." These are actual comments from studies of the relationship.

The public relations director of a midwest company neatly pinpointed this attitude. An attractive, blonde, 30-year-old Portia had been permanently assigned to his department. He had had a lot of problems with "getting through" to her. One night at dinner—she was not present—he caustically toasted her in these words: "Here's to my lawyer. I would love to fall into her arms provided I never fall into her hands."

Many lawyers have not been slow in reciprocating such sentiments. They speak of the public relations man in terms of "Madison Avenue" and "brainwashers." Some, as Carl Sandburg said of Ivy Lee, charge the public relations man with being a "paid liar." He is said to be "divorced from reality" and "a cloud-9 expert."

Glen Perry, former Director of Public Relations of DuPont Company, summed up the problem quite well when he wrote:

> ... the number of lawyers with the necessary knowledge and attitude is apparently no greater than the number of public relations men with a corresponding attitude towards the law and lawyers.[9]

Experience has shown, however, that if the public relations practitioner finds a lawyer with whom he is *simpatico,* this initial contretemps will disappear. The result will be a mutually happy relationship and a valuable and productive public relations/legal team.

THE PUBLIC RELATIONS/LEGAL TEAM

To create and maintain such a productive accommodation may not be easy for the public relations member of the public relations/legal team. It certainly is not a short-term chore.

The lawyer and the public relations executive differ widely in background, education, personality, and, above all, perspective. But we must also recognize the similarities. Both are well-educated, intelligent, and presumably reasonable people, having a broad interest in company or organization matters. Above all, both are communicators.

Then too, both the law and public relations deal with human behavior. Public relations supplements the law, which deals essentially with restraints on human conduct—both individual and corporate. These restraints are necessary to provide an orderly and balanced world. William Gaskill, former chairman of the PRSA accreditation program, has called public relations ... "a groping for the best balance between conflicting interests, to the end that laws will not have to be devised to contain human behavior."

---

[9] *Public Relations Law,* by Morton J. Simon, foreword, p. v.

We might almost be justified in saying that if the lawyer and the public relations practitioner achieve their common ideal, they will be delighted to discover that they have put themselves out of business.

Need for mutual respect and understanding. Most knowledgeable observers of the public relations/legal scene have concluded that the basic need for a productive public relations/legal team is *mutual respect* and *mutual understanding*. This, of course, is one of the commonplaces of human relations.

Creating this mutual respect and understanding takes time and real effort on both sides. It is unlikely to germinate in time of crisis or bloom without extended fertilization.

Each must make a serious effort to understand the other. Casual or occasional contacts will not do it. At the risk of overdramatization, the relationship must become a way of life if the result is to be an effective—even synergistic—public relations/legal team.

The approach and relationship must be prophylactic—to prevent mistakes, not to cure them after the event. Experience shows that this needs particular emphasis. As the Navy insists: BE FOREHANDED.

The public relations man cannot expect even the best-intentioned lawyer to react promptly and intelligently—above all, cooperatively—to a problem or situation that is thrown at him for the first time in a vacuum or in the heat of an immediate deadline. The lawyer should be briefed well in advance. Background, facts, purpose, format, and all other minutiae should be explored with him, and this must be done preliminarily. Give the lawyer time to evaluate, learn and, above all, think.

In short, the public relations man should do what he does best. He must communicate.

RECOMMENDATIONS IN BRIEF

The "nuts and bolts" of working with lawyers would be the subject of a lengthy chapter. Here, in brief compass, are recommendations for effecting mutual respect and understanding. Since this *Handbook* is directed to the public relations practitioner, these comments are unilateral only. Most of them could be matched by somewhat similar advice to the legal member of the team.

(1) Recognize the place of the law and the lawyer in the public relations scheme of things.

(2) Ask top management to make the public relations/legal relationship a basic, continuing fact of corporate life.

(3) Appoint the lawyer—whether company inside counsel or outside lawyer—to the Public Relations Committee or any *ad hoc* public relations task forces.

(4) Seek to avoid "lateral laryngitis." This term—apparently popularized by the American Management Association—dramatizes the frustrating inability to communicate directly and horizontally with one's opposite number—in this case, legal counsel.

(5) Define relative areas of authority and responsibility.

(6) Teach the lawyer the public relations business.

(7) Demonstrate the importance of the "two-way street" concept.

(8) Work at the public relations/legal relationship until it becomes almost a way of life.

(9) Stake out for the lawyer major or continuing public relations problems or campaigns and do it well in advance.

(10) Avoid "crisis communications."

(11) Organize the specific logistics of the relationship and put them in writing.

(12) Arrange a "24-hour watch" with your legal department as a safeguard against crisis demands.

(13) Avoid "pride of authorship" between the two parties. This does not mean that both must agree on everything. As Walter Lippman said, "Where all think alike, no one thinks very much."

(14) Mutually select and indoctrinate "company spokesmen."

(15) Use the lawyer as a "listening post."

(16) Look to the lawyer for practical, as well as legal, solutions and answers.

(17) Stay on top of government relations with the lawyer.

(18) Let the lawyer steer the boat in financial public relations.

(19) Develop a very clear understanding with the lawyer on handling of consumer relations.

(20) Provide for mutual "security" precautions and provisions.

(21) Try to make the public relations/legal team both a synergistic and affirmative force in company policy and activities.

(22) Above all, THINK OF THAT MAN AS "MY LAWYER."

SECTION VII

Emerging Principles and Trends

55

Emerging Principles and Trends

Philip Lesly

It has become customary to decry the greater pace of scientific advancement than of man's ability to understand and cope with mankind. The great need to achieve the same degree of order in human relationships that is being attained in the physical world is common in the expressions of social scientists, churchmen, and others. They justifiably fear the rush of scientific knowledge is outpacing man's ability to cope with the changes created in the human world.

Evolvement of the principles now known about group attitudes, how they develop, and how they can be coped with is, accordingly, one of the significant events of the Twentieth Century. Because they have not been marked by spectacular explosions, propulsion of man into outer space, conquering of feared diseases, or easing of odious labor, they have attracted comparatively little attention. In some circles, techniques of influencing group attitudes are still looked at askance, as perhaps being not quite respectable.

However, considering that the principles of public relations began to evolve several years after the advent of the closed automobile, the pace of its development and acceptance has testified to its vital importance in the rapid changes of all aspects and locales of life.

Complexity of group attitudes. Public relations is one of the youngest of the basic disciplines. As a result, too little recognition is given to the great complexity in achieving any accurate knowledge, let alone control, of the attitudes of large masses of people. Any one person defies full understanding, or even knowledge, of the source of life itself, the forces that motivate it, or the drives that carry it through the myriad thoughts and emotions of a single day.

Just one person is a puzzle far greater to man's understanding than any inanimate challenge he has conquered. And not only is a large group of such individuals infinitely more complex than one person, but as has been recognized since the explorations in Gustave Le Bon's famous "The Crowd," published in 1895, the sum of complexity of a large group is greater than the multiplication of individuals involved.

Achieving knowledge of how a virus causes a disease and then finding a specific to destroy that virus is a miracle of man's capacity for creative and brilliant thought. But the virus is incomparably simpler a mechanism than the simplest of human beings, and the human being is infinitely simpler than the psychological group to which he belongs, in any given context.

It is encouraging that so much progress toward understanding what is involved in enabling groups to understand and cope with each other has been made in so short a time. It is even more encouraging that on the horizon can be seen promise of greater understanding in many areas of group psychology and communication. A few of those areas not otherwise treated in depth in this volume can be cited to indicate the direction in which thought is leading and to offer stimulus to further understanding and exploration.

THE INTANGIBLES IN A WORLD OF TANGIBLES

Emphasis in management of all kinds of organizations is increasingly on evaluating, measuring, and predicting. The growing complexity of all aspects of life has come into confluence with the computer, quantitative analysis, and other tools for coping with complexity.

But the major problems facing business today are mostly intangible, immeasurable, and not subject to factual analysis. This applies also to governments, institutions, and other organizations.[1]

• The main problem in production is no longer increasing the efficiency of our plants, but attitudes of the people whose jobs are to be changed or eliminated by more efficient methods.

• The principal obstacle to planning for growth, increased employment, and meeting the expectations of the public is not the availability of resources but the attitudes of conservationists, community organizations, and others who resist construction and technological innovation.

• The principal problem of growth through innovation is not organizing and administering development programs, but the reactions of the intended customers and dealers to the product.

• The personnel problem is not projecting a firm's manpower needs and standards, but persuading the best people to work for the company—and then to stay and do their best work.

• The financing problem is not financial planning for the company's funding, but the attitude of the stock market or other investors.

• The problem in advertising is not minutely analyzing the media, the timing, and the costs, but how to reach the minds and hearts of the audience.

• The problem of business acceptance is not only demonstrating that it operates in the public interest, but getting people to understand that its cornucopia works better when it is not unduly hampered by restraints.

All of these problems, and others, are in the minds of men—the most intangible, immeasurable, and unpredictable of all elements affecting a business.

Resistance of attitudes. Many of the recommendations that come out of hard-headed analysis of the "facts" are frustrated by existing attitudes. Not only are the analyses likely to be distorted by the lack of imput of attitudes, but the "answers" cannot be executed.

• The railroads' struggle to modernize is stalled by the attitudes of the public and government left over from the roads' old image as ruthless, giving undue support to unions' demands and bureaucracies' restrictions.

• When the facts add up to moving a plant or headquarters, the move is often blocked by opposition of employees.

• Growth or improved operations by acquisition or merger increasingly is prevented by the attitudes of the public and government officials, based on fear of concentrated power.

• Efforts to meet threats of new competition are hobbled by resistance of employees: department stores' night and Sunday hours, newspapers' efforts to automate typesetting and use mass-produced ads.

• Need to follow changing social patterns is blocked by lingering prejudices from past problems: efforts of major Illinois banks to follow population trends are balked by the law prohibiting branch banking.

• Meeting unfair competition: the public's readiness to have tax laws favor cooperatives and credit unions over their profit-making competitors.

• Technological innovation: delayed use of new materials and techniques because unions and activist groups block new methods or installations.

• Building excellence into the staff: employee and community sympathy for the weak but veteran employee; objection of career employees to bringing in outsiders rather than promoting from within.

Conflict of two electronic revolutions. The isolation of executives from the rest of society is abetted by what is no less than an electronic revolution—the impact of electronic data processing and automation.

The size and function of complex institutions demand that their managers organize for their goals, eliminate unplanned variables, and systematize their decision-making process. They must have "smooth operations" and "scientific management." This science of management is geared to data processing and automation—an electronic revolution.

On the other hand, a generation whose development has been dominated by the electronic revolution of television and films assumes an activist role on behalf of the "human feeling" of social objectives. They pit "human feelings" against the "inhumanity" of mechanisms and institutions. They get high visibility through instant and widespread picturing of emotional "human interest events." This force is attuned to the picture tube and movie camera—another electronic revolution.

The anomaly existing between those opposing products of an electronic age and those who demand the benefits that are made possible only by

---

[1] From "Effective Management and the Human Factor," by Philip Lesly—*Journal of Marketing,* April, 1965, pp. 1-4.

electronic facilities constitutes a major problem. Communication between the two forces is vital; and so is understanding by each of the nature of today's communications.

TREND AWAY FROM OVERSIMPLIFICATION

In the developing maturity of public relations there has been a succession of concepts that for a time evoked enthusiasm because they appeared to offer a simple means toward influencing desired audiences. It is a sign that the field is approaching true maturity, that these over-simplified panaceas are losing support and that new ones are being met with considerable skepticism as they appear.

Some of those that have risen to attention and been found to lack sufficient scope to present answers include:

(1) The concept of the "image" as the means toward recognition and acceptance. The idea that a "corporate image" can be developed to such a graphic state that the great majority of people the company is interested in will visualize it has faltered of its own inadequacies. It has been demonstrated that even the strongest corporate images are envisaged similarly by only a small fraction of any organization's public.

However, the effectiveness of sharply defining the traits and characteristics of an organization so that it can be more readily understood by its various publics continues to be important. Development and projection of these characteristics represent much of the functioning of a sound public relations program.

The most extreme efforts toward oversimplification of the image concept are found in organizations that seek to derive a visual symbol as if it alone is the corporate image. Many articles, monographs, and even books have been written about the visualization of an organization's image, oversimplifying the concept and misleading the efforts of the companies involved. The result has been a multiplicity of visual symbols so little different from each other that very few have any individual identification outside the companies involved.

The *visual* elements of what a company represents are vital, but they are not total.

(2) The oversimplified belief that sufficient exposure of an idea is an assured means of driving it into the public's consciousness and then into its acceptance.

(3) What might be called the "bulldozer technique" in public relations. This is the belief that if you spend enough money and have enough people on the payroll, you will accomplish your objectives. "Shove hard enough with enough resources behind you, and you can't fail," is the essence of this philosophy. Actually, there are innumerable instances in which a small group of talented people with limited budgets, but with creativeness and dedication, are greatly outperforming monolothic masses of men and funds.

(4) Various techniques of communication have become highly popular, taking on almost the essence of business fads, only to prove incapable of serving as cure-alls. They are gradually leveling off to a proper proportionate value in the list of resources available to the public relations man. At one time the open house was "the thing to do" for any company that felt it was enlightened about its public and community relations. Open houses became more and more elaborate, more and more common, and less and less effective because they were not carefully selected and set up to meet a specified need. Today the open house is an important public relations technique, but is used selectively by well-informed companies. The increasingly elaborate annual report was another technique that went through the over-development stage and then leveled off as one tool in the communications kit. Institutional advertising was oversold for a time, and continues to be expected to do far more than it is able, but is increasingly recognized for both its limitations and its values.

(5) Business managers have become increasingly alarmed about the damage done to their ability to perform their companies' functions as a result of encroachment by legislators and government agencies. Many executives attribute this to the low regard for business in the minds of the public; and that, in turn, is attributed to the public's lack of education in economics. The result has been a large number of business-financed programs intended to foster "economic education." Almost all of them have been ineffective, as evidenced by the continuing decline in the public's regard for business, because most of the principles of sound mass communication dealt with in this book have been violated.[2]

AWARENESS OF FALLACIES ABOUT COMMUNICATION

Recently there has been increased recognition of the limitations of many long-held beliefs about communication.

[2]"Why Economic Education Is Failing," by Philip Lesly, *Management Review,* Oct. 1976, pp. 17-23.

Many programs of communication are designed to "educate" the publics involved. In this sense, education is meant to mean the transfer of information from a knowing source into the minds of an unaware group. It is based on a faith that once people know the facts they will respond in precisely the way the source wants them to; that "they shall know the truth, and the truth shall make them free." Faith in this type of "education" is expressed in the famous dictum of H. G. Wells: "Human history becomes more and more a race between education and catastrophe."

The actualities demonstrate the fallaciousness of this faith. Drug education programs that inform people of the dangers have reached billions of people many times—yet many of them have become addicted. A nine-month saturation campaign to persuade people to use auto seat belts, conducted by the Insurance Institute for Highway Safety in a medium-sized city, had "no effect whatsoever." In fact, many people paid to have their seat belt buzzers disconnected or to have the belts removed entirely. There is high public awareness of the penalties of smoking, but the number of people who start smoking continues to be high. Intensive education about nutrition has been accompanied by massive consumption of unwholesome food and drink.

It is evident that education can take place only when the intended recipient is inclined to accept it and takes the trouble necessary to respond. Yet as more people go through the formal education process, the faith in "education" as a cure for ills continues to grow, in the face of evidence that it usually fails or causes more problems. Many social-engineering efforts, as well as campaigns by private organizations, are based on faith that somehow a formula will be found for transmitting the facts into the minds and hearts of the audience. Instead, the planning involved in conducting such programs requires intensive analysis of the psyche of the intended audience, as well as the highest levels of judgment and skill.

Faith in interchange. It has been widely believed that friction between groups of people is the result of separateness; that if only they could be brought together and "get to know each other" they would develop mutual respect and understanding. That is the principle behind "involvement" and "sitting down together," both of which have been concepts propounded as the means to resolve human conflicts.

However, like many rules this one is often untrue. Few groups are more "involved" with each other or understand each other so well as the Protestants and Catholics in Northern Ireland, the Turks and Greeks on Cyprus, the Jews and Arabs in the Middle East, the blacks and whites in Rhodesia . . . and millions of husbands and wives everywhere.

Close involvement often emphasizes differences more than similarities. Especially, *forced* interchange can lead to explosive opposition.

Interchange as a means of achieving understanding between groups is an important factor to consider; but the chances for making real progress must be assessed soberly and realistically. Where the groups have wide differences that their very nature prevents them from ceding, a realistic awareness of the impasse may be the only course of wisdom.

Anti-communication.[3] Communication that's intended to get somebody's support for ideas is like courtship. We want to win that person over with logic, ardor, charm, and persuasion.

Yet millions of people who think they are communicating are really repelling the objects of their intention. There are eight ways that people discommunicate when they think they are communicating:

- *The snobbery of jargon.* When we try to make others recognize we are in a different class, we use the language of our special field. We say things like "motivational deprivation" when we mean laziness. Language is supposed to be a bridge between people. Jargon digs chasms instead.

- *No-name names.*[4] There is a proliferation of company names that look and sound alike or like nothing at all: initials such as AMF, AMP, and ARA; coined names such as Ampex, Amrep, Amstar, and Amtel.

- *The lost art of expression.* Today most people have trouble expressing themselves because they never really learned how to write and because they never really learned how to read. Good use of language is one of the greatest achievements of civilization. Most people use language like underwear, merely to cover the subject; only a few use it like lingerie, to show it at its best.[5]

- *Putting art ahead of meaning.*[6] Illustration and design are supposed to help get a message across; but often the design is put ahead of the message, instead of being a vehicle for it. So we find corporate

---

[3]From "How We Discommunicate," by Philip Lesly, *Passages,* Feb. 1976, pp. 16-18.

[4]See "The Name as an Image Factor" later in this chapter.

[5]Lesly, Philip, *The People Factor: Managing the Human Climate,* Dow Jones-Irwin, Homewood, Ill., 1974, pp. 175-7.

[6]See Chapter 2.

signatures that cannot be read, signs that don't direct, and color combinations that lose the printing.

- *Deliberate destruction of communication.* Commercials blare, "Me and my RC . . . cause what's good enough for other folks ain't good enough for me." Suave actors talk of *pre*spiration. Punctuation, such as apostrophes, wanders in and out of likely and unlikely places. The attitude is growing that language that's almost right is okay; but "almost right" communication can be as ineffectual as an almost right 23-foot leap over a 25-foot chasm.
- *The temptation of "controlled communication."* Managers are inherently geared to seeing tangible things and to having control of what happens. They tend to be uneasy with communications that are invisible and that depend on how others use them, such as the press and broadcast outlets. So they are inclined to choose "controlled communication" to get across their ideas: ads they can see and approve in advance;[7] company publications;[8] bulletin board notices. Such overt messages can be effective in conveying information but are likely to be less effective in changing attitudes. They visibly tell the audience that they are efforts to impose opinions on them.
- *Euphemisms.* Many young people pride themselves on the forthrightness of their language. These same young people are asked by many organizations to accept such terms as "deaccession" for unloading a losing division; "early retirement" for discharge with reduced pay; "discontinued" or "laid off" for fired; "misappropriated" for stolen. Efforts to mislead through euphemisms not only fail in the long run; the oral or written insincerity repels today's cynical, suspicious, educated public audience.
- *Condescension.* When a communicator is eager to exhibit his or her own stature and superior intellect, he shows he is manipulating the audience, rather than serving it; he condescends to his readers or viewers. He shows off the big words he knows, uses foreign phrases without translations, or wallows in gobbledygook to avoid simple, clear statements.

The biggest cause of these sins of discommunication is thinking about oneself instead of the audience. Ego is singular, likely to be massaged in solitude. Communication is plural, involving interaction with others, and makes it possible to win over multitudes. Ego is the enemy of good communication.

THE CHANGING ROLE OF THE MEDIA[9]

For a whole network of reasons, the nature of the communications media has changed in the past generation—not only technologically, but in orientation and effect. The change is both the result and the cause of ferments in our society; and how it is accommodated will have much to do with the future nature of society.

In many ways, mass communication has progressed and improved more than any other aspect of modern living. Its impact, therefore, has been vastly increased and is now dominant in determining what course events shall take. Accordingly, it calls for constant review and evaluation. Public relations people must keep abreast of the media patterns constantly.

When there were only a few thought leaders and a few media, the individual medium tended to be highly personal. It was strongly marked with the personality of its moving force—a Greeley, a Hearst, a Pulitzer, a McCormick, a McClure, a Lorimer. Publishing a newspaper was possible and attractive for many men, so most people had a wide choice of papers and magazines.

Today the major media are institutions. Few of them are organs of a leader's personality. What goes into the press and over the air is now largely determined by the bent of the creative staffs. Creative people are, by definition, sensitive—and this often means they are critical of all about them. They see a world that puts greater store on solid (they would say, stolid) virtues and achievements than on their valued intangibles.

Dr. Donald W. MacKinnon of the Institute of Personality Assessment and Research at the University of California, Berkeley, has said:

"There is the necessity in the creative person for a certain amount of what the poets have called 'divine discontent.' "

The ferment of discontent with established patterns also is traceable to the history of many media people. When higher education attracted large numbers of young people, the established businesses and institutions were largely closed to the children of families not yet established. Accordingly, the women and non-WASPs who got college training and found the "establishment" barring

---

[7]See Chapter 47.
[8]See Chapter 15.

[9]Adapted from "Changing Media—a Challenge to Public Relations," *Public Relations Journal,* May, 1970, pp. 20-1.

them turned to avenues that were open—the media, as well as government, labor unions, social work, schools, and colleges. These institutions became largely staffed with well-educated, dedicated anti-establishment personnel. In turning from the "establishment," these young people also in many cases turned from the competitive system it represented to them. This was converted to rejection and scorn for the gross "practical" world.

Where the "media baron" who controlled voices of opinion in the past tended to be biased in favor of the *status quo,* many of the creative staffs of media today automatically favor anything that attacks it. In fact, there is a strong tendency on the part of some journalists to make over the world, and not just deal with events and interpretations of the news.

New forces of competition. First radio and then television heated up the competitive pressure among the media. Competition for audiences and, even more, for advertising support becomes more fierce constantly. Mass magazines find it hard to demonstrate their reasons for existence in a world of color television. Newspapers—even where there is a monopoly in a given city—find it harder to hold readers' attention and to keep advertising dollars ahead of rising costs. Costs of TV demand that audiences be vast so ad rates can be vaster. The pressure to grasp for attention—to sensationalize—intensifies.

In this climate, the reporter who produces a sensation is rewarded. The one who comes in with a solid but unspectacular report may find it hard to be appreciated. A media man who doesn't find a riot or crisis he can cover is tempted to wish for one.

The forces at work are augmented by the rapidly rising education and awareness of the public. A murder trial pales in interest when thousands are rioting or crowds shout for revolution. In other areas, such as science, the straight facts no longer are enough. Part of the reader's need is interpretation of the news. Especially in the print media, where space and time are available, it is the sensibility and sensitivity of the interpretation that mark the effective report.

Media as creators of news. All of the factors mentioned combine to alter greatly the role of the communications media. Where Hearst's ability to produce a war in 1898 was so exceptional it marked the history books, today the media are creating events at every turn. The TV broadcasters especially, apparently unaware of the great potency of their own medium, find it hard to recognize the impact of what they carry and are shocked when others question the consequences of treating equally such events as St. Patrick's Day parades and riots as spectacles.

The selection process, egged on by the hunger for sensation, crates "leaders" out of criminals who have minuscule followings—until the media anoint them.

This ability of the media to create "leaders" and "issues" by succumbing to the most unrestrained publicity hounds was noted as long ago as 1948 by Dr. Paul Lazarsfeld and Dr. Robert Merton of Columbia University in their paper "Mass Communication, Popular Taste and Organized Social Action":[10]

> "The mass media *confer* status on public issues, persons, organizations and social movements... Enhanced status accrues to those who merely receive attention in the media, quite apart from any editorial support. The mass media bestow prestige and enhance the authority of individuals and groups by *legitimatizing their status.* Recognition by the press or radio or newsreels testifies that one has arrived... that one's behavior or opinions are significant enough to require public notice... The audiences of mass media apparently subscribe to the circular belief: 'If you really matter, you will be the focus of mass attention, and if you *are* at the focus of mass attention, then surely you must really matter.'"

Now this process is accelerating in the area of issues and ideas. Countless problems in a rapidly changing and advancing society have been found by media—and some of them have been converted into crises.

Attention focusing on the media. While much that is remarkable and constructive has resulted from the media revolution, the force and importance of what has been happening inevitably has led to widespread concern. New looks at the role of the media have been called for from all elements of society. The ownership of many media by one organization, either locally or nationally; the right to renewal of broadcast licenses regardless of the caliber or type of programming offered; the question of balance in presentation of differing viewpoints; the nature and influence of some types of advertising—these and other matters are being questioned with increasing urgency. Inquiry is healthy, but there is always danger of suppression, of government influence on a free press, or of other aberrations.

---

[10]Reprinted in *Mass Culture; The Popular Arts in America,* edited by Bernard Rosenberg and David Manning White, The Free Press, New York, 1964.

New shifts in the media mix. The complexity in the media situation is further accentuated by trends that seem to reverse some of the patterns cited: The difficulties of the mass magazines, the pressure to break up large media combines and disperse influences of public opinion, the growing influence of publications reaching special-interest segments of the populace, and the appearance of new forms of media created by technology.

These trends may lead to many more media units—local cable TV stations, videotapes for rental or purchase, more media voices in many localities, expanded public broadcasting, more magazines, and newsletters devoted to specific interests. If so, they may bring a partial return of the personal, involved media owner who is close to his audience, sensitive to it, and influential with it.

It is clear that as great as the change has been in mass communications in just a few years, much more change is ahead. Old methods of dealing with them, based on the press release and the quiet event, are obsolete. Today's methods probably will also be obsolete before long. It will be one of public relations' greatest challenges to keep abreast of this multifaceted pattern.

THE NAME AS AN IMAGE FACTOR

The importance of concentrating on instilling readily identifiable characteristics of an organization into the minds of its publics is properly gaining recognition of management leaders. This accounts for the large number of changes in corporate names since 1950, a trend that seems to be continuing. It is difficult enough to get across the image of an organization without having it handicapped by a name that is inappropriate in any one of many ways.

This has led to a pell-mell, faddist rush toward "simplification" that has really bred confusion and difficulty. In an effort to derive names that are not at all misnomers, some companies have adopted names that are not names at all.

A random look at a list of companies big enough to be listed on the New York Stock Exchange reveals more than 50 with initials or coined names based on esoteric syllables. There are many others among smaller companies. Many of them are recognizable only by their own employees and a few other people. After years of trying, only a few companies with such coined names have succeeded in attaining distinctiveness in the minds of even sophisticated businessmen and financial specialists.

One of the basic principles of names is that the right degree of distinctiveness—not too difficult, but not commonplace or meaningless—is important if the owner of the name is to make a lasting impression.

It is easier to remember Martin Morrison than it is 384-1093. Henry Josephson is remembered more easily than John Johnson. It is easier to distinguish between Annotated Notes Company and Amplified Notions Systems than it is between ANC and ANS.

The loss of identity that can result from this lack of recognition can be costly. The name is the distillation of what the company is and stands for in people's minds. It is much more its "image" than any emblem or logotype. The recognition it creates affects its impression among prospective employees, potential investors, dealers, customers, and others. Coupon returns from direct-response advertisements decreased by 50 percent after Smith-Corona-Marchant changed its name to SCM Corporation.[11]

Factors in choosing a name. While there are many approaches to the selection of a new name, each of which has its proponents, it is important that the basic elements involved in the choice of a name be kept in mind during considerations. These include:

(1) It must be *euphonious*—pleasant to the ear, easy to say, not subject to such mispronunciation as is common with Uslife and Tesoto.

(2) It must be *memorable*—avoiding names that are too commonplace, such as "Smith," "National," "Universal," etc.; and easy to remember.

(3) It should create a feeling of *friendliness and warmth,* if possible; a good name of a person would be preferable to an institutional name like "Standard" or "Empire." The word "Corporation" is likely to create more resistance than "Company."

(4) It should be *timeless.* It must not only be effective and suitable for the present, but safe from any conceivable developments of the future. It should not be associated with any techniques, kind of product, or other factor that could be out-dated or limited by future events.

It is possible, for instance, that companies now using the name "National" will be embarrassed in their efforts to exploit world-wide markets; and, going further into the future, should these companies adopt "International" they may have to change later to "Interplanetary."

(5) The name should be *all-inclusive,* so it in no way limits future possibilities. For example, Hotpoint was a good name for an electric iron but

---

[11]The Gallagher Report, N.Y., Oct. 15, 1969.

Figure 55-1. Changes of corporate names are common and familiarizing people with a new name is difficult, but the former United Aircraft Corporation achieved awareness for its new name with print ads like this one and TV commercials. (See Chapter 47.)

somewhat anomalous on a refrigerator; Frigidaire is good for a refrigerator but not on a range. At the speed with which business and industry are developing, it is hardly possible now to predict what any company may be identified with thirty years in the future.

(6) It must be *unduplicated*—not only in its own business but, if possible, in any area of business. This is not only important in preventing confusion and legal complications; it can be devastating if a company in any line, having a similar name, should run into very unfavorable publicity.

(7) Similarly, the name must have *good associations* in the minds of all groups of people. It should not bring up unpleasant connotations or prejudices. As nearly as possible it should be a good "neutral" name.

(8) It should be *conducive to use* in a logotype, on labels, and in other printed forms. Some combinations of letters are had to distinguish at a glance or a distance, such as COATES, in which the capital "C" and capital "O" look so much alike.

(9) It should be *registerable* in all countries.

(10) It should have *quick acceptability*—not requiring a slow memorization or recognition process.

Despite the great attention being given to the name as an important image factor, there is no agreement on its role in marketing.

Exceptionally successful companies such as General Electric and IBM identify all products with the corporate name, feeling that its penetration fosters acceptance of each product. Equally successful companies such as Procter & Gamble and American Home Products subdue the corporate name and let each product develop acceptance under its own name.

The "umbrella-name" advocates point out that impressions much more massive than is possible for separate names accrue from total identification in advertising, publicity, cartons, truck signs, and other exposures.

The product-name advocates feel that the lack of success of one product or an unfavorable experience can too readily damage other products under the same corporate name. Products can be phased in and out of the market readily without affecting attitudes toward other products or the company. And a company can market products that compete with each other when they are named and marketed as competitors rather than as members of the same family.

Figure 55-2. Well-planned building projects convey the desired impression of an organization, as well as meeting its needs. This is the 850-foot sloping First National Bank of Chicago building. Adjacent is a landscaped plaza; a 32-story building is nearby.

THE EDIFICE AS A VISIBLE SYMBOL

Although North Americans have been in love with large or distinctive buildings for generations, it was not until recently that the great value of the symbolic building to a corporation's image has been widely recognized.

Early in the Twentieth Century the Woolworth Building in New York became known throughout the world, and helped make the company name distinctive. The Wrigley Building in Chicago was one of a few others that were overtly developed to focus distinction on their occupants. But the great majority of landmark buildings were, like the Flatiron in New York, not identified with any one firm. Even the major tenants in Rockefeller Center, such as RCA, were subdued in the identity of the whole development.

After World War II the erection of Lever House in New York and a series of distinctive regional headquarters offices of the Prudential Insurance Company awakened corporate managements to the possibilities. But while many firms erected buildings bearing their names, only a few achieved the distinctiveness and admiration that made their buildings stand out as widely recognized symbols. The Seagram Building in New York, the Deere headquarters in Moline, Illinois, the Connecticut General Life Insurance Company office in Hartford, the General Motors Research Center in Michigan, and the John Hancock Life Insurance Company building in Chicago have been among those that have achieved this symbolism.

Strong public interest in the total environment and the need for extensive facilities are moving companies toward complexes, rather than just buildings. The First National Bank of Chicago has developed an 850-foot sloping tower as its headquarters, a 32-story office building across the street, a two-story landscaped plaza with a four-sided mural by Chagall, and a huge fountain. The total complex is transforming the core of the city it is dependent on.

The next step may be toward whole environments, in which the company offices and facilities are the focus of a new community—inspired and motivated by the company, but not dependent on its paternalism.

Some companies have found pitfalls in their approaches to edifices. Architecture that sharply clashes with the character of the area and buildings that threaten to accent pollution or congestion have made their sponsors the objects of sharp attacks and boycotts. As in all other matters, sensitivity to the situation and attitudes involved is an essential ingredient of planning.

TRENDS AND FUTURE REQUIREMENTS

Increasingly it is important for the public relations person to help his or her organization anticipate and deal with future trends and developments, as well as present conditions. Sensitivity to what people are concerned with, research experience, and judgment combine to make the qualified public relations person better able to anticipate trends and to advise on courses of action than most other people.

For the intelligent and experienced person, the body lives in the present but the mind needs to live in the future.[12] What we do today is likely to have been largely determined by the time we do it—determined by our heritage, our training, our position, our outlook on the world. But what we do in the future will be largely determined by whether we let the future roll upon us, or we think about it and prepare ourselves for the shape it is likely to have.

Scarcely anywhere is this more true than in public relations. The greatest value of the public relations professional is in anticipating and shaping what is developing, not in reporting or coping with what has already been determined. By the time an organization is confronted with attitudes of its publics it is usually too late for public relations thinking to have an effect on them. Dealing with existing attitudes is important, but helping to shape and direct future attitudes is far more valuable.

In an era of widespread uncertainty, iconoclasm, and transformation, how can points of reference be found to serve as the foundation from which to detect the shape of the future?[13]

Here are five basics that can probably be counted on:

1. In every human society, no matter what else may wither or alter, the attitude of the people will determine what can and cannot be done. That has long been believed of Western democratic societies, but current events demonstrate its validity in such undemocratic societies as China, Russia, Africa, and Southeast Asia. We now know, from revelations about the underground in Nazi Germany during World War II, that even that most ruthless of controlled societies was permeated with dissent during the nation's life struggle. Stalin repeatedly felt the need to remove pockets of opposing attitudes, and the Russian people still fight their system. The Roman Catholic church is finding that when it loses rapport with the attitudes of millions of its members on a vital issue, its hold on them weakens. So whatever course our society may take, we can be sure the human climate will determine how it fares.

2. In human affairs, all excesses create their own demise. Nature hates untenable extremes as much as vacuums. The "1,000-year Reich" lasted 12 years because its excesses destroyed the stability necessary for any social system to continue. So extremism in the interest of any doctrine or dogma or discipline is certain to bring on its dissolution.

3. There will constantly be changes that create

---

[12]From Guest Editorial, *Public Relations Quarterly*, by Philip Lesly, Summer, 1976, p. 5.

[13]"The Problems in the Future," *ibid*, p. 10.

new challenges for those who must understand and deal with human attitudes. In today's volatile world there will be changes in technology, nature, demographics, ideas, tastes—all having impact on many aspects of our social structure and on each other. All these changes will create problems, needs, or opportunities for the organizations that employ or need skilled public relations people.

4. Excellence in mind and attitude ultimately will prevail over poor standards and destructive attitudes. If they should fail to prevail in North America, then those who have such standards and attitudes will surpass or conquer us.

5. Reality will prevail over wishfulness. It is still true that some people are smarter than others. There are limits to the resources that can be apportioned among people. Despite the ultimate expression of wishfulness—Alan Harrington's "Death is an imposition on the human race, and no longer acceptable"—man is mortal and still is subject to the consequences of his own neglect, his own delusions, and the ravages of time.

These verities provide some foundation for our speculations. We must constantly be sure that what we dream or plan remains in touch with these points, lest we build our castles on illusory horizons. But beyond these bases there seems to be little else that can be assumed. The expectations of futurologists have repeatedly been shattered by actual events—often while the binderies were still getting their prognostic volumes ready for distribution.

EVALUATION OF PUBLIC RELATIONS

Executives called on to utilize public relations services are rapidly increasing their understanding of the field. They are more and more aware of what its role can be, and what *cannot* be expected of it; how it should be evaluted, going far beyond the measurement of clippings and circulation; and how to judge the character and abilities of people who function in the field. This trend is the most heartening assurance that public relations will advance in standards, stature, and acceptance, since those who appropriate funds for it are becoming better able to sift out the ineffective, the misleading, and the inadequate.

Companies and organizations are basing their selection of public relations personnel or agencies on penetrating analyses of their skills as demonstrated in meeting challenging assignments, rather than on their persuasive oratory, graphic promises of results, and other irrelevant sales techniques.

Evaluation of services. The degree to which management is able to evaluate public relations services was demonstrated in a study made by Eugene Miller[14] in preparing a major report on public relations for *Business Week* magazine. He found the following seven criticisms of public relations most common among the management men he interviewed:

(1) The public relations man is too much of a "yes man" compared to many other of the staff persons who surround the top officers.

(2) The corporate brass often find the public relations man not very articulate at staff meetings. A certain shyness seems to set in.

(3) The public relations man has an inadequate grasp of business and economics generally. Of all the corporation staff people, he least understands business philosophy or basic marketing, production, or research.

(4) More specifically, the public relations man often doesn't understand the operations of the company he works for. He may have a good grasp of what is going on in marketing—perhaps labor relations. But he frequently comes up with a blank in the area of research and development, or finance.

(5) The public relations man frequently doesn't concern himself with the company's immediate problems. "My public relations man is talking about some sort of super-duper plant open house, when my immediate problem is upcoming labor negotiations. Why doesn't he give me a super-duper plan to help solve them?" asks one company vice-president.

(6) "In our company the department is known as the opera house. It has more prima donnas than the Metropolitan," was one comment.

(7) The public relations man is too sensitive on the point of whether his advice is taken or not. "My public relations man doesn't seem to get through his mind that his advice is only one of many pieces of advice and information I have to consider in making a decision."

Measurability. With business and other organizations moving precipitately toward using computers and other quantifying techniques to "get answers" and "organize" efficiently, there has been growing pressure to apply the same methods to public relations. Since this field deals with the most intangible

---

[14]See Chapter 11.

factors managers must cope with—human attitudes—the discomfort it can evoke in a man trained to be entirely practical and fact-oriented is understandable.

However, there is danger that the more effort that is made to apply standards of prediction and measurement to public relations, the more emphasis will be placed on the superficial and the more difficult it will be to make progress against the real problems.

There are several reasons for this:

1. The greatest resource of public relations is human intellect and creativeness. The very ability to perceive why people do not follow the expected patterns and how they might be reached with messages not projected previously is the greatest value a client can receive.

To the degree that direct measurements are attempted against these attributes, there is danger that the unremarkable and the undistinguished—what has been done before and therefore can be measured—will be emphasized at the expense of the unique and the excellent. If managements expect to be able to predict and measure quantitatively in public relations, public relations people will be inclined to confine themselves to things that are predictable and measurable, and the best thinking and creativity will be lost.

2. Public relations must deal with *changes* in attitude. It must lead its target, not follow it. The greatest source of problems and needs is *change*. If too much weight is given to what surveys and computer readouts show attitudes *were,* it is less likely that the public relations program will have an effect on what they *will be.*

3. In obtaining data for quantified judgments, it is necessary to probe into the minds of people. The human mind is murky and its ramifications multitudinous. And all the mental resources of the person are arrayed in defense of his private thoughts and feelings. It is not sound to assume that effective measurement of some attitudes indicates the possibility of accurately measuring all others. In any survey, interviewees' reactions are meaningful only when the subject is really meaningful to them: a major election, for instance. When queried about something less meaingful—such as acceptable profit margins of aluminum companies—they may answer, but the validity and stability of their answers—especially numerically and over a period of time—are dubious.

Tangible goals. While in cases where a very tangible goal of public relations work is involved the measurements can be more specific, it is extremely limiting and harmful to public relations to permit managements to feel that the tangible-goal program is the essence of public relations.

In every public relations program some sort of evaluation is called for. Usually this is a judgment by the client and the practitioner as to what progress is being made toward the objectives that have been clearly established. Aside from this, the differences are far greater than the similarities. No two programs should even be thought to be alike; it is individual differences and the relationships of human attitudes that make good public relations necessary and meaningful. To apply patterns from other programs is like using IBM cards to substitute for human relationships on a college campus or in a company's personnel program.

MOVES TOWARD PROFESSIONALISM

Five major factors have retarded the maturity of public relations as a profession:

1. It has grown very rapidly in response to needs. With effective sources of training developing much more slowly, many unqualified persons—often with unsound motives—have called themselves public relations specialists and offered their services. In many cases, they have been able to prosper, though damaging confidence in the field and its practices among many of those they have dealt with.

2. It covers an exceedingly wide scope. People with skills in arranging special events or in editing a company publication, for instance, are public relations practitioners. People who encounter such specialists, however, often do not understand the difference between a special range of experience and skill and the entire field. There is considerable difference between an opthalmologist and a psychiatrist—both of whom must have M.D. degrees—and often there is an equal difference between persons who have concentrated on separate aspects of public relations.

3. There have been forces within the field and outside that have created misunderstanding. Because journalists tend to interpret anything dealing with communication as a form of journalism, many writers have had a narrow view of public relations. Many articles have been based on the preconceived premise that "public relations" is a pseudo-journalist's snobbish term for trying to

"use" the press. As public relations has developed and many of its practitioners have prospered, this prejudice has sometimes been tinged with resentment. While treatment of public relations has tended to improve gradually, it is still among the most stubbornly distorted subjects covered by the press in general.

Some practitioners, in turn, have tended to create an aura of mystery about the field, to aggrandize their stature and to glorify talents supposedly only they can provide. This has included sweeping promises to make any business tycoon an international personage; assurances that social and economic tides can be reversed merely through propaganda "magic"; and claims of solving a great industry's problems by forming a committee and holding a conference. Propounding of terms like "engineering of consent" to describe a public relations man's functions, that imply both omnipotence and manipulation of the public, has aroused fears of intellectuals and public officials.

4. The fact that the best public relations service is often intangible and comparatively immeasurable has often made it easier for the charlatan to obtain an assignment than the sound practitioner. The man or organization that spells out specific promises where none can be made; who finds out what the prospect will buy and then develops his presentation accordingly, rather than on what sound judgment calls for; the periodic report that stresses visible items—selected press clippings and circulation figures, regardless of their relations to the problem and objective—these often appeal to the practical-minded management executive who is not trained to understand the nuances of public relations.

5. Until recently there has been little enforcement of any standards that practitioners are expected to meet.

Sources of criticism. Practices harmful to respect for public relations have been of two general types: those that result in widespread attention to malpractices, and those that are not exposed but still undermine confidence in the field. This may be said of any field of endeavor, from law and college teaching to operating subways. In the case of public relations, the first group has been far less numerous than the second, but the publicized exposes have been deeply impressed on the minds of many people.

They have included investigations of the Securities and Exchange Commission into stock promotion practices; investigations by the U.S. Senate into efforts of a few practitioners to foster foreign interests in the United States without listing themselves with the State Department, as required by law; and the monumentally publicized habit of the Watergate gang of using "public relations" and "pr" as terms for their dirty tricks and efforts to delude the public. None of the gang was truly a public relations man and none of the practices they attributed the terms to was acceptable among professionals in this field.

The fact that these three scandals involved less than twenty individuals—some of whom were exonerated—does not lessen their impact on the many thousands of sound and ethical practitioners.

More numerous are the lesser and less-visible abuses: attempting to suborn writers or broadcasters to carry publicity material or suppress unfavorable news; misleading prospective clients in sales presentations with almost-promises of results that cannot be obtained or predicted; seeking to get a client by calumniating a competitor; misrepresenting the size of the firm's staff or the clients it serves; falsifying or distorting reports to clients, and others.

As in almost all fields, the most common failing of practitioners is assuming assignments they are not qualified to perform. For this and all other reasons, the leaders in the field have long sought means of educating potential clients and employers so they will be inoculated against deception, and an enforceable set of standards and ethics to be applied to anyone seeking to function in this field.

Ethics and standards. In 1954 the Public Relations Society of America adopted a mild code of professional standards for its members. This was strengthened in 1959 and amended in 1963 and 1977. The text of this code appears in the Appendix.

The consultants in Great Britain in 1969 formed the Public Relations Consultants Association. It set up a code of practice that includes this clause often discussed by counselors in other countries but not enacted:

"12) A member firm shall not submit to a potential client detailed proposals for a public relations campaign or programme before appointment by that client without payment of a reasonable fee. This does not preclude a member firm from giving information about the services it can provide, or its suitability for the assignment or the general approach it would recommend."

This is aimed at the practice among some prospective clients of asking six to twenty-five firms to submit "proposals" as fully developed as possible, with no compensation to those not selected. In some cases, the list is then "narrowed down" to several who are asked to make further proposals before a selection is made. The British group feel that since this practice is not permitted in the true professions of medicine, law, architecture, and engineering, public relations cannot aspire to true professionalism until it forestalls such widespread competitive presentations.

In 1963, following extensive exposure of practices by a few public relations men in efforts to boost the market prices of clients' stocks, PRSA named a committee to work out with the Securities and Exchange Commission a specific code applying to financial public relations. The text of this code also appears in the Appendix.

Accreditation and licensing. In the early 1960's the Counselors Section of the PRSA began exploring plans to accredit counselors who met specified qualifications of training and reputation. When the plan was presented to the governing body of PRSA, non-counselor members feared that such accreditation for counselors only would give the impression such counselors had superior status to employees of corporations and other organizations. Since they out-numbered counselors, they voted to make the accreditation plan applicable to the entire PRSA membership.

While this program, effective with accreditation of the first group of members in 1965, is a step forward, it will be some time before its effectiveness can be evaluated. New applicants for membership must now agree to go through the accreditation procedure. Since it is administered by PRSA, which depends on membership for its revenues, there is a natural tendency to avoid any affront to a member or discouragement to a prospective member. This tends to set standards down to the base level of the membership's standards and abilities, rather than up to the levels to which the best practitioners aspire.

Another method of establishing standards is licensing by government. This has been written into law in Brazil, for instance. However, because restriction by government of opinion-directed activities could become a tool of a strong government to limit free speech, licensing has had few advocates in the United States. Journalists, broadcasters, and other communicators are not licensed.

While public relations goes through its process of maturing, the best means of raising standards and protecting the public interest will continue to be educating users of the service, the press, and the public on the true nature of the field. The reputation of the practitioner among clients and the best of his contemporaries is the surest measure of his stature and integrity.

GROWING NEED FOR BROAD SCOPE

For a time it appeared that the trend in the public relations field might be similar to that in other increasingly complex disciplines, toward development of specialists in the various phases. A number of such specialties were charted by enterprising workers in the field, such as financial public relations, community relations, government relations, and public affairs.

However, the indivisibility of a company's impression on the people it deals with; the fact that communications do not stop at imaginary lines between publics but inevitably overlap; and the practical advantage of dealing with all elements involved in an organization's non-selling communications have increased the need for full-scope public relations people as well as the specialists.

Adding increasingly to the requirements is the international scope of many organizations' relationships, carrying the need for a breadth well beyond the borderlines of the United States.

As a result, there is need for many intensified and specialized talents, but coordinated and integrated so they work effectively together and meet all the requirements of the client organization. This calls for either a large and expensive internal staff, including a good many specialists, some of whose talents will be required only part of the time; a broad public relations organization that can provide the talents and skills in all the necessary areas; or an internal staff augmented by the broad experience, judgment, and skills of an exceptional counsel. In many cases, a combination of the internal staff and the broad external organization is meeting the needs.

Accordingly, the opportunities in public relations are growing in both intensified specialization and broad over-all knowledge and talent. The way ahead for success for the individual can come from either direction.

In a world that at times seems to be tenuously held together by too-little-understood principles of group attitudes, the challenge and opportunities for the field that specializes in understanding and developing group attitudes still appear to be in their infancy.

Appendix

Bibliography

Note: Lists of publications dealing with working with Washington (federal government) appear in Chapter 5; on Research and Fact Finding in Chapter 36; and media lists and directories in Chapters 36, 38, 39, 40, 41, 42, and 43.

PUBLIC RELATIONS

Adams, Alexander B., *Handbook of Practical Public Relations.* Thomas Y. Crowell, New York, 1970.

Bernays, Edward L., *Biography of an Idea.* Simon and Schuster, New York, 1965.

Bernays, Edward L., *Public Relations.* University of Oklahoma Press, Norman, 1970.

Budd, John F. Jr., *An Executive's Primer on Public Relations.* Chilton, Philadelphia, 1969.

Bullock, Robert P., *School-Community Attitude Analysis for Educational Administrators.* Ohio State University, Columbus, 1959.

Canfield, Bertrand R., and F. Moore, *Public Relations.* 5th Ed. Richard D. Irwin, Homewood, Ill., 1973.

Center, Allen, *Public Relations Practices: Case Studies.* Prentice-Hall, Englewood Cliffs, N.J., 1975.

The Climate of Public Relations, two radio programs, 1965. Multigraphed copies available, The Philip Lesly Co.

Conversations on Public Relations, a series of four radio programs (pamphlet), The Philip Lesly Co., Chicago, 1967.

Critical Issues in Public Relations. Hill and Knowlton, New York, 1975.

Currah, Philip, *Setting Up a European Public Relations Operation.* Business Books Ltd., London, 1975.

Cutlip, Scott M., and Allen H. Center, *Effective Public Relations.* 4th Ed. Prentice-Hall, Englewood Cliffs, N.J., 1971.

Fairman, Milton, *The Practice of Public Relations.* (Booklet). Foundation for Public Relations Research and Education, New York, 1973.

Gilbert, W. H., ed., *Public Relations in Local Government.* International City Management Assn., Washington, D.C., 1975.

Golden, L.L.L., *Only by Public Consent.* Hawthorn Books, New York, 1968.

Henry, Kenneth, *Defenders and Shapers of the Corporate Image.* College and University Press, New Haven, 1972.

Hiebert, Ray, *Courtier to the Crowd* (story of Ivy Lee). Iowa State Univ. Press, Ames, 1966.

Hill, John W., *The Making of a Public Relations Man.* McKay, New York, 1963.

How to Start and Improve a PR Program. National School Boards Assn., Evanston, Ill., 1975.

Kelley, Stanley, *Professional Public Relations and Political Power.* Johns Hopkins Press, Baltimore, 1956.

Kobre, S., *Successful Public Relations for Colleges and Universities.* Hastings, N.Y., 1974.

Kurtz, Harold, *Public Relations for Hospitals: A Practical Handbook.* Thomas, New York, 1969.

Lendt, David L., *The Publicity Process.* Iowa State University Press, Ames, Iowa, 1975.

Lerbinger, Otto, *Designs for Persuasive Communications.* Prentice-Hall, Englewood Cliffs, N.J., 1972.

Lesly, Philip, *Public Relations in Action.* Ziff-Davis, Chicago, 1947.

Lesly, Philip, *You Are in Public Relations.* Pamphlet, National Research Bureau, Burlington, Iowa, 1966.

Lesly, Philip, *Having Your Say About the Future.* Pamphlet. National Research Bureau, Burlington, Iowa, 1971.

Managing Corporate External Relations. The Conference Board, New York, 1976.

Marcus, Bruce W., *Competing for Capital.* Wiley-Interscience, New York, 1975.

Marshall, Sol H., *Public Relations Basics for Community Organizations.* Creative Book Co., Hollywood, Calif., 1975.

Newsom, Doug and Alan Scott, *This Is PR: The Realities of Public Relations.* Wadsworth, Belmont, Calif., 1976.

Nolte, L. W., *Fundamentals of Public Relations.* Pergamon Press Ltd., Oxford, England, 1974.

Pimlott, J.A.R., *Public Relations and American Democracy.* Princeton University Press, Princeton, N.J., 1951.

Public Relations: Comprehensive Bibliography 1964-72. R.L. Bishop, ed., Foundation for Public Relations Research and Education, New York, 1974.

Public Relations for the Smaller Company. Research Institute of America, Mt. Kisco, N.Y., 1974.

Schmidt, F. and H.M. Weiner, *Public Relations in Health and Welfare.* Columbia Univ. Press, New York, 1966.

Simon, Morton J., *Public Relations Law.* Appleton-Century-Crofts, New York, 1969.

Simon, Raymond, *Perspectives in Public Relations.* University of Oklahoma Press, Norman, 1966.

Steinberg, Charles S., *The Creation of Consent: Public Relations in Practice.* Hastings, N.Y., 1975.

Walker, Albert, *Status and Trends of Public Relations Education in U.S. Senior Colleges and Universities.* (Booklet). Foundation for Public Relations Research and Education, New York, 1975.

Weiner, Richard, *Professional's Guide to Public Relations Services.* Prentice-Hall, Englewood Cliffs, N.J., 1975.

Who's Who in Public Relations, Robert L. Barbour and Adrian A. Paradis, Editors, PR Publishing Co., Exeter, N.H., 1976.

Woodress, Fred, *Public Relations for Community/Junior Colleges.* Interstate Publishers, Danville, Ill., 1976.

PUBLIC RELATIONS PERIODICALS

Channels. (Health and Welfare). Public Relations Society of America, 845 3d Ave., New York, N.Y. 10022. Monthly.

Communications for Health. Box A-G Port Jeff. Sta., New York 11776. Monthly.

Corporate Public Issues, P.O. Box 318, Old Greenwich, Conn. 06870. Semi-monthly.

Editor's Newsletter. Box 243 Lenox Hill Sta., New York, N.Y. 10021. Monthly.

Managing the Human Climate, by Philip Lesly, 33 N. Dearborn St., Chicago, Ill. 60602. Bimonthly.

Jack O'Dwyer's Newsletter, 271 Madison Ave., New York, N.Y. 10016. Weekly.

Practical Public Relations, P.O. Box 3861, Rochester, N.Y. 14610. Semi-monthly.

PR Reporter, Dudley House, P.O. Box 600, Exeter, N.H. 03833. Weekly.

Public Opinion Quarterly, Columbia U. Press, 510 Journalism Bldg., 116th St. & Broadway, New York, N.Y. 10027.

Public Relations Journal, 845 Third Avenue, New York, N.Y. 10022. Monthly.

Public Relations News, 127 East 80th St., New York, N.Y. 10022. Weekly.

Public Relations Quarterly, 44 W. Market St., Rhinebeck, N.Y. 12572.

Public Relations Review, College of Journalism, University of Maryland, College Park, Md. 20742. Bimonthly.

PUBLIC AFFAIRS

Adrian, Charles F., *Governing Our Fifty States and Their Communities,* McGraw-Hill, New York, 1972.

Adrian, Charles F., *State and Local Government.* McGraw-Hill, New York, 1972.

Athos, Anthony G., and Robert E. Coffey, *Behavior in Organizations: A Multidimensional View.* Prentice-Hall, Englewood Cliffs, N.J., 1968.

Berelson, Bernard and Gary Steiner, *Human Behavior.* Harcourt, Brace & World, New York, 1967.

Berelson, Bernard and Morris Janowitz, *Reader in Public Opinion and Communication* (2nd Edition). The Free Press, N.Y., 1966.

Brayman, Harold, *Corporate Management in a World of Politics.* McGraw-Hill, New York, 1969.

Cross, F.L. and R.W. Ross, *Corporate Communicator's Guide for Environmental Control.* Technomic, Westport, Conn., 1974.

Deakin, James, *The Lobbyists.* Public Affairs Press, Washington, 1966.

Klapper, Joseph T., *Effects of Mass Communication.* Free Press, New York, 1960.

Lazarsfeld, Paul F., Bernard Berelson and Hazel Gaudet, *The People's Choice.* Columbia University Press, New York, 1960.

LeBon, Gustave, *The Crowd.* Macmillan, New York, 1925; Ernest Benn, London, 1952.

Lerbinger, Otto and Albert J. Sullivan, (eds.), *Information, Influence and Communication.* Basic Books, New York, 1965.

Lippmann, Walter, *Public Opinion.* Macmillan, New York, 1965.

Lippmann, Walter, *The Public Philosophy.* Little, Brown, Boston, 1955.

McLuhan, Marshall, *Understanding Media.* McGraw-Hill, New York, 1964.

Riesman, David, *The Lonely Crowd.* Yale University Press, 1950.

Turner, Henry A., *American Democracy: State and Local Government.* Harper & Row, New York, 1970.

Ujifusa, Grant, Douglas Matthews and Michael Barone, *The Almanac of American Politics.* E.P. Dutton & Co., New York, 1975.

Wattenberg, Ben J., *The Real America: A Surprising Examination of the State of the Union*. Doubleday, New York, 1974.

PUBLICITY

Bloomenthal, H., *Promoting Your Cause*. Crowell, New York, 1971.

Brody, W. Austin, *Keeping Your Church in the News*. Fleming H. Revell Co., Westwood, N.J., 1959.

Crockett, W. David, *Promotion and Publicity for Churches*. Morehouse-Barlow Co., New York, 1974.

Daubert, H.E., *Industrial Publicity*. Wiley, New York, 1974.

Dowdy, Augustus W., Jr., *Phone Power*, Judson Press, Valley Forge, Pa., 1975.

Hall, Babette, *Public Relations, Publicity, Promotion*. Washburn, N.Y., 1970.

Klein, Ted and Fred Danzig, *How to Be Heard: Making the Media Work for You*. Macmillan, N.Y., 1974.

Kotler, Philip, *Marketing for Nonprofit Organizations*. Prentice-Hall, Englewood Cliffs, N.J., 1975.

Liebert, E.; Sheldon, B., *Handbook of Special Events for Nonprofit Organizations*. Association Press, N.Y., 1972.

PR Aids' Party Line. 221 Park Ave., South, New York, N.Y. 10003. Weekly.

Weiner, Richard, *Professional's Guide to Publicity*. Richard Weiner, New York, 1975.

PUBLIC OPINION AND POLLING

Carlson, Robert O., *Communications and Public Opinion: A Public Opinion Quarterly Reader*. Praeger, N.Y., 1975.

Edison, Michael and Susan F. Herman, *Public Opinion Polls*. Franklin Watts, Inc., New York, 1972.

The Facts About Political Polls. U.S. News and World Report, v. 77, October 7, 1974; 34, 37.

Gallup, George, *The Sophisticated Poll Watcher's Guide*. Opinion Press, Princeton, N.J., 1972.

Issacs, Stephen, *The Pitfalls of Polling*. Columbia Journalism Review, May/June 1972; 28-34.

Merrill, John C. and Ralph L. Lowenstein, *Media, Messages and Men, New Perspectives in Communication*. David McKay Co., Inc., New York, 1971.

Scammon, Richard M. and Ben J. Wattenberg, *The Real Majority*. Coward-McCann, New York, 1970.

Shaw, David, *Political Polls: How to Avoid the Distortions*. Los Angeles Times, January 3, 1975: 1, 3, 10, 11.

Stein, Robert, *Media Power*. Houghton Mifflin, Boston, 1972.

Stevens, G.E., *Public Opinion Polling*. Richards Rosen Press, New York. n.d.

COMMUNICATIONS

Blum, Eleanor, *Basic Books in the Mass Media*. University of Illinois Press, Urbana, Ill., 1972.

Emery, Edwin and others, *Introduction to Mass Communications*. Dodd, Mead Co., New York, 1973.

Ewing, David W., *Writing for Results: In Business, Government & the Professions*. Wiley-Interscience, New York, 1974.

Morris, John D., *Make Yourself Clear! Morris on Business Communication*. McGraw-Hill, N.Y., 1962.

Sigband, Norman B., *Communication for Management and Business*. Scott, Foresman, Chicago, 1976. (2nd edition).

Steinberg, Charles S., editor, *Mass Media and Communication*. Hastings House, New York, 1972.

Wales, LaRae H., *A Practical Guide to Newsletter Editing and Design*. Iowa State U. Press, Ames, 1976.

PROPAGANDA

Brown, J.A.C., *Techniques of Persuasion from Propaganda to Brainwashing*. Penguin, Baltimore, 1963.

Davison, W. Phillips, *International Political Communication*. Praeger, New York, 1965.

DeFleur, Melvin L., *Theories of Mass Communication*. David McKay Co., New York, 1970.

Efron, Edith, *The News Twisters*. Nash, Los Angeles, 1971.

Ellul, Jacques, *Propaganda*. Alfred A. Knopf, New York, 1965.

Gordon, G.N., *Persuasion: Theory and Practice of Manipulative Communication*. Hastings House, New York, 1971.

Lerbinger, Otto, *Designs for Persuasive Communication*. Prentice-Hall, Englewood Cliffs, N.J., 1972.

MANAGEMENT AND POLICY

Ackerman, Robert W., *The Social Challenge to Business*. Harvard University Press, 1975.

Anshen, Melvin, (ed.), *Managing the Socially Responsible Corporation*. Macmillan, New York, 1974.

Auger, Bertrand Y., *How to Run Better Business Meetings*. Business Services Press, St. Paul, 1966.

Carvell, Fred J., *Human Relations in Business*. Macmillan, New York, 1975.

Champion, Dean J., *The Sociology of Organizations*. McGraw-Hill, New York, 1975.

Christopher, William F., *The Achieving Enterprise*. American Management Associations, New York, 1974.

Corporate Directors' Handbook. SEC Reporter, Washington, D.C., 1974.

Davis, Keith and Robert L. Blomstrom, *Business and Society: Environment and Responsibility*. McGraw-Hill, New York, 1975.

Drucker, Peter, *Management: Tasks, Responsibilities, Practices*. Harper, 1974.

Finkel, Coleman, *Professional Guide to Successful Meetings*. Successful Meetings Magazine, New York, 1976.

Gellerman, Saul W., *The Human Factor in Organizations*. Penguin, Baltimore, 1974.

Herzberg, F., *Work and the Nature of Man*. World Publishing Company, New York, 1966.

Heyel, Carl, (Ed.), *The Encyclopedia of Management*. Van Nostrand Reinhold, New York, 1973.

Illich, John, *The Art and Skill of Successful Negotiation*. Prentice-Hall, Englewood Cliffs, N.J., 1973.

Jacoby, Neil H., *Corporate Power and Social Responsibility: A Blueprint for the Future*. Macmillan, New York, 1973.

Leavitt, Harold J., *Managerial Psychology*. University of Chicago Press, Chicago, Ill., 1972.

Lesly, Philip, *The People Factor: Managing the Human Climate*. Dow Jones-Irwin, Homewood, Ill., 1974. (Available from The Philip Lesly Company, Chicago.)

Linowes, David F., *The Corporate Conscience*. Hawthorn Books, New York, 1974.

Maslow, Abraham, *Motivation and Personality*. Harper & Row, New York, 1954.

McGregor, Douglas, *The Human Side of Enterprise*. McGraw-Hill, N.Y., 1960.

Mitchell, Ewan, *Businessman's Guide to Speech Making and to the Laws and Conduct of Meetings*. International Publications Service, New York, 1968.

Moore, Wilbert E., *The Conduct of the Corporation*. Random House, New York, 1962.

New York Times Financial and Business News Editors, *How to Read and Understand Financial and Business News*. Doubleday, Garden City, New York (n.d.).

Roalman, A.R. (Editor), *Investor Relations Handbook*. Amacom, New York, 1974.

Sethi, S. Prakash, *Up Against the Corporate Wall; Modern Corporations and Social Issues of the Seventies*. Prentice-Hall, Englewood Cliffs, N.J., 1974.

Steiner, George A., *Business and Society*. Random House, New York, 1975.

Zausner, Martin, *Corporate Policy and the Investment Community*. Ronald, New York, 1968.

POLITICAL PUBLIC RELATIONS

Agranoff, Robert, (ed.), *The New Style and Technique of Election Campaigns*. Holbrook Press, Boston, 1972.

American Federation of Labor-Congress of Industrial Organizations. Committee on Political Education. *How to Win*. Washington, D.C., 1972.

Atkins, Chester G., *Getting Elected: A Guide to Winning State and Local Office*. Houghton Mifflin, Boston, 1973.

Bloom, M.H., *Public Relations and Presidential Campaigns*. Crowell, N.Y., 1973.

Bruno, Jerry and Jeff Greenfield, *The Advance Man*. Morrow, New York, 1971.

Chartrand, Robert L., *Computers and Political Campaigning*. Spartan Books, New York, 1972.

Hiebert, Ray et al, *The Political Image Merchants: Strategies in the New Politics*. Campaign Workers Handbook. Acropolis Books, Washington, D.C., 1971.

Napolitan, Joseph, *The Election Game and How to Win It*. Doubleday, New York, 1972.

Nimmo, Dan, *The Political Persuaders: The Techniques of Modern Election Campaigns*. Prentice-Hall, Englewood Cliffs, N.J., 1970.

O'Brien, Lawrence, Robert J. Dole and Rogers C.B. Morton, *The Political Image Merchants*. Acropolis, Washington, D.C., 1971.

Parkinson, Hank, *Winning Political Campaigns with Publicity*. Campaign Associates, New York, 1973.

Parkinson, Hank, *Winning Your Campaign: A Nuts-and-Bolts Guide to Political Victory.* Prentice-Hall, Englewood Cliffs, N.J., 1970.

Roll, Charles W., and Albert H. Cantril, *Polls: Their Use and Misuse in Politics.* Basic Books, New York, 1972.

Rosenbloom, David L., *The Election Men: Professional Campaign Managers and American Democracy.* Quadrangle Books, New York, 1973.

Schwartzman, Edward, *Campaign Craftsmanship: A Professional's Guide to Campaigning for Elective Office.* Universe Books, New York, 1973.

Shadegg, Stephen, *The New How to Win an Election.* Taplinger, New York, 1972.

Simpson, Dick W., *Winning Elections: A Handbook for Participatory Politics.* Swallow Press, Chicago, 1972.

Totaro, Ronald, *How to Conduct a Political Campaign with the Systematic Analysis Study System.* Vantage Press, New York, 1971.

JOURNALISM

Alexander, Louis, *Beyond the Facts.* Gulf, Houston, 1975.

Ashley, Paul P., *Say It Safely: Legal Limits in Publishing, Radio and Television* (rev. ed.). U. of Washington, Seattle, 1976.

Bagdikian, Ben H., *The Information Machines: Their Impact on Men and the Media.* Harper & Row, New York, 1971.

Gehman, Richard, *How to Write and Sell Magazine Articles.* Harper & Row, New York, 1959.

McNaughton, Harry H., *Proofreading & Copyediting.* Hastings House, Philadelphia, 1973.

Meredith, Scott, *Writing to Sell.* Harper & Row, New York, (3d Edition), 1974.

Sheehan, Paul V., *Reportorial Writing.* Chilton, Radnor, Pa., 1972.

Tebbel, John, *The American Magazine.* Hawthorn Books, New York, 1969.

Tebbel, John, *The Media in America.* Crowell, New York, 1974.

Editors of UPI Broadcast Services, *United Press International Broadcast Stylebook.* UPI, New York.

Williamson, Daniel R., *Feature Writing for Newspapers.* Hastings House, Philadelphia, 1975.

Wolfe, Tom, *The New Journalism.* Harper & Row, New York, 1973.

TELEVISION AND RADIO

Bittner, John R., and Denise Bittner, *Radio Journalism.* Prentice-Hall, Englewood Cliffs, N.J., 1977.

Brown, Les, *Television: The Business Behind the Box.* Harcourt Brace Jovanovich, New York, 1971.

Diamont, Lincoln, *The Broadcast Communications Dictionary.* Hastings House, New York, 1974.

If You Want Air Time: A Handbook for Publicity Chairmen. National Association of Broadcasters, Washington, D.C. (Pamphlet).

Lewis, Carolyn, *Politicians on TV: The Good, Bad and Awful.* Washingtonian, v. 10, March 1975: 157-162.

Mayer, Martin, *About Television.* Harper & Row, New York, 1972.

Mickelson, Sig., *The Electric Mirror: Politics in an Age of Television.* Dodd, Mead & Co., New York, 1972.

Mitchell, Curtis, *Cavalcade of Broadcasting.* Follett, Chicago, 1970.

Price, Monroe and John Wicklein, *Cable Television: A Guide for Citizen Action.* Pilgrim Press, Philadelphia, 1972.

Schwartz, Tony. *The Responsive Chord.* Anchor Press-Doubleday, Garden City, N.Y., 1974.

Television Contacts, 1975-76. Larami, 151 E. 50th St., New York 10022.

The Video Handbook, Media Horizons, New York, 1972.

INTERNAL COMMUNICATIONS

Anderson, Walter G., *Handbook of Business Communications.* New York, 1975.

Bently, Garth, *Editing the Company Publication.* Harper & Row, N.Y., 1972.

Carter, Robert M., *Communication in Organizations.* Gale Research Co., Detroit, 1972.

Case Studies in Organizational Communication. McGraw-Hill, New York, 1975.

Coffin, Royce, *The Negotiator: A Manual for Writers.* American Management Associations, New York, 1973.

Darrow, Ralph, *House Journal Editing.* Interstate Printers, Danville, Ill., 1975.

Gebbie Press House Magazine Directory. National

Research Bureau, Burlington, Iowa. Every three years.
Goldhaber, G., *Organizational Communication.* W.C. Brown, Dubuque, Ia., 1974.
Heyel, C., *How to Communicate Better with Workers.* Clemprint Inc., Concordville, Pa. (n.d.).
Vordomon, George T. and Patricia B. Vordomon, *Communication in Modern Organizations.* John Wiley & Sons, New York, 1973.

FILMS AND AUDIO/VISUAL

Babin, Pierre, ed., *The Audiovisual Man.* Geo. A. Pflaum, Publisher, 1970.
Baddeley, W. Hugh, *The Technique of Documentary Film Production.* 3d Edition. Hastings House, N.Y., 1973.
Bunyan, John and James Crimmins, *Television and Management.* Knowledge Industry Publications, White Plains, N.Y., 1977.
Hack, John, *How to Make Audiovisuals.* Convention Press, Nashville, 1973.
Hayett, William, *Display and Exhibit Handbook.* Van Nostrand Reinhold Co., New York, 1967.
Jensen, Mary and Andrew, *Audiovisual Idea Book for Churches.* Augsburg Publishing House, Minneapolis, 1974.
Jones, G. William, *Landing Rightside Up in TV and Film.* Abingdon Press, Nashville, 1973.
Klein, Walter J., *The Sponsored Film.* Hastings House, N.Y., 1976.
Millerson, Gerald, *Basic Television Staging.* Hastings House, N.Y., 1974.
Millerson, Gerald, *The Techniques of Television Production.* Hastings House, New York, 1972.
Nisbett, Alec, *The Technique of the Sound Studio.* Hastings House, N.Y., 1973.
The Video Bluebook. Knowledge Industry Publications, White Plains, New York, 1975.
Westmoreland, Bob, *Teleproduction Shortcuts: A Manual for Low-Budget Television in a Small Studio.* University of Oklahoma Press, Norman, 1974.
Wolfe, Betty, *The Banner Book.* Morehouse-Barlow Co., New York, 1974.
Wyman, Raymond, *Mediaware: Selection, Operation and Maintenance.* William C. Brown Company, Dubuque, Iowa, 1969.

GRAPHIC ARTS, PRINTING AND PRODUCTION

Bowman, W., *Graphic Communication.* John Wiley & Sons, New York, 1967.

Ceynor, Marvin E., editor, *Creativity in the Communicative Arts.* Whitston Publishing, New York, 1974.
Enrick, Norbert L., *Effective Graphic Communications.* Auerback Publishers, Princeton, N.J., 1972.
Gillis, Don, *The Art of Media Instruction.* Crescendo Book Publications, Dallas, 1973.
Hurley, Gerald D. and Angus McDougall, *Visual Impact in Print.* American Publishers Press, Chicago, 1971.
Moller-Brockmann, Josef, *Grahic Artist and His Design Problems.* Hastings House, New York, 1968.
Murgio, Matthew P., *Communications Graphics.* Van Nostrand Reinhold, New York, 1969.
Pilditch, James, *Communications by Design: A Study in Corporate Identity.* McGraw-Hill, New York, 1970.
Production Yearbook. Colton Press, New York. (Annual).
Rosen, Ben, *The Corporate Search for Visual Identity.* Van Nostrand Reinhold, New York, 1970.
Spencer, Herbert, *The Visible World.* Book Dept., Graphic Arts Monthly, Chicago, 1969.
Turnbull, Arthur T., and R.N. Baird, *Graphics of Communication.* Holt, Rinehart & Winston, New York, 1968.
Wales, La Rae H., *A Practical Guide to Newsletter Editing and Design.* Iowa State University Press, Ames, Iowa, 1976.
White, Jan V., *Editing by Design.* R.R. Bowker, New York, 1974.

SEMANTICS AND USAGE

Ayer Public Relations and Publicity Style Book. Ayer Press, Philadelphia, Pa., 1974.
Benjamin, Robert L., *Semantics and Language Analysis.* Bobbs-Merrill, Indianapolis, 1969.
Bernstein, Theodore M., *The Careful Writer.* Atheneum, New York, 1965.
Blake, R.H. and E.O. Haroldson, *A Taxonomy of Concepts in Communications.* Hastings House, N.Y., 1975.
Boettinger, Henry M., *Moving Mountains: The Art and Craft of Letting Others See Things Your Way.* Macmillan, New York, 1969.
Condon, John C., *Semantics and Communication.* Macmillan, New York, 1966.
Evans, Bergen and Cornelia Evans, *A Dictionary of Contemporary American Usage.* Random House, New York, 1957.

Flesch, Rudolf, *The Art of Readable Writing.* Harper & Row, New York, 1974.

Follett, Wilson, *Modern American Usage.* Hill & Want, New York, 1968.

Fowler, H.W., *A Dictionary of Modern English Usage.* 2nd Ed., Oxford University Press, New York, 1965.

Gordon, George N., *The Language of Communication, a Logical and Psychological Examination.* Hastings House, New York, 1970.

Hayakawa, S.I., *The Use and Misuse of Language.* Premier, N.Y. (n.d.).

Kierzek, John M. and Gibson Walker, *Handbook of Writing and Revision.* Macmillan, New York, 1967.

Korzybski, Alfred, *Science and Sanity.* Science Press, Lancaster, Pa., 1958.

Leggett, Glenn, C. David Mead and William Charvat, *Handbook for Writers* (Seventh Edition). Prentice-Hall, Englewood Cliffs, N.J. 1978.

Meadow, Charles T., *Sounds and Signals— How We Communicate.* Westminster Press, Philadelphia, 1975.

Mencken, Henry Louis, *The American Language.* Alfred Knopf, New York, 1963.

Morris, William and Mary Morris, *Harper Dictionary of Contemporary Usage.* Harper & Row, New York and Evanston, 1975.

Newman, Edwin, *Strictly Speaking.* Warner, New York, 1975.

Newman, Edwin, *A Civil Tongue.* Bobbs-Merrill, New York, 1976.

New York Times *Manual of Style,* New York, 1977.

Postman, Neil, Charles T. Weingartner, and Terence P. Morgan, *Language in America.* Pegasus, New York, 1970.

Strunk, William Jr., and E.B. White, *The Elements of Style.* Macmillan, New York, 1959.

University of Chicago *Manual of Style.* University of Chicago Press, Chicago, 1969.

U.S. Government Printing Office Style Manual. U.S. Government Printing Office, Washington, D.C., 1973.

Wentworth, Harold and Stuart Berg Flexner, *Dictionary of American Slang* (2d Edition). Crowell, New York, 1975.

Winkler, G.P., *The Associated Press Stylebook.* The Associated Press, New York.

PUBLIC SPEAKING

Howell, William S., and Ernest G. Bormann, *Presentational Speaking for Business and the Professions.* Harper & Row, New York, 1971.

Jay, Antony, *The New Oratory.* American Management Associations, N.Y., 1971.

Larson, Orvin, *When It's Your Turn to Speak.* Harper & Row, New York, 1971.

Tacey, William S., *Business and Professional Speaking.* William C. Brown, Dubuque, Ia., 1975, 2d Edition.

ADVERTISING

Advertising Federation of America, *Books for the Advertising and Marketing Man;* a classified bibliography. Bureau of Research and Education, New York. Revised Periodically.

Barton, Roger, (Ed.), *Handbook of Advertising Management,* McGraw-Hill, New York, 1970.

Controversy Advertising. (Group Authorship). Hastings House, N.Y., 1977.

Kleppner, Otto, *Advertising Procedure.* Prentice-Hall, Englewood Cliffs, N.J., 1970.

Riso, Ovid, *Advertising Cost Control Handbook.* Van Nostrand Reinhold, New York, 1973.

Riso, Ovid, (Ed.), *Sales Promotion Handbook.* The Dartnell Corporation, Chicago, 1973.

Sethi, S. Prakash, *Advocacy Advertising and Large Corporations.* Lexington Books/Heath, Lexington, Mass. 1977.

Simon, Julian, *The Management of Advertising.* Prentice-Hall, Englewood Cliffs, N.J., 1971.

Wright, John S., Daniel S. Warner and Willis L. Winter, Jr., *Advertising.* McGraw-Hill, New York, 1971.

FUND RAISING

Phillips, E. Hereward, *Fund Raising Techniques and Case Histories.* International Publications Service, New York, 1969.

Seymour, Harold J., *Designs for Fund Raising.* McGraw-Hill, New York, 1966.

Sheridan, Philip G., *Fund Raising for the Small Organization.* J.B. Lippincott, Philadelphia, 1968.

Glossary

Acetate. Transparent plastic sheet used in layouts. Also, base of photographic film.

Advance. Story, feature, or speech manuscript distributed before the event.

Advertising. Persuasive material that is presented to the public as acknowledged appeal of an identified party. It is almost always paid for, and therefore fully controlled in context, presentation, medium, and time by the appealing party. In some instances, an item may be called either advertising or publicity, such as posters, brochures, and industrial motion pictures.

Agate. A type size, 5½ points. There are 14 agate lines to an inch. The agate line is the standard unit of measurement for advertising space.

Air Brush. An art process widely used for retouching photographs, applied with aid of compressed air and an air brush. Also used by many illustrators to obtain interesting tone effects.

Air Check. Tape made of TV or radio content when it is aired.

Air Time. Starting time of a TV or radio program.

Alignment. Arrangement of type so that the bottom of the characters are in a straight line. May also be applied to positioning of type and illustrations for pleasing effect.

Angle. Particular emphasis of a story or broadcast; also called "slant."

Annual Report. A financial statement by management, required by the Securities and Exchange Commission. Frequently summarized and translated into layman's language for distribution to stockholders and interested media.

Answer Print. Print of a motion picture film used to check quality, before final printing.

Antique-Finish Paper. A stock with a soft, fluffy surface used primarily for type matter. Will take wood cuts and line illustrations but not halftones, except in the very highest grades. This stock varies widely in grade.

Art. All types of illustration in any medium.

Ascender. The element of a lower case letter extending above the body of the letter such as in b, d, h.

Attitude. The composition of a person's bent on any issue or question, made up from all the influences that have built up throughout his lifetime. Usually unexpressed.

Audience. Denotes the group or groups to whom the public relations program, or any part thereof, is directed.

Author's Alterations. Changes made in subject matter after proofs have been submitted; changes not due to errors by the typesetter. Author's alterations are far more costly than original composition and are charged in addition to original rates.

Backgrounder. A document prepared to provide the facts and significance underlying a subject, as a means of "backgrounding" an editor or writer.

Backtiming. Figuring from end of a public relations program or broadcast, to determine how all segments will be scheduled.

Back Up. When one side of a sheet has been printed and the reverse side is being printed, it is said to be backed up.

Balloon. A device most commonly used in cartoons and comics to connect the dialogue with the speaker within the area of the illustration.

Bank. A table on which galleys rest in a composing room.

Banner Head. Headlines set in large type and usually extending all the way across the top of a page.

Bearers. Extra metal on an engraving or metal strips placed around type forms to strengthen and protect them during electrotyping.

Beat. 1. An area or subject that a medium assigns to a given reporter or department, such as the criminal courts or boating. 2. An exclusive story; a "scoop."

Beeper. Device attached to a telephone that "beeps" every 14 seconds, as required by FCC, to indicate conversation is recorded. Also, recorded telephone interview on TV or radio.

Behavior Pattern. A recurrent way of acting toward a given object or in a given situation.

Ben Day. A process, named after its originator, that enables photo-engravers to produce a variety of shadings in line plates. This process reduces the amount of artwork necessary to obtain the effects desired and makes it possible for the engraver to prepare a line cut rather than the more expensive halftone.

Blanking Out or Breaking for Color. Forms run in two or more colors must be broken or separated and spacing material must be inserted where lines have been lifted to print in different colors.

Bleed. When printed matter is trimmed so that illustrations run off the edges of the sheet, it is said to bleed. At least one-eighth of an inch should be added on all bleed sides of an illustration to facilitate trimming and assure a proper bleed.

"Blow Up." Increase the size of any visual item by photographic reproduction.

Blurb. Short description of story or article, usually used to promote it.

Body Type. As distinguished from *display* type used in headlines, body type is that used for the text. Rarely is body type larger than 14 points in size; rarely should it be in less than 8-point size for readability, in public relations work. The body type of this book is 10-point, leaded 2 points and the body type of this glossary is 10-point, leaded 1 point.

Boiler Plate. Cast-metal reproductions of newspaper stories and illustrations, sent by syndicates to small newspapers that have limited facilities for typesetting. Often full pages of boiler plate are used by small country papers, to fill in the space not occupied by local items or advertisements.

Boldface Type. A blacker, heavier type than its regular or medium counterpart in any given type face. The elements are made thicker for boldface than the normal width for the regular face, to make the matter stand out from the surrounding copy. The headings of sections in the text of this book are boldface type.

Bond Paper. Paper ranging in grade from a low-grade sulphite to 100 per cent rag content. Used mainly for office stationery.

Booklet. A printed piece of six or more pages, with a paper cover and prepared as a bound unit, usually by stapling. (See *Brochure*.)

Boomerang-Effect. In propaganda, when the affected individual reacts in the opposite from the expected way.

Box. A newspaper item enclosed within printed borders.

Bridge. Phrase or sentence connecting two stories or segments of a telecast.

Broadside. A printed piece intended for quick reading and motivation to quick action. Printed on one side of a single sheet.

Brochure. A printed piece containing six or more pages. More elaborate than a booklet.

Burnishing. Mechanical act of spreading dots in a halftone to change the tone of certain areas to deepen the hue.

Business Publications. Periodicals directed primarily to business and financial groups.

By-Line. Signature of the author on a newspaper or magazine story.

Cable Television (CATV). Also called Community Antenna Television. A means of transmitting signals to receivers through direct cable connections rather than over the air.

Camera Copy. Copy ready for reproduction by offset or lithography.

Campaign. An organized effort to poll, formulate, or alter the opinion of any group or groups on a selected subject.

Candids. Unposed but effective photographs.

Caps. Capital letters.

Caption. Descriptive matter accompanying an illustration. Also referred to as a *cut-line*.

Casting Off or **Scaling.** Estimating the space that copy set in a given type size will occupy.

Catalogue. A book of reference, including a description and, if possible, an illustration of products and other pertinent data, such as instructions for their use and care.

Cathode Ray Tube (CRT). Electronic vacuum tube with screen on which information, story material, or images can be displayed.

Cell. Also photocell. Optical reader.

Center Spread. The two facing center pages of a publication appearing on a continuous sheet.

Channel. A place on television dial where a station can be received. Also, in communication, one of avenues for reaching an audience.

Character. A single unit of type, such as a letter, number, or punctuation mark.

Chase. Metal frame placed around a type form.

Cheesecake. Photographs depending for their appeal on display of feminine sex appeal. "Leg art."

Circular. A mailing piece or free-distribution item, usually one sheet. An item intended for widespread, inexpensive distribution.

Circulation. For print media, number of copies put into the hands of readers; often substantially less than readership because of multiple use of each copy. In broadcasting, number of people who regularly or often view or listen to a station.

Class Publications. Periodicals designed to appeal to particular, well-defined groups, interested in certain limited subjects.

CLC. In typesetting, capital and lower-case letters.

Client. Organization or individual employing public relations counsel or other service.

Clip. In broadcasting, a short segment taken from

the whole or to be spliced in. In print media, a clipping.

Clipping Returns. Clippings of stories or other published material mentioning a specific subject, taken from newspapers, magazines, trade journals, specialized publications, and/or house organs. Most frequently these are obtained from commercial clipping services that supply clippings from numerous publications for a flat rate per clipping.

Clipsheet. A printed page of stories and/or illustrations, sent to publications so they may clip out any item they may wish to use. Combines a number of releases into one mailing and provides editors with a quick means of judging story-value and length.

Coated Paper. Enamelled stock coated with a mixture of casein, china clay, or other finish to give paper a hard, smooth finish suitable for fine halftone reproduction.

Cold Composition. Typesetting without molten metal. Includes typewriting and photocomposition.

Colophon. A few lines at the end of a book telling who designed the book, who printed it, and what type faces and paper stock were used. Rarely done at present except for especially fine editions. Also used as term for the imprint of a publishing house.

Color. (1) To exaggerate or distort. (2) Background or mood material to accompany factual report. (3) Colored art or printing.

Column Rule. Printed vertical line between columns of type.

Combination Plate. The combining of a halftone and line plate in one engraving.

Combination Publication. A publication distributed both to an organization's own employees or members and to outside groups or individuals.

Comic Book. A leaflet or magazine using the comic strip method to tell its purpose.

Communication. v. The transaction of conveying thought from one party or group to another.

Communications. n. The processes of conveying thought from one party or group to another. Also, the thought so conveyed.

Community. The adjacent geographical area influenced and affected by company policy and production.

Composition. Setting type. Also, arrangements of the elements in a paragraph.

Condensed. Type with a narrower face than the regular face.

Conference Report. A summary of the points discussed, actions taken, and assignments made at a conference among various members of an organization, or between members of the organization and its counsel.

Conservation. Support of the public's existing opinion and preventing it from changing.

Consumerism. The composite of movements and causes purporting to protect the consumer in the purchase of goods and services, product safety, and other matters.

Continuity Strip. A form of advertisement that simulates in appearance a newspaper comic strip and tells a complete story in plot sequence.

Control Group. Group in which the members are chosen for their characteristics or opinions. Often, a group not exposed to a test that is used as a comparison to a test group in equating results.

Conversion. To sway public opinion from one side of an issue to another.

Copy. Written material, such as press releases, the text of booklets, broadcast material, or a magazine article.

Copy Desk. Editors' center at newspaper, magazine, TV or radio station where copy is edited and headlines written.

Copyreader. Editor who reads and corrects copy and usually writes headlines.

Correspondent. Out-of-town or traveling reporter.

Coverage. Extent of distribution of publicity or opinion-affecting material.

Cover Stock. Sturdy papers used for pamphlet and booklet covers, posters, memo cards, announcement cards, and similar purposes.

Cropping. Changing the proportions or size of an illustration to eliminate unnecessary or undesirable background or to enable the reproduction to fit into a specific space.

Crystallization. Bringing into public consciousness previously vague or subconscious attitudes.

Cut. A term most often used for an engraving of an illustration, either line or screened, to be used in letterpress printing. A cut can be made of metal, wood, as in wood engravings, or a plate with a raised printing surface made from a matrix, etc.

Cutline. Photo caption.

Cylinder Press. A press with a cylinder around which the paper travels as it is pressed against the printing form.

Dateline. Line at start of a story giving point of origin and date.

Deadline. Time when story must be completed.

Dealer Imprint. Name and address of dealer printed

GLOSSARY

on leaflet, pamphlet, poster, or similar matter, usually in space set aside for this purpose.

Debrief. Originally, to interrogate a serviceman after return from combat area. Now includes interviewing members of an organization on their readings of public attitudes.

Deckle-Edge. Ragged edge of a sheet of paper.

Delete. "Take out" or "omit" from copy.

Demographics. Various characteristics of an audience—age, sex, size of family, economic status.

Descender. The element of a lower case letter extending below the body of the letter as in g, j, p, q, and y.

Display Face. Type or hand lettering, normally larger than 14 points, used for headlines.

Documentary. Informational film or television show with a unified subject or purpose.

Double Truck. Same as center spread when two pages are in chapter of publication and on same sheet. Otherwise, two full facing pages.

Drop-In Ads. Advertising messages that are added to regular advertisements of a different character.

Dry-Brush Drawing. A drawing made with ink or paint that is thick and dry, usually on coarse board.

Dub. To transcribe one medium onto another, such as sound from a tape onto soundtrack of a film or videotape.

Dummy. Sheets of paper cut and folded to the size of a proposed printing job. Layouts can be drawn on the dummy and finished dummy may be made from proofs to portray how the finished job will appear.

Duographs or **Duotones.** Two halftone plates made from a one-color illustration; etched to produce two-tone effect.

Ears of a Newspaper. Boxes or messages appearing at the upper left- and right-hand corners of publications alongside the masthead.

Editorialize. Inject opinion into a news story.

Electrostatic Copier. A machine employing a process by which paper is given an electrostatic charge to which a powder adheres.

Electrotypes (or Electros). Printing plates made by electrolysis from original composition or plates. They are made from wax or lead molds. They are much cheaper than original and duplicate photoengravings. When long runs or several copies of plates or forms are required, it is a wise economy to order electros and hold the original material for future electrotyping. In preparing material for distribution to a large number of newspapers, in which the expense of shipping would be an additional cost factor, *mats* or *flongs* should be used instead of electros.

Eleemosynary Institution. An institution that is dependent on or supported by charity.

Element. Any line in the face of a type.

Em. The square of the body of any given type. Usually refers to the pica em, which is 12 points square.

Embossing. Pressing a piece of paper between two dies so that the impression is made to stand above the surface of the rest of the sheet.

En. Half an em.

Enamelled Stock. See *Coated Paper*.

English Finish (E.F.). A paper smoother and less bulky than antique. Has a hard, even, unpolished surface suitable for printing 100- to 120-line screen halftones by letterpress. Also suitable for gravure printing. Widely used for folders, booklets, magazines, and house organs.

Engraving. A plate, usually zinc or copper, that has been etched (with acid in most cases) to obtain a raised surface for printing by letterpress. Engravings are reproductions of either line illustrations or halftones (screened).

Also called photoengravings because they are made by being brought into contact with film negatives of illustrations, engravings in commercial usage refer almost solely to letterpress, although in the past the term "engraving" more properly was used to refer to the intaglio processes.

Etching Proofs. Sharp, clean proofs from which the zinc etchings can be made.

Exclusive. Article, story, or broadcast show limited to one medium or network.

Extended or **Expanded.** Extra wide typeface.

External Publication. A publication issued by an organization to people outside its own employee or membership groups, such as to customers, the local community, the financial world, etc.

Extra Condensed. Especially compressed typeface.

Face. The uppermost part of a piece of type. The printing surface. Also used to differentiate one style of type from another.

Facsimile. An exact copy or reproduction of something, usually produced by a mechanical or photographic process from the original. Also the electronic process of transmitting exact copies of printed or photographic material over long distances. Also called **fax.**

Fact Sheet. A document containing essential facts, usually in non-narrative form, on a given subject.

Family. All of the series of one type face in all its variations.

False Front. An organization created to give the appearance of support for a cause from a segment of the populace it does not represent.

Feature. (1) A story based more on interest or background than on news. (2) The main topic of interest in a story.

Feed. Electronic signal sent from the source to other outlets.

File. Send story by wire or electronic means.

Filler. A short bit of copy used in making up the pages of a publication to fill small spaces.

Fill-In Stories. Press releases drafted at a central point for filling in of specific information locally or on a great many separate individuals. Local dealers may be quoted and their stores cited; or promotions of members of the armed forces may be processed for hometown papers.

Financial Analyst. A specialist in studying and evaluating securities. May be with a brokerage house, bank, institutional investor, or investment counselor.

"Flack." A press agent. Standard in entertainment business, usually derogatory elsewhere.

Flag. Front page title of a newspaper.

Flagship Station. The major, usually program-originating, station of a broadcasting network.

Flong. See *Matrix*.

Flyer. A mailing piece prepared to announce or promote new merchandise, a sale, special offer, or an event.

FM. Frequency modulation; broadcasting in higher frequency bands that are freer from distortions and static than **AM** (amplitude modulation).

Fold. Where the page of a newspaper is folded in half.

Folder. A printed piece of four pages. Also a four-page heavy-paper container for other printed materials.

Folio. Page number.

Follow-Up. A broadcast or story that follows a news report; also known as second- or third-day story.

Font. An assortment of type face in one size.

Form. Pages of type and illustrations locked in a rectangular iron frame called a *chase*.

Format. Size, shape, and general make-up of a publication.

Foundry Proofs. See *Etching Proofs*. Characterized by heavy borders of black foundry rules.

Four-Color Process. Reproduction of full-colored illustrations by the combination of plates for yellow, blue, red, and black ink. All colored illustrations are separated photographically into these four primary colors. The four-color process is applicable to the letterpress, offset, and gravure processes.

Frame. (1) Single picture in film footage. (2) 1/30 of a second in TV, 1/24 of a second in film. (3) A single illustration on a storyboard.

Franchise-Building Services. Activities aimed at firmly establishing an organization's purposes in the minds of various publics—building a "franchise" with them for carrying on its functions.

Free-Lance. An unaffiliated writer, photographer, cameraman, artist, or other person who is available on assignment or contract basis.

Freeze. Single frame of film used as a still picture.

"Gag." A created event, sometimes fictitious, developed by a press agent to seek media coverage.

Galley Proofs. Proofs not made up in page form, but drawn from the type as it stands in galley trays following composition, or as it is reproduced from cold type.

Ghosted View. An X-ray view of the subject of an illustration.

"Ghost Writer." One who writes speeches, articles, or other manuscripts that will be presented as the work of his employer or client.

Glossy Print. A smooth, shiny-surfaced photograph. Most suitable form for reproduction. Also called "glossy."

Good Will. The favorable attitude of other persons or groups toward any person, institution, or group.

Grain. The direction in which the fibers of paper lie. Paper folds best with the grain. Against the grain it is likely to crack or fold irregularly. Also, fuzziness in a photograph or film.

Grapevine. Informal word-of-mouth process of disseminating information or rumors.

Graphics. Illustrative material in all media.

"Grass Roots." The dispersed membership or constituency of an organization throughout a geographical area, such as a country or a region. The anonymous, scattered holders of opinions or attitudes.

Gravure. A form of intaglio printing.

Halftone. A screened reproduction of a photograph, painting, or drawing.

Hand Composition. Type set by hand.

Hand Lettering. Lettering drawn by hand as distinguished from typeset letters.

Handout. Publicity release, especially when it is widely distributed rather than given as an exclusive.

"Hard Sell." Overt, forceful effort to persuade, such as advertising about a product's merits or a direct argument on behalf of an idea.

Head. Headline or title of a story.

Headnote. Short text before beginning of an article, usually featuring its highlights and information about the author.

Highlight Halftone. A halftone in which whites are intensified by dropping out the dots, usually by hand tooling.

Hold. Refrain from publishing or broadcasting until authorization is given.

Hold for Release. Material not to be printed or broadcast until a designated time or under specified conditions.

Home-Town Stories. Stories, prepared for the local newspapers, of individuals who are participating in an event or activity.

House Magazine. Internal publication.

Human Interest. Feature material appealing to emotions, such as humor, sympathy, or passion.

"Image." The subconscious impression a person has of an organization, institution, or person. Based on the interaction of all exposures he has had to the subject of the image. A "corporate image" is the supposed impression toward a company held in common by a whole public.

Imposition. Preparing a form for printing so that all parts will be in correct position when printed.

Initial Letter. First letter in a block of copy, usually equal to two or three times the depth of a line of the copy. Used as an ornament and attention getter, frequently in another color.

Input. Information fed into a data processing system. By extension, information obtained in the process of human considerations.

Insert. Printed matter prepared for enclosure with letters. Also, new material inserted into a story already written.

Institutional Investors. Non-personal holders of blocks of securities: mutual funds, insurance companies, pension funds, banks, universities, etc.

Intaglio Printing. A process in which the design is scratched, engraved, or etched into the plate, "dug down" below the general level of the metal and filled with ink, so the transfer will show only the design. **Kinds of Intaglio:** rotogravure, engraving (in the strict sense).

Internal Communications. Communications with personnel or membership of a company or organization.

Internal Publication. A publication directed to the personnel or membership of a company or organization.

Interviewer. A person who asks respondents the questions specified on a questionnaire in an opinion or market survey. Also, a person who seeks information for media use—a newspaper reporter, a television or radio panel show moderator, etc.

Job Press. Press taking small forms, normally under 25x38 inches.

Jump and **Jump Head.** Continuation of a story on a later page in a publication, and the head put on the continuation.

"Junket." A trip for press people at the expense of the organization seeking publicity. Usually based on need to see what is distant from press centers, such as a new plant, a new resort, or a convention. Many media will not accept payment of expenses for such trips.

Justification. The arrangement of type and spacing in a line so that type completely fills a line and is the same length as adjoining lines.

Kicker. A short line over the headline.

Kill. To eliminate part or all of a story or to discontinue a program or broadcast.

Kinescope. A film made of a transmitted television picture.

L.C. Lower-case letters. The small letters in the alphabet.

Laid Paper. Paper with a watermarking having appearance of slight parallel vertical or horizontal ridges.

Layout. An outline for presentation of material for publication or reproduction within the confines of the previously designated format.

Lead. (pronounced "leed"). The beginning of a newspaper story. Also, a tip on a potential story.

Lead. (pronounced "led"). A thin strip of metal, usually lead alloy, placed upright between lines of type to spread them apart, in order to give a less compact appearance on the printed surface. Leads can be 1, 2, or 3 points thick, and are less than "type-high" so that they do not print. Ten-point type lines separated by 2-point leads, for example, are said to be "10-point leaded 2 points." (See also *slug*.)

Leaders (pronounced "leed-ers"). Dots used to direct the eye from one part of the copy to another.

Leaflet. A printed piece, usually of four pages.

Leg Man. Reporter who goes after information and phones or wires it to office.

Letterpress. A printing process in which the ink is applied to raised type and plates and then applied to the paper by direct pressure.

Letterspacing. Placing thin spaces between letters.

Light Pen. Tube with photocell used to edit or revise text stored in computer and displayed on cathode ray tube.

Line Function. In a large organization the "line" structure is the operating force, such as managers and personnel of manufacturing plants or officers of combat units in the armed forces. A function of this line is something to be executed, rather than basic planning.

Lineprinter. Computer-related device for printing out complete lines of copy from the memory bank.

Linotype. Machine that sets full lines of type in metal.

Lithographic Printing. Transferring an inked image from a smooth surface to paper by a chemical (mutual repulsion of grease and water) process. Kinds of lithographic printing: Planography, offset lithography, offset printing, photo-offset.

Lithography. Printing from a flat surface.

Live. Performed or reported now; not recorded.

Localize. Make specific references to a locality in a mass-distributed story or broadcast.

Logotype or **Ligature.** Combination of two or more letters on the same body such as fi, ff, fl. Company trade names prepared on one base, usually a zinc etching, generally are called logos.

Long Shot (**LS**). Photo or film shot from a distance.

Machine Finish (M.F.). Paper that has not been calendered. Cheapest paper that will take halftones well. Has dull finish.

Make-Ready. Preparing forms on press for printing.

Make-Up. Putting type and engravings in proper positions in printing form.

Management. Those persons charged with the responsibilities of determining company or organization policy and planning and directing operations.

Management Chart. A diagram that illustrates the lines of responsibility and authority within an organization.

Manual. A compilation of directions and instructions in book or booklet form.

Markup. Proof with corrections and changes indicated.

Mass Publications. Periodicals having a wide variety of appeal and a large, general circulation.

Masthead. Name of publication and staff, usually boxed and appearing in each issue.

Mat or **Matrix.** A papier-mâché impression of a printing plate, from which a lead casting can be made to reproduce the material on the original plate.

Matte. Dull finish on illustrations. Needed to prevent glare from stills on television.

Media. Avenues through which public relations messages are transmitted. Common media (singular is "medium") include newspapers, magazines, radio, books, music, paintings, cartoons, posters, leaflets, brochures, speeches, window displays, car cards, trade or business papers, envelope stuffers, calendars, house publications, motion pictures, slide films, television.

Merchandising. Promotion of a product or idea by making it attractive, easier to buy, and/or more desirable.

Microwave Relay. Sending broadcasts from one point to another by ultra high frequency signals.

Mimeographing. A process for reproducing typewritten or hand-worked material by use of a wax stencil on a rotary-operated machine. Effective up to about 2,000 copies from one stencil.

Mock-Up. A scale model used for study, testing, or instruction.

Model. (1) A person employed to pose in photographs, style shows, or other activities. (2) A representation of large entity, to provide a smaller, inexpensive means of visualizing it. A model of a new skyscraper, for instance, may be shown in a company's lobby or used in photography to approximate the appearance of the building.

Model Release. A document signed by a model allowing use of pictures of the model.

Monitor. (1) TV receiver used to watch broadcasts or closed-circuit signals. (2) To review a broadcast station's content.

Morgue. The department of a publication that contains clippings, reference materials, illustrations, and other source materials. It sometimes

GLOSSARY

incorporates the traditional library of reference works.

Multigraphing. A trademarked process for making numerous copies of typewritten or hand-drawn material. More closely resembles hand typing than does mimeographing.

Multilithing. A process for reproducing large numbers of copies of typewritten material.

Multiple-Channel Approach. Impressing an idea or subject on an audience by utilizing many types of media and communications, to "surround" them with it.

Multiplier Effect. Using a communications device that stimulates many others to disseminate the same information. For example, a folder of press stories that members of an organization in many areas use with local media.

Newsletter. A publication in letter-size format, usually issued periodically.

Network. Linkup of two or more broadcast stations to carry the same material.

Newsprint. The paper on which most newspapers are printed. Also used for inexpensive printed material.

Offset. (1) A process of lithography. (2) When the ink on one printed sheet smudges or marks the back of the sheet on top of it. This can be prevented by slip-sheeting.

Op Ed. Opposite editorial. The page facing the editorial page in newspapers. Some are now devoted in part to statements from non-staff sources.

Open End. Broadcast material in which time is left at beginning or end for addition of material by the station.

Open House. An event in which a company invites its employees, dealers, suppliers, and/or its community to visit it and see how it operates. A device of employee, stockholder, supplier, dealer, and/or community relations.

Opinion. A person's view on an issue or subject as he articulates it. More conscious than an *attitude*.

Optical Center. A point equidistant from the left and right sides of a sheet of paper and five-eighths of the way from the bottom.

Optical Reader. Electronic reader of printed material.

Outline. The skeleton or gist of an article or a program.

Outtake. Filmed or taped material not used in the final program.

Overline. See *kicker*.

Overrun. Printing trades practice permits delivery and charge for up to 10 per cent more than the quantity of printed matter ordered.

Overset. Excess typeset material, beyond what is published.

Over the Counter. Stocks not sold on a registered exchange.

"Over the Transom." Pertaining to material submitted to a medium without its request. Unsolicited offerings.

Page Proof. Proof of the type and engraved matter as it will appear in final page form.

Pamphlet. A printed piece of a few pages, with a paper cover. Often interchangeable with "leaflet," except that a pamphlet may contain more pages than the word "leaflet" will permit.

Panel. An area of type different in size, weight, or design from the text and usually wholly or partially surrounded by text. Also, a group of persons used in research to provide information repeatedly. Also, a group sharing discussion on a subject at a meeting.

Paste-up. A dummy.

Perforating. Punching small holes in paper, making it easy to detach a part of the sheet.

Photo Composition. A method of setting type photographically to produce proofs on paper or film without the need for handling and inking metal types.

Photo-Offset. A printing process by which the image is first transferred to a rubber blanket and then from the blanket to the paper.

Photo-Montage. A layout of photographs in which the pictures blend into each other to give the effect of unity.

Photoprint. Reproduction of a printed, typewritten, or other document by any of a number of photographic copying processes.

Photostat. A trademarked device for making photographic copies of drawings, maps, text.

Pica. Basic printing measure of 12 points.

Picturephone. Telephone service providing simultaneous transmission of voice and picture.

Pied Type. Type that is all mixed up.

"Pitch." The idea that the source wants to get across to his audience. To "make your pitch" is to present your argument.

"Pix." Photographs.

Planograph. An inexpensive offset printing process. Also, any piece of printed material produced by this process.

Planting. Placing publicity material with the media.

Plate. Any engraving or electrotype used to reproduce artwork in printing. The term "plate" is also applicable to the printing surfaces in gravure and offset.

Plug. A free and favorable reference.

The Point and the Pica. The standard unit of measure used by printers is the point. It is 0.01384 inch. For most purposes, consider that 72 points equal one inch. The pica is exactly 12 points. Thus there are 6 picas to the inch. Lengths of type lines are specified in picas. Half picas are used, never quarters or thirds of a pica. Sizes of type and amounts of leading are specified in points.

Policy. The basic tenets of an organization that determine the pattern of its attitude and activities.

Poll. A survey of the attitudes, opinions, and/or desires of a specified group of people.

Position Paper. A document that presents an organized exposition of an organization's position on a given issue. It may be used with the media, with government bodies, or in other ways.

Posture of Receptivity. Readiness of a person to receive and respond to communications from a given source.

Precinct Principle. Organization of a campaign through delegation of local responsibilities to chosen leaders in each community, as in the precincts of a city in a political campaign.

Presentation. Offering of a program or services at a meeting. May involve written materials, graphic displays, films, or other materials.

Press Agentry. Seeking publicity by creating news of a flighty or dubious sort.

Press Conference. A meeting called to inform members of the press about an event or news subject, and to provide them an opportunity to ask questions and explore their areas of interest in the subject.

Prestige. The reputation and standing of a person, institution, or group.

Pretesting. Sampling techniques in a survey to be confident they are right before setting up the complete survey pattern.

Price-earnings Level or Ratio. Multiple of stock market price of security on basis of its current earnings per share. For example, a stock selling at $100 and having current after-tax earnings of $10 a year would be at a 10-to-1 price-earnings level.

Prime Time. Broadcast hours when the potential audience is largest—usually weekday evenings.

Process Plates. Sets of two, three, or four plates for printing in colors. Colors are laid on paper one over another.

Program. The planned outline of activities for a campaign.

Promotion. Special activities designed and intended to create and stimulate interest in a person, product, organization, or cause.

Proof. Inked impression of type and engraved matter. The process of taking the impression is called "pulling a proof."

Propaganda. An effort to influence the opinion of others.

Proposal. Materials organized to offer plans for a program or services. A proposal may be used at a presentation or submitted by mail or hand delivery.

Proxy. Written authorization given by a stockholder to someone else to vote his stock.

Proxy Fight. Combative effort by a stockholder or group to win the voting support of stockholders holding the controlling number of shares.

Proxy Statement. Document required by government regulation and stock exchanges, detailing for stockholders all information pertinent to a request for their vote or proxy on any question or group of questions to be acted on at a meeting of stockholders.

Public (plural, Publics). Any group of individuals that a public relations program seeks to influence. A committee of three may be a public; so may a firm's stockholders, its employees, its customers, its community; so may a legislature, the entire nation, the world.

Public Relations. All activities and attitudes intended to judge, adjust to, influence, and direct the opinion of any group or groups of persons in the interest of any individual, group, or institution. Also helping an organization and its publics accommodate to each other.

Publicity. A technique of public relations. A message purposefully planned, executed, and distributed through selected media to further the particular interest of the client without specific payment to media.

Puffery. Exaggeration or unsubstantiated material appearing in publicity.

Puff-Sheet. A publication that survives by consciously giving favorable mentions to advertisers and others who aid it financially.

Pulp. Term used to describe magazines printed on rough, wool-pulp paper, as contrasted with "slicks," which are magazines printed on coated or calendered stock.

Punch. Emphasis or vigor in story or broadcast material.

Quads. Blank pieces of metal less than type high used to fill out a line of type.

Quarterly Report. Statement of a company's sales and earnings experience for three months. Issued for first, second, and third quarters of the year. Often contains information on other developments in the quarter reported.

Query. Written inquiry to an editor or broadcaster outlining a proposed story or treatment.

Questionnaire. The body of questions asked of persons interviewed in a survey of attitudes, opinions, intentions, desires, activities.

Quoins (pronounced "coins"). Metal wedges used in locking up a form.

Quote. (1) A quotation used in a story. (2) Quotation mark. (3) A price estimate.

Rear Screen Projection. Projection of transparencies behind a speaker or newscaster so they will be seen as background.

Recap. Recapitulation of subject matter, series, or program.

Reduce. Decrease the size of any visual item in reproducing it.

Relief Printing. When the design on the block or plate is raised above the general level, so that when the roller charged with ink is passed over the surface the ink can touch only the raised portions, the process is called relief, or letterpress, printing.

Register. The correct position in which a form is to print. In color printing it means the exact position for superimposition of each color in order to blend the colors properly.

Registrar. An agent or officer of a corporation appointed to keep a record of its securities and to certify that the name on each certificate issued is that of the owner of record. Often a bank or trust company.

Release. n. A manuscript prepared for issuance to the press or broadcast media.
v. To issue material to the press or broadcast media.

Release Date. The time and day on which information issued to the press and broadcast media is to be exposed to public view. A release date is justified when it coincides with an occurrence that has not yet taken place, such as a speech.

Reprint. A second or new impression of a printed work (book, magazine or newspaper article, chart or graph, picture or map, and the like). If a photographic process is used, the subject may be enlarged ("blown up") for framing, window display, or poster; or reduced. Additions or deletions can readily be made before reprinting.

Respondent. The person of whom questions are asked in a survey.

Retouch. To improve by artwork the definition of photographs for halftone reproduction.

Reverse. To run printed material (especially cuts) with white type on a dark background. Also, in making a cut from a picture, to turn over the negative so that everything falls in an opposite direction.

Review. Commentary on event, art, or performance.

Rewrite Man. Journalist who writes stories from material provided by others.

Roman Type. Most commonly used kind of type as distinguished from Text, Script, and Gothic. Roman type, distinguished by serifs, comes in modern and old-style groups.

R.O.P. Color. Run-of-press use of color in newspapers; added color or full-color materials (advertisements or illustrations) produced on regular press run at same time as black.

Rotary Press. Press that prints from curved stereotypes bolted to a cylinder.

Rotogravure. Printing by means of a sensitized copper cylinder on which the image to be reproduced is etched. "Roto" is the familiar abbreviation.

Rough. Preliminary draft of manuscript or visualization of graphic.

Rough Cut. First editing of film before effects, titles, and sound have been added.

Roundup. Story prepared from material derived from various sources.

Routing. Cutting out a part of plate or engraving so it will not print.

Rule. Thin strip of type-high metal that makes a line on paper.

S. and S.C. Sized and super-calendered paper.

Saddle Stitching. Binding pages by stitching with wire through fold.

Sample. The portion of the total population involved in a survey, of whom questions are asked. The sample is intended to be representative of the total population involved.

Sans Serif. Letters without serifs.

Scaling. Measuring and marking illustrations for engravings.

Security Analyst. Financial analyst.

Segue (say'-gway). An uninterrupted transition, as when one scene moves directly into another in a motion picture.

Selective Attention. Singling out particular objects from among many for concentration of the mind.

Selective Reinforcement. Tendency to pick out of many ideas or messages those that confirm an opinion or attitude already held.

Self-Cover. Printed matter in booklet form without a protective cover.

Self-Mailer. Printed folder prepared for mailing without an envelope.

Series. All the fonts of one kind of type.

Serifs. Small decorative lines on letters at the ends of elements. The most distinguished feature of some faces. The lines, or "flares," at the ends of the elements in the individual letters of the text and display type used for this book are properly called serifs.

Shelter Books. Magazines that feature home furnishings.

Sidebar. A secondary story that accompanies a main news story or feature article, sometimes in a box set into the larger story.

Side Stiching. Method of stitching thick booklets by pressing wire staples from the front side of the booklet and clinching in back. Pages cannot be opened flat.

Signature. (1) The formalized construction of a company's name as it appears on stationery, advertisements, and other printed material. Often used interchangeably with **logotype**.
(2) A printed sheet containing 4, 8, 12, 16 or 32 pages, folded into one unit and forming a portion of a book or pamphlet.

Silhouette or Outline Halftone. Halftone in which all background has been removed.

Silk Screen. A stencil process using fine cloths that have been painted with an impermeable surface except where color is to come through.

Silver Print. Proof, taken on sensitized paper, of negative for offset plate. Used as final proof before plates are made. Sometimes referred to as a Vandyke, or simply "blues."

Simulcast. Simultaneous transmission over television and radio.

Sizing. See *scaling*.

Slant. Emphasis given in a story or program.

Slick. A publication published on coated, smooth paper.

Slidefilm (or film strip). A continuous strip of film in which the frames are presented in a fixed sequence, but not simulating motion. Usually accompanied by a recorded sound track that is synchronized with the succession of the film frames.

Slides. Individual film frames that are projected onto a screen to serve as visual accompaniment to an oral presentation.

Slip-Sheet. Paper placed between sheets of printing to prevent offsetting or smudging.

Slug. Lead thicker than 4 points. Used between lines of type.

Slug Lines. Words placed at the upper left of a story to identify the story during typesetting and make-up of a publication.

Soft News. Feature news or news that has no immediate timeliness.

"Soft Sell." Indirect, subtle effort to persuade without overt presentation of arguments on the issue. Motivation by indirect techniques.

Spike. To kill copy.

Split Play. Treatment of a news event in which one side of an issue is presented prominently first, and the other side not until later. Often results from second party being unprepared or late in issuing its information.

Split Run. Publication in part of the total circulation of a newspaper or magazine.

Split Screen. Two or more images shown simultaneously in a TV transmission.

Spread. An advertisement, group of related photographs, or copy that occupies two facing pages in a publication, usually without separation by "gutters," and usually printed from a single plate.

Squib. A short story in a newspaper or magazine. Sometimes, a short second heading that tells more about a long story.

Staff Function. Analysis, planning, or communications by an organization's headquarters, as opposed to the execution of tasks by the line or divisional forces.

Standing Head or Matter. Headings or type used repeatedly.

Stereotype. Plate cast by pouring molten metal into a matrix or flong. An inexpensive form of duplicating plates used generally by newspapers.

Stet. Proofreader's designation to let copy stand—to disregard change marked previously.

Stock Letters (or stories, etc.). Letters prepared at a central office that are provided to members or others in various areas for their dissemination.

Story "Angle" or "Peg." The distinctive interest element that makes a story notable or newsworthy.

Storyboard. Sequence of roughs depicting the continuity of television program contact or commercials.

Straight Matter. Copy without any display lines.

"Street Name." Securities that are held for the in-

GLOSSARY

vestor by his broker, and not identified with him, are listed on the stock registrations in the broker's name. "Street names" may be a shield of secrecy for buying up blocks in seeking to gain control of the company.

"String Man." A reporter in a given area who is available on call to cover stories for a medium headquartered elsewhere.

Stuffer. A printed piece intended for insertion into pay envelopes, packages delivered to customers, with bills and receipts, or any other item that provides a medium of delivery.

"Stunt." A created event developed by a press agent to evoke publicity.

Style Book. Manual setting up standards for handling copy—i.e., spelling, capitalization, abbreviations, word usages, and so on.

Subhead. Small heading within a news story or article to break up solid type mass and catch reader's eye.

Surprint. Superimposing type or lettering upon an illustration. This method retains the type as a solid, unbroken by screen.

Survey. An analysis of a market or state of opinion among a specified group of persons, groups, or institutions.

Tabloid. A newspaper format, smaller than standard size, and usually having five columns per page, each page being slightly more than half the size of a standard paper.

Takeover Bid. An effort to assume control of a publicly held company without the approval of the management. This may be through election by stockholders of a controlling number of directors, or through purchase of a controlling proportion of the shares.

Talent. Actors, performers, musicians, models—usually in television or motion pictures.

Tally Light. Red light on TV camera indicating its picture is being transmitted.

Teaser. Material that stimulates interest in forthcoming media content without providing specifics.

Telecommunications. Long-distance transmission of signals.

Teletype. An electronic system of transmitting information in typewritten form. Used in operation of the various public relations newswires, as well as by the Associated Press and United Press International.

Teletypesetting. Setting type from punched tape, enabling one source to provide exact typeset material to many linotype locations.

Tender Offer. Offer to purchase a designated number of shares of a corporation at a specified price by a specified date. This is often, but not always, intended to acquire enough shares to control the corporation.

Terminal. A place in a communication system where information can either leave or enter.

Test Group. A group selected for reaction to or use of a product or an idea.

Testing. To sample the opinion or acceptance of a carefully selected and well-defined area or group on any particular product, event, or question. Tabulated results frequently serve as the basis for determining the direction of a larger campaign.

Text. The body of any written material—the copy.

Threshold of Consciousness. The point at which a given subject passes out of the mass of unperceived subjects into the awareness of the individual.

Tie-In. A promotional technique used to describe the joint (or combined) activities of two or more organizations on one project.

Tint Block. Solid color area on a printed piece.

"Tipping-In." A printing process used to insert or attach extra pages or other items. Example: pages 5 and 6 of a ten-page booklet are "tipped-in"; a swatch in a textile catalog is also "tipped-in."

Trade Publications. Periodicals dealing with matters of interest to a particular trade or industry.

Transfer Agent. An office, usually a bank or trust company, that acts for a corporation in transferring stock from one owner to another.

Transparency. A plastic or film reproduction, through which light can be projected to show its full contents on a screen. Color transparencies are commonly used in making color plates for printing.

Trim. (1) In publications, reduce length of copy. (2) In printing, cutting pages to final size. *Trim size* is the dimension of the final printed item.

Type Page. The printed area on a page. The area around the type page is the margins. Inside margins, adjacent to the fold, are called gutters.

Typo. Typographical error.

UHF (ultra high frequency). The added band of television broadcast channels in the U.S., added to the 2-to-12 group to provide added outlets.

U. and l.c. Upper and lower case; capitals and small letters.

Underrun. Printing trades practice permits an allowance of 10 per cent less than the total printing order as completion of an order. Normally, the printer provides for an overrun, but excessive spoilage in printing or in binding may cause a slight shortage.

Update. Bring the information in a story up-to-date.

Upper Case. Another term for capital letters.

Vandyke. See *Silver print*.

Varitype. A form of typewriter with many alternate type fonts.

VHF (very high frequency). The original band of television broadcast channels in the U.S., 2 through 12.

Video. The visual television signal.

Videophone. Combined telephone and television transmission, by which voice and sight of the two parties are received at each end.

Videotape. A recording of the video and sound of television subject matter.

Vignette. Feature, usually a sidebar, providing a humorous, poignant, etc., look at a subject.

Vignetted Halftone. A halftone without clearly defined edges. Tones soften gradually until they completely fade out.

VIP. Very important person.

Visual Display Terminal (VDT). Displays copy selected from computer memory and allows editing.

Visual Scanner. Optical scanner.

Wash Drawing. Water color or diluted India ink brush drawing that requires halftone reproduction.

Watermark. Identification mark left in texture of paper, which can be seen when held up to the light.

White Paper. A document prepared as an argument in behalf of an organization on a given issue. It may be more argumentative than a position paper.

Widow. A short line at the end of a paragraph, leaving unprinted "white space." Permissible except when used in first line of column.

Women's Publications. Periodicals designed to be of special interest to women, with subject matter selected accordingly.

Wood Cuts. Wooden printing blocks with impression carved by hand. Forerunner to zinc etchings.

Working Drawings. Final drawings, usually black and white, prepared for use by engraver, as compared with original sketch showing how final art will appear.

Work Print. Print of a film used for first editing.

Wrong Font (w.f.). Letter from one font of type mixed with another.

Zinc Etching. A line engraving etched in zinc.

Codes of Ethics

Code of the Public Relations Society of America

This Code was adopted in April 1977 by the PRSA Assembly. It replaces a similar Code of Professional Standards for the Practice of Public Relations previously in effect since 1954, strengthened by amendments in 1959 and 1963.

Declaration of Principles

Members of the Public Relations Society of America base their professional principles on the fundamental value and dignity of the individual, holding that the free exercise of human rights, especially freedom of speech, freedom of assembly and freedom of the press, is essential to the practice of public relations.

In serving the interests of clients and employers, we dedicate ourselves to the goals of better communication, understanding and cooperation among the diverse individuals, groups and institutions of society.

We pledge:

To conduct ourselves professionally, with truth, accuracy, fairness and responsibility to the public;

To improve our individual competence and advance the knowledge and proficiency of the profession through continuing research and education;

And to adhere to the articles of the Code of Professional Standards for the Practice of Public Relations as adopted by the governing Assembly of the Society.

Articles of the Code

These articles have been adopted by the Public Relations Society of America to promote and maintain high standards of public service and ethical conduct among its members.

1. A member shall deal fairly with clients or employers, past and present, with fellow practitioners and the general public.

2. A member shall conduct his or her professional life in accord with the public interest.

3. A member shall adhere to truth and accuracy and to generally accepted standards of good taste.

4. A member shall not represent conflicting or competing interests without the express consent of those involved, given after a full disclosure of the facts; nor place himself or herself in a position where the member's interest is or may be in conflict with a duty to a client, or others, without a full disclosure of such interests to all involved.

5. A member shall safeguard the confidences of both present and former clients or employers and shall not accept retainers or employment which may involve the disclosure or use of these confidences to the disadvantage or prejudice of such clients or employers.

6. A member shall not engage in any practice which tends to corrupt the integrity of channels of communication or the processes of government.

7. A member shall not intentionally communicate false or misleading information and is obligated to use care to avoid communication of false or misleading information.

8. A member shall be prepared to identify publicly the name of the client or employer on whose behalf any public communication is made.

9. A member shall not make use of any individual or organization purporting to serve or represent an announced case, or purporting to be independent or unbiased, but actually serving an undisclosed special or private interest of a member, client or employer.

10. A member shall not intentionally injure the professional reputation or practice of another practitioner.

However, if a member has evidence that another member has been guilty of unethical, illegal or unfair practices, including those in violation of this Code, the member shall present the information promptly to the proper authorities of the Society for action in accordance with the procedure set forth in Article XIII of the Bylaws.

11. A member called as a witness in a proceeding for the enforcement of this Code shall be bound to appear, unless excused for sufficient reason by the Judicial Panel.

12. A member, in performing services for a client or employer, shall not accept fees, commissions or any other valuable consideration from anyone other than the client or employer in connection with those services without the express consent of the client or employer, given after a full disclosure of the facts.

13. A member shall not guarantee the achievement of specified results beyond the member's direct control.

14. A member shall, as soon as possible, sever relations with any organization or individual if such relationship requires conduct contrary to the articles of this Code.

An Official Interpretation of The PRSA Code of Professional Standards for the Practice of Public Relations As It Applies to Financial Public Relations

In 1963 the PRSA Board of Directors approved the following interpretation as it applies to financial public relations practice which is defined as "that area of public relations which relates to the dissemination of information that affects the understanding of stockholders and investors generally concerning the financial position and prospects of a company, and includes among its objectives the improvement of relations between corporations and their stockholders." This interpretation, which was prepared for the PRSA Board by the Society's Legal Counsel, an Advisory Committee working with the Securities and Exchange Commission and the PRSA Committee on Standards of Professional Practice, is rooted directly in the Code and has the full force of the Code behind it. A violation of any one of the following ten points should be subject to the same procedures and penalties as a violation of the Code.

1. It is the responsibility of the member practicing financial public relations to know and understand the rules and regulations of the SEC and the laws which it administers and the other laws, rules and regulations affecting financial public relations and to act in accordance with their letter and spirit. (See paragraph 2 of the Code.)

2. It shall be the objective of such member to follow the policy of full disclosure of corporate information, except in such instances where such information is of a confidential nature. The purpose of this objective is to enable an accurate evaluation of the company by the investing public and not to influence the price of securities. Such information should be accurate, clear and understandable. (See paragraphs 1 and 2 of the Code.)

3. Such member shall observe the confidential nature of certain of the information he has access to because of his employment and shall take every precaution to make sure this information is not used in a manner detrimental to his client's or employer's best interests. (See paragraph 5 of the Code.)

4. Such member shall disclose or release information promptly so as to avoid the possibility of any use of the information by an insider for personal gain. In general, such member should make every effort to comply with the spirit and intent of the "Timely Disclosure" provisions of the New York Stock Exchange Company Manual. Information deemed not confidential but which is not subject to a formal release shall be available to all on an equal basis. (See paragraphs 1 and 2 of the Code.)

5. Such member shall exercise reasonable care to ascertain the facts correctly and to disseminate only information which he believes to be accurate and adequate. Such member shall use reasonable care to avoid the issuance or release of predictions or projections of financial or other matters lacking adequate basis in fact. (See paragraph 7 of the Code.)

6. Such member shall act promptly to correct false or misleading information or rumors concerning his client's or employer's securities or business whenever he has reason to believe such information or rumors exist. (See paragraphs 1, 2, and 7 of the Code.)

7. Such member shall clearly identify to the investing public the sources of any communication for which he is responsible, including the name of the client or employer on whose behalf the communication is made. (See paragraph 8 of the Code.)

8. Such member shall not exploit the information he has gained as an insider for personal gain. However, this is not intended to prohibit a member from making bona fide investments in his company's or client's securities in accordance with normal investment practices. (See paragraphs 1 and 4 of the Code.)

9. Such member shall not accept compensation which would place him in a position of conflict with his duty to his client, employer or the investing

public. Specifically, such member shall not accept a contingent fee or a stock option from his client or employer unless part of an over-all plan in favor of corporate executives, nor shall he accept securities as compensation at a value substantially below market price. (See paragraph 4 of the Code.)

10. Such member shall so act as to maintain the integrity of channels of public communication and to observe generally accepted standards of good taste. He shall as a minimum observe the publicly announced standards published by organizations representing the media of communications. (See paragraph 6 of the Code.)

Institute of Public Relations (Great Britain)
Code of Professional Conduct

1. **Standards of professional conduct**
   A member, in the conduct of his professional activities, shall respect the public interest and the dignity of the individual. It is his personal responsibility at all times to deal fairly and honestly with his client or employer, past or present, with his fellow members, with the media of communication and with the public.

2. **Dissemination of information**
   A member shall not knowingly or recklessly disseminate false or misleading information, and shall use proper care to avoid doing so inadvertently. He has a positive duty to maintain integrity and accuracy.

3. **Media of communication**
   A member shall not engage in any practice which tends to corrupt the integrity of the media of communication.

4. **Undisclosed interests**
   A member shall not be a party to any activity which deliberately seeks to dissemble or mislead by promoting a disguised or undisclosed interest whilst appearing to further another. It is his duty to ensure that the actual interest of any organization with which he may be professionally concerned is adequately declared.

5. **Confidential information**
   A member shall not disclose (except upon the order of a court of competent jurisdiction) or make use of information given or obtained in confidence from his employer or client, past or present, for personal gain or otherwise, without express consent.

6. **Conflict of interests**
   A member shall not represent conflicting or competing interests without the express consent of the parties concerned after full disclosure of the facts.
   A member having a financial interest in an organization shall not recommend the use of that organization nor make use of its services on behalf of his client or employer, without declaring his interest.

7. **Sources of payment**
   A member, in the course of his professional services to his employer or client, shall not accept payment either in cash or kind for those services from any other source without the express consent of his employer or client.

8. **Payment contingent upon achievements**
   A member shall not negotiate or agree to terms with a prospective employer or client on the basis of payment contingent upon specific future public relations achievements.

9. **Supplanting another member**
   A member seeking employment or new business by direct and individual approach to a potential employer or client shall take all reasonable steps to ascertain whether that employment or business is already carried out by another member. If so, it shall be his duty to advise the other member in advance of any approach he proposes to make to the employer or client concerned. (Nothing in this clause shall be taken as inhibiting a member from the general advertisement of his services.)

10. **Rewards to holders of public office**
    A member shall not offer or give any reward to a Member of Parliament, of either House, or to any member of a local authority or other public body, or to any other person holding public office, in return for furthering the interests of the member, his client or employer, either without disclosure of those interests by, or in a manner inconsistent with the public responsibilities of, the MP or other office-holder concerned.

11. **Employment of Members of Parliament**
    A member who employs a Member of Parliament, of either House, in connection with Parliamentary matters, whether in a consultative or executive capacity, shall disclose

this fact, and also the object of the employment to the General Secretary of the Institute, who shall enter it in a register kept for the purpose. A member of the Institute who is himself a Member of Parliament shall be directly responsible for disclosing or causing to be disclosed to the General Secretary any such information as may relate to himself. (The register referred to in this clause shall be open to public inspection at the offices of the Institute during office hours.)

12. **Injury to other members**
    A member shall not maliciously injure the professional reputation or practice of another member.

13. **Instruction of others**
    A member who knowingly causes or permits another person or organization to act in a manner inconsistent with this Code or is party to such action shall himself be deemed to be in breach of it.

14. **Reputation of the profession**
    A member shall not conduct himself in any manner detrimental to the reputation of the Institute or the profession of public relations.

15. **Upholding the Code**
    A member shall uphold this Code, shall cooperate with fellow members in so doing and in enforcing decisions on any matter arising from its application. If a member has reason to believe that another member has been engaged in practices which may be in breach of this Code, it shall be his duty to inform the Institute. It is the duty of all members to assist the Institute to implement this Code, and the Institute will support any member so doing.

(Effective November 22, 1970)

International Public Relations Association
Code of Conduct
(adopted in Venice, May 1961)

A. Personal and Professional Integrity

1. It is understood that by personal integrity is meant the maintenance of both high moral standards and a sound reputation.
   By professional integrity is meant observance of the Constitution, rules and, particularly, the Code as adopted by IPRA.

B. Conduct Towards Clients and Employers

1. A member has a general duty of fair dealing towards his clients or employers, past and present.
2. A member shall not represent conflicting or competing interests without the express consent of those concerned.
3. A member shall safeguard the confidences of both present and former clients or employers.
4. A member shall not employ methods tending to be derogatory of another member's client or employer.
5. In performing services for a client or employer a member shall not accept fees, commission or any other valuable consideration in connection with those services from anyone other than his client or employer without the express consent of his client or employer, given after a full disclosure of the facts.
6. A member shall not propose to a prospective client or employer that his fee or other compensation be contingent on the achievement of certain results: nor shall he enter into any fee agreement to the same effect.

C. Conduct Towards the Public and the Media

1. A member shall conduct his professional activities with respect for the public interest and for the dignity of the individual.
2. A member shall not engage in any practice which tends to corrupt the integrity of channels of public communication.
3. A member shall not intentionally disseminate false or misleading information.
4. A member shall at all times seek to give a faithful representation of the organization which he serves.

5. A member shall not create any organization to serve some announced cause but actually to serve an undisclosed special or private interest of a member or his client or his employer, nor shall he make use of it or any such existing organization.

D. Conduct Towards Colleagues

1. A member shall not intentionally injure the professional reputation or practice of another member. However, if a member has evidence that another member has been guilty of unethical, illegal or unfair practices, including practices in violation of this Code, he should present the information to the Council of IPRA.
2. A member shall not seek to supplant another member with his employer or client.
3. A member shall cooperate with fellow members in upholding and enforcing this code.

Associations

International and Regional Public Relations Societies

INTERNATIONAL PUBLIC RELATIONS ASSOCIATION (IPRA)
20 Quai Gustave-Ador, 1207 Geneva, Switzerland P.O. BOX: 1211 Geneva 6 TEL: (022) 36. 81. 81. & 36. 94. 89. TELEX: 27744

INTERNATIONAL ASSOCIATION OF POLITICAL CONSULTANTS
Nassau Ouwerkestraat 14, The Hague, The Netherlands

PUBLIC RELATIONS CONSULTANTS ASSOCIATION, Ltd. (PRCA)
IPA Building, 44 Belgrave Square, London SWIX 8QS England. TEL: (01) 235-6225 & (01) 235-4404

EUROPEAN FEDERATION OF PUBLIC RELATIONS (CERP)
12, Avenue du Rond-Point, B-1330 Rixensart, Belgium. TEL: (02) 53. 52. 39

INTER-AMERICAN FEDERATION OF PUBLIC RELATIONS ASSOCIATIONS (FIARP)
Apartado 50. 359, Caracas, 105, Venezuela

PAN PACIFIC PUBLIC RELATIONS FEDERATION (PPPRF)
c/o Roy J. Leffingwell, Esq., 625 Lolani Avenue, Honolulu, Hawaii, U.S.A.

National Public Relations Societies

ARGENTINA	Public Relations Association of Argentina (AARP): Avenida de Mayo 1157, piso 1°, Buenos Aires, Republic of Argentina. TEL: 37-0061
AUSTRALIA	Public Relations Institute of Australia (PRIA): P.O. BOX: 868 Sydney, N.S.W., Australia
BELGIUM	Centre Belge des Relations Publiques (CBRP): Rue du Sceptre, 61, Bruxelles 1040, Belgique. TEL: (02) 647 .23 .59 Belgian Institute for Information and Documentation: 3, Rue Montoyer, B-1040 Bruxelles, Belgique
BRAZIL	Public Relations Association of Brazil (ABRP): Rua Augusta 2676, 18°/conj. 184, 01000 Sao Paulo, Brazil. TEL: 282-8397
CANADA	Canadian Public Relations Society, Inc. (CPRS): Suite 640, 220 Laurier Avenue W., Ottawa KIP 529, Ontario, Canada. TEL: 1613-232-1222
CHILE	Chilean Institute of Public Relations (ICRP): Moneda 1160 piso 11°, Santiago de Chile. TEL: 89554
REPUBLIC OF CHINA	Chinese Public Relations Association (CPRA): House 1, Lane 3, Linyi Street, Taipei, Taiwan, Republic of China
COLOMBIA	Colombian Society of Public Relations (SCRP): Apartado Aereo 29572, Bogota, Colombia

ASSOCIATIONS

DENMARK	Danish Public Relations Association (DPRK): Rodovre Centrum 111, DK - 2610 Rodovre, Denmark
ECUADOR	Public Relations Association of Ecuador (AERP): Casilla 6193, Guayaquil, Ecuador
FINLAND	Public Relations Society of Finland (PRSF): Tiedotusmiehet ry, Kivihaantie 7, 00310 Helsinki 31, Finland.
FRANCE	Association Francaise des Relations Publiques (AFREP): 8, Rue Jean-Goujon, 75008 Paris, France. TEL: 359. 52. 41
FED. REPUBLIC OF GERMANY	Deutsche Public Relations Gesellschaft E. V. (DPRG): 5 Koln, Rudolf-Platz 9, Federal Republic of Germany
GHANA	Public Relations Association of Ghana (PRAG): P.O. BOX: 6475, Accra, Ghana
GREAT BRITAIN	The British Institute of Public Relations (IPR): 1 Great James Street, London WCIN 3DA
GREECE	Hellenic Public Relations Society (HPRS): 15 Alexandrou Soutsou Street, Athens, 134, Greece.
HONG KONG	Public Relations Association of Hong Kong, Limited (PRAHK): GPO BOX: 1264, Hong Kong, South East Asia
REPUBLIC OF INDIA	Public Relations Society of India (PRSI): UCO Building, 5 Parliament Street, New Delhi 1; and c/o Air India - Niemal - 241/242 Backbay Reclamation, Nairman Point, Bombay 1, India
IRAN	Public Relations Society of Iran (PRSI): Ziba Building, 255 Sa'adi Avenue, (North), P.O. BOX: 692, Teheran, Iran
IRELAND	Public Relations Institute of Ireland (PRII): c/o Miss Gladys MacNevin, 50 Waterloo Road, Dublin 4
ISRAEL	Public Relations Association of Israel (PRAI): P.O. BOX: 6321, Tel Aviv, Israel
ITALY	Federazione Italiana Relazioni Pubbliche (FERPI): Palazzo del Toro, Corso Vittorio Emmanuelle 376 - Milano 20122, and Via Filippo Corridoni 6, Rome
JAPAN	Public Relations Society of Japan (PRSJ): Isehan Building, 3-7, 8-chome Ginza, Chuo-ku, Tokyo 104. TEL: 572-1267
KENYA	Public Relations Society of Kenya (PRSK): P.O. BOX: 30123, Nairobi, Kenya
LEBANON	The Lebanese Public Relations Association (LPRA): c/o Middle East Business Services & Research Corporation, P.O. BOX: 2400 Beirut
MALAYSIA	Institute of Public Relations, Malaysia (IPRM): P.O. BOX: 636 Kuala-Lumpur
MEXICO	Mexican Association of Public Relations (AMRP): Avenida Bajo California 245, 8°, piso 804, Mexico II - D.F. TEL: 564-61-30
NETHERLANDS	Nederlands Genootschap voor Public Relations (NGPR): Raamweg 44, The Hague, Holland. TEL: (070) 46. 70. 49

NETHERLANDS ANTILLES	Netherlands Antilles Public Relations Association (NAPRA): Fokkerweg 7, Curacao, Netherlands Antilles. TEL: 54311. P.O. BOX: 777
NEW ZEALAND	Public Relations Institute of New Zealand (PRINZ): P.O. BOX: 10-086 Wellington, New Zealand
NIGERIA	Nigerian Institute of Public Relations (NIPR): P.O. BOX: 6103 Lagos
NORWAY	Norwegian Public Relations Society (NPRS): Nedre Ullern Terrace 10, Oslo 2
REPUBLIC OF PANAMA	Panamanian Association of Public Relations Professionals (APPRP): Apartado 4431, Zone 5, Panama
PARAGUAY	Paraguayan Association of Public Relations Professionals (APPRP): Oliva y 14 de Maya, 8° piso, Asuncion, Paraguay. TEL: 41285/43548
PERU	Federacion Peruana de Relacionistas (FPR): Avenida Guzman Blanco 240, Of. 1301, Apartado 10, Lima 120
PHILIPPINES	Public Relations Society of the Philippines (PRSP): P.O. BOX: 3474, Manilla, the Philippines
PORTUGAL	Sociedade Portuguesa de Relacoes Publicas (SOPREP): Avenida Miguel Bombarda 133 - 7°B, Lisboa
ARAB REPUBLIC OF EGYPT	Arab Public Relations Society (APRS): 15, Emad El-Din Street, Cairo, Egypt. P.O. BOX: 821, Cairo. TEL: 911819/900257
RHODESIA	Rhodesian Institute of Public Relations (RIPR): P.O. BOX: 3895 Salisbury
SINGAPORE	Institute of Public Relations of Singapore (IPRS): P.O. BOX: 3800, Singapore
SPAIN	Agrupacion Espanola de Relaciones Publicas (AERP): San Elias, 11 desp. 101-102, Barcelona 6. TEL: 218.0054
	Asociacion National de Tecnicos en Relaciones Publicas (formerly CENERP): Eurobuilding, Juan Ramon Jiminez, 8, Madrid 16, Spain. TEL: 457.91.94
REPUBLIC OF SOUTH AFRICA	Public Relations Institute of South Africa (PRISA): 307 Hampstead House, 46 Biccard Street, Braamfontein, Johannesburg 2000, Transvaal, South Africa. P.O. BOX: 31390, Braamfontein 2017, Tvl., S.A. TEL: 724.3091 & 724.6379/9
SWEDEN	Swedish Public Relations Association (Sveriges PR Forening): Stureplan 4, S- 114 35 Stockholm, Sweden. TEL: (08) 83. 97. 49
SWITZERLAND	Swiss Society of Public Relations (SSPR): Kasinoplatz 8, 3011 Bern
TANZANIA	Public Relations Association of Tanzania (PRAT): P.O. BOX: 1246, Dar-Es-Salaam
UNITED STATES OF AMERICA	Public Relations Society of America (PRSA): 845 Third Avenue, New York 10022, U.S.A.
URUGUAY	Uruguayan Association of Public Relations (AURP): San Jose 1280, escritorio 4, Uruguay. TEL: 912938

VENEZUELA Public Relations Association of Venezuela (ARPV):
Edificio Centro Villasmil - 8° piso, No: 802-Esquina Puente
Victoria, Caracas. TEL: 54-70-21 (Extension: 192)

Specialized Associations

ACCE Communications Council
c/o St. Louis Commerce
10 Broadway
St. Louis, Mo. 63102

Agricultural Relations Council
18 South Michigan Avenue
Chicago, Ill. 60603
(312) 346-1387

American Association of Minority Consultants
c/o Charles A. Davis & Associates
2400 South Michigan Avenue
Chicago, Ill. 60616
(312) DA 6-4140

American Association of Political Consultants
633 Third Avenue, Suite 1330
New York, N.Y. 10017
(212) 687-2725

American Business Communication Association
317b David Kinley Hall
University of Illinois
Urbana, Ill. 61801
(217) 333-1007

American Jewish Public Relations Society
515 Park Avenue
New York, N.Y. 10022
(212) PL 2-0600

American Medical Writers Association
5272 River Road, Suite 290
Bethesda, Md. 20016
(301) 986-9119

American Society for Hospital Public Relations
840 N. Lake Shore Drive
Chicago, Ill. 60611
(312) 645-9492

Bank Marketing Association
309 West Washington Street
Chicago, Ill. 60606
(312) 782-1442

Baptist Public Relations Association
460 James Robertson Pkwy.
Nashville, Tenn. 37219
(615) 244-2355

College Sports Information Directors of America
c/o Princeton University
Princeton, N.J. 08540
(609) 452-3568

Council for Advancement and Support of Education (CASE)
One Dupont Circle, Room 600
Washington, D.C. 20036
(202) 659-3820

Industrial Communication Council
P.O. Box 3970
Grand Central Post Office
New York, N.Y. 10017
(415) 894-2305

Industrial Publicity Association
c/o Vincent J. Biunno
Worthington Corporation
401 Worthington Avenue
Harrison, N.J. 07029

International Association of Business Communicators
2108 Braewick Circle
Akron, Ohio 44313
(216) 836-3255

Library Public Relations Council
c/o Alice Norton
Box 516
Ridgefield, Conn. 06877
(203) 438-4064

National Investor Relations Institute
1629 K Street, N.W.
Washington, D.C. 20036
(202) 223-4725

National School Public Relations Association
1801 N. Moore Street
Arlington, Va. 22209
(703) 528-5840

Public Affairs Council
1220 16th St., N.W.
Washington, D.C. 20036
(202) 232-8844

Public Relations Student Society of America
c/o Public Relations Society of America
845 Third Ave.
New York, N.Y. 10022
(212) 751-1940

Publishers' Publicity Association
c/o Kate S. Wilson
Hammond, Inc.
Maplewood, N.J. 07040
(212) 962-0210

Railroad Public Relations Association
American Railroads Building
Washington, D.C. 20036
(202) 293-4194

Religious Public Relations Council
475 Riverside Drive - Room 1031
New York, N.Y. 10027
(212) 870-2013

Society of Consumer Affairs Professionals in Business
1430 K Street, N.W., Suite 301
Washington, D.C. 20005
(202) 393-3270

Women Executives in Public Relations
c/o Ms. Retha Odom
Shell Oil Company
50 West 50th Street
New York, N.Y. 10020
(212) 262-6983

Women in Communications, Inc.
8305-A Shoal Creek Blvd.
Austin, Texas 78758
(512) 452-0119

Index

A

Abstract thinker, 15
Accreditation, 614
"Action Course in Practical Politics," 33
Activism, 507-508
Activist groups, 52
Adjustment, 7
Administrative public relations, 591
Adventures in Negro History, 91
Ad Systems, Inc., 195
Advertising:
   alerting public to issue, 496
   broadcasters, 307
   broadcast media, 498-499
   conveying information, 495-496
   effective uses, 495-496
   financial and educational, 109
   financial organizations, 246
   ineffective uses, 499, 502-503
   institutional, 253
   performing needed public service, 496
   political candidates, 348
   publications, 623
   public issue, 593-594
   special nature, 494
   utilities, 220-221
AFL-CIO News, 100
Afro-American's Quest for Education, 91
Agnew, Spiro, 314
Agricultural magazines, 458
Almanacs, 377
American Alumni Council, 284, 288
American Association of Industrial Editors, 174-175
American Banker, 45
American Cancer Society, 268
American College Public Relations Association, 284, 288
American Council on Education, 285
American Gas Association, 222
American Indian, 88
American Jewish Public Relations Society, 281
American Management Association, 598
American Meat Institute, 238
American Music Conference, 422
American Newspaper Publishers Association, 428

American Red Cross, 265, 268
American Society of Association Executives, 243
American Society of Travel Agents, 334
American Trade Association Executives, 243
American Traveler's Guide to Negro History, 91
America's Education Press, 398
AMPAC, 86
Analysis, 383-385
Anderson, David, 282
Animal Farm, 21
Annual meeting of shareholders, 120, 123-124
Annual reports:
   accounting changes, 120
   balance sheet interpretation, 118
   dealer relations, 195
   employee edition, 165
   employees, 118
   extra mailings, 114-115
   illustrating 118-120
   maps, 118
   operating expenses, 118
   operating results, 118
   organization, 118
   outline and continuity, 115, 118
   preparing, 112-115
   products or services, 118
   stockholders, 118
   translations, 112
Annual Youth Conference, 222
Anti-Trust Division, 418
Approvals, 403-404
Aristotle, 97, 314
Armour, Norbert F., 260
Armstrong, Richard A., 51
Asians, 351, 352
Associated Church Press, 281
Associated Merchandising Corporation Employee Opinion Survey Program, 260
Associated Press, 45
Associated Release Service, 395, 512
Association of Regional Religious Communicators, 282
Associations:
   broadcasting, 306

Associations: (*cont'd.*)
   business and professional, 230-244
   (*see also* Business and professional association)
   commercial, 97
   education, 284, 288
   Encyclopedia of Associations, 398
   federations, 231
   industry, 61, 62, 97
   professional, 97, 98, 231
   public affairs, 36
   religious, 281
   single-purpose, 98
   state government, 58-59
   trade, 62, 97, 98, 188, 190, 231
   travel, 335
Aszling, Richard A., 198
Attacks, handling, 425-426
Auctions, 480
Audience, public television, 477
Audience-participation shows, 469
Audio aids, 492-493
Audio cassette, 492
Audio/visual, publications, 622
Audio-visuals, 295-296
Aun, Emil Michael, 319
Austria, 351
Auto manufacturers, 351
Awards, 309
Ayer Directory of Publications, 428, 520
Ayer's Directory of Newspapers and Periodicals, 397-398, 434, 448

B

Bacon's Publicity Checker, 397, 448
Bacon's Publicity Distribution Service, 395
Baker, Robert K., 300
Ball, Sandra J, 300
Baptist Public Relations Association, 281
Barbour, Robert L., 423
"Basic Business-Consumer Relations Code," 232
Bastien, Brian, 283
Bateman, J. Carroll, 230, 315
Baton, 92
Batten, W.M., 201
Baus, Herbert, 391, 428, 448, 460, 517
Beatty, Robert O., 313

Before-and-after reading, 362-363
Belgians, 351
Bell and Howell Company, 285
Bell System, 221
Belson, Walter W., 44, 46
Berelson, 13, 14, 16, 20
Bernays, Edward L., 19
Better Business Bureaus, 207
Better Home Furnishing Council of Greater Chicago, 499
Bible, 277
Bibliographical publications, 377-378
Billboards, 273
Billing methods, 582
Black community, 88, 89, 90, 91, 92, 93, 95
Black Panthers, 20
Block, Lillian, 282
Blumenthal, W. Michael, 28
Board of Directors, participation, 575
Boards, public affairs, 31
Bookkeeping, 588
Books, public relations values, 329-330
Books and other publications:
    arranging for publication, 460-461
    cartoon booklets, 462-463
    mini, 461-462
    paperback, 461-462
    purchase of copies, 461
    reading rack booklets, 464
    special, 463-464
    subsidy, 461
    syndication, 462
    underwriting, 460-461
Boulding, Kenneth E., 285
Boxoffice, 485
Boy Scouts of America, 265, 266, 268, 269, 270, 275
Boyd, John, 107
Boys Clubs of America, 258
Branch operations, 585
Brayman, Harold, 156, 318
Briggs, Kenneth, 282
British, 352, 354, 355
Broadcast, 271
Broadcast and composite reports, 414-415
Broadcast coverage, 474-475
Broadcast Education Association, 310
Broadcasters:
    activism, 467
    advertising, 307
    ambassadors to community, 305-306
    be understood, 306
    building broadcasting, 310
    charting course, 306
    developing the plan, 305
    governments, 309-310
    interested, 305
    involving community, 308-309
        awards and citations, 309
        community relations, 308
        contests, 309
        direct mail, 309

Broadcasters: (*cont'd.*)
        exhibits, 309
        Speakers' Bureau, 308-309
    media, 338-339, 466, 467
    non-commercial radio and television stations, 306
    professional standards, 310
    promotion, 307-308
    publicity, 307
    Research Department, 306
    scope of station plans, 306-308
Broadcasting:
    diversified effort, 473-474
    religion, 282
    source file, 471-473
Broadcasting Yearbook, 398, 491
Broadcast media, advertising, 498-499
Brochures, 195, 327, 329
Broide, Mace, 80
Brookings Institution, 33
Brown, David, 320
Brown, J.A.C., 13, 14, 15
Brownstone Renovation Movement, 255
Budgeting:
    nonprofit organization, 271
    tourists, 333
Budgets, public affairs, 35
Buildings, 609-610
Bulletin boards, 165
Bulletins, painted, 514
Bulletins and newsletters, 270
Bull horns, electronic, 424
Bumper stickers, 513
Bureau of National Affairs, 45
Bureaus, press clipping, 409-414
Business:
    associations, 231
    groups, 160-161
    information, 378-379
    publications, 126-127
Business and professional association:
    agencies exerting influence, 231
    aim toward action, 241-242
    analysis, 237
    "Basic Business-Consumer Relations Code, 232
    bringing together allied forces, 242
    definition, 237
    differences from corporate public relations, 242-244
        personal qualities of executive, 244
        relationship to purposes, 243
        reports to members, 244
    establishing objectives, 237-238
    "federations," 231
    identification of publics, 237
    industry data, 240-241
    implementing program, 239
    marketing values of research, 242
    mutual interest, 231
    opinion research, 241

Business and professional association: (*cont'd.*)
    organizing for public relations, 232-235
        employment of counsel, 234
        financing, 234
        purposes, 235
        staff, 233
    periodic evaluations, 239
    planning program, 238-239
    "professional societies or associations," 231
    social problems in our country, 231-232
    steps in developing program, 235-239
    techniques, 239-242
    "trade or business associations," 231
    trade press editor as friend, 242
    two kinds of research, 240
Business and society, 28
Business-Consumer Relations Code, 232
Business groups, 520-521
Business magazines, 458-459
Business Week, 15, 205, 325, 611
Buttons, lapel, 513
Butts, Virginia, 299
By-lined articles, 327-328

C

Cafeteria news, 164
Call, Harvey, 98, 99
Cameraman, 427
Camp Fire Girls, 265
"Campaign Finance," 33
Campaign organization, 341
Campaigns, political, 85-86
Campbell, Rodney, 15
Canada, 351, 354
Canadian magazines, 455
Candidates (*see* Political candidates)
Cantril, Hadley, 368
Career training:
    broadcasters, 310
    public affairs, 30
Carlson, Robert O., 361
Carnegie Foundation for Advancement of Teaching, 285
Carter, Jimmy, 80, 199
Cartoon booklets, 462-463
Case histories, 327
Cassettes, 492
Catholic Journalist, 281
Catholic Press Association, 281
Catholic Press Directory, 281, 282, 398
Caveat emptor, 199
Central Intelligence Agency of United States, 352
Chain, national, 251-252
Chambers of Commerce, 61, 62
Chandler, Russell, 282
Chanel, 352

INDEX

Change:
　criticism as signal, 37-38
　defining direction, 38
　directing course, 11
　management, directories, 127
　reporting, 23
　role of public relations, 38-39
Charges, counsel, 580-582
Charts, 492
Chase, Stuart, 13
Chase Direct Mail Service Corporation, 395
Chase Manhattan, 246
Chicago Daily News, 302
Chicago Sun-Times, 282, 302
China, 352
Chronicles, 281
Chronologies, 377
"Church at Jackrabbit Junction," 281
Church groups, 519-520
Cincinnati Enquirer, 282
Citations, 309
Citizens' Conference on State Legislatures, 63
City magazines, 457-458
Civil rights organizations, 91
Clark, Gerda, 255
Class magazines, 454
Clearinghouse on Corporate Social Responsibility, 232
Clipping bureaus, 409-414, 451, 588
Clipsheets, 439, 440
Clothes Magazine, 251
Clubs:
　investment, 132-133
　political, 84
Code Authority of National Association of Broadcasters, 310
Columns, regular, 330
Come-and-see tours, 273
Commercial associations, 97
Commission on Consumer Product Safety, 231
Committee on Program Evaluation, 298
Committees:
　political action, 86
　public affairs, 31
"Common Situs" picketing bill, 96, 100-101, 103
Communication:
　acceptability, 22
　activism, 507-508
　advertising, 494-503
　arranging for approvals, 403-404
　bank checks carrying messages, 513
　behavior, influence, 22-23
　broadcast and composite report, 414-415
　bumper stickers, 513-514
　community relations, 75-77
　compatibility, 22
　condescension, 21, 605

Communication: (*cont'd.*)
　"controlled," 20-21, 605
　controlling rumors, 408-409
　conviction and motivation, 22
　corporate public relations department, 569
　dealer relations, 193, 194-196
　direct, 504-516
　displays, 515-516
　educational institutions, 291-295 (*see also* Educational institutions)
　effective and ineffective, 13-15
　　believing what comforts psyche, 13
　　fidelity of message, 13
　　group membership, 14
　　harmony between needs and desires, 13
　　needs of individual, 13
　　predisposition of recipient, 13
　　skill and experience, 13
　　susceptibility, 14
　　varying receptivity, 14-15
　employee, 162-165 (*see also* Employee relations and communications)
　euphemisms, 21, 605
　extension home economists, 512
　factors determining effectiveness, 15-22
　　direction to specific audience, 20
　　discommunication, 20-22
　　discretionary and imposed exposure, 20
　　diversity of mental "bents," 16
　　focusing key point, 20
　　graphic, action orientation, 17
　　importance given to subject, 17-18
　　increased education, 15
　　mental posture of audience, 15
　　"multiple-channel approach," 19-20
　　negative opinion or indifference, 18
　　"posture of receptivity," 18
　　reaction to events disguise effects, 20
　　selection of media, 18, 20
　　sophisticated, skeptical audiences, 15-16
　　"source effect," 18
　　"threshold of consciousness," 18-19
　　two-step flow, 16-17
　　visibility, 17, 22
　fairs and exhibits, 515
　fallacies about, 603-605
　forms, 12-13
　inserts, 513
　intensity, 22
　internal, publications, 621-622
　jargon, 21, 604
　jokes, 513
　lapel buttons, 513
　letters, 509-511 (*see also* Letters)
　lost art of expression, 21, 604
　mail, retailers, 259
　mailgrams, 513

Communication: (*cont'd.*)
　media of publicity, 408
　multinational business, 350-352
　names that communicate nothing, 21, 605
　new, but a step backward, 21-22
　news and publicity, 392-393
　newsletters, 511-512
　organizing files, 404
　persuasiveness, 22
　planning publicity, 393-403 (*see also* Publicity)
　planning publicity program, 391-392
　post cards, 511
　preparations for communicating, 391-415
　press clipping bureaus, 409-414
　product publicity, 407-408
　"promotion," 391
　public address systems, 516
　publications, 619
　publicity (*see* Publicity)
　putting art ahead of, 20, 604-605
　religion and religious groups, 280
　retailers, 253, 258, 259
　rubber stamp, 513
　schools as medium, 524-525
　signs, 514-515
　slogan, 513
　speakers' bureaus, 504-507
　special events, 404-407
　stamping mass mailings, 513
　stickers, 513
　stockholders, 112
　symbols, 513
　telephone, 507
　variety of impressions, 22
　visibility, 22
　word of mouth, 508-509
Communications Act of 1934, 304, 309
Communist bloc, 352
Community, 278
Community:
　broadcasting, 308-309
　good will, 9
　public television and radio, 478-479
Community Antenna Television, 465-466
Community Leader Tours, 205
Community organizations, 265
Community relations:
　action, 73-75
　　case studies, 73-74
　　overcoming imagined fears, 74-75
　　preconditioning for change, 74
　applied, 69-79
　communicating, 75-77
　　health and safety programs, 75-76
　　publicity content, 76-77
　　selecting publicity outlets, 76
　community, 65, 66-68, 78-79
　　coming into or leaving, 78-79
　　continuing familiarization, 78-79

650 INDEX

Community relations: (cont'd.)
    needs, 68
    speaks out, 66
    strengths and weaknesses, 67-68
    structure, 66-67
    term, 65
  ecology, term, 64-65
  environment, 65
  evaluating, 77-78
    assuring continuity, 78
    keeping abreast, 77-78
  expert advice, 70
  importance to business, 65
  organizing, 71-73
    community relations man, 72
    companywide involvement, 71-72
    determining assignments, 72-73
    volunteers, 72
  planning, 69-70
    channeling resources, 69-70
    new employment practices, 70
    value of inquiries, 70
  priorities, 68
  retailer, 253, 259
  today, 64
  trends, 79
  utilities, 216-219
    community health, welfare, educational and cultural interests, 219
    industrial development, 216
    low- and middle-income families, 216-219
    minority group hiring and training, 219
  what's at stake for business, 65-66
  you've come a long way, 68-69
Community Resource Volunteers, 254
Companies:
  active, 61
  helping others, 161
  multi-state, 57
  one-state, 56-57
Company publications:
  aims, 167-168
  changing trends, 175
  "combination," 168
  corporate public relations department, 570
  design, 170-171
  distribution, 173-174
  "employee," 168, 173-174
  "external," 169
  feedback mechanisms, 172-173
  format, 169-170
  frequency, 173
  kind of editor, 170
  kind of material, 171-172
  legal counsel, 168
  letterpress or offset, 170
  "market testing," 171
  photographs, 171
  professional help, 174-175
  responsibility, 168

Company publications: (cont'd.)
  source of information, 168
  sources of material, 172
  what kind, 168-169
Complaint system, nonprofit organization, 270-271
Computerized mailing services, 434-435
Computers, 466
Concrete thinker, 15
Conference Board, 29, 30, 31
Conference of Consumer Organizations, 208
Conference Proceedings, 281
Confidentiality, counsel, 584-585
Congressional Directory, 41
Congressional Quarterly, 41
Congressional Record, 42, 344
Consultants, 35-36, 58, 62, 190
"Consumer Education Forums," 69
Consumerism, 34, 159, 199, 212, 214-215
Consumer Federation of America, 208
Consumer magazine, 448
Consumer publications, 195
Consumer relations:
  challenges, 202
  code, 208
  development of consumerism, 199-201
  forestalling and handling consumer complaints, 205, 207-208
  involving consumers, 203, 205
  participation by community leaders, 205
  President Kennedy's message, 200
  response by business, 201-202
  state and local activity, 201
  types of programs, 202-203
  volume of legislation, 200-201
Consumers, satisfying, 197
Consumers Report, 208
Contacts, 451
Content analysis, 362
Contests, broadcasters, 309
Continental Illinois, 246
Conviction, 22
Cook, C.W., 201
Cook, William W., 370
Cooper, Martin M., 481
COPE, 86
Cordiner, Ralph J., 97
Cornell, George W., 282
Corporate approach, 97-98
Corporate identity systems, 224, 226
Corporate program information, 61-62
Corporate public relations, 242-244
Corporate public relations department:
  Board of Directors participation, 575
  community relations, 570
  corporate donations, 570
  corporate publicity, 570
  education relations, 570
  employee publications, 570
  functions, 570
  government relations, 570
  guest relations, 570

Corporate public relations department: (cont'd.)
  organization, 571-574
  policy, 570
  product publicity, 570
  public relations in corporate organization 570-571
  public relations promotion programs, 570
  role of public relations firm, 575
  role of public relations in corporation, 567-568
  salaries, 574-575
  scope of public relations function, 568-570
    advice and counsel, 568-569
    communications service, 569
    promotion, 569-570
    research, 569
  speakers bureau, 570
  stockholder relations, 570
Corporation:
  priorities, 386-387
  public affairs, 29
Corporation for Public Broadcasting, 477
Correspondents, 585
Council for Advancement and Support of Education, 284
Council of Better Business Bureaus, 207
Council of State Governments, 63
Counsel:
  background, 576-577
  branch offices, 585
  branch operations, 585
  businessman, 585
  clippings, 588
  contacts with clients, 588
  correspondents, 585
  educating client, 583-584
  establishing working pattern, 583-584
  how he works with client, 577
  internal functions of firm, 588
  limitations, 579-580
  mailing lists, 588
  open-book policy, 584-585
  organizing staff, 585
  organizing to serve client, 582-583
  payments, 580-582
    billing methods, 582
    overhead, 582
    personnel, 582
    variations in charges, 581-582
  presentations and proposals, 587
  reciprocal arrangements, 585
  reports, 588
  resigning an account, 587-588
  sales activities, 586-587
  size of organization, 586
  specializing, 585
  what he has to offer, 577-579
  who is, 576-577
  work is confidential, 584-585
Counselor, 281

INDEX

Couric, John M., 304
Courier, 392
Created news, 392
Criminal Fraud Statute, 199
Criticism, 37-38, 613
Crowley, Susan, 282
Customers, good will, 10

D

Daily newspapers, 165, 428-432
Daily News Record, 251
Daily Variety, 485
Darion, Sid, 283
Dart, John, 282
Davison, W. Phillips, 14, 22
Daytonian, 258
Dayton's, 253-255
Dealer relations:
  content of dealer communications, 196
  dealer communications media, 194-196
    annual reports, 195
    articles in trade and consumer publications, 195
    brochures, 195
    executive speech reprints, 195
    external house publications, 194
    newsletters, 194
    news releases, 195
    other printed media, 194-195
    special mailers, 195
    special situations, 195-196
  importance, 192
  knowing the organization, 193
  researching the audience, 193
  role of communications, 193
  satisfying consumers, 197
  training and customer service, 196-197
Dealers, good will, 10
Deception, dangers, 593
Democracy in America, 230
Democratic Congressional Campaign Manual, 347
Denmark, 351
Department of Health, Education and Welfare, 313
Department store, local, 252
Depth survey, 363
Derus Media Service, 395
Dial-the-News, 164
Dichter, Ernst, 38
Digests, 456
Dimock, 314
Direct communications, 504-516
Direct mail, 100, 309, 327
Directories:
  "House Magazines," 175
  management changes, 127
  religions, 281-282
Director of Public Relations, 5
Directory, 281
Directory of College Student Press in America, 525
Directory of Newspaper and Magazine Personnel and Data, 398
Directory of Professional Photography, 398
Directory of Professional Writers, 451
Disasters, 423
Disclosure, 133-134, 140-148, 343 (*see also* Financial public relations)
Discounter, 255
Discover America Travel Organizations, Inc., 335
Disk recordings, 492-493
Displays, 515-516
Distributors, TV film, 473
Distribution services, 437-438
Documentary, 468
Dodge, Sherwood, 241
Donations:
  corporate, 570
  politics, 86-87
Dramatic programs, 469
Drucker, Peter, 198, 201

E

Ecology, term, 64-65
Economic illiteracy, 246
Economist of London, 355
Edifice, symbol, 609-610
Edison Electric Institute, 222, 224
Editor and Publisher, 398
Editor and Publisher International Yearbook, 283, 397, 428, 432, 434
Editors, 282-283, 320, 448-451
Education:
  financial public relations, 110
  political and economic, 33-34
Educational advertising, 109
Educational devices, mass, 4-5
Educational institutions:
  at policy level, 287
  changing attitudes, 285
  changing constituencies, 297
  communication with students, 293-295
  explaining change, 286
  external publics, 296-297
  forces for change, 285
  formula for survival, 285
  handling crises, 297-298
  in public spotlight, 287
  internal publics, 291-293
    channels of communication, 292
    communications in crises, 292
    complex communication, 291-292
    education's, 293
    how to combat rumors, 292-293
    internal communications program, 292
    match audience and message, 293
  nature of university, 286
  new techniques, 295-296
    attainable goals, 296
    audio-visuals, 295-296
Educational institutions: (*cont'd.*)
    changing technology, 296
    generation gap, 296
    new uses of telephone, 296
  program evaluation, 298
  qualifications, 291
  university, 287-291
    basic organizational structures, 288-289
    broadened responsibilities, 289, 291
    commitment and cooperation, 288
    faculty attitudes, 287
    Greenbrier Report, 288
    inventory of resources, 289
    semantic problems, 287-288
Education groups, 521
Education of public, 10
Education relations, 570
Educators, reaching, 479
Effectiveness studies, 362
Eisenhower, Dwight, 28
Elected officials, 55
Electric "spectacular displays," 514
Electronic bull horns, 424
Electronic revolutions, 602-603
Electronics in publicity program, 301
Electrowriters, 493
Ellsworth, Henry L., 319
Elton, Reuel, 243
Emancipation Proclamation, 315
Emergencies, handling, 422-426
Emergency public relations, nonprofit organization, 275-276
Emerson, Ralph Waldo, 159
Employee communications, retailers, 258
Employee publications (*see* Company publications)
Employee relations and communications:
  annual report, 165
  bulletin boards, 164
  cafeteria news, 164
  daily newspapers, 165
  dial-the-news, 164
  increasing challenges, 165
  in-plant exhibits, 165
  interests of employees, 163
  local newspapers, 165
  meetings with, 163
  monthly publication, 164
  newsletters, 164
  news publications, 164-165
  open houses, 165
  quarterly magazine, 164
  radio news schedules, 164-165
  techniques, 163-165
  teletype networks, 164
  television, 165
  utilities, 219-220
  weekly publications, 165
Employment Clearing House, 310
Employment practices, 70
Encyclopedia of Associations, 398
Encyclopedias, 376-377

Endorsement articles, 327
Englishmen, 354
Engravings, 557-560
Entertainment programs, 469
Environment:
 problems, 34
 term, 65
 utilities, 215-216
Environmental Affairs, Department, 222
Environmental Protection Agency, 596
Equal Employment Opportunities Commission, 231
Ernst and Ernst, 597
Ethics and standards, 613-614
Ethnic media and publications, 89-90, 91-95
Euphemisms, 21
Europeans, 351, 352
Evaluation, 7, 611-612
Evangelical Press Association, 281
Evening Star, 45
Excess profits tax, 156
Executive, 55, 244
Executive speech reprints, 195
Exhibits, 165, 309, 515
Extension home economists, 512
External company publications, 459

F

Fabun, Don, 166
Facsimile, 493
Fact-finding:
 almanacs and chronologies, 377
 bibliographical publications, 377-378
 encyclopedias and reference books, 376-377
 free materials, 374
 government, 379-380
 how to do research, 376
 information services, 374-376
 knowledge of sources, 373-375
 people, institutions, media, 380-382
 procedure, 374-375
 qualitative distinctions, 372-373
 reducing element of chance, 371-372
 sources of business information, 378-379
 sources of information, 374
 statistics, 382
Fact sheets, 328-329
"Fairness Doctrine," 594
Fairs, 515
Falcon Seaboard, 158
Farm groups, 519
Feature news, 392
Features, 327-328
Feature syndicates, 435-436
Feature Writer and Syndicate Directory, 400, 451
Federal Bar Association, 590
Federal Communications Commission, 306, 309
Federal Department of Consumers, 200

Federal government:
 change in climate, 41
 counseling management on policies, 43
 foreign agent registration, 48
 information gathering, 42-43
 information sources, 49-50
 interpreting government actions, 43
 interpreting organization's actions, 43-44
 investigations and hearings, 46-47
 lobbying, 48
 support of sales, 45
 taking advocacy position, 44
 tools and techniques, 41
 who does public relations work, 48-49
 working with news media, 44-45
Federalist Papers, 190
Federal Register, 42
Federal Regulation of Lobbying Act, 594
Federal Reserve Board, 43
Federal Trade Commission, 43, 199, 594
Federations, 231
Feedback, 7
Fellowship of Christians in Arts, Media and Entertainment, 281
Files, 404
Films:
 foreign audiences, 352
 movies, 481-485 (*see also* Movies)
 publications, 622
 religion, 282
 school use, 525
 slidefilms and slides, 491-492
 sponsored motion pictures, 486-490
 travel, 339
 TV releases and other films, 490-491
Financial Analysis Societies, National Federation of, 130-131
Financial columns, syndicated, 127
Financial organizations:
 advertising, 246
 basic principles and differences, 245-247
 buildings, 246
 changes in social patterns, 248-249
 distinctiveness, 246
 explosion of demand, 247-248
 forums, 246-247
 graphics, 246
 implications for other institutions, 249
 particular needs, 245
 publications, 246
 respected personalities, 246
 services, 246
 visibility, 245, 246
Financial publications, 126-127
Financial public relations:
 advertising, 109
 annual meeting of stockholders, 109
 annual reports, 112-120 (*see also* Annual reports)
 changes increase need, 106-107
 dealing with press, 128
 describing management, 111

Financial public relations: (*cont'd.*)
 directories for management changes, 127
 disclosure, 133-134, 140-148
  explanation of Exchange policies, 142-147
  guides, 133-134
  outline of Exchange policies, 140, 142
  public announcements, 147-148
  SEC requirements, 148
 financial profile, 111
 four basic publics, 111
 homecomings, 134
 investment clubs, 132-133
 liaison with executive management, 108
 long-term effectiveness, 135
 news wires, 133
 open houses, 134
 personnel, requisites, 108-110
 post annual meeting report, 124
 primary investment services, 127-128
 program, establishing, 110-111
 proxy fights, 109, 133
 publications, 109, 120, 126-128
 publicity, 108, 126
 regional meetings of stockholders, 109
 registration period publicity, 128-129
 reporting requirements, 149-155
 search for effective programs, 107
 security analysts, 109, 129-132 (*see also* Security analysts)
 seminar courses, 110
 shareholder annual meetings, 120, 123-124
 shareholder surveys, 134-135
 special services to stockholders, 109
 statistical bureaus, financial, 127-128
 stockholder correspondence, 108
 stockholder letters, 125-126
 stockholder surveys, 108
 syndicated columns, 127
 takeover efforts, 136-140
  basic differences, 136-137
  defenses against proxy flight, 137
  public relations activities, 139-140
  strategic defenses, 138-139
  tender offers, 137-138
 tender offers, 109, 133
 twelve financial publics, 107-108
 vocal stockholders, 123-124
Financial statistical bureaus, 127-128
First National Bank of Chicago, 246
Fisher, Lester, 302
Flannel boards, 492
Flesch, Rudolph, 527
Food and Drug Administration, 199, 596
Food and Drug Law, 200
Forbes, 567
Ford, Gerald, 96, 100, 200, 314
Foreign agent registration, 48
Foreign Language Press of America, 398
Foreign trade, 352
Fort Lauderdale News, 98
Fortune, 198, 325, 567

INDEX

Forums, 246, 524-525
Foundation for Public Relations Research and Education, 590
4-H, 258
Fraternal groups, 521
Frederick Douglass Years, 91
Freedom of Information Act, 312
French, 352, 354
Frey, Donald N., 285
Front projectors, 492
FTC Act, 596
Fulbright, J. William, 299, 300, 591
Funding laws, 342-344 (*see also* Political candidates)
Fundraising:
  nonprofit organization, 273-275
  political candidates, 344
  publications, 623

G

Galbraith, John Kenneth, 36, 37, 38
Gallup, George, 366
Gallup Poll, 366, 367, 533
Gardner, John W., 201
Gaskill, William, 597
Gaudet, 16
Gebbie Press House Magazine Directory, 398
General Television Network, 418
Generation gaps, 296
Germans, 351, 354, 355
Gibson, D. Parke, 88
Girl Scouts of U.S.A., 265, 268, 269
Giveaways, 408
Glenn, John, 336
Good will, 6, 8, 9, 10
Government:
  acceptance of public relations, 320-321
  broadcasting, 309-310
  building public image, 314-315
  federal, 40-50 (*see also* Federal government)
  forces for change, 37-39
    criticism, 37-38
    direction of change, 38
    role of public relations, 38-39
  freedom of information, 312-313
  good will, 10
  information programs, 319-321
  information sources, 379-380
  international public relations, 352
  low in public relations, 591
  needs for restraint, 314
  negative reactions, 318
  news management, 315
  nonprofit organizations, 265
  our way of life, 97
  public affairs, 32-33
  publics, 315-319
  role of public relations, 313-315
  state, 51-63 (*see also* State government)
  utilities, agencies and officials, 220

Government: (*cont'd.*)
  voting, politics and government, 81-82
  Watergate, 313
Government Printing Office, 42
Government relations, 570
Gow, Ronald, 192
Graphic arts, publications, 622
Graphic Arts Research Department, 558
Graphics and printing, 537-566 (*see also* Printing)
Greenbrier Report, 288
Groups:
  business, 520-521
  church, 519-520
  consumer, 67 (*see also* Community relations)
  education, 521
  farm, 519
  fraternal and service, 521
  interlocking effect, 523-524
  labor, 521
  minority, and allies, 521
  schools, 524-525
    films, 525
    forums, 524-525
    presentations, 524-525
  veterans', 519
  welfare, 522-523
  women's groups, 518-519
Guest relations, 570
"Guidelines for Corporate Political Action Committees," 33
Guide to Recurrent and Special Government Statistics, 63
Gulf Oil Corporation, 478
Gutenberg, Johann, 277

H

Haener, Harold F., 252
Hagerty, James C., 313
Hamilton, Alexander, 190
Handbook on Church Public Relations, 280
Harlow, Rex F., 499
Harrington, Alan, 611
Harsch, Joseph C., 82
Hart, Philip, 201
Harvard Business Review, 502
Hattal, Alvin M., 49
Hawver, Carl F., 311
Health and Safety Service, 276
Hearings, 46-47
Hearst Metrotone, 491
Hechinger, Fred, 285
Hefty, Robert W., 176
Heins, Lester F., 282
Henry, Patrick, 313
Hersh, Seymour, 300
Heyns, Roger W., 285
HFD Retailing Home Furnishings, 251
"History of Medicine," 302
Hobby magazines, 456-457

Hollywood Reporter, 485
Homecomings, 134
Home economists, extension, 512
Hoobler, G.I., 157
Hopkinson, Tom M., 27
Hospitality suites, 449
House Committee on Government Operations, 313
"House Magazines," 175
"How to Get Things Changed," 65
Hudson, Howard Penn, 40
Hyer, Marjorie, 282

I

"If You Want Air Time," 283
Illustrated general magazines, 453
Illustrations, newspaper, 443-447
Ilott, Pamela, 283
"Image," 8, 603
Imdrim case, 596
Independent samples, 368
Indian, American, 88
Industrial associations, 61, 62, 97
Industrial publications, 271, 273
Industrial Relations Center, 260
Industry, good will, 10
Industry associations, 61, 62, 97
Industry relations:
  being helpful to others, 159-161
  consumerism, 159
  helping other companies, 161
  good conduct, 158
  improving, 157-159
  interests of public, 160
  need for cooperation, 156-157
  other systems, 158
  pollution, 158-159
  public relations assistance, 161
  sales benefits, 160
  Warner and Swasey, 157
  work with business groups, 160-161
"Inefficiency in America," 199
Influential groups, 517-525 (*see also* Groups)
Information banks, 466
Information programs, 468
Information source:
  broadcasting, 471-473
  company publications, 174-175 (*see also* Company publications)
  ethnic media and publications, 89-90, 91-95
  extension home economists, 512
  fact-finding, 375-382
    almanacs, chronologies, 377
    bibliographical publications, 377-378
    business information, 378-379
    encyclopedias and reference books, 376-377
    government, 379-380

Information source: (cont'd.)
    people, institutions, and media, 380-382
    services, 375-376
    statistics, 382
  Federal Bar Association, 590
  federal government, 49-50
  financial public relations, 126-128
  free materials available, 374
  government, 319-320
  influential groups, 517-525
    business, 520-521
    church, 519-520
    education, 521
    farm, 519
    fraternal and service, 521
    labor, 521
    veterans', 519
    women's, 519
  knowledge of sources is essential, 373
  lists, 395-398, 509
  minority groups, and allies, 521
  "morgue," 415
  movies, 485
  newsletters, 512
  newsreel footage, library, 491
  press clipping bureaus, 409-414
  public affairs, 35
  Public Relations Law, 592
  publications (*see* Publications)
  roster of sources, 374
  schools, 524, 525
  services, 395-398
  sponsored motion pictures, 487, 489
  utilities, checklist, 226-229 (*see also* Utility and its public)
  welfare, 522-523
  working with state government, 61-63
"Information Specialists," 319
In loco parentis, 296
Inserts, 513
Institute of Personality Assessment and Research, 385
Institutional magazines, 457
Institutions, information sources, 380-382
Intellectual magazines, 456
Interfaith organizations, 281-282
Internal communications, publications, 621-622
Internal house magazines, 459
Internal Revenue Service, 44
International public relations:
  determining local posture, 355
  developing need, 350-352
  differing outlooks, 354
  functioning abroad, 353-357
  government's activities, 352
  identifying with local interests, 355-356
  major considerations, 354-356
  major publics, 355
  multinational business communication, 350-352

International public relations: (cont'd.)
  increased importance of foreign trade, 352
  lessening of price as factor, 351-352
  successful appeals to U.S. market, 351
  understanding differing attitudes, 351
  staff and counsel abroad, 356-357
  universal differences, 354
  values/ethics, 355
International Public Relations Association, 353, 357
International public relations operations, 595
Interstate Commerce Act in 1887, 97
Interstate Commerce Commission, 199
Interviewing:
  independent samples, 368-369
  mail, 368
  panels, 369
  personal, 368
  telephone, 368
  television, 470-471
Investigations, 46-47
Investment clubs, 132-133
Investment services, 127-128
Investor relations, retailers, 259
Involvement, 268
Irwin, James W., 518
Issues, campaign, 346-347
Italy, 351, 354

J

Jacobson, 298
Japanese, 351, 352, 355
Jargon, 21, 604
Jefferson, Thomas, 96, 299, 313
Johnson, Lyndon B., 312
Joint Budget Committee, 280
Jones, Reginal E., 28
Journalism, publications, 621
Journal of Broadcasting, 310
Journals of Commerce, 434
Jungle, 199
Justice Department, 231
Juvenile magazines, 455-456

K

Kallsen, Loren J., 486
Karson, Stanley G., 232
Katz, Elihu, 18
Kaufman, Ben L., 282
Kefauver, Estes, 200
Kelly, Robert A., 267
Kennedy, J.F., 17, 20, 200, 348, 594
Kiplinger Washington Editors, 45
Kiplinger Washington Letter, 511, 523
Klapper, 15, 16
Klein, Herbert, 314
Kohl, Peggy, 205
Koyen, Kenneth, 332

Kraft, John F., 340
Krugman, Herbert E., 18

L

Labor, problems, 9
Labor groups, 521
Labor matters:
  background "briefing," 179-180
  guarding proprietary information, 179
  handling the strike, 183-184
  how to help newsmen, 181-182
  local activities, 182-183
  organizing for job, 182-183
  preparing for negotiations, 178-179
  principal responsibilities, 180-181
  public relations, 177
  reporting results, 183
  restless employee, 177-178
  timing, 178
Laissez faire, 199
Landis, James, 528
Language and good taste, 301-302
Lapel buttons, 513
Larson, Roy, 282
"Lateral laryngitis," 598
Latin America, 352, 354
Law:
  administrative public relations matters, 591
  areas of concern, 591
  broad basic premises, 589-590
  dangers of deception, 593
  day-to-day operational public relations activities, 591
  genetic force, 590-591
  government attitudes, 591
  government regulation, 591
  government relations, 591
  increasing public relations interest, 590-591
  international operations, 595
  lawyer/law dichotomy, 597
  liability, 596-597
  lobbying, 594
  practitioner in politics, 594
  public issue advertising, 593-594
  public relations and litigation, 595-596
  public relations/legal team, 597-598
  recommendations in brief, 598
  relative degree of legal danger, 592-593
  research materials, 594-595
  tabulation of specific legal areas, 592
Laws, 314
Lazarsfeld, 16, 606
League of Women Voters, 62
Le Bon, Gustave, 601
Lee, Ivy, 19, 597
Legislative organizations, 62-63
Legislator, 54, 265
Legislature, 54
Leslie, John W., 291

INDEX

Lesly, Philip, 3, 12, 38, 99, 136, 245, 273, 279, 350, 383, 391, 428, 460, 465, 494, 504, 511, 591, 601
Letters:
  approach, 509-510
  contents, 510
  continuity, 510
  enclosures, 510
  etiquette, 510-511
  lists, 509
  outward form and appearance, 510
  testing, 510
  timing, 510
Levitt, Theodore, 18
Lewis, Harold R., 312
Liability, 596
Licensing, 614
Lincoln, 315
Linotron high speed typesetter, 277
Lippman, Walter, 598
Lists, 395-399, 509, 588
Litigation, 595-596
Little, Ernest, 590
Lobbying, 48, 594
Local newspapers, 165
"Look Up and Live" series, 281
Los Angeles Times, 282, 303
Low-income families, utilities, 216-219
Lyons, William A., 215

M

McCrory, James, 315, 319
McGraw-Hill, 45
McLuhans, Marshall, 425
MacKinnon, Donald W., 385, 578, 605
MacNaughton, Donald S., 477
Madison, James, 96
Magazine-format programs, 469
Magazines:
  agricultural, 458
  business, 458-459
  Canadian, 455
  city and state, 457-458
  class, 454
  classifications, 451-459
  clipping bureaus, 409-414, 451, 588
  company publications (*see* Company publications)
  consumer, 448
  dealer relations, 194
  dealing with editors, 448-451
    contacting local magazine outlets, 449
    established writers, 451
    free lance articles, 451
    hospitality suites, 449
    press conferences or showings, 449
    product demonstrations, 449-450
    queries, 449
    releases and photographs, 450-451
    special entertainments, 449-450
    tours, 450
    writing editor, 449

Magazines: (*cont'd.*)
  visits to editor, 449
  digests, 456
  employee (*see* Company publications)
  external company, 459
  general, 451-453
  institutional, 457
  intellectual, 456
  internal house, 459
  invited to "tie-in" stores, 262
  juvenile, 455-456
  men's, 455
  Merchandising Magazine, 408
  minority groups, 90
  news and illustrated, 453
  newsletters, 456
  nonprofit organization, 271
  Pacific Travel News, 335
  quarterly, 164
  references, 448
  represented in Washington, 45
  special, 453-457
  sport and hobby, 456-457
  timing, 451
  trade publications, 251, 458
  weekly newspaper, 453
  women's and home, 454-455
Magnetic boards, 492
Magnuson-Moss Act, 593
Mail:
  direct, 100, 309, 327
  retailers, 259
Mail interviewing, 368
Mailers, dealer relations, 195
Mailgrams, 513
Mailing lists, 395-399, 509, 588
Mailing services, 433-434
Maldon, 354-355
Management by objective, 268
Management changes, directories, 127
Management publications, 620
Managing the Human Climate, 112, 511
Manpower, 319
Marketing:
  advertising, 187
  consultants, 190
  corporate identity, 190-191
  establishing favorable climate, 191
  explaining publicity to executives, 191
  long-term business development, 187
  merchandising publicity to employees, 191
  new public relations role, 186-190
  organization, 191
  personnel, 188
  product planning, 191
  promotional process, 190-191
  publicity and salesman, 191
  representing public interest, 187-188
  role of public interest, 185-186
  special events, 191
  third party endorsement, 191

Marketing: (*cont'd.*)
  trade associations, 188, 190
  truth, 187
Marshall, E.G., 478
Martineau, Pierre, 499
Marxist countries, 354
Maverick, Maury, 528
Mayer, Terry, 250
Media:
  attacks, handling, 425-426
  attention focusing on, 606
  broadcast, 338-339, 466, 467, 498-499
  changing role, 605-607
  creator of news, 606
  criticism, 299-300
  dealer communication, 194-196
  disasters, 423
  educational institutions, 295, 296
  emergencies, handling, 422-426
  ethnic, 89-90
  exclusive story, 420-421
  handling inquiries from, 421-422
  individual, work with, 394-395
  information sources, 380-382
  keys to relationships, 427
  letter, 418
  mass, 16
  memo, 419
  movies, 481-485 (*see also* Movies)
  multiple-channel approach, 19
  new forces of competition, 606
  new shifts in mix, 607
  news conferences, briefing, introductions, 417-420
  newswires, 419
  nonprofit organization, 268, 271-273
  patterns of working with, 417
  press showings, 420
  professional organization, 325
  publicity, 408
  selection, 18
  slidefilms and slides, 491-492
  sovereignty, 416-417
  sponsored motion pictures, 486-490
  telegram, 419
  telephone, 419
  television, 17
  TV releases and other films, 490-491
  utilities, 220-221
  visual and/or audio aids, 492-493
Media Distribution Services, 395
Mediamatic Calendar of Special Editorial Issues, 398
Megapaper, 164
Membership Directory, 281
Membership List of Society of Magazine Writers, 398
Men's magazines, 455
Menswear, 251
Mentions, 326
Merchandising Magazine, 408
Merton, Robert, 606
Middle-income families, utilities, 216-219

Miles, Thomas W., 48
Milk Industry Foundation, 242
Miller, Eugene, 105, 611
Minibooks, 461-462
Minneapolis Star, 282
Minority groups:
   attitudes, understanding, 88-89
   civil rights organizations, 91
   community relations, 89
   confrontation, 88-89
   creating target material, 91-95
   employment, 89
   hiring and training, 219
   media, 89-90
   organizations, 521
   organization's position, 89-90
   press relations, 89
   publicity, 89, 91
   research, 89
   servicing their media, 90
   telling the story, 90
   25 million members, 88
   working with, 90-91
Minority/urban interests, 33
Mitchell, Broadus, 190
Mollenhoff, 311, 315
Money, nonprofit organization, 273-275
Money making, political candidates, 344
Monroe, James, 190
Monthly publication, 164
Moss, John, 313
Motion pictures:
   sponsored, 486-490
   travel, 339
Motivation, 22
Motivation in Advertising, 499
Motivation research, 368
Movie Business: American Film Industry Practice, 485
Movies:
   books, helpful, 485
   new pattern of film as medium, 481-482
   publicity opportunities today, 482-485
      in-film promotion, 483
      locations, 483
      people, 485
      potential, 485
      product, 485
      release-related tie-ins, 483-485
      taking advantage, 485
      timing, 485
   sponsored motion pictures, 486-490
   trade journals, 485
Movies and Society, 485
Moynihan, Daniel P., 37, 509
Multinational business communication, 350
Murphy, Thomas, 202

N

NACBA—Gram, 281
NACBA Ledger, 281

Nader, Ralph, 28, 36, 199, 201
Name:
   choosing, 607, 609
   image factor, 607-609
   neutral, 21, 605
National Association of Broadcasters, 283, 306, 308, 310
National Association of Church Business Administrators, 281
National Association of Free Lance Photographers, 400
National chain, 251
National Civic Review, 63
National Commission on the Causes and Prevention of Violence, 300
National Communications Council for Human Services, 266, 269
National Conference of Christians and Jews, 282
National Conference of State Legislatures, 63
National Council of Churches, 281
National Democratic Committee chairman, 347
National Directory of Newsletters and Reporting Services, 398
National Directory of Weekly Newspapers, 434
National Federation of Financial Analysts Societies, 130-131
National Geographic, 45, 337, 478
National Investor Relations Institute, 110
National Labor Relations Board, 418
National Municipal League, 63
National organizations, 62
National program underwriting, 477-478
National Radio Month, 308
National Religious Broadcasters, 282
National Research Bureau, 283, 400, 464
National Retail Merchants Association, 260, 261, 262
Nation's Business, 45
NC News Service, 282
Negroes, 88, 89, 90, 91, 92, 93, 95
Nelson, Paul R., 537
Network news staffs, radio-TV, 45, 49
Networks, 471
New Dayton Express, 75
New Hollywood: American Movies in '70's, 485
Newmyer, Arthur G., 43
News and publicity, 392-393
News Bureaus in U.S., 398
News editors, 427
Newsfilm release, 490-491
News Letter, 282
Newsletter on Newsletters, 512
Newsletters, 45, 164, 194, 262, 270, 281, 329, 456, 511-512, 540
News magazines, 453
News media, federal government, 44-45
Newsmen, how to help, 181-182

Newspaper as Advertising Medium, 428
Newspaper Guild, 302
Newspapers:
   acquisitions, 303
   analyzing the problem, 300
   annual editions, 432
   automobile sections, 432
   back copies, 302
   "beats," 430-431
   books, 432
   cartoon, 429
   city desk, 429
   clipsheets, 439, 440
   columnists, 430
   comics, 430
   company publications (*see* Company publications)
   computerized mailing, 433-434
   court beats, 431
   criticism of media, 299-300
   daily, 428
   distribution services, 437-438
   drama and movie sections, 432
   editorial page, 429
   educational editions, 432
   electronics, 301
   employees, 164-165
   feature syndicates, 434-436
   financial page, 431-432
   home and garden sections, 432
   home-town press, 432-434
   language and good taste, 301-303
   letter to editor, 429
   mechanics of press publicity, 441-443
   minority groups, 90
   news syndicates, 434-435
   nonprofit organization, 271
   "op ed" pages, 429
   periodic editions, 432
   permissions, 302
   photographs and illustrations, 443-447
   photograph syndicates, 436-437
   photography files, 447
   plant tours, 302
   political beats, 431
   press book or kit, 439, 441
   press' sensitivity, 303
   publicity, 301, 428-447
   public relations, 299-303
   public relations newswires, 438-439
   public service bureau, 302
   public service reporting, 300
   range of responsibility, 303
   real estate sections, 432
   religions publicity, 431
   role changing, 300-301
   special business editions, 432
   special classifications, 434
   special editions, 432
   special events, 302-303
   specialized sections, 429-430
   standard of excellence, 303
   state page or state edition, 430

INDEX 657

Newspapers: (cont'd.)
   Sunday, 428, 431
   television-radio section, 432
   travel sections, 432
   wire services, 301
   withholding bad news, 303
News publications, 164-165
News releases, 195, 326, 540-541
News services, 45
News shows, 468
Newsweek, 49, 202, 282
News wires, 133, 438-439
Newton, Hugh C., 96
New York Convention and Visitors Bureau, 335
New York Times, 34, 45, 101, 139, 202, 208, 251, 278, 282, 285, 300, 302, 303, 327, 392
1984, by G. Orwell, 21
Nixon, Richard, 52, 313, 314, 315, 318
Nominating process, 84-85
Nonprofit organization:
   board of directors, 264
   budgeting, 271
   clientele, 265
   community, 265
   complaint system, 270-271
   contributors, 265
   emergency public relations, 275-276
   government and legislators, 265
   internal public relations, 270
   involvement, 268
   kit for affiliates, 269
   management by objective, 268
   media, 271-273
      billboards, 273
      broadcast, 271
      check sheet, 273
      industrial publications, 271, 273
      magazines, 271
      making material work overtime, 273
      newspapers, 271
   media analysis, 268
   members, 264-265
   metropolitan coordination, 273
   newsletters and bulletins, 270
   perspective, 276
   prime publics, 264-265
   public relations and policy making, 266-267
   raise money, 273-275
      organization structure, 274-275
      organizing campaign, 274
   related, 265
   special events, 273
   speakers' bureau, 271
   staff, 264
   successful public relations, 267-271
   surveys, 267-268
   training volunteers and staff, 269-270
   volunteer agencies, 268-269
   volunteers, 265
North Americans, 354

O

O'Brien, Lawrence, 347
O'Dwyers Directory of Corporate Communications, 567, 571, 575
O'Malley, Patrick, 302
Occupational Safety and Health Act, 41
Occupational Safety Health Administration, 34, 231
Office for Films and Broadcasting, 282
Office of Institutional Advancement, 289
Officials:
   elected, 55
   non-elected, 55-56
Olivetti, 351
Ombudsman, 294
On The Track, 92
Opaque projectors, 492
Open-book policy, 584-585
Open houses, 134, 165, 273
Opinion leaders, 16
Opinion research, 241
Orange Disc, 478
Organization handbook, 41
Organizations:
   community, 265
   consumer, 198-208
   developing religious public relations, 280-281
   financial, 245-249 (*see also* Financial organizations)
   foster a cause, 98
   influential groups, 517-525 (*see also* Groups)
   interfaith, 281-282
   legislative, 62-63
   national, 62
   nonprofit, 263-276 (*see also* Nonprofit organization)
   press clipping bureaus, 409-414
   professional, 322-331 (*see also* Professional organization)
   public affairs, 35
   related, 265
   seminar courses, 110
   services, 395-398
   state, 62
   tourist, 332
   travel, 334-336
Orwell, George, 21
Ostling, Richard, 282
Outdoor Advertising Association of America, 514
Overhead, 582
Overhead projectors, 492

P

PAC, 86, 87
Pacific Area Travel Association, 335
Pacific Travel News, 335
Packaging, 256
Painted bulletins, 514

Panels, 368, 369
Panel shows, 469
Panel survey, 363
Paperback books, 461-462
Parade, 336
Party structure, 345-346
Patrick, Ruth, 78
Payments, counsel, 580-582
Pay-TV, 466
Peak, Wilbur J., 64
Penar, Diane, 302
People, information sources, 380-382
Periodicals:
   information on state government, 63
   public affairs, 35
   public relations, 618
   trade, 251
Perry, Glen, 190, 597
Personal drop-off, 368
Personal interviewing, 368
Personnel Division Merit Award, 260
Peterson, Esther, 205
Philippines, 355-356
Phillips, David J., 37
Photographers, 400, 427
Photographs:
   magazines, 450-451
   newspaper, 443-447
Photograph syndicates, 436-437
Photography files, 447
Planning, 385-386
Plant Relocation, Case History of a Move, 79
Plant tours, 302
Plato, 314
Player, Willis, 353
Pledge nights, 480
Police Athletic League, 258
Policy:
   formulating, 7, 11
   publications, 620
Political Action Committees, 343
Political candidates:
   campaign organization, 341-342
   candidate, 344-345
      categories, 345
      deciding approach, 345
   effects of funding laws, 342-344
      dealing with politicians, 344
      disclosure, 343
      federal money, 343
      independent outlays, 343
      limits, 343
   focusing interest on candidate, 342
   fund raising, money making, 344
   issues, 346-348
      benefits of research, 347-348
      use of surveys, 346-347
   party structure, 345-346
   reaching the voter, 342
   tools, 348-349
      advertising agency, 348
      avoiding shackles, 349

658 INDEX

Political candidates: (cont'd.)
    importance of theme, 348-349
    public relations in campaign, 348
Political public relations, publications, 620-621
Politics, 314
Politics:
    campaign, 85-86
    civic service, 81
    clubs, 84
    committees, 86
    donations, 86-87
    good business, 81
    nominating, 84-85
    political parties, 82-83
    precinct, 83-84
    voting, politics and government, 81-82
    your role, 87
Polling, publications, 619
Polls, 101, 103 (*see also* Support, public)
Pollution, 158-159
Porter, Sylvia, 432
Post, 45
Post annual meeting report, 124
Post cards, 511
Poster panels, 514
Power leaders, 17
Powers, Martin, 319
Practitioner in politics, 594
Praeger, Howard A., 211
PR Aids' Party Line, 451
Precinct, 83-84
Prejudices, overcoming, 9
Presentations, 524-525, 587
Press:
    annual reports, 114, 115
    financial public relations, 128, 132
    information on state government, 63
    travel and tourism, 336, 338
Press book, 439, 441
Press clipping bureaus, 409-414, 451, 588
Press Club, 45
Press kits, 328-329, 420, 439, 441, 541
Press publicity, mechanics, 441-443
Press release, 45, 90
Press room, 424
Prestige, 8
Pre-test, 363
Primary investment services, 127-128
Principles and trends:
    accreditation and licensing, 614
    away from oversimplification, 603
    changing role of media, 605-607
    complexity of group attitudes, 601
    conflict of electronic revolutions, 602-603
    edifice as visible symbol, 609-610
    ethics and standards, 613-614
    evaluation of public relations, 611-612
    fallacies about communication, 603-605
        anti-communication, 604-605
        faith in interchange, 604
    future requirements, 610-611

Principles and trends: (cont'd.)
    growing need for broad scope, 614
    intangibles, 601-603
    moves toward professionalism, 612-614
    name, image factor, 607-609
    resistance of attitudes, 602
    sources of criticism, 613
Printing:
    announcements, 538
    annual report, 538
    answer set, 538
    award, 538
    bleed, 538
    book, 538
    booklet, 538
    broadside, 538
    brochure, 538
    brownlines, 538-539
    bulletin, 539
    camera ready copy, 539
    catalog, 539
    chromalin, 539
    circular, 539
    clipsheet, 539
    cold type, 539
    color separations, 539
    comic book, 539
    computer cards, 539
    computer letters, 539
    computer typesetting, 539
    "C" prints, 539
    cropping, 559
    distribution, 542-543
        bulk third-class matter, 543
        express mail, 542
        first-class matter, 542
        fourth-class matter, 543
        priority mail, 542
        second-class matter, 542
        third-class matter, 543
        time and appropriateness, 542
    employee manual, 540
    engravings, 557-560
        halftones, 557-558, 560
        line, 558-559
        surprint, 560
        zinc, 558
    facsimile, 540
    fact sheet, 540
    flip cards, 540
    folded sheet, or folder, 538
    house organ, 540
    illustrated letter, 540
    insert, 540
    instruction book, 540
    invitations, 540
    key numbers, 540
    labels, 540
    leaf, 538
    leaflet, 540
    mechanical, 540
    memorandum, 540
    negatives, 540

Printing: (cont'd.)
    newsletter, 540
    news release, 540-541
    pamphlet, 541
    paper backs, 541
    paper sizes, 562
    paper stocks, comparison chart, 563-564
    personalized letters, 541
    photostats, 541
    posters, 541
    preparing copy, 546-548
        artwork, 547
        layout, 547-548
        tips, 547
    press kit, 541
    press type, 541
    processes and techniques, 543-546
        copiers, 546
        intaglio, 545-546
        letterpress, 543-544
        "office duplicator" equipment, 546
        offset lithography, 544-545
        planography, 545
        rotogravure, 546
        sheet-fed gravure, 546
        silk screen, 546
    publications, 622
    questionnaire, 541
    release on photograph, 541
    reports, 541
    reproduction proofs, 541
    retouch, 541
    return card, 541
    run-of-press, 541-542
    scanners, 542
    self-mailer, 542
    sheet, 538
    sizing or scaling illustration, 559
    space and copy fitting, 554-557
        character count, 557
        word count, 554, 556-557
    transparencies, 542
    types, 549-554
        agate, 550
        amount of ledding, 554
        ems, 550
        faces, 550
        families, 550
        font, 550
        gothic, 549
        italic, 549
        ledding a line, 550
        measuring and calculating, 550, 554
        pica, 550
        proofreading, 550
        Roman, 549
        sans serif, 549
        script, 549
        series, 550
        slugs, 550
        text, 549
    typography, 548-549
        electric typewriters, 549

INDEX

Printing: (cont'd.)
    handlettering, 549
    photo composition, 549
    press type, 549
    teletypesetting, 548-549
  welcome booklet, 542
  what to use when, 538-542
  why important, 537-538
Priorities, hypothetical corporation, 386-387
Probability sampling, 367
Producers, TV film, 473
Product demonstrations, 449
Production, publications, 622
Product publicity, 407-408, 570
Professional associations, 97, 98, 231
Professionalism, 612-614
Professional organization:
  attracting top-caliber personnel, 324
  books, 329-330
  by-lined articles and features, 327-328
  cost effectiveness, 324
  credibility, 324
  endorsement articles (case histories), 327
  fact sheets and press kits, 328-329
  getting job done, 330-331
  marketing strategy needed, 323-324
    ethical considerations, 323-324
  newsletters and brochures, 329
  news releases, 326
  periodic audit, 326
  prestige by association, 324
  quotes, mentions, short items, 326
  regular columns, 330
  reprints, brochures, other direct mail, 327
  research projects, 328
  round tables, 330
  seminars, 330
  speeches, 330
  sponsored meetings, 330
  start with plan, 324-326
  visibility, 324
Professional's Guide to Public Relations Services, 395
Professional societies or associations, 231
Profile survey, 362
Programming, radio and television:
  self-produced, syndicating, 471
  service, 472
  types, 467
Projectors, 492
Promotion:
  broadcasters, 307-308
  corporate public relations, 569-570
  public television and radio, 479
  term, 391
Promotion Exchange, 262
Propaganda, publications, 619
Propaganda program, 99-100
Proposals, 587
Prout, Charles H., 567
Proxy fights, 109, 133, 137

PR Reporter, 571, 575
Prudential Insurance, 477
Public address systems, 516
Public affairs:
  associations and nonprofit institutions, 36
  budgets, 35
  business and society, 28
  career training, 30
  central coordination, 31
  changing directions, 29-30
  committees and boards, 31
  consultants, 35-36
  consumerism, 34
  corporate role, 29
  environmental problems, 34
  government relations, 32-33
  historical background, 27-28
  how to organize, 30-32
  information sources, 35
  major components, 32-34
  minority/urban interests, 33
  one top staff executive, 31
  personnel, 32
  political and economic education, 33-34
  problems and barriers, 34-35
  public issues, 34
  regional representation, 31-32
  relationship to public relations, 30
  social audit, 28-29
  trends for tomorrow, 36
  what it accomplishes, 36
Public Affairs Council, 62
Public Affairs Monitor, 72
Publication, arranging, 460-461
Publications:
  advertising, 623
  audio/visual, 622
  bibliographical, 377-378
  books and other publications, 460-464 (*see also* Books and other publications)
  broadcasting, 310
  business, 126-127, 458-459
  communications, 619
  company, 166-175, 570 (*see also* Company publications)
  dealer relations, 194-195
  educational institutions, 295
  external company, 459
  films, 622
  financial, 126-127
  financial organizations, 246
  foreign audiences, 352
  fund raising, 623
  graphic arts, 622
  industrial, 271
  internal communications, 621-622
  journalism, 621
  magazines (*see* Magazines)
  management and policy, 620
  megapapers, 164
  minority groups, 90

Publications: (*cont'd.*)
  monthly, 164
  news, 164-165
  political public relations, 620-621
  printing, 622
  production, 622
  propaganda, 619
  public affairs, 618-619
  publicity, 619
  public opinion and polling, 619
  public relations, 617-618
  public relations periodicals, 618
  public speaking, 623
  reliable sources of lists, 395-398
  religious, 281, 282, 283
  semantics and usage, 622-623
  state government, 62-63
  stockholder, 109, 120
  television and radio, 621
  trade, 45, 195, 458-459
  weekly, 165
Public affairs, publications, 618-619
Public Broadcasting Service, 477, 478
Public issue advertising, 593-594
Public issues, 34
Publicist, 433
Publicity:
  approvals, 403-404
  billing, 402
  broadcast and composite reports, 414-415
  budget, 399-402
  cartoon booklets, 462-463
  characteristics of good publicity staff, 416
  corporate public relations department, 570
  distribution to smaller newspapers, 400-401
  entertainment, 401
  fee, 399
  files, 404
  film footage, 400
  lists, 395-399
  local, 394
  magazines, (*see also* Magazines)
  mailing, 401
  mats, 400
  media, 408, 416-427 (*see also* Media)
  messenger, 401
  mileage, 401
  models, 401-402
  movies, 481-485 (*see also* Movies)
  national, 394
  news, 392-393
  newspapers, 428-447 (*see also* Newspapers)
  photographs, 399-400
  planning, 393-403
    make lists, 395-399
    make the budget, 399-402
    plan work with individual media, 394-395

660 INDEX

Publicity: (cont'd.)
    research, 393-394
    schedule the activity, 402-403
    set objective, 394
  planning program, 391-392
  press clipping bureaus, 409-414
  product, 407-408
  production of copy, 401
  publications, 619
  regional, 394
  religious, 431
  rumors, 408-409
  schedule activity, 402-403
  sectional, 394
  services, 395-399
  special events, 404-407
  television and radio, 465-475 (*see also* Television and radio)
  three forms of work, 417
Publicity, How to Get It, 251
Publicity experts, 48
Public opinion, publications, 619
Public opinion surveys, 362
Public relations:
  accomplishments, 8
  accreditation and licensing, 614
  adjustment in age of revolutions, 4-5
  analysts, planning, programming, 383-387
  attitudes, 6, 7
  benefits, 8-11
    attacks, forestalling, 9-10
    change, directing course, 11
    community, 9
    customers, 10
    dealers, 10
    education of public, 10
    government, 10
    group attitudes toward organization, 10-11
    image, 8
    industry, 10
    labor problems, 9
    misconceptions, overcoming, 9
    personnel, 10
    policy, formulation and guidance, 11
    prejudices, overcoming, 9
    prestige, 8
    promotion of products, 8-9
    society, viability, 11
    stockholders, 9
    suppliers, 10
    supporters, 10
  carrying out planned activities, 7
  corporate department, 567-575
  counsel, 576 (*see also* Counsel)
  criticism, 613
  definition, 4, 40
  development, 3-4
  emerging principles and trends, 601-614 (*see also* Principles and trends)
  ethics and standards, 613-614
  evaluation, 611-612

Public relations (cont'd.)
    measurability, 611-612
    services, 611
    tangible goals, 612
  feedback, evaluation, adjustment, 7
  forces for change, 38-39
  good will, 6, 8, 9, 10
  mass educational devices, 4-5
  need for broad scope, 614
  opinion, analyzing state, 7
  policy formulation, 7, 11
  problems, anticipating, 7
  professionalism, 612-614
  serves organizations, 6
  universe, 7-8
  who works, 5-6
  workers, developing, 6
  working together, 5
Public Relations Aids, 395
Public Relations Consultants Association, 613
Public Relations Handbook, 44, 46, 273
Public Relations Journal, 45, 49, 190, 285, 315, 590, 591
Public Relations Law, 590, 592
"Public Relations Problem Solving Sequence," 267
Public Relations Quarterly, 48
Public Relations Review, 320
Public Relations Society of America, 48, 613
Public service announcements, 480
Public service bureau, 302
Public-service shows, 468
Public speaking, publications, 623
Public support, 96-104 (*see also* Support, public)
Public television and radio, 476-480 (*see also* Television and radio)
Public Utilities Advertising Association, 222

Q

Quarterly magazine, 164
Questionnaire, 367
Quota sampling, 367
Quotes, 326

R

Radio, 45, 47, 49, 90, 114, 115, 254, 271, 283, 342, 465-475, 476-480 (*see also* Television and radio)
Radio news schedules, 164
Radio station, non-commercial, 306
Radock, Michael, 284
Ragan, Bill, 49
Railroad Community Committees, 239
Readership, writing for, 526-536 (*see also* Writing for readership)
Reading rack booklets, 464
Rear projectors, 492

Reciprocal arrangements, 585
Red China, 352
Reddy Kilowatt, 222
Reedy, George, 315
Reference books, 376-377
Reference Guide to Tender Offers, 138
Registration period, 128-129
Releases, 450
Religion and religious groups:
  broadcasting and films, 282
  developing standards, 278-279
  financing program, 280
  gathering the facts, 279-280
  interfaith organizations, 281-282
  organizations can help, 280-281
  organizing program, 279-280
  periodicals, 282
  professional associations, 281
  religion editors of secular material, 282-283
  setting up communication center, 280
Religion in American Life, Inc., 281
Religious Communication Congress, 278
Religious News Service, 282
Religious publicity, 431
Religious Public Relations Council, Inc., 281
Religious Public Relations Handbook, 278, 281
Remodeling, 262
Reporters, 427
Reporting:
  public service, 300
  requirements, 149-155
  services, 45
Reports, 588
Reprints, 327
Research:
  before-and-after reading, 362-363
  clarify questions, 361
  confirms, 361
  content analysis, 362
  corporate public relations department, 569
  cost of survey, 369
  depth survey, 363
  effectiveness studies, 362
  evaluating, 364
  fact-finding, 376
  first questions to ask, 366
  guidelines and techniques, 366-369
  how to use tools, 363-364
  importance of know-how, 369
  ingredients of surveys, 366-369
  interviewing, 368-369
    independent samples, 368
    mail, 368
    panels, 368, 369
    personal, 368
    personal drop-off, 368-369
    telephone, 368
  legal aspects of use, 594-595
  many techniques available, 362-364

INDEX

Research: (cont'd.)
  marketing values, 242
  new directions, 364-365
  panel survey, 363
  planning publicity, 393-394
  political candidates, 347-348
  pre-test, 363
  probability sampling, 367
  profile survey, 362
  public opinion surveys, 362
  purposes and types, 361-365
  questionnaire, 367-368
    dealing with complex issues, 367
    designing, 367
    getting at the "why," 368
    intensity of opinion, 368
    motivation research, 368
  quota sampling, 367
  reorients, 361
  retailers, 253
  sample, 367
  secondary analysis, 362
  Stapel Scalometer, 368
  trend survey, 362
  two kinds, 240
Research Department, 306
Research projects, 328
Resigning an account, 587-588
Response Analysis of Princeton, 214
Retailers:
  appealing to youth, 256-258
  characteristics of retailing, 250-251
  communications by mail, 259
  community relations, 253, 259
  defining store's distinctiveness, 255-256
  discounter, 255
  emergency situations, 260-262
  employee communications, 258
  gearing to current events, 255
  institutional advertising, 253
  internal communications, 253
  local department store, 252-255
  investor relations, 259
  magazine tie-ins and editorial credits, 262
  minority group relations, 259-260
  national chain, 251-252
  packaging and visible symbols, 256
  remodeling, 262
  research, 253
  sales-support publicity and promotion, 254
  specialty shop, 255
  storewide and department events, 253
  store-wide promotions and events, 258-259
  trade periodicals, 251
  types of programs, 251-255
  visibility and identity, 250
  windows as image builders, 256
Reuters, 45
Reynolds, Milton, 408
Rich, Raymond, 273

Robertson, Rebel L., 263
Rockefeller, Nelson, 314
Role of Political Parties, U.S.A., 82
Roosevelt, Franklin, 200, 315, 528
Rosenbloom, Morris Victor, 42, 313
Ross, T.J., 568
Rostin, Leo, 319
Rothchild, Phillip, 318
Round tables, 330
Rourke, Francis E., 314
Rowland, A. Westley, 289
Rubber stamps, 513
Rubin, Bernard, 313, 314
Ruder, William, 314
Rumors, 408-409
Rush, Barbara, 302
Rush, Benjamin, 302
Russia, 352

S

Sain, Kenneth, 302
Salaries, 574-575
Sales activities, 586-587
Sales benefits, 160
Salinger, Pierre, 315
Sample, survey, 367
Samples and giveaways, 408
Sandler Institutional Films, 525
Saxon, David S., 285
Scandanavia, 351, 356
Schmidt, W. James, 79
Scholastic Magazines, 524
Schonfeld, Eugene, 107
Schools, medium of communication, 524-525
Scotch distillers, 352
"Screen News Digest," 491
Scripts, 471, 475
SEC Act, 597
Secondary analysis, 362
Securities and Exchange Acts, 110
Securities and Exchange Commission, 43, 199, 231, 418
Security analysts:
  communicating with, 129-130
  credibility, 131
  functions, 131
  list of major societies, 130-131
  meetings, 132
  needs, 131
  press, 132
  working with, 109
Semantics, publications, 622-623
Seminars:
  Federal Bar Association, 590
  financial public relations, 110
  professional organization, 330
Service groups, 521
Services, 395-399
Seventeen Magazine, 255, 256
Seventh-Day Adventists, 281

Shapiro, Mike, 310
Shareholder annual meetings, 120, 123-124
Shareholder surveys, 134
Shooting an Elephant and Other Essays, 21
Short-wave radio, 424
Show business formats, 469
Signs, 514-515
Silver Anvil Awards, 477
Simon, Morton J., 589
Sinclair, Upton, 199
Slidefilms and slides, 491-492
Slogans, 513
Social audit, 28-29
Social patterns, changes, 248-249
Social Science in Public Relations, 499
Society, 11
Society of Consumer Affairs Professionals in Business, 207, 208
Sorensen, Ted, 319
Source effect, 18
Sources (*see* Information sources)
Space satellites, 466
Spanish-speaking people, 88, 89, 90, 91
Speakers' Bureaus, 271, 308-309, 504-507, 570
"Speak Up" program, 163
Special-events shows, 469
Special-interest magazines, 453-457
Specialty shop, 255
Speeches, 330
Spitzer, 318
Sponsored motion pictures:
  contracting, budgeting, paying, 487-488
  developing script, 488
  distribution, 489-490
  distributors, 489
  how to begin, 487
  post-production, 488-489
  pre-production, 489
  production, 488-489
  production directories, 487
  selecting producer, 487
  Sport and hobby magazines, 456-457
Spot news, 392
Standard Periodical Directory, 398, 448
Standard Rate and Data Service, 398, 448
Standards, ethics and, 613-614
Stapel, Jan, 368
Stapel Scalometer, 368
State government:
  approaches to relations, 56
  components of successful program, 61
  elected officials, 55
  gain management support, 60
  getting started, 61
  influencing executive, 55
  information, 61-63
    additional sources, 63
    corporate program, 61-62
    legislative organizations, 62-63
    national organizations, 62
    state government, 62-63
    state organizations, 62

State government: (cont'd.)
  inventory company's political resources, 61
  need, 51-52
  non-elected officials, 55-56
  political climate of state(s), 61
  profile of company, 61
  prognosis, 52-54
  relations, 54-55
  surveillance, 59-60
    company's *ad hoc* system, 60
    monitoring system for capitals, 60
    private legislative information services, 59-60
  techniques, 56-69
    associations, 58-59
    consultants, 58
    line personnel, 57-58
    multi-state company, 57
    one-state company, 56-57
    people, 59
    professional staff lobbyists, 57
    satellite groups, 59
State magazines, 457-458
State organizations, 62
State University of New York, 289
Stations, radio and television, 472-473, 476, 479-480
Statistical bureaus, financial, 127-128
Statistics, information sources, 382
Steiner, 13, 14, 20
Stetler, C. Joseph, 47
Stickers, 513
Stockholder relations, 570
Stockholders:
  annual meeting, 109
  annual report, 118
  communications, 112
  correspondence, 108
  good will, 9
  letters, 125-126
  publications, 109, 120
  questionnaire, 134-135
  regional meetings, 109
  special services, 109
  surveys, 108
  vocal, 123-124
Stone, Mary E., 65
Strauss, Bert, 65
Strike, handling, 183-184
Subsidy, 461
Sugar, 101
Suggs, Jim, 280
Sunday newspapers, 428, 431
Sunday New York Times, 164
Suppliers, good will, 10
Support, public:
  corporate approach, 97-98
  government, 96-97
  organizations to foster cause, 98
  polls, 101, 103
    influencing legislation, 101, 103
    influencing public opinion, 103

Support, public: (cont'd.)
  membership development, 101
  policy and strategy guidance, 101
  propaganda program, principles, 99-100
    dedicated staff, 99
    define problem, 99
    direct mail, 100
    focus on problem, 99
    honest program, 99-100
    know public opinion, 99
    let Congress know, 100
    planning, 99
    policies simple, 99
    strong backing for staff, 99
    take case to people, 100
    "tight" staff, 99
  public opinion campaign, 100-101
  timing and execution, 103-104
  winning, 98-99
Supporters, good will, 10
Surveys:
  interviewing, 368-369
  nonprofit organizations, 267-268
  political issues, 346-347
  questionnaire, 367-368
  sample, 367
Swart, Charles M., 273
Symbols, 513
Syndicated financial columns, 127
Syndicate Directory, 283, 398
Syndicates (*see* Newspapers)
Syndication of books, 462

T

Taft-Hartley Act, 96, 98
Takeover efforts, 136-137
Talk programs, 469
Technology, changing, 296
Tele-lectures, 493
Telephone:
  educational institutions, 296
  public relations device, 507
Telephone interviewing, 368
Telephone switchboard, 424
Telephone utilities, 221-222
Teletype networks, 164
Teletype services, 133
Television, 45, 47, 49, 165, 254, 271, 283, 342, 352, 465-475, 482
Television and radio:
  approaching broadcasting people, 469-470
  arranging for broadcasts, 468-469
  audience-participation shows, 469
  broadcasters and activism, 467
  capitalizing on broadcast coverage, 474-475
  community antenna television, 465
  diversified broadcasting effort, 473-474
  documentary, 468
  entertainment programs, 469

Television and radio: (cont'd.)
  film for television, 471
  information banks, computers, facsimile systems, 466
  information programs, 468-469
  interviews, TV, 470-471
  magazine-format programs, 469
  news and feature stories, 471
  news shows, 468
  panel shows, 469
  pay-TV, 466
  personnel, 468
  public, 476-480
    audience, 477
    community programs, 479
    Corporation for Public Broadcasting, 477
    local and national opportunities, 476-478
    local stations, 479-480
    local underwriting, 480
    National program underwriting, 477-478
    pledge nights and auctions, 480
    promotion, 479
    Public Broadcasting Service, 477
    public service announcements, 480
    radio, 480
    reaching educators, 479
    reaching the community, 478, 479
    stations, 476-477
    underwriting costs and practices, 479
  publications, 621
  publicity, 465-475
  publicizing broadcast, 475
  public-service shows, 468
  recorded interview, 471
  scripts, 471, 475
  secondary uses for broadcast material, 475
  show business formats, 469
  source file on broadcasting, 471-473
  space satellites, 466
  special-events shows, 469
  still photographs of guest, 475
  structure of broadcast media, 467
  syndicating self-produced programming, 471
  talk programs, 469
  think programs, 468
  types of programming, 467-468
  variety and dramatic programs, 469
  videotapes, 466, 475
  working with broadcast media, 466
Television Factbook, 398
Television Information Office, 308
Television newsfilm release, 490-491
Television Quarterly, 310
Television stations, non-commercial, 306
Tender offers, 109, 133, 137-138
Thorkelson, Wilmar L., 282
Threshold of consciousness, 18-19
Thurston, Robert N., 185

Time, 199, 282, 314
Tocqueville, Alexis de, 230
Tourism (*see* travel and tourism)
Tours:
    come-and-see, 273
    editors, 450
    plant, 302
Trade, foreign, 352
Trade associations, 62, 97, 98, 188, 190, 231
Trade periodicals, 251
Trade press editor, 242
Trade publications, 45, 195, 458-459
Training, broadcasters, 310
Travel and tourism:
    broadcast media, 338-339
    budgeting to attract tourists, 333
    motion pictures, 339
    other services of press, 338
    pictures, 336-337
    planning press coverage, 336
    publicity content, 336
    scheduling, 334
    selecting theme, 334
    working with travel organizations, 334-336
Trends and principles, 601-614
Trend survey, 362
Types, 549-554 (*see also* Printing)
Typesetter, 277
Typography, 548-549 (*see also* Printing)

U

Ulrich's Periodicals Directory, 398
"Understanding Economics," 33
Underwood, Don C., 215
Underwood, Jordan Associates, 222
Underwriting:
    books, 460-461
    costs and practices, 479
    national program, 477-478
United Kingdom, 354
United Methodist Communications, 281
United Press International, 45
United States Government Organization Manual, 41
United States Information Agency, 352
United States Travel Service, 335
United Way of America, 268
Universe of public relations, 6, 7-8
University, nature, 286 (*see also* Educational institutions)
University of California, 285, 578, 605
University of Colorado, 285
University of Michigan, 287, 294, 298
Urban interests, 33
Usage, publications, 622-623
U.S. Dept. of Commerce, 63
U.S. Government Organizations Manual, 398
U.S. News and World Report, 45, 297

Utilities and its public:
    advertising, 220-221
    business and social peers, 220
    checklist, 226-229
        community relations, 226-227
        customer information, 227-228
        employee information, 228
        public information, 227
        stockholder information, 228-229
    communities served, 213
    community health, welfare, educational and cultural interests, 219
    consumerism, 214-215
    corporate identity systems, 224, 226
    customers, 213
    employee relations, 214, 219-220
    environment, 215-216
    financial community, 213
    government agencies and officials, 220
    industrial development, 216
    intra-industry relations, 222
    low- and middle-income families, 216-219
    media relations, 220-221
    meeting growth with adequate supply, 222-224
    minority group hiring and training, 219
    public participation in planning, 224
    "public," word, 211
    regulatory agencies, 213
    relations with many publics, 212-214
    strategy and techniques, 224-226
    telephone, 221-222
    trade allies, 213-214
    unique nature of utilities, 212-214

V

Variety, 45
Variety programs, 469
Varilla, Joseph A., 162
Veterans' organizations, 519
Video cassette, 492
Videoconference Networks, Inc., 418
Videotapes, 466, 475
Visual aids, 492-493
Vocal activists, 17
Voice of America, 352
Volkswagen, 351, 352
Voting, 81-82

W

Wall Street Journal, 139, 199, 325, 434
Waples, Douglas, 14
Ward, Barbara, 311
Warner and Swasey, 157
Washington, George, 315
Washington Cover-Up, 315
Washington Information Directory, 41
Washington Post, 282
Watergate, 313, 344, 613

WATS, 422
Watson, Thomas, 340
Wayfarer, 93
Weber, Max, 311
Weekly newspaper magazines, 453
Weekly publications, 165
Weinberger, Casper, 201
Welfare groups, 522-523
Wells, H.G., 604
Wells Fargo, 246
West Germany, 352
Whaley-Eaton, 523
White, Mel, 320
Whitman, Edmund S., 79
Wilbur, Marvin C., 277
Will, George, 49
Wire services, 301
Women, 200
Women's and home magazines, 454-455
Women's groups, 518-519
Women's Wear Daily, 251
Word of mouth, 508-509
Workers, 5-6
Working Press of Nation, 283, 398, 400, 448
World Association for Christian Communication, 280
World Magazine, 478
World Tourist Organization, 332
World Traveler, 478
Writers' Market, 448
Writing for readership:
    achieving good readership, 526-535
    evils of fancy talk, 535
    summary, 535-536
    why we need good readership, 526

XYZ

Yale Review, 528
Yearbook of American and Canadian Churches, 282
You and the Political Organization, 82
Young, Charles P., 138
Young, Jeane R., 476
Young, John Orr, 495
Youth groups, 258